Texas Real Estate Finance

Second Edition

Texas Real Estate Finance

Second Edition

Tom J. Morton

RMU, CRA
Residential Financial Consultant

Scott, Foresman and Company

Glenview, Illinois
London, England

I would like to dedicate this book to my wife, Annette, without whose help and reassurance this book would not have been possible.

ISBN: 0-673-16656-2

1 2 3 4 5 6 - MVN - 90 89 88 87 86 85

Preface

The purpose of this text is to give the student of real estate a practical look at Texas real estate finance. This text can also be of great aid to licensees, both salespersons and brokers, as a ready reference. This book, because of its straightforward manner, should be helpful to any individual interested in the financing of his or her own home.

Like the first edition of *Texas Real Estate Finance*, this second edition is practical in nature and reviews the latest mortgage instruments commonly used in Texas and the programs available for the financing of residential real estate through the federal government, the state of Texas, primary lenders and the secondary market. The hands-on approach to the procedures of loan application, processing, and underwriting is illustrated in this second edition by more than 240 figures and sample forms currently used in Texas.

The main difference between this text and other texts dealing with real estate finance is that it is a "nuts and bolts" approach that is simple, clear and step-by-step. Additionally, it is an in-depth study of both federal and Texas mortgage programs. Finally, it is the only finance book that deals with Texas specifically.

As an integral part of this text, many of the standard forms are illustrated and explained. The understanding of these forms is vital to the real estate practitioner.

During the 1981 session of the Texas legislature, several amendments were passed affecting the Texas Real Estate License Act. One of these amendments outlined the courses of study required for licensure. Real estate finance was one of the courses named. In addition to the naming of these courses, the legislation outlined minimum subject matter to be covered (monetary systems, primary lenders and secondary money markets, sources of mortgage loans, federal government programs, loan applications, processes and procedures, closing costs, alternative financial instruments, the Equal Credit Opportunity Act, the Community Reinvestment Act and the state housing agency). This text deals with all of this material in depth.

This book is intended to convey general information about the field of real estate finance and is not a legal interpretation of any federal, state or local rules, regulations or statutes, or any rules of a lending institution or a secondary marketer. For any legal interpretation, you should contact an attorney of your choice.

Acknowledgments

I would like to express my deep appreciation to the following persons who have either given advice, answered many questions, or supplied valuable information that made this book possible.

Ms. Betty J. Armbrust, President, Real Estate Prep, Inc., Denver, Colorado

Mr. Tom Bacon, Retired, Public Information Office, Department of Housing and Urban Development, Washington, D.C.

Ms. Sharon C. Benson, Professor of Business and Real Estate, Shoreline Community College, Seattle, Washington

Mr. Ronald G. Bliss, Vice-President, Regional Manager, Mortgage Guaranty Insurance Corporation, Dallas, Texas

Mr. Tom Bond, Director, Information Services, State Board of Insurance, State of Texas, Austin, Texas

Mr. Jim Hodge, Mercantile Mortgage Corporation of Texas, Houston, Texas

Mr. Jim Breslin, Mortgage Guaranty Insurance Corporation, Milwaukee, Wisconsin

Mrs. Jimmie Ham, Residential Loan Manager, Justice Mortgage, Dallas, Texas

Mr. Cal Harrison, Regional Manager Multifamily/Project Loans, Federal Home Loan Mortgage Corporation, Dallas, Texas

Ms. Nancy Harucki, Legislative Assistant, U.S. Congressman Manuel Lujan, New Mexico, Washington, D.C.

Mr. John Keating, Assistant Professor, Business Administration, Tarrant County Junior College, Fort Worth, Texas

Ms. Annette Kolis, Attorney-Advisor, Federal Home Loan Bank Board, Office of Community Investment, Washington, D.C.

Mr. Karl P. Kuehn, El Paso Community College, El Paso, Texas

Mr. Thomas S. LaMalfa, Senior Analyst, Secondary Market, Mortgage Guaranty Insurance Corporation, Milwaukee, Wisconsin

Dr. Robert Lyon, Education Division, Texas Real Estate Research Center, Texas A & M University

Mr. D. B. McKinney, Executive Vice President, Mortgage Investment Company, El Paso, Texas

Ms. Elinor Maskell, Arizona Department of Real Estate, Phoenix, Arizona

Mr. Larry Mumford, Chief Mortgage Credit, Department of Housing and Urban Development, Regional Office, Fort Worth, Texas

Mr. George W. Ratterman, Vice President, Jones Real Estate Colleges, Denver, Colorado

Mr. R. D. Smith, Regional Economist, Department of Housing and Urban Development, Regional Office, Fort Worth, Texas

Mr. Robert L. Stanley, Robert L. Stanley and Associates, Appraisers, Houston, Texas

Ms. Charlotte Sterling, Corporate Relations, Federal National Mortgage Corporation, Washington, D.C.

Mr. Dean Stout, Real Estate Instructor, Richland College of Dallas Community College District, Dallas, Texas

Mr. Jim Williams, Texas Department of Community Affairs, Austin, Texas

Mr. Timothy S. Wolf, Librarian, Mortgage Bankers Association of America, Washington, D.C.

Contents

1 MONEY AND REAL ESTATE 1
   European Beginnings 1
   Colonial Times 1
   Federal Reserve System 2
   HUD, the VA, and Other Agencies 8
   Interest Rates 8
   Texas Usury Law 10

2 MORTGAGES AND MORTGAGE INSTRUMENTS 13
   Definition 13
   History 13
   Three Theories of Mortgages 14
   Categories of Mortgages 14
   Types of Mortgages 14
   Alternative Mortgages 16
   Standard Mortgages 16
   Homestead and Community Property Laws 19
   Standard Mortgage Instruments 20

3 ALTERNATIVE MORTGAGE INSTRUMENTS 46
   Background 46
   Comptroller of the Currency Adjustable-Rate Mortgage
   (ARM) 54
   Federal Home Loan Bank Board Adjustable Rate Mortgage
   (ARM) 54
   National Credit Union Administration's ARM 56
   Standard ARM Instruments 57
   Convertible ARM Note 71
   Adjustable-Rate Mortgage Rates 71
   Buydown Mortgage (Temporary) 78
   Graduated-Payment Mortgage (GPM) 80
   Graduated-Payment Adjustable-Rate Mortgage (GPARM) 82
   Growing Equity Mortgage 85
   Shared-Appreciation Mortgage 91
   Renegotiable-Rate Mortgage (RRM) 98
   Reverse Annuity Mortgage (RAM) 99
   Price-Level Adjusted Mortgage (PLAM) 101

4 MORTGAGE LENDERS—INSTITUTIONAL (PRIMARY)
   LENDERS 103
   Definition 103
   Intermediation and Disintermediation 103
   Amount of Mortgage Debt 104
   Distribution of Debt by Lenders 104

Savings and Loan Associations   107
Commercial Banks   113
Life Insurance Companies   115
Mutual Savings Banks   116

5   COMMUNITY REINVESTMENT   118
Purpose   119
Significance to the Real Estate Industry   119
Requirements of the Act and Federal Regulations   119
Assessing the Performance of the Institution   121
Qualifying Governmental Programs   122
Home Mortgage Disclosure Act   123
Summary   126

6   NONINSTITUTIONAL LENDERS   127
The Mortgage Broker   131
The Future of Mortgage Lending   131
Credit Unions   132
Pension Funds   134
Alternative Mortgage Transaction Parity Act of 1982   135

7   PROGRAMS OF HUD-FHA   136
Homeowners Loan Corporation (HOLC)   136
History of FHA   136
HUD-FHA Programs   137
Major Loan Reforms   138
Advantages of FHA   139
Disadvantages of FHA   140
Negotiated Interest Rate   140
One-Time Mortgage Insurance Premium (MIP)   141
Alternative Mortgage Instruments   166
Mortgage Instruments for Section 245   170
Assumptions/Release of Liability   174

8   OTHER GOVERNMENTAL PROGRAMS   179
Veterans Administration   179
Farmers Home Administration (FmHA)   196
Texas Veterans Land Program   197
Texas Veterans Housing Assistance Program   198
State Housing Agencies   199
Texas Family Farm and Ranch Security Program   209
Federal Land Banks   209

9 CONVENTIONAL LOANS AND PRIVATE MORTGAGE INSURANCE 211
   Comparison of Conventional vs. Governmental Loans 211
   Private Mortgage Insurance 221
   PMI Premiums 223

10 THE SECONDARY MARKET, PART 1 228
   A Few Definitions 228
   Purpose of the Secondary Market 228
   Major Secondary Markets 229
   Federal National Mortgage Association (Fannie Mae) 229

11 THE SECONDARY MARKET, PART 2 281
   Federal Home Loan Mortgage Corporation (FHLMC) 281
   FHLMC Source of Funds 281
   The Government National Mortgage Association (GNMA) 302

12 QUALIFYING THE PROPERTY 314
   Property Appraisal 314
   Standard Appraisal Reports 322
   National Association of Review Appraisers 343

13 BORROWER QUALIFICATION 344
   Why Qualify Your Buyer? 344
   Initial Buyer Qualification 345
   Income and Debt Analysis 352

14 LOAN PROCESSING AND UNDERWRITING 375
   Loan Application 375
   Verification Forms 395
   Loan Packaging or Collation 401
   Loan Underwriting or Approval 405

15 LOAN CLOSING 407
   Definition 407
   Overview of the Closing Process 407
   Real Estate Settlement Procedures Act (RESPA) 408
   Truth-in-Lending Law 409
   Setting the Closing 412
   Mortgage Lenders Closing Procedures 418
   Closing Instructions 422
   Closing Costs 422

16 CREATIVE FINANCING METHODS   433
    Definition   433
    Wraparound Mortgage   433
    Blended Yield Mortgage   435
    Balloon Mortgage   435
    Participation Mortgage   436
    Equity Participation Mortgage   436
    Owner Financing   438
    Second Mortgages   438
    Land Leasing   439

APPENDICES
    A. Monthly Payment Factors for $1000 Loan Amounts   440
    B. Outstanding Loan Balance Factors—Section 245, Plan III   442
    C. Factors for Calculating Monthly Payments—Section 245, Plan III   455
    D. Growing Equity Mortgage with increasing payments for 10 years at 2.00 and 3.00 percent each year   456
    E. HUD-FHA Mortgage Insurance Programs   459
    F. Farmers Home Administration Loan Programs   462
    G. Federal Home Loan Mortgage Corporation Approved PMI Companies   464
    H. Samples of Completed Appraisal Forms   465
    I. Worksheets for Borrower Qualification   470
    J. HUD-FHA Effective Income Guidelines   473

Glossary   476

Index   485

Texas
Real Estate Finance

Second Edition

1 Money and Real Estate

In this chapter we will briefly cover the history of real estate from the time of our earliest ancestors to the present. We will also cover the development of the monetary system in the United States.

Upon completion of the chapter you should be able to do the following:

★ State how the ownership of real estate has developed.

★ Outline the Federal Reserve System and give a broad outline of how it works.

★ Explain how the management of the money supply can affect the financing of real estate.

★ Describe how interest rates are established and the effect of state usury laws on those interest rates.

EUROPEAN BEGINNINGS

At first, men and women were nomadic and had no need to own or finance real estate. The concept of ownership did not start until we began to cultivate crops and develop the idea that we would want the exclusive right to use of the land.

This exclusive right, in earlier times, was usually not held by just one person, but by a group of persons or a tribe. The actual ownership or title to the land was held by the leader. This form of ownership gave birth to the feudal system.

Under the feudal system, the leader or ruler would allow persons to farm a parcel of land, and in return the persons would share a portion of the crop with the leader and would also help the leader defend any attack on the leader's dominion.

It was not until the late 1200s that there was a major change in this system. This change was that a landholder could pass title to an heir. Prior to this concept, upon the death of the landholder, ownership of the land would revert back to the ruler and all of the heirs of the landholder could be forced to vacate.

The concepts of property ownership as we know it today did not evolve until the Industrial Revolution, before which time people or workers did not have the ability to earn or accumulate money. Once this was possible, the workers wanted to provide their families with shelter on property to which they had acquired title through purchase, rather than be controlled by the whims of a leader or ruler.

COLONIAL TIMES

The Pilgrims were drawn to the New World not only by the pursuit of religious freedoms, but also by the desire to own land. In the New World, the ability to acquire land was only limited by a person's ability to clear the land and defend it.

Along with ownership of land came the need for capital, or money, to purchase goods for the colonists' homes and businesses. This gave birth to the need for the saving of monies. The initial step was the formation of informal clubs or associations. Here the members could make regular payments into the treasury of the club or association. The funds that accumulated in the treasury were used to make lump sum payments to the survivors upon the death of a member. A member could also go to the treasury of the club and make a withdrawal or receive a loan.

These informal clubs or associations were the foundation for many modern institutions that are vital to the financing of real estate in the United States. One of the first of these institutions, the Presbyterian Ministers Fund, was formed in Pennsylvania in 1759. Its purpose was to insure the lives of the ministers and their wives. This is the oldest life insurance company in the United States, and it still exists today, now named the Presbyterian Annuity and Life Insurance Company. It was not until 1835 that New England Mutual, the first of the current type of life insurance company, was formed. As a source of funds for the financing of real estate, life insurance companies have been around a relatively short time.

Attempt at a Banking System

As the colonies grew and declared their independence from England, there was a need for a banking system. So in 1781, the Bank of North America was established. It was chartered by the Pennsylvania legislature and incorporated by the Continental Congress, thus making it the oldest commercial bank in North America.

The Bank of North America served its purpose, but as the United States grew there was a need for a banking system throughout the young nation. The first attempt at this system was the establishment of the First Bank of the United States, which operated from 1791 to 1811, when it was disbanded. The next attempt at a national banking system was in 1816, when the Second Bank of the United States was established. This bank continued in operation until 1836.

There was no federal regulation of the banking system from 1836 until 1913. During this time, each state issued its own currency and there was no single legal tender for the United States. Attempts to control the currency finally led to the establishment of the Federal Reserve System, which had its beginnings with the establishment of the Federal Bank in 1913.

FEDERAL RESERVE SYSTEM

There are two major purposes of the "Fed" or Federal Reserve System: to supply reserve funds when needed, and to control bank and consumer credit. The latter is the most important to the financing of real estate, as we will discuss later in this chapter.

The system is composed of twelve Federal Reserve Districts, each of the districts with a Federal Reserve Bank. With the Fed having not a central bank, but district banks located throughout the United States, it can better respond to the different economic needs of the various areas of the nation.

Many of the Federal Reserve Banks also operate Federal Reserve Branch Banks or offices. The purpose of the branch banks or offices is to further break down the districts in order to better serve the financial needs of the individual districts.

A map showing the boundaries of each Federal Reserve district and any branch office boundary is shown in Figure 1-1. The address of each of the Federal Reserve Banks and their branches, if any, is shown in Figure 1-2.

Board of Directors

The Federal Reserve Banks are not under the control of any governmental agency, but each Reserve Bank is under a Board of Directors. The board is composed of twelve members who represent business, the banking industry, and the general public in their Federal Reserve District. The directors are classified as A-, B-, or C-Class Directors. Class A members can come from the banking community of the district, Class B members can represent the borrowers of the district, and Class C Directors will represent the general public. Both Class B and Class C Directors cannot in any way be connected to the banking industry, including the owning of bank stocks.

The members of the board are primarily chosen by the banking community in the district. The Class A and Class B Directors are elected by the member banks, and the selection process sees that all sizes of banks are represented. The Class C members are selected by the Board of Governors of the Federal Reserve.

As in any other corporation, the Board of Directors selects the president and the vice-president, and the board of the Reserve Bank will choose the members of boards of any branch bank established in their district. This process, therefore, insures that the branch

Figure 1-1. The Federal Reserve System

Boundaries of Federal Reserve Districts and Their Branch Territories

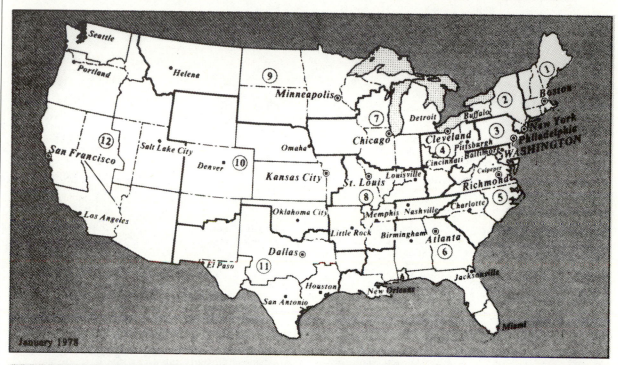

January 1978

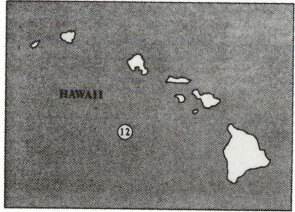

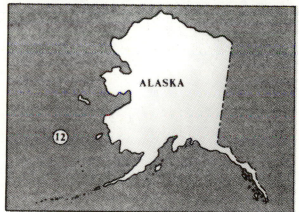

LEGEND

—— Boundaries of Federal Reserve Districts

—— Boundaries of Federal Reserve Branch Territories

⭐ Board of Governors of the Federal Reserve System

◉ Federal Reserve Bank Cities

• Federal Reserve Branch Cities

· Federal Reserve Bank Facility

Source: U.S., Board of Governors of the Federal Reserve System, *Federal Reserve Bulletin—September, 1981*, vol. 67, no. 9, p. A78.

Figure 1-2.   *Federal Reserve Banks, Branches, and Offices*

FEDERAL RESERVE BANK, branch, or facility Zip	Chairman Deputy Chairman	President First Vice President	Vice President in charge of branch
BOSTON* 02106	Robert P. Henderson Thomas I. Atkins	Frank E. Morris James A. McIntosh	
NEW YORK* 10045	John Brademas Gertrude G. Michelson	Anthony M. Solomon Thomas M. Timlen	
Buffalo 14240	M. Jane Dickman		John T. Keane
PHILADELPHIA 19105	Robert M. Landis Nevius M. Curtis	Edward G. Boehne Richard L. Smoot	
CLEVELAND* 44101	William H. Knoell E. Mandell de Windt	Karen N. Horn William H. Hendricks	
Cincinnati 45201	Vacant		Charles A. Cerino
Pittsburgh 15230	Milton G. Hulme, Jr.		Harold J. Swart
RICHMOND* 23219	William S. Lee Leroy T. Canoles, Jr.	Robert P. Black Jimmie R. Monhollon	
Baltimore 21203	Robert L. Tate		Robert D. McTeer, Jr.
Charlotte 28230	Henry Ponder		Albert D. Tinkelenberg
Culpeper Communications and Records Center 22701			John G. Stoides
ATLANTA 30301	John H. Weitnauer, Jr. Bradley Currey, Jr.	Robert P. Forrestal Jack Guynn	
Birmingham 35283	Martha A. McInnis		Fred R. Herr
Jacksonville 32231	Jerome P. Keuper		James D. Hawkins
Miami 33152	Sue McCourt Cobb		Patrick K. Barron
Nashville...........37203	C. Warren Neel		Jeffrey J. Wells
New Orleans 70161	Sharon A. Perlis		Henry H. Bourgaux
CHICAGO* 60690	Stanton R. Cook Edward F. Brabec	Silas Keehn Daniel M. Doyle	
Detroit 48231	Russell G. Mawby		William C. Conrad
ST. LOUIS...........63166	W. L. Hadley Griffin Mary P. Holt	Theodore H. Roberts Joseph P. Garbarini	
Little Rock 72203	Sheffield Nelson		John F. Breen
Louisville 40232	Sister Eileen M. Egan		James E. Conrad
Memphis...........38101	Patricia W. Shaw		Paul I. Black, Jr.
MINNEAPOLIS 55480	William G. Phillips John B. Davis, Jr.	E. Gerald Corrigan Thomas E. Gainor	
Helena.............59601	Ernest B. Corrick		Robert F. McNellis
KANSAS CITY........64198	Doris M. Drury Irvine O. Hockaday, Jr.	Roger Guffey Henry R. Czerwinski	
Denver 80217	James E. Nielson		Wayne W. Martin
Oklahoma City 73125	Patience Latting		William G. Evans
Omaha 68102	Robert G. Lueder		Robert D. Hamilton
DALLAS 75222	Robert D. Rogers John V. James	Robert H. Boykin William H. Wallace	
El Paso 79999	Mary Carmen Saucedo		Joel L. Koonce, Jr.
Houston 77252	Paul N. Howell		J. Z. Rowe
San Antonio........78295	Lawrence L. Crum		Thomas H. Robertson
SAN FRANCISCO.....94120	Caroline L. Ahmanson Alan C. Furth	John J. Balles Richard T. Griffith	
Los Angeles 90051	Bruce M. Schwaegler		Richard C. Dunn
Portland 97208	Paul E. Bragdon		Angelo S. Carella
Salt Lake City 84125	Wendell J. Ashton		A. Grant Holman
Seattle 98124	John W. Ellis		Gerald R. Kelly

*Additional offices of these Banks are located at Lewiston, Maine 04240; Windsor Locks, Connecticut 06096; Cranford, New Jersey 07016; Jericho, New York 11753; Utica at Oriskany, New York 13424; Columbus, Ohio 43216; Columbia, South Carolina 29210; Charleston, West Virginia 25311; Des Moines, Iowa 50306; Indianapolis, Indiana 46204; and Milwaukee, Wisconsin 53202.

SOURCE: U.S., Federal Reserve System, Board of Governors, *Federal Reserve Bulletin*—March 1984, vol. 70 no. 3, p. A87.

banks reflect the needs of the area that the branch serves.

Board of Governors

The Board of Governors has supervisory control over all of the Reserve Banks throughout the system. The members are appointed by the President of the United States with the advice and consent of the Senate. The board is composed of seven individuals who each serve for a term of fourteen years. These appointments are staggered so that only one term expires every other year. In order for the board to be truly representative of the whole system, the President tries to appoint only one member from each district.

The board has as one of its duties to publish the *Federal Reserve Bulletin*. This monthly publication gives information on the state of the economy in the nation and the world. The board also publishes reports on studies or research done for or under the authority of the Fed. One of the important groups of figures released each week by the Fed is "Federal Reserve Data." These figures reflect the changes in the weekly averages of member banks' reserves and other related items. These weekly figures also report the change in the basic money supply in the United States.

In addition to reporting weekly changes, the board can set the interest rate that member banks will have to pay when borrowing monies from the Fed. This rate is very important to the real estate industry, because banks use this rate to establish the *prime rate* (the rate their most credit-worthy customer would pay). The prime rate is usually the basis for the cost of builders' interim funds and for the rate that you and I will pay for our car loans and loans for business operations. Besides the above, the board may raise or lower the reserve requirements of the member banks. This requirement will affect the amount of money the banks will have available to loan: the lower the requirement, the more money the banks will have for loans; the higher the requirement, the less money the banks will have for loans.

Member Banks

How does a bank become a member of the Federal Reserve System? Any national bank must belong, and any state bank that wishes may join. For a bank to join, it must buy stock in the Federal Reserve Bank System and agree to abide by the rules and rulings of the Federal Reserve. It must also meet the reserve requirements established from time to time to meet the fiscal policy of the Fed.

About 40 percent or 5758 of the 14,497 banks in the United States now belong to the Federal Reserve System. Even though this percentage may seem small, most of the larger banks are members, and member banks control approximately 71 percent of all bank deposits.

For the past several years membership in the Federal Reserve has been on the decline. This decline has been of concern to many economists because the Fed will not be able to control the supply of money or the rate of inflation as effectively as it might if the majority of the depository institutions were members. Realizing this problem, Congress passed the Depository Institutions Deregulation and Monetary Control Act of 1980, which was signed by the President and became law on March 31, 1980. This act comprises ten titles affecting many areas of operations of the depository institutions. One of the most important titles is Title I, which greatly strengthens the Fed's control over nonmember banks by requiring them to meet the reserve requirements set by the Fed. This requirement will be phased in over eight years. It has been estimated that this will bring approximately 8900 nonmember banks under control of the Fed.

Open Market Committee

The implementation of the change of the money supply is the responsibility of the Open Market Committee. The Federal Reserve Open Market Committee is presently composed of twelve members; five of the members are chosen by the Board of Governors and the remainder come from the twelve Federal Reserve Districts. With only seven members left to be chosen, you can see that not all of the banks get to choose a member singly. In fact, only the Reserve Bank of New York gets to choose a member by itself.

The committee members meet on a regular basis, usually the third Tuesday of the month, in an unannounced location to establish what action they should take to carry out the fiscal policy of the board. The decision they reach is not announced to the general public, but the decisions of the Open Market Committee are published on a delayed basis in the *Federal Reserve Bulletin.* The reason for this is to hinder speculation on government securities and the U.S. dollar. The decision is carried out through a small staff that operates within the Federal Reserve Bank in New York. If the decision of the committee is to increase the supply of money, a member of the staff contacts a dealer who is licensed to deal in government securities, and the dealer is given a check, drawn on the U.S. Treasury, to buy government securities. The check is then deposited into a member bank, thus increasing the supply of money available to the banking system in general. If the decision is to reduce the money supply, the committee makes recommendations to the Board of Governors to increase the reserve requirements or take any other action they may deem necessary.

Measurement of the Money Supply

One of the more important functions of the Federal Reserve is to control the supply of money in the hands of the public, as well as the amount held in bank accounts, both demand-type accounts and thrift deposits. The Fed must know the amount in bank accounts in order to manage the money supply. This measurement will tell if they must either increase or decrease the amount of money in circulation.

To measure the money supply, the Fed relies on information supplied by the member banks. From these figures, the Fed arrives with the following measurements of the money supply:

M1-A – Consists of private checking-account deposits at commercial banks plus cash in the public hands. This is similar to the old M1 measurement, which was once the primary guideline for the Fed. This figure is averaging approximately $370 billion.

M1-B – Consists of M1-A plus all NOW (negotiated order of withdrawal) accounts, ATS (automatic transfer service), credit union share accounts, and demand deposits at thrift institutions.

There are two additional measurements that should be mentioned:

M2 – Consists of M1-B plus money market mutual fund shares, savings deposits at all depository institutions, and all small time deposits at all depository institutions. (For the purpose of this measuring device, a small time deposit is one of less than $100,000.) This measurement also contains overnight Eurodollar deposits held by U.S. nonbank residents at Caribbean branches of U.S. banks.

M3 – Consists of M2 plus large time deposits at all depository institutions. These are deposits of $100,000 or more.

The measurements are reported each week by the member banks and the resulting figures are released each week and are published usually on each Friday. These figures are compared with the previous week and either an increase or decrease is noted. If there is an increase in either M1-A or M1-B that exceeds the guidelines set by the Fed, the Fed can take measures to slow or halt the growth in these two areas.

How Does the Fed Control the Supply of Money?

Many experts disagree on the Fed's attempts to control the supply of available money. Some feel that the economy should be allowed to operate by the law of supply and demand, and others feel that the economy or the supply of money should be strictly regulated. The system that is used, in this author's opinion, is probably the best of both worlds. The economy is allowed to grow within certain guidelines through the law of supply and demand, and if the growth rate exceeds these limits the Fed then steps in to slow things down by using one or more tools available to them. The major tools or combination of tools they may use are as follows:

1. Change the reserve requirements

2. Change the discount rate

Each member bank must set aside a certain percentage of its deposits in a reserve account. These reserves have a twofold purpose: (1) to have monies in reserve in case the bank finds itself short of funds to meet the demand of depositors, and (2) to control the amount of monies available to the bank for the purpose of making loans.

For example, if the discount rate is 5 percent and the bank opens a new account in the amount of $1000, it will have to put 5 percent, or $50, into the reserve account, thus leaving it $950 to use for loans and the operation of the bank.

How does the Fed use this tool? Let's assume the Fed feels that at the present time the economy is growing too fast and is feeding inflation and it wants to shrink the supply of money available to the banks. All it has to do is raise the reserve rate requirement, and the banks must then make deposits to their reserve accounts to meet the new requirement. For example, a small bank has deposits of $2 million and the reserve requirement is 5 percent. That means the bank has to have $100,000 on account with the Fed. Now the Fed feels that there is too much money to loan, so it doubles the reserve requirement to 10 percent. The bank must immediately double the amount of money on account at the Fed. This takes another $100,000 out of the hands of the bank and leaves it less money available to loan. This would not only be true for this small bank, but for all of the banks in the system, thus reducing the money available rapidly and in large amounts. We then go back to the law of supply and demand. With the supply reduced, the interest rate should increase and, it is hoped, the demand will slow.

Another tool available to the Fed is to change the discount rate. The discount rate is the rate the Fed charges its member banks to borrow money. Why would a bank need to borrow? Whenever a bank has more commitments due than it has in cash available, it can use monies in its reserve account with the Fed. If in doing this the balance in a bank's reserve account drops below that required by the Fed, the bank must borrow to bring it into compliance. It's not surprising that some experts refer to the Fed as the "Bankers' Bank"!

How can the discount rate be used to control the economy? That's simple. If it costs the banks more to borrow money, this cost will be passed along to the consumer in the form of higher interest rates, or if the rate is lowered, the consumer *should* get the benefit of lower interest rates.

There is a good example of how the use of increasing the reserve requirements and an increase in the discount rate can affect the economy. In the fall of 1979, the economy was in runaway inflation. Inflation was at an annual rate of 13 to 14 percent and the Fed felt that it had to do something quickly. So it raised the discount rate a full 1 percent, thus causing the interest rate to shoot up and cut the amount of money available. The real estate industry saw the interest rate on single-family loans go to 13 to 13.5 percent, if you could find a lender with funds to loan.

Effects of Money Supply Management

These major tools of money supply management can be used by the Fed to cause either *tight money* or *easy money*. Tight money is the policy of the Fed that makes money expensive (high interest rates). This is usually a restrictive policy, with high discount rates and increased reserve requirements. Thus, the money supply is reduced and, usually, the demand remains about the same: business still needs money to operate and to buy raw materials for production; the demand for housing goes on, but usually at a reduced rate. With about the same number of people pursuing a smaller number of dollars, the interest rate increases until the demand starts to fall.

A good example of this policy happened during the third quarter of 1979 and continued into 1982, when the Fed instituted a strong tight-money policy to try to stop inflation and stabilize the dollar. During this time of tight money we also saw the mood of the world change toward the Fed. Most of the world felt that the Fed would not keep with the tight-money policy due to the unpopularity of this policy and political pressures. They therefore thought inflation in the United States would continue to run wild. So the world turned to precious metals, and the price of gold and silver shot to all-time records. Gold sold for over $800 per ounce.

Even though the Fed came under attack, it continued its policy of tight money into 1982 and the inflation rate in the United States was reduced. Gold was less in demand, thus the price fell and gold was traded in the fourth quarter of 1981 in the $350- to $450-per-ounce range.

With the price of gold falling and interest rates staying relatively high due to the Fed's tight-money policy, the demand by foreign investors for the American dollar increased.

Thus, the value of the dollar increased against many foreign currencies.

Easy money is just the opposite of tight money. The Fed's easy-money policy is to reduce the reserve requirements and lower the discount rate. This is usually implemented in a time of recession; the Fed uses this policy to stimulate the economy. It increases the supply of money, thus making it easier for business and individuals to get credit. As credit becomes available, companies can expand, hire more people, and increase salaries. As these monies go into the banks and thrift institutions, it tends to make more money available, and thus the cycle begins again.

How can these policies affect the real estate industry? In the second half of 1979, when the Fed started a tight-money policy, we saw the interest rates start to shoot up on builders' interim loans (those loans made to builders to construct homes), making the builders' costs go up, and thus the cost of the houses went up. In some cases, the rates got so high that builders were forced out of business. Mortgage rates were forced up as the cost of funds to mortgage lenders increased. As the rates increased, many states were forced out of the mortgage market as rates reached or exceeded state usury laws. (We will discuss usury laws later in the chapter.) These are only a few of the problems that can be brought about by a tight-money policy.

HUD, THE VA, AND OTHER AGENCIES

The Fed is not the only federal body that can have an effect on the monetary system or on the movement of money to the real estate industry.

Probably the federal agencies most familiar to us in the real estate industry are the Department of Housing and Urban Development (HUD) and the Veterans Administration, (VA). HUD—through the Federal Housing Administration (FHA)—and the VA have the most direct effect of any governmental agencies by the establishment of interest rates that affect either government-insured or VA-guaranteed loans. In addition to the setting of the interest rates, the FHA, through its loan insurance programs, can have a major effect on the real estate market. We will review these programs in depth later in this text. Some of the other agencies that can have a direct or indirect effect on real estate are listed below:

Small Business Administration   This agency through its involvement in the community reinvestment program and its ability to make disaster loans to home owners, can have an effect on the real estate market.

Government Services Agency   This agency has the responsibility of overseeing the real estate and buildings of the federal government. It can affect the value of real estate in a given market by acquiring or disposing of land or buildings.

The Federal Land Bank and the Farmers Home Administration   These are both active in the financing of farms, farmland, and rural housing.

The Federal National Mortgage Association and the Government National Mortgage Association   These two agencies have a strong influence over the very important secondary market. They will be discussed in depth in Chapters 10 and 11.

The Congress of the United States   This one body, in one vote, can undo all of the work that any other agency has done to either stabilize the economy or to institute programs that will aid a segment of the real estate industry. An example would be if HUD, through the FHA, wanted to institute a program that would aid a lagging housing market, and it went to Congress for funding: if Congress does not feel the program is good, it does not vote the funds, and the program is dead no matter how badly needed.

Most of these agencies will be discussed in depth in later chapters.

INTEREST RATES

One of the most important factors affecting the financing of real estate is the amount of yield that an investor can receive. This yield is translated into the interest rate a mortgage will bear or the rate of return guaranteed. The higher the rate, the more likely the investor will make the loan. The factor of risk must also be considered.

Most investors seek the highest rate of return with the least amount of risk. The real estate mortgage is an investment that has a low-risk level, for it is usually secured by real property that can be sold and the investor is relatively sure of getting the monies back.

Taking the previous paragraph into consideration, it would seem that investors would be standing in line to make first-lien mortgages on real property. But this is not necessarily true, for we are working in a free market economy where industry, government, and many others are trying to convince the investors that they also are a good investment. Competition for funds brings into play the most important factor that affects the interest rates in the United States—the law of supply and demand.

The Law of Supply and Demand

If the supply of money remains basically the same and the demand stays about the same, interest rates do not vary substantially. That was the case for many years in real estate financing.

But in the last decade we have seen the federal government need monies. This need has come about because the federal government has not been able to finance its operation through the monies derived from the federal income tax. So where does the government get the money to operate? From the same source that all other persons look to when seeking financial help: the public.

With this increase in demand for lendable funds, only one thing can happen to the interest rates: they will go up. If this demand decreases, the interest rates should go down. This is a very simple explanation of the law of supply and demand.

Interest Rate Indicators

A real estate professional must have an idea of the present trend in mortgage rates. Some of the indicators are explained below.

$100,000 certificate of deposit rate   As we learned earlier in this chapter, certificates of deposit, or CDs, are included in the measurement of the money supply and are very important. The certificate of deposit rate is the rate that banks and thrift institutions will pay a person who will deposit at least $100,000 in a CD for a minimum of three months and a maximum of one year.

This is the most volatile of all the rate indicators, for the rate can change every day, if not every hour. Why is such a rate of any concern to the real estate professional? Because this rate will tell what has to be paid for the use of the money for a given time. The lending institutions can use this rate as a basis for calculating the rate they will charge the general public. For example, if the institution has to pay 11 percent to use $100,000 for twelve months, it will not lend the money to you or me for any less than 11 percent. It usually will seek a rate of at least 2 percent over the costs of funds or, in this example, 13 percent. These rates are published daily in such papers as *The Wall Street Journal*. It is wise to review this rate regularly, for if the trend is up, you can expect that banks and savings and loan associations will soon start to raise rates. If the trend is down, the institutions should in the near future lower rates.

Fed fund rate   The Fed fund rate is the rate that one commercial bank charges another bank for the short-term use of reserves. This term may be as short as overnight. The minimum loan is $1 million. Banks have need for such funds if for the previous day they have funded a large number of loan commitments and find themselves short of the needed reserves to meet their reserve requirement. This rate during the first part of 1984 was approximately 11 percent. The Fed fund rate is used by some banks to establish their prime rate: the higher the Fed fund rate, the higher the prime rate.

Prime rate   The prime rate is defined as the rate a commercial bank will charge its most credit-worthy customer. Each bank may set its own prime rate, but usually the major banks on the East and West Coasts set a rate and the rest of the nation follows. As mentioned above, some banks use the Fed fund rate to establish prime. For example, if the Fed fund rate is 11 percent and the banks like to receive 2 percent above the cost of funds, this would set a prime rate of 13 percent. How can a prime rate affect the financing of real estate? First of all, it will affect the cost of funds for the interim financing of construction of homes; second, it will affect the cost to mortgage companies of their warehouse lines of credit. We will discuss both of these later in the text.

U.S. Government Securities   Many lenders are using the yield on selected U.S. Government Securities to establish the interest rate on several different types of mortgages secured by real property. The most commonly used yield is the Treasury Constant Maturities. These rates are reported by the Federal Reserve for 1-, 2-, 3-, 5-, 7-, 10-, 20-, and

30-year U. S. Treasury Securities. These yields are published in *Federal Reserve Statistical Release* number H.15(519). The lenders feel if, for example, they can loan money to the federal government for thirty years and receive a return of 12.50 with no risk, then this becomes a "safe rate," which means that the repayment is almost guaranteed. Thus, if you or I wish to borrow monies for thirty years, the lender will charge a rate that will be in excess of the current rate on the 30-year securities. If the current rate is 12.50 percent, the lender will add additional yield to the 12.50 to cover the risk of foreclosure. Let us assume the lender will add 1.5 percent to the current rate; thus the rate that we will be charged is 12.50 plus 1.5 percent or 14.00 percent.

TEXAS USURY LAW

In the *Glossary of Mortgage Banking Terms* compiled by the Mortgage Bankers Association of America, usury is defined as "a maximum legal rate, established by state law, for interest, discounts or other fees that may be charged for the use of money. The ceiling may vary depending on the nature of the loan."

The implementation of usury laws by many states has affected the flow of capital into the state. For example, if the current national lending rate on mortgages secured by real property was 13.5 percent and a state legislature had enacted a statute making it illegal to charge more than 12 percent on a mortgage, then there would be no real estate mortgages made in that state.

Texas is presently working under a usury law adopted by the 67th Texas Legislature in 1981. This law amends the law that limited the interest rate on any written contract in Texas to 12 percent. The original law was to remain in effect until September 1981 and if the legislature had not passed the amendment, the maximum rate would have reverted to 10 percent.

The new law provides for a floating interest rate ceiling on written contracts with a maximum of 24 percent. The rate that will be allowed at any time for any written contract is based on the auction rate of 26-week U.S. Treasury bills. To calculate the maximum allowable interest rate, the auction rate is multiplied by 2. This auction is held weekly and is reported in many of the major newspapers and in the "money rate" section of *The Wall Street Journal.* In addition to the new ceiling, the law requires the consumer credit commissioner to

publish in the *Texas Register* the annualized, quarterly, and monthly interest rate ceilings. This is also a change, for in the previous law the rate was based on a different indicator and the savings and loan commissioner published the rate.

Since the 26-week U.S. Treasury bill auction is held on Monday of every week unless it is a federal holiday, the rate could change weekly. For example, if the result of the latest auction places the 26-week rate at 12.25 percent, the maximum would be $12.25 \times 2 = 24.50$ percent. Since this exceeds the maximum permitted rate of 24 percent, the rate would be published as 24 percent. With this information, it is possible to keep up with the movement in the maximum rate by checking each week for the results of the 26-week auction.

The usury law, in addition to outlining the method to be used to establish the usury rate for Texas, also requires the Consumer Credit Commissioner to publish on a regular basis the maximum interest rates that may be charged on certain types of credit transactions. This information is published in the *Texas Register.* An example of the information published is shown in Figure 1–3.

Even though the Texas legislature passed a usury law, the effect and scope of the law is severely limited by the passage of the federal Depository Institutions Deregulation and Monetary Control Act of 1980. This is the same law that was mentioned earlier in this chapter. Title V of this law preempts any state law that limits the amount of interest, discount points, finance charges, or other charges that will apply to certain types of mortgages.

Most important to the real estate industry is that the law exempted from any state usury law any first-lien mortgage on residential real property, any first lien on stock in a residential cooperative housing corporation where the loan, mortgage, or advance is used to finance the acquisition of stock in the cooperative, or any first lien on residential manufactured housing made or executed after March 31, 1980.

It should be noted that if a state wishes it can pass legislation or certify that the voters of the state have voted in favor of any provision, constitutional or otherwise, that states expressly that the state does not wish the provision of the act to apply in that state.

It should be further noted that when the original act became effective on April 1, 1980, the term *lender* was defined to be any lender approved by the Secretary of Housing and Urban Development for participation in any

Figure 1-3.   *Rate Ceilings*

Type of Rate Ceilings Effective Period (Dates are Inclusive)	Consumer[3] Agricultural/ Commercial[4] thru $250,000	Commercial[4] over $250,000
Indicated (Weekly) Rate—Article 1.04(a)(1) 01/23/84-01/29/84	18.00%	18.00%
Monthly Rate— Article 1.04(c)[1] 01/01/84-01/31/84	18.31%	18.31%
Standard Quarterly Rate—Article 1.04(a)(2) 01/01/84-03/31/84	18.00%	18.00%
Retail Credit Card Quarterly Rate— Article 1.11[3] 01/01/84-03/31/84	18.00%	N/A
Lender Credit Card Quarterly Rate— Article 15.02(d)[3] 01/01/84-03/31/84	17.92%	N/A
Standard Annual Rate— Article 1.04(a)(2)[2] 01/01/84-03/31/84	18.00%	18.00%
Retail Credit Card Annual Rate— Article 1.11[3] 01/01/84-03/31/84	18.00%	N/A
Annual Rate Applicable to Pre-July 1, 1983, Retail Credit Card and Lender Credit Card Balances with Annual Implementation Dates from 01/01/84-03/31/84	18.00%	N/A
Judgment Rate— Article 1.05, §2 02/01/84-02/29/84	10.00%	10.00%

(1) For variable rate commercial transactions only.
(2) Only for open-end credit as defined in Texas Civil Statutes, Article 5069-1.01(f).
(3) Credit for personal, family, or household use.
(4) Credit for business, commercial, investment, or other similar purpose.

   Issued in Austin, Texas, on January 16, 1984.

   TRD-840532   Sam Kelly
                     Consumer Credit Commissioner

SOURCE: Office of Consumer Credit Commissioner, State of Texas; *Texas Register*—January 20, 1984, p. 430.

mortgage insurance program under the National Housing Act. The Housing and Community Development Act of 1980 in Section 324 made several amendments to the Depository Institutions Deregulation and Monetary Control Act of 1980, but one of the most important of all of the amendments was that the definition of a lender was expanded to include the following language: ". . . and any individual who finances the sale or exchange of residential real property which such individual owns and which such individual occupies or has occupied as his principal residence."[1] This means that if a person wishes to sell his or her principal residence with a first lien mortgage, the transaction will be exempt from state usury.

   With these exemptions in mind, the present

Texas usury law has limited effect on the residential real estate market, primarily affecting, then, second mortgages and contracts for deed.

REVIEW QUESTIONS

1. Trace the development of financing of real estate in the United States.

2. Name and define the two basic money supply measurements used by the Federal Reserve.

3. What is the purpose of the Federal Reserve?

4. How does the Federal Reserve implement its policy concerning the money supply?

5. What are the tools the Fed uses to control the supply of money?

6. Explain the difference between a tight money policy and an easy money policy.

7. Name three other government agencies besides the Fed that may have a direct or indirect effect on the real estate market.

8. Name and explain the most important factor that affects interest rates in the United States.

9. Name and explain two interest rate indicators a real estate professional may use to predict future interest rates.

10. Define the term *usury* and give a brief explanation of the Texas Usury Law and how has it been affected by federal legislation.

NOTE

1. Public Law 96-399, October 8, 1980 (Housing and Community Development Act of 1980), Usury Provisions, Section 324(e).

2 Mortgages and Mortgage Instruments

LEARNING OBJECTIVES

In this chapter we will look in depth at the types of mortgages and standard instruments that are in common use in Texas. We will study the standard mortgage instruments of the Federal National Mortgage Association/Federal Home Loan Mortgage Corporation, the Veterans Administration, and the Federal Housing Administration.

Upon completion of the chapter you should be able to do the following:

★ Define the term *mortgage*.

★ Outline the early history of mortgages.

★ Explain the theories of mortgages.

★ List the categories and types of mortgages.

★ Thoroughly describe the mortgage instruments in common use in Texas.

DEFINITION

In *Webster's Eighth New Collegiate Dictionary*, mortgage is defined as "a conveyance of property . . . on condition that the conveyance becomes void on payment or performance according to stipulated terms."

In this chapter, we are going to see how this definition relates to mortgage instruments used in Texas. The primary mortgage instruments in this state are the note and the deed of trust.

HISTORY

The word *mortgage* has its roots in Latin and means *dead pledge*. In English common law there were two forms of property transfer when the property was used to secure a debt. One was known as *mortuum vadium*, so named because under the law the lender was entitled to all of the fruits of the land such as rents, minerals, and profits, thus making the land "dead" to the borrower. The second form, called *vivum vadium*, was more desirable. Under this form, the fruits of the land were still dead to the borrower, but they applied to the repayment of the loan. Out of these forms came the modern mortgage instruments.

In any transfer of property in Texas where the property is used as security for the debt, there are two distinct instruments used: the *promissory note* and the *deed of trust*. The note is the instrument that creates a personal indebtedness and defines the repayment terms of the debt, such as when payments are due, any late charges, and prepayment.

The deed of trust or mortgage is the procedural instrument of the transaction. The two instruments are similar in that they outline the requirements placed on the borrower and the lender. Some of the requirements or conditions that may be outlined in the mortgage or deed of trust are as follows:

1. How payments made by the borrower will be applied by the lender

2. The responsibility of the borrower for the maintenance of the property

3. Under what conditions the existing mortgage on the property may be assumed

4. The procedure that will be used to foreclose on the property if the borrower fails to make the required payments and the note goes into default

The major difference between a mortgage and a deed of trust is that the deed of trust introduces a third party—the trustee—into the transaction. The sole function of the trustee, not the lender, is to institute foreclosure proceedings if the note goes into default. These procedures involving a trustee are usually nonjudicial proceedings. With this power given to the trustee by the deed of trust, the trustee is said to have "naked title" to the property, but the true title rests in the hands of the borrower. The trustee is appointed, for the most part, by the lender and is usually the attorney who drew up the original note and deed of trust. There are exceptions to this rule. In Colorado, for example, there is only one trustee who may be used and this person is an elected county official, known as the Public Trustee.

It should be noted that the use of the deed of trust or mortgage as the procedural document is established by each state. A listing of the states and the procedural document used for one- to four-family transactions is shown in Figure 2–1.

THREE THEORIES OF MORTGAGES

There are three theories of mortgages used in the United States. In some states, more than one theory is used.

The Lien Theory

The lien theory is the most widely used theory in the United States—over 50 percent of the states, including Texas, use it. Under the lien theory, the title to the property remains with the borrower and the mortgage becomes an "encumbrance" or "cloud" on the title. Upon repayment of the debt, the encumbrance or cloud is removed from the property title.

The Title Theory

Under the title theory, the borrower passes title to the lender, subject to conditions. One of the conditions is usually the repayment of the debt. When the debt is paid, the title reverts to the owner. There are fourteen states that use this theory. These states are located along the East Coast and are primarily the original thirteen colonies.

The Intermediate Theory

The intermediate theory is a combination of the two theories mentioned above. In this theory, when the property is used as security, the mortgage becomes a lien on the property. If the borrower does not make the payments and the mortgage goes into default, the title passes to the lender, who then forecloses on the property. This theory is used in seven states.

CATEGORIES OF MORTGAGES

Now that we have discussed the theories of mortgages, let us identify the four broad categories of mortgages: conventional, VA, FHA, and housing bond. Each of these categories will be covered in detail in later chapters.

Conventional mortgage—Conventional mortgage commonly refers to any mortgage that is neither insured nor guaranteed by the United States government.

FHA mortgage—This mortgage is insured from loss by the FHA.

Veterans Administration guaranteed mortgage—A portion of this mortgage is guaranteed by the VA.

The Housing Bond Mortgage—This mortgage is any mortgage—conventional, FHA, or VA—that is funded by the sale of tax-exempt bonds issued by any state or political subdivision of a state.

TYPES OF MORTGAGES

There are many types of mortgages. They can, however, be divided into two distinct groups: *alternative mortgages* and *standard mortgages*. Alternative mortgages are mortgages where at least one of the four basic character-

Figure 2-1. Procedural Documents

STATE	DOCUMENT USED	STATE	DOCUMENT USED
Alabama	Mortgage	Nebraska	Mortgage
Alaska	Mortgage	Nevada	Deed of Trust
Arizona	Mortgage and Deed of Trust	New Hampshire	Mortgage
Arkansas	Mortgage	New Jersey	Mortgage
		New Mexico	Mortgage
California	Deed of Trust	New York	Mortgage
Colorado	Deed of Trust	North Carolina	Mortgage
Connecticut	Mortgage	North Dakota	Mortgage
Delaware	Mortgage	Ohio	Mortgage
D.C.	Deed of Trust	Oklahoma	Mortgage
		Oregon	Deed of Trust and Mortgage
Florida	Mortgage		
		Pennsylvania	Mortgage
Georgia	Deed of Trust	Puerto Rico/Virgin Islands	Mortgage
Hawaii	Mortgage	Rhode Island	Mortgage
Idaho	Deed of Trust	South Carolina	Mortgage
Illinois	Mortgage	South Dakota	Mortgage
Indiana	Mortgage		
Iowa	Mortgage	Tennessee	Deed of Trust
		Texas	Deed of Trust
Kansas	Mortgage		
Kentucky	Mortgage	Utah	Deed of Trust or Mortgage
Louisiana	Mortgage	Vermont	Deed of Trust and Mortgage
		Virginia	Deed of Trust
Maine	Mortgage		
Maryland	Mortgage	Washington	Deed of Trust/Mortgage
Massachusetts	Mortgage	West Virginia	Deed of Trust
Michigan	Mortgage	Wisconsin	Mortgage
Minnesota	Mortgage	Wyoming	Mortgage
Mississippi	Deed of Trust		
Missouri	Deed of Trust		
Montana	Deed of Trust and Mortgage		

SOURCE: Milwaukee, Wis., MGIC Investment Corporation, *The MGIC Guide to Secondary Marketing—March 1981*, pp. VIII-6-VIII-7.

istics of a mortgage is varied. Those character-istics are:

1. Amount of the principal

2. Interest rate

3. Payments, varied by time or amount

4. Repayment term

With a standard mortgage, characteristics 2 through 4 do not change. The amount of principal, however, decreases with each payment.

ALTERNATIVE MORTGAGES

Alternative mortgages are normally referred to as AMIs (alternative mortgage instruments). The AMI type of mortgage is becoming more common in the real estate industry as interest rates continue to increase and funds for real estate financing become less available. The most important factor that makes this type of mortgage appeal to the lender is that it allows the lender's return from the mortgage to keep up with the prevailing interest rate. It appeals to the borrower because many of the AMIs allow the borrower to qualify for a larger mortgage amount, by making the initial monthly payments lower and increasing them over a specified time as the borrower's income increases. Some of the more common AMIs are as follows:

Graduated payment mortgage (GPM)
Adjustable-rate mortgage (ARM)
Renegotiable-rate mortgage (RRM)
Growing equity mortgage (GEM)

These and many of the newest AMIs will be discussed in detail in Chapter 3.

STANDARD MORTGAGES

As a professional in the real estate industry, you should have a thorough understanding of each of the standard mortgages described below.

Budget Mortgage

Budget mortgage is another name for the standard fixed-term, fixed-rate real estate mortgage. The name is derived from the fact that the payments are constant over the life of the loan, thus the borrower may budget for or plan on a fixed payment. In addition to the fixed-payment feature of the loan, the borrower starts to build equity from the first payment. With the budget mortgage, the principal and interest (P & I) portion of the payment does not vary. The only variable in the payment is the amount that is needed to pay the taxes, insurance, private mortgage insurance, if any, and any other fees that if not paid may affect the title to the property. It should be noted that the amount that will be collected for the aforementioned or escrows is the total amount due each year divided by 12.

Since the borrower starts to build equity with the first month's payment, let us review how we would calculate the amount that would be credited to principal reduction and what portion of the payment would go to the payment of the interest charges for the first three payments of a 30-year, fixed-rate, fixed-term loan. The mortgage amount is $85,000; the interest rate is 13.25 percent. The first step is to calculate the monthly payment. This can be done using several methods: a payment book, a financial calculator, or the use of monthly payment factors. For this example, we are going to use the monthly payment factor. The monthly payment factor may be defined as an amount that is necessary to repay a loan of $1000 at a specific interest rate for a specific number of years. In this example we need the factor of a 30-year loan at 13.25. In Appendix A, the monthly payment factors (MPFs) are listed for 15-, 20-, 25- and 30-year mortgages for interest rates from 7 percent to 17 percent. Find the proper interest rate of 13.250 percent in the first column, then go across the row under the proper heading that describes the term—30 years or 360 months—in the far right column. The MPF is 11.2577. This means that we will repay the loan at the rate of $11.2577 per $1000 borrowed. To calculate the monthly payment (P & I only), we would multiply the monthly payment factor (MPF) times the loan amount divided by 1000, or

$$\text{MPF} \times \frac{\text{Loan Amount (LA)}}{\$1000} = \text{Monthly Payment}$$

For our example we would then insert the proper numbers in the formula:

$$\$11.2577 \times \frac{\$85,000}{1000} = \$956.9045$$

Thus, the monthly payment for P & I only would equal $956.9045 or $956.91.

Now let us calculate the amount of the first payment that will go to pay the interest charges and the amount of the payment that will be credited to principal reduction. First, the interest payment. We calculate the amount of interest that would be charged on the loan amount for a full year.

$$\$85,000 \times 13.250\% = \$11,262.50$$

Since we only need the amount for one month, we would divide this amount by 12 months or:

$$\frac{\$11,262.50}{12} = \$938.54$$

Therefore, the interest payment for the first payment would be $938.54 and the remainder of the total payment of $956.91 — that is, $956.91 minus $938.54 or $18.37 — would be credited to principal reduction. Thus, the balance on the loan would be the original loan amount minus the $18.37 or $84,981.63. If you would like to calculate the amount of principal reduction for the second payment you would follow the same steps of multiplying the new loan amount by the annual interest rate of 13.250 percent (.13250) to get the annual interest that would be paid, dividing that answer by 12 to get the monthly interest rate, then subtracting that amount from the total P & I payment of $956.91, giving the amount that would go to principal reduction:

1. Annual interest
   $$\$84,981.63 \times 13.250\% = \$11,260.06589$$
2. Monthly Interest Charge
   $$\frac{\$11,260.07}{12} = \$938.34$$
3. Principal Reduction
   $$\$956.91 - \$938.34 = \$18.57$$

These calculations show that in the first years of the loan the majority of the payments go to the payment of interest. Many times a borrower will ask, "How much will I pay back on my loan?" This is simple to calculate. Multiply the monthly payment for P & I times the total number of payments, or in this example $956.91 × 360 monthly payments for a total of $344,487.60 or approximately 4 times the amount borrowed.

Also let us calculate the amount of interest that would be paid over the term of a loan. Using the previous figure of $344,487.60, or the total amount repaid for the 30-year $85,000 loan. What portion of the total repayment would be interest? All that has to be done is to subtract the original loan amount from the total amount repaid or:

$$\$344,487.60 - \$85,000 = \$259,487.60$$

With these simple steps and the monthly payment factors, a real estate professional has the ability to calculate the above for any fixed-rate (from 7 to 17 percent), fixed-term (15-, 20-, 25-, or 30-year) mortgage.

Package Mortgage

A package type of self-amortizing mortgage takes the budget mortgage one step further. It is not only secured by the real property, but it includes some of the appliances and other items that are a part of the structure to be financed. The items that are often included in the package mortgage are stoves, ovens, dishwashers, carpet, heating, and air conditioning. One reason to include such easily removed items in a mortgage is that the lender is better able to protect the investment. The property is more sellable with these items in place. An important advantage for the borrower is that he or she can include the cost of these items in the mortgage and, therefore, be able to budget their cost.

The Blanket Mortgage (with release clause)

A blanket mortgage with release clause is normally used for financing the purchase and development of land or subdivisions. Under the blanket mortgage, the developer has the opportunity to include more than one piece of property, usually subdivision lots, with the ability to release a lot from the mortgage as it is sold. This means, for example, if a developer has a subdivision with 100 lots financed under a blanket mortgage with release clause, as the developer sells one of the lots, the developer pays off 1/100 of the total mortgage. The lender will release the parcel or lot from the mortgage, thus giving the person purchasing the lot clear title. Without the release clause capability, the developer would have to sell all 100 lots before clear title could be issued for any of the lots.

The Open-End Mortgage

As the name implies, there is no end to the open-end mortgage, for it has no due date. The balance is usually not paid off and can be as little as one dollar. Thus, the mortgage is still alive and the lender can lend funds without having to start the procedures of a new loan; the collateral for the original loan is still used for the new funds. This type of loan is primarily used to finance agriculture in rural areas, where the lenders are quite familiar with the borrowers and their financial capabilities. It has some use in today's real estate market.

Wrap or Wraparound Mortgage

As the name implies, a wraparound mortgage is used to include an existing mortgage on a piece of real property, thus wrapping the new financing around, or including, the existing mortgage. The wrap is usually at a higher interest rate than the existing mortgage, but the interest rate is usually less than the rate charged on new mortgages. This type of mortgage will be discussed in detail in Chapter 16.

Purchase-Money Mortgage or Owner-Financed Mortgage

With a purchase-money or owner-financed type of first-lien mortgage, the seller will execute a first-lien mortgage (that is, the first recorded mortgage on real property) for the remainder of the purchase price, after the prospective buyer has made the required down payment. This type of mortgage will also be explained in further detail in Chapter 16.

Second Mortgages or Junior Mortgages

As the name implies, second or junior mortgages are inferior to the first lien. The priority of the mortgages is established by the recording date: the mortgage that is recorded first is the first lien, the mortgage that is recorded second is the second, and so on. This priority becomes very important if a property is to be foreclosed against, because the mortgages will be paid off in the order of recording.

These types of mortgages are frequently used when a piece of real property is sold on assumption. An assumption sale involves the purchaser assuming the loan of the seller and paying the seller his or her equity in the property. For example, the seller wishes to sell a piece of real property for $60,000. If the mortgage has a balance of $40,000, the owner has an equity of $20,000. The lender will allow the purchaser to assume the existing mortgage and the purchaser can execute a second mortgage with the seller in the amount of $10,000. The purchaser, then, is only required to give the seller $10,000 in cash.

Construction Mortgage

A construction mortgage is used for the initial construction of a home or building, and it is sometimes called an *interim loan* or *interim financing*. Unlike other types of mortgages, it is funded as the work is completed on the improvement or home. These fundings are sometimes called *draws*. The interim lender usually makes periodic inspection of the construction site to see that the construction is progressing as scheduled.

This is a high-risk loan, unless the builder has a purchaser for the home or building, and therefore the interest rates are usually high. The rate is usually based upon the prime rate. The lender will charge anywhere from 1 to 6 percent above prime. If the prime rate is 13 percent, as it was in the third quarter of 1984, builders would have to pay anywhere from 14 to 19 percent interest on the construction loan, thus adding to the cost of the house. The term of these loans is relatively short, from as little as ninety days for a simple project to as long as three years for a major office building.

Contract for Deed

The contract for deed is not a true mortgage. It is mentioned in this section only because it is used in some types of transactions. As its name implies, it is a contract, and if the purchaser meets all of the provisions of the contract, he or she *may* sometime in the future get a deed to the property. A contract for deed has been used in the past to sell recreational land where the developer, due to previous financing, cannot give clear title to the property until the previous financing is paid and released. It is also used to sell low-quality rental property to the present tenant.

There are some severe drawbacks to this type of financing, including the following:

The contract for deed normally is not recorded, thus allowing a less-than-honest developer to sell a piece of property more than once.

A title policy may not be secured on the property.

Most severely, even though the purchaser makes all of the payments in good faith, he or she may not be able to receive clear title due to insanity of the seller or a death, divorce, or bankruptcy concerning the seller or a member of his or her family.

Recognizing all of the possible dangers to a purchase of recreational or resort-type lots, the federal government, through HUD, established the Office of Interstate Land Sales Registration with the passage of the Interstate Land Sales Full Disclosure Act in 1969. The purpose of the act was to police the sale of land by developers in subdivisions of fifty lots or more for lots less than five acres. Under the act, each developer must prepare and submit an Office of Interstate Land Sales Property Report Form.

This report requires the developer to answer certain questions and supply certain information. The developer must supply this report to the prospective purchaser before he or she signs any contract. If the purchaser does not receive a copy of the report prior to or at the time he or she enters into a contract with the seller, the purchaser may terminate the contract by notice to the seller. The purchaser must sign a statement that he or she has received a copy of the property report.

Deed of Trust Mortgage

The deed of trust mortgage is the most commonly used mortgage to secure payment of a debt secured by real property in Texas. As was discussed earlier in this chapter, Texas uses the lien theory of mortgages—the title to the property stays with the borrower and the mortgage becomes a cloud or charge on the title of the property. With the deed of trust, the title to the property securing the debt stays in the name of the borrower. But as the name implies, there is a third party to the transaction, the trustee, who is granted limited title. This is sometimes called "naked" or "dormant" title. The trustee is usually appointed by the lender, with the right of substitution.

With a deed of trust mortgage, there are actually two instruments involved. One is the deed of trust, which is a procedural document that actually names the trustee. The second document is the promissory note.

As discussed earlier, the trustee is given a limited title to the property and that lies dormant until there is necessity to foreclose. The trustee is the only person who has the right to initiate the foreclosure procedures. The process of foreclosure is started by the lender notifying the trustee that the borrower has not met the payment obligations of the note or is not in compliance with the covenants of the deed of trust and, therefore, the note has gone into default. The trustee is asked to start foreclosure procedures as outlined in the deed of trust.

Why was the deed of trust selected for use in Texas? Due to the Texas community property law, both husband and wife own the property. In the state of Texas, however, until the equal rights movement, women did not have the same legal rights or accountability as men, thus creating a doubt as to the outcome of court-ordered sale. For lenders to be encouraged to make a first-lien mortgage on real property in Texas, the state adopted the use of the deed of trust mortgage, which allows the trustee to sell the property without court proceedings when the note goes into default.

HOMESTEAD ACT AND COMMUNITY PROPERTY

Texas is one of several states that have both homestead and community property statutes. At this time we should review the major provisions of each.

Homestead Act

In Texas a homestead can be defined as the place of residence of either a family or single adult that is protected by law from forced sale by creditors. There are three exceptions, however, as outlined in Article 15, Section 50 of the state constitution:

Section 50. The homestead of a family, or of an unmarried adult, male or female, shall be, and is hereby protected from forced sale, for the payment of all debts except for the purchase money thereof, or a part of such purchase money, the taxes due thereon, or for work and material used in constructing improvements thereon, and in the last case only when the work and material are contracted for in writing, with the consent of both spouses, in the case of a family homestead, given in the same manner as is required in making a sale and conveyance of the homestead; nor may the owner or claimant of the property claimed as homestead, if married, sell or abandon the homestead without the consent of the other spouse, given in such manner as may be prescribed by law. No mortgage, trust deed, or other lien on the homestead shall ever be valid, except for the purchase money therefor, or improvements made thereon, as hereinbefore provided, whether such mortgage or trust deed, or other lien, shall have been created by the owner alone, or together with his or her spouse, in case the owner is married. All

Right To Repay," deals with the prepayment of the loan by the borrower. You will note that the borrower is given the right to make payments of principal at any time before they are due, but the borrower must notify the lender if he or she wishes to do so. In addition, the borrower is given the right to make full prepayment or partial prepayment without any prepayment charges. The note is specific as to how the lender will apply any prepayment, and that is to reduce the principal amount owed. One very important fact is stated in this section: Even though a borrower may make, for example, five payments at one time, it does not change the due date of the next scheduled payment.

Paragraph 5 deals with state usury laws. This paragraph states that if there is an interpretation of a state law setting the maximum loan charges that may be collected, and the amounts being collected are more than is allowed, then the note holder must bring the loan into compliance either by reducing the amount owed or paying a sum directly to the borrower.

Paragraph 6 of the note deals with the borrower not making payments on time or as required. Section A allows the lender to collect a late payment. The note states that if the note holder has not received the full amount of any monthly payment by the end of _____ calendar days after the due day of the payment, the lender may charge a late fee, which is normally 4 percent of the principal and interest payment. Normally the lender will insert 15 days in the blank. Section B is self-explanatory. Section C deals with the notices that may be sent to the borrower. The lenders will normally follow the steps as outlined in this section. You will note that the notice may be either delivered or mailed to the borrower. Section D is self-explanatory. Section E allows the lender to recover not only the amount owed by the borrower, but also all of the lenders' expenses incurred in the enforcement of the note, including reasonable attorneys' fees.

Paragraph 7 outlines the procedures that will be followed in the giving of notice. One change should be pointed out. In the old note, notice had to be sent by certified mail return receipt. This is not the case with the new note. Therefore, the note implies that notice is given by simply placing a letter in a mailbox.

Paragraph 8 (Figure 2–3), states that all persons signing the note are equally responsible for the repayment of the note. In addition, if a person or persons take over the note, that person or persons are responsible for the repayment of the note. According to the last

portion of this paragraph, the lender is given the right to enforce its rights against each person individually or against all persons on the note. Paragraph 9 states that the note is secured by a deed of trust of even date or with the same date. The paragraph further states under what conditions the borrower may be required to make payment in full. You will note there is an example of one of the conditions in the deed of trust that may cause the lender to call the note due and payable. The example deals with an assumption of the property used as security for the note and deed of trust.

The Deed of Trust.   Let us now examine the deed of trust (Figure 2-4) that must accompany the note. This document is referred to in the note.

The deed of trust is the instrument that will outline the procedures to be followed during the life of the mortgage. The first page of the standard FNMA/FHLMC Deed of Trust indicates the date of the instrument. It identifies the grantor or borrower, the trustee, and the beneficiary or the lender. This section, therefore, identifies all three parties to the deed. The borrower grants and conveys to the trustee the power of sale of the property that is used to secure the property. As stated early in this chapter, the trustee may not sell the property until he or she is notified that: (1) the borrower has not made the payment in accordance with the note, or (2) the note is in default.

In the third paragraph of the first page of the deed, the borrower states or covenants that he or she has the capacity to grant and convey the property and will defend the title of the property against any claims and demands other than the exceptions that are listed in a title policy.

The remainder of the deed of trust contains the covenants or the rules to be followed by all parties. These covenants are divided into two parts. The first is the uniform covenants. This means that these covenants are the same in all standard FNMA/FHLMC uniform instruments. Thus, if you sign a standard FNMA/FHLMC deed of trust in Texas, or any other state, the uniform covenants are the same.

The second group of covenants is the non-uniform covenants. This section is added to the deed of trust to make it conform to the laws of Texas covering real property. The most important of these covenants is covenant 19, which outlines the procedures for foreclosure.

Figure 2-3.   Texas Fixed-Rate Note, page 2

8. OBLIGATIONS OF PERSONS UNDER THIS NOTE

If more than one person signs this Note, each person is fully and personally obligated to keep all of the promises made in this Note, including the promise to pay the full amount owed. Any person who is a guarantor, surety or endorser of this Note is also obligated to do these things. Any person who takes over these obligations, including the obligations of a guarantor, surety or endorser of this Note, is also obligated to keep all of the promises made in this Note. The Note Holder may enforce its rights under this Note against each person individually or against all of us together. This means that any one of us may be required to pay all of the amounts owed under this Note.

9. WAIVERS

I and any other person who has obligations under this Note waive notice of intention to accelerate, except as provided in Section 6 (C) above, and the rights of presentment and notice of dishonor. "Presentment" means the right to require the Note Holder to demand payment of amounts due. "Notice of dishonor" means the right to require the Note Holder to give notice to other persons that amounts due have not been paid.

10. UNIFORM SECURED NOTE

This Note is a uniform instrument with limited variations in some jurisdictions. In addition to the protections given to the Note Holder under this Note, a Mortgage, Deed of Trust or Security Deed (the "Security Instrument"), dated the same date as this Note, protects the Note Holder from possible losses which might result if I do not keep the promises which I make in this Note. That Security Instrument describes how and under what conditions I may be required to make immediate payment in full of all amounts I owe under this Note. Some of those conditions are described as follows:

Transfer of the Property or a Beneficial Interest in Borrower. If all or any part of the Property or any interest in it is sold or transferred (or if a beneficial interest in Borrower is sold or transferred and Borrower is not a natural person) without Lender's prior written consent, Lender may, at its option, require immediate payment in full of all sums secured by this Security Instrument. However, this option shall not be exercised by Lender if exercise is prohibited by federal law as of the date of this Security Instrument.

If Lender exercises this option, Lender shall give Borrower notice of acceleration. The notice shall provide a period of not less than 30 days from the date the notice is delivered or mailed within which Borrower must pay all sums secured by this Security Instrument. If Borrower fails to pay these sums prior to the expiration of this period, Lender may invoke any remedies permitted by this Security Instrument without further notice or demand on Borrower.

WITNESS THE HAND(S) AND SEAL(S) OF THE UNDERSIGNED.

....(Seal)
-Borrower

....(Seal)
-Borrower

....(Seal)
-Borrower

[Sign Original Only]

Figure 2-4.   Texas Single-Family Deed of Trust

——————————————— [Space Above This Line For Recording Data] ———————————————

DEED OF TRUST

THIS DEED OF TRUST ("Security Instrument") is made on ....,
19............ The grantor is ....
.... ("Borrower"). The trustee is ....
...., whose address is
....
("Trustee"). The beneficiary is ....,
which is organized and existing under the laws of ....,
and whose address is ....
.... ("Lender").
Borrower owes Lender the principal sum of ....
.... Dollars (U.S. $...). This debt is evidenced by
Borrower's note dated the same date as this Security Instrument ("Note"), which provides for monthly payments, with the
full debt, if not paid earlier, due and payable on ....
This Security Instrument secures to Lender: (a) the repayment of the debt evidenced by the Note, with interest, and all
renewals, extensions and modifications; (b) the payment of all other sums, with interest, advanced under paragraph 7 to
protect the security of this Security Instrument; and (c) the performance of Borrower's covenants and agreements under
this Security Instrument and the Note. For this purpose, Borrower irrevocably grants and conveys to Trustee, in trust,
with power of sale, the following described property located in .... County, Texas:

which has the address of ...., ...,
                                                          [Street]   [City]
Texas .... ("Property Address");
                    [Zip Code]

TOGETHER WITH all the improvements now or hereafter erected on the property, and all easements, rights,
appurtenances, rents, royalties, mineral, oil and gas rights and profits, water rights and stock and all fixtures now or
hereafter a part of the property. All replacements and additions shall also be covered by this Security Instrument. All of the
foregoing is referred to in this Security Instrument as the "Property."

BORROWER COVENANTS that Borrower is lawfully seised of the estate hereby conveyed and has the right to grant
and convey the Property and that the Property is unencumbered, except for encumbrances of record. Borrower warrants
and will defend generally the title to the Property against all claims and demands, subject to any encumbrances of record.

THIS SECURITY INSTRUMENT combines uniform covenants for national use and non-uniform covenants with
limited variations by jurisdiction to constitute a uniform security instrument covering real property.

TEXAS—Single Family—FNMA/FHLMC UNIFORM INSTRUMENT   Form 3044 12/83

Figure 2-5.   **Texas Single-Family Deed of Trust Covenants 1-7**

UNIFORM COVENANTS.   Borrower and Lender covenant and agree as follows:

   1.   Payment of Principal and Interest; Prepayment and Late Charges.   Borrower shall promptly pay when due the principal of and interest on the debt evidenced by the Note and any prepayment and late charges due under the Note.

   2.   Funds for Taxes and Insurance.   Subject to applicable law or to a written waiver by Lender, Borrower shall pay to Lender on the day monthly payments are due under the Note, until the Note is paid in full, a sum ("Funds") equal to one-twelfth of: (a) yearly taxes and assessments which may attain priority over this Security Instrument; (b) yearly leasehold payments or ground rents on the Property, if any; (c) yearly hazard insurance premiums; and (d) yearly mortgage insurance premiums, if any. These items are called "escrow items." Lender may estimate the Funds due on the basis of current data and reasonable estimates of future escrow items.

   The Funds shall be held in an institution the deposits or accounts of which are insured or guaranteed by a federal or state agency (including Lender if Lender is such an institution). Lender shall apply the Funds to pay the escrow items. Lender may not charge for holding and applying the Funds, analyzing the account or verifying the escrow items, unless Lender pays Borrower interest on the Funds and applicable law permits Lender to make such a charge. Borrower and Lender may agree in writing that interest shall be paid on the Funds. Unless an agreement is made or applicable law requires interest to be paid, Lender shall not be required to pay Borrower any interest or earnings on the Funds. Lender shall give to Borrower, without charge, an annual accounting of the Funds showing credits and debits to the Funds and the purpose for which each debit to the Funds was made. The Funds are pledged as additional security for the sums secured by this Security Instrument.

   If the amount of the Funds held by Lender, together with the future monthly payments of Funds payable prior to the due dates of the escrow items, shall exceed the amount required to pay the escrow items when due, the excess shall be, at Borrower's option, either promptly repaid to Borrower or credited to Borrower on monthly payments of Funds. If the amount of the Funds held by Lender is not sufficient to pay the escrow items when due, Borrower shall pay to Lender any amount necessary to make up the deficiency in one or more payments as required by Lender.

   Upon payment in full of all sums secured by this Security Instrument, Lender shall promptly refund to Borrower any Funds held by Lender. If under paragraph 19 the Property is sold or acquired by Lender, Lender shall apply, no later than immediately prior to the sale of the Property or its acquisition by Lender, any Funds held by Lender at the time of application as a credit against the sums secured by this Security Instrument.

   3.   Application of Payments.   Unless applicable law provides otherwise, all payments received by Lender under paragraphs 1 and 2 shall be applied: first, to late charges due under the Note; second, to prepayment charges due under the Note; third, to amounts payable under paragraph 2; fourth, to interest due; and last, to principal due.

   4.   Charges; Liens.   Borrower shall pay all taxes, assessments, charges, fines and impositions attributable to the Property which may attain priority over this Security Instrument, and leasehold payments or ground rents, if any. Borrower shall pay these obligations in the manner provided in paragraph 2, or if not paid in that manner, Borrower shall pay them on time directly to the person owed payment. Borrower shall promptly furnish to Lender all notices of amounts to be paid under this paragraph. If Borrower makes these payments directly, Borrower shall promptly furnish to Lender receipts evidencing the payments.

   Borrower shall promptly discharge any lien which has priority over this Security Instrument unless Borrower: (a) agrees in writing to the payment of the obligation secured by the lien in a manner acceptable to Lender; (b) contests in good faith the lien by, or defends against enforcement of the lien in, legal proceedings which in the Lender's opinion operate to prevent the enforcement of the lien or forfeiture of any part of the Property; or (c) secures from the holder of the lien an agreement satisfactory to Lender subordinating the lien to this Security Instrument. If Lender determines that any part of the Property is subject to a lien which may attain priority over this Security Instrument, Lender may give Borrower a notice identifying the lien. Borrower shall satisfy the lien or take one or more of the actions set forth above within 10 days of the giving of notice.

   5.   Hazard Insurance.   Borrower shall keep the improvements now existing or hereafter erected on the Property insured against loss by fire, hazards included within the term "extended coverage" and any other hazards for which Lender requires insurance. This insurance shall be maintained in the amounts and for the periods that Lender requires. The insurance carrier providing the insurance shall be chosen by Borrower subject to Lender's approval which shall not be unreasonably withheld.

   All insurance policies and renewals shall be acceptable to Lender and shall include a standard mortgage clause. Lender shall have the right to hold the policies and renewals. If Lender requires, Borrower shall promptly give to Lender all receipts of paid premiums and renewal notices. In the event of loss, Borrower shall give prompt notice to the insurance carrier and Lender. Lender may make proof of loss if not made promptly by Borrower.

   Unless Lender and Borrower otherwise agree in writing, insurance proceeds shall be applied to restoration or repair of the Property damaged, if the restoration or repair is economically feasible and Lender's security is not lessened. If the restoration or repair is not economically feasible or Lender's security would be lessened, the insurance proceeds shall be applied to the sums secured by this Security Instrument, whether or not then due, with any excess paid to Borrower. If Borrower abandons the Property, or does not answer within 30 days a notice from Lender that the insurance carrier has offered to settle a claim, then Lender may collect the insurance proceeds. Lender may use the proceeds to repair or restore the Property or to pay sums secured by this Security Instrument, whether or not then due. The 30-day period will begin when the notice is given.

   Unless Lender and Borrower otherwise agree in writing, any application of proceeds to principal shall not extend or postpone the due date of the monthly payments referred to in paragraphs 1 and 2 or change the amount of the payments. If under paragraph 19 the Property is acquired by Lender, Borrower's right to any insurance policies and proceeds resulting from damage to the Property prior to the acquisition shall pass to Lender to the extent of the sums secured by this Security Instrument immediately prior to the acquisition.

   6.   Preservation and Maintenance of Property; Leaseholds.   Borrower shall not destroy, damage or substantially change the Property, allow the Property to deteriorate or commit waste. If this Security Instrument is on a leasehold, Borrower shall comply with the provisions of the lease, and if Borrower acquires fee title to the Property, the leasehold and fee title shall not merge unless Lender agrees to the merger in writing.

   7.   Protection of Lender's Rights in the Property; Mortgage Insurance.   If Borrower fails to perform the covenants and agreements contained in this Security Instrument, or there is a legal proceeding that may significantly affect Lender's rights in the Property (such as a proceeding in bankruptcy, probate, for condemnation or to enforce laws or regulations), then Lender may do and pay for whatever is necessary to protect the value of the Property and Lender's rights in the Property. Lender's actions may include paying any sums secured by a lien which has priority over this Security Instrument, appearing in court, paying reasonable attorneys' fees and entering on the Property to make repairs. Although Lender may take action under this paragraph 7, Lender does not have to do so.

   Any amounts disbursed by Lender under this paragraph 7 shall become additional debt of Borrower secured by this Security Instrument. Unless Borrower and Lender agree to other terms of payment, these amounts shall bear interest from the date of disbursement at the Note rate and shall be payable, with interest, upon notice from Lender to Borrower requesting payment.

Figure 2-6.   *Texas Single-Family Deed of Trust Covenants 8-18*

If Lender required mortgage insurance as a condition of making the loan secured by this Security Instrument, Borrower shall pay the premiums required to maintain the insurance in effect until such time as the requirement for the insurance terminates in accordance with Borrower's and Lender's written agreement or applicable law.

8. Inspection.   Lender or its agent may make reasonable entries upon and inspections of the Property. Lender shall give Borrower notice at the time of or prior to an inspection specifying reasonable cause for the inspection.

9. Condemnation.   The proceeds of any award or claim for damages, direct or consequential, in connection with any condemnation or other taking of any part of the Property, or for conveyance in lieu of condemnation, are hereby assigned and shall be paid to Lender.

In the event of a total taking of the Property, the proceeds shall be applied to the sums secured by this Security Instrument, whether or not then due, with any excess paid to Borrower. In the event of a partial taking of the Property, unless Borrower and Lender otherwise agree in writing, the sums secured by this Security Instrument shall be reduced by the amount of the proceeds multiplied by the following fraction: (a) the total amount of the sums secured immediately before the taking, divided by (b) the fair market value of the Property immediately before the taking. Any balance shall be paid to Borrower.

If the Property is abandoned by Borrower, or if, after notice by Lender to Borrower that the condemnor offers to make an award or settle a claim for damages, Borrower fails to respond to Lender within 30 days after the date the notice is given, Lender is authorized to collect and apply the proceeds, at its option, either to restoration or repair of the Property or to the sums secured by this Security Instrument, whether or not then due.

Unless Lender and Borrower otherwise agree in writing, any application of proceeds to principal shall not extend or postpone the due date of the monthly payments referred to in paragraphs 1 and 2 or change the amount of such payments.

10. Borrower Not Released; Forbearance By Lender Not a Waiver.   Extension of the time for payment or modification of amortization of the sums secured by this Security Instrument granted by Lender to any successor in interest of Borrower shall not operate to release the liability of the original Borrower or Borrower's successors in interest. Lender shall not be required to commence proceedings against any successor in interest or refuse to extend time for payment or otherwise modify amortization of the sums secured by this Security Instrument by reason of any demand made by the original Borrower or Borrower's successors in interest. Any forbearance by Lender in exercising any right or remedy shall not be a waiver of or preclude the exercise of any right or remedy.

11. Successors and Assigns Bound; Joint and Several Liability; Co-signers.   The covenants and agreements of this Security Instrument shall bind and benefit the successors and assigns of Lender and Borrower, subject to the provisions of paragraph 17. Borrower's covenants and agreements shall be joint and several. Any Borrower who co-signs this Security Instrument but does not execute the Note: (a) is co-signing this Security Instrument only to mortgage, grant and convey that Borrower's interest in the Property under the terms of this Security Instrument; (b) is not personally obligated to pay the sums secured by this Security Instrument; and (c) agrees that Lender and any other Borrower may agree to extend, modify, forbear or make any accommodations with regard to the terms of this Security Instrument or the Note without that Borrower's consent.

12. Loan Charges.   If the loan secured by this Security Instrument is subject to a law which sets maximum loan charges, and that law is finally interpreted so that the interest or other loan charges collected or to be collected in connection with the loan exceed the permitted limits, then: (a) any such loan charge shall be reduced by the amount necessary to reduce the charge to the permitted limit; and (b) any sums already collected from Borrower which exceeded permitted limits will be refunded to Borrower. Lender may choose to make this refund by reducing the principal owed under the Note or by making a direct payment to Borrower. If a refund reduces principal, the reduction will be treated as a partial prepayment without any prepayment charge under the Note.

13. Legislation Affecting Lender's Rights.   If enactment or expiration of applicable laws has the effect of rendering any provision of the Note or this Security Instrument unenforceable according to its terms, Lender, at its option, may require immediate payment in full of all sums secured by this Security Instrument and may invoke any remedies permitted by paragraph 19. If Lender exercises this option, Lender shall take the steps specified in the second paragraph of paragraph 17.

14. Notices.   Any notice to Borrower provided for in this Security Instrument shall be given by delivering it or by mailing it by first class mail unless applicable law requires use of another method. The notice shall be directed to the Property Address or any other address Borrower designates by notice to Lender. Any notice to Lender shall be given by first class mail to Lender's address stated herein or any other address Lender designates by notice to Borrower. Any notice provided for in this Security Instrument shall be deemed to have been given to Borrower or Lender when given as provided in this paragraph.

15. Governing Law; Severability.   This Security Instrument shall be governed by federal law and the law of the jurisdiction in which the Property is located. In the event that any provision or clause of this Security Instrument or the Note conflicts with applicable law, such conflict shall not affect other provisions of this Security Instrument or the Note which can be given effect without the conflicting provision. To this end the provisions of this Security Instrument and the Note are declared to be severable.

16. Borrower's Copy.   Borrower shall be given one conformed copy of the Note and of this Security Instrument.

17. Transfer of the Property or a Beneficial Interest in Borrower.   If all or any part of the Property or any interest in it is sold or transferred (or if a beneficial interest in Borrower is sold or transferred and Borrower is not a natural person) without Lender's prior written consent, Lender may, at its option, require immediate payment in full of all sums secured by this Security Instrument. However, this option shall not be exercised by Lender if exercise is prohibited by federal law as of the date of this Security Instrument.

If Lender exercises this option, Lender shall give Borrower notice of acceleration. The notice shall provide a period of not less than 30 days from the date the notice is delivered or mailed within which Borrower must pay all sums secured by this Security Instrument. If Borrower fails to pay these sums prior to the expiration of this period, Lender may invoke any remedies permitted by this Security Instrument without further notice or demand on Borrower.

18. Borrower's Right to Reinstate.   If Borrower meets certain conditions, Borrower shall have the right to have enforcement of this Security Instrument discontinued at any time prior to the earlier of: (a) 5 days (or such other period as applicable law may specify for reinstatement) before sale of the Property pursuant to any power of sale contained in this Security Instrument; or (b) entry of a judgment enforcing this Security Instrument. Those conditions are that Borrower: (a) pays Lender all sums which then would be due under this Security Instrument and the Note had no acceleration occurred; (b) cures any default of any other covenants or agreements; (c) pays all expenses incurred in enforcing this Security Instrument, including, but not limited to, reasonable attorneys' fees; and (d) takes such action as Lender may reasonably require to assure that the lien of this Security Instrument, Lender's rights in the Property and Borrower's obligation to pay the sums secured by this Security Instrument shall continue unchanged. Upon reinstatement by Borrower, this Security Instrument and the obligations secured hereby shall remain fully effective as if no acceleration had occurred. However, this right to reinstate shall not apply in the case of acceleration under paragraphs 13 or 17.

Figure 2-7.   **Texas Single-Family Deed of Trust Covenants 19-27**

NON-UNIFORM COVENANTS. Borrower and Lender further covenant and agree as follows:

19. Acceleration; Remedies. Lender shall give notice to Borrower prior to acceleration following Borrower's breach of any covenant or agreement in this Security Instrument (but not prior to acceleration under paragraphs 13 and 17 unless applicable law provides otherwise). The notice shall specify: (a) the default; (b) the action required to cure the default; (c) a date, not less than 30 days from the date the notice is given to Borrower, by which the default must be cured; and (d) that failure to cure the default on or before the date specified in the notice will result in acceleration of the sums secured by this Security Instrument and sale of the Property. The notice shall further inform Borrower of the right to reinstate after acceleration and the right to bring a court action to assert the non-existence of a default or any other defense of Borrower to acceleration and sale. If the default is not cured on or before the date specified in the notice, Lender at its option may require immediate payment in full of all sums secured by this Security Instrument without further demand and may invoke the power of sale and any other remedies permitted by applicable law. Lender shall be entitled to collect all expenses incurred in pursuing the remedies provided in this paragraph 19, including, but not limited to, reasonable attorneys' fees and costs of title evidence.

If Lender invokes the power of sale, Lender or Trustee shall give notice of the time, place and terms of sale by posting and recording the notice at least 21 days prior to sale as provided by applicable law. Lender shall mail a copy of the notice of sale to Borrower in the manner prescribed by applicable law. Sale shall be made at public vendue between the hours of 10 a.m. and 4 p.m. on the first Tuesday in any month. Borrower authorizes Trustee to sell the Property to the highest bidder for cash in one or more parcels and in any order Trustee determines. Lender or its designee may purchase the Property at any sale.

Trustee shall deliver to the purchaser Trustee's deed conveying indefeasible title to the Property with covenants of general warranty. Borrower covenants and agrees to defend generally the purchaser's title to the Property against all claims and demands. The recitals in the Trustee's deed shall be prima facie evidence of the truth of the statements made therein. Trustee shall apply the proceeds of the sale in the following order: (a) to all expenses of the sale, including, but not limited to, reasonable Trustee's and attorneys' fees; (b) to all sums secured by this Security Instrument; and (c) any excess to the person or persons legally entitled to it.

If the Property is sold pursuant to this paragraph 19, Borrower or any person holding possession of the Property through Borrower shall immediately surrender possession of the Property to the purchaser at that sale. If possession is not surrendered, Borrower or such person shall be a tenant at sufferance and may be removed by writ of possession.

20. Lender in Possession. Upon acceleration under paragraph 19 or abandonment of the Property, Lender (in person, by agent or by judicially appointed receiver) shall be entitled to enter upon, take possession of and manage the Property and to collect the rents of the Property including those past due. Any rents collected by Lender or the receiver shall be applied first to payment of the costs of management of the Property and collection of rents, including, but not limited to, receiver's fees, premiums on receiver's bonds and reasonable attorneys' fees, and then to the sums secured by this Security Instrument.

21. Release. Upon payment of all sums secured by this Security Instrument, Lender shall release this Security Instrument without charge to Borrower. Borrower shall pay any recordation costs.

22. Substitute Trustee. Lender, at its option and with or without cause, may from time to time remove Trustee and appoint, by power of attorney or otherwise, a successor trustee to any Trustee appointed hereunder. Without conveyance of the Property, the successor trustee shall succeed to all the title, power and duties conferred upon Trustee herein and by applicable law.

23. Subrogation. Any of the proceeds of the Note used to take up outstanding liens against all or any part of the Property have been advanced by Lender at Borrower's request and upon Borrower's representation that such amounts are due and are secured by valid liens against the Property. Lender shall be subrogated to any and all rights, superior titles, liens and equities owned or claimed by any owner or holder of any outstanding liens and debts, regardless of whether said liens or debts are acquired by Lender by assignment or are released by the holder thereof upon payment.

24. Partial Invalidity. In the event any portion of the sums intended to be secured by this Security Instrument cannot be lawfully secured hereby, payments in reduction of such sums shall be applied first to those portions not secured hereby.

25. Waiver of Notice of Intention to Accelerate. Borrower waives the right to notice of intention to require immediate payment in full of all sums secured by this Security Instrument except as provided in paragraph 19.

26. Riders to this Security Instrument. If one or more riders are executed by Borrower and recorded together with this Security Instrument, the covenants and agreements of each such rider shall be incorporated into and shall amend and supplement the covenants and agreements of this Security Instrument as if the rider(s) were a part of this Security Instrument. [Check applicable box(es)]

☐ Adjustable Rate Rider   ☐ Condominium Rider   ☐ 2–4 Family Rider

☐ Graduated Payment Rider   ☐ Planned Unit Development Rider

☐ Other(s) [specify]

27. Purchase Money; Vendor's Lien; Renewal and Extension. [Complete as appropriate]

BY SIGNING BELOW, Borrower accepts and agrees to the terms and covenants contained in this Security Instrument and in any rider(s) executed by Borrower and recorded with it.

....(Seal)
—Borrower

....(Seal)
—Borrower

———————————————— [Space Below This Line For Acknowledgment] ————————————————

First, let us review some of the more important uniform covenants (Figure 2–5).

Covenant 1. This is the payment covenant in which the borrower agrees to make the payments on time and to pay any late charges as outlined in the note accompanying the deed of trust.

Covenant 2. Paragraph one of covenant 2 allows the lender to set up an escrow account until the note is paid in full. The escrow payment is due on the same day the monthly principal and interest payment is due. The amount of the payment is equal to one-twelfth of the taxes and assessments, which may affect the title or take priority over the deed of trust. In addition, the lender may collect one-twelfth of the annual premium for hazard insurance. This assures the lender that there is insurance coverage for any loss due to the nonpayment of taxes or loss due to lack of insurance coverage of the structure. This has an advantage for the homeowner in that he or she does not have to make one large payment at the end of each year to cover both the taxes and insurance. This paragraph also allows the lender to collect one-twelfth of the annual premium for mortgage insurance, if any is required.

Also in this covenant, the lender is required to keep the funds collected in an institution that is insured or guaranteed by an agency of a state government. It provides that the lender may not charge the borrower for holding the funds, applying the funds, or supplying the borrower with an accounting of the funds.

Paragraph three of this covenant outlines the procedures to be followed if there is an excess in the account after all of the taxes and so on have been paid. If there are insufficient funds in the account to meet the necessary payments, the deed declares what the lender must do to notify the borrower that there is a deficiency. The paragraph further states that the borrower has 30 days to make the necessary payment to bring the account to the required amount.

The last paragraph of this covenant specifies procedures to be followed regarding the balance in the escrow account when the loan is paid in full.

Covenant 3. This covenant indicates how the payments made by the borrower must be applied by the lender, unless otherwise dictated by law or agreed to by all parties in the deed of trust.

Covenant 4. Here the deed outlines the responsibility of the borrower as to the payment of any taxes, assessments, and other charges, fines, and impositions on the property that may, as the covenant says, "attain priority over this Security Instrument, and lease hold payments or ground rents, if any."

Covenant 5. This part deals with hazard insurance that the borrower must carry on the property securing the debt, as mentioned in the deed of trust. This covenant also states that the borrower may choose the carrier, but the carrier or insurance company must be acceptable to the lender. The last section of the covenant outlines the procedures to be followed in case of loss to the property, and how any proceeds paid by the insurance shall be applied to the restoration or repair of the property. The final paragraph of the covenant states that "unless the Lender and Borrower otherwise agree in writing, any applications of proceeds to principal shall not extend or postpone the due date of the monthly payments referred to in paragraphs 1 and 2 — or change the amount of the payments."

Covenant 6. Here the borrower is charged with the responsibility for maintenance of the property.

Covenant 7. Covenant 7 indicates that if the borrower fails to perform the covenants and agreements, or if any action or proceeding is commenced which materially affects the lenders interest in the property, including but not limited to, eminent domain, insolvency, action can be taken by the lender to protect the investment, including entry to the property to make any necessary repairs. As outlined in the last paragraph of this covenant, any monies, plus interest, disbursed by the lender shall become part of the indebtedness of the borrower unless some other arrangement is made in writing between the borrower and the lender.

Covenant 8. (Figure 2–6) This covenant allows the lender, with proper notice and reason for an inspection, to enter onto the property.

Covenant 9. Here the deed outlines the action that will be taken if the property is taken by condemnation. The first sentence declares that any proceeds of any award or claim of damages having to do with condemnation are assigned to the lender.

The second paragraph of this covenant states that if the property is taken in total, all awards will be applied to the mortgage secured by the deed of trust, and if there is any excess, the excess will be paid to the borrower. The second part of this paragraph outlines the procedures to be followed if the property is only partially taken.

Covenant 14. Covenant 14 sets the procedures for notification (for foreclosure, acceleration, inspection, etc.) and states how that notice must be given unless otherwise specified by law. The lender is to notify by certified mail, return receipt requested, and mailing or delivering the notice to the borrower at the property address or to an address designated by the borrower (by notice to the lender). The borrower, in order to give notice to the lender, must also send or deliver such notice certified mail, return receipt requested, to the lender's address or to another address the lender may designate (by notice to the borrower). (Actually, it is a good idea that *all* inquiries to the lender by you or your clients be sent by this method.)

Covenant 17. This is one of the more important paragraphs to the real estate professional, because it outlines the procedures to be followed by the borrower if he or she wishes to sell, by assumption, the property secured by a standard FNMA/FHLMC Deed of Trust.

This covenant has been revised. The revision was brought about by changes in federal laws covering the assumption of some conventional mortgages. According to the first paragraph, if all or any part of the property or any interest in the property is sold or transferred, the borrower must notify the lender. If the transfer or sale is completed without the express written approval of the lender, the lender, at the lender's option, may require the immediate repayment of all sums with interest. The second paragraph outlines the procedures that will be followed if the lender does exercise the option to require immediate repayment of the loan.

Covenant 18. This covenant outlines the procedure to be followed by the borrower to "reinstate" once the lender has enforced the foreclosure provisions of the deed of trust. You will note that the last sentence of the covenant states, "However, this right to reinstate shall not apply in the case of acceleration under paragraphs (Covenants) 13 and 17." These two paragraphs deal with legislation affecting lender's rights and assumption or the transfer of the property.

Covenant 19. (Figure 2–7). This covenant is used to bring the power of sale clause in the deed of trust into compliance with the laws of Texas. The law is very specific as to the methods to be used. In brief, a notice of sale must be posted at least twenty-one days prior to the day of the sale. The day of sale is set by law as the first Tuesday of the month. This notice must be posted at the courthouse in the county where the property is located. If the property is located in more than one county, a notice is to be posted at the courthouse door

in each of the counties. In addition, the law is specific as to when and where the sale will be held: the sale must be in public view and between 10 a.m. and 4 p.m.

In addition to the notice posted at the courthouse door, the trustee must notify the borrower at least 21 days prior to the sale by certified mail. But before this notice of sale is sent to the borrower and posted, an additional notice is required to be sent to the borrower as per covenant 14 of the deed of trust, to outline the following:

1. The breach

2. The action required to cure such breach

3. A date, not less than thirty days from the date the notice is mailed to the borrower, by which such breach must be cured

4. That failure to cure such breach on or before the date specified in the notice will result in acceleration of the sums secured by the deed of trust and sale of the property

This section also outlines the type of deed to be delivered by the trustee to the purchaser of the property at a trustee sale.

Covenant 21. This paragraph requires the lender to supply to the borrower a release upon the repayment of the monies advanced by the lender. The lender may not charge for the release, but the borrower shall pay for all charges for the recording of the release. The filing of the release is very important, for until the release is filed, the real property records will show that there is a lien against the property. The filing of the release is normally the responsibility of the borrower.

Covenant 26. This new covenant, entitled "Riders to this Security Instrument," is used as a checklist and to indicate which of the listed riders will accompany the deed of trust. The borrower will need to sign each of the riders that will accompany the deed of trust. The first two riders listed in covenant 26 will be discussed in Chapter 3.

If the property used as security is a condominium, the condominium rider (Figure 2–8) will be made a part of the deed of trust. The first section of the rider makes reference to the note and the deed of trust, gives the address of the property and names the condo project. The next portion of the rider, entitled "Condominium Covenants," is in addition to the covenants listed in the deed of trust.

The planned unit development rider (Figure 2–9) will be used if the property used as secu-

Figure 2-8.   FNMA/FHLMC Condominium Rider

CONDOMINIUM RIDER

THIS CONDOMINIUM RIDER is made this .... day of ...., 19........, and is incorporated into and shall be deemed to amend and supplement the Mortgage, Deed of Trust or Security Deed (the "Security Instrument") of the same date given by the undersigned (the "Borrower") to secure Borrower's Note to .... (the "Lender") of the same date and covering the Property described in the Security Instrument and located at:

....
[Property Address]

The Property includes a unit in, together with an undivided interest in the common elements of, a condominium project known as:

....
[Name of Condominium Project]

(the "Condominium Project"). If the owners association or other entity which acts for the Condominium Project (the "Owners Association") holds title to property for the benefit or use of its members or shareholders, the Property also includes Borrower's interest in the Owners Association and the uses, proceeds and benefits of Borrower's interest.

CONDOMINIUM COVENANTS. In addition to the covenants and agreements made in the Security Instrument, Borrower and Lender further covenant and agree as follows:

A. Condominium Obligations. Borrower shall perform all of Borrower's obligations under the Condominium Project's Constituent Documents. The "Constituent Documents" are the: (i) Declaration or any other document which creates the Condominium Project; (ii) by-laws; (iii) code of regulations; and (iv) other equivalent documents. Borrower shall promptly pay, when due, all dues and assessments imposed pursuant to the Constituent Documents.

B. Hazard Insurance. So long as the Owners Association maintains, with a generally accepted insurance carrier, a "master" or "blanket" policy on the Condominium Project which is satisfactory to Lender and which provides insurance coverage in the amounts, for the periods, and against the hazards Lender requires, including fire and hazards included within the term "extended coverage," then:

(i)   Lender waives the provision in Uniform Covenant 2 for the monthly payment to Lender of one-twelfth of the yearly premium installments for hazard insurance on the Property; and

(ii)   Borrower's obligation under Uniform Covenant 5 to maintain hazard insurance coverage on the Property is deemed satisfied to the extent that the required coverage is provided by the Owners Association policy.

Borrower shall give Lender prompt notice of any lapse in required hazard insurance coverage.

In the event of a distribution of hazard insurance proceeds in lieu of restoration or repair following a loss to the Property, whether to the unit or to common elements, any proceeds payable to Borrower are hereby assigned and shall be paid to Lender for application to the sums secured by the Security Instrument, with any excess paid to Borrower.

C. Public Liability Insurance. Borrower shall take such actions as may be reasonable to insure that the Owners Association maintains a public liability insurance policy acceptable in form, amount, and extent of coverage to Lender.

D. Condemnation. The proceeds of any award or claim for damages, direct or consequential, payable to Borrower in connection with any condemnation or other taking of all or any part of the Property, whether of the unit or of the common elements, or for any conveyance in lieu of condemnation, are hereby assigned and shall be paid to Lender. Such proceeds shall be applied by Lender to the sums secured by the Security Instrument as provided in Uniform Covenant 9.

E. Lender's Prior Consent. Borrower shall not, except after notice to Lender and with Lender's prior written consent, either partition or subdivide the Property or consent to:

(i)   the abandonment or termination of the Condominium Project, except for abandonment or termination required by law in the case of substantial destruction by fire or other casualty or in the case of a taking by condemnation or eminent domain;

(ii)   any amendment to any provision of the Constituent Documents if the provision is for the express benefit of Lender;

(iii)   termination of professional management and assumption of self-management of the Owners Association; or

(iv)   any action which would have the effect of rendering the public liability insurance coverage maintained by the Owners Association unacceptable to Lender.

F. Remedies. If Borrower does not pay condominium dues and assessments when due, then Lender may pay them. Any amounts disbursed by Lender under this paragraph F shall become additional debt of Borrower secured by the Security Instrument. Unless Borrower and Lender agree to other terms of payment, these amounts shall bear interest from the date of disbursement at the Note rate and shall be payable, with interest, upon notice from Lender to Borrower requesting payment.

BY SIGNING BELOW, Borrower accepts and agrees to the terms and provisions contained in this Condominium Rider.

....(Seal)
-Borrower

....(Seal)
-Borrower

MULTISTATE CONDOMINIUM RIDER—Single Family—**FNMA/FHLMC UNIFORM INSTRUMENT**   Form 3140 12/83

Figure 2-9. **FNMA/FHLMC *Planned Unit Development Rider***

PLANNED UNIT DEVELOPMENT RIDER

THIS PLANNED UNIT DEVELOPMENT RIDER is made this .... day of ...., 19........, and is incorporated into and shall be deemed to amend and supplement the Mortgage, Deed of Trust or Security Deed (the "Security Instrument") of the same date, given by the undersigned (the "Borrower") to secure Borrower's Note to ....
.... (the "Lender") of the same date and covering the Property described in the Security Instrument and located at:
....
[Property Address]

The Property includes, but is not limited to, a parcel of land improved with a dwelling, together with other such parcels and certain common areas and facilities, as described in ....
....
....

(the "Declaration"). The Property is a part of a planned unit development known as ....
....
[Name of Planned Unit Development]

(the "PUD"). The Property also includes Borrower's interest in the homeowners association or equivalent entity owning or managing the common areas and facilities of the PUD (the "Owners Association") and the uses, benefits and proceeds of Borrower's interest.

PUD COVENANTS. In addition to the covenants and agreements made in the Security Instrument, Borrower and Lender further covenant and agree as follows:

A. PUD Obligations. Borrower shall perform all of Borrower's obligations under the PUD's Constituent Documents. The "Constituent Documents" are the : (i) Declaration; (ii) articles of incorporation, trust instrument or any equivalent document which creates the Owners Association; and (iii) any by-laws or other rules or regulations of the Owners Association. Borrower shall promptly pay, when due, all dues and assessments imposed pursuant to the Constituent Documents.

B. Hazard Insurance. So long as the Owners Association maintains, with a generally accepted insurance carrier, a "master" or "blanket" policy insuring the Property which is satisfactory to Lender and which provides insurance coverage in the amounts, for the periods, and against the hazards Lender requires, including fire and hazards included within the term "extended coverage," then:

(i) Lender waives the provision in Uniform Covenant 2 for the monthly payment to Lender of one-twelfth of the yearly premium installments for hazard insurance on the Property; and

(ii) Borrower's obligation under Uniform Covenant 5 to maintain hazard insurance coverage on the Property is deemed satisfied to the extent that the required coverage is provided by the Owners Association policy.

Borrower shall give Lender prompt notice of any lapse in required hazard insurance coverage provided by the master or blanket policy.

In the event of a distribution of hazard insurance proceeds in lieu of restoration or repair following a loss to the Property or to common areas and facilities of the PUD, any proceeds payable to Borrower are hereby assigned and shall be paid to Lender. Lender shall apply the proceeds to the sums secured by the Security Instrument, with any excess paid to Borrower.

C. Public Liability Insurance. Borrower shall take such actions as may be reasonable to insure that the Owners Association maintains a public liability insurance policy acceptable in form, amount, and extent of coverage to Lender.

D. Condemnation. The proceeds of any award or claim for damages, direct or consequential, payable to Borrower in connection with any condemnation or other taking of all or any part of the Property or the common areas and facilities of the PUD, or for any conveyance in lieu of condemnation, are hereby assigned and shall be paid to Lender. Such proceeds shall be applied by Lender to the sums secured by the Security Instrument as provided in Uniform Covenant 9.

E. Lender's Prior Consent. Borrower shall not, except after notice to Lender and with Lender's prior written consent, either partition or subdivide the Property or consent to:

(i) the abandonment or termination of the PUD, except for abandonment or termination required by law in the case of substantial destruction by fire or other casualty or in the case of a taking by condemnation or eminent domain;

(ii) any amendment to any provision of the "Constituent Documents" if the provision is for the express benefit of Lender;

(iii) termination of professional management and assumption of self-management of the Owners Association; or

(iv) any action which would have the effect of rendering the public liability insurance coverage maintained by the Owners Association unacceptable to Lender.

F. Remedies. If Borrower does not pay PUD dues and assessments when due, then Lender may pay them. Any amounts disbursed by Lender under this paragraph F shall become additional debt of Borrower secured by the Security Instrument. Unless Borrower and Lender agree to other terms of payment, these amounts shall bear interest from the date of disbursement at the Note rate and shall be payable, with interest, upon notice from Lender to Borrower requesting payment.

BY SIGNING BELOW, Borrower accepts and agrees to the terms and provisions contained in this PUD Rider.

....(Seal)
-Borrower

....(Seal)
-Borrower

MULTISTATE PUD RIDER—Single Family—**FNMA/FHLMC UNIFORM INSTRUMENT**   Form 3150 12/83

rity for a loan is located in a planned unit development (PUD). A PUD may be defined as a large area that has a comprehensive land development plan. These are sometimes large townhouse developments. The contents of this rider is very similar to the condominium rider.

If the property used as security for the loan is a duplex, triplex, or fourplex, the lender will require the execution of the 2–4 Family Rider (Assignment of Rents). Paragraph A of the rider (Figure 2–10) states that the borrower will not try to get the zoning changed on the property without first securing the written consent of the lender to the proposed change. Paragraph C requires the borrower to secure rent loss insurance in addition to any other insurance required by the deed of trust. One additional paragraph that should be mentioned is paragraph F, Assignment of Rents. This paragraph requires the borrower to unconditionally assign and transfer to the lender all of the rents and revenues of the property. It should be noted that until the lender gives notice of breach of one of the covenants or the borrower does not make the payments in a timely manner, the lender will allow the borrower to collect the rents and receive any other revenues from the property. These collections are made as trustee for the benefit of the borrower and lender. The next section outlines the steps to be followed or actions that will be taken if the lender gives notice of a breach of any of the covenants of the deed.

FHA Note and Deed of Trust

Another of the important uniform documents that the real estate professional needs to be familiar with is the FHA Note and Deed of Trust. We will start with the FHA Note, Form 9181, revised September 1970 (Figure 2–11).

The Note. The first section of this note is similar to the FNMA/FHLMC Note in that it identifies the lender and states that the borrower "promises to pay," thus making it a promissory note. The first paragraph also outlines the amount to be repaid, the interest rate, the monthly payment with interest, and on what date the first and last payments are due, and finally states that the payments, except for the last payment, will be due on the first of the month. It should be pointed out that this paragraph contains a very important phrase, "if not sooner paid." Without this phrase, this note or any other note may not be prepaid.

One major difference between this note and the FNMA/FHLMC one is that there is no mention of any late charges or any grace period for payment. This note says that the payments are due on the first of each month. If a payment that is missed is not made prior to the due date of the next payment, at the option of the lender the note may become immediately due and payable without notice. This section further states that if the note goes into default and foreclosure is instituted, the borrower will pay an additional amount equal to 10 percent of the remaining balance as attorneys' fees.

In the last sentence of the note, reference is made to the deed of trust, similar to the FNMA/FHLMC Note. But, there is one difference. In the FHA Note, the property to be conveyed to the trustee is described.

As one can see, the FHA Note, Form 9181, is less complicated than the FNMA/FHLMC Note. If you would like to have a copy of this instrument, they are available from any mortgage lender who originates FHA mortgages.

The Deed of Trust. Now, let us review the FHA, or HUD, Deed of Trust (Figures 2–12, 2–13, and 2–14). The form that we are using is HUD Form 92181M, dated May 1984. This document was formerly known as FHA Form 2181M. At the time of this writing, this is the only form approved for insurance under the one-to-four-family provisions of the National Housing Act. This form is to be used for mortgages that call for the periodic mortgage insurance premium payments. When one first looks at this form in comparison to the FNMA/FHLMC Deed of Trust, one can see that the HUD document is not as easy to read and is more legalistic in its wording.

The first section of the deed is similar to the FNMA/FHLMC deed in that this section identifies the parties to the transaction, and the borrower transfers the property and all improvements to the property to the trustee. The HUD deed is more explicit in that it mentions heating, plumbing, refrigeration, lighting fixtures, and equipment now and hereafter attached to the property as being covered by this deed of trust.

Section 2 of the HUD deed of trust restates paragraph one and two of the note, outlining the amount borrowed, the interest rate, the monthly payment including interest, the due date of the first and last payment, and finally how the note can go into default.

Section 3 of the deed is the covenant section. It is different from the FNMA/FHLMC deed in that it is not divided into conforming and nonconforming covenants. We will now

Figure 2-10. **FNMA/FHLMC 2- to 4-Family Rider (Assignments of Rents)**

2-4 FAMILY RIDER
(Assignment of Rents)

THIS 2-4 FAMILY RIDER is made this .... day of .... , 19 .... , and is incorporated into and shall be deemed to amend and supplement the Mortgage, Deed of Trust or Security Deed (the "Security Instrument") of the same date given by the undersigned (the "Borrower") to secure Borrower's Note to .... (the "Lender") of the same date and covering the property described in the Security Instrument and located at:

....
[Property Address]

2-4 FAMILY COVENANTS. In addition to the covenants and agreements made in the Security Instrument, Borrower and Lender further covenant and agree as follows:

A. USE OF PROPERTY; COMPLIANCE WITH LAW. Borrower shall not seek, agree to or make a change in the use of the Property or its zoning classification, unless Lender has agreed in writing to the change. Borrower shall comply with all laws, ordinances, regulations and requirements of any governmental body applicable to the Property.

B. SUBORDINATE LIENS. Except as permitted by federal law, Borrower shall not allow any lien inferior to the Security Instrument to be perfected against the Property without Lender's prior written permission.

C. RENT LOSS INSURANCE. Borrower shall maintain insurance against rent loss in addition to the other hazards for which insurance is required by Uniform Covenant 5.

D. "BORROWER'S RIGHT TO REINSTATE" DELETED. Uniform Covenant 18 is deleted.

E. ASSIGNMENT OF LEASES. Upon Lender's request, Borrower shall assign to Lender all leases of the Property and all security deposits made in connection with leases of the Property. Upon the assignment, Lender shall have the right to modify, extend or terminate the existing leases and to execute new leases, in Lender's sole discretion. As used in this paragraph E, the word "lease" shall mean "sublease" if the Security Instrument is on a leasehold.

F. ASSIGNMENT OF RENTS. Borrower unconditionally assigns and transfers to Lender all the rents and revenues of the Property. Borrower authorizes Lender or Lender's agents to collect the rents and revenues and hereby directs each tenant of the Property to pay the rents to Lender or Lender's agents. However, prior to Lender's notice to Borrower of Borrower's breach of any covenant or agreement in the Security Instrument, Borrower shall collect and receive all rents and revenues of the Property as trustee for the benefit of Lender and Borrower. This assignment of rents constitutes an absolute assignment and not an assignment for additional security only.

If Lender gives notice of breach to Borrower: (i) all rents received by Borrower shall be held by Borrower as trustee for benefit of Lender only, to be applied to the sums secured by the Security Instrument; (ii) Lender shall be entitled to collect and receive all of the rents of the Property; and (iii) each tenant of the Property shall pay all rents due and unpaid to Lender or Lender's agent on Lender's written demand to the tenant.

Borrower has not executed any prior assignment of the rents and has not and will not perform any act that would prevent Lender from exercising its rights under this paragraph F.

Lender shall not be required to enter upon, take control of or maintain the Property before or after giving notice of breach to Borrower. However, Lender or a judicially appointed receiver may do so at any time there is a breach. Any application of rents shall not cure or waive any default or invalidate any other right or remedy of Lender. This assignment of rents of the Property shall terminate when the debt secured by the Security Instrument is paid in full.

G. CROSS-DEFAULT PROVISION. Borrower's default or breach under any note or agreement in which Lender has an interest shall be a breach under the Security Instrument and Lender may invoke any of the remedies permitted by the Security Instrument.

BY SIGNING BELOW, Borrower accepts and agrees to the terms and provisions contained in this 2-4 Family Rider.

....(Seal)
-Borrower

....(Seal)
-Borrower

MULTISTATE 2-4 FAMILY RIDER—FNMA/FHLMC Uniform Instrument   Form 3170 12/83

Figure 2-11.   FHA Note

DEED OF TRUST NOTE

$, Texas.
                                                                    , 19

FOR VALUE RECEIVED, the undersigned promise(s) to pay to the order of

                                                            the sum of
                                            Dollars ($),

with interest at the rate of   per centum (%) per annum on the unpaid balance, interest payable monthly as it accrues, both principal and interest to be paid at the office of
in
in monthly installments of
Dollars ($) each, including interest, one on the first day of each month hereafter commencing on the first day of   , 19   , and continuing until the principal and interest are fully paid, except that the final payment of principal and interest, if not sooner paid, shall be due and payable on the first day of

   If default be made in the payment of any installment under this note, and if the default is not made good prior to the date of the next such installment, at the option of the holder, this note shall become immediately due and payable without notice and the lien given to secure its payment may be foreclosed. Failure to exercise this option shall not constitute a waiver of the right to exercise it in the event of any subsequent default. All past due installments of principal and interest shall bear interest from maturity at the above rate. If this note is placed in the hands of an attorney for collection, or is collected through the Probate Court or the Bankruptcy Court or through other legal proceeding, the undersigned promise(s) to pay, as attorney's fees, an additional amount equal to ten per centum (10%) of the amount then owing on this note.

   The undersigned and all endorsers, and all persons liable or to become liable on this note, waive demand, protest and notice of demand, protest and nonpayment and consent to any and all renewals or extensions in the time of payment hereof.

   This note is secured by Deed of Trust of even date herewith, executed by the undersigned to
                                             Trustee(s), conveying property as follows:

_____   _____
          (Address)
_____   _____
          (Address)
_____   _____
          (Address)
_____   _____
          (Address)

HUD-99181 (8-81)
GPO 885-810

Figure 2-12. HUD-FHA Deed of Trust, page 1

DEED OF TRUST
MIP

This form is used in connection with mortgages insured under the one-to-four family programs of the National Housing Act which provide for periodic Mortgage Insurance Premium payments.

STATE OF TEXAS)
) ss:
COUNTY OF)

This Indenture, made and entered into by and between

of the County of

in the State of Texas, hereinafter called the Grantors, and

, Trustee(s), of

, hereinafter called the Trustee:

Witnesseth: That the Grantors for and in consideration of the sum of Ten Dollars ($10.00) and other valuable consideration in hand paid, the receipt whereof is hereby acknowledged, and the further consideration, uses, purposes and trusts herein set forth and declared, have granted, bargained, sold and conveyed, and by these presents do grant, bargain, sell and convey unto the said Trustee, and unto his successors in the trust hereby created and his assigns, forever, all of the following described real estate together with all the improvements thereon and hereafter placed thereon situated in the County of

, State of Texas, to wit:

To Have and To Hold the above-described premises, together with all the rights, hereditaments, and appurtenances in anywise appertaining or belonging thereto, including all heating, plumbing, refrigeration and lighting fixtures and equipment now or hereafter attached thereto or used in connection therewith, unto the said Trustee, his successors in this trust and his assigns, forever. And the Grantors do hereby bind themselves and their heirs, executors, administrators, and legal representatives, to warrant and forever defend all and singular the said premises unto the said Trustee, and unto his successors in this trust, and his assigns, forever, against any person who lawfully claims or shall claim the same or any part thereof.

This conveyance is made in trust to secure the payment of the principal sum of

Dollars ($),

as evidenced by a certain promissory note of even date herewith executed by the Grantors, payable to the order of

, the terms of which are incorporated herein by reference, together with interest at the rate of per centum (%) per annum on the unpaid balance, both interest and principal being payable monthly as it accrues at the office of

, in

in monthly installments of Dollars

($) each, including interest, one on the first day of each month hereafter, commencing on the first day of , 19 , and continuing until the principal and interest are fully paid, except that the final payment of principal and interest, if not sooner paid, shall be due and payable on the first day of

The note also provides that if default is made in the payment of any installment thereunder, and if the default is not made good prior to the due date of the next such installment, at the option of the holder, the note shall become immediately due and payable without notice, and that this lien may be foreclosed. Failure to exercise this option is not to constitute a waiver of the right to exercise it in the event of any subsequent default. If the note is placed in the hands of an attorney for collection, or is collected through the Probate Court or the Bankruptcy Court or through other legal proceedings, the makers thereof agree to pay reasonable attorney's fees.

The Grantors covenant as follows:

1. That they will pay the principal of and interest on the note secured hereby in accordance with the terms thereof. Privilege is reserved to pay the debt in whole, or in an amount equal to one or more monthly payments on the principal that are next due on the note, on the first day of any month prior to maturity; provided, however, that written notice of an intention to exercise such privilege is given at least thirty (30) days prior to prepayment.

2. That, together with and in addition to such payments of principal and interest, they will pay to the holder of the note, on the first day of each month until the note is fully paid, the following sums:

(a) An amount sufficient to provide the holder hereof with funds to pay the next mortgage insurance premium if this instrument and the note secured hereby are insured, or a monthly charge (in lieu of a mortgage insurance premium) if they are held by the Secretary of Housing and Urban Development, as follows:

(I) If and so long as said note of even date and this instrument are insured or are reinsured under the provisions of the National Housing Act, an amount sufficient to accumulate in the hands of the holder one (1) month prior to its due date the annual mortgage insurance premium, in order to provide such holder with funds to pay such premium to the Secretary of Housing and Urban Development pursuant to the National Housing Act, as amended Regulations thereunder; or

(II) If and so long as said note of even date and this instrument are held by the Secretary of Housing and Urban Development, a monthly charge (in lieu of a mortgage insurance premium) which shall be in an amount equal to one-twelfth (1/12) of one-half (1/2) per centum of the average outstanding balance due on the note computed without taking into account delinquencies or prepayments;

Previous Edition is Obsolete

STATE OF TEXAS
HUD-92181M (5-84)
(24 CFR 203.17(a))

Figure 2-13. HUD-FHA Deed of Trust, page 2

(b) A sum equal to the ground rents, if any, next due, plus the premiums that will next become due and payable on policies of fire and other hazard insurance covering the property covered by this Deed of Trust, plus taxes and assessments next due on the premises covered hereby (all as estimated by the holder of the note), less all sums already paid therefor divided by the number of months to elapse before one month prior to the date when such ground rents, premiums, taxes, and assessments will become delinquent, such sums to be held by the holder of the note in trust to pay said ground rents, premiums, taxes, and special assessments, before the same become delinquent; and

(c) All payments mentioned in the two preceding subsections of this paragraph and all payments to be made under the note secured hereby shall be added together, and the aggregate amount thereof shall be paid by the Grantors each month in a single payment to be applied by the holder of the note to the following items in the order set forth:

(I) premium charges under the contract of insurance with the Secretary of Housing and Urban Development, or monthly charge (in lieu of mortgage insurance premium), as the case may be;
(II) ground rents, if any, taxes special assessments, fire, and other hazard insurance premiums;
(III) interest on the note secured hereby; and
(IV) amortization of the principal of said note.

Any deficiency in the amount of such aggregate monthly payment shall, unless made good by the Grantors prior to the due date of the next such payment, constitute an event of default under this Deed of Trust. The holder of the note may collect a "late charge" not to exceed four cents (4¢) for each dollar ($1) of each payment more than fifteen (15) days in arrears to cover the extra expense involved in handling delinquent payments.

(3) If the total of the payments made by the Grantors under (*b*) of paragraph 2 preceding shall exceed the amount of the payments actually made by the holder of the note for ground rents, taxes, assessments, or insurance premiums, as the case may be, such excess, if the loan is current, at the option of the Grantor, shall be credited on subsequent payments to be made by the Grantors, or refunded to the Grantors. If, however, the monthly payments made by the Grantors under (*b*) of paragraph 2 preceding shall not be sufficient to pay ground rents, taxes, assessments, and insurance premiums as the case may be, when the same shall become due and payable, then the Grantors shall pay to the holder of the note any amount necessary to make up the deficiency, on or before the date when payment of such ground rents, taxes, assessments, or insurance premiums shall be due. If at any time the Grantors shall tender to the holder of the note, in accordance with the provisions thereof, the full payment of the entire indebtedness represented thereby, the holder of the note shall, in computing the amount of such indebtedness, credit to the account of the Grantors all payments made under the provisions of (*a*) of paragraph 2 hereof which the holder of the note has not become obligated to pay to the Secretary of Housing and Urban Development, and any balance remaining in the funds accumulated under the provisions of (*b*) of paragraph 2 hereof. If there shall be a default under any of the provisions of this Deed of Trust resulting in a public sale of the premises covered hereby or if the property is otherwise acquired after default, the holder of the note shall apply, at the time of the commencement of such proceedings or at the time the property is otherwise acquired, the balance then remaining in the funds accumulated under (*b*) of paragraph 2 preceding, as a credit against the amount of principal then remaining unpaid under the note secured hereby, and shall properly adjust any payments which shall have been made under (*a*) of paragraph 2.

4. That they have a good and merchantable title in fee simple to the premises hereby conveyed, free and clear from all encumbrances, with full right and authority to convey the same, and will warrant and defend the title against the claims of all persons whomsoever.

5. That they will pay all taxes, assessments, water rates and other governmental or municipal charges, fines, or impositions, for which provision has not been made hereinbefore, and in default thereof the holder of the note secured hereby may pay the same; and the Grantors will promptly deliver the official receipts therefor to the said holder.

6. That they will keep the improvements now existing or hereafter erected on the said premises, insured as may be required from time to time by the holder of the note against loss by fire and other hazards, casualties, and contingencies in such amounts and for such periods as may be required by the holder of the note and will pay promptly, when due, any premiums on such insurance provision for payment of which has not been made hereinbefore. All insurance shall be carried in companies approved by the holder of the note and the policies and renewals thereof shall be held by the holder of the note and have attached thereto loss payable clauses in favor of and in form acceptable to the holder of the note. In event of loss they will give immediate notice by mail to the holder of the note, who may make proof of loss if not made promptly by the party of the first part, and each insurance company concerned is hereby authorized and directed to make payment for such loss directly to the holder of the note instead of to the party of the first part and the holder of the note jointly, and the insurance proceeds, or any part thereof, may be applied by the holder of the note at its option either to the reduction of the indebtedness hereby secured or to the restoration or repair of the property damaged. In event of foreclosure of this Deed of Trust or other transfer of title to the said premises in extinguishment of the indebtedness secured hereby, all right, title, and interest of the party of the first part, in and to any insurance policies then in force shall pass to the purchaser or grantee.

7. That they will not suffer any lien superior to the lien hereby created to attach to or be enforced against the premises covered hereby and will keep the said premises in as good order and condition as they are now and will not commit or permit any waste, impairment, or deterioration of said premises or any part thereof.

8. That all awards of damages in connection with condemnation proceedings involving the premises or any part thereof shall be paid to the holder of the note secured hereby. Such awards shall be applied to the amount due under said note in amounts equal to the next maturing installment or installments of principal and any balance shall be credited to the escrow account. Such payment will not relieve the Grantors from making regular monthly payments commencing on the first day of the first month following the date of receipt of the award. The holder of the note is hereby authorized in the name of the Grantor to execute and deliver valid acquittances for such awards and to appeal from such awards.

9. That they hereby assign to the holder of the said note any and all rents on the premises covered hereby and authorize said holder to take possession of the premises at any time there shall be any default in the payment of the debt hereby secured or in the performance of any obligation herein contained and to rent the same for the account of the Grantors and to deduct from such rents all costs of collection and administration and to apply the remainder of such rents on the debt hereby secured.

10. That in the event the ownership of the premises covered hereby or any part thereof becomes vested in a person other than the Grantors, the holder of the note secured hereby may, without notice to the Grantors, deal with such successor or successors in interest with reference to this Deed of Trust and to the debt hereby secured in the same manner as with the Grantors without in any way vitiating or discharging the Grantors' liability hereunder or upon the debt hereby secured. No sale of the premises covered hereby and no forbearance on the part of the holder of the said note and no extension of the time for the payment of the debt hereby secured, given by said holder shall operate to release, discharge, modify, change, or affect the original liability of the Grantors either in whole or in part.

11. That the holder of the said note shall have the right to pay any taxes, assessments, water rates, and other governmental or municipal charges, fines or impositions which are to be paid under paragraph 5 hereof, and to make any payments hereinabove provided to be made by the Grantors under subsections (a) and (b) of paragraph 2 hereof, and any amount so paid by the said holder shall then be added to the principal debt named herein and bear interest at the rate set forth in the note secured hereby, payable monthly from the date of such payment and be secured by this Deed of Trust the same as said principal debt and interest thereon; and the said holder shall at its option be entitled to be subrogated to any lien, claim, or demand paid by it or discharged with the money advanced by it and secured by this Deed of Trust, which amount advanced shall be payable on demand, or as may be otherwise agreed in writing between the parties hereto either before, at the time, or after making such advances.

12. That they do hereby expressly waive and renounce the benefit of all laws now existing or that may hereafter be enacted providing for any appraisement before sale of any of the premises hereby granted, commonly known as Appraisement laws, and also the benefit of all laws that may be hereafter enacted in any way extending the time for the enforcement of the collection of the debt hereby secured or creating or extending a period of redemption from any sale made in collecting said debt, commonly known as Stay laws and Redemption laws, and the Grantors hereby agree and contract that the laws of the State of Texas, save as above excepted, now in force relative to the collection of the debt hereby secured and the application to the payment thereof are expressly adopted and made a part hereof.

13. That, as additional and collateral security for the payment of the note secured hereby and the indebtedness hereinbefore described, they hereby assign to the owner of said debt all of the profits, revenues, royalties, rights and benefits accruing under all oil, gas or mineral leases now on said property, or which may hereafter be placed thereon, and the lessee or assignee or sublessee is hereby directed on production of this Deed of Trust or certified copy thereof, to pay said profits, revenues, royalties, rights and benefits to the owner of said debt; this provision to become effective, however, only upon default in the conditions and terms of this Deed of Trust or the note hereby secured, or prior to such default, upon notice to the lessee of such oil, gas or mineral lease, and to terminate and become null and void upon payment of the indebtedness hereby secured.

14. The Grantors further agree that should this Deed of Trust and the note secured hereby not be eligible for insurance under the National Housing Act within from the date hereof (written statement of any officer of the Department of Housing and Urban Development or authorized agent of the Secretary of Housing and Urban Development dated subsequent to the time from the date of this Deed of Trust, declining to insure said note and this Deed of Trust, being deemed conclusive proof of such ineligibility), the Trustee or the holder of the note may, at its option, declare all sums secured hereby immediately due and payable.

If the Grantors shall well and truly pay, or cause to be paid, the note hereby secured, and other indebtedness that may be owing, and do keep and perform each and every covenant, condition, and stipulation herein and in the said note contained, then these presents shall become null and void; otherwise to be and remain in full force and effect; but if default shall be made in any payment, or part thereof, under the said note, or if for any reason (other than the fault of the holder of the note) the fire or other hazard insurance is canceled or discontinued, or if the Grantors shall fail to keep or perform any of the covenants, conditions or stipulations herein, then the said note, together with all accrued interest thereon and all other sums secured hereby, shall, at the option of the holder of the said note, become at once due and payable without demand or notice, and the Trustee hereunder shall be, and is hereby, authorized and empowered, when requested so to do by the holder of said note after such default, to sell the premises covered hereby at public auction to the highest bidder for cash, between the hours of ten o'clock A.M. and four o'clock P.M. of the first Tuesday in any month, at the door of the County Court House in the county in which said premises, or any part thereof, are situated, after advertising the time, place, and terms of said sale and the premises to be sold by posting, or causing to be posted, for at least twenty-one (21) consecutive days prior to the date of said sale written or printed notice thereof at the courthouse door of the county in which the sale is to be made, and if the real estate is in more than one county, one notice shall be posted at the courthouse door of each county in which the real estate is situated. In addition to the posted notice as set forth above, no foreclosure under Power of Sale herein contained shall be held unless the holder of the indebtedness herein secured shall at least 21 days preceding the date of sale serve written notice of the proposed sale by certified mail on each debtor obligated to pay such indebtedness according to the records of such holder. The Grantors do hereby authorize and empower said Trustee, and each and all of his or its successors in this trust, to sell said premises, together, or in lots or parcels, as such Trustee shall deem expedient, and to execute and deliver to the purchaser or purchasers of said premises good and sufficient deeds of

Figure 2-14. HUD-FHA Deed of Trust, page 3

conveyance thereof by fee simple title, with covenants of general warranty, and the title of such purchaser or purchasers, when so made by the Trustee, the Grantors bind themselves to warrant and forever defend; and to receive the proceeds of said sale which shall be applied as follows:

First - To the payment of all necessary actions and expenses incident to the execution of said trust, including a reasonable fee to the Trustee, not exceeding two and one-half per centum (2 1/2%) of the gross proceeds of the sale of said premises.

Second - To the payment of said note, to the amount of the principal sum and accrued interest legally due thereon, all other sums secured hereby, and to the payment of attorney's fees as in said note provided.

Third - The remainder, if any there shall be, after payment of said costs, expenses and attorney's fees, and the principal and interest legally due on said note, and all other sums secured hereby and other sums agreed to be paid by the Grantors, shall be paid to the Grantors.

It is further agreed that if default be made in any payment, or part thereof, under the said note, the holder of the note may at his option, without demand or notice, request the Trustee hereunder, and the Trustee shall be, and is, hereby authorized and empowered to proceed with foreclosure in satisfaction of such item as if under a full foreclosure, conducting the sale as herein provided and without declaring the unmatured portion of the debt due. It is agreed that such sale shall not in any manner affect the unmatured part of the debt secured by this Deed of Trust, but as to such unmatured part this Deed of Trust shall remain in full force and effect just as though no sale had been made under the provisions of this paragraph. It is further agreed that several sales may be made without exhausting the right of sale for any unmatured part of the debt secured. The proceeds of said sale shall be applied as provided in sections First and Second above and the remainder, if any there shall be, shall be applied as a credit on the unpaid balance of principal of the debt hereby secured; said credit will not operate to reduce the amount of the regular monthly payments to principal and interest, but will serve solely to accelerate the maturity of the mortgage.

The deed or deeds which shall be given by said Trustee to the purchaser or purchasers at such sale, shall be prima facie evidence of the truth of all the recitals therein as to default in the payment of said note, or of interest due thereon, or of the sums thereunder and hereunder due, the request to the said Trustee to sell, the advertisement or posting of such sale, the proceedings at such sale, the facts, if any, authorizing a substitute Trustee to act in the premises, and everything necessary to the validity of such sale.

The Grantors specifically agree that after any sale under this Deed of Trust they shall be mere tenants at sufferance of the purchaser of said property at the Trustee's sale, and that the purchaser shall be entitled to immediate possession thereof, and that if the Grantors fail to vacate the premises immediately, the purchaser may, and he shall have the right to go into any justice court in the precinct or county in which the property is located and file an action in forcible entry and detainer, which action shall lie against the Grantors as tenants at sufferance. The remedy is cumulative of any and all remedies the purchaser may have hereunder or otherwise.

In case of the death of the Trustee herein or of any substitute Trustee appointed hereunder, or the refusal, failure or inability of any Trustee or any substitute Trustee for any reason to act hereunder, or in the event the holder of the note shall deem it desirable to remove without cause the Trustee or any substitute Trustee and appoint another to execute this trust, then in either or any of said events the holder of the note shall have the right, and is hereby authorized and empowered to appoint by instrument in writing a substitute Trustee in lieu of the Trustee herein named, or in lieu of any substitute Trustee, who shall thereupon become vested with and succeed to all the title, power, and duties hereby conferred upon the Trustee named herein, the same as if said substitute Trustee had been named original Trustee by this instrument. All estates, title, rights, powers and duties herein given to Trustee(s) or imposed upon them are given and imposed upon Trustees joint and severally, and to the survivors of such Trustees, and may be exercised by any one or more than one, or all of such Trustees, as if any such Trustee or Trustees so acting were sole Trustee hereunder and the Grantors herein do hereby ratify and confirm any and all acts which Trustees or any of them, may do in the premises by virtue thereof or hereof.

In the event any item, items, terms, or provisions contained in this instrument are in conflict with the laws of the State of Texas, this instrument shall be affected only as to its application to such item, items, terms, or provisions, and shall in all other respects remain in full force and effect. It is understood and agreed that in no event and upon no contingency shall the maker or makers of the note secured hereby, or any party liable thereon or therefor, be required to pay interest in excess of the rate allowed by the laws of the State of Texas. The intention of the parties being to conform strictly to the Usury Laws now in force, any of said contracts for interest shall be held to be subject to reduction to the amount allowed under said Usury Laws as now or hereafter construed by the courts having jurisdiction.

The note secured hereby is [primarily secured by the Vendor's Lien retained in the Deed of even date herewith conveying the property to Grantors, which Vendor's Lien has been assigned to Lender, this Deed of Trust being additional security therefore. * [in renewal and extension, but not in extinguishment, of that certain indebtedness described as follows:] *

*Delete bracketed clauses as appropriate.

The covenants herein contained shall bind, and the benefits and advantages shall inure to, the respective heirs, executors, administrators, successors and assigns of the parties hereto. Whenever used, the singular number shall include the plural, the plural the singular, and the use of any gender shall be applicable to all genders.

Witness   hand(s) this   day of   , A.D.19

_____   _____

_____   _____

_____   _____

THE STATE OF TEXAS   )
COUNTY OF   )

Before Me, the undersigned authority, on this day personally appeared

known to me to be the person(s) whose
name(s)   subscribed to the foregoing instrument, and acknowledged to me that   executed the same for
the purposes and consideration therein expressed.

Given under my hand and seal of office this   day of   , A.D.19

_____
Notary Public in and for   County, Texas

THE STATE OF TEXAS   )
COUNTY OF   )

I,   , Clerk of the County Court of
County, Texas, do hereby certify that the within instrument with its certificate of authentication was filed for registration in my office on
the   day of   , 19   , at   o'clock   .M., and
duly recorded on the   day of   , 19   , at   o'clock   .M., in Vol.
, Page   , of records of   for said County.

Witness my hand and seal of office, at   , the day and date last
above written.

_____
Clerk County Court   County, Texas

By _____ Deputy

GPO 907-568

review some of the more important covenants, starting with covenant 1.

Covenant 1. This is the repayment covenant. The borrower declares that he or she will repay the principal with interest. There is, however, a very important statement contained in this covenant, and that is, "Privilege is reserved to pay the debt in whole . . ." This allows the borrower to prepay the loan at any time. It should be noted that if the borrower wishes to pay the note in full, he or she must give notice at least 30 days prior to prepayment. If this is not done, the lender can collect up to 30 days of interest. This 30-day interest charge is considered by some to be a prepayment penalty.

Covenant 2. Covenant 2 sets up the escrow account. Subparagraphs a and b define what will be collected and paid on the first of each month. In addition to the taxes, insurance, ground rent, or any other assessments, the covenant mentions that the borrower must pay on a monthly basis a sum sufficient to accrue annually to pay for the federal mortgage insurance premium. Subparagraph c states how the monthly payment, made by the borrower, will be applied: first, the premium for the federal mortgage insurance will be paid; second, taxes, insurance, special assessments, and ground rents, if any, will be paid; third, interest on the mortgage will be paid; and fourth, amortization of the principal will be paid. The final paragraph, paragraph 3, outlines what is to be done if there is an overage in the escrow account or a deficiency in the account.

Covenant 6 (Figure 2-13). Another important covenant is covenant 6. This covenant is similar to covenant 5 of the FNMA/FHLMC Deed, in that it requires the borrower to have insurance on all improvements now on the property and those added in the future. In addition, the insurance carrier must be approved by the lender. In case of loss, the covenant states that the borrower must notify the lender by mail immediately. The last part of this covenant outlines how payments, made by insurance carriers, may be applied by the lender. In normal practice, the insurance carrier will issue any payment for loss jointly to the borrower and the lender.

Covenant 7. Covenant 7 charges the borrower to see that no lien that will be superior to this deed will be executed against the property and to keep the property in good repair and not permit any waste, impairment, or deterioration of the property.

Covenant 8. Here, the HUD Deed of Trust deals with condemnation and how any awards will be applied by the lender. The covenant states such awards will be applied to the balance owed the lender and any excess will be applied to the escrow account. The credit of the funds in no way relieves the borrower from making the regular monthly payment, unless the award is sufficient to pay off the mortgage.

Covenant 10. Covenant 10 states that if the ownership of the property becomes vested in a person other than the grantor or borrower, the lender will without notice to the borrower deal with the successor or successors, and the borrower will not be released from liability from the obligation with such a transfer. The covenant also outlines under what other conditions the original borrower will not be released from his or her obligation.

Covenant 14 (Figure 2-14). This longest of all the covenants covers several topics. The first is quite important. If the note and deed of trust are not eligible for insurance under the National Housing Act within a specific time limit, usually 60 days, the noteholder or the trustee, at his or her option, may declare all sums secured to be immediately due and payable. The second paragraph outlines the foreclosure procedure to be followed if the borrower does not uphold the covenants of the deed of trust. The foreclosure procedure in this deed of trust is identical to the FNMA/FHLMC procedure. In addition to the procedures being outlined, the deed of trust states how the proceeds of a foreclosure sale will be applied. This covenant also allows for the substitution of a new trustee.

If the deed of trust is to be used to secure a loan that calls for a one-time mortgage insurance premium, it must be altered and a mortgage insurance premium rider must be executed (Figure 2-15). You will note that the rider amends the deed of trust in several places by removing any reference to the monthly collection of the mortgage insurance premium in covenants, or paragraphs, two and three. In addition, the rider adds language to paragraphs 14 and 15.

VA Note and Deed of Trust

The final two instruments that will be dealt with in this chapter are the Veterans Administration Note and Deed of Trust. At the time of this writing, the only forms approved for use with a Veterans Administration mortgage are those shown.

The Note. The VA note (Figure 2-16) is very similar to the HUD note. To avoid redundancy,

Figure 2-15. HUD Mortgage Insurance Premium Rider

MORTGAGE INSURANCE PREMIUM RIDER

This Mortgage Insurance Premium Rider, dated the _____ day of
_____, 19___, amends the Deed of Trust of even date executed
by the undersigned in the following manner:

1. Subsection (a) of Paragraph 2 is deleted.

2. Subsection (c)(I) of Paragraph 2 is deleted.

3. In the third sentence of Paragraph 3, the words "all
payments made under the provisions of (a) of paragraph 2 hereof which the
holder of the note has not become obligated to pay to the Secretary of
Housing and Urban Development and" are deleted.

4. The last sentence of Paragraph 3 is amended by inserting a
period after ". . . then remaining unpaid under the note secured hereby"
and by deleting the rest of the sentence.

5. Paragraph 14 is amended by adding the following sentence at
the end of the first paragraph:

> "This option may not be exercised when the ineligibility
> for insurance under the National Housing Act is due to
> the holder of the note's failure to remit the mortgage
> insurance premium to the Department of Housing and
> Urban Development."

6. The following paragraph 15 is added:

> "In the event that any portion of the lien is found
> not to be valid as against the homestead, all pay-
> ments under the note shall be first applied to that
> portion which is declared to be invalid as against
> the homestead."

BY SIGNING BELOW, the undersigned agrees to the foregoing changes in
the Deed of Trust.

_____

_____

Figure 2-16. VA Note

VA Form 26-6341a (Home Loan)
Oct. 1979 . Use Optional. Section
1810, Title 38, U.S.C. Acceptable
to Federal National Mortgage
Association.

TEXAS

DEED OF TRUST NOTE

, Texas.
, 19   .

For Value Received, the undersigned promise(s) to pay to the order of

the sum of

Dollars ($),
with interest at the rate of   per centum (%) per annum on
the unpaid balance, interest payable monthly as it accrues, both principal and interest to be paid at the
office of

in
or at such other place as the holder may designate in writing, in monthly installments of
Dollars ($) each, including interest,
one on the first of each month hereafter commencing on the first day of   , 19   , and
continuing until the principal and interest are fully paid. except that the final payment of principal and
interest, if not sooner paid, shall be due and payable on the first day of   ,   .

Privilege is reserved to prepay at any time, without premium or fee, the entire indebtedness or any
part thereof not less than the amount of one installment, or one hundred dollars ($100.00), whichever
is less. Prepayment in full shall be credited on the date received. Partial prepayment, other than on an
installment due date, need not be credited until the next following installment due date or thirty days
after such prepayment, whichever is earlier.

If any deficiency in the payment of any installment under this note is not made good prior to the due
date of the next such installment, at the option of the holder, this note shall become immediately due and
payable without notice and the lien given to secure its payment may be foreclosed. Failure to exercise this
option shall not constitute a waiver of the right to exercise it in the event of any subsequent default. All
past due installments of principal and interest shall bear interest from maturity at the above rate. If
collection on this note is made through a Probate Court or a Bankruptcy Court, or other appropriate legal
proceedings, or if after default this note is placed in the hands of an attorney at law for collection, the
undersigned promise(s) to pay all costs of such collection, including attorney fees, if actually incurred,
not to exceed   per centum (%) of the amount owing on this note at the
time of filing claim hereon or date of default, whichever is earlier.

The undersigned and all endorsers waive demand, protest and notice of demand, protest and nonpayment and consent to any and all renewals or extensions in the time of payment hereof.

This note is secured by Deed of Trust of even date herewith, executed by the undersigned to

trustee(s) conveying the following-described property, and by

_____
(Mechanic's lien, contractor's, vendor's lien, etc.)

----
* (the indebtedness evidenced hereby being in renewal and extension of that secured by said mechanic's
lien) :

Address:

_____   _____

_____   _____

_____   _____

_____   _____

*Note.—Strike words in parentheses if a vendor's lien.

we will review only the major difference between these two notes.

The first sentence of the second paragraph of the VA note includes the following: "Privilege is reserved to prepay at any time, without premium or fee, the entire indebtedness or any part thereof . . ." Similar wording is included not in the HUD note, but in the HUD deed of trust. This paragraph of the VA note deals exclusively with the payment of the mortgage and states how payment in full or partial payment will be credited. This is the only major difference in the VA note and the HUD note.

The Deed of Trust. Let us now review the accompanying VA deed of trust (Figure 2–17) by comparing it to the HUD deed of trust. Even though the wording is not identical, the HUD deed and the VA Deed are parallel in construction. With that in mind, we will cover the major differences.

The first of these differences appears in covenant 2 (Figure 2–18). In the VA deed, all mention of the National Housing Act and mortgage insurance has been omitted. The rest of this covenant is similar to the HUD document. It covers the setting up of an escrow account, the items to be collected, and the application of the collected funds.

The next difference appears in covenant 8, which deals with condemnation proceedings. The wording is different than in the HUD deed and does not state that the payment of the awards for condemnation does not relieve the borrower from making the regular monthly payment.

Covenant 12 (Figure 2–19) of the VA deed is the next difference. Neither this covenant nor any of the wording appears in the HUD deed. This covenant states that the holder of the note (the lender) shall, for any funds advanced by the lender, be able to execute a supplemental note or notes. This covenant outlines some examples of when a lender could advance funds and states the interest rate these funds will carry and the payment schedule. The covenant further states that if the parties are not able to agree on the maturity or length of the note, the sums advanced shall be due and payable thirty days after demand by the lender.

The addition of the above covenant to the VA deed causes some other covenants to change in numerical sequence. Thus, covenant 13 in the VA deed corresponds to covenant 12 in the HUD deed. Another difference between the two deeds is that in the VA deed of trust, the first paragraph of covenant 14 is used as covenant 13 in the HUD deed. The remainder of covenant 14 in the VA deed is identical to covenant 14 in the HUD deed, except that, once again, all mention of the National Housing Act and mortgage insurance has been omitted from the VA deed. This is due to the fact that VA loans are not insured. However, a portion of the loan is guaranteed by the Veterans Administration.

At the present time, there are efforts underway for HUD and the Veterans Administration to agree on a common form for the note and mortgage and/or deed of trust for all states. The first of the common forms will be introduced in Maryland, and the rest of the common forms are to be introduced on a state-by-state basis as soon as possible.

This completes our review of the three more important notes and deeds of trust: the FNMA/FHLMC, the HUD, and finally, the VA note and deed of trust. The reason for the review is to give you, the real estate professional, or the homeowner, an idea of the rights and duties of a homeowner. In addition, a real estate professional needs to have a broad concept of the deed to know if a piece of property may be sold on assumption and, if so, the terms of such a sale, if there is a prepayment penalty, and, finally, if the original borrower will be released from the obligation if the note is assumed.

REVIEW QUESTIONS

1. Explain the differences among the three theories of mortgages.

2. Define *alternative mortgage instrument* and give three examples.

3. Explain the difference between an open-end mortgage and a package mortgage.

4. Define *mortgage*.

5. Explain the difference between a note and a deed of trust.

6. Explain the major differences between the FNMA/FHLMC note, the VA note, and the FHA note.

7. Name and define the categories of mortgages.

8. Name and explain some of the major covenants found in the FNMA/FHLMC deed of trust.

Figure 2-17.   VA Deed of Trust

VA Form 26-6341 (Home Loan)
Rev. March 1983, Use Optional.
Section 1810, Title 38 U.S.C.
Acceptable to Federal National
Mortgage Association   TEXAS

DEED OF TRUST

STATE OF TEXAS
COUNTY OF   } *ss:*

THIS INDENTURE, made and entered into by and between

of the County of
in the State of Texas, hereinafter called the Grantors, and

Trustee(s), of
, hereinafter called the Trustee:

WITNESSETH: That the Grantors for and in consideration of the sum of Ten Dollars ($10.00) and other valuable consideration in hand paid, the receipt whereof is hereby acknowledged, and the further consideration, uses, purposes and trusts herein set forth and declared, have granted, bargained, sold and conveyed, and by these presents do grant, bargain, sell and convey unto the said Trustee, and unto his successors in the trust hereby created and his assigns, forever, all of the following described real estate together with all the improvements, thereon and hereafter placed thereon situated in the County of
State of Texas, to wit:

together with all fixtures now or hereafter attached to or used in connection with the premises herein described and in addition thereto the following described household appliances, which are, and shall be deemed to be, fixtures and a part of the realty, and are a portion of the security for the indebtedness herein mentioned:

TO HAVE AND TO HOLD the above-described property, with all the rights, hereditaments, and appurtenances now or here-after in anywise appertaining or belonging thereto, unto the said Trustee, his successors in this trust and his assigns, forever. And the Grantors do hereby bind themselves and their heirs, executors, administrators, and legal representatives, to warrant and forever defend all and singular the said premises unto the said Trustee, and unto his successors in this trust, and his assigns, forever, against any person who lawfully claims or shall claim the same or any part thereof.

This conveyance is made in trust to secure the payment of the principal sum of
Dollars ($), as evidenced by a certain promissory note
of even date herewith executed by the Grantors payable to the order of

together with interest at the rate of

per centum (%) per annum on the unpaid balance, both interest and principal
being payable monthly as it accrues at the office of
in   , or such other place as the holder of the note may designate in writing
in monthly installments of   Dollars ($)
each, including interest, one on the first day of each month hereafter, commencing on the first day of   , 19   ,
and continuing until the principal and interest are fully paid, except that the final payment of principal and interest, if not sooner paid,
shall be due and payable on the first day of   . The note also provides that if any deficiency in the
payment of any installment is not made good prior to the due date of the next such installment, at the option of the holder, the note
shall become immediately due and payable without notice, and that this lien may be foreclosed.   Failure to exercise this option is not to
constitute a waiver of the right to exercise it in the event of any subsequent default.   If collection on the note is made through
Probate Court or a Bankruptcy Court, or other appropriate legal proceedings, or if after default the note is placed in the hands
of an attorney at law for collection, the makers thereof agree to pay all costs of such collection, including attorney fees, if actually
incurred not to exceed   per centum   %)
of the amount owing on the note at the time of filing claim thereon or date of default whichever is earlier.

Figure 2-18. VA Deed of Trust, Covenants 1-11

The Grantors covenant as follows:

1. They will pay the principal of and interest on the note secured hereby in accordance with the terms thereof. Privilege is reserved to prepay at any time, without premium or fee, the entire indebtedness or any part thereof not less than the amount of one installment, or one hundred dollars ($100.00), whichever is less. Prepayment in full shall be credited on the date received. Partial prepayment, other than on an installment due date, need not be credited until the next following installment due date or thirty days after such prepayment, whichever is earlier.

2. Together with and in addition to such payments of principal and interest, they will pay to the holder of the note, as trustee (under the terms of this trust as hereinafter stated), on the first day of each month until the note is fully paid, the following sums:

(*a*) A sum equal to the ground rents, if any, next due, plus the premiums that will next become due and payable on policies of fire and other hazard insurance covering the property covered by this Deed of Trust, plus taxes and assessments next due on the premises covered hereby (all as estimated by the holder of the note and of which Grantors are notified), less all sums already paid therefor divided by the number of months to elapse before one month prior to the date when such ground rents, premiums, taxes, and assessments will become due and payable, such sums to be held by the holder of the note in trust to pay said ground rents, premiums, taxes, and special assessments, before the same become delinquent.

(*b*) All payments mentioned in the preceding subsection of this paragraph and all payments to be made under the note secured hereby shall be added together, and the aggregate amount thereof shall be paid by the Grantors each month in a single payment to be applied by the holder of the note to the following items in the order set forth:

(I) ground rents, if any, taxes, special assessments, fire, and other hazard insurance premiums;

(II) interest on the note secured hereby; and

(III) amortization of the principal of said note.

Any deficiency in the amount of such aggregate monthly payment shall, unless made good by the Grantors prior to the due date of the next such payment, constitute an event of default, under this Deed of Trust. At the option of the holder of the note, Grantors will pay a "late charge" not exceeding four per centum (4%) of any installment when paid more than fifteen (15) days after the due date thereof to cover the extra expense involved in handling delinquent payments, but such "late charge" shall not be payable out of the proceeds of any sale made to satisfy the indebtedness secured hereby, unless such proceeds are sufficient to discharge the entire indebtedness and all proper costs and expenses secured hereby.

3. If the total of the payments made by the Grantors under (*a*) of paragraph 2 preceding shall exceed the amount of payments actually made by the holder of the note, as trustee, for ground rents, taxes, assessments, or insurance premiums, as the case may be, such excess shall be credited by the holder of the note on subsequent payments to be made by the Grantors for such items or, at the option of the holder of the note, as trustee, shall be refunded to the Grantors. If, however, the monthly payments made by the Grantors under (*a*) of paragraph 2 preceding shall not be sufficient to pay ground rents, taxes, assessments, and insurance premiums, as the case may be, when the same shall become due and payable, then the Grantors shall pay to the holder of the note, as trustee, any amount necessary to make up the deficiency. Such payments shall be made within thirty (30) days after written notice from the holder of the said note stating the amount of the deficiency, which notice may be given by mail. If at any time the Grantors shall tender to the holder of the note, in accordance with the provisions thereof, the full payment of the entire indebtedness represented thereby, the holder of the note, as trustee, shall, in computing the amount of such indebtedness, credit to the account of the Grantors any balance remaining in the funds accumulated under the provisions of (*a*) of paragraph 2 hereof. If there shall be a default under any of the provisions of this Deed of Trust resulting in a public sale of the premises covered hereby or if the property is otherwise acquired after default, the holder of the note, as trustee, shall apply, at the time of the commencement of such proceedings or at the time the property is otherwise acquired, the amount then remaining in the funds accumulated under (*a*) of paragraph 2 preceding, as a credit on the interest accrued and unpaid and the balance to the principal then remaining unpaid on the note secured hereby.

4. They have a good and merchantable title in fee simple (or such other estate, if any, as is stated herein) to the premises hereby conveyed, free and clear from all encumbrances except as herein otherwise recited, with full right and authority to convey the same, and will warrant and defend the title against the claims of all persons whomsoever.

5. They will pay all taxes, assessments, water rates and other governmental or municipal charges, fines, or impositions, for which provision has not been made hereinbefore, and in default thereof the holder of the note secured hereby may pay the same; and the Grantors will promptly deliver the official receipts therefor to the said holder.

6. They will continuously maintain hazard insurance, of such type or types and amounts as the holder of the note may from time to time require, on the improvements now or hereafter on the said premises, and except when payment for all such premiums has theretofore been made under (*a*) of paragraph 2 hereof, they will pay promptly when due any premiums therefor. All insurance shall be carried in companies approved by the holder of the note and the policies and renewals thereof shall be held by the holder of the note and have attached thereto loss payable clauses in favor of and in form acceptable to the holder of the note. In event of loss they will give immediate notice by mail to the holder of the note, who may make proof of loss if not made promptly by the Grantors, and each insurance company concerned is hereby authorised and directed to make payment for such loss directly to the holder of the note instead of to the Grantors and the holder of the note jointly, and the insurance proceeds, or any part thereof, may be applied by the holder of the note at its option either to the reduction of the indebtedness hereby secured or to the restoration or repair of the property damaged. In event of foreclosure of this Deed of Trust, or other transfer of title to the said premises in extinguishment of the indebtedness secured hereby, all right, title, and interest of the Grantors in and to any insurance policies then in force shall pass to the purchaser or grantee.

7. They will not suffer any lien superior to the lien hereby created to attach to or be enforced against the premises covered hereby and will keep the said premises in as good order and condition as they are now and will not commit or permit any waste, impairment, or deterioration of said premises or any part thereof.

8. If the premises covered hereby or any part thereof shall be condemned and taken under the power of eminent domain, all damages and awards for the property so taken to the amount then unpaid on the indebtedness hereby secured, shall be paid to the holder of the note secured hereby. The amount so paid to such holder shall be credited on the indebtedness secured hereby and may, at the option of the said note holder, be applied to the last maturing installments.

9. They hereby irrevocably and specifically assign to the holder of the said note any and all rents on the premises covered hereby but so long as no default exists in the Grantors' obligations under this Deed of Trust or in the indebtedness secured hereby, the Grantors may collect and retain the rents, revenues, profits, and income from the property above described, except as provided in paragraph 14 hereof. Immediately upon any default in respect to any payment due, however its maturity is brought about, or in respect to any covenant herein, Grantors hereby authorize said holder, at its option, to take possession of the premises and to rent the same for the account of the Grantors and to deduct from such rents all costs of collection and administration and to apply the remainder of such rents on the debt hereby secured.

10. In the event the ownership of the premises covered hereby or any part thereof becomes vested in a person other than the Grantors, the holder of the note secured hereby may, without notice to the Grantors, deal with such successor or successors in interest with reference to this Deed of Trust and to the debt hereby secured in the same manner as with the Grantors without in any way vitiating or discharging the Grantors' liability hereunder or upon the debt hereby secured. No sale of the premises covered hereby and no forbearance on the part of the holder of the said note and no extension of the time for the payment of the debt hereby secured, given by said holder shall operate to release, discharge, modify, change, or affect the original liability of the Grantors either in whole or in part, nor shall the full force and effect of the lien of this instrument be altered thereby.

11. The holder of the said note shall have the right to pay any taxes, assessments, water rates, and other governmental or municipal charges, fines or impositions which are to be paid under paragraph 5 hereof, and to make any payments hereinabove provided to be made by the Grantors under subsection (*a*) of paragraph 2 hereof, and any amount so paid by the said holder shall then be added to the principal debt named herein and bear interest at the rate provided for in the principal indebtedness, payable monthly from the date of such payment and be secured by this Deed of Trust the same as said principal debt and interest thereon; and the said holder shall at its option be entitled to be subrogated to any lien, claim, or demand paid by it or discharged with the money advanced by it and secured by this Deed of Trust, which amount advanced shall be payable thirty (30) days after demand, or as may be otherwise agreed in writing between the parties hereto either before, at the time, or after making such advances.

12. Upon the request of the holder of the said note the Grantors shall execute and deliver a supplemental note or notes for the sum or sums advanced by the holder of the said note for the alteration, modernization, improvements, maintenance, or repair of said premises, for taxes or assessments against the same and for any other purpose authorized hereunder. Said note or notes shall be secured hereby on a parity with and as fully as if the advance evidenced thereby were included in the note first described above. Said supplemental note or notes shall bear interest at the rate provided for in the principal indebtedness and shall be payable in approximately equal monthly payments for such period as may be agreed upon by the creditor and debtor. Failing to agree on the maturity, the sum or sums so advanced shall be due and payable 30 days after demand by the creditor. In no event shall the maturity extend beyond the ultimate maturity of the note first described above.

13. They do hereby expressly waive and renounce the benefit of all laws now existing or that may hereafter be enacted providing for any appraisement before sale of any of the premises hereby granted.

14. As additional and collateral security for the payment of the note secured hereby and the indebtedness hereinbefore described, they hereby assign to the owner of said debt all of the profits, revenues, royalties, rights and benefits accruing under all oil, gas or mineral leases now on said property, or which may hereafter be placed thereon, and the lessee, assignee, sublessee or purchaser of production, is hereby directed on production of this Deed of Trust or certified copy thereof, to pay said profits, revenues, royalties, rights and benefits to the owner of said debt; this provision to become effective, however, only upon default in the conditions and terms of this Deed of Trust or the note hereby secured, or prior to such default, upon notice to the party obligated to pay same; and to terminate and become null and void upon payment of the indebtedness hereby secured.

Figure 2-19.   VA Deed of Trust, Covenants 12-14

If the Grantors shall well and truly pay, or cause to be paid, the note hereby secured, and any other indebtedness secured hereby, and shall keep and perform each and every covenant, condition, and stipulation herein and in said note or notes contained, then these presents shall become null and void; otherwise to be and remain in full force and effect; but if default shall be made in any payment, or part thereof, under the said note, or other indebtedness secured hereby or if for any reason (other than the fault of the holder of the note) the fire or other hazard insurance is canceled or discontinued, or if the Grantors shall fail to keep or perform any of the covenants, conditions or stipulations herein, then the said note, together with all accrued interest thereon and all other sums secured hereby, shall, at the option of the holder of the said note, become at once due and payable without demand or notice, and the Trustee hereunder shall be, and is hereby, authorized and empowered, when requested so to do by the holder of said note after such default, to sell the premises covered hereby at public auction to the highest bidder for cash, between the hours of ten o'clock A.M. and four o'clock P.M. of the first Tuesday in any month, at the door of the County Court House in the county in which said premises, or any part thereof, are situated, after advertising the time, place, and terms of said sale and the premises to be sold by posting, or causing to be posted, for at least twenty-one (21) days preceding the date of said sale written notice thereof at the courthouse door of the county in which the real estate is situated or, if the real estate is in more than one county, at the courthouse doors of every county in which the real estate is situated, and after the holder of said note shall have served written notice of said sale by certified mail, at least twenty-one (21) days preceding the date of sale, on each debtor obligated to pay such Indebtedness according to the records of such holder; provided that service of such notice shall be deemed completed by its deposit, enclosed in a postpaid wrapper, addressed to such debtor at the most recent address shown by the holder's records, in a post office or official depository under the care and custody of the United States Postal Service; and the Grantors do hereby authorize and empower said Trustee, and each and all of his or its successors in this trust, to sell said premises, together, or in lots or parcels, as such Trustee shall deem expedient, and to execute and deliver to the purchaser or purchasers of said premises good and sufficient deeds of conveyance thereof by fee simple title, with covenants of general warranty, and the title of such purchaser or purchasers, when so made by the Trustee, the Grantors bind themselves to warrant and forever defend; and to receive the proceeds of said sale which shall be applied as follows:

FIRST—To the payment of all necessary actions and expenses incident to the execution of said trust, including a reasonable fee to the Trustee, not exceeding two and one-half per centum (2½%) of the gross proceeds of the sale of said premises.

SECOND—To the payment of said note, to the amount of the principal sum and accrued interest legally due thereon, all other sums secured hereby, and to the payment of attorney's fees as in said note provided.

THIRD—To the reimbursement of the Veterans Administration for any sums paid by it on account of the guaranty or insurance of the indebtedness secured hereby.

FOURTH—The remainder, if any there shall be, after payment of said costs, expenses and attorney's fees, and the principal and interest legally due on said note, and all other sums secured hereby and other sums agreed to be paid by the Grantors, shall be paid to the Grantors.

The deed or deeds which shall be given by said Trustee to the purchaser or purchasers at such sale, shall be prima facie evidence of the truth of all the recitals therein as to default in the payment of said note, or of interest due thereon, or of the sums thereunder and hereunder due, the request to the said Trustee to sell, the advertisement or posting of such sale, the proceedings at such sale, the facts, if any, authorizing a substitute Trustee to act in the premises, and everything necessary to the validity of such sale even though such recitals are general and in the form of legal conclusions; and the purchaser or purchasers named in any such Deed, and all persons subsequently dealing with the property purported to be thereby conveyed, shall be fully protected in relying upon the truthfulness of such recitals.

After a sale under this Deed of Trust, Grantors shall be mere tenants at sufferance of the purchaser at said sale. The purchaser shall be entitled to immediate possession and may enforce said right by appropriate action. This remedy is cumulative of any and all remedies the purchaser may have hereunder or otherwise.

All estates, titles, rights, powers and duties herein given to Trustees, or imposed upon them, are given and imposed upon Trustees jointly and severally, and to the survivors of such Trustees, and may be exercised by any one or more than one, or all of such Trustees, as if any such Trustee or Trustees so acting were sole Trustee hereunder and the Grantors herein do hereby ratify and confirm any and all acts which Trustees or any of them, may do in the premises by virtue thereof or hereof.

In case of the death of the Trustee herein or of any substitute Trustee appointed hereunder, or the refusal, failure or inability of any Trustee or any substitute Trustee for any reason to act hereunder, or in the event the holder of the note shall deem it desirable to remove without cause the Trustee or any substitute Trustee and appoint another to execute this trust, then in either or any of said events the holder of the note shall have the right, and is hereby authorized and empowered to appoint by instrument in writing a substitute Trustee in lieu of the Trustee herein named, or in lieu of any substitute Trustee, who shall thereupon become vested with and succeed to all the title, power, and duties hereby conferred upon the Trustee named herein, the same as if said substitute Trustee had been named original Trustee by this instrument and any conveyance executed by him, including the recitals therein contained, shall have the same effect and validity as if executed by the Trustee named herein.

Failure of the holder of the indebtedness to exercise any option available under the terms of this instrument or the note or notes secured hereby, shall not consitute a waiver of its right to exercise the same upon any subsequent default.

If the indebtedness secured hereby be guaranteed or insured under Title 38, United States Code, such Title and Regulations issued thereunder and in effect on the date hereof shall govern the rights, duties and liabilities of the parties hereto, and any provisions of this or other instruments executed in connection with said indebtedness which are inconsistent with said Title or Regulations are hereby amended to conform thereto.

In the event any item or provision herein is violative of the laws of the State of Texas, this instrument shall be affected only as to its application to such item or provision and shall in all other respects remain in full force and effect. In no event and upon no contingency shall the maker or makers of the note secured hereby, or any party liable thereon or therefor, be required to pay interest at a rate which would be violative of any law of the State of Texas. The intention of the parties is to conform strictly to such Usury Laws as may apply to the loan secured by this instrument. If any law, applicable to this loan, limiting the amount of permissible interest or other charges to be collected, as such law may now or hereafter be interpreted, renders any charge provided for in this Deed of Trust or in the Note violative of such law as the result of prepayment of the indebtedness, acceleration of the maturity thereof, or for any other reason, such charge is hereby reduced to the extent necessary to eliminate such violation.

The indebtedness secured hereby is in renewal and extension, but not in extinguishment of that certain existing indebtedness described as follows:

9. List the three exceptions to homestead protection in the state of Texas.

10. Outline two covenants that are common to the FHA, VA, and FNMA/FHLMC deeds of trust.

PROBLEMS

1. What are the monthly payment factors for the following:

   a. A loan with a 20-year term and 12.250 percent interest rate

   b. A loan with a 15-year term and 11.125 percent interest rate

   c. A loan with a 30-year term and 14.750 percent interest rate

2. Calculate the principal and interest (P&I) payment of each of the following loans:

   a. $45,250 loan, 30-year term at 12.250 percent

   b. $62,500 loan, 20-year term at 13.375 percent

   c. $174,550 loan, 15-year term at 16.625 percent

3. Calculate the total amount that would be paid by the borrower on loans *a* and *c* in question 2.

4. Calculate the total amount of interest that would be paid by the borrower for loans *a* and *c* in question 2.

5. An $80,000 standard mortgage at 12.375 percent may be amortized in 20 years on a fixed monthly payment of _____ per month.

   a. Calculate the monthly payment.

   b. Calculate the amount of interest that will be in the first payment.

   c. Calculate the amount of interest paid in the second month.

   d. Calculate the amount of principal reduction in the third month.

3 Alternative Mortgage Instruments

LEARNING OBJECTIVES

In this chapter we will review the major alternative mortgage instruments that are presently being used in the financing of the real estate transaction.

Upon completion of this chapter, you should be able to do the following:

★ Define an alternative mortgage instrument.

★ Define many of the major alternative mortgages in use.

★ Define two variations of the graduated-payment mortgage.

★ List the major differences in the adjustable rate mortgage and the adjustable mortgage loan.

★ Define the methods to calculate escrow funds for a buy-down mortgage.

BACKGROUND

As mentioned in Chapter 2, the alternative mortgage instrument is one of the two basic types of mortgage instruments. (The other type is the standard mortgage instrument.) The alternative mortgage instrument is the type of mortgage in which at least one of the four basic mortgage characteristics varies. The importance of AMIs has grown in the last few years because the increase in interest rates means fewer persons can qualify for housing. In the past, AMIs were thought to be a creative method of financing the real estate transaction, but today they are becoming the standard.

In December 1978 the Federal Home Loan Bank Board had published a final rule that would allow federally chartered savings and loan associations to originate, participate in, or purchase certain types of alternative mortgage instruments. After the FHLBB received comments from the general public, it made the regulations effective January 1, 1979. These regulations then allowed savings and loans to originate, purchase, or participate in the variable-rate mortgage, graduated-payment mortgage, and reverse-annuity mortgage.

This regulation was amended several times to allow the savings and loans not only to make the mortgages listed previously, but also to make the renegotiable rate mortgage.

In late 1980, the FHLBB published proposed regulations that allowed federally chartered savings and loans to make the shared-appreciation mortgage and the graduated-payment adjustable mortgage.

But in the second quarter of 1981, both the FHLBB and the comptroller of the currency adopted regulations that drastically changed the types of alternative mortgages that federally chartered savings and loans and the federally chartered banks were allowed to originate and purchase, and/or in which they were allowed to participate.

With the adoption of these regulations, the previously authorized renegotiable-rate mortgage (RRM) and the variable-rate mortgage (VRM) have been canceled. In the place of the

RRM and the VRM, the comptroller of the currency allows national banks to originate, purchase, or participate in the adjustable-rate mortgage, and the FHLBB allows the savings associations to originate, purchase, or participate in the adjustable mortgage loan. However, RRMs and VRMs are of course still offered by other lenders.

A discussion of the old FHLBB rules governing the canceled RRM and the VRM is included in this chapter to give some insight into these RRMs and VRMs offered by other lenders.

Then in the early part of 1983, after the passage of federal legislation, both the Comptroller of the Currency and the Federal Home Loan Bank Board implemented new regulations that allowed more flexibility for both the federally chartered banks and savings and loan associations; in particular, the adjustable-rate mortgages. The changes instituted by the Comptroller of the Currency deleted any reference to limitations on the amount of adjustment or frequency of adjustment. Thus, the adjustable-rate mortgages offered by the federally chartered banks and savings and loans are very similar.

In this chapter, we will examine all of the listed AMIs as well as other types of commonly used AMIs. In addition, we will review some of the variations of the graduated-payment mortgages presently being made by some of the mortgage lenders in Texas.

COMPTROLLER OF THE CURRENCY ADJUSTABLE-RATE MORTGAGE (ARM)

With the cost of funds increasing in 1980 and 1981, the comptroller of the currency proposed a type of mortgage instrument that would allow all national banks to design an adjustable-rate mortgage that would meet the needs of the banks and the needs of the banks' customers. So on September 29, 1980, the Office of the Comptroller of the Currency published in the *Federal Register* a proposed regulation that would allow adjustable-rate mortgage lending by all national banks.

The comment period on this regulation was to expire on November 28, 1980, but since the Federal Home Loan Bank Board was also interested in a similar type of mortgage instrument, the comment period was extended to December 30, 1980, allowing the Office of the Comptroller of the Currency and the Federal Home Loan Bank Board to hold joint hearings on the proposed regulation.

As a result of these hearings and other comments received by the comptroller of the currency, a regulation was adopted on March 27, 1981, allowing the national banks to make, purchase, or participate in the adjustable-rate mortgage. Then on June 2, 1982, the comptroller of the currency published a proposed rule that would amend the existing ARM regulation. According to the introductory information, the proposed rule was to make the ARM conform more to the Federal Home Loan Bank Board's Adjustable Mortgage Loan (AML) and the National Credit Union Administration's ARM. Both of these mortgages will be discussed later in this chapter.

On March 7, 1983, the proposed rule was issued as a Final Rule by the Comptroller of the Currency (COC). We will examine the revised regulation in some depth, for this type of mortgage has become a very widely used mortgage to finance the residential real estate transaction. For example, according to the Federal Home Loan Bank Board in May 1984, the ARM makes up over one half of all of the single-family conventional loans. With this figure in mind, as a real estate professional, you must be as familiar as possible with the major provisions of the Comptroller of the Currency's ARM.

Definition of the ARM

First we need to define the ARM. According to the regulation, an adjustable-rate mortgage is

> *any loan made to finance or refinance the purchase of and secured by a lien on a one-to-four-family dwelling, including a condominium unit, cooperative housing unit, or a mobile home, where such loan is made pursuant to an agreement intended to enable the lender to adjust the rate of interest from time to time.*[1]

Thus, the ARM may include mortgages that have the rate adjusted periodically. It will also include fixed-rate mortgages that have the feature of rate adjustment by the mortgage having a demand feature or by the maturity of the note at a time prior to the end of the total amortization period. For example, if a borrower secures a mortgage on a home with a term of thirty years, but the note has a "call option" at the end of each seven-year period and the national bank has agreed to refinance the note at a different interest rate, the loan would be governed by this regulation.

Major Provisions

Rate change index   According to Section 29.3 of the regulation, the changes in the interest rate on an ARM are to be linked or tied to an index. This index is to be specified in the original loan documents. For example, a 50-basis point (1 basis point = .01 percentage point) or one-half of 1 percent change in the index normally will be transferred into a 50-basis point change in the same direction in the note interest rate. The section further states that the bank may use any interest rate index or measure of market interest rates that can be easily confirmed by the borrower and is beyond the control of the bank. Thus, a bank located in El Paso may use the prime rate of a New York bank or a government security. Both of these indexes meet the requirements of this section.

In the previous regulations, the banks were required to choose among several indexes listed in the regulation, but the Comptroller felt that a broad choice of indexes was necessary if the banks are to design ARM loans that meet both the need of the consumer and the bank. We should also consider the method or time of the selection of the initial index value and rate change value of the index or how the interest rate will be established at time of adjustment. The time of determination of the initial value can be of grave importance to the real estate professional. If you are working with a client in times of rising interest rates, the sooner the initial interest rate index can be established, the lower the interest rate your client will have to pay. The previous regulation required that the initial index value be the most recent available value at the time of closing or at the time the bank commits to make or purchase the ARM. This requirement has been removed. Thus, when contacting lenders in your area you must establish with the lender when the initial value of the index will be established. If at all possible, have the lender establish the initial value at the time of loan application.

In addition to the problem of rising interest rates, the COC has raised another concern: by not indicating when the initial index value is to be determined, the bank could select an index value that would allow the bank to attract borrowers with an unrealistically low interest rate. Borrowers might then be in for a sizable rate change at the first rate adjustment. It should be noted that the increase would not relate to changes in current market rates. It should be further noted that the COC has stated in the regulation that the banks are not to use the flexibility in determining the initial rate to offer a short-term bargain rate for the specific purpose of attracting borrowers. Thus, as a real estate professional, you should check with each of the banks in your area to see when each establishes the initial index value.

The establishment of the value of the interest rate index at the time of adjustment has also been revised with the new regulation. In the past, the interest rate index had to reflect a basis-point-for-basis-point change in the interest rate. Thus, if the index moved 3 basis points, the interest rate on the note moved in the same amount. This requirement has been replaced with the requirement that the relationship between the interest rate index and the interest rate on the ARM be outlined in the loan documents.

The new regulations no longer require the lender to base the rate change on the most recent index available at the time the borrower is notified of a rate change. Now, the lender can base the new or adjusted rate on the most recent available value of the index at the time of notification or at the time the actual rate is changed. Thus, the bank is no longer required to give the borrower notice at any time prior to the rate adjustment date. The process as to the notification of rate change is outlined in the note. As a real estate professional, you should find a lender that gives the borrower at least 30 days prior notice of rate change.

Rate changes   According to section 29.4 of the rule, there is no limitation on the amount or frequency that the rate on the ARM may be changed. Thus, the rate could be adjusted daily, but this is not likely due to the cost of such changes to the bank. According to the COC, even though the majority of the restrictions on the interest rate changes have been removed, the new regulation requires the interest rate changes be made in accordance with the procedures specified in the original loan documents. But the COC does require that the procedures must cover certain aspects of the interest rate change. According to the explanation of this section of the rule, the COC requires that the original loan document must cover the frequency of the rate change and the method of implementing the rate change (that is, through changes in the monthly payment, changes in the loan balance, or both). In addition, the loan documents must state or outline any other rules relating to rate changes that the bank might impose—such as rounding the interest rate to the nearest one-eighth of 1 percent, caps or limits on the magnitude of the rate or payment change, any carry over of changes in the excess of such limitations, or any mandatory and optional interest rate adjustments. It should be noted that this rule does not in any way prohibit banks from establishing limits on the frequency and amount of interest rate adjustments.

Amortization   The next section of the rule is entitled Amortization Requirements (Section 29.5). This section of the rule, which set the amortization requirements of the ARM, was deleted from the rule on September 9, 1983. Thus, the banks have no requirements for amortization for the ARM. Therefore, these mortgages may have negative amortization. Negative amortization may be defined as the process of making monthly payments that are not sufficient to pay all of the interest due. The difference between the interest due and the amount paid with the monthly payment is added to the outstanding balance of the loan. Thus, a borrower will owe more money than they borrowed. It should be noted that this section of the rule allows for no principal reduction for the first 21 years of the loan, thus negative amortization could happen for several years.

Prepayment fees   Section 29.6 of the rule, Prepayment Fees, allows the lender to charge a prepayment fee, regardless of any state law that prohibits or limits such fees. According to the COC in *Supplemental information: special analyses (Federal Register*/vol. 48, no. 45/ Monday, March 7, 1983/ Rules and Regulations), the banks are not prohibited from charging a fee for the interest rate or payment adjustment. This is to be outlined in the original loan documents.

Assumption   There is no section in the new rule relating to the assumption of the ARM. With the passage of Public Law 97-320, the Garn-St. Germain Depository Institutions Act of 1982, Section 314, has rendered such a provision in the rule unnecessary because the law provides statutory preemption of state laws that limit or prohibit the enforcement of due-on-sale clauses by lenders. This law did not affect Texas in that we have no such laws.

Disclosure–initial   As with any other alternative mortgage instrument, the bank is required to give a disclosure to the prospective borrower. The regulation in section 29.7 requires the bank to give a disclosure when it either gives written information about an ARM or at the time of application. It would be advisable for a person interested in the ARM to secure a copy of the ARM disclosure before the time of application in order to better understand the ramifications of the ARM.

In addition to the requirement as to the time the disclosure is to be given, the rule requires that the disclosure contain the following information:

1. The disclosure must indicate that the interest rate may change and a brief description of the general nature of an ARM.

2. It must list the index that will be used and at least one readily available source in which the index is published.

3. A chart showing the value of the index for the past 10 years using a semi-annual basis. For example, the rate as of June and December of each of the years as shown in Figure 3–1.

4. In addition to naming the index, the disclosure must state the frequency of adjustment of the interest rate and the payment.

5. A statement that, if appropriate, the initial annual payment of principal and interest may be different than the payment required to amortize the loan over the term of the loan. This portion must also state the effect this will have on the amortization of the loan. In other words, there must be information on any negative amortization.

6. A description of the method that will be used to implement an interest rate change, including, if appropriate to the loan, an example of negative amortization and balloon payments.

7. A statement, if required, relating to the refinancing of demand or short-term loans as well as prepayment and assumption.

Figure 3–1.   Adjustable-Rate Mortgage Indexes (Monthly Rate for June and December 1969–80)

	Mortgage Rates on Previously Occupied Homes	3-Year Treasury Rates	6-Month Treasury Rates		Mortgage Rates on Previously Occupied Homes	3-Year Treasury Rates	6-Month Treasury Rates
1969:				*1975:*			
June	7.64%	6.83%	6.725%	June	8.86%	7.17%	5.463%
December	8.08%	8.10%	7.788%	December	9.09%	7.43%	5.933%
1970:				*1976:*			
June	8.19%	7.84%	6.907%	June	8.82%	7.32%	5.784%
December	8.12%	5.75%	4.848%	December	8.90%	5.68%	4.513%
1971:				*1977:*			
June	7.38%	6.32%	4.890%	June	8.78%	6.39%	5.198%
December	7.51%	5.27%	4.199%	December	8.93%	7.30%	6.377%
1972:				*1978:*			
June	7.36%	5.64%	4.270%	June	9.27%	8.30%	7.200%
December	7.45%	6.01%	5.287%	December	9.85%	9.33%	9.397%
1973:				*1979:*			
June	7.64%	6.83%	7.234%	June	10.46%	8.95%	9.062%
December	8.46%	6.81%	7.444%	December	11.59%	10.71%	11.847%
1974:				*1980:*			
June	8.66%	8.15%	8.232%	June	12.88%	8.91%	7.218%
December	9.39%	7.24%	7.091%	December	13.15%	13.65%	14.700%

SOURCE: "Rules and Regulations," *Federal Register*, March 27, 1981, vol. 46, no. 59, p. 18947.

8. A description of any fees that will be charged at the time of interest rate or payment adjustment or for the prepayment of the outstanding principal balance as well as an explanation on how these fees will be calculated.

9. A statement of the fees that will be charged by the bank or any other person connected with the loan, including fees that will be due at loan closing.

10. Finally, the disclosure must contain a worse-case example showing the effect on the P & I payment on a $10,000 loan if the interest rate increases at the rate of 1 percent every 6 months.

An example of a possible initial ARM disclosure is shown in Figure 3–2.

Disclosure—scheduled adjustment   In addition to the initial disclosure, the regulation or rule requires the banks to supply the borrower with a rate or payment change notice. The regulation requires the bank to supply this to the borrower not later than one day after a rate change is implemented or, if the rate change includes a change in payment, the bank is required to supply a notice to the borrower at least 25 days prior to the due day of the first payment at the new level. The written change notice will contain the following items:

1. The disclosure must give the current and previous interest rate as well as the values of the index for both payments.

2. If there is a cap or ceiling on the amount the payment or interest rate may increase and the bank has had to forego any increase, a statement must be included if any of the increase has been or will be carried over to the next adjustment period.

3. The bank must disclose the amount of the payment after the implementation of the interest rate change. If this payment is different from the payment required to pay off the loan over the remaining term, the bank must also disclose this fact and show the payment that would be required to pay off the loan.

Figure 3–2. **Model Form for Initial Adjustable-Rate Mortgage Disclosure**

Important Mortgage Loan Information—
Please Read Carefully

If you wish to apply for an Adjustable-Rate Mortgage (ARM) loan with _____ National Bank, you should read the information below concerning the difference between this mortgage and other mortgages with which you may be familiar.

General Description of Adjustable-Rate Mortgage Loan

THE LOAN OFFERED BY _____ NATIONAL BANK IS AN ADJUSTABLE-RATE MORTGAGE. ITS INTEREST RATE WILL CHANGE [fill in frequency] BASED ON MOVEMENTS OF AN INTEREST RATE INDEX. YOUR MONTHLY PAYMENTS WILL INCREASE IF THE INTEREST RATE RISES OR DECREASE IF THE INTEREST RATE FALLS. BECAUSE FUTURE MOVEMENTS OF THE INDEX ARE RELATED TO MARKET CONDITIONS THAT CANNOT BE PREDICTED, IT IS IMPOSSIBLE TO KNOW IN ADVANCE HOW MUCH YOU WILL HAVE TO PAY, EITHER EACH MONTH OR OVER THE LIFE OF THE LOAN. INTEREST RATE AND PAYMENT CHANGES WILL BE MADE ACCORDING TO CERTAIN RULES THAT ARE EXPLAINED BELOW.

Key Terms of _____ *National Bank's Adjustable Rate Mortgage*

The following outline of the terms on ARM's offered by _____ National Bank is intended for easy reference only. You will find other essential information in this disclosure statement and in the loan note itself.

Loan Term . . . .
Frequency of rate changes . . . .
*[Grace period before first rate change . . . .]
Interest rate index . . . .
Maximum rate change at one time . . . .
Maximum rate change over life of loan . . . .
*[Minimum rate change at one time . . . .]
*[Minimum increments of rate change . . . .]
*[Prepayment fee . . . .]
Assumability [assumable, not assumable *or* at lender's discretion] . . . .
Possibility of increasing loan balance [yes *or* no] . . . .

*Bracketed items and footnotes are instructions to national banks or contain optional language to be selected as appropriate.

How Your Adjustable-Rate Mortgage Would Work

Starting Interest Rate

The starting interest rate offered by _____ National Bank on an ARM will be specified [at loan closing, when we make a loan commitment to you, other] based on market conditions at that time.

Frequency of Interest Rate Changes

Your interest rate will be reviewed every _____ beginning _____ after the date on which you take out your loan, and may increase or decrease at those times based on changes in the index.

Index for Measuring Interest Rate Changes

The index to which your interest rate will be tied is _____ .
Information on this index is published monthly in _____ . The table below shows a ten-year history of movements of this index. This does not necessarily indicate how the index may perform in the future.

10-Year History of _____ Index

Date	Index	Change from preceding rate
1/1/x0	. . . .	
7/1/x0	. . . .	
1/1/x1	. . . .	
	* * * * *	
7/1/x9	. . . .	

Figure 3–2.   *continued*

Size of Interest Rate Changes

The interest rate on your ARM will increase or decrease based on movements in the index. A change in the index of 1 percentage point will be translated into a 1 percentage point change of the same direction in your ARM interest rate. However, no single change in the interest rate will be more than _____ percentage points no matter how much the index may have moved. [Also, there will be no change in your interest rate if the index moves less than _____ percentage points.] All changes will be in increments of _____ percentage points.]

Mandatory and Optional Rate Changes

Decreases in your interest rate warranted by decreases in the index will always be automatic within the rules for maximum [and minimum] changes. However, increases warranted by increases in the index may be forgone at the bank's option. If the bank forgoes an interest rate increase, we may take it at a later interest rate change date, unless doing so would conflict with the carryover rule described below.

Carryover of Unused Index Changes

Changes in the index not passed on to you as changes in your ARM interest rate will be carried over to the next interest rate change date. This can happen when the index has moved more than the maximum permitted change (_____ percentage points) [or less than a minimum permitted change (_____ percentage points)] or when the bank has forgone an interest rate increase to which it is entitled. The carryover is the amount by which the net index change exceeds the net interest rate change since the loan was made. The net change is the difference between the interest rate (or index) on a given date and the interest rate (or index) on the date the loan was made. In addition to new index changes, index changes carried over may be passed on to you at the next rate adjustment date as a change in your ARM interest rate. However, we may not pass these carryovers on to you to the extent they have been offset by an opposite movement in the index as of that date. Also, if the total of the new index change and the carryover still exceeds the maximum permitted change (_____ percentage points) [or is less than a minimum permitted change (_____ percentage points)] the excess must be carried over again.

[The following example may be included at the bank's option:

An example shows how this carryover rule works. Suppose the index increases by 1.60 percentage points during the first period, but your rate change is limited by the rules to 1.00 percentage point. The remaining .60 percentage point would be carried over, so that at your next rate change date:

If the index in the new period had *stayed the same*, your mortgage rate would *still rise* by .60 percentage point.

If the index had decreased by .20 percentage point your mortgage rate would *still rise* by .40 percentage point (the difference between the increase that was carried over and the decline).

If the index had *decreased* by 1.0 percentage point your mortgage rate would *decrease by only* .40 percentage point (again, the difference between the new decrease and the carried over increase).

If the index had *increased* by .70 percentage point, your mortgage rate would increase by only 1.0 percentage point because of the 1.0 percentage point limit, *but* there would be a *new carryover* of .30 percentage point into the next rate change period (the difference between the 1.0 percentage point limit and the 1.30 percentage points justified by the old carryover plus the index change).]

Payment Changes

Changes in the interest rate on your mortgage will mean that your monthly payment will change to an amount sufficient to repay your loan over its life at the new interest rate.

Notice of Rate Changes

_____ National Bank will send you notice of any rate change at least 30 days before it becomes effective. The notice will tell you how the index has changed and how your interest rate and payment schedule will be affected. This notice will also be sent whenever the bank forgoes an interest rate increase it is permitted to take [and/but not] when the index has not changed at a rate adjustment date. All interest rate changes will be based on index information available at the time the notice is sent, rather than when the rate change goes into effect.

Prepayment Penalty

You may prepay an ARM in whole or in part without penalty at any time after the first notice of index movement has been sent to you [or, if the index has not changed, any time after the last date on which such a notice would have been sent]. This prepayment may be a lump sum payment of all or part of the remaining debt or may be in the form of larger monthly payments than required under the terms of the loan. _____ National Bank imposes a penalty charge of _____ for prepayments prior to the first rate change notice date.

Assumption of Mortgage Loan

Your ARM may be assumed by a purchaser of your home who meets our credit standards. [We have the right to change the loan terms, including the interest rate, upon assumption, and we may also charge the purchaser assumption fees.]

Figure 3–2. *continued*

Fees

   You will be charged fees by _____ National Bank and by other persons in connection with the origination of an ARM. We will give you an estimate of these fees within 3 days after receiving your loan application. However, _____ National Bank will not charge you any finance or processing fees at the time of any rate adjustment.

How Rapidly Rising Interest Rates Could Affect Your Adjustable-Rate Mortgage Loan

   The following table shows the effect a 10 percentage point increase in the index rate, taken as rapidly as possible, would have on monthly payments on a $10,000 ARM made at a starting interest rate of _____%. To figure the equivalent potential payment increases for your mortgage, simply multiply the payments in the table times 2 for a $20,000 loan, times 3 for a $30,000 loan, etc.

   [The table that follows would apply to an ARM with interest rate adjustments occurring every six months, a one percentage point periodic interest rate limit, an aggregate interest rate cap in excess of 10 percentage points, and an initial contract interest rate of 10%. Lender should insert relevant example.]

Payments No.	Year No.	Interest rate (percent)	Amount of payments
1 to 6	1	10.0	$ 87.76
7 to 12		11.0	95.18
13 to 18	2	12.0	102.71
19 to 24		13.0	110.34
25 to 30	3	14.0	118.04
31 to 36		15.0	125.81
37 to 42	4	16.0	133.63
43 to 48		17.0	141.49
49 to 54	5	18.0	149.39
55 to 60		19.0	157.32
61 to 360	6+	20.0	165.27

Source: "Rules and Regulations," *Federal Register*, March 27, 1981, vol. 46, no. 59, pp. 18945-946.

4. The disclosure must contain a statement regarding any fees that would be charged if the borrower, upon notice of the increase in interest rate or payment increase, wishes to repay the loan in full.

Disclosure—unscheduled adjustment

The bank must notify the borrower if the ARM contains the provision for a payment increase for reasons other than a change in the index. This is referred to by some banks as the unscheduled payment increase provision. This usually will occur if there is negative amortization and it exceeds the amount authorized in the original loan documents.

1. This notice, like this disclosure for scheduled adjustment, must be in writing and sent at least 25 days prior to the date the new payment may take effect.

2. The notice must contain an explanation of the reason or circumstances that led to the change in the payment.

3. The notice must indicate the amount of the new payment after the adjustment.

4. Also if the borrower wishes to pay off the loan before the payment changes are implemented, the notice must indicate any fees that would be charged.

Balloon and demand ARMs

Under the new rule or regulations of the COC, the banks are authorized to make balloon and short-term ARMs. According to the rule, balloon loans are defined as any loan to finance or refinance the purchase of a 1- to 4-family dwelling that is payable without any amortization by the term that is less than the amortization period. For example, a borrower could have a 1-year ARM with a term of 5 years, but the payments are based on a 30-year amortization schedule.

A demand ARM according to the rule or regulation is any loan to finance or refinance the purchase of a 1- to 4-family dwelling secured by a deed of trust that is payable upon demand of the bank. The demand feature may be related to a date or circumstance. This may be, for example, if the market interest rate exceeds the rate on the note by more than 3 points. One possible use is as a builders' interim loan, in which case the event would be the sale of the property by the builder.

FEDERAL HOME LOAN BANK BOARD ADJUSTABLE RATE MORTGAGE (ARM)

As was mentioned in the section on the adjustable-rate mortgages, the Federal Home Loan Bank Board was interested in a similar type of mortgage that would allow the federally chartered savings and loan associations (S and Ls) to make loans that would reflect the associations' cost of funds and assure the associations a fair return on monies lent. So after soliciting comments from the general public, the savings and loan associations, the building industry, and any group that had an interest in this type of mortgage, the FHLBB published a regulation effective on April 30, 1981, allowing the federally chartered S and Ls to make, purchase, participate in, or otherwise deal in an adjustable mortgage loan instrument. It should be noted again that, with the issuance of this regulation, the FHLBB has replaced the regulation allowing federally chartered savings and loan associations to make the renegotiable-rate mortgage and the variable-rate mortgage. With the issuance of the regulation, the FHLBB has preempted all state laws that would directly or indirectly restrict a federally chartered association or a federally chartered savings bank from making an ARM. This includes any state law that would limit charging interest on interest.

The Federal Home Loan Bank Board followed the lead of the Comptroller of the Currency and revised the original regulations allowing the federally chartered S and Ls to make an adjustable-rate mortgage. In the original regulations, the Federal Home Loan Bank Board (FHLBB) had called their adjustable mortgage an adjustable mortgage loan (AML), but the revised regulation, effective August 16, 1983, deletes all references to the name or initials. This does not mean that the federal S and Ls may not originate this type of loan, but only that the specific name has been deleted. Thus, many of the associations have adopted the name *adjustable-rate mortgage* and we now have some standardization in the field.

As with the previous ARM, we will review this regulation in some detail because there are some differences and because most S and Ls are presently offering an ARM. The portion of the FHLBB's regulations that will be reviewed in this section is 545.33, Home Loans. The FHLBB authorizes a mortgage with an adjustment feature with a term of 40 years and a maximum loan-to-value ratio of 100 percent of the market value.

Major Provisions

Rate or payment change   The regulation adopted by the FHLBB contains no provision to limit the amount that the interest rate or the payment may change. The regulation also does not limit the frequency of rate and/or payment adjustment, thus the adjustment could be as often as every day if the selected index changes that often. According to the FHLBB, the associations need the flexibility to design the frequency and amount of increase to meet the demands of their particular market, and the FHLBB believes that, in order to build public confidence in the ARM, lenders will adopt limitations on the amount and frequency of change due to competition in the market place. It has been proven that those in the secondary market who will purchase the ARM will require such limitations on the rate and/or payment increases.

The only restriction placed on the adjustment in section 545.33e(1) is that the adjustment to the interest rate shall correspond directly to the movement in an interest-rate index. It should be noted that the association may decrease the interest rate at any time.

Rate change indexes   As mentioned in the previous section, the adjustment must be tied to an interest-rate index.

In addition, the regulations allow an S and L to use a regional or national index that measures the rate of inflation as well as an index that measures the rate of change in the consumer disposal income. As with the Comptroller of the Currency regulations, the index must be readily available to the borrower and beyond the control of the association.

The regulation gives the associations the additional option of being able to use any combination of indexes or a moving average of index values as an index. Also, the association may use more than one index during the term of the loan.

As with the COC ARM regulations, the index that will be used to adjust the interest rate will be named in the original documents and selected by the lender.

Prepayment   The regulation states that for an association to charge a prepayment fee, the association must have included a prepayment charge in the original loan documents as well as having disclosed this fact to the borrower. If the original loan documents make no mention of a prepayment fee it is felt that the borrower has the right to prepay in part or in whole without penalty.

As a real estate professional, you will therefore need to contact the savings and loan associations in your area to see which of them do or will charge a prepayment fee.

Assumption The FHLBB regulation makes no reference to assumption, thus leaving the question of assumption up to the local association. It is therefore, important for the real estate professional to be familiar with the policies of each of the associations in his or her area.

Negative amortization Under the new regulations, the FHLBB permits negative amortization. This can occur when the payment is not sufficient to pay the interest due. The amount of interest not paid by the monthly payment will be added to the loan balance. This is called *capitalized interest.* The associations are authorized to allow negative amortization for a period of 10 years after loan closing. To reduce the effects of negative amortization, the associations may extend the term of the loan to 40 years; and if this is not sufficient, the association can institute a "catch-up" payment.

The catch-up payment may be either the payment of cash necessary to allow the amortization of the loan over the remaining term without an increase in the payment, or the payment may be increased to a level sufficient to amortize the loan over the remaining term. For example, if the loan had been in negative amortization for a period of 5 years, if the extension of the term was insufficient to pay off the outstanding loan balance in the term remaining, and if the borrower did not wish to make a cash payment, then the payment would have to be increased to a level to pay off the loan in the remaining term. According to the FHLBB, after the 10-year initial period there must be a catch-up payment scheduled every 5 years to be sure the mortgage is fully amortized over the remaining term. There is one exception to this requirement—if the association imposes a limit to the amount of negative amortization. This limitation is that the loan balance may never exceed 125 percent of the original appraisal price of the property being used as security for the loan.

Adjustable loan disclosures As with the Comptroller of the Currency regulations, there are two required disclosures for the S and L making the ARM. The first disclosure will be given to the borrower not later than 3 days

after the receipt of a written application by the association and will contain the following:

1. *Term of the loan to maturity,* thus the disclosure would state 20, 30, or 40 years.

2. *Initial interest rate on the loan,* if known, or the manner in which the initial rate will be established. Normally an association will not know the interest rate unless the association is making the loan against a commitment. Usually the association will state in the disclosure that the interest rate will be set at the time of a commitment and that the interest rate may change prior to the closing due to changes in the market conditions.

3. *Amount of the initial monthly payment,* if known, and an explanation of how the association will establish an amortization schedule for the loan. This must include how the association calculates the amount of each payment and what portion of each payment will be credited to interest. In other words, the association must explain that it has established an amortization schedule for the loan.

4. *Full explanation of how the interest rate, payment, loan balance, or term to maturity may be adjusted.* This will include the identification of the index or indexes that will be used as the interest rate index. In addition, the disclosure must give information about the sources where the value of the index or indexes used may be obtained by the borrower. Finally, this section must explain how the adjustment of one item, such as the interest rate, may affect the others, such as the payment.

5. *Information that will be contained in the notice of adjustment.*

6. *Description of all contractual contingencies,* if necessary, under which the loan may become due or that may result in forced sale of the property. This does not include the borrowers breach or failure to pay. This only deals with such items as a reverse annuity mortgage, or if the mortgage has a demand feature. An example would be if the interest rate on the mortgage fell below a certain level, the mortgage would be due and payable.

7. *Statement whether the mortgage is a balloon mortgage with an adjustable interest*

rate or a partially amortized loan, and, unless the association unconditionally obligates itself to refinance the loan, that a large payment will be due at the maturity of the loan and that the association is under no obligation to refinance the loan. Also, there must be a statement regarding the association's right to call the loan after a specific number of years. Once again the association is under no obligation to refinance the loan.

8. *Statement whether the loan will have a prepayment penalty or fee.*

9. *Statement whether there will be an escrow of funds* because many lenders escrow monies for taxes, insurance, and mortgage insurance. The disclosure must also state the purpose of the escrow and how the amount of the escrow payment was established.

10. *An example of the interaction of all of the variable features of the ARM over a period of time.*

Disclosure–adjustment   The regulation requires a notice to be sent to the borrower at least 30 days, but not more than 120 days, before the adjustment of the payment. If the loan has the interest rate changing more frequently than the payment, no notice is required prior to the payment change. The regulation does not state what information must be contained in the notice.

Payment-capped mortgages   Many of the associations are offering the adjustable mortgage with a payment cap. Normally, these capped mortgages may be divided into two types. The first is the *interest-rate-capped* mortgage, which limits the amount that the interest may increase, thus limiting the amount the monthly payment may increase. The second type is the *payment-capped mortgage*. With this type of mortgage, the interest rate on the loan is adjusted to reflect changes in the index; but to avoid any sharp increase in the monthly payment, the increase in the monthly payment is limited.

Capped mortgages sometimes have a carry-over provision. This provision allows the association or lender to carry over to the next adjustment period an increase not allowed by the cap; but normally, the lender can only take the amount that is not offset by an opposite movement in the index. For example, if the lender carried forward 0.50 or one-half of 1 per-

cent to the next adjustment period, and if at the next adjustment date the index had fallen one full percentage point, the lender could only have to lower the interest rate by one-half of 1 percent (the amount carried over).

NATIONAL CREDIT UNION ADMINISTRATION'S ARM

Before we leave the discussion of the ARM, we should review the ARM authorized by the National Credit Union Administration (NCUA). On July 22, 1981, the NCUA implemented a rule allowing all federally chartered credit unions to make an adjustable-rate mortgage.

On June 11, 1981, the NCUA board invited public comment on a proposal to allow the federal credit unions to make the ARM. According to NCUA, the majority of the comments received were favorable, but there were several recommendations. These recommendations were incorporated into a proposed rule that was published for comment on December 1, 1981. Now let us review some of the major provisions of the final rule.

Definition

The final rule defines the adjustable-rate mortgage as

a mortgage loan which permits the periodic adjustment of the rate of interest on the loan in response to the movement of an index which was agreed upon in advance by the borrower and the Federal credit union.[2]

One can see that, by this definition, the ARM loan authorized is similar to those authorized by the FHLBB and the Comptroller of the Currency.

Interest Rate Index

According to section (e) of the rule, the Federal credit union may use any index whose movement is beyond the control of the credit union and is readily verifiable by the borrower. One can see that this is similar to the wording contained in the FHLBB and COC rule authorizing the Federal savings and loans and Federal banks to make the ARM. As was mentioned in the definition, the index to be used must be agreed upon in advance by the union and the borrower. Thus, this indicates that the index to be used is a negotiable item, and must be shown in the original loan documents.

As with the ARM, any increase or decrease in the face interest rate of the mortgage must be reflected in a corresponding movement in the index. All decreases indicated by movement in the index are mandatory except for certain limitations:

1. The decrease is offset by an amount of a previously indicated increase not taken at that time and postponed or carried over.

2. The decrease exceeds any limitation or cap on the amount the interest rate may increase or decrease.

3. The indicated decrease is less than one eighth of a percent

4. If there is a decrease that would move the interest rate to a level that is lower than a minimum rate which was agreed upon between the union and the borrower in advance of the execution of the original loan documents

Frequency of Adjustments

According to the rule, the interest rate of the mortgage may be adjusted as often as every 30 days as long as the adjustment is based on the movement of the index.

Implementation of Adjustments

The final rule states that the adjustment in the interest rate may be implemented through the increasing of the monthly payment, negative amortization, extension of the loan term, maturity, or a combination of any of these methods. It should be noted that the rule does allow for an adjustment cap. Thus, the amount of increase or decrease may be limited. This must be contained in the original loan documents and negotiated prior to the execution of the original loan documents.

If the option of extension of loan term or maturity is used, the rule states that no adjustment may cause the maturity to exceed forty years.

Disclosures

Initial or application disclosure The proposed rule issued for public comment had two suggestions for initial disclosure. One of the proposed methods of disclosure was that the

disclosure be made in accordance with the provision of the Truth-in-Lending Act (Regulation Z). The second method proposed would require the unions to make the disclosures contained in the Truth-in-Lending Act, but within 3 days of the application, and in addition to the information required to be disclosed by the Truth-in-Lending Act, the union would have to disclose the following:

1. The index to be used

2. How often an increase or decrease may occur

3. How any increase or decrease may be calculated

After receiving comments and reviewing the regulations implementing the new Truth-in-Lending Simplification Act, NCUA felt that the initial disclosure should be made, in form and content, similar to that required for an adjustable-rate mortgage under Regulation Z. It should be noted that NCUA did state that, if the credit union does not use the form suggested by the Truth-in-Lending Act, the union may develop its own form, but it must be a "plain language" form.

Rate and payment adjustments There is no requirement that the borrower be notified of any payment or rate change, but NCUA feels that the union will, in its normal business activities, provide some type of notification to the borrower.

Costs or Fees

As with the other ARM, the regulation states that the borrower may not be charged any fees or costs in conjunction with the regularly scheduled interest rate and/or payment adjustment.

STANDARD ARM INSTRUMENTS

Now that we have reviewed some of the major ARMs authorized and learned that the lenders have a great deal of flexibility in the structuring of the ARM, there is a trend to the standardization of the ARM. The leaders of this standardization are two of the larger secondary marketers (a secondary marketer is a corporation, business, or individual that purchases closed real estate loans), the Federal National Mortgage Association (FNMA or Fannie Mae), and the Federal Home Loan

Mortgage Corporation (FHLMC). Since these two organizations purchase a large share of the ARMs, as with the standard mortgage, we will review their instruments.

Texas Adjustable-Rate Note

The notes that will be reviewed in this section are those issued by Fannie Mae/FHLMC as of December 1983, with four notes in the series. All of these notes will use U.S. Treasury Securities as an index.

Adjustable-rate note (1 year index-payment cap)

This note is shown in Figures 3–3 through 3–6. The top of the first page of the note (Figure 3–3) states in bold type that the note contains provisions that allow the interest rate and monthly payment to change. Also the borrower may be able to limit the monthly payment increase to 7.5 percent each year.

Section 1 is identical to the fixed-rate note reviewed in Chapter 2. It states that the borrower promises to pay to the lender an amount with interest.

Section 2 states that the interest will be charged on the unpaid balance and at a yearly rate of _____ percent, as well as stating that the interest rate will change in accordance with Section 4 of the note.

Section 3 is divided into three subsections. Subsection A, Time and Place of Payments, is identical to the Texas fixed-rate note. Subsections B and C are unique to this note. Subsection B, Amount of My Initial Monthly Payment, will state the payment in dollars. Since this is an adjustable-rate note and is adjusted every year, subsection C states that the interest rate and payment will change.

In subsection A of section 4, Interest Rate and Monthly payment change; Borrowers Right to Limit Payment, the change date is established for the first change and as the subsection states, the interest rate will change on that day every year thereafter.

Subsection B of the section establishes the interest-rate index that will be used. For this note and all of the Fannie Mae/FHLMC Texas adjustable-rate notes, the index will be either the 1-, 3-, or 5-year Treasury securities. Since this note will be adjusted annually, the 1-year Treasury security will be used as the index for this note. As you will notice, the note is specific. The index will be the weekly average yield of the 1-year Treasury security. As we learned in our study of the ARM disclosures,

the lender must identify what will be used as the current index. This information is also contained in this subsection.

In subsection C, Calculation of Changes (Figure 3–4), you will note that the lender will calculate the new interest rate by adding a certain spread or yield to the current index. In addition, this subsection allows the lender to round the interest rate to the nearest one-eighth. Using the new interest rate and the remaining term, the lender will calculate the new monthly payment that would be required to pay the loan off over the remaining term.

Subsections D and E are self-explanatory. Subsections F, G, and H deal with limiting the increase of the monthly payment by the borrower and the effect that this limiting may have on the unpaid balance of the loan. You will note that this note contains a limit on the amount of negative amortization. This limit is contained in subsection H of section 4 and it limits the negative amortization to 125 percent of the original amount borrowed. This means that if you borrowed $100,000, the maximum balance allowed under this paragraph is $125,000. This subsection also states that if a loan balance exceeds the limit, the monthly payment will increase to a level to pay off the loan over the remaining term of the loan.

Section 5, Borrower's Right to Repay, is similar to the fixed-rate note explained earlier in Chapter 2.

Section 7, Borrower's Failure to Pay as Required (Figure 3–5), gives the lender the right to charge a late charge if the payment is not received usually by the 15th of the month. In addition, it states that if they do not pay on the date the payment is due, the borrower will be in default and, if the borrower does go into default, the lender may send a notice that the borrower is in default. Finally, in this section the borrower agrees to pay the lender for his or her costs in enforcing the note.

The remainder of the note is very similar to the fixed rate note and is self-explanatory.

There are three additional notes in this series of Texas adjustable-rate notes. The only difference in two of the remaining notes is that they use the 3- and the 5-year Treasuries as the index. The note using the 3-year Treasury is shown in Figures 3–7 through 3–10.

The last of the standard Texas adjustable-rate notes is one that uses the 3- or 5-year Treasury security as the index, but without the option of limiting the amount the monthly payment may increase. This note is shown in Figures 3–11 through 3–14.

Figure 3–3. **Fannie Mae/FHLMC Adjustable-Rate Note (1-year index), page 1**

ADJUSTABLE RATE NOTE
(1 Year Index—Payment Cap)
THIS NOTE CONTAINS PROVISIONS ALLOWING FOR CHANGES IN MY INTEREST RATE AND MY MONTHLY PAYMENT. I MAY LIMIT MY MONTHLY PAYMENT INCREASES TO 7½% EACH YEAR IF THE PROVISIONS OF THIS NOTE PERMIT ME TO DO SO.

.... , 19 .... , ...

[City]   [State]

....

[Property Address]

1. BORROWER'S PROMISE TO PAY

In return for a loan that I have received, I promise to pay U.S. $.......................... (this amount is called "principal"), plus interest, to the order of the Lender. The Lender is ....

....

I understand that the Lender may transfer this Note. The Lender or anyone who takes this Note by transfer and who is entitled to receive payments under this Note is called the "Note Holder."

2. INTEREST

Interest will be charged on unpaid principal until the full amount of principal has been paid. I will pay interest at a yearly rate of ....%. The interest rate I will pay will change in accordance with Section 4 of this Note.

The interest rate required by this Section 2 and Section 4 of this Note is the rate I will pay both before and after any default described in Section 7(B) of this Note.

3. PAYMENTS

(A) Time and Place of Payments

I will pay principal and interest by making payments every month.

I will make my monthly payments on the first day of each month beginning on ...., 19 .... I will make these payments every month until I have paid all of the principal and interest and any other charges described below that I may owe under this Note. My monthly payments will be applied to interest before principal. If, on ...., ... , I still owe amounts under this Note, I will pay those amounts in full on that date, which is called the "maturity date."

I will make my monthly payments at ....

.... or at a different place if required by the Note Holder.

(B) Amount of My Initial Monthly Payments

Each of my initial monthly payments will be in the amount of U.S. $.......................... . This amount may change.

(C) Monthly Payment Changes

Changes in my monthly payment will reflect changes in the unpaid principal of my loan and in the interest rate that I must pay. The Note Holder will determine my new interest rate and the changed amount of my monthly payment in accordance with Section 4 of this Note.

4. INTEREST RATE AND MONTHLY PAYMENT CHANGES; BORROWER'S RIGHT TO LIMIT PAYMENT

(A) Change Dates

The interest rate I will pay may change on the first day of ...., 19 .... , and on that day every 12th month thereafter. Each date on which my interest rate could change is called a "Change Date."

(B) The Index

Beginning with the first Change Date, my interest rate will be based on an Index. The "Index" is the weekly average yield on United States Treasury securities adjusted to a constant maturity of 1 year, as made available by the Federal Reserve Board. The most recent Index figure available as of the date 45 days before each Change Date is called the "Current Index."

TEXAS ADJUSTABLE RATE NOTE—1 Year Treasury Index—Single Family—**FNMA/FHLMC Uniform Instrument**   Form 3401.44 12/83

Figure 3-4.   Fannie Mae/FHLMC Adjustable-Rate Note (1-year index), page 2

If the Index is no longer available, the Note Holder will choose a new index which is based upon comparable information. The Note Holder will give me notice of this choice.

(C) Calculation of Changes

Before each Change Date, the Note Holder will calculate my new interest rate by adding .... percentage points (................. %) to the Current Index. The Note Holder will then round the result of this addition to the nearest one-eighth of one percentage point (0.125%). This rounded amount will be my new interest rate until the next Change Date.

The Note Holder will then determine the amount of the monthly payment that would be sufficient to repay the unpaid principal that I am expected to owe at the Change Date in full on the maturity date at my new interest rate in substantially equal payments. The result of this calculation is called the "Full Payment." It will be the new amount of my monthly payment unless I choose the amount permitted by Section 4(F) below.

(D) Effective Date of Changes

My new interest rate will become effective on each Change Date. I will pay the amount of my new monthly payment beginning on the first monthly payment date after the Change Date until the amount of my monthly payment changes again.

(E) Notice of Changes

The Note Holder will deliver or mail to me a notice of any changes in my interest rate and the amount of my monthly payment before the effective date of any change. The notice will include information required by law to be given me and also the title and telephone number of a person who will answer any question I may have regarding the notice.

(F) Borrower's Right to Limit Monthly Payment

Unless Sections 4(H) and 4(I) below will not permit me to do so, I may choose to limit the amount of my new monthly payment following a Change Date to the amount I have been paying multiplied by the number 1.075. This amount is called the "Limited Payment." **If I choose a Limited Payment as my monthly payment, I must give the Note Holder notice that I am doing so at least 15 days before my first new monthly payment is due.**

(G) Additions to My Unpaid Principal

If I choose to pay the Limited Payment, my monthly payment could be less than the amount of the interest portion of the monthly payment that would be sufficient to repay the unpaid principal I owe at the monthly payment date in full on the maturity date in substantially equal payments. If so, each month that the Limited Payment is less than the interest portion, the Note Holder will subtract the Limited Payment from the amount of the interest portion and will add the difference to my unpaid principal. The Note Holder will also add interest on the amount of this difference to my unpaid principal each month. The interest rate on the interest added to principal will be the rate required by Section 4(C) above.

(H) Limit on My Unpaid Principal; Increased Monthly Payment

My unpaid principal can never exceed a maximum amount equal to one hundred twenty-five percent (125%) of the principal amount I originally borrowed. My unpaid principal could exceed that maximum amount if I pay a Limited Payment. If so, on the date that my paying my Limited Payment would cause me to exceed that limit, I will instead begin paying a new monthly payment until the next Change Date. The new monthly payment will be in an amount which would be sufficient to repay my then unpaid principal in full on the maturity date at my current interest rate in substantially equal payments.

(I) Required Full Payment

Beginning with the first monthly payment after the final Change Date, I will pay the Full Payment as my monthly payment.

5.   BORROWER'S RIGHT TO PREPAY

I have the right to make payments of principal at any time before they are due. A payment of principal only is known as a "prepayment." When I make a prepayment, I will tell the Note Holder in writing that I am doing so.

I may make a full prepayment or partial prepayments without paying any prepayment charge. The Note Holder will use all of my prepayments to reduce the amount of principal that I owe under this Note. If I make a partial prepayment, there will be no changes in the due dates of my monthly payments unless the Note Holder agrees in writing to those changes. My partial prepayment may reduce the amount of my monthly payments after the first Change Date following my partial prepayment. However, any reduction due to my partial prepayment may be offset by an interest rate increase.

6.   LOAN CHARGES

If a law, which applies to this loan and which sets maximum loan charges, is finally interpreted so that the interest or other loan charges collected or to be collected in connection with this loan exceed the permitted limits, then: (i) any such loan charge shall be reduced by the amount necessary to reduce the charge to the permitted limit; and

Figure 3–5. Fannie Mae/FHLMC Adjustable-Rate Note (1-year index), page 3

(ii) any sums already collected from me which exceeded permitted limits will be refunded to me. The Note Holder may choose to make this refund by reducing the principal I owe under this Note or by making a direct payment to me. If a refund reduces principal, the reduction will be treated as a partial prepayment.

7. BORROWER'S FAILURE TO PAY AS REQUIRED

(A) Late Charges for Overdue Payments

If the Note Holder has not received the full amount of any monthly payment by the end of .... calendar days after the date it is due, I will pay a late charge to the Note Holder. The amount of the charge will be .... % of my overdue payment of principal and interest. I will pay this late charge promptly but only once on each late payment.

(B) Default

If I do not pay the full amount of each monthly payment on the date it is due, I will be in default.

(C) Notice of Default

If I am in default, the Note Holder may send me a written notice telling me that if I do not pay the overdue amount by a certain date, the Note Holder may require me to pay immediately the full amount of principal which has not been paid and all the interest that I owe on that amount. That date must be at least 30 days after the date on which the notice is delivered or mailed to me.

(D) No Waiver By Note Holder

Even if, at a time when I am in default, the Note Holder does not require me to pay immediately in full as described above, the Note Holder will still have the right to do so if I am in default at a later time.

(E) Payment of Note Holder's Costs and Expenses

If the Note Holder has required me to pay immediately in full as described above, the Note Holder will have the right to be paid back by me for all of its costs and expenses in enforcing this Note to the extent not prohibited by applicable law. Those expenses include, for example, reasonable attorneys' fees.

8. GIVING OF NOTICES

Unless applicable law requires a different method, any notice that must be given to me under this Note will be given by delivering it or by mailing it by first class mail to me at the Property Address above or at a different address if I give the Note Holder a notice of my different address.

Any notice that must be given to the Note Holder under this Note will be given by mailing it by first class mail to the Note Holder at the address stated in Section 3(A) above or at a different address if I am given a notice of that different address.

9. OBLIGATIONS OF PERSONS UNDER THIS NOTE

If more than one person signs this Note, each person is fully and personally obligated to keep all of the promises made in this Note, including the promise to pay the full amount owed. Any person who is a guarantor, surety or endorser of this Note is also obligated to do these things. Any person who takes over these obligations, including the obligations of a guarantor, surety or endorser of this Note, is also obligated to keep all of the promises made in this Note. The Note Holder may enforce its rights under this Note against each person individually or against all of us together. This means that any one of us may be required to pay all of the amounts owed under this Note.

10. WAIVERS

I and any other person who has obligations under this Note waive notice of intention to accelerate, except as provided in Section 7(C) above, and the rights of presentment and notice of dishonor. "Presentment" means the right to require the Note Holder to demand payment of amounts due. "Notice of dishonor" means the right to require the Note Holder to give notice to other persons that amounts due have not been paid.

11. UNIFORM SECURED NOTE

This Note is a uniform instrument with limited variations in some jurisdictions. In addition to the protections given to the Note Holder under this Note, a Mortgage, Deed of Trust or Security Deed (the "Security Instrument"), dated the same date as this Note, protects the Note Holder from possible losses which might result if I do not keep the promises which I make in this Note. That Security Instrument describes how and under what conditions I may be required to make immediate payment in full of all amounts I owe under this Note. Some of those conditions are described as follows:

Transfer of the Property or a Beneficial Interest in Borrower. If all or any part of the Property or any interest in it is sold or transferred (or if a beneficial interest in Borrower is sold or transferred and

Figure 3–6.   *Fannie Mae/FHLMC Adjustable-Rate Note (1-year index), page 4*

Borrower is not a natural person) without Lender's prior written consent, Lender may, at its option, require immediate payment in full of all sums secured by this Security Instrument. However, this option shall not be exercised by Lender if exercise is prohibited by federal law as of the date of this Security Instrument. Lender also shall not exercise this option if: (a) Borrower causes to be submitted to Lender information required by Lender to evaluate the intended transferee as if a new loan were being made to the transferee; and (b) Lender reasonably determines that Lender's security will not be impaired by the loan assumption and that the risk of a breach of any covenant or agreement in this Security Instrument is acceptable to Lender.

To the extent permitted by applicable law, Lender may charge a reasonable fee as a condition to Lender's consent to the loan assumption. Lender may also require the transferee to sign an assumption agreement that is acceptable to Lender and that obligates the transferee to keep all the promises and agreements made in the Note and in this Security Instrument. Borrower will continue to be obligated under the Note and this Security Instrument unless Lender releases Borrower in writing.

If Lender exercises the option to require immediate payment in full, Lender shall give Borrower notice of acceleration. The notice shall provide a period of not less than 30 days from the date the notice is delivered or mailed within which Borrower must pay all sums secured by this Security Instrument. If Borrower fails to pay these sums prior to the expiration of this period, Lender may invoke any remedies permitted by this Security Instrument without further notice or demand on Borrower.

WITNESS THE HAND(S) AND SEAL(S) OF THE UNDERSIGNED.

....(Seal)
-Borrower

....(Seal)
-Borrower

....(Seal)
-Borrower

[*Sign Original Only*]

Figure 3–7.   Fannie Mae/FHLMC Adjustable-Rate Note (3-year index), page 1

ADJUSTABLE RATE NOTE

(3 Year Index—Payment Cap)

THIS NOTE CONTAINS PROVISIONS ALLOWING FOR CHANGES IN MY INTEREST RATE AND MY MONTHLY PAYMENT. I MAY LIMIT MY MONTHLY PAYMENT INCREASES TO 7½% EACH YEAR IF THE PROVISIONS OF THIS NOTE PERMIT ME TO DO SO.

.... , 19........ .... , ...
| | |
|[City]|[State]|

....
[Property Address]

1. BORROWER'S PROMISE TO PAY

In return for a loan that I have received, I promise to pay U.S. $ .... (this amount is called "principal"), plus interest, to the order of the Lender. The Lender is ....

I understand that the Lender may transfer this Note. The Lender or anyone who takes this Note by transfer and who is entitled to receive payments under this Note is called the "Note Holder."

2. INTEREST

Interest will be charged on unpaid principal until the full amount of principal has been paid. I will pay interest at a yearly rate of .... %. The interest rate I will pay will change in accordance with Section 4 of this Note.

The interest rate required by this Section 2 and Section 4 of this Note is the rate I will pay both before and after any default described in Section 10(B) of this Note.

3. PAYMENTS

(A) Time and Place of Payments

I will pay principal and interest by making payments every month.

I will make my monthly payments on the first day of each month beginning on .... , 19 .... I will make these payments every month until I have paid all of the principal and interest and any other charges described below that I may owe under this Note. My monthly payments will be applied to interest before principal. If, on .... , ... , I still owe amounts under this Note, I will pay those amounts in full on that date, which is called the "maturity date."

I will make my monthly payments at .... or at a different place if required by the Note Holder.

(B) Amount of My Initial Monthly Payments

Each of my initial monthly payments will be in the amount of U.S. $ .... This amount may change.

(C) Monthly Payment Changes

Changes in my monthly payment will reflect changes in the unpaid principal of my loan and in the interest rate that I must pay. The Note Holder will determine my new interest rate and the changed amount of my monthly payment in accordance with Section 4 of this Note.

4. INTEREST RATE AND MONTHLY PAYMENT CHANGES

(A) Change Dates

The interest rate I will pay may change on the first day of .... , 19 .... , and on that day every 36th month thereafter. Each date on which my interest rate could change is called a "Change Date."

(B) The Index

Beginning with the first Change Date, my interest rate will be based on an Index. The "Index" is the weekly average yield on United States Treasury securities adjusted to a constant maturity of 3 years, as made available by the Federal Reserve Board. The most recent Index figure available as of the date 45 days before each Change Date is called the "Current Index."

If the Index is no longer available, the Note Holder will choose a new index which is based upon comparable information. The Note Holder will give me notice of this choice.

(C) Calculation of Changes

Before each Change Date, the Note Holder will calculate my new interest rate by adding .... percentage points (.................. %) to the Current Index. The Note Holder will then round the

TEXAS ADJUSTABLE RATE NOTE—3 Year Treasury Index—Single Family—**FNMA/FHLMC Uniform Instrument**   Form 3403.44 12/83

Figure 3–8.   Fannie Mae/FHLMC Adjustable-Rate Note (3-year index), page 2

result of this addition to the nearest one-eighth of one percentage point (0.125%). This rounded amount will be my new interest rate until the next Change Date.

The Note Holder will then determine the amount of the monthly payment that would be sufficient to repay the unpaid principal that I am expected to owe at the Change Date in full on the maturity date at my new interest rate in substantially equal payments. The result of this calculation is called the "Full Payment." It will be the new amount of my monthly payment unless I choose the amount permitted by Section 5 below.

(D) Effective Date of Changes

My new interest rate will become effective on each Change Date. I will pay the amount of my new monthly payment beginning on the first monthly payment date after the Change Date until the amount of my monthly payment changes again.

5.   BORROWER'S RIGHT TO LIMIT MONTHLY PAYMENT; REQUIRED FULL PAYMENT

(A) Calculation of Graduated Limited Payment

I may choose to limit the amount of my new monthly payment following a Change Date if my new interest rate would cause the monthly payment I have been paying to increase by more than seven and one-half percent (7.5%). **If I choose to limit the amount of my monthly payment, I must give the Note Holder notice that I am doing so at least 15 days before my first new monthly payment is due.** When I do so, on the first monthly payment date after the Change Date I will begin paying a new monthly payment which will be equal to the amount I have been paying each month for the preceding twelve months multiplied by the number 1.075. Thereafter, on each of the first two anniversaries of my new monthly payment effective date, my monthly payment will again increase to an amount equal to the amount I have been paying each month for the preceding twelve months multiplied by the number 1.075. These amounts are called the "Graduated Limited Payments."

Even if I have chosen to limit my monthly payment, Section 5(B), 5(C) or 5(D) below may require me to pay a different amount.

(B) Reduced Monthly Payment

A Graduated Limited Payment could be greater than the amount of a monthly payment which then would be sufficient to repay my unpaid principal in full on the maturity date at my current interest rate in substantially equal payments. If so, on the date my paying a Graduated Limited Payment would cause me to pay more than the lower amount, I will instead then begin paying the lower amount as my monthly payment until the next Change Date.

(C) Increased Monthly Payment

My paying a Graduated Limited Payment could cause my unpaid principal to exceed the limit stated in Section 6(B) below. If so, on the date that my paying my monthly payment would cause me to exceed that limit, I will instead begin paying a new monthly payment until the next Change Date. The new monthly payment will be in an amount which would be sufficient to repay my then unpaid principal in full on the maturity date at my current interest rate in substantially equal payments.

(D) Required Full Payment

Beginning with the first monthly payment after the final Change Date, I will pay the Full Payment as my monthly payment.

6.   INCREASES IN THE PRINCIPAL AMOUNT TO BE PAID

(A) Additions to My Unpaid Principal

If I choose to pay Graduated Limited Payments, my monthly payment could be less than the amount of the interest portion of the monthly payment that would be sufficient to repay the unpaid principal I owe at the monthly payment date in full on the maturity date in substantially equal payments. If so, each month that the amount of my monthly payment is less than the interest portion, the Note Holder will subtract the amount of my monthly payment from the amount of the interest portion and will add the difference to my unpaid principal. The Note Holder will also add interest on the amount of this difference to my unpaid principal each month. The interest rate on the interest added to principal will be the rate required by Section 4(C) above.

(B) Limit on My Unpaid Principal

My unpaid principal can never exceed a maximum amount equal to one hundred twenty-five percent (125%) of the principal amount I originally borrowed.

7.   NOTICE OF CHANGES

The Note Holder will deliver or mail to me a notice of any changes in my interest rate and the amount of my monthly payment before the effective date of any change. The notice will include information required by law to be given me and also the title and telephone number of a person who will answer any question I may have regarding the notice.

Figure 3–9.   Fannie Mae/FHLMC Adjustable-Rate Note (3-year index), page 3

8.   BORROWER'S RIGHT TO PREPAY

I have the right to make payments of principal at any time before they are due. A payment of principal only is known as a "prepayment." When I make a prepayment, I will tell the Note Holder in writing that I am doing so.

I may make a full prepayment or partial prepayments without paying any prepayment charge. The Note Holder will use all of my prepayments to reduce the amount of principal that I owe under this Note. If I make a partial prepayment, there will be no changes in the due dates of my monthly payments unless the Note Holder agrees in writing to those changes. My partial prepayment may reduce the amount of my monthly payments after the first Change Date following my partial prepayment. However, any reduction due to my partial prepayment may be offset by an interest rate increase.

9.   LOAN CHARGES

If a law, which applies to this loan and which sets maximum loan charges, is finally interpreted so that the interest or other loan charges collected or to be collected in connection with this loan exceed the permitted limits, then: (i) any such loan charge shall be reduced by the amount necessary to reduce the charge to the permitted limit; and (ii) any sums already collected from me which exceeded permitted limits will be refunded to me. The Note Holder may choose to make this refund by reducing the principal I owe under this Note or by making a direct payment to me. If a refund reduces principal, the reduction will be treated as a partial prepayment.

10.   BORROWER'S FAILURE TO PAY AS REQUIRED

(A) Late Charges for Overdue Payments

If the Note Holder has not received the full amount of any monthly payment by the end of .... calendar days after the date it is due, I will pay a late charge to the Note Holder. The amount of the charge will be .... % of my overdue payment of principal and interest. I will pay this late charge promptly but only once on each late payment.

(B) Default

If I do not pay the full amount of each monthly payment on the date it is due, I will be in default.

(C) Notice of Default

If I am in default, the Note Holder may send me a written notice telling me that if I do not pay the overdue amount by a certain date, the Note Holder may require me to pay immediately the full amount of principal which has not been paid and all the interest that I owe on that amount. That date must be at least 30 days after the date on which the notice is delivered or mailed to me.

(D) No Waiver By Note Holder

Even if, at a time when I am in default, the Note Holder does not require me to pay immediately in full as described above, the Note Holder will still have the right to do so if I am in default at a later time.

(E) Payment of Note Holder's Costs and Expenses

If the Note Holder has required me to pay immediately in full as described above, the Note Holder will have the right to be paid back by me for all of its costs and expenses in enforcing this Note to the extent not prohibited by applicable law. Those expenses include, for example, reasonable attorneys' fees.

11.   GIVING OF NOTICES

Unless applicable law requires a different method, any notice that must be given to me under this Note will be given by delivering it or by mailing it by first class mail to me at the Property Address above or at a different address if I give the Note Holder a notice of my different address.

Any notice that must be given to the Note Holder under this Note will be given by mailing it by first class mail to the Note Holder at the address stated in Section 3(A) above or at a different address if I am given a notice of that different address.

12.   OBLIGATIONS OF PERSONS UNDER THIS NOTE

If more than one person signs this Note, each person is fully and personally obligated to keep all of the promises made in this Note, including the promise to pay the full amount owed. Any person who is a guarantor, surety or endorser of this Note is also obligated to do these things. Any person who takes over these obligations, including the obligations of a guarantor, surety or endorser of this Note, is also obligated to keep all of the promises made in this Note. The Note Holder may enforce its rights under this Note against each person individually or against all of us together. This means that any one of us may be required to pay all of the amounts owed under this Note.

13.   WAIVERS

I and any other person who has obligations under this Note waive notice of intention to accelerate, except as provided in Section 10(C) above, and the rights of presentment and notice of dishonor. "Presentment" means the right to require the Note Holder to demand payment of amounts due. "Notice of dishonor" means the right to require the Note Holder to give notice to other persons that amounts due have not been paid.

Figure 3–10.   Fannie Mae/FHLMC Adjustable-Rate Note (3-year index), page 4

14. UNIFORM SECURED NOTE

This Note is a uniform instrument with limited variations in some jurisdictions. In addition to the protections given to the Note Holder under this Note, a Mortgage, Deed of Trust or Security Deed (the "Security Instrument"), dated the same date as this Note, protects the Note Holder from possible losses which might result if I do not keep the promises which I make in this Note. That Security Instrument describes how and under what conditions I may be required to make immediate payment in full of all amounts I owe under this Note. Some of those conditions are described as follows:

Transfer of the Property or a Beneficial Interest in Borrower. If all or any part of the Property or any interest in it is sold or transferred (or if a beneficial interest in Borrower is sold or transferred and Borrower is not a natural person) without Lender's prior written consent, Lender may, at its option, require immediate payment in full of all sums secured by this Security Instrument. However, this option shall not be exercised by Lender if exercise is prohibited by federal law as of the date of this Security Instrument. Lender also shall not exercise this option if: (a) Borrower causes to be submitted to Lender information required by Lender to evaluate the intended transferee as if a new loan were being made to the transferee; and (b) Lender reasonably determines that Lender's security will not be impaired by the loan assumption and that the risk of a breach of any covenant or agreement in this Security Instrument is acceptable to Lender.

To the extent permitted by applicable law, Lender may charge a reasonable fee as a condition to Lender's consent to the loan assumption. Lender may also require the transferee to sign an assumption agreement that is acceptable to Lender and that obligates the transferee to keep all the promises and agreements made in the Note and in this Security Instrument. Borrower will continue to be obligated under the Note and this Security Instrument unless Lender releases Borrower in writing.

If Lender exercises the option to require immediate payment in full, Lender shall give Borrower notice of acceleration. The notice shall provide a period of not less than 30 days from the date the notice is delivered or mailed within which Borrower must pay all sums secured by this Security Instrument. If Borrower fails to pay these sums prior to the expiration of this period, Lender may invoke any remedies permitted by this Security Instrument without further notice or demand on Borrower.

WITNESS THE HAND(S) AND SEAL(S) OF THE UNDERSIGNED.

....(Seal)
-Borrower

....(Seal)
-Borrower

....(Seal)
-Borrower

[*Sign Original Only*]

Figure 3–11.   FHLMC Adjustable-Rate Note (3- or 5-year index, no payment cap), page 1

ADJUSTABLE RATE NOTE
(3 or 5 Year Index—No Payment Cap)

THIS NOTE CONTAINS PROVISIONS ALLOWING FOR CHANGES IN MY INTEREST RATE AND MY MONTHLY PAYMENT. IF MY INTEREST RATE INCREASES, MY MONTHLY PAYMENTS WILL BE HIGHER. IF MY INTEREST RATE DECREASES, MY MONTHLY PAYMENTS WILL BE LOWER.

.... , 19 .... , ...

[City]   [State]

....

[Property Address]

1. BORROWER'S PROMISE TO PAY

In return for a loan that I have received, I promise to pay U.S. $ .... (this amount is called "principal"), plus interest, to the order of the Lender. The Lender is ....
....

I understand that the Lender may transfer this Note. The Lender or anyone who takes this Note by transfer and who is entitled to receive payments under this Note is called the "Note Holder."

2. INTEREST

Interest will be charged on unpaid principal until the full amount of principal has been paid. I will pay interest at a yearly rate of .... %. The interest rate I will pay will change in accordance with Section 4 of this Note.

The interest rate required by this Section 2 and Section 4 of this Note is the rate I will pay both before and after any default described in Section 7(B) of this Note.

3. PAYMENTS

(A) Time and Place of Payments

I will pay principal and interest by making payments every month.

I will make my monthly payments on the first day of each month beginning on .... , 19 .... I will make these payments every month until I have paid all of the principal and interest and any other charges described below that I may owe under this Note. My monthly payments will be applied to interest before principal. If, on .... , ... , I still owe amounts under this Note, I will pay those amounts in full on that date, which is called the "maturity date."

I will make my monthly payments at ....
....
 or at a different place if required by the Note Holder.

(B) Amount of My Initial Monthly Payments

Each of my initial monthly payments will be in the amount of U.S. $ .... This amount may change.

(C) Monthly Payment Changes

Changes in my monthly payment will reflect changes in the interest rate that I must pay. The Note Holder will determine my new interest rate and the changed amount of my monthly payment in accordance with Section 4 of this Note.

4. INTEREST RATE AND MONTHLY PAYMENT CHANGES

(A) Change Dates

The interest rate I will pay may change on the first day of .... , 19 .... , and on that day every .... th month thereafter. Each date on which my interest rate could change is called a "Change Date."

TEXAS ADJUSTABLE RATE NOTE—3 or 5 Year Treasury Index—Single Family—**FHLMC Uniform Instrument**   Form 3301.44 12/83

Figure 3–12.   FHLMC Adjustable-Rate Note (3- or 5-year index, no payment cap), page 2

(B) The Index

Beginning with the first Change Date, my interest rate will be based on an Index. The "Index" is the weekly average yield on United States Treasury securities adjusted to a constant maturity of .... years, as made available by the Federal Reserve Board. The most recent Index figure available as of the date 45 days before each Change Date is called the "Current Index."

If the Index is no longer available, the Note Holder will choose a new index which is based upon comparable information. The Note Holder will give me notice of this choice.

(C) Calculation of Changes

Before each Change Date, the Note Holder will calculate my new interest rate by adding .... percentage points (.................. %) to the Current Index. The Note Holder will then round the result of this addition to the nearest one-eighth of one percentage point (0.125%). This rounded amount will be my new interest rate until the next Change Date.

The Note Holder will then determine the amount of the monthly payment that would be sufficient to repay the principal I am expected to owe at the Change Date in full on the maturity date at my new interest rate in substantially equal payments. The result of this calculation will be the new amount of my monthly payment.

(D) Effective Date of Changes

My new interest rate will become effective on each Change Date. I will pay the amount of my new monthly payment beginning on the first monthly payment date after the Change Date until the amount of my monthly payment changes again.

(E) Notice of Changes

The Note Holder will deliver or mail to me a notice of any changes in my interest rate and the amount of my monthly payment before the effective date of any change. The notice will include information required by law to be given me and also the title and telephone number of a person who will answer any question I may have regarding the notice.

5. BORROWER'S RIGHT TO PREPAY

I have the right to make payments of principal at any time before they are due. A payment of principal only is known as a "prepayment." When I make a prepayment, I will tell the Note Holder in writing that I am doing so.

I may make a full prepayment or partial prepayments without paying any prepayment charge. The Note Holder will use all of my prepayments to reduce the amount of principal that I owe under this Note. If I make a partial prepayment, there will be no changes in the due dates of my monthly payments unless the Note Holder agrees in writing to those changes. My partial prepayment will reduce the amount of my monthly payments after the first Change Date following my partial prepayment. However, any reduction due to my partial prepayment may be offset by an interest rate increase.

6. LOAN CHARGES

If a law, which applies to this loan and which sets maximum loan charges, is finally interpreted so that the interest or other loan charges collected or to be collected in connection with this loan exceed the permitted limits, then: (i) any such loan charge shall be reduced by the amount necessary to reduce the charge to the permitted limit; and (ii) any sums already collected from me which exceeded permitted limits will be refunded to me. The Note Holder may choose to make this refund by reducing the principal I owe under this Note or by making a direct payment to me. If a refund reduces principal, the reduction will be treated as a partial prepayment.

7. BORROWER'S FAILURE TO PAY AS REQUIRED

(A) Late Charge for Overdue Payments

If the Note Holder has not received the full amount of any monthly payment by the end of .... calendar days after the date it is due, I will pay a late charge to the Note Holder. The amount of the charge will be .... % of my overdue payment of principal and interest. I will pay this late charge promptly but only once on each late payment.

(B) Default

If I do not pay the full amount of each monthly payment on the date it is due, I will be in default.

Figure 3-13.   FHLMC Adjustable-Rate Note (3- or 5-year index, no payment cap), page 3

(C) Notice of Default

If I am in default, the Note Holder may send me a written notice telling me that if I do not pay the overdue amount by a certain date, the Note Holder may require me to pay immediately the full amount of principal which has not been paid and all the interest that I owe on that amount. That date must be at least 30 days after the date on which the notice is delivered or mailed to me.

(D) No Waiver by Note Holder

Even if, at a time when I am in default, the Note Holder does not require me to pay immediately in full as described above, the Note Holder will still have the right to do so if I am in default at a later time.

(E) Payment of Note Holder's Costs and Expenses

If the Note Holder has required me to pay immediately in full as described above, the Note Holder will have the right to be paid back by me for all its costs and expenses to the extent not prohibited by applicable law. Those expenses include, for example, reasonable attorneys' fees.

8.   GIVING OF NOTICES

Unless applicable law requires a different method, any notice that must be given to me under this Note will be given by delivering it or by mailing it by first class mail to me at the Property Address above or at a different address if I give the Note Holder a notice of my different address.

Any notice that must be given to the Note Holder under this Note will be given by mailing it by first class mail to the Note Holder at the address stated in Section 3(A) above or at a different address if I am given a notice of that different address.

9.   OBLIGATIONS OF PERSONS UNDER THIS NOTE

If more than one person signs this Note, each person is fully and personally obligated to keep all of the promises made in this Note, including the promise to pay the full amount owed. Any person who is a guarantor, surety or endorser of this Note is also obligated to do these things. Any person who takes over these obligations, including the obligations of a guarantor, surety or endorser of this Note, is also obligated to keep all of the promises made in this Note. The Note Holder may enforce its rights under this Note against each person individually or against all of us together. This means that any one of us may be required to pay all of the amounts owed under this Note.

10.   WAIVERS

I and any other person who has obligations under this Note waive notice of intention to accelerate, except as provided in Section 7(C) above, and the rights of presentment and notice of dishonor. "Presentment" means the right to require the Note Holder to demand payment of amounts due. "Notice of dishonor" means the right to require the Note Holder to give notice to other persons that amounts due have not been paid.

11.   UNIFORM SECURED NOTE

This Note is a uniform instrument with limited variations in some jurisdictions. In addition to the protections given to the Note Holder under this Note, a Mortgage, Deed of Trust or Security Deed (the "Security Instrument"), dated the same date as this Note, protects the Note Holder from possible losses which might result if I do not keep the promises which I make in this Note. That Security Instrument describes how and under what conditions I may be required to make immediate payment in full of all amounts I owe under this Note. Some of those conditions are described as follows:

Transfer of the Property or a Beneficial Interest in Borrower. If all or any part of the Property or any interest in it is sold or transferred (or if a beneficial interest in Borrower is sold or transferred and Borrower is not a natural person) without Lender's prior written consent, Lender may, at its option, require immediate payment in full of all sums secured by this Security Instrument. However, this option shall not be exercised by Lender if exercise is prohibited by federal law as of the date of this Security Instrument. Lender also shall not exercise this option if: (a) Borrower causes to be submitted to Lender information required by Lender to evaluate the intended transferee as if a new loan were being made to the transferee; and (b) Lender reasonably determines that Lender's security will not be impaired by the loan assumption and that the risk of a breach of any covenant or agreement in this Security Instrument is acceptable to Lender.

Figure 3–14.   FHLMC Adjustable-Rate Note (3- or 5-year index, no payment cap), page 4

To the extent permitted by applicable law, Lender may charge a reasonable fee as a condition to Lender's consent to the loan assumption. Lender may also require the transferee to sign an assumption agreement that is acceptable to Lender and that obligates the transferee to keep all the promises and agreements made in the Note and in this Security Instrument. Borrower will continue to be obligated under the Note and this Security Instrument unless Lender releases Borrower in writing.

If Lender exercises the option to require immediate payment in full, Lender shall give Borrower notice of acceleration. The notice shall provide a period of not less than 30 days from the date the notice is delivered or mailed within which Borrower must pay all sums secured by this Security Instrument. If Borrower fails to pay these sums prior to the expiration of this period, Lender may invoke any remedies permitted by this Security Instrument without further notice or demand on Borrower.

WITNESS THE HAND(S) AND SEAL(S) OF THE UNDERSIGNED.

....(Seal)
-Borrower

....(Seal)
-Borrower

....(Seal)
-Borrower

[*Sign Original Only*]

Deed of Trust Rider   With each of the adjustable-rate notes, a deed of trust will be executed.

The deed of trust that will be executed is the standard fixed-rate deed of trust. In addition to the deed of trust, each of the adjustable-rate notes has an accompanying deed of trust rider. We will not review each of the riders; only the adjustable-rate rider that accompanies the 1-year index note-payment cap will be shown (Figures 3–15 and 3–16).

If you would like to secure a complete set of the notes and deed of trust riders, contact any Federal National Mortgage Association or Federal Home Loan Mortgage Corporation approved lender in your area.

CONVERTIBLE ARM

There is one additional type of ARM and accompanying note that should be discussed: the convertible ARM. This type of ARM was developed to counteract many borrowers' fear of the uncertainty of future increases in the interest rate on their mortgages.

With this type of ARM, the borrower is given the option to convert to a fixed-term, fixed-rate mortgage. This conversion may be a one-time option or the lender may offer the borrower an option to convert on any adjustment date. This conversion is normally offered only on the 3- or 5-year ARMs. Thus, if the borrower has a 3-year ARM with a conversion option at the first adjustment date, the borrower could opt to convert to a fixed-rate, fixed-term 27-year mortgage at the first adjustment date. If the convertible ARM gave the option of conversion at any adjustment date and the borrower opts to convert on the second adjustment date, then the borrower would have a fixed-rate, fixed-term 24-year mortgage.

Why would a borrower opt to convert? The borrower might opt to convert if the interest rate, at the time of adjustment, had fallen to a level at which the borrower felt he or she could make the payments. For example, if a borrower had received an ARM in August 1984 when the rates on the 3- and 5-year ARMs were in the 12- to 13-percent range, then at the first adjustment date, when the rate on a fixed-term, fixed-rate mortgage had fallen to 11 percent, a conversion may have been a good option.

Convertible ARM Note

The Federal Home Loan Mortgage Corporation has developed a standard note for this type of ARM. A convertible ARM note for Texas, using the 3- or 5-year Treasuries as an index, is shown in Figures 3–17 through 3–19. This note is similar to the ARM notes reviewed in the previous section. There is one major difference: paragraph 5, Conversion to Fixed Interest Rate. Section A indicates on which change date the borrower will be allowed to convert. This could be the first or the first, second, and third or any change dates specified in this section. Section B states how the fixed rate will be established. Finally, in section C, borrowers are advised that, if they should convert, they will have to sign a document as evidence of the modification of the note.

ADJUSTABLE-RATE MORTGAGE INTEREST RATES

How are the interest rates for some ARMs established? In reviewing the regulations of the COC, FHLBB, and the National Credit Union Administration, we learned that lenders are free to choose an interest-rate index, with certain limitations. After reviewing the standard Texas ARM notes and deed of trust riders, we learned that the Federal National Mortgage Association and the Federal Home Loan Mortgage Corporation have established the interest rate index as the 1-, 3-, and 5-year federal securities. If a lender therefore wishes to sell an ARM to either of these secondary marketers, they must use these indexes.

With this information, the real estate professional should keep up with the movement of these indexes. This can be done very easily by a simple request to the Federal Reserve Board, Publications Services, 20th and Constitution Ave., NW, Washington, D.C. 20551, requesting Federal Reserve Statistical Release H.15 (519), Selected Interest Rates (shown in this text as Figure 3–20). The cost of this publication is free.

The most important section to the real estate professional is the section U.S. Government Securities and, in particular, the part of the section entitled "Treasury Constant Maturities." Here the maturities for the 1-, 3-, 5-, 7-, 10-, 20-, and 30-year securities are shown. You

Figure 3–15.   *Fannie Mae/FHLMC Multistate Adjustable-Rate Rider (1-year index, payment cap), page 1*

ADJUSTABLE RATE RIDER
(1 Year Index—Payment Cap)

THIS ADJUSTABLE RATE RIDER is made this .... day of .... , 19 .... , and is incorporated into and shall be deemed to amend and supplement the Mortgage, Deed of Trust or Security Deed (the "Security Instrument") of the same date given by the undersigned (the "Borrower") to secure Borrower's Adjustable Rate Note (the "Note") to .... (the "Lender") of the same date and covering the property described in the Security Instrument and located at:

....
[Property Address]

THE NOTE CONTAINS PROVISIONS ALLOWING FOR CHANGES IN THE INTEREST RATE AND THE MONTHLY PAYMENT. THE BORROWER MAY LIMIT MONTHLY PAYMENT INCREASES TO 7½% EACH YEAR IF THE PROVISIONS OF THE NOTE PERMIT IT.

ADDITIONAL COVENANTS. In addition to the covenants and agreements made in the Security Instrument, Borrower and Lender further covenant and agree as follows:

A. INTEREST RATE AND MONTHLY PAYMENT CHANGES

The Note provides for an initial interest rate of .... %. The Note provides for changes in the interest rate and the monthly payments, as follows:

4.   INTEREST RATE AND MONTHLY PAYMENT CHANGES; BORROWER'S RIGHT TO LIMIT PAYMENT

(A) Change Dates

The interest rate I will pay may change on the first day of .... , 19 .... , and on that day every 12th month thereafter. Each date on which my interest rate could change is called a "Change Date."

(B) The Index

Beginning with the first Change Date, my interest rate will be based on an Index. The "Index" is the weekly average yield on United States Treasury securities adjusted to a constant maturity of 1 year, as made available by the Federal Reserve Board. The most recent Index figure available as of the date 45 days before each Change Date is called the "Current Index."

If the Index is no longer available, the Note Holder will choose a new index which is based upon comparable information. The Note Holder will give me notice of this choice.

(C) Calculation of Changes

Before each Change Date, the Note Holder will calculate my new interest rate by adding .... percentage points (................. %) to the Current Index. The Note Holder will then round the result of this addition to the nearest one-eighth of one percentage point (0.125%). This rounded amount will be my new interest rate until the next Change Date.

The Note Holder will then determine the amount of the monthly payment that would be sufficient to repay the unpaid principal that I am expected to owe at the Change Date in full on the maturity date at my new interest rate in substantially equal payments. The result of this calculation is called the "Full Payment." It will be the new amount of my monthly payment unless I choose the amount permitted by Section 4(F) below.

(D) Effective Date of Changes

My new interest rate will become effective on each Change Date. I will pay the amount of my new monthly payment beginning on the first monthly payment date after the Change Date until the amount of my monthly payment changes again.

(E) Notice of Changes

The Note Holder will deliver or mail to me a notice of any changes in my interest rate and the amount of my monthly payment before the effective date of any change. The notice will include information required by law to be given me and also the title and telephone number of a person who will answer any question I may have regarding the notice.

(F) Borrower's Right to Limit Monthly Payment

Unless Sections 4(H) and 4(I) below will not permit me to do so, I may choose to limit the amount of my new monthly payment following a Change Date to the amount I have been paying multiplied by the number 1.075. This amount is called the "Limited Payment." **If I choose a Limited Payment as my monthly payment, I must give the Note Holder notice that I am doing so at least 15 days before my first new monthly payment is due.**

(G) Additions to My Unpaid Principal

If I choose to pay the Limited Payment, my monthly payment could be less than the amount of the interest portion of the monthly payment that would be sufficient to repay the unpaid principal I owe at the monthly payment date in full on the maturity date in substantially equal payments. If so, each month that the Limited Payment is less than the interest portion, the Note Holder will subtract the Limited Payment from the amount of the interest portion

Figure 3–16.   ***Fannie Mae/FHLMC Multistate Adjustable-Rate Rider (1-year index, payment cap), page 2***

and will add the difference to my unpaid principal. The Note Holder will also add interest on the amount of this difference to my unpaid principal each month. The interest rate on the interest added to principal will be the rate required by Section 4(C) above.

(H) Limit on My Unpaid Principal; Increased Monthly Payment

My unpaid principal can never exceed a maximum amount equal to one hundred twenty-five percent (125%) of the principal amount I originally borrowed. My unpaid principal could exceed that maximum amount if I pay a Limited Payment. If so, on the date that my paying my Limited Payment would cause me to exceed that limit, I will instead begin paying a new monthly payment until the next Change Date. The new monthly payment will be in an amount which would be sufficient to repay my then unpaid principal in full on the maturity date at my current interest rate in substantially equal payments.

(I) Required Full Payment

Beginning with the first monthly payment after the final Change Date, I will pay the Full Payment as my monthly payment.

B. TRANSFER OF THE PROPERTY OR A BENEFICIAL INTEREST IN BORROWER

Uniform Covenant 17 of the Security Instrument is amended to read as follows:

Transfer of the Property or a Beneficial Interest in Borrower. If all or any part of the Property or any interest in it is sold or transferred (or if a beneficial interest in Borrower is sold or transferred and Borrower is not a natural person) without Lender's prior written consent, Lender may, at its option, require immediate payment in full of all sums secured by this Security Instrument. However, this option shall not be exercised by Lender if exercise is prohibited by federal law as of the date of this Security Instrument. Lender also shall not exercise this option if: (a) Borrower causes to be submitted to Lender information required by Lender to evaluate the intended transferee as if a new loan were being made to the transferee; and (b) Lender reasonably determines that Lender's security will not be impaired by the loan assumption and that the risk of a breach of any covenant or agreement in this Security Instrument is acceptable to Lender.

To the extent permitted by applicable law, Lender may charge a reasonable fee as a condition to Lender's consent to the loan assumption. Lender may also require the transferee to sign an assumption agreement that is acceptable to Lender and that obligates the transferee to keep all the promises and agreements made in the Note and in this Security Instrument. Borrower will continue to be obligated under the Note and this Security Instrument unless Lender releases Borrower in writing.

If Lender exercises the option to require immediate payment in full, Lender shall give Borrower notice of acceleration. The notice shall provide a period of not less than 30 days from the date the notice is delivered or mailed within which Borrower must pay all sums secured by this Security Instrument. If Borrower fails to pay these sums prior to the expiration of this period, Lender may invoke any remedies permitted by this Security Instrument without further notice or demand on Borrower.

BY SIGNING BELOW, Borrower accepts and agrees to the terms and covenants contained in this Adjustable Rate Rider.

....(Seal)
-Borrower

....(Seal)
-Borrower

Figure 3–17.   FHLMC Convertible ARM Note (3- or 5-year Treasury Index), page 1

CONVERTIBLE ARM NOTE

(3 or 5 Year Index—No Payment Cap)

THIS NOTE CONTAINS PROVISIONS ALLOWING FOR CHANGES IN MY INTEREST RATE AND MY MONTHLY PAYMENT. IF MY INTEREST RATE INCREASES, MY MONTHLY PAYMENTS WILL BE HIGHER. IF MY INTEREST RATE DECREASES, MY MONTHLY PAYMENTS WILL BE LOWER. ON THE CHANGE DATE(S) SPECIFIED BELOW, I MAY CONVERT MY ADJUSTABLE RATE LOAN INTO A FIXED RATE, LEVEL PAYMENT, FULLY AMORTIZING LOAN.

_____, 19 ____ _____, _____
                                              [City]   [State]

_____
[Property Address]

1. BORROWER'S PROMISE TO PAY

In return for a loan that I have received, I promise to pay U.S. $ _____ (this amount is called "principal"), plus interest, to the order of the Lender. The Lender is _____
_____.

I understand that the Lender may transfer this Note. The Lender or anyone who takes this Note by transfer and who is entitled to receive payments under this Note is called the "Note Holder."

2. INTEREST

Interest will be charged on unpaid principal until the full amount of principal has been paid. I will pay interest at a yearly rate of _____%. The interest rate I will pay will change in accordance with Section 4 of this Note.

The interest rate required by this Section 2 and Section 4 of this Note is the rate I will pay both before and after any default described in Section 8(B) of this Note.

3. PAYMENTS

(A) Time and Place of Payments

I will pay principal and interest by making payments every month.

I will make my monthly payments on the first day of each month beginning on _____, 19____. I will make these payments every month until I have paid all of the principal and interest and any other charges described below that I may owe under this Note. My monthly payments will be applied to interest before principal. If, on _____, _____, I still owe amounts under this Note, I will pay those amounts in full on that date, which is called the "maturity date."

I will make my monthly payments at _____
_____ or at a different place if required by the Note Holder.

(B) Amount of My Initial Monthly Payments

Each of my initial monthly payments will be in the amount of U.S. $ _____. This amount may change.

(C) Monthly Payment Changes

Changes in my monthly payment will reflect changes in the interest rate that I must pay. The Note Holder will determine my new interest rate and the changed amount of my monthly payment in accordance with Section 4 of this Note.

4. INTEREST RATE AND MONTHLY PAYMENT CHANGES

(A) Change Dates

The interest rate I will pay may change on the first day of _____, 19____, and on that day every _____th month thereafter. Each date on which my interest rate could change is called a "Change Date."

(B) The Index

Beginning with the first Change Date, my interest rate will be based on an Index. The "Index" is the weekly average yield on United States Treasury securities adjusted to a constant maturity of _____ years, as made available by the Federal Reserve Board. The most recent Index figure available as of the date 45 days before each Change Date is called the "Current Index."

If the Index is no longer available, the Note Holder will choose a new index which is based upon comparable information. The Note Holder will give me notice of this choice.

(C) Calculation of Changes

Before each Change Date, the Note Holder will calculate my new interest rate by adding _____ percentage points (_____%) to the Current Index. The Note Holder will then round the result of this addition to the nearest one-eighth of one percentage point (0.125%). This rounded amount will be my new interest rate until the next Change Date.

The Note Holder will then determine the amount of the monthly payment that would be sufficient to repay the principal I am expected to owe at the Change Date in full on the maturity date at my new interest rate in substantially equal payments. The result of this calculation will be the new amount of my monthly payment.

TEXAS—CONVERTIBLE ARM NOTE—3 or 5 Year Treasury Index (No Payment Cap)—Single Family—**FHLMC Uniform Instrument**   2/84

Figure 3–18. *FHLMC Convertible ARM Note (3- or 5-year Treasury Index), page 2*

(D) Effective Date of Changes

My new interest rate will become effective on each Change Date. I will pay the amount of my new monthly payment beginning on the first monthly payment date after the Change Date until the amount of my monthly payment changes again.

(E) Notice of Changes

The Note Holder will deliver or mail to me a notice of any changes in my interest rate and the amount of my monthly payment before the effective date of any change. The notice will include information required by law to be given me and also the title and telephone number of a person who will answer any question I may have regarding the notice. If I may convert my loan as provided in Section 5 of this Note, the notice will also include the following information:

(i) the fixed interest rate I will pay if I choose to convert my loan into a fixed interest rate loan;

(ii) the amount of my new monthly payment at the fixed rate of interest; and

(iii) a date, not more than 15 days from the date the notice is given, by which I must execute and deliver to Lender a document in the form that Lender may require evidencing the modification of the Note to provide for a fixed interest rate.

5. CONVERSION TO FIXED INTEREST RATE

(A) My Option to Convert

On the _____ Change Date(s), I may convert the adjustable rate loan evidenced by this Note into a fixed interest rate loan to be fully repaid in substantially equal monthly payments of principal and interest over the remaining term of the loan.

(B) My Fixed Rate of Interest and Monthly Payments

If I choose to convert to a fixed interest rate, the Note Holder will set the fixed rate of interest that I will pay at a rate equal to the sum of (i) the Federal Home Loan Mortgage Corporation's Required Net Yield for 60-day delivery of 30 year, fixed rate mortgages available 45 days prior to the Change Date on which I exercise my option to convert, plus (ii) three-eighths of one percentage point (.375%). If no such Required Net Yield is available, the Note Holder will determine the fixed interest rate by using a comparable figure. The new fixed interest rate will become effective on the Change Date on which I convert to a fixed interest rate.

My monthly payments at the new fixed interest rate will begin as of the first monthly payment after the Change Date on which I convert. The monthly payment will be the amount that is necessary to repay in full the principal I am expected to owe at that Change Date in substantially equal payments on the maturity date at my fixed interest rate.

(C) How to Convert

If I choose to convert, I will be required to sign and deliver to the Note Holder the document evidencing the modification of the Note within the period set in the Note Holder's notice as provided in Section 4(E) above. If I do not do this within the specified period, I will not have an option to convert unless I can exercise another option on other Change Dates as indicated in Section 5(A). In that case, the interest rate that I will pay will continue to adjust in accordance with Section 4.

6. BORROWER'S RIGHT TO PREPAY

I have the right to make payments of principal at any time before they are due. A payment of principal only is known as a "prepayment." When I make a prepayment, I will tell the Note Holder in writing that I am doing so.

I may make a full prepayment or partial prepayments without paying any prepayment charge. The Note Holder will use all of my prepayments to reduce the amount of principal that I owe under this Note. If I make a partial prepayment, there will be no changes in the due dates of my monthly payments unless the Note Holder agrees in writing to those changes. My partial prepayment will reduce the amount of my monthly payments after the first Change Date following my partial prepayment. However, any reduction due to my partial prepayment may be offset by an interest rate increase.

7. LOAN CHARGES

If a law, which applies to this loan and which sets maximum loan charges, is finally interpreted so that the interest or other loan charges collected or to be collected in connection with this loan exceed the permitted limits, then: (i) any such loan charge shall be reduced by the amount necessary to reduce the charge to the permitted limit; and (ii) any sums already collected from me which exceeded permitted limits will be refunded to me. The Note Holder may choose to make this refund by reducing the principal I owe under this Note or by making a direct payment to me. If a refund reduces principal, the reduction will be treated as a partial prepayment.

8. BORROWER'S FAILURE TO PAY AS REQUIRED

(A) Late Charges for Overdue Payments

If the Note Holder has not received the full amount of any monthly payment by the end of _____ calendar days after the date it is due, I will pay a late charge to the Note Holder. The amount of the charge will be _____% of my overdue payment of principal and interest. I will pay this late charge promptly but only once on each late payment.

(B) Default

If I do not pay the full amount of each monthly payment on the date it is due, I will be in default.

(C) Notice of Default

If I am in default, the Note Holder may send me a written notice telling me that if I do not pay the overdue amount by a certain date, the Note Holder may require me to pay immediately the full amount of principal which has not been paid and all the interest that I owe on that amount. That date must be at least 30 days after the date on which the notice is delivered or mailed to me.

(D) No Waiver by Note Holder

Even if, at a time when I am in default, the Note Holder does not require me to pay immediately in full as described above, the Note Holder will still have the right to do so if I am in default at a later time.

Figure 3–19.   FHLMC Convertible ARM Note (3- or 5-year Treasury Index), page 3

(E) Payment of Note Holder's Costs and Expenses

If the Note Holder has required me to pay immediately in full as described above, the Note Holder will have the right to be paid back by me for all of its costs and expenses to the extent not prohibited by applicable law. Those expenses include, for example, reasonable attorneys' fees.

9.   GIVING OF NOTICES

Unless applicable law requires a different method, any notice that must be given to me under this Note will be given by delivering it or by mailing it by first class mail to me at the Property Address above or at a different address if I give the Note Holder a notice of my different address.

Any notice that must be given to the Note Holder under this Note will be given by mailing it by first class mail to the Note Holder at the address stated in Section 3(A) above or at a different address if I am given a notice of that different address.

10.   OBLIGATIONS OF PERSONS UNDER THIS NOTE

If more than one person signs this Note, each person is fully and personally obligated to keep all of the promises made in this Note, including the promise to pay the full amount owed. Any person who is a guarantor, surety or endorser of this Note is also obligated to do these things. Any person who takes over these obligations, including the obligations of a guarantor, surety or endorser of this Note, is also obligated to keep all of the promises made in this Note. The Note Holder may enforce its rights under this Note against each person individually or against all of us together. This means that any one of us may be required to pay all of the amounts owed under this Note.

11.   WAIVERS

I and any other person who has obligations under this Note waive notice of intention to accelerate, except as provided in Section 8(c) above, and the rights of presentment and notice of dishonor. "Presentment" means the right to require the Note Holder to demand payment of amounts due. "Notice of dishonor" means the right to require the Note Holder to give notice to other persons that amounts due have not been paid.

12.   UNIFORM SECURED NOTE

This Note is a uniform instrument with limited variations in some jurisdictions. In addition to the protections given to the Note Holder under this Note, a Mortgage, Deed of Trust or Security Deed (the "Security Instrument"), dated the same date as this Note, protects the Note Holder from possible losses which might result if I do not keep the promises which I make in this Note. The Security Instrument describes how and under what conditions I may be required to make immediate payment in full of all amounts I owe under this Note. Some of those conditions are described as follows:

Transfer of the Property or a Beneficial Interest in Borrower. If all or any part of the Property or any interest in it is sold or transferred (or if a beneficial interest in Borrower is sold or transferred and Borrower is not a natural person) without Lender's prior written consent, Lender may, at its option, require immediate payment in full of all sums secured by this Security Instrument. However, this option shall not be exercised by Lender if exercise is prohibited by federal law as of the date of this Security Instrument. Lender also shall not exercise this option in connection with any sale or transfer occurring prior to a conversion to a fixed interest rate if: (a) Borrower causes to be submitted to Lender information required by Lender to evaluate the intended transferee as if a new loan were being made to the transferee; and (b) Lender reasonably determines that Lender's security will not be impaired by the loan assumption and that the risk of a breach of any covenant or agreement in this Security Instrument is acceptable to Lender.

To the extent permitted by applicable law, Lender may charge a reasonable fee as a condition to Lender's consent to the loan assumption. Lender may also require the transferee to sign an assumption agreement that is acceptable to Lender and that obligates the transferee to keep all the promises and agreements made in the Note and in this Security Instrument. Borrower will continue to be obligated under the Note and this Security Instrument unless Lender releases Borrower in writing.

If Lender exercises the option to require immediate payment in full, Lender shall give Borrower notice of acceleration. The notice shall provide a period of not less than 30 days from the date the notice is delivered or mailed within which Borrower must pay all sums secured by this Security Instrument. If Borrower fails to pay these sums prior to the expiration of this period, Lender may invoke any remedies permitted by this Security Instrument without further notice or demand on Borrower.

WITNESS THE HAND(S) AND SEAL(S) OF THE UNDERSIGNED.

_____ (Seal)
                                                                          - Borrower

_____ (Seal)
                                                                          - Borrower

_____ (Seal)
                                                                          - Borrower

[Sign Original Only]

Figure 3–20.   Federal Reserve Statistical Release

FEDERAL RESERVE statistical release

H.15 (519)

SELECTED INTEREST RATES
Yields in percent per annum

For immediate release
APRIL 30, 1984

Instruments	APR 23	APR 24	APR 25	APR 26	APR 27	Week ending APR 27	Week ending APR 20	MAR
FEDERAL FUNDS (EFFECTIVE) 1/	9.63	9.55	10.67	10.63	10.49	9.98	10.37	9.91
COMMERCIAL PAPER 2/3/								
1-MONTH	10.20	10.16	10.17	10.13	10.15	10.16	10.23	9.81
3-MONTH	10.26	10.19	10.24	10.20	10.18	10.21	10.22	9.83
6-MONTH	10.31	10.24	10.30	10.28	10.24	10.27	10.26	9.86
FINANCE PAPER PLACED DIRECTLY 2/								
1-MONTH	9.84	9.89	10.15	9.97	10.13	10.00	10.04	9.76
3-MONTH	9.93	9.91	9.93	9.91	9.92	9.92	9.83	9.54
6-MONTH	9.88	9.85	9.85	9.85	9.85	9.86	9.80	9.38
BANKERS ACCEPTANCES (TOP RATED) 2/								
3-MONTH	10.35	10.30	10.20	10.20	10.25	10.26	10.26	9.88
6-MONTH	10.40	10.35	10.30	10.30	10.35	10.34	10.33	9.91
CDS (SECONDARY MARKET)								
1-MONTH	10.24	10.25	10.23	10.22	10.24	10.24	10.28	9.91
3-MONTH	10.49	10.50	10.43	10.42	10.46	10.46	10.42	10.08
6-MONTH	10.88	10.88	10.84	10.81	10.81	10.84	10.76	10.37
EURODOLLAR DEPOSIT (3-MONTH) 4/	10.94	10.94	10.88	10.88	10.81	10.89	10.89	10.40
BANK PRIME LOAN 1/ 5/	12.00	12.00	12.00	12.00	12.00	12.00	12.00	11.21
DISCOUNT WINDOW BORROWING 1/ 6/	9.00	9.00	9.00	9.00	9.00	9.00	9.00	8.50
U.S. GOVERNMENT SECURITIES								
TREASURY BILLS 2/								
AUCTION AVERAGE (ISSUE DATE)								
3-MONTH				9.64		9.64	9.80	9.44
6-MONTH				9.74		9.74	9.92	9.58
1-YEAR							9.86	9.68
SECONDARY MARKET								
3-MONTH	9.65	9.65	9.63	9.54	9.71	9.64	9.76	9.52
6-MONTH	9.77	9.78	9.76	9.74	9.90	9.79	9.86	9.66
1-YEAR	9.99	9.98	9.98	9.97	10.08	10.00	9.98	9.67
TREASURY CONSTANT MATURITIES 7/								
1-YEAR	10.97	10.95	10.97	10.93	11.06	10.98	10.94	10.59
2-YEAR	11.78	11.73	11.79	11.77	11.89	11.79	11.69	11.31
3-YEAR	12.10	12.06	12.04	12.02	12.17	12.08	11.99	11.59
5-YEAR	12.49	12.46	12.45	12.42	12.55	12.47	12.38	12.02
7-YEAR	12.69	12.66	12.64	12.60	12.72	12.66	12.58	12.25
10-YEAR	12.80	12.75	12.69	12.67	12.79	12.74	12.66	12.32
20-YEAR	12.83	12.78	12.74	12.72	12.84	12.78	12.73	12.45
30-YEAR	12.82	12.75	12.71	12.68	12.82	12.76	12.70	12.38
COMPOSITE								
OVER 10 YEARS (LONG-TERM) 8/	12.31	12.29	12.23	12.21	12.32	12.27	12.21	11.90
CORPORATE BONDS (MOODYS), SEASONED								
ALL INDUSTRIES	13.69	13.71	13.70	13.70	13.72	13.70	13.60	13.33
AAA	12.92	12.94	12.96	12.94	13.00	12.95	12.79	12.57
BAA	14.42	14.41	14.40	14.41	14.40	14.41	14.37	13.99
STATE & LOCAL BONDS (MOODYS), AAA				9.55		9.55	9.50	9.41
CONVENTIONAL MORTGAGES 9/					13.73	13.73	13.67	13.39

1. WEEKLY FIGURES ARE AVERAGES OF 7 CALENDAR DAYS ENDING ON WEDNESDAY OF THE CURRENT WEEK;
   MONTHLY FIGURES INCLUDE EACH CALENDAR DAY IN THE MONTH.
2. QUOTED ON BANK-DISCOUNT BASIS.
3. RATES ON COMMERCIAL PAPER PLACED FOR FIRMS WHOSE BOND RATING IS AA OR THE EQUIVALENT.
4. FOR INDICATION PURPOSES ONLY.
5. RATE CHARGED BY BANKS ON SHORT-TERM BUSINESS LOANS.
6. RATE FOR THE FEDERAL RESERVE BANK OF NEW YORK.
7. YIELDS ON ACTIVELY TRADED ISSUES ADJUSTED TO CONSTANT MATURITIES. SOURCE: U.S. TREASURY.
8. UNWEIGHTED AVERAGE OF ALL ISSUES OUTSTANDING OF BONDS NEITHER DUE NOR CALLABLE IN LESS THAN 10 YEARS,
   INCLUDING SEVERAL VERY LOW YIELDING "FLOWER" BONDS.
9. CONTRACT INTEREST RATES ON COMMITMENTS FOR FIRST MORTGAGES. SOURCE: FHLBC.

NOTE: WEEKLY AND MONTHLY FIGURES ARE AVERAGES OF DAILY RATES, EXCEPT FOR STATE & LOCAL BONDS
      AND CONVENTIONAL MORTGAGES, WHICH ARE BASED ON THURSDAY AND FRIDAY FIGURES, RESPECTIVELY.

SOURCE: U.S., Federal Reserve System, Board of Governors, Federal Reserve Statistical Release—April 30, 1984.

will note that the yields are shown for each day of the week. In the case of this release, it covers the period of April 23rd through the 27th. Also, the average yields are shown for the week of the 27th as well as the previous week; and, finally, the average yield for the previous month is shown in the last column.

How do some lenders use this information to set the rate on certain ARMs? Let us assume that you have taken a client to a lender and are hoping to get a 3-year ARM. A lender tells you which index will be used. It is the previous month's average of the 3-year Treasury. In reviewing the statistical release shown (Figure 3–20), we find that the average yield on the 3-year Treasury is 11.59. This is what some lenders refer to as a *safe rate*, which means that the lender could loan the money to the federal government and receive a return of 11.59 percent with no risk of loss. Since there is risk with our loan, the lender will add spread or a risk factor. For example, the lender tells us they will add 2.5 percent to the yield. Thus, the rate that will be paid by the borrower will be the 11.59 percent plus the 2.5 percent or 14.09, but since most lenders round up to the nearest one-eighth, the rate would be 14.125 or 14 1/8 percent.

This is a simple explanation of how many of the lenders establish the interest rate on ARMs that use the Treasury securities as an interest-rate index.

BUYDOWN MORTGAGE (TEMPORARY)

A buydown mortgage (BDM) is a fixed-term, fixed-rate mortgage that has an effective interest rate below the note rate. This reduction is accomplished by the use of an escrow account and is sometimes referred to as a 3-2-1 or a step mortgage.

The reason for this type of mortgage is to lower the interest rate the borrower will pay in the first few years of the mortgage, especially the interest rate the borrower would pay in the first year of the mortgage. The importance of reducing the interest rate is that it will take less income for the borrower to qualify for the loan. It should be noted that the lender will receive the full principal and interest (P & I) payment as called for in the note, but there is no negative amortization since the difference between the payment made by the borrower and the amount received by the lender is taken from an escrow fund that is established at closing.

Buydown Period

The buydown period can be any length. What is meant by the *buydown period?* This is the period that the borrower will be paying an interest rate below the note rate. There is no fixed buydown period. It can be as short as 3 years or as long as 10 years, but many of those who purchase mortgages in the secondary market have limited the period to 3 years.

Buydown Interest Rate

Many times the real estate professional will see the buydown advertised as 3-2-1, which means that the first year's effective interest rate to the borrower or the rate that will be used to qualify the borrower will be 3 percentage points below the market rate offered by the lender. Thus, the second year the rate on the borrower's effective rate would be 2 points below the rate on the note; and finally in the third year of the mortgage, the borrower would be paid an effective rate of 1 percent below the rate on the note. Thus, with this type of mortgage, the borrower would not pay the full note rate until the 37th payment or at the beginning of the fourth year. Why is it important to lower the first-year interest rate? This is the rate the lender will use to qualify the borrower.

In late 1983 and early 1984, many builders and lenders started to offer *deep buydowns* extending over 5 to 10 year. For example, a builder might offer an 8-6-4-2 buydown. Many of the mortgage insurers and purchasers of mortgages in the secondary market felt that this deep buydown may in a few years expose the borrower to payment shock. Under this program, the borrower would be qualified at a rate 8 percentage points below the note rate. Let us assume the note rate was 13.250; the borrower would be qualified at 13.250 percent less 8 percent or 5.25 percent. This rate would increase in the second year to 13.250 less 6 percent or 7.25 percent and so on through the 4-year buydown period.

Many of those who either buy mortgages in the secondary market or insure conventional mortgages have set the maximum buydown that may be used to qualify the borrower as 3 below the rate expressed on the note regardless of the amount of the actual buydown.

Calculation of Buydown Funds

In this section we will review the methods that may be used to calculate the funds necessary to secure a temporary buydown for a client.

One question that always is asked is who may pay the buydown funds? According to many lenders as well as the Federal Housing Administration and the Veterans Administration, the funds can be provided by anyone. Most lenders will not require a gift letter from the borrower if a third party should provide a portion of the buydown fund. Thus the seller, builder/developer, buyer, or any other person can provide the funds. The buydown funds are in addition to any other discount points or any other fee in connection with the loan.

Now let us assume we are working with a client—either the buyer or seller—and that the client is interested in a buydown mortgage (BDM). The mortgage amount will be $86,550 with a term of 30 years and an interest rate of 14.125 percent. First we will need to calculate the monthly payment for the mortgage at 14.125 percent. This can be done by consulting Appendix A and finding the monthly payment factor for a 30-year loan at 14.125. We then multiply the monthly payment factor, 11.9477, by the loan amount expressed in thousands or:

$$11.9477 \times \frac{\$86,550}{1,000} = \$1,034.07 \text{ (P \& I)}$$

This will be the amount of the P & I payment the lender will receive each month, irrespective of the amount the borrower pays.

The second step is to calculate the interest rate the borrower will be paying for each of the 3 years.

Year 1 of the buydown is the note rate less 3 percent or
$14.125 - 3 = 11.125$
This will be the rate that will be used to qualify the borrower.

Year 2 of the buydown is the note rate less 2 percent or
$14.125 - 2 = 12.125$

Year 3 of the buydown is the note rate less 1 percent or
$14.125 - 1 = 13.125$

The third step is to calculate the actual dollars that will be required to fund or to be placed in escrow to supplement the borrower's payment to the level required by the lender or $1,034.07. This amount may be calculated using two different methods. One method is sometimes referred to as the *fast-and-dirty method.* Using this method, we add up the percent of buydown each year, in this case

3 + 2 + 1 or a total of 6 percent. This amount is then multiplied by the loan amount or the loan amount is multiplied by each of the percentages.

$86,550 × 3 percent = $2596.50
$86,550 × 2 percent = $1731.00
$86,550 × 1 percent = $ 865.50

Total required $5193.00

The second method used to calculate the buydown funds is sometimes referred to as the *actual cash method.* With this method, the actual difference between the monthly payment made by the borrower and the monthly required by the lender is calculated for each year of the buydown. This would be calculated as follows:

Year 1
Interest rate paid by borrower: 11.125
Monthly payment of borrower: $840.63
Monthly payment required by lender: $1,034.07
difference between payments:
$1,034.07 − $840.63 = $193.44 × 12
          = $2321.28

Year 2
Interest rate paid by borrower: 12.125
Monthly payment of borrower: $898.60
Monthly payment required by lender: $1,034.07
Difference between payments:
$1,034.07 − $898.60 = $135.47 × 12
          = $1625.64

Year 3
Interest rate paid by borrower: 13.125
Monthly payment of borrower: $965.88
Monthly payment required by lender: $1034.07
Difference between payments:
$1034.07 − $965.88 = $68.19 × 12
          = $818.28

Total of buydown funds:
$2321.28 + $1625.64 + $818.28 = $4765.20

You will note there is a difference between the two figures of approximately $427.80. The supplier of the buydown funds, therefore, would seek a lender that calculates the buydown funds using the actual cash method.

Some of the lenders as well as some of the secondary marketers will allow the use of the present value of money (PVM). A simple definition of the present value of money is the amount of money that would need to be deposited today to equal a specified amount at the end of a certain period if the funds drew interest at a defined rate. In this case, we would use a time frame of 3 years with the interest compounded monthly.

How does this relate to the buydown? Given that the lenders who allow the use of PVM have set the interest rate at 5.25 percent compounded monthly, how much money would actually have to be placed in the account at the time of closing? To calculate this amount we multiply the amount required by the factor 0.857697, the factor given in a commonly found PVM table. This factor will always be this value for monies compounded monthly at the rate of 5.25 percent. Thus, to find the actual amount needed at closing you would multiply the amount of the escrow deposit by the factor:

$$\$5,193.00 \times 0.857697 = \$4454.02$$

As a real estate professional, you will need to ask any lender that will be offering your client a buydown the method used to calculate the buydown funds and if the lender will be using the present value of money. If the lender says that the PVM will be used, your next question is what will be the compounding rate and frequency.

GRADUATED-PAYMENT MORTGAGE (GPM)

The most common type of GPM is the FHA 245 insured mortgage. This FHA GPM will be explained in depth in Chapter 7. In this section, we will review the conventional GPM and in particular the GPM that is authorized by the FHLBB, which defines a GPM in this manner:

A graduated payment mortgage loan is a fixed-rate loan on which the monthly payments begin at a level lower than that of a level-payment fixed-rate loan. During a period the length of which is fixed at loan origination (the graduation period), the monthly payment amount gradually rises to a level sufficient to amortize the remaining principal balance over the remaining term of the loan.[3]

Graduation Period—Rate and Frequency

The FHLBB has authorized federally chartered savings and loan associations to make the GPM. As with the GPM insured by FHA, the savings and loans can offer several plans of graduation with a maximum graduation period of ten years.

Prior to the Federal Home Loan Bank Board issuing a final rule on July 12, 1981, a section of which revised the graduated-payment mortgage, the federally chartered thrifts were limited to the types of GPM they could originate and purchase, or in which they could participate. This rule, then, canceled all such restrictions. According to Section 1 of the rule, the rate and frequency of payment adjustments will be at any rate or frequency that is contained in the initial loan documents. It should be noted that the changes in the GPM rule canceled the requirement that payments could not change more than once a year. The new rule now allows the federally chartered thrifts to change the payments as often as every 30 days, but the GPM rule change does limit the maximum period for graduations of the monthly payment to a maximum of 10 years.

Therefore, as a real estate professional, you must be very familiar with the conventional GPMs offered by the thrifts in your area. As with the ARM, the types offered by each lender can vary widely.

Disclosures

As with many of the other AMIs authorized by the FHLBB, an applicant for a conventional GPM must also be given a disclosure notice at the time the savings and loan receives the application. The disclosure notice should be in a form and should contain the basic information of the GPM disclosure notice illustrated in Figure 3–21.

Underwriting

As with the FHA-insured GPM, the underwriting or loan approval is based on the first year's payment, thus allowing the borrower to qualify for a larger mortgage than if he or she had applied for a standard fixed-payment mortgage.

Figure 3–21. **Graduated-Payment Mortgage Disclosure**

Information About the Graduated-Payment Mortgage

You have received an application form for a graduated-payment mortgage (GPM). The GPM differs from a level-payment mortgage in the following respect: during the early years of the loan, monthly payments are lower than they would be on a level-payment mortgage and are not sufficient to cover the interest being charged on the loan. As a result, the outstanding principal balance on the GPM loan actually increases somewhat during these years.

To compensate for the initial, lower payments, monthly payments increase gradually each year during a period of up to 10 years (the "graduation period") until they reach a level sufficient to pay all interest and principal by the end of the loan term. The length of the graduation period and limitations on the rate of increase of monthly payments are fixed at loan origination.

Payment amounts may not be changed more than once a year, and first change may not occur sooner than one year after the date of the first regular loan payment.

You have the right to convert this mortgage, at any time you choose, to a level-payment mortgage instrument, provided that you are then eligible for such mortgage under the association's normal underwriting standards. You may not be charged any fees or penalties if you convert to a level-payment mortgage bearing the same interest rate and outstanding maturity as the GPM. Such a mortgage has a fixed interest rate and level payments sufficient to pay all interest and principal by the end of the loan term.

Example of Operation of GPM

Consider a $50,000 GPM that has an interest rate of [*lender's current commitment rate*] percent, a graduation period of _____ years, and a term of _____ years. The monthly payments in the first _____ years of the mortgage (the graduation period) will be as shown in the following table, which reflects a _____ percent graduation. After the _____ year, the payment will remain constant; it will not be increased beyond the level paid in the _____ year.

Year	Principal at year-end	Monthly Payment

By comparison, a $50,000 level-payment mortgage with the same interest rate and for the same term would carry a monthly payment of $_____ , and the remaining principal balance at the end of the [*number corresponding to year in which graduation period on above GPM would end*] year would be $ _____ .

Texas Graduated-Payment Mortgage

In addition to the FHA-insured mortgage, VA-guaranteed mortgage, and the GPM approved by the FHLBB, there are conventional GPMs that may be originated by state-chartered savings and loan associations under Texas Savings and Loan Department rules. These rules are as follows:

1. The Texas GPM may have a maximum graduation period of 10 years provided the loan is structured to amortize both principal and interest in a period not to exceed 40 years.

2. Monthly payments during the first 5 years of the mortgage shall be enough to pay interest, insurance and "government charges assessable for the period of payment."

3. In regard to the repayment of the principal amount, the monthly payments must be sufficient to cover the items mentioned above and an amount sufficient to repay the principal amount in a period not to exceed 50 years.

4. After the first 10 years of the mortgage, the payment must be sufficient to amortize the remaining principal amount in a term not to exceed 30 years.

Graduated-Payment Mortgage Variations

The pledged savings account mortgage and the escrow advance mortgage are two additional types of conventional loans that are variations of the GPM and will also allow a lower initial monthly payment with the provision for periodic increase in the monthly payments at prescribed intervals.

Pledged savings account mortgage (PSAM)
This is a type of mortgage where part of the borrower's down payment is used to fund a pledged savings account, which is used to reduce the monthly payments of the

borrower for a specified number of years. The PSAM, in other words, is just another type of graduated-payment mortgage. The use of the pledge savings account can reduce the borrower's monthly payment up to 25 percent in the first year after origination. The PSAM is authorized by the FHLBB, thus allowing federally chartered savings and loan associations to make it. The most common PSAM is marketed by the FLIP Mortgage Corporation of Newtown, Pennsylvania. FLIP is an acronym for Flexible Loan Insurance Program.

The PSAM combines the lower initial payments of the GPM for the homebuyer with level or full payments for the lender, and the seller gets the full amount of the agreed sales price. With the borrower able to get the lower initial payments, he or she can have a lower annual income and qualify for a higher mortgage.

The PSAM requires the borrower to make a down payment equal to 10 percent of the sales price. Since the majority of the down payment is deposited in a pledged savings account, the loan-to-value ratio (LTV) may be as high as 99 percent. As noted earlier, federally chartered savings and loans are normally limited to making loans with a maximum loan-to-value ratio of 95 percent. The regulation has been amended to allow the federally chartered savings and loans to make loans with LTVs in excess of 95 percent if the excess percentage of 95 percent is secured by a pledged savings account and if the following are met:

1. The loan amount does not exceed the purchase price of the property or the appraised value, whichever is the lesser

2. The funds in the pledged account are those of the borrower

3. The savings and loan association makes certain disclosures to the borrower

Another type of the PSAM is the Action!® Mortgage offered by the Mortgage Guaranty Insurance Corporation. Under the Action!® Mortgage, once again the majority of the down payment is used to fund a pledged interest-bearing savings account that is used to supplement the borrower's monthly payment for a period of 5 years. Thus, the borrower's out-of-pocket payment for the first 5 years of the mortgage is less than the monthly payment of the fixed-payment mortgage. Also, the Action!® Mortgage assumes that the borrower's income will increase a sufficient amount each year to match the increase of the payment, and by the sixth year of the mortgage the borrower's income will be sufficient to match the payment beginning with the sixth year. An example of how the Action!® Mortgage works is given in Figure 3–22.

Escrow advance mortgage   Under this type of mortgage, the initial monthly payments are lower because for the first few years the homebuyer is only paying a portion of the escrow payments for taxes. The reduction can be as much as 20 percent for the initial year. Since the borrower is only paying a portion of the tax escrow, the lender will make up the difference by making advances that equal the amount not paid by the borrower. The advances are added to the principal mortgage amount and are repaid by the borrower over the remaining years of the mortgage.

One type of the escrow advance mortgage is marketed by the Mortgage Guaranty Insurance Corporation and called the MAGIC® Payment Mortgage. Under this program, the borrower's monthly payments gradually increase over a 5-year period, and beginning in the sixth year the payments increase to a level sufficient to pay off the mortgage in full, including the advances made by the lender.

Some of the other features of the MAGIC® Payment Mortgage Program are as follows:

1. Maximum term is 30 years

2. Initial loan-to-value ratio is between 80 and 90 percent

3. Advances made by the lender over the 5-year graduation period may not raise the loan-to-value ratio above 95 percent

4. Mortgage insurance will be purchased for the portion of the mortgage above a loan-to-value ratio of 80 percent

The MAGIC Payment Mortgage Program has been approved by the Texas Savings and Loan Department for use by Texas-chartered savings and loan associations.

GRADUATED-PAYMENT ADJUSTABLE-RATE MORTGAGE (GPARM)[5]

The graduated-payment adjustable-rate mortgage (GPARM) is a hybrid mortgage that combines the rate adjustment features of the ARM with the graduated-payment feature of the graduated-payment mortgage.

Figure 3–22.   *Action!® Mortgage Example*[4]

The example below is based on these assumptions

$54,000 selling price with 10% down payment
30 year mortgage at 10¼%
The down payment is to be applied so that the borrower's out-of-pocket P&I payment will increase 7.5% from year 1 to
   year 2.
$810 annual real estate tax estimate
$150 annual hazard insurance estimate

The Action! Mortgage will allocate the homebuyer's down payment as follows:

$5,400 down payment
−$1,150 applied to purchase

$4,250 savings account balance at start

The Action! Mortgage payment schedule (example)

Beginning Year	Homebuyer's Out-of-Pocket Payment	Pledged Savings Account Withdrawal	Total Monthly Principal & Interest
1st	$344.54*	$129.05	$473.59
2nd	$370.35	$103.24	$473.59
3rd	$396.16	$ 77.43	$473.59
4th	$421.97	$ 51.62	$473.59
5th	$447.78	$ 25.81	$473.59
6th and thereafter	$473.59	$ 0.00	$473.59

*Borrower's monthly payment of Principal and Interest will increase by $25.81 each of first 5 years.

The FHLBB issued proposed rules for this type of mortgage on October 10, 1980, and, while studying the AML, had considered the possibility of incorporating the GPAML into the final rule authorizing the AML. But, the FHLBB decided that all of the ramifications of such an incorporation had not been explored. Thus, the GPAML was still under study and a final rule authorizing the GPAML was to be issued in the future.

Since the spring of 1976, the Federal Home Loan Bank Board has been studying the use of the alternative mortgage instrument in order to meet the needs of the homeowners during different financial phases of their lives. The study has resulted in the introduction of the graduated-payment mortgage, the variable-rate mortgage, and the last of the approved types, introduced on April 3, 1980, the renegotiable-rate mortgage.

A study done by the FHLBB staff, entitled *Improving the Ability of Thrifts to Write Variable Rate Mortgages,* had proposed that the natural extension of the GPM and the RRM would be the graduated-payment adjustment mortgage. Under the GPAML, the payments would start at a lower rate than a conventional mortgage and graduate up. In addition to the payments increasing, the interest rate can also increase. Thus, the GPAML would differ from a conventional mortgage in two respects. First, the payments in the early years of the GPAML would be lower than on a standard fixed-rate mortgage or even on a mortgage with an adjustable interest rate. Thus, these GPAML payments would not be sufficient to cover the interest charges on the loan. In other words, for the first few years of the GPAML, the loan would be in negative amortization (that is, the loan balance would actually increase). The second difference is that the interest rate could be adjusted either up or down at specific intervals. The monthly payments, then, could increase from not only the prescribed payment increase, but also from an increase in the interest rate.

On July 22, 1981, the Federal Home Loan Bank Board issued a final rule allowing federally chartered savings and loan associations and federally chartered mutual savings banks to purchase, participate, or otherwise deal in the GPAML.

Then, as you learned earlier in this chapter, the FHLBB made a major revision to the lending regulations affecting the federally chartered savings and loan associations and the mutual savings banks. Since the revision deleted all reference to the term *adjustable mortgage loan,* but does authorize the associations to make a loan with both the features of rate adjustment and payment adjustment, the loan is now referred to as a graduated-payment adjustable-rate mortgage (GPARM).

Interest-Rate Index

The interest-rate index for the GPARM must meet the same requirement as stated in the FHLBB rule for the ARM. The index must be beyond the control of the lending association and readily verifiable by the borrower; but as with the ARM, the lenders as well as the secondary market are for the most part using the U.S. Treasury securities for indexes on the GPARM.

Adjustments: Payment and Interest Rate

Payment   The monthly payment for principal and interest could not increase during the period of graduation more than the percent agreed upon at the time of application. For example, if the payment graduation was agreed to be 3 percent per year for 10 years, this amount could not be increased later in the mortgage.

Interest rate   As with the ARM, the GPARM monthly payment may be adjusted due to change in the interest rate, which may be as often as monthly. So, for the first ten years of the mortgage, the payment will be increased as per the graduation schedule outlined in the original loan documents and by the amount the interest rate index warrants a change. There is no limitation to the amount the monthly payment may either increase or decrease from one adjustment period to the next. As with the ARM, the payment adjustment due to an index change may be as often as once a month.

Now let us examine how a GPARM can work and the effects of a graduation of the monthly payment and an interest rate index change. For this example, we will use a $50,000 mortgage with a 95 percent loan-to-value ratio and an initial interest rate of 13 percent. We will assume a payment graduation of 7.5 percent for the first 5 years of the mortgage and the interest rate will be adjusted every 3 years.

The effects of the graduation and interest-rate adjustment is shown in Figure 3–23. From this illustration, we can see that the first year's monthly payments are not sufficient to pay all of the interest, as per a GPM, and the ending balance for year one is $51,447.13. Since the original loan documents call for an increase or graduation in the monthly payment of 7.5 percent, the monthly payment in the second year will increase to $460.20 and the payments will increase again in the third year by 7.5 percent to $494.72. Then, at the end of the third year, we not only must increase the payments by the amount of the graduation, but also change the interest rate that is scheduled for an adjustment. In this case, the index indicates an increase of 1.5 percent. The interest rate, therefore, will increase to 14.5 percent. Combining both the graduation and the interest rate, we can see that the payment will increase to $585.75 or an increase of 18.4 percent from the previous year. In addition, we can see that the outstanding principal balance has increased to

Figure 3–23.   Example of the GPARM for a $50,000 mortgage, 5 year/7.5 percent per year graduation, interest rate adjustment every 3 years.

Year	Balance at End	Rate	Monthly Payment	Payment Increase
1	$51,447.13	13%	$428.09	-0-%
2	52,684.89	13	460.20	7.5
3	53,653.66	13	494.72	7.5
4	54,456.40	14.5	585.75	18.4
5	54,819.95	14.5	629.68	7.5
6	54,633.87	14.5	676.91	7.5
7	54,018.53	16	776.08	14.65
8	53,297.15	16	776.08	-0-
9	52,451.50	16	776.08	-0-
10	51,479.28	17.5	839.64	8.19

$54,456.40. This negative amortization continues through the fifth year with the maximum outstanding loan balance of $54,819.95.

As with the ARM, the FHLBB feels the mortgage will not exceed the 125 percent ratio even though the mortgage is in negative amortization for the first few years. Thus, the borrower will not have to put any additional money down. This is the thinking of the FHLBB, but some lenders may require the borrower to make a larger down payment and use the highest balance as the amount to establish the down payment. For example, in Figure 3–23, the mortgage was in negative amortization for the first 5 years and the outstanding loan balance increased from the initial $50,000 to $54,819.95; thus, the lender may require the borrower to put down an initial amount equal to the amount of negative amortization, $4,819.95, and the initial down payment of approximately $2,631 for a total down payment of $7,450.95. If the lender would require that the negative amortization be included in the down payment, the initial loan-to-value ratio would be approximately 86 percent.

The FHLBB also requires that the borrower maintain private mortgage insurance during any period that the loan exceeds 90 percent of the value of the security property. It should be noted that this is a requirement of the FHLBB, but many lenders may require the private mortgage insurance during any period that the loan exceeds 80 percent of the value of the property used as security.

Catch-Up Payment

As with the ARM, the GPARM rule requires that a catch-up payment be scheduled. A catch-up payment is an increase in the monthly payment to a level sufficient to amortize the remaining principal balance over the remaining life of the mortgage. This payment will increase irrespective of any payment increase limitation contained in the original loan documents. Let us review what effect this catch-up payment will have on our example. At the end of the fifth year, the outstanding principal balance is $54,819.95 and the payment beginning with the sixth year is $676.91. Since the original term of the mortgage was 30 years and payments have been made for 5 full years, the remaining original term is 25 years. The required monthly payment to amortize the remaining principal balance over the remaining term of 25 years is $680.95. Thus, the payment is insufficient to amortize the remaining principal balance. Now, the lender has two

choices: one is to increase the payment by some $4.04 per month or, as the rule allows, the lender can extend the term of the mortgage up to a maximum of 40 years from the date of the closing of the loan. If the lender would extend the term of the mortgage, the $676.91 payment would be sufficient with no increase.

Adjustment Notification

The FHLBB requires savings and loan associations making the GPARM to give notice of a rate adjustment at least 30 days prior to the adjustment, but not more than 120 days prior to any change in the interest rate. In addition, the savings and loan associations are required to send a written notice to the borrower. The borrower would have the right to prepay the mortgage in full without penalty at any time after the savings and loan has notified the borrower of the first interest increase.

Disclosure Requirement

As with the RRM, VRM, and SAM, the lender will give the prospective borrower a disclosure notice similar to the one illustrated in Figure 3–24.

GROWING EQUITY MORTGAGE (GEM)

As with the other AMIs, the growing equity mortgage (GEM) is another attempt to reduce the effects of the high interest rates of the 1980s. First, let us define the GEM. The GEM is a fixed-rate, first-lien mortgage in which the monthly payment increases at a specific rate for a specified number of years. The increase, instead of a specific rate, may be based on a specified index. The first year's payments are based on the face rate of the mortgage and all increases in payments will be credited to principal reduction. From this definition, we can see that the GEM is a type of GPM, but does not have the feature of negative amortization.

Advantages

First, let us review the advantages to the borrower. One advantage was mentioned above: there is no negative amortization. A second advantage to the borrower is that since the first year's payments are based on the face rate to amortize over 30 years, the initial monthly payment of principal and interest is contributing to principal reduction. Thus, any increase in the payment will be credited to

Figure 3–24.   *Graduated Payment Adjustable-Rate Mortgage Disclosure*

IMPORTANT INFORMATION ABOUT THE GRADUATED PAYMENT ADJUSTABLE RATE MORTGAGE – PLEASE READ CAREFULLY

You have received an application form for a graduated payment adjustable rate mortgage loan ("GPARM"). The GPARM may differ from other mortgages with which you are familiar.

General Description of Graduated Payment Adjustable Rate Mortgage

The graduated payment adjustable mortgage loan is a flexible loan instrument on which the scheduled monthly payment amount at the beginning of the loan term is insufficient to fully amortize the loan. Within ten years of the date of the closing of the loan, and at least every five years after that, the payment amount must be adjusted to a level that will fully amortize the loan. The interest rate on a GPARM may be adjusted by the lender from time to time. Such adjustments will result in increases or decreases in your payment amount, in the outstanding principal loan balance, in the loan term, or in all three (see discussion below relating to these types of adjustments). Federal regulations place no limit on the amount by which the interest rate may be adjusted either at any one time or over the life of the loan, or on the frequency with which it may be adjusted. Adjustments to the interest rate must reflect the movement of a single, specified index (see discussion below). This does not mean that the particular loan agreement you sign must, by law, permit unlimited interest-rate changes. It merely means that, if you desire to have certain rate-adjustment limitations placed in your loan agreement, that is a matter you should negotiate with the lender. You may also want to make inquiries concerning the loan terms offered by other lenders on GPARMs to compare the terms and conditions.

Another flexible feature of the GPARM is that the regular payment amount, in addition to being increased because it was too small to fully amortize the loan at the beginning of the loan term, may be increased or decreased by the lender from time to time to reflect changes in the interest rate. Again, Federal regulations place no limitations on the amount by which the lender may adjust payments at any one time, or on the frequency of payment adjustments. If you wish to have particular provisions in your loan agreement regarding adjustments to the payment amount, you should negotiate such terms with the lender prior to entering such an agreement.

A third flexible feature of the GPARM is that the outstanding principal loan balance (the total amount you owe) may be increased or decreased from time to time when, because of adjustments to the interest rate or because the payment amount was too small at the beginning of the loan term to fully amortize the loan, the payment amount is either too small to cover interest due on the loan, or larger than is necessary to pay off the loan over the remaining term of the loan.

The final flexible feature of the GPARM is that the loan term may be lengthened or shortened from time to time, corresponding to an increase or decrease in the interest rate. When the term is extended in connection with a rate increase, the payment amount does not have to be increased to the same extent as if the term had not been lengthened. In no case may the total term of the loan exceed 40 years.

Page 1 of 3

Figure 3–24. *continued*

Index

Adjustments to the interest rate of a GPARM must correspond directly to the movement of an index, subject to such rate-adjustment limitations as may be contained in the loan contract. If the index has moved down, the lender must reduce the interest rate by at least the decrease in the index. If the index has moved up, the lender has the right to increase the interest rate by that amount. Although taking such an increase is optional by the lender, you should be aware that the lender has this right and may become contractually obligated to exercise it.

[Name and description of index to be used for applicant's loan, initial index value (if known) or date of initial index value, a source or sources where the index may be readily obtained by the borrower, and the high and low index rates during the previous calendar year.]

Key terms of   Federal Savings and Loan Association's graduated payment adjustable rate mortgage

Following is a summary of the key terms of the type of GPARM to be offered to you. This summary is intended for reference purposes only. Important information relating specifically to your loan will be contained in the loan agreement, which alone will establish your rights under the loan plan.

[Provide summary of key terms of the loan, including the loan term, over what period and by what amounts the payment will be adjusted to fully amortize the loan, the frequency of rate changes, the frequency of payment changes, the maximum rate change, if any, at one time, the maximum rate change, if any, over the life of the loan, the maximum payment change, if any, at one time, minimum increments, if any, of rate changes, and whether there will be adjustments to the principal loan balance, in the following format:

Loan term . . . .
Graduation period . . . .
Rate of payment increases during graduation period . . . .
Frequency of payment increases during graduation
period . . . .
Frequency of rate changes . . . . (etc.)]

How Your Graduated Payment Adjustable Rate Mortgage Would Work

Initial Interest Rate

The initial interest rate offered by _____ Federal Savings and Loan Association on your GPARM will be established and disclosed to you on [commitment date, etc.] based on market conditions at the time.

[Insert a short description of each of the key terms of the type of GPARM to be offered to the borrower, using headings where appropriate.]

Figure 3–24.   continued

Notice of payment adjustments

_____ Federal Savings and Loan Association will send you notice of an adjustment to the payment amount at least 30 but not more than 120 days before it becomes effective. [Describe what information the notice will contain.]

Prepayment penalty

You may prepay a GPARM in whole or in part *without penalty at any time* during the term of the loan.

Fees

You will be charged fees by _____ Federal Savings and Loan Association and by other persons in connection with the origination of your GPARM. The association will give you an estimate of these fees after receiving your loan application. However, you will not be charged any costs or fees in connection with any regularly-scheduled adjustment to the interest rate, the payment, the outstanding principal loan balance, or the loan term initiated by the lender.

Example of operation of your type of GPARM

[Set out an example of the operation of all of the features of the type of GPARM to be offered to the borrower, including, where appropriate, the use of a table.]

principal reduction. Thus, the loan will be repaid in less than 30 years saving the borrower many dollars in interest expense.

A third advantage is that since the lender or investor will have funds tied up for fewer years, the face interest rate is usually below the prevailing market rate for a fixed-rate, fixed-term mortgage.

The lender will also receive several advantages for the GEM. One is that the loanable funds will be tied up for fewer years. A second advantage is that since the borrower's equity is rapidly increasing, there is less likelihood of default. Finally, many of the standard notes and mortgages/deeds of trust can be used for the conventional GEM with only slight modifications.

Graduation Period—Rate and Frequency

There is no set rate and frequency of graduation with the GEM as there is with the negative amortization GPM, but the normal range of rate of graduation is 3 to 5 percent per year for a period of 5 to 10 years. For example, HUD-FHA will issue mortgage insurance on GEMs with a 2 or 3 percent increase for a period of ten years. This GEM will be discussed in detail in Chapter 7. VA will also guarantee certain types of GEMs, which will be discussed in Chapter 8. The rate and frequency of the graduation will be set at the time of origination and will be outlined in the original loan documents.

Underwriting

As with the GPM and many of the other AMIs, the underwriting is based on the initial or first year's payments. Since the GEM will normally have a rate below market, the borrower will be able to qualify for a larger loan amount.

GEM Example and Comparison to a Fixed-Rate, Fixed-Term Mortgage

For this example we will use a fixed-rate, fixed-term mortgage of $75,000 with an interest rate of 15.50 percent and a term of 30 years. The GEM will be structured identically, but the payment will be increased by 3.5 percent per year for a period of 10 years. It should be noted that the 10-year period will not begin until the end of the first year, thus the graduation period will be year 2 through 11. The GEM is shown in Figure 3–25 and the conventional mortgage is shown in Figure 3–26.

Now let us do our comparison. We can see that the monthly payments for the GEM increase annually, but for the conventional mortgage the payments remain constant. With the payments increasing and all of the increase being credited to principal reduction, we can see that the GEM is paid in full in 12 years and 10 months. When this is compared to the conventional mortgage, the principal has only been reduced by $4,639.83.

Another interesting comparison is that over the 12-year, 10-month period, the conventional borrower has paid some $146,032.23 in interest and with the GEM, the borrower will have paid $109,618.67 or 75 percent of the conventional amount with over 50 percent of the interest paid during the first five years.

GEM Appeal

This type of mortgage would appeal to the persons or family who have decided that this is the home of their choice and would like to live there for the rest of their lives. For example, a GEM might appeal to a person being transferred into a job where he or she will finish his or her career and hope to retire at that present location. In some cases, the GEM would appeal to the young homebuyer who owns his or her own business and the home meets all of the present and anticipated needs of his or her family.

Growing Equity Variations

There are several variations that are offered by lenders to the GEM. Sometimes the GEM is referred to as an early ownership mortgage (EOM). This variation is identical to the example and the GEM mentioned in the previous section. The major variation is the step GEM or step EOM. The mortgage still allows the borrower to build equity rapidly through the usual increase in the P & I portion of the total monthly payment, but the beginning of the increase does not start with the second year of the mortgage. The payment increase does not start until later, say in the third, fourth, fifth, or eighth year of the loan. One reason for the delay in the increase is to allow the new homebuyer to get settled in the home. Another reason for seeking a delay in the payment increases is that the borrower may know that for several years their expenses will be high and will reduce in three, four, or five years. An example would be a family that has a child in college who will graduate in three or four years; thus their expenses would decrease. The increases for this type of GEM are calculated

Figure 3–25.   Growing Equity Loan

Year	Monthly Payments	Interest Paid	Principal Paid	Remaining Balance
1	978.39	11,616.42	124.26	74,875.74
2	1,012.63	11,565.25	586.31	74,289.42
3	1,048.08	11,436.06	1,140.90	73,148.52
4	1,084.76	11,213.45	1,803.67	71,344.85
5	1,122.72	10,879.34	2,593.30	68,751.55
6	1,162.02	10,412.57	3,531.67	65,219.88
7	1,202.69	9,788.34	4,643.94	60,575.94
8	1,244.78	8,977.66	5,959.70	54,616.23
9	1,288.35	7,946.57	7,513.63	47,102.60
10	1,333.45	6,655.40	9,346.00	37,756.60
11	1,380.12	5,057.75	11,503.69	26,252.90
12	1,380.12	3,142.39	13.419.05	12.833.85
12 + 6	1,380.12	755.25	7,525.47	5.308.38
12 + 8	1,380.12	875.45	10,165.51	2,668.33
12 + 9	1,380.12	909.95	11,511.17	1,322.71
12 + 10	1,339.81	917.01	1,322.71	- 0 -

Total Principal Paid =   75,000.00

Total Payments $184,618.67
Less Principal Reduction   − 75,000.00

TOTAL INTEREST   109,618.67

Figure 3–26.   Conventional Loan

Year	Monthly Payments	Interest Paid	Principal Paid	% Principal Repaid	Remaining Balance
1	978.39	11,616.42	124.26	0.17	74,875.74
2	978.39	11,595.73	144.95	0.36	74,730.79
3	978.39	11,571.59	169.09	0.58	74,561.70
4	978.39	11,543.76	197.24	0.85	74,364.46
5	978.39	11,510.92	230.08	1.16	74,134.38
6	978.39	11.447.29	268.39	1.52	73,865.99
7	978.39	11,427.61	311.07	1.93	73,552.91
8	978.39	11,370.80	365.20	2.42	73,187.72
9	978.39	11,314.67	426.01	2.99	72,761.71
10	978.39	11,243.74	496.94	3.65	72.264.77
11	978.39	11,161.01	579.67	4.42	71,685.09
12	978.39	11,064.49	676.19	5.32	71,008.90
12 + 6	978.39	5,491.13	379.21	5.83	70,629.68
12 + 8	978.39	7,314.87	512.25	6.00	70,496.65
12 + 9	978.39	8,225.46	580.05	6.10	70,428.85
12 + 10	978.39	9,135.16	648.74	6.19	70,360.16

Total Principal Paid = 4,639.83

Total Payments (12 years and 10 months @ 978.39) $150.672.06
Less Principal Reduction   − 4,639.83

TOTAL INTEREST   146,032.23

in the same manner as a regular GEM; they are only deferred.

GEM Standard Note

As with the standard mortgage and the ARMs there has been an effort to standardize the loan documents, in particular the note. Once again, one of the larger secondary marketers, Fannie Mae, has led the way and has introduced a uniform growing equity note. The Fannie Mae Uniform Instrument is shown in Figures 3–27 and 3–28.

The first portion of this note is very similar to the standard fixed-rate note shown in Chapter 2. The major difference occurs in section 4, Monthly Payment Calculations. Subsection A of the section states the amount of the first-year principal and interest payment and then it states the method and amount by which the monthly payment will increase. For example, you are working with a client that is interested in a GEM. This GEM will have an annual payment increase of 3 percent per year for a period of 10 years, beginning with the second year of the mortgage. To calculate the monthly payments for years 2 through 11, you would first calculate the first year's payment and then multiply that value by 1.03 or you could turn to Appendix D, find the table for a GEM with a 3 percent increase for 10 years and locate the proper interest rate. Listed below the interest rate for the loan are the monthly payment factors for years 1 through 11. Subsection B deals with how the increase in the payment will be credited. You will note that the subsection shows the amount of the first-year monthly payment and also states the number of years it would take to repay the loan if the payments did not increase. The next sentence states that all increases to the monthly payment will be used to reduce the unpaid principal balance. As was shown in the GEM example, the term of the loan can be reduced with the application of the increase in the payment. The remainder of the note is similar to the Texas fixed-rate note.

SHARED-APPRECIATION MORTGAGE (SAM)[6]

A *shared-appreciation mortgage* (SAM) is a mortgage in which the borrower agrees to share in the appreciation of the property. In return for the equity position, the lender will give the borrower an interest rate that is below the rate charged for a standard mortgage.

The primary reason for the Federal Home Loan Bank Board to authorize federally chartered savings and loans to make the SAM is that the lower the interest rate, the lower the monthly payment, and thus the income of the borrower can be less to qualify for the mortgage.

In addition to the lower interest rate, the SAM differs from the standard mortgage in two other ways. First, the payments are based on an amortization period for up to forty years, but the mortgage is due and payable no later than the tenth year with guaranteed refinancing. Second, the SAM has a contingent interest feature. *Contingent interest* can be defined as an interest charge, assessed by the lender making the mortgage, that is equal to a specified percentage of the property's net appreciation over the life of the mortgage.

In regard to the percentage of the appreciation that the lender may require to make the mortgage, most of the lenders charge 30 percent.

It should be noted that if the contingent interest is due and payable prior to the sale of the property, the borrower may pay the contingent interest in full, or the amount of the mortgage and the contingent interest can be refinanced by the lender at the prevailing market rates.

Net Appreciated Value

How do we calculate net appreciation or the net appreciated value? It may be figured by two methods, depending on whether the loan goes to maturity and is prepaid in full or the property is sold or transferred. If the property is sold or transferred, the lender making the mortgage may choose to accept the net sales price as the determination of the market value. According to some lenders, the *net selling price* is the gross selling price of the property less certain selling expenses such as real estate commissions, advertising, transfer fees, legal fees, and escrow and recording fees.

If the lender does not wish to accept the net sales price or if the loan matures or the borrower pays the loan in full prior to the maturity date, the market value would be established by an appraisal. The appraiser is agreed upon by both the borrower and the lender from a list of appraisers who have done appraisals for the lender. If the borrower and the lender cannot agree on a single appraiser, then the borrower and the lender will each select an appraiser and the market value will be the average of the two appraisals.

After the market value is established by the appraisal method, the net appreciated value

Figure 3–27.   Fannie Mae Multistate Growing Equity Note, page 1

GROWING EQUITY NOTE

This Note requires an increase in the amount of my monthly payment each year.

...., 19........   ...., ...
                                                                        [City]   [State]

....
                                          [Property Address]

1. BORROWER'S PROMISE TO PAY

In return for a loan that I have received, I promise to pay U.S. $.. (this amount is called "principal"), plus interest, to the order of the Lender. The Lender is ....

.... I understand that the Lender may transfer this Note. The Lender or anyone who takes this Note by transfer and who is entitled to receive payments under this Note is called the "Note Holder."

2. INTEREST

Interest will be charged on unpaid principal until the full amount of principal has been paid. I will pay interest at a yearly rate of ....%.

The interest rate required by this Section 2 is the rate I will pay both before and after any default described in Section 7(B) of this Note.

3. TIME AND PLACE OF PAYMENTS

I will pay principal and interest by making payments every month.

I will make my monthly payments on the .... day of each month beginning on ...., 19........ I will make these payments every month until I have paid all of the principal and interest and any other charges described below that I may owe under this Note. My monthly payments will be applied to interest before principal. If, on ...., ..., I still owe amounts under this Note, I will pay those amounts in full on that date, which is called the "maturity date."

I will make my monthly payments at ....

.... or at a different place if required by the Note Holder.

4. MONTHLY PAYMENT CALCULATIONS

(A) Yearly Increases

My first .... monthly payments will each be in the amount of U.S. $.. On the first day of ...., 19........, and on each anniversary of that date, I will begin paying a new monthly payment which will be equal to the amount I have been paying multiplied by the number 1.0........ I will pay the new amount of my monthly payment until it changes in accordance with this Section 4.

The Note Holder will give me notice of each change in the amount of my monthly payment before the effective date of any change.

(B) Effect of Increased Payments

Each of my first .... monthly payments will be in an amount that would be sufficient to fully repay my loan in .... years at the interest rate required by Section 2 above in substantially equal payments. Each remaining monthly payment will be greater than this amount. The Note Holder will apply the difference between these two amounts to reduce my unpaid principal balance.

5. BORROWER'S RIGHT TO PREPAY

I have the right to make payments at any time before they are due. A payment of principal only is known as a "prepayment." When I make a prepayment, I will tell the Note Holder in writing that I am doing so.

I may make a full prepayment or partial prepayments without paying any prepayment charge. The Note Holder will use all of my prepayments to reduce the amount of principal that I owe under this Note. If I make a partial prepayment, there will be no changes in the due date or in the amount of my monthly payment unless the Note Holder agrees in writing to those changes.

6. LOAN CHARGES

If a law, which applies to this loan and which sets maximum loan charges, is finally interpreted so that the interest or other loan charges collected or to be collected in connection with this loan exceed the permitted limits, then: (i) any such loan charge shall be reduced by the amount necessary to reduce the charge to the permitted limit; and (ii) any sums already collected from me which exceeded permitted limits will be refunded to me. The Note Holder may choose to make this refund by reducing the principal I owe under this Note or by making a direct payment to me. If a refund reduces principal, the reduction will be treated as a partial prepayment.

7. BORROWER'S FAILURE TO PAY AS REQUIRED

(A) Late Charge for Overdue Payments

If the Note Holder has not received the full amount of any monthly payment by the end of .... calendar days after the date it is due, I will pay a late charge to the Note Holder. The amount of the charge will be ....% of my overdue payment of principal and interest. I will pay this late charge promptly but only once on each late payment.

(B) Default

If I do not pay the full amount of each monthly payment on the date it is due, I will be in default.

(C) Notice of Default

If I am in default, the Note Holder may send me a written notice telling me that if I do not pay the overdue amount by a certain date, the Note Holder may require me to pay immediately the full amount of principal which has not been paid and all the interest that I owe on that amount. That date must be at least 30 days after the date on which the notice is delivered or mailed to me.

MULTISTATE GROWING EQUITY NOTE—Single Family—**FNMA Uniform Instrument**   Form 3255 12/83

Figure 3–28. **Fannie Mae Multistate Growing Equity Note, page 2**

(D) No Waiver By Note Holder

Even if, at a time when I am in default, the Note Holder does not require me to pay immediately in full as described above, the Note Holder will still have the right to do so if I am in default at a later time.

(E) Payment of Note Holder's Costs and Expenses

If the Note Holder has required me to pay immediately in full as described above, the Note Holder will have the right to be paid back by me for all of its costs and expenses in enforcing this Note to the extent not prohibited by applicable law. Those expenses include, for example, reasonable attorneys' fees.

8. GIVING OF NOTICES

Unless applicable law requires a different method, any notice that must be given to me under this Note will be given by delivering it or by mailing it by first class mail to me at the Property Address above or at a different address if I give the Note Holder a notice of my different address.

Any notice that must be given to the Note Holder under this Note will be given by mailing it by first class mail to the Note Holder at the address stated in Section 3 above or at a different address if I am given a notice of that different address.

9. OBLIGATIONS OF PERSONS UNDER THIS NOTE

If more than one person signs this Note, each person is fully and personally obligated to keep all of the promises made in this Note, including the promise to pay the full amount owed. Any person who is a guarantor, surety or endorser of this Note is also obligated to do these things. Any person who takes over these obligations, including the obligations of a guarantor, surety or endorser of this Note, is also obligated to keep all of the promises made in this Note. The Note Holder may enforce its rights under this Note against each person individually or against all of us together. This means that any one of us may be required to pay all of the amounts owed under this Note.

10. WAIVERS

I and any other person who has obligations under this Note waive the rights of presentment and notice of dishonor. "Presentment" means the right to require the Note Holder to demand payment of amounts due. "Notice of dishonor" means the right to require the Note Holder to give notice to other persons that amounts due have not been paid.

11. UNIFORM SECURED NOTE

This Note is a uniform instrument with limited variations in some jurisdictions. In addition to the protections given to the Note Holder under this Note, a Mortgage, Deed of Trust or Security Deed (the "Security Instrument"), dated the same date as this Note, protects the Note Holder from possible losses which might result if I do not keep the promises which I make in this Note. That Security Instrument describes how and under what conditions I may be required to make immediate payment in full of all amounts I owe under this Note. Some of those conditions are described as follows:

Transfer of the Property or a Beneficial Interest in Borrower. If all or any part of the Property or any interest in it is sold or transferred (or if a beneficial interest in Borrower is sold or transferred and Borrower is not a natural person) without Lender's prior written consent, Lender may, at its option, require immediate payment in full of all sums secured by this Security Instrument. However, this option shall not be exercised by Lender if exercise is prohibited by federal law as of the date of this Security Instrument.

If Lender exercises this option, Lender shall give Borrower notice of acceleration. The notice shall provide a period of not less than 30 days from the date the notice is delivered or mailed within which Borrower must pay all sums secured by this Security Instrument. If Borrower fails to pay these sums prior to the expiration of this period, Lender may invoke any remedies permitted by this Security Instrument without further notice or demand on Borrower.

WITNESS THE HAND(S) AND SEAL(S) OF THE UNDERSIGNED.

.... (Seal)
-Borrower

.... (Seal)
-Borrower

.... (Seal)
-Borrower

[Sign Original Only]

will be established by subtracting from the market value the following:

1. The original cost of the property

2. The cost of any capital improvements made to the property

3. The cost of the appraisal or appraisals needed to establish the market value

The original cost of the property is calculated by adding to the cost of the property any of the following:

1. Commissions

2. Cost of title search or title insurance

3. Legal, appraisal, and inspection fees

4. Payments to clear prior liens

Loan Term

The term of the SAM is normally a maximum of 10 years. The reason for the relatively short term is twofold:

1. If the term of the SAM was 30 years and the borrower held the SAM to maturity, the net appreciation of the property could be so great that the borrower could not be able to afford the cost of refinancing and thus would have to sell his or her home to pay the contingent interest.

2. With the increasing cost of money to the lenders, the holding of a below-market interest rate loan by a lender to the 30-year maturity could have an adverse impact on the profits of the lender.

Refinancing

Because of the relatively short term of the SAM, some lenders provide for guaranteed refinancing of the outstanding principal amount of the SAM plus the full amount of the contingent interest if the loan is not paid in full or the property is sold prior to the maturity of the mortgage. The borrower may be allowed to choose the type of mortgage for refinancing the SAM. The mortgage may be a fixed-rate or a flexible-payment mortgage other than a SAM.

The minimum term of the refinancing of the SAM is 30 years, and all of the fees associated with the refinancing of the property may be borne by the lenders, except the cost of the appraisal and that is to be paid by the borrower.

If the borrower should decide to refinance, unless the interest rates have fallen below those of the original SAM, the borrower's monthly payment may increase greatly.

Disclosures

Some lenders provide two disclosures. The first disclosure is at the time of application and the second disclosure will be sent to the borrower at least 90 days prior to the maturity of the mortgage. These disclosures are shown in Figures 3–29 and 3–30.

SAM Appeal

The SAM will probably be more attractive to the first-time homebuyers who do not have sufficient funds for a large down payment, and who traditionally do not reside for a long time in their first house and thus will sell prior to the term of the original SAM. Often, the first-time homebuyer is looking for a reduced payment; the following example will illustrate how the SAM can meet this desire.

Let's assume that the prospective homebuyer is looking for a mortgage of $50,000 with a term of 30 years, using a standard fixed-rate mortgage. With an interest rate of 13 percent, the monthly principal and interest payment would be $553.10. If the prospective borrower would use the SAM and give the lender a contingent interest covenant that would be equal to 30 percent of the appreciation and the lender would in turn give the borrower an interest rate of 9.5 percent, the monthly P & I payment would be reduced to $420.43. Let's assume that the taxes and insurance on the subject property would be $1000 per year or $83.33 per month. The total payments would be $634.43 for the fixed-rate mortgage and $503.76 for the SAM. In the underwriting of the mortgage, if the standard 25 percent rule is used, the borrower would need an income of $30,549 to qualify for the fixed-rate mortgage; but using the SAM, the annual income is reduced to $24,181. Thus, more borrowers could qualify to purchase homes using the SAM.

VARIABLE-RATE MORTGAGE (VRM)

A *variable-rate mortgage* can be defined as a long-term mortgage whose interest rate is adjusted at set intervals using a prescribed reference, or index rate, to establish the rate. In other words, with this type of alternative

Figure 3–29. *Disclosure Sent to Borrower at Time of Application*

Information About the Appreciation Mortgage

You have received an application form for an appreciation mortgage. The appreciation mortgage differs from other mortgages commonly in use in that there are two elements used in calculating interest with the appreciation mortgage. The first element of interest is fixed at the beginning of the loan and is paid over the term of the loan as part of the monthly installment. The second element of interest is contingent in nature, based upon the amount of the increased value of the residence securing the loan between the time of purchase and either the maturity or payment in full of the loan or the sale or transfer of the property. The amount of Contingent Interest which you will pay cannot be determined at this time.

The contingent interest on the shared appreciation mortgage is equal to a percentage of the appreciation of the property not to exceed 40%, as agreed to by the borrower and lender. Contingent interest is payable on the earlier of the maturity or payment in full of the loan or the sale or transfer of the property. The obligation to pay contingent interest will diminish the amount of appreciation realized by you on the property. The attached table shows examples of the total cost of a shared appreciation mortgage and comparison with conventional mortgages. Contingent interest is calculated as follows:

Market value of the property [The association may choose to use the amount realized on the sale or transfer of the property as a measure of market value.]

  – (less) Cost of the property to you [This amount includes certain costs paid by you incident to the purchase. In the event that the loan will be used to refinance the property the cost of the property will be determined by the market value as of the time that the loan is made.].

  – (less) Cost of capital improvements made by you [You will be required to provide proof of such costs.].

  – (less) Cost of appraisal [If used to determine market value.].

  = (equals) Net appreciated value.

  × (times) Percentage of net appreciated value to be paid by the borrower.

  = (equals) Total Contingent Interest.

If the property is not sold prior to the maturity of the loan, the lender must offer to refinance the outstanding obligation on the loan, including any contingent interest. The lender must offer refinancing using any fully amortizing mortgage instrument with a term of at least 30 years. You may request a loan with a shorter term. Refinancing may be by use of any home mortgage loan being made by the association at the time of refinancing under terms and conditions, including interest rates, then prevailing for home mortgage loans. If the association offers more than one type of loan for refinancing, you may choose between them. The association may not look to the forecast of your income in offering to refinance. However, as a condition of refinancing, the association may require that you satisfy any claims against your property arising since making of the original loan. The interest rate and specific terms of any refinancing are subject to then-prevailing market conditions. The interest rate and monthly payment on renewal cannot be determined at this time.

Use of the appreciation mortgage may have income tax or estate planning consequences. For further information, consult your accountant, attorney or other financial advisor.

[A side-by-side comparison of a SAM and a comparable standard mortgage instrument (with a fixed interest rate, level payments and full amortization) must be made in the following format. The initial property value, loan amount, fixed interest rate and ratio for sharing appreciation do not have to be exactly the same as the loan for which the applicant is applying, but must be similar enough to permit a fair comparison.].

financing, the term of the mortgage remains constant and with each payment the principal balance declines. The only variable is the interest rate, which can either increase or decrease, based on the prescribed interest rate index.

Interest Rate Indexes[7]

There are two basic types of interest rate indexes:

1. *Cost of funds index,* based on the cost of funds, or what the lender has to pay to depositors on savings accounts

2. *Mortgage-rate index,* based on the average of interest charged in the market place

Three cost of funds indexes that could be used are:

1. *The lenders own cost of funds, as calculated by the institution.* This index fails to meet one of the very desirable criteria: that the index be calculated and published by a reputable source and not subject to the influence of the lender.

2. *The average cost of funds of the insured institutions located in a city or state* as calculated by the Federal Home Loan Bank Board.

3. *The average cost of funds of FSLIC-insured institutions in the United States,* as calculated by the Federal Home Loan Bank Board twice each year.

Figure 3–29. continued

Examples of Total Cost of a Shared Appreciation Mortgage [Initial property value[1]]

A number not to exceed 40

Loan amount — percentage of appreciation to lender	Monthly[2] interest	Contingent[3] interest	Total interest cost
5-year life:			
Conventional mortgage at _____ % interest			
Shared appreciation mortgage at:			
[x] % fixed interest[2] and 5% property appreciation			
[x] % fixed interest[2] and 10% property appreciation			
[x] % fixed interest[2] and 15% property appreciation			
10-year life:			
Conventional mortgage at _____ % interest			
Shared appreciation mortgage at:			
[x] % fixed interest[2] and 5% property appreciation			
[x] % fixed interest[2] and 10% property appreciation			
[x] % fixed interest[2] and 15% property appreciation			

[1]This chart assumes that no improvements to the property are made by the borrower. The cost of such improvements would be deducted from appreciation prior to calculating contingent interest.
[2]A fixed rate of interest of [x] % is assumed. The fixed rate on your loan may not be the same.
[3]Contingent interest equal to [number not to exceed 40] percent of net appreciated value is assumed. The rate on your loan may not be the same. This chart assumes that there are no costs incident to sale. Such costs are deducted prior to calculating interest.

Date Received: _____
Borrower Signature: _____
Lending Officer: _____

SOURCE: "Proposed Rules," *Federal Register*, October 8, 1980, vol. 45, no. 197, p. 66806.

Rate Adjustment[8]

Some VRMs written in the United States have a limit to the amount that the interest rate may be increased. The regulations covering the rate adjustments state that any increase in rate based on the rate index can be made at the option of the lender, but any decrease in interest rate based on the rate index is mandatory and must be made.

Some VRM loan documents allow the rate to be adjusted only once a year or less often with a maximum adjustment of 0.5 percent each year and a maximum increase of 2.5 percent over the life of the mortgage. The Federal Home Loan Bank Board, prior to the cancellation of the VRM, had proposed the following amendments to their original rate adjustment rules:

1. The rate may be adjusted every 6 months after the first regular monthly loan payment

2. Once the adjustment period has been established, its length may not be altered (for example, if a savings and loan established 12 months as the period between the first regular monthly payment and the first interest-rate adjustment, the savings and loan could not in the future shorten the period between adjustments to, say, 6 months or lengthen the period to 24 months)

3. The maximum rate adjustment would have been changed to a maximum of 0.5 percent every six months, with a maximum increase or decrease of 5 percent over the life of the mortgage

It should be noted that some lenders may use these rate adjustment limitations.

Rate Change Notification[9]

Prior to the lender either increasing or decreasing the interest rate, the loan documents may require the lender to give the borrower notice. Some documents may state that the borrower

Figure 3–30.   Disclosure Sent to Borrower at Least 90 Days Before Mortgage Matures

NOTICE

Your loan with _____ Federal Savings and Loan Association, secured by a [mortgage/deed of trust] on the property located at [address], is due and payable on [no earlier than 90 days from date of notice]. Unless you choose to refinance the loan as set forth below, the outstanding indebtedness on your loan shall be payable on [no earlier than 90 days from date of notice]. The outstanding indebtedness on your loan on that date shall consist of the principal balance of [actual principal balance] and contingent interest in the amount of [number not to exceed 40] percent of the amount of appreciation on the property since the beginning of the loan. The amount of appreciation is determined by subtracting from the value of the property as of the date the loan is due (i) the cost of the property to you, (ii) the cost of improvements made by you, and (iii) the cost of appraisal to determine the value of the property.

The appraisal shall be performed by an appraiser selected by you and the association from a list of appraisers who have made appraisals accepted by the Federal Home Loan Mortgage Corporation or the Federal National Mortgage Association. You may obtain a copy of this list from the association. In the event that you do not agree with the association on the selection of an appraiser, you and the association shall each select an appraiser from the list and the market value shall be determined by an average of the two appraisals. In the event that you do not select an appraiser within 30 days from receipt of this notice, the appraisal shall be performed by an appraiser selected by the association.

The association is required to provide you with the opportunity to refinance the entire amount due with a loan for a term of not less than 30 years. Refinancing may be by use of any home mortgage loan presently being made by the association, including [specify types of loans being made], under current terms and conditions, including interest rates. The association may not look to the forecast of your income in offering to refinance the loan. However, as a condition of refinancing, the association may require that you satisfy any claims against your property arising since the making of the original loan. You may contact the association regarding the terms and conditions of such refinancing.

For further information with regard to this notice, please contact [title and telephone number of association employee.]

SOURCE: "Proposed Rules," *Federal Register*, October 8, 1980, vol. 45, no. 197, p. 66806.

must be notified 30 days prior to a change in the interest rate when the 1-year adjustment period is used. The instruments may also prohibit prepayment penalties for 90 days after receipt of the notice.

Prior to the cancellation of the VRM regulations, the FHLBB felt that the 30-day notice of adjustment was insufficient. Therefore, the FHLBB had proposed an increase in the notice period to 60 days, with a maximum of 90 days notice prior to the change in interest rate. The FHLBB had also proposed dropping any prepayment penalty at any time after commencement of the notice period for the first interest rate adjustment period.

Extension of Loan Maturity[10]

A VRM may allow the borrower to extend the term of a VRM up to a maximum of one third of the original term in order to lessen or avoid any increase in payment due to the increase in interest rates.

The FHLBB had proposed a change to this regulation that would still allow the extension of the term, but would limit the extension to a maximum of 10 years. The reduction, however, could not be to such an extent that it would have reduced the payments to an amount below the original monthly payment.

Offer of Fixed-Rate Payment Mortgage[11]

The canceled regulations covering the VRM required lenders to offer eligible prospective borrowers a standard mortgage. This regulation was adopted by the FHLBB originally due to the concern it had about the newness of the VRM. After the adoption of the regulations and the experience gained by S and Ls offering the VRM, particularly those located in California, the FHLBB was satisfied that the required disclosures were sufficient to protect the consumer, and therefore it had proposed to delete this requirement.

Disclosure Requirements[12]

As mentioned above, the FHLBB had proposed to drop the requirement to offer the fixed-rate mortgage to prospective borrowers applying for a VRM. Since the association would no longer have been required to offer a fixed-rate mortgage, the side-by-side comparison and full-term worst-case schedule would no longer have been required. These would have been replaced by an example of the effects of a maximum increase allowed at the first adjustment and the maximum possible rate change, both up and down, over the life of the mortgage. An example of such a disclosure is shown in Figure 3–31.

Figure 3–31. Variable-Rate Mortgage Disclosure

Information About the Variable-Rate Mortgage

You have received an application form for a variable-rate mortgage ("VRM"). The VRM differs from the fixed-rate, fixed-payment mortgage with which you may be familiar. Instead of having an interest rate that is set at the beginning of the mortgage and remains the same, the VRM has an interest rate that may increase or decrease as frequently as once each six months. This means that the amount of your monthly payment may also increase or decrease.

The term of the VRM is _____ years. The interest rate may be adjusted every _____ months (the "adjustment period").

Adjustments to the interest rate are based on changes in an index rate. The index used is computed by the Federal Home Loan Bank Board, an agency of the Federal government. The index is based on the national average cost of funds to institutions the accounts of which are insured by the Federal Savings and Loan Insurance Corporation.

At the time of adjustment of the interest rate, if the index has moved to a level higher than it was at the beginning of the mortgage, the lender has the right, subject to the limitations described in the paragraph below, to adjust the interest rate to a rate equalling the original interest rate plus the increase in the index rate. Although taking such an increase is optional with the lender, you should be aware that the lender has this right and may become contractually obligated to exercise it.

If the index has moved down, the lender must at the time of adjustment reduce the original interest rate by the decrease in the index rate. No matter how much the index rate increases or decreases, THE LENDER, AT THE TIME OF ADJUST-MENT, MAY NOT INCREASE OR DECREASE THE INTEREST RATE ON YOUR VRM LOAN BY AN AMOUNT GREATER THAN _____ OF ONE PERCENTAGE POINT PER ADJUSTMENT PERIOD, AND THE TOTAL INCREASE OR DECREASE OVER THE LIFE OF THE MORTGAGE LOAN MAY NOT BE MORE THAN _____ PERCENTAGE POINTS.

If the interest rate increases, you have the right to extend the maturity of the loan by up to 10 years, although the loan may not be lengthened to such an extent that the monthly loan payments would be reduced below the original monthly payment amount. In addition, you have the right to prepay the loan in part or in full without penalty at any time after notification of the first interest rate increase or decrease. This notification, which also sets out the new interest rate, monthly payment amount, and remaining principal balance, must be sent to you at least 60 but not more than 90 days prior to adjustment of the interest rate.

Example of Operation of VRM

The maximum interest-rate increase at the end of the first adjustment period, which is _____ months long, is _____ percentage points. On a $50,000 VRM with a term of _____ years and an original interest rate of [*lender's current commitment rate*] percent, this rate change would increase the monthly payment (principal and interest) from $_____ to $_____ . Using the same example, the highest interest rate you might have to pay over the life of the mortgage would be _____ percent, and the lowest would be _____ percent.

SOURCE: *Proposed Amendments—Alternative Mortgage Instruments*, 12 CFR, Part 545 (October 23, 1980), FHLBB.

Texas Approval of VRM

The Texas Savings and Loan Commissioner has approved the VRM; thus, the loan can be made by a Texas-chartered savings and loan association. In regard to the VRM, the commission has promulgated the following rule.

The index of the interest rate will be the "average cost of funds to FSLIC-insured institutions-all districts-index" as computed by the Federal Home Loan Bank Board and published in the Federal Home Loan Bank Board Journal, *or any other index that the Commissioner shall approve.*

RENEGOTIABLE-RATE MORTGAGE (RRM)

The *renegotiable-rate mortgage* (RRM), sometimes called the rollover mortgage, can be defined as a series of short-term loans issued for terms of 3 to 5 years each, secured by a long-term mortgage. The short-term loans are automatically renewable for the entire term of the long-term mortgage.

Background[13]

The RRM is a variation of the variable-rate mortgage and had its origin in Canada as early as 1930. Most residential mortgages in Canada are financed using this type of mortgage. It is commonly referred to as the 5-year rollover, or the renegotiable-rate mortgage. In Canada prior to 1969, all government-guaranteed mortgages were written as fixed-term mortgages of not less than 25 years. But in 1969, the laws were changed to allow the government-guaranteed loans in Canada to be made as RRMs, or rollovers, for a term of 5 years, and secured by a long-term mortgage for a period of not less than 25 years. In the first full year the RRMs were authorized, 58 percent of the real estate mortgages guaranteed by the Canadian government were RRMs. This percentage continued to increase until, by 1976, nearly 98 percent of the real estate loans guaranteed by the Canadian government were RRMs.

The RRMs have not been used extensively in the United States, and if they were used, they were used to finance commercial property. In late 1979, the Federal Home Loan Bank Board proposed an amendment to its lending regulations authorizing federally chartered savings and loan associations to make the RRM mortgage. The reason for the proposed change was to allow the savings and loan associations to have the flexibility to make mortgages that would meet the rise and fall of the interest rates in the 1980s. This rule became effective on April 3, 1980. In mid-1980, the FHLBB proposed amendments to the rules that would standardize the RRM and make it similar to the VRM. These amendments, however, were not implemented. Instead, the FHLBB instituted the AML.

Interest-Rate Index

As with the VRM, the interest rate on the RRM may change during the term of the mortgage. As was noted earlier, there are several indexes that may be used to establish the interest rate on the RRM at the time of the first renewal. The Federal Home Loan Bank Board, when it allowed the RRM, authorized the use of the following index:

The index to be used for calculating the adjustment in the interest rate for a RRM is the national average mortgage rate for all major lenders for the purchase of previously occupied homes.

This index is published monthly in the *Federal Home Loan Bank Board Journal*. It is also released to certain publications on a regular basis. You will note that the index may be different for a RRM when compared to a VRM.

Rate Adjustment

As was noted, the rate on the RRM is to be adjusted at a specific time, every 3 to 5 years. As with the VRMs, the RRMs are written with a provision that limits the amount of rate adjustment. Also, as with the VRMs, the RRMs normally state that the increase in the interest rate is made at the option of the lender. If the index reflects a decrease in the interest rate, however, the lender is normally mandated to make the decrease.

In regard to the amount of the rate adjust-ment, many RRMs limit the rate increase or decrease to a maximum of 0.5 to 1.0 percent per year of the loan term with a maximum increase or decrease over the life of the mortgage of 5 percent.

Extension of Loan Maturity

Some RRMs contain no provision that permits the borrower to extend the term of the RRM to reduce the effect of a rate increase. But it should be noted that some lenders may allow the borrower to extend the term up to 10 years. Normally, though, the extension cannot reduce the monthly payment to a level below the original monthly payments.

Rate Adjustment Notification

As with the VRM, the loan documents normally require the lender to give notice to the borrower. Some documents require that the notice be given 60 or 90 days prior to any change in the interest rate. This notice is to be given at any time the rate is changed, either up or down.

Disclosure Requirement for the RRM

As with the VRM, the lender is required to give the prospective borrower information about the RRM, normally at the time of receipt of an application. An example of such a form is illustrated in Figure 3–32.

REVERSE ANNUITY MORTGAGE (RAM)

The reverse annuity mortgage is not a true mortgage, but it is a method by which homeowners can obtain income based on the equity in their homes. The RAM is especially helpful to older families who have a home paid in full and wish to secure the value of the property in regular monthly income without having to sell the property and move.

The RAM was authorized by the Federal Home Loan Bank Board on January 1, 1979. The FHLBB did not formulate specific rules governing the RAM, but it requires that each type of RAM must be submitted to the FHLBB for approval on a case-by-case basis.

It should be noted that because of Texas law, the RAM may not be able to be used.

The FHLBB, though, has issued broad guidelines to insure adequate consumer protection and to guide the S and Ls in the formulation of RAMs. Some of the broad guidelines are:

Figure 3–32.   Renegotiable-Rate Mortgage Disclosure

Information About the Renegotiable-Rate Mortgage

You have received an application form for a renegotiable-rate mortgage ("RRM"). The RRM differs from the fixed-rate mortgage with which you may be familiar. In the fixed-rate mortgage the length of the loan and the length of the underlying mortgage are the same, but in the RRM the loan is short-term (3-5 years) and is automatically renewable for a period equal to the mortgage (up to 30 years). Therefore, instead of having an interest rate that is set at the beginning of the mortgage and remains the same, the RRM has an interest rate that may increase or decrease at each renewal of the short-term loan. This means that the amount of your monthly payment may also increase or decrease.

The term of the RRM loan is _____ years, and the length of the underlying mortgage is _____ years. The initial loan term may be up to six months longer than later terms.

The lender must offer to renew the loan, and the only loan provision that may be changed at renewal is the interest rate. The interest rate offered at renewal is based on changes in an index rate. The index used is computed monthly by the Federal Home Loan Bank Board, an agency of the Federal government. The index is based on the national average contract rate for all major lenders for the purchase of previously-occupied, single-family homes.

At renewal, if the index has moved higher than it was at the beginning of the mortgage, the lender has the right to offer a renewal of the loan at an interest rate equalling the original interest rate plus the increase in the index rate. This is the maximum increase permitted to the lender. Although taking such an increase is optional with the lender, you should be aware that the lender has this right and may become contractually obligated to exercise it.

If the index has moved down, the lender *must* at renewal reduce the original interest rate by the decrease in the index rate. No matter how much the index rate increases or decreases, THE LENDER, AT RENEWAL, MAY NOT INCREASE OR DECREASE THE INTEREST RATE ON YOUR RRM LOAN BY AN AMOUNT GREATER THAN _____ OF ONE PERCENTAGE POINT PER YEAR OF THE LOAN, AND THE TOTAL INCREASE OR DECREASE OVER THE LIFE OF THE MORTGAGE MAY NOT BE MORE THAN _____ PERCENTAGE POINTS.

As the borrower, you have the right to prepay the loan in part or in full without penalty at any time after the beginning of the notice period of the first interest rate adjustment. To give you enough time to make this decision, the lender, at least ninety (90) but not more than one-hundred twenty (120) days before interest rate adjustment, will send a notice stating the date of adjustment, the principal balance as of that date, the new interest rate and the monthly payment amount. If you elect not to pay the loan in full by the due date, the interest rate will be adjusted to the new rate. You will not have to pay any fees or charges at the time of interest rate adjustment.

The *maximum* interest-rate increase at the first renewal is _____ percentage points. On a $50,000 mortgage with an original term of _____ years and an original interest rate of [*lender's current commitment rate*] percent, this rate change would increase the monthly payment (principal and interest) from $_____ to $_____ . Using the same example, the highest interest rate you might have to pay over the life of the mortgage would be _____ percent, and the lowest would be _____ percent.

Source: Draft Final Rule, 12 CFR, Chapter V, Subchapter C, Part 545–Operations, p. 11, FHLBB, Washington, D.C.

1. Guaranteed refinancing of the RAM at any fixed term

2. Prepayment without penalty at any time during the loan term

3. A 7-day "cooling off period" after the loan commitment

4. Disclosures from the savings and loan, to include the following:

   a. Information pertaining to payments to and from the borrower

   b. A description of any contractual items or actions that could force the sale of the property used to secure the loan

   c. Information concerning any purchased annuity plan fees, charges, and interest rate

   d. A statement advising the borrower to consult with the appropriate authorities regarding tax and estate-planning consequences of the RAM.

Basic Types of RAMs

The two basic types of RAMs are the *rising-debt RAM* and the *fixed-debt RAM.*

The rising-debt RAM is the most common. With this type of RAM, the lender agrees to pay the borrower an annuity on a regular basis, usually monthly. Thus, with each payment the debt of the homeowner increases. The total indebtedness of the borrower is usually payable upon a certain event such as the sale of the property, the death of the borrower, or the loan-to-value reaching a certain percentage, or at some specific date.

The fixed-debt RAM is one in which the principal balance of the debt is established immediately and does not change over either the life of the debt or the life of the borrower.

There are many variations of either of these two basic types of RAMs and they can be tailored to the needs of a prospective borrower.

PRICE-LEVEL ADJUSTED MORTGAGE (PLAM)

The *price-level adjusted mortgage* (PLAM) type of AMI has been used in South America and Israel since the early 1970s, but has seen only limited use in the United States.

The PLAM can be defined as a mortgage that has a periodic adjustment in the principal as well as in the interest rate. Both may be adjusted monthly or annually. The PLAM, as opposed to the other AMIs, is affected by the actual rate of inflation rather than by an expected rate of inflation; the interest rate and the principal balance are adjusted by the actual rate of inflation. The interest rate for the PLAM is established by the investor's or lender's real rate of return, plus the actual rate of inflation as measured by a specific inflation rate index. This rate is sometimes referred to as the *nominal interest rate.* For example, if the investor seeks a real rate of return of 3 percent, and the inflation rate is running at the rate of 10 percent by the referenced index, the rate of the PLAM would be 13 percent, but if the inflation rate was at only 4 percent, the rate on the PLAM would only be 7 percent.

In addition to the adjustment to the interest rate on the PLAM, the outstanding principal balance is also increased by the indexed rate of inflation. For example, if a person borrows an initial $30,000 using the PLAM and the inflation rate was 10 percent for the first year, the principal balance would increase by $3000, thus making the outstanding balance approximately $33,000 at the end of the first year. The rationale behind this increase is that the value of the property used to secure the mortgage is also increasing at the same rate, as is the income of the borrower.

One can see that the advantage to the borrower under a PLAM is that under the standard type of mortgage the lender or investor will hedge against inflation by charging a higher interest rate. For example, if the lender expects that inflation will continue at a rate of 12 percent for the next several years, the lender will charge an interest that will be at least equal to and probably more than the inflation rate. The PLAM will take into consideration the variation in the inflation rate.

The major disadvantage to the borrower under a PLAM is that, if the borrower's income or the appreciation of the home price does not keep up with inflation, the borrower could possibly not make the increased monthly payments and the value of the property would not be sufficient, if sold, to pay off the outstanding balance of the mortgage.

Like the other AMIs we have examined, the PLAM is approved by the Federal Home Loan Bank Board.

REVIEW QUESTIONS

1. Define the term *alternative mortgage instrument.*

2. Define the interest indexes that may be used to establish the rate on the variable-rate mortgage.

3. Define the term *net appreciation* as related to the shared appreciation mortgage.

4. What is another name for the *renegotiable-rate mortgage,* and what country pioneered this type of mortgage?

5. What are the two variations to the graduated-payment mortgage that will also allow for a reduced initial monthly payment?

6. Outline the development of the AMIs by the Federal Home Loan Bank Board.

7. Explain the *carry-over rule* and give an example.

8. Name a source for many of the approved or suggested interest rate indexes.

9. Name two types of AMIs that no longer are authorized to be made by federally chartered savings and loan associations.

PROBLEMS

1. You are working with a client who has expressed an interest in an adjustable-rate mortgage. Since your client will not be in the house more than 4 years, he has indi-

cated that either a 1-, 3-, or 5-year ARM would be acceptable. You have contacted several lenders in your area and found that they use Treasury-constant maturities as interest rate indexes, plus a 2.125 percentage spread, as well as one-half of 1 percent servicing fee.

Using the information contained in the Federal Reserve Statistical Release (Figure 3–20), calculate the interest rate for the:

A. 1-year ARM

B. 3-year ARM

C. 5-year ARM

2. You have a listing that has been on the market for approximately two months and the seller has asked about a price reduction. Instead you have suggested that they offer a seller 3-2-1 buydown. The value of the home is $110,500 and 95 percent financing is available. The current interest rate on a 95 percent loan is 13.750 percent and the term is 30 years.

You will need to calculate the following:

A. Amount of down payment

B. Loan amount

C. Amount of the monthly payment for the interest rate of 13.75 percent

3. Referring to problem 2, and using the actual-cash method, calculate the following:

A. Buydown funds for the first year

B. Buydown funds for the second year

C. Buydown funds for the third year

D. Required value of the funds the seller will have to pay. (According to the lender, they will be using the present value of money, 5.25 percent compounded monthly for 3 years.)

NOTES

1. 12 CFR Part 29 – Adjustable-Rate Mortgages, Section 29.2, "Rules and Regulations," *Federal Register*, March 27, 1981, vol. 46, no. 59, p. 18943.

2. U.S., National Credit Union Administration, *Advance Copy – Final Rules and Regulations*, July 31, 1981, p. 22.

3. U.S., Federal Home Loan Bank Board, "Proposed Amendments, Alternative Mortgage Instruments," Code of Federal Regulations, October 23, 1980, Part 545, no. 80-653.

4. Milwaukee, Wis., Mortgage Guaranty Insurance Corporation, *Action!® Mortgage: A Simple GPM Program That Works*, rev. 1, p. 4.

5. Most of this section is based on material from *Federal Register*, October 8, 1980, vol. 45, no. 197, pp. 66789-801.

6. Most of this section is based upon material from U.S., Federal Home Loan Bank Board, *The Federal Home Loan Bank Board Journal*, November 1980, vol. 13, no. 11, pp. 11–15.

7. Most of this section is based upon material from U.S., Federal Home Loan Bank Board, *The Federal Home Loan Bank Board Journal*, August 1980, vol, 13, no. 8, pp. 4–5.

8. Most of this section is based upon material from U.S., Federal Home Loan Bank Board, "Proposed Amendments, Alternative Mortgage Instruments," Code of Federal Regulations, October 23, 1980, Part 545, no. 80-653.

9. ibid.

10. ibid.

11. ibid.

12. ibid.

13. U.S., Federal Home Loan Bank Board, Michael L. Unger, "Abstract VII, The Canadian Mortgage Market and the Renegotiable Term Mortgages," *Alternative Mortgage Instruments Research Study, Volume 1.*

4

Mortgage Lenders—
Institutional
(Primary) Lenders

LEARNING OBJECTIVES

In this chapter we will discuss the institutional, or primary, lenders in the United States and Texas. We will also examine the four basic institutional lenders: savings and loan associations, commercial banks, mutual savings banks, and life insurance companies. Upon completion of the chapter you should be able to do the following:

★ Define *institutional lender*.

★ Outline the amount of mortgage debt and distribution of the debt by type of lender.

★ Select the proper institutional lender to use in a particular lending situation.

★ Explain the lending policies of the various institutional lenders in Texas.

DEFINITION

uses it's dep. to reinvest

An *institutional lender* is a lender that meets the following two criteria: (1) the lender is highly regulated by either federal or state agencies and, in some cases, by both agencies; and (2) it is an institution or depository that pools funds from individuals and/or companies and reinvests these funds in some type of securities, such as real estate loans. In other words, an institutional lender uses its deposits, or income, to make real estate loans.

INTERMEDIATION AND DISINTERMEDIATION

Whenever institutional lenders, or any lenders who accumulate funds from outside sources, are discussed, two important terms must be understood. One is *intermediation*, the term used for the gathering of funds by a lender and then the lending or supplying of the funds to a borrower. Thus, the lender is serving as an intermediary, or go-between, between persons with funds and the person who needs funds. As we shall see in this chapter, this process is very important to the real estate industry.

The opposite of intermediation is *disintermediation*. This is the taking out or the withdrawal of funds from the institutional lender and the reinvesting in some other savings instrument with a higher yield. Disintermediation was a very important action that happened during the recession of 1979-1981. Depositors were withdrawing their savings from the savings associations in record amounts in order to try to keep up with inflation. The term became frequently used during the recession, and it has a great impact on the real estate market. The more disintermediation, the less funds there are available to lenders to make real estate loans.

Now that we have some idea of what an institutional lender is, let us see how mortgage loans are distributed among the institutional lenders.

AMOUNT OF MORTGAGE DEBT[1]

The residential mortgage debt, or the amount of residential credit, since 1950 has been growing faster than any other form of credit. The total amount of the credit debt has risen from $427 billion in 1950 to $5,639.3 billion at the end of 1982. This is over a tenfold increase. Accordingly, the residential debt rose during the same period, but at an even faster pace. In 1950, the total outstanding residential debt was $54.5 billion. By the end of 1982, the preliminary figures show this debt to have risen more than twenty times to $1,253.9 billion, or over 22 percent of the total outstanding credit in the United States. The only other debt of similar magnitude is the national debt. At the end of 1982, the federal debt was $1,370.7 billion. When we compare this to the national debt in 1950 of $218.4 billion, one can see that the national debt is not growing nearly as fast as the residential debt.

How does the residential debt break down according to types of loans? The 1- to 4-family homes make up a major portion of the debt. They account for $1,105.6 billion of the total debt of $1,253.9 billion. The remainder of the debt is to finance the construction or the purchase of multifamily units. Using Figure 4–1, we can compare the residential mortgage loans not only to the national debt, but also to the credit of consumers, state and local governments, and mortgages on commercial properties. This comparison shows that not only is residential credit the largest, it is also the fastest growing. This rapid growth points out the Great American Dream of everyone wanting to own a home.

The volatility of residential credit is quite evident when a year-to-year comparison is made as is illustrated in Figure 4–2. One can see that in 1970 the annual increase of residential credit declined to only 6.7 percent due to the credit crunch in that year. In the late 1960s and early 1970s, the annual increase continued to rise until the recession of 1974 and 1975. The annual increase was only 7.9 percent in 1974 and decreased even further in 1975 to 7.6 percent. In the following year, the rate of increase jumped to 11.8 percent. The decreases in the annual increase reflect the decrease or disintermediation of the loanable funds from the *thrift institutions*. Thrift institutions are savings and loan associations, mutual savings banks, and credit unions.

DISTRIBUTION OF DEBT BY LENDERS

Now that we have examined the amount of the mortgage debt and how it is divided among various types of real estate loans, let us look at how this debt is divided among the various types of lenders.

As of the end of 1982, the major source of mortgage credit was the savings and loan associations. The savings and loans accounted for 36.2 percent of all of the one- to four-family

Figure 4–1. Growth In Selected Types of Credit (in billions of dollars)

Type of Credit	1960	1982*	Increase
Total Credit Outstanding	$779.9	$5,639.3	$4,859.4
Residential Mortgage Loans:			
One- to Four-family Homes	141.9	1,105.6	963.7
Apartments	20.3	148.3	128.0
Total	162.2	1,253.9	1,091.7
Corporate and Foreign Bonds	90.2	563.7	473.5
State and Local Government Obligations	70.8	429.7	358.9
Consumer Credit	65.1	424.7	359.6
Mortgages on Commercial Properties	32.4	294.7	262.3
Federal Debt	243.1	1,370.7	1,127.6

Note: Components may not add to totals due to rounding.
*Preliminary.

SOURCE: Federal Reserve Board: United States League of Savings Associations. Reprinted with permission from United States League of Savings Associations, *'83 Savings and Loan Sourcebook*, p 23.

Figure 4–2. **Total Residential Mortgage Loans Outstanding (in billions of dollars)**

Year	Total Residential Debt	Annual Increase†	Percentage Increase†	Year	Total Residential Debt	Annual Increase†	Percentage Increase†	Year	Total Residential Debt	Annual Increase†	Percentage Increase†
1960	$162.7	$12.2	9.8%	1971	$397.6	$39.8	11.1%	1976	$ 661.0	$ 69.6	11.8%
1965	258.7	19.2	9.7	1972	454.1	56.5	14.2	1977	768.4	107.4	16.2
1970	357.8	19.8	6.7	1973	509.5	55.2	12.2	1978	885.5	117.1	15.2
				1974	549.4	40.1	7.9	1979	1,005.1	119.6	13.5
				1975	591.4	42.0	7.6	1980	1,097.5	92.4	9.2
								1981	1,202.0	104.5	9.5
								1982*	1,253.9	51.9	4.3

*Preliminary.
†1960, 1965 and 1970 increases are five-year annual averages.

SOURCE: Federal Reserve Board. Reprinted with permission from United States League of Savings Associations, *'81, '82, and '83 Savings and Loan Sourcebook*.

loans made in the United States. The savings and loan associations also are the single largest holders of mortgages on multifamily dwellings, accounting for 24.4 percent of all mortgages.

The importance of the savings and loan associations can be seen in Figure 4–3. One can see that for residential loans, the nearest competitor to the S and Ls are the commercial banks, who at the end of 1982 had outstanding $177.1 billion in first-lien mortgages on one- to four-family dwellings. When comparing this to the amount of loans outstanding by the S and Ls, one can see that the S and Ls had more than two times the dollar amount outstanding at the end of 1982.

Looking further at the distribution of the residential mortgages outstanding, one can see that even when combined, mutual savings banks with $63.7 billion in one- to four-family loans, the life insurance companies with $17.0 billion in loans outstanding, and commercial banks, still do not equal the loans outstanding or made by the S and Ls by the end of 1982.

In Figure 4–4, one can see that since 1960 the S and Ls have been the leader, but there

Figure 4–3. **Mortgage Loans Outstanding, by Type of Property and Lender, Year-End 1980*** **(in billions of dollars)**

Lender	Residential Properties			Commercial Properties	Farm Properties	Total Mortgage Loans
	1- to 4-family	Multi-family	Total			
Savings Associations	$ 400.6	$ 36.2	$ 436.7	$ 45.5	†	$ 482.2
Commercial Banks	177.1	15.8	193.0	100.3	$ 8.5	301.7
Mutual Savings Banks	63.7	14.9	78.7	15.2	†	93.9
Life Insurance Companies...	17.0	19.1	36.1	92.3	12.9	141.3
All Others	447.2	62.3	509.4	41.4	85.7	636.6
Total	$1,105.6	$148.3	$1,253.9	$294.7	$107.1	$1,655.8

Note: Components may not add to totals due to rounding.
*Preliminary.
†Less than $50 million.

Sources: Federal Home Loan Bank Board; Federal Reserve Board. Reprinted with permission from United States League of Savings Associations, *'83 Savings and Loan Sourcebook*, p. 24.

Figure 4–4.   One- to Four-Family Mortgage Loans Outstanding, by Lender (billions of dollars)

Year-end	Savings Associations	Mutual Savings Banks	Commercial Banks	Life Insurance Companies	Federally Supported Agencies†	All Others	Total
1960	$ 55.4	$20.6	$ 19.2	$24.9	$ 7.1	$ 14.7	$ 141.9
1965	94.2	33.8	30.4	29.6	6.6	25.9	220.5
1970	124.5	42.1	42.3	26.8	24.7	37.7	298.1
1971	141.0	43.4	48.0	24.6	30.5	40.8	328.3
1972	165.6	46.2	57.0	22.3	36.1	45.0	372.2
1973	187.1	48.8	68.0	20.4	41.9	49.3	415.5
1974	201.0	49.2	74.8	19.0	52.0	55.2	451.2
1975	223.9	50.0	77.0	17.6	66.0	60.5	495.0
1976	260.8	53.1	86.2	16.1	77.6	66.9	560.7
1977	310.7	57.6	105.1	14.7	96.3	73.4	657.8
1978	356.1	62.3	129.2	14.4	119.6	89.0	770.6
1979	394.3	66.1	149.5	16.2	154.1	110.9	891.1
1980	419.8	67.5	160.3	17.9	183.2	138.3	987.0
1981	433.1	68.2	170.0	17.2	205.4	166.7	1,060.6
1982*	400.6	63.7	177.1	17.0	274.4	172.8	1,105.6

*Preliminary.
†Includes mortgage pools.

SOURCE: Federal Reserve Board. Reprinted with permission from United States League of Savings Associations, *'83 Savings and Loan Sourcebook*, p. 25.

are some interesting trends that have been developing in the past few years. One is that the commercial banks are starting to make more of these types of loans. This is seen if we compare the mortgages held by these banks in 1965 to those held in 1982, as illustrated in Figure 4–5. The most dramatic change, however, has come in the percentage of the outstanding loans held by the insurance companies, which has dropped from 13.4 percent in 1965 to 1.5 percent in 1982. Another

major change is the role of federally supported agencies – the Federal National Mortgage Association, the Government National Mortgage Association, and the Federal Home Loan Bank System. In Figure 4–5, one can see that these agencies have increased their percentage of outstanding loans over eight times since 1965 and this trend will probably continue for the next few years. The reason is that these agencies do not have to rely on the money from depositors. They can sell bonds in the

Figure 4–5.   Mortgage Loans Outstanding on 1- to 4-Family Homes by Type of Lender, Year-End 1965 and 1983

Lender	Percent of Debt	
	1965*	1983†
Savings Associations	42.7%	32.1%
Mutual Savings Banks	15.3%	7.8%
Commercial Banks	13.8%	15.1%
Life Insurance Companies	13.4%	1.3%
Federally Supported Agencies	3.0%	27.9%

*SOURCE: Federal Home Loan Bank Board; Federal Reserve. Reprinted with permission from United States League of Savings Associations, *1979 Savings and Loan Fact Book*, p. 32.

†SOURCE: U.S., Federal Reserve, *Federal Reserve Bulletin*, February 1984, p. A39.

open market secured by first-lien mortgages to raise money for mortgages.

When studying the outstanding mortgages on multifamily properties, one can see that the S and Ls still are the leader with $36.2 billion outstanding at the end of 1982, as shown in Figure 4–3. Looking further at this figure, one can see that for commercial property loans outstanding, the commercial banks and the insurance companies are the leaders.

Now that we have looked at the amount of the mortgage credit outstanding and how it is distributed among the major lenders in the United States, let us examine the major institutional lenders. We will cover the development and the number of each in the United States.

SAVINGS AND LOAN ASSOCIATIONS

As we learned in Chapter 1, the savings and loan associations had their roots in colonial times with the formation of informal clubs or associations. The members of these groups would pool their funds in a central treasury, and the money was lent to the members for various needs. These clubs, or pools of funds, had no regulation, and therefore most went bankrupt, usually due to the borrowers not repaying the loans. It is not until 1831 that we find the beginnings of the modern-day savings and loan associations, then called building associations. These associations were formed for the specific purpose of accumulating funds from the general public in order to supply funds for the construction of homes. The first loan made by a building association was for the amount of $375, and it was to be repaid at the rate of $4.90 per month. All of the early savings and loan associations were regulated by the states in which they were located. Federal regulation was nonexistent before the Depression. In 1932, with the passage of the Federal Home Loan Bank Act, the Federal Home Loan Bank Board was established to oversee the operations of the savings and loan associations. The activity of the FHLBB is similar to that of the Federal Reserve. As with the banks and the Federal Reserve, all federally chartered savings and loan associations must belong to the FHLBB. All state-chartered associations may join if they wish.

The Federal Home Loan Bank Board organization is similar to that of the Federal Reserve in that the United States is divided into twelve districts with each district having a district bank. The districts are shown in Fig-

ure 4–6, with the address and the area served listed in Figure 4–7.

As with the Federal Reserve, the Federal Home Loan Bank Board has a board, but the board for the FHLBB is somewhat smaller in that it has only three members. In addition to being smaller, the President of the United States appoints all three persons with the advice and consent of the Senate. The term for each member is four years. Since these positions are political appointments, the law requires that no more than two of the board members be from the same political party.

The Federal Home Loan Bank Board office is in Washington, D.C., and has the responsibility of chartering and regulating all federal savings associations and overseeing the operation of the Federal Savings and Loan Insurance Corporation (FSLIC) and the Federal Home Loan Mortgage Corporation (FHLMC).

Another important piece of legislation implemented as a result of the Depression was the National Housing Act of 1934. In addition to this act establishing the Federal Housing Administration, it established the Federal Savings and Loan Insurance Corporation. The purpose of this corporation was to insure the savings accounts in savings and loan associations. As with the Federal Home Loan Bank Board, the federally chartered savings and loan associations must belong to this corporation, but the state-chartered associations may join if they wish. As illustrated in Figure 4–8, as of the end of 1982 only 490 of the 3833 total savings associations were not insured by the FSLIC. As of 1980, the FSLIC insured any account in a participating S and L up to a limit of $100,000.

In reviewing the history of the S and Ls, we should examine the types of charters and forms of ownership. All of the savings and loan associations were originally founded as mutual associations. With this type of ownership, the depositors are the owners of the association. The associations did not sell stock, therefore they did not have stockholders. This form of ownership has undergone some change in the last few years as some of the federally chartered savings and loan associations have been allowed to sell stock to the general public and have become public-held corporations.

The distribution by state of all of the federally chartered S and Ls and their assets as of December 31, 1982, is given in Figure 4–9.

Now that we have briefly covered the history of the savings and loan associations in the United States, let us see how many there are in Texas and review their lending policies.

Figure 4–6.   Federal Home Loan Bank Districts

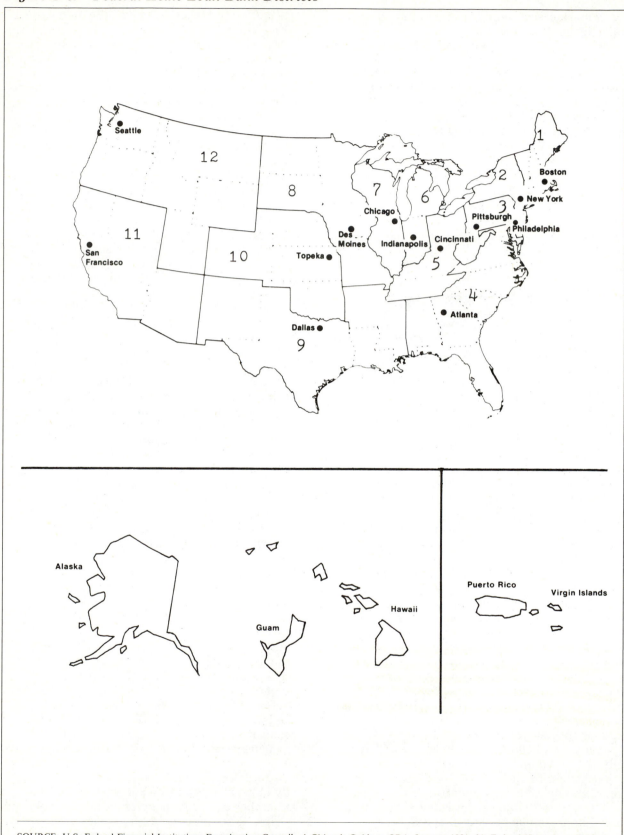

SOURCE: U.S. Federal Financial Institutions Examination Council, *A Citizen's Guide to CRA*, January 1981, 31. Federal Home Loan Bank Board, *Federal Home Loan Bank Board Journal*, February 1984, p. 45.

Figure 4–7. Federal Home Loan Bank Districts

1. **Federal Home Loan Bank of Boston**

   Raymond H. Elliott, President
   Post Office Box 2196
   Boston, Massachusetts 02106
   Connecticut, Maine, Massachusetts, New Hampshire, Rhode Island, and Vermont

   District Director-Examinations: Charles E. Seaman

2. **Federal Home Loan Bank of New York**

   Bryce Curry, President
   One World Trade Center, Floor 103
   New York, New York 10048
   New Jersey, New York, Puerto Rico, and Virgin Islands

   District Director-Examinations: Leonard Nightingale

3. **Federal Home Loan Bank of Pittsburgh***

   Eugene M. Calnan, President
   11 Stanwix St., 4th Floor, Gateway Center
   Pittsburgh, Pennsylvania 15222
   Delaware, Pennsylvania, and West Virginia

   District Director-Examinations: Norman L. Giancola

4. **Federal Home Loan Bank of Atlanta**

   Carl O. Kamp, Jr., President
   Post Office Box 56527
   Atlanta, Georgia 30343
   Alabama, District of Columbia, Florida, Georgia, Maryland, North Carolina, South Carolina, and Virginia

   District Director-Examinations: Lamar Heath

5. **Federal Home Loan Bank of Cincinnati**

   Charles Lee Thiemann, President
   Post Office Box 598
   Cincinnati, Ohio 45201
   Kentucky, Ohio, and Tennessee

   District Director-Examinations: John F. Saalman

6. **Federal Home Loan Bank of Indianapolis**

   Ronald R. Morphew, President-Secretary
   1350 Merchants Plaza, South Tower
   115 West Washington Street
   P.O. Box 60
   Indianapolis, Indiana 46206
   Indiana and Michigan

   District Director-Examinations: Ervin Berlinger

   ***Philadelphia Branch Office**
   One Franklin Plaza—Suite 200
   Philadelphia, Pennsylvania 19102

7. **Federal Home Loan Bank of Chicago**

   Leo B. Blaber, Jr., President
   111 East Wacker Drive
   Chicago, Illinois 60601
   Illinois and Wisconsin

   District Director-Examinations: John P. Valek

8. **Federal Home Loan Bank of Des Moines**

   Donald F. Roby, President
   907 Walnut Street
   Des Moines, Iowa, 50309
   Iowa, Minnesota, Missouri, North Dakota, and South Dakota

   District Director-Examinations: Bernard C. Zimmer

9. **Federal Home Loan Bank of Dallas**

   Joseph E. Settle, President
   Post Office Box 619026
   Dallas, Texas 75261-9026
   Arkansas, Louisiana, Mississippi, New Mexico, and Texas

   District Director-Examinations: William G. Ball

10. **Federal Home Loan Bank of Topeka**

    Kermit Mowbray, President
    Post Office Box 176
    Topeka, Kansas 66601
    Colorado, Kansas, Nebraska, and Oklahoma

    District Director-Examinations: Max L. Johnson

11. **Federal Home Loan Bank of San Francisco**

    James M. Cirona, President
    Post Office Box 7948
    San Francisco, California 94120
    Arizona, Nevada, and California

    District Director-Examinations: Paul F. Bowman

12. **Federal Home Loan Bank of Seattle**

    James R. Faulstich, President
    600 Stewart Street
    Seattle, Washington 98101
    Alaska, Hawaii and Guam, Idaho, Montana, Oregon, Utah, Washington, and Wyoming

    District Director-Examinations: James L. Brazil

SOURCE: Federal Home Loan Bank Board, *Federal Home Loan Bank Board Journal*, February 1984, p. 45.

S and Ls in Texas

As of the end of 1983, according to the Texas Savings and Loan Association, a nonprofit Texas corporation, there were 54 federally chartered and 216 state-chartered savings and loan associations in Texas. All but two of the state-chartered S and Ls were insured by the Federal Savings and Loan Insurance Corporation. In addition, these 270 savings and loan associations had more than $39.9 billion in real estate loans outstanding at the end of 1983. When comparing the assets of the associations, Texas ranks fourth in the United States, as shown in Figure 4–9. The state-chartered associations are regulated by the Savings and Loan Department of Texas, which is a part of the State Finance Commission.

This agency has the responsibility of setting the policy for and chartering the state-chartered savings and loan associations. As we learned earlier in this chapter, the federally

Figure 4–8.   Number and Assets of Savings Associations, by Charter

| Year-end | Federally Chartered† | State-chartered | | | Grand Total |
		Total	FSLIC-insured	Noninsured‡	
1960	1,873	4,447	2,225	2,222	6,320
1965	2,011	4,174	2,497	1,677	6,185
1970	2,067	3,602	2,298	1,304	5,669
1971	2,049	3,425	2,222	1,203	5,474
1972	2,044	3,254	2,147	1,107	5,298
1973	2,040	3,130	2,123	1,007	5,170
1974	2,060	2,963	2,081	882	5,023
1975	2,048	2,883	2,030	853	4,931
1976	2,019	2,802	2,025	777	4,821
1977	2,012	2,749	2,053	696	4,761
1978	2,000	2,725	2,053	672	4,725
1979	1,989	2,695	2,050	645	4,684
1980	1,985	2,628	2,017	611	4,613
1981	1,907	2,385	1,872	513	4,292
1982*	1,727	2,106	1,616	490	3,833

Millions of Dollars

| Year-end | Federally Chartered† | State-chartered | | | Grand Total |
		Total	FSLIC-insured	Noninsured‡	
1960	$ 38,511	$ 32,965	$ 28,919	$ 4,046	$ 71,476
1965	66,715	62,865	57,861	5,004	129,580
1970	96,259	79,924	74,386	5,538	176,183
1971	114,229	91,794	85,755	6,039	206,023
1972	135,925	107,202	100,424	6,778	243,127
1973	152,240	119,665	112,557	7,108	271,905
1974	167,671	127,874	120,552	7,322	295,545
1975	195,410	142,823	134,849	7,974	338,233
1976	225,763	166,144	157,409	8,735	391,907
1977	261,920	197,321	188,078	9,243	459,241
1978	298,195	225,347	215,115	10,232	523,542
1979	323,058	255,904	245,049	10,855	578,962
1980	348,461	281,368	270,004	11,364	629,829
1981	407,351	256,816	243,717	13,099	664,167
1982*	483,898	222,147	208,765	13,382	706,045

*Preliminary.
†All federally chartered associations are insured by the Federal Savings and Loan Insurance Corporation.
‡Includes the assets of institutions insured by the Co-operative Central Bank of Massachusetts, the Maryland Savings-Share Insurance Corporation, the North Carolina Savings Guaranty Corporation, the Ohio Deposit Guarantee Fund and the Pennsylvania Savings Association Insurance Corporation.

SOURCE: Federal Home Loan Bank Board; United States League of Savings Associations. Reprinted with permission from the United States League of Savings Associations. *'83 Savings and Loan Sourcebook*, p. 37.

chartered savings and loans in Texas are regulated by the Federal Home Loan Bank Board headquartered in Dallas, Texas.

Lending Policy

Savings and loan associations keep a large portion of their assets in mortgages secured by real estate. At the end of 1982, 36.2 percent of the mortgages held by associations were on 1- to 4-family homes. If one wished to include the 24.4 percent of loans made on multifamily dwellings, the total share of the associations' portfolio devoted to the financing of housing

would be 60.6 percent. These figures show that the S and Ls are an important factor in the financing of housing in the United States.

These associations usually make loans in an area of influence. This area can vary with each association. An association located in a major metropolitan market may make loans within so many miles of its office or branch offices. This can be as little as two and as much as thirty miles. Associations do not like to make loans in areas where they do not have experience or to builders that they have not made loans to in the past.

What type of loans do savings and loan

Figure 4–9. **Number of Assets of Savings Associations, by State, December 31, 1982***

State	Number of Associations	Total Assets (Millions)	Per Capita Assets	State	Number of Associations	Total Assets (Millions)	Per Capita Assets
Alabama	38	$ 5,229	$1,326	Montana	12	$ 1,124	$1,403
Alaska	5	408	932	Nebraska	27	5,872	3,702
Arizona	10	8,730	3,052	Nevada	7	2,696	3,060
Arkansas	48	5,180	2,261	New Hampshire	13	1,272	1,338
California	171	152,907	6,185	New Jersey	170	31,005	4,169
Colorado	43	9,687	3,181	New Mexico	28	3,096	2,278
Connecticut	38	7,609	2,413	New York	89	23,808	1,348
Delaware	15	262	435	North Carolina	157	13,200	2,193
District of Columbia	8	3,598	5,702	North Dakota	7	2,688	4,012
Florida	116	55,673	5,345	Ohio	325	43,037	3,988
Georgia	71	11,822	2,096	Oklahoma	55	7,168	2,256
Guam	2	75	667	Oregon	22	7,704	2,908
Hawaii	8	4,676	4,704	Pennsylvania	288	26,422	2,227
Idaho	9	1,179	1,222	Puerto Rico	11	2,983	904
Illinois	295	48,394	4,227	Rhode Island	4	879	917
Indiana	131	10,760	1,967	South Carolina	45	7,056	2,203
Iowa	60	7,692	2,648	South Dakota	18	1,190	1,722
Kansas	71	8,206	3,408	Tennessee	81	7,933	1,706
Kentucky	79	6,381	1,740	Texas	288	44,515	2,913
Louisiana	119	10,217	2,342	Utah	15	5,019	3,230
Maine	17	678	598	Vermont	5	273	528
Maryland	159	12,693	2,976	Virginia	75	12,969	2,362
Massachusetts	133	8,014	1,386	Washington	45	11,240	2,648
Michigan	53	23,506	2,581	West Virginia	25	1,835	942
Minnesota	40	11,005	2,663	Wisconsin	88	13,108	2,751
Mississippi	51	3,005	1,178	Wyoming	12	1,067	2,126
Missouri	96	16,765	3,386	Entire U.S.	3,833	$706,045	$3,034

Note: Components do not add to totals because of differences in reporting dates and accounting systems.
*Preliminary.

SOURCE: Bureau of the Census; Federal Home Loan Bank Board; United States League of Savings Associations. Reprinted with permission from United States League of Savings Associations, *'83 Savings and Loan Sourcebook*, p. 36.

associations make? As stated earlier, the associations make the majority of their loans as real estate loans on homes. These loans are usually held to 95 percent of the appraised value of the home except for those loans insured by the government or by private mortgage insurance or guaranteed by the Veterans Administration. The terms of the loans made by these associations are normally 30 years. This term has been extended to forty years. In addition to the standard mortgage, savings and loan associations are allowed to use the alternative mortgage instruments. The authorized alternative mortgage instruments were discussed in Chapter 3.

Texas-chartered S and Ls As mentioned earlier, the Texas-chartered savings and loan associations are under the control of the Savings and Loan Department. This department has authorized the S and Ls to make certain types of real estate mortgages secured by a mortgage, deed of trust, or any other type of instrument that will create or constitute a first

lien mortgage on real estate, including loans for manufactured housing (mobile homes).

In the following section we will review the promulgated rule of the Savings and Loan Section of the Texas Finance Commission and the Texas Savings and Loan Commissioner as required by Article 342-114, V.T.C.S., and Senate Bill 149 that was passed during the Regular Session of the 68th Texas Legislature, 1983.

The rules covering the making of real estate loans by Texas-chartered savings and loan associations are found in Chapter 65, Loans and Investments, as amended through April 16, 1984. The portion of this chapter that is most important to the Texas real estate professional begins with Rule 65.2, Real Estate Loans, and is divided into several sections.

Section 1 of the rule is the authority of the associations to make, purchase, or participate in loans secured by a mortgage, deed of trust, or other instrument creating a first lien on real estate. In addition, this section establishes the maximum loan-to-value ratio. According to the section, Texas associations may loan up to 100 percent of the appraised value of the property or sales price, whichever is less.

Section 2 of the rule section states that all loans made by Texas associations shall be repaid in monthly installments of principal and interest within a period of 40 years. Thus, the maximum term for a standard real estate loan made by a Texas association is 40 years.

In addition, this section of the rule allows the Texas associations to make the following types of loans:

1. Standard loans that are payable in annual, semiannual, or quarterly payments, but the term on these mortgages is reduced to 20 years.

2. Balloon loans secured by real estate, but the loans must provide for the payment of interest on at least a semiannual basis and the term on the balloon loan is limited to five years.

3. Adjustable-rate mortgage and the graduated-payment mortgage.

4. Interim construction loans. The interim loan may be made with or without monthly payments of principal and interest, but as with the balloon loan previously mentioned, there must be semiannual payment of interest. The maximum term for the interim loan is 36 months.

Texas associations also have the authority to make wraparound mortgages. According to Rule 65.3, the associations may make, purchase, or participate in a wraparound as long as the loan meets certain requirements. Those requirements are as follows:

1. The wrap is secured by a lien on improved real estate. Thus, the associations may not make wraps on raw land.

2. The amount of the wrap equals the remaining balance on the existing loan plus the amount of the funds advanced by the wrap lender.

3. The amount of the monthly payment must be equal to the amount of the monthly payment on the original loan.

4. The wraparound loan agreement must require the wraparound lender to make the payments due on the original as long as the payments on the wraparound loan are made.

In addition, the Texas associations are allowed to make home improvement, consumer, and manufactured housing loans. This authority is explained in Rule 65.6. The total rule will not be reviewed. Section 1, Property Improvement Loans, allows the association to make this type of loan for the purpose of "maintenance, repair, modernization, improvements, and equipment of real estate." There is no mention of maximum term or loan amount. Section (2), Equity Loans, allows any Texas association to make or purchase loans secured by a second or subordinate liens on real estate. The rule does state that the maximum loan amount shall not exceed the owners equity in the property as determined by a qualified appraisal. Section 7, Manufactured Home Loans, allows the Texas association to make loans secured by a manufactured home under either the association's regular mortgage loan authority (as long as the unit is permanently affixed to real property and is taxed as real property) or under the Tangible Property Loan authority.

Finally, the Texas associations may make or purchase participations in loans secured by real estate provided that the amount of loans made to any one individual does not exceed the net worth of the association.

Federally chartered S and Ls   Prior to the implementation of Title VI of the Depository Institutions Deregulation and Monetary Control Act of 1980 and the Garn-St. Germain Depository Institutions Act of 1982, the federally chartered savings and loan associations were somewhat limited. On November 10, 1980, however, the lending restrictions were somewhat liberalized, based on Title VI mentioned above. Then, with the implementation of the final rule on August 16, 1982, entitled Home Loan Amendments Adjustment Net Worth, the lending authority was liberalized even further. Some of the major changes are as follows:

1. All statutory dollar limits on home loans secured by real estate, including loans on apartments, have been removed. In addition, the Federal Home Loan Bank Board eliminated the maximum dollar amount for home improvement loans.

2. Federally chartered associations are now permitted to make loans up to 100 percent of the appraised value of the property. The changes now require the board of directors of each association to establish the loan-to-value ratios that will be used for each type of loan secured by real property.

3. Associations are now permitted to make nonhome or nonprincipal residence loans with loan-to-value ratios in excess of 90 percent, but the board of directors must approve each of these loans.

4. Associations now have the authority to make commercial loans up to 100 percent of the value if authorized by the board of directors of the associations. Also, the percent of commercial mortgages that can be made by an association has been increased from 20 percent to 40 percent of the association's assets.

5. Under the previous regulations, the Federal Home Loan Bank Board required that residential mortgages not exceed 80 percent of the value of the property unless the mortgage was insured by FHA or guaranteed by the Veterans Administration, or was insured by an approved private mortgage insurance company. This percentage has been increased to 90 percent of the value, thus making the 90-percent loan the basic home mortgage. The board has also increased the multifamily loan limit from 80 percent to 90 percent.

6. The board has authorized federal associations to make 40-year loans instead of the previous 30-year maximum.

7. Federal associations are no longer prohibited from making junior or second mortgages. The only restriction on the S and Ls making the junior mortgage is that they maintain sufficient documentation to indicate that the combined first and second liens on the property do not exceed the prescribed loan-to-value ratio.

In addition to the authorized AMIs and the loans mentioned above, the federal associations have the authority to make construction loans, home improvement loans and loans on manufactured housing. Before we leave this discussion, it should be mentioned that the federal- as well as the state-chartered S and Ls have the authority to make FHA-insured loans and Veterans Administration guaranteed loans.

COMMERCIAL BANKS

As we learned in Chapter 1, the development of commercial banks can also be traced to colonial times, with the first being founded in 1781. Commercial banks were for the most part chartered by the states, with very little federal regulation. The first attempt at federal regulation of commercial banks came with the passage of the National Bank Act in 1863. It continued in 1913 with the establishment of the Federal Reserve Bank, whose purpose it was to administer and regulate federally chartered banks.

There were no major changes in the national banking system until the Great Depression, when nearly one half of the commercial banks in the United States failed. As a result of these failures, Congress passed the Banking Act of 1933 which, as one of its provisions, established the Federal Deposit Insurance Corporation. The purpose of the Corporation was to insure the accounts held by commercial banks. As with membership in the Federal Reserve, membership in FDIC is mandatory for all national banks, but any state-chartered bank may be insured by FDIC if it will adhere to the banking practices outlined in the act. Over 95 percent of all commercial banks are insured by FDIC.

As with any other thrift institution, a commercial bank serves as a depository of funds and as an institution where money may be borrowed. The commercial bank has two sources of funds: *demand deposits* and *time deposits*. Demand deposits are deposits that are held in accounts that the customer, or depositor, may withdraw without notice. An example of such an account is a checking account. A time deposit can be defined as an account or certificate of deposit that cannot be drawn against before a specific notice is given or before a specific date. If these funds are withdrawn, there will be a penalty imposed.

Most commercial banks are operated as corporations and are owned by stockholders. They are operated for the benefit of the stockholders of the corporation. Commercial banks operate under either a federal charter or a state charter. If the bank operates under a federal charter, it is known as a national bank and it must be a member of the Federal Reserve and FDIC. If the bank is operating under a state charter, the bank will be a state bank and it will operate under the control of a state agency. In May of 1983, there were 14,497 commercial banks in the United States.

Real Estate Loan Policy

Since the majority of the deposits in these banks are demand-type deposits and can be withdrawn quickly, most commercial banks are not interested in making long-term commitments. Thus, most banks are not a good source of long-term real estate loans. They are more interested in the short-term, high-yield type of loan, such as automobile and other consumer loans.

Banks are an excellent source of funds for the interim or construction loan, especially if the builder or borrower has arranged for permanent financing prior to making application for the interim loan.

There have been some recent changes, however, in the thinking of the larger banks. Some have started to make long-term, first-lien mortgages. This is not due to the change in the type of deposits the banks are receiving, but to the growth of the secondary markets. (We will discuss the secondary market in Chapters 10 and 11.) With the growth of these markets, the banks can make the long-term mortgage and sell it in the secondary market. Thus, the bank can derive income from the loan origination fee, from the servicing of the loan and, finally, from selling a loan with *participation*. In a participation sale of a mortgage, only a portion of the principal is sold to another lender and the bank can receive interest income on the portion of the principal not sold.

With the preceding in mind, one can see that commercial banks are a good source for the interim loan or short-term financing. In the near future, they may play a more important role in the long-term financing of real estate.

Federally chartered banks The federal agency charged with the responsibility of chartering and overseeing the operation of the national banks is the Comptroller of the Currency and, in particular, the Administrator of National Banks. Prior to April 14, 1983, the national banks had statutory restrictions on their ability to make and/or participate in real estate loans. The importance of April 14, 1983, was the effective date contained in the Garn-St. Germain Depository Institutions Act of 1982. This legislation removed all statutory restrictions on real estate lending by national banks. The limits that were removed included loan-to-value ratios, aggregate limits, amortization, and maturity. In the place of the statutory limits, the act provides that the real estate lending policy of the national banks be subject to term, conditions, and limitations prescribed by the Comptroller of the Currency (COC).

On March 10, 1983, the COC published for comment in the *Federal Register* a proposed rule regarding real estate lending by national banks. After both the effective date of the Act and the proper comment period, the COC published a final rule in the *Federal Register* on September 9, 1983, which was also the effective date of the rule. The rule as adopted is intended to enhance the ability of national banks to develop real estate lending products or loan programs.

The final rule as adopted removes all restrictions of

1. Any mention of loan-to-value limitations on the amount a bank may loan relative to the appraised value or sales price of the property that will serve as security for the loan.

2. The requirements that certain loans follow a scheduled reduction of principal and that certain loans must mature in 30 years. (Thus the banks can structure the majority of their loans to any maturity and/or amortization they wish.)

3. The required amortization and other requirements for loans secured by leasehold and on constructions.

The final rule does not affect the rule or regulations allowing the national banks to make, purchase, or participate in the ARM, as mentioned in Chapter 3.

The final rule as passed is Part 34, Real Estate Lending, and is divided into three sections. The first section is entitled General and Scope. Paragraph *a* of this section gives the national banks the authority to make, arrange, purchase, or sell loans secured by liens on real estate. The scope paragraph states that the national banks have the authority to make real estate loans, including those secured by condominiums, leaseholds, cooperatives, forest tracts, construction project loans, and land sale contracts.

The second section of the rule is entitled Applicability of Law. Paragraph a of this section exempts the national banks from any state law that limits the ability of the national banks to make or participate in real estate loans in their respective states. Paragraph b of the section requires the national banks making real estate loans to comply with all federal laws and federal regulations that relate to disclosure.

The final section of the rule lists loans that are not considered to be real estate loans according to the COC.

In reviewing the three sections of the final rule, the real estate professional can see that the national banks are completely free to structure real estate loans as they wish with little or no restrictions.

Texas-chartered banks　As with the S and Ls, Texas has the authority to charter banks to operate in the state of Texas. The agency responsible for the chartering and regulations of the banks in Texas is the Banking Department of Texas, which is a part of the State Finance Commission. The authority for the Banking Department of Texas is Article 16 of the Texas Constitution of 1876. The General Provision of the Article states that the "legislature shall, by general laws, authorize the incorporation of corporate bodies with banking and discounting privileges, and shall provide for a system of State supervision regulation and control of such bodies which will adequately protect and secure the depositors and creditors thereof."

With this authority, the Banking Department has promulgated rules and regulations based on the laws passed by the Texas Legislature. The section of the rules that govern the ability of state banks to make real estate loans is contained in the regulations in the section entitled Real Estate Loan Regulations. This regulation is divided into five sections.

Section 11.1 is entitled Real Estate Loans. According to this section, the Banking Section of the Finance Commission has determined that no rules relating to margin requirements, repayment programs, or terms for real estate loans are necessary.

Section 11.2, Wraparound Mortgage, allows Texas chartered banks to make a wraparound loan if the bank has the right to prepay at anytime the existing first lien.

The third section, 11.3, Constructions Loans, allows the Texas-chartered banks to make construction loans. This rule limits the term of a construction loan on a residential or farm building to a maximum of 30 months. If the funds will be used to construct a commercial building where there is a takeout or permanent financing is available, the term of the banks construction loan may not exceed 60 months.

The fifth section, 11.5, Loans That Are Not Real Estate Loans, is self-explanatory. It lists certain types of loans that are classified as non real estate loans.

As with the national banks, the Texas-chartered banks are basically free to engage in real estate lending with little or no restrictions. Thus, the real estate professional must be very familiar with the lending practices for each state bank in his or her area.

LIFE INSURANCE COMPANIES[2]

As do the other institutional lenders, the life insurance companies have their roots in colonial times. At the end of 1982, there were 2048 legal reserve life insurance companies in operation in the United States. The most rapid growth of the life insurance companies came after World War II. In 1900, there were only 84 companies in operation. By 1905, the number had increased to 126. The trend for growth continued at the same pace, and by 1930 there were 438 companies in existence. By 1940, the number had grown to 444. Then in the 1950s, the rapid growth started. The number of companies had grown to 649 in 1950 and in just five years, this number had almost doubled to 1,107. During the 1960s, the industry grew from 1,441 in 1960 to 1,773 by 1969. The 1970s saw a slowing of the growth pattern with only the addition of 16 new companies by 1977, for a total of 1,789.

Life insurance companies can be organized as either mutuals or stock companies. The mutual life insurance company is a company that is owned by the policyholders and the policyholders share in the profits of the company through the reduction of premiums. If the life insurance company is a stock company, like any other corporation it is operated for the benefit and profit of the stockholders. No matter what the type of life insurance company, all life insurance companies are regulated by the state in which they do business. This means, for example, that if a life insurance company has its main office in Maine and wishes to do business in Texas, it must seek a license or the authority from the State Board of Insurance in Texas before it may do business in Texas.

If you would like more information on life insurance companies, the American Council of Life Insurance prepares a *Life Insurance Fact Book* each year that reviews the industry in depth.

Mortgage Lending in the United States

Life insurance company holdings in mortgages at the end of 1982 amounted to $142.0 billion, or 24.1 percent of their total assets. Real estate mortgages have always been a very attractive investment for life insurance companies because of the safety (secured by real property), good yields, or returns to the company, and favorable maturities. Insurance companies are looking for a longer maturity of their investments because they can, through the use of mortality tables, predict very accurately the deaths of their policyholders; thus they can predict the need for cash. With the regular payments of mortgage loans, they can predict the income from their mortgage loan portfolios. For these reasons, life insurance companies rank third among the major institutional lenders.

During the 1950s, life insurance companies were heavily involved with residential loans, but they have reduced this type of loan dramatically in the past twenty years. In 1958, the residential mortgage represented approximately 60 percent of the mortgages they held. By 1968 this percentage had dropped to 41 percent, and by the end of 1982 this type of loan was a mere 11.7 percent of the total mortgages outstanding. This dramatic reduction in the 1- to 4-family loans reflected a change in the investment policy of the life insurance companies from 1- to 4-family loans to the nonresidential loan. These nonresidential loans are loans secured by commercial, industrial, and institutional types of properties. This type of loan has risen from only 23 percent of the total outstanding loans in 1958 to 65.8 percent in 1982.

Mortgage Lending in Texas

Since a life insurance company is controlled by the state in which it operates, the type of real estate loans that can be made is set either by the state agency that oversees the operation of the life insurance companies or by the state legislature by the enactment of laws. In Texas, the legislature passes laws that set the type of real estate loans that can be made by life insurance companies. During the 1979 session of the Texas legislature, Part II, Article 3.39 of the Insurance Code was amended "to provide that domestic life insurance companies may loan any of their funds and accumulations on first liens upon real estate."

There were some limitations placed on the loan-to-value ratios of the loans:

1. A loan on unimproved land may not exceed 75 percent of the value of the land or real estate.

2. A loan on real estate with improvements may not exceed 90 percent of the real estate and improvements, except if the portion of the loan above 80 percent of the value of the real estate and improvements is insured by a mortgage insurance company that is licensed to operate in Texas. With mortgage insurance, the maximum amount of the loan may be increased to 95 percent of the value of the real estate and improvements.

This section of the Insurance Code also limits the amount of all real estate loans to any one corporation, partnership, company, or individual to no more than 10 percent of the admitted assets of the life insurance company. This section further provides that a single loan on real estate secured by a first lien may not exceed 5 percent of the admitted assets of the life insurance company.

Life insurance companies in Texas are also allowed to make loans on leasehold estates in real property and the improvements made to the property provided that the duration of the loan does not exceed a period equal to four-fifths of the unexpired term of the leasehold and provided that the unexpired term of the leasehold extends ten years beyond the term of the loan. This means that if a leasehold has 40 years to run, the maximum term of a loan would be four-fifths of 40 years, or 32 years. Due to the second requirement, however, the leasehold must extend 10 years beyond the end of the mortgage. The maximum term for this loan, therefore, is 30 years.

The code further states that the loan-to-value ratios stated in the code do not apply to any loan that is either insured or partially guaranteed by an agency of the federal government. These are exempt from the restrictions.

MUTUAL SAVINGS BANKS

Mutual savings banks are a unique type of thrift institution. They operate much like savings and loan associations, but in some areas offer the services of commercial banks. The mutuals were established along the same lines as the savings institutions of Europe. Prior to the early 1800s, most of the commercial banks would not accept deposits from individuals, and the workers had no place to deposit small sums of money. So the mutuals were established. As the name implies, mutuals are owned by the depositors.

A mutual savings bank is chartered by the state in which it operates and is subject to the banking rules of that state. In some cases, mutual savings banks will join the Federal Deposit Insurance Corporation and/or the Federal Home Loan Bank Board. Then, in addition to the state authority, they are subject to federal regulations.

The majority of the approximately 500 mutual savings banks are located on the East Coast, primarily in Massachusetts, New York, Connecticut, Maine, New Hampshire, New Jersey, Pennsylvania, Rhode Island, Vermont, Maryland, and Delaware. There are a few mutual savings banks in states such as Wisconsin, Washington, Indiana, Oregon, and Alaska, but no mutuals operate in Texas. So, why should we even discuss this type of lender? They are important to Texas because of their investment policy and their location. As we noted, most of the associations are located along the East Coast, where the building of single-family homes has slowed. The amount of deposits in these institutions, however, is still strong. The mutuals, therefore, are looking to make secure investments, and one of the most secure investments is in first lien mortgages secured by real estate. So the mutuals, through correspondence, are looking at the rapid growth areas to invest in mortgages. Since the investment policy of the mutuals is quite conservative, they normally will not make loans on real estate at more than 80 percent of the value or sales price, whichever is lower. In some states, the mutuals may not make loans of more than 50 percent of the value, unless the loan is insured or has some type of guarantee. Thus, with the advent of the FHA insured loan and VA guaranteed loan, the mutuals were able to expand the number of loans they were able to originate or purchase through their correspondence. With this correspondence relationship in mind, we can see why these mutuals are important to Texas. These institutions have large pools of funds to loan, but the activity or need for loans in their area of operation has been slowing due to the movement of people from the East Coast to the Sunbelt, and to Texas in particular. So the mutuals have been either purchasing loans from other thrift institutions in Texas or through their correspondence have been originating FHA and VA loans in Texas.

If you would like more information, about mutual savings banks, a good source is the annual *Mutual Savings Bank Fact Book*.

REVIEW QUESTIONS

1. Define the terms *intermediation* and *disintermediation*.

2. Briefly describe the lending policies of savings and loan associations, life insurance companies, and commercial banks in Texas.

3. What is the source of the loanable funds in the United States?

4. In your opinion, how will real estate be financed in the future?

5. Why are mutual savings banks important to Texas?

6. Why have commercial banks just started to enter into the financing of real estate?

7. Which of the institutional lenders would be a source of funds to finance a single-family dwelling, a hospital, an office building, and to provide a building loan?

NOTES

1. Most of this section is based on material from United States League of Savings Associations, *'83 Savings and Loan Sourcebook*.

2. Most of this section is based on material from American Council of Life Insurance, *1983 Life Insurance Fact Book*.

5 Community Reinvestment

LEARNING OBJECTIVES

In this chapter we will briefly review the Community Reinvestment Act (CRA), the Home Mortgage Disclosure Act, and the provisions of these acts that could affect you as a real estate professional.

Upon completion of this chapter you should be able to do the following:

★ Outline the history of the Community Reinvestment Act (CRA).

★ Identify the institutions that are covered by the CRA.

★ List some of the major requirements of the CRA as they apply to the affected institutions.

★ Name and explain some of the major programs that can apply to an institution's compliance to the CRA.

★ Outline the requirements of the Home Mortgage Disclosure Act.

BACKGROUND

The concept of community reinvestment was contained in Title VIII of the Housing and Community Development Act of 1977. This section was entitled the "Community Reinvestment Act of 1977." Section 802 of the act outlines Congress' intent in regard to community reinvestment and meeting the needs of the communities served by a financial institution. The Community Reinvestment Act expanded the responsibility of the financial institutions to meet not only the deposit needs of the community they serve, but also the credit needs of the community. The act also required the appropriate federal financial supervisory agency to use its authority when examining a financial institution, to encourage the institution to meet the credit needs of the community.

Section 804 of the Community Reinvestment Act allows the federal financial supervisory agency, in connection with the regular examination of the institution, to assess the institution's record of meeting the credit needs of the entire community served by the institution, including the needs of low- and moderate-income families.

At this time, let us define the federal financial supervisory agencies as they pertain to the Community Reinvestment Act. According to Section 803 of the act, the term *federal financial supervisory agency* refers to the:

1. Comptroller of the Currency

2. Board of Governors of the Federal Reserve System

3. Federal Deposit Insurance Corporation

4. Federal Home Loan Bank Board and the Federal Savings and Loan Insurance Corporation

From this list of federal supervisory agencies, one can see that the majority of the financial institutions in the United States—including national banks, state banks that are insured

118

by FDIC or are members of the Federal Reserve System, and savings and loan associations insured by FSLIC — are covered by the Community Reinvestment Act.

The Community Reinvestment Act has been implemented by the major financial supervisory agencies by the issuance of federal regulations.

PURPOSE[1]

The purpose of the act and the regulations issued by the supervisory agencies is to encourage the financial institutions to meet the credit needs of their communities, including low- and moderate-income families. The act and the regulations also guide the financial institutions as to how the supervisory agencies will assess an institution's record in meeting those credit needs. The programs offered to meet these needs should be consistent with safe and sound operation of the institutions.

SIGNIFICANCE TO THE REAL ESTATE INDUSTRY

The major significance of CRA to the real estate industry is that the act requires the federally supervised financial institutions to meet the credit needs of the community they serve. These credit needs are not just consumer loans or home-repair loans, but loans for the financing of housing and redevelopment of the community, particularly in predominantly low- to moderate-income areas. Thus, the act can serve the agent working in any city that has a need for the expansion of housing and facilities for families with low to moderate income.

REQUIREMENTS OF THE ACT AND FEDERAL REGULATIONS

The Community Reinvestment Act and the associated regulations contain many provisions, but the following are the four basic requirements that all institutions covered by the regulations must meet:

1. Define the area or community served

2. List the types of credit offered

3. Post a public notice stating that the institution is reviewed by a federal supervisory agency

4. Prepare a Community Reinvestment Act statement and give notice that the statement is available for public inspection.

Community Reinvestment Act Statement

Requirement 4, above, is that the lender must prepare a Community Reinvestment Act statement. This statement can be of great assistance to the real estate professional, for it will give insight into the financial institution's activities to aid the housing and community needs of low- to moderate-income families and the whole community that the institution serves. Now let us look at some of the major portions of the CRA statement.

First, the CRA statement must contain these items:

1. The institution must define its community by specific boundaries and illustrate it by a map. The institution must also describe the method it used to determine its community.

2. The institution is required to state the types of credit it is making available to the persons in its community.

3. The institution must maintain a file containing the comments from the general public about the performance of the institution in meeting or not meeting the credit needs of the community.

4. The CRA statement should contain a copy of the public notice posted in the lobby of the institution. The information and language of this notice is prescribed by a federal regulation. The required notice for those institutions under the jurisdiction of the Federal Home Loan Bank Board is shown in Figure 5-1.

In addition to the required information contained in the CRA statement, the institution *may* include, and is encouraged by the supervisory agencies to include, the following information:

(1) A description of how its current efforts, including special credit-related programs, help to meet community credit needs;

(2) A periodic report regarding its record of helping to meet community credit needs; and

Figure 5–1.   Community Reinvestment Act Notice

The Federal Community Reinvestment Act (CRA) requires the Federal Home Loan Bank Board to evaluate our performance in helping to meet the credit needs of this community, and to take this evaluation into account when deciding on certain applications submitted by us. Your involvement is encouraged.

You may obtain our current CRA statement for this community in this office. [Current CRA statements for other communities served by us are available at our home office, located at _____ .]

You may send signed, written comments about our CRA statement(s) or our performance in helping to meet community credit needs to (title and address of institution official) and to (title of officer), Federal Home Loan Bank of _____ _____ (address). Your letter, together with any response by us, may be made public.

You may look at a file of all signed, written comments received by us within the past 2 years, any responses we have made to the comments, and all CRA statements in effect during the past 2 years at our office located at (address). [You also may look at the file about this community at (name and address of designated office).]

You may ask to look at any comments received by the Federal Home Loan Bank of _____ _____ .

You also may request from the Federal Home Loan Bank of _____ an announcement of applications covered by the CRA filed with the Federal Home Loan Bank Board.

SOURCE: *Code of Federal Regulations*, Title 12—Banks and Banking: Section 563e.6, Public Notice, p. 752.

(3) A description of its efforts to ascertain the credit needs of its community, including efforts to communicate with members of its community regarding credit services.[2]

Now that we have reviewed the major provisions of the act and the related federal regulations, let us look at the methods that an institution may use to designate or define its community. The federal regulations set forth three methods that may be used by the institutions:

1. *Existing boundaries*, such as the boundaries of a standard metropolitan statistical area or counties in which the institution is located or has branch offices. A smaller institution may designate an area inside the larger metropolitan area as its community.[3]

2. *Effective lending territory*. This method is defined as "that local area or areas around each office or group of offices where it makes a substantial portion of its loans and all other areas equidistant from its offices as those areas."[4]

3. The third method of establishing the community is described in the regulations as follows: "An institution may use other reasonably delineated local area that meets the purposes of the Community Reinvestment Act (CRA) and does not exclude low- and moderate-income neighborhoods."[5]

Of the three methods, the most meaningful to the real estate professional is the effective lending territory method, the plotting of a

sampling of the actual loans that have been made by the institution in the area. This method will best define the actual area of operation and specialization of the institution.

The second type of information in the CRA statement that will be of importance to the real estate professional is the information regarding the type of credit extended by the institution. The regulations require the institution to list the specific types of credit granted in certain categories. The categories that are listed in the regulations are as follows:

1. Residential loans for 1- to 4-family residences

2. Residential loans for five or more dwelling units

3. Loans for housing rehabilitation

4. Loans for home improvement

5. Loans for financing small businesses

6. Community development loans

7. Commercial loans

8. Consumer loans

From this list, the real estate professional can pair the proper institution to the proper type of loan. For example, if you are working with a client who specializes in the purchase of properties that need rehabilitation, you would look for an institution that makes rehabilitation loans and serves the community in which the property is located.

These are the two main areas of the CRA statement that will be of help to the real estate professional. Being familiar with the CRA statements of the institutions in your community will be a service to your clients, for you will be better able to counsel them about the financing available through federally supervised financial institutions.

ASSESSING THE PERFORMANCE OF THE INSTITUTION

As mentioned earlier, the Community Reinvestment Act gives the supervisory agency that examines the institution the authority to assess the institution's performance in helping to meet the credit needs of its entire community, including the low- and moderate-income neighborhoods.

The supervisory agencies will review the institution's CRA statement and any signed written comments retained by the institution regarding their credit-granting activities. The supervisory agency, in addition to reviewing the above information, will review many areas of the institution's operation in order to assess the institution's performance. Some of the items reviewed are as follows:

How the institution ascertained the credit needs of the entire community

The geographic distribution of the credit extended and denied

The institution's participation, including investments, in local community development and redevelopment programs and projects

The institution's origination of residential loans, housing rehabilitation loans, and home improvement loans, or the purchase of these types of mortgages made in the institution's community

The institution's participation in government-insured, -guaranteed, or -subsidized loan programs for housing, small businesses, or small farms in the institution's community

Because the above items are reviewed by the federal supervisory agencies, financial institutions are more prone to make these types of mortgages, thus making it easier to get financing in low- to moderate-income neighborhoods.

One example of a financial institution being willing to participate in such loan programs was a rehabilitation loans program in low- to moderate-income areas of Houston. The program was passed by the Houston city council and was signed as an ordinance in February 1979. Entitled Rehabilitation Loan Agreement, the program was an agreement between the city of Houston and a group of financial institutions for a 2-year pilot project to establish the feasibility of a program of rehabilitation loans in which the city of Houston would guarantee the repayment of any loan made under the provisions of the program. The financial institutions taking part in the agreement would make available a total of $1 million at all times during the program for making rehabilitation loans.

Under this program, both owner- and nonowner-occupied property was eligible and the properties were to be located in areas that had a great deal of substandard property and were inside the Houston city limits.

The amount, term, and interest rate on these loans were as follows:

Owner-Occupied Property

Type A: A single-unit residential structure occupied by the owner

Loan Amount: $12,000
Interest Rate: 3%
Loan Period: 15 years

Type B: A residential dwelling structure containing two to four units, one of which is occupied by the owner

Loan Amount: The lesser of $5,000 per unit or $20,000
Interest Rate: 3%
Loan Period: 15 years

Investor-Owned Property

Type A: One or more unattached single-unit dwelling structures, none of which is occupied by the owner

Loan Amount: The lesser of $12,000 per unit or $50,000
Interest Rate: 6%
Loan Period: 15 years

Type B: A dwelling containing two or more attached units, none of which are occupied by the owner

Loan Amount: The lesser of $5,000 per unit or $50,000
Interest Rate: 6%
Loan Period: 15 years

*Type C: A dwelling structure containing
five or more attached units,
whether or not one is occupied by
the owner*

Loan Amount: The lesser of $5,000
                   per unit or $50,000
Interest Rate: 6%
Loan Period: 15 years

In addition to the immediate effects on the
financial institutions not meeting obligations
under the Community Reinvestment Act, it
may have an effect on the institution if it
should wish to expand. The community reinvestment regulations governing the institutions also state that an institution's
performance shall be taken into account if it
makes application for insurance under FDIC
or FSLIC for addition of a savings and loan
association branch office, for relocation of a
main office or branch, for merger or consolidation, or for acquisition of assets or assumption
of liabilities of another institution. In other
words, the involvement of a financial institution in community reinvestment is quite
important.

The importance of community development
can be further shown in that the Federal
Home Loan Bank Board now requires any federally chartered savings and loan association
that invests more than 2 percent of its assets
in a service corporation to also make an
investment in the community. The regulation
requires that if the savings and loan invests
2.5 percent of its assets in the service corporation, it must invest at least 0.5 percent of its
total assets in community, inner-city, or community development investments. If the
association invests as much as is authorized
by the regulation (3 percent of its assets) in a
service corporation, it must invest a sum equal
to 1 percent of its assets in investments that
serve primarily community, inner-city, or community development purposes.

*The Federal Home Loan Bank Board
believes investments that would qualify
as primarily related to "community,
inner-city, and community development
purposes" would be substantially directed
at programs for development, preservation, and revitalization of low- and
moderate-income areas, both urban and
rural.[6]*

Thus, the savings and loan institutions are
again required to invest in the community and
to help the low- to moderate-income areas of
the community.

In determining whether an investment
qualifies as primarily related to "community,
inner-city, and community development purposes," the board would consider:

1. Whether the investment demonstrates substantial involvement in innovative loans
which contribute to the development,
preservation, or revitalization of either
urban or rural communities; or

2. Whether the investment meets community
development and housing needs and priori-
ties, principally for low- and moderate-
income areas, or contributes to the elimination of slums or blight; or

3. Whether the investment demonstrates commitment to participate in government- or
privately sponsored programs aimed at
community development, preservation, or
revitalization; or

4. Whether the investment involves a local
partnership aimed at assisting existing residents in neighborhoods experiencing rein-
vestments.[7]

QUALIFYING GOVERNMENTAL PROGRAMS

The following governmental programs can
help financial institutions meet the requirements of the Community Reinvestment Act:

1. Urban Development Action Grants

2. Urban Homesteading

3. Community Development Block Grants

4. Neighborhood Reinvestment Corporations;
Title VI

5. Section 203(b) 1- to 4-Family Mortgage
Insurance (HUD)

6. Section 245, Graduated Payment Mortgage (HUD)

7. Section 221(d)(3) and (4) Multifamily
Rental Housing for Low- and Moderate-
Income Families (HUD)

8. Section 235 Revised (HUD)

9. Section 312 Housing Rehabilitation Loans
(HUD)

10. Section 8 Housing Assistance Payments Programs (HUD)

11. Title I Home Improvement Loan Insurance (HUD)

12. Section 502, Single-Family Rural Housing Loans Guaranteed by Farmers Home Administration

13. Section 7(a), Direct, Immediate Participation and Guaranteed Loans (SBA)

14. Section 502, Local Development Companies Loan Program (SBA)

15. Veterans Administration Single-Family Guarantee (VA).

Although this is not a complete list, if any of the listed governmental programs are implemented by a financial institution, they will aid the institution in meeting the requirements of the Community Reinvestment Act. Some of these programs will be of more use to the real estate professional in rural areas than in urban ones.

HOME MORTGAGE DISCLOSURE ACT

Another important piece of legislation that has affected the financial institutions in the field of community reinvestment is the Home Mortgage Disclosure Act (HMDA), which requires that financial institutions located in standard metropolitan statistical areas (SMSAs) disclose information about home mortgages and home improvement loans they make.

The HMDA was amended by the Housing and Community Development Act of 1980, it requires the compilation and disclosure of loan data by calendar year rather than by fiscal year. All of the data must now be reported by census tract and county rather than census tract and zip code. The amendment further requires that a standard disclosure format be used and that a central repository be established in each SMSA in the United States.

The act requires any depository institution with assets in excess of $10 million to make the required disclosures. State-chartered institutions are exempt from the provisions of the HMDA.

Some of the major provisions of the act are:

1. *Compilation of loan data.* Each institution shall compile data on loans by the number

and dollar amount of home purchase and home improvement loans that the institution both originates and purchases each calendar year beginning with 1981.

2. *Disclosure format.* The institution will use the prescribed format shown in Figures 5-2 and 5-3.

3. *Reporting area.* All loan data reported by the institution will be by SMSA, with the SMSA further divided into census tracts. This means that each loan will be shown by the broad area of the SMSA and then as to the particular census tract inside the SMSA where the property is located.

4. *Types of loans.* The regulations require the institution to report loans by the following types:

   a. FHA, VA, and FmHA loans on 1- to 4-family dwellings

   b. Other home mortgages (conventional) on 1- to 4-family dwellings

   c. Home improvement loans on 1- to 4-family dwellings

   d. Total purchase and home improvement loans on dwellings with four or more families

   e. Loans made to either purchase or improve properties that were not to be used as the primary residence of the borrower

In addition to the provisions outlined above, the act requires that the institution make the information available to the general public. Thus, the institutions are required to have a copy of the Disclosure Statement available at their home offices as well as at least one branch office located in each of the SMSAs in which the institution has shown activity in the previous 12-month period. To gain access to an institution's statement, one must make a request to the institution in person at any office of the institution during normal office hours. If a person requests a copy of the statement and if the institution has copying capabilities, the institution may charge a reasonable price for the copying service.

This law is another effort of the U.S. Congress to see that the financial institutions meet the total credit needs of all segments of the communities they serve. It also makes

Figure 5–2. Mortgage Loan Disclosure Statement, page 1

FRB HMDA-1
OMB No. 7100-0090
Approval expires September 1984

MORTGAGE LOAN DISCLOSURE STATEMENT

Report for loans made in 19 ____

This report is required by law (12 U.S.C. 2801–2811 and 12 CFR 203).

Depository Institution

Enforcement Agency for this Institution

Name _____

Address _____

Name _____

Census tract series used: ____ 1970 series ____ 1980 series

SMSA (location of property) _____

PART A—ORIGINATIONS

SECTION 1—LOANS ON PROPERTY LOCATED WITHIN THOSE SMSAs IN WHICH INSTITUTION HAS HOME OR BRANCH OFFICES

CENSUS TRACT (in numerical sequence) where property located or COUNTY (name) where property located	Loans on 1 - to - 4 family dwellings						Loans on Multi-family Dwellings for 5 or more families (home purchases and home improvement) D		Addendum Item: Non-occupant Loans on 1 - to - 4 family dwellings E	
	Home Purchase Loans				Home Improvement Loans C					
	FHA, FmHA, and VA A		Other ("Conventional") B							
	No. of Loans	Principal Amount (Thousands)	No. of Loans	Principal Amount (Thousands)	No. of Loans	Principal Amount (Thousands)	No. of Loans	Principal Amount (Thousands)	No. of Loans	Principal Amount (Thousands)
SMSA TOTAL										

SECTION 2—LOANS ON ALL PROPERTY LOCATED ELSEWHERE

Source: "Rules and Regulations," *Federal Register*, January 7, 1982, vol. 47, no. 4, p. 753.

Figure 5-3. Mortgage Loan Disclosure Statement, page 2

PART B—PURCHASES

SECTION 1—DATA FOR PROPERTY LOCATED WITHIN THOSE SMSAs IN WHICH INSTITUTION HAS HOME OR BRANCH OFFICES

CENSUS TRACT (in numerical sequence) where property located or COUNTY (name) where property located	Loans on 1 - to - 4 family dwellings							Loans on Multi-family Dwellings for 5 or more families (home purchases and home improvement)		Addendum Item: Non-occupant Loans on 1 - to - 4 family dwellings	
	Home Purchase Loans				Home Improvement Loans						
	FHA, FmHA, and VA		Other ("Conventional")								
	A		B		C		D		E	
	No. of Loans	Principal Amount (Thousands)	No. of Loans	Principal Amount (Thousands)	No. of Loans	Principal Amount (Thousands)	No. of Loans	Principal Amount (Thousands)	No. of Loans	Principal Amount (Thousands)
SMSA TOTAL										

SECTION 2—LOANS ON ALL PROPERTY LOCATED ELSEWHERE

available to the public information indicating whether the institution is truly meeting the needs of its community. As a real estate professional, this information required by the HMDA can help you find the institutions that may assist you in financing properties in low- to moderate-income areas.

SUMMARY

Community reinvestment is a concept designed to help large cities throughout the United States, particularly cities with declining areas in the inner city and elsewhere. The program will have the greatest effect on cities with a population of 200,000 or more. Community reinvestment can be of great assistance to the real estate professional who is working in the inner city or the transitional areas of a city. Even if you are not working in these areas, you should become familiar with the efforts of the financial institutions in your area to meet the requirements of the Community Reinvestment Act.

REVIEW QUESTIONS

1. Outline the history of the Community Reinvestment Act.

2. Identify the financial institutions covered by the CRA.

3. Name and explain some of the major requirements placed on the financial institutions by the CRA.

4. Give the major purpose of the Community Reinvestment Act.

5. Explain how the Community Reinvestment Act statement of a financial institution can aid the real estate professional.

6. Name and explain the three methods used by a financial institution to define its community.

7. List some of the guidelines used by the supervisory agencies to judge the performance of financial institutions.

8. Examine the Community Reinvestment Act statements of several financial institutions in your area and assess in your opinion how well the institutions are meeting the credit needs of their community.

NOTES

1. Most of this section is based upon material from the *Code of Federal Regulations*, Title 12, Parts 25.2, 228.2, 344.2, and 563e.2, January 1, 1980, pp. 276, 757, 294, and 750.
2. *Code of Federal Regulations*, Title 12, Part 284.4(c)(1), (2), and (3), January 1, 1980, p. 758.
3. *Code of Federal Regulations*, Title 12, Part 563e.3(b)(1), January 1, 1980, p. 750.
4. *Code of Federal Regulations*, Title 12, Part 563e.3(b)(2), January 1, 1980, p. 750.
5. *Code of Federal Regulations*, Title 12, Part 563e.3(b)(3), January 1, 1980, pp. 750–51.
6. Federal Home Loan Bank Board, *Draft of Code of Federal Regulations*, Title 12, Part 545, undated, p. 2.
7. Federal Home Loan Bank Board, *Draft of Code of Federal Regulations*, Title 12, Part 545, undated, pp. 2–3.

6 Noninstitutional Lenders

LEARNING OBJECTIVES

In this chapter, we will discuss the noninstitutional lenders. A noninstitutional lender is not as strictly regulated as the institutional lender, or may have no regulation at all by either the federal or state government. For our purposes, we will examine mortgage bankers, mortgage brokers, credit unions, and pension and retirement funds as noninstitutional lenders.

When you have completed your study of this chapter, you should be able to do the following:

★ Explain the difference between a mortgage banker and a mortgage broker.

★ Outline the lending policy of credit unions in Texas.

★ Briefly explain each of the areas of operation of a mortgage banker.

★ Identify the sources of income for a mortgage banker.

MORTGAGE COMPANIES

The common name for a mortgage company is *mortgage banker*. The term *mortgage banker* would imply that this type of lender is like the institutional one because the banker would accumulate funds through deposits and then loan these accumulated funds to the general public, but this is not the case. The modern mortgage banker is an intermediary and can be defined as "a firm or individual active in the field of Mortgage Banking. Mortgage Bankers, as local representatives of regional or national institutional lenders, act as correspondents between lenders and borrowers."[1]

History[2]

As with all of the other lenders in the United States, the origins of the mortgage banker, sometimes referred to as a mortgage company, can be traced back to a European counterpart. The modern mortgage banker, however, was nonexistent before the Civil War and those that began after the Civil War were primarily involved with the financing of farms. The majority of the operation of the lenders was in the Midwest, the Ohio Valley. The loans were of low loan-to-value ratio, usually 40 to 50 percent. The loans were not amortized over the term of the loan, but had a balloon payment, meaning the entire principal was due at the end of the term. Interest on these loans was payable either quarterly or semiannually. Like the mortgage bankers of today, these lenders were not making loans to keep in their portfolios. They were made for sale to institutional lenders or wealthy individuals.

The industry grew rapidly until the Great Depression. The reason for the bankruptcy of many mortgage bankers during the Depression was that they guaranteed the loans sold to the investors. This guarantee was not a true guarantee, but was more the custom of the industry. On a loan that went into default, the investor could choose between two plans: either the mortgage banker would substitute a new loan, or the mortgage banker would buy back the loan. As this practice grew, the companies were called, simply, *mortgage guarantee companies*. As with all of the other major financial operations, these were located primarily in New York City. As the economy in the late 1920s and early 1930s started to decline, many of the mortgages held by these guarantee companies went into default. More and more investors asked the companies to buy back the loans rather than substitute new loans. Many of the companies did not have the cash to do so and thus had to declare bankruptcy.

Why were there so many defaults during the Depression? Even though the borrower could keep a job, the problem came about at the end of the term, when the loan was to be refinanced. The term of a home loan at that time was normally 5 years, with no guarantee of refinancing. The Depression brought a severe lack of funds, and therefore the borrower could not refinance, nor did the borrower have the funds to repay the loan in total. The loan, therefore, went into default.

To help such persons keep their homes and to stop foreclosure, the federal government established the Homeowners' Loan Corporation in 1933. The purpose of this federal agency was to purchase the home that had been foreclosed, refinance the loan, and then have the homeowner repay the loan on a monthly basis. This was the beginning of the amortized mortgage.

The industry did not grow much until after World War II. Because of all of the people returning from the war, and because the thrift institutions had a large amount of savings on deposit, the housing industry and therefore the mortgage bankers grew overnight. Another reason for the rapid growth of the mortgage banking industry was the advent of the Federal Housing Administration. FHA-insured mortgages provided three very important elements that helped develop a national mortgage market: dependability, transferability, and minimal risk. This brings us to current mortgage banking. The industry as we know it today owes its growth to the decision of the insurance companies to engage in national lending because of the mortgage insurance provided by the FHA. With this growth of the mortgage market and the continued demand for housing, the mortgage banking industry has grown from small family operations to large corporations operating in several states. How important the mortgage bankers are to the financing of housing, particularly in the areas of the FHA and the VA,

was illustrated in 1983 when mortgage bankers originated over 78 percent of all FHA and VA loans in the United States.

Regulation

There is no direct regulation of the mortgage banking industry. This means that neither the state of Texas nor the federal government has the ability to regulate this group of lenders in the same fashion as a bank, a savings and loan association, or a mutual savings bank. The only state laws that may affect a mortgage banker are laws governing the formation of corporations and/or partnerships. The only way that a mortgage banker is subject to federal review is if the lender is an approved FHA lender or Fannie Mae seller/servicer. Then, the lender is subject to periodic audits. To strengthen its hold on the mortgage bankers, the Department of Housing and Urban Development has issued guidelines on how lenders are to handle problems with the borrower. Furthermore, the passage of federal laws involving equal credit and other antidiscrimination has affected the mortgage banker as well as other lenders. But, for the most part, they have remained relatively free of governmental control.

Lending Policy

Mortgage bankers conduct their lending operations rather differently from other lenders in that they normally lend not their own money, but the money of others through the use of commitments. These commitments are issued by the source of funds, such as savings and loans, insurance companies, Fannie Mae, or FHLMC, the latter two being the largest source of these commitments. So, the mortgage company only implements the underwriting, or lending policies, of the institution issuing the commitment. For example, if a Texas-based mortgage company serves as a correspondent for a life insurance company that is licensed to operate or has its home office in Georgia, the mortgage banker must make the real estate loans in accordance with Georgia laws governing the operation of life insurance companies.

Mortgage Banker Operations

The operation of the mortgage banker is similar to the operation of any other lender, except that the mortgage banker has no savings accounts or other sources of funds, as do institutional lenders. Rather, the mortgage banker originates the loans and sells them in the secondary market, or has previously arranged for an investor to purchase the loans. When making these loans, the mortgage banker executes seven steps:

1. Loan origination

2. Loan processing

3. Loan underwriting

4. Loan closing

5. Loan warehousing

6. Packaging and shipping

7. Loan servicing

Loan origination The process of loan origination is the solicitation of mortgages from realtors, builders, and so forth. The persons who actively seek to make loans on real property are sometimes called *loan solicitors* or *loan officers*, and these persons call on the real estate firms or builders. The loan officers seek clients or sources of loans, in order to fill commitments or to replace the loans that are paid off. These are the salespersons for the mortgage banking industry. As a real estate salesperson, you will become familiar with these persons as they come to your office and ask for the mortgages of the firm or from the individual salespersons. In the mortgage banking field, these loans are called *spot loans*. In Texas, there is no license required for a person to become a loan solicitor.

Loan processing Loan processing is the actual gathering of the information that will enable the mortgage banker either to approve or reject the loan, based on the applicant or the property. This process is divided into two parts. First, the application is taken on a standard application form. Second, along with the application, additional forms are completed to allow the mortgage banker to verify the credit, employment, and financial condition of the applicant. (The application form and verification forms will be discussed in Chapter 14.) The processing of a loan can take as little as a week or as long as 6 months. Loan processing has been complicated by the passage of several laws such as the Equal Credit Opportunity Act, the Real Estate Settlement Procedure Act, and the Fair Credit Reporting Act. These will be reviewed later in this text.

Loan underwriting Loan underwriting is defined as the "analysis of risk and the matching of it to an appropriate rate of return."[3] In other words, the process of underwriting is to see if the applicant, as well as the property, meets the requirements of the lender or investor. Since the mortgage banker deals with several investors, it is the underwriter's task to match the loan application to the proper investor. For example, a mortgage banker may have an investor that will make only 80 percent loan-to-value ratio loans on frame houses that are less than 3 years old. It would be foolish to submit to this investor a 90 percent loan of this type because it would be rejected.

With the growth of the conventional secondary market, primarily through the Federal National Mortgage Association and the Federal Home Loan Mortgage Corporation, the mortgage banking industry has adopted the two income ratios of these organizations for underwriting many conventional mortgages. These ratios are the income-to-total-house-payment ratio and the income-to-long-term-debt (including the total house payment) ratio. In addition to the ratios of Fannie Mae and FHLMC, many mortgage bankers will only make mortgages that conform to the mortgage amounts acceptable to Fannie Mae and FHLMC. With the adoption of these standards, it is easier for the mortgage banker to sell a package of conventional loans if all of the mortgages conform to the underwriting guidelines set forth by Fannie Mae and FHLMC. The underwriting guidelines for Fannie Mae and FHLMC will be discussed in Chapter 13.

Loan closing After all of the documents relating to the borrower and the property have been received, they will be checked to see that they conform to the lender's underwriting guidelines. If so, a letter is then issued to the borrower stating that the loan has been approved. The mortgage banker will then set a closing date for the transaction. It is hoped that the date set by the mortgage banker is on or before the date specified in the contract. Prior to the closing or the conclusion of the transaction, the mortgage banker will prepare or have prepared the necessary documents required by the investor or the person purchasing the loan, to be signed by the parties to the transaction. In addition to these documents, the mortgage banker will send to the closing agent a set of instructions to be followed at the time of closing. These instructions will be discussed in detail in Chapter 15.

Loan warehousing Loan warehousing is the borrowing of funds by the mortgage banker for a short term in order to fund the loan prior to the investor or lender actually purchasing or funding the loan. The warehousing loan is usually made at a commercial bank, using the closed mortgages as collateral. Some banks require a copy of the commitment agreement from the investor. Without this ability, the mortgage banker could not fund the loan at closing or within 24 hours. The reason for this is that the investors do not buy loans one at a time, but in a package usually amounting to $1 million. This could be weeks later.

In using this warehouse line of credit, the mortgage banker hopes that the bank will charge an interest rate that is less than the rate on the mortgage and thus allow the mortgage banker a slight margin of profit. But in some cases, the rate on the warehouse loan is more than that charged on the mortgage. The mortgage banker then will lose money on the mortgage while it is in the warehouse. If, for example, the face interest rate on the mortgage is 12 percent and the warehouse loan rate is 14 percent, it is costing the mortgage banker 2 percent until the loan is delivered to the investor. Normally, the mortgage banker will absorb the loss, but in some cases the mortgage banker will pass this charge along, usually to the borrower, as a warehouse fee. During the high short-term interest rates of late 1979 through 1980, this was being done by many lenders in Texas.

Packaging and shipping As stated above, loans are shipped in a group, and this group is usually called a *package*. This package of loans will always conform to the requirements of the investor who is buying the loans. Normally, the package, when sold to the investor, will state the average loan-to-value ratio and the average term. Prior to the loans being packaged for shipment, a person in the mortgage company will, upon receipt of the closing papers from the closing agent, check to see whether all of the lender's instructions have been followed and all of the documents have been signed. If all things are in order, he or she will place the closed loans in a package for shipment to the investor.

Loan servicing After the loan is packaged and shipped to the investor, the mortgage banker still can perform one more function for the investor, and that is to service the loan. This servicing of the loan is the most profitable of all of the operations. Since many of the investors, including Fannie Mae, do not have a servicing function in their operation, they will pay the originator of the loan to service the loan. What is involved in servicing the loan? It may include any or all of the following:

1. The collection of the monthly payment, the application of principal and interest, and the establishment of the escrow account where the proper amount is credited each month for taxes, insurance, and any other required fees.

2. Making the necessary payments on time for the taxes and insurance, including hazard insurance and private mortgage insurance, if any.

3. Acting for the investor in the event of loss due to fire or storm damage. In the case of condemnation procedures, the servicer will receive all awards to be applied to the loan balance and pay all fees and taxes.

4. Providing the borrower, as per the deed of trust or mortgage, with an annual statement of all collections and disbursements from the escrow account, including all taxes and interest paid. This information is to be used by the borrower for federal and state income tax returns.

5. In case of default of the borrower, the mortgage banker or the trustee will handle all of the steps to foreclose against the borrower and secure the property for the investor.

For all of these services, the mortgage banker is paid a fee, usually no less than three-eighths of 1 percent of the loan balance. This amount may seem small, but it represents a major source of income to the mortgage banker.

Mortgage Bankers' Income

The major source of the mortgage banker's income is the servicing of loans. The mortgage banker can also earn income from other sources.

Origination fee This is a fee charged for taking the application, processing, closing, and any other operation that is necessary to get the loan on the books of the mortgage banker and into the servicing portfolio. This origination fee is also the source of payment of the loan officer who is in the field generating loans. The origination fee is usually 1 percent of the loan amount, but when dealing with a mortgage lender for the first time, it is good to ask the loan officer what his or her company charges for origination, prior to your sending a client.

Insurance sales   Some of the mortgage bankers, in addition to making loans, are licensed by the Texas Insurance Commission either to sell insurance or accept a commission from an insurance company. If the mortgage company is licensed to sell insurance, it will usually have a separate insurance company established. The mortgage banker will ask applicants if they have an insurance company they wish to use. If not, the mortgage company will place the required insurance with the insurance company that is owned by the mortgage company. If the mortgage company does not have an insurance company, it will recommend that the applicant use a company that has agreed to pay the mortgage banker a fee or commission for all clients referred to the insurance company.

Real estate sales   Some of the larger mortgage bankers have set up, in addition to insurance companies, real estate firms. These firms usually will sell new homes in subdivisions that are financed by the mortgage banker, but they may also engage in the resale market. One such mortgage banker with a large real estate sale operation is First Mortgage of Texas, located in Houston.

Real estate development   This, for the larger mortgage bankers, is a major source of income. Here, the mortgage banker buys large tracts of land, subdivides, and develops the land for sale to builders. A good example of this is Clear Lake City, near Houston, a development of First Mortgage of Texas. The development and sales of such subdivisions is usually done through the real estate or development company of the mortgage banker.

Gains made from the sales of mortgages
This income is derived when a mortgage banker can sell to an investor mortgages that have a higher yield than is required. For example, an investor issues a commitment to a mortgage banker requiring a yield of 10.50 percent. The interest rate that is in the market place goes to 11.50 percent. The mortgage banker makes the loans at the prevailing rate and then sells them to the investor at the required yield of 10.50 percent. The mortgage banker, then, will be able to keep the dollars generated by the spread, or the difference,

between the 10.50 required yield and the 11.50 yield on the mortgages. This spread will be in addition to the servicing fee paid by the investor.

THE MORTGAGE BROKER

A term sometimes used incorrectly to describe a mortgage banker is *mortgage broker*. The mortgage broker is much like a stockbroker, in that he or she is a specialist in matching persons with money to loan with persons who need to borrow money. His or her services are normally used for the unusual or large loans; for example, the loan on a large office building. For these services, the mortgage broker is paid a fee ranging from one-fourth of 1 percent to 1 percent of the loan amount. Mortgage brokers differ from mortgage bankers in that the broker does not usually originate the loan or have anything to do with processing the loan, closing the loan, or servicing the loan. Nor does the broker have the financial ability to actually fund the loan. A mortgage banker may sometimes act as a mortgage broker, but the true mortgage broker will never act as a mortgage banker. The mortgage broker is in no way involved in the mortgage after the commitment is issued by the lender.

THE FUTURE OF MORTGAGE LENDING

The future of the mortgage banking industry is limitless. As the need for housing continues to grow, the need for mortgage money will also continue to grow. The only limitation on the growth of the industry will be the leadership in the industry. Since the savings and loan associations are the major source of mortgage funds and are now seeking the higher yields of short-term lending, the mortgage bankers will be called on more and more to seek investors that will make the 30-year straight amortization mortgage.

Another factor that will work in the favor of the mortgage banker in the future is the vast number of contacts that have been made by them in the financial field. It is easy for them to move capital from areas of the country with an excess of funds to those areas that are in need of loanable funds.

One of the major problems facing the mortgage banking industry is the lack of trained or knowledgeable personnel. (This need is not unique to the mortgage banking industry.) A person in real estate sales may find that mortgage banking is a good alternate career. The future for the industry as a whole is very bright.

CREDIT UNIONS

The credit union is a mutual type of financial institution where all of the depositors are stockholders in the credit union. Usually, the credit union is founded by a group of individuals who have a common interest. For example, one of the largest credit unions organized to serve the employees involved in education is the Houston Area Teachers Credit Union. This credit union is open to any full-time or part-time employee of a public school, college, or university. In some cases, students attending a college or university are eligible for membership. A credit union can be chartered by either the federal government or the government of the state in which it operates.

The credit unions that are federally chartered are under the control of the Federal Credit Union Act of 1934. This act set forth operating standards and also set the maximum interest rates a credit union could charge. The rate was set at 12 percent and remained at that maximum until the act was amended in July 1981 to allow credit unions to charge up to 21 percent on all loans.

The provisions of the Federal Credit Union Act are administered through the National Credit Union Administration (NCUA). NCUA has its headquarters in Washington, D.C., but, like the Federal Reserve and the Federal Home Loan Bank Board, NCUA has several regional offices that serve various sections of the United States. A map showing the regional structure and the addresses of the regional offices is shown in Figure 6-1. If you are interested, you may secure a list of the federally chartered credit unions in your state by contacting the regional office serving your state.

In addition to the federally chartered credit unions, the states will also charter credit unions. These will be under the supervision of an agency of the state in which the credit union is located and will operate in accordance with the laws of that state.

Real Estate Lending

The following review will be for the federally chartered credit unions.

The regulation covering the real estate lending policy of federally chartered credit unions is contained in the Code of Federal Regulations Title 12, Chapter 7, National Credit Union Administration, beginning with section 701.21-6.

Maximum loan-to-value ratio   Any federally chartered credit union with assets of $2 million or more, and other smaller credit unions with prior written consent, may make real estate loans secured by a first lien on residential property with a maximum loan-to-value ratio of 95 percent as long as the portion of the loan above 90 percent is covered by private mortgage insurance. The exceptions to this rule are loans insured or guaranteed by any agency of a state or the federal government.

Maximum term   The maximum term for a loan secured by real property is 30 years. The regulations further state that these mortgages should have a term of at least twelve years.

Type of properties   The regulation states that the mortgage shall be made to finance or refinance a 1- to 4-family dwelling and that the dwelling shall be used as the principal residence of a member of the federal credit union making the loan.

Sales price limitation   Under the regulation, the sales price of the real estate and improvements shall not exceed 150 percent of the median sales price of residential property in the area in which the property to be used as security for a loan is located.

Interest rate   As stated earlier, the maximum interest rate allowed is 21 percent. It is important to remember that this is the maximum and the actual rate charged by an individual credit union may be less.

Other requirements   All conventional mortgages made by the federally chartered credit unions will be executed on the latest Fannie Mae/FHLMC approved instruments for the state in which the property is located and will *not* contain any prepayment penalty. Insured or guaranteed mortgages originated by the unions will be on the approved instruments of the agency issuing the insurance or guarantee. All fixed-rate, fixed-term mortgages are required to contain a due-on-sale clause. An appraisal on an approved form must be prepared and signed prior to the making of any conventional mortgage. In the case of an insured or guaranteed mortgage, the appraisal must be on a form approved by the insuring or guaranteeing agency.

Figure 6-1.   National Credit Union Administration

National Credit Union Administration

Region, director, address, and phone

Region I:

Bernard Ganzfried
441 Stuart St.
Boston, MA 02116
617-223-6807

Region II:

Carl Zysk
228 Walnut St.
Harrisburg, PA 17108
717-782-4595

Region III:

Stephen Raver
1365 Peachtree St., NE
Atlanta, GA 30309
404-881-3127

Region IV:

Robert E. Boon
234 N. Summit St.
Toledo, OH 43604
419-259-7511

Region V:

Ray Motsenbocker
515 Congress Ave.
Austin, TX 78701
512-397-5131

Region VI:

Earl Bradley
2 Embarcadero Center
San Francisco, CA 94111
415-556-6277

Source: U.S., Office of the Federal Register, National Archives and Records Service, General Services Administration, *United States Directory of Federal Regional Structures 1980-1981*, May 1, 1980, p. 125.

Interest rate adjustment mortgages All of the federally chartered credit unions have been given the ability to make, purchase, or participate in mortgages that have the feature of interest-rate adjustment. These were reviewed in Chapter 3.

Texas-Chartered Credit Unions

As for the credit unions chartered by the state of Texas, they are controlled by the state Credit Union Department. It is the responsibility of this department to enforce the provisions of the Texas Credit Union Act.

The Credit Union Act of Texas allows credit unions to make first lien mortgages secured by real estate, subject to the following restrictions:

1. *Maximum loan-to-value ratio.* On improved property, the maximum loan-to-value ratio is 95 percent of the sales price or appraised value, whichever is less. On all real estate loans that are secured by unimproved property, the maximum loan-to-value ratio is 80 percent of the sales price or appraised value, whichever is less.

2. *Maximum term.* The maximum term for a loan secured by improved property is 40 years from the date the loan is made, and for loans secured by unimproved property the term is not to exceed 20 years.

3. *Other requirements.*

   a. No credit union may make a real estate loan without an appraisal on the property by an appraiser approved by the union.

   b. The union must be furnished a title policy in the principal amount of the loan issued by a title insurance company licensed to operate in Texas or a written opinion by an attorney as to the quality of the title to the property. Most of the credit unions are requesting the title policy.

   c. The credit union must be supplied an insurance policy covering the improvements to the property protecting them from loss by fire and extended coverage. The policy must be in an amount equal to the appraised value of the improvements.

   d. All documents involved in the making of a real estate loan must be promptly filed in the county records in the county where the property is located.

These are the majority of the requirements for the making of real estate loans by credit unions with deposits in excess of $500,000. If you have specific questions regarding these requirements or those of credit unions with less than $500,000 in deposits, contact a credit union near you or the state Credit Union Department:

Credit Union Department of the
State of Texas
914 East Anderson Lane
Austin, Texas 78753

Credit unions in Texas, in the past, have tended to make only short-term real estate loans. That trend, however, has been undergoing change, and credit unions will grow in importance as a source of real estate loans.

PENSION FUNDS

Pension and retirement funds are not a major source of financing real estate, but they are included in this section to make the real estate professional aware of another available source of funds. The money that is accumulated in these types of funds is for the future use of the participants in the fund. The overriding investment philosophy of the funds, then, is security.

It was not until the passage of the Employee Retiree Income Security Act of 1974 that those persons responsible for the operation of these funds were mandated to exercise care in the selection of their investments. They must ensure that the investments are widespread, in order to keep the funds' assets from being placed into one area or type and increasing the chance of loss. The funds have traditionally been invested in stocks and bonds, but with the recent poor showing of these investments, pension funds have been looking for other areas in which to invest. One is the financing of real estate. One of the major forms of real estate financing by these funds is the purchase of GNMA mortgage-backed securities. Some of the major funds are now exploring the possibilities of financing commercial properties and are trying to acquire experienced people for this purpose.

ALTERNATIVE MORTGAGE TRANSACTION PARITY ACT OF 1982

Before we leave the discussion of lenders both the institutional and noninstitutional, the above mentioned federal law should be reviewed. This law is Title VIII of the Garn-St. Germain Depository Institutions Act of 1982.

Findings

According to the findings of the Congress of the United States, the volatility and dynamic changes in the interest rates have limited the ability of the housing creditors to offer and provide to the public the fixed-term, fixed-rate mortgage. This means that the alternative mortgage instruments have become vital to ensure an adequate supply of mortgage money throughout the 1980s. To meet this need, many of the federal financial supervisory agencies, such as the Federal Home Loan Bank Board and the Comptroller of the Currency, passed regulations allowing the federally chartered institutions to make several types of AMIs.

These regulations only allowed the federally chartered institutions to make the AMI and many states had not passed such regulations allowing the institutions in many of the states to engage in a wide variety of AMIs.

Purpose

The purpose of this Title VIII, then, is to eliminate the discriminatory impact of those regulations on the nonfederally chartered housing creditors and to provide them the ability to make, purchase, and enforce the alternative mortgage transaction. The act does state that the AMI must be in compliance with the regulations issued by the federal agencies. It should be noted this authority is given to any state-chartered housing creditor, irrespective of any state law, regulation, court decision, and constitution. Thus, the federal government has preempted the state in the area of AMIs. In Texas, the state-chartered banks, savings and loan associations, and credit unions can make any AMI that is authorized to be made by a federally chartered bank, savings and loan association, or credit union.

REVIEW QUESTIONS

1. Explain the difference between a mortgage banker and a mortgage broker.

2. In your opinion, what are the three major sources of income for a mortgage banker? Explain.

3. Define the term *mortgage servicing* and briefly outline three functions that would be included in the servicing of a loan.

4. Contact several credit unions in your area to see if they are federally or state-chartered. Do they make real estate loans, and, if they do, what is their lending policy?

5. Explain why pension and retirement funds may turn to the financing of real estate.

NOTES

1. Mortgage Bankers Association of America, *Mortgage Banking Terms—A Working Glossary*, 3d ed., Washington, D.C.: January 1978, p. 68.

2. Most of this section is based on material from Mortgage Bankers Association of America, *Evolution of an Industry*, Washington, D.C.: 1973.

3. Mortgage Bankers Association of America, *Mortgage Banking Terms—A Working Glossary*, 3d ed., Washington, D.C.: January 1978, p. 108.

7 Programs of HUD-FHA

LEARNING OBJECTIVES

In this chapter we will examine the mortgage insurance programs of the Federal Housing Administration.

Upon the completion of this chapter you should be able to do the following:

★ Define the basic programs of FHA.

★ Define the major loan reforms established by FHA.

★ Calculate the maximum loan amount available through several FHA programs.

★ List and define the advantages of FHA insured loans.

★ Define *FHA aquisition cost*.

HOMEOWNERS LOAN CORPORATION (HOLC)

Before the Depression, there were very few governmental programs available for the financing of real estate. For the person who wished to purchase a single-family dwelling, there was no government help. As with many other types of investment, the Depression saw the housing industry collapse and millions of people lose their homes due to foreclosure. Realizing the problem of foreclosures, the administration of Franklin D. Roosevelt set up several agencies that would help the homeowner.

The Homeowners Loan Corporation (HOLC) was one of the programs that was established in 1933. The HOLC was to help the homeowner out of the crisis by either refinancing mortgages that were delinquent or purchasing those loans that had gone into default. HOLC put the homeowners back into their homes and set up monthly payments that could be afforded. This agency was later phased out and in its place was created the Federal Housing Administration (FHA).

HISTORY OF FHA

The Federal Housing Administration was created by the passage of the National Housing Act of 1934. With the passage of the Department of Housing and Urban Development Act, Public Law 89-174, all of the functions, powers, and duties of FHA were transferred to the control of the secretary of HUD. FHA was initially established as an experimental agency to help the national housing industry through the creation of a mutual fund for insuring mortgages made by private lenders. Many of the agencies that were created during the post-Depression era have disappeared—but not the FHA. It has become a self-sustaining and standard-setting agency for the federal government.

The purpose of FHA is threefold: (1) to upgrade the nation's housing standards; (2) to promote wider homeownership; and (3) to provide continuing and sound methods of financing home mortgages. But the majority of the financial community that was active in the financing of real estate looked upon FHA as governmental intrusion into the private financing of real estate, and it was not accepted as an answer to the housing problems.

The federal government was determined to make FHA a strong force in the financing of real estate. In 1938, the federal government set up an agency to sell bonds in the open market. The funds raised would be used to purchase mortgages insured by FHA from private lenders. The agency created for this purchase was the Federal National Mortgage Association (Fannie Mae). This made the federal insurance of mortgages even more attractive and was the birth of the secondary market as we know it today. The advent of Fannie Mae allowed lenders to sell mortgages that met the insurance requirements of FHA.

It must be remembered that FHA is not a lender. It does not make loans. FHA issues an insurance policy on loans that meet the underwriting requirements of the National Housing Act. This insurance policy ensures the lender that if the loan goes into default, FHA will make the loan good by taking the property and paying off the lender either in cash or with debentures guaranteed by the United States government.

FHA does appraise the property, and if the property is under construction, it can inspect the property throughout construction. In addition to the appraisal and approval of the property, FHA will approve the borrower. If the property and the borrower meet the underwriting requirements, FHA will insure the loan.

The insurance issued by FHA is called mutual mortgage insurance, and FHA now charges either one-half of 1 percent per annum on the unpaid balance or a one-time lump sum, either paid as a lump sum at closing or financed as part of the loan. This charge is referred to as MIP, or the mortgage insurance premium. This insurance should not be confused with any other type of insurance, such as mortgage payment insurance carried on the borrower. The FHA insurance protects the lender from loss.

Since HUD-FHA was founded to serve all of the United States, the headquarters is in Washington, D.C. The United States has been divided into ten regions and these regions have further been divided with the establishment of area offices to make FHA more responsive to the needs of the different areas of the country.

Texas is part of Region VI, with the headquarters for the region in Fort Worth. In addition to the Regional Office, there are HUD offices located in several Texas cities:

Fort Worth Regional Office
221 West Lancaster
Fort Worth, Texas 76113-2905
(817) 870-5431

Dallas Area Office
5555 Griffin Square
Dallas, Texas 75202
(214) 767-8308

Houston Service Office
Two Greenway Plaza East, Suite 200
Houston, Texas 77046-0294
(713) 954-6821

Lubbock Service Office
Federal Office Building
1205 Texas Avenue
Lubbock, Texas 79401-4001
(806) 743-7265

San Antonio Area Office
Washington Square
800 Dolorosa
San Antonio, Texas 78285-3301
(512) 229-6781

HUD-FHA PROGRAMS

The National Housing Act of 1934 that created the Federal Housing Administration and its programs divided these programs into major categories called *titles* and these were further subdivided into sections. The section numbers are the identifying numbers that the real estate professional uses when referring to FHA programs. Before we review some of the more commonly used sections of the National Housing Act, let us review some of the general rules that apply to most programs.

1. FHA will approve loans on 1- to 4-family dwellings, in subdivisions, planned unit development condominiums, and in rural areas.

2. The maximum term of most loans is 30 years.

3. There is no maximum sales price, but the buyer can pay no more than the FHA appraisal unless the borrower pays cash for the difference between the FHA-appraised value and the sales price. If the appraised price is lower than the sales price, this will affect the maximum amount of loan FHA

will authorize. The only maximum under any of the FHA programs is the loan amount. This amount is set by the U.S. Congress and the secretary of HUD.

4. The maximum interest rate that can be charged on any FHA loan is either set by the secretary of HUD or is negotiated between the borrower and the lender. The negotiated rate applies to all FHA-insured mortgages except those insured under Section 235. No lender may exceed either the rate set or the negotiated rate at the time of funding.

5. Normally, the borrower must occupy the property, but there are sections of the National Housing Act that will allow loans on nonowner occupied property. If you have a question about one of these programs, you should contact the HUD-FHA office nearest you or a lender that is familiar with the programs of HUD-FHA.

6. FHA usually does not allow any secondary financing on the property when making a new loan.

7. FHA requires that an escrow account be established and that the taxes, insurance on the property, principal and interest, and any other fees or assessments that can affect the title to the property be collected monthly.

This chapter will examine the major programs of Titles I and II. We will cover the major programs that you as a real estate professional will use on a regular basis. Appendix E outlines many of the other programs available through HUD-FHA.

MAJOR LOAN REFORMS

In addition to the introduction of mortgage insurance, FHA also introduced major loan reforms.

Fully amortized mortgages   Before the formation of FHA, most mortgages were like balloon mortgages, with all of the principal due at the term of the mortgage. In some cases, the mortgages were interest only with the interest payment due annually, and the full amount of principal due at the end of the term. The life of the mortgage prior to FHA was as little as three years, but FHA extended the term of

the mortgages to as long as twenty years, with the payments due on a monthly basis. These payments were level payments. Each monthly payment was the same; only the amount applied to principal and interest changed.

Higher loan-to-value ratios   Prior to FHA, the loans on property were usually based on 50 to 60 percent of the sales price. FHA raised the loan-to-value ratio to 80 percent of value, a very high ratio for that time. Many lenders also had objections to the high loan-to-value ratio, saying that the investment was not covered by sufficient value even though the loan was insured for 100 percent.

Lower down payments   The advent of the higher loan-to-value ratio meant a lower down payment to the homebuyer and thus made housing available to more of the general public.

Lower interest rates   In keeping with the investment policy that the lower the risk the lower the return, the FHA loan usually has a lower interest rate than the conventional loan. The reason is that the lender is protected from loss by the FHA insurance.

Escrow accounts   Prior to the FHA-insured loan, the person receiving the loan was responsible for seeing that all taxes were paid on time and that there was insurance on the property. As with most people, they did not make allowances for the once-a-year payments, and in many cases the property was lost due to a tax lien. Often the property was damaged by fire and the owner did not have insurance to cover the loss. FHA, with the advent of the escrow account, made sure that the lender was less likely to lose the property due to a tax lien and made sure that there was insurance coverage on the property. This was also an advantage for the property owner in that he or she did not have to make one lump sum payment for taxes and insurance, but would set aside one-twelfth of the cost each month.

Minimum property standards   FHA was the first lender or insurer of mortgages to set minimum standards for the property. These standards have constantly been upgraded to make sure that the property securing the mortgage is safe, sanitary, and livable. The standards covered such things as the amount of insulation, the arrangement of rooms, the number of baths, and the type of wiring used in a house. Some have referred to these standards as a *national housing code*. The requirements of FHA were basically the same no matter where in the United States the property is located.

Then with the passage of the Housing and Urban-Rural Recovery Act of 1983 and the signing of the legislation on November 30, 1983, Title IV, Program Amendments and Extensions, Part A, Subpart 1, Section 405, entitled Minimum Property Standards, all of the HUD-FHA minimum property standards for all types of properties other than manufactured housing were basically eliminated. Paragraph (2) of this section did keep in place the energy conservation portion of the minimum property standards. The paragraph states that the energy performance requirements developed and established by the Secretary of Housing and Urban Development under this subsection for newly constructed homes, other than manufactured homes, shall be effective as the energy performance requirements of the minimum property standards in effect as of September 30, 1982.

The section further states that the Secretary of Housing and Urban Development may require that any property to be insured under any section of this Act, excluding manufactured housing, shall comply with one of the nationally recognized model building codes, or with any state or local code that is based on these model codes.

Standard borrower qualifications Lenders, prior to the advent of FHA, had no firm guidelines for the qualifying of the borrower, thus allowing the lender to set the rule for each person or applicant. They could have refused the applicant for any reason. Sometimes a loan was refused due to the type of work, marital status, race, or religion of the applicant. The standards for qualifying the borrower will be discussed in depth in Chapter 13.

ADVANTAGES OF FHA

There are several advantages of FHA. One advantage is with the higher loan-to-value ratio, the borrower is required to make a lower down payment. The down payment may be as little as 3 percent of the appraised value, but the usual down for the standard fixed-term, fixed-rate mortgage insured by FHA is 3 percent of the first $25,000 of appraised value and 5 percent of the amount in excess of $25,000 to the maximum loan amount that will be insured by FHA in a specific area.

The 3 and 5 percent method of calculating the required down payment applies to properties that have been constructed for one year or more or were constructed under FHA inspection. For those homes that are less than one year old or were not inspected during construction by FHA and/or VA, the required down payment is 10 percent of the value. Even though there is a difference in the down payment, the maximum loan amount is the same.

The usual down payment is 3 and 5 percent, but it may vary with some of the programs available through FHA. As stated earlier, the easing of the down payments from approximately 50 percent allowed more people to purchase homes. Since the loans of FHA are relatively safe and possible loss to the lender is reduced, these loans usually have an interest rate that is below that charged on conventional mortgages or those loans with no governmental backing. With a lower interest rate, the monthly payments are lower, thus allowing a person to qualify for a greater loan amount with no increase in income. The effect that interest rates can have on the amount of the loan was dramatically illustrated in the high interest rates of late 1979 and into 1981. During this period, rates shot up from approximately 9.5 percent to over 18 percent. It was estimated that, with residential mortgage interest rates at 18 percent, only 5 percent of the population could afford housing.

FHA also pioneered allowing a person to assume an existing mortgage without a penalty or escalation of the interest rate. This escalation of interest and a penalty for the assumption of a mortgage still exist today for some types of conventional mortgages. FHA felt that with America being a mobile society, the transfer of property should be made as easy as possible and one way was to allow those mortgages meeting the standards of FHA to be assumable.

Probably one of the most important mortgage reforms instituted by FHA was to allow the borrower to pay off the mortgage prior to the due date of the mortgage without any prepayment penalty or prepayment premium. This lack of prepayment penalty is now a standard feature of all mortgages insured by FHA, but the penalty still can be found in many conventional mortgages. As a real estate professional, you need to know which conventional lenders in your area have prepayment penalties.

As mentioned in the previous section, one of the reforms instituted by FHA was minimum property standards. This is important to a purchaser of a new home in that they assure that the property has been inspected on a periodic basis and has been certified to conform to a minimum set of standards.

DISADVANTAGES OF FHA

Like all programs, the FHA loan has advantages as well as disadvantages. This section will discuss the major disadvantages.

The first disadvantage is that the seller, as with a conventional loan, in some cases may have to pay a discount or points to have a property financed through FHA. Since the interest rate on an FHA loan is usually below the market rate for conventional mortgages, sometimes the interest on FHA is too much below the conventional market and thus lenders are not interested in making FHA loans even though the risk is less. In order for the lender to be interested, he will require the seller to pay additional money up front. This money is usually expressed as a percentage of the loan, called *points*. Each point is equal to 1 percent of the loan amount. These points may be paid by the seller or buyer. These discount points can range from 1 to as many as 15. Thus, if a person wishes to sell a house and the FHA loan is $51,000, each point of discount that is charged by the lender will cost the seller $510, or 1 percent of the loan amount.

In the past, a disadvantage of an FHA loan was that the amount of time for FHA loan approval was rather long. In the past, HUD-FHA required that upon completion of the application and after all of the supporting data had been received, these materials must be sent to the nearest FHA underwriting office. After the materials were received, checked, and found to have no major errors, FHA would issue conditional commitment or conditional approval. This process was very time consuming and could take as long as 6 months in rare cases and usually took 6 weeks. Then on February 23, 1983, the Department of Housing and Urban Development implemented the Direct Endorsement Program. This gave to lenders that meet certain requirements the ability to give in-house approval on FHA-insured loans. Thus, the program cut the time required for loan approval. As a real estate professional, you should contact the FHA office serving your area and secure a list of the mortgage lenders in your area that have met the requirements of the HUD-FHA Direct Endorsement Program allowing them to give in-house approval of mortgages insured by FHA.

The final major disadvantage to the FHA program is that if the property does not meet the minimum standards, prior to the final approval of the loan, the property must be brought to the minimum. This cost can range from a few dollars to several thousand. The cost of repairs is usually borne by the seller, thus making this a disadvantage to the seller. In some instances, sellers will not sell their property FHA-insured because they know that it will not meet the minimum standards. From the purchaser's point of view, however, it is an advantage.

NEGOTIATED INTEREST RATE

Until the passage of the Housing and Community Development Act of 1980, the interest rates for all of the mortgages insured by HUD-FHA were set by the Secretary of HUD. The Act allowed a certain portion of the mortgages insured under Section 203(b) to have an interest rate that was freely negotiated between the borrower and the lender, with certain limitations. The program met with success and, with the passage of the Housing and Urban-Rural Recovery Act of 1983, Section 424 (entitled Elimination of Requirement That Federal Housing Administration Interest Rates Be Set By Law), allows the interest rate for all of the mortgage insurance programs—except for mortgage insured under sections 235 and 232—to be negotiated between the lender and the borrower. In addition, the act now allows the borrower to pay discount points. In the past, the borrower was prohibited from paying any of the discount points so many sellers refused to sell his or her home using FHA-insured financing. Thus, the FHA-insured mortgage is similar to the conventional mortgage in that the borrower has the opportunity to shop for the best interest rate and the seller and borrower can now negotiate who will or will not pay any of the discount points charged in conjunction with any FHA-insured loan.

The only requirement that has been placed on any person, company, or corporation originating an FHA-insured mortgage that has a negotiated interest rate is that the originator must supply to the borrower a disclosure statement. This disclosure must state that the interest rate is not set by the Department of Housing and Urban Development and that the interest rate, any points charged, or any commitment fee are items to be agreed upon by the borrower and lender. According to HUD, the statement is to be delivered to the borrower prior to the borrower's execution of the Borrowers Certification on the application HUD Form 92900.1. A copy of the statement is shown in Figure 7–1.

ONE-TIME MORTGAGE INSURANCE PREMIUM (MIP)

Before we start the discussion of the major programs, the one-time mortgage insurance premium (MIP) should be discussed since it applies to all mortgages insured under sections 203(b), the standard FHA mortgage; 203(i) mortgage insurance on loans in outlying areas; 203(n) mortgage insurance on single units in cooperatives; and 245, the graduated-payment mortgage. It should be noted that section 234(c), mortgages on condominium units, is exempt from the requirement of the one-time mortgage insurance premium.

Prior to September 1, 1983, the mortgage insurance premium was collected for all FHA insurance programs with the monthly payment and was paid once each year as with any other insurance policy. When the program was implemented, there was much confusion over the several methods to calculate the required premium. Then with section 423 of the Housing and Urban-Rural Recovery Act of 1983, several changes were made to the original program. According to this section, the one-time MIP is exempt from loan-to-value ratio and maximum mortgage restriction. Thus, the MIP can be added to the mortgage amount even though it is at the maximum allowed for an area. For example, if the maximum mortgage in an area is $85,000 and your client is applying for the maximum mortgage, the required MIP can be added totally to the mortgage amount even though it will exceed the maximum mortgage amount for the area.

Figure 7–1. Disclosure Statement

Disclosure Statement

This statement regarding the interest rate and discount points that you may pay on a mortgage insured by the Department of Housing and Urban Development (HUD) must be delivered to you prior to execution of the Borrowers Certification on application Form HUD-92900.1.

HUD does not establish the interest rate for mortgage loans to be insured or set either a maximum or minimum on the interest rate or on discount points that may be paid by you. This means that you can pay such interest rates and discount points, as well as a commitment fee to guarantee availability of the terms for a specific period of time, as you and the lender agree upon. The seller can pay the discount points, or a portion thereof, if you and the seller agree to such an arrangement.

It is important for you to understand that the interest rate, any discount points and the length of time the lender will honor the loan terms are all freely negotiable with the lender. Lenders may agree to offer the loan terms for a definite period of time (i.e., 30, 60 or 90 days), or may refuse to do so. Lenders may require payment of a commitment fee for binding themselves for a definite period to make the loan, or to make the loan on fixed terms, or to limit the extent to which such terms may change. Keep in mind that your agreement with the seller will also affect the date you can close the loan.

The terms of your agreement with the lender will determine the degree, if any, that the interest rate and discount points may change before closing. Any increase in the discount points which you as the purchaser are going to pay or an increase of more than one percent in the interest rate requires reprocessing of the loan approval by HUD (or, in Direct Endorsement cases, by the lender). If the lender determines to seek such a reprocessing, it will be necessary for the lender to obtain your signature on a new application. If, after reprocessing, it is determined that you remain eligible from a credit risk standpoint, the conditions of your agreements with the lender and the seller may require you to complete the transaction or lose your deposit.

YOU MUST BE CERTAIN THAT YOU UNDERSTAND THE TRANSACTION. SEEK PROFESSIONAL ADVICE IF YOU ARE UNCERTAIN.

Signed: _____

Date: _____

SOURCE: U.S., Department of Housing and Urban Development, Fort Worth Regional Office, Forth Worth, Texas, Housing Division *Circular Letter* No. 84-3—April 13, 1984.

Under the one-time program a borrower has two options: either pay the premium in cash at closing or finance 100 percent of the premium. It is important that the real estate professional understand how to figure the premium. As with other programs of HUD-FHA, a schedule of premiums is published. The premiums currently in effect are shown in Figure 7-2.

You will note that there are two sets of premiums: one for the borrower who wants to pay the premium in total and one for the borrower who wants to finance 100 percent of the premium. In addition, you will notice the premium increases as the term of the mortgage increases. The reason is that the longer the term the more the risk of loss. FHA charges a higher premium for longer term mortgages. Let us work through an example of how to figure an MIP premium. You are working with a client who is interested in a mortgage insured under Section 203(b), therefore the MIP has to be paid to FHA in one lump sum. Your client does not wish to pay cash for the premium and is seeking insurance for an $85,550 mortgage. What would be the required MIP? Let us assume that your client wants a 30-year mortgage. We go to Figure 7-2 to the column entitled "More than 25" and find, for 100-percent financing, a factor of .03800. Then multiply the mortgage amount by the factor or:

$$85,550 \times .03800 = \$3,250.90$$

This would give the required premium that would be added to the mortgage amount, thus giving a total mortgage amount of $88,800.90, but according to the Department of Housing and Urban Development's Mortgagee Letter 84-8, "when the MIP is financed, you round the mortgage amount down to the nearest dol-

lar". Following these instructions, the mortgage in this example would be rounded down to $88,800.00.

Since the entire MIP is collected at closing, the regulations governing this program require the refund of any unused portion of the MIP. According to Title 24, Code of Federal Regulations, Section 203.283, HUD will refund to the mortgagor unearned MIP if the contract of insurance is terminated before the maturity of the mortgage. In other words, if the mortgage is paid off prior to the maturity date on the mortgage. FHA must refund the remainder of the MIP.

In addition to the refund of any unearned MIP, Title 24, Code of Federal Regulations, Section 203.423, provides that HUD may distribute to the mortgagor a share of the participating reserve account in accordance with sound financial and actuarial practice. Therefore, a person may be due a refund on the unearned or unused portion of the MIP as well as a share of the reserve account. The Department of Housing and Urban Development, on April 2, 1984, published *Mortgagee Letter* 84-9. This letter shows how HUD will calculate both the amount of unearned premiums and distributive shares that will be forwarded to anyone who terminates any FHA-insured mortgage covered by the One-time Mortgage Insurance Premium. Figure 7-3 shows the chart that will be used to calculate the refund of unearned premium for mortgages of 12 percent. Figure 7-4 shows a chart indicating how FHA will figure the distributive shares for insurance terminations occurring in 1984. Therefore, FHA will issue a new chart for each year.

According to HUD, the lender and/or the originator must notify the borrowers who have a mortgage insured under Section 203 of the National Housing Act (including 245 Graduated Payment Mortgage) of the possi-

Figure 7-2.   One-Time MIP Factor Table

One-Time MIP Factor Table				
		Repayment Term in Years		
Portion of MIP Financed	*Less than 18*	*18 to 22*	*23 to 25*	*More than 25*
100%	.02400	.03000	.03600	.03800
0%	.02344	.02913	.03475	.03661

SOURCE: U.S., Department of Housing and Development, *Mortgagee Letter 84-8*—March 30, 1984, p. 2.

Figure 7–3. Refunds of Unearned Premiums

Refunds of Unearned Premiums

The following table illustrates the amount of unearned premium refunds to those persons whose mortgages were insured by FHA under the one-time premium system. The calculations are based on an annual contract interest rate of 12 percent. Those holding mortgages with other contract interest rates will get slightly different refund amounts.

End of policy year unearned premium refund per thousand dollars of insured mortgage amount (including amount of MIP financed).

Term of Loan in Years

Policy Year	15	20	25	30
1	$21.80	$27.70	$34.00	$34.30
2	18.90	24.80	31.60	29.70
3	15.10	20.70	27.30	23.90
4	11.70	16.70	22.50	18.90
5	8.70	13.20	18.00	15.00
6	6.30	10.20	14.10	11.90
7	4.40	7.90	11.00	9.50
8	3.00	6.00	8.50	7.70
9	2.00	4.60	6.70	6.40
10	1.30	3.50	5.30	5.40
11	0.70	2.70	4.30	4.70
12	0.40	2.00	3.50	4.10
13	0.10	1.50	2.90	3.60
14		1.00	2.30	3.20
15		0.70	1.90	2.80
16		0.40	1.50	2.40
17		0.20	1.20	2.10
18		0.10	0.90	1.80
19			0.60	1.50
20			0.40	1.30
21			0.20	1.00
22			0.10	0.80
23			0.00	0.60
24				0.40
25				0.30
26				0.20
27				0.10
28				0.00
29				
30				

Because the table's figures are calculated for the last month of each policy year, mortgagors prepaying before the end of the policy year will receive refunds somewhat larger than those listed above.

SOURCE: U.S., Department of Housing and Urban Development, *Mortgagee Letter 84-9*, April 2, 1984, attachment #1.

bility of a refund of unearned premiums and/or distributive shares. According to HUD's *Mortgagee Letter* 84-9, the lender must make this notification at the time of loan application and at the time of insurance termination. This includes loan pay off. Figure 7–5 shows the Homeowners' Fact Sheet that is to be used for the notification. If a borrower sells his or her home on an assumption, it is vital that the borrower let the lender know of any address changes because, if the person who assumed the FHA mortgage pays off the mortgage, the original borrower may be eligible for a refund.

In all cases where the MIP is to be included in the mortgage, the Assistant General Council, Home Mortgage Division of the Department of Housing and Urban Development, has approved the following to be included in all FHA-insured mortgages secured by a deed of trust in Texas.

In the event that any portion of the lien is found not to be valid as against the homestead, all payments under the note shall be first applied to that portion which is declared to be invalid as against the homestead.

Figure 7–4.   Distributive Shares

Distributive Shares

Distributive shares are dependent on the future performance of mortgages insured by FHA. Distributive shares will be paid only if future experience is favorable, i.e. future insurance terminations and/or losses are less than HUD expects. HUD hopes to be able to pay shares to mortgagors in future, but this cannot be guaranteed.

Annually, near the end of the calendar year, HUD determines distributive shares that would be payable to mortgagors whose mortgage insurance may be terminated during the following year. Using FHA insurance in force data of the previous March 31 as a basis, HUD actuarially computes a share factor per thousand dollars of the original mortgage amount for each group of mortgages, i.e. the same endorsement year and term. Subsequently, when the FHA insurance is terminated on an individual mortgage, the applicable share factor, if any, is multiplied by the mortgage amount to calculate the amount of share payable. If, there is no applicable share factor at time of termination, no share is payable.

Listed below are the share factors (per $1,000 of the original mortgage amount) to be used for insurance terminations occurring in 1984, by endorsement year and term. Note that *N/A* means the term is no longer applicable for the endorsement year and *0* means no share factor was declared for the endorsement year.

Endorsement Year	40 Yr Term	35 Yr Term	30 Yr Term	25 Yr Term	20 Yr Term
1953	N/A	N/A	91.56	N/A	N/A
1954	N/A	N/A	91.40	N/A	N/A
1955	N/A	N/A	90.95	N/A	N/A
1956	N/A	N/A	90.22	N/A	N/A
1957	N/A	N/A	90.79	N/A	N/A
1958	N/A	N/A	90.23	75.97	N/A
1959	N/A	N/A	89.34	76.37	N/A
1960	N/A	N/A	87.47	75.83	N/A
1961	91.67	91.67	84.75	74.40	N/A
1962	88.65	88.65	82.47	73.24	N/A
1963	85.48	85.48	79.99	71.79	45.11
1964	82.16	82.16	77.31	70.06	41.24
1965	78.71	78.71	74.45	68.08	34.30
1966	75.90	75.90	72.22	66.65	24.47
1967	72.44	72.44	69.29	60.38	8.46
1968	0	69.06	56.38	42.52	0
1969	0	65.80	39.66	31.87	0
1970	0	62.11	25.90	25.14	0
1971	0	56.79	5.65	10.07	0
1972	0	41.08	0	0	0
1973	0	15.34	0	0	0
1974	0	18.81	0	0	0
1975	0	27.30	0	8.90	0
1976	0	17.23	0	5.27	0
1977-84	0	0	0	0	0

SOURCE: U.S., Department of Housing and Urban Development, *Mortgagee Letter 84-9*—April 2, 1984, Attachment #2.

Section 203(b) Home Mortgage Insurance

This section of the National Housing Act is the oldest and the most commonly used of all of the HUD-FHA programs. For insurance under this section, the properties must meet the minimum property standards but there are no special qualifications for the borrowers. Any individual who has a good credit record and can demonstrate the ability to make the required down payment and the payments on the mortgage can be approved.

This program, as well as the other HUD-FHA single-family insurance programs, is available for use in all areas, both rural and urban, provided that the market exists for the property. Full mortgage insurance is available for properties that are approved prior to the beginning of construction or are completed for more than one year. Those properties that are under construction or that have been com-

pleted less than one year, if not covered by a homeowner warranty, can be approved for insurance, but only to a maximum of 90 percent of the value and closing cost up to the maximum loan available.

The following maximum loan amounts were established by Congress in December 1979:

One-family	$67,500
Two-family	$76,000
Three-family	$92,000
Four-family	$107,000

Since 1980, with the passage of the Housing and Community Development Act, Public Law 96-399 allows the secretary of HUD to increase these maximum mortgage amounts on an area-by-area basis annually. This authority to increase mortgage amounts on mortgages insured under Section 203(b) was implemented for the first time on November 20, 1980, by

Figure 7–5.   Homeowners' Fact Sheet

Homeowner's Fact Sheet

Mortgage Insurance Premium (MIP) Refunds and Distributive Shares

---

Refunds of Unearned One-Time MIP

When a mortgage insurance premium is paid in a one time payment at the time of mortgage closing, the borrower will be eligible for a refund of any unearned premium if the insurance is terminated prior to maturity of the mortgage with no insurance claim involved. HUD began the one-time premium system September 1, 1983 for a limited number of insurance programs. If you are not sure that the MIP was paid in full at loan closing, ask your lender. You do not need to be the original borrower to be eligible for a refund.

How Are MIP Refund Amounts Determined?

HUD determines the amount of the premium refund by multiplying the insured mortgage amount at the time the mortgage was insured by the applicable premium refund factor for mortgages insured in the year the mortgage was endorsed for insurance. The applicable premium refund factor is determined each year, taking into account projected salaries and expenses, prospective losses generated by insurance claims and expected future payments of premium refunds. As an *example*, a borrower with a $50,000 30-year term mortgage at 12 percent interest paid off after five years would receive a refund of approximately $760 (50 × 15.20). At the end of ten years, the refund would be approximately $275 (50 × 5.50), and after 20 years, approximately $65 (50 × 1.30), would be refunded. Mortgages with different interest rates will get slightly different refund amounts.

Distributive Shares

A distributive share is a payment to a homeowner out of any existing participating reserves of the Mutual Mortgage Insurance (MMI) Fund. HUD analyzes the total reserves of the MMI Fund in terms of its expected income and expenses. Reserves in excess of what is needed to cover expected expenses are participating reserves. You are eligible for a distributive share if:

1. Your mortgage is insured under any MMI Fund Section of the Act. Most Section 203 mortgages (including 245 Graduated Payment Mortgages) are in the MMI Fund.

2. Your mortgage insurance is terminated by payment in full, voluntarily terminated, or terminated by default that does not result in a claim to HUD.

3. Your mortgage (at time of termination of the FHA insurance) is part of a group of mortgages for which HUD has determined that a distributive share amount is payable (mortgages are grouped by mortgage characteristics such as year endorsed for insurance and term to maturity).

How Are Distributive Share Amounts Determined?

Each year in December, HUD determines the amount to be paid on eligible cases, from each group, terminating in the following year. Groups with low loss experience are more likely to receive a distributive share than groups with higher losses. In no case will a distributive share be greater than the premiums paid on the mortgage. Currently, a distributive share for a 30-year mortgage is authorized only when a mortgage has been insured for twelve years or more at the time of termination. As an example, a $10,000, 30 year term mortgage, endorsed in 1970 and terminated in 1984 would pay a share of $259.00 (10 × 25.90). A similar mortgage endorsed in 1968 would pay a share of $563.80 (10 × 56.30).

Payment of MIP Refund And/Or Distributive Shares

1. When termination of the FHA insurance is required before maturity of a mortgage, the lender submits a Form HUD-2344, Lenders Request For Termination of Home Mortgage Insurance, to HUD. For maturities the lender responds to HUD's request for confirmation that the mortgage is paid in full. In either instance the lender provides HUD with the current name(s) and address of the borrower (mortgagor).

2. HUD determines if a refund of MIP and/or distributive share is due. If a payment is due, HUD sends a claim form to the borrower for signature and return to HUD. This form is normally sent within 90 days after termination.

3. After receipt of the signed form, HUD has the payment mailed to the borrower. Payment is normally made within 45 days after receipt of the claim form.

4. For those qualifying for payment, it is important that a forwarding address be provided to the lender at the time of mortgage insurance termination so that HUD can send the claim form to the proper location. *The borrower should verify that the lender furnished a current mailing address to HUD.*

Assumptions

When an FHA-insured mortgage is assumed, the insurance continues in force and there will be no refund or unearned premiums or distributive shares. In the case where the original borrowers financed the one-time MIP, the assumptors assume the payments of the remaining MIP as a part of the total mortgage payment. On the other hand, when the original borrowers paid the one-time MIP in cash, they would not be able to recover from HUD that portion which might be considered unearned premiums unless they negotiate with the assumptors in a side agreement. HUD will not become involved in these negotiations.

Borrower Inquiries

Requests for information should be forwarded to: U.S. Department of Housing and Urban Development/Director, Mortgage Insurance Accounting and Servicing, OFA/Attn: Insurance Operations Division/Washington, DC 20410

Include the FHA Case Number for the mortgage, date the HUD insurance was terminated, and whether your inquiry pertains to *Refund of One-Time MIP* or a *Distributive Share*. Please wait 90 days after termination of FHA insurance before submitting an eligibility inquiry.

SOURCE: U.S., Department of Housing and Urban Development, *Mortgagee Letter 84-9*—April 2, 1984, Attachment #3.

then Secretary Moon Landrieu. The current adjustment of the maximum mortgage for areas of Texas is shown in Figure 7–6.

If the area in which you live is not listed, the maximum mortgage amount that will be insured is the amount that was authorized by the Congress in 1979. These amounts may change annually. To find the present maximum mortgage amount for your area, contact any FHA-approved lender or the nearest office of HUD.

The down payment for Section 203(b), as mentioned earlier in this chapter, is calculated one of three ways. The method to be used is dependent on the value of the home to be purchased. Prior to the passage and implementation of Section 424 of the Housing and Urban-Rural Recovery Act of 1983, there had been only one way to calculate the down payment for a mortgage insured under Section 203(b). Section 424 states that

if the mortgage to be insured covers a property on which there is a one- to four-family residence to be occupied as the principal residence of the owner, and the appraised value of the property, as of the date of the mortgage is accepted for insurance, does not exceed $50,000, the principal obligation may not be in an amount to exceed 97 percent of the value.

Since the loan-to-value ratio can be as much as 97 percent, the borrower would only be required to make a down payment equal to 3 percent of the value. It should be noted that according to *Mortgagee Letter 84-8*, Office of the Assistant Secretary for Housing–Federal Housing Commissioner, dated March 30, 1984, the term *appraised value of the property* has always been interpreted as the appraised value of the property plus closing costs.

The second method of calculating the down payment is for homes with a value in the excess of $50,000 and was the only method used for many years before the implementation of the down-payment calculation for modestly priced homes. The method used to calculate the down payment for a home with a value exceeding $50,000 is as follows:

3 percent of the first $25,000 of value and closing costs, plus

5 percent of the value and closing costs in excess of $25,000 to the maximum loan available.

You will notice that in calculating the down payment, the closing costs are included. When the closing costs are included, HUD-FHA

refers to this as the *acquisition cost* of the property. The closing costs that are to be used when figuring the acquisition cost are the average for your area. The HUD-FHA office will furnish you with a schedule of closing costs used in your area or you can call a mortgage lender that originates HUD-FHA loans who will be glad to furnish you with the estimated closing costs.

An example of the information that will be furnished by your local HUD office is illustrated in Figure 7–7. For example, if you are selling real estate in Coppell and your client would like to purchase a home valued at $87,500, the acquisition cost of this home would be the sales price of $87,500 plus the estimated FHA closing cost of $1450 or $88,950. It is important when dealing with FHA to know the difference between the value of the home and the acquisition cost of the property.

Now let us calculate the down payment for the home in Coppell. According to FHA, first we take 3 percent of the first $25,000 of value and closing costs:

$25,000 × 3 percent = $750

Second, FHA tells us to take 5 percent of the value and closing costs in the excess of $25,000 to the maximum loan amount:

$88,950 − $25,000 = $63,950
$63,950 × 5 percent = $3197.50

Then to get the calculated down payment we would add the two subtotals:

$3197.50 + $750.00 = $3947.50

What then would be the maximum loan that would be insured by FHA on this home? To calculate this there are two methods. First we could subtract the calculated down payment from the acquisition cost of the home or:

$88,950 − $3947.50 = $85,002.50

It should be noted that FHA will only make loans in even $50 amounts. According to FHA, you always round down to the nearest $50. For this example, we would round the loan amount down to $85,000, thus reducing the loan amount by $2.50. This amount is then added to the down payment or:

$3947.50 + $2.50 = $3950.00

The second method used to calculate the maximum loan amount and the down payment

Figure 7–6. Schedule of Section 203(b) Area-Wide 1- to 4-Family Mortgage Limits

For any market area in Texas not listed below, the following maximum mortgage limits shall apply: $67,500 for a one-family unit; $76,000 for a two-family unit; $92,000 for a three-family unit; and $107,000 for a four-family unit.

Market area designation and local jurisdictions	Mortgage limits			
	1-family and condominium unit	*2-family*	*3-family*	*4-family*
Region VI				
HUD Field Office: Dallas Office				
Dallas, TX PMSA Collin County .... Dallas County Denton County Ellis County Kaufman County Rockwall County	$90,000	$101,300	$122,650	$142,650
Sherman-Denison, TX MSA Grayson County	$78,000	$88,000	$106,500	$124,000
HUD Field Office: Fort Worth Office				
Ft. Worth-Arlington, TX PMSA Johnson County .... Parker County Tarrant County	$90,000	$101,300	$122,650	$142,650
HUD Field Office: Houston Office				
Houston, TX PMSA Brazoria County .... Fort Bend County Harris County Liberty County Montgomery County Waller County	$90,000	$101,300	$122,650	$142,650
HUD Field Office: Lubbock Office				
Amarillo, TX MSA Potter County .... Randall County	$68,500	$77,000	$93,500	$108,500
Lubbock, TX MSA Lubbock County	$70,000	$78,500	$95,500	$110,500
Midland, TX MSA Midland County	$70,000	$78,500	$95,500	$110,500
HUD Field Office: San Antonio Office				
Austin, TX MSA Hays County .... Travis County Williamson County	$90,000	$101,300	$122,650	$142,650
San Antonio, TX MSA Bexar County .... Comal County Guadalupe County	$82,750	$93,250	$113,250	$130,700
Corpus Christi, TX MSA Nueces County .... San Patricio County	$70,000	$78,500	$95,500	$110,500

SOURCE: "Rules and Regulations," *Federal Register*, May 22, 1984, vol. 49, no. 100, p. 21525.

Figure 7-7.   FHA Schedule of Closing Costs

SCHEDULE OF CLOSING COSTS FOR USE IN
THE FORT WORTH REGIONAL OFFICE AND DALLAS OFFICE

Market Price of Property	Total Closing Costs	Market Price of Property	Total Closing Costs
$10,000	$ 700	$ 86,000	$1400
$11,000	$ 700	$ 87,000	$1450
$12,000	$ 700	$ 88,000	$1450
$13,000	$ 750	$ 89,000	$1450
$14,000	$ 750	$ 90,000	$1450
$15,000	$ 750	$ 91,000	$1450
$16,000	$ 750	$ 92,000	$1500
$17,000	$ 750	$ 93,000	$1500
$18,000	$ 800	$ 94,000	$1500
$19,000	$ 800	$ 95,000	$1500
$20,000	$ 800	$ 96,000	$1500
$21,000	$ 800	$ 97,000	$1550
$22,000	$ 800	$ 98,000	$1550
$23,000	$ 850	$ 99,000	$1550
$24,000	$ 850	$100,000	$1550
$25,000	$ 850	$101,000	$1550
$26,000	$ 850	$102,000	$1600
$27,000	$ 850	$103,000	$1600
$28,000	$ 900	$104,000	$1600
$29,000	$ 900	$105,000	$1600
$30,000	$ 900	$106,000	$1600
$31,000	$ 900	$107,000	$1600
$32,000	$ 900	$108,000	$1650
$33,000	$ 900	$109,000	$1650
$34,000	$ 950	$110,000	$1650
$35,000	$ 950	$111,000	$1650
$36,000	$ 950	$112,000	$1650
$37,000	$ 950	$113,000	$1700
$38,000	$ 950	$114,000	$1700
$39,000	$1000	$115,000	$1700
$40,000	$1000	$116,000	$1700
$41,000	$1000	$117,000	$1700
$42,000	$1000	$118,000	$1750
$43,000	$1000	$119,000	$1750
$44,000	$1050	$120,000	$1750
$45,000	$1050	$121,000	$1750
$46,000	$1050	$122,000	$1750
$47,000	$1050	$123,000	$1800
$48,000	$1050	$124,000	$1800
$49,000	$1050	$125,000	$1800
$50,000	$1100	$126,000	$1800
$51,000	$1100	$127,000	$1800
$52,000	$1100	$128,000	$1800
$53,000	$1100	$129,000	$1850
$54,000	$1150	$130,000	$1850
$55,000	$1150	$131,000	$1850
$56,000	$1150	$132,000	$1850
$57,000	$1150	$133,000	$1850
$58,000	$1150	$134,000	$1900
$59,000	$1200	$135,000	$1900
$60,000	$1200	$136,000	$1900
$61,000	$1200	$137,000	$1900
$62,000	$1200	$138,000	$1900
$63,000	$1200	$139,000	$1950
$64,000	$1250	$140,000	$1950
$65,000	$1250	$141,000	$1950
$66,000	$1250	$142,000	$1950
$67,000	$1250	$143,000	$1950
$68,000	$1250	$144,000	$2000
$69,000	$1250	$145,000	$2000
$70,000	$1250	$146,000	$2000
$71,000	$1300	$147,000	$2000
$72,000	$1300	$148,000	$2000
$73,000	$1300	$149,000	$2000
$74,000	$1300	$150,000	$2050
$75,000	$1300	$151,000	$2050
$76,000	$1350	$152,000	$2050
$77,000	$1350	$153,000	$2050
$78,000	$1350	$154,000	$2050
$79,000	$1350	$155,000	$2100
$80,000	$1350	$156,000	$2100
$81,000	$1400	$157,000	$2100
$82,000	$1400	$158,000	$2100
$83,000	$1400	$159,000	$2100
$84,000	$1400	$160,000	$2150
$85,000	$1400		

Mortgage lenders requiring a complete breakdown of the individual closing costs can call the Valuation Branch at (817) 870-5538.

is to multiply the first $25,000 of value and closing costs by 97 percent and then to multiply all of the value and closing costs in excess of $25,000 to the maximum loan amount by 95 percent. Let us use the same home as in the previous example and calculate the loan amount and the required down payment.

The value of the home is $87,500 plus the estimated closing cost of $1450 or $88,950. First, let us multiply $25,000 times 97 percent or

$25,000 × 97 percent = $24,250

Second, we will multiply all of the value in excess of $25,000 to the maximum loan amount by 95 percent or in this case:

$88,950 − $25,000 = $63,950
$63,950 × 95 percent = $60,752.50

To calculate the maximum loan amount add the two values together:

$24,250 + $60,752.50 = $85,002.50

Once again we would need to round down to the nearest $50 or $85,000.00. This is the same amount as was previously calculated. Then to figure the down payment, subtract the maximum loan amount from the acquisition cost and again the down payment will equal $3950.00.

The third method is the method used by some mortgage lenders as well as some Loan Specialists in the Mortgage Credit section of some of the HUD-FHA offices. With this method, the value or basis of the property is multiplied by 95 percent; then $500 is added to the answer. It should be noted that the "basis" can either be the acquisition cost of the property or the value of the property as established from an earnest money contract. Let us use the same example as in the previous two methods. The value of the home is $87,500 plus the estimated closing costs of $1,450, or $88,950. First let us multiply $88,950 times 95 percent or

$88,950 × 95 percent = $84,502.50

Then $500 is added to the $84,502.50 or

$84,502.50 + $500.00 = $85,002.50

Once again we would round down to the nearest $50 or $85,000.00. This is the same amount that was determined using the other two methods.

As outlined earlier in this chapter, the maximum term for a loan insured under this section is 30 years. Prior to the passage of the Housing and Community Development Act of 1980, the term of the FHA 203(b) mortgage was either 30 years or three-quarters of the remaining economic life, whichever was less. Section 333 of the act deleted all references to remaining economic life as one of the criteria for determining the maximum term for an insurable FHA mortgage. This deletion was made in several programs, including any mortgage insured under Section 203(b) of the National Housing Act.

203(b) Veteran This is a special program for veterans through FHA. This program should not be confused with the Veterans Administration guaranteed home loan that will be discussed in the next chapter. This program is sometimes called 203(b) Vet mortgage insurance. For a veteran to qualify under this program, it is best for the veteran to have used up all of his or her entitlement under the program authorized by the Veterans Administration. Furthermore, the veteran must have served for 90 consecutive days on active duty. In some cases the veteran who served less than 90 days may be allowed to use the plan if the Secretary of Defense will certify that the veteran served on hazardous duty. In addition to the service requirements, the veteran must have received a discharge other than dishonorable.

This insurance program is only available for single-family dwellings and the veteran must reside in the dwelling. The insurance will not cover mortgages on duplexes, triplexes, or fourplexes. The mortgage term for this program is 30 years. The maximum loan amount for the 203(b) Vet mortgage insurance is $67,500, or the same as the limit for a single-family dwelling under the regular 203(b).

The major difference in this program and the standard 203(b) program is the amount of down payment. Under the FHA Vet insurance program, the veteran pays no down payment of either the first $25,000 of value and closing costs, or $25,000 plus prepaid expenses less $200, whichever is less. It should be noted that the $200 is the minimum closing cost for 203(b) Vet . The veteran will pay 5 percent of the value and closing costs on the excess above $25,000 to the maximum of $67,500.

One additional advantage of FHA Vet insurance is that a veteran can use the program more than once.

With the FHA Vet program, a veteran can actually afford the same house as under 203(b), but the amount of front money, or the money needed for the down payment, is less. For example, a veteran would like to purchase a house valued at $54,700 with an estimated closing cost of $1000, equaling an acquisition cost of $55,700. The veteran would be required to make a down payment calculated as follows:

No down on the first $25,000	0
5% of the excess of $25,000, or $55,700 minus $25,000 = $30,700 × 5%	$1535
Total down payment	$1535

The amount of money that would be needed for the down payment under 203(b) would be calculated as follows:

3% of first $25,000	$750
5% of the excess of $25,000, or $30,700	$1535
Total down payment	$2285

From this comparison, one can see that a veteran can save $750 in down payment, but the $750 will be added to the mortgage balance. The dollar savings may not seem significant, but the loan-to-value ratio changes significantly. Under 203(b), the loan-to-value ratio is approximately 96 percent, whereas under the 203(b) Vet, this ratio is increased to 97 percent.

In regard to the loan amount, FHA will only insure loans that are rounded down to the nearest $50. The maximum loan that FHA would insure on the previous two examples would be:

203(b)

Acquisition costs	$55,700
Less down payment	$ 2,285
Loan amount	$53,415

The actual loan amount when rounded down to the nearest $50 would be $53,400. The $15 dropped from the loan amount would have to be added to the down payment, making it $2300.

203(b) Vet

Acquisition costs	$55,700
Less down payment	$ 1,535
Loan amount	$54,165

Using the same criteria, rounding down to the nearest $50, the actual loan amount would be $54,150. Once again, the amount that the loan is reduced will be added to the down payment, thus making it $1550.

There is one additional method that may be used to calculate the maximum mortgage. This method is similar to the last method shown in the previous portion of this chapter. With this method for 203(b) Vet, the basis of the property is multiplied by 95 percent; but instead of adding $500, you will add $1250. This $1250 includes the first $750 of the down payment that is added to the loan amount. Using the same acquisition cost of $55,700, this amount, then, is multiplied by 95 percent or

$$\$55,700 \times 95 \text{ percent} = \$52,915.00$$

Then the $1250 is added to this amount or

$$\$52,915 + \$1250 = \$54,165.00$$

Once again this amount is rounded down to the nearest $50 or $54,150. This is the same amount that was calculated in the other method used to calculate the maximum loan amount.

Buy down   Under this program HUD will allow the seller/builder to set up an escrow account to be used to reduce the monthly payment of the buyer/borrower.

This represents a change in HUD's policy regarding any gift or contribution of monies to the buyer of a property. Prior to the issuance of HUD's Mortgagee Letter 81-23, in June 1981, HUD held that any such gift and/or contribution was an inducement to the buyer to purchase a property. HUD felt that the loan-to-value ratio was also reduced.

With the issuance of the Mortgagee Letter, HUD revised its policy to allow the institution of the buydown program. Under this program, the interest rate is reduced in the early years of the mortgage with the establishment of an escrow account to supplement the monthly payment made by the buyer.

According to HUD, this program will allow more people to become eligible for mortgages, particularly first-time homebuyers.

The program will use the reduced initial payment as the basis for underwriting the mortgage and is available under Sections 203, 234(c) and 245(a) plan IV of the National Housing Act.

The program authorized is subject to the following rules:

1. The mortgage loan must be a level payment, unsubsidized mortgage. Both new and existing homes are eligible for this procedure.

2. The payments to reduce the interest chargeable to the buyer shall run for a minimum of 3 years.

3. The assistance payments will not diminish the normally required Monthly P & I payments by more than the payment which would be calculated on a mortgage with an interest rate which is 3 percentage points less than the interest rate on the mortgage. For example, on a $15\frac{1}{2}$ percent mortgage, the assistance payment could not reduce the amount the mortgagor would pay below the monthly payment on a $12\frac{1}{2}$ percent mortgage. Any scheduled reductions of the assistance payments during this period must be uniform and must occur on the annual anniversary date of the mortgage payment.

4. Payments will be made by the escrow agent. The escrow agreement must require the escrow agent to make the payments to the mortgagee which is the holder of the mortgage, or its servicing agent.

5. The agreement may provide for reversion of undistributed escrow funds to builder/seller if the property is sold by the borrower or the mortgage is prepaid in full. At the option of the builder/seller, the agreement may also provide that assistance payments will be made for the benefit of buyers who assume the mortgage.

6. Repayment of escrow funds may not be required.

7. In order that the buyer may be fully protected, the funds must be held in an escrow account with a financial institution which is not the originating or servicing mortgagee and is supervised by a federal or state agency. (All banks and savings associations are supervised financial institutions.) This will insure the availability of the funds and preclude any possibility that the buyer will be forced to make the payments called for in the note prior to the scheduled termination of the escrow. However, if, for some unforeseen reason the escrow payments are not forthcoming, it is the mortgagor's responsibility to make the total payment set forth in the mortgage note.

8. In the event of foreclosure, the claim for mortgage insurance benefits will be reduced by the amount of the remaining escrow only if the mortgagee has received the balance of the escrow at the time of the claim. The escrow agreement must provide that, should the mortgage be foreclosed, the balance remaining in the escrow account must be immediately paid to the mortgagee which acquired title to the property.

9. Applications will be processed on the basis of the reduced mortgage payment for the first year.

10. Firm commitments involving applications in which underwriting has been based on the reduced monthly payment must contain a condition which requires assurance that the funds described in the approved plan have been placed in escrow prior to or at closing and meet the requirements set forth herein.

In these particular situations the acquisition cost shall not be reduced to reflect the amount of cash placed in escrow for the benefit of the buyer. The mortgage will be computed on our estimate of value plus closing costs or acquisition cost, whichever is the lesser.

Applications involving escrow arrangements which do not meet *all* of the above criteria are to be processed with the monthly assistance payments considered as a strong compensating factor. In these instances, there will be no commitment requirement for evidence that the funds have been placed in escrow.[1]

Section 221(d)(2) Homeowner Assistance for Low- and Moderate-Income Families

Section 221(d)(2) of the National Housing Act provides mortgage insurance for the purchase of homes by low- and moderate-income families and by families displaced by government action or by major disaster declared by the President of the United States. HUD-FHA has not set an income maximum. As long as the applicant meets one of the other qualifications, the income can be any amount. This is particularly true for those people displaced by governmental action or by natural disaster. The program can also be used to finance the rehabilitation of substandard properties, but, in regard to this type of property, HUD-FHA will have to be supplied with a certificate showing that the property meets the minimum housing standards after rehabilitation.

The terms of the loans insured by this section are divided into three categories. The first category is for displaced families. The normal term is 30 years, but terms of 35 or 40 years are authorized if the person or family cannot qualify for a 30-year term. This means that if the applicant's income is insufficient to meet the 30-year payment, it may be extended to 35 or 40 years to help the applicant qualify. For other than displaced families, the normal term is 30 years, but if the applicant is unacceptable under the 30-year term, it may be extended to 35 or 40 years. Also, the house must have been built under HUD-FHA or VA inspections. The last category is for other than HUD-FHA existing construction. For this type, the maximum term is 30 years.

The maximum loan amounts that can be insured under this section are divided into two categories. One is for normal or average cost areas and the second is for properties located in areas designated by HUD-FHA as areas of high cost. These costs refer to the cost of construction. The current maximum loan amounts for a normal cost area are as follows:

1-family unit	$31,000
2-family unit	$35,000
3-family unit	$48,600
4-family unit	$59,400

The maximum of $31,000 for a 1-family unit is increased to $36,000 if the property is occupied by a family of 5 or more and the property has 4 or more bedrooms. In areas where the costs so require, the above limits can be increased up to the following:

1-family unit	$36,000
2-family unit	$45,000
3-family unit	$57,600
4-family unit	$68,400

As before, if the 1-family unit is occupied by a family of 5 or more and the property has 4 or more bedrooms, the maximum loan amount is increased to $42,000.

In Texas, each of the HUD-FHA offices is responsible for the designations of areas of high costs. In general, all areas of Texas are allowed to make above the minimum and in some counties, HUD-FHA allows the amount of the mortgage to be increased to the maximum loan allowed for high-cost areas. To find the maximum loan allowed in your area, you will need to contact a HUD-FHA lender in your area or the nearest HUD-FHA office.

Loan-to-value ratios   The loan-to-value ratios under this section are calculated as follows:

1. Displaced families

   A. For properties approved by HUD-FHA prior to construction or completed 1 year or more, the loan-to-value ratio is 100 percent of either the sum of the FHA estimate of value and closing costs, or the sum of the FHA estimate of value, closing costs, and prepaids, less $200 per unit, whichever is less.

   B. For construction completed less than 1 year, the maximum loan-to-value ratio is 90 percent of the sum of the HUD-FHA estimate of value and closing costs.

   C. For the rehabilitation of property, the loan-to-value ratio is 100 percent of either the HUD-FHA estimate of value before rehabilitation, plus closing costs, plus the estimated costs of rehabilitation, or, the HUD-FHA estimate of value, plus the prepaid expenses, plus the closing costs minus $200 per unit, whichever is less.

2. Low- to moderate-income families

   A. One unit

      1. For properties approved by HUD-FHA prior to construction or completed more than one year, HUD-FHA uses the following method to calculate the loan-to-value ratio. The loan-to-value ratio is either 100 percent of the sum of the HUD-FHA estimate of value and closing costs, or 97 percent of the sum of the HUD-FHA estimate of value and closing costs, plus prepaids, whichever is less.

      2. For construction completed less than one year, the ratio is 90 percent of the sum of the HUD-FHA estimate of value and closing costs.

   B. 2- to 4-family units

      1. For construction completed more than one year, or approved by HUD-FHA prior to construction, the ratio is figured identically to the method used for 203(b). It is 97 percent of the first

$25,000 of estimated value and closing costs and 95 percent of the excess of $25,000 in estimated value and closing costs to the maximum loan amount.

2. For construction completed less than one year, the maximum loan is calculated in the same manner as Section 203(b), or 90 percent of the estimated value and closing costs.

3. For rehabilitation, the maximum loan-to-value ratio is figured using the same method as outlined for the displaced family.

Even though Section 221(d)(2) indicates that the loan-to-value ratio can be 100 percent in some cases, the prospective homeowner is required to make a minimum cash investment in the property. This cash investment may not be less than 3 percent of the total cost of acquisition and may include items of prepaid expenses.

Section 221(d)(2) was designed to aid the homeowner displaced by urban renewal. In the past three years, this program has become less important to the real estate professional.

Section 235(i) (Revised): Homeownership Assistance for Low- and Moderate-Income Families

Section 235(i) provides for insurance and interest subsidies to low- and moderate-income families to enable these families to afford safe and sanitary housing that meets HUD-FHA standards.

This housing can either be new construction or substantially rehabilitated single-family units, with the construction or rehabilitation approved by HUD-FHA on or after October 17, 1975.

For the purpose of this section, *substantially rehabilitated* is defined as the improvement of a unit in deteriorating or substandard condition to a decent, safe, and sanitary level meeting HUD-FHA standards for mortgage insurance. One other measure of substantial rehabilitation is that the cost of the rehabilitation must be at least 25 percent of the value of the property after the completion of the rehabilitation.

The latest amendments to the National Housing Act allow insurance to be issued on an existing dwelling or a family unit in an existing condominium project which meets HUD-FHA standards.

Under this program, HUD-FHA can make supplemental payments for eligible families directly to the mortgage lender in an amount that will reduce the payment for the homeowner to a level that would equal an interest rate of 4 percent. For example, if the prevailing interest rate on all HUD-FHA insured loans is $13\frac{1}{2}$ percent, then HUD-FHA can make payments for the homeowner that would reduce the payment equal to a principal and interest payment on a 4 percent mortgage. What does this mean in real dollars? Say an applicant wishes to get a loan in the amount of $35,000 and the interest rate is $13\frac{1}{2}$ percent. The payment for principal and interest would be $400.89. If the applicant, however, qualifies for the 235 subsidy, the payment would be reduced to a 4 percent level, or $167.30 per month. It must be pointed out that the 4 percent interest rate is the maximum subsidy that is allowed under this section.

As with other sections, HUD-FHA has maximum loan amounts for which it can issue insurance. As with Section 221(d)(2), the loan amounts are divided into two categories: one for the normal-cost areas and another for high-cost areas. The maximum will vary if the house has three or four bedrooms. The loan amounts authorized in the 1980 Housing and Community Development Act are as follows:

	Normal Cost	High Cost
3-bedroom house	$40,000	$47,500
4-bedroom house with 5 or more people	$47,500	$55,000
2-family dwellings	$55,000	$61,250

In Texas, the HUD-FHA maximum loan limit is set at the maximum (high cost). To find the maximum loan available in your area, contact an approved HUD-FHA lender or the nearest HUD-FHA office.

The maximum loan amount in your area will also establish the maximum sales price. The guidelines state that the sales price may be up to, but not exceed, 120 percent of the maximum mortgage amount. In some cases, this will require a greater cash investment by the buyer to reduce the purchase price down to the maximum. Another stipulation regarding sales price is that no property may be purchased under Section 235 at a price, excluding closing costs, which exceeds the FHA estimate of value.

This section also requires a buyer to make a minimum cash investment. This amount shall be 3 percent of the acquisition cost and is to be paid in cash by the buyer. As explained in the previous paragraph, the buyer can put down any amount of money he or she wishes, but 3 percent is the minimum.

In addition to the minimum investment and the type of property, this section also limits the amount of income a person or family may be making in order to qualify for the subsidies. These incomes will vary with each area of Texas and the size of the family. Contact any approved FHA lender for the income limits in your area.

There is one additional requirement placed on the applicant by Section 811 of the Housing and Community Development Act of 1974. It requires that HUD-FHA provide counseling and advice to Section 235 homeowners. This counseling and advice will deal with such subjects as home maintenance, financial management, and any other subjects to assist the homeowner in improving housing conditions and meeting the responsibilities of home-ownership.

To keep any area from becoming too concentrated with Section 235 homeowners, as occurred under the program prior to the present revision, the revised Section 235 states that no subdivision, neighborhood, or single residential area shall have over 40 percent of the homes assisted by Section 235. This 40 percent rule is applicable to the sum of vacant lots plus built-upon lots within a tract under centralized control.

Furthermore, the 235 mortgage is assumable. The person who is planning to assume such a loan must qualify under the same requirements as the original borrower. One fact should be noted regarding the assumption: even though the person assuming the mortgage is anticipating no subsidy payments and will make the regular principal and interest payments, there will be no reduction in the premium charges for the mortgage insurance. This factor will increase the regular payment slightly, for the insurance premium on Section 235 is set at 0.7 percent instead of the 0.5 percent as charged on other HUD-FHA insured loans.

Section 245(a): Federal Mortgage Insurance for Graduated Mortgages

The graduated-payment mortgage was authorized under Section 245 of the National Housing Act and was implemented in November 1976 under provision of the Housing and Community Development Act of 1974. It was not until the passage of the Housing and Community Development Act of 1977, however, that we find the present form of the Graduated-Payment Mortgage (GPM). HUD's objective with the GPM was to develop and promote new methods of mortgage financing that would allow early homeownership for families with stable incomes and a potential to grow in the future. The GPM allows these homeowners to make lower payments in the initial years of the mortgage and for the payments to increase gradually over a specified time.

The GPM is likely to appeal to the first-time homebuyer, but is not limited to the first-time buyer in the middle-income range because it allows homebuyers to tailor their monthly installments to present income and the future growth potential of that income. As with any of the other mortgage insurance programs of HUD, the program is open to all persons or families that have good credit and show the ability to make the necessary initial investment and the potential to make the monthly payments. They must also show that they have, or expect to have, enough steady and increasing income to make the future mortgage payments.

How does the GPM work?   Simply stated, the GPM is a mortgage where the early payments are low and rise over a period of time. It should be noted that the early payments of a GPM are not sufficient to cover the amount needed to amortize the loan fully, so the homeowner is borrowing additional monies that are added to the principal balance to be paid back in the future. To state this another way, it is said that the GPM for the first few years is in negative amortization.

Persons applying for the GPM must be aware that the monthly payments to principal and interest will increase each year for the next 5 to 10 years depending upon which of the GPM plans is selected. Applicants should also be aware that over the life of the mortgage, they will pay more interest than if they had secured a level-payment loan. Finally, any persons who will use the GPM must be made aware that they will have to make a larger down payment than those required under Section 203(b) or a level-term mortgage.

As stated earlier in this section, there are several GPM plans available to the prospective homebuyer. The GPM offers 5 separate plans. The 5 basic GPM plans vary the rate of the annual monthly payment increase from 2 percent per year to 7.5 percent per year and vary the number of years over which the payments will increase from 5 to 10 years.

The following will give the percent of increase and the number of years of increase for each plan:

Plan I – The payment will increase at the rate of 2.5 percent per year for 5 years.

Plan II – The payment will increase at the rate of 5 percent per year for 5 years.

Plan III – The payment will increase at the rate of 7.5 percent per year for 5 years.

Plan IV – The payment will increase 2 percent per year for 10 years.

Plan V – The payment will increase 3 percent per year for 10 years.

It is important to note that the monthly payments only increase yearly, not monthly, and that at the end of either the fifth or tenth year the payments are level and are higher than those of a level or straight amortized mortgage. The reason for the higher payment, as stated previously, is that the homeowner has been in negative amortization and is now starting to repay the funds borrowed.

Of all the plans listed, Plan III has become the most popular, for it allows the lowest initial monthly payment. This can be easily illustrated when comparing the monthly payments on a mortgage of $50,000 with an interest rate of 9 percent for a term of thirty years (see Figure 7–8). Since the homebuyers are qualified based on the first year's monthly payment and other housing expenses, one can see that under Plan III the prospective homebuyer would need a lesser income to qualify.

The GPM has the same term as mortgages insured under Section 203(b), that is, up to a maximum of 30 years. The interest on these loans is set by the Secretary of Housing and Urban Development. The premium for the mortgage insurance is similar to Section 203(b) or 0.5 percent.

The maximum loan amount under Section 245(a) is the same as 203(b), thus it is set area-by-area, but the loan must be calculated for

each sales price, according to Section 203.45 of HUD regulations. The maximum mortgage amount shall not exceed the lesser of the following:

1. 97 percent of the first $25,000 of value and closing costs, plus 95 percent of the remaining value and closing costs

2. "An amount which, when added to all deferred interest pursuant to the financing plan selected, shall not exceed 97 percent of the appraised value of the property covered by the mortgage as of the date the mortgage is accepted for insurance. However, if the mortgagor is a veteran, the mortgage amount, when added to all deferred interest pursuant to the financing plan selected, shall not exceed the applicable limits prescribed for veterans under Section 203(b). It is necessary therefore, to compute the allowable loan amount both on the basis of the method applicable to Section 203(b) as well as on the basis of 97 percent of the value including deferred interest."[2]

To better understand the meaning of these methods, let us work through an example. We assume the following:

HUD Value	$70,000
Closing Costs	$1,250
Acquisition Cost	$71,250

As per the regulation, the maximum loan amount will be the lesser of the two methods, or:

Criterion I

97 percent of $25,000	$24,250
95% of the remaining ($46,250)	$43,937.50
Calculated maximum loan	$68,187.50

Figure 7–8. Monthly Payment (P & I)—Section 245(a)

Year	203(b)	I	II	III	IV	V
1	$402.50	$366.22	$333.53	$303.94	$355.97	$334.47
2	$402.50	$375.38	$350.21	$326.74	$363.09	$344.51
3	$402.50	$384.76	$367.72	$351.24	$370.35	$354.84
4	$402.50	$394.38	$386.11	$377.59	$377.76	$365.49
5	$402.50	$404.24	$405.41	$405.91	$385.32	$376.45
6	$402.50	$414.35	$425.68	$436.35	$393.02	$387.75
7	$402.50	$414.35	$425.68	$436.35	$400.88	$399.38
8	$402.50	$414.35	$425.68	$436.35	$408.90	$411.36
9	$402.50	$414.35	$425.68	$436.35	$417.07	$423.70
10	$402.50	$414.35	$425.68	$436.35	$425.42	$436.41
11-30	$402.50	$414.35	$425.68	$436.35	$433.92	$449.50

Since HUD-FHA will only insure loans rounded down to the nearest $50, the actual maximum loan is $68,150.00.

Now let us review Criterion II. The initial calculation is different from Criterion I in that we take 97 percent of the total cost plus the closing costs, or 97 percent of $71,250, resulting in $69,112.50. Then this value is divided by the highest outstanding balance loan factor. This factor is used to calculate the highest loan balance that will occur. These factors will change each time the interest rate either increases or decreases or a different plan is selected. For this example, we will use the factor for 12 percent interest and Plan III. On the fifth page of the table in Appendix B (discussed in more detail below) that value is 1078.7082. Therefore, $69,112.50 divided by 1078.7082 is $64,070.00. In this case, the lesser of the two criteria is Criterion II, thus establishing the maximum loan as $64,050.

Now let us review how an increase in the interest rate will affect the maximum loan for this same piece of property. In this case, the interest rate will be 13.5 percent. The calculation for Criterion I will remain the same as in the example above. Under Criterion II, however, the calculation will change because of the change in the interest rate. We still begin with 97 percent of $71,250, or $69,112.50. Then we divide $69,112.50 by the highest outstanding loan balance factor for Plan III with an interest rate of 13.5 percent, or 1095.1195. This results in a maximum loan of $63,109.55. In this case, we can see that Criterion II is the lesser and the maximum loan amount is reduced to $63,100 by some $950, when the interest rate is increased to 13.5 percent.

The highest outstanding loan balance factors for Plan III, the most commonly used plan, are shown in Appendix B. The appendix lists these factors for interest rates from 7.75 to 17.50 and is broken down in one-quarter percent steps. To find a factor using these tables, first locate the appropriate interest rate at the top of the column, then find the underlined factor listed below it. This is the highest outstanding balance factor at that interest rate. For example, if the present interest rate is 13.75 percent and the client is interested in Plan III, first find the pages in Appendix B for interest rates from 12.75 to 15.00 percent. Then, look for the 13.75 interest rate below which you will find the underlined factor appears as the sixtieth payment and is 1097.6900. This factor would be used to calculate the maximum loan amount.

You will note that this table not only gives the maximum outstanding balance factor, but also the factors to be used to calculate the out-standing principal balance of the mortgage at any time over the life of the mortgage. For example, if you as a real estate professional have listed a home financed by a GPM Section 245(a) with an interest rate of 10.00 percent using Plan III and the present owner has just made the fortieth payment, the factor for that payment is 1051.3538. This factor would then be multiplied by the original loan amount (in thousands) to get the present outstanding principal balance. For example, if the original loan amount was $50,000, the balance would be $50 \times 1051.3538 = \$52,567.69$.

Now that we have figured the maximum loan that is available on this property, let us calculate the required down payment. Using the maximum loan for 13.5 percent interest, the prospective homeowner would have the following required down payment:

Acquisition price	$71,250
Maximum loan amount as calculated earlier	$63,100
Required down payment	$ 8,150

How does this down payment compare with the required down payment under Section 203(b)?

97% of the first $25,000	$24,250
95% of remaining $46,250	$43,937.50
Maximum loan	$68,187.50
	or
	$68,150.00

In order to get the required down payment, we will subtract the maximum loan amount from the acquisition cost:

Acquisition cost	$71,250
Maximum loan amount	$68,150
Required down payment	$ 3,100

From this example, one can see that under Section 245, the required down payment is substantially increased—from $3100 under Section 203(b) to $8,150 under Section 245(a). It also must be remembered that the down payment is not all of the initial investment the prospective homebuyer may be required to make. The additional cost will include the required prepaids, and if the seller does not wish to pay the closing costs, the buyer will also have these expenses.

Now that we have figured the maximum loan amount and the required down payment, we need to learn how to calculate the first year's monthly payment, for this will be the payment that will be used to qualify the client.

The monthly payment is divided into two basic portions: (1) the amount of the payment to be applied to interest charges and principal reduction, and (2) the amount to be escrowed to pay the taxes, insurance, and any other fees that may affect the title to the property. In the following we will discuss how to calculate the first item. Once again using Plan III, this time with an interest rate of 10.75, the monthly payment is calculated by multiplying the original loan amount by a factor. These factors are shown in Appendix C. Turning to this appendix and looking for the proper interest rate under Plan III, we find that the factor for the first year is 7.1277. Multiply this factor by the original loan amount (expressed in thousands) and obtain a monthly payment for principal and interest of:

$$7.1277 \times 50.00 = \$356.385 \text{ or } \$356.39$$

With this table, one can calculate the monthly payment (excluding escrows) for a Plan III mortgage at any time during the term of the mortgage.

Section 245(b)

In addition to the standard Section 245, Congress has authorized an additional 245 program. This program in no way alters the existing Section 245(a), but it creates an all-new mortgage insurance program. This section is presently known as Section 245(b). This section will permit the principal obligation of the mortgage to rise during the mortgage to an amount higher than the initial appraised value of the property.

This program of insurance will have the following limitations. First, insurance under this section will only be issued on the properties approved by HUD-FHA prior to the start of construction or substantial rehabilitation, or on properties under construction involving Section 203(b) that are covered by an approved insured-homeowner warranty plan.

The program is limited to 50,000 mortgages or 10 percent of the original principal balance of all mortgages on 1- to 4-family dwellings insured by HUD in the previous fiscal year, whichever is greater.

This program is available only to prospective homebuyers who have not held title to property within the 3-year period preceding their application for a Section 245(b) GPM. The homebuyer must sign a statement to this effect.

Also, this program is limited to applicants for mortgage insurance who could not reasonably afford to purchase their home under the original Section 245 or other FHA insurance programs.

This program is limited to two plans, in contrast to the 5 plans offered under the original 245 program. The two programs are as follows:

1. The payments will increase at the rate of 4.9 percent per year for a period of 10 years.

2. The payments will increase at the rate of 7.5 percent per year for a period of 5 years.

Maximum mortgage amounts will be established locally. This established limit may not exceed the maximum mortgage amount for Section 203(b).

The FHA field offices have been given formulas that will be used to calculate the maximum loan amounts for both plans. The formulas are based on the face interest rate of the mortgage. Some of the formulas are illustrated in Figure 7–9. In regard to the amount of down payment or investment required, there are formulas to calculate these amounts. According to Mortgagee Letter 80-33 from the Office of the Assistant Secretary for Housing—Federal Housing Commissioner, formulas shown in Figure 7–9 will be used to calculate the minimum down payments for the two plans authorized. In other words, you will have to figure the amount of the down payment under Section 203(b) for the amount of the loan for which your client is making application and also multiply the acquisition cost by the proper percentage to see which is larger.

This section has certain limits as to the amount the mortgage balance may increase. There are two limitations, but the one that will have the greatest effect is that the mortgage amount may increase to an amount that, when all of the deferred interest is added, can never exceed 113 percent of the original appraised value of the home, or 97 percent of the projected value of the property. The projected value is determined by increasing the value of the property at a rate not to exceed 2.5 percent per year during the period when the payments of the mortgage are increasing.

Growing Equity Mortgage (GEM)

On June 4, 1982 the Department of Housing and Urban Development issued a memorandum announcing the growing equity mortgage. According to the memo, Section 245(a) of the National Housing Act authorizes the insuring of mortgages with varying rates

Figure 7–9.   *Loan-to-value (LTV) Ratio Tables and Cash Investment for Section 245(b)*

7½ Percent for 5 Years

	11½%*	12%	13%	14%
Maximum insurable loan non-veteran as well as veteran	Lesser of 203(b) limits or 96.98% of value	Lesser of 203(b) limits or 96.86% of value	Lesser of 203(b) limits or 96.63% of value	Lesser of 203(b) limits or 96.29% of value
Minimum investment requirements non-veteran loans only	Greater of 203(b) requirement or 3.02% of acquisition cost	Greater of 203(b) requirement or 3.14% of acquisition cost	Greater of 203(b) requirement or 3.37% of acquisition cost	Greater of 203(b) requirement or 3.71% of acquisition cost

*At rates less than 11½ percent, the maximum insurable mortgage will be limited by the 203(b) loan-to-value and cash investment ratios. At rates falling between those listed above, use the loan-to-values for the next higher rate. For example, if the rate is 11⅞ percent, use the loan-to-value ratio at 12 percent.

4.9 Percent for 10 Years

	12%*	13%	14%
Maximum insurable loan non-veteran as well as veteran	Lesser of 203(b) limits or 96.76% of value**	Lesser of 203(b) limits or 96.08% of value	Lesser of 203(b) limits or 94.43% of value
Minimum investment requirements non-veteran loans only	Greater of 203(b) requirement or 3.24% of acquisition cost	Greater of 203(b) requirement or 3.92% of acquisition cost	Greater of 203(b) requirement or 5.57% of acquisition cost

*At rates less than 12 percent, the maximum insurable mortgage will be limited by the 203(b) loan-to-value and cash investment ratios. If the interest rate falls between the amounts shown, the loan-to-value ratio will be the same as the next highest rate. For example, if the rate is shown as 12½ percent, use the loan-to-value ratios at 13 percent.

**Value means the HUD estimate of value including closing cost.

SOURCE: U.S. Department of Housing and Urban Development, Office of the Assistant Secretary for Housing—Federal Housing Commissioner, *Mortgagee Letter 80-33—August 7, 1980*, p. 3.

of amortization, both negative and positive. In the previous section, we reviewed the graduated-payment mortgage with negative amortization. In this section, we review the growing equity mortgage (GEM), also insured under Section 245(a). One major difference is that the GEM allows for accelerated amortization.

First, we should define *growing equity mortgage*. This mortgage is very similar to the GEM discussed in Chapter 3 and the definition is very similar. A GEM can be defined as a first-lien mortgage secured by real property, with a fixed interest rate, where the first-year payment is based on a 30-year amortization of the mortgage amount and the fixed-interest rate. The remaining monthly payments increase at a specified amount for a specified number of years, with all increase credited to principal balance. What is the difference then? For example, with this GEM the number of available plans for payment increase is limited.

According to the HUD, with the scheduled increase in monthly payments credited to principal reduction, the term of the mortgage is shortened. Even though the first-year payment is based on a 30-year amortization, the term of the mortgage is dramatically shortened. The actual term of the mortgage will be determined by the amount of the annual payment increase and the interest rate. Since the term of the mortgage is greatly shortened and the lender's funds are tied up for a shorter period, normally the interest rate on the GEM is below the current rate on 30-year fixed-rate mortgages.

After working under the original GEM memo dated June 4, 1982, for about two years, the Department of Housing and Urban Development on May 8, 1984, published a final rule for the Growing Equity Mortgage. The effective date of the rule was June 13, 1984. The rule allows the GEM to be insured under sections 203 mortgage insurance for certain 1- to 4-family dwellings and 1-family condominium units under Section 234(c) of the National Housing Act.

Authorized Payment Increases

According to the final rule, after the initial period (normally the first year), the monthly payment may increase either every year or every two years, or at such intervals as may be approved by the HUD. HUD in the final rule has limited the maximum payment increase from one year to the next. This limit is 5 percent. In the original memo, HUD had set only two increases, 2 or 3 percent per year for a period of 10 years. Thus, with the final rule, the payments may increase at any rate 1, 1.5, 2, etc., with the limit of five percent. There is no mention of a maximum or minimum period for the increase.

Term   The term of the GEM is limited to the term shown in Appendix D. For example, if the GEM is increasing at the rate of 2.00 percent per year and the interest rate is 15.50, the term in months listed at the bottom of the column is 197 months or 16 years and 5 months. Therefore, even though the initial monthly payment is calculated for a term of 30 years, the actual term is only 16 years and 5 months. If you review each of the interest rates for each of the plans, you can see that the term for the GEM varies for each interest rate.

Down payment   According to the HUD, because there is no negative amortization the down payment will be calculated in the same manner as for Section 203(b).

Monthly payments   As with the GPM, HUD-FHA has prepared tables for the calculation of the GEM monthly payments. Appendix D shows the monthly payment factors. It should be noted that the monthly payment factors are only for the P & I portion of the payment. You will have to add the utilities, maintenance, and taxes to get the total housing expenses.

For example, if you are working with a client who is interested in a $64,500 insured mortgage and the GEM interest rate is 14.75, you would calculate the first year's principal and interest payment as follows: For the 2.00 percent increase, GEM principal-and-interest payment, read across the column headings in Appendix D (with increasing payments for ten years at 2.00 percent each year) until you find the interest rate 14.75. Look down that column on the line opposite year 1: the factor listed is 12.444757. The factor is then multiplied by the loan amount in thousands or 64.50. This gives 802.686 or $802.69.

This procedure would then be repeated for the 3.00 percent increase plan. It could then be decided which of the plans would best suit your client.

Application and underwriting   When making application for the GEM, the standard HUD-FHA application will be used, but the applicant will be required to sign a *GEM Certification*, shown in Figure 7–10.

Figure 7–10.   GEM Certification

GEM Certification

I/We certify that I/we fully understand the obligation I/we am/are undertaking, that my/our mortgage payment to principal and interest will start at $ _____ and will increase by __ % each year for 10 years to a maximum payment of $ _____ at the end of the 10th year. I/we understand that the __ % increase for the first 10 years of my/our mortgage is being used to reduce my/our outstanding principal balance.

Principal Interest   Mortgage Insurance Premium

$ _____ During the 1st note year $ _____ During the 1st note year
$ _____ During the 2nd note year $ _____ During the 2nd note year
$ _____ During the 3rd note year $ _____ During the 3rd note year
$ _____ During the 4th note year $ _____ During the 4th note year
$ _____ During the 5th note year $ _____ During the 5th note year
$ _____ During the 6th note year $ _____ During the 6th note year
$ _____ During the 7th note year $ _____ During the 7th note year
$ _____ During the 8th note year $ _____ During the 8th note year
$ _____ During the 9th note year $ _____ During the 9th note year
$ _____ During the 10th note year $ _____ During the 10th note year
$ _____ During the 11th note year $ _____ During the 11th note year
         and thereafter   and thereafter

In addition I/we will be required to make payment toward taxes, hazard insurance and other costs of homeownership.

Also, I/we certify that I/We have been advised of the present maximum FHA interest rate for 30-year level payment mortgages, which is __ %.

Signed

_____
Mortgagor

_____
Mortgagor

Source: U.S., Department of Housing and Urban Development, Seattle Area Office, Seattle, Washington, *Circular Letter No. 82-08—June 18, 1982.*

All underwriting of the GEM will be based on the first year's payment. The actual process of underwriting the loan will be discussed in Chapter 14.

Note and deed of trust   As with the negative amortization mortgages insured under Section 245(a), the standard HUD-FHA note and deed of trust must be altered. One of the major modifications is the inclusion of the subtitle "With Increasing Monthly Installments" on both the note and the deed of trust. The note will also show the schedule of payments. These modifications are shown in Figures 7-11 and 7-12.

Temporary Mortgage Assistance Payments Program (TMAP)

The Housing and Community Development Act of 1980 revised Section 230 of the National Housing Act to authorize the Secretary of Housing and Urban Development to make all or part of the mortgage payments on such a mortgage directly to the lender on behalf of the homeowner.

Homeowner eligibility   Before a homeowner can be eligible for the program, the secretary must determine that the temporary mortgage assistance payments, or TMAPs, are necessary to avoid foreclosure, and that the homeowner will be able to meet the following:

1. Resume full mortgage payments within 36 months after the beginning of the TMAP or upon the termination of the TMAP

2. In addition to making the regular monthly payment on the mortgage, be able to start the repayment of all funds advanced under the TMAP at the time designated by the Secretary of Housing and Urban Development

3. Be able to repay the mortgage by its maturity date or by a later date established by the secretary

Amount of payments   TMAPs can be made in an amount that is equal to the total monthly mortgage payment. The initial payment under the TMAP may include an amount that will bring the mortgage current. It should be noted that this payment may not exceed the amount established by the secretary deemed necessary to supplement the amount the homeowner can contribute toward the total monthly mortgage payment.

Payment period   TMAPs can be made for an initial period of 18 months and any period of default. The period can be extended by the secretary for a period not to exceed an additional eighteen months. The primary reason for the extension is to keep the mortgage from going into foreclosure. There must be a reasonable expectation that, with the extension, the homeowner will be able to repay the mortgage as well as all of the funds advanced under the TMAP.

Repayment of the TMAP   The funds advanced under the TMAP are regarded as a loan and are required to be repaid by the homeowner receiving the TMAP. The term of the repayment will be set by the secretary and may include any monies paid by the secretary to the lender for expenses incurred in conjunction with the delinquency of the mortgage. The secretary may require that interest be charged on the amount advanced under the TMAP, but the interest rate shall not exceed the interest rate established for mortgages insured under Section 203(b) at the time the TMAP assistance is approved. It should also be noted that these interest charges are exempt from any state or local usury law.

Section 234(c): Mortgage Insurance for Condominium Units

Section 234(c) was originally designed to insure only mortgages on condominiums in HUD-approved projects. This authority, however, has been expanded. With the passage of the Housing and Community Development Amendments of 1979, HUD, through FHA, was allowed to insure mortgages on individual units in a condominium project that were built without HUD-FHA project approval and inspection during construction. The purpose of this authority is to provide FHA insurance on the resale of the units that were conventionally financed, in order to help in the resale of these units.

For the project to qualify for this program it must meet the following requirements:

1. All units were built for conventional financing

2. The project has been under construction for at least 1 year

3. Eighty percent of the units are sold or have intent or contracts to be sold to owner occupants

Figure 7–11.   GEM Note

| This form is used in connection with mortgages insured under the one-to four-family provisions of the National Housing Act. | **NOTE** | FHA CASE NO. |

SECTION 245
APPROVED FORM

Rev. 6-80

(To be used with Deed or Trust or Mortgage)
WITH INCREASING MONTHLY INSTALLMENTS

, Washington.
, 19

$

FOR VALUE RECEIVED, the undersigned promise(s) to pay to the order of

the principal sum of
Dollars

($), with interest from date at the rate of
per centum (%) per annum on the balance remaining from time to time unpaid. The said
principal and interest shall be payable at the office of

in

, or at such other place as the holder may designate, in writing, in monthly
installments of

$	during the 1st Note Year	$	during the 7th Note Year
$	during the 2nd Note Year	$	during the 8th Note Year
$	during the 3rd Note Year	$	during the 9th Note Year
$	during the 4th Note Year	$	during the 10th Note Year
$	during the 5th Note Year	$	during the 11th Note Year
$	during the 6th Note Year		and thereafter,

commencing on the first day of   , 19   , and on the first day of each month thereafter, until the
principal and interest are fully paid, except that the final payment of the entire indebtedness evidenced hereby, if
not sooner paid, shall be due and payable on the first day of

If default be made in the payment of any installment under this note, and if such default is not made good prior to
the due date of the next such installment, the entire principal sum and accrued interest shall at once become due
and payable at the option of the holder of this note. Failure to exercise this option shall not constitute a waiver of
the right to exercise the same in the event of any subsequent default. If any suit or action is instituted to collect
this note or any part thereof the undersigned promise(s) and agree(s) to pay, in addition to the costs and disbursements provided by statute, a reasonable sum as attorney's fees in such suit or action.

The undersigned, whether principal, surety, guarantor, endorser, or other party hereto, agrees to be jointly and
severally bound, severally hereby waive demand, protest and notice of demand, protest and nonpayment, and
expressly agree that this note or any payment thereunder may be extended from time to time and consent to the
acceptance of further security, including other types of security, all without in any way affecting the liability of
such parties.

_____   _____

_____   _____

_____

Source: U,S., Department of Housing and Urban Development, Seattle Area Office, Seattle, Washington, *Circular Letter No.*
82-08—June 18, 1982.

Figure 7–12.   *GEM Deed of Trust*

STATE OF WASHINGTON

DEED OF TRUST

> This form is used in connection with deeds of trust insured under the one- to four-family provisions of the National Housing Act.

WITH INCREASING MONTHLY INSTALLMENTS

THIS DEED OF TRUST, is made this _____ day of _____ , 19 ____ ,

BETWEEN _____ , as Grantor,

whose address is _____ ;

and _____ , as Trustee,

whose address is _____ ;

and _____

_____ , as Beneficiary,

whose address is _____

Grantor hereby irrevocably grants, bargains, sells and conveys to Trustee in trust, with power of sale, the following described property in _____ County, Washington:

TOGETHER WITH all the tenements, hereditaments, and appurtenances now or hereafter thereunto belonging or in anywise appertaining, and the rents, issues and profits thereof.

THIS DEED IS FOR THE PURPOSE OF SECURING PERFORMANCE of each agreement of Grantor herein contained and payment of the sum of _____ Dollars ($ _____),

with interest thereon according to the terms of a promissory note of even date herewith, payable to Beneficiary or order and made by Grantor, and also such further sums as may be advanced or loaned by Beneficiary to Grantor, or any of their successors or assigns, together with interest thereon at such rate as shall be agreed upon.

The Grantor covenants and agrees as follows:

1. That he will pay the indebtedness secured hereby, Privilege is reserved to pay the debt in whole, or in an amount equal to one or more monthly payments on the principal that are next due on the note, on the first day of any month prior to maturity: *Provided, however,* That written notice of an intention to exercise such privilege is given at least thirty (30) days prior to prepayment.

2. Grantor agrees to pay to Beneficiary together with and in addition to the monthly payments of principal and interest payable under the terms of the note secured hereby, on the first day of each month until said note is fully paid, the following sums:

     (a) An amount sufficient to provide the Beneficiary with funds to pay the next mortgage insurance premium if this instrument and the note secured hereby are insured, or a monthly charge (in lieu of a mortgage insurance premium) if they are held by the Secretary of Housing and Urban Development, as follows:

         (I) If and so long as said note and this instrument are insured or are reinsured under the provisions of the National Housing Act, an amount sufficient to accumulate in the hands of the Beneficiary one (1) month prior to its due date the annual mortgage insurance premium, in order to provide the Beneficiary with funds to pay such premium to the Secretary of Housing and Urban Development pursuant to the National Housing Act, as amended, and applicable regulations thereunder; or

         (II) If and so long as said note and this instrument are held by the Secretary of Housing and Urban Development, a monthly charge (in lieu of a mortgage insurance premium) which shall be in an amount equal to one-twelfth (1/12) of one-half (1/2) per centum of the average outstanding balance due on said note computed without taking into account delinquencies or prepayments;

     (b) A sum, as estimated by the Beneficiary, equal to the ground rents, if any, and the taxes and special assessments next due on the premises covered by this Deed of Trust, plus the premiums that will next become due and payable on such insurance policies as may be required under paragraph 9 hereof, satisfactory to Beneficiary, Grantor agreeing to deliver promptly to Beneficiary all bills and notices therefor, less all sums already paid therefor divided by the number of months to elapse before one (1) month prior to the date when such ground rents, premiums, taxes and assessments will become delinquent, such sums to be held by the Beneficiary in trust to pay said ground rents, premiums, taxes and special assessments; and

     (c) All payments mentioned in the two preceding subsections of this paragraph and all payments to be made under the note secured hereby shall be added together and the aggregate amount thereof shall be paid by the Grantor each month in a single payment to be applied by Beneficiary to the following items in the order set forth:

         (I) premium charges under the contract of insurance with the Secretary of Housing and Urban Development, or monthly charge (in lieu of mortgage insurance premium), as the case may be:

         (II) ground rents, if any, taxes, special assessments, fire and other hazard insurance premiums;

         (III) interest on the note secured hereby; and

         (IV) amortization of the principal of said note.

     Any deficiency in the amount of any such aggregate monthly payment shall, unless made good by the Grantor prior to the due date of the next such payment, constitute an event of default under this Deed of Trust. The arrangement provided for in paragraph 2 is solely for the added protection of the Beneficiary and entails no responsibility on the Beneficiary's part beyond the allowing of due credit, without interest, for the sums actually received by it. Upon assignment of this Deed of Trust by the Beneficiary, any funds on hand shall be turned over to the assignee and any responsibility of the assignor with respect thereto shall terminate. Each transfer of the property that is the subject of this Deed of Trust shall automatically transfer to the Grantee all rights of the Grantor with respect to any funds accumulated hereunder.

Replaces FHA-2189T, which may be used.   HUD-92189T (3-79)

Source: U.S., Department of Housing and Urban Development, Seattle Area Office, Seattle, Washington, *Circular Letter No. 82-08—June 18, 1982.*

4. The developer or declarant has no remaining interest (there is one exception to this: if the construction or conversion has not reached a level where the developer or declarant no longer has an interest, but the document of the development or conversion contains a provision for such a phasing out of the developer, the project may qualify)

To make application under this program of mortgage insurance, the person will make application on the standard FHA application form and supply some additional exhibits which must accompany the application. (This information is only required to accompany the first application in a project.)

The number of required exhibits depends on whether the project was approved by Fannie Mae or VA. Approval by FHLMC will not be recognized by FHA. For projects which have only FHLMC approval, you will need to contact your local FHA office for approval requirements.

HUD has prepared a listing (Figure 7–13) of the documents that must accompany the first application for mortgage insurance in such a condominium project. You will notice that under the portion of the figure dealing with conventional or Fannie Mae approval, it lists the information for project approval and unit appraisal.

Under the section dealing with VA-approved projects, HUD-FHA will require no information or documents; but for the individual unit appraisal HUD-FHA will require certain information. Figure 7–13 also shows what is needed when making application for mortgage insurance for a resale in a HUD-approved project.

The maximum loan amount under Section 234(c) is identical to that of Section 203(b) and that is $67,500, unless the secretary of HUD has designated an area to be a high-cost area and has increased the maximum mortgage amount. Those areas so designated by the secretary are shown in Figure 7–6.

Under this program, mortgages on both owner-occupied and nonowner-occupied units are eligible for mortgage insurance. If the borrower is a resident of the complex, HUD will allow the borrower to purchase up to three units as a nonowner occupant.

It should be noted that many lenders will not usually offer to help either the applicant or the Homeowners Association in getting HUD's approval for a condominium project because the lender could expend a large amount of time and will not be given an exclusive approval (that is, other HUD-FHA

approved lenders will be able to make loans in the project). As a real estate professional you may be helped in making condominium sales if you work with a project to secure HUD-FHA approval.

Mobile Home or Manufactured Housing Loans

As the demand and cost of housing constantly increase, many prospective homebuyers are looking for alternatives. One that has been selected by many is mobile homes or manufactured housing. The real estate professional must have some knowledge of the methods for financing manufactured housing. Probably one of the best finance methods is through HUD-FHA.

Under Title I, Section 2, of the National Housing Act, HUD-FHA is authorized to offer mortgage insurance on mobile homes or manufactured housing that meets HUD-FHA standards.

This mortgage insurance is available to anyone who demonstrates the ability to make the cash investment and the mortgage payment and has good credit. One of the major restrictions placed on this program is that the mobile home must be the primary residence of the applicant. HUD has defined the primary residence as one in which the applicant lives at least nine months of the year.

Under this program, HUD-FHA will insure loans to the maximums shown in Figure 7–14.

In addition to the limits shown in Figure 7–14, HUD will allow insurance on a maximum loan of up to $13,500 for a "suitably developed" manufactured home lot. HUD also allows the basic maximum loan amounts for manufactured homes on improved lots to be increased by an additional $7500 in areas that can show there is such a need to meet the higher cost of land acquisition, site development, and construction of a permanent foundation. Another important change authorized by HUD allows the inclusion of garages, patios, carports, and comparable appurtenances as part of manufactured home loans and combination loans as long as the loan is secured by a first lien. Finally HUD will allow the refinancing of presently owned manufactured home lots through the combination program. The combination program allows for the financing of both a manufactured home and the lot on which it will be placed.

In addition to the mortgage insurance issued under Title I, HUD will also issue mortgage insurance on manufactured housing under Title II, Section 203(b). The mortgage

Figure 7–13. **Required Exhibits for Existing Condominiums**

REQUIRED EXHIBITS FOR EXISTING CONDOMINIUMS

	Existing Not HUD Approved	Existing Resale in HUD Approved Project
I. CONVENTIONAL or FANNIE MAE APPROVED		
1. PROJECT APPROVAL		
a. Master Deed or Declaration of Condominium with recording date, include any amendments	X	
b. By-Laws of the Condominium Association	X	
c. Recorded project plat, map and/or air lot survey	X	
d. Management Agreement	AA	
e. Articles of Incorporation of the Condominium Association	X	
f. Attorney's certification that legal documents meet HUD objectives or evidence Fannie Mae has approved the Project	X	
g. Mortgagee Certification that the project construction is over one year old	X	
h. Certification the Declarant's rights have expired or have been waived	X	
i. Certification that at least 80% of the units are owner-occupied	X	
j. Current financial statement (or budget) of the condominium project (including reserves for replacement expected life of Assets)	X	
k. Statement signed by Office of Board of Directors of Council of Co-owners specifying any existing or pending special assessments and any pending litigation affecting the condominium	X	
l. Minutes of last two Council of Co-owners meetings	X	
2. UNIT APPRAISAL		
a. HUD 92800	X	X
b. Mortgagees certification that there have been no changes to the legal or organizational documents since HUD approved letter		X
II. VA APPROVED		
No project exhibits required for preapproval.	After Project Acceptances by VA	
UNIT APPRAISAL		
a. HUD 92800 Application		X
b. Copy of VA Approval Letter or Loan Guaranty Letter indicating approval by VA		X

FOOTNOTE:
1. Submit a single set of documents which will not be returned.
2. Legend: X Required   AA if Applicable
3. Section 1: Organizational documents one-time submission for the project, drafts are not acceptable.
4. Section 2: Exhibits will accompany the first appraisal requests. Once project approved, only Section 2 items need be submitted.

SOURCE: U.S. Department of Housing and Urban Development, Seattle Area Office, Seattle, Washington, *Circular Letter No. 81-26 — October 29, 1981,* Attachment I.

Figure 7–14. **HUD-FHA Maximum Loans**

	Loan Amount	Term
Singular modular	$40,500	20 years, 32 days
Double modular	40,500	20 years, 32 days
Manufactured home on lot	54,000	20 years, 32 days

insurance under Section 203(b) will be issued for both proposed and existing construction as long as the unit meets certain requirements. Some of the requirements for proposed construction are as follows:

1. The unit must have a floor area of not less than 400 square feet

2. The unit must be owner occupied and the title to the land, or the leasehold, shall be vested to the owner occupant

3. The unit must be classified and taxed as real property by the state in which the unit is located

4. The unit must bear a seal or identification that the unit complies with HUD's mobile home construction and safety standards

5. Only units built after June 15, 1976, may be used as security for a mortgage to be insured under Title II Section 203(b)

6. The unit must be permanently affixed to a foundation

7. The wheels, axles, and hitch or tongue must be removed

8. The unit must have the required crawl space between the bottom of the unit and the ground (according to HUD, the minimum crawl space is 18 inches). HUD requires access to the crawl space and requires that crawl space to be ventilated

9. As with the other types of construction, HUD will require the proposed construction to be inspected (HUD now requires a minimum of two inspections: a foundation inspection and a final inspection)

The following are some of the requirements for mortgage insurance if the unit is to be insured as existing construction:

1. The unit must have a floor area of not less than 400 square feet

2. The unit must be owner occupied similar to the requirements under proposed construction

3. The unit must be permanently affixed to a foundation with the wheels, axles, and hitch or tongue removed

4. The unit must be connected to permanently installed utilities that are protected from freezing

5. HUD will require the unit to be constructed after June 15, 1976, and bear the proper identification as to the construction meeting the HUD mobile home requirements

6. The unit must have the proper crawl space similar to the requirements for proposed construction

7. HUD will not insure units that have a basement if the unit is located in a federally designated flood area

These are only some of the requirements. Before working with a client seeking a unit financed with a mortgage insured by HUD under Title II, Section 203(b), you should contact any HUD-approved lender or your nearest HUD office.

Since this mortgage is insured under Section 203(b), the maximum loan amounts are the same as shown earlier in this chapter. The term for these mortgages is also the same as that listed for Section 203(b).

This completes our discussion of the more important programs of mortgage insurance available through HUD-FHA. A synopsis of other HUD-FHA mortgage insurance programs is found in Appendix E. If you have any questions regarding any of these programs listed in Appendix E, contact an approved HUD-FHA lender or the HUD-FHA office nearest you.

ALTERNATIVE MORTGAGE INSTRUMENTS

The Housing and Urban-Rural Recovery Act of 1983, Public Law 98-181, in Title IV, Subpart 4, entitled Alternative Mortgage Instruments, authorizes the Department of Housing and Urban Development to insure various kinds of alternative mortgage instruments.

Section 443 of the Act amends Title II of the National Housing Act, by adding a new section 251 which, subject to certain limitations, allows HUD to insure the adjustable-rate mortgage (ARM). On June 6, 1984, HUD published in the *Federal Register*, in the Rule and Regulation section, an interim rule providing for and setting forth the requirements of the ARM that HUD will insure.

On July 18, 1984, the Department of Housing and Urban Development issued Mortgagee Letter 84-16. The subject of the letter was the insurance of adjustable-rate mortgages on single-family properties, section 251 of the National Housing Act. This mortgage letter was sent to all HUD-approved lenders and outlined and amplified the information contained in the *Federal Register*.

According to the rule and letter, ARMs will be insured under section 203(b), 203(k) rehabilitation mortgages, or section 234(c) single-family condominium units. These can only be loans secured by owner occupied dwellings. Direct Endorsement lenders can originate ARMs only under sections 203(b) and 234(c).

Interest-Rate Index

According to the rule, all changes in the interest rate charged on an ARM must be based on the change in the weekly average yield on the 1-year U.S. Treasury Securities. As we learned in Chapter 3, the weekly averages are published in the Federal Reserve Statistical Release H. 15 (519).

Frequency of Interest and Payment Adjustments

According to the rule, interest-rate adjustments must occur annually, except for the first adjustment. The rule states that the first adjustment may not occur sooner than 1 year from the due date of the first monthly payment, but the lender does have the option to wait or postpone the first adjustment up to 18 months after the due date of the first monthly payment. This ability to defer the first payment adjustment allows the homebuyer some additional time before the first adjustment, since normally the first year after moving into a home is rather expensive due to purchasing draperies, putting in a yard and landscaping, etc. An adjustment in payment, particularly an increase, could be a hardship on the borrower.

In regard to the adjustment of the payment, the rules require that the payment be adjusted at the same time the interest rate is adjusted. Thus, there is no possibility for negative amortization.

Adjustment Limitations

According to the rule, the adjustments must be made annually and the maximum change either upward or downward in the annual change is 1 percent. In addition, the rule limits the amount of change over the life of the mortgage to 5 percent above or below the initial contract interest rate.

Calculation of Adjustments

The initial interest rate charged for an ARM insured under any of the authorized sections will be a rate that is agreed upon by the borrower and the lender.

According to the Supplementary Information that accompanied the rule, section III, b, states that there are two methods that may be used to calculate the adjustment to the initial interest rate. One method is to use the change in the index alone to adjust the initial rate. For example, if the initial rate used 11.00 percent and the index goes from 11 percent to 12 percent in 1 year, the borrower's interest note rate would also increase from 11 percent to 12 percent.

With the second method, the borrower and the lender once again agree on an initial interest rate. In addition, they agree on a margin to be used in conjunction with any adjustment. For example, the parties agree that all future interest rates will be based on the index plus 2 percent. If a borrower and lender agree on an initial interest rate of 11.5 percent, then at the time of the first adjustment the index is 10.00 percent plus the 2.00 percent margin; the new rate would be 12.00 percent. Thus, the borrower's rate would increase to 12.00 percent. Since most conventional lenders use the margin method to establish the interest rate, the Government National Mortgage Association will only allow this type of ARM in any pool of mortgages it purchases.

Carryover Requirements

The rule does provide for the mandatory carryover of changes in the index that, because of the annual ceiling limitations, cannot be translated into changes in the interest rate for the loan. For example, assume that a mortgage contains an initial interest rate of 11 percent and uses a margin of 1 percent for the calculation of the annual rate adjustment.

At the time of the first adjustment, for this example, the index has increased from 11 to 13 percent. Because of the 1-percent annual ceiling, the rate on the note would only be adjusted by one percent. Thus, the unapplied 1 percent would be carried over to the next adjustment date and would be applied in whole or in part at that time.

Let us assume that at the time of the second annual adjustment the index did not change and was still 13 percent. The rate on the mortgage would still go up by 1 percent due to the carryover from the first annual adjustment. If instead at the second annual adjustment the rate had increased by only one-half of 1 percent. The rate would have still gone up 1 percent, due to the carryover from the previous adjustment period and then the one-half of one percent would be carried over to the next adjustment date.

Let us now assume there was a 1 percent decrease in the index at the time of the second adjustment, the interest rate on the mortgage would stay the same because of the offset by the one percent carry over from the first annual adjustment. What would be the effect of a 2-percent decrease in the index? Since there is a limit of 1 percent, the note rate would be reduced by 1 percent and there would be a negative 1 percent carryover to the next adjustment date.

Since there is a maximum 5-percent increase or decrease, the borrower is assured that the rate on this example would never be more than 17 percent and could be as low as 7 percent.

Buydown

HUD-FHA allows the use of a buydown with the ARM, but according to Mortgagee Letter 84-16, issued by the Department of Housing and Urban Development on July 18, 1984, if there is a temporary buydown FHA will only treat it as a compensating factor. FHA will do its underwriting on the initial interest rate. For example, if the initial rate on an ARM to be insured is 12 percent and the rate is "bought down" to 9 percent with a 3-2-1 buydown, FHA will do its underwriting based on the 12 percent. Additionally all portions of the disclosure will be predicated on the initial interest rate or 12 percent.

Disclosure

As with the conventional ARM, the HUD interim rule requires that the lender shall explain fully and in writing to the borrower certain aspects of the ARM. This disclosure according to the rule is called a *pre-loan disclosure*. According to the rule, this is to be done no later than on the date the lender pro-

vides an application to a prospective borrower. The disclosure is to explain the nature of the ARM. In addition, the borrower is to certify that he or she understands the nature of the ARM. The rule requires that the pre-loan disclosure must include the following items:

1. Indicate that the interest rate on the loan may change, and explain how changes in the interest rate correspond to changes in the interest-rate index, including the impact of a carryover adjustment.

2. Identify the interest-rate index, the source of the index, as well as a source where the borrower can verify the value and movement of the index.

3. Indicate the annual frequency that the interest rate and payments will be adjusted and the length of the interval before the first rate and payment adjustment. For example, indicate that the lender will not make the first adjustment until 14 months after the due date of the first payment.

4. Show a hypothetical monthly payment schedule that displays the maximum potential increase in the monthly payments to the borrower over the first 5 years of the mortgage. This is referred to as a *worst-case scenario*. An example of such a scenario is shown in Figure 7-15.

Figure 7-15 shows a worst-case scenario for a $50,000 ARM indexed to the 1-year Treasury bills with a yield of 10 percent, and the lender is requiring a 1 percent margin or a face interest rate of 11 percent for the first year of the loan. The index will rise at the rate of 1 percent per year for 5 years. In the sixth year and beyond, the index is presumed to remain at the initial rate plus 5 percent (or the maximum the interest rate may increase for the HUD ARM). A table similar to the one shown in Figure 7-15 is to be exhibited as part of the ARM disclosure.

The ARM disclosure also must contain an example showing the effect of the carryover operation. A sample of such an example is shown in Figure 7-16. This figure uses the same mortgage information as in the previous example. In reviewing the figure, we see that

Figure 7–15.   HUD ARM Worst-Case Scenario

"Worst Case" Scenario

Policy year	Contract interest rate	Monthly payment	End of year balance
1.	11	$476.17	$49,794.55
2.	12	514.06	49,590.17
3.	13	552.01	49,401.83
4.	14	590.13	49,225.49
5.	15	628.35	49,057.89
6.	16	666.65	48,895.83
7.	16	666.65	48,705.83
8.	16	666.65	48,483.10
9.	16	666.65	48,221.99
10.	16	666.65	47,915.89
11.	16	666.65	47,557.07
13.	16	666.65	46,643.34
14.	16	666.65	46,065.30
15.	16	666.65	45,387.68
16.	16	666.65	44,593.34
17.	16	666.65	43,662.15
18.	16	666.65	42,570.55
19.	16	666.65	41,290.91
20.	16	666.65	39,790.83
21.	16	666.65	38,032.31
22.	16	666.65	35,970.84
23.	16	666.65	33,554.22
24.	16	666.65	30,721.32
25.	16	666.65	27,400.39
26.	16	666.65	23,507.36
27.	16	666.65	18,943.67
28.	16	666.65	13,593.79
29.	16	666.65	7,322.28
30.	16	666.65	.00

SOURCE: "Rules and Regulations," *Federal Register*, June 6, 1984, vol. 49, no. 110, p. 23583.

Figure 7–16.   Effect of Carryover

Effect of "Carryover"

Policy year	Contract interest rate	Monthly payment	End of year balance	Year end change in index value
1.	11	$476.17	$49,794.55	+2
2.	12	514.06	49,590.17	0
3.	13	552.01	49,401.83	+.5
4.	13.5	571.00	49,207.33	−3
5.	12.5	533.62	48,939.85	+1.5
6.	12	515.45	48,609.46	....

SOURCE: "Rules and Regulations," *Federal Register*, June 6, 1984, vol. 49, no. 110, p. 23583.

at the end of year 1 the index had increased by 2 percent, but with the one percent limit the rate on the mortgage will only increase to 12 percent and the one percent additional will be carried over to the next adjustment date. Then at the end of the second year there was no change in the index, but the interest rate on the mortgage still increased by the amount of the carryover or 1 percent. At the end of the third year the index had increased by one-half of 1 percent; thus the rate on the mortgage increased by the same amount since there was no carryover from the previous year. By the end of the fourth year the index had declined by 3 percent, once again since there is a 1-percent limit to both the increases and decreases, the rate will only be reduced by 1 percent or to 12.5 percent. The remaining 2 percent will be carried forward to the next year. Then according to the figure, the index had increased by 1.5 percent and we had a 2 percent decrease carryover from the previous year. The net change, then, is a negative one-half of 1 percent. Thus, the note rate would drop to 12 percent.

In addition to the pre-loan disclosure, the rule requires the lender to supply to the borrower an *annual disclosure*. This disclosure is to be provided to the borrower at least 30 days prior to any adjustment to the borrower's monthly payment and must advise the borrower of the following:

1. The new mortgage interest rate as well as the new monthly payment.

2. The current index value and the method used to calculate the new interest rate.

3. Finally, if applicable, any amount the interest rate has been affected by carryover from any previous adjustment period.

Authorized AMIs

In addition to the adjustable-rate mortgage, subpart 4 allows HUD to issue mortgage insurance on the indexed mortgage (a type of price level adjustable mortgage), the graduated payment mortgage for multifamily housing, and the shared appreciation mortgage for both single- and multiple-family housing. It should be noted that HUD is authorized to insure these types of mortgages, but HUD will have to develop the rules and regulations for each and publish them for public comment. So it could be several years before these AMIs will be available.

MORTGAGE INSTRUMENTS FOR SECTION 245

The standard HUD Note and Deed of Trust was reviewed in Chapter 2. These standard documents can be used with many of the programs of HUD-FHA, but some of the programs will require these documents to be modified. Any mortgage insured under section 245(a) and (b) will require modified standard instruments.

Both the note and the deed of trust will have to be modified. First let us review the modification to the mortgage instrument. In all states under the document caption or title, the following must be added in all caps: "WITH DEFERRED INTEREST AND INCREASING MONTHLY INSTALLMENTS." The second modification to the mortgage instrument in all states is the addition of the following: "DEFERRAL OF INTEREST MAY INCREASE THE PRINCIPAL BALANCE TO $_____." The location of this additional statement will depend on available space in the mortgage, but it should be as close as possible to the section identifying the amount of the mortgage. These modifications are illustrated in Figure 7–17. In some states there will not be room in this section of the mortgage instrument and the addition of the "DEFERRAL OF INTEREST" will be placed in the margin of the document and asterisks will be placed in the proper area of the mortgage, as illustrated in Figure 7–18.

The modifications to the note are more detailed. The first modification to the note is similar to the first modification to the deed of trust. A similar statement is added below the caption or title. The statement to be added in all caps is "WITH DEFERRED INTEREST AND INCREASING MONTHLY PAYMENTS."

The second modification to the note occurs in the space where the monthly payment is given. Instead of a dollar amount, the following statement will be added: "ACCORDING TO SCHEDULE A." The final change or modification to the note is the following addition: "DEFERRED INTEREST SHALL BE ADDED TO THE PRINCIPAL BALANCE MONTHLY AND SHALL INCREASE THE PRINCIPAL BALANCE TO NOT MORE THAN $_____." This statement should be added as shown in Figure 7–19, but if there is not sufficient room for this statement, it may be added as an attachment.

The monthly payments as shown in Schedule A will be added to the front of the note in the large space provided (illustrated in Chap-

Figure 7–17. Deed of Trust, Example 1

4240.2 REV CHG	

APPENDIX 4

STATE OF ARIZONA
FHA Form No. 2101 DT
Revised October 1975

EXAMPLE 1

> This form is used in connection with deeds of trust insured under the one- to four-family provisions of the National Housing Act.

DEED OF TRUST

WITH DEFERRED INTEREST AND INCREASING MONTHLY INSTALLMENTS
With Assignment of Rents

THIS DEED OF TRUST, made this _____ day of _____, 19____,

BETWEEN _____

_____, as TRUSTOR,

(Street and number)   *(City)*   *(State)*

_____, as TRUSTEE, and

_____, as BENEFICIARY,

WITH POWER OF SALE, described as:

TOGETHER WITH the rents, issues, and profits thereof, SUBJECT, HOWEVER, to the right, power, and authority hereinafter given to and conferred upon Beneficiary to collect and apply such rents, issues, and profits;

FOR THE PURPOSE OF SECURING Performance of each agreement of Trustor herein contained and payment of the sum of $ _____ with interest thereon according to the terms of a promissory note of even date herewith, payable to Beneficiary or order and made by Trustor. DEFERRAL OF INTEREST MAY INCREASE THE PRINCIPAL BALANCE TO $ _____.

1. Privilege is reserved to pay the debt secured hereby in whole or in an amount equal to one or more principal payments next due on the note, on the first day of any month prior to maturity, provided written notice of intention so to do is given at least thirty days prior to prepayment.

2. Trustor agrees to pay to Beneficiary in addition to the monthly payments of principal and interest payable under the terms of said note, on the first day of each month until said note is fully paid, the following sums:

    a. An amount sufficient to provide the holder hereof with funds to pay the next mortgage insurance premium if this instrument and the note secured hereby are insured, or a monthly charge (in lieu of a mortgage insurance premium) if they are held by the Secretary, Department of Housing and Urban Development, as follows:

       (I) If and so long as said note of even date and this instrument are insured or are reinsured under the provisions of the National Housing Act, an amount sufficient to accumulate in the hands of the holder one (1) month prior to its due date the annual mortgage insurance premium, in order to provide such holder with funds to pay such premium to the Secretary, Department of Housing and Urban Development pursuant to the National Housing Act, as amended, and applicable Regulations thereunder; or

       (II) If and so long as said note of even date and this instrument are held by the Secretary, Department of Housing and Urban Development, a monthly charge (in lieu of a mortgage insurance premium) which shall be in an amount equal to one-twelfth (1/12) of one-half (1/2) per centum of the average outstanding balance due on the note computed without taking into account delinquencies or prepayments;

    b. An installment of the ground rents, if any, and of the taxes and special assessments levied or to be levied against the premises covered by this Deed of Trust; and an installment of the premium or premiums that will become due and payable to renew the insurance on the premises covered hereby against loss by fire or such other hazard as may be required by Beneficiary in amounts and in a company or companies satisfactory to Beneficiary; trustor agreeing to deliver promptly to Beneficiary all bills and notices therefor. Such installments shall be equal respectively to one-twelfth (1/12) of the annual ground rent, if any, plus the estimated premium or premiums for such insurance, and taxes and assessments next due (as estimated by Beneficiary) less all installments already paid therefor, divided by the number of months that are to elapse before one month prior to the date when such premium or premiums and taxes and assessments will become delinquent. Beneficiary shall hold such payments in trust to pay such ground rents, premium or premiums and taxes and special assessments before the same become delinquent; and

    c. All payments mentioned in the two preceding subsections of this paragraph and all payments to be made under the note secured hereby shall be added together and the aggregate amount thereof shall be paid each month in a single payment to be applied by Beneficiary to the following items in the order set forth:

       (I) premium charges under the contract of insurance with the Secretary, Department of Housing and Urban Development, or monthly charge (in lieu of mortgage insurance premium), as the case may be;
       (II) grounds rents, taxes, special assessments, fire and other hazard insurance premiums;
       (III) interest on the note secured hereby; and
       (IV) amortization of the principal of said note.

    Any deficiency in the amount of any such aggregate monthly payment shall, unless made good prior to the due date of the next such payment, constitute an event of default under this Deed of Trust.

Source: U.S., Department of Housing and Urban Development, *The Graduated Payment Mortgage Program—A HUD Handbook*, June 1978, Appendix 4, p. 4.

Figure 7–18.   Deed of Trust, Example 2

```
                                                              4240.2 REV CHG

                                                              APPENDIX 4
```

STATE OF MARYLAND
FHA FORM NO. 2127M   EXAMPLE 2
Rev. June 1975

```
                                        This form is used in connection
                                        with deeds of trust insured under
                                        the one- to four-family provisions
                                        of the National Housing Act.
```

DEED OF TRUST

WITH DEFERRED INTEREST AND INCREASING MONTHLY INSTALLMENTS

THIS DEED, made this   day of   , 19   , by and between
                                                                                              ,
party of the first part and   , Trustee,
as hereinafter set forth, party of the second part:

WHEREAS, the party of the first part is justly indebted unto

                                                    , a corporation organized and existing
under the laws of   , in the principal sum of
                                        Dollars ($), with interest from
date at the rate of   per centum (%) per annum on the
unpaid balance until paid, for which amount the said party has signed and delivered a certain promissory note bearing even
date herewith and payable in monthly installments of ACCORDING TO THE SCHEDULE ATTACHED TO SAID NOTE
                                        Dollars ($ x), commencing on the first day
of   , 19   , and on the first day of each month thereafter until the principal and interest are fully paid, except that the final payment of principal and interest, if not sooner paid, shall be due and payable on
the first day of   ,   **
AND WHEREAS, the party of the first part desires to secure the prompt payment of said debt, and interest thereon,
the same shall become due and payable, and all costs and expenses incurred in respect thereto, including
incurred or paid by the said party of the second part or substituted Trustee, or by any person hereby
litigation at law or in equity which may arise in respect to this trust or the property hereinafter
may be advanced as provided herein, with interest on all such costs and advances from

WITNESSETH, that the party of the first part, in consideration of the
States of America, to
in hand paid by the party of the second part, the
hereby acknowledged, has granted and conveyed, and
successors and assigns, the following-described
Maryland, known and distinguished as

** DEFERRAL OF INTEREST MAY INCREASE THE PRINCIPAL BALANCE TO $

together with all the improvements in anywise appertaining, and all the estate, right, title, interest, and claim, either at law or
in equity, or otherwise however, of the party of the first part, of, in, to, or out of the said land and premises.
    By the execution of this instrument, Mortgagors, Grantors or parties of the first part (whichever applies) certify and
acknowledge that prior thereto they have received both a fully executed agreement as to the contractural rate of interest and
a loan disclosure statement in connection with the loan secured hereby both as required by Article 49 of the Annotated Code
of Maryland.
    TO HAVE AND TO HOLD the said property and improvements unto the party of the second part, its successors and
assigns
```

IN AND UPON THE TRUSTS, NEVERTHELESS, hereinafter declared; that is to say: IN TRUST to permit said party
of the first part, or assigns, to use and occupy the said described land and premises, and the rents, issues, and profits thereof,
to take, have, and apply to and for                                    sole use and benefit, until default be made in the
payment of any manner of indebtedness hereby secured or in the performance of any of the covenants as hereinafter
provided.
    AND upon the full payment of all of said note and the interest thereon, and all moneys advanced or expended as herein
provided, and all other proper costs, charges, commissions, half-commissions, and expenses, at any time before the sale
hereinafter provided for to release and reconvey the said described premises unto the said party of the first part or assigns, at
cost. Prior to the execution and delivery of any partial or complete release, each trustee
shall be entitled to charge and receive a fee of $5.00, plus 50 cents for Notary's fee, for each release. The right to charge and
receive said fee shall be limited to two Trustees.

Source: U.S., Department of Housing and Urban Development, *The Graduated Payment Mortgage Program—A HUD Handbook*, June
1978, Appendix 4, p. 5.
```

Figure 7–19.   Mortgage Note

FHA FORM NO. 9122
Revised July 1970

EXAMPLE 3

This form is used in connection
with mortgages insured under the
one- to four-family provisions of
the National Housing Act.

MORTGAGE NOTE

FHA CASE NO.

WITH DEFERRED INTEREST AND INCREASING MONTHLY INSTALLMENTS

$ _____   , Kentucky.
                                                               , 19   .

   FOR VALUE RECEIVED, the undersigned promise(s) to pay to the order of

the principal sum of   Dollars
($), with interest from date at the rate of
per centum (%) per annum on the unpaid balance until paid. Principal and interest
shall be payable at the office of
                                              in
or at such other place as the holder hereof may designate in writing, in monthly installments of
ACCORDING TO SCHEDULE A ATTACHED   xxxxbxxxxx$ x),
commencing on the first day of   , 19   , and on the first day of each month thereafter, until the principal and interest are fully paid, except that the final payment of the entire indebtedness evidenced hereby, if not sooner paid, shall be due and payable on the first day of   ,
          . DEFERRED INTEREST SHALL BE ADDED TO THE PRINCIPAL BALANCE MONTHLY AND
SHALL INCREASE THE PRINCIPAL BALANCE TO NOT MORE THAN $ _____ .
   If default be made in the payment of any installment under this note, and if such default is not made
good prior to the due date of the next such installment, the entire principal sum and accrued interest
shall at once become due and payable without notice at the option of the holder of this note. Failure to
exercise this option shall not constitute a waiver of the right to exercise the same in the event of any
subsequent default.

   The undersigned, whether principal, surety, guarantor, endorser, or other party hereto, agree(s) to be
jointly and severally bound, and severally hereby waive demand, protest, and notice of demand, protest,
and nonpayment.

_____   _____

_____   _____

_____

SCHEDULE A

$_____ during the 1st note year
_____ during the 2nd note year
_____ during the 3rd note year
_____ during the 4th note year
_____ during the 5th note year
_____ during the 6th note year and thereafter

8/78   HUD-Wash., D.C.
                                 Page 6

Source: U.S., Department of Housing and Urban Development, *The Graduated Payment Mortgage Program—A HUD Handbook*, June
1978, Appendix 4, p. 6.

ter 2). HUD-FHA has specified the form that will be used for Schedule A for Plans I, II, and III as well as Plans IV and V. This form is illustrated in Figure 7–20.

It should be noted that the maximum principal balance to be shown on both the note and deed of trust is calculated by using the highest outstanding balance factor. These factors of Plan III are shown in Appendix B. To find the dollar amount that will be placed in the blank in the statement "MAY INCREASE THE PRINCIPAL BALANCE TO $_____," you would turn to Appendix B, locate the proper interest rate, look for the underlined factor, and multiply the original principal balance (in thousands) by the factor. This will give the highest outstanding balance.

ASSUMPTIONS/RELEASE OF LIABILITY

According to the HUD handbook *Administration of Insured Mortgages*, there are four basic types of mortgage assumptions, but only three will be of interest to most real estate professionals. These three types of assumptions are the simple assumption, Form-2210 without substitution of mortgagor, and Form-2210 with release of liability.

1. Simple assumption. With this type of assumption the original borrower is not released from any liability to the federal government.

2. Form-2210 assumption without substitution of mortgagor. The Form 2210 and the supporting forms are filled out, and the original borrower is not released from liability to the federal government.

3. Form-2210 assumption with release of liability and substitution of mortgagor. Here the proper forms are completed and the original borrower is not only "formally" released from liability, but the person assuming the loan is substituted as the mortgagor.

With type 2, the original borrower normally will still appear as mortgagor on the note, whereas with type 3 the assumptor will replace the original borrower on the note. Let us review each of the three very briefly.

Simple assumption As the name implies, this is simply that the person assuming the loan pays the seller his or her equity and takes up the monthly payments. Neither the lender nor FHA is notified of the change and the

Figure 7–20. Schedule A

<table>
<tr><td colspan="2" align="center">PAYMENT SCHEDULE</td></tr>
<tr><td>*(for Plans I, II, III)*</td><td>*(for Plans IV, V)*</td></tr>
<tr><td align="center">*SCHEDULE A*</td><td align="center">*SCHEDULE A*</td></tr>
<tr><td>$_____ during the 1st note year</td><td>$_____ during the 1st note year</td></tr>
<tr><td>$_____ during the 2nd note year</td><td>$_____ during the 2nd note year</td></tr>
<tr><td>$_____ during the 3rd note year</td><td>$_____ during the 3rd note year</td></tr>
<tr><td>$_____ during the 4th note year</td><td>$_____ during the 4th note year</td></tr>
<tr><td>$_____ during the 5th note year</td><td>$_____ during the 5th note year</td></tr>
<tr><td>$_____ during the 6th note year and thereafter</td><td>$_____ during the 6th note year</td></tr>
<tr><td></td><td>$_____ during the 7th note year</td></tr>
<tr><td></td><td>$_____ during the 8th note year</td></tr>
<tr><td></td><td>$_____ during the 9th note year</td></tr>
<tr><td></td><td>$_____ during the 10th note year</td></tr>
<tr><td></td><td>$_____ during the 11th note year and thereafter</td></tr>
</table>

SOURCE: U.S. Department of Housing and Urban Development, *The Graduated Payment Mortgage Program—A HUD Handbook, June 1978*, Appendix 4, p. 2.

original borrower is still liable to the federal government for the repayment of the mortgage. If the person who assumed the mortgage should fail to make the payments in a timely manner and the mortgage goes into foreclosure, the original borrower will be the person the lender and the government will look to for payment. Thus, the original borrower will possibly have a foreclosure on his or her credit record. It should be noted that unless the original borrower has made some provision, the foreclosure notice will be sent to the property address. In addition, if the property is sold at a foreclosure sale for less than the mortgage amount, the lender and/or the federal government may file a judgment against the original borrower and not the person living in the house.

Form-2210 assumption without substitution of mortgagor

With this type of assumption the Form 2210 is completed (Figure 7–21) along with all of the supporting documentation. According to the handbook, the lender will only complete the form along with an FHA application. In addition, the lender will secure a credit report and verify the deposits and employment of the person or persons assuming the mortgage. This information is then sent to the Mortgage Credit Section of the nearest FHA office. After reviewing all of the documents and determining whether the person or persons assuming the loan meet the underwriting guidelines, FHA will issue a release of the original borrower from any liability to the federal government or to the lender.

Form 2210 assumption with release of liability and substitution of mortgagor or borrower

With this type of assumption the Form 2210, the HUD application, and all of the supporting material—once again including the verification of bank accounts, employment, and credit report—are sent to the nearest HUD office. The assumptor is reviewed as if he or she were receiving a new loan. It is important to note that even though the person assuming the loan in effect is making application and is being reviewed as if seeking a new loan, the interest rate on the approved loan does not change. This is different from some conventional loans. If the person assuming the loan meets the underwriting requirements of HUD-FHA, the original borrower will be released from his or her liability and the person or persons assuming the loan is substituted as the mortgagor or borrower. The lender will supply to the original borrower and coborrower page 2 of Form 2210, Approval of

Purchaser and Release of Seller (Figure 7–22). In addition, a release of the seller is also filed in the county clerks office in the county where the property is located.

This release of liability may be very important to the seller or sellers if they make application for a new FHA-insured loan. In addition, if the person defaults on the mortgage, the seller is not in any way financially obligated for the loan and no deficiency judgments will be taken against the seller if the mortgage goes into foreclosure.

REVIEW QUESTIONS

1. Identify by section number and explain the basic mortgage insurance programs of HUD-FHA.

2. Define the term *acquisition cost* and give an example.

3. Name and explain at least three advantages of mortgages insured by HUD-FHA.

4. What is the only fee that the borrower may pay when the mortgage is insured by HUD-FHA?

5. What is the current rate for mortgages insured by HUD-FHA?

6. What are the current discount points charged for mortgages insured under section 203(b) and section 245(a) and (b)? If there is a difference in the discount points charged, give your reasons for the difference.

7. For the purposes of section 221(d)(2), is your city located in a high-cost area? If so, what is the maximum mortgage that can be insured on a single-family dwelling?

8. Explain the graduated-payment mortgage (GPM). Is there more than one plan available under Sections 245(a) and 245(b)?

PROBLEMS

1. Calculate the required one-time mortgage insurance premium for the following FHA-insured mortgages:

   a. $84,550, 15-year mortgage; the borrower wishes to finance 100 percent of the MIP.

Figure 7–21.   Request for Credit Approval of Substitute Mortgagor

Request For Credit Approval of Substitute Mortgagor

U.S. Department of Housing and Urban Development
Office of Housing
Federal Housing Commissioner

OMB No. 2502-0036 (Exp. 12/31/86)

Instructions: This form is for use in cases involving the release of a Mortgagor from liability for a deficiency occuring as a result of foreclosure. Submit original only to HUD.

Case Number	Section of the National Housing Act
	☐ 203 ☐ _____

Mortgagee *(Name, Address & Zip Code)*	Property Address *(Street, City & State)*

Seller *(Name, Address & Zip Code)*	Purchaser *(Name, Address & Zip Code)*
	Social Security No.

A. Mortgagee's Request for Substitution:

It is requested that the above named purchaser be accepted as Mortgagor and the Seller released from financial responsibility for a deficiency occurring as a result of foreclosure.

A HUD Form 92900, Mortgagor's Application for Credit Approval, with required exhibits is submitted herewith and the statements contained therein are true and complete to the best knowledge and belief of the undersigned.

Title of the Above Property:	Monthly Mortgage Payment *(Total Principal, Interest, M.I.P., Ins., Taxes, and any ground Rent or Special Assessments)* $	Remaining Term of Mortgage Months	Face Amount of Original Mortgage $
☐ Has been ☐ Will be Transferred Transferred		Purchaser is or will be Owner-Occupant ☐ Yes ☐ No	Current Balance $
Mortgage — ☐ Is ☐ Is Not Current	Date of First Payment *(Original)*	Date of Next Scheduled Payment	Insured under Escrow ☐ Commitment Procedure
Date	Name and Title of Officer By:		

B. Consent by the Federal Housing Commissioner

The above named Purchaser is acceptable as a Mortgagor and, subject to compliance with the following conditions, if any, and the issuance of Form 2210-1 to the Seller, consent is given to the release of the Seller from Financial liability for a deficiency occurriing as a result of foreclosure in connection with the above numbered loan. Form 2210-1 shall not be executed by the mortgagee until the sale to the above named Purchaser is concluded and conditions specified below are met.

Specific Conditions

Date	Authorized Agent By:

Note to Mortgagee

A copy of this form has not been retained by HUD in its files. Within 30 days of change, you are required to submit to HUD, Form 92080, Mortgage Record Change, to the Office of Finance and Accounting, Department of Housing and Urban Development, Att: Receipts and Deposits, Washington, D.C. 20410.

Replaces FHA-2210, which is obsolete

HUD-2210 **(4-84)**
(HB 4155.1)

SOURCE: U.S. Department of Housing and Urban Development, *Administration of Insured Home Mortgages—A HUD Handbook*, August 1983, Appendix 3.

Figure 7–22.   Approval of Purchaser and Release of Seller

Approval of Purchaser and Release of Seller	U.S. Department of Housing and Urban Development Office of Housing — Federal Housing Commissioner

Case Number	Section of the National Housing Act ☐ 203 ☐ _____

Mortgagee *(Name, Address & Zip Code)*	Property Address *(Street, City & State)*

Seller *(Name, Address & Zip Code)*	Purchaser *(Name, Address & Zip Code)*

This will acknowledge that the above-named seller has sold the propety described above to the purchaser named.

The credit of the purchaser has been examined and approved by HUD. The seller is hereby released from any financial obligation arising in connection with the security instruments executed in the above numbered case. No deficiency judgment will be taken against the seller if the HUD insured mortgage covering the subject property is foreclosed.

If the seller should apply for a HUD insured loan on another property, this release should be delivered to the Mortgage Lender through whom the application for such loan is made.

_____
Mortgagee

_____
By

_____
Date

Note: This document should be retained by seller.

Replaces FHA-2210.1 which is obsolete.   HUD-2210-1 (4-84)
                                                          (HB-4155.1)

SOURCE: U.S. Department of Housing and Urban Development, *Administration of Insured Home Mortgages—A HUD Handbook*, August 1983, Appendix 4.

b. $54,500, 20-year mortgage; the borrower wishes to pay cash for the MIP.

c. $88,950, 30-year mortgage; the borrower wishes to finance all of the MIP.

2. You find in listing one of your client's homes that they have an FHA-insured mortgage that includes a one-time MIP premium. The mortgage is in year 4, has a term of 30 years, and the remaining balance is $82,212.43. Using Figure 7–3, calculate the amount of refund they may possibly receive.

3. Using the information supplied in this chapter, calculate the required down payment and maximum mortgage amount for a 30-year mortgage, to be insured under section 203(b) for a home valued at $89,550.

4. Using the information in question 3, calculate the MIP for 100 percent financing, the loan amount including the MIP, and the monthly payment for the loan using an interest rate of 12.875.

5. You have a buyer who has made an offer on a home and wishes to finance the purchase using an FHA-GPM Plan III mortgage. The value of the home is $76,550 and the current interest rate is 12.250 for the FHA-GPM Mortgage. Calculate the following:

A. Maximum mortgage amount.

B. Required down payment.

C. First-year monthly payments (P & I only).

D. Loan balance after the forty-fourth payment.

6. While working floor time, you received a call from a prospective buyer who is interested in purchasing a home using an FHA-GEM, with an annual payment increase of 3 percent per year for 10 years. The value of the house the person is interested in is $90,000 and the term is 30 years. In checking the quote sheets in the office, you find that GEMs have an interest rate of 12.250. Also, the buyer wants to finance the MIP. Calculate the following:

A. Required down payment.

B. Maximum loan amount.

C. Required MIP.

D. Monthly payment for the first and third years.

NOTES

1. U.S., Department of Housing and Urban Development, Fort Worth Service Office, *Circular Letter No. 81-6*, June 19, 1981, p. 2.
2. U.S., Department of Housing and Urban Development/FHA, HUD-H-318(3), *Lending and Selling with a Graduated Payment Mortgage*, December 1978, p. 8.

8 Other Governmental Programs

LEARNING OBJECTIVES

Besides HUD-FHA, there are other agencies of the federal and state governments that either guarantee or make mortgages on family dwellings in urban and/or rural areas. The agencies we will examine here are the Veterans Administration, the Farmers Home Administration, the Texas Veterans Land Board, the Federal Land Bank, and the Texas Housing Agency.

Upon completion of this chapter you should be able to do the following:

★ Define and explain the loan guaranty benefits of the Veterans Administration.

★ Explain the advantages and disadvantages of loans guaranteed by the Veterans Administration

★ Explain the basic program available through the Farmers Home Administration for rural housing.

★ Outline the Texas Veterans Land Program.

VETERANS ADMINISTRATION

The Veterans Administration is similar to FHA in that VA does not usually make loans, but VA does have the ability to make direct loans in some rural or small communities where VA has determined that private mortgage financing is not available. Whereas FHA insures 100 percent of the loan, VA only guarantees a portion of the loan. This ability to guarantee a portion of an eligible veteran's loan was made possible when Congress passed the Serviceman's Readjustment Act of 1942. This act has been amended several times, but the loan guaranty section of the act has basically remained the same. Under the provision of the act, the VA can presently guarantee up to 60 percent of the loan, or $27,500, whichever is less. Later in this chapter we will discuss the guaranty and the maximum loan, but first let us examine the advantages and disadvantages of a Veterans Administration guaranteed loan.

Advantages

The advantages of the VA loan guaranty are very similar to the advantages of an FHA-insured loan.

Low interest rates   As with the FHA-insured mortgage, the VA-guaranteed loan interest rate is usually less than the interest rate on conventional loans. The reason for the lower interest rate is that the lender is protected from loss by a guaranty from the Veterans Administration. If there is a difference between the VA rate and the conventional rate, many lenders will charge discount points to the seller.

No down payment   One of the major differences between the FHA and VA is that with the VA loan, the eligible veteran normally does not have to make any down payment. The seller is allowed to pay all of the closing costs as well as all of the prepaids. In other words, a veteran can move into a home with no cash investment.

Borrower qualification   Under the VA guaranty program, the borrower qualifications are less strenuous and less formal than under the FHA-insured loan. These qualifications will be discussed in detail in Chapter 13.

No prepayment penalty   As with the FHA-insured mortgage, the borrower may pay off the loan on or before the due date and the VA does not allow the lender to charge a penalty.

Loans are assumable   As with the FHA loans, loans guaranteed by the VA are usually assumable. There is, however, a drawback or penalty to the veteran regarding assumption: the veteran in some cases may not be released from the liability for the mortgage and may not be able to qualify for another VA guaranty mortgage.

Disadvantages

We have discussed the major advantages for the veteran in using the VA guaranty, but as with any program there are disadvantages. Like the advantages, the disadvantages are very similar for FHA- and VA-guaranteed loans.

Discount points   As with the FHA loans, points are usually charged by the lenders who make the VA-guaranteed loan. The reason for these points is the same as for the FHA loan. They are used to bring the yield on the VA-guaranteed mortgage in line with other mortgages. The points may not be paid by the veteran. The law allows the veteran to pay only for the origination of the loan and this fee may not exceed 1 percent of the loan amount. So the only person to whom the discount points are a disadvantage is the seller. For this reason, when the discount points are at a high level, many sellers are reluctant to sell to a veteran wishing to use his "GI loan."

Processing time   Since the VA is a government agency, the time for the application to be approved is sometimes longer than for conventional loans. This is only true if the lender making the loan is not a *supervised lender*. According to Section 500(b) of the Servicemen's Readjustment Act, the Veterans Administration classifies any lender that is subject to examination and supervision by an agency of the United States or any state government including the District of Columbia as a supervised lender. These lenders have the authority to make a VA home loan which the Veterans

Administration must automatically guarantee. Examples of such supervised lenders are savings and loan associations, commercial banks, and life insurance companies. Therefore, the disadvantage of processing time applies to the nonsupervised lenders, such as mortgage companies, for they must submit the completed application and all of the supporting information to the nearest VA office for approval.

Guarantee Fee   The Veterans Administration now charges a fee to issue a guarantee on any loan that meets the requirements of the Veterans Administration. This fee is sometimes called a *guarantee fee* or a *VA-funding fee*. The fee is currently 1 percent of the loan amount. Thus, if the loan amount was $95,000, the fee would be $950.

One can see that the majority of the disadvantages of a VA loan are not major and in most cases are not disadvantages to the veteran, but to the person selling the property.

Eligible Veterans

Not all veterans are eligible to take advantage of the VA's loan guaranty program, and as a real estate professional you must know the eligibility requirements for a VA loan guaranty. Only those veterans who served on active duty during one of the following periods may be eligible. (One additional fact to be remembered is that only active duty counts—not active duty for training.)

World War II   To qualify, a veteran must have served on active duty for at least 90 days and must have a discharge under conditions other than dishonorable or have been released with less than 90 days of service due to a service-connected disability. This service must have been not before September 16, 1940, and no later than July 25, 1947.

Cold War Era   The Veterans Housing Amendments Act of 1976 extended the home loan guaranty to those who served during the period that is sometimes referred to as the Cold War Era. For a veteran to qualify under these amendments, he or she must either have served for at least 181 days and received a discharge or have been released under conditions other than dishonorable, or have been released with less than 181 days due to a service-connected disability. This service must have occurred after July 25, 1947, and prior to June 27, 1950.

Korean Conflict   To be eligible under the Korean Conflict, a veteran must have served on active duty for 90 days or more and have been either discharged or released from active duty under conditions other than dishonorable. If any portion of the 90 days of service was during the period of June 27, 1950, to January 31, 1955, or if a veteran was released from service due to service-connected disability with less than 90 days, the veteran is still eligible.

Noncombat   To be eligible under this category, a veteran must have served for a period of continuous active duty for a period of 181 days or more, and the active duty must have been after January 31, 1955, and prior to August 5, 1964. In addition, a veteran must have been discharged or released from active duty under conditions other than dishonorable or have been released or discharged due to a service-connected disability.

Vietnam Era   For veterans to be eligible under the Vietnam Era benefits, they must have served on active duty between August 5, 1964, and May 7, 1975, for a period of 90 days or more and have been discharged or released under conditions other than dishonorable, or have been released or discharged with less service due to a service-connected disability.

Noncombat   For service after September 7, 1982, to the present a veteran must have served on active duty for two years or more and have been either discharged or released from active duty under conditions other than dishonorable. Or, if a veteran was released from service due to a service-connected disability with less than two years, the veteran is still eligible.

Current active duty   Under the present law a person on active duty for 180 or more days, even though not discharged or released from service, is eligible while his or her service continues without breaks.

In addition to the veterans being eligible, an unmarried surviving spouse of a veteran who served during any of the above periods is eligible if the veteran died while on active duty or as a result of a service-connected disability. Spouses of service personnel who have been missing in action, captured in the line of duty by a hostile force, or forcibly detained or interned by a foreign government or power for a period of more than 90 days are also eligible for a VA-loan guarantee.

Certificate of Eligibility

When dealing with a veteran in the purchase of a home or mobile home, the only true way to establish the eligibility and the amount of entitlement available is for the veteran to secure a Certificate of Eligibility from the Veterans Administration. A sample certificate is shown in Figure 8–1.

If the veteran was released from active service after August 1973, he or she should have received a certificate showing the amount of entitlement available. If the veteran has not used any of his or her entitlement and the amount of entitlement shown on the back of the certificate is less than $27,500, the veteran should have the certificate updated. This can be done by the veteran by sending the Certificate of Eligibility along with a completed VA Form 26-1880 (Figure 8–2) to the nearest VA office.

If the veteran was released prior to August 1973, the following procedure should be followed to secure a Certificate of Eligibility. If the veteran has never been issued a certificate in the past, he or she can go to any VA office with a copy of his or her separation papers (Defense Department Form 214, sometimes referred to as a DD-214) or discharge papers and meet with the guarantee section. Usually the certificate will be issued at that time.

If the veteran has had a previous certificate issued and it has been lost, he or she should complete VA Form 26-1880 and bring or mail it with the separation papers to the guarantee section of the nearest VA office. The veteran must fill out sections 7A through 8C of the form.

One other problem may arise: the veteran may have lost his or her separation papers. Without the separation papers, the VA will not issue a certificate. If this is the case, prior to October 19, 1981, the veteran had only one option – to fill out a Request Pertaining to Military Records (Figure 8–3) and mail it to the proper agency as listed on the reverse side of the form. After the military records were received, the veteran would fill out VA Form 26-1880, attach a copy of the separation papers, and either mail it or take it to the nearest VA office. The VA cut this lengthy process on October 19, 1981, when it published a final regulation in the Federal Register that again allows the VA to accept a copy of a veteran's discharge papers as long as the copy was certified by a public custodian of records as a true and exact copy.

According to the VA, this regulation was

Figure 8–1.   VA Certificate of Eligibility (both sides)

DUPLICATE

Certificate of Eligibility

VA Veterans Administration
7739765

FOR LOAN GUARANTY BENEFITS

NAME OF VETERAN (First, Middle, Last)		SERVICE SERIAL NUMBER/SOCIAL SECURITY NUMBER
Thomas Jackson MORTON		05-412-667
ENTITLEMENT CODE	BRANCH OF SERVICE	DATE OF BIRTH
Code 3 10/63	Army	10/29/37

IS ELIGIBLE FOR THE BENEFITS OF CHAPTER 37, TITLE 38, U.S. CODE, AND HAS THE AMOUNT OF ENTITLEMENT SHOWN AS AVAILABLE ON THE REVERSE, SUBJECT TO THE STATEMENT BELOW, IF CHECKED.

☐   Valid unless discharged or released subsequent to date of this certificate. A certification of continuous active duty as of date of note required.

ADMINISTRATOR OF VETERANS AFFAIRS

J Bewley
(Signature of Authorized Agent)

Regional Office
Albuquerque, N.M.

July 16, 1981
Date Issued

(Issuing Office)

"THIS IS A DUPLICATE CERTIFICATE OF ELIGIBILITY ISSUED UPON THE REQUEST OF THE VETERAN"

DO NOT WRITE ON THIS SIDE—FOR VA USE ONLY

LOAN NUMBER (Include amount if direct loan)	ENTITLEMENT			DATE AND INITIALS OF VA AGENT
	USED		AVAILABLE	
		OTHER		
			27,500	
LH 93897 NM 12/79	$25,000	-----	$2,500	7/16/81 *JB*

NOTE: The figure shown as available entitlement represents the portion of a loan which may be guaranteed or insured by VA to a lender. For information about maximum loan amounts, see VA Pamphlets 26-4 and 26-71-1, or contact the nearest VA office for further information.

Available entitlement is subject to reduction if VA incurs actual liability or loss on the loan(s), if any, listed below, obtained by the veteran with the assistance of loan benefits derived from military service in WW II or the Korean conflict.			REDUCED		
OUTSTANDING LOAN NUMBER(S)	DATE	INITIALS OF VA AGENT	ITEM	DATE	INITIALS OF VA AGENT

VA FORM **26-8320**
DEC 1980

SUPERSEDES VA FORM 26-8320, FEB 1979,
WHICH WILL NOT BE USED.

Figure 8–2.   *VA Form 26-1880*

☆ GPO: 1983-396-608

Form Approved
OMB No. 2900-0086

Veterans Administration

	VETERANS ADMINISTRATION ATTN: LOAN GUARANTY DIVISION
REQUEST FOR DETERMINATION OF ELIGIBILITY AND AVAILABLE LOAN GUARANTY ENTITLEMENT TO	

NOTE: Please read instructions on reverse before completing this form. If additional space is required attach separate sheet.

1. FIRST - MIDDLE - LAST NAME OF VETERAN	2A. ADDRESS OF VETERAN *(No., Street or rural route, City or P.O., State and ZIP Code)*

2B. VETERAN'S DAYTIME TELEPHONE NO. *(Include Area Code)*	3. DATE OF BIRTH	

4. MILITARY SERVICE DATA *(ATTACH PROOF OF SERVICE – SEE INSTRUCTIONS ON REVERSE (Paragraphs F and G.1))*

PERIOD OF ACTIVE SERVICE		NAME *(Show your name exactly as it appears on your separation papers (DD214) or Statement of Service)*	SERVICE NUMBER *(Enter Social Security No., if appropriate)*	BRANCH OF SERVICE
DATE FROM	DATE TO			
A.				
B.				
C.				
D.				

5A. WERE YOU DISCHARGED, RETIRED OR SEPARATED FROM SERVICE BECAUSE OF DISABILITY OR DO YOU NOW HAVE ANY SERVICE-CONNECTED DISABILITIES? ☐ YES ☐ NO *(If "Yes," Complete Item 5B)*	5B. VA FILE NUMBER C-	6. IS A CERTIFICATE OF ELIGIBILITY FOR LOAN GUARANTY PURPOSES ENCLOSED? ☐ YES ☐ NO *(If "No," Complete Items 7A and 7B)*
7A. HAVE YOU PREVIOUSLY APPLIED FOR A CERTIFICATE OF ELIGIBILITY FOR VA LOAN PURPOSES? ☐ YES ☐ NO *(If "Yes," give location of VA office(s))*	7B. HAVE YOU PREVIOUSLY RECEIVED SUCH A CERTIFICATE? ☐ YES ☐ NO *(If "Yes," give location of VA office(s))*	7C. THE CERTIFICATE OF ELIGIBILITY PREVIOUSLY ISSUED TO ME HAS BEEN LOST OR STOLEN. IF RECOVERED IT WILL BE RETURNED TO THE VA *(Check if applicable)* ☐

8. HAVE YOU PREVIOUSLY ACQUIRED PROPERTY WITH THE ASSISTANCE OF A GI LOAN? ☐ YES ☐ NO *(If "Yes," complete Items 9 through 18. Please attach a separate sheet if more than one loan is involved. If "No," skip to Items 19 through 21.)*	9. ADDRESS OF REGIONAL OFFICE(S) WHERE LOAN WAS OBTAINED *(City and State)*

10. STATE TYPE(S) AND NUMBER OF LOAN(S) *(Home, Mobile home, Condominium, Direct, Farm, Business, etc.)*	11. ADDRESS(ES) OF PROPERTY PREVIOUSLY PURCHASED WITH GUARANTY ENTITLEMENT	12. DATE YOU PURCHASED THE PROPERTY(IES)
13. DO YOU NOW OWN THE PROPERTY DESCRIBED IN ITEM 11? ☐ YES ☐ NO *(If "Yes," do not complete Items 14 through 18)*	14. DATE(S) THE PROPERTY WAS SOLD	15. IS THERE ANY UNDERSTANDING OR AGREEMENT WRITTEN OR ORAL, BETWEEN YOU AND THE PURCHASERS THAT THEY WILL RECONVEY THE PROPERTY TO YOU? ☐ YES ☐ NO

NOTE: It will speed processing if you can complete Items 16, 17, and 18.

16. NAME AND ADDRESS OF LENDER(S) TO WHOM LOAN PAYMENTS WERE MADE	17. LENDER'S LOAN OR ACCOUNT NUMBER
	18. VA LOAN NUMBER(S)

I certify that the statements herein are true to the best of my knowledge and belief.

19. SIGNATURE OF VETERAN	20. DATE SIGNED

FEDERAL STATUTES PROVIDE SEVERE PENALTIES FOR FRAUD, INTENTIONAL MISREPRESENTATION, CRIMINAL CONNIVANCE OR CONSPIRACY PURPOSED TO INFLUENCE THE ISSUANCE OF ANY GUARANTY OR INSURANCE BY THE ADMINISTRATOR.

THIS SECTION FOR VA USE ONLY

DATE CERTIFICATE ISSUED AND DISCHARGE OR SEPARATION PAPERS AND VA PAMPHLETS GIVEN TO VETERAN OR MAILED TO ADDRESS SHOWN BELOW	TYPE OF DISCHARGE OR SEPARATION PAPERS RETURNED	INITIALS OF VA AGENT	STATION NUMBER

VA FORM 26-1880, JUN 1982   DO NOT DETACH

IMPORTANT · You must complete Item 21 since the Certificate of Eligibility along with all discharge and separation papers will be mailed to the address shown in Item 21 below. If they are to be sent to you, your current mailing address should be indicated, or if they are to be sent elsewhere, the name and address of such person or firm should be shown in Item 21.

The amount of loan guaranty entitlement available for use is endorsed on the reverse of the enclosed Certificate of Eligibility. This certificate must be returned to the VA at the time a loan application or loan report is submitted.

NOTE - PLEASE DELIVER THE ENCLOSED PAMPHLETS AND DISCHARGE OR SEPARATION PAPERS TO THE VETERAN PROMPTLY

VA FORM JUN 1982 **26-1880**   SUPERSEDES VA FORM 26-1880, JUN 1981, WHICH WILL NOT BE USED.   627735

DO NOT DETACH

- -

◀ 21. PLEASE BE SURE THAT NAME AND ADDRESS ARE ENTERED IN THE SPACE INDICATED TO INSURE PROMPT DELIVERY OF DOCUMENTS

Figure 8-3.   Request Pertaining to Military Records

REQUEST PERTAINING TO MILITARY RECORDS

Please read Privacy Act Statement and instructions on reverse. If more space needed, attach additional sheets.

DATE OF REQUEST

SECTION I—INFORMATION NEEDED TO LOCATE RECORDS *(Furnish as much information as possible)*

1. NAME USED DURING SERVICE *(Last, first, middle)*   2. SOCIAL SECURITY NO.   3. DATE OF BIRTH   4. PLACE OF BIRTH

For an effective records search, it is important that ALL periods of service be shown below.

ACTIVE SERVICE—PAST AND PRESENT

5. BRANCH OF SERVICE *(Show also last organization, if known)*	6. DATES OF ACTIVE DUTY — Date Entered / Date Released	7. Check One — Officer / Enlisted	8. SERVICE NUMBER DURING THIS PERIOD

RESERVE SERVICE—PAST AND PRESENT IF NONE, CHECK ☐ NONE

9. BRANCH OF SERVICE	10. DATES OF MEMBERSHIP — Beginning Date / Ending Date	11. Check One — Officer / Enlisted	12. SERVICE NUMBER DURING THIS PERIOD

NATIONAL GUARD MEMBERSHIP IF NONE, CHECK ☐ NONE

13. ARMY 14. AIR 15. State 16. ORGANIZATION	17. DATES OF MEMBERSHIP — Beginning Date / Ending Date	18. Check One — Officer / Enlisted	19. SERVICE NUMBER DURING THIS PERIOD

20. IS SERVICE PERSON DECEASED? ☐ NO ☐ YES *(If "Yes" enter date:)*   DATE OF DEATH

21. IS (Was) INDIVIDUAL A MILITARY RETIREE OR FLEET RESERVIST? ☐ NO ☐ YES

SECTION II—REQUEST

1. EXPLAIN WHAT INFORMATION OR DOCUMENTS YOU NEED OR CHECK ITEMS 2 OR 3 BELOW

2. ☐ CHECK THIS BOX IF YOU NEED A STATEMENT OF SERVICE ONLY

3. LOST SEPARATION DOCUMENT REPLACEMENT REQUESTED *(Check One)*

☐ REPORT OF SEPARATION (DD Form 214 or equivalent) ISSUED IN _____ *(Yr.) (This contains information normally needed to determine eligibility for benefits. It may be furnished only to the veteran, his surviving next of kin, or to his representative with veteran's signed release authorization—item 6.)*

☐ DISCHARGE CERTIFICATE ISSUED IN _____ *(Yr.) (This shows only date and character of discharge and is of little value in determining eligibility for benefits. It may be issued only to veterans discharged honorably or under honorable conditions, or, if deceased, to the surviving spouse.)*

3A. HOW WAS SEPARATION DOCUMENT LOST?

4. PURPOSE FOR WHICH INFORMATION OR DOCUMENTS ARE NEEDED *(Explain)*

5. REQUESTER IS *(Check proper box)* ☐ PERSON IDENTIFIED IN SECTION 1 ☐ SURVIVING SPOUSE ☐ NEXT OF KIN *(Show relationship)* ☐ OTHER *(Specify)*

5A. SIGNATURE OF REQUESTER

6. RELEASE AUTHORIZATION, IF REQUIRED *(Read instruction J on reverse)* I hereby authorize release of the requested information/documents to the addressee shown at right.

7. REQUESTER *(Please type or print complete return address. Include ZIP code)*

6A. SIGNATURE OF VETERAN *(If signed by other than veteran, complete 6B)*

6B. RELATIONSHIP TO VETERAN

180-104

STANDARD FORM 180 (REV. 1-76)
Prescribed by GSA
FPMR 101-11.410-7

implemented as a means to cut the time required to establish a veteran's eligibility if his or her DD-214 had been lost.

Service personnel presently on active duty for 180 days or more may also apply for a Certificate of Eligibility by submitting a Statement of Service with any supporting material to the nearest VA office. The VA will process the request and either mail the certificate to the service person or he or she may go by the office and pick it up.

The importance of the Certificate of Eligibility cannot be overemphasized. Without a certificate the VA will not guarantee a veterans loan. In most cases a lender will not even start the processing of a VA loan application without the veteran having the Certificate of Eligibility.

If you have any questions regarding a veteran's eligibility, you should contact any VA-approved lender or the nearest VA office in Texas:

Houston:
VA Regional Office
2515 Murworth Dr.
Houston, Texas 77211

Lubbock:
VA Local Office
U.S. Courthouse and Federal Building
1205 Texas Ave.
Lubbock, Texas 79401

San Antonio:
VA Local Office
307 Dwyer Ave.
San Antonio, Texas 78285

Waco:
VA Regional Office
1400 North Valley Mills Drive
Waco, Texas 76710

These offices will have an eligibility section, which will be of great assistance when inquiring about the VA Home Loan Guaranty program.

The Loan Guaranty or Veterans Entitlement

Standard home loan The Veterans Administration loan guaranty is the amount of the loan expressed as either a dollar amount or a percent of the loan. This amount is referred to as the *veterans entitlement*. This entitlement or loan guaranty for home loans is now $27,500 or 60 percent of the loan, whichever is less.

As we stated earlier, the amount of entitlement available to the veteran will establish the maximum loan the veteran can get with no money down. The Veterans Administration has set no maximum loan, only the maximum guaranty. The lending industry has set the maximum loan with no money down as roughly four times the veterans entitlement. This means that a veteran with the full entitlement of $27,500 or 60 percent can usually get a maximum loan of four times $27,500, or $110,000 with no money down.

This does not say the veteran will automatically get the $110,000 loan. The veteran must meet the underwriting requirements of the VA. From this formula of four times the veterans entitlement, the lenders are making a 75 percent loan-to-value ratio loan. If the VA is guaranteeing $27,500 of a $110,000 loan, the lender's exposure to loss is $82,500, or 75 percent. If a veteran wishes to secure a VA-guaranteed loan in excess of four times the entitlement, most mortgage lenders require the veteran to put down 25 percent of the excess, thus keeping the loan-to-value ratio at 75 percent. For example, a veteran wishes to purchase a home for $125,000 and has the full entitlement of $27,500. Using the industry standard of four times the entitlement, the maximum loan with no money down would be $110,000. With a loan amount of $110,000 and purchase price of $125,000 we see the veteran must make up the difference with a down payment of $15,000 (although some lenders will only require a down payment of 25 percent of the excess $15,000, or $3750). Even with a down payment, the veteran has a small cash investment in relation to the total value of the house.

As stated earlier, the present entitlement is 60 percent of the loan amount up to a maximum of $27,500, but the entitlements have increased over the years as the value of houses have increased. The increases in the entitlements will be outlined later in this chapter.

In addition to the purchase of new homes, the loan guaranty may be used for the following:

1. To refinance existing mortgages or other liens of record on homes owned and occupied by the eligible veteran

2. To finance the alterations, repairs, or improvements on homes already owned and occupied by an eligible veteran

3. To purchase individual residence units in certain condominium projects

Graduated-payment mortgage loan   On October 17, 1981, the President of the United States signed Public Law 97-66 that permitted the Veterans Administration to guarantee loans with a graduated-payment feature. The VA-GPM is limited to the purchase of single-family dwellings and does include the purchase of new and existing, not previously occupied, homes and condominiums in VA-approved projects. It should be noted that the VA-GPM may not be used for refinancing an existing debt, alterations, repair or improvements. The GPM also may not be used for the purchase of manufactured housing or a lot or both.

Only one method of graduated-payment amortization is now authorized. The plan is based on Plan III Section 245 of the Department of Housing and Urban Development.

A major difference between this loan and the standard VA loan is a required down payment. The amount of this payment will be reviewed later in this section.

The features and requirements of the VA-GPM, as follows, are based on the information contained in DVB Circular 26-81-36 dated November 12, 1981. The veteran's down payment must be paid in cash from the veteran's own resources. The property must have a remaining economic life of at least thirty years to be eligible to be used as security for the VA-GPM. As with the FHA underwriting, the first year's payments will be used as the basis for underwriting. The DVB circular states that in the cases where the veteran's present income is marginal and some doubt exists as to whether his or her income will increase to keep pace with the increased payments, the VA will disapprove the application. The actual underwriting guidelines for the Veterans Administration will be reviewed in Chapter 13. The maximum entitlement under the VA-GPM is the same as under the standard VA home loan: $27,500 or 60 percent of the loan amount, whichever is smaller.

Now that we have reviewed some of the provisions of the VA-GPM, let us see how the VA will compute the maximum loan amount, the required down payment and the monthly payment.

The maximum loan amount for the VA-GPM is calculated by using either one of two methods allowed by VA. The method that will be used is determined by whether the home to be purchased is a new home or a used home.

If the home to be purchased is a new home, according to VA, the veteran must make a down payment equal to 2.5 percent of the value as established by VA. The document used to establish value by VA is the Certificate of Reasonable Value and is normally referred to as a CRV. In other words, this is the name that VA has given to the appraisals done by VA. For this example, the veteran is interested in a new home and the CRV has established the value of the home as $65,000. To calculate the required down payment, multiply the CRV times 2.5 percent or

$$\$65,000 \times 2.5 \text{ percent} = \$1625$$

For this home, the veteran must make a down payment of $1625 and, as mentioned previously, the down payment must be paid in cash from the veteran's own resources.

If the home is a used home, the method used to calculate the down payment is similar to the method used to calculate the down payment for the FHA-GPM. According to VA, only Plan III of the FHA-GPM may be used. We would use, therefore, the tables shown in Appendix B to calculate the maximum loan amount and the required down payment. Using an interest rate of 14.50 percent, we turn to Appendix B and find the interest rate of 14.50 percent and find the highest outstanding loan-balance factor. This underlined value is 1105.1441. If the value of the property has been established by the CRV as $65,000, we would then divide the CRV value of the property by this factor:

$$\frac{65,000}{1105.1441} = 58.815859$$

Next, this is multiplied by $1000 to get the maximum loan amount of $58,815.86. Accordingly, the $58,815.86 will be rounded down to the nearest $50. Thus, the maximum loan amount would be $58,800.00.

To calculate the required down payment, one would subtract the maximum loan amount from the CRV value of the property. In this example, the down payment would be calculated as:

CRV	$65,000
Less maximum loan amount	$58,800
Required down payment	$ 6,200

One can see that, to qualify for this program, a veteran must have a substantial down payment. This program would appeal to the veteran who has saved a rather large amount for a down payment and has not reached his or her potential highest income.

Since this program is similar to the 245, the monthly payments are calculated as they are for the FHA 245. To calculate the monthly payment, we would turn to Appendix C and locate the proper interest rate, in this case 14.50, and locate the proper factor for the first year's payment. We find the factor is 9.5621. Calculate the first year's payment (principal and interest only) by multiplying the original principal balance (in thousands) by this factor:

$$58.815 \times 9.5621 = \$562.39$$

To calculate the monthly payments for the second, third, fourth, fifth, and each year thereafter, multiply the original principal balance by the proper factor given in the table.

There is one additional requirement: the veteran must sign a statement which must accompany the application or the automatic loan report from a supervised lender. This statement is as follows:

I fully understand that because of the graduated-payment loan obligation I am undertaking, my mortgage payment excluding taxes and insurance will start at $_____$ and will increase by 7.5 percent each year for 5 years to a maximum payment of $_____$ and the mortgage balance will increase to no more than $_____$ at the end of the _____ year. The maximum total amount by which the deferred interest will increase the principal is $_____$. Monthly installments will be due according to the following schedule:

$_____ during the 1st year of the loan
$_____ during the 2nd year of the loan
$_____ during the 3rd year of the loan
$_____ during the 4th year of the loan
$_____ during the 5th year of the loan
$_____ during the 6th year of the loan and every year thereafter[1]

Buydown mortgages On April 16, 1982, the Administrator of Veterans Affairs authorized the VA to guarantee mortgages that have a temporary mortgage interest-rate buydown. It should be noted that this buydown feature may only be used with the standard fixed-rate, fixed-payment mortgage. Thus, the interest rate buydown may not be combined with the graduated payment mortgage. In the past, the VA has reduced the value of properties when the seller or builder/developer would offer an "inducement" to the veteran to purchase a home. According to the VA, the buydown rate mortgage has, due to market conditions and the acceptance of the secondary market, become a useful tool for the financing of homes. The VA, therefore, will not reduce the reasonable value of a property if financed by a buydown mortgage that meets certain requirements. Some of the major requirements are as follows:

1. The assistance or buydown payments will run for a minimum of 3 years and a maximum of 5 years

2. The buydown payments must remain constant for 12 months

3. The annual increase in the monthly payments must be equal or approximately equal

4. The buydown funds will be held by a third party escrow agent and must be beyond the reach of the seller or builder/developer and lender, unless the mortgage is purchased by Fannie Mae who will take custody of the funds

5. The buydown funds may not revert to the seller or builder/developer

6. If the property is sold on an assumption, the buydown will continue

Growing equity mortgage (GEM) At approximately the same time as HUD-FHA announced the growing equity mortgage, the Veterans Administration also announced that they would guarantee a GEM. The VA stated that the GEMs are being guaranteed under the authority of DVB Circular 26-82-17, but the VA GEM is not in all respects identical to the GEM of HUD-FHA.

The GEM has previously been defined in Chapters 3 and 7. Please see these chapters if you need to review the definition.

VA has authorized two basic types of GEMs. In one, the payment increases at a rate not to exceed 4 percent per year for the first 10 years of the mortgage; the second type is a GEM where the annual payment increase is based on a percentage of the Department of Commerce index that measures per capita, after-tax disposable personal income. VA has stated that if the GEM is based on the Department of Commerce index, the loan documents must be written in such a manner to limit the annual payment increase to a maximum of 5 percent. Here, we can see one of the major differences. HUD, at the present time, does not offer the "Indexed GEM."

The term for the VA GEM is similar to the HUD-FHA GEM in that the interest rate and the amount of annual increase will determine the term of the mortgage. Underwriting for the VA GEM is similar to the HUD-FHA GEM in that it is generally based on the first-year payments. An interesting statement in the VA literature on the GEM is that it hopes the lenders will "cooperate" with veteran borrowers who may have difficulty with the increased payments in the later years of the mortgage. In order to reinforce this hope, VA has cited VA Regulation 4314. This regulation provides for the extension or reamortization of a VA-guaranteed loan to prevent or cure a default. Another major difference between the HUD-FHA and the VA GEM is that VA requires all lenders wishing to offer the GEM to submit the proposed GEM to VA for approval. The lenders must submit a detailed description of the GEM, a proposed loan disclosure statement, loan documents, and the acknowledgment statement to be signed by the veteran-borrower. This acknowledgment must explain the effect of the GEM on the borrower's future monthly payments.

There is one additional fact that should be mentioned. VA will not allow the GEM to be used in conjunction with the graduated-payment mortgage. If you want more information on the VA GEM or a list of lenders in your area making the VA-guaranteed GEM, you should contact the nearest VA Loan Guarantee Office.

Manufactured Housing Loan Guarantee

VA, like FHA, can guarantee loans secured by manufactured housing that is classified as either personal property or as real property. This was not true until the President signed into law Public Law 98-223 on March 2, 1984.

The Section entitled "Loan Guaranties for Manufactured Homes Permanently Affixed to Lots" amends chapter 37 of title 38 allowing the Veterans Administration to issue a guar-

antee for the purchase or the refinancing of a loan secured by a manufactured unit. The section further states that the unit must meet two requirements before the guarantee may be issued and they are:

1. The manufactured home is or will be permanently attached or affixed to a lot that is owned or will be owned by the veteran making application for the guarantee.

2. As so permanently affixed, the home is regarded, by the laws of the state in which the home is located, as real property and is taxed as real property.

In other words, an eligible veteran with his or her full entitlement can now secure, from most lenders, a maximum loan with no money down of $110,000 on a manufactured housing unit including a lot if the unit is permanently affixed to the lot and is classified as real property according to the real property laws of Texas.

If the unit is not permanently affixed to the ground and is not considered as real property, the present entitlement or guarantee is 50 percent of the value or $20,000, whichever is less. In regard to the maximum loan amount with no money down, there is no standard for mobile homes as there is for single-family dwellings. In order to secure the maximum in your area of Texas, call several lenders, particularly savings and loan associations, and the larger mobile home dealers in your area.

Partial Use of Entitlement

Home loan   Even though a veteran has previously purchased a home and has used his entitlement, he or she may still be able to purchase a second home using a second VA loan while still owning the previous home. Even if the first home was sold on assumption where the veteran is still liable, he or she may possibly be able to secure another home using VA. In order for you as the real estate professional to see if the veteran can purchase the second home, you must establish the following:

1. When the first home was purchased

2. The VA entitlement or guaranty at the time of purchase

The maximum guaranty has been increased steadily since 1944, in the following amounts:

Date	Maximum Entitlement
Before 1945	$2,000
December 28, 1945	50% of the loan or $4,000
July 12, 1950	60% of the loan or $7,500
May 7, 1968	60% of the loan or $12,500
December 31, 1974	60% of the loan or $17,500
October 1, 1978	60% of the loan or $25,000
October 1, 1980	60% of the loan or $27,500

After establishing the date of the original loan and the amount of entitlement at that time, we then subtract the veterans entitlement at the time of the loan from the amount of entitlement at the present time. For example, a veteran purchased a home in 1967 for $30,000. First we must establish the veteran's entitlement in 1967. It was 60 percent of the loan amount to a maximum $7500. Now let us figure the amount of entitlement used by the veteran at the time the home was purchased:

$30,000 × 60% = $18,000 or $7500, whichever is lower

We can see that the veteran had used all of the original entitlement at the time he or she purchased the first home.

Can the veteran now purchase a second home without being released from the liability of the first home? The answer is yes. How much loan can the veteran expect with no money down? First, we will subtract the entitlement at the time of the original loan from the entitlement in effect today:

Entitlement in effect today	$27,500
Entitlement in effect at time of original loan	−$ 7,500
Remaining entitlement	$20,000

The amount of the maximum loan with no money down is calculated by multiplying the amount of the remaining entitlement by a factor of 4:

$20,000 × 4 = $80,000 maximum loan with no money down

Let us take the same veteran as in the previous example. Instead of purchasing an $80,000 home, however, the veteran wishes to purchase an $82,000 home. What would be the veteran's down payment?

We figured that the maximum loan with no money down was $80,000. Using the rules that most lenders follow, we would calculate the down payment as 75 percent of the sales price plus the remaining entitlement or:

Sales price	$82,000
	×75%
	$61,500
Remaining entitlement	$20,000
Maximum loan	$81,500

This, then, requires a down payment of $500. This is one method used by lenders to figure the down payment required.

Some lenders use the method outlined earlier in the chapter for new loans to calculate the down payment required on a partial use of entitlement. If this were the case, the calculation would be as follows:

Sales price	$82,000
Maximum loan with no money down, $20,000 × 4	$80,000
Difference	$ 2,000

Lenders require the veteran to put down 25 percent of the excess, or

$2000 × 25% = $500.

Mobile homes   If the veteran wishes to purchase a second mobile home, the Va rules are different. If a veteran has obtained a prior VA loan for the purchase of a mobile home, any remaining entitlement may not be used to purchase a second mobile home unless the veteran has disposed of the previously purchased mobile home.

Release of Liability and Reinstatement of Entitlement

Even though the veteran can apply for a second VA-guaranteed loan using the remainder of the entitlement, there is only one way for a veteran to get the full entitlement after once purchasing a home using the VA guaranty, and that is through the release of liability and the requesting of reinstatement of entitlement.

Release of liability   First, let us discuss the process of release of liability. Release of liability can be accomplished in one of three ways.

First, a veteran who is selling his or her home that is financed with a VA guaranty may be released from the liability to the government provided the loan is current, the buyer is obligated contractually to purchase the property and to assume the veteran's liability, and the VA is satisfied that the purchaser is a good credit risk.

Second, the veteran can be released from the liability of a VA-guaranteed loan if the purchaser of the veteran's property is also a veteran who is qualified and will substitute his or her own entitlement to assume the loan.

The third method of release of liability is for the home to be sold, and the purchaser to secure a new loan, and the veteran to pay off the VA-guaranteed loan. Upon payment of the loan, the veteran will secure evidence that the loan is paid off and submit this evidence to the VA with a request for release of liability. Normally the VA will release the veteran from the liability.

Restoration of entitlement   Prior to the passage of the Veterans Housing Act of 1974, even though a veteran had been released from the liability of a VA-guaranteed loan, he or she could never again apply for another VA loan. Now, a veteran may qualify for the restoration of full entitlement if the property has been disposed of, the prior loan has been paid in full, and the government has been released from the guaranty. It should be noted that even though the veteran has been released from liability to the government on a loan, the government is still liable to the lender for the guaranty until the loan is paid off.

There is one additional method for the veteran to be restored to full entitlement, as mentioned earlier: if the property is sold by assumption and the person assuming the property is a veteran who is willing and qualified to substitute his or her entitlement, the veteran may be restored to full entitlement.

Procedures for Release and Reinstatement of Entitlement

If you are working with a seller who has a VA-guaranteed loan, have the veteran contact the Loan Guarantee Section of the nearest VA office. The veteran will need to supply to the VA the loan number, the address of the property, and the veteran's name. Upon supplying this information, VA will send the necessary forms directly to the veteran with instructions. It should be noted that the mortgage lender is not involved in the process and there is no need to contact the lender.

The veteran seller will complete the VA form entitled *Application for Release From Personal Liability to the Government on A Home Loan.* This form is shown in Figure 8–4, along with the veteran's Certificate of Eligibility. In addition the Veteran will need to complete VA Form 26-1880 (which was illustrated earlier in Figure 8–2).

According to the VA, when the above forms are submitted to VA, there must be a certified check or money order payable to the Veterans Administration to pay for a credit report (about $35.00).

If a veteran assumes the mortgage, he or she will complete a Statement of Purchaser or Owner Assuming Seller's Loan, VA Form 26-6382 (Figure 8–5); Financial Statement, VA Form 26-6807 (Figure 8–6); Important Notice (Figure 8–7) as well as completing Part I of the supplied copies of the Request For Verification of Employment and Request For Verification of Deposit. In addition, the veteran assumptor must supply his or her Certificate of Eligibility. Thus if the person who is assuming the loan is a veteran, has sufficient entitlement, is approved by the VA, and is willing to substitute his or her entitlement, the veteran seller will have his or her full entitlement.

If the person or persons assuming the VA-guaranteed loan is not a veteran, he or she will still complete all of the forms mentioned in the previous paragraph. The main difference is that the nonveteran purchaser will not have a Certificate of Eligibility.

After receiving the required information, VA will underwrite or review the purchaser as they would an application for a new loan. It should be noted that this is true whether or not the person or persons assuming the loan is a veteran. VA, after reviewing the credit and employment and finding that there are sufficient funds available to assume the loan, will then send a letter to the veteran stating that the VA has tentatively approved the veteran's request for release of liability with or without reinstatement of entitlement. In this letter, the VA will request one copy of the recorded deed containing an assumption clause.

Assumption clause   The *LG Bulletin # 7–84,* issued by the Veterans Administration, Regional Office, Waco, Texas, on January 12, 1984, states that for properties located in

Figure 8-4.   Application for Release from Personal Liability

Form Approved
OMB No. 76-RO425

VETERANS ADMINISTRATION
APPLICATION FOR RELEASE FROM PERSONAL LIABILITY TO THE GOVERNMENT ON A HOME LOAN

INSTRUCTIONS· Please complete this form fully and accurately and return it to the office of the Veterans Administration shown below. Enclose remittance (certified check or money order) payable to the Veterans Administration for a credit report on the person(s) who will assume or who has already assumed liability on your home loan. NOTE: Use of this form does not effect the seller's liability to the lender. See VA Pamphlet 26-5, Pointers for the Veteran Homeowner, Chapter 4. See Section II for Privacy Act Information.

SECTION I – *To be completed by Veterans Administration*

RETURN TO

ADDRESS *(Complete)*
Veterans Administration
ATTN: Loan Guaranty Officer

1. VA LOAN NO.

SECTION II – *To be completed by the Seller*

PRIVACY ACT INFORMATION - No release of liability may be granted unless this form has been completed and received (38 U.S.C. 1817). This form provides information that is used in determining whether VA can approve a request for release of liability to the Government on a loan. Any disclosure of the information outside the VA will only be made as permitted by law.

2A. FIRST NAME - MIDDLE NAME - LAST NAME OF SELLER *(Type or print)*

3. ADDRESS OF PROPERTY WHICH IS SECURITY FOR THE LOAN FROM WHICH YOU WISH TO BE RELEASED FROM LIABILITY *(If rural property give directions to locate it)*

2B. MAILING ADDRESS OF SELLER *(Number and street or rural route, City or P.O., State and ZIP Code.)*

4. INFORMATION ABOUT PURCHASER OR OWNER OF PROPERTY WHO WILL ASSUME YOUR LOAN

A. FIRST NAME - MIDDLE NAME - LAST NAME OF ASSUMER OF LOAN *(Type or print)*

B. MAILING ADDRESS OF ASSUMER OF LOAN *(Number and street or rural route, City, or P.O., State and ZIP Code)*

5A. STATUS OF SALE TRANSACTION *(Check one)*

☐ HAVE AGREED ON PURCHASE PRICE BUT NO SALE HAS BEEN COMPLETED AND NO CONTRACT OR DEED SIGNED *(complete Item 5B)*

☐ NO SALE HAS BEEN COMPLETED BUT CONTRACT FOR SALE HAS BEEN SIGNED AND COPY IS ATTACHED *(Complete Item 5B)*

☐ SALE HAS BEEN COMPLETED AND DEED EXECUTED AND DELIVERED TO PURCHASER *(Complete Item 5C)*

5B. AGREED PURCHASE PRICE
$

5C. SALE PRICE
$

6. PAYMENT ENCLOSED FOR CREDIT REPORT *(Check one)*
☐ MONEY ORDER   ☐ CERTIFIED CHECK

7A. NAME OF LENDER WHO HOLDS YOUR MORTGAGE *(If unknown, enter "Unknown")*

7B. ADDRESS OF LENDER

8A. NAME OF FIRM OR COMPANY TO WHOM YOU MAKE YOUR PAYMENTS ON YOUR LOAN *(If same as Lender, enter "same")*

8B. ADDRESS OF FIRM OR COMPANY

8C. LENDER'S LOAN NO. *(If known)*

9. ASSESSMENTS AND OR OTHER LIENS OUTSTANDING

A. AMOUNT	B. PURPOSE *(Streets, sidewalks, sewers, etc.)*	C. HOW PAYABLE

IMPORTANT—If the property identified in Item 3 above is located in Massachusetts, Connecticut, Maryland, Illinois, Missouri, Nevada, California or the Commonwealth of Puerto Rico, complete Item 10A. For properties located in all other states, complete Item 10B.

10A. DOES THE PURCHASER OF YOUR PROPERTY AGREE TO SIGN THE ASSUMPTION AGREEMENT IF YOUR APPLICATION IS APPROVED? *(Answer "Yes" if you and your purchaser have already executed the VA approved Agreement Creating Liability to holder and to U.S.)*
☐ YES ☐ NO *(If "No", return this form and all other forms sent to you)*

10B. DOES THE PURCHASER OF YOUR PROPERTY AGREE TO SIGN THE ASSUMPTION AGREEMENT IF YOUR APPLICATION IS APPROVED? *(Answer "Yes" if your purchaser has already assumed personal liability by a VA approved clause in the deed and attach a copy of the deed showing date and place of recordation)*
☐ YES ☐ NO *(If "No", return this form and all other forms sent to you)*

11. HAVE YOU DELIVERED VA FORMS 26-6382 AND 26-6807 TO YOUR PURCHASER FOR COMPLETION AND FORWARDING TO THE VETERANS ADMINISTRATION?
☐ YES ☐ NO *(If "No", explain)*

12. DATE | 13. SIGNATURE OF SELLER

VA FORM
AUG 1979 **26-6381**

EXISTING STOCKS OF VA FORM 26-6381, FEB 1976, WILL BE USED.

607990

Figure 8–5.   Statement of Purchaser or Owner Assuming Loan

Form Approved
OMB No. 76-R0426

VETERANS ADMINISTRATION

STATEMENT OF PURCHASER OR OWNER ASSUMING SELLER'S LOAN

INSTRUCTIONS - Please complete this form and the VA Form 26-6807, Financial Statement, and return to the office of the Veterans Administration shown below. These forms are for submission in connection with the application for release from liability to the Government on a home loan filed with this office by the seller in Item 3 and in connection with an application for substitution of entitlement by a veteran purchaser and the veteran-seller. In substitution of entitlement cases, also submit VA Form 26-8106, Statement of Veteran Assuming GI Loan.

PRIVACY ACT INFORMATION - No release of liability of the veteran-seller may be granted unless this form has been completed and received (38 U.S.C. 1817). This form provides information that is used in determining whether VA can approve the seller's request for release of liability to the Government on the loan. Any disclosure of the information outside the VA will only be made as permitted by law.

SECTION I

RETURN TO

1. ADDRESS (Complete)	2. LOAN NUMBER
	3. FIRST NAME - MIDDLE NAME - LAST NAME OF SELLER (Type or print)
	4. COMPLETE PROPERTY ADDRESS

SECTION II – (To be completed by purchaser)

I understand and agree that the attached Financial Statements are for use of the Veterans Administration and the lender who holds the mortgage on the property which I am purchasing or have purchased from the above-named seller. I also understand that the Veterans Administration will not examine the title to this property and that it is my responsibility to determine that such title is acceptable to me. It is further understood that the release of the seller from liability to the Government on the loan or substitution of entitlement is conditioned upon my assuming all of the liabilities and obligations of the above seller arising out of the loan. This includes the liability of the seller to reimburse the Veterans Administration for any amount it may hereafter be required to pay or for any loss it suffers as a result of the making, guaranty, or insurance of the seller's loan. I will assume, or have already assumed all of the liability of the above seller arising out of the loan by written agreement in such form as the Veterans Administration requires.

5. INFORMATION ON PURCHASER AND SALE OF PROPERTY

A. NAME OF PURCHASER (First - middle - last) (Type or print)	B. ARE YOU A VETERAN	C. SERVICE SERIAL NO.	D. PRICE I HAVE AGREED TO PAY OR HAVE PAID FOR THE PROPERTY
	(If "Yes," complete Item 5C) ☐ YES ☐ NO		$

E. IS AMOUNT IN ITEM 5D GREATER THAN UNPAID BALANCE ON SELLER'S LOAN?	F. PAYMENT OF DIFFERENCE BETWEEN PURCHASE PRICE AND UNPAID BALANCE ON SELLER'S LOAN (Check one)
(If "Yes" complete Item 5F) ☐ YES ☐ NO	☐ THE DIFFERENCE WILL BE PAID (OR HAS BEEN PAID) AT THE TIME PROPERTY IS (WAS) TRANSFERRED BY ME IN CASH WITHOUT BORROWING ANY PORTION THEREOF ☐ IT WILL BE (OR WAS) NECESSARY FOR ME TO BORROW ALL OR A PORTION OF THE DIFFERENCE (If checked, complete Items 6A thru 6G)

6. TERMS OF SALE (If additional space is needed, use reverse)

A. AMOUNT OF CASH PAID OR TO BE PAID	B. AMOUNT BORROWED (Item 5F)	C. SOURCE OF FUNDS BORROWED (Name and address)

D. IS (WAS) MORTGAGE OR DEED OF TRUST GIVEN SELLER OR OTHER PERSON?	E. AMOUNT OF OR BALANCE OF MORTGAGE OR DEED OF TRUST	F. SECURITY FOR AMOUNT BORROWED (Item 6B) (If other than mortgage or deed of trust)
☐ YES ☐ NO	$	

G. TERMS OF REPAYMENT OF AMOUNT BORROWED (Item 6B)

AMOUNT OF PAYMENT	PAYMENTS MADE
$	☐ MONTHLY ☐ OTHER (Specify)

7. LIST YOUR ADDRESSES FOR PAST 5 YEARS

A. ADDRESSES (No. and street or rural route, P.O. Box, City, State and ZIP Code)	B. DATES

8. DATE	9. SIGNATURE OF PURCHASER

VA FORM
DEC 1979   **26-6382**

SUPERSEDES VA FORM 26-6382, AUG 1978,
WHICH WILL NOT BE USED

607145

Figure 8–6.   *VA Financial Statement, page 1*

Form Approved
OMB No. 2900-0047

VA Veterans Administration	FINANCIAL STATEMENT	1 FILE NO. C–	2 LOAN NO.

IMPORTANT: Type or print all entries in ink. If more space is needed for any item continue under Section VI, "Remarks," or attach separate sheets. If there is a coborrower or coapplicant who is not the spouse of the borrower applicant, a separate financial statement should be completed by that person.

SECTION I   GENERAL INFORMATION

3. NAME AND PRESENT MAILING ADDRESS OF BORROWER/APPLICANT (Include ZIP Code)	4. HOME TELEPHONE NO. (Include Area Code)	5. DATE OF BIRTH
	6. MARITAL STATUS OF BORROWER APPLICANT ☐ MARRIED ☐ UNMARRIED ☐ SEPARATED	7. SOCIAL SECURITY NO. OF BORROWER/APPLICANT
8. NAME OF SPOUSE	9. SPOUSE'S DATE OF BIRTH 10. SOCIAL SECURITY NO. OF SPOUSE	11. AGE(S) OF DEPENDENT(S)

12A. BORROWER/APPLICANT *If you do not wish to complete Items 12B and 12C, please initial here* ▶	INITIALS	13A. SPOUSE *If you do not wish to complete Items 13B and 13C, please initial here* ▶	INITIALS
12B. RACE/NATIONAL ORIGIN ☐ AMERICAN INDIAN ALASKAN NATIVE ☐ ASIAN, PACIFIC ISLANDER ☐ BLACK *(Not Hispanic)* ☐ HISPANIC ☐ WHITE *(Not Hispanic)*	**12C. SEX** ☐ FEMALE ☐ MALE	**13B. RACE NATIONAL ORIGIN** ☐ AMERICAN INDIAN ALASKAN NATIVE ☐ ASIAN, PACIFIC ISLANDER ☐ BLACK *(Not Hispanic)* ☐ HISPANIC ☐ WHITE *(Not Hispanic)*	**13C. SEX** ☐ FEMALE ☐ MALE

14. PLEASE CHECK THE APPROPRIATE BOX(ES). IF ONE OR MORE ARE CHECKED THIS CREDIT STATEMENT MUST INCLUDE INFORMATION CONCERNING THE BORROWER/APPLICANT'S SPOUSE (OR FORMER SPOUSE IF BOX "D" IS CHECKED). IF NO BOXES ARE CHECKED NO INFORMATION CONCERNING THE SPOUSE NEED BE FURNISHED.

☐ A. THE SPOUSE IS OR WILL BE JOINTLY OBLIGATED WITH THE BORROWER APPLICANT ON THE LOAN.

☐ C. THE BORROWER APPLICANT IS MARRIED AND THE PROPERTY SECURING THE LOAN IS LOCATED IN A COMMUNITY PROPERTY STATE.

☐ B. THE BORROWER APPLICANT IS RELYING ON THE SPOUSE'S INCOME AS A BASIS FOR REPAYMENT OF THE LOAN.

☐ D. THE BORROWER/APPLICANT IS RELYING ON ALIMONY, CHILD SUPPORT, OR SEPARATE MAINTENANCE PAYMENTS FROM A SPOUSE OR FORMER SPOUSE AS A BASIS FOR REPAYMENT OF THE LOAN.

SECTION II   EMPLOYMENT AND FINANCIAL STATUS

15. COMPLETE RECORD OF EMPLOYMENT FOR YOURSELF AND SPOUSE *(Start with present position and work back 2 years)*

		A. NAME AND ADDRESS OF EMPLOYER	B. DATES (Month, year) FROM / TO	C. KIND OF JOB *(Mechanic, stenographer, etc.)*	D. WORK TELEPHONE NO.
BOR-ROWER/APPLI-CANT	(1)		PRESENT TIME		
	(2)				
SPOUSE	(1)		PRESENT TIME		
	(2)				

16. MONTHLY INCOME *(Include income from business or property after deduction of expenses. Disclosure of child support, alimony and maintenance income is optional.)*	A. GROSS SALARY *(Before payroll deductions)*	BORROWER APPLICANT	SPOUSE	C. OTHER *(Specify)*	BORROWER APPLICANT	SPOUSE
		$	$			
	B. PENSION OR COMPENSATION			D. TOTAL MONTHLY INCOME	$	$

17. ASSETS

A. CASH IN BANK *(Checking and savings accounts, building and loan accounts, etc.)*	$	F. SAVINGS BONDS *(Current value)*	$
B. CASH ON HAND		G. STOCKS AND OTHER BONDS *(Current value)*	
C. FURNITURE AND HOUSEHOLD GOODS *(Resale value)*		H. REAL ESTATE OWNED *(Resale value)*	
D. AUTOMOBILES *(Resale value)*		I. OTHER ASSETS *(Itemize)*	
MAKE YEAR MODEL			
E. TRAILERS, BOATS, CAMPERS *(Resale value)*		J. TOTAL ASSETS	$

18. DEBTS

NOTE: DETAILS FOR INSTALLMENT CONTRACTS AND OTHER DEBTS *(Show here ALL debts which you are required to pay in regular monthly installments, such as car, television, washing machine, payments to dealers, banks, finance companies, repayment of money borrowed for any purpose, doctor bills, hospital bills, etc. Include any alimony, child support, or separate maintenance obligations you are required to pay. If additional space is needed, use Section VI, or attach separate sheet. Do not include living expenses. If repayment of a debt is not on a monthly basis, write "0" in Column E and describe arrangements to repay in "Remarks")*

ITEM NO.	NAME AND ADDRESS OF CREDITOR *(Include ZIP Code)* A.	DATE AND PURPOSE OF DEBT *(Include account number, if available)* B.	ORIGINAL AMOUNT OF DEBT C.	UNPAID BALANCE D.	AMOUNT DUE MONTHLY E.	AMOUNT PAST DUE *(If any)* F.
(1)			$	$	$	$
(2)						
(3)						
(4)	TOTAL ▶		$	$	$	$

VA FORM 26-6807
SEP 1982

EXISTING STOCKS OF VA FORM 26-6807, MAR 1981, WILL BE USED.

PRIVACY ACT INFORMATION

The information requested on this form is used in loan servicing and in evaluating an application for release of liability and substitution of entitlement if applicable. No determination can be made unless a completed financial statement has been submitted (38 U.S.C. 1802, 1817 and 1820). Failure to provide the information will deprive VA of information needed in reaching decisions which could affect you. You are not required to furnish your Social Security number, but are urged to do so. Specifically, your Social Security number is requested under authority of 38 U.S.C. 1802, 1817 and 1820. It is requested for use as a personal identifier to assist VA in obtaining your most recent address in the event your loan becomes past due. Responses may be disclosed outside the VA only if the disclosure is authorized under the Privacy Act, including the routine uses identified in VA system of records, 55VA26, Loan Guaranty Home, Condominium and Mobile Home Loan Applicant Records and Paraplegic Grant Applicant Records - VA, published in the Federal Register.

VOLUNTARY INFORMATION FOR GOVERNMENT MONITORING PURPOSES

The information in Items 12A, 12B, 12C and 13A, 13B and 13C is requested by the Federal Government to monitor compliance by VA as a lender with Equal Credit Opportunity and Fair Housing laws. The law provides that a lender may neither discriminate on the basis of this information nor on whether or not it is furnished.

Figure 8–6.   (continued) VA Financial Statement, page 2

NOTICE TO APPLICANTS

This is notice to you as required by the Right to Financial Privacy Act of 1978 that the Veterans Administration Loan Guaranty Service or Division has a right of access to financial records held by a financial institution in connection with the consideration or administration of assistance to you. Financial records involving your transaction will be available to the Veterans Administration Loan Guaranty Service or Division without further notice or authorization but will not be disclosed or released to another Government Agency or Department without your consent except as required or permitted by law.

SECTION III - CREDIT REFERENCES AND OTHER FINANCIAL INFORMATION

19. NAME AND ADDRESS OF FIRMS OR BANKS WITH WHOM YOU HAVE DONE BUSINESS

A.	B.
C.	D.

20. IF YOU ARE RENTING PREMISES YOU NOW OCCUPY, COMPLETE A, B AND C

A. MONTHLY RENTAL	B. UTILITIES INCLUDED?	C. NAME AND ADDRESS OF PERSON OR FIRM RENTAL PAID TO
$.	☐ YES ☐ NO	

21A. HAVE YOU EVER BEEN ADJUDICATED BANKRUPT?	21B. DATE ADJUDICATED BANKRUPT	22A. HAVE YOU HAD A GI LOAN?	22B. NAME OF VA OFFICE WHERE LOAN WAS PROCESSED
☐ YES ☐ NO *(If "Yes," complete Item 21B)*		☐ YES ☐ NO *(If "Yes," complete Item 22B)*	

SECTION IV - REAL ESTATE OWNED

(Show ALL real estate owned. Use this sheet to provide information for one property. If you own more than one property use separate blank sheets to provide the same items of information for each of your other properties.)

23. ADDRESS OF PROPERTY (Number, street, city, county, State)	24. TYPE OF PROPERTY (House, farm, etc.)	25. PURCHASE PRICE	26. CURRENT MARKET VALUE OF PROPERTY
		$	$

27. NAME AND ADDRESS OF MORTGAGEE (If mortgaged)	28. ORIGINAL AMOUNT OF MORTGAGE	29. UNPAID BALANCE
	$	$

30. FREQUENCY OF MORTGAGE PAYMENTS (If payment is not by regular amortization plan, explain in Section VI, "Remarks")	31. AMOUNT OF MORTGAGE PAYMENT	32. STATUS OF LOAN (Check)	33. AMOUNT OF DELINQUENCY (If any)
☐ MONTHLY ☐ QUARTERLY ☐ SEMI-ANNUALLY ☐ ANNUALLY	$	☐ CURRENT ☐ DELINQUENT	$

34. OTHER LIENS AGAINST PROPERTY, IF ANY	35. DO YOU OCCUPY THE PROPERTY?	36. NAME OF OCCUPANTS OTHER THAN YOURSELF AND DEPENDENTS
$	☐ YES ☐ NO	

37. IF PROPERTY IS RENTED, WHAT ARE THE RENTAL TERMS?	38. NAME OF PERSON PAYING RENT IF OTHER THAN OCCUPANT	39. AMOUNT OF AVERAGE MONTHLY INCOME YOU RECEIVE FROM THIS PROPERTY IN EXCESS OF OPERATING EXPENSES
$ PER		$

SECTION V - ADDITIONAL DATA

40. NAME AND ADDRESS OF NEAREST RELATIVE NOT LIVING WITH YOU *(Include telephone number if available)*

SECTION VI - REMARKS

41. USE THIS SPACE AND ADDITIONAL SHEETS, IF NECESSARY TO SUPPLY ANY OTHER PERTINENT INFORMATION AND TO CONTINUE YOUR ANSWER TO PREVIOUS ITEMS. INDICATE ITEM NUMBER TO WHICH YOUR COMMENTS APPLY.

SECTION VII - CERTIFICATIONS

I (WE) AFFIRM that the information contained herein is true, correct, and complete to the best of my (our) knowledge and belief.

42A. SIGNATURE OF BORROWER/APPLICANT	42B. DATE	43A. SIGNATURE OF SPOUSE	43B. DATE

PENALTY - The law provides severe penalties which include fine or imprisonment, or both, for the willful submission of a statement or evidence of a material fact, knowing it to be false.

☆U.S. Government Printing Office 1982—361-489/2617

Figure 8–7.   Notice Accompanying Application to Assume a Loan

VA LH# _____ (ROL)

IMPORTANT NOTICE

(To be executed by Assumer of Loan)

The enclosed VA Form 26-6382 and 6807 represent my application to assume the indebtedness on this loan and permit VA to consider releasing the current owner from further liability.

I realize it may be necessary for VA to contact employers, former employers, creditors, depositories and landlords to verify information submitted on my financial statement.

My signature below authorizes full disclosure of any and all information sought by VA in connection with my application.

X _____

Date: _____   Signature of Assumer-Applicant

SSN# _____

X _____

Signature of Spouse

SSN# _____

Texas an assumption clause that is acceptable is:

"As a part of the consideration for this conveyance, the Grantees herein expressly assume and agree to pay the balance owing on that certain promissory note dated _____, 19_____, in the original principal sum of $ _____, secured by and fully described in the Deed of Trust of even date therewith recorded in Vol. _____, Page _____, Deed of Trust Records of _____ County, Texas, and hereby expressly assume the obligation of (name of veteran) under the terms of the instruments creating said loan to indemnify the Veterans Administration to the extent of any claim payment arising from the guaranty or insurance of the indebtedness above mentioned, this agreement of assumption being evidenced by their acceptance of this deed."

As one can see, the process of release of liability and the reinstatement of entitlement is not automatic and both the veteran seller and the purchaser—either a veteran or nonveteran—must follow very specific steps. If you have any questions, have the veteran seller contact the nearest VA office.

Maximum Loan and Term

Under the VA home-loan guaranty and mobile home loan guaranty, there is no maximum loan. Most lenders use the rough rule of four times the veterans entitlement as the maximum loan with no money down.

One should note that the VA will not issue a guaranty on a loan that exceeds the value established by the Certificate of Reasonable Value (CRV). The CRV is the VA appraisal and will be discussed in depth later in this text.

The maximum term for a VA loan is as follows:

1. Home loan: 30 years and 32 days.

2. Mobile home loans:

   a. New single-wide unit with or without lot—20 years and 32 days

   b. Lot only—20 years and 32 days

   c. New double-wide unit with or without lot—20 years and 32 days

   d. Used mobile home—the term may not exceed those listed above or the remaining physical life of the mobile home as established by the VA, whichever is less

FARMERS HOME ADMINISTRATION (FmHA)

The Farmers Home Administration (FmHA) serves as a rural credit agency for the Department of Agriculture and was established during the administration of Franklin D. Roosevelt to aid the farmers devastated by the depression. The agency has had several names since its beginning in 1935, but it was not until Congress passed the Farmers Home Administration Act of 1946 that the agency received its name and purpose as we know them today. The purpose of FmHA is to serve eligible families and residents of rural communities of the United States with credit and technical help. FmHA has many loan programs available, but this section will deal with only one of the major programs for the financing of rural homes. Some of the other programs available through FmHA are outlined in Appendix F.

The agency, as are many other government agencies, is headquartered in Washington, D.C., with each state having a state office. The state office has the responsibility of coordinating the FmHA's programs in that state. The state office for Texas is in Temple at the following address:

Farmers Home Administration
W.R. Poage Building
101 South Main
Temple, Texas 76501

In addition to a state office in each state, branch offices are usually located in each county. In Texas, there are 148 of these county offices.

Section 502—Rural Housing Mortgages

The objective of Section 502 loans is to enable eligible individuals or families who live in rural areas to obtain adequate, modest, decent, safe, and sanitary homes and related facilities.

The 502 loan may be for the following purposes:

1. To purchase, construct, or relocate a dwelling and related facilities if the dwelling is to be used as his or her permanent home

2. To purchase a suitable building site for a home if the applicant does not own a suitable site

3. To purchase essential equipment for use in the home such as a range, refrigerator, or clothes washer or dryer

4. To install heaters or approved solar systems, and storm cellars and similar protective structures

For the 502 program, FmHA has established income limits for a family for each of the states. The income figures used are referred to as adjusted incomes. The adjusted income for this program is calculated as follows: the total gross income of the family or individual, less a 5 percent deduction, less $300 per child member of the household. For example, let us figure the annual adjusted income for a family of four with a total gross income of $16,500 living in the Panhandle region of Texas. The calculation for two adults and two minor children would be as follows:

Total gross income	$16,500
less 5 percent	−$825
less $300 per child	−$600
Annual adjusted income	$15,075

For that region of Texas, the low income maximum is $15,000; thus, this family could possibly qualify for a 502 loan.

The 502 loans are limited to rural areas of the United States. According to FmHA, a rural area is defined as:

1. Open country that is not associated or part of an urban area

2. Any town, city, or village which has the following population:

   a. 10,000 or less if the town, city, or village is rural in character

   b. A population in the excess of 10,000, but less than 20,000, that is not part of a Standard Metropolitan Statistical Area or has a serious lack of mortgage funds for low- and moderate-income households.

For areas in Texas that possibly will meet this criteria, you should contact the office of the Texas FmHA director.

In addition to income limitations, there are limitations to the size of the home that can be financed under this program. According to the regulations, new dwellings should be designed to fit the needs of the applicant and may have 3 bedrooms and 1 1/2 baths. All new dwellings will contain no more than 1200 square feet of living area. Existing dwellings must be structurally sound, functionally adequate, and in good repair or able to be placed in good repair with the funds loaned. The footage requirement for the existing dwelling is flexible in order to adjust to the size of the housing available.

Under this program, the interest rate on these loans is based on the family's ability to repay the loan. For the interest rate range, you will need to contact the nearest FmHA office. Under this program, FmHA will loan up to 100 percent of the FmHA appraised value of the site and the improvements if the new home was built with inspections made by HUD-FHA, FmHA, or the VA. The FmHA will also make loans up to 100 percent of the appraised value of homes and improvements made to a home that is over one year old. The maximum term of the loan under this program is 30 years.

TEXAS VETERANS LAND PROGRAM

The Texas Veterans Land Program was established by the Texas legislature in 1949 to help veterans buy land with a small down payment and low interest rate mortgages. This program is unique to Texas and has been used by thousands of veterans to purchase land both in and out of a subdivision.

Who may use the program? The legislature has established the following rules:

1. The applicant must have served ninety days or more on active duty in the military services of the United States since September 16, 1940.

2. The applicant must have been a resident of the state of Texas on entering into active duty status or have been a resident of Texas for the past 5 years.

3. The applicant must have established Texas as his or her state residence.

4. The applicant must have received any discharge other than dishonorable from military service.

5. The applicant must not have previously used the right to purchase land under the provision of this program.

6. The unmarried surviving spouse of a Texas veteran who died while on active duty may also be eligible for the program.

The program has certain limitations and restrictions as to the amount of land. Those restrictions are:

1. The tract of land that the veteran wishes to purchase must contain at least 10 acres with a clear title.

2. The property must be located inside the confines of Texas.

3. The property must be described.

4. The property must have at least a 30-foot-wide access to a public road.

5. If the land is located inside an existing or proposed subdivision, the veteran must contact the Veteran Land Board. It is the policy of the board not to purchase more than 5 lots from any one person or developer.

The Texas legislature has authorized a 40-year mortgage with semi-annual payments. The veteran is required to pay 5 percent of the purchase price as down payment. In addition, the board has established the following fees: (1) an application fee of $25.00; (2) an appraisal and contract fee of $190; (3) legal and closing fees at a maximum of $130; and (4) the interest rate as established based upon the cost of funds. The funds for the program are raised by the sale of bonds as authorized by the Texas legislature.

These mortgages have no prepayment penalty, and after the mortgage has reached the third year the mortgage may be assumed by anyone, veteran or nonveteran. If the person is not a veteran, however, the interest rate will escalate.

The board has established the maximum available loan through this program at $20,000.

If you should want more information on this program, contact the Veteran Land Board, Stephen F. Austin Building, Austin, Texas, 78701, or telephone 1-800-252-VETS.

TEXAS VETERANS HOUSING ASSISTANCE PROGRAM

The Texas Veterans Housing Assistance Program was established by the 68th Texas Legislature in 1983 with the passage of the Veterans Housing Assistance Act. Since the act would require an amendment to the constitution of Texas, it was placed on the ballot of the general election of November 1983 as Proposition 7. As a result of the vote, the proposition was passed and the program began in January 1984.

It should be noted that the Veterans Land Program and the Veterans Housing Assistance program are two different programs. As we learned in the section on the land program, it is to help the veteran purchase land, whereas the Texas Veterans Housing Assistance Program (VHAP) is to assist a veteran in the purchase of a principal residence.

Eligibility Requirements

Section 177.5 (b) states that a veteran loan applicant is eligible to participate in the program if he or she:

1. is a citizen of the United States of America;

2. is a bona fide resident of Texas at the time of an application;

3. has completed 90 continuous days of active duty, unless sooner discharged by reason of service connected disability, in the Army, Navy, Air Force, Coast Guard, or Marine Corps after September 16, 1940;

4. has been honorably discharged from military service;

5. was a bona fide resident of Texas at the time of entering the service or has been a resident of the state for 5 years prior to making application for a loan; and

6. has not previously participated in the Veterans Housing Assistance Program or the Veterans Land Program.

The last of the requirements is very important. If a veteran has received a loan under the Veterans Land Program, he or she is not eligible for a VHAP loan.

In addition, it should be pointed out that if the husband and wife are both veterans who qualify for the program, each may make application and receive a loan or one may apply under the land program and one under the VHAP program. Thus, they could get help from Texas to purchase the land as well as help build or purchase a home.

Application Procedure

After the veteran has selected a home, he or she will then go to an approved lending institution. This means the lender has been approved by the Veteran Land Board to participate in the program. As with the land program, there is an application fee. At the present time, the fee is $25.00. This fee and the complete application form are sent to the Veterans Land Board. Then, once the application is approved, the board will notify the veteran and the lender that the veteran is approved and the length of time that the funds will be reserved by the board for use by the veteran. Thus, the approval is like any other approval and issuing of a commitment.

Types of Homes that Qualify

According to the requirements of the program the funds may only be used to purchase a principle residence or in other words the veterans homestead. The home that the veteran purchases can either be an existing home or may be a new home. The home does not have to be the first home of the veteran, but as mentioned earlier the home must be the veterans homestead. In addition, there is no limit to the amount of acreage bought with the home.

At the present time, the proceeds of the loan may be used to purchase a single-family dwelling or a condominium unit only, but according to the board they are seeking a ruling from the Internal Revenue Service as to whether the program may be extended to include the purchase of a duplex, triplex, and fourplex units.

Loan Amount and Down Payment

The maximum loan amount authorized under the VHAP program is $20,000 and the loan will be funded to the lender that will be making the veteran's loan. If the veteran is seeking a loan in the amount of $90,000, the VHAP will fund up to $20,000; the lender, then, would have to fund $70,000. It should be noted that the $20,000 may not be used in the place of a down payment.

According to the information from the Veterans Land Board, if the veteran is seeking a conventional loan or an FHA-insured loan, the veteran will be required to make the minimum down payment; but if the veteran is seeking a VA-guaranteed loan, the vet would not be required to make a down payment. Thus, the veteran could secure the $110,000 no-money-down loan from VA and also the $20,000 VHAP loan—if qualified, he or she could receive a loan totaling $130,000 with no money down. Another example would be if the veteran is seeking to purchase a home using an FHA-insured loan, the maximum loan amount would be increased, in the Dallas area, from $90,000 to $110,000 with the same down payment.

Terms

The maximum term of a VHAP loan is 30 years and the monthly payments for the VHAP loan will be made with the veterans regular monthly payment.

The lender and the VHAP will *share* a first lien on the property. This is sometimes referred to as a concurrent first lien. In addition, FHA and VA require that there be a Deed of Trust Rider. A sample of the Deed of Trust Rider is shown in Figures 8-8 and 8-9. You will note that the first paragraph of the rider makes reference to the two notes that are secured by the deed of trust and the rider.

If the VHAP loan is to be made in conjunction with a conventional loan that will be sold to Fannie Mae, then the lender will execute a deed of trust rider as shown in Figures 8-10 and 8-11 as well as a *Seller Warranty and Indemnification Agreement, Texas Veterans' Housing Assistance Program* (Figure 8-12). Thus, the VHAP may be combined with a con-

ventional loan as well as an FHA insured and a VA Guaranteed loan.

Assumptions

According to the guidelines of the program, a veteran must reside in the home for 3 years before the mortgage may be assumed. If the veteran must sell prior to the end of the 3-year period, the loan must be paid off with some exceptions. Some of the exceptions are:

Death of the veteran purchaser

Bankruptcy of the veteran

Financial incapacity of the veteran

Forced sale of the home due to:

1. divorce and property settlement
2. move required due to a change in the employment of the veteran or veteran's spouse
3. condemnation of the property through no fault of the veteran.

If the veteran has lived in the home for the required 3 years or has had to sell the property due to one of the exclusions, then the requirements for an assumption are:

1. The payment of interest and principal is current.

2. The party wishing to assume the loan must meet the qualification requirements of the participating lending institution.

3. The assumption agreement must be on forms approved by the administrator and the board and must be executed by the chairman of the Veteran's Land board.

As with the Texas Veterans' Land Program, if you would like more information on the VHAP, contact the Veterans Land Board, Austin, Texas 78701 or call 1-800-252-VETS.

STATE HOUSING AGENCIES

The first state housing agency was established in the state of New York when the state legislature authorized the creation of the New York Housing Finance Agency in 1960. The authority sold its first tax-exempt bonds in 1961.

Texas has joined the other 49 states in the formation of state housing agencies for the

Figure 8–8.   Veterans' Housing Assistance Program Deed of Trust Rider, page 1

VETERANS LAND BOARD

VETERAN'S HOUSING ASSISTANCE PROGRAM

DEED OF TRUST RIDER

The rights and obligations of the parties to the Deed of Trust (the "Deed of Trust") to which this Rider is attached and the two promissory notes described below (the "Notes") which it secures are expressly made subject to this Rider. In the event of any conflict between the provisions of this Rider and the provisions of the Deed of Trust or Notes, the provisions of this Rider shall control. To the extent that they are not modified by this Rider, all the terms, conditions and other provisions of the Deed of Trust and Notes remain in full force and effect.

1. The Loan secured by the Deed of Trust (the "Mortgage Loan") is evidenced by two promissory notes of the Grantor (the "Borrower") as follows:

(i) The Program Note, dated as of _____, 19___, in the original principal amount of $_____ (not to exceed $20,000), bearing interest at the rate of 9.97% per annum and due in 360 equal monthly installments; and

(ii) The Participant Note, dated the date of the Program Note, in the original principal amount of $_____, bearing interest at the rate _____% per annum and due in 360 equal monthly installments.

2. The interests of the respective holders of the Notes in the Mortgage Loan and the collateral securing such loan shall be equal and ratable, computed on a pro rata basis according to the outstanding principal balances of the Program Note and the Participant Note at the time of computation, and neither shall have priority over the other; provided that any amounts applied to pay less than all amounts then due shall be applied first to pay interest on a pro rata basis according to the respective amounts of interest then owing and thereafter shall be applied to pay other amounts according to principal balances. In the events that a holder of one of the Notes shall at any time receive cash or other property on account of the Mortgage loan, including property received due to any right of set-off with respect to any balance or balances in an account or accounts maintained by the Borrower, such property will be applied to the liabilities of the Borrower under the Notes on a pro rata basis as herein provided. The holders of the Notes will make such disposition and arrangements with each other, either by way of distribution, assignment of claims, subrogation or otherwise, as will result in such holders receiving ratably equal payment on all liabilities of the bor-rower with respect to the Mortgage Loan, in accordance with their respective participating interests therein.

3. Under the terms of the Deed of Trust, if the Borrower does not occupy the property purchased with the proceeds of such loan as his principal years from the date of the purchase of such property, or if he shall lease, transfer, sell or convey, in whole or in part, his interest in such property, the Veterans Land Board of the State of Texas, as holder of the Program Note,

SOURCE: U.S., Department of Housing and Urban Development, Fort Worth Regional Office, Regional Housing Commissioner, *Circular Letter No. 84-3* — April 13, 1984.

Figure 8-9.   Veterans' Housing Assistance Program Deed of Trust Rider, page 2

may require escalation of the interest rate on the Program Note or acceleration and immediate payment of principal of and interest due on the Program Note, and/or may pursue such other remedy or course of action as it may deem appropriate and in the best interest of the Veterans' Housing Assistance Program.

    4. This rider shall be binding upon and inure to the benefit of the parties to the Deed of Trust and their respective successors and assigns.

NOTICE TO BORROWER:

THIS DOCUMENT MODIFIES THE TERMS OF THE DEED OF TRUST. DO NOT SIGN IT UNLESS YOU HAVE READ AND UNDERSTOOD IT.

    I hereby consent to the modifications of the terms of the Deed of Trust which are contained in this Rider.

    Dated this _____ day of _____, 19____.

Borrower's   Borrower's
Signature_____ Signature_____
Printed_____ Printed_____

THE STATE OF TEXAS   S
                                S
COUNTY OF _____ S

    BEFORE ME, the undersigned, a Notary Public in and for The State of Texas, on this day personally appeared _____
_____
known to me to be the person(s) whose name (s) is (are) subscribed to the foregoing instrument, and acknowledged to me that he (she) (they) executed the same for the purposes and consideration therein expressed.

    GIVEN UNDER MY HAND AND SEAL OF OFFICE, this _____ day of _____
_____, 19____.

                                    _____
                                    Notary Public
                                    in and for THE STATE OF TEXAS

My Commission Expires:

_____

This instrument was prepared by:_____
Address:_____

0607S-843

SOURCE: U.S., Department of Housing and Urban Development, Fort Worth Regional Office, Regional Housing Commissioner, *Circular Letter No. 84-3*—April 13, 1984.

Figure 8–10.   *Veterans' Housing Assistance Program Deed of Trust Rider for Conventional Loan, page 1*

Veterans Land Board
Veterans' Housing Assistance Program

DEED OF TRUST RIDER
(for conventional loans)

The rights and obligations of the parties to the Deed of Trust (the "Deed of Trust") to which this Rider is attached and the two promissory notes described below (the "Notes") which it secures are expressly made subject to this Rider. In the event of any conflict between the provisions of this Rider and the provisions of the Deed of Trust, the provisions of this Rider shall control. To the extent that they are not modified by this Rider, all the terms, conditions and other provisions of the Deed of Trust remain in full force and effect. This Rider is made a part of the Deed of Trust. The term "Borrower" as used in this Rider shall mean the Grantor(s) and Borrower(s) specified in the Deed of Trust.

A.   The fourth paragraph of the first page of the Deed of Trust, commencing with the words **"To secure,"** is hereby deleted and the following is substituted therefor:

"To secure to Lender the repayment of indebtedness evidenced by the following Borrower's notes:

(i)   [Complete the following description of note originated for sale to Veterans Land Board under Veterans' Housing Assistance Program.] Borrower's Note, dated _____ , in the principal sum of _____ Dollars ($ _____) (not to exceed $20,000), with interest thereon, providing for monthly installments of principal and interest, with the balance of the indebtedness, if not sooner paid, due and payable on _____ ; the payment of all other sums with interest thereon, advanced in accordance herewith to protect the security of this Deed of Trust; and the covenants and agreements of Borrower herein contained; and the repayment of any future advances, with interest thereon, made to Borrower by Lender pursuant to paragraph 21 hereof (herein "Future Advances"). This note is designated "Note A" and the payee and any subsequent holder of said Note A is designated "Beneficiary A".

(ii)   [Complete the following description of note evidencing remainder of loan.] Borrower's Note, dated the date of Note A, in the principal sum of _____ Dollars ($ _____), with interest thereon, providing for monthly installments of principal and interest, with the balance of the indebtedness, if not sooner paid, due and payable on _____ ; the payment of all other sums with interest thereon, advanced in accordance herewith to protect the security of this Deed of Trust, and the covenants and agreements of the Borrower herein contained; and the repayment of any future advances with interest thereon, made to Borrower by Lender pursuant to paragraph 21 hereof (herein "Future Advances"). This Note is designated "Note B" and the payee and any subsequent holder of said Note B is designated "Beneficiary B".

The mortgage loans secured by this Deed of Trust and evidenced by Note A and Note B are hereinafter collectively referred to as the "Mortgage Loan."

B.   The interest of the respective holders of Note A and Note B in the Mortgage Loan and collateral securing such loan shall be of equal priority and ratable, computed on a pro rata basis according to the outstanding principal balances of Note A and Note B at the time of computation; provided that any amounts applied to pay less than all amounts then due, including amounts payable under paragraph 2 of this Deed of Trust entitled "Funds for Taxes and Insurance," shall be applied first to pay amounts specified in such paragraph 2 of this Deed of Trust, then to pay interest on a pro rata basis according to the respective amounts of interest then owing and thereafter shall be applied to pay other amounts according to principal balances. In the event that a holder of one of the Notes shall at any time receive cash or other property on account of the Mortgage Loan, including property received due to any right of set-off with respect to any balance or balances in an account or accounts maintained by the Borrower, such property will be applied to the liabilities of the Borrower under the Notes on a pro rata basis as herein provided. In the event any advance permitted under this Deed of Trust is made by Beneficiary B, Beneficiary B shall have the right to immediate reimbursement by Beneficiary A of Beneficiary A's pro rata share of such advance.

C.   The word "Lender" in this Deed of Trust shall mean both Beneficiary A and Beneficiary B together, the rights and powers of each such Beneficiary being set out in this Rider. As long as Note B has not been paid in full, including principal, interest and any advances, then Beneficiary B shall have the exclusive rights and powers of Lender under this Deed of Trust, including but not limited to the power to appoint a substitute Trustee, to take actions for the protection of Lender's security as set forth in paragraph 7 of this Deed of Trust, to direct the Trustee to exercise the powers and remedies set forth in paragraphs 17, 18, 19 and 20 of this Deed of Trust, including acceleration of both Note A and Note B in the event of a default under the provisions of either Note or this Deed of Trust, to hold a Trustee's sale in accordance with the provision of this Deed of Trust and the laws of the State of Texas or to bring a foreclosure action in a competent court in the name of both Beneficiary A and Beneficiary B, to modify this Deed of Trust to the extent allowed by applicable law, to convey by special warranty deed property securing the Mortgage Loan to a mortgage insurer and to release the lien of this Deed of Trust upon payment and discharge of all sums secured hereby. Beneficiary B may, at its option, designate an attorney-in-fact with the power and authority to execute any instruments reasonably necessary and appropriate for any actions authorized herein. If Note B has been paid in full, then all rights and powers of Lender hereunder shall inure to the benefit of Beneficiary A.

D.   In the event the Borrower does not occupy the property purchased with the proceeds of the loan evidenced by Note A as Borrower's principal residence for a period of three years from the date of the purchase of such property, or if Borrower shall lease, transfer, sell or convey, in whole or in part, Borrower's interest in such property, the Veterans Land Board of the State of Texas, as holder of Note A, may, to the extent permitted by applicable law, require escalation of the interest rate on Note A or acceleration and immediate payment of principal of and interest due on Note A, and may pursue such other remedy or course of action as it may deem appropriate and in the best interest of the Veterans' Housing Assistance Program; provided, however, this paragraph D shall only be applicable to Note A and shall not be in limitation of any rights under paragraph 17 of the Deed of Trust of the holder of Note B with respect to acceleration of the principal of and interest due on Note B, and provided further, that the provisions of this paragraph D shall be subject to the provisions of paragraph C hereof, that any rights and powers of Lender, including the right and power to direct foreclosure as provided in paragraph 18 of this Deed of Trust, shall be the exclusive right and power of Beneficiary B as long as Note B has not been paid in full.

6330(4-84)

SOURCE: Federal National Mortgage Association, Dallas, Texas, memo, *FNMA's Special Purchase Requirements for Loans Originating Under the Texas Veterans' Housing Assistance Program*, April 11, 1984.

Figure 8–11.   Veterans' Housing Assistance Program Deed of Trust Rider for Conventional Loan, page 2

E. Any default under Note A shall constitute a default under Note B and, conversely, any default under Note B shall constitute a default under Note A, provided that so long as Note B has not been paid in full, the exercise of any remedies shall be at the option of Beneficiary B as provided in paragraph C hereof.

F. This Rider shall be binding upon and inure to the benefit of the parties to the Deed of Trust, including Beneficiary A and Beneficiary B, and their respective succcessors and assigns.

NOTICE TO BORROWER:

THIS DOCUMENT MODIFIES THE TERMS OF THE DEED OF TRUST. DO NOT SIGN IT UNLESS YOU HAVE READ AND UNDERSTOOD IT.

I hereby consent to the modifications of the terms of the Deed of Trust which are contained in this Rider.

Dated this _____ day of _____ , 19 _____ .

Borrower's
Signature _____

Printed _____

Borrower's
Signature _____

Printed _____

THE STATE OF TEXAS

COUNTY OF _____

BEFORE ME, the undersigned, a Notary Public in and for The State of Texas, on this day personally appeared _____
_____ known to me to be the person(s) whose name(s) is(are) subscribed to the foregoing instrument, and acknowledged to me that he(she) (they) executed the same for the purposes and consideration therein expressed.

GIVEN UNDER MY HAND AND SEAL OF OFFICE, This _____ day of _____ , 19 _____ .

_____
Notary Public
in and for THE STATE OF TEXAS

My Commission Expires:

_____

This instrument was prepared by:_____

Address:_____

SOURCE: Federal National Mortgage Association, Dallas, Texas, memo, *FNMA's Special Purchase Requirements for Loans Originating Under the Texas Veterans' Housing Assistance Program*, April 11, 1984.

Figure 8–12.   Seller Warranty and Indemnification Agreement—Texas Veterans' Housing Assistance Program

SELLER WARRANTY AND INDEMNIFICATION AGREEMENT
TEXAS VETERANS' HOUSING ASSISTANCE PROGRAM

FNMA Loan No._____

Loan Amount (Note "B"):_____

Borrower:_____

Property:_____

For and in consideration of the purchase by the Federal National Mortgage Association (herein called "FNMA") of the loan identified above and other good and valuable consideration, the receipt and sufficiency of which are hereby acknowledged, without limitation or impairment of any warranty contained in the FNMA Mortgage Selling and Servicing Contract, _____ (herein called "Lender"), hereby makes to FNMA the warranties hereinafter set forth:

1.   That Lender has entered into a fully executed Mortgage Origination, Sale and Servicing Guide for the Texas Veterans' Housing Assistance Program, (herein called "TVLB Guide") which is in full force and effect and has not been amended or terminated at the time of loan funding by FNMA.

2.   The combined total of the face amount of the Program Loan (evidenced by Note "A") and the Participant Loan (evidenced by Note "B") do not exceed FNMA's maximum loan amount as stated in the FNMA Lending Guide.

3.   A Deed of Trust Rider in the form attached hereto has been executed by the Borrower(s) and filed of record in the Deed of Trust records of the jurisdiction where the property is located. Such recording information as well as a specific reference to such Rider has been set forth in the description of the lien in the Mortgagee Policy of Title Insurance.

4.   The Participant Loan will be sold, assigned, and serviced solely in accordance with the FNMA Mortgage Selling and Servicing Contract, as amended from time to time by FNMA's Selling Guide, Lending Guide and Servicing Guide.

5.   The "Mortgage Loan", as defined in the TVLB Guide, will be serviced solely by the Lender. In the event servicing of either Note "A" or Note "B" is transferred by the Lender; or Note "A" or Note "B" severally or jointly are sold by the holders of such notes; or servicing is terminated for any reason by the holder of Note "A" and/or Note "B", the provisions of Section 8.09 of the TVLB Guide shall prevail.

6.   FNMA shall not be liable in any respect for the holder of Note "A"'s pro rata share of any expenditure, including but not limited to, foreclosure fees, repairs of the property securing the deed of trust, or advances due to deficiencies in the amount of escrow payments.

_____

LENDER

SOURCE: Federal National Mortgage Association, Dallas, Texas, memo, *FNMA's Special Purchase Requirements for Loans Originating Under the Texas Veterans' Housing Assistance Program*, April 11, 1984.

sole purpose of generating funds through the sale of tax-exempt bonds secured by first-lien mortgages to provide mortgages to low- and moderate-income families. These mortgages are used to purchase housing that is safe and decent.

Texas Housing Agency

The Texas Housing Agency was established by the sixty-sixth session of the legislature through legislation signed by Governor W. P. Clements, Jr. on June 14, 1979.

The agency is empowered to issue tax-exempt mortgage revenue bonds. These funds can be used to purchase mortgages currently in the lending institutions' portfolios, to purchase new mortgage loans on real property originated by qualified lenders, or to make direct loans to qualified housing sponsors who are recommended by a lender.

The purpose of the agency is fivefold:

1. to increase the supply of sanitary and safe housing units for eligible families;

2. to provide short- and long-term mortgage financing of housing at affordable rates;

3. to support, encourage, and supplement private industry resources that provide housing units for the eligible families;

4. to help implement the goals and objectives of the Texas State Housing Plan; and

5. to operate the agency without requiring assistance from state tax revenues.

The Texas Housing Agency published the rules and regulations for its first loan program in the *Texas Register* on September 9, 1980. This program was called the 1980 Series A Program. The agency issued its first bonds on November 6, 1980 in the amount of $150 million of single family mortgage bonds. The bonds had a rate of 9.8 percent and the rate charged to the borrower was 11.2 percent.

To qualify for a mortgage under this issue, the Housing Agency set the following limitations:

1. The income was limited to a maximum of $25,000 for a family of two, plus an additional $1000 for each family member in excess of two. For example, a family of four with two adults and two children could have a maximum income of:

2 adults	$25,000
2 children @$1000 each	$ 2,000
Maximum income	$27,000

2. The maximum loan amount authorized under this issue was $67,500.

3. The mortgages could only be used to purchase single-family housing.

4. The Housing Agency reserved 25 percent of the funds for families whose adjusted gross income was $19,500 or less for two persons and $1000 for each member in excess of two.

Then in April 1983, the agency announced its 1983 Single-Family Mortgage Purchase Program. The Texas Housing Agency (THA) sold approximately $90 to $200 million of single-family revenue bonds. Then on August 25, 1983, the THA announced the details of the program. According to the information supplied by THA, the agency had $217,000,000 available to purchase qualifying mortgages originated by participating lenders. The interest rate for these mortgages was 10.79 percent and according to THA these funds would fund approximately 4500 mortgages.

The THA, according to requirements, designated certain areas of the state as targeted areas. These areas are targeted for special assistance. In these targeted areas, a higher purchase price limitation applies and the applicant need not be a first-time homebuyer.

In addition, there were three sets of financial restrictions that applied to the program. These restrictions were:

1. For homes in nontargeted areas of Texas, the applicant must not have owned a home within the past 3 years.

2. An individual applicant must have had an adjusted gross income in 1982 of less than $33,000. If the applicant (or applicants) is a family, the limitation was increased to $42,000.

3. Finally, there was a maximum sales price for homes that might be eligible for this program. These limits are shown in Figure 8–13.

The interest rate that was charged to the borrower was 10.71 percent and the program had the provision for a buydown. This buydown was not the standard 3-2-1, but was a 2.5

Figure 8–13.   Texas Housing Agency Maximum Purchase Price Limits

Maximum Purchase Price Limits

	NON-TARGETED AREAS		TARGETED AREAS	
	New	*Existing*	*New*	*Existing*
Austin SMSA (1)	$ 95,370	$ 81,180	$104,040	$ 88,560
Dallas/Fort Worth SMSA (2)......	112,420	105,820	122,640	115,440
Houston SMSA (3)...............	89,650	104,830	97,800	114,360
San Antonio SMSA (4)	87,560	84,590	95,520	92,280
ALL OTHER AREAS (5).........	80,410	55,990	87,720	61,080

Counties in each SMSA:

(1) Hays, Travis and Williamson
(2) Collin, Dallas, Denton, Ellis, Hood, Johnson, Kaufman, Parker, Rockwall, Tarrant and Wise
(3) Brazoria, Fort Bend, Harris, Liberty, Montgomery and Waller
(4) Bexar, Comal and Guadalupe

below-the-note rate, or a qualifying rate of 8.29 percent; then in the second year the rate increased to 9.08 percent; and in the third, the rate increased to 9.91 percent.

On April 18, 1984, the Texas Housing Agency announced its intention to proceed with the 1984 Single-Family Mortgage Purchase Program. The THA intended to sell $238 million of single-family mortgage revenue bonds to purchase mortgages secured by qualified owner-occupied residences in Texas. The interest rate to the borrower under the 1984 issue was 12.25 percent. It should be noted that the requirements for the 1984 program are almost identical to those of the 1983 program. In other words, the loan amounts and the income requirements were the same as well as the buydown. If you would like information on any of the programs offered by the THA, contact the Texas Housing Agency, P.O. Box 13941 Capital Station, Austin, Texas 78711-3941.

The underwriting guidelines that were adopted by the agency were those of the FHA/VA, Fannie Mae, or FHLMC.

The agency did not actually originate the mortgages under this program, but issued commitments to lenders to purchase mortgages that met all of the requirements set forth by the agency in the commitments issued to the lenders. This type of program is known as a forward commitment program. In this type of program, the agency issues a commitment to the participating lender to purchase mortgages in a specific amount that meets the guidelines of the agency.

There is another type of mortgage program that may be used by the Texas Housing Agency. This is the loan-to-lenders program.

Under this program, the Housing Agency would loan funds to the lenders who wish to participate in the program, with the stipulation that the funds would be used to make mortgages on housing that meets the guidelines set by the Housing Agency.

Federal Regulation

Prior to the passage of the Omnibus Reconciliation Act of 1980, there had been no federal regulations governing either a state housing agency or any governmental body in the issuances of tax-exempt bonds secured by mortgages on single-family dwellings.

When this legislation became law on December 31, 1980, it placed several limitations on the issuance of such bonds. One of the limitations was that the maximum amount of bonds that could be issued per year in a state was set at either $200 million or 9 percent (whichever is higher) of the average of all mortgages originated in the state for the past three years.

In 1983 using 9 percent of all mortgages originated in Texas, the Internal Revenue Service calculated that for the whole state of Texas there could be some $1.014 billion of single-family mortgage revenue bonds issued, which was to include all of the bonds issued by the Texas Housing Agency as well as those issued by either a city or county government in Texas.

Some of the other major restrictions are listed below:

1. *Principal residency requirement.* The law requires that any residence purchased with funds from a sale of bonds be used as the primary residence of the borrower.

2. *3-year requirement.* The act further requires that the borrower must not have been a homeowner within the last 3 years.

3. *Purchase price limitations.* The law has set the maximum purchase price for homes as 90 percent of the average purchase price in the preceding year in the Standard Metropolitan Statistical Area (SMSA) in which the mortgage is placed.

4. *New mortgage requirement.* The law states that a mortgage funded by tax-exempt bond funds may only be used for a new mortgage and may not be used to acquire or replace an existing mortgage unless it is a construction loan, bridge loan, or similar temporary initial financing.

5. *Assumption of mortgages.* Individuals assuming a mortgage originally financed with tax-exempt bonds must meet the residency requirement, the 3-year requirement, and the purchase price requirement.

6. *Terminations of tax-free status of bonds.* In one of its more important provisions, the law allows for the issuance of single-family, owner-occupied bonds as tax-free bonds for a period of 4 years, and any interest paid on such bonds after that date will be taxable. This date is generally considered to be January 31, 1987.

One major change that has been brought about by the passage of this legislation is that the VA and FHA have had to modify their note and deed of trust to comply with restriction 5 listed above. As our review of the standard HUD and VA note and deed of trust revealed, neither of these sets of documents contained any assumption or due-on-sale clause. Restriction 5 states that any person or persons assuming a mortgage financed through the sale of tax-exempt bonds must meet certain requirements. HUD and VA have issued instructions allowing for the inclusion of a due-on-sale clause in mortgages financed by tax-exempt bonds. On October 23, 1981, the Veterans Administration issued its regulation allowing for the inclusion of due-on-sale in mortgages guaranteed by the VA and funded through the sale of tax-exempt bonds. According to the regulation, the veteran must be fully informed by the lender or the state housing agency that the veteran's ability to sell his or her property by assumption is restricted. The veteran must sign a statement indicating that he or she is aware of the restriction. The Veterans Administration has suggested the format in Figure 8-14.

On April 29, 1981, the Department of Housing and Urban Development issued to all of its offices instructions that were later updated on December 23, 1981. These instructions permit the inclusion of a due-on-sale clause, allowing the acceleration of a mortgage financed through the sale of tax-exempt bonds (1) if the property is sold to an unqualified buyer, (2) if the property is not occupied by the borrowers because it is being rented or has been purchased by others, or (3) because of fraud by

Figure 8-14. Veteran's Consent Form—Due-on-Sale

Your home purchase is being financed with a mortgage made available with the assistance of _____ Housing Authority. This mortgage is made at an interest rate below what is usually being charged. Because of this you cannot sell your home to a person ineligible for assistance from the Housing Authority, unless you pay your loan in full. If you sell your home to a party ineligible for the Housing Authority's assistance and allow the buyer to make your payments for you (assume your loan), the Housing Authority may refuse to allow the sale and demand immediate full repayment of the loan. This could result in foreclosure or repossession of the property. If the lender takes your home through a foreclosure of the mortgage because of this, VA will not be able to help you. In addition, VA may have to pay a claim to the Housing Authority for any loss incurred on your loan. You may then be obligated to the VA for any claim paid by the VA to the Housing Authority.

You may avoid such actions by paying your loan in full when you sell your home or by making certain that any person who purchases your home and takes over your payments meets the necessary qualifications established by the Housing Authority. Those requirements are: (Complete as appropriate for the particular housing assistance program).

_____   _____
Date   Veteran's signature

SOURCE: Veterans Administration, Department of Veterans Benefits, DVB Circular 26-81-34, Due-on-Sale Provisions—October 23, 1981, pp. 1-2.

the borrowers or misrepresentation by the borrowers. The instructions state that the borrower must be given thirty days to correct that situation before the due-on-sale is implemented. The mortgage must contain an addendum for due-on-sale, and reference to this addendum must be made in the mortgage. The suggested format for the addendum is shown in Figure 8–15.

In addition to the issuance of single-family bonds, the Texas Housing Agency issues tax-exempt revenue bonds to provide funds to purchase mortgages secured by multi-family structures. According to THA for a development to be eligible, it must meet the following requirements:

1. The development must be located in Texas.

2. All units in the development must be made available for rental by the general public, subject to some income restrictions. Thus a developer may not rent to just one group such as adults, the elderly, or any other groups.

3. The development must have at least 50 dwelling units.

4. The entire development, whether consisting of one or more buildings, must be owned by only one developer and also operated as one project.

5. Construction must commence no later than six months after the issuance of bonds and the project must be completed no later than 36 months after the issuance of the bonds.

These are only a few of the major requirements. If you would like more information on the program, contact the Texas Housing Agency at the address mentioned earlier in this section.

City and County Housing Agency

In addition to the State of Texas having the authority to issue the mortgage revenue bonds, any type of government in the state may issue such bonds. Many of the cities and counties in Texas have done so. An example is The Dallas County Housing Finance Corporation. In August 1984, it made available some $51 million to purchase mortgages secured by single-family dwellings to be occupied by qualified borrowers.

Some of the major provisions of the program were:

1. The property must be owner-occupied.

2. The purchaser may not have owned a home in the past 3 years.

3. The maximum income allowable under the program was $40,000 based on the adjusted gross income on the 1983 tax return.

Figure 8–15.   HUD Mortgage Addendum for Due-on-Sale

ADDENDUM

As long as this mortgage is held by _____ (NAME OF AGENCY) _____
the lender may, at lender's option, declare all sums secured by this mortgage to be immediately due and payable if:

    (I) All or any part of the property is sold or transferred by borrower without lender's prior written consent, other than a transfer by devise, decent or operation of law;
    (II) Borrower fails to occupy the property described in this mortgage without lender's prior written consent; or
    (III) Borrower omits or misrepresents a fact in an application for this mortgage; or
    (IV) This mortgage ceases to be covered by private mortgage insurance.

SOURCE: U.S. Department of Housing and Urban Development, *Memorandum: Mortgages Financed by State and Local Governmental Agencies—Use of "Due-on-Sale" Clauses*, December 23, 1981, p. 4.

4. The purchase price of a home to be purchased through this program could not exceed the following:

   A. In nontargeted areas of Dallas, the maximum purchase price for an existing home was $98,268 and for a new home the maximum was $98,801.

   B. The term of the mortgage was 30 years.

   C. The borrower was required to make a minimum investment in the property of 5 percent. Thus, the maximum loan was 95 percent of the maximum purchase price.

   D. The interest rate on the mortgages was a fixed-rate of 12.10 percent.

Thus as a real estate professional, you will need to contact both the city and county government in the area of your operation and see if they have or will in the future offer any of these types of funds.

TEXAS FAMILY FARM AND RANCH SECURITY PROGRAM

This program was authorized by the Texas legislature in 1969 and was approved by the voters of Texas in November 1969. The Family Farm and Ranch Security Act authorizes the establishment of a program by the state of Texas to issue guarantees to lenders on loans used for the purchase of farm and ranch land. The program is administered by the Texas Department of Agriculture.

The primary purpose of this program is to assist qualified people who can demonstrate a need for help in purchasing farm or ranch land in Texas. This land must be used to either expand an existing farm or ranch or enter into the operation of a farm or ranch.

Under this program, the state Secretary of Agriculture is authorized to guarantee loans made by the seller of land and/or private lenders up to 90 percent of the loan amount.

Eligibility Requirements

The applicant must:

1. Be a citizen of the United States

2. Have been a resident of the state of Texas for the past 5 years

3. Have education or training or experience in the type of farming or ranching for which the land is to be used

4. Along with his or her spouse and children, have a net worth of less than $100,000, excluding the value of a residential homestead

5. Meet the credit standard set forth by the Secretary of Agriculture

6. Not be related within the second degree by affinity or third degree by consanguinity to any member of the Farm and Ranch Security Advisory Board, the Commissioner of Agriculture, the Deputy or Assistant Commissioner, or the Administrator of the Department of Agriculture

According to the Texas Department of Agriculture, the following criteria will be used by the department in the approval of an application for a loan guarantee under this program.

1. The meeting of all requirements listed in the previous section;

2. The degree to which the farming and/or ranching will be the applicant's primary occupation;

3. The extent to which the applicant demonstrates the need for the guaranty to acquire the farm or ranch land;

4. The economic feasibility of the loan based on the present and projected financial history of the applicant

The other requirements for the program were published in the *Texas Register*, on September 28, 1984. For more information contact the Texas Department of Agriculture, Family Farm and Ranch Security Program, P. O. Box 12874, Austin, Texas 78711.

FEDERAL LAND BANKS

The Federal Land Banks were established by the passage of the Federal Farm Loan Act of 1916. The present activities of the banks and associations are authorized by the Farm Credit Act of 1971. This act supersedes all previous laws governing the operation of the banks. There is not one central bank; the United States is divided into twelve districts, each with its own bank.

The primary purpose of the Federal Land Banks is to provide a dependable and permanent source of loanable funds—at reasonable rates—to the agricultural community. The banks were originally funded by the federal government, but the original legislation contained a provision allowing the banks to be owned by its borrowers through the Federal Land Bank Association. All of the initial money advanced to the banks was repaid by 1947. Today the banks are owned completely by the borrowers or customers of the banks.

The banks make primarily agricultural loans to farmers, ranchers, and legal entities as defined by the banks. The banks will make loans for the purpose of purchasing, remodeling, building, refinancing, and improving a home. The amount of the loan or mortgage will be based on the agricultural holdings or assets of the borrower.

The term of the mortgages will range from five to forty years, with payments made annually, semiannually, quarterly, or monthly. Any loan from a bank may be repaid at any time without penalty. The interest rate on a loan from a Federal Land Bank will be a variable rate based on the bank's cost of funds. As was noted earlier, the banks receive no funds from the federal government, thus they must secure their funds from the open market. The variable-rate feature of the bank's loans allows them to react quickly to the changes in the nation's money markets. According to the banks, it allows them to provide the funds at the lowest possible rate. In regard to the loan-to-value ratio of Federal Land Bank loans, they are authorized to make loans that do not exceed 85 percent of the appraised value of the real estate used as security. For more information, contact the nearest Federal Land Bank and they will supply you with data on the present loan programs available and current interest rates.

REVIEW QUESTIONS

1. List and explain three advantages of a VA-guaranteed loan.

2. Which veterans are eligible for VA loan benefits?

3. Explain how a veteran can secure a Certificate of Eligibility.

4. Define the term *entitlement* and the amount of a veteran's entitlement as it refers to VA home loans and VA mobile home loans.

5. Explain how a veteran can secure a release of liability and the reinstatement of his or her entitlement.

6. Name and explain the basic home loan program of the Farmers Home Administration.

7. State the purposes of the Texas Housing Agency.

8. Explain how federal legislation has affected state housing agencies.

9. Explain how a veteran may be able to secure more than one VA-guaranteed home loan.

PROBLEMS

1. A buyer with whom you are presently working is seeking a VA-guaranteed loan for $109,550. What would be the VA funding or guarantee?

2. What would be the required down payment for a veteran to secure a VA-GPM in the amount of $99,950? The current interest rate on a VA guarantee loan is 14.750 percent. The veteran is making an offer for a used home.

3. Calculate the monthly payments for a VA growing equity mortgage where the monthly payments increase by 3 percent per year for 10 years, for years 1 through 11.

4. Calculate the maximum loan, with no money down, that a veteran could receive after securing a VA-guaranteed loan in 1966. The loan in 1966 has not been paid off.

5. Calculate the required down payment a veteran may have to pay if he or she is seeking a home with a CRV of $133,550. The veteran has full entitlement available.

NOTES

1. U.S., Veterans Administration, *Graduated Payment Mortgage Loans*, DVB Circular 26-81-36, November 12, 1981, p. 20420.

9

Conventional Loans and Private Mortgage Insurance

LEARNING OBJECTIVES

In this chapter we will discuss the conventional loan and lenders, as well as private mortgage insurance. Upon completion of this chapter you should be able to do the following:

★ Define *conventional mortgage*.

★ Choose the best type of mortgage, either government-backed or conventional.

★ Explain private mortgage insurance and why it is important to the conventional lender.

CONVENTIONAL LOANS

A *conventional loan* may be defined as a loan that is neither insured nor guaranteed by any agency of a state or the federal government. In Texas, then, any loan that is not insured by FHA, guaranteed by VA, or made by the Texas Land Board is a conventional loan.

Until the advent of FHA, the Farmers Home Administration, the Veterans Administration, and state housing agencies, conventional loans were the only type of real estate loans made. These loans were made by commercial banks, savings and loan associations, and in some sections of the nation by mutual savings banks. Prior to the advent of the mortgage banker, most conventional loans were made by savings and loan associations. Life insurance companies were also a source of real estate loans. As was stated earlier in the text, most of these loans had low loan-to-value ratios, in some cases as low as 50 percent of the value. The term was short, usually three to five years, with no escrow for taxes, insurance, or other fees or assessments that could affect the title to the property. With the advent of the FHA-insured loan with its long amortization, level monthly payments, and other reforms, the conventional lenders did adopt many of the reforms of FHA. One of the major reforms that was not adopted by the conventional lenders was the higher loan-to-value ratio. The reason for this was that many of the institutional lenders by law could not make a loan that had a loan-to-value ratio above 75 percent. This was true until the advent of private mortgage insurance. Private mortgage insurance (PMI) allows the lender to make loans up to a loan-to-value ratio of 95 percent, which will be discussed in depth later in this chapter.

COMPARISON OF CONVENTIONAL vs. GOVERNMENTAL LOANS

In the previous two chapters the advantages and disadvantages were listed for FHA and VA loans. This will not be done for the conventional loan. Rather, the conventional loan will be compared to the VA- and FHA-insured mortgages. As a real estate professional, you must be able to help your client select the best financing possible. To do this, you must be able to compare the financing available and advise your client. The following comparisons will be made: loan limits, processing time, interest rates, down payments or loan-to-value ratios, assumption procedures, prepayment penalties, loan fees, and underwriting guidelines.

Loan Limits

Unlike governmental loans the conventional loans or lenders have no set loan limits. This limit is usually set by the investor. For example, if the company originating the loan is a lender using the funds of an investor, the investor will set the loan limit. If the investor that has issued the commitment is the Federal National Mortgage Association (Fannie Mae) or the Federal Home Loan Mortgage Corporation (FHLMC), the limit on the mortgage is set by the U.S. Congress, (which will be outlined in Chapters 10 and 11).

If the investor is an insurance company, the loan limits will be different from that of Fannie Mae and FHLMC. The insurance companies usually only make loans with a low loan-to-value ratio in amounts in the excess of the Fannie Mae and FHLMC limits. For example, the present limit on Fannie Mae/FHLMC loans is $115,300. Normally the insurance companies will make loans at approximately $115,300+. For a conventional loan, the best method to determine the current loan limits is to contact lenders in your area.

Processing Time

The processing time on a conventional loan is sometimes less than for a government-insured or government-guaranteed loan. Usually, the originator of the conventional loan has been given the underwriting guidelines of the investor and is allowed to approve any loan that, in the opinion of the originator, meets the guidelines. This is even true for conventional loans that are to be sold to Fannie Mae. This allows a lender to give in-house approval on Fannie Mae loans.

The actual processing time for a conventional loan can take as little as a week if all of the information to be verified is from local sources. This faster processing time is one of the major factors that will make the conven-tional mortgage more attractive to your clients.

Interest Rates

The interest rate on conventional loans is set in the marketplace and is affected greatly by supply and demand, unlike the interest rate on VA loans. The VA rates are set by the government and reflect only slightly the interest rates in the marketplace. Interest rates on conventional loans can be different for the amount of the loan and the loan-to-value ratio. In some cases, the lower the ratio—that is, 80 percent or less—the lower the interest rate.

One of the major factors that will affect the interest rate on a conventional loan is the source of the funds. For example, an Austin mortgage company is using a commitment from a savings and loan located in California that has a cost of funds of 10.250 percent. This savings and loan will not allow a mortgage lender to make a loan at the same rate as the savings and loan is paying to its depositors. The S and L will usually like to receive a yield at least 2 to 3 percent above the cost of funds or a rate of 12.250 to 13.250 percent. Usually the conventional loans made by insurance companies or by mortgage bankers using a commitment from an insurance company will have a lower interest rate because the cost of funds to the insurance company is less.

When comparing the interest rates on conventional mortgages to government-insured or guaranteed mortgages, one must also compare one additional item: the amount of discount points being charged. As stated earlier, one point is equal to 1 percent of the loan amount. Each point increases the yield (effective interest rate) to the investor one eighth of 1 percent. For example, if a government-insured loan has a face interest rate of 11.5 percent, but the investor wishes a return of 12.5 percent, the lender would have to charge eight points ($1/8 \times 8 = 8/8$ or 1%).

Usually the interest rate on the government-insured loan is lower, but the discount or points are higher. For example, when the rate on FHA/VA loans was 11.5 percent and the rate on the conventional loans was between 12 and 12.75 percent, the points charged by some lenders on FHA/VA loans ranged between four and six points, as compared to one to three points on the conventional loan. One thing that should be noted is that like the FHA loan, the buyer can pay any or all of the points being charged. So if you are the agent for the seller, possibly the conventional loan would be an advantage.

Down Payments

When comparing the down payment required on the conventional loan to that required on either the FHA or VA loan, the conventional down payment is more. For example, the minimum down payment required by most of the conventional lenders is 5 percent, as compared to the FHA, which only requires a down payment of 3 percent on the first $25,000 and 5 percent on the remaining amount up to the maximum loan amount. For VA, most lenders require no money down on loans up to four times the veteran's entitlement.

Let us work through an example of the down payment required on a property with a sales price of $70,000. For this example, let us assume that the closing costs for the borrower are zero and the maximum FHA loan amount for the area is $67,500.

First, the conventional loan, using a lender that will make a 95 percent loan, requires a down payment of 5 percent:

Sales price	$70,000
Down payment 5% of sales price	−$ 3,500
Loan amount	$66,500

Second, let us calculate the FHA down payment with the acquisition cost of $70,000:

Acquisition cost (sales price + closing costs)	$70,000
Down payment 3% of first $25,000 = $750 5% of the remaining, or 5% of ($70,000 − $25,000) = 5% of $45,000 = $2,250	
Total down payment	$ 3,000
Loan amount	$67,000

This would be possible since the present maximum FHA loan on a single-family dwelling is $67,500.

Finally, what is the down payment required for the VA-guaranteed loan? We will assume the veteran has all of his or her entitlement of $27,500 available. Using the factor of four times the entitlement for the maximum loan with no money down, let us calculate as follows:

Entitlement	$27,500
Loan factor	×4
Maximum loan with no money down	$110,000

Thus for the home in question, the veteran would have no down payment requirement.

From this comparison of the minimum conventional down payment to FHA and VA, one can see that the FHA and VA down payments are less. One must remember that the loan limit on the FHA is lower than most of the conventional loans including those loans purchased by Fannie Mae and FHLMC. The VA loan program is not open to all buyers.

Assumptions

As we noted in the previous chapters, the FHA and VA loans are assumable and the procedure is rather easy. The conventional loan is not always assumable. As a real estate professional, when dealing with a conventional lender you should ask if the loan can be assumed and what the procedure will be. There is no standard procedure, but since the advent of Fannie Mae and FHLMC and the standard note and deed of trust, those lenders that use the forms and have adopted their procedures may allow the mortgage to be assumed and the original borrower to be released from liability. The conventional lender will usually charge an assumption fee that will range from a few dollars to a certain percentage of the remaining loan balance. In some cases, the lender may try to increase the yield on the mortgage at the time of assumption under the due-on-sale clause of the mortgage. At the present time, this practice is done in Texas.

It should be noted that Fannie Mae began enforcing the due-on-sale provision on all conventional loans originated after November 10, 1980 that are owned by Fannie Mae. This includes when the ownership of property is transferred using a wraparound or second mortgage by an institutional lender. This provision requires on mortgages that are assumed that the assumptor make application and his or her credit will be checked, and that the interest rate will be adjusted to the market interest rate. The due-on-sale provision will be enforced unless there is a state law or a court decision that makes this practice illegal. Seventeen states outside of Texas have passed laws or their courts have made rulings that have halted or amended this practice.

In these seventeen states where a lender

cannot fully enforce the due-on-sale, sometimes referred to as the acceleration-upon-sale provision of the mortgage or deed of trust, the lender may require that the note be modified and a call option rider executed by the borrower be attached to either the mortgage or deed of trust.

This call option rider in effect makes the note have a term of seven years, with the term of the mortgage or deed of trust thirty years. A sample call option rider is shown in Figure 9-1. One can see that the provision of the call option rider allows the lender, at the lender's option, to declare the total outstanding sum of the mortgage due and payable in full. If the borrower is unable to pay the amount due, the lender can then notify the trustee to start foreclosure proceedings, or the lender on his own may institute the remedies permitted in the state where the property is located. It should be noted that in addition to the mortgage or deed of trust, the note must also be altered to include additional wording similar to that added to either the mortgage or deed of trust. This additional information is shown in Figures 9-2 and 9-3.

Some lenders have further amended their assumption procedure by requiring both parties to the assumption to execute a form entitled, "Modification and Assumption Agreement With Release." A copy of a form that may be used in Texas is shown in Figures 9-4, 9-5, and 9-6.

Once again, when dealing with a conventional lender, be sure to have a thorough knowledge of the lender's assumption policies and procedures so that you may be able to properly advise your client.

Prepayment Penalties

In comparing the conventional to the FHA or VA mortgages, neither the FHA nor VA mortgage has any mention of a prepayment penalty. The conventional mortgage, however, may have such a penalty. If the conventional lender is using the Fannie Mae/FHLMC standard note and deed of trust, there is a mention of a prepayment penalty, but many of the lenders using these forms do not implement the penalty. If the mortgage is sold to Fannie Mae or FHLMC, even though the note makes reference to a penalty, after September 1979 the penalties will not be charged. In addition to not charging the penalty, all lenders selling mortgages to Fannie Mae and FHLMC after July 1, 1984, are required to use the revised note and deed of trust that deletes the penalty completely.

Usually, if the loan is originated by or sold to an insurance company, there will be a prepayment penalty. Normally these penalties are graduated. That means the penalty is more in the first years of the mortgage and is reduced over the life of the mortgage. For example, the penalty may be 3 percent of the loan balance if the loan is paid off in the first five years; then the penalty may be reduced to 2 percent of the balance if the mortgage is paid off in the next five years; and finally, it may be reduced to 1 percent of the loan balance if the loan is paid off prior to the thirtieth year or the term of the loan. This is only an example and is not the only form of penalty. So, as a real estate professional, when you are suggesting a conventional lender to your client, you should know whether the lender has a penalty and, if so, what the penalty is.

Loan Fee or Origination Fee

First, we should define the term loan fee or origination fee. This is the fee charged by the lender for taking the loan application, processing the application, and all of the other operations required to close the loan. This fee should not be confused with the other fees that are connected with the processing of the loan application, such as appraisal fee, credit report fee, attorney fees, and so forth. Only the origination fee is paid directly to the lender for services. The FHA and the VA limit this fee to 1 percent of the loan amount, but there is no such limitation on most conventional loans. The lenders can charge any amount for this fee. The charge is usually expressed as a percentage of the loan amount. On the normal single-family dwelling, the loan fee will be 1 percent, but the fee may be increased for two- to four-family dwellings. This is done by some conventional lenders if they feel loan application and processing will be involved and will require additional persons and/or time. This fee, as with any of the fees charged on a conventional loan, may be paid by either party to the transaction, but the origination fee is usually paid by the purchaser. When dealing with conventional lenders, you should find out what the lender is charging for a loan origination fee and who may pay the fee.

Loan Programs Available

As outlined in the previous chapter, FHA in particular has many loan programs available, but many of the conventional lenders may not

Figure 9–1. Call Option Rider

CALL OPTION RIDER

THIS RIDER is made this . . . . .day of . . . . ,
19 . . . . . ., and is incorporated into and shall be deemed to amend and supplement the Mortgage, Deed of Trust, or
Deed to Secure Debt (the "Security Instrument") of the same date given by the undersigned (the "Borrower") to secure
Borrower's Note to . . . .
. . . . (the "Lender") of the same date (the "Note") and covering the property described in the
Security Instrument and located at:

. . . .
(Property Address)

ADDITIONAL COVENANT. In addition to the covenants and agreements made in the Security Instrument,
Borrower and Lender further covenant and agree as follows:

A. Lender's Call Option. During the thirty day period beginning on a date seven years from the
date of the Note, Lender shall have the option to require payment in full of the sums secured by the Security Instrument. If Lender elects to exercise this call option, notice of such election shall be given to Borrower who shall pay
all such sums to Lender on the payment date specified in the notice, which date shall be at least 60 days from the date
of mailing. If Borrower fails to pay such sums when due, Lender may invoke any remedies permitted by the Security
Instrument.

IN WITNESS WHEREOF, Borrower has executed this Call Option Rider.

_____
— Borrower

_____
— Borrower

9/80

Figure 9–2.   Fannie Mae Note (front)

NOTE

US $ . . . ., Arizona
City

. . . ., 19 . . . .

     FOR VALUE RECEIVED, the undersigned ("Borrower") promise(s) to pay . . . .
. . . ., or order, the principal sum of
. . . . .Dollars, with
interest on the unpaid principal balance from the date of this Note, until paid, at the rate of . . . .
. . . . .percent per annum. Principal and interest shall be payable at . . . .
. . . ., or such other place as the Note holder may
designate, in consecutive monthly installments of . . . .
. . . . .Dollars (US $ . . . .), on the . . . .
. . . . .day of each month beginning . . . ., 19 . . . . . Such monthly installments
shall continue until the entire indebtedness evidenced by this Note is fully paid, except that any remaining indebtedness, if not sooner paid, shall be due and payable on . . . .

     If any monthly installment under this Note is not paid when due and remains unpaid after a date specified by a
notice to Borrower, the entire principal amount outstanding and accrued interest thereon shall at once become due
and payable at the option of the Note holder. The date specified shall not be less than thirty days from the date such
notice is mailed. The Note holder may exercise this option to accelerate during any default by Borrower regardless of
any prior forbearance. If suit is brought to collect this Note, the Note holder shall be entitled to collect all reasonable
costs and expenses of suit, including, but not limited to, reasonable attorney's fees.

     Borrower shall pay to the Note holder a late charge of . . . . .percent of any monthly
installment not received by the Note holder within . . . . .days after the installment is due.

     Borrower may prepay the principal amount outstanding in whole or in part. The Note holder may require that
any partial prepayments (i) be made on the date monthly installments are due and (ii) be in the amount of that
part of one or more monthly installments which would be applicable to principal. Any partial prepayment shall be
applied against the principal amount outstanding and shall not postpone the due date of any subsequent monthly
installments or change the amount of such installments, unless the Note holder shall otherwise agree in writing.

     Presentment, notice of dishonor, and protest are hereby waived by all makers, sureties, guarantors and endorsers
hereof. This Note shall be the joint and several obligation of all makers, sureties, guarantors and endorsers, and shall
be binding upon them and their successors and assigns.

     Any notice to Borrower provided for in this Note shall be given by mailing such notice by certified mail addressed
to Borrower at the Property Address stated below, or to such other address as Borrower may designate by notice to
the Note holder. Any notice to the Note holder shall be given by mailing such notice by certified mail, return receipt
requested, to the Note holder at the address stated in the first paragraph of this Note, or at such other address as may
have been designated by notice to Borrower.

     The indebtedness evidenced by this Note is secured by a Deed of Trust, dated . . . .
. . . ., and reference is made to the Deed of Trust for rights as to acceleration of the indebtedness
evidenced by this Note.

See reverse side of this Note for provision concerning option to call.

. . . .

. . . .

. . . .
       Property Address   *(Execute Original Only)*

  —1 to 4 Family—8/79—**FNMA/FHLMC UNIFORM INSTRUMENT**

Figure 9–3.   Fannie Mae Note (back)

During the thirty day period beginning on a date seven years from
the date of this Note, the Note holder shall have the option to
require payment in full of the entire principal amount outstanding
and any accrued interest thereon. If the Note holder elects to
exercise this call option, notice of such election shall be given
to Borrower who shall pay such principal and interest in full to
the Note holder on the payment date specified in the notice, which
date shall be at least 60 days from the date of mailing.

Date:

_____   _____

                                                    _____

                                                    _____

Figure 9–4.   *Modification and Assumption Agreement with Release, page 1*

MODIFICATION AND ASSUMPTION AGREEMENT WITH RELEASE

THIS AGREEMENT is made this _____ day of _____, 19_____, between

_____
(here "BORROWER"),

_____
(here "ASSUMER"), and

XYZ Mortgage Co., a corporation organized and existing under the laws of the state of Texas, whose address is 1114 Fifth St., Dallas, Texas, (here "LENDER"),

for a modification, assumption, and release with respect to that promissory note dated _____, in the original amount of $_____, bearing interest at the rate of _____ percent per annum, secured by a mortgage or deed of trust (here "security instrument"), dated _____, made by BORROWER to _____ _____ recorded in _____ secured by the property described in Exhibit "A" hereto, located in the County of _____, State of _____, which has the address of _____
(here "PROPERTY ADDRESS");   (street)   (city)   (state and zip code)

WHEREAS, LENDER acquired the note and security instrument described above by an assignment dated _____ and recorded in _____ ;

WHEREAS, BORROWER is indebted to LENDER under the note and security instrument described above, payable in _____ monthly installments of $_____ due on the _____ day of each month; and

WHEREAS, BORROWER desires to sell and ASSUMER desires to purchase such property subject to such indebtedness and to assume the unpaid principal owing to LENDER, but such security instrument requires the written consent of LENDER prior to any sale or transfer of all or any part of such property, and a sale or transfer without consent of LENDER would constitute a default under such security instrument, and BORROWER and ASSUMER wish to obtain the consent of LENDER to such sale or transfer.

NOW, THEREFORE, for and in consideration of the granting of such consent by LENDER and of the benefits flowing to each of the parties hereto, BORROWER and ASSUMER do agree as follows:

1. As of the date of the transfer of the property on _____ , or as a result of such transfer, payments of principal and interest on the indebtedness are current, and the unpaid principal balance of the indebtedness to LENDER is $_____ as of such date, subject to payment of all checks in process of collection.

2. The terms of the note evidencing such indebtedness are hereby modified by increasing the rate of interest payable thereunder to _____ percent per annum, effective on _____ . Such indebtedness shall, beginning on _____ and continuing thereafter, be payable in monthly installments of $_____ per month together with any amounts required for escrow deposits. The dates on which payments are due shall remain unchanged.

1 of 3

Figure 9–5. *Modification and Assumption Agreement with Release, page 2*

3. ASSUMER hereby assumes such indebtedness as modified in paragraph 2 above, and shall hereafter make all monthly payments as called for therein. If this Agreement is entered into after the date of the transfer of the property, ASSUMER agrees and tenders herewith an amount necessary to make the loan current as modified in paragraph 2. Further, ASSUMER agrees to abide by all provisions of such note and of the security instrument securing such indebtedness as described above, excepting as specifically modified by this agreement. In the event of any default by ASSUMER under the terms of such note or such security instrument, LENDER may exercise all remedies available to it under the terms of such note or security instrument, including an action at law against ASSUMER to collect any monies due under the note, and exercise of the remedies contained in NON-UNIFORM COVENANT 19 of the security instrument. ASSUMER hereby acknowledges that LENDER has made all disclosures to ASSUMER as may be required under the Consumer Credit Protection Act of 1968 and Regulation Z (Title 12, part 226, Code of Federal Regulations).

4. BORROWER hereby relinquishes and transfers to ASSUMER all BORROWER'S interest in any monies which may be held by LENDER as escrow deposits for the purposes of application to taxes, assessments, fire or other insurance premiums, or any other purposes for which deposits are being required by LENDER. ASSUMER assumes the liability for payment of any unpaid taxes, assessments, fire, or other insurance and agrees to continue making monthly deposits for such purposes if required by LENDER.

5. LENDER hereby consents to the sale and transfer of such property to ASSUMER by BORROWER, hereby accepts ASSUMER as its obligor, and shall amend its records to indicate the transfer of such indebtedness from the name of BOR-ROWER to the name of ASSUMER, and LENDER shall henceforth in all respects treat ASSUMER as its borrower. LENDER hereby releases BORROWER from all obligations or liabilities under such note or security instrument. All other terms of this agreement to the contrary notwithstanding, the remedies contained in NON-UNIFORM COVENANT 19 of the security instrument shall remain in full force and effect in accordance with their terms.

6. ASSUMER agrees that the granting of consent by LENDER to this transfer shall not constitute a waiver of the restrictions on transfer contained in such security instrument, and such restrictions shall continue in full force and any future transfer or sale by ASSUMER without the written consent of LENDER shall constitute a default of the terms of such security instrument, and LENDER, at its option, may exercise all remedies available to it under the terms of such note and security instrument.

7. Wherever the words "BORROWER" or "ASSUMER" are used in this agreement, they shall represent the plural as well as the singular, the feminine and neuter genders as well as the masculine, and shall include heirs, successors or assigns.

IN WITNESS WHEREOF, the parties have executed this agreement on the day and year first above written.

BORROWER(S):   ASSUMER(S):

_____   _____

_____   _____

                                        XYZ Mortgage Co.

Attest: _____   By _____
              Secretary   President

2 of 3

Figure 9–6.   Modification and Assumption Agreement with Release, page 3

ACKNOWLEDGMENT - BORROWER(S)

STATE OF TEXAS
COUNTY OF

BEFORE ME, the undersigned authority, on this day personally appeared _____ known to me to be the person(s) whose name(s) _____ subscribed to the foregoing instrument, and acknowledged to me that ____ he ____ executed the same for the purposes and considerations therein expressed.

GIVEN UNDER MY HAND AND SEAL OF OFFICE, this _____ day of _____ , 19 ____ .

_____
Notary Public

My commission expires: _____

ACKNOWLEDGMENT - ASSUMER(S)

STATE OF TEXAS
COUNTY OF

BEFORE ME, the undersigned authority, on this day personally appeared _____ known to me to be the person(s) whose name(s) _____ subscribed to the foregoing instrument, and acknowledged to me that ____ he ____ executed the same for the purposes and consideration therein expressed.

GIVEN UNDER MY HAND AND SEAL OF OFFICE, this ____ day of _____ , 19____ .

_____
Notary Public

My commission expires: _____

ACKNOWLEDGMENT - XYZ Mortgage Co.

STATE OF TEXAS
COUNTY OF

BEFORE ME, the undersigned authority, on this day personally appeared _____ known to me to be the person whose name is subscribed to the foregoing instrument as _____ President of the XYZ Mortgage Co., a party thereto, and acknowledged to me that he executed the same as _____ President for the said XYZ Mortgage Co. and as the act and deed of XYZ Mortgage Co., a corporation, for the purposes and consideration therein expressed and in the capacity therein stated.

GIVEN UNDER MY HAND AND SEAL OF OFFICE, this ____ day of _____ , 19____ .

_____
Notary Public

My commission expires: _____

have such a wide selection. As a real estate professional, you should have knowledge of the conventional lenders and the types of loans that each makes. For example, some of the conventional lenders will only make loans on property that is built by a builder who has received his interim financing from the lender. Some savings and loan associations will only make loans within the city in which they have offices and in some cases will limit their loan operation to within a specific radius of the offices of the association. This limiting of the area of operation is a rule of the S and L and not of the Federal Home Loan Bank Board.

Underwriting Guidelines

In comparing the underwriting guidelines of the conventional loan to those of the FHA or VA, the FHA or VA guidelines are rather specific and are set by regulation of the FHA or VA, whereas there are no set guidelines for the conventional loan. Each conventional lender sets the guidelines it wishes to use. Some lenders are more lenient than others. Some lenders rely more on the income and the potential increase of the income, some are more interested in the past credit history of the applicant, and others are more interested in the property that will serve as security for the mortgage.

The above is true for all mortgages that will not be sold to Fannie Mae and/or FHLMC. Mortgages that will be sold to either of these corporations must meet their strict underwriting guidelines. There is a growing trend among the conventional lenders to use the income and other guidelines of Fannie Mae and FHLMC for the qualification of the conventional borrower.

The informed real estate professional will be familiar with the underwriting guidelines of the conventional lenders in his or her area. This will allow the salesperson to better match the borrower to the proper lender.

Selection of a Conventional Lender

From the previous paragraphs, one can see that the selection of the proper conventional lender for a client is an involved process and should be done with great care. A real estate salesperson should look at all of the conventional lenders and not just at the interest rate. The salesperson who selects a lender based only on the interest rate may be doing a disservice to his or her client.

Also, the policies of a conventional lender can change from time to time. One reason for this change may be that the lender has a commitment from a different investor and the underwriting guidelines of that investor are different, thus the lender must change its policies. So it is important, then, for you to check the conventional market on a continuing basis, for what was true last week may not be true this week.

When dealing with the conventional mortgage, one thing must be kept in mind: because a client is rejected by one conventional lender does not mean that the client will be rejected by all of the conventional lenders. Each lender has its own set of rules for accepting or rejecting a loan application. This is not true for VA or FHA loans. If either the VA or the FHA rejects the application, there is usually little hope of getting the application approved by the other.

PRIVATE MORTGAGE INSURANCE

Private mortgage insurance may be defined as an insurance policy issued from a licensed company to an approved lender, protecting that lender from financial loss due to the default of a borrower. This insurance is issued only on first-lien mortgages that are secured by improved residential property. Usually the insurance is only issued on mortgages that exceed 80 percent of the appraised value of the property.

History

Private mortgage insurance (PMI) is not a new idea. It can be traced to companies that issued such policies since the late 1800s. Most of these companies were located in New York City and normally issued their insurance not on single-family dwellings, but on commercial buildings. Prior to the Depression, the industry was made up of only private companies. There was little regulation of these insurance companies, and as with many companies, they either went into bankruptcy or stopped operation as a result of the Depression.

Out of the reform instituted during the Roosevelt era, the federal government entered the mortgage insurance business with the formulation of the FHA. The FHA was the only source of mortgage insurance until 1957, when the Wisconsin Insurance Commission issued a license to the Mortgage Guaranty Insurance Corporation. This was the beginning of the PMI industry as we know it today. Currently there are several companies licensed to issue PMI in the United States. Even though there are many companies licensed to issue PMI, the giant of the industry is still Mortgage Guaranty Insurance Corporation (MGIC).

Two events that happened in the early 1970s greatly enhanced the PMI industry. The first was in 1970, when Congress passed the Emergency Home Finance Act of 1970. One of the provisions of this act, which went into effect in 1971, allowed Fannie Mae to purchase conventional loans in excess of the 75 percent loan-to-value ratio where either the seller kept a 10 percent participation or the loan was insured by a PMI company that was approved by Fannie Mae. This LTV (loan-to-value) has been amended to 80 percent.

The second event that was of significance to the PMI industry occurred in 1972 when the Federal Home Loan Bank Board allowed savings and loan associations to make 95 percent loan-to-value loans on single-family dwellings as long as the amount of the loan above 75 percent was insured by a PMI company. Thus 75 percent as the basic loan for S and Ls was modified to 80 percent, and as of August 1980 the basic loan for S and Ls has been increased to 90 percent by the Federal Home Loan Bank Board. The PMI companies approved by FHLMC are listed in Appendix G.

It should be noted that the passage and/or enactment of the above-mentioned laws and regulations was the basis that made PMI a viable alternative to FHA insurance.

This ends our discussion of the history of the PMI industry. If you have any questions, contact the nearest office of one of the PMI companies listed in the appendix or any PMI-approved lender in your area.

PMI Coverage

Types of properties   As a real estate professional, you should have knowledge of the types of properties and the amount of insurance that is available. All PMI companies will normally issue policies on first lien mortgages on a 1- to 4-family dwelling that is used as a primary residence where the loan does not exceed 95 percent of the appraised value. Some PMI companies will issue mortgage insurance on a mortgage for a second home or a leisure home. In this case, the loan may not exceed 90 percent of the appraised value. Some PMI companies will issue insurance on mortgages of 1- to 4-family dwellings that are not the primary residence, but are held as investment property. For the investment property, the loan-to-value ratio generally should not exceed 80 percent. Not only will PMI com-

panies issue insurance on single-family dwellings, but some of the companies will issue mortgage insurance on manufactured housing. To get the details on this coverage, you will have to contact the various PMI companies to see if they issue this type of insurance.

Insurance issued   Many references have been made to issuance of insurance by the PMI company on mortgages, but what is the coverage of the insurance? First, it should be made very clear that PMI insurance is not the same as the insurance issued by FHA. PMI does not insure 100 percent of the mortgage, but only a portion of the mortgage. What portion of the mortgage is insured? The PMI companies are limited by law to the maximum percent of the loan they can insure. In Texas, for example, this maximum is 100 percent.

The normal protection for a fixed-term, fixed-rate mortgage is between 20 and 30 percent, and for an adjustable-rate mortgage the coverage is between 20 and 35 percent. This protection is available on a high loan-to-value ratio loan of 80 percent or more and issued almost exclusively on 90 to 95 percent loans. With this type of coverage available, institutions that are limited to a maximum loan-to-value ratio of 75 percent are able to make 95 percent loans. With the 25 percent coverage on a fixed-term, fixed-rate 95 percent loan on a home selling for $70,000, the lender would have the following risk:

Sales price	$70,000
Loan amount—95%	$66,500
Borrower's down payment	$ 3,500
Loan amount	$66,500
PMI coverage	×25%
Total PMI coverage	$16,625

Thus, the lender's exposure on the property would be the sales price, less the down payment, less the insurance coverage, or:

$70,000 − $3500 − $16,625 = $49,875

When the items are subtracted from the sales price and the lender's exposure of $50,000 is divided by the sales price, the lender is actually making a 71.25 percent loan.

$$\frac{\$49,875}{\$70,000} \times 100 = 71.25\%$$

In addition to the 25 percent coverage on the fixed-rate loans, many of the PMI companies offer 12-, 16-, 17-, 20-, and 30-percent coverage. In regard to the adjustable-rate mortgage, many of the companies offer 20-, 25-, 30-, and 35-percent coverage.

These are the standard coverages that many of the lenders will require on many of the loans they originate or fund. If the mortgage is to be sold to Fannie Mae or FHLMC, however, the required coverages are as follows:

Fixed-rate mortgage

91 to 95% loans	22% coverage .5% DN
86 to 90% loans	17% coverage -10%
81 to 85% loans	12% coverage 15%
80% and under	No coverage

Loans with possible negative amortization

91 to 95% loans	25% coverage
All other loan-to-value ratios	20% coverage

One can see that normally Fannie Mae and FHLMC require less coverage, thus increasing the lender's exposure slightly.

Let us use the same example as before and calculate the lender's exposure to loss through Fannie Mae or FHLMC.

Sales price	$70,000
95% loan	$66,500
Required down payment	$ 3,500
Loan amount	$66,500
PMI coverage	× 22%
Total PMI coverage	$14,630

Once again, the lender's exposure to loss would be the sales price, less the down payment, less the PMI coverage, or:

$70,000 − $3,500 − $14,630 = $51,870

This would have the lender actually making a 74.1 percent loan, increasing the lender's exposure by less than 3 percent.

The coverages discussed above are only the basic coverages and many are available. You as a real estate professional, however, will normally deal only with the coverages outlined above.

PMI PREMIUMS

As the PMI companies' operations are regulated by the State of Texas, so are the rates they can charge. The following discussion of rates is based on the rates established by the State Board of Insurance as of July 1984. The

premiums allowed to be charged for coverage of a standard mortgage are shown in Figure 9–7, and the allowable premiums for mortgage insurance on adjustable-rate mortgages with and without negative amortization are shown in Figure 9–8.

In the following section, we will review the method that you as a real estate professional may use to calculate the cost of private mortgage insurance for the first year premium and the method used to calculate the renewal premiums. First, the calculations using the standard coverage plans. Let us assume a home with a value of $110,000 and the borrower is applying for a 95-percent 30-year loan at 14.50 percent. Thus, the loan amount would be $104,500. For this example, the mortgage will be sold to Fannie Mae, who requires 22 percent mortgage insurance coverage on loans with a loan-to-value ratio of 95 percent.

In Figure 9–7, find the column labelled Coverage and look down the column until you find 22 percent. There you will see several loan-to-value ratios; find the 91–95 percent and look across the row to the first-year premium or .80 of 1 percent. Thus, to calculate the first-year premium, multiply the loan amount by the percentage or:

$104,500 × 0.008 = $836.00

This would be the premium that would be collected at closing to pay for the first-year cost of the private mortgage insurance.

Then, to calculate the renewal premiums for the mortgage insurance, you will use the percent that is shown in the column entitled Renewal Premiums. In our example the percent is one fourth of 1 percent. To calculate the required premium, multiply the percentage times the balance at the end of the first year. It should be noted that many of the lenders will use the original loan balance to establish the renewal premium. For example, since the original balance was $104,500, the lender would multiply that by the renewal premium or:

$104,500 × 0.0025 = $261.25

Since the premium is collected as part of the monthly payment, the $261.25 is divided by 12 or:

$$\frac{\$261.25}{12} = \$21.77$$

Therefore $21.77 would be added to the monthly payment for the mortgage insurance. The

Figure 9–7.   Texas Rates for Private Mortgage Insurance—Standard Mortgage

Coverage	LTV	1st Yr. Premium	Renewal Premiums
30%	91–95%	1.25%	.25%
	86–90%	.90%	.25%
	81–85%	.70%	.25%
	80% & under	.50%	.25%
25%	91–95%	1.00%	.25%
	86–90%	.75%	.25%
	81–85%	.50%	.25%
	80% & under	.35%	.25%
22%	91–95%	.80%	.25%
	86–90%	.55%	.25%
	81–85%	.45%	.25%
20%	91–95%	.75%	.25%
	86–90%	.50%	.25%
	81–85%	.35%	.25%
	80% & under	.25%	.25%
17%	86–90%	.40%	.25%
	81–85%	.30%	.25%
	80% & under	.20%	.20%
16%	91–95%	.625%	.25%
12%	86–90%	.25%	.25%
	81–85%	.15%	.15%
	80% & under	.14%	.14%

SOURCE: Mortgage Guaranty Insurance Corp. *Operating Manual*, February 1984, Premium Rates.

proper way to calculate the renewal premium would be to calculate the loan balance at the end of the first year and then multiply that value times the renewal premium. In our example the loan balance at the end of the first year is $104,282.49. Multiply that amount by the renewal percentage and divide the answer by 12 or:

$$\$104{,}282.49 \times .0025 = \frac{\$260.71}{12} = \$21.73$$

Thus, there is very little difference in the first year of the loan. Should the lender then use the original loan amount to calculate the premium for the *life* of the policy, this will cost the borrower unnecessary additional premiums.

If you were working with a client who was going to make application for an adjustable-rate mortgage, then you must find out if the loan will have negative amortization or not. The reason is that this will determine which of the adjustable-rate mortgage tables you would use. It should be noted that if the ARM is to be sold to Fannie Mae, Fannie Mae requires that the Negatively Amortizing Loans chart be used. The reason is that the new Fannie Mae ARM notes allow the borrower to cap his or her payment at any adjustment date. If the borrower in the previous example was seeking an ARM that was to be sold to Fannie Mae to calculate the PMI premiums we would use the premium table with negative amortization. The first year premium would be calculated by multiplying the loan amount by 1.15 percent or

$$\$104{,}500 \times 0.0125 = \$1306.25$$

Figure 9–8. Texas Rates for Private Mortgage Insurance (PMI) for Adjustable-Rate Mortgages

NORMALLY AMORTIZING LOANS

Minimum Coverage	LTV	1st Year Premium	Renewal Premiums
25%	91–95%	1.00%	.35%
20%	81–90% 80% & under	.50% .35%	.35% .35%

NEGATIVELY AMORTIZING LOANS

Minimum Coverage	LTV	1st Year Premium	Renewal Premiums
25%	91–95%	1.15%	.35%
20%	81–90% 80% & under	.70% .35%	.35% .35%

SOURCE: Mortgage Guaranty Insurance Corp., *Operating Manual*, February 1984, Premium Rates.

which would be collected at closing. Then the renewal premiums would be calculated by multiplying the balance by 0.0035.

It should be noted that all of these calculations and rates are for owner-occupied properties. For investor or second-home rates, you will need to contact one of the private mortgage insurance companies listed in Appendix G or contact any lender that makes or originates conventional loans.

In addition to the annual plan, most of the PMI companies offer several single payment plans. The single payment plan allows the purchase of a policy for terms of from 3 years up to 15 years. For the plans available, contact any lender or PMI company in your area.

There are major differences in the coverage and premiums of PMI and the mortgage insurance issued by FHA. One of the major differences is that PMI insurance is not for the life of the loan, as is FHA mortgage insurance. Once the loan balance reaches the 80 percent loan-to-value ratio based on the original sales or appraised price, the PMI insurance coverage may be dropped and the premium is discontinued. This usually takes approximately 19 years.

It should be noted that even though the lender is ordering or requesting the insurance coverage, the borrower will pay the cost of the PMI insurance.

Application for PMI

Each of the PMI companies has its own procedures for the application of coverage. Usually the lender will submit a completed loan package to the PMI company. Using the form of the investor or those supplied by the PMI company, the PMI company will review the materials and approve or disapprove the borrower based on the materials.

Normally the PMI companies will have standard underwriting guidelines concerning the relationship of the total monthly income to the total mortgage payment, including all escrows and any fees that may affect the title to the property. In addition to the ratio of the total monthly income to mortgage payment, the PMI companies will review the ratio of the total monthly income to the total long-term obligations of the borrower, including the total mortgage payment. In most cases, the PMI companies define *long-term obligation* as any obligation that will take ten or more months to pay off.

The PMI company will review the credit history of the borrower, his and/or her work record, and any other factor that may affect the borrower's ability or willingness to repay the obligations. Some of these factors are court judgments, pending lawsuits, and bankruptcy.

The PMI company will also review the property that will serve as the security for the mortgage. The economic life of the property will be checked to see if it is sufficient to support the term of the loan. Also considered is whether the property can be sold rapidly if it is taken back, and whether it is an existing construction or proposed construction. These are only a few of the guidelines that are used by the PMI companies. If you would like further information, you may contact a PMI company and they will be able to supply you with the in-depth underwriting guidelines they use.

If all of the underwriting guidelines are met and the PMI company will issue the requested coverage, the originating lender will be notified by phone, and later a written confirmation of the approval will be furnished. This underwriting procedure will normally take only one or two days. One can see that the underwriting by the PMI companies is a great deal faster than that of FHA, which can take many weeks.

Claims Payment

When a lender has notified the PMI company that an insured loan is in default as per the procedures of the PMI company, the insuring company has two ways of handling the claim. First, the company can pay the lender the full amount of the remaining loan balance. If this is done, the PMI company will take title to the property and then dispose of the property. Second, the PMI company can pay the lender as per the coverage purchased (20, 25, or 10 percent of the loan balance) plus other expenses in the policy of the PMI company, and the lender will then dispose of the property.

Claims under insurance issued by a PMI company are handled differently from claims filed against FHA mortgage insurance. The FHA will pay the lender the outstanding loan balance either in cash or debentures secured by the United States Treasury and FHA will take the property.

Benefits of PMI Coverage

One can see that there are many benefits for both the borrower and the lender with the purchase of PMI coverage. Some of the benefits to the *lender* are listed below:

1. The PMI insurance allows the lender to make 90 and 95 percent loans and to sell these loans in the secondary market

2. With the ability to make higher loan-to-value ratio loans, the amount of possible loans is expanded

3. The lender can secure an additional amount of security for the loan at no extra cost

4. The processing time and the issuance of the insurance commitment is usually faster from a PMI company than the FHA.

Advantages for the *borrower* include the following:

1. The borrower has the ability to purchase a home with a conventional loan with as little as 5 percent down payment

2. With the need for less money down, the borrower can buy a home sooner and sometimes larger than expected

3. The processing time for the insurance commitment is usually faster than with the FHA

4. The payment of the insurance premiums is for a shorter period than FHA

usually 20% equity into it *over life of loan*

Other Services Offered by PMI Companies

In addition to the insurance of conventional loans, some of the PMI companies offer other services to the lender and the real estate industry. The most important of these services is operation of a secondary market department or facility. This department of a PMI company helps lenders locate sources of either funds to loan or commitments to purchase loans. In effect, this will bring together those with funds to loan and those who need funds to loan.

Some PMI companies have branched out and offer a wide range of financial services. For example, the parent company of Mortgage Guaranty Insurance Corporation offers commercial mortgage insurance, municipal bond insurance, and officer's and director's insurance.

REVIEW QUESTIONS

1. Define the term *conventional loan*.

2. Compare the loan limits, processing time, and down payments for a conventional loan to those of VA- and FHA-insured loans.

3. Contact a lender in your area and inquire as to the assumption procedures and cost charged by a conventional lender.

4. If you presently own a home and have a mortgage on that home, outline the prepayment penalties in your note and deed of trust.

5. Define the term *origination fee*. What is the usual fee charged by lenders in your area?

6. Name and define the items that you feel are important in the selection of a conventional lender.

7. What is private mortgage insurance?

8. Explain the insurance coverage issued by a PMI company and give an example.

9. What are the premiums charged by PMI companies in your area?

10. How may a PMI company pay claims filed by an insured lender?

PROBLEMS

1. Calculate a lender's exposure on a home valued at $94,550 and 5 percent down. The lender requires 30-percent coverage.

2. Calculate the first-year premium on the following loan: purchase price of the home $105,550; $91,820 loan amount, with 22 percent coverage

3. Calculate the amount that would be added to the monthly payment to pay the first renewal premium for the loan example in problem 2.

10

The Secondary Market, Part 1

LEARNING OBJECTIVES

In this chapter we will discuss the secondary market in general, and in particular the conventional mortgage purchase programs of the Federal National Mortgage Association.

Upon completion of this chapter you should be able to do the following:

★ Define the term *secondary market* as it relates to mortgage lending.

★ Identify the primary secondary markets.

★ Outline some of the major mortgage purchase programs of the Federal National Mortgage Association.

★ Outline the methods used by the Federal National Mortgage Association to generate funds for the purchase of mortgages.

A FEW DEFINITIONS

First, we should define the term *secondary market*. The secondary market is the market in which closed real estate loans are bought and sold.

When discussing the secondary market, one must understand that there is also a *primary market*. The primary market can be defined as those lenders that originate the loan and process the loan. These lenders are referred to as *primary lenders*. Many of the primary lenders do not wish to keep the closed loans in their portfolios and keep their funds tied up. They, therefore, will sell the loan in the secondary market. It should be noted that the secondary market is not like the stock market; it is not as organized, regulated, or structured. As a primary lender, normally you cannot call up a mortgage broker as you can a stockbroker and sell a mortgage. How mortgages are sold in the secondary market will be discussed later in this chapter.

Among those investors that are purchasing real estate loans in the secondary market are insurance companies, savings and loan associations, commercial banks, title companies, other private companies and individuals, and agencies of the federal government. It should be noted that some of the companies that purchase loans in the secondary market also operate in the primary market as originating lenders.

PURPOSE OF THE SECONDARY MARKET

The primary purpose of the secondary market is to move funds from an area of the country with a surplus of capital for real estate loans to an area of the country that has a deficiency of capital for real estate loans. Since the supply of money is never static or in balance in all sections of the nation, the need for money and the supply of money is always changing. The secondary market tries to keep things in balance. For example, a mortgage banker in Midland has a large demand for loans due to a rapid influx of families to that area. Since mortgage companies normally do not lend their own funds, they will turn to the secondary market for help. The mortgage banker will call financial institutions in sections of the country that have a large supply of loanable funds, but do not have a great demand for real estate loans; or, the mortgage banker can secure a commitment from one of the government or quasi-government agencies that purchase loans.

How does a mortgage banker or any other lender keep up with the area of the country that has a surplus of funds? This is done by either a person or several people in the company who keep in contact with other lenders throughout the United States. Usually, there is a surplus of funds in savings institutions in Florida and the Midwest. The wise primary lender tries to keep up with the institutions in those areas in order to secure funds.

MAJOR SECONDARY MARKETS

There are three organizations that are the heart of the secondary market and purchase most of the real estate loans in the secondary market. These are the Federal National Mortgage Association (FNMA), the Government National Mortgage Association (GNMA), and the Federal Home Loan Mortgage Corporation (FHLMC). These organizations, particularly Fannie Mae, gave birth to a national secondary market. GNMA and FHLMC will be reviewed in depth in the next chapter.

FEDERAL NATIONAL MORTGAGE ASSOCIATION (FNMA)[1]

Prior to the Great Depression, there was no secondary market as we know it today. The first attempt at a secondary market was the creation of the Home Owners Loan Corporation (HOLC) with the enactment of the Home Owners' Loan Act of 1933. The purpose of this corporation was to help home owners refinance an existing loan that was in danger of going into foreclosure or being taken due to back taxes. This agency is no longer in existence.

As we learned earlier, the Federal Housing Administration was created with the passage of the National Housing Act of 1934. In addition to the creation of FHA, Title III, Section 301 allowed the establishment of secondary market facilities for home mortgages and also provided that the operations of this secondary market would be financed with private capital, to the maximum extent possible. This was the authority under which Fannie Mae was subsequently created, thus beginning the modern secondary market.

The actual creation of the corporation was not until February 10, 1938, upon the request of the President under the authority of Title III of the National Housing Act. When the secondary marketing corporation was founded it was not known as the Federal National Mortgage Association, but was named the National Mortgage Association of Washington. The name was changed on April 5, 1938, to the Federal National Mortgage Association. At this time, the operations of Fannie Mae were controlled by the Reconstruction Finance Corporation. The control of Fannie Mae remained under this federal agency until September 1950, when the control of the operations was shifted to the Housing and Home Finance Agency. This agency was the forerunner to the Department of Housing and Urban Development. Then in 1965, when the Department of Housing and Urban Development was created, the control of Fannie Mae was transferred to HUD.

The final and most major change to the operations of Fannie Mae came about in 1968 with the passage of the 1968 amendments to the National Housing Act. Under Section 801 of these amendments, Fannie Mae was partitioned into two separate and distinct corporations. One of these corporations was to be known as the Federal National Mortgage Association and was to be a government-chartered, shareholder-owned, for-profit corporation. Fannie Mae would continue to operate in the secondary market as authorized by the National Housing Act. The other corporation was to be known as the Government National Mortgage Association, and the ownership and control of this corporation was to remain with the government. Today, GNMA is under the control of the Department of Housing and Urban Development.

In the amendments of 1968, Fannie Mae was to be responsible for its own operations and management after a period of transition. This transition was to be completed on or after May 1, 1970. According to Section 801, Fannie Mae could not be classified as a separate corporation responsible for its own operations until at least one-third of the common stock was owned by persons or institutions in the mortgage lending business, home construction industry, real estate industry, or other related industries. This one-third ownership of the stock was to be established by the Board of Directors of Fannie Mae in concurrence with the Secretary of Housing and Urban

Development. The board found that the necessary stock was being held by the specified industries in February 1970, and the Secretary of HUD concurred with such findings on May 21, 1970, thus establishing Fannie Mae as a privately owned and controlled corporation with a public purpose.

The Purpose of Fannie Mae

The purposes, or functions, of Fannie Mae were established by the enactment of the Fannie Mae Charter Act of 1954 and became effective in August 1954. These purposes are listed below:

1. To establish a secondary market operation for the purpose of buying and selling real estate mortgages

2. To help in the financing of special housing programs and to help ease the effect of adverse economic conditions on the housing market

3. To manage and liquidate the Fannie Mae mortgage portfolio with the least adverse effect on the mortgage market and the federal government

In 1968, the second and third purposes were transferred to GNMA.

Governmental Interaction[2]

Even though Fannie Mae is a private corporation and is listed on the New York Stock Exchange, it still has a close relationship to the federal government—in particular to HUD and the Treasury Department. Since Fannie Mae has been given some advantages by the federal government with the passage of the Fannie Mae Charter Act and other laws, it is also subject to some governmental supervision and control.

Let's discuss some of the advantages accorded to Fannie Mae. First, the Secretary of the Treasury has the authority to purchase up to $2.25 billion of Fannie Mae outstanding debts. This authority has become known as a *treasury backstop authority*, although it has never been used. It should be noted that the debt of Fannie Mae is not an obligation of the federal government, nor is it guaranteed by the federal government. The debt is solely an obligation of Fannie Mae. Even though Fannie Mae is a private corporation, its obligations, along with the obligations of federally owned corporations, are known as *federal agency securities.*

The second advantage accorded to Fannie Mae is that its stock is exempt from the federal registration requirements and other laws enforced by the Securities and Exchange Commission.

Another advantage is that although Fannie Mae is required to pay federal corporate income tax, it is exempt from all state and local taxes except for real estate taxes.

Finally, all issues of notes and debentures or other obligations of Fannie Mae are issued through and payable by the Federal Reserve Banks. Any service that is rendered by a Reserve Bank is paid for by Fannie Mae. All of the obligations sold by Fannie Mae are legal investments for federally supervised institutions, as well as for many state-supervised institutions.

Along with these advantages, Fannie Mae has accepted some forms of federal supervision and regulation. Five of the fifteen members of the Fannie Mae Board of Directors are appointed by the President of the United States. Three of the five must be selected as follows: one from the home building industry, one from the mortgage lending industry, and one from the real estate industry. The remaining ten directors are elected by the Fannie Mae stockholders.

The Secretary of HUD has the authority to see that a reasonable portion of Fannie Mae's mortgage purchases is related to the national goal of providing adequate housing for low- and moderate-income families. It should be noted that these loans are to provide Fannie Mae a reasonable economic return.

The Secretary of Housing and Urban Development has certain regulatory powers over Fannie Mae. This means that the secretary has the power to make and enforce regulations to see that Fannie Mae accomplishes the purposes of the Federal National Mortgage Association Charter Act, subject to being overseen by the Congress of the United States.

All issuance of debt by Fannie Mae must be approved by the Secretary of the Treasury. It should be noted that the largest borrower of funds is the United States Treasury, and in some years Fannie Mae is the second largest borrower of funds. The activities of the two need to be coordinated, thus the issuance of Fannie Mae debt obligations is approved by the Secretary of the Treasury, who reviews the debt obligations as to the maturities and rates of interest.

The Secretary of HUD may examine and audit the Fannie Mae books and require Fannie Mae to make reports as the Secretary of HUD deems necessary.

These are the principal forms of federal supervision or control of Fannie Mae. In addition to direct federal supervision, the Secretary of HUD has the power to issue regulations that have a direct effect on Fannie Mae and its operation. These regulations were revised in 1978; three of the revisions were as follows:

1. To establish, within the authority granted under the Fannie Mae Charter Act, standards and goals for the secondary marketing operations of Fannie Mae

2. To set forth regulations that would insure that Fannie Mae is complying with the non-discrimination statutes

3. To provide for annual audits of the books and financial transactions of Fannie Mae

The first revision is one of the more significant changes, for it provides for goals to be established for Fannie Mae regarding the purchase of mortgages on properties in the inner-city areas of standard metropolitan statistical areas, as well as the purchase of conventional mortgages on housing of low- and moderate-income families.

Fannie Mae's Corporate Offices

The National Housing Act in Title III requires that Fannie Mae maintain its principal office in the Washington, D.C. area. It is located at 3900 Wisconsin Avenue NW, Washington, D.C. In addition to that home office, Fannie Mae operates five regional offices. Texas is under control of the Southwestern Regional Office, located in Dallas, Texas. The address of the office is

Fannie Mae Southwestern Region
2001 Bryan Tower
Dallas, Texas 75201
(214) 744-0311

Fannie Mae Source of Funds

Since Fannie Mae is in the business of purchasing loans, it must have funds to accomplish this function, and it derives these funds from the capital market.

One source of Fannie Mae funds is the sale of debt instruments. These instruments are either short- or long-term. The long-term instruments usually take the form of a debenture and the short-term instruments are in the form of short-term discount notes. The debenture is a debt obligation that, when issued, is not secured by any tangible asset, but by the soundness or financial strength of Fannie Mae. An example of such a debenture offering is shown in Figure 10–1. As we learned earlier in the chapter, all of the obligations of Fannie Mae are viewed by the market as federal agency securities and have for many years been looked upon favorably by the financial community. Since most assets of Fannie Mae are in the form of secured real estate loans, most members of the financial community feel there is little chance of default by Fannie Mae. In addition to all of the assets being secured real estate loans, Fannie Mae also has the ability to call on the Treasury of the United States for the purchase of a portion of its debt.

In regard to the term of the debt instruments of Fannie Mae, the short-term notes are issued for a term of from 30 days to 360 days. The debentures are issued for a term of 1 year to 25 years.

In addition to the borrowing of funds, Fannie Mae also has portfolio income. This portfolio income is not only derived from interest on mortgages, but also from discounts on mortgages.

One other method that may be used by Fannie Mae to raise capital is the selling of stock in the corporation. Even though Fannie Mae has close ties with the federal government, it is still a private corporation and has the right to issue stock, as any other corporation would.

A new method used by Fannie Mae to provide funds to the mortgage market is through the issuance and guaranty of Conventional Mortgage Pass-Through Securities. The purpose of this program is to tap the long-term investor market, including pension funds, which have traditionally invested little or nothing in mortgages. In other words, this is an additional means that Fannie Mae can use to support the mortgage market without itself purchasing loans. Under this program, Fannie Mae will issue guaranteed securities representing an undivided fractional interest in a pool of conventional first lien mortgages. These securities will be similar to those guaranteed by the Government National Mortgage Association.

Figure 10–1. Fannie Mae Debenture Offering

Federal National Mortgage Association
3900 WISCONSIN AVENUE, N.W., WASHINGTON, D.C. 20016

News Release

For further information contact: Paul Paquin   (202) 537-7115

<u>FOR IMMEDIATE RELEASE</u>   <u>WEDNESDAY, SEPTEMBER 3, 1980</u>   #4264

DEBENTURE OFFERING

Date of Release: WEDNESDAY, SEPTEMBER 3, 1980

Date of Offering: THURSDAY, SEPTEMBER 4, 1980

Price: Par

Issue Date	Term	Interest Rate	Amount (in millions)	Maturity Date	Date of First Interest Payment (then-semiannually)
9/10/80	1 year 4 mos.	10.90%	$400	1/11/82	1/11/81

Uses to Which Proceeds will   The net proceeds of this offering
be Put: will be used to partially redeem
                                the $400,000,000 7.50% and the
                                $650,000,000 8.75% debentures that
                                mature on September 10, 1980.

Debentures will be issued in book-entry form only. The minimum
purchase is $10,000 and multiples of $5,000 thereafter. The
offering is being made through FNMA's Vice President and Fiscal
Agent, John J. Meehan, 100 Wall Street, New York, assisted by
a nationwide selling group of recognized security dealers.

The issues which are offered tomorrow will be free to trade at
12:00 NOON Eastern Daylight Time.

The GNMA securities program will be explained in Chapter 11. There is one major difference between the "certificates" issued by GNMA and the "securities" of Fannie Mae. Since GNMA is a federal agency, its "certificates" are guaranteed by the federal government, whereas the "securities" issued by Fannie Mae carry no such guarantee, but only the guarantee of Fannie Mae. The guarantee issued by Fannie Mae is for the full and timely payment of principal and interest on the 25th of each month.

The mortgages that will be used as the collateral for these securities are grouped or packaged into what is referred to as a pool. The mortgages that are grouped or pooled must meet or conform to certain specifications, which are essentially the same as those pertaining to loans purchased for Fannie Mae's own portfolio:

1. The property used to secure the mortgage must be a single-family or 2- to 4-family dwelling

2. Each mortgage in the pool must have an original term of no more than 30 years

3. All mortgages in the pool that have a loan-to-value ratio in excess of 80 percent must be insured by private mortgage insurance issued by a private mortgage insurance company approved by Fannie Mae and authorized by the state in which the property is located to issue such mortgage insurance

These are the major specifications that each of the mortgages must meet prior to being included in a pool of mortgages. For *all* of the requirements, you should contact a Fannie Mae-approved lender.

There are now two types of pools authorized to be packaged. One type of pool is called a *single-user pool.* With this type of pool, the lender packages a number of mortgages that meet all of the specifications and that equal $1 million or more. The second type of pool is a *multiple pool* in which loan packages—minimum $1 million each, from more than one lender—are combined to back a single security offering.

The minimum face amount for a certificate of ownership of an undivided fractional interest in one of these pools is $25,000, with additional interests sold in multiples of $5000, thus making these "securities" available to the general public, corporations, pension funds and financial institutions.

Fannie Mae Loan Approval

Prior to the purchase of a mortgage by Fannie Mae, the mortgage must meet certain criteria. For most FHA/VA mortgages, if the mortgage has been insured by FHA or has been issued a guaranty by the Veterans Administration, Fannie Mae will purchase it without reviewing its credit and property underwriting.

For conventional mortgages, before December 1, 1981, when Fannie Mae instituted a major change in the approval process, there were two methods for conventional approval. This change was that Fannie Mae would no longer require, or even offer, the option of "prior approval," prior to the purchase of a mortgage from an approved lender. It should be noted that Fannie Mae refers to its approved lenders as approved seller/servicers. This was a major change in the approval procedures of Fannie Mae. Before this change, all lenders without a "Fannie Mae Delegated Underwriter" had to submit all mortgage applications with all of the documents to Fannie Mae for approval either before the closing of the mortgage or when the loans were submitted for purchase. For example, if a mortgage company located in Brownsville originated a mortgage to be sold to Fannie Mae, the mortgage company would have to mail the application along with all of the supporting data to the Fannie Mae regional office in Dallas for prior approval. The mailing and approval process at the regional office could take as long as two weeks. If this time is added to the normal processing time, one can see that the prior approval method could be rather time consuming.

With the implementation of the change allowing the lenders to give *in-house* approval, the processing and approval time can be cut significantly. As with any other delegation of authority, Fannie Mae has placed some requirements on the seller/servicer. One of the major requirements is that the lender must establish internal procedures to monitor credit, appraisals of property, underwriting requirements, and the accuracy of appraisals and all supporting documents that will accompany any application used in the underwriting of a mortgage loan.

As with any other program, there are certain limitations. Fannie Mae may require newly approved lenders to submit to Fannie Mae credit and property documents for an underwriting review prior to the purchase of mortgages for a limited period of time. The purpose of this is for Fannie Mae to see if the lender is following the underwriting guidelines of Fannie Mae. The only other exception to the program are those lenders that are "under sanction" by Fannie Mae.

The importance of this change in the Fannie Mae procedures cannot be overemphasized for it has streamlined the processing and approval of loans to be sold to Fannie Mae. This streamlining will be of great value to the real estate professional due to the ability for closer coordination with the lender on necessary information for the underwriting of the mortgage and thus for faster approval.

Mortgage Purchase Programs

Fannie Mae, since its beginning, has had the ability to purchase mortgages on one- to four-family dwellings. It never mattered whether the property was new or existing construction, but there once was the requirement that the mortgage had to be either insured or guaranteed by an agency of the federal government. This meant that Fannie Mae was limited to the purchase of only FHA or VA mortgages. This limitation was lifted by the passage of an amendment to the Charter Act in July 1970. It was not until February 1972, however, that Fannie Mae purchased its first conventional mortgage. The purchase of conventional loans has increased at a rapid rate and today represents approximately one-half of the mortgages purchased by Fannie Mae. In relation to the total portfolio of Fannie Mae, conventional mortgages represent approximately one half. In regard to the size and importance of the purchase of mortgages by Fannie Mae, its portfolio of purchased mortgages had grown to over $78.3 billion by the end of 1983.

Let us now examine the major conventional mortgage purchase programs available through Fannie Mae.

Single family home   Fannie Mae will purchase conventional mortgages on single-family homes or units on a spot basis located in subdivisions, de minimis PUD projects, and in Fannie Mae-approved condominiums or PUDS. (A de minimis PUD may be defined as a Planned Unit Development in which the common areas, if removed from the PUD, would have little or no effect on the value of the individual units or reduce the enjoyment of the homeowners.) In addition to the homes listed previously, Fannie Mae will purchase mortgages on detached, semi-detached, row, or townhouse structures.

Fannie Mae has set no minimum remaining term for the fixed-rate mortgages it purchases,

but has set the maximum term as thirty years. Fannie Mae accepts conventional mortgages with loan-to-value ratios as high as 95 percent. On a loan of 80 percent or less, Fannie Mae does not require any PMI coverage. Such coverage, down to 75 percent of value, is required on higher loan-to-value ratio loans. The maximum loan amount, irrespective of loan-to-value ratio, for a single-family dwelling is $115,300.

With the passage of the Housing and Community Development Act of 1980, the maximum single-family loan amount is to be adjusted as of January 1 of each year. This practice began January 1, 1981. The act states that the maximum limitation will be increased by an amount equal to the percentage of increase in prices for new and existing homes based upon a survey conducted by the Federal Home Loan Bank Board for the previous twelve months, as measured October to October.

Fannie Mae allows second liens on the property used as security for the first lien mortgage to be purchased provided that the following conditions are met:

1. The second must be junior to the mortgage that Fannie Mae is purchasing.

2. The terms of the second mortgage must be fully disclosed to Fannie Mae.

3. When the amount of the first and second liens are combined, they may not exceed certain loan-to-value limitations. If Fannie Mae holds the second and the first is held by another investor, for owner-occupied property the ratio is limited to 80 percent, and 70 percent for second homes and investment properties. If the second or subordinate financing is held by some other investor, the maximum combined loan-to-value ratio for owner-occupied property is increased to 95 percent and for second homes or investment property the loan-to-value ratio is increased to 90 percent. In addition, for the second homes and investment properties, the unpaid balance on the first lien may not exceed 80 percent of the property's value. Thus, the second mortgage on the investment property may not exceed 10 percent of the value of the property.

4. The monthly payments required to repay a subordinate lien must remain constant for a period of twelve months. If the monthly

payment will change from one 12-month period to the next, the increase may not exceed 7.5 percent of the previous monthly payment.

5. If the subordinate lien does not require a monthly payment, the lien may not have a term, maturity, or call option date of less than 5 years.

This use of secondary financing is not allowed by all conventional lenders and can be important to a client.

Prior to June 22, 1981, Fannie Mae would only purchase mortgages on single-family dwellings that would serve as the primary residence of the applicant. This policy was revised allowing Fannie Mae to purchase conventional mortgages secured by nonowner-occupied single-family dwellings under any commitments issued on or after June 22, 1981. The maximum loan-to-value ratio authorized is 80 percent and the maximum term is 30 years. Fannie Mae will, at the time of purchase of a nonowner-occupied mortgage, charge an additional commitment fee of 1.5 percent and will require an additional yield of one half of one percent above the yield on the commitment. This means that if the lender will sell the mortgage to Fannie Mae under a commitment that requires a yield of 13.50, Fannie Mae will add 0.50 percent making the yield 14.0.

In addition to purchasing conventional mortgages on nonowner-occupied single-family dwellings, Fannie Mae will now purchase conventional mortgages secured by single-family dwellings in resort areas. Before Fannie Mae will purchase such a mortgage, there are certain criteria that must be met, including the following:

1. The property is suitable for year-round occupancy.

2. The property is occupied by the borrower or the borrower intends to rent the property for long-term use. According to Fannie Mae, if the property is to be rented, it will have to be demonstrated that there is a rental market for year-round occupancy.

Buydown interest rate mortgage   In May 1981, Fannie Mae offered for the first time a conventional mortgage purchase program other than the traditional fixed-rate, fixed-payment, fixed-term mortgage. This new mortgage is a conventional mortgage that will allow the interest rate to be bought down with the payment of a lump sum when the mortgage is closed.

This buydown mortgage is a type of graduated-payment mortgage, with no negative amortization, in that the initial monthly payments made by the borrower are lower than a fixed-payment mortgage of the same amount. The buyer is qualified on the basis of the lower bought-down payment. The difference in the monthly payments is made up from the monies furnished by the borrower, seller, homebuilder, borrowers' parents, or anyone else at the time of origination. This feature of the buydown mortgage is similar to the pledged account mortgage, which was discussed in Chapter 3.

Fannie Mae will purchase conventional mortgages secured by a home or unit on new or existing property that is subject to interest rate buydown (fixed rate or Plans 6, 10, and 11 of the Adjustable-Rate Mortgage Purchase Program), provided the buydown plan meets the following characteristics:

1. The buydown period is limited to a minimum term of 1 year and a maximum of 10 years.

2. The payments for a buydown period must be constant over each 12-month period of the buydown. Thus, the payments may not increase, for example, every 3 months.

3. If the buydown calls for the payments to increase annually, the borrowers' effective interest rate cannot increase more than 1 percent a year (for example, the 3-2-1 buydown).

4. If the buydown is a level-plan buydown, the payments do not change annually, but rather every two years. For example, the maximum effective interest-rate increase is limited to 2 percent per adjustment period. A 4-2-1 buydown, therefore, would be as follows: the first 2 years the effective rate would be 4 percent below the note rate; beginning with the third year of the buydown, the rate would be 2 percent below note rate; beginning with the fifth year, the rate would be 1 percent below the note rate; and then, beginning with the seventh year, the borrower would pay note rate.

5. When the seller is the source of the buydown funds, there are certain limitations to the amount the seller may contribute without the funds being considered as a sales

concession. It should be noted that Fannie Mae, when calculating the actual cash contribution of the seller toward the buydown funds, does not include any origination fees and closing costs paid by the seller. The limitations are:

A. If the loan-to-value ratio is greater than 90 percent, the maximum the seller may pay is 6 percent of the value or sales price, whichever is less. For example, if a property has a value of $80,000, the maximum the seller could pay before it is considered a sales concession would be $80,000 × 6 percent, or $4,800.

B. If the loan-to-value is 90 percent or less, the maximum the seller may pay is increased to 10 percent of the value or sales price, whichever is less. Thus, using the example from above, the maximum the seller could pay would be $80,000 × 10 percent or $8,000.

6. Buydown funds from any source other than the seller or builder are unlimited. For example, the additional funds may be provided by the buyer's employer. Through a corporate relocation plan, they could be combined with the funds provided by the seller or builder.

7. The buydown plan must be a written agreement. The funds that will be held by the lender will represent the total funds required to fund the buydown less a 5 1/4 percent discount, compounded monthly calculated on a present value of money basis.

It should be noted that the buydown funds will not be refunded to the borrower. The only interest that the borrower has is to have them applied to the payments of the note as per the buydown agreement. The payments will not be used to make any past-due payments. If the property is sold or the mortgage is paid off during the term of the buydown, the remaining buydown funds will be disposed of as follows:

1. If the mortgage is paid in full, the remaining funds will be credited to principal reduction.

2. If the mortgage goes to foreclosure, the remaining funds will also be credited to principal reduction.

3. If the property is sold and the mortgage is assumed, the funds will continue to be used to fund the buydown as per the original terms of the buydown.

In regard to number 3 above, normally if the mortgage is assumable and if the buydown has a remaining term of 1 year or more, Fannie Mae will use the reduced interest rate for loan approval. If the term of the buydown is less than 1 year, Fannie Mae will use the face or note rate for loan approval. These are some of the major rules or requirements that a buydown plan must meet prior to Fannie Mae's purchase.

Fannie Mae will allow the use of a second mortgage to secure the buydown funds. In other words, the seller can pay the buydown funds at closing, but at the closing the buyer executes a second in the amount of the buydown funds. The requirements for the buydown second are the same as mentioned earlier in this chapter.

Now that we have reviewed the major provisions of the Fannie Mae buydown mortgage, let us see how such a mortgage may work. A sample buydown plan is shown Figure 10-2, part 1. Figure 10-2, part 2, shows how a subordinate or a second lien may be used in conjunction with the buydown funds.

2- to 4-family homes   Under this mortgage purchase program, Fannie Mae will purchase mortgages secured by duplexes, triplexes, and fourplexes. It should be emphasized that the property does not have to be occupied by the borrower, thus making this program ideal for the small investor who is interested in these types of properties. Fannie Mae is one of the few secondary marketers that will purchase mortgages on these types of properties.

As with the single-family purchase program, Fannie Mae will purchase mortgages on 2- to 4-family dwellings that are under construction, existing, or proposed for construction. The structures can be detached, semi-detached, row or townhomes, in a subdivision or Planned Unit Development, or in a de minimis PUD. This program is not available to units located in condominiums. This program is excellent for use in the rehabilitation of properties in the inner cities and declining areas of a city.

The maximum mortgage amounts for this Fannie Mae program underwent a major revision with the passage of the Housing and Community Development Act of 1980. Prior to the passage of the legislation, the maximum loan amount was keyed to the number of

Figure 10–2. Part 1: Examples of Buydown Plans That Are Satisfactory to Fannie Mae

1. A builder wishes to offer a buydown plan to assist prospective purchasers to meet the mortgage payments on a 15.50% mortgage. The builder proposes a three-year graduated mortgage payment plan, that will effectively give the home purchaser a 12.50% interest rate payment for the first year; 13.50% for the second year and 14.50% for the third year. Starting with the mortgage's 37th payment the mortgage instrument's stated mortgage payments, based on a 15.50% rate, will become the complete responsibility of the mortgagor.

EXAMPLE:

Loan Amount	$50,000
Interest Rate	15.50%
Mortgage Term	30 years
Level Monthly Payment	$652.26

Cost first year	= $1423.56	(at $118.63 per month)
Cost second year	= $ 954.60	(at $79.55 per month)
Cost third year	= $ 479.74	(at $39.98 per month)
Total cost to builder	$2857.92	

The Mortgage Payment Schedule:

Monthly Pmts. Nos.	Borrower's Pmt.	Buydown Pmt.	Total Mtg. Pmt.
1-12	$533.63	$118.63	$652.26
13-24	$572.71	$ 79.55	$652.26
25-36	$612.28	$ 39.98	$652.26
37-360	$652.26	–0–	$652.26

Note: In this example the borrower's first twelve monthly payments under the buydown plan change to $572.71 in the second twelve-month phase. This is an increase of $39.08 which represents a 7.3% increase. The change from the second to the third twelve-month phase represents a 6.9% increase and from the third to the fourth represents a 6.5% increase. The amount of these increases does not exceed the FNMA 7½ % guideline, so the plan is acceptable.

2. Using the same facts described above, a home seller wishes to offer a level or straight buydown of 2% per year for the first three years.

The Mortgage Payment Schedule:

Monthly Pmts. Nos.	Borrower's Pmt.	Buydown Pmt.	Total Mtg. Pmt.
1-36	$572.71	$ 79.55	$652.26
37-360	$652.26	–0–	$652.26

Note: In this example the payment increase ($652.26 - $572.71) is $79.55 or 13.9%. Since the year-to-year increase from year 2 to year 3 does not exceed 15%, this plan also would be acceptable to FNMA.

Total Cost to home seller
   ($79.55 × 36 Months) = $2,863.80

SOURCE: Federal National Mortgage Association, memo, May 26, 1981.

Figure 10–2.   Part 2: Example of Subordinate Financing to Secure Buydown

Assuming that the value of a property is $56,000, the following is an example of a plan which would be acceptable to FNMA:

FNMA First Mortgage

Loan Amount	$50,000
Interest Rate	15.50%
Mortgage Term	30 years
Monthly Pmt.	$652.26
Total Builder Buydown	$2,857.92

Second Mortgage

Loan Amount	$3,000
Interest Rate	12%
Mortgage Term	5 years
Level Mortgage Pmt.	$30.00

(interest only)

Balloon – $3,000, due and payable after 5 years.

In the buydown example shown on Exhibit I, the developer and purchaser agreed that the lump sum of $2,857.92 (say $3,000) would be in the form of a second mortgage that provided for regular monthly interest payments of $30.00 per month (12.00% per annum) with the total principal due (balloon payment) at the end of five years. This second mortgage ($3,000) when added to the first mortgage ($50,000) resulted in a combined loan-to-value percent of 94.64% based upon the sale price of $56,000. This example of a second mortgage used to secure a buydown would be acceptable to FNMA because:

1. The sum of the first and the second mortgage equals no more than 95% of value.

2. Monthly payments remain constant.

3. In this case, there is no change in second mortgage payments.

4. The maturity date of this non-amortizing plan is the minimum 5 years.

SOURCE: Federal National Mortgage Association, memo, May 26, 1981.

bedrooms in each of the units. The current multifamily maximum mortgage amounts are as follows:

2-family dwelling	$147,500
3-family dwelling	$178,200
4-family dwelling	$221,500

As with the mortgage limits for the single-family loan maximum, the limits for the 2- to 4-family program are to be adjusted on January 1 each year using the results of the survey of major lenders conducted by the Federal Home Loan Bank Board for a twelve-month period.

As stated earlier, this program is available to the investor wishing to buy this type of property for rehabilitation and resale or for rental. The maximum loan and terms for the nonowner-occupant is 80 percent loan-to-value ratio and the maximum term is 30 years. The maximum loan available for the owner-occupant is somewhat different from that of the nonowner-occupant. The maximum term of the owner-occupant loan is still 30 years, but the maximum loan-to-value ratio is 95 percent.

This program of Fannie Mae, as with the single family program, allows for both subordinate financing and refinancing. The subordinate or second financing allowed on the 2- to 4-family mortgage purchase program is the same as that allowed under the single-family mortgage purchase program.

In addition to the increases in the mortgage amounts, there are some other differences that should be noted with this program. The first is that, in addition to the applicant's regular income, Fannie Mae will recognize and count the operating income derived from the property toward the income used to qualify the applicant. Fannie Mae will not use the total income produced by the property, but will use an amount referred to as *operating income*. Operating income is calculated as the economic rent of the property or the total amount of rent possible from the property, less certain expenses. The expenses to be deducted are expenses for vacancy/credit loss and expenses for the operation of the property, which will include replacement reserves and mortgage payments. Fannie Mae has prepared Form 216 for the calculation of these expenses, shown in Figure 10-3. Fannie Mae also requires an additional 1.5 percent commitment fee at the time of loan delivery and a 0.50 percent additional yield on 2- to 4-family loans for nonowner occupants.

The second major difference is the appraisal report that is required for the 2- to 4-family dwelling. Fannie Mae requires the appraisal on its Form 1025, entitled Appraisal Report—Small Residential Income Property. Also required to accompany the appraisal are the appraiser's comments on the information contained in the operating statement prepared by the applicant.

One final difference is that Fannie Mae will require a statement from the appropriate agency that the structure meets the minimum standards of the area. For example, if the property is located in Houston, Fannie Mae must be supplied with a certificate from the Housing Code Enforcement Department of the City of Houston, indicating that the property meets Houston's minimum property standards.

A word of caution in regard to the two- to four-family program: The Southwest Regional Office of Fannie Mae was receiving an increasing number of submissions for newly established or proposed subdivisions devoted primarily to this type of property. The regional office has issued Circular Letter No. 80-17, covering the requirements for securing the approval of the subdivisions prior to Fannie Mae purchase of any loans in the subdivision. If you are working with a developer or investor who wishes to rehabilitate larger housing in the inner-city, it may also be important to contact a Fannie Mae-approved seller/servicer in your area or the Southwest Regional Office of Fannie Mae in Dallas to see if a subdivision approval will be necessary.

Condominium and PUD Unit Mortgage Purchase Program

As with many other Fannie Mae mortgage purchase programs, this program has undergone a major revision and streamlining. Prior to Fannie Mae Program Announcement Number 6 on November 16, 1981, there had been two purchase programs for these types of mortgages. One was for mortgages secured by condominium or PUD units located in projects that had been approved by Fannie Mae prior to the start of construction, and the other was a program for the purchase of mortgages located in existing projects.

According to Fannie Mae's *Lending Guide* (Chapter 3, "Conventional Projects") Fannie Mae will still purchase unit mortgages in two types of condo or PUD projects. You will note that Fannie Mae still divides the projects into two types, but they have divided the projects on different lines. Now Fannie Mae classifies the project according to (1) whether the majority of the units in the project are owned as principal residences and second homes or (2)

Figure 10–3.   Fannie Mae Operating Income Statement for 2- to 4-Family Property

FEDERAL NATIONAL MORTGAGE ASSOCIATION

OPERATING INCOME STATEMENT — 2-4 Family Property

DATE: _____

PROPERTY ADDRESS _____ (Street) _____ (City, State, Zip)

RENT SCHEDULE :

UNIT No. 1 _____ ROOMS _____ BEDRMS _____ BATHS @ $ _____ PER MONTH

UNIT No. 2 _____ ROOMS _____ BEDRMS _____ BATHS @ $ _____ PER MONTH

UNIT No. 3 _____ ROOMS _____ BEDRMS _____ BATHS @ $ _____ PER MONTH

UNIT No. 4 _____ ROOMS _____ BEDRMS _____ BATHS @ $ _____ PER MONTH

TOTAL _____ ROOMS _____ BEDRMS _____ BATHS $ _____ PER MONTH

UTILITY EXPENSE :

	ON OWNER	ON TENANT
ELECTRICITY	☐	☐
HEATING	☐	☐
COOKING	☐	☐
HOT WATER	☐	☐
WATER	☐	☐
SEWER	☐	☐

ANNUAL INCOME AND EXPENSE PROJECTION FOR NEXT 12 MONTHS	BY APPLICANT	INITIAL ADJUSTMENTS BY SELLER'S UNDERWRITER	FINAL ADJUSTMENTS BY SELLER'S UNDERWRITER
INCOME			
ANNUAL RENTAL @ 100% OCCUPANCY	$_____	$_____	$_____
OTHER INCOME	+_____	_____	_____
TOTAL	$_____	_____	_____
LESS OWNER-OCCUPANT UNIT (UNIT No. ___)	−_____	_____	_____
TOTAL	$_____	_____	_____
LESS VACANCY/RENT LOSS	−_____ (%)	_____ (%)	_____ (%)
EFFECTIVE GROSS INCOME	$_____	$_____	$_____
EXPENSES (OMIT OWNER-OCCUPANT EXPENSES)			
HEATING (_____)	$_____	$_____	$_____
COOKING (_____)	_____	_____	_____
HOT WATER (_____)	_____	_____	_____
ELECTRICITY	_____	_____	_____
WATER/SEWER	_____	_____	_____
CASUAL LABOR	_____	_____	_____
INTERIOR PAINT / DECORATING	_____	_____	_____
GENERAL REPAIRS / MAINTENANCE	_____	_____	_____
MANAGEMENT EXPENSE	_____ (%)	_____ (%)	_____ (%)
SUPPLIES	_____	_____	_____
EQUIPMENT REPLACEMENT-SEE SCHEDULE	_____	_____	_____
CARPETING REPLACEMENT-SEE SCHEDULE	_____	_____	_____
MISCELLANEOUS	_____	_____	_____
	_____	_____	_____
	_____	_____	_____
	_____	_____	_____
	_____	_____	_____
	_____	_____	_____
TOTAL OPERATING EXPENSES	$_____	$_____	$_____

*** THIS FORM MUST BE REPRODUCED BY SELLERS ***   PAGE 1 OF 2   FNMA Form 216 Nov. 79

Figure 10–3.   continued

OPERATING INCOME RECONCILIATION

$_____ − \$_____ = \$_____ ÷ 12 = \$_____$ OPERATING INCOME PER MONTH
(EFFECT. GROSS INC.) − (OPERATING EXPENSES) = (OPERATING INCOME)   (ENTER ON LINE 34 of FNMA FORM 1008)

REPLACEMENT RESERVE SCHEDULE

EQUIPMENT:		BY APPLICANT	INITIAL ADJUSTMENTS	FINAL ADJUSTMENTS
STOVES / RANGES	@ \$____ ea. ÷ ___ YRS X ___ UNITS =	\$____	\$____	\$____
REFRIGS.	@ \$____ ea. ÷ ___ YRS X ___ UNITS =	\$____	\$____	\$____
D. WASHER	@ \$____ ea. ÷ ___ YRS X ___ UNITS =	\$____	\$____	\$____
A/C UNITS	@ \$____ ea. ÷ ___ YRS X ___ UNITS =	\$____	\$____	\$____
C. WASHER/DRYER	@ \$____ ea. ÷ ___ YRS X ___ UNITS =	\$____	\$____	\$____
HW HEATER	@ \$____ ea. ÷ ___ YRS X ___ UNITS =	\$____	\$____	\$____
(OTHER)	@ \$____ ea. ÷ ___ YRS X ___ UNITS =	\$____	\$____	\$____
(OTHER)	@ \$____ ea. ÷ ___ YRS X ___ UNITS =	\$____	\$____	\$____
TOTAL		\$____	\$____	\$____

CARPETING:				
(UNITS) ____ TOTAL SQ. YDS. @ \$____ PER SQ. YD. ÷ ___ YRS. =		\$____	\$____	\$____
(PUBLIC AREAS) ____ TOTAL SQ. YDS. @ \$____ PER SQ. YD. ÷ ___ YRS. =		\$____	\$____	\$____
TOTAL		\$____	\$____	\$____

APPRAISER INSTRUCTIONS

The subject 2-4 family property is being considered for a mortgage application. Operating income is defined as a property's gross monthly rent less allowances for rental income of an owner-occupant's unit (if applicable), for vacancy/rent loss and operating expenses (including replacements and management expenses and excluding the pro-rata expenses attributable to an owner-occupant's unit) but before deductions for taxes, hazard insurance, mortgage insurance and the mortgage's monthly principal and interest charges. Operating income as used in this analysis does not meet the characteristics of net operating income as the term is commonly used and is intended for credit underwriting purposes only. As part of your appraisal instructions you are requested to comment upon the reasonableness of the projected operating income. If applicable, the property's past two year-end operating statements are attached to assist you in your analysis.

UNDERWRITER NAME   UNDERWRITER SIGNATURE   DATE

APPRAISER'S COMMENTS

APPRAISER   DATE

PAGE 2 OF 2

whether the majority of the units are owned as investment type properties or nonowner occupied properties.

Before we leave this discussion, let us define, according to Fannie Mae, the requirement for a project to be classified as a principal residence or second home project. Such a project is so defined if 70 percent or more of the units are owner-occupied as principal residences or second homes. Thus, the investment type of project would be one in which less than 70 percent of the units are principal residences or second homes.

According to Fannie Mae, this distinction of the project will determine the type of approval that will be required. Fannie Mae has established three classifications of condo or PUD project approval: type A, type B, and type C.

Type A approval   Type A approval applies to existing projects that have only *spot-loan* business available. This means that Fannie Mae will purchase loans on an individual unit basis. It should be noted that the purchase of spot loans in condominium projects or Planned Unit Development (PUD) is a significant change for Fannie Mae. Before this change, Fannie Mae would not normally purchase any spot loans in a condominium or PUD project. The lender, and not Fannie Mae, has the responsibility of determining the acceptability of a project for this type of approval.

Type B approval   Type B approval, according to Part 1 of Chapter 3, applies to existing projects that meet certain eligibility and underwriting criteria. Once again, the lender is given the responsibility of determining the acceptability of a project for this type of approval.

Type C approval   The final approval type is the type C approval. This type of approval applies to any project that does not meet the requirements for a type A or type B approval. This type of project may be existing, proposed, or under construction. Unlike the two previous types of approval, Fannie Mae will determine the acceptability of a type C project.

Now that we have reviewed the three classifications of project approval, let us review some of the basic eligibility criteria for each of the approvals.

First for the type A project approval, the project must meet the following:

1. The project may not be subject to any additional phases or the annexation of any additional undeveloped or developed land. Thus,

the boundaries of the project must be firm and not subject to change.

2. The project must be complete, this includes all units built, common areas and facilities, including those that are part of an umbrella association.

3. Fannie Mae additionally requires that at least 90 percent of all of the units in the project must have been sold and closed. Since this is a type A project, at least 70 percent of the units sold and closed must be occupied by the owners or be 2nd homes.

4. In regard to how the ownership of the units is held, Fannie Mae requires that the title to the units in the project be owned in fee-simple, rather than leasehold estates.

5. The control of the homeowners' association must have been turned over to the owners of the units in the project.

6. Finally, Fannie Mae will require that the project be properly insured against loss as outlined by Fannie Mae.

In addition, the lender is not required to do a full, detailed underwriting analysis of the project. The lender can warrant that the project meets the same underwriting criteria that is specified for a type B project.

The type B approval is valuable for principal residences and second home projects only. If a project is given this type of approval, Fannie Mae will not limit the number of mortgages it will purchase from the project. The basic requirements for the type B approval are the same as the type A approval in regard to phasing and annexation, completion of the project, control of the homeowners' association, how title is held to each of the units, and insurance requirements. There is one major difference that deals with the percent of the units sold. According to section 102, of Chapter 3 of the *Lending Guide*, at least 70 percent of all units in the project must have been sold, or under contract to be sold, to owner-occupant principal residents or second home purchasers. Since the lender is asked to confirm that the project is well managed and in good condition, both physically and financially, the lender will review and approve the actual financial and physical condition of the project, the operating budget of the project, and any management agreement.

These two approvals are the most important to the real estate professional. If you have a condo or PUD project that meets the requirements of either the type A or type B approval and is not Fannie Mae approved if, by working through a Fannie Mae-approved lender, you can get the project approved. This will make funds available for the resale of units in the project. Thus the project will be a good source of listings and sales. It should be noted that many lenders do not like to use this plan for they are not given an exclusive approval by Fannie Mae; thus, any approved Fannie Mae lender may make loans in the project. Many lenders, therefore, will require the real estate professional to do a great deal of the work in gathering the required information.

The final approval is the type C approval. Under this type of approval Fannie Mae does all of the evaluation and approval. This type of approval will normally be used for a new project prior to construction. The documentation is involved and detailed. For more information on this type of an approval contact any Fannie Mae-approved lender in your area. If none of the lenders you contact is willing to work with you, contact the Southwest Regional Office and they will assist you in finding a lender who will.

Refinance/Resale Program. On March 30, 1981, Fannie Mae offered for the first time the Refinance/Resale Program to all Fannie Mae-approved seller/servicers. First let us review the refinance portion of the program. As with other refinancing programs in Texas, there are certain conditions that have been imposed by Fannie Mae. Because of the Homestead Act and other Texas state laws, Fannie Mae will only purchase any refinance mortgage in Texas that meets the following conditions outlined in Fannie Mae Circular Letter No. 81-7:

1. The loan is either (a) secured by non-homestead property or (b) secured by a homestead property, with the borrower's proceeds used for the sole purpose of paying off perfected improved liens on the property as well as the balance of the pre-existing first mortgage thereon; and

2. The mortgagee's title policy is in such substance and form as promulgated by the Texas State Board of Insurance to assure full protection to Fannie Mae and to comply with Section 314 of the Fannie Mae Conventional Home Mortgage Selling Contract Supplement.

From these conditions, one can see that in

Texas the program has rather limited usage and can only be used to refinance an existing first mortgage or any loan for the specific purpose of making improvements to the property.

The second portion of the program, the resale program, can be used very effectively in Texas. Under this program, a person wishing to purchase property using a wraparound or a second mortgage can, if the existing first-lien mortgage is owned by Fannie Mae, combine both the existing mortgage and the second or wraparound into a new first-lien mortgage from Fannie Mae with an interest rate that normally will be below the present market level. (The rate is a function of the balance, rate, and remaining term of the old loan, and the amount and term of the new loan.) In other words, this is a type of blended-yield mortgage or BYM. The program does require a minimum interest rate on the new mortgage of 11 percent.

Let us work through an example of how the Refinance Program may work, as illustrated in Figure 10-4.

The actual interest rate or yield on the refinance mortgage will be established by Fannie Mae, but Fannie Mae has published a Fannie Mae Refinance/Resale Mortgage Yield Estimating Table as a guide. An excerpt of this table, shown in Figure 10-5, allows a lender or real estate salesperson to estimate the yield that will be required on a refinance mortgage.

This table is to be used for estimating purposes only. For the actual yield on resale mortgages, you will have to contact an approved Fannie Mae seller/servicer, who in turn will contact Fannie Mae for the actual yield.

One very important fact should be emphasized. Fannie Mae will not enforce the acceleration-upon-sale (due-on-sale) provision on conventional mortgages originated under this program—either to refinance or upon the resale of a home where Fannie Mae owns the mortgage—if the transfer of ownership occurs within one year from the date of the resale/refinance mortgage. It should be noted that the nonenforcement of the acceleration-upon-sale provisions is limited to increase in note rate, but the provision of credit underwriting of the person or persons acquiring title to the property will still be enforced.

As with the other single-family loan purchase programs of Fannie Mae, the maximum term for this program is 30 years, with a maximum loan-to-value ratio of 95 percent for owner-occupied principal residences. For the purchase of second homes or investment property, the maximum term remains the same,

Figure 10–4.   Fannie Mae Resale Finance Program Example

The Thorntons plan to buy a house that is selling for $94,750, and they've checked different ways of financing its purchase. When they asked about getting a new, 30-year loan, the lender quoted them a rate of 16%; their monthly principal and interest payments, after putting 5% or $4,750 down, would be $1,210.28. Since the existing $41,592.01 VA-guaranteed loan on the house is assumable, they looked into taking over the payments on that mortgage and getting a $48,407.99 second mortgage at 18% for 10 years. The payments on the existing loan are $338.36 a month and payments on the new second mortgage would be $872.24, for a total of $1,210.60. Since the existing loan is owned by FNMA, they had one other option: a FNMA Resale Finance mortgage. They could get a $90,000 resale loan at 13.4 percent, with monthly payments of $1023.79, $186.49 a month less than a new first mortgage and $186.81 a month less than assuming the old loan and getting a new second mortgage.

	Existing Mortgage	*Resale Mortgage*	*New Mortgage*	*Old First And New Second Mortgage*	
Amount	$41,592.01	$90,000	$90,000	$41,592.01	(First)
				+48,407.99	(Second)
Rate	8.5%	13.4%	16%	8.5%	(First)
				18.00%	(Second)
Monthly Payment	$338.36	$1,023.79	$1,210.28	$338.36	(First)
				+872.24	(Second)
				$1,210.60	

Source: Federal National Mortgage Association news release, "FNMA's Refinance/Resale Finance Program."

Figure 10–5.   Fannie Mae Refinance/Resale Mortgage Yield Estimating Table

Old Note Rate and Loan Amounts		*New Mortgage Amount ($,000)*								
		20	30	40	50	60	70	80	90	98.5
7%	10,000	12.600	14.250	15.100	15.600	15.875	16.125	16.300	16.500	16.600
	15,000	10.100*	12.600	13.875	14.600	15.100	15.500	15.700	15.875	16.100
	25,000	—	9.200*	11.375	12.600	13.500	14.000	14.500	14.800	15.100
7½%	10,000	12.875	14.500	15.200	15.700	16.000	16.200	16.375	16.500	16.600
	15,000	10.500*	12.875	14.100	14.750	15.200	15.600	15.800	16.000	16.100
	25,000	—	9.625*	11.700	12.875	13.625	14.200	14.625	15.000	15.200
8%	20,000	—	11.200	12.800	13.750	14.375	14.875	15.200	15.500	15.625
	30,000	—	—	10.375*	11.875	12.800	13.500	14.000	14.375	14.700
	40,000	—	—	—	9.875*	11.200	12.125	12.800	13.375	13.700
8½%	20,000	—	11.600	13.100	14.000	14.600	15.000	15.300	15.600	15.750
	30,000	—	—	10.800*	12.200	13.100	13.700	14.200	14.600	14.875
	40,000	—	—	—	10.375*	11.600	12.500	13.100	13.600	13.900
9%	20,000	—	11.800	13.250	14.100	14.700	15.100	15.375	15.625	15.800
	30,000	—	—	11.100	12.375	13.250	13.875	14.375	14.700	15.000
	40,000	—	—	—	10.600*	11.800	12.625	13.250	13.750	14.100
9½%	30,000	—	—	11.375	12.600	13.500	14.100	14.500	14.800	15.100
	40,000	—	—	—	11.000	12.100	12.875	13.500	13.900	14.200
	50,000	—	—	—	10.700*	11.700	12.400	13.000	13.375	
10%	30,000	—	—	11.700	12.875	13.700	14.250	14.625	15.000	15.200
	40,000	—	—	—	11.300	12.375	13.100	13.700	14.100	14.400
	50,000	—	—	—	—	11.100	12.000	12.700	13.250	13.600

To estimate FNMA's minimum required yield on a new Refinance/Resale Mortgage, find the note rate and mortgage amount in the left column which most nearly approximate a mortgagor's old loan characteristics and read across to the yield under the new mortgage amount nearest that requested by the mortgagor.

*Minimum yield 11%.

Source: Federal National Mortgage Association, memo, *Resale and refinance program*, May 12, 1981.

but the loan-to-value ratio is reduced to 80 percent. The loan amounts for this program are the same as for the single and 2- to 4-family purchase programs.

In reference to the fees that a lender may charge for this program, Fannie Mae states that the lender may not charge an origination fee of more than 3 percent of the loan amount. It should be noted this origination does not cover nor does it include any of the following:

1. Any discount fees the lender must pay to Fannie Mae, when the interest rate on the refinance/resale mortgage is below the yield required by Fannie Mae.

2. The expenses for such items as a credit report, appraisal, commitment fees charged by Fannie Mae, or any fees or charges paid by the lender to warehouse the mortgage prior to the purchase by Fannie Mae.

These are only a portion of the additional fees that are not included.

Second Mortgage Purchase Program   On November 30, 1981, Fannie Mae initiated a program of purchasing second mortgages in Texas. With this program, Fannie Mae will purchase second mortgages from lenders that have experience in the origination of second mortgages.

Fannie Mae has issued, jointly with the Federal Home Loan Mortgage Corporation, a note and deed of trust. These Fannie Mae/ FHLMC forms are identified by a title appearing at the bottom of the page of the note and the first page of the deed of trust. The identification information will be: Name of the State — Home Improvement — Date of the form — Fannie Mae/FHLMC Uniform Instrument. A sample of the Texas note and deed of trust authorized for use with the second mortgage purchase program is illustrated in Figures 10–6 through 10–11.

In addition to the creation of a uniform note and deed of trust, Fannie Mae has created a due-on-transfer rider. This document is shown in Figure 10–12. This due-on-transfer rider must accompany any second mortgage sold to Fannie Mae.

Fannie Mae will purchase conventional second mortgages on 1- to 4-family homes including units in a condominium project and/or a planned unit development. Accordingly, the underlying first lien can be either a conventional, VA-guaranteed, or FHA-insured mortgage.

The maximum loan-to-value ratio authorized under this program for both owner-occupied principal residences and second homes is:

1. The first and second lien combined outstanding principal balance may not exceed 80 percent of the property's value.

2. If the property is a second home or an investment property, the first and second liens' combined outstanding principal balance may not exceed 70 percent of the property's value.

In addition to the maximum loan-to-value ratio, Fannie Mae has set the following maximum terms:

1. If the mortgage is fully amortizing over the term of the mortgage, the term may be from 3 to 15 years.

2. If the mortgage is not fully amortizing, the term of the mortgage may be from 5 to 15 years, but the payments may be calculated as if the mortgage were to be repaid in 30 years. It should be noted that with this type of amortization schedule, the borrower will have a lump sum payment due at the end of the 5- to 15-year term.

Prior to the implementation of the Secondary Mortgage Enhancement Act of 1984 on October 3, 1984, the maximum loan amount that Fannie Mae could purchase under this program was the same as those for the first-lien purchase programs. According to the act, the maximum loan amount that Fannie Mae can now purchase cannot exceed 50 percent of the 1-family loan amount. At the time this text was written, that amount was $115,300. Thus, one half of that amount is $57,650. Since the one family loan amount changes annually, so will the maximum loan amount for the second mortgage purchase program. It should be noted that this limit applies regardless of whether or not Fannie Mae owns or has an interest in the first lien on the property. If Fannie Mae owns or has an interest in the first, the combined loan amount of the first and second may not exceed $115,300.

One very important fact should be noted at this time: in addition to second mortgages originated by approved lenders, purchase-money second mortgages that are taken back by a home seller may also be eligible for purchase under this program. To be eligible, the second mortgage must be originated by a Fannie Mae-approved second lender according to Fannie Mae's second mortgage guidelines and

Figure 10–6.   Fannie Mae/FHLMC Home Improvement Note, page 1

NOTE

...., 19..........   ...., Texas
City

....
Property Address   *City*   *State*   *Zip Code*

1. BORROWER'S PROMISE TO PAY

In return for a loan that I have received, I promise to pay U.S. $ ....
(this amount will be called "principal"), plus interest, to the order of the Lender. The Lender is ....
.... I understand that the Lender may transfer this
Note. The Lender or anyone who takes this Note by transfer and who is entitled to receive payments under this Note will
be called the "Note Holder."

2. INTEREST

I will pay interest at a yearly rate of ....%.
Interest will be charged on that part of principal which has not been paid. Interest will be charged beginning on the
date of this Note and continuing until the full amount of principal has been paid.

3. PAYMENTS

I will pay principal and interest by making payments each month of U.S. $ ....
I will make my payments on the .... day of each month beginning on ...., 19.......... I will
make these payments every month until I have paid all of the principal and interest and any other charges, described below,
that I may owe under this Note. If, on ...., ..., I still owe amounts under
this Note, I will pay all those amounts, in full, on that date.
I will make my monthly payments at ....
.... or at a different place if required by the Note Holder.

4. BORROWER'S FAILURE TO PAY AS REQUIRED

(A) Late Charge for Overdue Payments

If the Note Holder has not received the full amount of any of my monthly payments by the end of ....
calendar days after the date it is due, I will pay a late charge to the Note Holder. The amount of the charge will be
......................% of my overdue payment, but not less than U.S. $ .... and not more than
U.S. $ .... I will pay this late charge only once on any late payment.

(B) Notice From Note Holder

If I do not pay the full amount of each monthly payment on time, the Note Holder may send me a written notice
telling me that if I do not pay the overdue amount by a certain date I will be in default. That date must be at least 10 days
after the date on which the notice is mailed to me or, if it is not mailed, 10 days after the date on which it is delivered to me.

(C) Default

If I do not pay the overdue amount by the date stated in the notice described in (B) above, I will be in default. If I am
in default, the Note Holder may require me to pay immediately the full amount of principal which has not been paid and all
the interest that I owe on that amount.
Even if, at a time when I am in default, the Note Holder does not require me to pay immediately in full as described
above, the Note Holder will still have the right to do so if I am in default at a later time.

(D) Payment of Note Holder's Costs and Expenses

If the Note Holder has required me to pay immediately in full as described above, the Note Holder will have the
right, to be paid back for all of its costs and expenses to the extent not prohibited by applicable law. Those expenses include,
for example, reasonable attorneys' fees.

5. THIS NOTE SECURED BY A DEED OF TRUST

In addition to the protections given to the Note Holder under this Note, a Deed of Trust, dated ....
...., 19.........., protects the Note Holder from possible losses which might result if I do not keep
the promises which I make in this Note. That Deed of Trust describes how and under what conditions I may be required to
make immediate payment in full of all amounts that I owe under this Note.

6. BORROWER'S PAYMENTS BEFORE THEY ARE DUE

I have the right to make payments of principal at any time before they are due. A payment of principal only is known
as a "prepayment." When I make a prepayment, I will tell the Note Holder in a letter that I am doing so. A prepayment of
all of the unpaid principal is known as a "full prepayment." A prepayment of only part of the unpaid principal is known as
a "partial prepayment."

TEXAS—HOME IMPROVEMENT—1/80—**FNMA/FHLMC UNIFORM INSTRUMENT**

Figure 10-7.   Fannie Mae/FHLMC Home Improvement Note, page 2

I may make a full prepayment or a partial prepayment without paying any penalty. The Note Holder will use all of my prepayments to reduce the amount of principal that I owe under this Note. If I make a partial prepayment, there will be no delays in the due dates or changes in the amounts of my monthly payments unless the Note Holder agrees in writing to those delays or changes. I may make a full prepayment at anytime. If I choose to make a partial prepayment, the Note Holder may require me to make the prepayment on the same day that one of my monthly payments is due. The Note Holder may also require that the amount of my partial prepayment be equal to the amount of principal that would have been part of my next one or more monthly payments.

7. BORROWER'S WAIVERS

I waive my rights to require the Note Holder to do certain things. Those things are: (A) to demand payment of amounts due (known as "presentment"); (B) to give notice that amounts due have not been paid (known as "notice of dishonor"); (C) to obtain an official certification of nonpayment (known as a "protest"). Anyone else who agrees to keep the promises made in this Note, or who agrees to make payments to the Note Holder if I fail to keep my promises under this Note, or who signs this Note to transfer it to someone else also waives these rights. These persons are known as "guarantors, sureties and endorsers."

8. GIVING OF NOTICES

Any notice that must be given to me under this Note will be given by delivering it or by mailing it by certified mail addressed to me at the Property Address above. A notice will be delivered or mailed to me at a different address if I give the Note Holder a notice of my different address.

Any notice that must be given to the Note Holder under this Note will be given by mailing it by certified mail to the Note Holder at the address stated in Section 3 above. A notice will be mailed to the Note Holder at a different address if I am given a notice of that different address.

9. RESPONSIBILITY OF PERSONS UNDER THIS NOTE

If more than one person signs this Note, each of us is fully and personally obligated to pay the full amount owed and to keep all of the promises made in this Note. Any guarantor, surety, or endorser of this Note (as described in Section 7 above) is also obligated to do these things. The Note Holder may enforce its rights under this Note against each of us individually or against all of us together. This means that any one of us may be required to pay all of the amounts owed under this Note. Any person who takes over my rights or obligations under this Note will have all of my rights and must keep all of my promises made in this Note. Any person who takes over the rights or obligations of a guarantor, surety, or endorser of this Note (as described in Section 7 above) is also obligated to keep all of the promises made in this Note.

....
Borrower

....
Borrower

....
Borrower

(Sign Original Only)

Figure 10–8.　Fannie Mae/FHLMC Purchase Money Deed of Trust

PURCHASE MONEY DEED OF TRUST

THIS DEED OF TRUST is made this .... day of ....,
19........, among the Grantor, ...
.... (herein "Borrower"), ...
.... (herein "Trustee"), and the Beneficiary,
...., a corporation organized and
existing under the laws of ....,
whose address is ....
.... (herein "Lender").

BORROWER, in consideration of the indebtedness herein recited and the trust herein created, irrevocably grants and conveys to Trustee, in trust, with power of sale, the following described property located in the County of ...., State of Texas:

which has the address of.., ...,
　　　　　　　　　　　　　　　　　　　　[Street]　　　　　　　　　　　　　　　　　　　　　　　　　[City]
Texas...(herein "Property Address");
　　　　　[Zip Code]

TOGETHER with all the improvements now or hereafter erected on the property, and all easements, rights, appurtenances and rents (subject however to the rights and authorities given herein to Lender to collect and apply such rents), all of which shall be deemed to be and remain a part of the property covered by this Deed of Trust; and all of the foregoing, together with said property (or the leasehold estate if this Deed of Trust is on a leasehold) are hereinafter referred to as the "Property";

TO SECURE to Lender the repayment of the indebtedness evidenced by Borrower's note dated ....
.... and extensions and renewals thereof (herein "Note"),
in the principal sum of U.S. $ ...., with interest thereon,
providing for monthly installments of principal and interest, with the balance of the indebtedness, if not sooner paid, due
and payable on ....; the payment of all other sums,
with interest thereon, advanced in accordance herewith to protect the security of this Deed of Trust; and the performance
of the covenants and agreements of Borrower herein contained.

Borrower covenants that Borrower is lawfully seised of the estate hereby conveyed and has the right to grant and convey the Property, and that the Property is unencumbered, except for encumbrances of record. Borrower covenants that Borrower warrants and will defend generally the title to the Property against all claims and demands, subject to encumbrances of record.

UNIFORM COVENANTS. Borrower and Lender covenant and agree as follows:

1. Payment of Principal and Interest. Borrower shall promptly pay when due the principal and interest indebtedness evidenced by the Note and late charges as provided in the Note.

2. Funds for Taxes and Insurance. Subject to applicable law or a written waiver by Lender, Borrower shall pay to Lender on the day monthly payments of principal and interest are payable under the Note, until the Note is paid in full, a sum (herein "Funds") equal to one-twelfth of the yearly taxes and assessments (including condominium and planned unit development assessments, if any) which may attain priority over this Deed of Trust and ground rents on the Property, if any, plus one-twelfth of yearly premium installments for hazard insurance, plus one-twelfth of yearly premium installments for mortgage insurance, if any, all as reasonably estimated initially and from time to time by Lender on the basis of assessments and bills and reasonable estimates thereof. Borrower shall not be obligated to make such payments of Funds to Lender to the extent that Borrower makes such payments to the holder of a prior mortgage or deed of trust if such holder is an institutional lender.

If Borrower pays Funds to Lender, the Funds shall be held in an institution the deposits or accounts of which are insured or guaranteed by a Federal or state agency (including Lender if Lender is such an institution). Lender shall apply the Funds to pay said taxes, assessments, insurance premiums and ground rents. Lender may not charge for so holding and applying the Funds, analyzing said account or verifying and compiling said assessments and bills, unless Lender pays Borrower interest on the Funds and applicable law permits Lender to make such a charge. Borrower and Lender may agree

Figure 10-9. *Fannie Mae/FHLMC Purchase Money Deed of Trust, Covenants 2-10*

in writing at the time of execution of this Deed of Trust that interest on the Funds shall be paid to Borrower, and unless such agreement is made or applicable law requires such interest to be paid, Lender shall not be required to pay Borrower any interest or earnings on the Funds. Lender shall give to Borrower, without charge, an annual accounting of the Funds showing credits and debits to the Funds and the purpose for which each debit to the Funds was made. The Funds are pledged as additional security for the sums secured by this Deed of Trust.

If the amount of the Funds held by Lender, together with the future monthly installments of Funds payable prior to the due dates of taxes, assessments, insurance premiums and ground rents, shall exceed the amount required to pay said taxes, assessments, insurance premiums and ground rents as they fall due, such excess shall be, at Borrower's option, either promptly repaid to Borrower or credited to Borrower on monthly installments of Funds. If the amount of the Funds held by Lender shall not be sufficient to pay taxes, assessments, insurance premiums and ground rents as they fall due, Borrower shall pay to Lender any amount necessary to make up the deficiency in one or more payments as Lender may require.

Upon payment in full of all sums secured by this Deed of Trust, Lender shall promptly refund to Borrower any Funds held by Lender. If under paragraph 16 hereof the Property is sold or the Property is otherwise acquired by Lender, Lender shall apply, no later than immediately prior to the sale of the Property or its acquisition by Lender, any Funds held by Lender at the time of application as a credit against the sums secured by this Deed of Trust.

3. Application of Payments. Unless applicable law provides otherwise, all payments received by Lender under the Note and paragraphs 1 and 2 hereof shall be applied by Lender first in payment of amounts payable to Lender by Borrower under paragraph 2 hereof, then to interest payable on the Note, and then to the principal of the Note.

4. Prior Mortgages and Deeds of Trust; Charges; Liens. Borrower shall perform all of Borrower's obligations under any mortgage, deed of trust or other security agreement with a lien which has priority over this Deed of Trust, including Borrower's covenants to make payments when due. Borrower shall pay or cause to be paid all taxes, assessments and other charges, fines and impositions attributable to the Property which may attain priority over this Deed of Trust, and leasehold payments or ground rents, if any.

5. Hazard Insurance. Borrower shall keep the improvements now existing or hereafter erected on the Property insured against loss by fire, hazards included within the term "extended coverage", and such other hazards as Lender may require and in such amounts and for such periods as Lender may require.

The insurance carrier providing the insurance shall be chosen by Borrower subject to approval by Lender; provided, that such approval shall not be unreasonably withheld. All insurance policies and renewals thereof shall be in a form acceptable to Lender and shall include a standard mortgage clause in favor of and in a form acceptable to Lender. Lender shall have the right to hold the policies and renewals thereof, subject to the terms of any mortgage, deed of trust or other security agreement with a lien which has priority over this Deed of Trust.

In the event of loss, Borrower shall give prompt notice to the insurance carrier and Lender. Lender may make proof of loss if not made promptly by Borrower.

If the Property is abandoned by Borrower, or if Borrower fails to respond to Lender within 30 days from the date notice is mailed by Lender to Borrower that the insurance carrier offers to settle a claim for insurance benefits, Lender is authorized to collect and apply the insurance proceeds at Lender's option either to restoration or repair of the Property or to the sums secured by this Deed of Trust.

6. Preservation and Maintenance of Property; Leaseholds; Condominiums; Planned Unit Developments. Borrower shall keep the Property in good repair and shall not commit waste or permit impairment or deterioration of the Property and shall comply with the provisions of any lease if this Deed of Trust is on a leasehold. If this Deed of Trust is on a unit in a condominium or a planned unit development, Borrower shall perform all of Borrower's obligations under the declaration or covenants creating or governing the condominium or planned unit development, the by-laws and regulations of the condominium or planned unit development, and constituent documents.

7. Protection of Lender's Security. If Borrower fails to perform the covenants and agreements contained in this Deed of Trust, or if any action or proceeding is commenced which materially affects Lender's interest in the Property, then Lender, at Lender's option, upon notice to Borrower, may make such appearances, disburse such sums, including reasonable attorneys' fees, and take such action as is necessary to protect Lender's interest. If Lender required mortgage insurance as a condition of making the loan secured by this Deed of Trust, Borrower shall pay the premiums required to maintain such insurance in effect until such time as the requirement for such insurance terminates in accordance with Borrower's and Lender's written agreement or applicable law.

Any amounts disbursed by Lender pursuant to this paragraph 7, with interest thereon, at the Note rate, shall become additional indebtedness of Borrower secured by this Deed of Trust. Unless Borrower and Lender agree to other terms of payment, such amounts shall be payable upon notice from Lender to Borrower requesting payment thereof. Nothing contained in this paragraph 7 shall require Lender to incur any expense or take any action hereunder.

8. Inspection. Lender may make or cause to be made reasonable entries upon and inspections of the Property, provided that Lender shall give Borrower notice prior to any such inspection specifying reasonable cause therefor related to Lender's interest in the Property.

9. Condemnation. The proceeds of any award or claim for damages, direct or consequential, in connection with any condemnation or other taking of the Property, or part thereof, or for conveyance in lieu of condemnation, are hereby assigned and shall be paid to Lender, subject to the terms of any mortgage, deed of trust or other security agreement with a lien which has priority over this Deed of Trust.

10. Borrower Not Released; Forbearance By Lender Not a Waiver. Extension of the time for payment or modification of amortization of the sums secured by this Deed of Trust granted by Lender to any successor in interest of Borrower shall not operate to release, in any manner, the liability of the original Borrower and Borrower's successors in interest. Lender shall not be required to commence proceedings against such successor or refuse to extend time for payment or otherwise modify amortization of the sums secured by this Deed of Trust by reason of any demand made by the original Borrower and Borrower's successors in interest. Any forbearance by Lender in exercising any right or remedy hereunder, or otherwise afforded by applicable law, shall not be a waiver of or preclude the exercise of any such right or remedy.

11. Successors and Assigns Bound; Joint and Several Liability; Co-signers. The covenants and agreements herein contained shall bind, and the rights hereunder shall inure to, the respective successors and assigns of Lender and Borrower, subject to the provisions of paragraph 15 hereof. All covenants and agreements of Borrower shall be joint and several. Any Borrower who co-signs this Deed of Trust, but does not execute the Note, (a) is co-signing this Deed of Trust only to grant and convey that Borrower's interest in the Property to Trustee under the terms of this Deed of Trust, (b) is not personally liable on the Note or under this Deed of Trust, and (c) agrees that Lender and any other Borrower hereunder may agree to extend, modify, forbear, or make any other accommodations with regard to the terms of this Deed of Trust or the Note

Figure 10–10.   Fannie Mae/FHLMC Purchase Money Deed of Trust, Covenants 11–17

without that Borrower's consent and without releasing that Borrower or modifying this Deed of Trust as to that Borrower's interest in the Property.

12. Notice. Except for any notice required under applicable law to be given in another manner, (a) any notice to Borrower provided for in this Deed of Trust shall be given by delivering it or by mailing such notice by certified mail addressed to Borrower at the Property Address or at such other address as Borrower may designate by notice to Lender as provided herein, and (b) any notice to Lender shall be given by certified mail to Lender's address stated herein or to such other address as Lender may designate by notice to Borrower as provided herein. Any notice provided for in this Deed of Trust shall be deemed to have been given to Borrower or Lender when given in the manner designated herein.

13. Governing Law; Severability. The state and local laws applicable to this Deed of Trust shall be the laws of the jurisdiction in which the Property is located. The foregoing sentence shall not limit the applicability of Federal law to this Deed of Trust. In the event that any provision or clause of this Deed of Trust or the Note conflicts with applicable law, such conflict shall not affect other provisions of this Deed of Trust or the Note which can be given effect without the conflicting provision, and to this end the provisions of this Deed of Trust and the Note are declared to be severable. As used herein, "costs", "expenses" and "attorneys' fees" include all sums to the extent not prohibited by applicable law or limited herein.

14. Borrower's Copy. Borrower shall be furnished a conformed copy of the Note and of this Deed of Trust at the time of execution or after recordation hereof.

15. Transfer of the Property or a Beneficial Interest in Borrower. If all or any part of the Property or an interest therein is sold or transferred by Borrower (or if a beneficial interest in Borrower is sold or transferred and Borrower is not a natural person or persons but is a corporation, partnership, trust or other legal entity) without Lender's prior written consent, excluding (a) the creation of a lien or encumbrance subordinate to this Deed of Trust which does not relate to a transfer of rights of occupancy in the property, (b) the creation of a purchase money security interest for household appliances, (c) a transfer by devise, descent or by operation of law upon the death of a joint tenant or (d) the grant of any leasehold interest of three years or less not containing an option to purchase, Lender may, at Lender's option, declare all the sums secured by this Deed of Trust to be immediately due and payable.

If Lender exercises such option to accelerate, Lender shall mail Borrower notice of acceleration in accordance with paragraph 12 hereof. Such notice shall provide a period of not less than 30 days from the date the notice is mailed within which Borrower may pay the sums declared due. If Borrower fails to pay such sums prior to the expiration of such period, Lender may, without further notice or demand on Borrower, invoke any remedies permitted by paragraph 16 hereof.

Lender may consent to a sale or transfer if: (1) Borrower causes to be submitted to Lender information required by Lender to evaluate the transferee as if a new loan were being made to the transferee; (2) Lender reasonably determines that Lender's security will not be impaired and that the risk of a breach of any covenant or agreement in this Deed of Trust is acceptable; (3) interest will be payable on the sums secured by this Deed of Trust at a rate acceptable to Lender; (4) changes in the terms of the Note and this Deed of Trust required by Lender are made, including, for example, periodic adjustment in the interest rate, a different final payment date for the loan, and addition of unpaid interest to principal; and (5) the transferee signs an assumption agreement that is acceptable to Lender and that obligates the transferee to keep all the promises and agreements made in the Note and in this Deed of Trust, as modified if required by Lender. To the extent permitted by applicable law, Lender also may charge a reasonable fee as a condition to Lender's consent to any sale or transfer.

Borrower will continue to be obligated under the Note and this Deed of Trust unless Lender releases Borrower in writing.

NON-UNIFORM COVENANTS. Borrower and Lender further covenant and agree as follows:

16. Acceleration; Remedies. Except as provided in paragraph 15 hereof, upon Borrower's breach of any covenant or agreement of Borrower in this Deed of Trust, including the covenants to pay when due any sums secured by this Deed of Trust, Lender prior to acceleration shall give notice to Borrower and to any other person required by applicable law as provided in paragraph 12 hereof specifying: (1) the breach; (2) the action required to cure such breach; (3) a date, not less than 10 days from the date the notice is mailed to Borrower, by which such breach must be cured; and (4) that failure to cure such breach on or before the date specified in the notice may result in acceleration of the sums secured by this Deed of Trust and sale of the property. The notice shall further inform Borrower of the right to reinstate after acceleration and the right to bring a court action to assert the nonexistence of a default or any other defense of Borrower to acceleration and sale. If the breach is not cured on or before the date specified in the notice, Lender, at Lender's option, may declare all of the sums secured by this Deed of Trust to be immediately due and payable without further demand and may invoke the power of sale and any other remedies permitted by applicable law. Lender shall be entitled to collect all reasonable costs and expenses incurred in pursuing the remedies provided in this paragraph 16, including, but not limited to, reasonable attorneys' fees.

If Lender invokes the power of sale, Lender or Trustee shall give notice of the time, place and terms of sale by posting written notice at least 21 days prior to the day of sale at the courthouse door in each of the counties in which the Property is situated. Lender shall mail a copy of the notice of sale to Borrower in the manner prescribed by applicable law. Such sale shall be made at public vendue between the hours of 10 o'clock a.m. and 4 o'clock p.m. on the first Tuesday in any month. Borrower authorizes Trustee to sell the Property to the highest bidder for cash in one or more parcels and in such order as Trustee may determine. Lender or Lender's designee may purchase the Property at any sale.

Trustee shall deliver to the purchaser Trustee's deed conveying indefeasible title to the property so sold with covenants of general warranty. Borrower covenants and agrees to defend generally the purchaser's title to the property against all claims and demands. The recitals in the Trustee's deed shall be prima facie evidence of the truth of the statements made therein. Trustee shall apply the proceeds of the sale in the following order: (a) to all reasonable costs and expenses of the sale, including, but not limited to, reasonable Trustee's and attorneys' fees and costs of title evidence; (b) to all sums secured by this Deed of Trust; and (c) the excess, if any, to the person or persons legally entitled thereto.

If the Property is sold pursuant to this paragraph 16, Borrower or any person holding possession of the Property through Borrower shall immediately surrender possession of the property to the purchaser at such sale. If possession is not surrendered, Borrower or such person shall be a tenant at sufferance and may be removed by writ of possession.

17. Borrower's Right to Reinstate. Notwithstanding Lender's acceleration of the sums secured by this Deed of Trust due to Borrower's breach, Borrower shall have the right to have any proceedings begun by Lender to enforce this Deed of Trust discontinued at any time prior to the earlier to occur of (i) the fifth day before sale of the Property pursuant to the power of sale contained in this Deed of Trust or (ii) entry of a judgment enforcing this Deed of Trust if: (a) Borrower pays Lender all sums which would be then due under this Deed of Trust and the Note had no acceleration occurred; (b) Borrower cures all breaches of any other covenants or agreements of Borrower contained in this Deed of Trust; (c) Borrower pays all reasonable expenses incurred by Lender and Trustee in enforcing the covenants and agreements of Borrower contained in this Deed of Trust, and in enforcing Lender's and Trustee's remedies as provided in paragraph 16

Figure 10–11.   Fannie Mae/FHLMC Purchase Money Deed of Trust, Covenants 18–21

hereof, including, but not limited to, reasonable attoneys' fees; and (d) Borrower takes such action as Lender may reasonably require to assure that the lien of this Deed of Trust, Lender's interest in the Property and Borrower's obligation to pay the sums secured by this Deed of Trust shall continue unimpaired. Upon such payment and cure by Borrower, this Deed of Trust and the obligations secured hereby shall remain in full force and effect as if no acceleration had occurred.

18. Assignment of Rents; Appointment of Receiver; Lender in Possession. As additional security hereunder, Borrower hereby assigns to Lender the rents of the Property, provided that Borrower shall, prior to acceleration under paragraph 16 hereof or abandonment of the Property, have the right to collect and retain such rents as they become due and payable.

Upon acceleration under paragraph 16 hereof or abandonment of the Property, Lender, in person, by agent or by judicially appointed receiver shall be entitled to enter upon, take possession of and manage the Property and to collect the rents of the Property including those past due. All rents collected by Lender or the receiver shall be applied first to payment of the costs of management of the Property and collection of rents, including, but not limited to, receiver's fees, premiums on receiver's bonds and reasonable attorneys' fees, and then to the sums secured by this Deed of Trust. Lender and the receiver shall be liable to account only for those rents actually received.

19. Release. Upon payment of all sums secured by this Deed of Trust, Lender shall release this Deed of Trust without charge to Borrower. Borrower shall pay all costs of recordation, if any.

20. Substitute Trustee. Lender, at Lender's option, with or without cause, may from time to time remove Trustee and appoint a successor trustee to any Trustee appointed hereunder by an instrument recorded in the county in which this Deed of Trust is recorded. Without conveyance of the Property, the successor trustee shall succeed to all the title, power and duties conferred upon the Trustee herein and by applicable law.

21. Subrogation. Any of the proceeds of the Note used to take up outstanding liens against all or any part of the Property have been advanced by Lender at Borrower's request and upon Borrower's representation that such amounts are due and are secured by valid liens against the Property. Lender shall be subrogated to any and all rights, superior titles, liens and equities owned or claimed by any owner or holder of any outstanding liens and debts, regardless of whether said liens or debts are acquired by Lender by assignment or are released by the holder thereof upon payment.

22. Partial Invalidity. In the event any portion of the sums intended to be secured by this Deed of Trust cannot be lawfully secured hereby, payments in reduction of such sums shall be applied first to those portions not secured hereby. In the event that any applicable law limiting the amount of interest or other charges permitted to be collected is interpreted so that any charge provided for in this Deed of Trust or in the Note, whether considered separately or together with other charges that are considered a part of this Deed of Trust and Note transaction, violates such law by reason of the acceleration of the indebtedness secured hereby, or for any other reason, such charge is hereby reduced to the extent necessary to eliminate such violation. The amounts of such interest or other charges previously paid to Lender in excess of the amounts permitted by applicable law shall be applied by Lender to reduce the principal of the indebtedness evidenced by the Note, or, at Lender's option, be refunded.

23. Purchase Money Deed of Trust; Vendor's Lien. The funds lent to Borrower under the Note secured hereby were used to pay all or part of the purchase price of the Property. The Note secured hereby also is primarily secured by the Vendor's Lien retained in the deed of even date herewith conveying the Property to Borrower, which Vendor's Lien has been assigned to Lender, this Deed of Trust being additional security therefor.

**REQUEST FOR NOTICE OF DEFAULT
AND FORECLOSURE UNDER SUPERIOR
MORTGAGE OR DEEDS OF TRUST**

Borrower and Lender request the holder of any mortgage, deed of trust or other encumbrance with a lien which has priority over this Deed of Trust to give Notice to Lender, at Lender's address set forth on page one of this Deed of Trust, of any default under the superior encumbrance and of any sale or other foreclosure action.

IN WITNESS WHEREOF, Borrower has executed this Deed of Trust.

....
-Borrower

....
-Borrower

STATE OF TEXAS, ... County ss:

BEFORE ME, the undersigned, a Notary Public in and for said County and State, on this day personally appeared ....

....

known to me to be the persons whose names are subscribed to the foregoing instrument, and acknowledged to me that they executed the same for the purposes and consideration therein expressed.

GIVEN UNDER MY HAND AND SEAL OF OFFICE, this .... day of ....,19...

....
Notary Public

———————— (Space Below This Line Reserved For Lender And Recorder) ————————

Figure 10–12.   Fannie Mae/FHLMC Due-on-Transfer Rider

DUE-ON-TRANSFER RIDER

Notice: This rider adds a provision to the Security Instrument allowing the Lender to require repayment of the Note in full upon transfer of the property.

This Due-On-Transfer Rider is made this .... day of ...., 19........., and is incorporated into and shall be deemed to amend and supplement the Mortgage, Deed of Trust, or Deed to Secure Debt (the "Security Instrument") of the same date given by the undersigned (the "Borrower") to secure Borrower's Note to .... (the "Lender") of the same date (the "Note") and covering the property described in the Security Instrument and located at:

....
(Property Address)

AMENDED COVENANT. In addition to the covenants and agreements made in the Security Instrument, Borrower and Lender further covenant and agree as follows:

A. TRANSFER OF THE PROPERTY OR A BENEFICIAL INTEREST IN BORROWER

Uniform Covenant 16 of the Security Instrument is amended to read as follows:

16. Transfer of the Property or a Beneficial Interest in Borrower.   If all or any part of the Property or an interest therein is sold or transferred by Borrower (or if a beneficial interest in Borrower is sold or transferred and Borrower is not a natural person or persons but is a corporation, partnership, trust or other legal entity) without Lender's prior written consent, excluding (a) the creation of a lien or encumbrance subordinate to this Security Instrument which does not relate to a transfer of rights of occupancy in the property, (b) the creation of a purchase money security interest for household appliances, (c) a transfer by devise, descent or by operation of law upon the death of a joint tenant or (d) the grant of any leasehold interest of three years or less not containing an option to purchase, Lender may, at Lender's option, declare all the sums secured by this Security Instrument to be immediately due and payable.

If Lender exercises such option to accelerate, Lender shall mail Borrower notice of acceleration in accordance with paragraph 12 hereof. Such notice shall provide a period of not less than 30 days from the date the notice is mailed within which Borrower may pay the sums declared due. If Borrower fails to pay such sums prior to the expiration of such period, Lender may, without further notice or demand on Borrower, invoke any remedies permitted by paragraph 17 hereof.

Lender may consent to a sale or transfer if: (1) Borrower causes to be submitted to Lender information required by Lender to evaluate the transferee as if a new loan were being made to the transferee; (2) Lender reasonably determines that Lender's security will not be impaired and that the risk of a breach of any covenant or agreement in this Security Instrument is acceptable; (3) interest will be payable on the sums secured by this Security Instrument at a rate acceptable to Lender; (4) changes in the terms of the Note and this Security Instrument required by Lender are made, including, for example, periodic adjustment in the interest rate, a different final payment date for the loan, and addition of unpaid interest to principal; and (5) the transferee signs an assumption agreement that is acceptable to Lender and that obligates the transferee to keep all the promises and agreements made in the Note and in this Security Instrument, as modified if required by Lender. To the extent permitted by applicable law, Lender also may charge a reasonable fee as a condition to Lender's consent to any sale or transfer.

Borrower will continue to be obligated under the Note and this Security Instrument unless Lender releases Borrower in writing.

IN WITNESS WHEREOF, Borrower has executed this Due-On-Transfer Rider.

....(Seal)
-Borrower

....(Seal)
-Borrower

DUE-ON-TRANSFER RIDER-Second Mortgage—4/82-**FNMA UNIFORM INSTRUMENT**

executed on the Fannie Mae-approved forms, including the due-on-transfer rider.

In addition to the purchase of fixed-payment second mortgages, Fannie Mae will also purchase second mortgages with a buydown feature. As with the buydown program for the first mortgage purchase program Fannie Mae requires that the loan documents only reflect the permanent payment term rather than the terms of the buydown plan. Also the terms of the buydown must be disclosed to the appraiser so that it can be made a part of the appraisal if the buydown is not a common practice for the area or otherwise would affect the value of the property. Also Fannie Mae requires the buydown plan must be reduced to writing. The agreement must state that the funds are nonrefundable and that the borrower's only right and interest in the funds is to have them applied to the monthly payments as per the agreement. As with the first-lien buydown, the funds may not be used to pay back due payments and that if the mortgage is paid off or if the property is sold the remaining funds should be used to reduce the outstanding loan balance.

Fannie Mae has set up certain requirements that a second mortgage buydown plan must meet.

1. The buydown period is limited to a minimum of one year and a maximum of 12 years.

2. If the buydown plan calls for graduated payments, the payment must remain constant for a period of 12 months. Thus, the payments could not be increased quarterly.

3. The maximum increase in the borrower's effective interest rate for a graduated-payment buydown is limited to one percent per year.

4. If the buydown is a *level buydown plan,* where the payment changes every 2 years or longer, the borrower's effective interest rate may not increase by more than 2 percent.

5. The buydown funds can come from any source, but if the seller is the source of the funds, the seller cannot contribute more than 6 to 10 percent of the property's sales price or appraised value, whichever is less. The percent will depend on the loan-to-value ratio of the loan. For example, if the loan-to-value is less than 90 percent, the seller could contribute up to 10 percent of the sales price or appraised value, whichever is less.

Rehabilitation Mortgage Plan

With Announcement 83-31, dated October 25, 1984, Fannie Mae announced an enhancement to their Rehabilitation Mortgage Plan. Prior to the announcement, only supervised lenders that had accounts insured by FDIC or FSLIC could participate in the program. With this program change, other lenders are eligible to participate in the program provided the lender is:

Approved by Fannie Mae

Demonstrates the ability and expertise to originate and supervise this type of loan

Approved by the Southwest Regional Office to use and/or participate in the plan

According to the announcement, any conventional first mortgage that meets the normal criteria of Fannie Mae is eligible to be sold to Fannie Mae under this program.

Purpose   The purpose of this plan is to make long-term financing available for the purchase (or refinance) and rehabilitation of existing 1- to 4-family properties through a single lender. According to the announcement, Fannie Mae will purchase mortgages on properties in their as-is condition, but the mortgage amount will be based on the "as completed" value. Thus, the person wishing to purchase an older property and rehabilitate the property can secure the funds for the property as well as the repairs from one lender at one interest rate.

Loan-to-value ratios   If the property is to be an owner-occupied property, the maximum loan to value ratio is 95 percent if a new loan and 90 percent if for refinancing. If the property is a second home or investment property the maximum is 80 percent.

Maximum loan amounts   These are the same as the conventional mortgage purchase program: single-family dwelling, $115,300; 2-family dwelling, $147,500; 3-family dwelling, $178,200; and for a 4-family dwelling, $221,500.

Special deposit account   Upon the closing of a rehabilitation loan, the lender and the borrower will establish an account and deposit the difference between the as-is cost of the property and the completed value of the property. The purpose of the account is to fund the rehabilitation work on the property. According to the announcement, the account is to be an interest-bearing account and all of the interest earned on the funds in the account will be credited to the borrower. It should be noted that all withdrawals from the account will be made through the originating lender. Also, all work is to be completed within 12 months after Fannie Mae has purchased the loan. If there is any excess in the account after all of the repairs have been completed, the excess will be credited to principal reduction.

If you have a client who is interested in the purchase and rehabilitation of older homes, this is an excellent program. Once again if you contact several lenders and they either refuse to make or indicate no knowledge of the program, contact the Southwest Regional Office and they will supply you with information regarding lenders that have expressed an interest in the program.

Adjustable-Rate Mortgage Purchase Program

On June 25, 1981, Fannie Mae announced its program to purchase adjustable-rate mortgages beginning August 7, 1981. In the initial program Fannie Mae purchased eight different ARM's based on five different indexes.

According to the original rule of the program, any standard ARM or plan was to be based on one of the five approved indexes listed below:

6-month U.S. Treasury bills

1-year U.S. Treasury Securities

3-year U.S. Treasury Securities

5-year U.S. Treasury Securities

Federal Home Loan Bank Board series of closed loans (which translates to the monthly average contract interest rate charged by all lenders on mortgage loans for previously occupied homes)

As Fannie Mae gained more experience in the purchase of ARM's, there have been many changes in this initial purchase program. Today Fannie Mae will purchase ARM's under only four plans. These are referred to as the *Standard Plans (ARM)*. According to the Fannie Mae Lending Guide, part 5, section 501, these plans are defined as follows:

ARM Plan 9   This plan is tied to the weekly average yield of the 1-year Treasury securities. The plan calls for a payment adjustment every 12 months or at the same time the interest

rate is adjusted. When the payment and the interest rate are adjusted at the same time there will be no negative amortization.

It should be noted that with Plan 9, Fannie Mae does allow the lender to offer to the borrower the option of limiting the payment change to a maximum of 7.5 percent. If this is done there is a possibility of negative amortization. It should be noted that this 7.5 percent limitation affects any increase.

ARM Plan 10   This plan is tied to the weekly average of the 3-year Treasury securities. The plan requires that the interest rate and payment be adjusted every 36 months or 3 years. As with Plan 9, Plan 10 allows the lender to offer to the borrower the option of limiting the amount of payment increase. The limitation for this plan is also 7.5 percent.

ARM Plan 11   This plan is tied to or uses the weekly average of the 5-year Treasury securities as an index. With this plan, the interest rate and payment will adjust either upward or downward every 60 months or 5 years. As with the other two plans, the lender may offer the 7.5 percent payment adjustment cap.

ARM Plan 6 resale and refinance   As the name implies, this is the only ARM plan that may be used in conjunction with the resale and refinance program mentioned earlier in the chapter. This is similar to Plan 11 in that it uses the weekly average of the 5-year Treasury securities as an index. One major difference in this plan is that the first interest rate adjustment is limited to a maximum change of 2.5 percent no matter how much the index changes. After the first adjustment there is no limit to the amount the interest and payment may change.

It should be noted that these are the Standard Plans offered by Fannie Mae. Fannie Mae will purchase any other plan, but only on a negotiated basis.

Mortgage term and amount   The maximum term for the ARM is similar to the standard mortgage in that the term is 30 years. In regard to the maximum mortgage amount, the ARM limits are identical to those of the standard mortgage:

1-family	$115,300
2-family	$147,500
3-family	$178,200
4-family	$221,500

Maximum loan-to-value ratio   The loan-to-value ratios for the ARM are similar to those of the standard mortgage:

Owner-occupied principal residence	95 percent
Owner-occupied refinance	90 percent
Second home or investment property	80 percent

Interest rate adjustment   According to Fannie Mae, the interest rate is to be calculated by adding a specified margin to the most recent index figure available 45 days before the interest rate change date. It should be noted that the calculated interest rate will be rounded to the nearest 1/8 of a percent. At the time this text was written Fannie Mae required the following margins:

1-year ARM	1.00
3-year ARM	1.20
5-year ARM	1.40

Note that is a *net yield*. Net yield is defined as the required yield less any servicing fee. Once again at the time of the writing of this text, Fannie Mae suggested a minimum servicing fee of 1/2 of 1 percent for the ARM. For example, to calculate the interest rate for a Plan 9 ARM or the 1-year ARM, we would find the rate or constant maturity of the 1-year Treasury securities. This information is available from the Federal Reserve statistical release H.15(519). Let us assume the current yield is 11.52 on the securities. Then we would add the specified margin for the 1-year ARM or 1.00, giving us a net yield of 12.52. Then we would add the minimum servicing of 1/2 of 1 percent for a gross yield of 13.02. Since Fannie Mae allows the lender to round to the nearest 1/8 of a percent, the interest rate on the mortgage could be rounded up to 13.125.

Payment calculation   After the new interest rate is calculated then the monthly payment is established. The payment will be the amount necessary to amortize the outstanding principal balance over the remaining term of the mortgage. If the borrower has chosen to limit the payment change to a maximum of 7.5 percent then the increase will be limited to the previous year's payment multiplied by the factor 1.075. For example if the previous year's P and I payment is $981.25, then the maximum payment increase for the next adjustment date would be $981.25 × 1.075 or $1054.84. If for example, the actual increase of

the monthly payment on the adjustment date is more than the capped payment, the borrower may wish to make the higher payment, thus avoiding negative amortization.

Negative amortization   Fannie Mae limits the amount of negative amortization on the mortgages they will purchase. According to the *Lending Guide*, Fannie Mae limits the negative amortization to 125 percent of the original mortgage amount. For example, if the original mortgage amount is $100,000 the mortgage amount when negative amortization is added cannot exceed $125,000. When this happens, the monthly payment will be increased to a level to amortize the mortgage over the remaining term of the mortgage.

Interest-rate buydowns   Fannie Mae will purchase ARM's that have an interest-rate buydown feature. The interest-rate buydown can either be of a permanent or temporary nature. If the buydown is a permanent type, this can apply to all ARM plans. If the buydown is temporary, only the plans based on the 3 and 5 year Treasuries may include the buydown. In addition Fannie Mae has placed some limitations of the buydown for the 3- and 5-year ARM. For both of these plans, the temporary buydown must end 12 months prior to the initial payment adjustment date. Thus, for the 3-year ARM, the maximum buydown period is 2 years. The buydown period for the 5-year ARM is limited to a term of 4 years.

Underwriting   Any ARM purchased by Fannie Mae will be underwritten using the initial interest rate and the standard income ratios and property standards.

Graduated-Payment Adjustable-Rate Mortgage (GPARM) Purchase Program

On February 25, 1982, Fannie Mae announced its intention to purchase these types of mortgages. The GPARM's that were purchased under this initial program primarily used variations of three of the original eight ARM purchase programs mentioned in the previous section.

Graduation period and frequency   As with many of the other programs of Fannie Mae, the GPARM program has undergone revision and today Fannie Mae will purchase GPARMs that are variations of all four of the ARM Plans mentioned in the previous section. The graduation period for the GPARM based on the 1- or 3-year Treasury securities (plans 9 and 10) is 3 years; the graduation period for the GPARM based on the 5-year Treasury securities (plans 6 and 11) is 5 years. The amount of payment graduation or increase for each of the plans is 7.5 percent per year. Thus, for the GPARMs that have a graduation period of 3 years, the payments would increase 7.5 percent a year for 3 years.

As with the graduated-payment mortgage (GPM) discussed in previous chapters, the payments will change or graduate every 12 months and will increase by 7.5 percent.

Initial monthly payment   The initial monthly payments for each of the plans will be calculated to be an amount such that—when the 7.5 percent annual monthly payment increase is taken over the life of the graduation period—the monthly payment at the end of the authorized graduation period will be sufficient to pay off the outstanding principal balance over the remaining life of the mortgage. It should be noted that the initial monthly payment is calculated for the original interest rate and does not take into consideration any adjustments in the interest rate.

The calculation of this initial payment is complicated, so Fannie Mae has prepared a chart giving the monthly payment factors for the initial monthly payment for the 3- and 5-year graduation periods. This chart is shown in Figure 10–13.

If you are working with a client who has expressed interest in the GPARM, using this chart you could calculate the initial monthly payment for either of the GPARMs that can be sold to Fannie Mae. For example, the current interest rate on the GPARM is 14.750, and your client is interested only in the 3-year ARM, you would go to the section of the chart dealing with the 3-year graduation and find the 14.750 under the column entitled mortgage interest rate. The initial monthly payment factor is 10.5466. To calculate the amount of the payment, you would multiply this factor by the mortgage amount divided by 1000. For example, if your client is seeking an $85,550 loan the initial monthly P & I payment would be calculated as follows:

$$\frac{85,550}{1000} = 85.550 \times 10.5466 \text{ or } \$902.26$$

If your client is interested in the amount of the P & I payments in years 2 and 3, the second year's payment can be calculated by multiplying $902.26 by 1.075. Thus, the payment for the second year would be $969.93. The pay-

ment for the third year could be calculated by multiplying $969.93 by 1.075. It should be noted that the payments in the second and third year do not take into consideration any adjustment in the interest rate.

Negative amortization   Since the payments for the first few years of the GPARM are not sufficient to pay all of the interest charges, these loans will have negative amortization. To lessen the effective of the negative amortization, Fannie Mae has limited the amount of negative amortization to 125 percent of the original mortgage amount.

GPARM Note and Deed of Trust Rider   As with many of the other purchase programs of Fannie Mae, they have developed a standard form for the GPARM. The GPARM Notes for Texas are shown in Figures 10–14 through 10–22. The Deed of Trust Riders for the previous notes are shown in Figures 10–23 through 10–28.

Underwriting   Underwriting or borrower approval will be based on the initial interest rate; thus allowing the borrower to qualify for a larger loan.

Manufactured housing mortgage purchase program   On August 20, 1981, Fannie Mae instituted a program for the purchase of mortgages secured by manufactured housing units that are legally classified as real property. These mortgages can be sold to Fannie Mae through any of its mortgage purchase programs. According to Fannie Mae, the mortgages can be either VA guaranteed, FHA insured, or conventional. Any mortgage secured by manufactured housing must meet the following requirements:

A. The manufactured housing unit must be permanently affixed to a foundation and assume the characteristics of residential property.

B. If manufactured as a mobile unit, the wheels and axles must be removed when the unit is permanently sited.

C. The purchase of the land and home must represent a single real estate transaction under state law and must be evidenced by a recorded mortgage or deed of trust. (The combination of a chattel and real estate mortgage is not eligible.) The appropriate one- to four-family Fannie Mae/FHLMC Uniform Instruments, or

Figure 10-13. **Initial Monthly Payment Factors for GPARMs**

Three-Year Graduated Payment Factor Table Per $1000 — Initial Monthly Fixed Installment Factors

Mortgage Interest Rate	Monthly Installment Factor	Mortgage Interest Rate	Monthly Installment Factor
8.000	6.1015	13.000	9.3288
8.125	6.1763	13.125	9.4146
8.250	6.2514	13.250	9.5006
8.375	6.3268	13.375	9.5867
8.500	6.4026	13.500	9.6731
8.625	6.4788	13.625	9.7597
8.750	6.5553	13.750	9.8464
8.875	6.6321	13.875	9.9333
9.000	6.7093	14.000	10.0204
9.125	6.7868	14.125	10.1077
9.250	6.8646	14.250	10.1952
9.375	6.9428	14.375	10.2828
9.500	7.0212	14.500	10.3706
9.625	7.1000	14.625	10.4585
9.750	7.1791	14.750	10.5466
9.875	7.2585	14.875	10.6349
10.000	7.3381	15.000	10.7233
10.125	7.4181	15.125	10.8119
10.250	7.4984	15.250	10.9007
10.375	7.5789	15.375	10.9896
10.500	7.6597	15.500	11.0786
10.625	7.7408	15.625	11.1678
10.750	7.8222	15.750	11.2571
10.875	7.9038	15.875	11.3465
11.000	7.9857	16.000	11.4361
11.125	8.0679	16.125	11.5259
11.250	8.1503	16.250	11.6157
11.375	8.2330	16.375	11.7057
11.500	8.3159	16.500	11.7958
11.625	8.3991	16.625	11.8861
11.750	8.4824	16.750	11.9764
11.875	8.5661	16.875	12.0669
12.000	8.6499	17.000	12.1576
12.125	8.7340	17.125	12.2483
12.250	8.8184	17.250	12.3391
12.375	8.9029	17.375	12.4301
12.500	8.9876	17.500	12.5212
12.625	9.0726	17.625	12.6124
12.750	9.1578	17.750	12.7037
12.875	9.2432	17.875	12.7951
		18.000	12.8866

Five-Year Graduated Payment Factor Table Per $1000 — Initial Monthly Fixed Installment Factors

Mortgage Interest Rate	Monthly Installment Factor	Mortgage Interest Rate	Monthly Installment Factor
8.000	5.5101	13.000	8.5618
8.125	5.5799	13.125	8.6440
8.250	5.6500	13.250	8.7263
8.375	5.7206	13.375	8.8089
8.500	5.7915	13.500	8.8917
8.625	5.8628	13.625	8.9748
8.750	5.9344	13.750	9.0580
8.875	6.0064	13.875	9.1415
9.000	6.0788	14.000	9.2252
9.125	6.1516	14.125	9.3091
9.250	6.2246	14.250	9.3933
9.375	6.2981	14.375	9.4776
9.500	6.3719	14.500	9.5621
9.625	6.4460	14.625	9.6469
9.750	6.5204	14.750	9.7318
9.875	6.5952	14.875	9.8170
10.000	6.6704	15.000	9.9023
10.125	6.7458	15.125	9.9879
10.250	6.8216	15.250	10.0736
10.375	6.8976	15.375	10.1595
10.500	6.9740	15.500	10.2456
10.625	7.0507	15.625	10.3319
10.750	7.1277	15.750	10.4183
10.875	7.2050	15.875	10.5050
11.000	7.2826	16.000	10.5918
11.125	7.3605	16.125	10.6788
11.250	7.4387	16.250	10.7660
11.375	7.5172	16.375	10.8533
11.500	7.5960	16.500	10.9408
11.625	7.6750	16.625	11.0285
11.750	7.7543	16.750	11.1163
11.875	7.8339	16.875	11.2043
12.000	7.9138	17.000	11.2924
12.125	7.9939	17.125	11.3807
12.250	8.0743	17.250	11.4692
12.375	8.1549	17.375	11.5578
12.500	8.2358	17.500	11.6465
12.625	8.3169	17.625	11.7355
12.750	8.3983	17.750	11.8245
12.875	8.4800	17.875	11.9137
		18.000	12.0031

SOURCE: Federal National Mortgage Association, *The Fannie Mae Adjustable Rate Mortgage Workbook*, August 1983, p17

other documents acceptable to the Fannie Mae regional office, must be used for conventional loans, and the mortgage or deed of trust must include an identification of the unit by manufacturer, model, and serial number.

D. The required title insurance policy must identify the unit as part of the real property and must insure against any loss sustained should the manufactured home be determined not to be part of the real property and that the insured mort-

gage is prior and superior to all other recorded real property or personal property liens or claims.

E. The mortgage amount must not include the financing of furniture (except for kitchen/laundry appliances and carpeting), credit life insurance, property damage insurance, or any other form of insurance.

F. The unit and land package must be taxed as real property except that, in

Figure 10–14.   Fannie Mae Graduated Payment Note (1-year index), page 1

GRADUATED PAYMENT NOTE
(1 Year Index — Payment Cap)

This Note contains provisions allowing for changes in my interest rate and monthly payments. I may limit my monthly payment increases to 7½% each year if the provisions of this Note permit me to do so.

The principal amount I must repay will be larger than the amount I originally borrowed, but not more than 125% of the original amount.

...., 19 ...., Texas
                                                                                                [City]

....
[Property Address]

1. BORROWER'S PROMISE TO PAY
In return for a loan that I have received, I promise to pay U.S. $... plus any amounts added in accordance with Section 6 (B) below (the total amount is called "principal"), plus interest, to the order of the Lender. The Lender is..
.... I understand that the Lender may transfer this Note. The Lender or anyone who takes this Note by transfer and who is entitled to receive payments under this Note is called the "Note Holder."

2. INTEREST
(A) Interest Owed
Interest will be charged on unpaid principal until the full amount of principal has been paid. I will owe interest at a yearly rate of ....%. The interest rate I will pay will change in accordance with Section 4 (A) below on the first day of ...., 19 .... and on that day every 12th month thereafter. Each date on which my interest rate could change is called an "Interest Change Date."

(B) The Index
Beginning with the first Interest Change Date, my interest rate will be based on an Index. The "Index" is the weekly average yield on United States Treasury securities adjusted to a constant maturity of 1 year, as made available by the Federal Reserve Board. The most recent Index figure available as of the date 45 days before each Interest Change Date is called the "Current Index."

If the Index is no longer available, the Note Holder will choose a new index which is based upon comparable information. The Note Holder will give me notice of this choice.

(C) Interest After Default
The interest rate required by this Section 2 or Section 4 (A) below is the rate I will pay both before and after any default described in Section 10 (B) below.

3. TIME AND PLACE OF PAYMENTS
I will pay principal and interest by making payments every month.

I will make my monthly payments on the first day of each month beginning on ...., 19 ...... I will make these payments every month until I have paid all of the principal and interest and any other charges described below that I may owe under this Note. My monthly payments will be applied to interest before principal. If, on ...., ..., I still owe amounts under this Note, I will pay those amounts in full on that date, which is called the "maturity date."

I will make my monthly payments at ....
....
or at a different place if required by the Note Holder.

4. INTEREST RATE CHANGES AND FULL PAYMENT
(A) Calculation of New Interest Rate and Full Payment
Each of my first .... monthly payments could be less than a Full Payment. A "Full Payment" is the monthly amount sufficient to repay the amount I originally borrowed, or the unpaid principal balance of my loan as of an Interest Change Date, in full on the maturity date at the interest rate I am required to pay by Section 2 above or this Section 4 (A) in substantially equal payments. Beginning on the date of this Note, my first Full Payment will be U.S. $ .... until the first Interest Change Date.

Before each Interest Change Date, the Note Holder will determine a new Full Payment for my loan. The Note Holder will first calculate my new interest rate by adding .... percentage points (............%) to the Current Index. The Note Holder will then round the result of this addition to the nearest one-eighth of one percentage point (0.125%). This rounded amount will be my new interest rate until the next Interest Change Date. The Note Holder will then determine the amount of the monthly payment that would be sufficient to repay the unpaid principal that I am expected to owe on the Interest Change Date in full on the maturity date at my new interest rate in substantially equal payments. The result of this calculation is my new Full Payment.

Each new interest rate will become effective on each Interest Change Date, and each new Full Payment will become effective on the first monthly payment after the Interest Change Date.

(B) Required Full Payment
I will pay the Full Payment as my monthly payment beginning with my .... monthly payment unless I choose to limit the amount of my monthly payment as permitted by Section 6 (A) below.

5. GRADUATED MONTHLY PAYMENTS
My first .... monthly payments will each be in the amount of U.S. $...
On ...., 19 ...., and on the first anniversary of that date, I will begin paying a new monthly payment which will be equal to the amount I have been paying multiplied by the number 1.075. I will pay the

TEXAS GRADUATED PAYMENT NOTE—1 Year Treasury Index—Single Family—FNMA Uniform Instrument   Form 3701.44 12/83

Figure 10–15. Fannie Mae Graduated Payment Note (1-year index), page 2

new amount of my monthly payment until it changes in accordance with this Section 5, Section 4 (B) above or Section 6 or 7 below.

6. BORROWER'S RIGHT TO LIMIT MONTHLY PAYMENT

(A) Calculation of Limited Payment

Unless Sections 6 (C) and 6 (D) below will not permit me to do so, I may choose to limit the amount of my new monthly payment following the third and each later Interest Change Date to the amount I have been paying multiplied by the number 1.075. This amount is called the "Limited Payment." **If I choose a Limited Payment as my monthly payment, I must give the Note Holder notice that I am doing so at least 15 days before my first new monthly payment is due.**

(B) Additions to My Unpaid Principal

My monthly payment could be less than the amount of the interest portion of the monthly payment that would be sufficient to repay the unpaid principal I owe at the monthly payment date in full on the maturity date at my current interest rate in substantially equal payments. If so, each month that the amount of my monthly payment is less than the interest portion, the Note Holder will subtract the amount of my monthly payment from the amount of the interest portion and will add the difference to my unpaid principal. The Note Holder will also add interest on the amount of this difference to my unpaid principal each month. The interest rate on the interest added to principal will be the rate required by Section 2 or 4 (A) above.

(C) Limit on Unpaid Principal; Increased Monthly Payment

My unpaid principal can never exceed a maximum amount equal to one hundred twenty-five percent (125%) of the principal amount I originally borrowed. My unpaid principal could exceed that maximum amount if I pay a Limited Payment. If so, on the date that my paying my Limited Payment would cause me to exceed that limit, I will instead begin paying a new monthly payment until the next Interest Change Date. The new monthly payment will be in an amount which would be sufficient to repay my then unpaid principal balance in full on the maturity date at my current interest rate in substantially equal payments.

(D) Final Monthly Payments

Beginning with the first monthly payment after the final Change Date, I will pay the Full Payment as my monthly payment.

7. NOTICE OF CHANGES

The Note Holder will deliver or mail to me a notice of any changes in my interest rate and in the amount of my monthly payment before the effective date of any change. The notice will include information required by law to be given me and also the title and telephone number of a person who will answer any question I may have regarding the notice.

8. BORROWER'S RIGHT TO PREPAY

I have the right to make payments of principal at any time before they are due. A payment of principal only is known as a "prepayment." When I make a prepayment, I will tell the Note Holder in writing that I am doing so.

I may make a full prepayment or a partial prepayment without paying any prepayment charge. The Note Holder will use all of my prepayments to reduce the amount of principal that I owe under this Note. If I make a partial prepayment, there will be no delays in the due dates of my monthly payments unless the Note Holder agrees in writing to those delays. My partial prepayment may reduce the amount of my monthly payments after the first Interest Change Date following my partial prepayment. However, any reduction due to my partial prepayment may be offset by an interest rate increase or an addition to the unpaid principal.

9. LOAN CHARGES

If a law, which applies to this loan and which sets maximum loan charges, is finally interpreted so that the interest or other loan charges collected or to be collected in connection with this loan exceed the permitted limits, then: (i) any such loan charge shall be reduced by the amount necessary to reduce the charge to the permitted limit; and (ii) any sums already collected from me which exceeded permitted limits will be refunded to me. The Note Holder may choose to make this refund by reducing the principal I owe under this Note or by making a direct payment to me. If a refund reduces principal, the reduction will be treated as a partial prepayment.

10. BORROWER'S FAILURE TO PAY AS REQUIRED

(A) Late Charge for Overdue Payments

If the Note Holder has not received the full amount of any of my monthly payments by the end of .... calendar days after the date it is due, I will pay a late charge to the Note Holder. The amount of the charge will be ....% of my overdue payment of principal and interest. I will pay this late charge promptly but only once on any late payment.

(B) Default

If I do not pay the full amount of each monthly payment on the date it is due, I will be in default.

(C) Notice of Default

If I am in default, the Note Holder may send me a written notice telling me that if I do not pay the overdue amount by a certain date, the Note Holder may require me to pay immediately the full amount of principal which has not been paid and all the interest that I owe on that amount. That date must be at least 30 days after the date on which the notice is delivered or mailed to me.

(D) No Waiver By Note Holder

Even if, at a time when I am in default, the Note Holder does not require me to pay immediately in full as described above, the Note Holder will still have the right to do so if I am in default at a later time.

(E) Payment of Note Holder's Costs and Expenses

If the Note Holder has required me to pay immediately in full as described above, the Note Holder will have the right to be paid back by me for all of its costs and expenses in enforcing this Note to the extent not prohibited by applicable law. Those expenses include, for example, reasonable attorneys' fees.

11. GIVING OF NOTICES

Unless applicable law requires a different method, any notice that must be given to me under this Note will be given by delivering it or by mailing it by first class mail to me at the Property Address above or at a different address if I give the Note Holder a notice of my different address.

Any notice that must be given to the Note Holder under this Note will be given by mailing it by first class mail to the Note Holder at the address stated in Section 3 above or at a different address if I am given a notice of that different address.

Figure 10–16.   Fannie Mae Graduated Payment Note (1-year index), page 3

12. OBLIGATIONS OF PERSONS UNDER THIS NOTE

If more than one person signs this Note, each person is fully and personally obligated to keep all of the promises made in this Note, including the promise to pay the full amount owed. Any person who is a guarantor, surety, or endorser of this Note is also obligated to do these things. Any person who takes over these obligations, including the obligations of a guarantor, surety, or endorser of this Note, is also obligated to keep all of the promises made in this Note. The Note Holder may enforce its rights under this Note against each person individually or against all of us together. This means that any one of us may be required to pay all of the amounts owed under this Note.

13. WAIVERS

I and any other person who has obligations under this Note waive notice of intention to accelerate, except as provided in Section 10 (C) above, and the rights of presentment and notice of dishonor. "Presentment" means the right to require the Note Holder to demand payment of amounts due. "Notice of dishonor" means the right to require the Note Holder to give notice to other persons that amounts due have not been paid.

14. UNIFORM SECURED NOTE

This Note is a uniform instrument with limited variations in some jurisdictions. In addition to the protections given to the Note Holder under this Note, a Mortgage, Deed of Trust, or Security Deed (the "Security Instrument"), dated the same date as this Note, protects the Note Holder from possible losses which might result if I do not keep the promises which I make in this Note. That Security Instrument describes how and under what conditions I may be required to make immediate payment in full of all amounts I owe under this Note. Some of those conditions are described as follows:

Transfer of the Property or a Beneficial Interest in Borrower. If all or any part of the Property or any interest in it is sold or transferred (or if a beneficial interest in Borrower is sold or transferred and Borrower is not a natural person) without Lender's prior written consent, Lender may, at its option, require immediate payment in full of all sums secured by this Security Instrument. However, this option shall not be exercised by Lender if exercise is prohibited by federal law as of the date of this Security Instrument. Lender also shall not exercise this option if: (a) Borrower causes to be submitted to Lender information required by Lender to evaluate the intended transferee as if a new loan were being made to the transferee; and (b) Lender reasonably determines that Lender's security will not be impaired by the loan assumption and that the risk of a breach of any covenant or agreement in this Security Instrument is acceptable to Lender.

To the extent permitted by applicable law, Lender may charge a reasonable fee as a condition to Lender's consent to the loan assumption. Lender may also require the transferee to sign an assumption agreement that is acceptable to Lender and that obligates the transferee to keep all the promises and agreements made in the Note and in this Security Instrument. Borrower will continue to be obligated under the Note and this Security Instrument unless Lender releases Borrower in writing.

If Lender exercises the option to require immediate payment in full, Lender shall give Borrower notice of acceleration. The notice shall provide a period of not less than 30 days from the date the notice is delivered or mailed within which Borrower must pay all sums secured by this Security Instrument. If Borrower fails to pay these sums prior to the expiration of this period, Lender may invoke any remedies permitted by this Security Instrument without further notice or demand on Borrower.

WITNESS THE HAND(S) AND SEAL(S) OF THE UNDERSIGNED.

....(Seal)
-Borrower

....(Seal)
-Borrower

....(Seal)
-Borrower

[Sign Original Only]

Figure 10–17.   **Fannie Mae Graduated Payment Note (3-year index), page 1**

GRADUATED PAYMENT NOTE
(3 Year Index — Payment Cap)

This Note contains provisions allowing for changes in my interest rate and monthly payments. I may limit my monthly payment increases to 7½% each year if the provisions of this Note permit me to do so.

The principal amount I must repay will be larger than the amount I originally borrowed, but not more than 125% of the original amount.

...., 19 ...., Texas
                                                                               [City]

....
[Property Address]

1. BORROWER'S PROMISE TO PAY

In return for a loan that I have received, I promise to pay U.S. $.. plus any amounts added in accordance with Section 8 (A) below (the total amount is called "principal"), plus interest, to the order of the Lender. The Lender is...
.... I understand that the Lender may transfer this Note. The Lender or anyone who takes this Note by transfer and who is entitled to receive payments under this Note is called the "Note Holder."

2. INTEREST

    (A) Interest Owed

Interest will be charged on unpaid principal until the full amount of principal has been paid. I will owe interest at a yearly rate of ....%. The interest rate I will pay will change in accordance with Section 4 (A) below on the first day of ...., 19 ....and on that day every 36th month thereafter. Each date on which my interest rate could change is called an "Interest Change Date."

    (B) The Index

Beginning with the first Interest Change Date, my interest rate will be based on an Index. The "Index" is the weekly average yield on United States Treasury securities adjusted to a constant maturity of 3 years, as made available by the Federal Reserve Board. The most recent Index figure available as of the date 45 days before each Interest Change Date is called the "Current Index."

If the Index is no longer available, the Note Holder will choose a new index which is based upon comparable information. The Note Holder will give me notice of this choice.

    (C) Interest After Default

The interest rate required by this Section 2 or Section 4 (A) below is the rate I will pay both before and after any default described in Section 12 (B) below.

3. TIME AND PLACE OF PAYMENTS

I will pay principal and interest by making payments every month.

I will make my monthly payments on the first day of each month beginning on ...., 19 ...... I will make these payments every month until I have paid all of the principal and interest and any other charges described below that I may owe under this Note. My monthly payments will be applied to interest before principal. If, on ...., ..., I still owe amounts under this Note, I will pay those amounts in full on that date, which is called the "maturity date."

I will make my monthly payments at ....
....

or at a different place if required by the Note Holder.

4. INTEREST RATE CHANGES AND FULL PAYMENT

    (A) Calculation of New Interest Rate and Full Payment

Each of my first .... monthly payments could be less than a Full Payment. A "Full Payment" is the monthly amount sufficient to repay the amount I originally borrowed, or the unpaid principal balance of my loan as of an Interest Change Date, in full on the maturity date at the interest rate I am required to pay by Section 2 above or this Section 4 (A) in substantially equal payments. Beginning on the date of this Note, my first Full Payment will be U.S. $ .... until the first Interest Change Date.

Before each Interest Change Date, the Note Holder will determine a new Full Payment for my loan. The Note Holder will first calculate my new interest rate by adding .... percentage points (............%) to the Current Index. The Note Holder will then round the result of this addition to the nearest one-eighth of one percentage point (0.125%). This rounded amount will be my new interest rate until the next Interest Change Date. The Note Holder will then determine the amount of the monthly payment that would be sufficient to repay the unpaid principal that I am expected to owe on the Interest Change Date in full on the maturity date at my new interest rate in substantially equal payments. The result of this calculation is my new Full Payment.

Each new interest rate will become effective on each Interest Change Date, and each new Full Payment will become effective on the first monthly payment after the Interest Change Date.

    (B) Required Full Payment

I will pay the Full Payment as my monthly payment beginning with my .... monthly payment unless I choose to limit the amount of my monthly payment as permitted by Section 6 (A) below.

5. GRADUATED MONTHLY PAYMENTS

My first .... monthly payments will each be in the amount of U.S. $.. On ...., 19 ...., and on the first anniversary of that date, I will begin paying a new monthly payment which will be equal to the amount I have been paying multiplied by the number 1.075. I will pay the

---

TEXAS GRADUATED PAYMENT NOTE—3 Year Treasury Index—Single Family—**FNMA Uniform Instrument**   Form 3703.44 12/83

Figure 10–18.   Fannie Mae Graduated Payment Note (3-year index), page 2

new amount of my monthly payment until it changes in accordance with this Section 5, Section 4 (B) above or Section 6 or 7 below.

6. BORROWER'S RIGHT TO LIMIT MONTHLY PAYMENT

(A) Calculation of Graduated Limited Payment

I may choose to limit the amount of my new monthly payment following an Interest Change Date if my new interest rate would cause the monthly payment I have been paying to increase by more than seven and one-half percent (7.5%). **If I choose to limit the amount of my monthly payment, I must give the Note Holder notice that I am doing so at least 15 days before my first new monthly payment is due.** When I do so, on the first monthly payment date after the Interest Change Date I will begin paying a new monthly payment which will be equal to the amount I have been paying each month for the preceding twelve months multiplied by the number 1.075. Thereafter, on each of the first two anniversaries of the new monthly payment effective date, my monthly payment will again increase to an amount equal to the amount I have been paying each month for the preceding twelve months multiplied by the number 1.075. These amounts are called the "Graduated Limited Payments."

Even if I have chosen to limit my monthly payment, Section 6 (B), 6 (C) or 7 below may require me to pay a different amount.

(B) Reduced Monthly Payment

My Graduated Limited Payment could be greater than the amount of a monthly payment which then would be sufficient to repay my unpaid principal balance in full on the maturity date at my current interest rate in substantially equal payments. If so, on the date my paying a Graduated Limited Payment would cause me to pay more than the lower amount, I will instead then begin paying the lower amount as my monthly payment until the next Interest Change Date.

(C) Increased Monthly Payment

My paying a Graduated Limited Payment could cause my unpaid principal to exceed the limit stated in Section 8 (B) below. If so, on the date that my paying a monthly payment would cause me to exceed that limit, I will instead begin paying a new monthly payment until the next Interest Change Date. The new monthly payment will be in an amount which would be sufficient to repay my then unpaid principal balance in full on the maturity date at my current interest rate in substantially equal payments.

7. FINAL MONTHLY PAYMENTS

Beginning with the first monthly payment after the final Interest Change Date, I will pay the Full Payment as my monthly payment.

8. INCREASES IN THE PRINCIPAL AMOUNT TO BE PAID

(A) Additions to My Unpaid Principal

My monthly payment could be less than the amount of the interest portion of the monthly payment that would be sufficient to repay the unpaid principal I owe at the monthly payment date in full on the maturity date in substantially equal payments. If so, each month that the amount of my monthly payment is less than the interest portion, the Note Holder will subtract the amount of my monthly payment from the amount of the interest portion and will add the difference to my unpaid principal. The Note Holder will also add interest on the amount of this difference to my unpaid principal each month. The interest rate on the interest added to principal will be the rate required by Section 2 or 4 (A) above.

(B) Limit on My Unpaid Principal

My unpaid principal can never exceed a maximum amount equal to one hundred twenty-five percent (125%) of the principal amount I originally borrowed.

9. NOTICE OF CHANGES

The Note Holder will deliver or mail to me a notice of any changes in my interest rate and in the amount of my monthly payment before the effective date of any change. The notice will include information required by law to be given me and also the title and telephone number of a person who will answer any question I may have regarding the notice.

10. BORROWER'S RIGHT TO PREPAY

I have the right to make payments of principal at any time before they are due. A payment of principal only is known as a "prepayment." When I make a prepayment, I will tell the Note Holder in writing that I am doing so.

I may make a full prepayment or a partial prepayment without paying any prepayment charge. The Note Holder will use all of my prepayments to reduce the amount of principal that I owe under this Note. If I make a partial prepayment, there will be no delays in the due dates of my monthly payments unless the Note Holder agrees in writing to those delays. My partial prepayment may reduce the amount of my monthly payments after the first Interest Change Date following my partial prepayment. However, any reduction due to my partial prepayment may be offset by an interest rate increase or an addition to the unpaid principal.

11. LOAN CHARGES

If a law, which applies to this loan and which sets maximum loan charges, is finally interpreted so that the interest or other loan charges collected or to be collected in connection with this loan exceed the permitted limits, then: (i) any such loan charge shall be reduced by the amount necessary to reduce the charge to the permitted limit; and (ii) any sums already collected from me which exceeded permitted limits will be refunded to me. The Note Holder may choose to make this refund by reducing the principal I owe under this Note or by making a direct payment to me. If a refund reduces principal, the reduction will be treated as a partial prepayment.

12. BORROWER'S FAILURE TO PAY AS REQUIRED

(A) Late Charge for Overdue Payments

If the Note Holder has not received the full amount of any of my monthly payments by the end of .... calendar days after the date it is due, I will pay a late charge to the Note Holder. The amount of the charge will be ....% of my overdue payment of principal and interest. I will pay this late charge promptly but only once on any late payment.

(B) Default

If I do not pay the full amount of each monthly payment on the date it is due, I will be in default.

(C) Notice of Default

If I am in default, the Note Holder may send me a written notice telling me that if I do not pay the overdue amount by a certain date, the Note Holder may require me to pay immediately the full amount of principal which has not been paid and all the interest that I owe on that amount. That date must be at least 30 days after the date on which the notice is delivered or mailed to me.

Figure 10–19.   Fannie Mae Graduated Payment Note (3-year index), page 3

(D) No Waiver By Note Holder

Even if, at a time when I am in default, the Note Holder does not require me to pay immediately in full as described above, the Note Holder will still have the right to do so if I am in default at a later time.

(E) Payment of Note Holder's Costs and Expenses

If the Note Holder has required me to pay immediately in full as described above, the Note Holder will have the right to be paid back by me for all of its costs and expenses in enforcing this Note to the extent not prohibited by applicable law. Those expenses include, for example, reasonable attorneys' fees.

13. GIVING OF NOTICES

Unless applicable law requires a different method, any notice that must be given to me under this Note will be given by delivering it or by mailing it by first class mail to me at the Property Address above or at a different address if I give the Note Holder a notice of my different address.

Any notice that must be given to the Note Holder under this Note will be given by mailing it by first class mail to the Note Holder at the address stated in Section 3 above or at a different address if I am given a notice of that different address.

14. OBLIGATIONS OF PERSONS UNDER THIS NOTE

If more than one person signs this Note, each person is fully and personally obligated to keep all of the promises made in this Note, including the promise to pay the full amount owed. Any person who is a guarantor, surety, or endorser of this Note is also obligated to do these things. Any person who takes over these obligations, including the obligations of a guarantor, surety, or endorser of this Note, is also obligated to keep all of the promises made in this Note. The Note Holder may enforce its rights under this Note against each person individually or against all of us together. This means that any one of us may be required to pay all of the amounts owed under this Note.

15. WAIVERS

I and any other person who has obligations under this Note waive notice of intention to accelerate, except as provided in Section 12 (C) above, and the rights of presentment and notice of dishonor. "Presentment" means the right to require the Note Holder to demand payment of amounts due. "Notice of dishonor" means the right to require the Note Holder to give notice to other persons that amounts due have not been paid.

16. UNIFORM SECURED NOTE

This Note is a uniform instrument with limited variations in some jurisdictions. In addition to the protections given to the Note Holder under this Note, a Mortgage, Deed of Trust, or Security Deed (the "Security Instrument"), dated the same date as this Note, protects the Note Holder from possible losses which might result if I do not keep the promises which I make in this Note. That Security Instrument describes how and under what conditions I may be required to make immediate payment in full of all amounts I owe under this Note. Some of those conditions are described as follows:

Transfer of the Property or a Beneficial Interest in Borrower. If all or any part of the Property or any interest in it is sold or transferred (or if a beneficial interest in Borrower is sold or transferred and Borrower is not a natural person) without Lender's prior written consent, Lender may, at its option, require immediate payment in full of all sums secured by this Security Instrument. However, this option shall not be exercised by Lender if exercise is prohibited by federal law as of the date of this Security Instrument. Lender also shall not exercise this option if: (a) Borrower causes to be submitted to Lender information required by Lender to evaluate the intended transferee as if a new loan were being made to the transferee; and (b) Lender reasonably determines that Lender's security will not be impaired by the loan assumption and that the risk of a breach of any covenant or agreement in this Security Instrument is acceptable to Lender.

To the extent permitted by applicable law, Lender may charge a reasonable fee as a condition to Lender's consent to the loan assumption. Lender may also require the transferee to sign an assumption agreement that is acceptable to Lender and that obligates the transferee to keep all the promises and agree-ments made in the Note and in this Security Instrument. Borrower will continue to be obligated under the Note and this Security Instrument unless Lender releases Borrower in writing.

If Lender exercises the option to require immediate payment in full, Lender shall give Borrower notice of acceleration. The notice shall provide a period of not less than 30 days from the date the notice is delivered or mailed within which Borrower must pay all sums secured by this Security Instrument. If Borrower fails to pay these sums prior to the expiration of this period, Lender may invoke any remedies permitted by this Security Instrument without further notice or demand on Borrower.

WITNESS THE HAND(S) AND SEAL(S) OF THE UNDERSIGNED.

....(Seal)
                                                                        -Borrower

....(Seal)
                                                                        -Borrower

....(Seal)
                                                                        -Borrower

[Sign Original Only]

Figure 10–20.   Fannie Mae Graduated Payment Note (5-year index), page 1

GRADUATED PAYMENT NOTE
(5 Year Index — Payment Cap)

This Note contains provisions allowing for changes in my interest rate and monthly payments. I may limit my monthly payment increases to 7½% each year if the provisions of this Note permit me to do so.

The principal amount I must repay will be larger than the amount I originally borrowed, but not more than 125% of the original amount.

...., 19 ...., Texas
                                                                                          |City|

....
                                        |Property Address|

1. BORROWER'S PROMISE TO PAY

In return for a loan that I have received, I promise to pay U.S. $... plus any amounts added in accordance with Section 8 (A) below (the total amount is called "principal"), plus interest, to the order of the Lender. The Lender is..

.... I understand that the Lender may transfer this Note. The Lender or anyone who takes this Note by transfer and who is entitled to receive payments under this Note is called the "Note Holder."

2. INTEREST

(A) Interest Owed

Interest will be charged on unpaid principal until the full amount of principal has been paid. I will owe interest at a yearly rate of ....%. The interest rate I will pay will change in accordance with Section 4 (A) below on the first day of ...., 19 .... and on that day every 60th month thereafter. Each date on which my interest rate could change is called an "Interest Change Date."

(B) The Index

Beginning with the first Interest Change Date, my interest rate will be based on an Index. The "Index" is the weekly average yield on United States Treasury securities adjusted to a constant maturity of 5 years, as made available by the Federal Reserve Board. The most recent Index figure available as of the date 45 days before each Interest Change Date is called the "Current Index."

If the Index is no longer available, the Note Holder will choose a new index which is based upon comparable information. The Note Holder will give me notice of this choice.

(C) Interest After Default

The interest rate required by this Section 2 or Section 4 (A) below is the rate I will pay both before and after any default described in Section 12 (B) below.

3. TIME AND PLACE OF PAYMENTS

I will pay principal and interest by making payments every month.

I will make my monthly payments on the first day of each month beginning on ...., 19 ...... I will make these payments every month until I have paid all of the principal and interest and any other charges described below that I may owe under this Note. My monthly payments will be applied to interest before principal. If, on ...., ..., I still owe amounts under this Note, I will pay those amounts in full on that date, which is called the "maturity date."

I will make my monthly payments at ....

....

or at a different place if required by the Note Holder.

4. INTEREST RATE CHANGES AND FULL PAYMENT

(A) Calculation of New Interest Rate and Full Payment

Each of my first .... monthly payments could be less than a Full Payment. A "Full Payment" is the monthly amount sufficient to repay the amount I originally borrowed, or the unpaid principal balance of my loan as of an Interest Change Date, in full on the maturity date at the interest rate I am required to pay by Section 2 above or this Section 4 (A) in substantially equal payments. Beginning on the date of this Note, my first Full Payment will be U.S. $ .... until the first Interest Change Date.

Before each Interest Change Date, the Note Holder will determine a new Full Payment for my loan. The Note Holder will first calculate my new interest rate by adding .... percentage points (............%) to the Current Index. The Note Holder will then round the result of this addition to the nearest one-eighth of one percentage point (0.125%). This rounded amount will be my new interest rate until the next Interest Change Date. The Note Holder will then determine the amount of the monthly payment that would be sufficient to repay the unpaid principal that I am expected to owe on the Interest Change Date in full on the maturity date at my new interest rate in substantially equal payments. The result of this calculation is my new Full Payment.

Each new interest rate will become effective on each Interest Change Date, and each new Full Payment will become effective on the first monthly payment after the Interest Change Date.

(B) Required Full Payment

I will pay the Full Payment as my monthly payment beginning with my .... monthly payment unless I choose to limit the amount of my monthly payment as permitted by Section 6 (A) below.

5. GRADUATED MONTHLY PAYMENTS

My first .... monthly payments will each be in the amount of U.S. $... On ...., 19 ...., and on each of the first three anniversaries of that date, I will begin paying a new monthly payment which will be equal to the amount I have been paying multiplied by the number 1.075. I

TEXAS GRADUATED PAYMENT NOTE—5 Year Treasury Index—Single Family**—FNMA Uniform Instrument**   Form 3705.44 12/83

Figure 10–21.   Fannie Mae Graduated Payment Note (5-year index), page 2

will pay the new amount of my monthly payment until it changes in accordance with this Section 5, Section 4 (B) above or Section 6 or 7 below.

6. BORROWER'S RIGHT TO LIMIT MONTHLY PAYMENT

    (A) Calculation of Graduated Limited Payment

    I may choose to limit the amount of my new monthly payment following an Interest Change Date if my new interest rate would cause the monthly payment I have been paying to increase by more than seven and one-half percent (7.5%). **If I choose to limit the amount of my monthly payment, I must give the Note Holder notice that I am doing so at least 15 days before my first new monthly payment is due.** When I do so, on the first monthly payment date after the Interest Change Date I will begin paying a new monthly payment which will be equal to the amount I have been paying each month for the preceding twelve months multiplied by the number 1.075. Thereafter, on each of the first four anniversaries of the new monthly payment effective date, my monthly payment will again increase to an amount equal to the amount I have been paying each month for the preceding twelve months multiplied by the number 1.075. These amounts are called the "Graduated Limited Payments."

    Even if I have chosen to limit my monthly payment, Section 6 (B), 6 (C) or 7 below may require me to pay a different amount.

    (B) Reduced Monthly Payment

    My Graduated Limited Payment could be greater than the amount of a monthly payment which then would be sufficient to repay my unpaid principal balance in full on the maturity date at my current interest rate in substantially equal payments. If so, on the date my paying a Graduated Limited Payment would cause me to pay more than the lower amount, I will instead then begin paying the lower amount as my monthly payment until the next Interest Change Date.

    (C) Increased Monthly Payment

    My paying a Graduated Limited Payment could cause my unpaid principal to exceed the limit stated in Section 8 (B) below. If so, on the date that my paying a monthly payment would cause me to exceed that limit, I will instead begin paying a new monthly payment until the next Interest Change Date. The new monthly payment will be in an amount which would be sufficient to repay my then unpaid principal balance in full on the maturity date at my current interest rate in substantially equal payments.

7. FINAL MONTHLY PAYMENTS

    Beginning with the first monthly payment after the final Interest Change Date, I will pay the Full Payment as my monthly payment.

8. INCREASES IN THE PRINCIPAL AMOUNT TO BE PAID

    (A) Additions to My Unpaid Principal

    My monthly payment could be less than the amount of the interest portion of the monthly payment that would be sufficient to repay the unpaid principal in full on the maturity date in substantially equal payments. If so, each month that the amount of my monthly payment is less than the interest portion, the Note Holder will subtract the amount of my monthly payment from the amount of the interest portion and will add the difference to my unpaid principal. The Note Holder will also add interest on the amount of this difference to my unpaid principal each month. The interest rate on the interest added to principal will be the rate required by Section 2 or 4 (A) above.

    (B) Limit on My Unpaid Principal

    My unpaid principal can never exceed a maximum amount equal to one hundred twenty-five percent (125%) of the principal amount I originally borrowed.

9. NOTICE OF CHANGES

    The Note Holder will deliver or mail to me a notice of any changes in my interest rate and in the amount of my monthly payment before the effective date of any change. The notice will include information required by law to be given me and also the title and telephone number of a person who will answer any question I may have regarding the notice.

10. BORROWER'S RIGHT TO PREPAY

    I have the right to make payments of principal at any time before they are due. A payment of principal only is known as a "prepayment." When I make a prepayment, I will tell the Note Holder in writing that I am doing so.

    I may make a full prepayment or a partial prepayment without paying any prepayment charge. The Note Holder will use all of my prepayments to reduce the amount of principal that I owe under this Note. If I make a partial prepayment, there will be no delays in the due dates of my monthly payments unless the Note Holder agrees in writing to those delays. My partial prepayment may reduce the amount of my monthly payments after the first Interest Change Date following my partial prepayment. However, any reduction due to my partial prepayment may be offset by an interest rate increase or an addition to the unpaid principal.

11. LOAN CHARGES

    If a law, which applies to this loan and which sets maximum loan charges, is finally interpreted so that the interest or other loan charges collected or to be collected in connection with this loan exceed the permitted limits, then: (i) any such loan charge shall be reduced by the amount necessary to reduce the charge to the permitted limit; and (ii) any sums already collected from me which exceeded permitted limits will be refunded to me. The Note Holder may choose to make this refund by reducing the principal I owe under this Note or by making a direct payment to me. If a refund reduces principal, the reduction will be treated as a partial prepayment.

12. BORROWER'S FAILURE TO PAY AS REQUIRED

    (A) Late Charge for Overdue Payments

    If the Note Holder has not received the full amount of any of my monthly payments by the end of .... calendar days after the date it is due, I will pay a late charge to the Note Holder. The amount of the charge will be .... % of my overdue payment of principal and interest. I will pay this late charge promptly but only once on any late payment.

    (B) Default

    If I do not pay the full amount of each monthly payment on the date it is due, I will be in default.

    (C) Notice of Default

    If I am in default, the Note Holder may send me a written notice telling me that if I do not pay the overdue amount by a certain date, the Note Holder may require me to pay immediately the full amount of principal which has not been paid and all the interest that I owe on that amount. That date must be at least 30 days after the date on which the notice is delivered or mailed to me.

*Figure 10–22.   **Fannie Mae Graduated Payment Note (5-year index), page 3***

(D) No Waiver By Note Holder

Even if, at a time when I am in default, the Note Holder does not require me to pay immediately in full as described above, the Note Holder will still have the right to do so if I am in default at a later time.

(E) Payment of Note Holder's Costs and Expenses

If the Note Holder has required me to pay immediately in full as described above, the Note Holder will have the right to be paid back by me for all of its costs and expenses in enforcing this Note to the extent not prohibited by applicable law. Those expenses include, for example, reasonable attorneys' fees.

13. GIVING OF NOTICES

Unless applicable law requires a different method, any notice that must be given to me under this Note will be given by delivering it or by mailing it by first class mail to me at the Property Address above or at a different address if I give the Note Holder a notice of my different address.

Any notice that must be given to the Note Holder under this Note will be given by mailing it by first class mail to the Note Holder at the address stated in Section 3 above or at a different address if I am given a notice of that different address.

14. OBLIGATIONS OF PERSONS UNDER THIS NOTE

If more than one person signs this Note, each person is fully and personally obligated to keep all of the promises made in this Note, including the promise to pay the full amount owed. Any person who is a guarantor, surety, or endorser of this Note is also obligated to do these things. Any person who takes over these obligations, including the obligations of a guarantor, surety, or endorser of this Note, is also obligated to keep all of the promises made in this Note. The Note Holder may enforce its rights under this Note against each person individually or against all of us together. This means that any one of us may be required to pay all of the amounts owed under this Note.

15. WAIVERS

I and any other person who has obligations under this Note waive notice of intention to accelerate, except as provided in Section 12 (C) above, and the rights of presentment and notice of dishonor. "Presentment" means the right to require the Note Holder to demand payment of amounts due. "Notice of dishonor" means the right to require the Note Holder to give notice to other persons that amounts due have not been paid.

16. UNIFORM SECURED NOTE

This Note is a uniform instrument with limited variations in some jurisdictions. In addition to the protections given to the Note Holder under this Note, a Mortgage, Deed of Trust, or Security Deed (the "Security Instrument"), dated the same date as this Note, protects the Note Holder from possible losses which might result if I do not keep the promises which I make in this Note. That Security Instrument describes how and under what conditions I may be required to make immediate payment in full of all amounts I owe under this Note. Some of those conditions are described as follows:

Transfer of the Property or a Beneficial Interest in Borrower. If all or any part of the Property or any interest in it is sold or transferred (or if a beneficial interest in Borrower is sold or transferred and Borrower is not a natural person) without Lender's prior written consent, Lender may, at its option, require immediate payment in full of all sums secured by this Security Instrument. However, this option shall not be exercised by Lender if exercise is prohibited by federal law as of the date of this Security Instrument. Lender also shall not exercise this option if: (a) Borrower causes to be submitted to Lender information required by Lender to evaluate the intended transferee as if a new loan were being made to the transferee; and (b) Lender reasonably determines that Lender's security will not be impaired by the loan assumption and that the risk of a breach of any covenant or agreement in this Security Instrument is acceptable to Lender.

To the extent permitted by applicable law, Lender may charge a reasonable fee as a condition to Lender's consent to the loan assumption. Lender may also require the transferee to sign an assumption agreement that is acceptable to Lender and that obligates the transferee to keep all the promises and agreements made in the Note and in this Security Instrument. Borrower will continue to be obligated under the Note and this Security Instrument unless Lender releases Borrower in writing.

If Lender exercises the option to require immediate payment in full, Lender shall give Borrower notice of acceleration. The notice shall provide a period of not less than 30 days from the date the notice is delivered or mailed within which Borrower must pay all sums secured by this Security Instrument. If Borrower fails to pay these sums prior to the expiration of this period, Lender may invoke any remedies permitted by this Security Instrument without further notice or demand on Borrower.

WITNESS THE HAND(S) AND SEAL(S) OF THE UNDERSIGNED.

....(Seal)
                                                                                   -Borrower

....(Seal)
                                                                                   -Borrower

....(Seal)
                                                                                   -Borrower

[Sign Original Only]

Figure 10-23. Fannie Mae/FHLMC Adjustable Rate Rider (1-year index), page 1

ADJUSTABLE RATE RIDER
(1 Year Index—Payment Cap)

THIS ADJUSTABLE RATE RIDER is made this .... day of .... , 19 .... , and is incorporated into and shall be deemed to amend and supplement the Mortgage, Deed of Trust or Security Deed (the "Security Instrument") of the same date given by the undersigned (the "Borrower") to secure Borrower's Adjustable Rate Note (the "Note") to .... (the "Lender") of the same date and covering the property described in the Security Instrument and located at:

....
[Property Address]

THE NOTE CONTAINS PROVISIONS ALLOWING FOR CHANGES IN THE INTEREST RATE AND THE MONTHLY PAYMENT. THE BORROWER MAY LIMIT MONTHLY PAYMENT INCREASES TO 7½% EACH YEAR IF THE PROVISIONS OF THE NOTE PERMIT IT.

ADDITIONAL COVENANTS. In addition to the covenants and agreements made in the Security Instrument, Borrower and Lender further covenant and agree as follows:

A. INTEREST RATE AND MONTHLY PAYMENT CHANGES

The Note provides for an initial interest rate of .... %. The Note provides for changes in the interest rate and the monthly payments, as follows:

4. INTEREST RATE AND MONTHLY PAYMENT CHANGES; BORROWER'S RIGHT TO LIMIT PAYMENT

(A) Change Dates

The interest rate I will pay may change on the first day of .... , 19 .... , and on that day every 12th month thereafter. Each date on which my interest rate could change is called a "Change Date."

(B) The Index

Beginning with the first Change Date, my interest rate will be based on an Index. The "Index" is the weekly average yield on United States Treasury securities adjusted to a constant maturity of 1 year, as made available by the Federal Reserve Board. The most recent Index figure available as of the date 45 days before each Change Date is called the "Current Index."

If the Index is no longer available, the Note Holder will choose a new index which is based upon comparable information. The Note Holder will give me notice of this choice.

(C) Calculation of Changes

Before each Change Date, the Note Holder will calculate my new interest rate by adding .... percentage points (................. %) to the Current Index. The Note Holder will then round the result of this addition to the nearest one-eighth of one percentage point (0.125%). This rounded amount will be my new interest rate until the next Change Date.

The Note Holder will then determine the amount of the monthly payment that would be sufficient to repay the unpaid principal that I am expected to owe at the Change Date in full on the maturity date at my new interest rate in substantially equal payments. The result of this calculation is called the "Full Payment." It will be the new amount of my monthly payment unless I choose the amount permitted by Section 4(F) below.

(D) Effective Date of Changes

My new interest rate will become effective on each Change Date. I will pay the amount of my new monthly payment beginning on the first monthly payment date after the Change Date until the amount of my monthly payment changes again.

(E) Notice of Changes

The Note Holder will deliver or mail to me a notice of any changes in my interest rate and the amount of my monthly payment before the effective date of any change. The notice will include information required by law to be given me and also the title and telephone number of a person who will answer any question I may have regarding the notice.

(F) Borrower's Right to Limit Monthly Payment

Unless Sections 4(H) and 4(I) below will not permit me to do so, I may choose to limit the amount of my new monthly payment following a Change Date to the amount I have been paying multiplied by the number 1.075. This amount is called the "Limited Payment." **If I choose a Limited Payment as my monthly payment, I must give the Note Holder notice that I am doing so at least 15 days before my first new monthly payment is due.**

(G) Additions to My Unpaid Principal

If I choose to pay the Limited Payment, my monthly payment could be less than the amount of the interest portion of the monthly payment that would be sufficient to repay the unpaid principal I owe at the monthly payment date in full on the maturity date in substantially equal payments. If so, each month that the Limited Payment is less than the interest portion, the Note Holder will subtract the Limited Payment from the amount of the interest portion

MULTISTATE ADJUSTABLE RATE RIDER—1 Year Treasury Index—Single Family—**FNMA/FHLMC Uniform Instrument**   Form 3101 12/83

Figure 10–24.   Fannie Mae/FHLMC Adjustable Rate Rider (1-year index), page 2

and will add the difference to my unpaid principal. The Note Holder will also add interest on the amount of this difference to my unpaid principal each month. The interest rate on the interest added to principal will be the rate required by Section 4(C) above.

(H) Limit on My Unpaid Principal; Increased Monthly Payment

My unpaid principal can never exceed a maximum amount equal to one hundred twenty-five percent (125%) of the principal amount I originally borrowed. My unpaid principal could exceed that maximum amount if I pay a Limited Payment. If so, on the date that my paying my Limited Payment would cause me to exceed that limit, I will instead begin paying a new monthly payment until the next Change Date. The new monthly payment will be in an amount which would be sufficient to repay my then unpaid principal in full on the maturity date at my current interest rate in substantially equal payments.

(I) Required Full Payment

Beginning with the first monthly payment after the final Change Date, I will pay the Full Payment as my monthly payment.

B. TRANSFER OF THE PROPERTY OR A BENEFICIAL INTEREST IN BORROWER

Uniform Covenant 17 of the Security Instrument is amended to read as follows:

Transfer of the Property or a Beneficial Interest in Borrower. If all or any part of the Property or any interest in it is sold or transferred (or if a beneficial interest in Borrower is sold or transferred and Borrower is not a natural person) without Lender's prior written consent, Lender may, at its option, require immediate payment in full of all sums secured by this Security Instrument. However, this option shall not be exercised by Lender if exercise is prohibited by federal law as of the date of this Security Instrument. Lender also shall not exercise this option if: (a) Borrower causes to be submitted to Lender information required by Lender to evaluate the intended transferee as if a new loan were being made to the transferee; and (b) Lender reasonably determines that Lender's security will not be impaired by the loan assumption and that the risk of a breach of any covenant or agreement in this Security Instrument is acceptable to Lender.

To the extent permitted by applicable law, Lender may charge a reasonable fee as a condition to Lender's consent to the loan assumption. Lender may also require the transferee to sign an assumption agreement that is acceptable to Lender and that obligates the transferee to keep all the promises and agreements made in the Note and in this Security Instrument. Borrower will continue to be obligated under the Note and this Security Instrument unless Lender releases Borrower in writing.

If Lender exercises the option to require immediate payment in full, Lender shall give Borrower notice of acceleration. The notice shall provide a period of not less than 30 days from the date the notice is delivered or mailed within which Borrower must pay all sums secured by this Security Instrument. If Borrower fails to pay these sums prior to the expiration of this period, Lender may invoke any remedies permitted by this Security Instrument without further notice or demand on Borrower.

BY SIGNING BELOW, Borrower accepts and agrees to the terms and covenants contained in this Adjustable Rate Rider.

....(Seal)
                                                                                    -Borrower

....(Seal)
                                                                                    -Borrower

Figure 10–25.   Fannie Mae/FHLMC Adjustable Rate Rider (3-year index), page 1

ADJUSTABLE RATE RIDER
(3 Year Index—Payment Cap)

THIS ADJUSTABLE RATE RIDER is made this .... day of .... , 19 .... , and is incorporated into and shall be deemed to amend and supplement the Mortgage, Deed of Trust or Security Deed (the "Security Instrument") of the same date given by the undersigned (the "Borrower") to secure Borrower's Adjustable Rate Note (the "Note") to ....
.... (the "Lender") of the same date and covering the property described in the Security Instrument and located at:

....
[Property Address]

THE NOTE CONTAINS PROVISIONS ALLOWING FOR CHANGES IN THE INTEREST RATE AND THE MONTHLY PAYMENT. THE BORROWER MAY LIMIT MONTHLY PAYMENT INCREASES TO 7½% EACH YEAR IF THE PROVISIONS OF THE NOTE PERMIT IT.

ADDITIONAL COVENANTS. In addition to the covenants and agreements made in the Security Instrument, Borrower and Lender further covenant and agree as follows:

A. INTEREST RATE AND MONTHLY PAYMENT CHANGES

The Note provides for an initial interest rate of .... %. The Note provides for changes in the interest rate and the monthly payments, as follows:

4.   INTEREST RATE AND MONTHLY PAYMENT CHANGES

(A) Change Dates

The interest rate I will pay may change on the first day of .... , 19 .... , and on that day every 36th month thereafter. Each date on which my interest rate could change is called a "Change Date."

(B) The Index

Beginning with the first Change Date, my interest rate will be based on an Index. The "Index" is the weekly average yield on United States Treasury securities adjusted to a constant maturity of 3 years, as made available by the Federal Reserve Board. The most recent Index figure available as of the date 45 days before each Change Date is called the "Current Index."

If the Index is no longer available, the Note Holder will choose a new index which is based upon comparable information. The Note Holder will give me notice of this choice.

(C) Calculation of Changes

Before each Change Date, the Note Holder will calculate my new interest rate by adding ....
.... percentage points (.................%) to the Current Index. The Note Holder will then round the result of this addition to the nearest one-eighth of one percentage point (0.125%). This rounded amount will be my new interest rate until the next Change Date.

The Note Holder will then determine the amount of the monthly payment that would be sufficient to repay the unpaid principal that I am expected to owe at the Change Date in full on the maturity date at my new interest rate in substantially equal payments. The result of this calculation is called the "Full Payment." It will be the new amount of my monthly payment unless I choose the amount permitted by Section 5 below.

(D) Effective Date of Changes

My new interest rate will become effective on each Change Date. I will pay the amount of my new monthly payment beginning on the first monthly payment date after the Change Date until the amount of my monthly payment changes again.

5.   BORROWER'S RIGHT TO LIMIT MONTHLY PAYMENT; REQUIRED FULL PAYMENT

(A) Calculation of Graduated Limited Payment

I may choose to limit the amount of my new monthly payment following a Change Date if my new interest rate would cause the monthly payment I have been paying to increase by more than seven and one-half percent (7.5%). **If I choose to limit the amount of my monthly payment, I must give the Note Holder notice that I am doing so at least 15 days before my first new monthly payment is due.** When I do so, on the first monthly payment date after the Change Date I will begin paying a new monthly payment which will be equal to the amount I have been paying each month for the preceding twelve months multiplied by the number 1.075. Thereafter, on each of the first two anniversaries of my new monthly payment effective date, my monthly payment will again increase to an amount equal to the amount I have been paying each month for the preceding twelve months multiplied by the number 1.075. These amounts are called the "Graduated Limited Payments."

Even if I have chosen to limit my monthly payment, Section 5(B), 5(C) or 5(D) below may require me to pay a different amount.

(B) Reduced Monthly Payment

A Graduated Limited Payment could be greater than the amount of a monthly payment which then would be sufficient to repay my unpaid principal in full on the maturity date at my current interest rate in substantially equal

MULTISTATE ADJUSTABLE RATE RIDER—3 Year Treasury Index—Single Family—**FNMA/FHLMC Uniform Instrument**   Form 3103 12/83

Figure 10–26.   Fannie Mae/FHLMC Adjustable Rate Rider (3-year index), page 2

payments. If so, on the date my paying a Graduated Limited Payment would cause me to pay more than the lower amount, I will instead then begin paying the lower amount as my monthly payment until the next Change Date.

(C) Increased Monthly Payment

My paying a Graduated Limited Payment could cause my unpaid principal to exceed the limit stated in Section 6(B) below. If so, on the date that my paying my monthly payment would cause me to exceed that limit, I will instead begin paying a new monthly payment until the next Change Date. The new monthly payment will be in an amount which would be sufficient to repay my then unpaid principal in full on the maturity date at my current interest rate in substantially equal payments.

(D) Required Full Payment

Beginning with the first monthly payment after the final Change Date, I will pay the Full Payment as my monthly payment.

6. INCREASES IN THE PRINCIPAL AMOUNT TO BE PAID

(A) Additions to My Unpaid Principal

If I choose to pay Graduated Limited Payments, my monthly payment could be less than the amount of the interest portion of the monthly payment that would be sufficient to repay the unpaid principal I owe at the monthly payment date in full on the maturity date in substantially equal payments. If so, each month that the amount of my monthly payment is less than the interest portion, the Note Holder will subtract the amount of my monthly payment from the amount of the interest portion and will add the difference to my unpaid principal. The Note Holder will also add interest on the amount of this difference to my unpaid principal each month. The interest rate on the interest added to principal will be the rate required by Section 4(C) above.

(B) Limit on My Unpaid Principal

My unpaid principal can never exceed a maximum amount equal to one hundred twenty-five percent (125%) of the principal amount I originally borrowed.

7. NOTICE OF CHANGES

The Note Holder will deliver or mail to me a notice of any changes in my interest rate and the amount of my monthly payment before the effective date of any change. The notice will include information required by law to be given me and also the title and telephone number of a person who will answer any question I may have regarding the notice.

B. TRANSFER OF THE PROPERTY OR A BENEFICIAL INTEREST IN BORROWER

Uniform Covenant 17 of the Security Instrument is amended to read as follows:

Transfer of the Property or a Beneficial Interest in Borrower. If all or any part of the Property or any interest in it is sold or transferred (or if a beneficial interest in Borrower is sold or transferred and Borrower is not a natural person) without Lender's prior written consent, Lender may, at its option, require immediate payment in full of all sums secured by this Security Instrument. However, this option shall not be exercised by Lender if exercise is prohibited by federal law as of the date of this Security Instrument. Lender also shall not exercise this option if: (a) Borrower causes to be submitted to Lender information required by Lender to evaluate the intended transferee as if a new loan were being made to the transferee; and (b) Lender reasonably determines that Lender's security will not be impaired by the loan assumption and that the risk of a breach of any covenant or agreement in this Security Instrument is acceptable to Lender.

To the extent permitted by applicable law, Lender may charge a reasonable fee as a condition to Lender's consent to the loan assumption. Lender may also require the transferee to sign an assumption agreement that is acceptable to Lender and that obligates the transferee to keep all the promises and agreements made in the Note and in this Security Instrument. Borrower will continue to be obligated under the Note and this Security Instrument unless Lender releases Borrower in writing.

If Lender exercises the option to require immediate payment in full, Lender shall give Borrower notice of acceleration. The notice shall provide a period of not less than 30 days from the date the notice is delivered or mailed within which Borrower must pay all sums secured by this Security Instrument. If Borrower fails to pay these sums prior to the expiration of this period, Lender may invoke any remedies permitted by this Security Instrument without further notice or demand on Borrower.

BY SIGNING BELOW, Borrower accepts and agrees to the terms and covenants contained in this Adjustable Rate Rider.

....(Seal)
　　　　　　　　　　　　　　　　　　　　　　　　　　　　　-Borrower

....(Seal)
　　　　　　　　　　　　　　　　　　　　　　　　　　　　　-Borrower

Figure 10–27.   Fannie Mae/FHLMC Adjustable Rate Rider (5-year index), page 1

ADJUSTABLE RATE RIDER
(5 Year Index—Payment Cap)

THIS ADJUSTABLE RATE RIDER is made this .... day of .... , 19 .... , and is incorporated into and shall be deemed to amend and supplement the Mortgage, Deed of Trust or Security Deed (the "Security Instrument") of the same date given by the undersigned (the "Borrower") to secure Borrower's Adjustable Rate Note (the "Note") to ....
.... (the "Lender") of the same date and covering the property described in the Security Instrument and located at:

....
[Property Address]

THE NOTE CONTAINS PROVISIONS ALLOWING FOR CHANGES IN THE INTEREST RATE AND THE MONTHLY PAYMENT. THE BORROWER MAY LIMIT MONTHLY PAYMENT INCREASES TO 7½% EACH YEAR IF THE PROVISIONS OF THE NOTE PERMIT IT.

ADDITIONAL COVENANTS. In addition to the covenants and agreements made in the Security Instrument, Borrower and Lender further covenant and agree as follows:

A. INTEREST RATE AND MONTHLY PAYMENT CHANGES

The Note provides for an initial interest rate of .... %. The Note provides for changes in the interest rate and the monthly payments, as follows:

4. INTEREST RATE AND MONTHLY PAYMENT CHANGES

(A) Change Dates

The interest rate I will pay may change on the first day of .... , 19 .... , and on that day every 60th month thereafter. Each date on which my interest rate could change is called a "Change Date."

(B) The Index

Beginning with the first Change Date, my interest rate will be based on an Index. The "Index" is the weekly average yield on United States Treasury securities adjusted to a constant maturity of 5 years, as made available by the Federal Reserve Board. The most recent Index figure available as of the date 45 days before each Change Date is called the "Current Index."

If the Index is no longer available, the Note Holder will choose a new index which is based upon comparable information. The Note Holder will give me notice of this choice.

(C) Calculation of Changes

Before each Change Date, the Note Holder will calculate my new interest rate by adding ....
.... percentage points (................. %) to the Current Index. The Note Holder will then round the result of this addition to the nearest one-eighth of one percentage point (0.125%). This rounded amount will be my new interest rate until the next Change Date.

The Note Holder will then determine the amount of the monthly payment that would be sufficient to repay the unpaid principal that I am expected to owe at the Change Date in full on the maturity date at my new interest rate in substantially equal payments. The result of this calculation is called the "Full Payment." It will be the new amount of my monthly payment unless I choose the amount permitted by Section 5 below.

(D) Effective Date of Changes

My new interest rate will become effective on each Change Date. I will pay the amount of my new monthly payment beginning on the first monthly payment date after the Change Date until the amount of my monthly payment changes again.

5. BORROWER'S RIGHT TO LIMIT MONTHLY PAYMENT; REQUIRED FULL PAYMENT

(A) Calculation of Graduated Limited Payment

I may choose to limit the amount of my new monthly payment following a Change Date if my new interest rate would cause the monthly payment I have been paying to increase by more than seven and one-half percent (7.5%). **If I choose to limit the amount of my monthly payment, I must give the Note Holder notice that I am doing so at least 15 days before my first new monthly payment is due.** When I do so, on the first monthly payment date after the Change Date I will begin paying a new monthly payment which will be equal to the amount I have been paying each month for the preceding twelve months multiplied by the number 1.075. Thereafter, on each of the first four anniversaries of my new monthly payment effective date, my monthly payment will again increase to an amount equal to the amount I have been paying each month for the preceding twelve months multiplied by the number 1.075. These amounts are called the "Graduated Limited Payments."

Even if I have chosen to limit my monthly payment, Section 5(B), 5(C) or 5(D) below may require me to pay a different amount.

(B) Reduced Monthly Payment

A Graduated Limited Payment could be greater than the amount of a monthly payment which then would be sufficient to repay my unpaid principal in full on the maturity date at my current interest rate in substantially equal payments. If so, on the date my paying a Graduated Limited Payment would cause me to pay more than the lower amount, I will instead then begin paying the lower amount as my monthly payment until the next Change Date.

MULTISTATE ADJUSTABLE RATE RIDER—5 Year Treasury Index—Single Family—FNMA/FHLMC Uniform Instrument   Form 3105 12/83

Figure 10–28.   Fannie Mae/FHLMC Adjustable Rate Rider (5-year index), page 2

(C) Increased Monthly Payment

My paying a Graduated Limited Payment could cause my unpaid principal to exceed the limit stated in Section 6(B) below. If so, on the date that my paying my monthly payment would cause me to exceed that limit, I will instead begin paying a new monthly payment until the next Change Date. The new monthly payment will be in an amount which would be sufficient to repay my then unpaid principal in full on the maturity date at my current interest rate in substantially equal payments.

(D) Required Full Payment

Beginning with the first monthly payment after the final Change Date, I will pay the Full Payment as my monthly payment.

6.   INCREASES IN THE PRINCIPAL AMOUNT TO BE PAID

(A) Additions to My Unpaid Principal

If I choose to pay Graduated Limited Payments, my monthly payment could be less than the amount of the interest portion of the monthly payment that would be sufficient to repay the unpaid principal I owe at the monthly payment date in full on the maturity date in substantially equal payments. If so, each month that the amount of my monthly payment is less than the interest portion, the Note Holder will subtract the amount of my monthly payment from the amount of the interest portion and will add the difference to my unpaid principal. The Note Holder will also add interest on the amount of this difference to my unpaid principal each month. The interest rate on the interest added to principal will be the rate required by Section 4(C) above.

(B) Limit on My Unpaid Principal

My unpaid principal can never exceed a maximum amount equal to one hundred twenty-five percent (125%) of the principal amount I originally borrowed.

7.   NOTICE OF CHANGES

The Note Holder will deliver or mail to me a notice of any changes in my interest rate and the amount of my monthly payment before the effective date of any change. The notice will include information required by law to be given me and also the title and telephone number of a person who will answer any question I may have regarding the notice.

B. TRANSFER OF THE PROPERTY OR A BENEFICIAL INTEREST IN BORROWER

Uniform Covenant 17 of the Security Instrument is amended to read as follows:

Transfer of the Property or a Beneficial Interest in Borrower. If all or any part of the Property or any interest in it is sold or transferred (or if a beneficial interest in Borrower is sold or transferred and Borrower is not a natural person) without Lender's prior written consent, Lender may, at its option, require immediate payment in full of all sums secured by this Security Instrument. However, this option shall not be exercised by Lender if exercise is prohibited by federal law as of the date of this Security Instrument. Lender also shall not exercise this option if: (a) Borrower causes to be submitted to Lender information required by Lender to evaluate the intended transferee as if a new loan were being made to the transferee; and (b) Lender reasonably determines that Lender's security will not be impaired by the loan assumption and that the risk of a breach of any covenant or agreement in this Security Instrument is acceptable to Lender.

To the extent permitted by applicable law, Lender may charge a reasonable fee as a condition to Lender's consent to the loan assumption. Lender may also require the transferee to sign an assumption agreement that is acceptable to Lender and that obligates the transferee to keep all the promises and agreements made in the Note and in this Security Instrument. Borrower will continue to be obligated under the Note and this Security Instrument unless Lender releases Borrower in writing.

If Lender exercises the option to require immediate payment in full, Lender shall give Borrower notice of acceleration. The notice shall provide a period of not less than 30 days from the date the notice is delivered or mailed within which Borrower must pay all sums secured by this Security Instrument. If Borrower fails to pay these sums prior to the expiration of this period, Lender may invoke any remedies permitted by this Security Instrument without further notice or demand on Borrower.

BY SIGNING BELOW, Borrower accepts and agrees to the terms and covenants contained in this Adjustable Rate Rider.

....(Seal)
                                                                    -Borrower

....(Seal)
                                                                    -Borrower

those jurisdictions where real estate taxation is prohibited by law, Fannie Mae will consider submissions where the unit is taxed as personal property.

G. The Seller must obtain from the borrower, and retain in the loan file, a written "acknowledgement of intent" specifying that it is the borrower's intent that the unit be a fixture and part of the real property securing the mortgage. The form and content of this acknowledgement may be drafted by the Seller.[3]

There is no limitation regarding whether the home is a single-section or multi-section located on an individually owned lot, a leasehold estate that is acceptable to Fannie Mae, or in the case of a conventional mortgage, a lot in a subdivision, in an approved condominium project, PUD, or de minimus PUD. There are some limitations if the home is financed through VA or FHA: if the home is financed by FHA under Title I or guaranteed under the VA Mobile Home Program, the mortgage is not eligible for purchase.

On February 17, 1982, the Fannie Mae regional office in Dallas issued Circular Letter No. 82-1. This letter listed some additional program requirements. The major additional requirements concerned property guidelines. Some of the more important requirements are listed below:

1. The manufactured unit may be either a single-wide or double-wide, but a single-wide unit must be at least 12 feet wide and contain 700 square feet of living area.

2. Fannie Mae stated that only units built after June 15, 1976, will qualify as security for a mortgage to be sold to Fannie Mae.

3. In regard to the foundation for the unit, Fannie Mae has established the following guidelines:

    a. The foundation must be designed to the soil characteristics and sufficient to withstand wind loads of the individual site.

    b. Any foundation made from materials other than concrete or cement block must be approved by Fannie Mae.

4. Fannie Mae further requires that the manufactured property must be comparable to a house built on a standard lot in the local market place. According to Fannie Mae, this means that the units should have pitched roofs, covered front and rear entrances, in-place built steps and porches, and the exterior finish is to be either real or standard wood siding, stucco, brick, or a combination.

Prior to working with a client in your area, you should contact a Fannie Mae-approved lender for requirements in your area.

Energy Conservation Program

With Announcement 83-36, dated December 23, 1983, Fannie Mae made it easier for a homeowner to obtain financing for energy-efficient homes. Fannie Mae will purchase mortgages that include the cost of energy-saving components in the purchase price of the home. According to the Fannie Mae *Lending Guide,* section 423, lenders may include the actual cost of the improvements in the purchase price of the house, but there is a limit to the amount that may be included. The limit is 15 percent of the value of the property. Thus, if the property is valued at $65,500 the maximum that could be included would be $9825.

Eligible properties   Fannie Mae will purchase loans that are secured by 1- to 4-family properties that are older properties to be retrofitted, or new properties to be upgraded with energy saving features.

Delivery of loans to Fannie Mae   The lender has the option to sell and deliver the loans to Fannie Mae prior to the completion of the energy improvements or to wait until the improvements are complete.

If the lender opts to deliver the mortgage to Fannie Mae prior to the completion of the improvements, the lender will have to establish an *energy escrow account.* The lender will have the responsibility of managing the account and seeing that the improvements are completed 120 days after the closing of the loan.

Underwriting   It should be noted that the borrowers will be able to qualify for these mortgages with higher payment-to-income and debt-to-income ratios. The reason for the relaxing of the requirements is that less of the borrower's income will have to be used to pay utility bills.

Conventional Multifamily Purchase Program

On March 6, 1984, Fannie Mae announced the establishment of a conventional multifamily mortgage purchase program. This program is open to all lenders, but each lender in Texas must apply for approval by the Southwest Regional Office to sell or service the multifamily mortgages. According to the announcement, all multifamily mortgages sold under this program must be acceptable to other institutional lenders, as well as meeting other requirements.

Property qualifications   Each of the mortgages sold to Fannie Mae must be secured by a residential multifamily property. The property used as security must have five or more units. It should be noted that there is no maximum number of units for a project. There is a stipulation, however, that all of the units must be located on adjoining or contiguous property.

Repayment terms   Fannie Mae will only purchase multifamily mortgages with one of the following repayment terms.

Fixed-term mortgage – These are mortgages with a term of 15 years, but they will have a 10-year call option. The payments will be based on a 30-year amortization.

Balloon mortgages – These will be mortgages with a term of 3, 5, or 7 years, but the payments will be calculated on a different rate of amortization. This amortization term may be as long as 30 years.

Adjustable-rate mortgages – There are two ARMs authorized to be used in conjunction with this program and they are ARMs based on the 3- and 5-year Treasury securities. The borrower may opt for a 7.5 percent payment adjustment cap on either of the ARMs. Thus, there may be negative amortization; and if there is, the amount is limited to only 110 percent of the original principal balance. The term of the ARMs is 30 years with a call option in the 15th year.

Loan-to-value ratio   According to the announcement, the loan-to-value ratio cannot exceed 80 percent of the appraised value of the property.

Maximum loan amount   The maximum loan per unit is based on the number of bedrooms per unit. The maximum loan amounts for nonelevator structures are listed below:

Number of bedrooms	Maximum loan amount
0	$24,375
1	$27,000
2	$32,250
3	$39,750
4	$45,000

These are a few of the major requirements of this new program. Contact the Southwest Regional Office to secure the names of lenders in your area that are approved to participate in the program.

Due-On-Sale Enforcement

Before we conclude the discussion of the mortgage purchase programs of Fannie Mae, there should be a quick review of the due-on-sale policy of Fannie Mae. The policy is best summed up by the Fannie Mae Announcement, 83-04, dated February 15, 1983. According to this announcement, upon any transfer of property ownership on or after April 20, 1983, Fannie Mae will call conventional, fixed-rate, first and second mortgages due and payable. The announcement states that this policy applies to whole mortgages, mortgages purchased by Fannie Mae under a participation agreement with nonsupervised lenders, and any portfolio loans Fannie Mae has sold under a participation agreement. Also this policy applies to any mortgage or mortgages that were transferred from Fannie Mae's portfolio to form mortgage-backed securities.

The announcement further states that ARMs may be assumed on the existing loan contract terms so long as the assumptor or buyer is creditworthy; but if the assumptor's or buyer's credit is not satisfactory, and the ownership in the property is transferred, the debt will be accelerated.

In addition, the announcement states there are certain exceptions to this policy and the exceptions are as follows:

1. Mortgages Fannie Mae purchased under participation agreements with a supervised lender, such as a bank or savings and loan associations, for these lenders will continue to be subject to the due-on-sale policy of the supervisory agency.

2. Fannie Mae will continue to allow an assumption of all mortgages they own that were purchased under commitment dated prior to November 10, 1980, with exception. The exception is if the transferred property is financed, directly or indirectly, with a

wraparound or secondary financing from any institutional lender.

3. Any Fannie Mae resale/refinance mortgage may be assumed with the original contract terms for 1 year after the loan is closed, but the person or persons assuming the loan will be subject to credit check. The assumption must be closed 1 year from the original note date.

There are certain transactions that are not subject to this due-on-sale policy. Those transactions that are not affected by the policy are as follows:

Creation of a purchase money loan for household appliances.

Transfer of property by devise, descent, or operation of law on the death of a joint tenant or tenant by the entirety.

Establishment of a leasehold interest with a term of 3 years or less and does not contain an option to buy. The announcement does state that any lease with a stated term of three years or less but is renewable beyond the initial three-year term is not exempt.

If the transfer is to a person who will occupy or who does occupy the property, any transfer:

1. to a relative resulting from the death of the borrower;
2. where the spouse or child(ren) becomes an owner of the property; or
3. resulting from a divorce decree issued by a court, legal separation, or from an incidental property settlement agreement by which the spouse becomes owner of the property.

Any transfer into an *inter vivos* trust in which the borrower is and remains the beneficiary and occupant of the property.

This quick review of the due-on-sale policy of Fannie Mae is in no way complete. For further information contact any Fannie Mae-approved seller or servicer.

Home Mortgage Commitments

Before a lender may sell any mortgage under any of the purchase programs discussed previously in the chapter, the lender must secure or purchase commitments from Fannie Mae. When a lender purchases a commitment, the lender agrees to deliver a dollar amount of a specific type of loan on or before a specific date. In other words, a mortgage company will contact Fannie Mae and purchase a commitment to sell to Fannie Mae $1,000,000 of fixed-rate conventional mortgages to be delivered in 60 days. In the following section some of the major home mortgage purchase programs will be reviewed.

Mandatory delivery commitments
As the name implies, under this type of commitment the lender must deliver eligible mortgages or participation interest for the full amount of the commitment on or before the due date of the commitment.

Under this program a lender may purchase 30- or 60-day mandatory delivery commitments to sell to Fannie Mae eligible

FHA/VA fixed-rate mortgages,

FHA/VA graduated-payment mortgages,

Conventional fixed-rate first mortgages,

Conventional fixed-rate second mortgages, including participations,

Adjustable-rate mortgages, including participations, and

Participations in conventional fixed-rate first mortgages.

It should be noted that the yields for the mandatory commitment program may change without notice and the lender must always contact Fannie Mae to find the actual yield for a specific commitment.

Normally under this program, commitments are issued in even multiples of $1000. The minimum commitment for the program is as follows

Whole mortgages	$25,000
Second-mortgage participation	$100,000
First-mortgage participation	$250,000

With the whole mortgage minimum it would be possible for a lender to sell to Fannie Mae loans one at a time. According to Fannie Mae, there is no maximum commitment amount. Thus, the lenders have a great deal of flexibility in delivering or selling mortgages to Fannie Mae.

Because it would be impossible to get mortgages that would equal the exact dollar amount of a commitment purchased by a lender, Fannie Mae states that the lender must deliver an amount equal to at least 90 percent of the commitment amount. What if a lender may not be able to deliver the required 90 percent by the date of the commitment?

Fannie Mae states that failure to meet the delivery term of a commitment may result in the lender's contract with Fannie Mae being suspended or even terminated. The reason for this requirement is that, since Fannie Mae is not lending their own money, they must go into the open market and secure the monies to cover the commitments they have issued. So if a lender does not meet the requirements of a commitment, Fannie Mae has, nevertheless, incurred the expense of generating the capital to cover a commitment.

Commitment procedures   How does a lender secure a commitment from Fannie Mae? The lender may request or purchase a commitment by calling a special number at Fannie Mae, on any business day between the hours of 11:00 AM and 5:00 PM, Eastern Standard Time.

This is the most important commitment to the real estate professional for this is the commitment used by the majority of lenders. If at all possible, you as a real estate professional should keep up with the yields on these commitments because they can determine the interest rates in the market place. Fannie Mae releases the posted yields at the close of business each Friday. This information is supplied to a variety of publications. A sample of such a release is shown in Figure 10–29, parts 1, 2, and 3. Part 3 is the most important to the real estate professional.

You will notice that all of the yields are quoted as net. This means that the yields do not include the lenders' servicing fees. The first section of the release indicates the current yields for the ARMs, showing the current yield, the yield a week ago and the yield one year ago. Thus, from this information one could assume that rates are on the rise. Also in this section it states that there are optional graduated payment features available and shows the additional yield required if the graduated payment feature is used.

The second section shows the required yields for certain fixed-rate mortgages as well as second mortgages. As with the previous section, the present yield is compared to last week's yield and the yield 1 year ago. Thus, if you have been receiving this information, you will have some idea of the trends in interest rates for some of the more common mortgages.

Loan Participation Program   In order to simplify many of the Fannie Mae programs, Fannie Mae announced the Loan Participation Program on June 1, 1981. This program is a consolidation of two existing Fannie Mae pro-

grams: Urban Loan Participation, implemented on February 1, 1978, and the Rural Loan Participation program implemented on July 1, 1980. The reason for the consolidation is to simplify the procedures for both of these previous programs and allow for Fannie Mae's purchase of a participation in a pool of mortgages regardless of the location of the property.

Under this program Fannie Mae will purchase a participation, or an interest, in a pool of first or second mortgages. The amount of the participation can range from as little as 50 percent to a maximum of 95 percent of the pool. All of the mortgages in the pool must be secured by 1- to 4-family properties. In addition to the minimum percentage of participation, Fannie Mae has established a $250,000 minimum for the dollar amount for first mortgages and $100,000 for second mortgages that Fannie Mae will purchase in any pool of mortgages.

The underwriting requirements for mortgages in the pool are generally the same as for the conventional loan purchase program mentioned earlier in the chapter. One unique feature of the program is that the use of the standard Fannie Mae/FHLMC Uniform Note and Mortgage/Deed of Trust is suggested, but is not required. Also, many of the other procedures for the program have been streamlined. For example, Fannie Mae will purchase and fund a participation in a pool of mortgages upon receipt of a participation certificate, including a loan schedule, and will not review the loans prior to funding.

The program is available to any Fannie Mae-approved conventional lender or any institution that is either insured and supervised by an agency of the federal government or any state government.

Other commitments offered   Fannie Mae has several other commitments that it will issue. One of these commitments is the *standby commitment.* Under this commitment Fannie Mae issues an optional delivery commitment to purchase either FHA/VA, FHA/VA-GPM, or conventional fixed-rate and ARM mortgages on 1- to 4-family dwellings that are either proposed, under construction, or existing. These commitments are issued for 9 or 12 months in specified dollar amounts. Any time after the day of issuance, the lender may convert the commitment to a 30-day mandatory commitment at the prevailing yield on such commitments. Why is this type of commitment important to you as a person working in the field of real estate? For example, you are

Figure 10–29. Fannie Mae Minimum Yields, part 1

News Release

3900 Wisconsin Avenue, NW
Washington, DC 20016

Contact:

Number: **4969**

Date: **September 28, 1984**

FANNIE MAE'S WEEKLY YIELD REQUIREMENTS

WASHINGTON, DC -- The Federal National Mortgage Association (Fannie Mae - FNM/NYSE) today reported that its minimum yield required for conventional fixed-rate mortgages is 13.700 percent up from last week's rate of 13.650 percent.

Fannie Mae is a large investor in mortgages and its rates are reflective of new mortgages being originated by mortgage lenders throughout the nation.

The rate for five-year adjustable rate mortgages (ARMs) is 13.700 percent, down from last week's rate of 13.800 percent.

(more)

Figure 10-29. *(continued)* **Fannie Mae Minimum Yields, part 2**

-2-

The rate on one-year ARMs is 12.400 percent, down from last week's rate of 12.500 percent. The rate on three-year ARMs is 13.350 percent, down from last week's rate of 13.450 percent.

For standard FHA/VA mortgages, the required yield is 13.950 percent, up from last week's rate of 13.900 percent. The yield for graduated payment FHA/VA mortgages is 14.450 percent, up from last week's rate of 14.400.

The rate for second mortgages is 14.075 percent, up from last week's rate of 14.025 percent.

All Fannie Mae yields are quoted on a <u>net</u> basis servicing fees are not included.

Fannie Mae, a federally chartered, shareholder-owned corporation, is the nation's largest single supplier of home mortgage funds. It purchases mortgage loans from local lenders to replenish those institutions' supply of mortgage money.

# # #

Figure 10–29. (continued) **Fannie Mae Minimum Yields, part 3**

3   9/28/84

FANNIE MAE COMMITMENTS
CURRENT YIELDS

(All yields are net: servicing fees are not included.)

NOTE: Fannie Mae yields may change daily depending on market conditions.
This release reflects the posted yields at the close of business each
Friday and is provided for purposes of comparison only.

Adjustable Rate Mortgages (ARMs)*	Current Yield	Yield Week Ago	Yield Year Ago
1 year Treasury Index	12.400%	12.500%	11.200%
3 year Treasury Index	13.350	13.450	12.200
5 year Treasury Index	13.700	13.800	12.750

* Optional graduated payment also available. Yields are 0.25% higher
  for plans tied to 1-year and 3-year Treasury securities, and 0.50%
  higher for plans tied to the 5-year Treasury security.

30-Day Mandatory Delivery	Current Yield	Yield Week Ago	Yield Year Ago
Fixed-Rate Whole Loan			
Conventional	13.700%	13.650%	13.100%
Standard FHA/VA	13.950	13.900	13.350
FHA/VA Graduated Payment	14.450	14.400	13.850
Second Mortgages	14.075	14.025	13.475

Commitment and Purchase Volumes ($ Millions)

	Week Ending 9/28/84	Year to Date	Previous Year to Date
Commitments to Purchase for Portfolio	$ 660.1	$14,453.7	$14,257.1
Portfolio Purchases	296.7	12,164.4	12,762.1
Mortgage-Backed Securities Issued	325.8	9,903.3	11,108.3

working with a client who wishes to build a house that will take at least 4 months to complete. To be sure that there will be mortgage money available at the time of completion, you and your client may secure Fannie Mae standby commitment, thus assuring the money for the permanent financing.

REVIEW QUESTIONS

1. Define the term *secondary market.*

2. Name the major secondary marketers.

3. Outline the development of the Federal National Mortgage Association.

4. Define the term *governmental interaction* as it applies to Fannie Mae.

5. Outline the conventional single-family and 2- to 4-family mortgage purchase programs of Fannie Mae.

6. Name and explain at least four of the general characteristics of the Fannie Mae buydown interest rate mortgage purchase program.

7. Outline the general limitations for subordinate financing when used in conjunction with the financing of a single-family dwelling or a 2- to 4-family dwelling.

8. Define the term *operating income* as it applies to 2- to 4-family properties.

9. List the approved interest rate indexes and adjustment interval for the Adjustable-Rate Mortgage Purchase Program.

10. List four requirements that must be met by a mortgage to be purchased under the Manufactured Housing Mortgage Purchase Program.

NOTES

1. Most of this section is based on material from U.S. House of Representatives, 90th Congress, First Session, Committee on Banking and Urban Affairs, *Basic Laws and Authorities on Housing and Community Development,* revised through January 3, 1979, part 1, pp. 645-80.

2. Most of this section is based on material from Federal National Mortgage Association, *A Guide to Fannie Mae,* 1979, pp. 60-65.

3. Federal National Mortgage Association, Dallas, Texas, memo, *Manufactured Housing—August 20, 1981,* pp. 1-2.

11

The Secondary Market, Part 2

LEARNING OBJECTIVES

In this chapter we will discuss the two remaining major secondary marketers, the Federal Home Mortgage Corporation (FHLMC) and the Government National Mortgage Association (GNMA) as well as the Residential Funding Corporation.

Upon completion of this chapter you should be able to do the following:

★ Outline the development of GNMA and FHLMC.

★ Outline the operations of the two governmental agencies.

★ Outline the programs of the two agencies.

FEDERAL HOME LOAN MORTGAGE CORPORATION (FHLMC)

The Federal Home Loan Mortgage Corporation (FHLMC) was created in 1970 with the passage of the Emergency Home Finance Act of 1970. Under Section 305 of the act, FHLMC was authorized to purchase and make commitments to purchase residential mortgages from any federal home loan bank, the Federal Savings and Loan Insurance Corporation, or any financial institution where the deposits or accounts are insured by any agency of the federal government or an agency of any state government.

The Federal Home Loan Mortgage Corporation, sometimes called Freddie Mac or the Mortgage Corporation, is under the control of the Federal Home Loan Bank Board. The Mortgage Corporation is authorized to purchase or commit to purchase both conventional and FHA/VA mortgages. In recent years, however, it reduced its holding of FHA/VA mortgages and discontinued all purchases of FHA/VA mortgages on March 1, 1981. The conventional mortgages purchased by Freddie Mac can be secured by either single-family or two- to four-family units. These units can be located in any FHLMC-approved planned unit development or condominium.

Under Section 303 of Title III of the legislation, Freddie Mac was authorized to be incorporated and to be under the direction of a board of directors, with its principal office in Washington, D.C. It was also authorized to establish branch offices as needed. Freddie Mac now operates five regional offices. A map illustrating the five regions is shown in Figure 11–1, and the addresses of the regional offices and the states that each office serves are shown in Figure 11–2.

FHLMC SOURCE OF FUNDS

Freddie Mac received its initial capital, $100 million, through the sale of nonvoting common stock to the 12 Federal Home Loan Banks. As mentioned earlier in the text, the FHLBs are

Figure 11–1.   Mortgage Corporation Areas Served

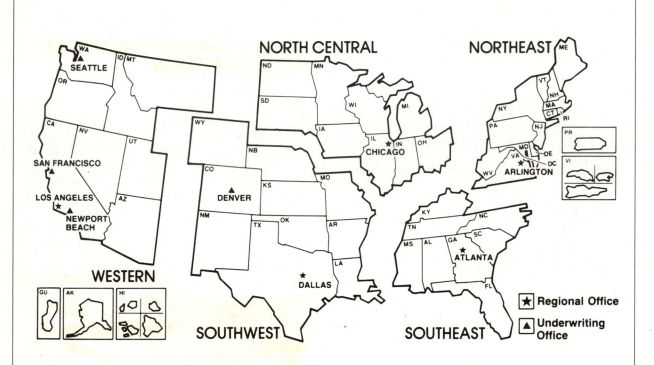

Source: Federal Home Loan Mortgage Corporation, *Announcement of a New Program from the Mortgage Corporation: ARM Invitation—Adjustable Rate Mortgage Mortgage Pilot Purchase Program*, July 1, 1981, p. 5.

Figure 11–2. Freddie Mac Offices Throughout the United States

NORTHEAST

Regional Office   (703) 685-2400
Federal Home Loan Mortgage Corporation
2001 Jefferson Davis Highway, Suite 901
Arlington, Virginia 22202

SOUTHEAST

Regional Office   (404) 659-3377
Federal Home Loan Mortgage Corporation
Peachtree Center, Cain Tower Building
Post Office Box 56566
Atlanta, Georgia 30343

NORTH CENTRAL

Regional Office   (312) 861-8400
Federal Home Loan Mortgage Corporation
111 East Wacker Drive, Suite 1515
Chicago, Illinois 60601

SOUTHWEST

Regional Office   (214) 387-0600
Federal Home Loan Mortgage Corporation
12700 Park Central Place, Suite 1800
Dallas, Texas 75251

Denver Underwriting Office   (303) 770-1435
Federal Home Loan Mortgage Corporation
Denver Technological Center
Building B-7
8000 East Prentice Avenue
Englewood, Colorado 80111

WESTERN

Regional Office   (213) 738-8200
Federal Home Loan Mortgage Corporation
3435 Wilshire Boulevard, Suite 1000
Los Angeles, California 90010

Seattle Underwriting Office   (206) 622-9904
Federal Home Loan Mortgage Corporation
600 Stewart Street, Suite 1315
Seattle, Washington 98101

San Francisco Underwriting Office   (415) 433-1822
Federal Home Loan Mortgage Corporation
600 California Street, Suite 311
San Francisco, California 94108

Newport Beach Underwriting Office   (714) 955-0322
Federal Home Loan Mortgage Corporation
4000 MacArthur Boulevard, Suite 4700
Newport Beach, California 92660

States and Territories

Connecticut, Delaware, District of Columbia, Maine, Maryland, Massachusetts, New Hampshire, New Jersey, New York, Pennsylvania, Puerto Rico, Rhode Island, Vermont, Virginia, Virgin Islands, West Virginia

Alabama, Florida, Georgia, Kentucky, Mississippi, North Carolina, South Carolina, Tennessee

Illinois, Indiana, Iowa, Michigan, Minnesota, North Dakota, Ohio, South Dakota, Wisconsin

Arkansas, Louisiana, Missouri, New Mexico, Oklahoma, Texas

*Colorado, Kansas, Nebraska, Wyoming

Arizona, California, Guam, Hawaii, Nevada, Utah

*Alaska, Idaho, Montana, Oregon, Washington

*Designated Sellers, as assigned by the Western Regional Office

*Designated Sellers, as assigned by the Western Regional Office

Source: Federal Home Loan Mortgage Corporation, *Announcement of a New Program from the Mortgage Corporation: ARM Invitation—Adjustable Rate Mortgage Pilot Purchase Program*, July 1, 1981, p. 4.

the central banks for the nation's federally chartered thrift institutions. The Federal Home Loan Bank Board, which consists of three members, supervises the operation of the FHLBs and regulates the operation of the member institutions. In addition, the three members serve as the board of directors of Freddie Mac. Then, in 1982 the Congress passed and the President signed legislation that allowed Freddie Mac to sell preferred stock.

In addition to the sale of stock, Freddie Mac also finances its operations through the sale of debt obligations. These debt obligations can either be long-term obligations, such as debentures, or short-term obligations, such as notes and lines of credit secured from commercial banks.

The majority of the funds to finance the operation and mortgage purchase programs of Freddie Mac come from the sale of *participation certificates* (PCs), and *guaranteed mortgage certificates*. These are mortgage backed securities that are sold to the general public. Sometimes these are called *pass throughs* because the payment of interest and principal reduction are passed through monthly as they are collected by Freddie Mac. The holder of a PC will receive one check each month, normally the 15th of the month.

These certificates represent an undivided interest in a pool of mortgages. These mortgages may be fixed-rate or adjustable-rate mortgages. These certificates are offered by Freddie Mac in the face amounts from $25,000 to $5,000,000. It should be noted that Freddie Mac may also offer these certificates in odd denominations between $25,000 and $50,000. Thus, it is possible to purchase a PC in the amount of $37,000.

FHLMC LOAN APPROVAL

Freddie Mac has given to all of its approved seller/servicers or lenders the authority to give prior approval or in-house approval for all types of loans that Freddie Mac will purchase.

SINGLE-FAMILY MORTGAGE PURCHASE PROGRAM

FHLMC will purchase mortgages secured by a 1- to 4-family dwelling consisting of a detached or semidetached, row, townhouse, a unit within a condominium project, or a unit located in a PUD. It should be noted that

FHLMC will not purchase mortgages in a Class I condominium project or PUD, unless 80 percent of the units sold have been sold to individuals for use as their primary year-round residence.

Freddie Mac has set the minimum term for a mortgage it will purchase as 10 years with a maximum term of 30 years. You will note that this is different from Fannie Mae. Freddie Mac will purchase mortgages with a loan-to-value ratio as high as 95 percent. It should be noted that, according to the FHLMC's *Sellers' Guide Conventional Mortgages,* the down payment must be paid from the borrower's cash or other equity. On loans with a loan-to-value in excess of 80 percent, Freddie Mac does require private mortgage insurance. Freddie Mac does require insurance on the amount of the loan in excess of 75 percent and will remain in effect until the mortgage loan amount is reduced to 80 percent or less of the original value.

The maximum loan amount, irrespective of the loan-to-value ratio, for a single-family dwelling is $115,300. You will note that this amount is identical to that of Fannie Mae. As with Fannie Mae this loan amount must be adjusted on January 1 of each year.

FHLMC permits a second lien on property used as security for the first-lien mortgage to be purchased provided that the following are met:

1. The second must be junior or inferior to the mortgage that FHLMC is purchasing.

2. The combined amount of the first and second may not exceed 95 percent of the value or sales price of the property, whichever is less, that will serve as security for the loan.

3. The second will have an amortization or maturity date not to exceed 30 years or less than 5 years. According to FHLMC, a second mortgage cannot mature, either automatically or under a call option, sooner than 5 years from the original date of the note.

4. The second mortgage may not have a prepayment premium.

5. The repayment of the second must be on a scheduled basis, such as quarterly, monthly, semiannually. In addition, the payments may be either graduated or variable. According to FHLMC, if the second is to have a fixed payment, the payment must be an amount to at least pay the interest due. Thus, the second may be an interest-

only second. If the second mortgage has a graduated-payment or variable interest rate, FHLMC states that the graduation or increase in the payment may not increase more than 8 percent from one year to the next and that the graduated payment must be structured in such a manner so that when all of the graduations are taken, the payment will be sufficient to repay the mortgage within the term of the mortgage.

6. The term of the secondary financing must be disclosed and included in the borrower's monthly housing expense.

Prior to May 31, 1983, FHLMC would only purchase loans on homes that would serve as the principal residence of the borrower. Then on June 1, 1983, Freddie Mac started the purchase of mortgages secured by nonowner occupied properties. Freddie Mac refers to these loans as *NOO loans*. Normally Freddie Mac limits the NOO loan to a loan-to-value ratio of 80 percent; but a loan with a loan-to-value ratio of 90 percent will be purchased if the amount of the loan above 65 percent of the loan-to-value ratio is covered by mortgage insurance from any Freddie Mac approved mortgage insurance company. According to Freddie Mac these NOO loans must come under one of the following two categories:

Second home – A 1-family dwelling, not 2- or 3-family dwellings, owned by an individual and usually occupied by the owner for some portion of the year. According to the Freddie Mac Memo dated May 13, 1983, there is no minimum amount of time that the owner must reside in the property. This, then, could be as little as 1 week. Thus, the property could be located in a resort area, such as Corpus Christi.

Investment property – A 1- to 4-family property owned by an individual and leased as a principal year-round residence. It should be noted that the property is never occupied by the owner.

Buydown Plans

Freddie Mac permits the use of a temporary buydown. This is a conventional loan whereby the interest rate paid by the borrower is reduced over the first few years of the mortgage with the payment of one lump sum at the time of closing.

This buydown option to the standard fixed-rate or ARM is a type of graduated-payment mortgage, but with no negative amortization

since the funds necessary to offset the effects of the lower initial monthly payments are placed in an account at the time of closing. The borrower is normally qualified on the basis of the lower bought-down payment. The reason that there is no negative amortization is that the difference in the actual payment and the payment made by the borrower is made up by making withdrawals from the monies supplied at the time of closing by the builder, seller, borrower's parents, or anyone else.

Freddie Mac will purchase conventional mortgages secured by a home or unit on new or existing property, either owner or nonowner occupied. These mortgages can be either fixed-rate or adjustable-rate mortgages, provided that the buydown plan meets the following requirements:

1. The amount of the buydown funds must include any funds used to pay any discount points, as well as any funds used to subsidize or buy down the borrower's effective interest rate. This means that if the builder will pay 3 points of discount, the dollar amount of the points must be included in any buydown offered by the builder or seller thus reducing the amount of funds that may be used for the buydown. For example, if the value of a home is $100,000 and you are working with a client who is seeking a $95,000 loan and the builder will pay 3 points or $2,850, this amount must be deducted from the maximum the builder can contribute toward a buydown.

2. The maximum funds that may be paid by the seller or its agent is 10 percent of the value or sales price of the property, whichever is less. If the funds are supplied by the buyer, relative, employer, or another similar source, there is no limit. This is similar to a provision in the Fannie Mae buydown program.

3. The increase in the borrower's principal and interest payment may not exceed 7.5 percent per year compounded annually. According to Freddie Mac's *Seller's Guide Conventional Mortgages* for a fixed-rate loan, increases in the borrower's P & I payment may be made annually or cumulatively over a longer period of time. For example, at the required 7.5 percent limit per year compounded, the payment could increase by 7.5 percent after 1 year, 15.56 percent after 2 years, 24.23 after 3 years and so on. It should be noted that Freddie

Mac requires the payment to adjust every year if the mortgage is an adjustable-rate mortgage.

4. There is to be no reference to the buydown plan in the mortgage documents.

5. The appraisal report adequately supports the use of the buydown in the area.

6. The buydown funds will be held by the originator of the loan and the funds will be placed in an insured account either in the name of the borrower or originator.

7. The borrower agrees in writing that if the buydown funds are in an account in his or her name, they will not assign, transfer, or close the account nor withdraw funds from the account during the term of the buydown agreement.

8. The borrower will also have to agree, in writing, that the funds in the buydown account will be applied automatically on a monthly basis to reduce the monthly payment as per the buydown agreement.

9. In the case of default or prepayment, unless the borrower agreed differently at the time of application, the remaining funds will not automatically be applied to principal reduction or the payment of any other charge connected with the mortgage.

2- to 4-Family Mortgage Purchase Program

FHLMC will also purchase loans secured by a duplex, triplex, or fourplex. The property can either be the principal residence of the owner or can be a nonowner occupied property. If the property is owner occupied and is a duplex, the owner will be required to make a down payment of 5 percent of the value or sales price, whichever is less; and if the dwelling is a triplex or fourplex, the owner occupant will be required to make a down payment equal to 10 percent of the value or closing costs, whichever is less. As with the loan secured by a single-family dwelling, the minimum term for one of these mortgages to be purchased by FHLMC is 10 years and the maximum term is 30 years.

As with the single-family purchase program, FHLMC will purchase mortgages on 2- to 4-family dwellings, that are under construction or already exist. The property to serve as security for the loan, as with the single-family

properties, may be either detached, semi-detached, a row dwelling, a townhouse, or a unit in a PUD project.

Prior to the passage of the Housing and Community Development Act of 1980, the maximum loan amount for these types of structures was based on the number of bedrooms in the structure, but with the passage and implementation of the act, this "bedroom method" of determining the maximum loan amount was deleted. The maximum loan amounts for 2-, 3-, and 4-family dwellings are reviewed annually. The current maximum loan amounts are as follows:

2-family dwelling	$147,500
3-family dwelling	$178,200
4-family dwelling	$221,500

Adjustable Rate Mortgage Purchase Program

On July 1, 1981, Freddie Mac announced its program to purchase adjustable-rate mortgages beginning July 15, 1981. This pilot program was the first in a series of programs instituted by the major secondary marketer to purchase the adjustable-rate mortgage. In this initial program Freddie Mac purchased ARMs that were based on or used as the index, namely *The Contract Interest Rate on Conventional Home Mortgage Loans Made for Previously Occupied Homes: National Average of All Major Types of Lenders.*

As Freddie Mac gained more experience in the purchase of the ARM, there have been changes in the initial program. Today, Freddie Mac will purchase ARMs based on three indexes. These indexes are:

1-Year Treasury Securities
3-Year Treasury Securities
5-Year Treasury Securities

Mortgage Term and Amount

The maximum term for the ARM is similar to the standard mortgage, 30 years. Likewise the ARM maximum mortgage or loan amounts are identical to those of the standard mortgages:

1-family	$115,300
2-family	$147,500
3-family	$178,200
4-family	$221,500

Maximum Loan-to-Value Ratio

The loan-to-value ratios for the ARM are similar to those of the standard mortgage:

Owner-occupied	95 percent
Nonowner-occupied	90 percent

Initial Interest Rate

The initial interest rate from any ARM purchased must have an initial net interest rate equal to the posted Freddie Mac required net yield. These required net yields are posted daily and if a lender sells an ARM with a net yield equal to the required net yield, Freddie Mac will purchase the loan with no discount points. Once again, the term *net yield* means a yield quoted without the .375 percent servicing fee. These yields are published by Freddie Mac weekly in a news release.

Interest-Rate Adjustment

According to Freddie Mac, the interest rate is to be calculated by adding a specified margin to the most recent index figure that is available 45 days before the interest rate change date. You will note that this is similar to the method used by Fannie Mae. Freddie Mac currently requires the following margins:

1-year ARM	1.00 percent
3-year ARM	1.20 percent
5-year ARM	1.40 percent

This means that the required net yield for an ARM to be sold to Freddie Mac is the value of the index plus the proper margin. Once again note that this is a net yield. Since this rate is less any lender's servicing fee, in order to get the minimum interest rate a lender may charge, you would have to add a servicing fee. The suggested servicing fee for a whole loan sold to Freddie Mac is currently 0.375 percent. Once again, the lender has the option to adjust the interest rate to the nearest one eighth of 1 percent.

Payment Cap

Freddie Mac offers a payment cap for each of the three approved ARMs. The CAP that is authorized at the present time is 7.5 percent per year. Thus, the borrower can be assured that his or her payment will not go up or down more than 7.5 percent from one year to the next. Unlike some of the other ARMs Freddie Mac does not have a carry-over rule. Thus,

any payment not taken by the lender will be added to the principal balance. Before we leave the discussion of payment caps, it must be noted that Freddie Mac does not offer any uncapped payments with the 1-year ARM.

Negative Amortization

Since Freddie Mac offers the payment cap on its ARMs, there is the possibility of negative amortization. Freddie Mac has limited the amount of negative amortization allowed in connection with the capped payment to a maximum of 125 percent. Once again, if the borrower has secured a loan in the amount of $100,000 using an ARM with a payment cap, the maximum negative amortization that will be allowed is $25,000, making the maximum loan balance $125,000.

Interest-Rate Buydown

As with the fixed-rate mortgages, Freddie Mac will purchase ARMs that have an interest-rate buydown. The buydown may either be of a permanent or temporary nature. If the buydown is a permanent type, it may be used with any one of the ARMs. If the buydown is temporary, only the ARMs based on the 3- and 5-year Treasuries may include the buydown. In addition to the limitations mentioned earlier in the chapter, Freddie Mac also requires that the temporary buydown must end 12 months prior to the first change date.

Underwriting

Any ARM purchased by Freddie Mac will normally be underwritten using the initial interest rate and the standard income ratios, unless it has no rate or payment cap, or it has a buydown of more than 2 percent below the indexed rate.

CONVENTIONAL MULTIFAMILY PURCHASE PROGRAM

Since 1972, Freddie Mac has offered a program to purchase loans secured by multifamily properties. Before we briefly review the program, what does Freddie Mac define as a multifamily property? According to Freddie Mac, it is any structure or structures that are designed principally for residential use and containing five or more family units.

The program has been constantly refined to meet the needs of the lenders and the borrower, with the last major change made in the latter part of August 1983. These changes offer two separate loan plans. The plans are called *Multifamily Loan Plan A* and *Multifamily Loan Plan B*.

Multifamily Loan Plan A

As was mentioned in the previous section, the property that will serve as security for the loan must have at least five units. The maximum loan amount will be based on the number and type of units contained in the project. According to part IV, section 2, paragraph 4.201, the maximum per unit mortgage amounts are shown in Figure 11-3.

The maximum mortgage that may be purchased under this plan is $7,500,000 and the minimum loan that will be purchased is $100,000.

Repayment term Freddie Mac will purchase mortgage that have a maturity of 10 to 30 years with a repayment period of 10 to 30 years. For example, you could sell a fixed-term, fixed-rate mortgage or a developer could sell a mortgage that could have a maturity or term of 10 years with payments that are based on a 30-year amortization schedule.

Loan-to-value ratio According to the Freddie Mac *Sellers' Guide,* the original amount of a multifamily mortgage must not exceed 80 percent of the appraised value of the project.

Occupancy Freddie Mac requires as of the deliver date of the mortgage to Freddie Mac that the project must be at an 80 percent occupied level, but if the 80 percent level does not generate sufficient income to cover the debt service and all other expenses, Freddie Mac will require a higher level until these outlays are covered. In other words, Freddie Mac will not purchase any mortgages on projects that are in negative cash flow (i.e., losing money).

Prepayment Freddie Mac will allow any mortgage purchased under this program to be repaid at any time, but the loan will be subject to a prepayment charge of a minimum of 6 months interest if the loan is repaid in the first 5 loan years or 1 percent of the remaining principal balance if the loan is prepaid after the fifth loan year to maturity.

Assumption Any mortgage purchased under this plan may not be assumed.

Documents If a lender wishes to sell a multifamily mortgage under this plan, the mortgage must be executed on the Fannie Mae/ FHLMC Uniform Multifamily Note, Deed of Trust, and Due-on-Transfer Rider. The multifamily note is shown in Figure 11-4. You will notice that the note has been modified. Paragraph four has been deleted and a new paragraph is to be added. According to the

Figure 11-3. **Maximum Per Unit Amount of Multifamily Mortgage**

(Nonelevator Structures)	
Family Unit — Bedrooms	**Maximum Mortgage Amounts per Unit**
0	$24,375
1	27,000
2	32,250
3	39,750
4	45,000

(Elevator Structures)	
Family Unit — Bedrooms	**Maximum Mortgage Amounts per Unit**
0	$28,125
1	31,500
2	38,625
3	48,375
4	54,697

Figure 11–4.   Fannie Mae/FHLMC Texas Multifamily Note, page 1

MULTIFAMILY NOTE

US $..   ...., Texas
                                                                                                                City

                                                                                    ...., 19 ......

FOR VALUE RECEIVED, the undersigned promise to pay ....
...., or order, the
principal sum of ....
.... Dollars, with interest on the unpaid principal balance from
the date of this Note, until paid, at the rate of......... percent per annum. The principal and interest shall be payable at
....,
....
in consecutive monthly installments of ....
....
Dollars (US $..) on the .... day of each month beginning
...., 19........., (herein "amortization commencement date"), until the entire indebtedness
evidenced hereby is fully paid, except that any remaining indebtedness, if not sooner paid, shall be due and payable
on ....

  If any installment under this Note is not paid when due, the entire principal amount outstanding hereunder and
accrued interest thereon shall at once become due and payable, at the option of the holder hereof. The holder hereof
may exercise this option to accelerate during any default by the undersigned regardless of any prior forbearance. In
the event of any default in the payment of this Note, and if the same is referred to an attorney at law for collection or
any action at law or in equity is brought with respect hereto, the undersigned shall pay the holder hereof all expenses
and costs, including, but not limited to, attorney's fees.

  If any installment under this Note is not received by the holder hereof within ....
calendar days after the installment is due, the undersigned shall pay to the holder hereof a late charge of..........
percent of such installment, such late charge to be immediately due and payable without demand by the holder
hereof. If any installment under this Note remains past due for .... calendar days or more,
the outstanding principal balance of this Note shall bear interest during the period in which the undersigned is in
default at a rate of .... percent per annum, or, if such increased rate of interest may not be collected from the
undersigned under applicable law, then at the maximum increased rate of interest, if any, which may be collected
from the undersigned under applicable law.

  On and after, but not prior to .... 19...... ("prepayment permitted date"), the
undersigned may make partial prepayments of principal without charge provided that the aggregate of such
prepayments does not exceed in any one loan prepayment year .... percent of the original principal amount of this
Note ("allowable prepayment"). For purposes of this paragraph, "loan prepayment year" means each twelve month
period beginning with the prepayment permitted date or an anniversary date thereof. Prepayments of principal which
in any loan prepayment year exceed the allowable prepayment ("excess prepayments") may be made provided that
the undersigned gives the holder hereof written notice of the full amounts to be prepaid at least
.... days prior to such prepayments and provided further that the undersigned pays to the
holder hereof together with each such prepayment (including prepayments occurring as a result of the acceleration by
the holder hereof of the principal amount of this Note, but excluding prepayments occurring because of the
application by the holder hereof of insurance or condemnation awards or proceeds pursuant to a Mortgage or Deed of
Trust securing this Note) a prepayment premium. In the first [..................................]* loan prepayment
year(s), the prepayment premium shall be an amount equal to .... percent of the excess prepayments. The
percentage used to calculate the prepayment premium shall decline by the number .... in the
.... loan prepayment year and in every [..................................]* loan prepayment
year thereafter until the percentage payable on excess prepayments is .... percent, which percentage shall be used
to calculate the prepayment premium which shall be payable on excess prepayments during the remaining term of this
Note.

  Prepayments shall be applied against the outstanding principal balance of this Note and shall not extend or
postpone the due date of any subsequent monthly installments or change the amount of such installments, unless the
holder hereof shall agree otherwise in writing. The holder hereof may require that any partial prepayments be made
on the date monthly installments are due and be in the amount of that part of one or more monthly installments which
would be applicable to principal.

  From time to time, without affecting the obligation of the undersigned or the successors or assigns of the
undersigned to pay the outstanding principal balance of this Note and observe the covenants of the undersigned
contained herein, without affecting the guaranty of any person, corporation, partnership or other entity for payment of
the outstanding principal balance of this Note, without giving notice to or obtaining the consent of the undersigned,
the successors or assigns of the undersigned or guarantors, and without liability on the part of the holder hereof, the
holder hereof may, at the option of the holder hereof, extend the time for payment of said outstanding principal
balance or any part thereof, reduce the payments thereon, release anyone liable on any of said outstanding principal
balance, accept a renewal of this Note, modify the terms and time of payment of said outstanding principal balance,
join in any extension or subordination agreement, release any security given herefor, take or release other or
additional security, and agree in writing with the undersigned to modify the rate of interest or period of amortization
of this Note or change the amount of the monthly installments payable hereunder.

  * *Strike through bracketed clause(s) if not completed.*

TEXAS—Multifamily—1/77—**FNMA/FHLMC Uniform Instrument**

instructions issued by Freddie Mac, the new paragraph is to be added to the second page of the note beneath the signature lines and must be initialed by the borrower and/or borrowers. The second page of the note is shown in Figure 11-5. It should be mentioned that the borrower and/or borrowers must initial the deletion of paragraph four on page one of the note. The new prepayment paragraph is shown in Figure 11-6. The Multifamily Deed of Trust is shown in Figures 11-7 through 11-14. The Due-on-Transfer Rider is shown in Figure 11-15.

Multifamily Loan Plan B

As with plan A, the property that will serve as security for a loan that will be purchased under plan B must have 5 or more units. In addition, the maximum loan amount for plan B will be based on the same per unit limits mentioned in plan A. The minimum loan amount is identical to plan A, or $100,000. Here the similarity ends, for the maximum loan that will be purchased under plan B is $20,000,000.

Repayment term   Under this program Freddie Mac will purchase a multifamily loan with a term of 10 to 15 years. You will notice that the maximum term has been reduced from 30 years for plan A to 15 years for plan B, but the minimum is the same or 10 years. As with plan A, the payments may be based on an amortization of 10 to 30 years. Thus, if a loan purchased has a maturity or term of 15 years and the payments are based on an amortization of 30 years, there will be a balloon payment at maturity.

Loan-to-value ratio   The loan-to-value ratio for mortgages to be purchased under this plan is a maximum of 80 percent of the appraised value of the property.

Occupancy   The occupancy requirements for plan B are the same as those of plan A—80 percent or an occupancy level that will provide the income to meet debt service and other expenses.

Prepayment   There is a major difference in the prepayment policy of plan B. According to Freddie Mac's *Bulletin* dated August 23, 1983, partial or full payment of a loan purchased using plan B is not allowed for the first 54 months of the loan after delivery or purchase by Freddie Mac. Then after the 54th month,

the loan may be prepaid but there will be a prepayment charge. This charge will be equal to 1 percent of the remaining principal balance.

Assumptions   There is a major difference in the assumption policy of plan B from that of plan A. Plan B allows assumptions at any time with one condition and that is the credit of the assumptor is reviewed by Freddie Mac in accordance with the requirements listed in the *Sellers' Guide,* part IV, section 4, Underwriting Requirements. According to Freddie Mac, they will collect a nonrefundable assumption review fee equal to $750 or one twentieth of the loan amount; then if the assumptor is approved and the title is transferred, they will collect an assumption fee equal to 1 percent of the outstanding principal balance less the amount of the review fee collected initially.

Documents   As with plan A, if a lender wishes to sell a multifamily mortgage under plan B the lender will be required to use the Fannie Mae/FHLMC instruments shown earlier in this section. It should be noted that once again paragraph 4 of the note is to be deleted and in its place the paragraph shown in Figure 11-16 is added to the note. Once again, the borrower and/or borrowers must initial the deletion on page 1 of the note and the addition to the note shown on page 2 of the note.

MORTGAGE COMMITMENTS

Before any approved lender may sell any mortgage to Freddie Mac through any of the mortgage purchase programs discussed in this chapter, the lender must secure or purchase a commitment. Freddie Mac will issue commitments through three purchase programs. In the following section, the three purchase programs will be reviewed.

Immediate Delivery—Conventional Home Mortgages

As the name implies, if a lender purchases this type of commitment, he must deliver enough mortgages to equal the dollar amount of the purchased commitment. Under this commitment program, Freddie Mac will purchase 15- and 30-year fixed-rate mortgages; 1-, 3-, and 5-year ARMs; and home improvement loans. Under this commitment program, a lender may purchase commitments for 15- and 30-year fixed-rate and ARM loans. These commitments have terms that range from 0 to 10

Figure 11–5.   Fannie Mae/FHLMC Texas Multifamily Note, page 2

Presentment, notice of dishonor, and protest are hereby waived by all makers, sureties, guarantors and endorsers hereof. This Note shall be the joint and several obligation of all makers, sureties, guarantors and endorsers, and shall be binding upon them and their successors and assigns.

The indebtedness evidenced by this Note is secured by a Mortgage or Deed of Trust dated ...., and reference is made thereto for rights as to acceleration of the indebtedness evidenced by this Note. This Note shall be governed by the law of the jurisdiction in which the Property subject to the Mortgage or Deed of Trust is located.

Prior to the commencement of amortization, the undersigned shall pay the holder hereof interest only on the outstanding principal balance of this Note at the rate of .... percent per annum in consecutive monthly installments beginning ...., 19........, and on .... thereafter until the amortization commencement date, at which time any remaining interest payable pursuant to this paragraph (and not paid as a part of the first monthly installment of principal and interest) shall be paid. **

————
** *Strike through this paragraph if not applicable.*

TEXAS—Multifamily—1/77—FNMA/FHLMC Uniform Instrument

Figure 11–6.   Plan A Amendment to Multifamily Note, page 2

This Note may be prepaid, in whole or in part, at any time provided the above named Borrower(s) give(s) the holder hereof written notice of the full amounts to be prepaid at least _____* days prior to such prepayment and provided further that the above named Borrower(s) pay(s) to the holder hereof, together with each prepayment (excluding prepayment occurring as a result of the acceleration by the holder hereof of the principal amount of this Note, and of the application by the holder hereof of insurance or condemnation proceeds pursuant to a Mortgage or Deed of Trust securing this Note), a prepayment charge. During the first _____** loan years, the prepayment charge shall be an amount equal to the interest otherwise payable on that portion of the principal prepaid for a period of _____** months. Thereafter, the prepayment charge shall be an amount equal to _____*** of the principal prepaid.

Notice to Seller/Servicers:

*Lender's option.

**During the first five loan years, the prepayment charge must be equal to at least six months interest otherwise payable on the amount prepaid in order to meet the Freddie Mac minimum prepayment charge requirements and be eligible for purchase.

***After the first five loan years, the prepayment charge must be at least one percent (1.0%) of amount prepaid in order to meet the Freddie Mac minimum prepayment charge requirements and be eligible for purchase.

---

days to as long as 91 to 120 days. These commitments are offered daily. Thus, if a lender has a very active day and closes several loans, the lender could contact Freddie Mac and receive a commitment and deliver the closed loans the next day after closing. It should be noted that the shorter the commitment time, the lower the net rate required by Freddie Mac. The minimum amount of a commitment that will be sold by Freddie Mac is $100,000. Thus, a lender can sell to Freddie Mac one loan at a time if the dollar amount is sufficient.

Optional Delivery—Conventional Home Mortgages

Under this program, a lender may purchase a commitment to deliver mortgages to Freddie Mac in either 120 or 240 days. Unlike the immediate delivery program, lenders can make offers or purchase this type of commitment only one day a week and that day is Tuesday.

The lender is also limited to the number of offers he or she may submit. According to the current program guidelines, a lender may only submit one offer per delivery period or only one offer for 120 days delivery and one offer for 240 days delivery. The lender is also limited to a maximum dollar amount of each bid. The present limit is $5,000,000 with a minimum offer of $100,000.

Multifamily Purchase Programs

Under this type of purchase program, Freddie Mac offers two programs. One is the *immediate delivery program* and the other is a *prior approval purchase program.* As one would suspect, the first program is similar to the immediate delivery program for conventional

home loans in that the lender will immediately deliver to Freddie Mac a mortgage secured by a multifamily project. The lender can deliver either a plan A or plan B multifamily mortgage with this program. The second program is self-explanatory. Here, the lender requests that Freddie Mac approve the loan prior to its purchase of the mortgage. Once again the lender may use either plan A or plan B.

It is important for the real estate professional to keep up with the net yields required by Freddie Mac on the 15- and 30-year fixed-rate loans and the ARMs because this is the commitment that is used by many of the savings and loan associations. Freddie Mac makes it possible for the real estate professional to do this by receiving the weekly *Freddie Mac Commitment Activity,* a news release that is made available to all interested parties at no cost and released every Thursday to show the daily posted net yields that Freddie Mac requires for its commitment programs. Pages 1 and 2 of such a release are shown in Figures 11–17 and 11–18, but the most important of all of the pages is page 3, which is shown in Figure 11–19.

Page 3 shows the required yields for a 7-day period and will give a good indication of what the current rate is that will be charged by Freddie Mac approved lenders as well as the future trend of interest rates. You will note that the release lists each of the commitment programs, starting with the 30-year fixed-rate mortgage and ending with the multifamily mortgage.

You should then notice that the release shows a 5-day week from Thursday to Thursday. If you look at the required yields for the 30-year fixed-rate mortgage, the longer the commitment the higher the required yield. Thus, if a lender was to deliver a mortgage to

Figure 11–7.   *Fannie Mae/FHLMC Texas Multifamily Deed of Trust, page 1*

WHEN RECORDED MAIL TO

SPACE ABOVE THIS LINE FOR RECORDER'S USE

MULTIFAMILY DEED OF TRUST,
ASSIGNMENT OF RENTS AND SECURITY AGREEMENT
(Security for Construction Loan Agreement)

THIS DEED OF TRUST (herein "Instrument") is made this .... day of ...., 19........, among the Trustor/Grantor, ...
....,
whose address is ....
(herein "Borrower"), ...
.... (herein "Trustee"), and
the Beneficiary, ...
...., a .... organized and existing under the laws of
...., whose address is ....
....(herein "Lender").

BORROWER, in consideration of the indebtedness herein recited and the trust herein created, irrevocably grants, conveys and assigns to Trustee, in trust, with power of sale, [the leasehold estate pursuant to a lease (herein "ground lease") dated ...., between...
...., and...
...., recorded in ....
.... in and to*] the following described property located in
...., State of Texas:

* *Delete bracketed material if not completed.*

Figure 11–8.   Fannie Mae/FHLMC Texas Multifamily Deed of Trust, page 2

TOGETHER with all buildings, improvements, and tenements now or hereafter erected on the property, and all heretofore or hereafter vacated alleys and streets abutting the property, and all easements, rights, appurtenances, rents (subject however to the assignment of rents to Lender herein), royalties, mineral, oil and gas rights and profits, water, water rights, and water stock appurtenant to the property, and all fixtures, machinery, equipment, engines, boilers, incinerators, building materials, appliances and goods of every nature whatsoever now or hereafter located in, or on, or used, or intended to be used in connection with the property, including, but not limited to, those for the purposes of supplying or distributing heating, cooling, electricity, gas, water, air and light; and all elevators, and related machinery and equipment, fire prevention and extinguishing apparatus, security and access control apparatus, plumbing, bath tubs, water heaters, water closets, sinks, ranges, stoves, refrigerators, dishwashers, disposals, washers, dryers, awnings, storm windows, storm doors, screens, blinds, shades, curtains and curtain rods, mirrors, cabinets, panelling, rugs, attached floor coverings, furniture, pictures, antennas, trees and plants, and ....
....
.....................................; all of which, including replacements and additions thereto, shall be deemed to be and remain a part of the real property covered by this Instrument; and all of the foregoing, together with said property (or the leasehold estate in the event this Instrument is on a leasehold) are herein referred to as the "Property".

TO SECURE TO LENDER (a) the repayment of the indebtedness evidenced by Borrower's note dated .... (herein "Note") in the principal sum of ....
....Dollars, with interest thereon, with the balance of the indebtedness, if not sooner paid, due and payable on ...., and all renewals, extensions and modifications thereof; (b) the repayment of any future advances, with interest thereon, made by Lender to Borrower pursuant to paragraph 33 hereof (herein "Future Advances"); (c) the performance of the covenants and agreements of Borrower contained in a Construction Loan Agreement between Lender and Borrower dated ...., 19........., if any, as provided in paragraph 25 hereof; (d) the payment of all other sums, with interest thereon, advanced in accordance herewith to protect the security of this Instrument; and (e) the performance of the covenants and agreements of Borrower herein contained.

Borrower covenants that Borrower is lawfully seised of the estate hereby conveyed and has the right to grant, convey and assign the Property (and, if this Instrument is on a leasehold, that the ground lease is in full force and effect without modification except as noted above and without default on the part of either lessor or lessee thereunder), that the Property is unencumbered, and that Borrower will warrant and defend generally the title to the Property against all claims and demands, subject to any easements and restrictions listed in a schedule of exceptions to coverage in any title insurance policy insuring Lender's interest in the Property.

(page 2 of 8 pages)

Figure 11-9.   *Fannie Mae/FHLMC Texas Multifamily Deed of Trust, page 3*

Uniform Covenants. Borrower and Lender covenant and agree as follows:

1. PAYMENT OF PRINCIPAL AND INTEREST. Borrower shall promptly pay when due the principal of and interest on the indebtedness evidenced by the Note, any prepayment and late charges provided in the Note and all other sums secured by this Instrument.

2. FUNDS FOR TAXES, INSURANCE AND OTHER CHARGES. Subject to applicable law or to a written waiver by Lender, Borrower shall pay to Lender on the day monthly installments of principal or interest are payable under the Note (or on another day designated in writing by Lender), until the Note is paid in full, a sum (herein "Funds") equal to one-twelfth of (a) the yearly water and sewer rates and taxes and assessments which may be levied on the Property, (b) the yearly ground rents, if any, (c) the yearly premium installments for fire and other hazard insurance, rent loss insurance and such other insurance covering the Property as Lender may require pursuant to paragraph 5 hereof, (d) the yearly premium installments for mortgage insurance, if any, and (e) if this Instrument is on a leasehold, the yearly fixed rents, if any, under the ground lease, all as reasonably estimated initially and from time to time by Lender on the basis of assessments and bills and reasonable estimates thereof. Any waiver by Lender of a requirement that Borrower pay such Funds may be revoked by Lender, in Lender's sole discretion, at any time upon notice in writing to Borrower. Lender may require Borrower to pay to Lender, in advance, such other Funds for other taxes, charges, premiums, assessments and impositions in connection with Borrower or the Property which Lender shall reasonably deem necessary to protect Lender's interests (herein "Other Impositions"). Unless otherwise provided by applicable law, Lender may require Funds for Other Impositions to be paid by Borrower in a lump sum or in periodic installments, at Lender's option.

The Funds shall be held in an institution(s) the deposits or accounts of which are insured or guaranteed by a Federal or state agency (including Lender if Lender is such an institution). Lender shall apply the Funds to pay said rates, rents, taxes, assessments, insurance premiums and Other Impositions so long as Borrower is not in breach of any covenant or agreement of Borrower in this Instrument. Lender shall make no charge for so holding and applying the Funds, analyzing said account or for verifying and compiling said assessments and bills, unless Lender pays Borrower interest, earnings or profits on the Funds and applicable law permits Lender to make such a charge. Borrower and Lender may agree in writing at the time of execution of this Instrument that interest on the Funds shall be paid to Borrower, and unless such agreement is made or applicable law requires interest, earnings or profits to be paid, Lender shall not be required to pay Borrower any interest, earnings or profits on the Funds. Lender shall give to Borrower, without charge, an annual accounting of the Funds in Lender's normal format showing credits and debits to the Funds and the purpose for which each debit to the Funds was made. The Funds are pledged as additional security for the sums secured by this Instrument.

If the amount of the Funds held by Lender at the time of the annual accounting thereof shall exceed the amount deemed necessary by Lender to provide for the payment of water and sewer rates, taxes, assessments, insurance premiums, rents and Other Impositions, as they fall due, such excess shall be credited to Borrower on the next monthly installment or installments of Funds due. If at any time the amount of the Funds held by Lender shall be less than the amount deemed necessary by Lender to pay water and sewer rates, taxes, assessments, insurance premiums, rents and Other Impositions, as they fall due, Borrower shall pay to Lender any amount necessary to make up the deficiency within thirty days after notice from Lender to Borrower requesting payment thereof.

Upon Borrower's breach of any covenant or agreement of Borrower in this Instrument, Lender may apply, in any amount and in any order as Lender shall determine in Lender's sole discretion, any Funds held by Lender at the time of application (i) to pay rates, rents, taxes, assessments, insurance premiums and Other Impositions which are now or will hereafter become due, or (ii) as a credit against sums secured by this Instrument. Upon payment in full of all sums secured by this Instrument, Lender shall promptly refund to Borrower any Funds held by Lender.

3. APPLICATION OF PAYMENTS. Unless applicable law provides otherwise, all payments received by Lender from Borrower under the Note or this Instrument shall be applied by Lender in the following order of priority: (i) amounts payable to Lender by Borrower under paragraph 2 hereof; (ii) interest payable on the Note; (iii) principal of the Note; (iv) interest payable on advances made pursuant to paragraph 8 hereof; (v) principal of advances made pursuant to paragraph 8 hereof; (vi) interest payable on any Future Advance, provided that if more than one Future Advance is outstanding, Lender may apply payments received among the amounts of interest payable on the Future Advances in such order as Lender, in Lender's sole discretion, may determine; (vii) principal of any Future Advance, provided that if more than one Future Advance is outstanding, Lender may apply payments received among the principal balances of the Future Advances in such order as Lender, in Lender's sole discretion, may determine; and (viii) any other sums secured by this Instrument in such order as Lender, at Lender's option, may determine; provided, however, that Lender may, at Lender's option, apply any sums payable pursuant to paragraph 8 hereof prior to interest on and principal of the Note, but such application shall not otherwise affect the order of priority of application specified in this paragraph 3.

4. CHARGES; LIENS. Borrower shall pay all water and sewer rates, rents, taxes, assessments, premiums, and Other Impositions attributable to the Property at Lender's option in the manner provided under paragraph 2 hereof or, if not paid in such manner, by Borrower making payment, when due, directly to the payee thereof, or in such other manner as Lender may designate in writing. Borrower shall promptly furnish to Lender all notices of amounts due under this paragraph 4, and in the event Borrower shall make payment directly, Borrower shall promptly furnish to Lender receipts evidencing such payments. Borrower shall promptly discharge any lien which has, or may have, priority over or equality with, the lien of this Instrument, and Borrower shall pay, when due, the claims of all persons supplying labor or materials to or in connection with the Property. Without Lender's prior written permission, Borrower shall not allow any lien inferior to this Instrument to be perfected against the Property.

5. HAZARD INSURANCE. Borrower shall keep the improvements now existing or hereafter erected on the Property insured by carriers at all times satisfactory to Lender against loss by fire, hazards included within the term "extended coverage", rent loss and such other hazards, casualties, liabilities and contingencies as Lender (and, if this Instrument is on a leasehold, the ground lease) shall require and in such amounts and for such periods as Lender shall require. All premiums on insurance policies shall be paid, at Lender's option, in the manner provided under paragraph 2 hereof, or by Borrower making payment, when due, directly to the carrier, or in such other manner as Lender may designate in writing.

All insurance policies and renewals thereof shall be in a form acceptable to Lender and shall include a standard mortgage clause in favor of and in form acceptable to Lender. Lender shall have the right to hold the policies, and Borrower shall promptly furnish to Lender all renewal notices and all receipts of paid premiums. At least thirty days prior to the expiration date of a policy, Borrower shall deliver to Lender a renewal policy in form satisfactory to Lender. If this Instrument is on a leasehold, Borrower shall furnish Lender a duplicate of all policies, renewal notices, renewal policies and receipts of paid premiums if, by virtue of the ground lease, the originals thereof may not be supplied by Borrower to Lender.

In the event of loss, Borrower shall give immediate written notice to the insurance carrier and to Lender. Borrower hereby authorizes and empowers Lender as attorney-in-fact for Borrower to make proof of loss, to adjust and compromise any claim under insurance policies, to appear in and prosecute any action arising from such insurance policies, to collect and receive insurance proceeds, and to deduct therefrom Lender's expenses incurred in the collection of such proceeds; provided however, that nothing contained in this paragraph 5 shall require Lender to incur any expense or take any action hereunder. Borrower further authorizes Lender, at Lender's option, (a) to hold the balance of such proceeds to be used to reimburse Borrower for the cost of reconstruction or repair of the Property or (b) to apply the balance of such proceeds to the payment of the sums secured by this Instrument, whether or not then due, in the order of application set forth in paragraph 3 hereof (subject, however, to the rights of the lessor under the ground lease if this Instrument is on a leasehold).

If the insurance proceeds are held by Lender to reimburse Borrower for the cost of restoration and repair of the Property, the Property shall be restored to the equivalent of its original condition or such other condition as Lender may approve in writing. Lender may, at Lender's option, condition disbursement of said proceeds on Lender's approval of such plans and specifications of an architect satisfactory to Lender, contractor's cost estimates, architect's certificates, waivers of liens, sworn statements of mechanics and materialmen and such other evidence of costs, percentage completion of construction, application of payments, and satisfaction of liens as Lender may reasonably require. If the insurance proceeds are applied to the payment of the sums secured by this Instrument, any such application of proceeds to principal shall not extend or postpone the due dates of the monthly installments referred to in paragraphs 1 and 2 hereof or change the amounts of such installments. If the Property is sold pursuant to paragraph 27 hereof or if Lender acquires title to the Property, Lender shall have all of the right, title and interest of Borrower in and to any insurance policies and unearned premiums thereon and in and to the proceeds resulting from any damage to the Property prior to such sale or acquisition.

6. PRESERVATION AND MAINTENANCE OF PROPERTY; LEASEHOLDS. Borrower (a) shall not commit waste or permit impairment or deterioration of the Property, (b) shall not abandon the Property, (c) shall restore or repair promptly and in a good and workmanlike manner all

Uniform Covenants—Multifamily—1/77—FNMA/FHLMC Uniform Instrument   *(page 3 of 8 pages)*

Figure 11–10.   Fannie Mae/FHLMC Texas Multifamily Deed of Trust, page 4

or any part of the Property to the equivalent of its original condition, or such other condition as Lender may approve in writing, in the event of any damage, injury or loss thereto, whether or not insurance proceeds are available to cover in whole or in part the costs of such restoration or repair, (d) shall keep the Property, including improvements, fixtures, equipment, machinery and appliances thereon in good repair and shall replace fixtures, equipment, machinery and appliances on the Property when necessary to keep such items in good repair, (e) shall comply with all laws, ordinances, regulations and requirements of any governmental body applicable to the Property, (f) shall provide for professional management of the Property by a residential rental property manager satisfactory to Lender pursuant to a contract approved by Lender in writing, unless such requirement shall be waived by Lender in writing, (g) shall generally operate and maintain the Property in a manner to ensure maximum rentals, and (h) shall give notice in writing to Lender of and, unless otherwise directed in writing by Lender, appear in and defend any action or proceeding purporting to affect the Property, the security of this Instrument or the rights or powers of Lender.   Neither Borrower nor any tenant or other person shall remove, demolish or alter any improvement now existing or hereafter erected on the Property or any fixture, equipment, machinery or appliance in or on the Property except when incident to the replacement of fixtures, equipment, machinery and appliances with items of like kind.

If this Instrument is on a leasehold, Borrower (i) shall comply with the provisions of the ground lease, (ii) shall give immediate written notice to Lender of any default by lessor under the ground lease or of any notice received by Borrower from such lessor of any default under the ground lease by Borrower, (iii) shall exercise any option to renew or extend the ground lease and give written confirmation thereof to Lender within thirty days after such option becomes exercisable, (iv) shall give immediate written notice to Lender of the commencement of any remedial proceedings under the ground lease by any party thereto and, if required by Lender, shall permit Lender as Borrower's attorney-in-fact to control and act for Borrower in any such remedial proceedings and (v) shall within thirty days after request by Lender obtain from the lessor under the ground lease and deliver to Lender the lessor's estoppel certificate required thereunder, if any.   Borrower hereby expressly transfers and assigns to Lender the benefit of all covenants contained in the ground lease, whether or not such covenants run with the land, but Lender shall have no liability with respect to such covenants nor any other covenants contained in the ground lease.

Borrower shall not surrender the leasehold estate and interests herein conveyed nor terminate or cancel the ground lease creating said estate and interests, and Borrower shall not, without the express written consent of Lender, alter or amend said ground lease.   Borrower covenants and agrees that there shall not be a merger of the ground lease, or of the leasehold estate created thereby, with the fee estate covered by the ground lease by reason of said leasehold estate or said fee estate, or any part of either, coming into common ownership, unless Lender shall consent in writing to such merger; if Borrower shall acquire such fee estate, then this Instrument shall simultaneously and without further action be spread so as to become a lien on such fee estate.

7. USE OF PROPERTY.   Unless required by applicable law or unless Lender has otherwise agreed in writing, Borrower shall not allow changes in the use for which all or any part of the Property was intended at the time this Instrument was executed.   Borrower shall not initiate or acquiesce in a change in the zoning classification of the Property without Lender's prior written consent.

8. PROTECTION OF LENDER'S SECURITY.   If Borrower fails to perform the covenants and agreements contained in this Instrument, or if any action or proceeding is commenced which affects the Property or title thereto or the interest of Lender therein, including, but not limited to, eminent domain, insolvency, code enforcement, or arrangements or proceedings involving a bankrupt or decedent, then Lender at Lender's option may make such appearances, disburse such sums and take such action as Lender deems necessary, in its sole discretion, to protect Lender's interest, including, but not limited to, (i) disbursement of attorney's fees, (ii) entry upon the Property to make repairs, (iii) procurement of satisfactory insurance as provided in paragraph 5 hereof, and (iv) if this Instrument is on a leasehold, exercise of any option to renew or extend the ground lease on behalf of Borrower and the curing of any default of Borrower in the terms and conditions of the ground lease.

Any amounts disbursed by Lender pursuant to this paragraph 8, with interest thereon, shall become additional indebtedness of Borrower secured by this Instrument.   Unless Borrower and Lender agree to other terms of payment, such amounts shall be immediately due and payable and shall bear interest from the date of disbursement at the rate stated in the Note unless collection from Borrower of interest at such rate would be contrary to applicable law, in which event such amounts shall bear interest at the highest rate which may be collected from Borrower under applicable law.   Borrower hereby covenants and agrees that Lender shall be subrogated to the lien of any mortgage or other lien discharged, in whole or in part, by the indebtedness secured hereby.   Nothing contained in this paragraph 8 shall require Lender to incur any expense or take any action hereunder.

9. INSPECTION.   Lender may make or cause to be made reasonable entries upon and inspections of the Property.

10. BOOKS AND RECORDS.   Borrower shall keep and maintain at all times at Borrower's address stated below, or such other place as Lender may approve in writing, complete and accurate books of accounts and records adequate to reflect correctly the results of the operation of the Property and copies of all written contracts, leases and other instruments which affect the Property.   Such books, records, contracts, leases and other instruments shall be subject to examination and inspection at any reasonable time by Lender.   Upon Lender's request, Borrower shall furnish to Lender, within one hundred and twenty days after the end of each fiscal year of Borrower, a balance sheet, a statement of income and expenses of the Property and a statement of changes in financial position, each in reasonable detail and certified by Borrower and, if Lender shall require, by an independent certified public accountant.   Borrower shall furnish, together with the foregoing financial statements and at any other time upon Lender's request, a rent schedule for the Property, certified by Borrower, showing the name of each tenant, and for each tenant, the space occupied, the lease expiration date, the rent payable and the rent paid.

11. CONDEMNATION.   Borrower shall promptly notify Lender of any action or proceeding relating to any condemnation or other taking, whether direct or indirect, of the Property, or part thereof, and Borrower shall appear in and prosecute any such action or proceeding unless otherwise directed by Lender in writing.   Borrower authorizes Lender, at Lender's option, as attorney-in-fact for Borrower, to commence, appear in and prosecute, in Lender's or Borrower's name, any action or proceeding relating to any condemnation or other taking of the Property, whether direct or indirect, and to settle or compromise any claim in connection with such condemnation or other taking.   The proceeds of any award, payment or claim for damages, direct or consequential, in connection with any condemnation or other taking, whether direct or indirect, of the Property, or part thereof, or for conveyances in lieu of condemnation, are hereby assigned to and shall be paid to Lender subject, if this Instrument is on a leasehold, to the rights of lessor under the ground lease.

Borrower authorizes Lender to apply such awards, payments, proceeds or damages, after the deduction of Lender's expenses incurred in the collection of such amounts, at Lender's option, to restoration or repair of the Property or to payment of the sums secured by this Instrument, whether or not then due, in the order of application set forth in paragraph 3 hereof, with the balance, if any, to Borrower.   Unless Borrower and Lender otherwise agree in writing, any application of proceeds to principal shall not extend or postpone the due date of the monthly installments referred to in paragraphs 1 and 2 hereof or change the amount of such installments.   Borrower agrees to execute such further evidence of assignment of any awards, proceeds, damages or claims arising in connection with such condemnation or taking as Lender may require.

12. BORROWER AND LIEN NOT RELEASED.   From time to time, Lender may, at Lender's option, without giving notice to or obtaining the consent of Borrower, Borrower's successors or assigns or of any junior lienholder or guarantors, without liability on Lender's part and notwithstanding Borrower's breach of any covenant or agreement of Borrower in this Instrument, extend the time for payment of said indebtedness or any part thereof, reduce the payments thereon, release anyone liable on any of said indebtedness, accept a renewal note or notes therefor, modify the terms and time of payment of said indebtedness, release from the lien of this Instrument any part of the Property, take or release other or additional security, reconvey any part of the Property, consent to any map or plan of the Property, consent to the granting of any easement, join in any extension or subordination agreement, and agree in writing with Borrower to modify the rate of interest or period of amortization of the Note or change the amount of the monthly installments payable thereunder.   Any actions taken by Lender pursuant to the terms of this paragraph 12 shall not affect the obligation of Borrower or Borrower's successors or assigns to pay the sums secured by this Instrument and to observe the covenants of Borrower contained herein, shall not affect the guaranty of any person, corporation, partnership or other entity for payment of the indebtedness secured hereby, and shall not affect the lien or priority of lien hereof on the Property.   Borrower shall pay Lender a reasonable service charge, together with such title insurance premiums and attorney's fees as may be incurred at Lender's option, for any such action if taken at Borrower's request.

13. FORBEARANCE BY LENDER NOT A WAIVER.   Any forbearance by Lender in exercising any right or remedy hereunder, or otherwise afforded by applicable law, shall not be a waiver of or preclude the exercise of any right or remedy.   The acceptance by Lender of payment of any sum secured by this Instrument after the due date of such payment shall not be a waiver of Lender's right to either require prompt payment when due of all other sums so secured or to declare a default for failure to make prompt payment.   The procurement of insurance or the payment of taxes or other liens or charges by Lender shall not be a waiver of Lender's right to accelerate the maturity of the indebtedness secured by this Instrument, nor shall Lender's receipt of any awards, proceeds or damages under paragraphs 5 and 11 hereof operate to cure or waive Borrower's default in payment of sums secured by this Instrument.

(page 4 of 8 pages)

Figure 11–11. **Fannie Mae/FHLMC Texas Multifamily Deed of Trust, page 5**

14. ESTOPPEL CERTIFICATE. Borrower shall within ten days of a written request from Lender furnish Lender with a written statement, duly acknowledged, setting forth the sums secured by this Instrument and any right of set-off, counterclaim or other defense which exists against such sums and the obligations of this Instrument.

15. UNIFORM COMMERCIAL CODE SECURITY AGREEMENT. This Instrument is intended to be a security agreement pursuant to the Uniform Commercial Code for any of the items specified above as part of the Property which, under applicable law, may be subject to a security interest pursuant to the Uniform Commercial Code, and Borrower hereby grants Lender a security interest in said items. Borrower agrees that Lender may file this Instrument, or a reproduction thereof, in the real estate records or other appropriate index, as a financing statement for any of the items specified above as part of the Property. Any reproduction of this Instrument or of any other security agreement or financing statement shall be sufficient as a financing statement. In addition, Borrower agrees to execute and deliver to Lender, upon Lender's request, any financing statements, as well as extensions, renewals and amendments thereof, and reproductions of this Instrument in such form as Lender may require to perfect a security interest with respect to said items. Borrower shall pay all costs of filing such financing statements and any extensions, renewals, amendments and releases thereof, and shall pay all reasonable costs and expenses of any record searches for financing statements Lender may reasonably require. Without the prior written consent of Lender, Borrower shall not create or suffer to be created pursuant to the Uniform Commercial Code any other security interest in said items, including replacements and additions thereto. Upon Borrower's breach of any covenant or agreement of Borrower contained in this Instrument, including the covenants to pay when due all sums secured by this Instrument, Lender shall have the remedies of a secured party under the Uniform Commercial Code and, at Lender's option, may also invoke the remedies provided in paragraph 27 of this Instrument as to such items. In exercising any of said remedies, Lender may proceed against the items of real property and any items of personal property specified above as part of the Property separately or together and in any order whatsoever, without in any way affecting the availability of Lender's remedies under the Uniform Commercial Code or of the remedies provided in paragraph 27 of this Instrument.

16. LEASES OF THE PROPERTY. As used in this paragraph 16, the word "lease" shall mean "sublease" if this Instrument is on a leasehold. Borrower shall comply with and observe Borrower's obligations as landlord under all leases of the Property or any part thereof. Borrower will not lease any portion of the Property for non-residential use except with the prior written approval of Lender. Borrower, at Lender's request, shall furnish Lender with executed copies of all leases now existing or hereafter made of all or any part of the Property, and all leases now or hereafter entered into will be in form and substance subject to the approval of Lender. All leases of the Property shall specifically provide that such leases are subordinate to this Instrument; that the tenant attorns to Lender, such attornment to be effective upon Lender's acquisition of title to the Property; that the tenant agrees to execute such further evidences of attornment as Lender may from time to time request; that the attornment of the tenant shall not be terminated by foreclosure; and that Lender may, at Lender's option, accept or reject such attornments. Borrower shall not, without Lender's written consent, execute, modify, surrender or terminate, either orally or in writing, any lease now existing or hereafter made of all or any part of the Property providing for a term of three years or more, permit an assignment or sublease of such a lease without Lender's written consent, or request or consent to the subordination of any lease of all or any part of the Property to any lien subordinate to this Instrument. If Borrower becomes aware that any tenant proposes to do, or is doing, any act or thing which may give rise to any right of set-off against rent, Borrower shall (i) take such steps as shall be reasonably calculated to prevent the accrual of any right to a set-off against rent, (ii) notify Lender thereof and of the amount of said set-offs, and (iii) within ten days after such accrual, reimburse the tenant who shall have acquired such right to set-off or take such other steps as shall effectively discharge such set-off and as shall assure that rents thereafter due shall continue to be payable without set-off or deduction.

Upon Lender's request, Borrower shall assign to Lender, by written instrument satisfactory to Lender, all leases now existing or hereafter made of all or any part of the Property and all security deposits made by tenants in connection with such leases of the Property. Upon assignment by Borrower to Lender of any leases of the Property, Lender shall have all of the rights and powers possessed by Borrower prior to such assignment and Lender shall have the right to modify, extend or terminate such existing leases and to execute new leases, in Lender's sole discretion.

17. REMEDIES CUMULATIVE. Each remedy provided in this Instrument is distinct and cumulative to all other rights or remedies under this Instrument or afforded by law or equity, and may be exercised concurrently, independently, or successively, in any order whatsoever.

18. ACCELERATION IN CASE OF BORROWER'S INSOLVENCY. If Borrower shall voluntarily file a petition under the Federal Bankruptcy Act, as such Act may from time to time be amended, or under any similar or successor Federal statute relating to bankruptcy, insolvency, arrangements or reorganizations, or under any state bankruptcy or insolvency act, or file an answer in an involuntary proceeding admitting insolvency or inability to pay debts, or if Borrower shall fail to obtain a vacation or stay of involuntary proceedings brought for the reorganization, dissolution or liquidation of Borrower, or if Borrower shall be adjudged a bankrupt, or if a trustee or receiver shall be appointed for Borrower or Borrower's property, or if the Property shall become subject to the jurisdiction of a Federal bankruptcy court or similar state court, or if Borrower shall make an assignment for the benefit of Borrower's creditors, or if there is an attachment, execution or other judicial seizure of any portion of Borrower's assets and such seizure is not discharged within ten days, then Lender may, at Lender's option, declare all of the sums secured by this Instrument to be immediately due and payable without prior notice to Borrower, and Lender may invoke any remedies permitted by paragraph 27 of this Instrument. Any attorney's fees and other expenses incurred by Lender in connection with Borrower's bankruptcy or any of the other aforesaid events shall be additional indebtedness of Borrower secured by this Instrument pursuant to paragraph 8 hereof.

19. TRANSFERS OF THE PROPERTY OR BENEFICIAL INTERESTS IN BORROWER; ASSUMPTION. On sale or transfer of (i) all or any part of the Property, or any interest therein, or (ii) beneficial interests in Borrower (if Borrower is not a natural person or persons but is a corporation, partnership, trust or other legal entity), Lender may, at Lender's option, declare all of the sums secured by this Instrument to be immediately due and payable, and Lender may invoke any remedies permitted by paragraph 27 of this Instrument. This option shall not apply in case of

- (a) transfers by devise or descent or by operation of law upon the death of a joint tenant or a partner;
- (b) sales or transfers when the transferee's creditworthiness and management ability are satisfactory to Lender and the transferee has executed, prior to the sale or transfer, a written assumption agreement containing such terms as Lender may require, including, if required by Lender, an increase in the rate of interest payable under the Note;
- (c) the grant of a leasehold interest in a part of the Property of three years or less (or such longer lease term as Lender may permit by prior written approval) not containing an option to purchase (except any interest in the ground lease, if this Instrument is on a leasehold);
- (d) sales or transfers of beneficial interests in Borrower provided that such sales or transfers, together with any prior sales or transfers of beneficial interests in Borrower, but excluding sales or transfers under subparagraphs (a) and (b) above, do not result in more than 49% of the beneficial interests in Borrower having been sold or transferred since commencement of amortization of the Note; and
- (e) sales or transfers of fixtures or any personal property pursuant to the first paragraph of paragraph 6 hereof.

20. NOTICE. Except for any notice required under applicable law to be given in another manner, (a) any notice to Borrower provided for in this Instrument or in the Note shall be given by mailing such notice by certified mail addressed to Borrower at Borrower's address stated below or at such other address as Borrower may designate by notice to Lender as provided herein, and (b) any notice to Lender shall be given by certified mail, return receipt requested, to Lender's address stated herein or to such other address as Lender may designate by notice to Borrower as provided herein. Any notice provided for in this Instrument or in the Note shall be deemed to have been given to Borrower or Lender when given in the manner designated herein.

21. SUCCESSORS AND ASSIGNS BOUND; JOINT AND SEVERAL LIABILITY; AGENTS; CAPTIONS. The covenants and agreements herein contained shall bind, and the rights hereunder shall inure to, the respective successors and assigns of Lender and Borrower, subject to the provisions of paragraph 19 hereof. All covenants and agreements of Borrower shall be joint and several. In exercising any rights hereunder or taking any actions provided for herein, Lender may act through its employees, agents or independent contractors as authorized by Lender. The captions and headings of the paragraphs of this Instrument are for convenience only and are not to be used to interpret or define the provisions hereof.

22. UNIFORM MULTIFAMILY INSTRUMENT; GOVERNING LAW; SEVERABILITY. This form of multifamily instrument combines uniform covenants for national use and non-uniform covenants with limited variations by jurisdiction to constitute a uniform security instrument covering real property and related fixtures and personal property. This Instrument shall be governed by the law of the jurisdiction in which the Property is located. In the event that any provision of this Instrument or the Note conflicts with applicable law, such conflict shall not affect other provisions of this Instrument or the Note which can be given effect without the conflicting provisions, and to this end the provisions of this

(page 5 of 8 pages)

Figure 11–12.   Fannie Mae/FHLMC Texas Multifamily Deed of Trust, page 6

Instrument and the Note are declared to be severable. In the event that any applicable law limiting the amount of interest or other charges permitted to be collected from Borrower is interpreted so that any charge provided for in this Instrument or in the Note, whether considered separately or together with other charges levied in connection with this Instrument and the Note, violates such law, and Borrower is entitled to the benefit of such law, such charge is hereby reduced to the extent necessary to eliminate such violation. The amounts, if any, previously paid to Lender in excess of the amounts payable to Lender pursuant to such charges as reduced shall be applied by Lender to reduce the principal of the indebtedness evidenced by the Note. For the purpose of determining whether any applicable law limiting the amount of interest or other charges permitted to be collected from Borrower has been violated, all indebtedness which is secured by this Instrument or evidenced by the Note and which constitutes interest, as well as all other charges levied in connection with such indebtedness which constitute interest, shall be deemed to be allocated and spread over the stated term of the Note. Unless otherwise required by applicable law, such allocation and spreading shall be effected in such a manner that the rate of interest computed thereby is uniform throughout the stated term of the Note.

23. WAIVER OF STATUTE OF LIMITATIONS. Borrower hereby waives the right to assert any statute of limitations as a bar to the enforcement of the lien of this Instrument or to any action brought to enforce the Note or any other obligation secured by this Instrument.

24. WAIVER OF MARSHALLING. Notwithstanding the existence of any other security interests in the Property held by Lender or by any other party, Lender shall have the right to determine the order in which any or all of the Property shall be subjected to the remedies provided herein. Lender shall have the right to determine the order in which any or all portions of the indebtedness secured hereby are satisfied from the proceeds realized upon the exercise of the remedies provided herein. Borrower, any party who consents to this Instrument and any party who now or hereafter acquires a security interest in the Property and who has actual or constructive notice hereof hereby waives any and all right to require the marshalling of assets in connection with the exercise of any of the remedies permitted by applicable law or provided herein.

25. CONSTRUCTION LOAN PROVISIONS. Borrower agrees to comply with the covenants and conditions of the Construction Loan Agreement, if any, which is hereby incorporated by reference in and made a part of this Instrument. All advances made by Lender pursuant to the Construction Loan Agreement shall be indebtedness of Borrower secured by this Instrument, and such advances may be obligatory as provided in the Construction Loan Agreement. All sums disbursed by Lender prior to completion of the improvements to protect the security of this Instrument up to the principal amount of the Note shall be treated as disbursements pursuant to the Construction Loan Agreement. All such sums shall bear interest from the date of disbursement at the rate stated in the Note, unless collection from Borrower of interest at such rate would be contrary to applicable law in which event such amounts shall bear interest at the highest rate which may be collected from Borrower under applicable law and shall be payable upon notice from Lender to Borrower requesting payment therefor.

From time to time as Lender deems necessary to protect Lender's interests, Borrower shall, upon request of Lender, execute and deliver to Lender, in such form as Lender shall direct, assignments of any and all rights or claims which relate to the construction of the Property and which Borrower may have against any party supplying or who has supplied labor, materials or services in connection with construction of the Property. In case of breach by Borrower of the covenants and conditions of the Construction Loan Agreement, Lender, at Lender's option, with or without entry upon the Property, (i) may invoke any of the rights or remedies provided in the Construction Loan Agreement, (ii) may accelerate the sums secured by this Instrument and invoke those remedies provided in paragraph 27 hereof, or (iii) may do both. If, after the commencement of amortization of the Note, the Note and this Instrument are sold by Lender, from and after such sale the Construction Loan Agreement shall cease to be a part of this Instrument and Borrower shall not assert any right of set-off, counterclaim or other claim or defense arising out of or in connection with the Construction Loan Agreement against the obligations of the Note and this Instrument.

26. ASSIGNMENT OF RENTS; APPOINTMENT OF RECEIVER; LENDER IN POSSESSION. As part of the consideration for the indebtedness evidenced by the Note, Borrower hereby absolutely and unconditionally assigns and transfers to Lender all the rents and revenues of the Property, including those now due, past due, or to become due by virtue of any lease or other agreement for the occupancy or use of all or any part of the Property, regardless of to whom the rents and revenues of the Property are payable. Borrower hereby authorizes Lender or Lender's agents to collect the aforesaid rents and revenues and hereby directs each tenant of the Property to pay such rents to Lender or Lender's agents; provided, however, that prior to written notice given by Lender to Borrower of the breach by Borrower of any covenant or agreement of Borrower in this Instrument, Borrower shall collect and receive all rents and revenues of the Property as trustee for the benefit of Lender and Borrower, to apply the rents and revenues so collected to the sums secured by this Instrument in the order provided in paragraph 3 hereof with the balance, so long as no such breach has occurred, to the account of Borrower, it being intended by Borrower and Lender that this assignment of rents constitutes an absolute assignment and not an assignment for additional security only. Upon delivery of written notice by Lender to Borrower of the breach by Borrower of any covenant or agreement of Borrower in this Instrument, and without the necessity of Lender entering upon and taking and maintaining full control of the Property in person, by agent or by a court-appointed receiver, Lender shall immediately be entitled to possession of all rents and revenues of the Property as specified in this paragraph 26 as the same become due and payable, including but not limited to rents then due and unpaid, and all such rents shall immediately upon delivery of such notice be held by Borrower as trustee for the benefit of Lender only; provided, however, that the written notice by Lender to Borrower of the breach by Borrower shall contain a statement that Lender exercises its rights to such rents. Borrower agrees that commencing upon delivery of such written notice of Borrower's breach by Lender to Borrower, each tenant of the Property shall make such rents payable to and pay such rents to Lender or Lender's agents on Lender's written demand to each tenant therefor, delivered to each tenant personally, by mail or by delivering such demand to each rental unit, without any liability on the part of said tenant to inquire further as to the existence of a default by Borrower.

Borrower hereby covenants that Borrower has not executed any prior assignment of said rents, that Borrower has not performed, and will not perform, any acts or has not executed, and will not execute, any instrument which would prevent Lender from exercising its rights under this paragraph 26, and that at the time of execution of this Instrument there has been no anticipation or prepayment of any of the rents of the Property for more than two months prior to the due dates of such rents. Borrower covenants that Borrower will not hereafter collect or accept payment of any rents of the Property more than two months prior to the due dates of such rents. Borrower further covenants that Borrower will execute and deliver to Lender such further assignments of rents and revenues of the Property as Lender may from time to time request.

Upon Borrower's breach of any covenant or agreement of Borrower in this Instrument, Lender may in person, by agent or by a court-appointed receiver, regardless of the adequacy of Lender's security, enter upon and take and maintain full control of the Property in order to perform all acts necessary and appropriate for the operation and maintenance thereof including, but not limited to, the execution, cancellation or modification of leases, the collection of all rents and revenues of the Property, the making of repairs to the Property and the execution or termination of contracts providing for the management or maintenance of the Property, all on such terms as are deemed best to protect the security of this Instrument. In the event Lender elects to seek the appointment of a receiver for the Property upon Borrower's breach of any covenant or agreement of Borrower in this Instrument, Borrower hereby expressly consents to the appointment of such receiver. Lender or the receiver shall be entitled to receive a reasonable fee for so managing the Property.

All rents and revenues collected subsequent to delivery of written notice by Lender to Borrower of the breach by Borrower of any covenant or agreement of Borrower in this Instrument shall be applied first to the costs, if any, of taking control of and managing the Property and collecting the rents, including, but not limited to, attorney's fees, receiver's fees, premiums on receiver's bonds, costs of repairs to the Property, premiums on insurance policies, taxes, assessments and other charges on the Property, and the costs of discharging any obligation or liability of Borrower as lessor or landlord of the Property and then to the sums secured by this Instrument. Lender or the receiver shall have access to the books and records used in the operation and maintenance of the Property and shall be liable to account only for those rents actually received. Lender shall not be liable to Borrower, anyone claiming under or through Borrower or anyone having an interest in the Property by reason of anything done or left undone by Lender under this paragraph 26.

If the rents of the Property are not sufficient to meet the costs, if any, of taking control of and managing the Property and collecting the rents, any funds expended by Lender for such purposes shall become indebtedness of Borrower to Lender secured by this Instrument pursuant to paragraph 8 hereof. Unless Lender and Borrower agree in writing to other terms of payment, such amounts shall be payable upon notice from Lender to Borrower requesting payment thereof and shall bear interest from the date of disbursement at the rate stated in the Note unless payment of interest at such rate would be contrary to applicable law, in which event such amounts shall bear interest at the highest rate which may be collected from Borrower under applicable law.

Any entering upon and taking and maintaining of control of the Property by Lender or the receiver and any application of rents as provided herein shall not cure or waive any default hereunder or invalidate any other right or remedy of Lender under applicable law or provided herein. This assignment of rents of the Property shall terminate at such time as this Instrument ceases to secure indebtedness held by Lender.

Uniform Covenants—Multifamily—1/77—FNMA/FHLMC Uniform Instrument   *(page 6 of 8 pages)*

Figure 11–13.   *Fannie Mae/FHLMC Texas Multifamily Deed of Trust, page 7*

Non-Uniform Covenants. Borrower and Lender further covenant and agree as follows:

27. ACCELERATION; REMEDIES. Upon Borrower's breach of any covenant or agreement of Borrower in this Instrument, including, but not limited to, the covenants to pay when due any sums secured by this Instrument, Lender at Lender's option may declare all of the sums secured by this Instrument to be immediately due and payable without further demand and may invoke the power of sale and any other remedies permitted by applicable law or provided herein. Borrower acknowledges that the power of sale herein granted may be exercised by Lender without prior judicial hearing. Borrower has the right to bring an action to assert the non-existence of a breach or any other defense of Borrower to acceleration and sale. Lender shall be entitled to collect all costs and expenses incurred in pursuing such remedies, including, but not limited to, attorney's fees and costs of documentary evidence, abstracts and title reports.

If Lender invokes the power of sale, Lender or Trustee shall give notice of the time, place and terms of sale by posting written notice at least 21 days prior to the day of sale at the courthouse door in each of the counties in which the Property is situated. Lender shall mail a copy of the notice of sale to Borrower in the manner provided by applicable law. Trustee shall sell the Property according to the laws of Texas. Such sale shall be made at public vendue between the hours of 10 o'clock a.m. and 4 o'clock p.m. on the first Tuesday in any month. Borrower authorizes Trustee to sell the Property to the highest bidder for cash in one or more parcels and in such order as Trustee may determine. Lender or Lender's designee may purchase the Property at any sale.

Trustee shall deliver to the purchaser Trustee's deed conveying the Property so sold in fee simple with covenants of general warranty. Borrower covenants and agrees to defend generally the purchaser's title to the Property against all claims and demands. The recitals in Trustee's deed shall be prima facie evidence of the truth of the statements contained therein. Trustee shall apply the proceeds of the sale in the following order: (a) to all reasonable costs and expenses of the sale, including, but not limited to, reasonable Trustee's fees and attorney's fees and costs of title evidence; (b) to all sums secured by this Instrument in such order as Lender, in Lender's sole discretion, directs; and (c) the excess, if any, to the person or persons legally entitled thereto.

If the Property is sold pursuant to this paragraph 27, Borrower or any person holding possession of the Property through Borrower shall immediately surrender possession of the Property to the purchaser at such sale upon the purchaser's written demand. If possession is not surrendered upon the purchaser's written demand, Borrower or such person shall be a tenant at sufferance and may be removed by writ of possession or by an action for forcible entry and detainer.

28. RELEASE. Upon payment of all sums secured by this Instrument, Lender shall release this Instrument. Borrower shall pay Lender's reasonable costs incurred in releasing this Instrument.

29. SUBSTITUTE TRUSTEE. Lender at Lender's option, with or without cause, may from time to time remove Trustee and appoint a successor trustee to any Trustee appointed hereunder by an instrument recorded in the county in which this Instrument is recorded. Without conveyance of the Property, the successor trustee shall succeed to all the title, power and duties conferred upon the Trustee herein and by applicable law.

30. SUBROGATION. Any of the proceeds of the Note utilized to take up outstanding liens against all or any part of the Property have been advanced by Lender at Borrower's request and upon Borrower's representation that such amounts are due and are secured by valid liens against the Property. Lender shall be subrogated to any and all rights, superior titles, liens and equities owned or claimed by any owner or holder of any outstanding liens and debts, however remote, regardless of whether said liens or debts are acquired by Lender by assignment or are released by the holder thereof upon payment.

31. PARTIAL INVALIDITY. In the event any portion of the sums intended to be secured by this Instrument cannot be lawfully secured hereby, payments in reduction of such sums shall be applied first to those portions not secured hereby.

32. VENDOR'S LIEN; RENEWAL AND EXTENSION. The Note secured hereby is [primarily secured by the Vendor's Lien retained in the Deed of even date herewith conveying the Property to Borrower, which Vendor's Lien has been assigned to Lender, this Instrument being additional security therefor.]* [in renewal and extension, but not in extinguishment, of that certain indebtedness described as follows:]*
* *Delete bracketed clauses as appropriate.*

33. FUTURE ADVANCES. Upon request of Borrower, Lender, at Lender's option so long as this Instrument secures indebtedness held by Lender, may make Future Advances to Borrower. Such Future Advances, with interest thereon, shall be secured by this Instrument when evidenced by promissory notes stating that said notes are secured hereby. At no time shall the principal amount of the indebtedness secured by this Instrument, not including sums advanced in accordance herewith to protect the security of this Instrument, exceed the original amount of the Note (US $.................) plus the additional sum of US $.................

IN WITNESS WHEREOF, Borrower has executed this Instrument or has caused the same to be executed by its representatives thereunto duly authorized.

Borrower's Address:

Figure 11–14.   Fannie Mae/FHLMC Texas Multifamily Deed of Trust, page 8

CORPORATE ACKNOWLEDGMENT

THE STATE OF TEXAS, ... County ss:

BEFORE ME, the undersigned, a Notary Public in and for said County and State, on this day personally appeared ....
...., ... of ...., the
corporation that executed the foregoing instrument, known to me to be the person and officer whose name is subscribed to the
foregoing instrument, and acknowledged to me that the same was the act of the said corporation, and that he executed the same as
the act of such corporation for the purposes and consideration therein expressed and in the capacity therein stated.

GIVEN UNDER MY HAND AND SEAL OF OFFICE this .... day of ...., 19.........

....
Notary Public in and for

.... County, Texas.

INDIVIDUAL ACKNOWLEDGMENT

THE STATE OF TEXAS, ... County ss:

BEFORE ME, the undersigned, a Notary Public in and for said County and State, on this day personally appeared ....
....
...., known to me to be the person(s) whose name(s)...............................
subscribed to the foregoing instrument, and acknowledged to me that ....he......... executed the same for the purposes and
consideration therein expressed.

GIVEN UNDER MY HAND AND SEAL OF OFFICE this .... day of ...., 19.........

....
Notary Public in and for

.... County, Texas.

INDIVIDUAL LIMITED PARTNERSHIP ACKNOWLEDGMENT

THE STATE OF TEXAS, ... County ss:

BEFORE ME, the undersigned, a Notary Public in and for said County and State, on this day personally appeared ....
....
...., known to me to be general partner(s) of ....
...., the limited partnership that executed the foregoing instrument, and known to me
to be the person(s) who executed the foregoing instrument on behalf of said limited partnership, and .... acknowledged to me
that said limited partnership executed the same for the purposes and consideration therein expressed.

GIVEN UNDER MY HAND AND SEAL OF OFFICE this .... day of ...., 19.........

....
Notary Public in and for

.... County, Texas.

CORPORATE LIMITED PARTNERSHIP ACKNOWLEDGMENT

THE STATE OF TEXAS, ... County ss:

BEFORE ME, the undersigned, a Notary Public in and for said County and State, on this day personally appeared ....
...., known to me to be the .... of ....
...., the corporation that executed the foregoing instrument, and known to me to be
the person who executed the foregoing instrument on behalf of said corporation, said corporation being known to me to be general
partner of ...., the limited partnership that executed the
foregoing instrument, and acknowledged to me that such corporation executed the same as such general partner and that such limited
partnership executed the same for the purposes and consideration therein expressed.

GIVEN UNDER MY HAND AND SEAL OF OFFICE this .... day of ...., 19.........

....
Notary Public in and for

.... County, Texas.

Figure 11–15.   Multifamily Due-on-Transfer Rider

DUE-ON-TRANSFER RIDER

Notice: This rider adds a provision to the Instrument allowing the Lender to require repayment of the Note in full upon transfer of the property.

This Due-On-Transfer Rider is made this . . . . day of . . . . ,19 . . . . . . , and is incorporated into and shall be deemed to amend and supplement the Mortgage, Deed of Trust, or Deed to Secure Debt (the "Instrument") of the same date given by the undersigned (the "Borrower") to secure Borrower's Note to . . . . (the "Lender") of the same date (the "Note") and covering the property described in the Instrument and located at:

. . . .

(Property Address)

AMENDED COVENANT. In addition to the covenants and agreements made in the Instrument, Borrower and Lender further covenant and agree as follows:

A. TRANSFER OF THE PROPERTY OR A BENEFICIAL INTEREST IN BORROWER

Uniform Covenant 19 of the Instrument is amended to read as follows:

19. Transfer of the Property or a Beneficial Interest in Borrower. If all or any part of the Property or an interest therein is sold or transferred by Borrower (or if a beneficial interest in Borrower is sold or transferred and Borrower is not a natural person or persons but is a corporation, partnership, trust or other legal entity) without Lender's prior written consent, excluding
   (a) a transfer by devise, descent or by operation of law upon the death of a joint tenant or partner,
   (b) the grant of any leasehold interest in a part of the Property of three years or less (or such longer lease term as Lender may permit by prior written approval) not containing an option to purchase (except any interest in the ground lease, if this Instrument is on a leasehold),
   (c) sales or transfers of beneficial interests in Borrower provided such sales or transfers, together with any prior sales or transfers of beneficial interests in Borrower, but excluding sales or transfers under subparagraph (a) above, do not result in more than 49% of the beneficial interests in Borrower having been sold or transferred since commencement of amortization of the Note, or
   (d) sales or transfers of fixtures or any personal property pursuant to the first paragraph of paragraph 6 hereof,
Lender may, at Lender's option, declare all the sums secured by this Instrument to be immediately due and payable and Lender may invoke any remedies permitted by paragraph 27 of this Instrument.

Lender may consent to a sale or transfer if: (1) Borrower causes to be submitted to Lender information required by Lender to evaluate the transferee as if a new loan were being made to the transferee; (2) Lender reasonably determines that Lender's security will not be impaired and that the risk of a breach of any covenant or agreement in this Instrument is acceptable; (3) interest will be payable on the sums secured by this Instrument at a rate acceptable to Lender; (4) changes in the terms of the Note and this Instrument required by Lender are made, including, for example, periodic adjustment in the interest rate, a different final payment date for the loan, and addition of unpaid interest to principal; and (5) the transferee signs an assumption agreement that is acceptable to Lender and that obligates the transferee to keep all the promises and agreements made in the Note and in this Instrument, as modified if required by Lender. To the extent permitted by applicable law, Lender also may charge a reasonable fee as a condition to Lender's consent to any sale or transfer.

Borrower will continue to be obligated under the Note and this Instrument unless Lender releases Borrower in writing.

IN WITNESS WHEREOF, Borrower has executed this Due-On-Transfer Rider.

DUE-ON-TRANSFER RIDER—MULTIFAMILY—7/82—FHLMC UNIFORM INSTRUMENT

Figure 11–16.   Plan B Amendment to Multifamily Note, page 2

This Note may not be prepaid, in whole or in part, (excluding prepayments occurring as a result of application by the holder hereof of insurance or condemnation awards or proceeds pursuant to the Mortgage or Deed of Trust securing this Note) prior to the _____ day of _____ , 19_____* (the "permitted prepayment date"). Thereafter, the unpaid principal and accrued interest may be prepaid in whole or in part provided the above named Borrower(s) give(s) the holder hereof written notice of the full amount to be prepaid at least _____** days prior to each such prepayment and provided further that the above named Borrower(s) pay(s) to the holder hereof, together with each prepayment (excluding prepayments occurring as a result of the acceleration by the holder hereof of the principal amount of this Note and of application by the holder hereof of insurance or condemnation awards or proceeds pursuant to the Mortgage or Deed of Trust securing this Note), a prepayment charge equal to _____*** of the principal prepaid. The above named Borrower(s) acknowledge(s) that the prepayment prohibition is a material part of the consideration for this loan and that the Noteholder has a business need to avoid payment of principal prior to the permitted prepayment date.

Notice to Seller/Servicers:

*Prepayment must be prohibited for at least 54 months following delivery to Freddie Mac for purchase in order to meet Freddie Mac minimum prepayment requirements and be eligible for purchase.

**Lender's option.

***Prepayment charge must be equal to at least one percent (1.0%) of the principal prepaid in order to meet Freddie Mac minimum prepayment charge requirements and be eligible for purchase.

Freddie Mac in 5 days, the required net yield would be 14.36; but if the lender had secured a commitment to deliver in 91 to 120 days, the required net yield would have increased to 14.69. In addition, the real estate professional can compare the required net yield for the fixed-rate mortgages and the adjustable-rate mortgages. Once again, the yields quoted on the release are net and do not include the lender's servicing fee. If you will look at the bottom of page 3, it states that the yields are quoted at a net yield exclusive of the .375 percent servicing fee applicable for whole loans. With this in mind, what would be the yield that a lender would show on a 30-year mortgage that would be delivered to Freddie Mac under a 0- to 30-day delivery commitment dated July 25, 1984? First you would locate the proper mortgage and then the proper delivery under that mortgage, in this case that is the 0 to 30 delivery program under the 30-year mortgage. Then, you would come across to the proper date and find the net yield to be 14.36 percent. Since this is net yield, you would add the .375 percent servicing fee, giving a rate of 14.735 percent. Since the lender has the ability to round the rate to the nearest one eighth of 1 percent, the note rate would be increased to 14.75 percent.

THE GOVERNMENT NATIONAL MORTGAGE ASSOCIATION (GNMA)

The Government National Mortgage Association, sometimes known as Ginnie Mae, was created September 1, 1968, with the passage of an amendment to Title III of the National Housing Act. In the amendment in Section

302 of Title III, Fannie Mae was rechartered into two separate corporations: the Federal National Mortgage Association (FNMA) and a governmental corporation to be known as the Government National Mortgage Association (GNMA). GNMA is under the control of the Department of Housing and Urban Development. HUD is responsible for the establishment of all of the policies of, as well as responsible for all of the operations of GNMA. The Secretary of HUD was given the power to adopt, amend, or repeal any bylaws of the corporation governing the performance of the duties imposed by the enacting law.

Also included in the amendment was the authority to establish the position of President of the Government National Mortgage Association, in the Department of Housing and Urban Development. Section 308 of Title III, as amended in 1976, states that the President of the GNMA will be appointed by the President of the United States with the advice and consent of the Senate, and that the remaining executive officers of GNMA will be appointed by the Secretary of Housing and Urban Development.

The Functions of GNMA

The functions or purposes of GNMA are in three specific areas. One of the three functions of GNMA is the special assistance function. Under this function, GNMA will purchase whole loans, or participations in certain types of loans, in order to meet two statutory requirements: (1) the purchase of residential loans, originated under special housing programs for which the financing is not presently available through the normal sources in the

Figure 11-17.   Freddie Mac Commitment Activity, page 1

FOR IMMEDIATE RELEASE
July 26, 1984
CONTACT: TAMBREY MATTHEWS
                         (202) 789-4448

FREDDIE MAC COMMITMENT ACTIVITY

WASHINGTON, D.C. -- The net yield Freddie Mac requires on its purchases of 30-year fixed-rate mortgages for 30-day delivery was 14.36 percent on July 25, down from 14.47 percent on July 18, one week earlier.

A Freddie Mac spokesman said, "Continuing low inflation, despite large deficits and the strong economic expansion, may be contributing toward somewhat lower interest rates as investors reduce the premium required as protection from future inflation."

Freddie Mac's commitments to purchase mortgages over the past five business days totaled $1.4 billion in both its standard and Guarantor programs.

As of July 25, Freddie Mac has committed to purchase $15.4 billion in residential mortgages in 1984.

Commitments to sell Freddie Mac securities called Mortgage Participation Certificates (PCs) over the past five business days were $1.3 billion in both the standard and Guarantor programs. The average yield on PCs sold for settlement within 60 days was 13.86 percent for the week ending July 25 and 13.88 percent for the previous week ending July 18.

(more)

1776 G Street NW
PO Box 37248
Washington, DC 20013

Figure 11–18.   Freddie Mac Commitment Activity, page 2

FREDDIE MAC COMMITMENT ACTIVITY
July 26, 1984
PAGE TWO

Commitments in 1984 to sell PCs are $12.2 billion as of July 25.
Total commitments to sell PCs since inception of the program are
$97 billion.

The Guarantor program allows lenders to simultaneously sell
mortgage loans and purchase PCs representing undivided interests in
those same mortgages.

Freddie Mac is a publicly chartered corporation whose stock is
owned by savings institutions across the nation and is held in trust by
the Federal Home Loan Bank System. Its purpose is to increase mortgage
money for home loans and it does so by buying mortgages from local
lenders and reselling these mortgages as securities for investors around
the nation.

# # # # #

Figure 11–19.   Freddie Mac Commitment Activity, page 3

FREDDIE MAC COMMITMENT ACTIVITY
DAILY POSTED YIELDS*

PURCHASE PROGRAMS	07/19/84	07/20/84	07/23/84	07/24/84	07/25/84
30-year fixed-rate					
0- 10 day delivery	14.36	14.36	14.57	14.38	14.30
0- 30 day delivery	14.44	14.44	14.64	14.45	14.36
0- 60 day delivery	14.52	14.52	14.71	14.52	14.42
61- 90 day delivery	14.60	14.60	14.78	14.59	14.49
91-120 day delivery	14.69	14.69	14.85	14.66	14.56
120 day delivery-optional (A)				14.66	
120 day delivery-optional (B)				15.16	
240 day delivery-optional				15.67	
15-year fixed-rate					
0- 30 day delivery	14.31	14.31	14.45	14.25	14.21
0- 60 day delivery	14.38	14.38	14.51	14.31	14.28
61- 90 day delivery	14.46	14.45	14.58	14.38	14.34
91-120 day delivery	14.51	14.51	14.65	14.45	14.41
1-year ARM					
0- 30 day delivery	13.10	13.10	13.10	13.03	13.03
0- 60 day delivery	13.36	13.36	13.36	13.27	13.27
61- 90 day delivery	13.61	13.61	13.61	13.52	13.52
91-120 day delivery	13.86	13.86	13.86	13.76	13.76
120 day delivery-optional				13.76	
3-year ARM					
0- 30 day delivery	14.39	14.39	14.39	14.26	14.26
0- 60 day delivery	14.53	14.53	14.53	14.38	14.38
61- 90 day delivery	14.67	14.67	14.67	14.50	14.50
91-120 day delivery	14.81	14.81	14.81	14.61	14.61
120 day delivery-optional				14.61	
5-year ARM					
0- 30 day delivery	14.79	14.79	14.79	14.63	14.63
0- 60 day delivery	14.90	14.90	14.90	14.72	14.72
61- 90 day delivery	15.01	15.01	15.01	14.82	14.82
91-120 day delivery	15.13	15.13	15.13	14.92	14.92
120 day delivery-optional				14.92	
Home Improvement Loan (HIL)	14.52	14.52	14.71	14.52	14.42
Multifamily (Immediate Delivery)					
Plan A	14.81	14.81	15.02	14.83	14.74
Plan B	14.20	14.20	14.39	14.20	14.17
PC SALES		**1984 SETTLEMENT**			
Average Weighted Price-Aug	99.12	98.24	98.28	98.08	99.29
Average Weighted Yield-Aug	13.81	13.92	13.90	13.84	13.72
Average Weighted Price-Sept	99.00	98.17		98.30	99.18
Average Weighted Yield-Sept	13.88	13.96		13.88	13.78
Average Weighted Price-Oct	98.20	98.08	98.08		99.09
Average Weighted Yield-Oct	13.94	14.01	14.01		13.83

Commitment Volume 07/19/84 thru 07/25/84   (thousands)

Total Purchases	$1,367,772
Standard Program	$ 102,094
Guarantor Program	$1,265,678
Total Sales	$1,281,378
Standard Program	$ 15,700
Guarantor Program	$1,265,678

*Yields are quoted at a net yield exclusive of the .375% servicing fee applicable for whole loans.

open market; and (2) the purchase of, or the participation in, residential mortgages in order to stop or counter declines in mortgage lending or home construction. This function will be discussed in detail later in this chapter.

The second function is the management and liquidation function. Under this function, GNMA is authorized to be responsible for the orderly management and liquidation of mortgages acquired by Fannie Mae prior to the close of business on October 31, 1954. The dollar amount of these mortgages transferred to GNMA was $3,012,905,653.

> *GNMA was responsible for the management and liquidation of other mortgages, loans, and other obligations acquired and to be acquired, in an orderly manner, with a minimum of adverse effect upon the home mortgage market and minimum loss to the Federal Government.* [1]

Under this function, GNMA is also authorized to purchase mortgages on residential properties from any Federal agency and also to purchase any obligation offered by the Department of Housing and Urban Development. One other operation authorized under this function by the corporate charter is to guarantee the timely payment of principal and interest on securities that are backed by a pool of mortgages.

The ability to insure the timely payment of principal and interest allows GNMA to carry out its third major function: the mortgage backed securities program. This program will be covered later in this chapter.

Corporate Offices

As they require of Fannie Mae, the amendments to the National Housing Act require that the corporate headquarters of GNMA be located in Washington, D.C. The act also allows GNMA to maintain branch or regional offices, but at the present time GNMA now operates through the five regional offices of Fannie Mae. If you should have any questions about any of the programs of GNMA, contact the regional office nearest you.

Source of Funds

The major source of funds for the operation of GNMA is the U.S. Treasury, but GNMA also generates income from the following sources: sales of mortgages, commitment fees, fees charged for the processing of commitments,

and discount fees charged in some of the special assistance programs. These fees are sometimes referred to as income from operations.

Special Assistance Programs

History   When Fannie Mae was divided in 1968 into the two corporations, Fannie Mae was to continue its activities in the support of the secondary market in general, whereas GNMA was chartered to conduct or support specialized programs in the secondary market. This function of GNMA has come to be called the Special Assistance Function (SAF). The SAF is to support certain types of mortgages and the housing market in times of tight money, as well as to stimulate home construction when the industry is declining.

The original SAF was limited to the purchase of government-underwritten mortgages, but with the enactment of the Emergency Home Purchase Act of 1974, the function was expanded to include conventional mortgages. The President of the United States was given the authority, under Section 305 of the title, to institute a Special Assistance Program. The President,

> *after taking into account (1) the conditions in the building industry and the national economy and (2) conditions affecting the home mortgage investment market, generally, or affecting various types or classifications of home mortgages, or both, and after determining that such action is in the public interest, may under this section authorize the Association, for such period of time and to such extent as he shall prescribe, to exercise its powers to make commitments to purchase such types, classes, or categories of home mortgages (including participations therein) as he shall determine.*

This authority was later delegated to the Secretary of Housing and Urban Development by Executive Order No. 11732, approved July 30, 1973.

Eligible sellers or participants   For a lender to be eligible to sell to GNMA, the lender must meet certain requirements and execute a GNMA Seller Agreement, known as GNMA Form 301. In addition to the agreement, the GNMA will require the lender to have the ability to service the loans sold to GNMA either through a service agreement with a company specializing in the servicing of mortgage loans or through an in-house ability.

If the lender wishes to sell a HUD/FHA-insured loan or VA-guaranteed mortgage to GNMA through one of the special assistance programs, the lender must be an approved FHA or VA lender. If a lender wishes to sell a conventional mortgage to GNMA, the lender must be a lender who is approved by the Federal National Mortgage Association. These are just a few of the requirements for lenders who wish to sell to GNMA. If you are interested in all of the requirements, they are listed in detail in the Government National Mortgage Association's *Seller's Guide.*

Tandem programs The programs that are operated under the Special Assistance Function of GNMA are commonly referred to as *tandem programs.* The term *tandem* originated in 1970 because of several agreements between GNMA and Fannie Mae. Under these agreements, GNMA would agree to issue commitments to purchase mortgages through a special assistance program, then the commitment would be transferred to Fannie Mae, which would actually purchase the mortgage. If the return was below market or the rate established by Fannie Mae, GNMA would make up the difference. This practice of issuing the commitments and then selling to Fannie Mae is no longer done, but the term has remained and now refers to the purchase of below-market interest rate loans by GNMA and the selling of these loans to private investors. The ability to make this type of loan and to sell to private investors has a twofold benefit: it aids the housing market, and it reduces the amount of federal monies that must be used to support these types of loans.

In addition to the advantages of the tandem program outlined above, it is a great help to the building industry in that a builder wishing to build either single-family or multifamily units can arrange for the permanent financing of the housing prior to the start of construction, at below market rates. With the permanent financing established, the builder or developer can then arrange for the interim financing to construct the housing.

What are the steps to be followed in applying for a tandem program, or commitment?[2] The steps are as follows:

1. The builder or developer approaches a GNMA-approved seller in order to apply for a commitment from GNMA.

2. The approved GNMA seller approaches GNMA for a commitment.

(If the commitment is issued, it will be for a period of one year, if the structure in question is a single-family dwelling. The commitment can be for a period of 36 months for multifamily projects. If the commitment is on a single-family dwelling, the mortgage can be delivered to GNMA at any time during the one-year commitment period. If the lender does not wish to deliver the mortgage to GNMA, the lender will only be charged a commitment fee. This commitment fee at the present time is 1 percent of the loan amount.)

3. GNMA issues the commitment to the mortgage lender.

4. With a firm commitment from GNMA, the lender will then issue its commitment to the builder or developer to furnish the permanent financing for the structure upon completion.

5. The builder or developer will use that commitment from the mortgage lender to arrange for interim, or construction, financing.

6. After the construction is completed, the GNMA approved mortgage lender will make the permanent loan to the homebuyer.

After the mortgage lender has closed the permanent loan, the lender has three options:

1. Keep the mortgage as part of the lender's portfolio.

2. Sell the mortgage to a private investor and forfeit the commitment fee paid to GNMA.

3. Sell the mortgage to GNMA under the terms of the commitment, and then GNMA will sell the mortgage to a private investor.

This process is illustrated in Figure 11–20.

Special assistance program announcements Since the program of special assistance has been instituted, some twenty-seven announcements of programs have been instituted by action of the President of the United States or the Secretary of Housing and Urban Development. The first announcement had an effective date of November 1, 1954, and was for disaster housing mortgages. Under this announcement, GNMA would enter into contracts to purchase mortgages that were either insured by FHA or guaranteed by the VA, covering the financing of homes of victims of a

Figure 11–20.   Tandem Program Process

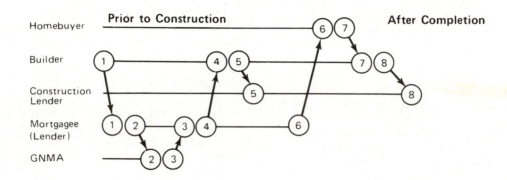

TANDEM PROGRAM PROCESS

Mortgagee Options

1. Retain mortgage
2. Sell mortgage to private investor
3. Deliver mortgage to GNMA; GNMA in turn sells loan to private investor

Source: Government National Mortgage Association, *Annual Report 1977*, Department of Housing and Urban Development, June 1978. Housing and Urban Development Publication: HUD-85-6N (2)

major disaster as determined by the President of the United States.

These are just 2 of the 27 announcements of programs. For further information regarding the other programs available through the SAF of GNMA, contact a GNMA Regional Office.

Mortgage-Backed Securities Program (MBS)

The Mortgage-Backed Securities Program, sometimes called *Pass-Throughs* or *Ginnie Maes,* was authorized by the 1968 amendment of the National Housing Act. The 1968 amendment, in section 804(b), added subsection (g) to section 306 of the National Housing Act. The first sentence of the subsection states that

> *The Association [GNMA] is authorized, upon such terms and conditions as it may deem appropriate, to guarantee the timely payment of principal of and interest on such certificates or other securities. . . (2) be based on or backed by a trust or pool comprised of mortgages which are insured under the National Housing Act or Title V of the National Housing Act of 1949, or which are insured or guaranteed under the Servicemen's Readjustment Act of 1944 . . . .*

The first MBS was issued in February 1970.

Purpose   The purpose of the MBS program is to attract investors to invest in the residential mortgage market by the offering of government-backed-and-guaranteed securities. The program has been a great success and, according to GNMA, over $80 billion of MBSs have been issued, thus making the program the third largest supplier of mortgage funds in the United States.

Under this program, the investor or the holder of an MBS is guaranteed the timely payment of principal and interest as per the terms of the MBS. The payment will be made by GNMA whether or not GNMA has received its payment from the originator of the mortgage. Thus, the MBS is one of the safest of all investments, for it is backed by the full faith and credit of the United States of America. In addition to the safety of the MBS, it has other advantages to the investor or purchaser. One such advantage is that the MBS has the highest yield of any federally guaranteed security. Another advantage to the purchaser is that the return on the MBS compares very favorably to the yields of corporate debt issues.

Eligible mortgages and pools   As stated earlier, mortgages that may serve as security for the MBS are limited by law. The mortgages that are authorized are mortgages on single-family dwellings either insured by FHA or guaranteed by Veterans Administration, mobile home loans that are either insured by FHA or guaranteed by the VA, and some multifamily project loans insured by FHA.

These mortgages are then packaged into a group of eligible mortgages, called a *pool.* Usually the mortgages in a pool will be of the same type yield. For example, all of the mortgages could be FHA-insured on single-family dwellings – a pool sometimes called a standard FHA pool.

In addition to the standard pool, additional pools have been authorized such as a graduated mortgage pool. This is a pool exclusively comprised of Section 245 FHA graduated payment mortgages.

GNMA has established the minimum size of the pools. For pools of FHA or VA single-family mortgages, the minimum is $1 million. For pools of multifamily project-construction loans or multifamily project loans, the minimum is $500,000. The minimum amount for a pool of mobile home loans is also $500,000.

Types of mortgage-backed securities   Presently, three types of mortgage-backed securities are authorized: pass-through, bond, and graduated payment mortgage-backed.

The *pass-through* security is further divided into two types of securities known as the *straight pass-through* and the *modified pass-through.* With the straight pass-through security, the purchaser will receive a proportionate share of the proceeds of the principal and interest as collected, less servicing fees and other costs approved by GNMA. On the other hand the modified pass-through security provides for the payment of the specified principal installment and a fixed rate of interest on the unpaid principal, whether or not these payments are collected from the borrower, and with all prepayments being passed through to the security holder. Both straight pass-through and modified pass-through securities must specify the dates that the payments are to be made to the holder of the security. This date of payment is usually the fifteenth of each month. The minimum amount of the straight and modified pass-through certificate is now $25,000 and may increase in $5,000 increments.

The second type of security authorized to be issued by GNMA is the bond type of security. As the name implies, this is a long-term security and it guarantees the payment of interest on a semiannual basis with principal reduction as per an agreed schedule outlined in the security agreement. This type of MBS has not been issued in large numbers, for the requirements for the mortgage lenders are rather high. GNMA now has the following requirement for any corporation, trust, partnership, or other entity to be able to issue the bond type security: the entity must have at least a net worth of $50 million in assets acceptable to GNMA and have the capacity to assemble acceptable and eligible mortgages to support the minimum pool size. The minimum pool size for the issuance of the bond type security is currently $100 million.

The third security is the graduated payment mortgage-backed security. As of March 29, 1979, GNMA was authorized to guarantee the timely payment of principal and interest on modified pass-through securities that are based on a pool of mortgages with unlevel monthly installments, or those mortgages that are insured under section 245 of the National Housing Act, provided that the graduated payment mortgages in the pool provide for level monthly installments beginning no later than the sixty-first payment. As with the pass-through and the modified pass-through, the minimum pool is $1 million and the minimum face amount of the securities is $25,000 and can be increased in $5,000 increments.

Eligible issuers of MBSs

According to Title 24, Chapter III, of the Code of Federal Regulations, to be eligible to issue securities an issuer must meet the following:

1. Be an approved FHA lender, in good standing

2. Be an approved Fannie Mae seller/servicer in current good standing with Fannie Mae

3. Have adequate experience, management capability, and facilities to issue and service mortgage-backed securities, as determined by GNMA

4. Maintain the minimum acceptable net worth in assets prescribed by GNMA

These are a few of the requirements for lenders. For more information as to the minimum requirements, you should contact the home office of GNMA or request a copy of the *Mortgage-Backed Securities Guide* from

GNMA Services Division
Room 6210
U.S. Department of HUD
Washington, D.C. 20410

Program outline   In the previous sections of this chapter we discussed the various aspects of the MBS program, from the history of the program and who can issue MBS, to the types of securities that can be issued. Now let us examine how the program works.

The first step is for the lender to apply to GNMA to become an approved issuer and at the same time apply for a commitment from GNMA for a guaranty of security. Once the approval and the commitment are issued, the mortgage lender starts either to originate the loans required to meet the minimum pool requirement, or if the lender wishes, to acquire mortgages from other lenders in sufficient amounts to make up the required pool. As we learned earlier, the minimum for the standard FHA pool is $1 million.

While the mortgage lender is either originating or acquiring the necessary mortgages, it is also making arrangements with a securities dealer to market the securities when they become available. When the mortgage lender has arranged for the steps above, the process begins (Figure 11–21).

Working through Figure 11–21, one can see that the process is divided into three different stages. In the first stage, the family buys a home and applies for a loan from VA, FHA, or FmHA. Upon approval of the loan, the mortgage lender makes the loan and the homeowners begin the payments.

In the second stage, this mortgage goes into the pool and the mortgage lender sets up the required escrow accounts. The mortgage documents are held in trust by a custodian. Once the pool of mortgages is assembled, the mortgage lender submits all of the required documents to GNMA. GNMA will review all of the documents and effect delivery of the securities within 20 calendar days.

In the third stage, once the review is completed, GNMA will prepare and deliver the securities to the securities dealer as per the mortgage lender's instructions. The securities dealer will sell the securities in the open market to the general public or institutions. When the securities are sold, the GNMA transfer agent is notified and the ownership of the securities is transferred to the purchaser.

Once the securities are sold, the mortgage lender or issuer of the securities is responsible for ensuring that the payment of principal and

Figure 11–21.   How the GNMA Mortgage-Backed Securities Program Works

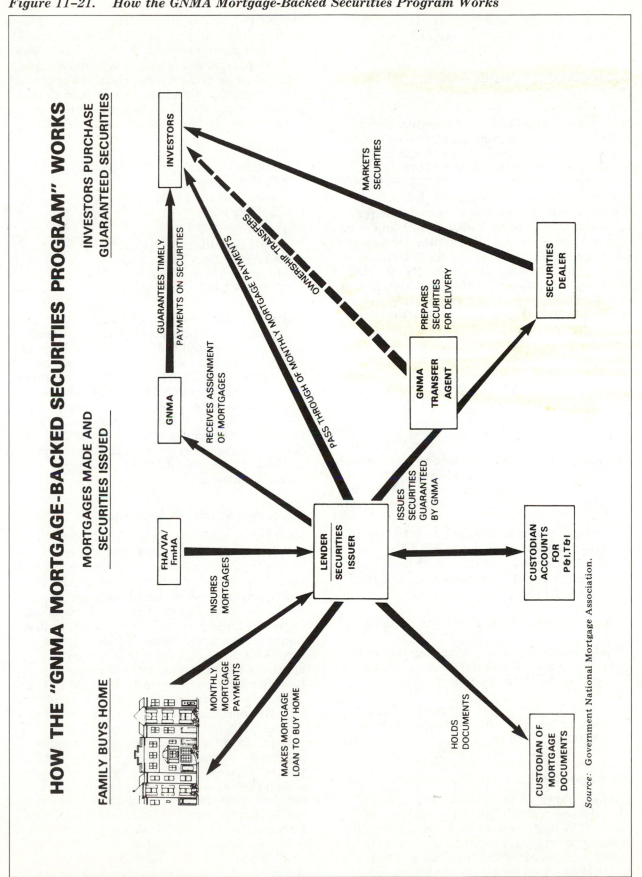

HOW THE "GNMA MORTGAGE-BACKED SECURITIES PROGRAM" WORKS

FAMILY BUYS HOME

MORTGAGES MADE AND
SECURITIES ISSUED

INVESTORS PURCHASE
GUARANTEED SECURITIES

INVESTORS

MARKETS
SECURITIES

GUARANTEES TIMELY
PAYMENTS ON SECURITIES

OWNERSHIP TRANSFERS

PASS THROUGH OF MONTHLY MORTGAGE PAYMENTS

RECEIVES ASSIGNMENT
OF MORTGAGES

GNMA

SECURITIES DEALER

PREPARES
SECURITIES
FOR DELIVERY

GNMA
TRANSFER
AGENT

FHA/VA/
FmHA

INSURES
MORTGAGES

LENDER
SECURITIES
ISSUER

ISSUES
SECURITIES
GUARANTEED
BY GNMA

MONTHLY
MORTGAGE
PAYMENTS

MAKES MORTGAGE
LOAN TO BUY HOME

HOLDS
DOCUMENTS

CUSTODIAN
ACCOUNTS
FOR
P&I, T&I

CUSTODIAN OF
MORTGAGE
DOCUMENTS

Source: Government National Mortgage Association.

interest is passed through to the investors, less any fees authorized by GNMA.

RESIDENTIAL FUNDING CORPORATION (RFC)

As mentioned earlier in this chapter, the secondary market is dominated by three major funding organizations: Federal National Mortgage Corporation, Federal Home Loan Mortgage Corporation, and the Government National Mortgage Association. Since these organizations are controlled by the Congress in regard to maximum loan amounts and other segments of their operations, they are somewhat limited and it is felt by some financial experts that these organizations are not able to meet all of today's funding requirements. So in 1982, Residential Funding Corporation was incorporated as a subsidiary of Norwest Mortgage, the former Banco Mortgage Company. RFC has established what they have called a "conduit" program. The purpose of the program is to provide a constant conduit of funds for the purchase of only conventional loans from approved lenders.

Approved Lenders

According to RFC before a lender may become a qualified *RFC Originating Lender*, RFC has established four basic requirements. A lender must have

1. Experience and be familiar with the origination of conventional and FHA/VA real estate loans, in accordance with accepted standards and demonstrate the use of prudent guidelines.

2. A current net worth of at least $250,000.

3. Submitted to RFC for review and approval of three years of audited financial statements of condition and income.

4. A letter of credit from a financial institution that is acceptable to RFC of at least $200,000.

Loan Approval

The loan approval process for RFC is somewhat different from that of Fannie Mae and FHLMC in that the lenders are not given in-house approval. According to RFC, once the lender has processed the loan and all required material has been gathered, the lender will

submit the loan package to the nearest RFC underwriting office. It should be noted that RFC does not underwrite the loans. RFC uses Mortgage Guaranty Insurance Corporation (MGIC) as its underwriter. Thus, the approved RFC originator would submit the loan to the nearest Texas MGIC underwriting office for RFC. There are two such offices in Texas:

MGIC
Carillon Tower East, Suite 610
13601 Preston Road
Dallas, Texas 75240
(214) 233-8639

MGIC
North Belt Place III Building
340 North Belt East, Suite 180
Houston, Texas 77060
(713) 448-7878

Then, after the loan is approved by MGIC, the lender is notified at which time the lender may close and fund the loan. As a real estate professional, you can see that if you are located in a city with a RFC underwriting office approval can be rather fast, but if you are located away from one of the underwriting offices the approval may be delayed. The reason is that the loan package must be forwarded to the underwriting office by some method of transportation that can sometimes be time consuming.

Mortgage Purchase Program

RFC will purchase loans secured by a 1- to 4-family dwelling consisting of a detached, semidetached, row, townhouse, unit in a condominium project (up to 3 stories), or PUD and approved manufactured housing. The dwelling can be an owner-occupied, vacation, or second home located in rural areas, or non-owner-occupied and located in an urban or rural area. Thus, RFC is not limiting its approved lenders to the type of properties that may be used as security for a loan. RFC has set the maximum term for a mortgage they will purchase as 30 years. RFC will purchase mortgages with a maximum loan-to-value ratio of 95 percent for owner-occupied properties and 80 percent for nonowner occupied properties. In regard to mortgage insurance for owner occupied properties, RFC requires coverage on all loans. Loans exceeding 80 percent loan-to-value ratio must carry PMI coverage to the 75 percent level and the insurance must remain in force until the loan reaches the 80 percent loan-to-value ratio. If the property that serves as security for the loan is a vacation/second home or is a non-owner-occupied dwelling, RFC requires 100 percent coverage of the loan for the full life of the loan.

For further information regarding any of the programs offered by RFC, contact any RFC-approved lender in your area or contact either the Dallas or Houston MGIC office to locate an approved lender in your area.

REVIEW QUESTIONS

1. Compare the loan approval procedures of Freddie Mac and Residential Funding Corporation.

2. Outline the second-lien requirements of Freddie Mac.

3. Discuss the buydown plan of Freddie Mac.

4. Outline the major feature of the Freddie Mac ARM purchase program.

5. Discuss the Mortgage Commitment programs offered by Freddie Mac.

6. What types of properties may serve as security for mortgages purchased by Residential Funding Corporation?

7. Explain the meaning of the term *net yield*.

8. Outline the mortgage purchase programs of the Government National Mortgage Association.

9. Explain the provisions of the Freddie Mac Multifamily Mortgage Purchase Program.

10. Outline the major mortgage purchase programs of the Government National Mortgage Association.

NOTES

1. U.S., Government National Mortgage Association, *Sellers' Guide*, 1974, Chapter 1, Section 501, p. 19.
2. U.S., Government National Mortgage Association, *Annual Report 1977*, Department of Housing and Urban Development, June 1978, HUD #85-6-N(2), p. 13.

12 Qualifying the Property

In this chapter we shall examine the various methods used to value property and look at the forms used by the Federal National Mortgage Association/Federal Home Loan Mortgage Corporation, the Federal Housing Administration, and the Veterans Administration to establish value.

Upon completion of this chapter you should be able to do the following:

★ Identify the major professional organizations for certification of appraisers.

★ Explain the three primary methods used to establish the value of real property.

★ Outline the major sections of the appraisal forms used by Fannie Mae/FHLMC, VA, and FHA.

This chapter is only an overview of the complex appraisal process. You will find a more in-depth study in a real estate appraisal course.

PROPERTY APPRAISAL

At the start of our discussion of the appraisal of property, the term *appraisal* must be defined. A simple definition is: an estimate of value of an adequately described piece of real property, as of a specific date, supported by the analysis of relevant data, by a trained professional appraiser, and usually in written form. The term *market value* must also be defined as it will be used throughout this chapter. Market value may be defined as the highest price that a property, when exposed to a competitive and open market for a reasonable time period, would bring to a seller who desires to sell, but is under no duress from an informed buyer who is ready, willing and able to pay for the property. In other words, market value is simply the price at which a seller is willing to sell and a buyer is willing to buy.

Professional Organizations

Our definition of appraisal referred to a trained professional appraiser, a person who has met the training and experience requirements of either of the major professional organizations that certify appraisers.

The first of the organizations is the Society of Real Estate Appraisers (SREA), which originated through the lending institutions. The Society of Real Estate Appraisers presently grants three designations: senior residential appraiser or SRA, senior real property appraiser or SRPA (for those appraisers who specialize in the appraisal of commercial property), and senior real estate analyst or SREA (the most prestigious designation given by the SREA). In addition to the training of and setting of standards for the industry, SREA publishes regular sales data for regions of the United States. The sales data books, sometimes referred to as *comp books*, list all of the closed transactions that were appraised by SREA members and serve as one of the best sources of information on current sales in a market. An example of one of the pages from an SREA book of Southern Texas is shown in Figure 12–1.[1]

Figure 12–1. Single-Family Residential Sales Data

MARKET DATA CENTER INC

SINGLE FAMILY RESIDENTIAL SALES DATA

COUNTY HARRIS

MAP CODE / CITY / CENSUS TRACT	UNIT	PROPERTY ADDRESS	$ SALE PRICE	TYPE	% CASH DOWN	% 1ST MTG	SALE DATE MO/YR	SALE CLOSED	LOT SIZE OR AREA	LOT ZONE	FLOOD ZONE	SITE INF	OBSOLESCENCE	WATER	SEWER	STYLE	STORIES	FLOOR PLAN	QUALITY	CONDITION	YEAR BUILT	ROOMS	BDRMS	OTHER ROOMS	BATHS FULL	BATHS HALF	SQ. FT. LIVING AREA	% BSMT AREA	% BSMT FINISH	A/C	PARKING	POOL	FIREPLACE	EQUIPMENT	REMODELED	OTHER IMP	HEATING	FUEL	TYPE CONSTR	EXT WALLS	TYPE ROOF	FLOORING	AMENITIES	LEASEHOLD	TYPE OWNER	TYPE IMP	
325 -J	24214	ROCKIN SEVEN DR	38,900	F			6-79	N	60X105	R	N		N	P	P	BUN	1	G	E		79	5	3		2		1,361	S		C	A2		1	RDG			A	G	F	X	C	C				S	
	24318	ROCKIN SEVEN DR	38,000	F			6-79	N	60X105	R	N		N	P	P	BUN	1	G	E		79	5	2		2		1,251	S		C	A1		1	RDG			E	E	F	X	C	C				S	
	24319	ROCKIN SEVEN DR	37,900	F			6-79	N	60X105	R	N		N	P	P	BUN	1	G	E		79	5	2		2		1,251	S		C	A1		1	RDG			E	E	F	X	C	C				S	
	24322	ROCKIN SEVEN DR	39,900	F			6-79	N	60X105	R	N		N	P	P	BUN	1	G	E		79	5	3		2		1,407	S		C	A1		1	RDG			E	E	F	X	C	C				S	
	24327	ROCKIN SEVEN DR	39,900	F			8-79	N	60X105	R	N		N	P	P	BUN	1	G	E		79	5	3		2		1,408	S		C	A1		1	RDG			E	E	F	X	C	C				S	
	24407	ROCKIN SEVEN DR	39,900	F			8-79	N	60X105	R	N		N	P	P	BUN	1	G	E		79	5	3		2		1,407	S		C	A1		1	RDG			E	E	F	X	C	C				S	
	24410	ROCKIN SEVEN DR	36,900	F			6-79	N	6,300	R	N		N	P	P	BUN	1	G	E		79	5	2		2		1,251	S		C	A1		1	RDG			E	E	F	X	C	C				S	
	24426	ROCKIN SEVEN DR	38,900	F			6-79	N	6,825	R	N		N	P	P	BUN	1	G	E		79	5	3		2		1,361	S		C	A1		1	RDG			E	E	F	X	C	C				S	
325 -L	2618	KILLDEER LN	50,700	F			7-79	N	60X117	R	N		N	P	P	BUN	1	G	E		79	6	3	DR	2		1,519	S		C	A2		1	RDG			E	E	F	X	C	C				S	
326 -Q	19803	SHADY HILL CR	42,000	C	24%	76%	11-78	Y	17,465	R	N		N	I	S		1	A	A	A	79	7	2	DR+OT	2		1,390	S		C	D2			X			A	E	F	W	C	C				S	
327 -Q	17422 N	BARKER ST	51,300	F			6-79	N	60X105	R	N		N	P	P	BUN	1	G	E		79	8	3	DR	2		1,682	S		C	A2			RDG			E	E	F	X	C	C				S	
327 -Y	16202	BARKLEA	70,600	C		80%	6-79	Y	150X350	R	N			P	P	COL	1	G	G	G	79	8	3	FR+DR+ATOT	2		2,009	S	U	C	G1		1	RDH		L	E	E	B	X	C	C	S			S	
328 -R	17110	LILLIAN LN	72,300	C		80%	7-79	Y	1.00	R	N			P	P	COL	1+	G	G	G	79	7	3	DR+AT+OT	2		2,026	S	U	C	H		1	RDH		L	E	E	B	X	C	C	S			S	
328 -S	14407	CYPRESS CREEK DR	54,400	C			4-79	N	64X105	R	Y		N	P	P	COL	2		A	A	79	6	3	DR+OT	2	1	1,512	S		C	A2			RDG			A	G	B	X	C	C				S	
	14811	CYPRESS MEADOW	70,100	C			4-79	N	65X100	R	N	V	N	P	P	BUN	2	A	A	A		11	4	FR+DR	2	1	2,420			C	D2		1	RDG		D	A	G	F	X	C	C	P		D	S	C
	14714	CYPRESS VALLEY	55,900	C			5-79	N	60X100	R			N	P	P	COL	2	G	A	A	79	6	3	DR	2	1	1,512			C	A2		1	RDG			A	G	C	X	C	C				S	C
	14802	CYPRESS VALLEY	47,900	V			6-79	N	60X100	R	N	W	N	P	P	COL	1	G	G	G		6	3	FR+DR	2		1,416	S		C	A2		1	RDG			A	G	F	X	C	C				S	
328 -T	15026	CYPRESS FALLS DR	58,000	V			7-79	N	58X100	R	N		N	P	P	RNC	1+	G	E	E	78	7	3	FR+DR	2	1	1,544	S		C	A2		1	RDG		L	A	G	F	X	C	C				S	
	14715	CYPRESS MEADOW	46,700	F			7-79	N	6,000	R	N		N		P	BUN	1	G	E		79	6	3	DR	2		1,452	S		C	A2		1	RDG			E	E	F	X	C	C				S	
	14407	CYPRESS SPRING	28,800	F			6-79	N	60X120		N	W	N	C	P	RNC	1		A	A	76	6	3	DR	2		1,530	S		C	D2		1	RDG		Z	A	E	F	X	C	C				S	
	14506	LOVETTA RD	47,900	V			8-79	N	63X120	R	N		N	P	P		1	G	G	G		6	3	DR+OT	2		1,445	S		C	A2		1	RDG		L	A	G	F	X	C	C				S	
328 -U	12930	BOWING OAKS DR	93,900	C			4-79	Y	11,500	R	N	VW	N	P	P	COL	2	A	A	A	79	10	4	FR+DR+BR	2	1	2,734	S		C	D3		1	RDG		PL	A	G	F	X	W	C				S	C
328 -V	12902	BELGRAVE	102,000	C			8-79	N	20,000	R	N	W	N	P	P	CON	1+	G	G	G	79	9	4	FR+DR	3	1	2,918			C	A3		1	RDG		P	A	G	F	X	W	C				S	C
	12818	BOWING OAKS	99,000	C		75%	6-79	Y	15,545	R	N	V	N	P	P	TUD	2	G	G	E	79	10	5	FR+DR+OT	2	1	3,003	S		C	D2		1	RDG		PL	A	E	F	L	W	C	TP			S	
	12866	BOWING OAKS	96,500	C		62%	6-79	Y	14,991	R	N	V	N	P	P	TUD	2	G	G	E	79	9	4	FR+DR+OT	2	1	2,788	S		C	D2		1	RDG		PL	A	E	F	L	W	C	TP			S	
	12907	BOWING OAKS	98,500	C			8-79	N	12,500	R	N	W	N	P	P		2	G	G	G	79	9	4	FR+DR	2	1	2,948			C	D2		1	RDG		P	A	G	F	X	W	C				S	C
	12918	BOWING OAKS	92,900	C			4-79	Y	77X144	R	N	W	N	P	P	COL	1+	A	A	G	79	9	4	FR+DR	2	1	2,662	S		C	D2		1	RDG		PL	A	G	F	X	W	C			D	S	C
	12926	BOWING OAKS	95,000	C		77%	6-79	Y	12,803	R	N	V	N	P	P	TUD	2	G	G	E	79	9	4	FR+DR+OT	2	1	3,017	S		C	D2		1	RDG		PL	A	E	F	L	W	C	TP			S	
	12807	FOREST MEADOW	100,600	C	20%	80%	6-79	Y	12,000		N		N	P	P	COL	2	G	G	G	79	10	4	DN+DR	2	1	2,784	S		C	D2		1	RDG			A	G	F	X	W	C				S	
	14406	LOUETTA RD	47,900	V			6-79	N	63X120	R	N		N	P	P	BUN	1	A	A	E	79	6	3	DR	2		1,447	S		C	A2		1	RDG			A	G	F	X	C	C				S	
328 -W	14923	CYPRESS GREEN	47,900	C			3-79	N	4,777	R	N	V	N	P	P	BUN	1	A	A	G		6	3	DR	2		1,448			C	A2		1	RDG		D	A	G	F	X	C	C	P		D	S	C
	14923	CYPRESS GREEN	48,300	V			8-79	N	45X100	R			N	P	P	BUN	1	A	A	G	79	7	3		2		1,445	S		C	A2		1	RDG			A	G	F	X	C	C				S	
	12802	FOREST MEADOW	106,000	C		52%	4-79	Y	15,950		N		N	P	P	TUD	1+	G	G	G	79	11	4	DN+DR	2	1	2,872	S		C	D2		1	RDG			A	G	F	X	W	C				S	
328 -Z	15139	CAROLS WY	86,900	C	20%	80%	8-79	Y	11,000	R	N	W	N	C	P	MED	1+	G	G	G	79	9	4	FR+DR+AT	2	1	2,407	S		C	A2		1	RDG		L	A	G	F	L	C	C	TP			S	
	12207	CAROLS WAY CR	72,000	C	21%	79%	7-79	Y	70X115	R	N	VW	N	C	P	CON	1	G	G	G	79	7	3	FR+DR+AT	2		1,835	S		C	A2		1	RDG		L	A	G	F	L	C	C	TP			S	
	12210	CAROLS WAY CR	86,500	C		80%	8-79	N	9,900	R	N		N	P	P	TUD	2	A	A	A	79	9	4	FR+DR	2	1	2,205	S		C	D2		1	RDG		LZ	A	E	F	X	W	C	TP			S	
	15210	CAROLS WAY DR	73,300	V			6-79	N	50X122	R	N		N	P	P	CON	1	G	G	E	79	7	3	FR+DR	2		1,943	S		C	A2		1	RDG			A	G	F	X	C	C				S	
	15003	CAROLSWAY	73,900	C	20%	80%	5-79	N	80X120		N	V	N	P	P	TUD	1+	G	G	G	78	9	4	FR+DR	2	1	1,924	S		C	A2		1	RDG			A	G	F	L	W	C	TP			S	
	14903	CYPRESS GREEN DR	64,500	V			8-79	N	9,477	R	N	W	N	P	P	COL	2	G	G	G		10	4	FR+DR	2		2,106	S		C	A2		1	RDG			A	G	F	X	C	C				S	
	15018	OAK BLUFF CT	78,900	C	37%	63%	6-79	Y	11,335	R	N		N	P	P		2	G	G	G		10	4	FR+DR+ATOT	2	1	2,260	S		C	D2		1	RDG		L	A	G	F	X	W	C				S	
	12207	OAK PARK DR	87,900	C		60%	7-79	N	9,481	R		V		P	P	GEO	2	G	G	E	79	8	4	FR+DR	2	1	2,293	S		C	D2		1	RDG		LZ	A	G	F	L	W	C	TP			S	
	12411	OAK PARK DR	81,500	C		80%	6-79	N	70X115	R	N	V	N	P	P	MED	2	A	A	E	79	8	4	FR+DR+OT	2	1	2,175	S		C	D2		1	RDG		LZ	A	G	F	L	W	C	CP			S	
	12411	OAK PARK DR	80,500	C	13%	87%	6-79	N	70X115	R	N	W	N	C	P	TUD	2	G	G	G	79	8	4	FR+DR+AT	2	1	2,150	S		C	D2		1	RDW		Z	A	G	F	L	W	C	TP			S	
	12415	OAK PARK DR	88,400	C	12%	88%	6-79	N	70X115	R	N	W	N	C	P	TUD	1+	G	G	G	79	9	4	FR+DR	2	1	2,198	S		C	D2		1	RDG		Z	A	G	F	L	W	C	TP			S	
	14910	ROSEHILL CT	75,000	C	20%	80%	8-79	N	80X120		N		N	P	P	HRN	2	G	A	G	79	8	4	FR+DR	2		2,467	S		C	D2		1	RDG		D	A	G	F	L	W	C				S	
	12415	ROSEHILL LN	70,500	C	11%	89%	8-79	Y	8,260	R	N	W	N	C	P	TUD	2	G	G	G	79	8	4	FR+DR+ATOT	2	1	2,299	S		C	D2		1	RDG		LZ	A	G	F	L	W	C	CP			S	
329 -L	17522	BONNIE SEAN	54,900	F			7-79	N	60X140	R	N		N	P	P	BUN	1	G	G	G	72	8	4	DN+DR	2		1,780	S		C	A2			RDG		F	E	E	F	X	W	C				S	
	9602	JAN GLEN	52,100	F			9-79	N	65X110	R	N	V	N	P	P	CON	1	A	A	A	73	7	3	FR+DR	2		1,800	S		C	D2		1	RDG		F	A	G	F	X	C	C				S	
329 -Q	16911	BALLYCASTLE	53,900	C		87%	6-79	Y	10,882	R	N	V	N	P	P	RNC	1	A	A	E	79	6	3	FR+DR	2		1,457	S		C	A2		1	RDG			A	G	F	X	C	C				S	
	17322	BARONSHIRE	45,600	V			9-79	N	65X120	R	N		N	P	P	COL	1	A	A	A	77	6	3	FR+DR	2		1,448	S		C	D2		1	RDG			A	E	F	L	C	C				S	
	17114	CAMBERWELL GREEN	58,600	F			7-79	N	65X120	R	N		N	P	P	BUN	1	G	E		79	8	4	DR	2		1,799	S		C	A2		1	RDG			A	G	F	X	C	C				S	
	9519	CHARTER RIDGE	62,500	C			7-79	N	65X115	R	N	V	N	P	P	CON	1	A	A	E	79	6	3	FR+DR	2		1,620	S		C	A2		1	RDG			A	G	F	X	C	C				S	C
	16303	HOLLOW ROCK	62,500	C			8-79	N	8,065	R	N		N	P	P	CON	1	A	A	G	79	6	3	FR+DR	2		1,620	S		C	A2		1	RDG		PF	A	G	F	X	C	C				S	C
	17007	KINGS WALK	55,000	V			7-79	N	65X120	R	N	V	N	P	P	HRN	1+	G	G	E	79	6	3	FR+DR	2	1	1,655	S		C	A2		1	RDG			A	G	F	X	C	C				S	
	9534	MAGNOLIA RIDGE	47,500	C			6-79	N	70X115	R	N	V	N	P	P	BUN	1	A	A	E	79	6	3	FR+DR	2		1,307	S		C	A2			RDG			A	G	F	X	C	C				S	C
	9606	MAGNOLIA RIDGE	54,500	C			6-79	N	66X115	R	N	V	N	P	P	TUD	1	A	A	E	79	6	3	FR+DR	2		1,526	S		C	A2		1	RDG			A	G	F	X	C	C				S	C
	9626	MAGNOLIA RIDGE	56,400	C			7-79	N	62X115	R	N		N	P	P	CON	1+	A	A	G	79	5	3	FR	2		1,489	S		C	A2		1	RDG			A	G	F	X	C	C	TP			S	C
	9510	THISTLE TR	54,500	C			6-79	N	8,057	R	N	V	N	P	P	TUD	1	A	A	E	79	6	3	FR+DR	2		1,526	S		C	A2		1	RDG			A	G	F	X	C	C				S	C
329 -R	9727	BITSAY	50,300	F			9-79	N	60X110	R	N		N	P	P	BUN	1	A	A	A	76	7	3	FR+DR	2		1,538	S		C	A2		1	RDG			A	G	F	X	C	C				S	
	9627	CRAIL	61,900	V			6-79	Y	60X110	R	N	V	N	P	P	BUN	1+	A	A	A	74	8	4	FR+DR	2		2,226	S		C	D2		1	RDG		L	A	G	F	L	W	C				S	
	9630	DORNOCH	73,500	V			8-79	N	60X100	R	N		N	P	P	BUN	1	G	G	G	74	9	5	FR+DR	2	1	2,318	S		C	A2		1	RDG		F	A	G	F	X	W	C				S	
	9710	HALKIRK	54,900	F			7-79	N	60X110	R	N		N	P	P	BUN	1	A	A	A	73	6	3	FR+DR	2		1,883	S		C	A2		1	RDG		L	A	G	F	X	W	C				S	
	9715	HALKIRK	52,900	V			6-79	N	6,600	R	N	V	N	P	P	BUN	1	A	A	A	75	6	3	FR+DR	2		1,517	S		C	A2		1	RDG			A	G	F	X	C	C				S	
	9419	KILRENNY	46,700	A			7-79	N	60X115		N		N	C	P	RNC	1	G	G	G	78	7	3	FR	2		1,556	S		C	A2		1	RDG		F	A	E	F	X	C	C				S	
	9635	KILRENNY	58,500	V			7-79	N	7,130	R	N	V	N	P		BUN	1	A	A	A	77	8	4	FR+DR	2		1,935	S		C	D2		1	RDG		L	A	G	F	X	W	C				S	
	9314	MAGNOLIA RIDGE	45,400	F			8-79	N	66X115	R	N		N	P	P	BUN	1	A	G	E	79	5	3		2		1,359	S		C	A2		1	RDG			A	G	F	X	C	C				S	
	9619	ORANGEVALE	40,600	V			6-79	N	61X110		N		N	P	P	BUN	1	G	E	E	78	5	3		2		1,674	S		C	A2		1	RDG			A	E	F	X	C	C				S	
329 -S	15622	TEN OAKS	105,800	C	20%	80%	7-79	N	11,964	R	N	V	N	P	P	TUD	2	G	G	G	79	10	4	FR+DR+OT	2	1	2,766	S		C	D2		1	RDG		PL	A	G	F	L	W	C	C+			S	
	15415	WINTERHAVEN	76,900	C	61%	39%	12-78	N	22,123	R	N	W	N	P	S	CON	1	G	A	G	78	6	3	FR	2		1,965	S		C	D2		1	RDG			A	G	F	X	C	C				S	
329 -T	16302	CHARTERSTONE DR	43,400	F			6-79	N	1,181	R	N		N	P	P	BUN	1	G	E		79	6	3	DR	2		1,257	S		C	A2		1	RDG			A	G	F	X	C	C				S	
	11818	OAKCROFT	127,000	C	20%	80%	4-79	Y	9,800	R	N	W	N	P	P	TUD	2	A	G	E	79	8	3	DN+DR	3	2	3,052	S		C	D2		1	RDG		Z	A	G	F	X	W	C	C+			S	
329 -U	9810	CHARTER RIDGE	44,700	F			8-79	N	70X121	R	N		N	P	P	BUN	2	G	G	G	79	6	3	DR	2		1,484	S		C	B2		1	RDG			A	G	F	X	C	C	P			S	
	9614	CHARTER RIDGE DR	61,900	F			9-79	N	60X115	R	N		N	P	P	BUN	1+	G	E		79	8	3	DR	2		2,011	S		C	A2		1	RDG			A	G	F	X	C	C				S	
	16307	HOLLOW ROCK DR	54,500	V			8-79	N	63X115	R	N		N	P	P	CON	1+	A	A	A	79	5	3		2		1,490	S		C	A2		1	RDG			A	E	F	X	C	C				S	
	9506	MAGNOLIA RIDGE	54,200	F			8-79	N	61X115	R	N		N	P	P	BUN	1	G	E		79	6	3	DR	2		1,521	S		C	A2		1	RDG			E	E	F	X	C	C				S	
	9806	SUGAR TREE CT	50,100	V			6-79	Y	9,188	R	N	W	N	P	P	COL	2	G	A	G		6	3	FR+DR	2		1,476	S		C	A2		2	RDG			A	G	F	X	C	C				S	
	9403	THISTLE TR	44,900	F			8-79	N	7,741							CON	1	A	A	A	79	6	3		2		1,360	S		C	A2		1	RDG			A	G	F	X	C	C				S	

** THE ABOVE DATA BELIEVED TO BE RELIABLE BUT ACCURACY IS NOT GUARANTEED

-- 5-- SOUTH TEXAS

325 -J / 329 -U

Source: SREA Market Data Center, Inc., South Texas Regional Center

When these books were originally published, they were available only to SREA members, but today they are available to real estate brokers. If you are interested in further information on the sales data books, contact either of the SREA Market Data Centers in Texas. The addresses for the centers are:

Northern Texas
SREA Market Data Center, Inc.
13771 N. Central Expressway, Suite 801
Dallas, Texas 75243

Southern Texas
SREA Market Data Center, Inc.
3223 Smith Street, Suite 312
Houston, Texas 77006

The second organization that issues designations to appraisers who meet its standards is the American Institute of Real Estate Appraisers (AIREA). This organization is a member group of the National Association of Realtors® and one of the requirements for membership in AIREA is that the person must be a member of the National Association of Realtors®. AIREA issues two designations: member, appraisal institute (MAI), and residential member (RM).

In addition to the issuance of these designations, AIREA is one of the leading publishers of books and articles about the field of appraisal. If you would like more information on AIREA, contact either your local board of Realtors® or the American Institute of Real Estate Appraisers at this address:

American Institute of
Real Estate Appraisers
430 North Michigan Ave.
Chicago, IL 60611

Appraisal Formats

The appraisal may take one of three forms: letter appraisal, narrative appraisal, or report appraisal.

The *letter appraisal*, as the name implies, will be a simple letter stating the value of the property and how the stated value was calculated.

The *narrative appraisal* will usually be in book form. The size of the narrative report will vary with the complexity of the property appraised. Usually this type of appraisal is used for the income type of property. The narrative appraisal report will have several sections. Some of the more common sections are as follows:

1. The introduction will contain a table of contents and a letter of transmittal to the firm that requested the appraisal. The transmittal letter will state the market value of the property to be appraised. If the subject property is a townhouse complex comprised of several different types of units, the transmittal letter will state the market value of each unit as of a specific date. For example:

As of January 1, 1983, it is our opinion that the present market value of the individual units are as follows:

Unit 101	$51,500
Unit 102	$54,350
Unit 203	$63,500

It should be noted that the value is expressed at the beginning of the narrative appraisal and all of the additional information is used to support this market value. The reason for this arrangement is that the narrative report can be as few as 10 pages to as many as 100. So with the value stated in the first few pages, a person reviewing the appraisal does not have to read the whole report.

2. The second section of the narrative is the description, analysis, and conclusion. In this section, the appraiser will describe the property to be appraised and the date of the appraisal. Some include a definition of market value.

3. The third section is the market survey. This gives information about the market in which the property is located. This market can be a whole city if the property described will be affected by the complete city, or it could be only a section of a city if the city is large.

4. The fourth section of the report is usually the qualitative study. In this section, the quality of the property is discussed. For example, if the property is a condo project, the report will analyze the common area, land use, parking facilities, recreational facilities if any, and finally the features of each of the different units in the project.

5. The final major section of the report is the valuation conclusions. In this section, the appraiser will establish the market value of each unit and certify the value as of the date of the report.

6. Some narrative reports will contain an addendum. In this section, the appraiser will furnish a set of photographs of the location of the property, floor plans of the units, a budget for operation of the project, and any other information that will help in the establishment of market value.

A table of contents of a narrative report is shown in Figure 12-2.

The final form an appraisal may take is the *report appraisal*. This is the format that is most commonly used for the appraisal of residential properties, including the 2- to 4-family dwelling and a unit in a condominium or PUD project. One such form is the standard Fannie Mae Form 1004. There are several other standard forms, which will be discussed in detail later in this chapter.

Basic Principles of Real Property Value

Before we examine the methods of establishing value, we should review some of the basic economic principles that affect the appraisal of property. These economic principles are sometimes referred to as the principles of value. Some of the more important principles are discussed below.

Supply and demand   As with any other product or commodity, the one principle that has the greatest effect on the value of property is supply and demand. For example, if there is a high demand for single-family dwellings in a certain area of a city and the builders and the real supply market cannot meet the demand, the prices of the dwellings in the area will escalate at a rapid rate. If there is an oversupply of homes in an area—more homes available than there are buyers—the prices in the area will decline in order to increase demand.

Conformity   The principle of conformity is that value is enhanced when the properties in a general area, such as a subdivision, generally have the same styling and the land is used generally for the same purpose. This principle can be illustrated with the following example. If a subdivision is comprised primarily of single-family dwellings in the price range of $60,000 to $80,000 and these homes are located on standard subdivision lots of 70 × 120 feet, a home that is built in the subdivision which costs $150,000 and sits on three-fourths of an acre lot is not in conformity, and financing could be a problem.

Substitution   This principle of value states that if there are several properties or products available that are substantially the same in quality, the product or property with the lowest price will be in the most demand. For example, let us say that in a subdivision there are two houses available: one is a resale and the other is a new home offered by the builder or developer. They are basically the same house, but the resale home is $1000 less than the one offered by the builder/developer. The resale will be of more interest to the buying public and can be in more demand.

Anticipation   This principle of value can be explained in the following manner: items are given value or the value is increased by the anticipation of value or benefit to be received in the future. For example, a house located in an area of a city that in the past has had the highest rate of appreciation for that city will have a greater value, and thus there will be more demand for homes in this area than for homes located in another area of the city, because the prospective buyer will anticipate a greater future value or greater appreciation.

Highest and best use   This principle of value to some experts in the field of appraisal is most important in establishing the value of land and/or improvements to the land. The highest and best use of the land at the time of the appraisal is the use that is most likely to produce the greatest return. Stated another way, the highest and best use is the most profitable use of the land. This principle can be illustrated as follows. A one-acre tract of land is located adjacent to a new industrial district and contains a single-family dwelling. In addition to the property being adjacent to the industrial district, across the back boundary there is a railroad spur and across the front of the property there has been built a new divided street leading into the industrial park. From this, it could be stated that the highest and best use of the property has changed from residential to commercial.

Contribution   *Market increase—* This principle of value can be defined as the amount of value that is added by the addition of an improvement to a property. For example, when a house is added to a lot in a subdivision, the addition of the house is an improvement and the value is greatly increased. It should be noted that all improvements do not increase the value in the same amount as the cost of the improvement. A good example is a swimming pool added to a

Figure 12-2.   Narrative Appraisal Report Table of Contents

TABLE OF CONTENTS

PART 1

INTRODUCTION

Title Page
Letter of Transmittal
Appraisal of the Value
Table of Contents
Summary of Salient Facts and Conclusions

PART II

DESCRIPTION, ANALYSIS AND CONCLUSIONS

Purpose of the Appraisal
Property Rights Appraised
Definition of Market Value
Function of the Appraisal
Date of the Appraisal
Zoning and Restrictions
Tax Ratio and Tax Rate
The Appraisal Process
Regional Data
City Data
Neighborhood Analysis
Neighborhood Map
Site Analysis
Site Location Map
Survey Site Plan
Highest and Best Use
Market Data Approach - Site Valuation
Land Value Analysis & Conclusion
Comparable Land Sales Map
Description of the Improvements
Cost Approach to Value
Schedule of the Cost Approach to Value
Income Approach to Value
   1. Comparable Rental Data
   2. Estimate of Economic Rent and Rental Schedule
   3. Reconstructed operating statements
   4. Discussion of Expenses
   5. Capitalizing of Net Income
      A. Ellwood Mortgage-Equity Technique
      B. Band of Investment Technique

ROBERT L. STANLEY
& Associates, Appraisers
HOUSTON, TEXAS

Figure 12-2.   *continued*

TABLE OF CONTENTS, Continued

Market Data Approach - Whole Property
Improved Sales Map
Correlation and Final Value Estimate

<u>PART III</u>

<u>ADDENDUM</u>

Appraiser's Certificate
Qualifications of Appraiser
Contingent & Limiting Conditions
Photographs
Building Plans/Square Footage Computation
Metes & Bounds Description

Source: Robert L. Stanley and Associates, Appraisers, Houston, Texas.

ROBERT L. STANLEY
& Associates, Appraisers
HOUSTON, TEXAS

single-family dwelling. If the home costs $80,000 and the owner builds a $10,000 pool, the property value will not increase in value by $10,000, but it will increase somewhat, depending on many factors.

Change   This principle of value states that all things change and that the change is inevitable. Change is constantly happening and cannot usually be reversed. For example, change is occurring in the make-up of the family in the United States, and this change is having an effect on the housing market throughout the nation. This change is inevitable due to outside forces such as the increase in gasoline prices and inflation.

Methods to Determine Property Value

There are three basic methods or approaches to determine the value of real property: the cost method, the market data method, and the income method. We will briefly examine each of the methods, and later in the chapter we will see how the methods are employed in the standard Fannie Mae/FHLMC appraisal reports.

Cost method   The cost method of establishing the market value can be described as taking the cost of reproducing or replacing the improvements to the land, adding the value of the land, and subtracting any depreciation. *Depreciation* is the loss of value of an asset. In our case it would be the loss of value of the improvements. For the cost method, this loss can include three forms of depreciation: physical deterioration, functional obsolescence, and economic obsolescence.

Physical deterioration   This loss of value is due to the wear and tear of use. This type of deterioration can be either curable or incurable. For example, if a home is in need of a new roof due to age, this would be a curable type of physical deterioration. But if the same house was in need of a foundation due to settling, the cost of the foundation may be prohibitive and the physical deterioration, then, would be incurable.

Functional obsolescence   This loss of value can be due to the design of the house, outdated equipment, or the lack of items that are now considered to be normal and expected in today's construction. Once again, functional obsolescence is either curable or incurable. An example of functional obsolescence is a home built along the Gulf Coast without air conditioning. This type of functional obsolescence

may be of the curable type if the cost is not prohibitive to add air conditioning and the house can be insulated in sufficient manner to cut the cost of operation of the central air conditioning. Another type of functional obsolescence would be a three-bedroom home with only one bath. This type of obsolescence may be of the incurable type if the house is so designed that the addition of a second bath is impossible.

Economic obsolescence   This loss of value is due to occurrences outside the property. For example, an apartment building was built in a quiet, secluded area just outside the city limits of a medium-size city. The city expands its limits to include the apartment building, and the adjacent area to the apartment building is zoned heavy industrial. This would be a factor affecting the value of the apartment building that has nothing to do with the property or the improvements.

The cost method of establishing the market value is primarily used for the appraisal of new or substantially rehabilitated property.

Market data method   This method of establishing market value is sometimes referred to as the *sales-comparison method*. In this method recently closed sales of comparable property are compared to the property that is being appraised. The comparable property is often simply called the *comparable*. When comparing properties, several factors are considered, including the following:

1. Proximity of the comparable to the property being appraised.

2. The date of the sale of the comparable. (The closer the date of the sale to the date of the appraisal, the better. If the sale is sometime in the past, the appraiser will adjust the sales price of the comparable.)

3. The design and room count of the comparable compared to that of the property to be appraised.

4. The quality of construction of the comparable compared to that of the property to be appraised.

When comparing the subject property to the comparables, the appraisers will make adjustments, either deducting dollars from the sales prices of the comparable properties where they are superior to the subject property, or adding dollars to the sales prices of the comparable properties where they are inferior.

When the standard appraisal form of Fannie Mae/FHLMC is reviewed later in this chapter, these and other areas of comparison will be shown.

When using the market data approach, the quality of the comparables is of the utmost importance, and most appraisers select them with great care. There are several sources for comparable properties, but the most widely used are those listed in the Society of Real Estate Appraisers sales data books. These books are published either monthly or quarterly and show all closed transactions where an SREA member made the appraisal. A sample page from one of the sales data publications was illustrated in Figure 12–1.

The market data method of determining value is used primarily for properties located in developed areas where there are sufficient and current closed sales to be used as comparables.

Income method   The third and final method used to establish the value of property is the income method. This approach is almost exclusively used to establish the value of income-producing properties. It uses the net operating income of the property to establish value.

The net operating income (NOI) is calculated as the gross potential income of the property, less the vacancy rate and credit loss, less operating expenses. The operating expenses are those items that will regularly occur, such as taxes, insurance, utilities, repairs, and maintenance. All expenses and income will be annualized.

The net operating income for a small apartment complex could be figured as follows:

Gross Potential Income	
5 units at $300.00 month	$18,000
Vacancy and Credit Loss	
6% of gross potential income	−1,080
Gross Possible Income	$16,920
Operating Expenses	
Includes the items listed above and should equal approximately 40% of the gross potential income	−7,200
Net Operating Income	$ 9,720

This calculation of the net operating income is referred to as a *proforma statement* of the complex. When dealing with income properties, the proforma statement is one of the more important elements used to establish value.

Using the information supplied in the proforma statement of the property, the value of the property can be established by using the NOI. One such method of establishing value is through *capitalization*. By this process, the appraiser can establish value by dividing the NOI by a *capitalization rate* or *cap rate*. This cap rate can change and can be based on several factors. Using our small apartment complex, we can establish the value by dividing the NOI by a cap rate. For example, using a cap rate of 14 percent, what would be the value of the property? We divide the NOI by the 14 percent cap rate.

$$\frac{\$9,720}{14\%} = \$69,428$$

The value or maximum sales price would be $69,428. Now, let us lower the cap rate to 10 percent and see how this will affect the value of the property.

$$\frac{\$9,720}{10\%} = \$97,200$$

From this cap rate example, one can see that the lower the cap rate, the higher the value or maximum sales price.

As mentioned above, the cap rate can be figured in several ways and most are very technical, but one may refer to the cap rate as the rate of return an investor is seeking from an investment.

Another method that is often used to calculate the value of a small apartment complex or a duplex, triplex, or fourplex is the *gross rent multiplier (GRM)* method. The GRM is a relationship between the monthly rent and the sales price and can be expressed as:

$$\frac{\text{Sales Price}}{\text{Gross Monthly Rent}} = \text{Gross Rent Multiplier (GRM)}$$

How can this be used to establish value for small income-producing properties?

For example, we are going to purchase a duplex for $85,500 and the monthly rent for both units is $800 per month. The appraiser would then search for properties that are similar to the subject property and calculate the GRM for those sales and apply the calculated GRM to the subject property.

During the search, the appraiser finds that there are several sales that are comparable to the subject and that the average GRM for these sales is 105. He then would apply the

GRM to the subject property to establish value:

$$Value = monthly\ rent \times GRM$$
$$or$$
$$= \$800 \times 105 = \$84,000$$

From this calculation, we can see that the value is approximately $1500 above the value established by the appraiser.

Now let us calculate the GRM for the subject property using the sales price of $85,500. As was stated earlier, the GRM is calculated by dividing the sales price by the monthly rent, so for our property the calculation would be:

$$\frac{\$85,500}{\$800} = 106.87$$

With this information, we can see that the GRM for the property we are interested in is approximately 1.87 above the average for comparable properties in the area.

This is not to say that the property is overpriced or that the rent is too low. The final value would take into consideration many other factors. This example was only intended to show how value could be established using the gross rent multiplier.

Fair Market Value

After all of the methods to establish value are completed, the appraiser will then establish the *fair market value* of the property. This is done by the correlation of the methods that apply to the property being appraised.

For example, if the property is a single-family dwelling located in a subdivision, the only methods that would apply would be the cost approach and the market data approach. Usually the value established by these methods should be close, but if the values are not close, the appraiser must then establish which method will be given emphasis.

STANDARD APPRAISAL REPORTS

Now that we have defined an appraisal, reviewed the standard appraisal formats, and discussed the methods to establish value, let us look at some of the standard forms used in the industry to report the value of property or to request establishing the value of real property with improvements.

We will examine the most common conventional appraisal reports, the standard forms

that have been developed by Fannie Mae and/or FHLMC. At the present time, there are three of these forms. The first is the Residential Appraisal Report, Fannie Mae Form 1004/FHLMC Form 70. Page one of this form is shown in Figure 12-3 and page two is illustrated in Figure 12-4. The second form is Fannie Mae Form 1025/FHLMC Form 72, the Appraisal Report—Small Residential Income Property. This form is illustrated in Figures 12-5 and 12-6. The third form developed by Fannie Mae/FHLMC is the Appraisal Report—Individual Condominium or PUD Unit. This form is numbered Fannie Mae Form 1073 and is shown in Figures 12-7 and 12-8.

Since the most widely used of the three forms is the Residential Appraisal Report or Form 1004/Form 70, this form will be covered in detail.

Residential Appraisal Report, Fannie Mae Form 1004/FHLMC Form 70[2]

This form is required on all properties that will serve as security for loans that will be sold to the Federal National Mortgage Association and the Federal Home Loan Mortgage Corporation, and it must be completed according to the guidelines set forth by each. In addition, many conventional lenders also require the use of this form. This report is brief and requires the appraiser to be concise in filling it out.

The first page of the report (Figure 12-3) is descriptive in nature, starting with the section that identifies the property and sales information. You will note that in the left margin it explains who is to fill out this section. The lender, then, is asked to supply the name of the borrower and the address of the property, as well as the legal description. The lender is to supply the name of the present owner and the terms of the sale.

The second section of the report is entitled "Neighborhood," and the appraiser is asked to furnish information about the neighborhood, beginning with the location of the property as rural, urban, or suburban. Second, the appraiser is asked to establish the growth rate of the area and the amount of the area that is built up. The appraiser is asked to give information concerning the present land use and to indicate if there will be any change in the present use, along with giving the price range of the homes in the area and the age of the structures in the neighborhood. In the final part of this section, the appraiser must rate, by the use of the grid, twelve factors that may affect the value of the property now or in the future.

Figure 12–3. Fannie Mae/FHLMC Residential Appraisal Report, page 1

RESIDENTIAL APPRAISAL REPORT

To be completed by Lender

Borrower		Census Tract	Map Reference	File No.

Property Address

City   County   State   Zip Code

Legal Description

Sale Price $ Date of Sale   Loan Term   yrs   Property Rights Appraised ☐ Fee ☐ Leasehold ☐ DeMinimis PUD

Actual Real Estate Taxes $ (yr) Loan charges to be paid by seller $ Other sales concessions

Lender/Client   Address

Occupant   Appraiser   Instructions to Appraiser

NEIGHBORHOOD

Location	☐ Urban	☐ Suburban	☐ Rural
Built Up	☐ Over 75%	☐ 25% to 75%	☐ Under 25%
Growth Rate ☐ Fully Dev.	☐ Rapid	☐ Steady	☐ Slow
Property Values	☐ Increasing	☐ Stable	☐ Declining
Demand/Supply	☐ Shortage	☐ In Balance	☐ Over Supply
Marketing Time	☐ Under 3 Mos.	☐ 4–6 Mos.	☐ Over 6 Mos.

Present Land Use ____% 1 Family ____% 2–4 Family ____% Apts. ____% Condo ____% Commercial
____% Industrial ____% Vacant ____%

Change in Present Land Use ☐ Not Likely ☐ Likely (*) ☐ Taking Place (*)
(*) From ____ To ____

Predominant Occupancy ☐ Owner ☐ Tenant ____% Vacant

Single Family Price Range $ ____ to $ ____ Predominant Value $ ____

Single Family Age ____ yrs to ____ yrs Predominant Age ____ yrs

	Good	Avg.	Fair	Poor
Employment Stability	☐	☐	☐	☐
Convenience to Employment	☐	☐	☐	☐
Convenience to Shopping	☐	☐	☐	☐
Convenience to Schools	☐	☐	☐	☐
Adequacy of Public Transportation	☐	☐	☐	☐
Recreational Facilities	☐	☐	☐	☐
Adequacy of Utilities	☐	☐	☐	☐
Property Compatibility	☐	☐	☐	☐
Protection from Detrimental Conditions	☐	☐	☐	☐
Police and Fire Protection	☐	☐	☐	☐
General Appearance of Properties	☐	☐	☐	☐
Appeal to Market	☐	☐	☐	☐

Note: FHLMC/FNMA do not consider race or the racial composition of the neighborhood to be reliable appraisal factors.
Comments including those factors, favorable or unfavorable, affecting marketability (e.g. public parks, schools, view, noise) ____

SITE

Dimensions ____ = ____ Sq. Ft. or Acres   ☐ Corner Lot

Zoning classification ____ Present improvements ☐ do ☐ do not conform to zoning regulations

Highest and best use: ☐ Present use ☐ Other (specify) ____

	Public	Other (Describe)	OFF SITE IMPROVEMENTS			
Elec.	☐		Street Access	☐ Public	☐ Private	Topo ____
Gas	☐		Surface ____			Size ____
Water	☐		Maintenance:	☐ Public	☐ Private	Shape ____
San.Sewer	☐		☐ Storm Sewer	☐ Curb/Gutter		View ____
						Drainage ____

☐ Underground Elect. & Tel. ☐ Sidewalk ☐ Street Lights   Is the property located in a HUD Identified Special Flood Hazard Area? ☐ No ☐ Yes

Comments (favorable or unfavorable including any apparent adverse easements, encroachments or other adverse conditions) ____

IMPROVEMENTS

☐ Existing ☐ Proposed ☐ Under Constr.   No. Units ____   Type (det, duplex, semi/det, etc.)   Design (rambler, split level, etc.)   Exterior Walls

Yrs. Age: Actual ____ Effective ____ to ____   No. Stories ____

Roof Material ____   Gutters & Downspouts ☐ None   Window (Type): ____   Insulation ☐ None ☐ Floor

☐ Storm Sash ☐ Screens ☐ Combination   ☐ Ceiling ☐ Roof ☐ Walls

☐ Manufactured Housing

Foundation Walls ____

BSMT   ____% Basement   ☐ Floor Drain   Finished Ceiling ____
☐ Outside Entrance   ☐ Sump Pump   Finished Walls ____
☐ Concrete Floor   ____% Finished   Finished Floor ____
Evidence of: ☐ Dampness ☐ Termites ☐ Settlement

☐ Slab on Grade ☐ Crawl Space

Comments ____

ROOM LIST

Room List	Foyer	Living	Dining	Kitchen	Den	Family Rm.	Rec. Rm.	Bedrooms	No. Baths	Laundry	Other
Basement											
1st Level											
2nd Level											

Finished area above grade contains a total of ____ rooms ____ bedrooms ____ baths. Gross Living Area ____ sq. ft. Bsmt Area ____ sq. ft.

INTERIOR FINISH & EQUIPMENT

Kitchen Equipment: ☐ Refrigerator ☐ Range/Oven ☐ Disposal ☐ Dishwasher ☐ Fan/Hood ☐ Compactor ☐ Washer ☐ Dryer ☐

HEAT: Type ____ Fuel ____ Cond. ____   AIR COND: ☐ Central ☐ Other ____ ☐ Adequate ☐ Inadequate

Floors	☐ Hardwood	☐ Carpet Over ____
Walls	☐ Drywall	☐ Plaster ____
Trim/Finish	☐ Good	☐ Average ☐ Fair ☐ Poor
Bath Floor	☐ Ceramic	☐ ____
Bath Wainscot	☐ Ceramic	☐ ____

Special Features (including energy efficient items) ____

ATTIC: ☐ Yes ☐ No ☐ Stairway ☐ Drop-stair ☐ Scuttle ☐ Floored
Finished (Describe) ____ ☐ Heated
CAR STORAGE: ☐ Garage ☐ Built-in ☐ Attached ☐ Detached ☐ Car Port
No. Cars ____ ☐ Adequate ☐ Inadequate   Condition ____

PROPERTY RATING

	Good	Avg.	Fair	Poor
Quality of Construction (Materials & Finish)	☐	☐	☐	☐
Condition of Improvements	☐	☐	☐	☐
Room sizes and layout	☐	☐	☐	☐
Closets and Storage	☐	☐	☐	☐
Insulation—adequacy	☐	☐	☐	☐
Plumbing—adequacy and condition	☐	☐	☐	☐
Electrical—adequacy and condition	☐	☐	☐	☐
Kitchen Cabinets—adequacy and condition	☐	☐	☐	☐
Compatibility to Neighborhood	☐	☐	☐	☐
Overall Livability	☐	☐	☐	☐
Appeal and Marketability	☐	☐	☐	☐

Yrs Est Remaining Economic Life ____ to ____ Explain if less than Loan Term

FIREPLACES, PATIOS, POOL, FENCES, etc. (describe) ____

COMMENTS (including functional or physical inadequacies, repairs needed, modernization, etc.) ____

FHLMC Form 70 Rev. 7/79   ATTACH DESCRIPTIVE PHOTOGRAPHS OF SUBJECT PROPERTY AND STREET SCENE   FNMA Form 1004 Rev. 7/79

Figure 12–4.   Fannie Mae/FHLMC Residential Appraisal Report, Valuation Section

VALUATION SECTION

Purpose of Appraisal is to estimate Market Value as defined in Certification & Statement of Limiting Conditions (FHLMC Form 439/FNMA Form 1004B). If submitted for FNMA, the appraiser must attach (1) sketch or map showing location of subject, street names, distance from nearest intersection, and any detrimental conditions and (2) exterior building sketch of improvements showing dimensions.

COST APPROACH

Measurements	No. Stories	Sq. Ft.
___ x ___	___ x ___	= ___
___ x ___	___ x ___	= ___
___ x ___	___ x ___	= ___
___ x ___	___ x ___	= ___
___ x ___	___ x ___	= ___

Total Gross Living Area (List in Market Data Analysis below) ___
Comment on functional and economic obsolescence: ___

ESTIMATED REPRODUCTION COST – NEW – OF IMPROVEMENTS:

Dwelling ___ Sq. Ft. @ $ ___ = $ ___
___ Sq. Ft. @ $ ___ = ___
Extras ___ = ___
Special Energy Efficient Items ___ = ___
Porches, Patios, etc. ___ = ___
Garage/Car Port ___ Sq. Ft. @ $ ___ = ___
Site Improvements (driveway, landscaping, etc.) ___ = ___
Total Estimated Cost New . . . . = $ ___

Less | Physical | Functional | Economic
Depreciation $ ___ | $ ___ | $ ___ = $ (___)
Depreciated value of improvements . . . . = $ ___
ESTIMATED LAND VALUE . . . . = $ ___
(If leasehold, show only leasehold value)

INDICATED VALUE BY COST APPROACH . . . $ ___

The undersigned has recited three recent sales of properties most similar and proximate to subject and has considered these in the market analysis. The description includes a dollar adjustment, reflecting market reaction to those items of significant variation between the subject and comparable properties. If a significant item in the comparable property is superior to, or more favorable than, the subject property, a minus (-) adjustment is made, thus reducing the indicated value of subject; if a significant item in the comparable is inferior to, or less favorable than, the subject property, a plus (+) adjustment is made, thus increasing the indicated value of the subject.

MARKET DATA ANALYSIS

ITEM	Subject Property	COMPARABLE NO. 1		COMPARABLE NO. 2		COMPARABLE NO. 3	
Address							
Proximity to Subj.							
Sales Price	$	$		$		$	
Price/Living area	$	$	∅	$	∅	$	∅
Data Source							
Date of Sale and Time Adjustment	DESCRIPTION	DESCRIPTION	+(–)$ Adjustment	DESCRIPTION	+(–)$ Adjustment	DESCRIPTION	+(–)$ Adjustment
Location							
Site/View							
Design and Appeal							
Quality of Const.							
Age							
Condition							
Living Area Room Count and Total	Total / B-rms / Baths	Total / B-rms / Baths		Total / B-rms / Baths		Total / B-rms / Baths	
Gross Living Area	Sq.Ft.	Sq.Ft.		Sq.Ft.		Sq.Ft.	
Basement & Bsmt. Finished Rooms							
Functional Utility							
Air Conditioning							
Garage/Car Port							
Porches, Patio, Pools, etc.							
Special Energy Efficient Items							
Other (e.g. fireplaces, kitchen equip., remodeling)							
Sales or Financing Concessions							
Net Adj. (Total)		☐ Plus; ☐ Minus $		☐ Plus; ☐ Minus $		☐ Plus; ☐ Minus $	
Indicated Value of Subject		$		$		$	

Comments on Market Data ___

INDICATED VALUE BY MARKET DATA APPROACH . . . . $ ___

INDICATED VALUE BY INCOME APPROACH   (If applicable) Economic Market Rent $ ___ /Mo. x Gross Rent Multiplier ___ = $ ___

This appraisal is made ☐ "as is" ☐ subject to the repairs, alterations, or conditions listed below ☐ completion per plans and specifications.

Comments and Conditions of Appraisal: ___

Final Reconciliation: ___

Construction Warranty ☐ Yes ☐ No   Name of Warranty Program ___ Warranty Coverage Expires ___

This appraisal is based upon the above requirements, the certification, contingent and limiting conditions, and Market Value definition that are stated in
☐ FHLMC Form 439 (Rev. 10/78)/FNMA Form 1004B (Rev. 10/78) filed with client ___ 19 ___ ☐ attached.

I ESTIMATE THE MARKET VALUE, AS DEFINED, OF SUBJECT PROPERTY AS OF ___ 19 ___ to be $ ___

Appraiser(s) ___ Review Appraiser (If applicable) ___
☐ Did ☐ Did Not Physically Inspect Property

FHLMC Form 70 Rev. 7/79   REVERSE   FNMA Form 1004 Rev. 7/79

Figure 12–5.   *Fannie Mae/FHLMC Small Residential Income Property Appraisal Report, page 1*

APPRAISAL REPORT—SMALL RESIDENTIAL INCOME PROPERTY   File No. ____

To be completed by Lender

Borrower		Census Tract	Map Reference
Property Address			
City	County	State	Zip Code
Legal Description			
Sale Price $	Date of Sale ____ Loan Term ____ yrs.	Property Rights Appraised: ☐ Fee ☐ Leasehold ☐ Other____	
Actual Real Estate Taxes $	(yr) Loan charges to be paid by seller $	Other sales concessions	
Lender/Client		Address	
Occupant	Appraiser	Instructions to Appraiser	

NEIGHBORHOOD

Location . . . . ☐ Urban . . . . ☐ Suburban . . . . ☐ Rural

Built-up . . . . ☐ Over 75% . . . . . ☐ 25% to 75% . . . ☐ Under 25%

Present land use . . . . ____% Condominiums ____% 1-Family ____% 2-4 Family

____% Apartments ____% Commercial ____% Vacant ____%

Change in present land use . . ☐ Not likely . . . . . ☐ Likely (*) . . . . . ☐ Taking Place(*)

(*) From ____ To ____

Property values . . . . ☐ Increasing . . . . ☐ Stable . . . . . . ☐ Declining

Housing demand/supply . . . . ☐ In balance . . . . ☐ Shortage . . . . . ☐ Oversupply

Predominant occupancy . . . ☐ Owner . . . . ☐ Tenant . . . . . . ____% Vacant

Single Family: Price range $ ____ to $ ____ Predominant $ ____

Age ____ yrs. to ____ yrs. Predominant ____ yrs

Typical multifamily bldg.   Type ____ No. Stories ____ No. Units ____

Age ____ yrs. Condition ____

Typical rents $ ____ to $ ____   ☐ Increasing ☐ Stable ☐ Declining

Est. neighborhood apt. vacancy ____% ☐ Decreasing ☐ Stable ☐ Increasing

Rent controls   ☐ No ☐ Yes   ☐ Not likely ☐ Likely

OVERALL RATING	Good	Avg.	Fair	Poor
Adequacy of Shopping.				
Adequacy of Utilities.				
Employment Opportunities				
Police and Fire Protection				
Recreational Facilities				
Property Compatibility				
Protection from Detrimental Conditions				
General Appearance of Properties				
Appeal to Market.				

	Distance	Access or Convenience
Public Transportation		
Employment Centers		
Shopping Facilities		
Grammar Schools		
Freeway Access		

Note: FHLMC/FNMA do not consider race or the racial composition of the neighborhood to be reliable appraisal factors.

Describe those factors, favorable or unfavorable, affecting marketability (incl. mkt. area population size & financial ability). ____

SITE

Dimensions ____ = ____ Sq. Ft. or Acres ☐ Corner Lot

Zoning classification ____ Present improvements ☐ do ☐ do not conform to zoning regulations

Highest and best use: ☐ Present use ☐ Other (specify)

	Public	Other (Describe)	OFF-SITE IMPROVEMENTS	
Elec.	☐	____	Street Access: ☐Public ☐ Private
Gas	☐	____	Surface ____
Water	☐	____	Maintenance ☐Public ☐Private
San.Sewer	☐	____	☐ Storm Sewer ☐ Curb/Gutter
	☐ Underground Elec. & Tel.		☐ Sidewalk ☐ Street Lights

Topo ____

Size ____

Shape ____

View ____

Drainage ____

Is the property located in a HUD Identified Special Flood Hazard Area? ☐No☐Yes

Comments (favorable or unfavorable conditions including any apparent adverse easements or encroachments) ____

DESCRIPTION OF IMPROVEMENTS

☐ Existing ☐ Proposed ☐ Under Construction Type: ☐ Elevator ☐ Walk-up ☐ Det. ☐ Semi-Det. ☐ Row   No. Stories ____

No. Bldgs. ____ No. Units ____ No. Rooms ____ No. Baths ____ Parking Spaces: No. ____ Type ____

Basic Structural System ____ Exterior Walls ____ Roof Covering ____

Foundation Walls ____ Basement ____% Finished ____% Describe use ____

Interior Walls ____ Floors ____ Bath Floor and Walls ____

Insulation ____ Adequacy ____ Adequacy of Soundproofing ____

Heating: ☐ Central ☐ Individual   Type ____ Fuel ____ Adequacy & Condition ____

Air Conditioning: ☐ Central ☐ Individual   Fuel ____ Make ____ Adequacy & Condition ____

Kitchen Cabinets, Drawers and Counter space ☐ Adequate ☐ Inadequate

Total No. Appliances: ____Range/Oven ____Fan/Hood ____Dishwasher

____ Disposal ____Refrigerator ____Washer ____Dryer ____Compactor

Water Heater(s) (make, capacity, fuel) ____

Plumbing Fixtures (make) ____

Electrical Service (amps per unit) ____

Security Features ____

Special Features (including energy efficient items) ____

OVERALL PROPERTY RATING	Good	Avg.	Fair	Poor
Quality of construction (materials and finish)				
Condition of improvements				
Room sizes and layout				
Closets and storage				
Plumbing—adequacy and condition				
Electrical—adequacy and condition				
Kitchen equipment—adequacy and condition				
Amenities and parking facilities				
Overall livability				
Appeal to market				

Age: Actual ____ yrs., Effective ____ yrs. to ____ yrs. Est. Remaining Economic Life ____ yrs. to ____ yrs. Explain if less than Loan Term

COMMENTS: (including functional or physical inadequacies, repairs needed, modernization, etc.) ____

COST APPROACH

ESTIMATED REPRODUCTION COST NEW

____ x ____ = ____ sq. ft. x ____ (Stories) = ____ sq. ft. x $ ____ $ ____

____ x ____ = ____ sq. ft. x ____ (Stories) = ____ sq. ft. x $ ____

____ x ____ = ____ sq. ft. x ____ (Stories) = ____ sq. ft. x $ ____

OTHER IMPROVEMENTS (Including special energy efficient items) ____

SITE IMPROVEMENTS ____

TOTAL ESTIMATED COST NEW OF IMPROVEMENTS . . . . $ ____

LESS DEPRECIATION: Physical $ ____ Functional $ ____ Economic $ ____

DEPRECIATED VALUE OF IMPROVEMENTS . . . . $ ____

ADD-ESTIMATED LAND VALUE (If leasehold, show only leasehold value – attach calculations) . . . . $ ____

INDICATED VALUE BY THE COST APPROACH ☐FEE SIMPLE ☐ LEASEHOLD . . . . $ ____

FHLMC Form 72 7/79
2-12 Units

ATTACH LAYOUT SKETCHES SHOWING UNIT ENTRIES, LOCATION MAP AND
DESCRIPTIVE PHOTOGRAPHS OF SUBJECT PROPERTY AND STREET SCENE

FNMA Form 1025 7/79
2-4 Units

Figure 12–6.   Fannie Mae/FHLMC Small Residential Income Property Appraisal Report, page 2

COMPARABLE RENTAL DATA

ITEM	COMPARABLE No. 1	COMPARABLE No. 2	COMPARABLE No. 3
Address			
Proximity to subject			
Rent survey date			
Description of property and conditions	No. Units ____ No. Vac. ____ Yr. Blt.: 19 ____	No. Units ____ No. Vac. ____ Yr. Blt.: 19 ____	No. Units ____ No. Vac. ____ Yr. Blt.: 19 ____

	Rm.Count Tot BR b	Size Sq. Ft.	Monthly Rent $ ¢ Rm	Rm.Count Tot BR b	Size Sq. Ft.	Monthly Rent $ ¢ Rm	Rm.Count Tot BR b	Size Sq. Ft.	Monthly Rent $ ¢ Rm
Individual unit breakdown									

Utilities, furniture and amenities incl. in rent			
Compare comps to subj.			

Utilities included in actual rents: ☐ Water ☐ Gas ☐ Heat ☐ Electric ☐ Air Conditioning ☐ _____

Utilities included in forecasted rents: ☐ Water ☐ Gas ☐ Heat ☐ Electric ☐ Air Conditioning ☐ _____

RENT SCHEDULE

No. of Units	Individual Unit Rm Count Tot. BR b	Total Rooms	Sq. Ft. Area Per Unit	No. Units Vacant	ACTUAL RENTS — Per Unit — Unfurnished	Furnished	Total Rents	FORECASTED RENTS — Per Unit — Unfurnished	Furnished	Per Sq. Ft. or Room	Total Rents
					$	$	$	$	$	$	$
TOTAL							$				$

Other Monthly Income (Itemize) _____ $ _____

Vacancy: Actual last yr. ____% Prev. yr. ____% Forecasted: ____% $ _____ Total Gross Monthly Forecasted Rent $ _____

Discuss rental concessions, forecasted rents _____

MARKET DATA ANALYSIS

ITEM	SUBJECT	COMPARABLE No. 1	COMPARABLE No. 2	COMPARABLE No. 3
Address				
Proximity to subject				
Price	$ ☐ Unf. ☐ F.	$ ☐ Unf. ☐ F.	$ ☐ Unf. ☐ F.	$ ☐ Unf. ☐ F.
Date of sale				

	Yr. Blt. 19 ____ No. Vac.: ____ No. of Units	Individual Unit Room Count Tot. BR b	Yr. Blt. 19 ____ No. Vac.: ____ No. of Units	Individual Unit Room Count Tot. BR b	Yr. Blt. 19 ____ No. Vac.: ____ No. of Units	Individual Unit Room Count Tot. BR b	Yr. Blt. 19 ____ No. Vac.: ____ No. of Units	Individual Unit Room Count Tot. BR b
Individual unit breakdown								

Compare to subject, including condition, terms of sale/financing				
Gross Bldg. Area (GBA)	sq. ft.	sq. ft.	sq. ft.	sq. ft.
Gross Monthly Rent	$	$	$	$
Gross Mo. Rent Mult. (1)				
Price Per Unit	$	$	$	$
Price Per Room	$	$	$	$
Price Per S.F. GBA	$ /sq. ft. GBA	$ /sq. ft. GBA	$ /sq. ft. GBA	$ /sq. ft. GBA

(1) Sale Price ÷ Gross Monthly Rent | Value Indication for Subject

Val. Per Unit $ _____ X _____ Units = $ _____ ; Val. Per S.F. G.B.A. $ _____ X _____ S.F. Bldg. Area = $ _____

Val. Per Rm $ _____ X _____ Rms = $ _____ ; G.R.M. _____ X _____ Total Monthly Rent = $ _____

Reconciliation: _____

INDICATED VALUE BY MARKET DATA APPROACH _____ $ _____

EXPENSE ANALYSIS

ANNUAL EXPENSE SUMMARY - (If for FNMA - Lender must prepare operating data on sep. form for appraiser to review, comment on & attach to appraisal)

			ACTUAL	FORECAST	CALCULATIONS OR COMMENTS
1. Utilities: ☐ Heat $ ____ ☐ Electric $ ____ ☐ Gas $ ____ ☐ Water & Sewer $ ____	Total:		$	$	
2. Real Estate Taxes $ ____ 3. Insurance $ ____	Total:				
4. Management $ ____ Salaries $ ____	Total:				
5. Maint. & Decor.$ ____ Repairs $ ____ Reserves $ ____	Total:				
6. Other ____	Total:				
TOTAL EXPENSES & REPLACEMENT RESERVES			$	$	

This appraisal is made ☐ "as is" ☐ subject to the repairs, alterations, or conditions listed below ☐ completion per plans and specifications.

Comments, Conditions and Final Reconciliation _____

This appraisal is based upon the above requirements, the certification, contingent and limiting conditions, and Market Value definition that are stated in

☐ FHLMC Form 439 (Rev. 10/78)/FNMA Form 1004B (Rev. 10/78) filed with client _____ 19 ____ ☐ attached.

I ESTIMATE THE MARKET VALUE, AS DEFINED, OF SUBJECT PROPERTY AS OF _____ 19 ____ to be $ _____

Appraiser(s) _____ Review Appraiser (If applicable) _____ ☐ Did ☐ Did Not Physically Inspect Property

FHLMC Form 72 7/79
2-12 Units

FNMA Form 1025 7/79
2-4 Units

Figure 12-7. Fannie Mae/FHLMC Condominium or PUD Unit Appraisal Report, page 1

APPRAISAL REPORT – INDIVIDUAL ☐CONDOMINIUM OR ☐PUD UNIT   File No.

To be completed by Lender

Borrower _____ Census Tract _____ Map Reference _____
Unit No. _____ Address _____ Project Name/Phase No. _____
City _____ County _____ State _____ Zip Code _____
Actual Real Estate Taxes $_____ (yr.) Sales Price $_____ Property Rights Appraised ☐Fee ☐Leasehold
Loan Charges to be Paid by Seller $_____ Other Sales Concessions _____
Lender/Client _____ Lender's Address _____
Occupant _____ Appraiser _____ Instructions to Appraiser _____
☐FNMA 1073A required   ☐FHLMC 465 Addendum A required   ☐FHLMC 465 Addendum B required

NEIGHBORHOOD

				NEIGHBORHOOD RATING	Good	Avg.	Fair	Poor
Location	☐Urban	☐Suburban	☐Rural	Adequacy of Shopping	☐	☐	☐	☐
Built Up	☐Over 75%	☐25% to 75%	☐Under 25%	Employment Opportunities	☐	☐	☐	☐
Growth Rate ☐Fully Developed	☐Rapid	☐Steady	☐Slow	Recreational Facilities	☐	☐	☐	☐
Property Values	☐Increasing	☐Stable	☐Declining	Adequacy of Utilities	☐	☐	☐	☐
Demand/Supply	☐Shortage	☐In Balance	☐Oversupply	Property Compatibility	☐	☐	☐	☐
Marketing Time	☐Under 3 Mos.	☐4–6 Mos.	☐Over 6 Mos.	Protection from Detrimental Cond.	☐	☐	☐	☐

Present Land Use ____% 1 Family ____% 2–4 Family ____% Apts. ____% Condo
____% Commercial ____% Industrial ____% Vacant
Change in Present Land Use ☐Not Likely ☐Likely* ☐Taking Place*
*From _____ To _____

					Good	Avg.	Fair	Poor
				Police and Fire Protection	☐	☐	☐	☐
				General Appearance of Properties	☐	☐	☐	☐
				Appeal to Market	☐	☐	☐	☐

Predominant Occupancy ☐Owner ☐Tenant ____% Vacant

	Distance	Access or Convenience			
Public Transportation		☐	☐	☐	☐
Employment Centers		☐	☐	☐	☐
Neighborhood Shopping		☐	☐	☐	☐
Grammar Schools		☐	☐	☐	☐
Freeway Access		☐	☐	☐	☐

Condominium: Price Range $____ to $____ Predominant $____
Age ____ yrs. to ____ yrs. Predominant ____ yrs.
Single Family: Price Range $____ to $____ Predominant $____
Age ____ yrs. to ____ yrs. Predominant ____ yrs.
Describe potential for additional Condo/PUD units in nearby area _____

Note: FHLMC/FNMA do not consider race or the racial composition of the neighborhood to be reliable appraisal factors.

Describe those factors, favorable or unfavorable, affecting marketability (e.g. public parks, schools, noise, view, mkt. area population size & financial ability)

SITE

Lot Dimensions (if PUD) _____ = _____ Sq. Ft. ☐Corner Lot Project Density When Completed as Planned _____ Units/Acre
Zoning Classification _____ Present Improvements ☐do ☐do not conform to zoning regulations.
Highest and Best Use: ☐Present Use ☐Other (specify) _____

	Public	Other (describe)	OFF-SITE IMPROVEMENTS	Project Ingress/Egress (adequacy) _____
Elec.	☐	_____	Street Access: ☐Public ☐Private	Topo _____
Gas	☐	_____	Surface: _____	Size/Shape _____
Water	☐	_____	Maintenance: ☐Public ☐Private	View Amenity _____
San. Sewer	☐	_____	☐Storm Sewer ☐Curb/Gutter	Drainage/Flood Conditions _____
	☐Underground Elec. & Tel.		☐Sidewalk ☐Street Lights	Is property located in a HUD Identified Special Flood Hazard Area? ☐No ☐Yes

COMMENTS (including any easements, encroachments or adverse conditions) _____

PROJECT IMPROVEMENTS

☐Existing Approx. Year Built 19___ Original Use _____
TYPE ☐Condo ☐PUD ☐Converted (19___)
☐Proposed ☐Under Construction
PROJECT ☐Elevator ☐Walk-up No. of Stories _____
☐Row or Town House ☐Other (specify) _____
☐Primary Residence ☐Second Home or Recreational

If Completed: No. Phases ___ No. Units ___ No. Sold ___
If Incomplete: Planned No. Phases ___ No. Units ___ No. Sold ___
Units in Subject Phase: Total ___ Completed ___ Sold ___ Rented ___
Approx. No. Units for Sale: Subject Project ___ Subject Phase ___
Exterior Wall _____ Roof Covering _____ Security Features _____
Elevator: No. ___ Adequacy & Condition ___ Soundproofing: Vertical ___ Horizontal ___
Parking: Total No. Spaces ___ Ratio ___ Spaces/Unit ___ Type ___ No. Spaces for Guest Parking ___
Describe common elements or recreational facilities _____
Are any common elements, rec. facilities or parking leased to Owners Assoc.? _____ If yes, attach addendum describing rental, terms and options.

PROJECT RATING	Good	Avg.	Fair	Poor
Location	☐	☐	☐	☐
General Appearance	☐	☐	☐	☐
Amenities & Recreational Facilities	☐	☐	☐	☐
Density (units per acre)	☐	☐	☐	☐
Unit Mix	☐	☐	☐	☐
Quality of Constr. (mat'l. & finish)	☐	☐	☐	☐
Condition of Exterior	☐	☐	☐	☐
Condition of Interior	☐	☐	☐	☐
Appeal to Market	☐	☐	☐	☐

SUBJECT UNIT

☐Existing ☐Proposed ☐Under Constr. Floor No. ___ Unit Livable Area ___ ☐Basement ___% Finished ___
Parking for Unit: No. ___ Type ___ ☐Assigned ☐Owned Convenience to Unit ___

Room List	Foyer	Liv	Din	Kit	Bdrm	Bath	Fam	Rec	Lndry	Other
Basement										
1st Level										
2nd Level										

Floors ☐Hardwood ☐Carpet over _____ ☐_____
Int. Walls ☐Drywall ☐Plaster ☐_____
Trim/Finish ☐Good ☐Average ☐Fair ☐Poor
Bath Floor ☐Ceramic ☐Wainscot ☐Ceramic ☐_____
Windows (type): _____ ☐Storm Sash ☐Screens ☐Combo
Kitchen Equip: ☐Refrig. ☐Range/Oven ☐Fan/Hood ☐Washer ☐Dryer
☐Intercom ☐Disposal ☐Dishwasher ☐Microwave ☐Compactor
HEAT: Type ___ Fuel ___ Cond. ___
AIR COND: ☐Central ☐Other ☐Adequate ☐Inadequate

UNIT RATING	Good	Avg.	Fair	Poor
Condition of Improvements	☐	☐	☐	☐
Room Sizes and Layout	☐	☐	☐	☐
Adequacy of Closets and Storage	☐	☐	☐	☐
Kit. Equip., Cabinets & Workspace	☐	☐	☐	☐
Plumbing - Adequacy and Condition	☐	☐	☐	☐
Electrical - Adequacy and Condition	☐	☐	☐	☐
Adequacy of Soundproofing	☐	☐	☐	☐
Adequacy of Insulation	☐	☐	☐	☐
Location within Project or View	☐	☐	☐	☐
Overall Livability	☐	☐	☐	☐
Appeal and Marketability	☐	☐	☐	☐
Est. Effective Age	___ to ___ yrs.			
Est. Remaining Economic Life	___ to ___ yrs.			

☐Earth Sheltered Housing Design ☐Solar Design/Landscape ☐Solar Space Heat/Air Cond. ☐Solar Hot Water
☐Flue Damper ☐Elec./Mech. Gas Furn. Ignition ☐Auto. Setback Thermostat ☐Dble./Triple Glazed Windows ☐Caulk/Weatherstrip
INSULATION (state R-Factor if known) ☐Walls ___ ☐Ceiling ___ ☐Floor ___ ☐Roof/Attic ☐Water Heater
If rehab proposed, do plans and specs provide for adequate energy conservation? ___ If no, attach description of modification needed.
ENERGY EFFICIENCY APPEARS: ☐High ☐Adequate ☐Low Energy Audit ☐Yes (attach, if available) ☐No
COMMENTS (special features, functional or physical inadequacies, modernization or repairs needed, etc.) _____

FHLMC Form 465 9/80   ATTACH DESCRIPTIVE PHOTOGRAPHS OF SUBJECT PROPERTY AND STREET SCENE   FNMA Form 1073 9/80

Figure 12-8. **Fannie Mae/FHLMC Condominium or PUD Unit Appraisal Report, page 2**

BUDGET ANALYSIS

Unit Charge $ _____ /Mo. x 12 = $ _____ /yr. ($ _____ /Sq. Ft./year of livable area). Ground Rent (if any) $ _____ /yr.

Utilities included in unit charge: ☐ None ☐ Heat ☐ Air Cond. ☐ Electricity ☐ Gas ☐ Water ☐ Sewer

Note any fees, other than regular Condo/PUD charges, for use of facilities _____

To properly maintain the project and provide the services anticipated, the budget appears: ☐ High ☐ Adequate ☐ Inadequate

Compared to other competitive projects of similar quality and design subject unit charge appears: ☐ High ☐ Reasonable ☐ Low

Management Group: ☐ Owners Association ☐ Developer ☐ Management Agent (identify) _____

Quality of Management and its enforcement of Rules and Regulations appears: ☐ Superior ☐ Good ☐ Adequate ☐ Inadequate

Special or unusual characteristics in the Condo/PUD Documents or otherwise known to the appraiser, that would affect marketability (if none, so state)

Comments

COST APPROACH

NOTE: FHLMC does not require the cost approach in the appraisal of condominium or PUD units.

Cost Approach (to be used only for detached, semi-detached, and town house units):

Reproduction Cost New _____ Sq. Ft. @ $ _____ per Sq. Ft. = ... $ _____

Less Depreciation: Physical $ _____ Functional $ _____ Economic $ _____ (_____)

Depreciated Value of Improvements: . . . . _____

Add Land Value (if leasehold, show only leasehold value—attach calculations) . . . . _____

Pro-rata Share of Value of Amenities . . . . $ _____

Total Indicated Value: ☐ FEE SIMPLE ☐ LEASEHOLD . . . . $ _____

Comments regarding estimate of depreciation and value of land and amenity package _____

MARKET DATA ANALYSIS

The appraiser, whenever possible, should analyze two comparable sales from within the subject project. However, when appraising a unit in a new or newly converted project, at least two comparables should be selected from outside the subject project. In the following analysis, the comparable should always be adjusted to the subject unit and not vice versa. If a significant feature of the comparable is superior to the subject unit, a minus (−) adjustment should be made to the comparable; if such a feature of the comparable is inferior to the subject, a plus (+) adjustment should be made to the comparable.

LIST ONLY THOSE ITEMS THAT REQUIRE ADJUSTMENT

ITEM	Subject Property	COMPARABLE NO. 1		COMPARABLE NO. 2		COMPARABLE NO. 3	
Address-Unit No. Project Name							
Proximity to Subj.							
Sales Price	$	$		$		$	
Price/Living Area	$	$		$		$	
Data Source							
	DESCRIPTION	DESCRIPTION	+(−)$ Adjustment	DESCRIPTION	+(−)$ Adjustment	DESCRIPTION	+(−)$ Adjustment
Date of Sale and Time Adjustment							
Location							
Site/View							
Design and Appeal							
Quality of Constr.							
Age							
Condition							
Living Area, Room Count and Total	Total B·rms Baths	Total B·rms Baths		Total B·rms Baths		Total B·rms Baths	
Gross Living Area	Sq. ft.	Sq. ft.		Sq. ft.		Sq. ft.	
Basement & Bsmt. Finished Rooms							
Functional Utility							
Air Conditioning							
Storage							
Parking Facilities							
Common Elements and Recreation Facilities							
Mo. Assessment							
Leasehold/Fee							
Special Energy Efficient Items							
Other (e.g. fireplaces, kitchen equip., remodeling)							
Sales or Financing Concessions							
Net Adj. (total)		☐Plus ☐Minus $		☐Plus ☐Minus $		☐Plus ☐Minus $	
Indicated Value of Subject		$		$		$	

Comments on Market Data Analysis _____

INDICATED VALUE BY MARKET DATA APPROACH _____ $ _____

INDICATED VALUE BY INCOME APPROACH (If applicable) Economic Market Rent $ _____ /Mo. x Gross Rent Multiplier _____ = $ _____

This appraisal is made ☐ "as is". ☐ subject to the repairs, alterations, or conditions listed below. ☐ subject to completion per plans and specifications.

Comments and Conditions of Appraisal _____

Final Reconciliation _____

Construction Warranty ☐ Yes ☐ No Name of Warranty Program _____ Warranty Coverage Expires _____

This appraisal is based upon the above requirements, the certification, contingent and limiting conditions, and Market Value definition that are stated in

☐ FHLMC Form 439 (Rev. 10/78)/FNMA Form 1004B (Rev. 10/78) filed with client _____, 19 ___. ☐ attached

I ESTIMATE THE MARKET VALUE, AS DEFINED, OF SUBJECT PROPERTY AS OF _____, 19 ____ to be $ _____

Appraiser(s) _____ Review Appraiser (if applicable) _____

Date Report Signed _____, 19 ____ ☐ Did ☐ Did Not Physically Inspect Property

FHLMC Form 465 9/80 REVERSE FNMA Form 1073 9/80

If the appraiser rates any of the items as either fair or poor, this opinion must be supported by facts in the comment section. For example, the appraiser could rate the convenience to shopping as fair, adding the following explanation: The convenience to shopping is adversely affected by the construction of a major thoroughfare causing the residents to have to travel an additional one mile to reach shopping. The construction will take at least eighteen months to complete.

In the third section of the report, the appraiser is asked to analyze the site of the property with regard to certain aspects that may affect the property value. The items to be reviewed include the following: zoning, if any; if no zoning, how the property standards will be maintained; utilities; off-site improvements; and the highest and best use.

The final section of the first page deals with the improvements to the property. The first part of the section asks that the appraiser review the improvements that are existing, proposed, or under construction and the type of improvements (single-family, duplex, etc.). The appraiser is also asked to describe the roofing material, type of foundation, insulation, and windows used in the house. The appraiser is asked to specify whether the improvement has a basement and if so to give a description. Next, the appraiser will give a room count and square footage of the improvement or house. The information furnished about the interior includes the finish and equipment to be included in the improvement. Also, the appraiser is asked to rate the property as compared to other similar properties, and once again any rating of fair or poor must be explained. Some lenders view "Appeal and Marketability" as one of the key ratings in this section.

Before we leave the discussion of this section of the appraisal report, it should be noted that the appraiser is asked to comment on any special features of the property. This is to include any energy-efficient items. In other words, the appraiser is asked to comment on the energy efficiency of the home, a very important factor as the cost of utilities continues to increase. The energy efficiency of the home may be increased by its design, use of solar heat, and materials designed to enhance the energy efficiency of the home. Some of the items that add to the efficiency of the home follow:

1. Insulation: using the minimum amounts of ceiling insulation that the Department of Energy considers desirable for homes, as well as exterior walls, roofs, under floors, and surrounding ducts and pipes.

2. The installation of an automatic setback thermostat.

3. Water heaters enclosed in an insulation blanket designed for use with either a gas or electric water heater.

4. The use of weather stripping and caulking to prevent air from escaping around openings such as windows and doors.

5. The use of double- or triple-glazed windows with weather stripping.

In addition, the lender may require the appraiser to complete or provide an addendum to the appraisal that may be used to identify, rate, and evaluate the property's energy related features. An example of such an addendum is shown in Figures 12–9 and 12–10.

You will note that on the first page of the addendum, the appraiser is asked to rate or appraise the insulation, windows and doors, heating and cooling system or systems. Finally, the appraiser is asked if there has been an energy audit made on the property. The appraiser is asked to rate the energy efficiency as high, adequate, or low. On page 2 or part 2 of the addendum, the appraiser is asked to estimate the value of the energy-saving items. Why is this so important? If the cost of utilities is reduced, many lenders will take the estimated savings into consideration and may allow more of the borrower's income to go toward the house payment, thus allowing the borrowers to qualify for more loan.

Let us continue our discussion of the Fannie Mae Form 1004/FHLMC Form 70. The second page of this report is the Valuation Section, Figure 12–4, where the appraiser will use the three approaches to value to establish the market value of the property. In the first half of this section, the appraiser gives the dimensions of the rooms and calculates the gross living area in the house. In the second or right half of this section, the appraiser is asked to estimate the reproduction costs of the improvements. The appraiser will figure the cost of the dwelling by multiplying the square feet of the dwelling by the cost per square foot to build a comparable dwelling. Then, the value of such items as porches, patios, garages/carports, and driveways is added to the value. If there is any depreciation to be deducted from the total reproduction cost, it is included and itemized and explained on the left side in

Figure 12-9.   Energy Addendum, page 1

ENERGY ADDENDUM—RESIDENTIAL APPRAISAL REPORT

This Energy Addendum is an optional report designed to assist appraisers in (1) describing the energy efficiency of the subject property and (2) estimating the value of energy-saving items in those instances when adequate comparable market data are not available. It may be used as an attachment to FHLMC Form 70, 72 and 465.

Borrower _____

Property address _____

PART I—Energy Checklist

In this section the appraiser should note the energy-efficient characteristics of the subject property and use these characteristics as a basis for rating the property's overall energy efficiency (high, adequate or low). The appraiser's rating of energy efficiency may be utilized by the lender to justify higher housing expense and total debt-to-income ratios for investment-quality loans.

The comment sections should be used to describe the specific features and the quality of installation of the energy-efficient item(s) or technique(s). For example, in the heating and cooling section below, if the Energy-efficient furnace box is checked by the appraiser, those features that make the furnace "energy efficient" should be explained.

INSULATION *(Check if present, state "R" value)*
- ☐ Attic/roof: R-_____
- ☐ Walls: R-_____
- ☐ Floors: R-_____
- ☐ Slab/perimeter: R-_____
- ☐ Foundation walls: R-_____
- ☐ Water Heater
- ☐ Heat/cooling ducts or pipes

Comments *(Describe quality and adequacy):* _____

WINDOWS AND DOORS
- ☐ Double (storm)/triple glazed windows
- ☐ Storm doors: On ____ of ____ doors
- ☐ Weatherstripping
- ☐ Caulking
- ☐ Other: _____

Comments *(Describe quality and adequacy):* _____

HEATING AND COOLING
a. Conventional equipment
- ☐ Automatic setback thermostat
- ☐ Automatic flue damper
- ☐ Energy-efficient furnace/air conditioner
- ☐ Energy-efficient water heater
- ☐ Special fireplace devices/features *(Describe in comments)*
- ☐ Wood burning stove
- ☐ Other: _____

Comments *(Describe quality and adequacy):* _____

b. Solar equipment or design
- ☐ Passive solar design/landscaping — exterior *(Describe features below)*
- ☐ Passive solar design — interior *(Describe features below)*
- ☐ Solar space heating/cooling   ☐ Back-up system
- ☐ Solar hot water heating
- ☐ Earth-sheltered housing design
- ☐ Other: _____

Comments *(Describe quality and adequacy):* _____

ENERGY RATING
Has an energy audit/rating been performed on the subject property?
- ☐ Yes *(Attach, if available)*   ☐ No   ☐ Unknown

Energy efficiency appears:
- ☐ High   ☐ Adequate   ☐ Low

General comments: _____

Date _____   Appraiser(s) signature(s) _____

FHLMC Form 70A   1/83

Figure 12–10.   Energy Addendum, page 2

This section is to be used for estimating the value of energy-saving items in those instances when adequate comparable market data are not available.

The value of the energy-saving items should be the lesser of:

(a) the present worth of the estimated savings in utility costs, as determined by capitalizing the savings at an interest rate not less than the current interest rate for home mortgages for a period which does not exceed the lesser of the item's expected physical life or seven years; or

(b) the installed cost of the energy-saving item or construction technique, less any physical, functional and economic depreciation.

As a matter of underwriting policy, FHLMC will limit the value contribution of the energy-saving items to five percent (5%) of the estimated value of the subject property.

VALUE CALCULATIONS *(Use additional forms if more than three items.)*

1. Description of item or construction technique _____

_____

Estimated monthly savings $ _____   Expected life _____ years

Source(s) of savings estimate _____

Use this space to show all calculations

   a. Present worth of estimated savings ....$_____

   b. Installed cost of item or technique (less any depreciation)................$_____

      Estimated value of item (the lesser of a or b) ....$_____ (1)

2. Description of item or construction technique _____

_____

Estimated monthly savings $ _____   Expected life _____ years

Source(s) of savings estimate _____

Use this space to show all calculations

   a. Present worth of estimated savings ....$_____

   b. Installed cost of item or technique (less any depreciation)................$_____

      Estimated value of item (the lesser of a or b) ....$_____ (2)

3. Description of item or construction technique _____

_____

Estimated monthly savings $ _____   Expected life _____ years

Source(s) of savings estimate _____

Use this space to show all calculations

   a. Present worth of estimated savings ....$_____

   b. Installed cost of item or technique (less any depreciation)................$_____

      Estimated value of item (the lesser of a or b) ....$_____ (3)

Estimated total value of item(s) or technique(s) *(The sum of (1), (2) and (3) above)* .... $_____

(In the market data analysis section of the appraisal report, you may enter the lesser of this figure or an amount not to exceed five percent of the value of the property.)

The appraiser has utilized acceptable valuation methodology in this analysis in order to develop an estimate of the present worth of the items and techniques contributing to the energy efficiency of the property. The results are subject to variance based on the effective use and maintenance of the items and the lifestyle of the occupants of the property.

Date _____   Appraiser(s) Signature(s) _____

FHLMC Form 70A   1/83   Reverse

PART II—Estimate of Value of Energy-Saving Items

the comment section. Finally, the value of the land is calculated and added to the depreciated value of the improvements to establish the value by the cost method.

Many conventional lenders as well as those who buy conventional mortgages in the secondary market have established as a rough rule of thumb that the "estimated land value" should not exceed 30 percent of the total value as shown on the line entitled *Indicated value by the cost approach.* Also many of the lenders have a rule that the cost approach is not a good way to establish the value of properties more than about five years old.

The Market Data Analysis section is provided for the appraiser to compare the subject property to similar properties that have been sold and closed in the general area. You will note that there is space provided for only three of the most comparable sales, but the appraiser may provide as many comparables as are believed necessary to establish the value of the subject property. The adjustment column should be noted. As mentioned earlier in the chapter, this is where the appraiser will make a dollar adjustment to the comparable to make it more comparable to the subject property. For example, if the comparable was sold 3 months prior to the appraisal and houses have been appreciating at the rate of $250 per month, he would adjust the sales price of the comparable up by $750. This would be shown as a plus in the adjustment column in the row entitled Date of Sale and Time Adjustment.

If there are any major adjustments or the appraiser has any comments about the Market Data Analysis, they will appear in the comment section. Next, the appraiser will establish the value of the property as calculated by the Market Data Analysis and will show this at the bottom of the section.

The next section of the report is Indicated Value by the Income Approach. This section is used only if the property is to be used as rental property or if any part of the property will be rented to generate income. As we learned earlier in this chapter, to calculate the value by this method, two estimates must be made. One is the monthly rent and the second is the gross rent multiplier (GRM). Once these items have been established, the value can be calculated by multiplying the rent by the GRM.

Following this, the report requires the appraiser to state if the appraisal for existing property is being made "requiring repairs" or in an "as is" condition. If repairs are required, the appraiser will list those to be made. If the property is proposed or under construction,

the appraiser will check the block stating the appraisal is being made subject to the completion of the property as per the submitted plans and specifications.

Normally if there are repairs to be made or if the appraisal is made on proposed construction or on a property under construction, many lenders will require some proof that the repairs have been made, the construction was done according to all plans or specifications, or the construction was completed. The usual method is for the appraiser or someone from the lender to inspect the property after completion and fill out some type of certification. A possible format for such a certification is shown in Figure 12–11. Thus, if you are working with a client who is purchasing a new home under construction, this may be required by the lender prior to the closing of the loan.

The next part is Final Reconciliation. Here, the appraiser states why more emphasis was given either to the cost approach or the market data approach. In the final statements of the report, the appraiser gives information regarding any warranties on the home, and then the market value of the property is stated as of a certain date. The appraisal is then signed by the appraiser. If there is a requirement for the appraisal to be reviewed, the reviewer will sign the appraisal and will state if the property was physically inspected by the reviewer.

This completes our overview of the standard Fannie Mae/FHLMC appraisal reports. For further study of the three forms, there are sample completed appraisal forms in Appendix H.

Federal Housing Administration and Veterans Administration

Congress, seeing the need for the reduction of forms used by the various federal agencies, mandated that all of the departments and agencies work together to develop common forms. One such effort for common forms was between the Department of Housing and Urban Development and the Veterans Administration. The first form developed was a common application for property appraisal and commitment.

This common form was placed in service on July 1, 1981, and according to the VA and FHA instructions, all prior forms were then to be destroyed. The new form is similar to the previous forms used by the VA and FHA, in that the form has an instruction sheet and a list of required exhibits that must be submitted with the application for property

Figure 12-11. *Satisfactory Completion Certificate*

SATISFACTORY COMPLETION CERTIFICATE

On _____ 19_____, the property situated at

_____

_____

_____

was appraised by me or _____.

The appraisal report was subject to: _____ satisfactory completion, _____ repairs, or_____

_____

I certify that I have reinspected subject property, the requirements or conditions set forth in the appraisal report have been met, and any required repairs or completion items have been done in a workmanlike manner.

Itemized below are substantial changes from the data in the appraisal report, and these changes do not adversely affect any property ratings or final estimate of value in the report:

_____ 19 _____   _____
Date   Inspector

FHLMC 442 Rev. 6/78

appraisal. The instruction sheet, for the most part, applies to both of the agencies; but the exhibits required are not the same. The instruction sheet, therefore, lists the required exhibits for FHA and VA separately.

There is one major difference with the new combined form: when the form is used as a Request for Determination of Reasonable Value (that is, a request for a VA appraisal), it will no longer show the number of square feet of improved living area. FHA-HUD, however, still has the requirement of showing this figure. According to HUD's Mortgagee Letter 81-21, June 2, 1981, any application submitted to FHA-HUD must have this information or the request will be rejected.

As with the previous forms used by FHA-HUD and VA, this is a multipage form and we shall review only those pages that may be of importance to you as a real estate professional or to your client. This review is being done to show the information that will be required to complete this form and to show where you may be able to help provide the necessary data.

The first page of the form is the Application for Property Appraisal and Commitment. This page is illustrated in Figure 12-12. Let us start at the top of the first page and work our way through the more important sections. In the same area as the title of the form, there is one important block if the form is to be used as a HUD application and that block is entitled, "HUD Section of Act." Here the type of mortgage insurance being applied for must be indicated. For example, if the mortgage is to be insured under section 203(b), this would be placed in the block. Sections 2, 3, and 4 will apply to both FHA and VA. Section 2, Property Address, and section 3, Legal Description, are self-explanatory; but section 4 may require your assisting the lender or originator. According to FHA/VA, title limitations and restrictive covenants may be, but are not limited to, easements, special assessments, mandatory homeowner associations, and so forth. Normally, the originator or lender will have this information, but it may be a good idea at the time of listing a piece of property to secure a copy of a title policy issued on the property, or any other document that may list any limitations to the title, and supply this information to the lender where your client is making application.

The next sections that may require you or your client to provide information are sections 6 through 8. In section 6, the size of the lot must be supplied. It would be advisable to indicate if it is a subdivision lot because some FHA offices will request this information. Sec-

tion 7 deals with the utilities to the property. If the property is located inside the corporate limits of a city, town, or village, the utilities will normally be public. Only if the property is located outside an incorporated area will additional information possibly be requested. Section 8 is very important. Here the equipment included in the house must be listed, for it will have an effect on the appraised value of the property. Normally, the VA will not include any equipment that is not indicated on the application.

Sections 9 through 15 deal with improvements to the real property. Sections 9 through 11 are self-explanatory. Section 12 is one that may be overlooked. For example, section 10 may indicate a detached type of building, but, as with section 9, there is no question whether the structure is a single-family or multifamily unit. Therefore, section 12 is the section that will indicate whether the building is a duplex, triplex, or fourplex.

The following sections starting with section 16 are very important to the real estate professional. If any sections are not completed or are completed with incorrect information, there is a strong possibility that the property will not be appraised. Normally, if the appraiser assigned by HUD or VA cannot readily make contact with the owner or his or her agent to gain access to the property, they will return the application to the person or organization originating the application. Therefore, make sure that the appraiser's access to the property is made as easy as possible. You may want to contact the originator of the application and get the name of the appraiser and arrange to meet him or her at the property in order to answer any questions or to gather any information that may be needed. Some real estate professionals, when meeting the FHA or VA appraiser, will also bring information on recently closed FHA or VA sales in the immediate area of the property. Immediate area is defined by some of the FHA or VA offices as an area of one square mile surrounding the property.

Section 29 will be filled out only if the property is new or proposed construction. Sections 30 through 37 are self-explanatory. The next large areas are the certifications to be completed and signed by the necessary party or parties.

After this page is completed, the lender will keep the last copy of the form for the files and the following action will be taken:

1. If the application is for FHA mortgage insurance, the lender will call the nearest FHA office and will be given a case number

Figure 12–12.   **VA Request for Determination of Reasonable Value/HUD Application for Property Appraisal and Commitment**

Form Approved
OMB No. 2900-0045

VA REQUEST FOR DETERMINATION OF REASONABLE VALUE (Real Estate)
HUD APPLICATION FOR PROPERTY APPRAISAL AND COMMITMENT

HUD Section of Act | 1. CASE NUMBER

2. PROPERTY ADDRESS *(Include ZIP Code and county)*

3. LEGAL DESCRIPTION

4. TITLE LIMITATIONS AND RESTRICTIVE COVENANTS
1. [ ] CONDOMINIUM 2. [ ] PLANNED UNIT DEVELOPMENT

5. NAME AND ADDRESS OF FIRM OR PERSON MAKING REQUEST/APPLICATION *(Include ZIP Code)*

6. LOT DIMENSIONS:
1. [ ] IRREGULAR: SQ/FT 2. [ ] ACRES:

7. UTILITIES (✓)	ELEC.	GAS	WATER	SAN. SEWER
1. PUBLIC				
2. COMMUNITY				
3. INDIVIDUAL				

8. EQUIP.
1. [ ] RANGE/OVEN 4. [ ] CLOTHES WASHER 7. [ ] VENT FAN
2. [ ] REFRIG. 5. [ ] DRYER 8. [ ] W/W CARPET
3. [ ] DISH-WASHER 6. [ ] GARBAGE DISP. 9. [ ]

9. BUILDING STATUS
1. [ ] PROPOSED 3. [ ] UNDER CONSTR.
2. [ ] SUBSTANTIAL REHABILITATION 4. [ ] EXISTING

10. BUILDING TYPE
1. [ ] DETACHED 3. [ ] ROW
2. [ ] SEMI-DETACHED 4. [ ] APT. UNIT

11. FACTORY FABRICATED?
1. [ ] YES 2. [ ] NO

12. NUMBER OF UNITS

13A. STREET ACCESS
1. [ ] PRIVATE
2. [ ] PUBLIC

13B. STREET MAINT.
1. [ ] PRIVATE
2. [ ] PUBLIC

14A. CONSTRUCTION WARRANTY INCLUDED?
1. [ ] YES 2. [ ] NO *(If "Yes" complete Items 14B and C also.)*

14B. NAME OF WARRANTY PROGRAM

14C. EXPIRATION DATE *(Month, day, year)*

15. CONSTR. COMPLETED *(Mo., yr.)*

16. NAME OF OWNER

17. PROPERTY:
[ ] OCCUPIED BY OWNER [ ] NEVER OCCUPIED [ ] VACANT [ ] OCCUPIED BY TENANT *(Complete Item 18 also)*

18. RENT *(If applic.)* $ /MONTH

19. NAME OF OCCUPANT

20. TELEPHONE NO.

21. NAME OF BROKER

22. TELEPHONE NO.

23. DATE AND TIME AVAILABLE FOR INSPECTION
[ ] AM [ ] PM

24. KEYS AT *(Address)*

25. ORIGINATOR'S IDENT. NO.

26. SPONSOR'S IDENT. NO.

27. INSTITUTION'S CASE NO.

28. PURCHASER'S NAME AND ADDRESS *(Complete mailing address. Include ZIP code.)*

EQUAL OPPORTUNITY IN HOUSING

NOTE – Federal laws and regulations prohibit discrimination because of race, color, religion, sex, or national origin in the sale or rental of residential property. Numerous State statutes and local ordinances also prohibit such discrimination. In addition, section 805 of the Civil Rights Act of 1968 prohibits discriminatory practices in connection with the financing of housing.

If HUD/VA finds there is noncompliance with any antidiscrimination laws or regulations, it may discontinue business with the violator.

29. NEW OR PROPOSED CONSTRUCTION – *Complete Items 29A through 29G for new or proposed construction cases only.*

A. COMPLIANCE INSPECTIONS WILL BE OR WERE MADE BY:
[ ] FHA [ ] VA [ ] NONE MADE

B. PLANS *(check one)*
[ ] FIRST SUBMISSION [ ] REPEAT CASE *(If checked complete Item 29C.)*

C. PLANS SUBMITTED PREVIOUSLY UNDER CASE NO.:

D. NAME AND ADDRESS OF BUILDER

E. TELEPHONE NO.

F. NAME AND ADDRESS OF WARRANTOR

G. TELEPHONE NO.

30. COMMENTS ON SPECIAL ASSESSMENTS OR HOMEOWNERS ASSOCIATION CHARGES

31. ANNUAL REAL ESTATE TAXES $

32. MINERAL RIGHTS RESERVED?
[ ] YES *(Explain)*
[ ] NO

33. LEASEHOLD CASES *(Complete if applicable)*
LEASE IS:
[ ] 99 YEARS
[ ] RENEWABLE
[ ] HUD/VA APPROVED

EXPIRES *(Date)*

ANNUAL GROUND RENT $

34. SALE PRICE OF PROPERTY $

35. REFINANCING – AMOUNT OF PROPOSED LOAN $

36. PROPOSED SALE CONTRACT ATTACHED
[ ] YES [ ] NO

37. CONTRACT NUMBER PREVIOUSLY APPROVED BY VA THAT WILL BE USED

CERTIFICATIONS FOR SUBMISSIONS TO HUD

In submitting this application for a conditional commitment for mortgage insurance, it is agreed and understood by the parties involved in the transaction, that if, at the time of application for a Firm Commitment, the identity of the seller has changed, the application for a Firm Commitment will be rejected and the application for a Conditional Commitment will be reprocessed upon request by the mortgagee.

It is further agreed and understood that in submitting the request for a Firm Commitment for mortgage insurance, the seller, the purchaser and the broker involved in the transaction shall each certify that the terms of the contract for purchase are true to his or her best knowledge and belief, and that any other agreement entered into by any of these parties in connection with this transaction is attached to the sales agreement.

BUILDER/SELLER'S AGREEMENT: All Houses: The undersigned agrees to deliver to the purchaser HUD's statement of appraised value. **Proposed Construction:** The undersigned agrees, upon sale or conveyance of title within one year from date of initial occupancy, to deliver to the purchaser Form HUD-92544, warranting that the house is constructed in substantial conformity with the plans and specifications on which HUD based its value and to furnish HUD a conformed copy with the purchaser's receipt thereon that the original warranty was delivered to him/her. **All Houses:** In consideration of the issuance of the commitment requested by this application, I (we) hereby agree that any deposit or down payment made in connection with the purchase of the property described above, whether received by the undersigned, or an agent of the undersigned, shall upon receipt be deposited in escrow or in trust or in a special account which is not subject to the claims of my creditors and where it will be maintained until it has been disbursed for the benefit of the purchaser or otherwise disposed of in accordance with the terms of the contract of sale.

Signature of: [ ] Mortgagee [ ] Builder [ ] Seller [ ] Other X_____ Date _____ 19___

MORTGAGEE'S CERTIFICATE: The undersigned mortgagee certifies that to the best of his/her knowledge, all statements made in this application and the supporting documents are true, correct and complete.

Signature and Title of Mortgage Officer: X_____ Date _____ 19___

CERTIFICATIONS FOR SUBMISSIONS TO VA

1. On receipt of "Certificate of Reasonable Value" or advice from the Veterans Administration that a "Certificate of Reasonable Value" will not be issued, we agree to forward to the appraiser the approved fee which we are holding for this purpose.

2. CERTIFICATION REQUIRED ON CONSTRUCTION UNDER FHA SUPERVISION *(Strike out inappropriate phrases in parentheses)*

I hereby certify that plans and specifications and related exhibits, including acceptable FHA Change Orders, if any, supplied to VA in this case, are identical to those (submitted to) (to be submitted to) (approved by) FHA, and that FHA inspections (have been) (will be) made pursuant to FHA approval for mortgage insurance on the basis of proposed construction under Sec.

38. SIGNATURE OF PERSON AUTHORIZING THIS REQUEST

39. TITLE

40. DATE

41. DATE OF ASSIGNMENT

42. NAME OF APPRAISER

WARNING Section 1010 of Title 18, U.S.C. provides: "Whoever for the purpose of . . . influencing such Administration . . . makes, passes, utters or publishes any statement knowing the same to be false . . . shall be fined not more than $5,000 or imprisoned not more than two years or both."

VA FORM 26-1805, AUG 1980
HUD FORM 92800-1

SUPERSEDES VA FORM 26-1805, AUG 1977, AND
HUD 92800, JUL 1979, WHICH WILL NOT BE USED.

VA/HUD FILE COPY 1

and the name of an appraiser who will make the appraisal. The lender will then forward the 7 remaining copies of the form to the appraiser. The appraiser will make the appraisal and return the completed form to FHA within 4 working days.

2. If the application is for a Certificate of Reasonable Value, the lender will forward the remaining 7 pages to the nearest VA Loan Guaranty office, which will assign an appraiser. The assigned appraiser will make the appraisal and return the completed application to the VA.

The next step in the process for either the FHA or VA occurs after the completed appraisal is received. It is reviewed and then the value of the property is approved. Once the appraisal and value is approved, HUD will issue a Conditional Commitment or VA will issue a Certificate of Reasonable Value. This is done by returning copies 2 (Requester's Copy) and 4 (Purchaser's Copy) to the originator or as indicated on the form (see Name and Address of Firm or Person Making Request/Application). Copy 3 will be missing because it is kept by HUD or VA. Copy 4 is shown in Figure 12–13. Pages 2 and 4 are identical.

Normally, the lenders or originators of the application or request will call the applicant to notify him or her of the results and to confirm that the Commitment or Certificate has been received. If possible, you should get a copy of the commitment or certificate and place it in the property file. This will allow you to build your own file of property values in your area.

Now let us review the major sections of the commitment or certificate of reasonable value. The top of the form will indicate whether it is a CRV or a Conditional Commitment. This was done when the first page was completed along with sections 1 through 13B. The information contained in sections 14 through 18 of the form are of the utmost importance to the parties to the transaction.

HUD Conditional Commitment   Let us review how these sections may be completed if the application is for FHA mortgage insurance. Section 14 will indicate the estimated value of the property, which should equal the sales price of the property. It should be noted that this is only the estimated value of the property and not the maximum loan amount that FHA will insure. The maximum loan amount will be established later. Section 15 will state the estimated remaining economic life of the property. Section 16 will give the

expiration date of the conditional commitment. Section 17 is the most important section of the commitment for it will establish the following:

1. Maximum mortgage amount

2. Term of the mortgage

3. If the value is an as-is value

4. Monthly expense estimates will be used by FHA to establish the monthly housing costs for borrower approval

5. Estimated closing costs, which will be used to establish the maximum loan amount (estimated closing costs are usually added to the estimated value of the property to establish the maximum loan amount)

It should be noted that if the sales price of the property exceeds the FHA-estimated value of the property, the purchaser has the right either to proceed with the purchase of the property or to cancel the contract. If the purchaser wishes to proceed with the sale, the purchaser will have to put down additional money.

An authorized agent of HUD will sign the commitment in block 19, indicate the date the commitment was issued in block 20, and, finally, the HUD office issuing the commitment will be shown in block 21.

Accompanying this conditional commitment will be one or more documents outlining the general commitment conditions. These conditions may be an explanation of the maximum mortgage amount and terms, the requirements for issuing a firm commitment, and the statement that all construction, repairs, or alterations proposed shall equal or exceed the FHA minimum property standards.

Either contained in the document mentioned above or in a separate document, FHA-HUD will indicate specific commitment conditions that must be met. These may include required termite control or the execution of a form from a health authority indicating an approval of the water supply and/or that a sewage disposal installation is required.

In addition, these conditions may include required repairs that must be made prior to the funding of the mortgage. These repairs may range from the replacement of broken panes of glass to a complete roof.

It must be stressed that all of these specific requirements must be met before HUD-FHA will issue any mortgage insurance on the property in question.

Figure 12–13. *VA Request for Determination of Reasonable Value/HUD Application for Property Appraisal and Commitment, Purchaser's Copy, page 4*

☐ VA CERTIFICATE OF REASONABLE VALUE		HUD Section of Act	1. CASE NUMBER
☐ HUD CONDITIONAL COMMITMENT			

2. PROPERTY ADDRESS *(Include ZIP Code and county)*	3. LEGAL DESCRIPTION	4. TITLE LIMITATIONS AND RESTRICTIVE COVENANTS
		1. ☐ CONDOMINIUM 2 ☐ PLANNED UNIT DEVELOPMENT

5. NAME AND ADDRESS OF FIRM OR PERSON MAKING REQUEST/APPLICATION *(Include ZIP Code)*	6. LOT DIMENSIONS:
	1. ☐ IRREGULAR: SQ/FT *2.* ☐ ACRES:

7. UTILITIES (√)	ELEC.	GAS	WATER	SAN. SEWER
1. PUBLIC				
2. COMMUNITY				
3. INDIVIDUAL				

8. E Q U I P.	*1.* ☐	RANGE/OVEN	*4.* ☐	CLOTHES WASHER	*7.* ☐	VENT FAN
	2. ☐	REFRIG.	*5.* ☐	DRYER	*8.* ☐	W/W CARPET
	3. ☐	DISH-WASHER	*6.* ☐	GARBAGE DISP.	*9.* ☐	

9. BUILDING STATUS	10. BUILDING TYPE	11. FACTORY FABRICATED?	12. NUMBER OF UNITS	13A. STREET ACCESS	13B. STREET MAINT.
1. ☐ PROPOSED *3.* ☐ UNDER CONSTR.	*1.* ☐ DETACHED *3.* ☐ ROW			*1.* ☐ PRIVATE	*1.* ☐ PRIVATE
2. ☐ SUBSTANTIAL REHABILITATION *4.* ☐ EXISTING	*2.* ☐ SEMI-DETACHED *4.* ☐ APT. UNIT	*1.* ☐ YES *2.* ☐ NO		*2.* ☐ PUBLIC	*2.* ☐ PUBLIC

14. ESTIMATED REASONABLE VALUE OF PROPERTY	15. REMAINING ECONOMIC LIFE OF PROPERTY IS ESTIMATED TO BE NOT LESS THAN.	16. EXPIRATION DATE	17. HUD COMMITMENT TERMS	
$	YEARS		A. MAXIMUM MORTGAGE AMOUNT	$

17. HUD COMMITMENT TERMS (cont.)	
B. NO. OF MONTHS	

18. ☐ This Certificate of Reasonable Value is valid only if VA Form 26-1843p showing VA General Conditions and the applicable Specific Conditions is attached.

C. NOTICE OF REJECTION	
D. "AS IS" VALUE	$

19. ADMINISTRATOR OF VETERANS AFFAIRS, BY *(Signature of authorized agent)*, OR HUD AUTHORIZED AGENT	20. DATE ISSUED	21. VA OR HUD OFFICE

E. MONTHLY EXPENSE ESTIMATE	
FIRE INSURANCE	$
TAXES	$

22. PURCHASER'S NAME AND ADDRESS *(Complete mailing address. Include ZIP Code.)*

CONDO. COMMUNITY EXPENSE	$
MAINTENANCE AND REPAIRS	$
HEAT AND UTILITIES	$
F. ESTIMATED CLOSING COST	$

G. ☐ EXISTING ☐ PROPOSED	*(See General Condition 3 on attachment.)*
H. IMPROVED LIVING AREA	SQ/FT

I. ☐ This Conditional Commitment is valid only if HUD Form 92800-5a showing HUD General Conditions and the applicable Specific Conditions is attached.

VA FORM 26-1843, AUG 1980   HUD FORM 92800-5   PURCHASER'S COPY 4

VA Certificate of Reasonable Value   Now let us review what sections of pages 2, 3, and 4 will be completed if the application is for a VA Certificate of Reasonable Value. Sections 1 through 13B will have been completed at the time of the initial application. Once the VA has reviewed the appraisal, the VA will fill out sections 14 through 16 and 18 through 21. Section 14 is the most important because it will give the VA's Estimate of Reasonable Value. This reasonable value is also the maximum loan amount for VA. FHA, to get the maximum loan amount, will normally combine the amount in section 14 and the estimated closing cost listed in section 17 I. Sections 15 and 16 are self-explanatory. As noted above, section 17 is not completed. Section 18 is then checked, an official of VA signs in section 19, and places a date in section 20.

If the sales price of the home is more than the amount listed in section 14, the veteran has two options: (1) to cancel the contract and all of the monies paid by the veteran will be returned or (2) to continue with the sale and make a down payment in the amount of the difference.

Use of VA-CRV by HUD-FHA   HUD-FHA will accept a current Veterans Administration Certificate of Reasonable Value (CRV) for both proposed and existing construction as an estimate of value in lieu of the standard FHA appraisal. It should be noted that FHA will not accept an expired CRV. If the CRV is about to expire, or will expire prior to completion of processing by FHA, the CRV will be considered an active or valid CRV until all of the HUD processing has been completed. The ability to convert a VA-CRV to be used by HUD-FHA can be very important to a real estate professional. For example, you represent a seller who had requested a VA-CRV on their home to establish the value of the property. Then instead of a veteran buyer, the buyer could qualify for an FHA-insured loan. The CRV on the property was current, therefore it could be converted to FHA, thus saving the time and expense of another appraisal.

Home Energy Checklist   In addition to the normal appraisal procedures, both VA and HUD now require that any existing home to be appraised must be appraised with regard to deficiencies in thermal protection. In other words, the appraiser will review the property noting any improvements that may be made to increase the energy efficiency of the home

and save the prospective homebuyer in heating and cooling expenses.

The agencies have developed a form for this review, The Home Energy Checklist. This form must now accompany all HUD Conditional Commitments and VA Certificates of Reasonable Value. The form is a multipage form and once again we will review only those pages that you or your client will normally see. The first page of the form (Figure 12–14) asks the appraiser to check for potential areas of energy savings. You will notice that these areas range from the simple installation of insulation wrap around the hot water heater to installation of storm windows and storm doors. The appraiser can make any additional suggestions that he or she feels will help the energy efficiency of the home. This form, along with the completed request for Conditional Commitment or Request for a Certificate of Reasonable Value, is returned to the HUD or VA office. Then, HUD or VA will return three pages to the lender. Page 3 of the form is for the lender and page 5 is to be returned, if the request is for a CRV, to the veteran making the request or, if the request is for a HUD commitment, to the person making application. The third copy would go to the other party to the transaction. Page 5 of the form is illustrated in Figure 12–15.

There is a note at the top of this page stating that the amount shown on the Conditional Commitment or CRV in section 14 may be increased if funds were expended for weatherization or energy conservation improvements to the property. When a request for an increase in the valuation is due to the expenditure of funds for energy conservation or weatherization, the increase will be made by one of the following methods:

1. $2,000 or less without a separate value determination.

2. From $2,001 to $3,500 if supported by a value determination made by a HUD-FHA review appraiser or staff appraiser. The value determination is normally made by desk review in house; however, some value determinations may require a field inspection of the property. The review appraiser shall make this inspection.

3. $3,501 or more subject to an inspection made by a HUD-FHA-approved fee appraiser/inspector. The lender will mail all proposals submitted by the homeowner concerning the addition of thermal protection improvements to the Field

Figure 12–14.   VA Home Energy Checklist, page 1

Form Approved
OMB No. 76-R0743

	HOME ENERGY CHECKLIST	CASE NUMBER
VA Veterans Administration	(Attachment to VA Form 26-1803, HUD Form 92800-5 and FmHA Form 1922-8)	

NOTE TO APPRAISER: The specific areas of the property listed below are those that have been identified as potential sites where home energy can be lost. Examine those areas listed and check each that, if corrected or improved, could result in energy and monetary savings for the homeowner.

IMPORTANT – Press hard. You are making five copies.

AREA(S) FOR POTENTIAL ENERGY SAVINGS *(Check each applicable box)*

☐ 1.   THERMOSTATS – Consideration should be given to clock thermostats.

☐ 2.   WATER HEATERS – Consideration should be given to an insulation wrap.

☐ 3.   HEATING/COOLING SYSTEM – Insulate ducts and pipes in unheated spaces.

☐ 4.   ATTIC – Attic and attic door should be insulated to the recommended level.

☐ 5.   FLOORS AND FOUNDATION WALLS – Adequate insulation is needed:

    ☐   A.   UNDER FLOORS   ☐   C.   CRAWL SPACE
    ☐   B.   AROUND BASEMENT   ☐   D.   FOUNDATION WALLS

☐ 6.   WINDOWS AND DOORS – Consideration should be given to installation of:

    ☐   A.   WEATHER-STRIPPING/CAULKING TO PREVENT AIR   ☐   C.   _____ STORM DOORS
            ESCAPES FROM OPENINGS *(Including pipes/ducts)*
    ☐   B.   _____ STORM WINDOWS   ☐   D.   DOUBLE OR TRIPLE GLAZED PRIME WINDOWS
                                                WITH WEATHER-STRIPPING

ADDITIONAL REMARKS PERTAINING TO ENERGY CONSERVATION

SIGNATURE OF APPRAISER	DATE

VA FORM
SEP 1980   **26-1803a**   VA 1

Figure 12–15.   VA Home Energy Checklist, page 5

| | Form Approved OMB No. 76-R0743 |

| **Veterans Administration** | **HOME ENERGY CHECKLIST** (Attachment to VA Form 26-1843 and HUD Form 92800-5) | CASE NUMBER |

NOTE: The amount of value shown in Item 14 of VA Form 26-1843/HUD Form 92800-5 may be increased by up to one of the following if such increase is expended for weatherization and/or energy conservation improvements to the property: (a) $2000, without a separate value determination; (b) $3500, if supported by a value determination by a designated appraiser; or, (c) more than $3500, subject to appraisal by VA or HUD, as applicable, and subsequent endorsement of the VA Certificate of Reasonable Value or HUD Conditional Commitment.

The specific areas of the property listed below are those that have been identified as potential sites where home energy can be lost. Examine those areas listed and check each that, if corrected or improved, could result in energy and monetary savings for the homeowner.

AREA(S) FOR POTENTIAL ENERGY SAVINGS *(Check each applicable box)*

☐ 1.   THERMOSTATS — Consideration should be given to clock thermostats.

☐ 2.   WATER HEATERS — Consideration should be given to an insulation wrap.

☐ 3.   HEATING/COOLING SYSTEM — Insulate ducts and pipes in unheated spaces.

☐ 4.   ATTIC INSULATION — See map below for location of the property and recommended minimum insulation.
CAUTION: Do not forget to consider ventilation.

☐ 5.   FLOORS AND FOUNDATION WALLS — Adequate insulation is needed:

☐ A. UNDER FLOORS
☐ B. AROUND BASEMENT
☐ C. CRAWL SPACE
☐ D. FOUNDATION WALLS

☐ 6.   WINDOWS AND DOORS — Storm windows are recommended in areas D, E and F for all fuels and for electric heat in areas B and C (see map below). Consideration should be given to installation of:

☐ A. WEATHER-STRIPPING/CAULKING TO PREVENT AIR ESCAPES FROM OPENINGS *(Including pipes/ducts)*
☐ B. _____ STORM WINDOWS
☐ C. _____ STORM DOORS
☐ D. DOUBLE OR TRIPLE GLAZED PRIME WINDOWS WITH WEATHER-STRIPPING

RECOMMENDED CEILING INSULATION BY ENERGY TYPE AND DEGREE-DAY ZONE

INSULATION CONVERSION TABLE		
R VALUE	EQUIVALENTS	
	BATT OR BLANKET	LOOSE-FILL
19	5½ – 6½ inches	6½ – 8¾ inches
22	6½ inches	7 – 9½ inches
30	9 inches	10 – 11 inches
38	12 inches	13 – 17 inches

The minimum amounts of ceiling insulation that the Department of Energy considers desirable for existing homes are listed below.

The amounts range from R-38 to R-19, according to heating degree-days and type of energy — gas, oil, or electricity — used for heating. Electricity is divided into two categories, resistance heat and the heat pump. The DOE minimums, as shown on the map, are:

Zone A   ((0-1000 degree-days) (Includes Hawaii and Puerto Rico)) — All energy types, R-19.
Zone B   (1001-2500 degree-days) — Gas, oil and electric heat pump, R-19. Electric resistance heat, R-22.
Zone C   (2501-3500 degree-days) — Gas, oil and electric heat pump, R-22. Electric resistance heat, R-30.
Zone D   (3501-6000 degree-days) — All energy types, R-30.
Zone E   (6001-7000 degree-days) — Gas and oil, R-30. All electric heat, R-38.
Zone F   ((7001 or more degree-days) (Includes Alaska)) — All energy types, R-38.

Duct and pipe insulation, and water heater insulation are recommended in all climate zones. Floor insulation is recommended for electric resistance heating in all zones with more than 2500 degree-days and for other energy sources and heat pumps in zones above 3500 degree-days; either R-19 or R-11 is recommended.

VA FORM
SEP 1980   **26-1843n**   VETERAN 5

Office for review. The appraiser/inspector must review the expense involved in adding the thermal improvements and determine what effect the improvements will have on value. This will be done by an on-site inspection. The fee appraiser/inspector will bill the lender for this service but the fee charged cannot exceed those charged for inspections in the geographical area. The lender is responsible for paying the fee appraiser/inspector for this service.[3]

It should be noted that HUD now requires the purchaser to indicate on the application for mortgage insurance that he or she has been given a copy of the Home Energy Checklist and understands the contents of the form.

Request for Reconsideration of Appraisals—HUD If, as a real estate professional, you are working with a seller and have either made an application for, or have had a buyer make an application for, a Conditional Commitment from HUD and the Estimated Value in section 14 of page 2 or 4 (Figure 12–13) is below the sales price thus affecting the maximum mortgage amount, there are procedures to request a reconsideration.

Usually, you will work with the lender or originator of the application to complete a Request for Reconsideration of FHA Appraisal. A sample of such a form used by the FHA Insuring Office in Dallas, Texas, is shown in Figure 12–16. All of the FHA Insuring Offices will have a similar form, and the basic information for each of the forms will be the same. You will note that the form calls for recent sales. Some of the offices have established any sale within six months of the application for commitment to be a recent sale. As you will notice, these must be sales and not appraisals. Some of the offices even take this one step further and state that these must be closed sales, not pending sales. If you are gathering information on sales for a request, you should submit only closed sales, even though your nearest insuring office does not state that the sales must be closed sales.

Prior to June 22, 1982, the only types of comparable sales that were acceptable to FHA were either FHA or VA sales, but with the issuance of Mortgagee Letter 82-10, Department of Housing and Urban Development, Office of the Assistant Secretary for Housing—Federal Housing Commissioner, that requirement has changed. According to the letter,

HUD procedures for establishing property values rely heavily on the market approach, which establishes an upper limit of value. In applying this approach, members of fee panels and HUD staff will be required to use the best available and most recent comparable sales which can be identified. At least two of the three comparable sales used in establishing value for mortgage insurance should have been financed conventionally, with the values assigned on the basis of the conventional mortgage closing amounts.

Thus, as a real estate professional in completing the Request for Reconsideration of FHA Appraisal, you should keep this in mind when selecting the comparables that you will submit. In many areas of Texas, having to use only one FHA-insured sale can make the job of completing the request a great deal faster and less involved.

After the request form is completed, the lender or originator of the original application will submit the request to the insuring office. The FHA office will review the request for reasonableness prior to the request going to the appraiser who made the original appraisal. It should be noted that there may be a fee charged for such reconsideration. So, prior to the submission of any request, you should check with the lender or originator. If there will be a fee charged, let your client know the amount of the fee and that the client may have to pay it.

Request for Reconsideration of Appraisals—VA According to the Veterans Administration's Appraisal Section in Washington, D.C., there is no written policy for requesting reconsideration of appraisal. It should be noted that some of the Loan Guaranty Offices have instituted a specific program. According to the Appraisal Section, any party to a transaction may request the reconsideration including any real estate agent representing either party to the transaction. The request will have to be made in writing and should include comparable sales data to support the request. Since there is no specific form to be used when making the request, you may wish to use a form similar to the one illustrated in Figure 12–16, but prior to making any request for reconsideration, you should contact the lender making the initial request or the VA Loan Guaranty section that is responsible for your area.

Figure 12–16.   Request for Reconsideration of FHA Appraisal to Dallas Insuring Office

VAL FORM #100
November 1979

REQUEST FOR RECONSIDERATION OF FHA APPRAISAL
DALLAS AREA OFFICE

NOTE: (Comparable sales must be dwellings similar in type and quality of construction in the same or comparable neighborhood)

Recent Sales (Within 6 months) --- (Not Appraisals) --- Submit Three (Minimum)

	Subject Property	Comp. No. 1	For FHA Use Only - +	Comp. No. 2	For FHA Use Only - +	Comp. No. 3	For FHA Use Only - +
FHA Case No.							
Address							
Lot Size							
Year Blt/Condition							
Date & type of sale							
Type of Roof							
Living Area Sq.Ft.							
No. of Stories							
No. of Rooms							
No. of Bedrooms							
No. of Baths							
W.B.F.P.							
Covered Patio							
Type Fencing							
Type of Cooling							
Type of Heat							
Type of Foundation							
Floor Covering							
Gar/CP # of Cars							
(1)Install'd Equip.							
(2)Personal Prop.							
Sale Price							
Other							
Total Adj.							
Net Adj.							
Remarks:							

(1) Built-in range, oven, dishwasher, disposal, etc.
(2) Rugs, drapes, free standing appliances, BBQ, swimming pool

DO NOT WRITE IN SPACES BELOW -FHA USE ONLY

REQUEST FOR RECONSIDERATION IS: ☐ Acceptable for reopening
☐ Unacceptable- return to Mortgage Company for correction

Initials: _____
Date: _____

The information herein is from our records, or was furnished to us, and to the best of my knowledge, is accurate.

_____
(Signature - Mortgagee only)

_____
(Title)

_____
Mortgagee Phone No.

_____
(Date)

NATIONAL ASSOCIATION OF REVIEW APPRAISERS (NARA)

Reference was made early in this chapter to the major professional organizations that *certify* appraisers. Now there is a national organization to aid and train persons who have the responsibility to *review* appraisals. This organization is the National Association of Review Appraisers, headquartered in Scottsdale, Arizona.

The association sponsors seminars throughout the United States to teach the latest and best methods to persons who review appraisals. In addition to sponsoring seminars, the NARA also publishes an *Appraisal Review Journal* that presents articles of interest to the review appraiser, as well as to the real estate industry. If you would like further information, contact the NARA headquarters at the address below:

National Association of Review Appraisers
National Headquarters
8715 Via De Commerico
Scottsdale, Arizona 85258

REVIEW QUESTIONS

1. Define the term *appraisal.*

2. Define the term *market value.*

3. Name and explain the basic formats of appraisals.

4. Name and explain four principles of real property value.

5. Name and explain the major methods used to determine property value.

6. Define and give examples of the term *functional obsolescence.*

7. Define and give an example of a proforma statement.

8. What are the three basic Fannie Mae and/or Freddie Mac standard appraisal reports?

9. Explain the major difference between the Fannie Mae/Freddie Mac appraisal reports and the reports of value used by VA and FHA.

10. What is meant by the abbreviation CRV?

NOTES

1. SREA Market Data Center, Inc., South Texas Regional Center, Sales Data, July-September 1979, p. 5.

2. Most of this section is based upon material from National Association of Review Appraisers, *Appraisal Review Journal,* Summer 1979, vol. 2, no. 2, pp. 47-55.

3. U.S., Department of Housing and Urban Development—Federal Housing Administration, Southeast Texas District, Houston, Texas, *HUD Circular Letter No. 81-9,* December 8, 1981, p. 1.

13 Borrower Qualification

LEARNING OBJECTIVES

In this chapter we will discuss how the real estate professional qualifies a buyer in order to best serve that buyer. After qualifying the buyer, the professional can select the proper price range of homes and give the buyer some idea of the amount of loan he or she will be able to make payments on according to the guidelines set forth by Fannie Mae, FHLMC, VA, FHA, and the Texas Housing Agency. We will also discuss the application forms used by Fannie Mae, FHLMC, VA, and FHA and the information the buyer will need to complete the application forms.

When you have completed your study of this chapter, you should be able to do the following:

★ Calculate the maximum loan a buyer may qualify for based on present income and using the income and long-term debt ratios of Fannie Mae, FHLMC, VA, and FHA.

★ Define the types of income that may be used to qualify a prospective buyer.

★ Define the term *net effective income.*

★ Explain the difference between the terms *monthly mortgage payment* and *total housing expenses* and explain how each relates to the qualifying of a prospective purchaser.

★ Outline the basic method of qualification used by FHA, VA, Fannie Mae, and FHLMC.

WHY QUALIFY YOUR BUYER?

Many real estate salespersons wait for the lender to qualify the borrower (after the buyer has selected a home to purchase) and hope that their buyer will qualify for the loan. The real estate professional in his or her first visit with the buyer can, however, gather information that will aid the professional in qualifying the prospective buyer. This qualification of the buyer is a help not only to the real estate salesperson, but also to the buyer. The buyer will have a better idea of the maximum mortgage amount that he or she can support with his or her present income.

Once the maximum mortgage is established and the buyer has determined the amount of money available for a down payment, the maximum sales price of a home that the prospective buyer can afford can be calculated. To establish the maximum sales price, the maximum loan amount and the amount of down payment are added together. For example, in your meeting with a prospective buyer, you learn that the maximum conventional loan your buyer can afford is $55,450 and he or she has $24,000 for the down payment. The maximum sales price is $79,450. You should explain to the buyer that the maximum loan amount is based on the current guidelines of the lenders in the area, not just your own guidelines, and for the prospective buyer to afford a home with a higher sales price, he or she must either make a larger down payment or be able to establish the existence of additional income that will meet the lenders' guidelines. Once again, you have informed the buyer as to the maximum affordable house price. If the buyer wishes to purchase a higher priced house, the buyer must meet the requirements mentioned.

In addition to knowing the maximum house price before seeing any property, the prospective homebuyer will then be familiar with the methods the lenders will use to establish whether the buyer can qualify for the mortgage. If you take the time—before you begin showing your prospective homebuyer any properties—to determine the maximum mortgage the buyer can qualify for, you can avoid many headaches for both you and your buyer. Many times the buyer will tell you the desired price range without really knowing how much home he or she can actually afford. If this is the case and the real estate salesperson takes the prospective buyer at the buyer's word and starts to show homes without first qualifying the buyer, there may be surprises for both you and your buyer. For example, you have as buyers a young couple who say they want an $80,000 house. You take them at face value and begin to show them homes in this price range. After looking at several, they find one that fits their needs and they make an offer. Let us assume the offer is accepted. Later, back at the office, you suggest several lenders to whom they may make application for the mortgage of $64,000. At application, however, they state that they only make $20,000 a year and have several long-term debts. This causes them not to qualify for the mortgage at time of application. This not only will cause you to lose a sale, but will make the mortgage lender less anxious to work with you again. The buyers will lose faith in your ability and turn to another agent. This is not to say that with your qualification of the buyer you will eliminate the possibility of rejection of your buyer by a lender, but it will greatly reduce the number of times your buyers are rejected.

INITIAL BUYER QUALIFICATION

Since one of the factors used by a lender to qualify a prospective buyer for a mortgage is income, we will discuss the significance of the prospective buyer's employment pattern and employment stability as well as the types of income that can be used to establish what the lender refers to as the *stable monthly income.*

Stable Monthly Income

The stable monthly income can be defined as "the borrower's gross monthly income from primary employment base earnings, plus recognizable secondary income."[1] Let us examine the factors that can affect the stable monthly income.

Pattern   First, you must establish the employment pattern of your prospective buyer. Has the person been a job hopper, jumping from one type of work or profession to another for no apparent reason? Lenders look for a pattern of full employment and job

changes that improve the applicant's and co-applicant's careers.

Stability   A second factor that is used to establish the ability of the borrower to repay a mortgage is employment stability—not only the stability of employment in the past, but the potential for future employment. When qualifying your buyer as to the stability of income, you should establish how long the prospective buyer has been employed in his or her present line of work and how long your buyer has been at his or her present job. Most conventional lenders have established a minimum of two years in the buyer's present line of work, with no minimum time on the present job. It should be noted that the important factor is the time in the present line of work. Americans have become mobile and, because the availability of jobs has decreased in some areas of the country while increasing in others, people change jobs more frequently now than in the past. For example, let us say that a prospective buyer has for the past several years been a lumber salesperson to the construction industry in New York state and due to the slowdown in construction in that area decided to move to Austin to seek better opportunities. In Austin, the prospective buyer was not able to get a job selling lumber to the construction industry, but was able to get a job selling appliances in a retail store. According to most lenders, the prospective buyer has not changed his or her line of work—sales.

In addition to the length of employment, the type of job or profession is important. For example, a person who is highly skilled as a tool and die maker will always be in demand and will have little worry in finding employment. Today, with advances in computer technology and the ever-expanding use of computers in industry, a person trained in computer science also will not have a problem finding employment. Other people thought to have stable employment are government employees, engineers, and other skilled people employed by large corporations.

One other factor that was once thought to affect the stability of income was the age of the applicant. Today, with the passage of federal antidiscrimination legislation, the age of the applicant cannot be used as a factor to establish the stability of the applicant's income. For example, in the past a person who was 45 years old would have had a difficult time securing a 30-year mortgage because many lenders would not make loans to a person where the term of the loan would extend past age 65, then the retirement standard. Thus, the 45-year-old person could only get a 20-year loan no matter what his or her profession.

We will discuss the different employment requirements for FHA, VA, Fannie Mae, and FHLMC later in this chapter.

Types of Income

Now that you have learned how to qualify your buyer as to the pattern and stability of employment, let us examine the types of income that can be used to establish the stable monthly income.

Salaries   This type of income is the easiest for you to establish and for the lender to verify. A prospective homebuyer who is employed by a company or corporation is usually paid a specific amount on a regular basis. The pay period can be weekly, biweekly, monthly, or bimonthly. This type of income is thought to be the most stable. If the prospective homebuyer is married and the spouse is employed, the income from the spouse will also count if the spouse has met the employment pattern and stability requirements of the lender. In the past, many lenders would discount, or in many cases eliminate, the salaried income of a woman if she was capable of having children, no matter what her profession or how long she had been employed. This practice was stopped with the passage of the Equal Credit Opportunity Act, and lenders are no longer allowed to discount income due to sex, age, or marital status.

Overtime   This type of income is standard to many jobs and can be counted toward the prospective homebuyer's stable monthly income. It must be proved by the homebuyer that the income has been regular in the past and that the chances are good that it will continue in the future. To establish that the overtime income has existed in the past, the prospective buyer may wish to supply copies of his or her paycheck stubs to the lender showing the overtime hours worked in the past year. To establish whether the overtime will continue, the mortgage lender will, when verifying the income of the applicant, ask the employer to state if there is a possibility of the overtime continuing. The verification forms used by FHA, VA, Fannie Mae, and FHLMC will be reviewed later in the chapter.

Bonus   This type of income can also be included in the establishment of the monthly stable income, if the prospective buyer can establish a pattern of payments of the bonus for at least the past two years. This can be done by supplying copies of Internal Revenue Form 1099 if no deductions were withheld from the bonus, or of Internal Revenue Form W-2 if there were deductions made for social security and income taxes. The employer will be asked if there is a possibility that the payment of bonus will continue.

Commissions   If the prospective homebuyer is paid by commissions only, or is self-employed, the lenders may require much more information. Usually, the lenders will require either an acceptable profit-and-loss statement and balance sheets for the 2 years preceding, or complete copies of signed federal income tax forms from the previous 2 years. If the homebuyer is self-employed and has recently formed a new company, many lenders will require the information outlined above and current financial statements on the business as well as verification of the employment of the homebuyer for the 2 previous years. A person on straight commission or royalty income for less than 2 years will have a difficult time securing a mortgage, in particular if the prospective buyer is a real estate salesperson on a straight commission basis.

Second job   Since more and more persons have second jobs, lenders are accepting them more and more as part of the stable monthly income if the prospective homebuyer can establish that the job has existed for at least 2 years and that the possibilities are good for the job to continue. An example of an acceptable buyer with a second job would be a police officer who in his or her off-duty hours has served as a security guard in several banks for the past 3 years. Since this type of second job is in the same field of work and the demand for security in banks is growing, the second job would not only provide extra money, but would be considered by lenders to be stable employment with excellent chances for continuing. Thus, the income would count toward the stable monthly income.

Dividend or interest income   This type of income can be counted if it is at least $100 per month and the investment that is providing the income is such that it cannot be sold or cashed in easily. This is true if the dividend or interest income is not the primary source of income. If the dividend or interest income is the primary source of the homebuyer's income, the lenders are going to require the homebuyer to show the source of income. If the income is dividend from stocks, the lender will request either copies of the stocks or a statement from the brokerage firm that is holding the stock as to the actual ownership of the stock and a summary of the stock performance for the past several years. If the income is from interest, once again the lender will ask the source of income. The lender may ask for copies of the certificates of deposit or a statement from the bank or institution holding the CDs as to ownership and the amount of interest paid. In addition to this information, the homebuyer will be asked to supply complete signed copies of his or her tax returns for the past several years.

Rental income   Rental income can be counted toward the stable monthly income, but many lenders give this type of income special consideration, reviewing it very closely. On many applications, the lenders provide space for rental income to be included, but require the prospective homebuyer to provide the following information:

1. The gross rental income from the property

2. The amount of the mortgage payment on the property

3. The amount of the taxes on the property

4. A realistic set of operating expenses for the property

When the information is provided, and prior to the lender approving the net operating income as part of the stable monthly income, some lenders will relate the net operating income to the type of property. For example, if the rental property is an efficiency apartment complex near a college and its tenants are college students, the lender may feel that the net operating income may not be constant. As one can see, there are no hard and fast rules as to whether any or all of the income from income producing properties will be used by a lender.

Child support or alimony payments   This type of income can be included in the determination of the stable monthly income if the applicant or co-applicant so wishes. Most

lenders will review the payment of such monies in regard to the following items:

Are the payments made as a result of a court order?

What is the length of time the payments have been made?

How regularly have the payments been made?

What measures are available to demand payments if payments are missed?

What are the ages of the children? Are the children all young and are the payments to be made for several years, or are the children near the age of consent?

Welfare assistance   This type of income may be counted by the prospective homebuyer if it is to be used as part of the income for repayment of the mortgage. In the past, most lenders discounted or disallowed this type of income as part of the stable monthly income, but this practice was stopped with the passage of the Equal Credit Opportunity Act. These payments, as with any other income, will be verified by the lender as to their amount and frequency.

Retirement income   Since the age of the borrower can no longer be used as a criterion for the granting of mortgages, more people are buying homes with the intention of retiring and financing the dwelling based on retirement income and personal savings. So income from social security and other pensions or trust funds can be used to establish the stable monthly income.

Source of Funds for Down Payment and Closing Costs   After the employment pattern and income of the prospective homebuyer is established, the next major item that should be determined is the source of funds for the down payment and closing. This information is necessary not only to establish the maximum house price, but to provide it for the lender who will ask the prospective homebuyer to supply it. There are two basic sources of the funds: from cash on hand (that is, bank accounts) or from the sale of property.

If the source is either a savings or checking account, the lender will verify with the bank or financial institution the date the account was opened and the average balance for at least the past 60 days. If the balance has seen a dramatic increase in the past sixty days, the lender will ask the prospective homeowner to explain the source of the additional funds. For example, say the balance in the account has been approximately $1000, but at the time of the verification the balance is $10,000. The lender will question the source of the additional funds. If the additional funds are a gift from the parents of an applicant, the lender will require a gift letter from the party giving the money. A form for such a letter is available from the lender or any attorney. If the additional funds are from a bequest from a will, a copy of the will and a letter from the administrator of the estate may be required.

If the additional cash is due to the sale of property and is so stated at the time of the application or in the initial meeting, the prospective homebuyer will be required to provide the lender with a copy of the earnest money contract if the transaction has not closed. If the transaction is closed, or upon closing, the prospective homebuyer must provide the lender with a copy of the closing statement, showing the proceeds to the seller and signed by all parties to the transaction. Some lenders will require a copy of the seller's proceeds check and a copy of the deposit slip.

These are only a few of the types of situations that may arise in determining the amount and source of the down payment and closing costs.

Emotional Needs for Housing

In addition to the prospective income and cash on hand, there are emotional needs for housing. As a real estate professional, you should have an insight to some of the more important needs.

Desire for homeownership During the initial qualification of your buyer, you need to establish the underlying desire for homeownership. There can be many reasons, including the following:

Nesting. This is important to the young who either have or are expecting a child.

Economic. To beat inflation or to use the home as a tax shelter.

Retirement. An older couple who has owned a large home is now looking for housing that meets the needs of an older couple and can serve as a home for their later years.

No matter what the emotional need of the prospective buyers, many lenders look to see the underlying desire for homeownership.

Desire to pay This emotional aspect is closely related to the income of the prospective homebuyer. Many of your prospects may be marginal in their ability to pay by mathematical analysis of their income. These prospective homebuyers, though, may have the desire to pay and are willing to make sacrifices in order to buy the home they want. This desire to pay can be shown by the past payment record of a previous mortgage. On the other hand, a person who has previously owned a home and has adequate income to meet the financial requirements of a mortgage may have a payment record which has not demonstrated the desire to pay, for example, payments may have been regularly late. Thus, in some cases the prospect with the desire to make payments will be given favorable consideration by lenders.

Liabilities

In addition to the income and emotional reason for buying, the next item that needs to be discussed with prospective homebuyers is their debts and/or obligations. These debts and/or obligations can be divided into two types: long-term and short-term. Most investors are interested in only the long-term debts, for they can have a major effect on a borrower's ability to repay the mortgage. Guidelines used by FHA, Fannie Mae, and FHLMC to determine what constitutes a long-term debt will be discussed later.

What are some of the typical debts that prospective homebuyers may have? We will describe some below.

Installment debts This type of debt can be payments made on a regular basis to department stores for a revolving charge account or a contract on appliances. It can also be payments made on bank credit where there is a continuous balance. Most families have a car loan or a bank loan that may be counted as a long-term debt.

Loans other than bank loans Many people are members of credit unions and have loans from the credit union that are used for many purposes. For example, they may be used to purchase stocks and sometimes to purchase recreational lots or acreage.

Comaker or endorser of a note In some cases a member of a family will have been a cosigner on a note or loan for one of the older children or a friend. This will have to be shown on the loan application of the homebuyer.

Child support or alimony   This type of court-enforced obligation of the prospective homebuyer can be the most major of the payments made apart from the mortgage payment. It should also be pointed out that with the changing divorce laws throughout the United States, in addition to the father being required to make child support payments, some women have been ordered to make child support payments to the father if he has been given custody of the children.

These are just a few examples of debts and obligations that may affect the ability of the prospective homebuyer to qualify for a mortgage.

Credit History

In addition to the verification of the borrower's income, employment, assets, and liabilities, the lenders will be interested in the past credit history of the borrower. As with employment and income, the lender will check the credit history of the borrower and/or coborrower for a minimum of 2 years.

As with many other aspects of the real estate transaction, there is a federal law that affects the investigation of a borrower's credit. The law that affects the reporting of credit information is the Fair Credit Reporting Act. Usually, the credit history of a borrower is reported to the lender or originator by the use of a Standard Factual Data Credit Report. A sample of such a report is shown in Figure 13–1.

Let us quickly review the factual credit report. The report can be divided into three sections as shown in Figure 13–1. Section 1 identifies the parties whose credit is being checked. It also shows the date of the report and the purpose of the report. The second section shows the date of birth, marital status, length of time at the present address, number of dependents, and employment of the applicant. Similar information is shown for the spouse. This information is supplied by the borrower and/or coborrower. In the Remarks portion of the section, the reporting agency is asked to amplify the employment history of the applicants if they had not been on the job at least 2 years. In paragraph 2 of this section, the reporting agency certifies that there has been a search of the public records for such items as judgments, bankruptcies, foreclosures, and other legal actions involving the borrower and the coborrower. In this case, there were none and this fact was noted in the proper block in this paragraph. Finally, in remark 3, the reporting agency certifies that it has checked the credit of the borrower and/or

coborrower and the results of that check are shown in section 3 of the report.

In the third section of the report is the credit record of the borrower and/or the coborrower. You will note that the trade name of the account is shown along with the date the account was opened. The date of the last sale is shown as well as the highest credit. In addition, the present balance on the account is shown. One of the more important areas to the mortgage lender is the column that shows amount past due. You will notice that the borrower and/or coborrower have $25.00 past due. The next column is Payment Terms. Here the amount and the frequency of the payment are given. For example for Nation Card, the payment is $30.00 per month. The final column, Paying Record, shows that they have one payment to Nation Card that is over 30 days late. The final portion of section three is where the credit reporting agency reports on the banking activities, employment, and residence of the borrower and/or coborrower.

One question that may be asked by a buyer about his or her credit is, How long does a bad entry stay on my credit report? According to the Fair Credit Reporting Act, section 605, entitled *Obsolete Information*, certain information may not be included on a credit report for a loan with a principal balance of $50,000 or less. According to this section, the time limits are as follows:

1. Cases under Title 11 of the U.S. Code or Bankruptcy Act that occur more than 10 years prior to the date of the credit report may not be included.

2. Suits and judgments may not be included in the report where the date of entry is more than 7 years or if sooner if the governing statutes of limitations has expired.

3. Paid tax liens where the date of payment is 7 years or more prior to the date of the credit report may not be included.

4. Accounts placed for collection or charged to profit and loss more than 7 years prior to the date of the credit report may not be included.

5. Any record of arrest, indictments, or convictions for a crime which from the date of disposition, release, or parole, happened more than 7 years before the date of the requested credit report may not be included.

6. Or any other adverse action that happened more than 7 years ago may not be included.

Figure 13–1.   Standard Factual Data Credit Report

STANDARD FACTUAL DATA REPORT   CONFIDENTIAL

Acct. No. __12345__   Wash. D.C. _____ **OFFICE**
Date __5/17/80__

Applicant's Name __DOE, JOHN A.__   **REPORT**
Applicant's Social   **FROM**
Security Number __123-45-6798__   *(If not city in heading)*   *(State whether former addr., etc.)*
Spouse's Name __MARY B. DOE__
Spouse's Social   No reference shall be made in this report
Security Number __987-65-4321__   to race, creed, color, or national origin.
Street Address __250 North Main Street__
City/State/ZIP Code __Anytown, Virginia 22000__   Date __5/17/80__ _____ 19____
Property __1685 Lane Street__   FHA CASE NUMBER _____
Address __Anywhere, Virginia__   VA LOAN NUMBER _____
                                                         Property Address __CONVENTIONAL MORTGAGE__
Credit report order from FHA ☐ or Mortgagee ☐   Dated _____
Credit report order from VA   ☐ or VA Lender ☐   Dated _____
Credit report order received by reporting agency   Date _____
Credit report mailed to FHA   ☐ or FHA Mortgagee ☐   Date _____
Credit report mailed to VA   ☐ or VA Lender ☐   Date _____

APPLICANT	Are name and address same as shown on request for report? If no, explain below.	Yes	Date of Birth: 1/15/50	Marital Status: Married	How long at present address: 1½ years, renting

Number of Dependents Including Self: __4__   Any record of separation or divorce? __No__

Present Employer and Kind of Business: __ABC Trucking Company__   Position Held: __Driver__   Since: __3/2/75__   Employment verified? If No, explain. ☒ Yes ☐ No Date: 5/80   Name of person verif. emp. __Miss Jones__
Has employment changed within past two years? __No__   Monthly Income __$1,292__   Income verified? If No, explain. ☒ Yes ☐ No

Present Employer and Kind of Business: __XYZ Packing Company__   Position Held: __Packer__   Since: __1 year__   Employment verified? If No, explain. ☒ Yes ☐ No Date: 5/80   Name of person verif. emp. __Mr. Smith__
Has employment changed within past two years? __Yes__   Monthly Income __$801.66__   Income verified? If No, explain. ☒ Yes ☐ No

REMARKS: 1. Amplify employment history on subject(s). (This report shall contain information as to previous employment location and salary, if there has been a change in employment within the past two years.)

2. The reporting bureau certifies that: (a) ☐ public records have been checked for judgments, foreclosures, garnishments, bankruptcies, and other legal actions involving the ☐ applicant's credit; ☐ spouse's credit with the results indicated below; or, (b) ☒ equivalent information has been obtained through the use of a qualified public records reporting service with the results indicated below. *(Give details.) (The records of real estate transfers which do not involve foreclosure may be excluded.)* If no public records to report, type "NONE" in the appropriate block(s).

applicant NONE	spouse NONE

3. The reporting bureau certifies that the subject's credit record in the payment of bills and other obligations has been checked: (a) through the credit accounts extended by combined minimum of 75% of the larger department stores and larger consumer and unsecured credit granters of the community in which the applicant(s) reside with the results indicated below; or, (b) through accumulated credit records of such credit granters of the community in which the applicant(s) reside with the results indicated below.

CREDIT RECORD

Trade Name	Orig. Acct. Opened	Date of Last Sale MO. YR.	High Credit	Balance Owing	Amount Past Due	Payment Terms	Paying Record
Nation Card	7/78	5/17/80	$ 848	$ 623	$25	$30/mo.	1X over 30 (J)
GMA CORP.	8/76	5/17/80	$6,248	$4,165	0	36x$173.55	As Agreed (J)
Dept. Store	7/76	4/80	$ 288	$ 28	0	$10/mo.	As Agreed (I)
Local Charge	6/75	4/80	$ 164	$ 52	0	$10/mo.	As Agreed (J)
U.S. Charge	4/75	2/80	$ 709	$ 373	0	$20/mo.	As Agreed (U)

The subject states the balance is now $245.

Landlord   Acme Realty Co. reports subject is tenant of record since 12/78 paying $250/mo. rental, promptly and satisfactorily.

Checking   First National Bank reports low 3 figure average balance, since 3/79, maintained satisfactorily.

Savings   First National Bank reports high 4 figure present savings balance. Account not rated.

BUSINESS-FINANCES: JOHN A. DOE is employed by the ABC Trucking Company as a Driver, since 3/2/75, earning $15,500 per annum, as verified by Miss Jones in Personnel. The subject's wife, Mary, is employed with the XYZ Packing Company, as a Packer, for the past one year, earning $801.66 per month, as verified by Mr. Smith, Supervisor. Prior to this, she was a housewife and not gainfully employed.

RESIDENCE: The subject is married to Mary, with three dependent children, ages 8, 6, and 2 years. They have resided at 250 North Main Street, Anytown, Virginia for the past 1½ years, where they are renting. See Landlord reference for details. Prior to this, the subject and family resided at 682 Pine Street, Elsewhere, Virginia for two years and rented.

As was mentioned in the first part of this discussion, these restrictions only apply to loans with a principal balance of less than $50,000. Many of the credit reporting agencies follow the above guidelines for all loans whether they are more or less than $50,000. In some cases, a local credit bureau will not report any information about arrest, indictment, or conviction for a crime.

Another common question is, What constitutes a problem on a credit report? The following are some good rules of thumb that have been adopted by many lenders:

1. No more than one 30- or 60-day late payment for a major installment debt. A major installment debt may be a car payment or any account with a balance in excess of $5,000.

2. No more than two 30- to 60-day late payments on small accounts. This type of account might be a department store charge.

3. No 30- to 60-day late payments showing on a mortgage payment record, unless extreme extenuating circumstances can be proven by the applicant.

4. Many lenders will not approve a mortgage loan for an applicant if the credit report shows any bankruptcies or repossessions, within the past 5 years. If either have occurred more than 5 years ago, many lenders will require that the applicant has established a record of good credit.

5. All liens, judgments, and accounts that have gone to collection must have been satisfied or paid in full.

If a person has any of these entries on his or her report, they are said to have derogatory credit information. This does not always mean that the person may never get credit, but that the applicant may have to provide a satisfactory written explanation stating the reason for the late or missed payments.

When dealing with a lender, it is not uncommon to find that many of the lenders will not discuss a credit report with an applicant until the applicant has received or has secured a copy of his or her credit report. The reason for this is that many lenders feel that if they discuss the credit prior to the applicant having a copy of the report, they then become a Credit Reporting Agency and must meet the requirements of the Fair Credit Reporting Act as it relates to a credit reporting agency.

Some lenders will even take this a step further and will not in any way discuss a credit report. Normally, if the lender will not discuss the report they will notify the applicant that they have received the report and there is information in the report that needs explanation. They will advise the applicant and/or coapplicant to contact the credit reporting agency for details. A possible reason for some lenders to adopt this policy is that many of the agreements between the credit reporting agencies and their buyers does not allow them to discuss any items on the report, but to refer all questions and explanations to the credit reporting agency. A possible second reason for their reluctance to discuss the report is that section 610—Conditions of Disclosure to Consumers in paragraph (c) states that "any consumer reporting agency shall provide trained personnel to explain to the consumer any information furnished to him pursuant to section 609." Since the lenders are not classified as credit reporting agencies and since they do not normally have trained credit reviewing personnel on their staff, they will refer all questions and explanations to the credit reporting agency that provided the report.

From this brief discussion one can see that the credit history could be an area that may delay the process of a loan application, particularly if the lender does not discuss any information on a credit report. A possible solution to the problem is to have your buyer, prior to completing a loan application, go to the credit reporting agency in your city and request to check the credit information that is on file. The consumer has a right to view the information with certain exceptions as per section 609, Disclosure to Consumers, of the Act. It should be noted that the consumer will not normally be given a copy of his or her credit report, but will be supplied with an abstract.

The abstract will have stamped or noted on it in some manner the following statement: Not For Credit Granting Purposes. In this way the person, before going to loan application, can find if there is any derogatory information or credit information that is not theirs on the report and correct or give an explanation before the lender requests a credit report. Also, they could take the abstract to loan application and when the person taking the application asks about credit, the applicant could give the lender a copy of the abstract. It should be noted that the lender will still order a credit report, but possibly if the lender questions any entry on the abstract, the lender could ask for clarification at the time of application rather than waiting to receive the credit report and having the buyer make explanations at the credit reporting agency.

One final item regarding the credit history of a buyer: if you are working with a buyer who is moving from another city, you may suggest to that person that they should have their credit transferred from the city they are leaving. There are two good reasons:

1. If the credit is not transferred, it is classified as an out-of-town credit report and normally the credit reporting agencies charge more for such a report.

2. Since the report has to come from outside or from another city, the time to get a report is usually longer, and could possible slow down loan approval.

INCOME AND DEBT ANALYSIS

In the past, many real estate professionals have used the formula for the amount of loan a person or family can qualify for as approximately 2.5 times the annual salary. No reference was made to the amount of debts that the person or family had, or how much of the income was used to satisfy those obligations. Today, there are no hard and fast rules used by all conventional lenders to establish ratios of housing cost to income and long-term debts to income. The ratios used by VA and FHA are used by all lenders for underwriting loans either insured by FHA or guaranteed by VA. If your buyer is going to apply for either a loan insured by FHA or guaranteed by VA, you should be able to show your buyer the method for income and debt analysis and be able to determine the approximate loan amount he or she will be able to repay, based on the information he or she supplied.

Conventional Guidelines

Many conventional lenders have adopted the income-to-payment and long-term-debt-to-income ratios of Fannie Mae/FHLMC for the underwriting of their loans. These guidelines are as follows:

Income-to-payment ratio   The maximum amount a person or family may spend for the monthly payment on housing is 28 percent of the total gross stable monthly income. The monthly payment will include the following: payments for principal and interest, the amount needed to pay for private mortgage insurance if required, an escrow amount collected monthly to cover the taxes and insurance on the property, and sufficient funds to pay any other fees that may affect title to the property. Such additional fees could be homeowners association fees or special assessments levied by a taxing authority for streets or curbs and gutters.

Many lenders will allow a higher monthly payment ratio if it can be shown that the borrower and the coborrower can devote more income to the cost of housing or if the property is constructed to be energy efficient. According to the *Seller's Guide—Conventional Mortgages*, issued by the Federal Home Loan Mortgage Corporation, higher monthly payment ratios may be appropriate if the following conditions are met:

(i) energy efficient property which reduces energy costs;

(ii) demonstrated ability of Borrower to devote a greater portion of income to basic needs, such as housing;

(iii) demonstrated ability of Borrower to maintain a good credit history, accumulate savings and maintain a debt-free position;

(iv) a larger down payment on the purchase of the property;

(v) Borrower's potential for increased earnings based on education, job training or time employed or practiced in his/her profession; and

(vi) Borrower's net worth being substantial enough to evidence ability to repay the mortgage regardless of income.[2]

Long-term debt-to-income ratio   According to the ratios in effect in 1984, the maximum amount of an applicant's income that could be spent for the payment of long-term debts was 36 percent. According to Fannie Mae/FHLMC, a long-term debt is any debt that extends beyond 10 months and must include the amount of the house payment as outlined above. The long-term debt must include any child support or alimony payments.

Now, let us work through a sample buyer qualification for a conventional mortgage. The information in Figure 13-2 is the basic information on our prospective homebuyers. Let us calculate whether they can qualify for the 90

Figure 13-2. **Loan Information for the Palmer family**

Buyer:	Mr. and Mrs. J.C. Palmer
Dependents:	1 child, age 14

Employment:

Mr. Palmer   employer—ABC Oil Field Equipment Co. (National)
job and years on job—Machinist 10 years experience
Salary—$13.50/hr, average work week 55 hrs. overtime is 1.5 times after 40 hrs

Mrs. Palmer   employer—XYZ Department Store (part-time)
job and years on job—Salesperson 2.5 years
salary—$500 per month

Obligations:

	Balance	Payment
Master Card	$500.00	$50.00/month
ABC Credit Union (auto)	$3,000.00	$120.00/month
Sears	$200.00	$50.00/month
Furniture Payment	$500.00	$100.00/month
Home Mortgage	$31,050.75	$525.00/month

Cash on Hand:

Checking	$1,500.00
Savings	$7,000.00

Real Estate:

Presently, the Palmers have a contract on their present home that will net them an additional $11,000 after closing costs and the sales commission are paid.

Loan Information:

Purchase Price of the House	$83,350
Amount of Down Payment (10%)	8,350
Loan Amount	$75,000
Interest Rate	14%
Term	30 years
Estimated Closing Costs: (including 2 point discount)	$3,000
Prepaids	$1,000

percent loan at 14 percent interest in the amount of $75,000.

Whenever you do a buyer qualification, as a real estate professional you should always use some type of qualifying worksheet. Such a worksheet is shown in Figure 13-3. You will notice the worksheet is divided into three sections. Section 1 deals with the gross monthly income and proposed monthly payment. Section 2 is where all of your buyer's long-term obligations are listed and finally the third section deals with move-in costs and source of

down payment and closing costs. In addition to being a reminder of all of the items that need to be checked in the qualification process, it will serve as a permanent record for future reference.

Using another qualification worksheet (Figure 13-4), let us see if the Palmers can qualify for the loan. Let us calculate their gross monthly income. Referring to our qualifying sheet, we see that it asks first for the borrowers' income. To calculate their income we would do the following:

Figure 13-3.   Conventional Loan Qualifying Worksheet

CONVENTIONAL LOAN QUALIFYING

Gross Monthly Income — *Proposed Monthly Payment*

Borrowers Income	$_____	Principal & Interest	$_____
Co-Borrower Income	$_____	Private Mort. Insurance	$_____
Overtime	$_____	Taxes	$_____
Part-time	$_____	Homeowners Insurance	$_____
Other	$_____	Home Owners Assoc	$_____
Total Income	$_____	Total First Mortgage Pymt . . .	$_____

Total Mortgage Pymt $_____ divided by total Income $_____ equals _____ % (cannot exceed 28%).

Obligations (Debts Lasting over 10 months)

Balance	Owed To	Purpose
$_____ @mo.	_____	_____
$_____ @mo.	_____	_____
$_____ @mo.	_____	_____
$_____ @mo.	_____	_____
$_____ @mo.	_____	_____
$_____ @mo.	_____	_____

Total Obligations $_____ + Total Mortgage Payment $_____ = Total Fixed Payment

$_____ Divided by Gross Income $_____ = _____ % (cannot exceed 36%)

Move-In Costs — *Source: Down Payment and Closing Costs*

Sales Price	$_____	Banks	$_____
Loan Amount	$_____	Savings	$_____
Required Down Pymt	$_____	Net from sale of Real Est . . .	$_____
Closing and Prepaids	$_____	Other (List)	$_____
Other	$_____		
Total Move-In	$_____	Total Available	$_____

The Total Available should equal or exceed the Total Move-In Costs.

Figure 13–4. Palmer's Conventional Loan Qualifying Worksheet

CONVENTIONAL LOAN QUALIFYING

Gross Monthly Income		*Proposed Monthly Payment*	
Borrowers Income	$ _2340.00_	Principal & Interest	$ _888.65_
Co-Borrower Income	$ _500.00_	Private Mort. Insurance	$ _15.62_
Overtime	$ _1316.25_	Taxes	$ _85.42_
Part-time	$_____	Homeowners Insurance	$ _29.17_
Other	$_____	Home Owners Assoc.	$_____
Total Income	$_4156.25_	Total First Mortgage Pymt. . .	$_1018.86_

1

Total Mortgage Pymt $ _1018.86_ divided by total Income $ _4156.25_ equals _24.5_ % (cannot exceed 28%).

Obligations (Debts Lasting over 10 months)

Balance		*Owed To*	*Purpose*
$ _500_	@mo. _50.00_	Mastercard	
$ _3000_	@mo. _120.00_	ABC Credit Union	Auto
$ _200_	@mo. _50.00_	Sears	
$ _500_	@mo. _100.00_		Furniture Payment
$_____	@mo. _____		
$_____	@mo. _____		

2

Total Obligations $ _170.00_ + Total Mortgage Payment $ _1018.86_ = Total Fixed Payment $ _1188.86_ Divided by Gross Income $ _4156.25_ = _28.6_ % (cannot exceed 36%)

Move-In Costs		*Source: Down Payment and Closing Costs*	
Sales Price	$ _83,350_	Banks	$ _1,500_
Loan Amount	$ _75,000_	Savings	$ _7,000_
Required Down Pymt	$ _8,350_	Net from sale of Real Est . . .	$ _11,000_
Closing and Prepaids	$ _4,000_	Other (List)	$_____
Other	$_____		
Total Move-In	$ _12,350_	Total Available	$ _19,500_

3

The Total Available should equal or exceed the Total Move-In Costs.

Mr. Palmer:

Weekly wages

40 hours × $13.50 = $540.00

Gross monthly income

$$\frac{\$540.00 \text{ per week} \times 52 \text{ weeks}}{12 \text{ months}} = \$2340.00$$

Thus, you would enter the $2340 on the first line. Next, enter Mrs. Palmer's salary on the second line. The third line of this section concerns overtime. Knowing that Mr. Palmer's overtime has been continual for the past 12 months and is very likely to continue in the future, we would include it in their gross monthly income. The amount of the overtime would be calculated as follows:

Weekly overtime

15 hours × $20.25 = $303.75

Monthly Overtime

$$\frac{\$303.75 \text{ per week} \times 52 \text{ Weeks}}{12 \text{ months}} = \$1316.25$$

Enter this amount on the overtime line. Add the three amounts for a total income of $4156.25.

Now, let us calculate the proposed monthly payment using the portion of the worksheet with the same title. The first line of this section is for the monthly principal and interest portion of the payment.

Once again, the Palmers' monthly P & I payment is based on a loan amount of $75,000 at 14 percent interest for 30 years.

To calculate the P & I payment, find the monthly payment factor for 14 percent, 30 years in Appendix A. In checking, you will find the factor is 11.8487. As you learned in Chapter 2, you will multiply this factor by the loan amount in thousands:

$$MP = \frac{\$75,000}{1000} \times 11.8487 = \$888.65$$

Thus, we would enter $888.65 as the monthly payment.

Because this is a 90-percent loan, there would be private mortgage insurance. The amount of private mortgage insurance would have to be calculated. As we learned earlier in the text, the renewal premium for PMI is calculated as the balance multiplied by one quarter of 1 percent divided by 12 or:

$$\frac{\$75,000 \times 0.0025}{12} = \$15.62$$

This amount, therefore, would be entered as the amount of the monthly PMI escrow.

Now the monthly escrow for taxes is figured. According to the city tax office, last year's taxes on the house were $1025.00. Thus, to get the estimated tax escrow divide the $1025.00 by 12 months or:

$$\frac{\$1025.00}{12} = \$85.42$$

Enter this amount on the line entitled Taxes.

Next you calculate the amount of the monthly escrow for insurance. In checking with other sales in the same area and in the same amount, you find that the premium will be approximately $350 per year. To get the amount of the monthly escrow, the $350 is divided by 12 or $29.17 per month, and this amount is entered on the sheet.

The final line is entitled Home Owners Assoc. Since there is not one in the area in which the Palmers are looking, we would then calculate the total payment by adding the four amounts for a total of $1018.86 and enter it on the proper line.

The total mortgage-payment-to-income ratio is calculated by using the final line of this section. As mentioned earlier, the total house payment may not exceed 28 percent of the Palmers' income. To calculate the ratio, the total monthly payment is divided by the total income of the Palmers or 24.5 percent. Thus the Palmers' proposed housing expense is below the maximum percentage allowed, and so far they will qualify for the loan.

There is one other ratio that we must calculate in order to see if the Palmers can qualify for the mortgage. This is the ratio of the long-term debts to their total income. Remember that Fannie Mae/FHLMC, as well as many conventional lenders, count any debt that will take 10 months or more as a long term debt. In section 2 of the Palmers' worksheet, we would list all of the debts. Of the debts listed, only two would be counted as long-term debts for a total of $170.00. This amount would be entered on the line Total Obligations. Then to this amount the proposed monthly payment is added:

$1018.86

$\underline{\ \ \ 170.00}$

$1188.86

Finally, to get the income-to-long-term-debt ratio as the worksheet indicates, the amount of the long-term debt is divided by the gross monthly income:

$$\frac{\$1188.86}{\$4156.25} = 28.6 \text{ percent}$$

Since the maximum that most conventional lenders will allow is 36 percent and the Palmers are below the maximum, they should qualify for the loan.

It must be noted that these ratios used to qualify the prospective homebuyer are not the only factors used by the lender. The credit of the prospective buyer must also be investigated, as well as his or her payment record of any previous mortgages. This type of investigation is normally only done by the lender.

The only other question that must be asked is whether the Palmers will have enough money available for the down payment and the closing costs. This then brings you to the third section of the form. It deals with the amount of the move-in cost and the source of the down payment and closing costs. First, the move-in costs. You will notice in this section you are asked first to enter the sales price of the home and, second, the loan amount; in this case, $83,350 and $75,000, respectively. Then the loan amount is subtracted from the sales price of the home giving you the down payment of $8,350. You are then asked to enter the amount of the estimated closing costs and prepaids—in this case it was given as $4,000. The required down payment and the estimated closing and prepaids are added together for a total move-in of $12,350. On the right-hand portion of the section, you are to enter the amount and source of the down payment and closing costs. On the line entitled Banks you would enter the $1500.00 in their checking account; on the line entitled Savings you would enter $7,000 as is listed on the original fact sheet. Finally, since they will be selling their previous home and will be netting approximately $11,000, you would enter that as the net from sale of real estate. When these three amounts are totaled, they have $19,500 available. As the worksheet states, the total available should equal or exceed the total move-in cost. In this case it does; therefore, the Palmers have sufficient cash available to close the transaction. From this initial qualification meeting, it is obvious that the Palmers are excellent prospects for a conventional mortgage.

Energy-efficient homes   As mentioned earlier in this section, if it can be demonstrated that a new home is energy efficient, then both Fannie Mae and Freddie Mac will allow a larger portion of a borrower's income to go toward his or her house payment.

According to Fannie Mae, there are two methods that may be used to establish if a home can be classified as energy efficient. The first method, which may apply to either a new or used home, involves an energy-efficiency rating made by an appraiser. Here, the appraiser is asked to evaluate the energy efficiency of the house. This is done by the use of FHLMC Form 70A, Energy Addendum-Residential Appraisal Report. The second method that may be used applies to new construction only. Any new home that is built in compliance with energy conservation programs classified by the National Association of Home Builders as meeting the NAHB Thermal Performance Guidelines may be acceptable as energy efficient. If the home is built meeting these specifications, there is no requirement for the FHLMC Form 70A.

The importance of a home being declared as energy efficient is that a larger portion of the borrower's income may go toward the house payment. According to Fannie Mae, for a fixed-term, fixed-rate mortgage the ratios can be increased from 28 percent and 36 percent to 30 percent and 38 percent.

Thus, the borrower can spend up to 30 percent of his or her gross stable monthly income for a house payment, and up to 38 percent of his or her income for long-term debts including the house payment. If the borrower is applying for an ARM that will be secured by an energy-efficient home, Fannie Mae will still allow 30 percent of the gross stable income to go toward housing expenses and 38 percent of the applicant's income to go toward the payment of long-term debts with one very major difference. Fannie Mae will count all debts in this ratio—even those that take 10 months or less to pay off. In other words, if the applicant has only debts that will pay off in 5 or 6 months, Fannie Mae will still count them in the qualifying process.

Finally, if the borrower is applying for a graduated-payment ARM secured by an energy-efficient home, Fannie Mae will only allow the total house payment to equal 28 percent of the borrower's total gross monthly income and only 36 percent of the borrower's income can go for any long-term debts. Once again, Fannie Mae will count all debts in this ratio.

Federal Housing Administration Guidelines

When qualifying a prospective buyer, FHA also uses a ratio of income to housing expense and income to long-term debts. However, FHA's method of qualifying the prospective homebuyer is very different from the conventional method outlined in the previous section. FHA does not use an income multiplier as many people in the real estate profession believe.

First of all, FHA uses a different monthly income base than the conventional guidelines. This base is called *net effective income* and is figured in a different manner. The same types of income can be counted and FHA uses the 2-year time frame as outlined previously, but that is where the similarity ends. The net effective income can be defined as the total gross income of the prospective homebuyer less federal withholding taxes.

FHA guidelines   Prior to June 22, 1983, FHA used the following guidelines for a borrower and/or coborrower to qualify for a FHA-insured loan. The FHA regulations stated that the mortgagor's income will be considered to be adequate if the total prospective housing expense did not exceed 35 percent of the mortgagor's net effective income, and if the total of the prospective housing expense and other recurring charges did not exceed 50 percent of the mortgagor's net effective income. Then on June 22, 1983, the Department of Housing and Urban Development, Office of The Assistant Secretary for Housing–Federal Housing Commissioner, issued Mortgagee Letter 82-10. In this Letter, the total housing expense ratio was increased to 38 percent and the long-term debt including the housing expense was increased to 53 percent. The most important change, in the opinion of lenders, was the portion of the letter that allowed the use of Veterans Administration's *residual income* approach for the approval of a borrower.

Before we start qualifying the Palmers for an FHA-insured loan, you will note several differences. First, the use of the term *total housing expense*. FHA defines the total housing expense as the monthly payment including:

1. Principal and interest payment

2. Hazard Insurance

3. Taxes, Special Assessments

4. Maintenance and Common Expenses

5. Heat and Utilities

Another major difference is FHA's definition of a long-term debt. According to FHA, a long-term debt is any debt that requires 12 or more months to pay off.

Finally, as was mentioned above, the FHA offices (and now with direct endorsement, many lenders), have the right to use the VA residual income. With this method of underwriting, the borrower and coborrower's gross monthly income is calculated and then all expenses—such as the total housing expense, income taxes, social security, and long-term debts—are subtracted. Then according to minimums set by FHA if there is a certain amount left over, the borrower and coborrower will be approved.

Now that we have looked at the methods used by FHA to qualify a borrower, let us start the qualification of the Palmers. As with conventional qualifying, you as a real estate professional should use some type of worksheet. Many of the lenders have many types of FHA-qualifying worksheets, but the best one to use is the one used by FHA and the lenders. This is the U.S. Department of Housing and Urban Development's Mortgage Credit Analysis Worksheet (Figure 13–5).

You will note that the worksheet is divided into six sections. Section I, Loan Data, is self-explanatory. Section II, Borrower's/Coborrower's Personal and Financial Status, asks about the borrower's and coborrower's age and occupation as well as the number of dependents. Also in this section, the amount of the mortgage insurance premium (MIP) is shown as well as how much is financed. Section III, Estimated Monthly Shelter Expenses, has us calculate the amount of the Total Fixed Payment and the settlement cost are outlined. Section IV is the section of the form where the net effective income of the borrower and coborrower is calculated. Section V of the worksheet deals with the debts and obligations of the borrower and coborrower. You will note there is a column where the underwriter is asked to indicate by placing a check those debts that will last or take 12 or more months to repay. The final section is section VI, Borrower Rating. The most important parts of this section to the real estate professional are the blanks 40 through 43.

Using the Mortgage Credit Analysis Worksheet, Figure 13–6, we will now qualify the Palmers. We will start with section I, space 2, the amount of the mortgage. As we learned in the chapter on HUD-FHA, we know that the Palmers can finance a portion of their closing costs. First, we must establish the acquisition cost. That is the value of the property plus the HUD estimated closing cost. For this problem let us use the estimated closing cost shown in Chapter 7, Figure 7–7.

Figure 13-5. HUD Mortgage Credit Analysis Worksheet

U.S. DEPARTMENT OF HOUSING AND URBAN DEVELOPMENT HOUSING — FEDERAL HOUSING COMMISSIONER **MORTGAGE CREDIT ANALYSIS WORKSHEET**		CASE NUMBER

SECTION I — LOAN DATA

1. NAME OF BORROWER AND CO-BORROWER	2. AMOUNT OF MORTGAGE $	3. CASH DOWN PAYMENT ON PURCHASE PRICE

SECTION II — BORROWER'S/CO-BORROWER'S PERSONAL AND FINANCIAL STATUS

4. BORROWER'S AGE	5. OCCUPATION OF BORROWER	6. MIP	7. TOTAL MIP	8. CURRENT MONTHLY RENTAL OR OTHER HOUSING EXPENSE

9. IS CO-BORROWER EMPLOYED?	10. CO-BORROWER'S AGE	11. OCCUPATION OF CO-BORROWER	12. MIP FINANCED	13. OTHER DEPENDENTS (a) Ages____ (b) Number____

SECTION III — ESTIMATED MONTHLY SHELTER EXPENSES (This Property)

FUTURE MONTHLY PAYMENTS	14. TERM OF LOAN (Months)	16. SETTLEMENT REQUIREMENTS	
15. (a) Principal and Interest	$	(a) Existing Debt (Refinancing ONLY)	$
(b) FHA Mortgage Insurance Premium	$	(b) Sale Price (Realty ONLY)	$
(c) Ground Rent (Leasehold ONLY)	$	(c) Repairs and Improvements	$
(d) TOTAL DEBT SERVICE (A + B + C)	$	(d) Closing Costs	$
(e) Hazard Insurance	$	(e) TOTAL ACQUISITION COST (A + B + C + D)	$
(f) Taxes, Special Assessments	$	(f) Mortgage Amount	$
(g) TOTAL MTG. PAYMENT (D + E + F)	$	(g) Borrower(s)' Required Investment (E minus F)	$
(h) Maintenance and Common Expense	$	(h) Prepayable Expenses	$
(i) Heat and Utilities	$	(i) Non-Realty and Other Items	$
(j) TOTAL HSG. EXPENSE (G + H + I)	$	(j) TOTAL REQUIREMENTS (G + H + I)	$
(k) Other Recurring Charges (explain)	$	(k) Amount paid ☐ cash ☐ other (explain)	$
(l) TOTAL FIXED PAYMENT (j + K)	$	(l) Amt. to be paid ☐ cash ☐ other (explain)	$
		(m) TOTAL ASSETS AVAILABLE FOR CLOSING	$

SECTION IV — MONTHLY EFFECTIVE INCOME / SECTION V — DEBTS AND OBLIGATIONS

SECTION IV — MONTHLY EFFECTIVE INCOME		ITEM	✓	Monthly Payment	Unpaid Balance
17. Borrower's Base Pay	$	25. State and Local Income Taxes		$	$
18. Other Earnings (explain)	$	26. Social Security/Retirement			
19. Co-Borrower's Base Pay	$	27. Child Care Expense/Support			
20. Other Earnings (explain)	$	28. Operating Exp., Other R.E.			
21. Income, Real Estate	$	29.			
22. TOTAL MONTHLY EFFECTIVE INCOME	$	30.			
23. Less Federal Tax	$	31.			
24. NET EFFECTIVE INCOME	$	32.			

SECTION VI — BORROWER RATING

		33.			
34. Borrower Rating		33. TOTAL		$	$
35. Credit Characteristics					
36. Adequacy of Eff. Income					
37. Stability of Eff. Income					
38. Adequacy of Available Assets					

39. FINAL ☐ Approve Application ☐ Reject Application	SECTION VII-RATIOS	40. Loan to Value Ratio ____% 41. Total Payment to Rental Value ____% 42. Debt Service to Rental Income ____%	43. ☐ Ratio of Net Effective Income to: Total Housing Expense ____% Total Fixed Payment ____%

44. REMARKS (Use reverse, if necessary)   First Time Home Buyer? ☐ Yes ☐ No

45. SIGNATURE OF EXAMINER	46. DATE

FORWARD TO MANAGEMENT SYSTEMS WITH HUD-92800-8   HUD-92900-WS (5-81)

Figure 13-6. Palmers' HUD Mortgage Credit Analysis Worksheet

U.S. DEPARTMENT OF HOUSING AND URBAN DEVELOPMENT HOUSING – FEDERAL HOUSING COMMISSIONER **MORTGAGE CREDIT ANALYSIS WORKSHEET**		CASE NUMBER

SECTION I – LOAN DATA

1. NAME OF BORROWER AND CO-BORROWER	2. AMOUNT OF MORTGAGE	3. CASH DOWN PAYMENT ON PURCHASE PRICE
Mr. and Mrs. J. C. Palmer	$84,078	$3,750

SECTION II – BORROWER'S/CO-BORROWER'S PERSONAL AND FINANCIAL STATUS

4. BORROWER'S AGE	5. OCCUPATION OF BORROWER	6. MIP 100%	7. TOTAL MIP $3,078	8. CURRENT MONTHLY RENTAL OR OTHER HOUSING EXPENSE $525.00
	Machinist			

9. IS CO-BORROWER EMPLOYED? Yes	10. CO-BORROWER'S AGE	11. OCCUPATION OF CO-BORROWER Salesperson	12. MIP FINANCED $3,078	13. OTHER DEPENDENTS (a) Ages 14 (b) Number 1

SECTION III – ESTIMATED MONTHLY SHELTER EXPENSES (This Property) / 14. TERM OF LOAN (Months) / 16. SETTLEMENT REQUIREMENTS

15.			
(a) Principal and Interest	$996.22	(a) Existing Debt (Refinancing ONLY)	$
(b) FHA Mortgage Insurance Premium	$	(b) Sale Price (Realty ONLY)	$83,350
(c) Ground Rent (Leasehold ONLY)	$	(c) Repairs and Improvements	$
(d) TOTAL DEBT SERVICE (A+B+C)	$996.22	(d) Closing Costs	$1,400
(e) Hazard Insurance	$43.00	(e) TOTAL ACQUISITION COST (A+B+C+D)	$84,750
(f) Taxes, Special Assessments	$103.00	(f) Mortgage Amount Less MIP	$81,000
(g) TOTAL MTG. PAYMENT (D+E+F)	$1142.22	(g) Borrower(s)' Required Investment (E minus F)	$3,750
(h) Maintenance and Common Expense	$77.00	(h) Prepayable Expenses	$1,000
(i) Heat and Utilities	$231.00	(i) Non-Realty and Other Items	$1,600
(j) TOTAL HSG. EXPENSE (G+H+I)	$1450.22	(j) TOTAL REQUIREMENTS (G+H+I)	$6,350
(k) Other Recurring Charges (explain)	$	(k) Amount paid ☐ cash ☐ other (explain)	$
(l) TOTAL FIXED PAYMENT (j+K)	$1450.22	(l) Amt. to be paid ☐ cash ☐ other (explain)	$
		(m) TOTAL ASSETS AVAILABLE FOR CLOSING	$19,500

SECTION IV – MONTHLY EFFECTIVE INCOME / **SECTION V – DEBTS AND OBLIGATIONS**

		ITEM	✓	Monthly Payment	Unpaid Balance
17. Borrower's Base Pay	$2340.00	25. State and Local Income Taxes		$	$
18. Other Earnings (explain)	$1316.25	26. Social Security/Retirement	✓	268.25	
19. Co-Borrower's Base Pay	$500.00	27. Child Care Expense/Support			
20. Other Earnings (explain)	$	28. Operating Exp., Other R.E.			
21. Income, Real Estate	$	29. Mastercard		50.00	500.00
22. TOTAL MONTHLY EFFECTIVE INCOME	$4156.25	30. ABC Credit Union	✓	120.00	3000.00
23. Less Federal Tax	$715.00	31. Sears		50.00	200.00
24. NET EFFECTIVE INCOME	$3441.25	32. Furniture		100.00	500.00
SECTION VI – BORROWER RATING		33. TOTAL		$588.25	$4200.00

34. Borrower Rating		39. FINAL	40. Loan to Value Ratio 96%	43. ☐ Ratio of Net Effective Income to:
35. Credit Characteristics		☐ Approve Application		
36. Adequacy of Eff. Income			41. Total Payment to Rental Value ___%	Total Housing Expense 43.1%
37. Stability of Eff. Income		☐ Reject Application	42. Debt Service to Rental Income ___%	Total Fixed Payment 52.7%
38. Adequacy of Available Assets				

44. REMARKS (Use reverse, if necessary) First Time Home Buyer? ☐ Yes ☒ No

Total Monthly Effective Income	$4,156.25
LESS	
Federal Tax	− 715.00
Total Housing Expense	− 1,450.22
Social Security	− 268.25
Long Term Debts	− 120.00
Balance for Family Support	$1,602.78

45. SIGNATURE OF EXAMINER	46. DATE

FORWARD TO MANAGEMENT SYSTEMS WITH HUD-92800-8   HUD-92900-WS (5-81)

Value of the property	$83,350
Estimated closing costs	1,400
Acquisition cost	$84,750

Next, we must calculate the mortgage amount. This is calculated as 97 percent of the first $25,000 of value and closing and 95 percent of all value and closing in excess of $25,000. In this case, it would be calculated as follows:

Acquisition cost

$84,750		
Less $25,000 × 97% =	$24,250.00	
$59,750 × 95% =	$56,762.50	
Total calculated loan amount	$81,012.50	

Also as we learned in the chapter on HUD, you always round down to the nearest $50.00 so the actual loan amount would be $81,000.00. It should be noted this property is located in Dallas and is in an area where the maximum loan amount is $90,000.

Block 3 of this section asked the amount of the cash down payment. To review, to calculate the down payment you would subtract the loan amount from the acquisition cost. In this case it would be calculated as follows:

Acquisition cost	$84,750
Less loan amount	(81,000)
Down payment	$ 3,750

This amount, $3,750, would be entered in block three.

The next area of the worksheet that is to be completed deals with MIP. For this example, the borrower wishes to finance 100 percent of the MIP. To calculate the amount of the MIP we would use the factor for 100 percent financing for a loan with a term in the excess of 25 years, which is 0.0038. Then, you would multiply the loan amount by this factor or:

Loan amount	$81,000
Factor	× 0.0038
	$ 3,078

This amount would be entered in blocks 7 and 12.

The only remaining block to be completed is block 2, the amount of the loan. Since the Palmers are going to finance 100 percent of the MIP you would add the MIP amount of $3,078 to the $81,000 loan and enter $84,078 in the block.

Now we will move to section III, Estimated Monthly Shelter Expenses, and enter the required information. First the principal and interest payment is the same as in the conventional qualifying and since the interest rate is the same, we will multiply the loan amount by the monthly payment factor of 11.8487.

$$\frac{\$84,078}{1000} \times 11.8487 = \$996.22$$

Then this amount will be entered in space 15(a). There will be no entries in 15(b) and (c). Then you would enter 996.22 in space 15(d), TOTAL DEBT SERVICE.

In space 15(e), Hazard Insurance, you will enter the amount that will be escrowed each month for insurance. Where do you get the proper number to be used? There is only one source and that is from HUD-FHA. On a regular basis, each of the HUD-FHA offices publishes an Insurance Schedule for its area. Such a schedule is shown in Figure 13–7. This schedule was issued by the Dallas Office. You or your broker should be on the mailing list to receive this information from the HUD-FHA office in your area. You will notice that this schedule is based on value of the property and type of construction, either frame or brick veneer (BV). The construction of the home the Palmers are buying is a brick veneer home. In this example, the value of the property is $84,750, so the nearest value is $85,000 and the required escrow is $43.00. This amount is entered in space 15(e).

The next space is for the amount of the monthly escrow for taxes. As with the insurance, each HUD-FHA office publishes a Tax Schedule and as with the insurance escrow, the amount shown on the tax schedule for your area is the only amount that may be used in your market. For the purpose of this example, a tax schedule issued by the Dallas HUD Office will be used (Figure 13–8).

Since the property is located in Dallas and in the Dallas Independent School District (ISD), the tax rate is $1.21 per $1,000 of value. Therefore, the monthly tax escrow would be calculated as:

$$\frac{\$84,750}{1,000} \times \$1.21 = \$102.54$$

HUD-FHA instructs the lenders to round the tax escrow to the nearest dollar or $103.00. This would be entered into space 15(f). Then total spaces 15(d), (e), and (f) to get the total mortgage payment. In this example, the payment would be $1142.22.

Figure 13–7.   Insurance Schedule Dallas County Towns

INSURANCE SCHEDULE

DALLAS COUNTY TOWNS

(Addison, Cockrell Hill, Dallas,
Duncanville, Garland, Grand Prairie,
Irving, Lancaster, Seagoville.)

**Insurance Expense per Month
Select Nearest Figure to Value**

VALUE	FRAME	B V	VALUE	FRAME	B V	VALUE	FRAME	B V
$10,000	7.00	5.00	41,000	30.00	21.00	71,000	52.00	36.00
11,000	8.00	6.00	42,000	31.00	21.00	72,000	53.00	36.00
12,000	9.00	6.00	43,000	31.00	22.00	73,000	53.00	37.00
13,000	9.00	7.00	44,000	32.00	22.00	74,000	54.00	37.00
14,000	10.00	7.00	45,000	33.00	23.00	75,000	55.00	38.00
15,000	11.00	8.00	46,000	34.00	23.00	76,000	55.00	38.00
16,000	12.00	8.00	47,000	34.00	24.00	77,000	56.00	39.00
17,000	12.00	9.00	48,000	35.00	24.00	78,000	57.00	39.00
18,000	13.00	9.00	49,000	36.00	25.00	79,000	58.00	40.00
19,000	14.00	10.00	50,000	37.00	25.00	80,000	58.00	40.00
20,000	14.00	10.00	51,000	37.00	26.00	81,000	59.00	41.00
21,000	15.00	11.00	52,000	38.00	26.00	82,000	60.00	41.00
22,000	16.00	11.00	53,000	39.00	27.00	83,000	61.00	42.00
23,000	17.00	12.00	54,000	39.00	27.00	84,000	61.00	43.00
24,000	18.00	12.00	55,000	40.00	28.00	85,000	62.00	43.00
25,000	18.00	13.00	56,000	41.00	28.00	86,000	63.00	43.00
26,000	19.00	13.00	57,000	42.00	29.00	87,000	64.00	44.00
27,000	20.00	14.00	58,000	42.00	29.00	88,000	64.00	44.00
28,000	20.00	14.00	59,000	43.00	30.00	89,000	65.00	45.00
29,000	21.00	15.00	60,000	44.00	30.00	90,000	66.00	45.00
30,000	22.00	15.00	61,000	45.00	31.00	91,000	66.00	46.00
31,000	23.00	16.00	62,000	45.00	31.00	92,000	67.00	46.00
32,000	23.00	16.00	63,000	46.00	32.00	93,000	68.00	47.00
33,000	24.00	17.00	64,000	47.00	32.00	94,000	69.00	47.00
34,000	25.00	17.00	65,000	47.00	33.00	95,000	69.00	48.00
35,000	26.00	18.00	66,000	48.00	33.00	96,000	70.00	48.00
36,000	26.00	18.00	67,000	49.00	34.00	97,000	71.00	49.00
37,000	27.00	19.00	68,000	50.00	34.00	98,000	72.00	49.00
38,000	28.00	19.00	69,000	50.00	35.00	99,000	72.00	50.00
39,000	28.00	20.00	70,000	51.00	35.00	100,000	73.00	50.00
40,000	29.00	20.00						

INSURANCE SCHEDULE FOR OTHER DALLAS COUNTY TOWNS

	FRAME	B V		FRAME	B V
Balch Springs	.97	.68	Hutchins	.74	.51
Carrollton	.57	.41	Mesquite	.73	.52
Cedar Hill	.57	.39	Richardson	.57	.41
Coppell	.88	.62	Rowlett	.88	.62
De Soto	.88	.62	Sachse	.88	.62
Farmers Branch	.51	.36	University Park	.54	.38
Ferris	.60	.42	Wilmer	.89	.62
Highland Park	.60	.43			

VAL FORM #60, Revised April 1982

Page 1 of 5

SOURCE: Department of Housing and Urban Development, Dallas Office, Dallas, Texas, Circular Letter 83-11 – November 7, 1983

The next two spaces deal with maintenance, heat, and utilities. Once again the HUD-FHA office in your area will supply schedules for these items. First for maintenance, a sample monthly maintenance and repair schedule is shown in Figure 13–9.

You will note that the schedule is not by value but size of home. For this example, the Palmers are looking at a home with 1900 square feet. So we find 1900 square feet and come across to the column for a brick veneer home and find $77.00. This is the HUD-FHA estimate and is to be entered in space 15(h). Finally, you must add an estimate for Heat and Utilities. Figure 13–10 shows the HUD-FHA estimate of average monthly expenses

Figure 13–8.   Tax Schedule—$1000.00 of Value

DALLAS COUNTY		COLLIN COUNTY	
Coppell	1.15	Allen	1.07
Addison	1.05	Anna	.60
Balch Springs	1.25	Blue Ridge	.77
Carrollton	1.07	Celina	.78
Cedar Hill	1.32	Dallas	1.12
Cockrell Hill	1.13	Fairview	.72
		Farmersville	.62
Dallas		Frisco	.74
		Josephine	.82
Dallas ISD	1.21	Lucas	.78
Coppell ISD	1.38	McKinney	1.22
Richardson ISD	1.34	Melissa	.80
		Murphy	.99
DeSoto	1.22	Parker	.85
Duncanville	1.26	Plano	1.07
Farmers Branch	1.04	Princeton	1.00
Garland ISD	1.17	Prosper	.68
Richardson ISD	1.23	Richardson	.98
		Royse City	2.25
Grand Prairie		Seis Lagos	1.90
		Westminster	1.65
Dallas County	1.20	Wylie	.95
Tarrant County	1.40		
		Rural Property	.62
Highland Park	.79		
Hutchins	1.84		
		ROCKWALL COUNTY	
Irving			
		Fate	
Irving ISD	1.15		
Coppell ISD	1.28	Rockwall ISD	1.78
		Royse ISD	2.47
Lancaster	1.34		
Mesquite	1.14	Heath	1.12
Richardson	1.14		
Rowlett	1.21	*McLendon-Chisholm*	
Sachse	1.09		
Seagoville	1.13	Rockwall ISD	.95
Sunnyvale	.69	Royse ISD	1.63
University Park	.83		
Wilmer	1.99	Rockwall	1.29
		Rowlett	1.18
Rural Property	.95	Royse City	2.38
DENTON COUNTY		Rural Property	.95
Carrollton	.93		
Dallas	1.57		

SOURCE: Department of Housing and Urban Development, Dallas Office, Dallas, Texas, Circular Letter 83-11—November 7, 1983

for utilities for the Dallas HUD-FHA office. Once again, this schedule is in square feet. You would find 1900 square feet and come across to the first column. This is for a home with walls and ceiling insulated and with central air conditioning (A/C). The HUD-FHA estimate is $231.00 per month and is entered in space 15(i). Now add up the values in space 15(g), (h), and (i) to get the total housing expense, or $1450.22.

Since there are no other recurring charges, block 15(k) will be left blank and the total housing expense would be moved down to block 15(l).

Next to be completed are the settlement requirements, blocks 16(a) through (m). Since the Palmers are not refinancing any debt, 16(a)

will be left blank. The sales price of the home is entered in block 16(b). Block 16(d) asks for the closing costs. This is the HUD estimated closing cost used to calculate the acquisition for this example; that amount is $1,400. Then blocks 16(b), (c), and (d) are added together to arrive at the acquisition cost or $84,750. Next, you will enter the loan amount less any MIP to be financed.

Block 16(g) is the amount of the Palmers' down payment or, as the form calls it, the borrower(s) required investment. As indicated on the worksheet the loan amount is subtracted from the acquisition cost to give the required investment of $3,750. Blocks 16(h) and (i) are self-explanatory; as per the fact sheet shown in Figure 13–2 we would enter the amount of

Figure 13–9.   Monthly Maintenance and Repair Schedule

Square Feet	Exterior Construction Wood Siding	Exterior Construction Brick-V, Asbestos, Aluminum
500	12.00	9.00
600	18.00	14.00
700	24.00	19.00
800	30.00	24.00
900	36.00	29.00
1000	42.00	34.00
1100	48.00	39.00
1200	54.00	44.00
1300	60.00	48.00
1400	67.00	53.00
1500	73.00	58.00
1600	79.00	63.00
1700	85.00	68.00
1800	91.00	73.00
1900	97.00	77.00
2000	103.00	82.00
2100	109.00	87.00
2200	115.00	92.00
2300	121.00	97.00
2400	127.00	102.00
2500	133.00	106.00
2600	139.00	111.00
2700	145.00	116.00
2800	151.00	121.00
2900	157.00	126.00
3000	162.00	131.00

SWIMMING POOL: Small & Plain 36.00
              Average w/ extras 60.00

Townhouses, Cluster homes and Condos which provide for exterior maintenance in their Home Owner's Association agreement should receive a 40% reduction in the M & R expenses shown in this schedule.

SOURCE: Department of Housing and Urban Development, Dallas Office, Dallas, Texas, Circular Letter 84-11 – April 4, 1984

the prepaids, $1,000, in block 16(h) and the closing costs of $1,600 in block 16(i). The total closing costs for the Palmers are $3,000 as shown in Figure 13–2; but since FHA will allow them to finance $1,400, line 16(d), their out-of-pocket expense for closing costs is $1,600.

If the borrower were paying all of the MIP, as the form indicates, that amount would be added to the other closing costs. To calculate the cash required to be paid by the Palmers, blocks 16(g), (h), and (i) are totaled and the total of $6,350 is entered in block 16(j).

If the Palmers had put up earnest money with a Title Company, the amount would be entered in block 16(k) and that would be subtracted from the amount shown in block 16(j). Finally, the amount of funds the Palmers have available for closing are entered in block 16(m). Since they will have approximately $19,500 available, they can pay the required amount with money left. Some of the real estate professionals, as well as mortgage lenders, who

use this form will regularly complete this section first. Then they will complete section III.

The next to be reviewed is section IV, Monthly Effective Income. Mr. Palmer's base income of $2,340 is entered in block 17, Borrower's Base Pay. Then in block 18, Mr. Palmer's overtime of $1,316.25 is entered. Both of the amounts were calculated in the previous portion of the chapter dealing with the conventional qualifying. Finally, Mrs. Palmer's income is entered in block 19, and the three values are totaled ($4,156.25) and entered in block 22. As was mentioned earlier, HUD-FHA uses net effective income to qualify. This is the gross monthly income less federal withholding for income tax. The amount of the withholding can come from either borrower's check stub or from the Employer's Tax Guide Circular E, which is supplied by the Internal Revenue Service.

Let us assume that for the Palmers, a married couple with one dependent or a total of 3 dependents, the monthly withholding is

Figure 13–10.   Average Monthly Expenses for Utilities

Average Monthly Expenses for Utilities		
Living Area	Utilities for Average Homes Including Central A/C	Utilities for Average Homes Without Central A/C
Square Feet	Walls & Ceiling — Insulated	Walls & Ceiling — Insulated
500	$119.00	$ 82.00
600	126.00	93.00
700	133.00	103.00
800	140.00	114.00
900	147.00	124.00
1000	154.00	135.00
1100	162.00	142.00
1200	173.00	151.00
1300	180.00	158.00
1400	186.00	165.00
1500	193.00	172.00
1600	203.00	177.00
1700	210.00	184.00
1800	223.00	193.00
1900	231.00	202.00
2000	240.00	209.00
2100	250.00	216.00
2200	259.00	225.00
2300	267.00	234.00
2400	275.00	240.00
2500	285.00	247.00
2600	296.00	255.00
2700	307.00	264.00
2800	328.00	276.00

Replaces VAL Form 91 (3-82) which is obsolete.

For a duplex: Use S.F. of One Unit
*Add 20% for homes without insulation.
**Reduce figure 20% for "Energy Efficient Homes".
***Utilization of Solar Energy requires Special Rate.

Revised March 1984

FTW/DAO 4150.1/4
(3-84)

SOURCE: Department of Housing and Urban Development, Dallas Office, Dallas, Texas, Circular Letter 84-4 — April 26, 1984

$715.00. To calculate the net effective income of the Palmers, the federal tax is subtracted from the total monthly effective income in block 22. The Palmers' net effective income is $3,441.25 which is entered in block 24.

Now you will complete section V, Debt and Obligations. Line 25 of the form is of no significance to the real estate professional in Texas for neither is collected in Texas. Block 26, Social Security/Retirement, will have to be completed. For an employed person, the social security rate is currently 7.05 percent of the first $39,960 of income, which would be equal to 7.05 percent of the first $3,300 on a monthly basis. With these figures in mind, many of the HUD-FHA offices use a maximum withholding for an individual employer of $233.00. The rate for a self-employed person is somewhat higher or 11.8 percent of the first $39,960 of income or a maximum of $389.00 per month.

It should be noted that these figures change on a regular basis and the new information can be gotten from the HUD-FHA office in your area or from the Internal Revenue Service. Now let us calculate the Palmers' social security tax. Mr. Palmer will come under the maximum of $233.00 and for Mrs. Palmer you would multiply her salary $500.00 times 7.05 percent or $35.25. These two values are added together and the total of $268.25 is entered in block 26. Next you enter all of the debts of the Palmers and indicate by a check which of the debts are considered by FHA as long-term debts. Since FHA considers a long-term debt to be a debt that takes 12 months or more to pay off, only two of the debts count — social security and the payment to the credit union — for a total of $388.25. Now you total up all of the payments and the total amount of the debt.

Next, you will calculate the majority of the information requested in section VII, Ratio. When you calculate the loan-to-value ratio, be sure to use the loan amount less any MIP to be financed. In this case, that amount is $81,000. Once again, to calculate the loan-to-value ratio, you will divide the value of the property into the loan amount:

$$\text{Loan-to-value} = \frac{\text{Loan amount}}{\text{Value}}$$

$$\frac{\$81,000}{84,750} = 95.57 \text{ or } 96 \text{ percent}$$

This is entered in block 40. Blocks 41 and 42 are of no value to you for an owner-occupied dwelling, but will be used for investment properties. Block 43 is very important for the majority of the previous calculations have been done in order to calculate these two ratios. First, for the ratio of total housing expense to net effective income, you will divide the total housing expense by the net effective income:

$$\frac{\text{Total housing expense}}{\text{Net effective income}}$$

$$\frac{\$1,450.22}{\$3,441.25} = 42.1 \text{ percent}$$

This figure is entered in the proper space. Next you will calculate the total fixed payment to net effective income ratio:

$$\frac{\text{Total fixed payments}}{\text{Net effective income}}$$

$$\frac{1450.22 + \$268.25 + 120.00}{\$3,441.25} = 53.42 \text{ percent}$$

The 53.42 percent is entered in the appropriate block. You will note that the housing ratio exceeds that authorized by HUD-FHA. With the issuance of the Mortgagee Letter 82-10 and the accompanying memos and, in particular, a memo from Secretary Pierce to all of the Regional Administrators, the qualifying guidelines were eased. Secretary Pierce stated that on March 29, 1982, President Reagan accepted the recommendation and announced that "we are easing existing guidelines to expand the number of potential homebuyers qualifying for FHA loans." So based on that statement, the FHA offices were directed that in determining the adequacy of a borrower's income, the borrower can be qualified using either the 38-53 ratios or the residual income method as used by the Veterans Administration.

Since the Palmers will not qualify using the 38-53 ratios, you would qualify them using the residual income method. As was mentioned earlier in the chapter, the residual method is where all of the expenses such as income tax, social security, total housing expense, and long-term debts are subtracted from the gross monthly income. Whatever is left is the residual income for family support. Each of the HUD-FHA offices has established minimum amounts. For example, the Dallas Office has established the following minimums based on the number of persons in the household:

Borrower only	$375
Borrower and coborrower	$500
Each dependent	$ 90

For the Palmers (a borrower, a coborrower, and one dependent) to qualify, they would need to have $590 residual income. To calculate the amount of residual in the Remarks portion, you would do the following:

Total monthly effective income	$4,165.25
Less	
Federal tax	− 715.00
Total housing expense	−1,450.22
Social security	− 268.25
Long-term debts	− 120.00
Residual income for family support	$1,611.78

Since the Palmers were only required to have $590 and they have $1,611.78, they would be approved for the loan.

It should be noted that many real estate professionals will normally only prequalify the borrower and/or coborrower using the residual method; one can see it is rather easy to qualify using this method. One additional fact is that either you or your broker must get the proper residual income figures for your area in order to be accurate in your FHA prequalifying.

Veterans Administration

As you learned in the HUD-FHA section, the Veterans Administration and HUD-FHA use the same method to qualify an applicant for a mortgage. Even though VA uses a similar method to qualify a veteran and spouse for a loan, there are some major differences.

One major difference is that the VA uses 6 months of payments as the rule to establish if a debt is a long-term debt, instead of FHA's 12 months. The VA will count any debt that is less than 6 months duration if the payment is of such an amount that it can cause severe impact on the family's ability to make the mortgage payment. For example, a debt of $500 which is to be paid back in 5 months would have to be counted as a long-term debt. If you are working with a buyer who has any monthly payment of $100 or more, even if for less than 6 months, that debt should be included in your estimate of his or her long-term debts.

A second major difference is that the VA does not use ratios as used in the conventional and FHA guidelines. Instead, VA uses the amount of money remaining after all of the appropriate monies are deducted from the total gross income of the family. This amount is referred to as the *balance for family support*. The VA feels that the income for the support of the family is a significant factor in determining whether the veteran has the ability to repay the loan. It should be noted that the VA uses no single factor in qualifying a veteran for a GI loan, but looks at many factors. The VA considers each case individually.

As with the conventional and HUD-FHA qualification, when qualifying a veteran for a VA-guaranteed loan, you should use some type of worksheet. As with the HUD-FHA insured loan, the conventional lenders have developed many different forms, but according to the Department of Veterans Benefits' DVB Circular 26-80-11, Change 5, September 7, 1983, the analysis of a veteran's income and credit acceptability for a VA loan must use VA Form 26-6393, Loan Analysis. The circular further states that the lenders may use this form for their own purposes for preapproval of a veteran. A copy of this form is shown in Figure 13-11. To be a true real estate professional, you should also use this form for your prequalifications.

You will note that the form is divided into six sections, A through F. The sections are similar to those of the FHA Mortgage Credit Analysis Worksheet. Now using a separate VA loan analysis sheet (Figure 13-12), let us work through a sample prequalification, using the Palmers as buyers. In section A, Loan Data, you would enter the name of your buyer. In this case it is Mr. Palmer.

The amount of the loan goes into space 2 of the section. Since VA allows a no-money-down loan, the Palmer's are applying for a loan in an amount equal to the value of the home. Since the Palmers are applying for a 100 percent loan, there would be nothing placed in space 3.

Now move to section B, Borrower's Personal and Financial Status. The information

requested in spaces 4 through 13 is self-explanatory and is taken from the Palmers' loan information shown in Figure 13-2.

With section C, Estimated Monthly Shelter Expenses, you will notice that VA uses the same method of calculating the monthly shelter expenses. They both not only include the principal and interest and escrow payments for insurance and taxes, but also maintenance and utilities. You will note that in space 14 the term of the loan is indicated as 30 years. Space 15 asks for the interest rate on the loan as well as the monthly principal and interest payment. The monthly payment for P & I would be calculated in the same manner as for the conventional and HUD-FHA loans:

$$\frac{\text{Loan amount}}{\$1,000} \times \begin{array}{l}\text{Monthly}\\ \text{Payment} =\\ \text{Factor}\end{array}$$

$$\frac{\$83,350 \times 11.8487}{\$1,000} = \$987.59$$

This amount is entered in space 15. Spaces 16, 17, 19, and 20 are similar to those on the HUD-FHA mortgage credit analysis worksheet and for the purposes of this example the same figures will be used. It is important for the real estate professional to know the exact figures that VA will use in your area. In order to have those figures, you should contact the VA regional office for your area of Texas and request the correct figures. Sometimes they are very similar to those used by HUD-FHA. After totaling all of the figures, the total estimated monthly shelter expenses equal $1441.59.

The next section, Debts and Obligations, as with the HUD-FHA worksheet, lists all of the Palmers' obligations; but there is a major difference. You will notice that three of the obligations count as long-term obligations. As mentioned earlier, a long-term debt for VA is any that takes 6 months or more to repay. That is why the MasterCard and the credit union debts are checked. The furniture payment will take less than 6 months, but VA will still count the payment because it is a major payment and will last through the first few months of the loan as was mentioned in the early paragraphs of this discussion.

The final section of the worksheet deals with the salaries of the applicants and the calculation of the Balance Available for Family Support. First, in line 32, the gross salary of the borrower and the spouse is listed and then is totaled. Lines 34, 35, 36, and 37 deal with

Figure 13-11.   VA Loan Analysis Form

LOAN ANALYSIS

LOAN NUMBER

SECTION A – LOAN DATA

1. NAME OF BORROWER	2. AMOUNT OF LOAN $	3. CASH DOWN PAYMENT ON PURCHASE PRICE $

SECTION B – BORROWER'S PERSONAL AND FINANCIAL STATUS

4. APPLICANT'S AGE	5. OCCUPATION OF APPLICANT	6. NUMBER OF YEARS AT PRESENT EMPLOYMENT	7. LIQUID ASSETS (CASH, SAVINGS, BONDS, ETC.) $	8. CURRENT MONTHLY RENTAL OR OTHER HOUSING EXPENSE $

9. IS SPOUSE EMPLOYED? ☐ YES ☐ NO	10. SPOUSE'S AGE	11. OCCUPATION OF SPOUSE	12. NUMBER OF YEARS AT PRESENT EMPLOYMENT	13. AGE OF OTHER DEPENDENTS

SECTION C – ESTIMATED MONTHLY SHELTER EXPENSES (This Property)

SECTION D – DEBTS AND OBLIGATIONS (Itemize and indicate by (✓) which debts considered in Section E, Line 41)

ITEMS	AMOUNT		ITEMS	✓	MO. PAYMENT	UNPAID BALANCE	
14. TERM OF LOAN YEARS		23.			$	$	
15. MORTGAGE PAYMENT (Principal and Interest)	$	24.					
16. REALTY TAXES		25.					
17. HAZARD INSURANCE		26.					
18. SPECIAL ASSESSMENTS		27.					
19. MAINTENANCE		28.					
20. UTILITIES (Including heat)		29.					
21. OTHER (HOA, Condo Fees, etc.)		30. JOB RELATED EXPENSE					
22. TOTAL	$	31. TOTAL			$	$	

SECTION E – MONTHLY INCOME AND DEDUCTIONS

ITEMS		SPOUSE	BORROWER	TOTAL	
32. GROSS SALARY OR EARNINGS FROM EMPLOYMENT		$	$	$	
33.	FEDERAL INCOME TAX				
34.	STATE INCOME TAX				
35. DEDUCTIONS	RETIREMENT OR SOCIAL SECURITY				
36.	OTHER (Specify)				
37.	TOTAL DEDUCTIONS	$	$	$	
38. NET TAKE HOME PAY					
39. PENSION, COMPENSATION OR OTHER NET INCOME (Specify)					
40. TOTAL (Sum of Lines 18 and 19)		$	$	$	
41. LESS THOSE OBLIGATIONS LISTED IN SECTION D WHICH SHOULD BE DEDUCTED FROM INCOME					
42. TOTAL NET EFFECTIVE INCOME				$	
43. LESS ESTIMATED MONTHLY SHELTER EXPENSE (Line 22)				$	
44. BALANCE AVAILABLE FOR FAMILY SUPPORT				$	

45. PAST CREDIT RECORD ☐ SATISFACTORY ☐ UNSATISFACTORY	46. DOES LOAN MEET VA CREDIT STANDARDS? (GIVE REASONS FOR DECISION UNDER "REMARKS," IF NECESSARY, E.G., BORDERLINE CASE) ☐ YES ☐ NO

47. REMARKS (Use reverse, if necessary)

SECTION F – DISPOSITION OF APPLICATION

☐ Recommend that the application be approved since it meets all requirements of Chapter 37, Title 38, U.S. Code and applicable VA Regulations and directives.

☐ Recommend that the application be disapproved for the reasons stated under "Remarks" above.

48. DATE	49. SIGNATURE OF EXAMINER

50. FINAL ACTION ☐ APPROVE APPLICATION ☐ REJECT APPLICATION	51. DATE	52. SIGNATURE AND TITLE OF APPROVING OFFICIAL

VA FORM OCT 1976   26-6393

Figure 13–12. **Palmer's VA Loan Analysis**

LOAN ANALYSIS		LOAN NUMBER	

SECTION A – LOAN DATA

1. NAME OF BORROWER	2. AMOUNT OF LOAN	3. CASH DOWN PAYMENT ON PURCHASE PRICE
Mr. J. C. Palmer	$ 83,350	$ none

SECTION B – BORROWER'S PERSONAL AND FINANCIAL STATUS

4. APPLICANT'S AGE	5. OCCUPATION OF APPLICANT	6. NUMBER OF YEARS AT PRESENT EMPLOYMENT	7. LIQUID ASSETS (CASH, SAVINGS, BONDS, ETC.)	8. CURRENT MONTHLY RENTAL OR OTHER HOUSING EXPENSE
	Machinist	10 YR	$ 19,500	$ 525.00

9. IS SPOUSE EMPLOYED?	10. SPOUSE'S AGE	11. OCCUPATION OF SPOUSE	12. NUMBER OF YEARS AT PRESENT EMPLOYMENT	13. AGE OF OTHER DEPENDENTS
☒ YES ☐ NO		Salesperson	2.5	14

SECTION C – ESTIMATED MONTHLY SHELTER EXPENSES *(This Property)*			SECTION D – DEBTS AND OBLIGATIONS *(Itemize and indicate by (√) which debts considered in Section E, Line 41)*			
ITEMS	**AMOUNT**		**ITEMS**	**√**	**MO. PAYMENT**	**UNPAID BALANCE**
14. TERM OF LOAN 30 YEARS			23. Mastercard	√	$ 50 00	$ 500 00
15. MORTGAGE PAYMENT *(Principal and Interest)*	$ 987 59		24. ABC Credit Union	√	120 00	3000 00
16. REALTY TAXES	103 00		25. Sears		50 00	200 00
17. HAZARD INSURANCE	43 00		26. Furniture Payment	√	100 00	500 00
18. SPECIAL ASSESSMENTS			27.			
19. MAINTENANCE	77 00		28.			
20. UTILITIES *(Including heat)*	231 00		29.			
21. OTHER *(HOA, Condo Fees, etc.)*			30. JOB RELATED EXPENSE			
22. TOTAL	$ 1441 59		31. TOTAL		$ 320 00	$ 4200 00

SECTION E – MONTHLY INCOME AND DEDUCTIONS

	ITEMS		SPOUSE	BORROWER	TOTAL
32.	GROSS SALARY OR EARNINGS FROM EMPLOYMENT		$ 500 00	$ 3656 25	$ 4156 25
33.		FEDERAL INCOME TAX	7 20	707 60	
34.		STATE INCOME TAX			
35.	DEDUCTIONS	RETIREMENT OR SOCIAL SECURITY	35. 25	233. 00	
36.		OTHER *(Specify)*			
37.		TOTAL DEDUCTIONS	$ 42. 45	$ 940. 60	$ 983. 05
38.	NET TAKE HOME PAY		457. 55	2715. 65	3173. 20
39.	PENSION, COMPENSATION OR OTHER NET INCOME *(Specify)*				
40.	TOTAL *(Sum of Lines 18 and 19)*		$ 457. 55	$ 2715. 65	$ 3173. 20
41.	LESS THOSE OBLIGATIONS LISTED IN SECTION D WHICH SHOULD BE DEDUCTED FROM INCOME				270. 00
42.	TOTAL NET EFFECTIVE INCOME				$ 2903. 20
43.	LESS ESTIMATED MONTHLY SHELTER EXPENSE *(Line 22)*				$ 1441. 59
44.	BALANCE AVAILABLE FOR FAMILY SUPPORT				$ 1461. 61

45. PAST CREDIT RECORD	46. DOES LOAN MEET VA CREDIT STANDARDS? (GIVE REASONS FOR DECISION UNDER "REMARKS," IF NECESSARY, E.G., BORDERLINE CASE)
☐ SATISFACTORY ☐ UNSATISFACTORY	☐ YES ☐ NO

47. REMARKS *(Use reverse, if necessary)*

SECTION F – DISPOSITION OF APPLICATION

☐ Recommend that the application be approved since it meets all requirements of Chapter 37, Title 38, U.S. Code and applicable VA Regulations and directives.
☐ Recommend that the application be disapproved for the reasons stated under "Remarks" above.

48. DATE	49. SIGNATURE OF EXAMINER

50. FINAL ACTION	51. DATE	52. SIGNATURE AND TITLE OF APPROVING OFFICIAL
☐ APPROVE APPLICATION ☐ REJECT APPLICATION		

VA FORM OCT 1976 26-6393

deductions from the salaries of the borrower and spouse. Line 33 is the amount of federal income tax that is withheld for Mrs. Palmer (it is $7.20). This figure was taken from the Employer's Tax Guide for a married person with three deductions making $500 per month. Mr. Palmer's deduction was derived from the same source. As you learned in the FHA qualification section, the social security deductions are 7.05 percent of the wages earned with a maximum of $233.00. So on line 38 the deductions are subtracted from the person's gross salary giving the net take-home pay. Then, since the Palmers have no other income, the totals are brought down to line 40. On line 41, "less those obligations listed in section D which should be deducted from income," the three monthly checks are totaled and entered. The $270.00 is subtracted from the $3173.90 and the remaining $2903.20 is entered on line 42. Then the amount of the estimated monthly shelter cost is entered on line 43 and subtracted from the remaining income and that amount, $1,461.61, is entered on line 44. This is the balance available for family support.

Now, the question is, Do the Palmers qualify for the loan? The answer to that question depends on the amount of income that the VA Loan Guaranty Section requires for your area. The amount will vary across the United States because each of the VA Regions sets the requirements for its area. In Texas, for example, the Loan Guaranty Section in Waco has set the following required levels for the amount that must be available for family support:

Veteran only	$350
Veteran and wife	$500
Each additional dependent	$ 90

The requirements of the Loan Guaranty Section located in Houston require:

Veteran only	$300
Veteran and wife	$600
Each additional dependent	$160

So one can see if the Palmers were located in the area served by the Waco Regional VA Loan Guaranty Section, they would only need $590; if they were located in the area under the control of the Houston Regional VA Loan Guaranty Section, they would need $760 left over for family support. Thus, since they have $1,461.61, they could easily qualify for the loan.

From this example, you can see how important it is to have accurate figures for the balance available for family support. Typically, the Veterans Administration is reluctant to give these figures out, but upon formal written request, they normally will release the figures for the area they serve.

It should be noted that in addition to the balance for family support, VA reviews the credit of the veteran as well as other factors. If you would like more information on the underwriting of loans by the VA, contact the Administrative Services office of your VA Regional Office and request a copy of DVB Circular 26-80-11, Change 5, "Credit Standards." This circular outlines the loan analysis procedures of the VA and will give you indepth information on the underwriting of VA loans secured by real property.

Texas Housing Agency

The final set of guidelines we wish to examine are those of the Texas Housing Agency. As mentioned earlier in the text, this agency is rather new and has as its purpose to provide financing for the housing industry in Texas. The agency usually establishes the guidelines for borrower qualifications with each of its mortgage purchase programs. The following guidelines were those used by the agency for the Single-Family Mortgage Purchase Program 1984.

Property   The agency would purchase mortgage loans on owner-occupied detached, attached single-family dwellings, residences in Texas.

Eligible borrowers   Those persons or families who would be eligible for these mortgages are borrowers whose adjusted gross income does not exceed $42,200 for a family of 2 or more or $33,000 for a single person.

The income period to be used is for the calendar year of 1983. According to the guidelines for the 1984 program, the adjusted gross income is to be established in the following manner:

The evidence of eligibility and adjusted gross income shall be the amount of adjusted gross income shown on the Federal Income Tax Form of the eligible borrower for 1983 or other evidence acceptable to the Texas Housing Agency.

Underwriting guidelines According to the guidelines set by the agency, each of the loans originated for sale to the agency will be underwritten with the ratios of 33% payment to income and 38% long-term debt to income.

If you have any questions regarding the underwriting guidelines of the Texas Housing Agency, you may contact any participating lender or the Texas Housing Agency at:

Texas Housing Agency
Earline Jewett, Executive Director
P.O. Box 13941
Austin, Texas 78711
(512) 475-0812

Self-Employed Individuals

Before leaving the discussion of borrower qualification, a brief discussion of the self-employed borrower should be included. First, what is a self-employed person? Many lenders define a self-employed person as anyone who has no federal withholding tax deducted from his or her earnings or a nonsalaried employee. Some lenders even take this a step further and include anyone who is a principal stockholder in a closely held or family corporation or a partner in a legal partnership even if a salary is drawn from the corporation or partnership. So if you are working with such an individual you will need to contact the lenders in your area to see if they classify the latter as self-employed. If you should have the opportunity to work with a self-employed or nonsalaried person, the following short discussion will aid you in counseling your buyer as to the additional information he or she will need to provide the lender or originator.

Conventional If your buyer is self-employed or nonsalaried and is seeking a conventional mortgage, many lenders will require the following information:

1. Signed federal tax return for the past 2 years with all supporting schedules.

2. If available, a current profit-and-loss statement and a current balance sheet. These should be prepared by an accountant. The financial statements must be in detail and show all of the assets and liabilities of the individual.

If your buyer is a principal or majority stockholder in a closely held corporation (in Texas a closely held corporation by some attorneys is

defined as one with less than 35 stockholders), in addition to the mentioned items, your buyer will have to supply the following additional information:

1. Signed federal tax returns on the corporation for the past 2 years.

2. Profit-and-loss Statement; if possible, it should be an audited year-to-date statement.

3. In addition some lenders will require a copy of the minutes of the corporate meeting authorizing the salary.

To establish the gross stable monthly income of the self-employed person, the lenders normally will take the taxable income indicated on the tax returns, add the 2 years together and divide by 2 to arrive at an annual salary, then divide the average by 12 to get a monthly salary. This has caused problems in the past for many professionals may have rather large incomes, but due to the sheltering of income will show a small taxable income. For example, let's say you are working with a person whose gross income was $250,000 but who, after expenses and legal tax shelters, only had a taxable income of $40,000. Many lenders will only use the $40,000 for loan purposes; thus reducing rather substantially the amount of loan they could receive.

In the past lenders would, if a self-employed person used real estate depreciation as a deduction, add an amount equal to the depreciation back into the income for loan purposes. For example, using the person in the previous paragraph, to reduce their taxable income they had claimed $100,000 of depreciation of real property. That $100,000 could be added to the $40,000 taxable income, thus giving them an income for loan purposes of $140,000.

If we are working with a self-employed buyer who is seeking a loan that may be sold to Fannie Mae, Fannie Mae has made some major policy changes regarding the underwriting of loans to self-employed persons. These changes were published in Fannie Mae Announcement No. 84-13, May 18, 1984. Fannie Mae still requires that the borrower's individual and business earnings must be documented for a period of 2 years prior to the date of the application. This can be done by the originator requesting signed federal income tax returns for 2 years. In addition,

Fannie Mae has asked the originators to provide financial statements for the same period as well as a year-to-date profit-and-loss statement.

The major changes in Fannie Mae's policy are in reference to the items that may be added to the adjusted gross income on the borrower's tax returns. Now Fannie Mae allows their approved seller/servicers to add to the borrower's adjusted gross income any of the following items to determine the qualifying income:

1. Depreciation of real property

2. Depreciation on personal property when it is not fully consumed during the current operating cycle. In order to be acceptable, personal property must be depreciated over its general acceptable useful life.

3. IRA/Keogh contributions

4. Interest income and dividend exclusions

5. Nontaxable pension income

6. Noncash losses

7. Nonrecurring losses

8. Adjustments to gross income (for example, the married couple's deductions)

The announcement further states that in cases where the business is less than 2 years old, the lender is asked to evaluate its potential for success.

HUD-FHA guidelines   The policy of HUD-FHA in regard to the income of self-employed persons or majority stockholders in a corporation are outlined in the U.S. Department of Housing and Urban Development, Handbook 4155.1 Revised, entitled *Mortgage Credit Analysis for Mortgage Insurance on One- to Four-Family Properties.* Chapter 3, Analysis of Credit Factors, section 2, Effective Income, gives the requirements for several types of income. As with conventional loans, HUD-FHA will accept, if the borrower is willing to supply, signed federal tax returns for a 2-year period prior to the date of the application. Paragraphs 3-13, 3-14, 3-15, 3-16 and 3-17 are the most important to the real estate professional who is working with a self-employed

person. The complete section 2, Effective Income, is shown in Appendix J.

Veterans Administration   The Veterans Administration requirements for a self-employed veteran seeking a VA-guaranteed loan are contained in the Veterans Administration *Lenders Handbook,* VA Pamphlet 26-7, Revised. The particular area of the handbook that contains information on the self-employed veteran is section D, Loan Processing Procedures; part 4, Credit Standards. This part is further divided into several sections. The most important to the real estate professional is section E, Monthly Income and Deductions, paragraph (f), entitled Self-Employment. This paragraph is shown below.

(f) Self-Employment. When a self-employed applicant has been in business a relatively short period of time (i.e., less than 2 years), sufficient information must be obtained to ascertain that the applicant has the training, experience and other qualifications necessary to be successful in the enterprise. Verification of the amount of income is accomplished by obtaining a profit and loss statement for the previous 12 months and a current balance sheet showing all assets and liabilities. Both will be prepared by an accountant based on the financial records. In some cases, the nature of the business or the content of the financial statement may necessitate an independent audit certified as accurate by the accountant. Depending on the situation, this data may be on the veteran and/or the business. When it is otherwise not possible to determine a self-employed applicant's qualification from an income standpoint, the applicant may wish to voluntarily offer to submit copies of complete income tax returns, including all schedules for the past 2 years, or for whatever additional period is deemed necessary to properly demonstrate a satisfactory earnings record. If the business is a corporation or partnership, a list of all stockholders or partners showing the interest each holds in the business will be required. Some cases may justify a written credit report on the business as well as the applicant. When the business is of an unusual type and it is difficult to determine the probability of its continued operation, explanations as to the function and

purpose of the business may be needed from the applicant and/or any other qualified party with the acknowledged expertise to express a valid opinion.

REVIEW QUESTIONS

1. Name and define three types of income that may be used to qualify a prospective homebuyer.

2. Define the term *net effective income*.

3. Define the term *gross stable monthly income*.

4. Explain the ratios of 28 percent and 36 percent.

5. Explain the difference between the terms *monthly mortgage payment* and *total housing expense*.

6. Define the term *long-term debts* according to Fannie Mae/FHLMC, VA, and FHA.

7. Give your reason for prequalifying the prospective homebuyer.

8. If a homebuyer wishes to use income from rental property, what information will a lender require?

9. Explain the 3 sections of a Factual Credit Report.

10. Explain the meaning of *obsolete information* as it relates to the Fair Credit Reporting Act.

11. Name and explain the qualification methods used by HUD-FHA.

12. Name and explain the most important 6 sections of the HUD-FHA Mortgage Credit Analysis Worksheet.

PROBLEMS

1. Using the material supplied in the text, prepare a conventional worksheet and a HUD-FHA Mortgage Credit Analysis for the borrower and coborrower described in the following section.

2. Calculate the amount of mortgage the given borrower and coborrower could secure using a 3-2-1 buydown.

Pertinent Qualifying Information

Borrower

Age 52
Married
2 dependents (12 and 16 years old)

Employment

Database analyst	
10 years	
Software company	
$2916.67	
Federal taxes	$443.50

Assets

Earnest money	$1,000
Checking account	$3,300
Savings account	$9,000
Automobile	$1,000
Automobile	$4,000
Household & personal	$47,500
Existing home	$84,250

Coborrower

Age 45
Married
None

Employment

Teacher	
15 years	
Public schools	
$22,000/9 months	
Federal taxes	$188.70

Liabilities

	PMT	Rem. Bal.
Department store	$35.00	$400.00
Department store	$50.00	$300.00
Department store	$45.00	$733.25
Retirement program	$50.00	
Life insurance	$25.00	
Automobile	$275.00	$2,725.73
Existing home	$485.00	$31,537.89

Present Home Expenses

First mortgage	$485.00
Hazard insurance	10.00
Real estate taxes	74.50
Total monthly payment	$569.50

Proposed Home

Sales price	$92,250
90-percent conventional loan	
Interest	14%
Term	30 years
Taxes	$1,084.00
Insurance	$400.00
Closing	$3,000.00
Prepaids	$300.00
2000 square feet	

Equity on existing home will equal approximately 90 percent of gross equity. Required PMI coverage is 25 percent. Sales price equals FHA value of property less estimated closing cost. Maximum FHA loan is $90,000.

NOTE

1. *Underwriting Guidelines, Home Mortgages*, Federal Home Loan Mortgage Corporation, July 1979, p. 12.

2. Federal Home Loan Mortgage Corporation, "Conventional Mortgages," Seller's Guide, Part 3, Section 4, p. 142.

14

Loan Processing and Underwriting

LEARNING OBJECTIVES

In this chapter we will discuss how loans are processed and, in general, how they are underwritten. In addition, we will review the application forms of Fannie Mae/FHLMC, FHA, and VA, as well as the information or items on the application forms that will be verified by the lender.

Upon completion of this chapter you should be able to do the following:

★ Define the term *underwriting*.

★ List the steps in the processing and underwriting of a real estate loan.

★ Recognize the application forms used by Fannie Mae/FHLMC, FHA, and VA.

★ Counsel a client on the information that will be needed by the lender to complete an application form.

LOAN APPLICATION

All loan processing and underwriting begins with an application. The application may be in several forms, but we will review only those forms used by Fannie Mae/FHLMC, FHA, and VA.

Usually the application is only completed after a face-to-face interview with an employee or agent of the lender, at which time the terms of the mortgage are discussed. The interest rate, term, loan-to-value ratio, and loan amount are established and agreed upon. Once these items have been established, the lender will proceed with the filling out of the loan application.

The loan application may take several forms, but there is basic information which is common to all applications:

1. Identification of the borrower and coborrower

2. Complete legal description of the property to be used as security for the mortgage

3. Exact amount of the loan the applicant is seeking

4. Term and interest rate of the loan

5. Purpose of the mortgage

6. Information regarding the finances and employment of the borrower and coborrower:

   a. *Employment.* They must supply their employment history for a period of at least two years. This information will include the name and address of the employer, job title, dates of employment, and their salaries at the time of leaving the employment if either the borrower or coborrower has had more than one employer.

   b. *Bank accounts.* The lenders will need information on all bank accounts of the borrower and coborrower. This information will include the account numbers, name and address of the institution, and balance at the time of application.

c. *Financial obligations.* The lender will also want information regarding all financial obligations of the borrower and coborrower. This will include all loans and long-term obligations as previously discussed in the chapter on qualifying the borrower.

d. *Other property.* If the borrower or coborrower owns any additional properties, the lender will need information regarding any loans against the property. If the property is held for investment purposes or if the property is rental property, the lender will ask for information regarding the monthly rental and expenses.

e. *Additional information.* The lender at the time of application may ask for any other information that will be necessary to make a lending decision.

It should be noted that the lender is also limited to the type of information which can be asked and used to make the lending decision. These limitations were placed on the mortgage lender by the passage of the Equal Credit Opportunity Act of 1975.

Equal Credit Opportunity Act (ECOA)

The Equal Credit Opportunity Act (ECOA) became law on October 25, 1975. It has been amended several times since its original passage, but the intent of the law remains the same. It was enacted to prohibit in a credit transaction any discrimination based on sex, marital status, age, race, color, country of national origin, or the receipt of income from public assistance programs. This law has a direct effect on the real estate industry in that it applies to anyone who regularly participates in the decision of whether to grant or extend credit. Thus, most mortgage lenders are covered by the provisions of ECOA.

One of the amendments to the act in 1978 had a major impact on the real estate industry and, in particular, the real estate professional who recommends a mortgage lender to a client. According to the change, if a salesperson recommends a lender to a client, and the client later feels that the lender has discriminated against him or her, the salesperson can in

some cases also be accused of discrimination, due to the actions of the lender.

ECOA outlines the questions and information that may be included on the application form, and section 202.5 of ECOA outlines the information that is prohibited on an application form. ECOA also makes the following prohibitions:

1. The lender may not seek information regarding the birth control practices or childbearing capacities of the borrower or coborrower.

2. The lender may not discount or exclude from consideration any income because of the source of the income.

3. The lender cannot refuse an applicant credit because the applicant cannot secure health, life, or accident insurance due to the age of the borrower or coborrower.

4. The lender cannot ask if the borrower or coborrower is divorced or widowed (but the lender can ask if the borrower or coborrower is married, unmarried, or separated).

5. The lender may not request information concerning the spouse or former spouse of the applicant, unless that person will be contractually liable for the repayment of the loan.

ECOA requires the lender to notify the borrower and coborrower as to the action taken by the lender within the following limits:

30 days after receiving a completed application and/or

30 days after the lender has taken adverse action on an application

Adverse action is the denial of credit by a lender. Notice of adverse action must give the reason for the denial of credit and the name and address of the federal agency that oversees compliance with ECOA by the credit-granting organization. An example of such a letter is shown in Figure 14–1. This is the format that is prescribed by Fannie Mae for use by an approved seller/servicer.

Real Estate Settlement Procedures Act (RESPA)

In addition to the Equal Credit Opportunity Act, there is additional federal legislation that has an effect on the application procedure for a real estate mortgage. It is the Real Estate

Figure 14-1. **Notice of Adverse Action**

FNMA CONVENTIONAL HOME MORTGAGE SELLING
APPENDIX A   CONTRACT SUPPLEMENT   FORM 1011

Consumer Disclosure Letter
(Equal Credit Opportunity Act/Fair Credit Reporting Act)

_____
(Date)

APPLICANT(S):_____
       (Type Full Name)   (City)   (State)

DESCRIPTION OF REQUESTED CREDIT:_____

_____

Dear (Name of Applicant):

This is to advise you that your recent application for an extension of credit has been submitted to Federal National Mortgage Association for their evaluation.

☐ 1. In compliance with Regulation "B" (Equal Credit Opportunity Act), you are advised that the application is being held pending further review or receipt of additional information. This notice of the status of your application is required to be given to you by the Federal Equal Credit Opportunity Act. We will notify you of the decision on your application as soon as possible.

☐ 2. In compliance with Regulation "B" (Equal Credit Opportunity Act), you are advised that the application has been declined. The decision to deny your application was based on the following reasons:

CREDIT
☐ No credit file
☐ Insufficient credit references
☐ Insufficient credit file
☐ Unable to verify credit references
☐ Garnishment, attachment, foreclosure,
     repossession or suit
☐ Insufficient income for total obligations
☐ Unacceptable payment record on previous
     mortgage
☐ Delinquent credit obligations
☐ Bankruptcy
☐ Information from a consumer reporting agency
☐ Lack of cash reserves

EMPLOYMENT STATUS
☐ Unable to verify employment
☐ Length of employment
☐ Insufficient stability of income

(SEE NEXT PAGE)   FNMA Form 1011
                              Rev. 7/77

Figure 14–1. *continued*

FNMA CONVENTIONAL HOME MORTGAGE SELLING

<u>APPENDIX A</u> CONTRACT SUPPLEMENT <u>FORM 1011</u>

INCOME
- ☐ Insufficient income for mortgage payments
- ☐ Unable to verify income

RESIDENCY
- ☐ Secondary residence

PROPERTY
- ☐ Unacceptable property
- ☐ Insufficient data-property
- ☐ Unacceptable appraisal
- ☐ Unacceptable leasehold estate

OTHER
- ☐ Insufficient funds to close the loan
- ☐ Credit application incomplete
- ☐ We do not grant credit to any applicant on the terms and conditions you request

3. DISCLOSURE OF USE OF INFORMATION OBTAINED FROM AN OUTSIDE SOURCE

☐ Disclosure inapplicable
☐ In compliance with Fair Credit Reporting Act, Section 615, your application was declined either wholly or partly because of:
   ☐ Information obtained in a report from a consumer reporting agency:

_____

(Full Name at Credit Bureau)   (Address & Telephone Number)

This information is obtained as a routine matter in connection with a mortgage application. Any questions you may have concerning this information should be addressed to the consumer reporting agency shown above, rather than to us.

   ☐ Information obtained from an outside source other than a consumer reporting agency. You have the right to make a written request of us for disclosure of the nature of this information. <u>However, to be honored, such written request must be received by us within 60 days from the date you received this notice.</u>

4. The Federal Equal Credit Opportunity Act prohibits creditors from discriminating against credit applicants on the basis of race, color, religion, national origin, sex, marital status, age (provided that the applicant has the capacity to enter into a binding contract); because all or part of the applicant's income derives from any public assistance program; or because the applicant has in good faith exercised any right under the Consumer Credit Protection Act. The Federal agency that administers compliance with this law concerning Federal National Mortgage Association is the Federal Trade Commission, Equal Credit Opportunity, Washington, D.C. 20580.

(SEE NEXT PAGE)

FNMA Form 1011
Rev. 7/77

Figure 14-1. continued

FNMA CONVENTIONAL HOME MORTGAGE SELLING

APPENDIX A   CONTRACT SUPPLEMENT   FORM 1011

5. Should you have any additional information which might assist us in evaluating your creditworthiness, please let us know. Thank you for applying.

This notification is given by us on behalf of Federal National Mortgage Association.

Notice ☐ delivered or   ☐ mailed on _____

_____

By: _____

_____
          (Address)

_____
(City)   (State)   (Telephone)

FNMA Form 1011
Rev. 7/77

Settlement Procedures Act, sometimes referred to as RESPA. This act was passed in 1974 and later amended in 1976.

Purpose of RESPA

According to the act, the purpose was to affect certain changes in the settlement procedures for residential real estate transactions that will result:

In more effective advance disclosure to the homebuyer and seller of settlement costs;

In the elimination of kickbacks or referral fees that tend to increase unnecessarily the costs of certain settlement services;

In a reduction in the amounts homebuyers are required to place in escrow accounts; and

In significant reform and modernization of local record keeping of land title information.

In this discussion only some of the portions of the Act dealing with the closing of the residential transactions will be discussed.

Federally Related Mortgage Loan

Reference is made throughout the act to a *federally related mortgage loan*, a definition of the term which is necessary to better understand the act. According to section 3, Definitions, the term *federally related mortgage loan* includes any loan (other than interim financing) that

Is secured by a first lien on residential real property designed principally for the occupancy of from one to four families; and

Is made in whole or part by a lender whose deposits or accounts are insured by either the FSLIC or FDIC or is made by a lender who is under the supervision of any agency of the Federal government; or

Is made in whole or in part or insured, guaranteed, or supplemented, or assisted in any way by any officer or agency of the Federal Government; or

Is intended to be sold by the originator to Fannie Mae, FHLMC or GNMA or to an institution that will sell the mortgage loan to FHLMC; or

Is made in whole or part by certain lenders who make or invest in residential real estate loans equaling more than $1,000,000 a year. It should be noted that the term lender or

creditor does not include any agency or institution of any state government.

From this definition, it is obvious that any FHA, VA, and the majority of conventional principal residence loans are covered by the act.

Exemption Transactions

According to regulation X, Section 3500.5, Coverage of RESPA, certain real estate transactions are exempt from the requirements of RESPA and regulation X. Those exemptions are:

A loan to finance the purchase or transfer of a property of 25 or more acres;

A home improvement loan, a loan to refinance, or any other loan where the proceeds are used to finance the purchase or transfer of legal title to the property;

A loan to finance the purchase of a vacant lot where none of the proceeds of the loan are to be used for the construction of a 1- to 4-family residential structure or for the purchase of a mobile home to be placed on the lot; or

An assumption, refinance or sale or transfer of property subject to a pre-existing loan, with one exception – the conversion of a construction loan to a permanent mortgage loan to finance the purchase by the first user; or

A permanent loan the proceeds of which will be used to finance the construction of a 1- to 4-family dwelling where the lot is already owned by the borrower or borrowers; or

A loan to purchase a property where the primary purpose of the purchase is for resale; or

The execution of a contract for deed where the legal title is not transferred upon execution.

The act does state that any loan to finance the acquisition of title pursuant to a contract for deed is a federally related loan. Therefore, the distinction is whether the legal title is conveyed to the purchaser.

RESPA covers most residential mortgages used to finance the purchase of 1- to 4-family properties. The statute is not designed to set the fees for the settlement services, but is designed to help the prospective buyer better understand the settlement procedure and to require lenders and settlement agencies to conform to certain practices.

Application Requirements

In regard to the application for a residential mortgage, RESPA requires the lender at the time of application or within 3 days to mail to the applicant and coapplicant a copy of an information booklet prescribed by the Department of Housing and Urban Development. The table of contents of such a booklet is illustrated in Figure 14-2.

The lender is required to supply the applicant and coapplicant with a "good faith estimate of settlement costs" at the time of application or within three days by mail. A common format for this estimate is shown in Figure 14-3.

In addition to these provisions, RESPA has provisions that will affect the closing of the transaction. These will be discussed in the next chapter.

Standard Application Forms

In the following section we will examine some of the standard loan application forms. Since most lenders require a face-to-face interview with the prospective homebuyer, the application is usually filled in at the time of this interview.

Federal National Mortgage Association/Federal Home Loan Mortgage Corporation Application

The form that will be reviewed in this section is Fannie Mae Form 1003/FHLMC Form 65, revised August 1978. In addition to establishing the secondary market, Fannie Mae/FHLMC has a responsibility to establish industry standards. Fannie Mae/FHLMC has, for example, set standardized forms. One such form is the application form shown in Figure 14-4. Because this form meets the requirements of ECOA, many conventional lenders have adopted it.

The importance of the application cannot be overstated, for the information supplied on this form will determine whether the loan is approved or rejected. Many times the loan has been rejected by an investor if the originator of the mortgage has not properly filled out the application or has omitted some supporting data. This supporting data will be discussed later in this chapter. Now let us review the main section of the application.

The first section of the application has to do with the type of mortgage being applied for: conventional, VA, or FHA. The interest rate and the term of the mortgage as well as the monthly payments are calculated, and finally the escrow or impounds are indicated.

Figure 14-2. *Table of Contents to Settlements Costs, A HUD Guide*

Contents

3 Introduction

Part I

4 What Happens and When
4 Shopping for Services
5 Role of the Broker
6 Negotiating a Sales Contract
7 Selecting an Attorney
8 Selecting a Lender
10 Selecting a Settlement Agent
10 Securing Title Services

Home Buyer's Rights

12 Information Booklet
12 Good Faith Estimates
13 Lender Designation of Settlement Service Providers
14 Disclosure of Settlement Costs One Day Before Closing and Delivery
15 Escrow Closing
15 Truth-in-Lending
16 Protection Against Unfair Practices
16 Kickbacks
17 Title Companies
17 Fair Credit Reporting
18 Equal Credit Opportunity
18 The Right to File Complaints

Home Buyer's Obligations

19 (Repayment of Loan and Maintenance of Home)

Part II

21 Specific Settlement Services
22 Uniform Settlement Statement
26 Settlement Costs Worksheet
33 Comparing Lender Costs
36 Calculating the Borrower's Transactions
39 Reserve Accounts
41 Adjustments between Buyer and Seller

Appendix

43 Appendix – Bibliography

Figure 14-3.   Good Faith Estimates

"GOOD FAITH ESTIMATES"
(Required by RESPA)

This list gives an estimate of most of the charges, based on the contract and/or general experience, that you will have to pay at the settlement of the loan. The figures shown, as estimated, are subject to change. The numbers listed on the left hand column of the estimated settlement charges correspond to the lines of the Uniform Settlement Statement (HUD-1), which will be used in the closing of your loan. The figures shown are based on the sales price and proposed mortgage amount as reflected by your loan application. For further explanation of the charges, consult your special information booklet.

ESTIMATED SETTLEMENT CHARGES

801	Loan Origination Fee (_____ %)	_____
803	Appraisal Fee	_____
804	Credit Report	_____
805	Lender's Inspection Fee	_____
806	Mortgage Insurance Application Fee	_____
901	Interest (*See Below)	_____
902	Mortgage Insurance Premium	_____
1105	Document Preparation	_____
1108	Title Insurance	_____
1201	Recording Fees	_____
1301	Survey	_____
		_____
		_____
		_____
		_____
	Total	$ _____

*This interest calculation represents the greatest amount of interest you could be required to pay at settlement. The actual amount will be determined by which day of the month your settlement is conducted. To determine the amount you will have to pay, multiply the number of days remaining in the month in which you settle, times $ _____ , which is the daily interest charge for your loan.

The Lender requires that _____ , Attorneys be used for mortgage loan document preparation. The name, address and telephone number of such firm is _____ _____ , and the services to be rendered by such firm will be document preparation for the mortgage loan closing. The above estimate of Lender for the document preparation is based upon the charge furnished by _____ , Attorneys. The firm of _____ _____ , Attorneys has a business relationship with Lender.

(   ) Check if applicable
The contract between you and the seller indicates to us that you will be required to pay a fixed amount of $ _____ for all charges imposed at settlement for the settlement services listed above. You are exempt from settlement disclosure under Section 3500.8(d)(2) of HUD Regulation X.

(   ) Check if applicable
The contract between you and the seller indicates to us that you will be required to pay no settlement charges. You are exempt from settlement disclosure under Section 3500.8(d)(1) of HUD Regulation X.

Source: **Mercantile Mortgage Corporation of Texas, 2714 Louisiana, Houston, Texas 77006**

Figure 14–4. **Fannie Mae/FHLMC Residential Loan Application, page 1**

RESIDENTIAL LOAN APPLICATION

MORTGAGE APPLIED FOR	☐ Conventional ☐ VA	☐ FHA	Amount $	Interest Rate %	No. of Months	Monthly Payment Principal & Interest $	Escrow/Impounds (to be collected monthly) ☐ Taxes ☐ Hazard Ins. ☐ Mtg. Ins. ☐

Prepayment Option

SUBJECT PROPERTY

Property Street Address	City	County	State	Zip	No. Units

Legal Description (Attach description if necessary)	Year Built

Purpose of Loan: ☐ Purchase ☐ Construction-Permanent ☐ Construction ☐ Refinance ☐ Other (Explain)

Complete this line if Construction-Permanent or Construction Loan ☛	Lot Value Data	Original Cost	Present Value (a)	Cost of Imps. (b)	Total (a + b)	ENTER TOTAL AS PURCHASE PRICE IN DETAILS OF PURCHASE.
	Year Acquired $	$	$	$		

Complete this line if a Refinance Loan	Purpose of Refinance	Describe Improvements [ ] made [ ] to be made
Year Acquired	Original Cost $	Amt. Existing Liens $		Cost: $

Title Will Be Held In What Name(s)	Manner In Which Title Will Be Held

Source of Down Payment and Settlement Charges

This application is designed to be completed by the borrower(s) with the lender's assistance. The Co-Borrower Section and all other Co-Borrower questions must be completed and the appropriate box(es) checked if ☐ another person will be jointly obligated with the Borrower on the loan, or ☐ the Borrower is relying on income from alimony, child support or separate maintenance or on the income or assets of another person as a basis for repayment of the loan, or ☐ the Borrower is married and resides, or the property is located, in a community property state.

BORROWER				CO-BORROWER			
Name		Age	School Yrs ___	Name		Age	School Yrs ___
Present Address	No. Years ___ ☐ Own ☐ Rent			Present Address	No. Years ___ ☐ Own ☐ Rent		
Street				Street			
City/State/Zip				City/State/Zip			
Former address if less than 2 years at present address				Former address if less than 2 years at present address			
Street				Street			
City/State/Zip				City/State/Zip			
Years at former address ☐ Own ☐ Rent				Years at former address ☐ Own ☐ Rent			
Marital Status ☐ Married ☐ Separated ☐ Unmarried (incl. single, divorced, widowed)	DEPENDENTS OTHER THAN LISTED BY CO BORROWER NO. / AGES			Marital Status ☐ Married ☐ Separated ☐ Unmarried (incl. single, divorced, widowed)	DEPENDENTS OTHER THAN LISTED BY BORROWER NO. / AGES		
Name and Address of Employer	Years employed in this line of work or profession? ___ years Years on this job ___ ☐ Self Employed*			Name and Address of Employer	Years employed in this line of work or profession? ___ years Years on this job ___ ☐ Self Employed*		
Position/Title	Type of Business			Position/Title	Type of Business		
Social Security Number***	Home Phone	Business Phone		Social Security Number***	Home Phone	Business Phone	

GROSS MONTHLY INCOME				MONTHLY HOUSING EXPENSE**			DETAILS OF PURCHASE	
Item	Borrower	Co-Borrower	Total		PRESENT	PROPOSED	Do Not Complete If Refinance	
Base Empl. Income	$	$	$	Rent	$		a. Purchase Price	$
Overtime				First Mortgage (P&I)		$	b. Total Closing Costs (Est.)	
Bonuses				Other Financing (P&I)			c. Prepaid Escrows (Est.)	
Commissions				Hazard Insurance			d. Total (a + b + c)	$
Dividends/Interest				Real Estate Taxes			e. Amount This Mortgage	( )
Net Rental Income				Mortgage Insurance			f. Other Financing	( )
Other† (Before completing, see notice under Describe Other Income below.)				Homeowner Assn. Dues			g. Other Equity	( )
				Other			h. Amount of Cash Deposit	( )
				Total Monthly Pmt.	$	$	i. Closing Costs Paid by Seller	( )
Total	$	$	$	Utilities			j. Cash Reqd. For Closing (Est.)	$
				Total	$	$		

DESCRIBE OTHER INCOME

☞ B—Borrower   C—Co-Borrower   NOTICE: † Alimony, child support, or separate maintenance income need not be revealed if the Borrower or Co-Borrower does not choose to have it considered as a basis for repaying this loan. | Monthly Amount $ |

IF EMPLOYED IN CURRENT POSITION FOR LESS THAN TWO YEARS COMPLETE THE FOLLOWING

B/C	Previous Employer/School	City/State	Type of Business	Position/Title	Dates From/To	Monthly Income
						$

THESE QUESTIONS APPLY TO BOTH BORROWER AND CO-BORROWER

If a "yes" answer is given to a question in this column, explain on an attached sheet.	Borrower Yes or No	Co-Borrower Yes or No	If applicable, explain Other Financing or Other Equity (provide addendum if more space is needed).
Have you any outstanding judgments? In the last 7 years, have you been declared bankrupt?			
Have you had property foreclosed upon or given title or deed in lieu thereof?			
Are you a co-maker or endorser on a note?			
Are you a party in a law suit?			
Are you obligated to pay alimony, child support, or separate maintenance?			
Is any part of the down payment borrowed?			

*FHLMC/FNMA require business credit report, signed Federal Income Tax returns for last two years, and, if available, audited Profit and Loss Statements plus balance sheet for same period.

**All Present Monthly Housing Expenses of Borrower and Co-Borrower should be listed on a combined basis.

***Neither FHLMC nor FNMA requires this information.

FHLMC 65 Rev. 8/78   FNMA 1003 Rev. 8/78

In the next section of the application, Subject Property, the property is identified by both a street address and a legal description. Next, the lender will need to know the purpose of the loan, whether it is to purchase, to construct, or to refinance existing financing. If the purpose is either to construct or to refinance, additional information is requested. The final portion of this section asks in whose names the title to the property will be held and in what manner the title will be held: fee simple, fee conditional, joint tenancy, and so forth. Therefore, you will need to tell the prospective homebuyer how the title can be held and help him or her arrive at a decision, or advise them of the lender's requirements as to how the title will be held.

The next sections have to do with the borrower and coborrower. Normally, a lender will not allow the borrower to give the information for the coborrower or vice versa. Both parties, therefore, must be present at the time of application. What information is required seems self-explanatory, but there are some important items that should be reviewed. The first is the applicant's present address. If either the borrower or coborrower has resided at his present address for less than 2 years, the lender will request the prior address to establish residency for the past two years. If the borrower or coborrower has rented, the lender will need the name and address of the landlord or rental agent to verify the residency and payment record of the borrower or coborrower. If the borrower or coborrower has owned or was purchasing a home and was making mortgage payments, he will have to supply the name and address of the mortgage lender as well as his account number, for the lender will verify the mortgage and payment record of the borrower and/or coborrower. The borrower and/or the coborrower will also need to furnish the names and addresses of employers for the past two years. These addresses should be accurate, for the lender will wish to verify the employment. If the address is incorrect, it can slow the processing of the application.

The next section of the application is divided into three sections: Gross Monthly Income, Monthly Housing Expenses, and Details of the Purchase. This section is self-explanatory and the information required is not difficult to furnish.

In the next section of the application, the borrower or coborrower describes other income, if any. Once again, sufficient information must be supplied to allow the lender to verify the income.

In the section entitled "If Employed in the Current Position For Less Than Two Years," the borrower and coborrower are given additional room to establish a 2-year work record; the information must be sufficient to allow the lender to verify the employment.

The final section of the first page is composed of several questions. If any question is answered "yes" by either the borrower or coborrower, the answer must be explained in depth.

The second page of the application (Figure 14-5) is devoted primarily to the financial and credit history of the borrower and coborrower. The first section is divided into two parts, the first being the assets and the second being the liabilities of the borrower or coborrower. The information that is requested needs no in-depth explanation here. It should be noted, however, that complete information for the installment debts is once again required; the lender verifying the credit of the borrower or coborrower will need this information for the credit-checking agency.

At the end of the liability and assets section there is a place for the borrower and coborrower to list all of the real estate they own. You will note that, after the address of the property, the borrower or coborrower must state whether the property is sold, whether a sale is pending, or whether the property is being held for rental purposes. If the property is sold, the lender will require a copy of a closing statement. If the sale is pending, the lender may request a copy of the earnest money contract and will not close the loan until a copy of the closing statement is furnished, if the sale proceeds are to be used as part of the down payment or for closing costs.

The next major section of the application is for previous credit references. Here the borrower will list any loans or charge accounts which have been paid in full to any credit-granting organization.

Immediately below the previous credit section is an agreement that the borrower and coborrower must sign. The borrower and coborrower at this time must declare their intent either to occupy or not to occupy the property. By signing the statement, the borrower and coborrower acknowledge that they can be punished by the federal government if they knowingly make any false statement.

Some of the information that is needed to determine if a lender is discriminating due to color, race, or sex is contained in the section Information for Government Monitoring Purposes. Since this information is not used in the processing or approval of a loan, the borrower and coborrower are not required to furnish the

Figure 14–5. **Fannie Mae/FHLMC Residential Loan Application, page 2**

This Statement and any applicable supporting schedules may be completed jointly by both married and unmarried co-borrowers if their assets and liabilities are sufficiently joined so that the Statement can be meaningfully and fairly presented on a combined basis; otherwise separate Statements and Schedules are required (FHLMC 65A/FNMA 1003A). If the co-borrower section was completed about a spouse, this statement and supporting schedules must be completed about that spouse also.   ☐ Completed Jointly   ☐ Not Completed Jointly

ASSETS / LIABILITIES AND PLEDGED ASSETS

Indicate by (*) those liabilities or pledged assets which will be satisfied upon sale of real estate owned or upon refinancing of subject property

Description	Cash or Market Value	Creditors' Name, Address and Account Number	Acct. Name If Not Borrower's	Mo. Pmt. and Mos. left to pay	Unpaid Balance
Cash Deposit Toward Purchase Held By	$	Installment Debts (include "revolving" charge accts)		$ Pmt./Mos.	$
Checking and Savings Accounts (Show Names of Institutions/Acct. Nos.)				/	
				/	
				/	
Stocks and Bonds (No./Description)				/	
				/	
Life Insurance Net Cash Value Face Amount ($)		Other Debts Including Stock Pledges		/	
SUBTOTAL LIQUID ASSETS	$			/	
Real Estate Owned (Enter Market Value from Schedule of Real Estate Owned)		Real Estate Loans			
Vested Interest in Retirement Fund					
Net Worth of Business Owned (ATTACH FINANCIAL STATEMENT)					
Automobiles (Make and Year)		Automobile Loans			
				/	
Furniture and Personal Property		Alimony, Child Support and Separate Maintenance Payments Owed To			
Other Assets (Itemize)				/	
		TOTAL MONTHLY PAYMENTS		$	
TOTAL ASSETS	A $	NET WORTH (A minus B) $		TOTAL LIABILITIES	B $

(left vertical label: STATEMENT OF ASSETS AND LIABILITIES)

SCHEDULE OF REAL ESTATE OWNED (If Additional Properties Owned Attach Separate Schedule)

Address of Property (Indicate S if Sold, PS if Pending Sale or R if Rental being held for income)		Type of Property	Present Market Value	Amount of Mortgages & Liens	Gross Rental Income	Mortgage Payments	Taxes, Ins. Maintenance and Misc.	Net Rental Income
			$	$	$	$	$	$
TOTALS →			$	$	$	$	$	$

LIST PREVIOUS CREDIT REFERENCES

B - Borrower C - Co-Borrower	Creditor's Name and Address	Account Number	Purpose	Highest Balance	Date Paid
				$	

List any additional names under which credit has previously been received _____

AGREEMENT. The undersigned applies for the loan indicated in this application to be secured by a first mortgage or deed of trust on the property described herein, and represents that the property will not be used for any illegal or restricted purpose, and that all statements made in this application are true and are made for the purpose of obtaining the loan. Verification may be obtained from any source named in this application. The original or a copy of this application will be retained by the lender, even if the loan is not granted. The undersigned ☐ intend or ☐ do not intend to occupy the property as their primary residence.

I/we fully understand that it is a federal crime punishable by fine or imprisonment, or both, to knowingly make any false statements concerning any of the above facts as applicable under the provisions of Title 18, United States Code, Section 1014.

_____ Date _____   _____ Date _____
Borrower's Signature   Co-Borrower's Signature

INFORMATION FOR GOVERNMENT MONITORING PURPOSES

Instructions: Lenders must insert in this space, or on an attached addendum, a provision for furnishing the monitoring information required or requested under present Federal and/or present state law or regulation. For most lenders, the inserts provided in FHLMC Form 65-B/FNMA Form 1003-B can be used.

FOR LENDER'S USE ONLY

(FNMA REQUIREMENT ONLY) This application was taken by ☐ face to face interview ☐ by mail ☐ by telephone

_____   _____
(Interviewer)   Name of Employer of Interviewer

FHLMC 65 Rev. 8/78   **REVERSE**   FNMA 1003 Rev. 8/78

requested information, but they must initial the section stating that they do not wish to furnish the information. A sample of the information that will be requested is shown in Figure 14–6.

Federal Housing Administration/Veterans Administration   This is the second of the major common forms and has been developed by FHA, VA, and the Farmers Home Administration. This application, HUD form 92900, will be used for any application for a HUD-FHA commitment for mortgage, VA, or FmHA loan guaranty after July 31, 1982. Any application submitted on any other form will be rejected.

First, let's review how the common form will be used by HUD-FHA and the information that will be required. Since this is a multipurpose form, it is an 8-page carbon form and contains pages for use by all three agencies. HUD-FHA only uses pages 1, 4–7, and 8. The real estate professional will only be interested in pages 1 (the application page) and 4 (the Certificate of Commitment for a HUD-insured mortgage).

Page 1 is the actual application and is shown in Figure 14–7. The first step is to indicate in the first line that this is an application for HUD-FHA mortgage insurance. The next block that will be filled out at the time of application is Block 3, the name and address of the borrower and/or coborrower. This information must be complete and must include the proper zip code. Blocks 4A, 4B, and 4C are not completed by the borrower. The lender supplies this information.

Blocks 5A through 5C and 6A through 6C are requirements of federal civil rights law. The lender must advise the applicants of this fact and that the information will not affect any lending decision of the lender or the issuance of mortgage insurance by HUD-FHA. If the lender and/or originator of the mortgage advises the applicant of the purpose for securing this information and the applicant refuses, the lender will then ask the applicant to initial the appropriate block. This will indicate to HUD-FHA that the information was not given by a decision of the applicant.

Block 7 is very important and must be complete and correct. The reason for including the property address, the name of the subdivision, the lot and block number, and the zip code is to make sure the application covers the correct property.

Blocks 8A through 8C deal with the terms

of the loan which will be insured by HUD-FHA. You will need to see that the loan amount and the interest rate are correct. The final block, 8C, states the term of the mortgage, normally thirty years unless the loan is a Growing Equity Mortgage or the borrower is making application for mortgage insurance that allows for an extended term.

Blocks 8D and 8E will only be filled out if the borrower/coborrower is to pay discount points. This completes our review of the top portion of the form that will apply to HUD-FHA.

The next portion of the form, Section I – Purpose, Amount, Terms of and Security for Proposed Loan – deals with the property and the repayment of the mortgage. Block 9A, Purpose of Loan, will tell HUD-FHA how the proceeds are to be used. There are 8 specific uses shown and the applicants will need to select the proper purpose. Applicants indicate in block 9B whether they will be an occupant or landlord. If the property used as security is a duplex, triplex, or fourplex and the borrower/coborrower will be living in one of the units, they will need to mark both landlord and occupant boxes.

Blocks 11 through 13 are self-explanatory.

Block 14, Estimated Taxes, Insurance and Assessments, items A through F, will be completed by the lender. The information that will be used for this block comes from fact sheets supplied by the nearest HUD-FHA office.

In block 15, the lender will complete the information required to establish the monthly payment. All of the amounts are then totaled.

In block 16 of section II, Personal and Financial Status of Applicant, HUD-FHA is establishing who will be obligated on the mortgage in addition to the borrower. Also, HUD-FHA wants to establish if the property is located in a state that has a community property law. Block D is checked if the borrower will rely on child support and/or alimony or separate maintenance from a spouse or former spouse for repayment of the loan. If so, HUD-FHA will require information on the spouse or former spouse. This source of funds to repay the mortgage can be true for either a male or female. As a good real estate salesperson, you should see if this type of income will be used for repayment of the loan and have the applicants gather the required information.

Blocks 17A through 17D and 18A through 18C are self-explanatory.

If the borrower/coborrower are presently making mortgage payments, HUD-FHA

Figure 14-6. Information for Government Monitoring Purposes

INFORMATION FOR GOVERNMENT MONITORING PURPOSES - INSERTS

The following are "camera-ready" versions of language which may be inserted to complete the "Information for Government Monitoring Purposes" section of the Residential Loan Application Form (FHLMC Form 65/FNMA 1003). The language in the first insert has been approved by both Federal Deposit Insurance Corporation and Federal Home Loan Bank Board.

Before printing an insert, it should be reviewed to assure conformity with state law. In particular, all lenders, who may be subject to a state fair housing or equal opportunity law which has monitoring requirements, should determine whether the applicable disclosure statement is in compliance with the legal requirements of that state.

INSERT FOR FHLBB OR FDIC REGULATED LENDERS

The following information is requested by the Federal Government if this loan is related to a dwelling, in order to monitor the lender's compliance with equal credit opportunity and fair housing laws. You are not required to furnish this information, but are encouraged to do so. The law provides that a lender may neither discriminate on the basis of this information, nor on whether you choose to furnish it. However, if you choose not to furnish it, under Federal regulations this lender is required to note race and sex on the basis of visual observation or surname. If you do not wish to furnish the above information, please initial below

BORROWER: I do not wish to furnish this information (initials)_____

RACE/ NATIONAL ORIGIN:
☐ American Indian, Alaskan Native ☐ Asian, Pacific Islander
☐ Black ☐ Hispanic ☐ White
☐ Other (specify) _____

SEX: ☐ Female ☐ Male

CO-BORROWER: I do not wish to furnish this information (initials)_____

RACE/ NATIONAL ORIGIN:
☐ American Indian, Alaskan Native ☐ Asian, Pacific Islander
☐ Black ☐ Hispanic ☐ White
☐ Other (specify) _____

SEX: ☐ Female ☐ Male

INSERT FOR LENDERS SUBJECT ONLY TO FEDERAL RESERVE SYSTEM REGULATION B

If this loan is for purchase or construction of a home, the following information is requested by the Federal Government to monitor this lender's compliance with Equal Credit Opportunity and Fair Housing Laws. The law provides that a lender may neither discriminate on the basis of this information nor on whether or not it is furnished. Furnishing this information is optional. If you do not wish to furnish the following information, please initial below.

BORROWER: I do not wish to furnish this information (initials) _____

RACE/ NATIONAL ORIGIN:
☐ American Indian, Alaskan Native ☐ Asian, Pacific Islander
☐ Black ☐ Hispanic ☐ White
☐ Other (specify) _____

SEX: ☐ Female ☐ Male

CO-BORROWER: I do not wish to furnish this information (initials) _____

RACE/ NATIONAL ORIGIN:
☐ American Indian, Alaskan Native ☐ Asian, Pacific Islander
☐ Black ☐ Hispanic ☐ White
☐ Other (specify) _____

SEX: ☐ Female ☐ Male

Note: This form will be amended in the event that the Comptroller of the Currency or the National Credit Union Administration issue regulations which are not accommodated by the insert "FOR LENDERS SUBJECT TO FEDERAL RESERVE SYSTEM REGULATION B." Until such time, lenders regulated by these agencies should continue to use the Regulation B insert. Before printing any insert, it should be reviewed to assure compliance with any applicable state legal requirements.

Figure 14–7.   HUD Form 92900, page 1

Form Approved
OMB No. 2900-0144

VA Application for Home Loan Guaranty ☐	USDA-FmHA Application for FmHA Guaranteed Loan ☐	HUD/FHA Application for Commitment for Insurance under the National Housing Act ☐	1. AGENCY CASE NUMBER ▲	2A. LENDER'S CASE NUMBER	2B. SECTION OF THE ACT (HUD Only)

3. NAME AND PRESENT ADDRESS OF BORROWER (Include ZIP Code)

5A. BORROWER: If you do not wish to complete Items 5B or 5C, please initial in the space to the right.   INITIALS

5B. RACE/NATIONAL ORIGIN
▲1 ☐ WHITE, NOT HISPANIC   4 ☐ ASIAN OR PACIFIC ISLANDER
2 ☐ BLACK, NOT HISPANIC   5 ☐ HISPANIC
3 ☐ AMERICAN INDIAN OR ALASKAN NATIVE

5C. SEX
▲1 ☐ MALE
2 ☐ FE-MALE

4A. NAME AND ADDRESS OF LENDER (Include ZIP Code)

6A. SPOUSE OR OTHER BORROWER: If you do not wish to complete Items 6B or 6C, please initial in space to the right.   INITIALS

6B. RACE/NATIONAL ORIGIN
▲1 ☐ WHITE, NOT HISPANIC   4 ☐ ASIAN OR PACIFIC ISLANDER
2 ☐ BLACK, NOT HISPANIC   5 ☐ HISPANIC
3 ☐ AMERICAN INDIAN OR ALASKAN NATIVE

6C. SEX
▲1 ☐ MALE
2 ☐ FE-MALE

4B. ORIGINATORS' I.D. (HUD Only)   4C. SPONSOR'S I.D. (HUD Only)

7. PROPERTY ADDRESS INCLUDING NAME OF SUBDIVISION, LOT AND BLOCK NO., AND ZIP CODE

8A. LOAN AMOUNT $	8B. INT. RATE %	8C. PROPOSED MATURITY YRS. MOS.

DISCOUNT: (Only if borrower to pay) ➤   8D. PERCENT %   8E. AMOUNT $

VA ONLY: Veteran and lender hereby apply to the Administrator of Veterans Affairs for Guaranty of the loan described here under Section 1810, Chapter 37, Title 38, United States Code to the full extent permitted by the veteran's entitlement and severally agree that the Regulations promulgated pursuant to Chapter 37, and in effect on the date of the loan shall govern the rights, duties, and liabilities of the parties.
HUD/FHA ONLY: Mortgagee's application for mortgagor approval and commitment for mortgage insurance under the National Housing Act.

SECTION I - PURPOSE, AMOUNT, TERMS OF AND SECURITY FOR PROPOSED LOAN

9A. PURPOSE OF LOAN - TO:
▲1 ☐ PURCHASE EXISTING HOUSE PREVIOUSLY OCCUPIED
2 ☐ FINANCE IMPROVEMENTS TO EXISTING PROPERTY
3 ☐ REFINANCE
4 ☐ PURCHASE NEW CONDO. UNIT
5 ☐ PURCHASE EXIST-ING CONDO. UNIT
6 ☐ PURCHASE EXISTING HOME NOT PREVIOUSLY OCCUPIED
7 ☐ CONSTRUCT A HOME - PRO-CEEDS TO BE PAID OUT DURING CONSTRUCTION
8 ☐ HUD ONLY – FINANCE COOP-PURCHASE

9B. HUD ONLY – BORROWER WILL BE
1 ☐ OCCUPANT   5 ☐ ESCROW COMMIT-MENT
2 ☐ LANDLORD
3 ☐ BUILDER
4 ☐ OPERATIVE BUILDER

10. VA ONLY – TITLE WILL BE VESTED IN:
☐ VETERAN   ☐ VETERAN AND SPOUSE
☐ OTHER (Specify)

11. LIEN: ☐ FIRST MORTGAGE ☐ OTHER (Specify)	12. ESTATE WILL BE: ☐ FEE SIMPLE ☐ LEASEHOLD (Show expiration date)	13. IS THERE A MANDATORY HOMEOWNERS ASSOC.? ☐ YES ☐ NO (If "Yes," complete Item 14F.)

14. ESTIMATED TAXES, INSURANCE AND ASSESSMENTS		15. ESTIMATED MONTHLY PAYMENT	
A. ANNUAL TAXES	$	A. PRINCIPAL AND INTEREST	$
B. AMOUNT OF HAZARD INSURANCE ON SECURITY		B. TAXES AND INSURANCE DEPOSITS	
C. ANNUAL HAZARD INSURANCE PREMIUM		C. OTHER	
D. ANNUAL SPECIAL ASSESSMENT PAYMENT			
E. UNPAID SPECIAL ASSESSMENT BALANCE			
F. ANNUAL MAINTENANCE ASSESSMENT		TOTAL	$

SECTION II - PERSONAL AND FINANCIAL STATUS OF APPLICANT

16. PLEASE CHECK APPROPRIATE BOXES! IF ONE OR MORE ARE CHECKED, ITEMS 18B, 21, 22 AND 23 MUST INCLUDE INFORMATION CONCERNING BORROWER'S SPOUSE (or former spouse if box "D" is checked). IF NO BOXES ARE CHECKED, NO INFORMATION CONCERNING THE SPOUSE NEED BE FURNISHED IN ITEMS 18B, 21, 22 AND 23.

A. ☐ THE SPOUSE WILL BE JOINTLY OBLIGATED WITH THE BORROWER ON THE LOAN
B. ☐ THE BORROWER IS RELYING ON THE SPOUSE'S INCOME AS A BASIS FOR REPAYMENT OF THE LOAN.
C. ☐ THE BORROWER IS MARRIED AND THE PROPERTY TO SECURE THE LOAN IS LOCATED IN A COMMUNITY PROPERTY STATE.
D. ☐ THE BORROWER IS RELYING ON ALIMONY, CHILD SUPPORT, OR SEPARATE MAINTENANCE PAYMENTS FROM A SPOUSE OR FORMER SPOUSE AS A BASIS FOR REPAYMENT OF THE LOAN.

17A. MARITAL STATUS OF BORROWER ▲ 1 ☐ MARRIED 3 ☐ UNMARRIED 2 ☐ SEPARATED	17B. MARITAL STATUS OF COBORROWER OTHER THAN SPOUSE ▲ 1 ☐ MARRIED 3 ☐ UNMARRIED 2 ☐ SEPARATED	17C. MONTHLY CHILD SUPPORT OBLIGATION $	17D. MONTHLY ALIMONY OBLIGATION $	18A. AGE OF BORROWER	18B. AGE OF SPOUSE OR COBORROWER	18C. AGE(S) OF DEPENDENT(S)

19. NAME AND ADDRESS OF NEAREST LIVING RELATIVE (Include telephone number, if available).	20A. CURRENT MONTHLY HOUSING EXPENSE $	20B. UTILITIES INCLUDED? ☐ YES ☐ NO

21. ASSETS		22. LIABILITIES (Itemize all debts)		
		NAME OF CREDITOR	MO. PAYMENT	BALANCE
A. CASH (Including deposit on purchase)	$			
B. SAVINGS BONDS - OTHER SECURITIES			$	$
C. REAL ESTATE OWNED				
D. AUTO				
E. FURNITURE AND HOUSEHOLD GOODS				
F. OTHER (Use separate sheet, if necessary)		JOB-RELATED EXPENSE (Specify)		
G. TOTAL	$	TOTAL	$	$

23. INCOME AND OCCUPATIONAL STATUS			24. ESTIMATED TOTAL COST	
ITEM	BORROWER	SPOUSE OR COBORROWER	ITEM	AMOUNT
A. OCCUPATION			A. PURCHASE EXISTING HOME	$
			B. ALTERATIONS, IMPROVEMENTS, REPAIRS	
B. NAME OF EMPLOYER			C. CONSTRUCTION	
			D. LAND (If acquired separately)	
C. NUMBER OF YEARS EMPLOYED			E. PURCHASE OF CONDOMINIUM UNIT	
			F. REFINANCE	
D. GROSS PAY	▲ MONTHLY $ HOURLY $	▲ MONTHLY $ HOURLY $	G. PREPAID ITEMS	
			H. ESTIMATED CLOSING COSTS	
E. OTHER INCOME (Disclosure of child support, alimony and separate maintenance income is optional.)	▲ MONTHLY $	▲ MONTHLY $	I. DISCOUNT (Only if borrower permitted to pay)	
			J. TOTAL COSTS (Add Items 24A through 24I)	
NOTE — If land acquired by separate transaction, complete Items 25A and 25B.			K. LESS CASH FROM BORROWER	
25A. DATE ACQUIRED $	25B. UNPAID BALANCE $		L. LESS OTHER CREDITS	
			M. AMOUNT OF LOAN	$

VA FORM 26-1802a, JAN 1982
HUD FORM 92900.1

SUPERSEDES VA FORM 26-1802a, APR 1979, WHICH WILL NOT BE USED.
HUD FORM 92900, JUL 1980, MAY BE USED FOR HUD PURPOSES.

VA/HUD COPY 1

wants to know the amount of their total monthly housing expense, which is entered in block 20A. This should include principal and interest, insurance, utilities and any other fees that may affect the title to the property. If the applicants are renters, HUD-FHA would like information regarding the monthly rent. Whether the monthly housing expense includes money for utilities is indicated in block 20B. Your clients should have all of this information at the time of application. If they do not, it could slow down the processing of the application.

In block 21 the applicant will need to list all assets that will show his or her financial strength. Each category in block 21 is explained below:

A. Cash—This should include all cash accounts in banks, credit unions, money market funds (if there is check writing capabilities). According to HUD-FHA, significant amounts of cash on hand should be supported by an explanation as to the source of such funds which could be the sale of a house, stocks or other items or by death of a relative.

B. Savings Bonds–Other Securities—If savings bonds are to be shown as an asset, the face value should be used unless a schedule of value was given at the time of purchase, in which case the actual value should be used. As for "other securities," HUD-FHA states that these are any assets that are readily converted to cash.

C. Real Estate Owned—This section is self-explanatory.

D. Auto—If an auto is listed as an asset, the amount listed should be based on the replacement value of the vehicle.

E. Furniture and Household Goods—If furniture and household goods are listed as an asset, the amount listed should be equal to the value of household goods listed in the homeowner's insurance policy, unless the goods are itemized and individually appraised.

F. Other—In this category the applicant should list any other item that has cash value and is not listed in section B. This would include jewelry, artwork, or any item for which the value can be established.

The borrower/coborrower lists in block 22 any liabilities or debts, including any real estate loans even though the property is to be sold. The borrower/coborrower also lists all retail accounts, including the name and address and the approximate balance and monthly payments. The borrower/coborrower will also list all bank loans or any other type of long-term debt that may adversely affect his or her credit status. One other important section is Job-Related Expense. Here, the borrower/coborrower should list any costs of child care, union dues, significant commuting costs, group hospitalization, or life insurance deducted from his or her check. These are not all of the job-related expenses, but only some examples. You will need to determine if your client has any of these expenses or any others.

In block 23 the borrower, spouse, or coborrower will have to supply employment and salary information for the past two years to indicate income and occupational status. It should be noted that only the primary employment should be listed on the application; any part-time, overtime, and secondary income must be listed separately and attached to the application.

The lender will determine the estimated total cost of the acquisition of the property and put it into block 24. This total cost will include all closing costs and prepaid items. From the total cost, the lender then deducts the amount of the down payment of the borrower/coborrower, which will give the amount of the loan. The amount in box 24M should be the same as the amount in box 8A of the application.

The next major section of the application is on the back of page 1, shown in Figure 14–8. The part of this page that applies to a HUD-FHA-insured loan is Section V—Borrowers Certification. This must be signed by both the borrower, and if there is one, the coborrower.

Question 1 of 31A asks if the borrower/coborrower owns or has sold any real estate in the past twelve months. If the answer is "yes," HUD-FHA wants information about the sales price and the original mortgage amount. HUD-FHA also wants to know if it was insured by HUD-FHA and, if so, the name and address of the lender. The remaining two questions are self-explanatory.

The next part that applies to a HUD-FHA insured loan, 31B, reminds the borrower/coborrower of his or her responsibility for repayment of the loan. This section also states that if the property is sold in any other manner than the mortgage having been paid in full, the original borrower/coborrower is still

Figure 14-8.   HUD Form 92900, page 2

SECTION III - LENDER'S CERTIFICATION *(Must be signed by lender)*

The undersigned lender makes the following certifications to induce the Veterans Administration to issue a certificate of commitment to guarantee the subject loan under Title 38, U.S. Code, or to induce the Department of Housing and Urban Development - Federal Housing Commissioner to issue a firm commitment for mortgage insurance under the National Housing Act.

26A.   The information furnished in Section I is true, accurate and complete.

26B.   The information contained in Section II was obtained directly from the borrower by a full-time employee of the undersigned lender or its duly authorized agent and is true to the best of the lender's knowledge and belief.

26C.   The credit report submitted on the subject borrower *(and spouse, if any)* was ordered by the undersigned lender or its duly authorized agent directly from the credit bureau which prepared the report and was received directly from said credit bureau.

26D.   The verification of employment and verification of deposits were requested and received by the lender or its duly authorized agent without passing through the hands of any third persons and are true to the best of the lender's knowledge and belief.

26E.   This application was signed by the borrower after Sections I, II and V were completed.

26F.   This proposed loan to the named borrower meets the income and credit requirements of the governing law in the judgment of the undersigned.

26G through 26I - TO BE COMPLETED OR APPLICABLE FOR VA LOANS ONLY.

26G.   The names and functions of any duly authorized agents who developed on behalf of the lender any of the information or supporting credit data submitted are as follows:

NAME	ADDRESS	FUNCTION	*(e.g., obtained information in Sec. II, ordered credit report, verification of employment, verif. of deposits, etc.)*

(1)

(2)

(3) ☐   *(Check box if all information and supporting credit data were obtained directly by the lender.)*

26H.   The undersigned lender understands and agrees that it is responsible for the acts of agents identified in item 26G as to the functions with which they are identified.

26I.   The proposed loan conforms otherwise with the applicable provisions of Title 38, U.S. Code, and of the regulations concerning guaranty or insurance of loans to veterans.

27. Date	28. Name of Lender	29. Telephone Number *(Include Area Code)*	30. Signature and Title of Officer of Lender

---

SECTION IV - NOTICE TO BORROWERS

PRIVACY ACT INFORMATION - The information requested in this form is authorized by 38 U.S.C. 1810 *(if VA)* and 12 U.S.C. 1701 et seq., *(if HUD/FHA)* and will be used in determining whether you qualify as a mortgagor. Any disclosure of information outside VA or HUD/FHA will only be made as permitted by law. Disclosure of this information is voluntary but no loan may be approved unless a completed application is received.

NOTICE TO BORROWERS - This is notice to you as required by the Right to Financial Privacy Act of 1978 that the VA or HUD/FHA has a right of access to financial records held by financial institutions in connection with the consideration or administration of assistance to you. Financial records involving your transaction will be available to VA and HUD/FHA without further notice or authorization but will not be disclosed or released to another Government Agency or Department without your consent except as required or permitted by law.

SECTION V - BORROWERS CERTIFICATION *(Must be signed by Borrower/s)*

31A.   COMPLETE FOR HUD/FHA INSURED MORTGAGE ONLY.

(1)   Do you own or have you sold, within the past 12 months, other real estate?   ☐ Yes ☐ No   Is it to be sold? ☐ Yes ☐ No   HUD/FHA Mortgage? ☐ Yes ☐ No   Sales Price $_____   Original Mortgage Amount $_____

Address: _____   Lender: _____

(2)   Have you ever been obligated on a home loan, home improvement loan or a mobile home loan which resulted in foreclosure, transfer of title in lieu of foreclosure or judgment? ☐ Yes ☐ No. If "Yes" give details including date, property address, name and address of lender, FHA or VA Case Number, if any, and reasons for the action.

(3)   If dwelling to be covered by this mortgage is to be rented, is it a part of, adjacent or contiguous to any project, subdivision, or group rental properties involving eight or more dwelling units in which you have any financial interest? ☐ Yes ☐ No ☐ Not to be rented. If "Yes" give details. Do you own four or more dwelling units with mortgages insured under any title of the National Housing Act? ☐ Yes ☐ No. If "Yes" submit form HUD-92561.

31B.   APPLICABLE FOR BOTH VA AND HUD. As a home loan borrower, you will be legally obligated to make the mortgage payments called for by your mortgage loan contract. The fact that you disposed of your property after the loan has been made WILL NOT RELIEVE YOU OF LIABILITY FOR MAKING THESE PAYMENTS. PAYMENT OF THE LOAN IN FULL IS ORDINARILY THE WAY LIABILITY ON A MORTGAGE NOTE IS ENDED.
Some home buyers have the mistaken impression that if they sell their homes when they move to another locality, or dispose of it for any other reasons, they are no longer liable for the mortgage payments and that liability for these payments is solely that of the new owners. Even though the new owners may agree in writing to assume liability for your mortgage payments, this assumption agreement will not relieve you from liability to the holder of the note which you signed when you obtained the loan to buy the property. Also, unless you are able to sell the property to a buyer who is acceptable to the VA or to HUD/FHA and who will assume the payment of your obligation to the lender, you will not be relieved from liability to repay any claim which the VA or HUD/FHA may be required to pay your lender on account of default in your loan payments. The amount of any such claim payment will be a debt owed by you to the Federal Government. This debt will be the object of established collection procedures.

I, THE UNDERSIGNED BORROWER(S) CERTIFY THAT:

(1)   I have read and understand the foregoing concerning my liability on the loan.

(2)   VA Only *(check applicable box)* ☐ Purchase or Construction Loan. I now actually occupy the above-described property as my home or intend to move into and occupy said property as my home within a reasonable period of time. ☐ Home Improvement or Refinancing Loan. I own and personally occupy as my home the property described in Item 7 of the Application.

(3)   Check applicable box *(not applicable for Home Improvement or Refinancing Loan)*, I have been informed that $_____ is ☐ the reasonable value of the property as determined by the VA, ☐ the statement of appraised value as determined by HUD/FHA. IF THE CONTRACT PRICE OR COST EXCEEDS THE VA REASONABLE VALUE OR HUD/FHA STATEMENT OF APPRAISED VALUE, COMPLETE EITHER ITEM (a) or (b), WHICHEVER IS APPLICABLE.

(a) ☐ I was aware of this valuation when I signed my contract and I have paid or will pay in cash from my own resources at or prior to loan closing a sum equal to the difference between the contract purchase price or cost and the VA or HUD/FHA established value. I do not and will not have outstanding after loan closing any unpaid contractual obligation on account of such cash payment;

(b) ☐ I was not aware of this valuation when I signed my contract but have elected to complete the transaction at the contract purchase price or cost. I have paid or will pay in cash from my own resources at or prior to loan closing a sum equal to the difference between contract purchase price or cost and the VA or HUD/FHA established value. I do not and will not have outstanding after loan closing any unpaid contractual obligation on account of such cash payment.

(4)   Neither I, nor anyone authorized to act for me, will refuse to sell or rent, after the making of a bona fide offer, or refuse to negotiate for the sale or rental of, or otherwise make unavailable or deny the dwelling or property covered by this loan to any person because of race, color, religion, sex or national origin. I recognize that any restrictive covenant on this property relating to race, color, religion, sex or national origin is illegal and void and civil action for preventive relief may be brought by the Attorney General of the United States in any appropriate U.S. District Court against any person responsible for the violation of the applicable law.

(5)   The Borrower certifies that all information in this application is given for the purpose of obtaining a loan to be insured under the National Housing Act, or guaranteed by the Veterans Administration and the information in Section II is true and complete to the best of his/her knowledge and belief. Verification may be obtained from any source named herein.

HUD ONLY {
(6)   For properties constructed prior to 1950 - I have received the brochure "Watchout for Lead Paint Poisoning" ☐ ☐ NA

(7)   ☐ I have read and understand the contents of the Home Energy Checklist attached to HUD-92800-4.
}

READ CERTIFICATIONS CAREFULLY - DO NOT SIGN UNLESS APPLICATION IS FULLY COMPLETED.	32. DATE	33. SIGNATURE OF BORROWER(S) *(Before signing, review accuracy of application and certifications.)*

Federal statutes provide severe penalties for any fraud, intentional misrepresentation, or criminal connivance or conspiracy purposed to influence the issuance of any guaranty or insurance by the VA or USDA-FmHA Administrator or the HUD/FHA Commissioner.

liable for the repayment of the mortgage. However, if HUD-FHA feels the buyer is acceptable, then HUD-FHA will release the original borrower/coborrower from the liability for repayment. The borrower is asked to certify that he or she has read and understands the section of the borrower/coborrower liability for repayment of the loan.

Statement 3 under 31B deals with the valuation and sales price. If the sales price is more than the value set by HUD-FHA, the borrower must attest to paying more than the established value and must agree that the difference will be paid in cash.

Next, the borrower/coborrower is asked to certify that renting or selling the property covered by an insured loan will not be denied due to race, creed, religion, sex, or national origin. The final statement is that the borrower/coborrower has made these statements in order to receive a home mortgage insured by the National Housing Act or VA and that the statements are true and complete to the best of his or her knowledge.

After the application is completed, the lender will give page 6 of the form to the borrower (Figure 14-9). The lender will then verify all of the information. Upon receipt of the completed verifications—if the lender feels that the borrower/coborrower and the property meet HUD-FHA requirements—the application, along with all of the necessary supporting documents, may be sent to HUD-FHA for approval. The lender will retain page 8 of the form. After HUD-FHA has reviewed all of the information and approves the application, the mortgage credit section of the HUD-FHA office will send the lender a Certificate of Commitment (Figure 14-10).

You will notice that sections 1 through 6E are identical to those on page 1 of the form. Since this is a multipage carboned form, these sections were filled out at the time the original application was completed.

Just below the first section is the statement where HUD-FHA accepts the note and the mortgage/deed of trust described in the first section, or will accept the note and mortgage/deed of trust as modified. The modifications, if any, are described just below the statement in the box entitled, "Modified and Accepted as Follows."

Another key section of this certificate is the box entitled, "Estimate of Value and Closing Costs." The estimate of value should equal the sales price of the property. Also, the lender will usually supply a copy of the certificate of commitment to the borrower/coborrower.

The VA will use pages 1-3, 6, and 8. Page 1 (Figure 14-7) will be filled out similarly for the VA as it was for HUD-FHA. We will, therefore, only review the differences. First, in the top section of the form, the box indicating that the application is for Home Loan Guaranty will be marked instead of the one indicating mortgage insurance or FmHA-guaranteed loan. The next difference occurs when box 2B is left blank with boxes 1 and 2A completed. Except for boxes 4B and 4C, boxes 3 through 8E are completed as per the discussion above.

Most of section I—Purpose, Amount, Terms of and Security for Proposed Loan—will be completed in the same manner as outlined for HUD-FHA. The one difference is that box 10 instead of box 9B will be completed. In section II, HUD-FHA did not require completing box 19. VA does require this information and will not process the application if this information is missing.

Page 2 of the application (Figure 14-8) has information that is to be filled out if the mortgage is to be guaranteed by the VA. HUD-FHA did not require the lender to complete Section III, but VA does require the lender to make the certifications. This is not signed by the borrower/coborrower.

In section V, Borrowers Certification, the veteran does not complete 31A, but does make the required certifications in 31B; then the borrower/coborrower signs in box 33. You will notice the statement just before box 32 tells the borrower/coborrower to read the certifications carefully and not to sign the applications unless the application is completely filled out.

After the application is completed, the lender will give page 6 to the borrower/coborrower and will retain page 8 since pages 6 and 8 are identical. The remainder of the application, less pages 4 and 5, is then sent along with all of the necessary supporting data to the VA for approval. Upon approval of VA, a completed page 2 (Figure 14-11) will be returned to the lender. Once again we see that the top portion of the Certificate of Commitment was completed at the time the application was completed. The only additional information added by the VA is under the heading, "For VA Use Only." Here, the VA will show the percent of guaranty. This is calculated by dividing $27,500 by the loan amount. For example, the veteran is purchasing a home with a CRV of $84,000. With no money down, the guaranty would be $27,500 divided by $84,000 or 32.7 percent guaranty. Once again the lender will normally give a copy of the certificate of commitment to the

Figure 14–9.   HUD Form 92900, page 6

Form Approved
OMB No. 2900-0144

VA Application for Home Loan Guaranty ☐	USDA-FmHA Application for FmHA Guaranteed Loan ☐	HUD/FHA Application for Commitment for Insurance under the National Housing Act ☐	1. AGENCY CASE NUMBER ▲	2A. LENDER'S CASE NUMBER	2B. SECTION OF THE ACT (HUD Only)

3. NAME AND PRESENT ADDRESS OF BORROWER (Include ZIP Code)	5A. BORROWER: If you do not wish to complete Items 5B or 5C, please initial in the space to the right.	INITIALS

5B. RACE/NATIONAL ORIGIN
▲1 ☐ WHITE, NOT HISPANIC   4 ☐ ASIAN OR PACIFIC ISLANDER
2 ☐ BLACK, NOT HISPANIC   5 ☐ HISPANIC
3 ☐ AMERICAN INDIAN OR ALASKAN NATIVE

5C. SEX
▲1 ☐ MALE
2 ☐ FE-MALE

4A. NAME AND ADDRESS OF LENDER (Include ZIP Code)

6A. SPOUSE OR OTHER BORROWER: If you do not with to complete Items 6B or 6C, please initial in space to the right.   INITIALS

6B. RACE/NATIONAL ORIGIN
▲1 ☐ WHITE, NOT HISPANIC   4 ☐ ASIAN OR PACIFIC ISLANDER
2 ☐ BLACK, NOT HISPANIC   5 ☐ HISPANIC
3 ☐ AMERICAN INDIAN OR ALASKAN NATIVE

6C. SEX
▲1 ☐ MALE
2 ☐ FE-MALE

4B. ORIGINATORS' I.D. (HUD Only)	4C. SPONSOR'S I.D. (HUD Only)

7. PROPERTY ADDRESS INCLUDING NAME OF SUBDIVISION, LOT AND BLOCK NO., AND ZIP CODE	8A. LOAN AMOUNT $	8B. INT. RATE %	8C. PROPOSED MATURITY YRS. MOS.
	DISCOUNT: (Only if borrower to pay) ➤	8D. PERCENT %	8E. AMOUNT $

VA ONLY: Veteran and lender hereby apply to the Administrator of Veterans Affairs for Guaranty of the loan described here under Section 1810, Chapter 37, Title 38, United States Code to the full extent permitted by the veteran's entitlement and severally agree that the Regulations promulgated pursuant to Chapter 37, and in effect on the date of the loan shall govern the rights, duties, and liabilities of the parties.
HUD/FHA ONLY: Mortgagee's application for mortgagor approval and commitment for mortgage insurance under the National Housing Act.

SECTION I - PURPOSE, AMOUNT, TERMS OF AND SECURITY FOR PROPOSED LOAN

9A. PURPOSE OF LOAN – TO:			9B. HUD ONLY – BORROWER WILL BE	10. VA ONLY – TITLE WILL BE VESTED IN:
▲1 ☐ PURCHASE EXISTING HOUSE PREVIOUSLY OCCUPIED	4 ☐ PURCHASE NEW CONDO. UNIT	7 ☐ CONSTRUCT A HOME - PROCEEDS TO BE PAID OUT DURING CONSTRUCTION	▲1 ☐ OCCUPANT 5 ☐ ESCROW COMMITMENT	☐ VETERAN ☐ VETERAN AND SPOUSE
2 ☐ FINANCE IMPROVEMENTS TO EXISTING PROPERTY	5 ☐ PURCHASE EXISTING CONDO. UNIT	8 ☐ HUD ONLY – FINANCE COOP-PURCHASE	2 ☐ LANDLORD 3 ☐ BUILDER	☐ OTHER (Specify)
3 ☐ REFINANCE	6 ☐ PURCHASE EXISTING HOME NOT PREVIOUSLY OCCUPIED		4 ☐ OPERATIVE BUILDER	

11. LIEN: ☐ FIRST MORTGAGE ☐ OTHER (Specify)	12. ESTATE WILL BE: ☐ FEE SIMPLE ☐ LEASEHOLD (Show expiration date)	13. IS THERE A MANDATORY HOMEOWNERS ASSOC.? ☐ YES ☐ NO (If "Yes," complete Item 14F.)

14. ESTIMATED TAXES, INSURANCE AND ASSESSMENTS		15. ESTIMATED MONTHLY PAYMENT	
A. ANNUAL TAXES		A. PRINCIPAL AND INTEREST	$
B. AMOUNT OF HAZARD INSURANCE ON SECURITY	$	B. TAXES AND INSURANCE DEPOSITS	
C. ANNUAL HAZARD INSURANCE PREMIUM		C. OTHER	
D. ANNUAL SPECIAL ASSESSMENT PAYMENT			
E. UNPAID SPECIAL ASSESSMENT BALANCE			
F. ANNUAL MAINTENANCE ASSESSMENT		TOTAL	$

SECTION II - PERSONAL AND FINANCIAL STATUS OF APPLICANT

16. PLEASE CHECK APPROPRIATE BOX(ES). IF ONE OR MORE ARE CHECKED, ITEMS 18B, 21, 22 AND 23 MUST INCLUDE INFORMATION CONCERNING BORROWER'S SPOUSE (or former spouse if box "D" is checked). IF NO BOXES ARE CHECKED, NO INFORMATION CONCERNING THE SPOUSE NEED BE FURNISHED IN ITEMS 18B, 21, 22 AND 23.

A. ☐ THE SPOUSE WILL BE JOINTLY OBLIGATED WITH THE BORROWER ON THE LOAN.
B. ☐ THE BORROWER IS RELYING ON THE SPOUSE'S INCOME AS A BASIS FOR REPAYMENT OF THE LOAN.
C. ☐ THE BORROWER IS MARRIED AND THE PROPERTY TO SECURE THE LOAN IS LOCATED IN A COMMUNITY PROPERTY STATE.
D. ☐ THE BORROWER IS RELYING ON ALIMONY, CHILD SUPPORT, OR SEPARATE MAINTENANCE PAYMENTS FROM A SPOUSE OR FORMER SPOUSE AS A BASIS FOR REPAYMENT OF THE LOAN.

17A. MARITAL STATUS OF BORROWER ▲	17B. MARITAL STATUS OF COBORROWER OTHER THAN SPOUSE ▲	17C. MONTHLY CHILD SUPPORT OBLIGATION	17D. MONTHLY ALIMONY OBLIGATION	18A. AGE OF BORROWER	18B. AGE OF SPOUSE OR COBORROWER	18C. AGE(S) OF DEPENDENT(S)
1 ☐ MARRIED 3 ☐ UNMARRIED 2 ☐ SEPARATED	1 ☐ MARRIED 3 ☐ UNMARRIED 2 ☐ SEPARATED	$	$			

19. NAME AND ADDRESS OF NEAREST LIVING RELATIVE (Include telephone number, if available).	20A. CURRENT MONTHLY HOUSING EXPENSE $	20B. UTILITIES INCLUDED? ☐ YES ☐ NO

21. ASSETS		22. LIABILITIES (Itemize all debts)		
		NAME OF CREDITOR	MO. PAYMENT	BALANCE
A. CASH (Including deposit on purchase)	$			
B. SAVINGS BONDS - OTHER SECURITIES			$	$
C. REAL ESTATE OWNED				
D. AUTO				
E. FURNITURE AND HOUSEHOLD GOODS				
F. OTHER (Use separate sheet, if necessary)		JOB-RELATED EXPENSE (Specify)		
G. TOTAL	$	TOTAL	$	$

23. INCOME AND OCCUPATIONAL STATUS			24. ESTIMATED TOTAL COST	
ITEM	BORROWER	SPOUSE OR COBORROWER	ITEM	AMOUNT
A. OCCUPATION			A. PURCHASE EXISTING HOME	$
			B. ALTERATIONS, IMPROVEMENTS, REPAIRS	
B. NAME OF EMPLOYER			C. CONSTRUCTION	
			D. LAND (If acquired separately)	
C. NUMBER OF YEARS EMPLOYED			E. PURCHASE OF CONDOMINIUM UNIT	
			F. REFINANCE	
D. GROSS PAY	▲MONTHLY $ HOURLY $	▲MONTHLY $ HOURLY $	G. PREPAID ITEMS	
			H. ESTIMATED CLOSING COSTS	
E. OTHER INCOME (Disclosure of child support, alimony and separate maintenance income is optional.)	MONTHLY $	MONTHLY $	I. DISCOUNT (Only if borrower permitted to pay)	
			J. TOTAL COSTS (Add Items 24A through 24I)	
			K. LESS CASH FROM BORROWER	
NOTE — If land acquired by separate transaction, complete Items 25A and 25B.			L. LESS OTHER CREDITS	
25A. DATE ACQUIRED	25B. UNPAID BALANCE $		M. AMOUNT OF LOAN	$

VA FORM 26-1802a, JAN 1982
HUD FORM 92900.6

SUPERSEDES VA FORM 26-1802a, APR 1979, WHICH WILL NOT BE USED.
HUD FORM 92900, JUL 1980, MAY BE USED FOR HUD PURPOSES.

DELIVER TO BORROWER - COPY 6

Figure 14–10. *HUD Certificate of Commitment sent to lender*

CERTIFICATE OF COMMITMENT (FOR HUD INSURED MORTGAGE)	1. AGENCY CASE NUMBER	2A. LENDER'S CASE NUMBER	2B. SECTION OF THE ACT *(HUD Only)*

3. NAME AND PRESENT ADDRESS OF BORROWER *(Include ZIP Code)*

4A. NAME AND ADDRESS OF LENDER *(Include ZIP Code)*

4B. ORIGINATOR'S I.D.   4C. SPONSOR'S I.D.

5. PROPERTY ADDRESS INCLUDING NAME OF SUBDIVISION, LOT AND BLOCK NO., AND ZIP CODE

6A. LOAN AMOUNT	6B. INT. RATE	6C. PROPOSED MATURITY
$	%	YRS. MOS.

DISCOUNT: *(Only if borrower to pay)* ➔   6D. PERCENT %   6E. AMOUNT $

☐ **ACCEPTED:** A note and mortgage described above or as modified below will be insured under the National Housing Act provided one of the mortgagors will be an owner-occupant and all conditions appearing in any outstanding commitment issued under the above case number and those set forth below are fulfilled.

IMPROVED FLOOR AREA = _____ square feet.

☐ MODIFIED AND ACCEPTED AS FOLLOWS	Mortgage Amount $	Interest Rate %	No. of Months	Monthly Payment $

ESTIMATE OF VALUE AND CLOSING COSTS

ADDITIONAL CONDITIONS

☐ 2544 - Builders warranty required.   ☐ Owner-occupancy NOT required. *(Delete (b) - Mtgrs. Cert.)*

☐ The property is to be insured under Section 221(d)(2); a code compliance inspection is required.

VALUE OF PROPERTY $_____

Closing Costs $_____

This is to certify, in compliance with the Right to Financial Privacy Act of 1978, that, in connection with any subsequent request for access to financial records for the purpose of considering or administering assistance to this applicant, the Department of Housing and Urban Development is in compliance with the applicable provisions of said Act.

DATE OF THIS COMMITMENT:

THIS COMMITMENT EXPIRES:

_____, 19 ____

_____ , 19   _____   _____
(Expiration Date)   *(Authorized Agent for the Federal Housing Commissioner)*   *(Field Office)*

INSTRUCTIONS TO MORTGAGEE - Forward to the HUD Field Office; (1) this commitment signed by the mortgagee and mortgagor; (2) a copy of the note or other credit instrument; (3) a copy of the mortgage or other security instrument; (4) a copy of the settlement statement, *(Form HUD-1)* signed by the mortgagee which itemizes all charges and fees collected by the mortgagee from the mortgagor and seller; and (5) HUD/FHA Mortgage Insurance Certificate completed with case number, Section of the National Housing Act, mortgage amount, property address, mortgagors' names and mortgagee's name and address. Attach Form HUD-92900 Supplement.

HUD 92900.4, JAN 1982   LENDER COPY 4

Figure 14–11.   VA Certificate of Commitment sent to lender

CERTIFICATE OF COMMITMENT (FOR VA LOAN GUARANTY)	1. AGENCY CASE NUMBER	2A. LENDER'S CASE NUMBER	2B. SECTION OF THE ACT (HUD Only)

3. NAME AND PRESENT ADDRESS OF BORROWER *(Include ZIP Code)*

4. NAME AND ADDRESS OF LENDER *(Include ZIP Code)*

5. PROPERTY ADDRESS INCLUDING NAME OF SUBDIVISION, LOT AND BLOCK NO., AND ZIP CODE	6A. LOAN AMOUNT $	6B. INT. RATE %	6C. PROPOSED MATURITY YRS. MOS.
	DISCOUNT: *(Only if borrower to pay)* ➡	6D. PERCENT %	6E. AMOUNT $

FOR VA USE ONLY *(To be completed by VA and returned to lender.)*

PERCENT OF GUARANTY %	CERTIFICATION OF ACTIVE DUTY STATUS AS OF DATE OF NOTE REQUIRED ☐ *(Applicable if checked)*

TERMS OF COMMITMENT

The documents submitted in connection with the loan described above on this certificate have been examined and the loan has been determined to be eligible under Chapter 37, Title 38, U.S.C., and the regulations effective thereunder.

Upon receipt of a duly executed "Certificate of Loan Disbursement"* showing full compliance with the applicable regulations, the Administrator will issue: A Loan Guaranty Certificate as indicated above on this Certificate; subject to any adjustment necessary under Section 36:4303(g) of the Regulations upon ascertainment of the exact principal amount of the loan, or upon submission of the loan disbursement report under Section 36:4305 thereof.

In the case of a joint loan as defined in Section 36:4307 of the Regulations the portion of such loan eligible for guaranty shall be as provided therein.

This Certificate of Commitment will expire and will be invalid 6 months from the date hereof, unless the loan described herein is closed prior to such expiration date.

*If the loan described above on this Certificate is made by the lending institution named herein this certificate need not be returned to the VA. Otherwise this certificate or a copy of the agreement assigning this certificate must accompany the Certificate of Loan Disbursement.

ADMINISTRATOR OF VETERANS AFFAIRS, BY *(Authorized Agent)*	ISSUING OFFICE	DATE

VA FORM
JAN 1982   **26-1866a**   LENDER COPY 2

borrower/coborrower. It is a good policy, though, to remind the borrower/coborrower to get a copy of this commitment.

VERIFICATION FORMS

As with the application forms, various lenders have forms to verify employment, income, deposits, mortgage loan payments, rental history, and credit. In this discussion we will examine those forms approved or authorized by Fannie Mae/FHLMC, FHA, and VA.

Verification of Employment and Income

Fannie Mae Form 1005, Request for Verification of Employment, is illustrated in Figure 14–12. The form is divided into three sections. The first section is to be completed by the lender. This section is usually completed at the time of application and is signed by the applicant. Normally the lender will have the applicant sign several of the forms, just in case the original form that is sent to the employer is lost. The second section of the form is to be completed by the present employer. The employer states that the applicant or co-applicant is still in his employment. You will notice that part II of Figure 14–12 is divided into two parts: employment record and pay data. As mentioned in Chapter 13, line 13 of the employment section inquires about the existence of overtime and/or bonuses, and, if they are paid, what the likelihood is of their continuance in the future. Part III of the form, Verification of Previous Employment, is to be filled out by the employer only if the person signing the request is no longer an employee. This form will be forwarded directly to the employer and upon its completion the employer will return the completed form directly to the lender. Do not ask the lender if you can hand carry the verification to help speed up approval; the statement at the bottom specifies that the form must be transmitted directly to the lender without passing through the hands of the applicant or any other party.

The second employment verification form to be reviewed is the one used by both FHA and VA, illustrated in Figure 14–13. This form is divided into four sections and requests basically the same information as the Fannie Mae form. There is one major difference and that is item 3, where FHA and VA require the lender to certify that the verification was sent directly to the employer and has not passed through the hands of any other party. As with the Fannie Mae form, the FHA/VA form part I is completed at the time of application and signed by the applicant.

Verification of Bank Accounts and Loans

Fannie Mae Form 1006, Request for Verification of Deposit, is shown in Figure 14–14. This form is divided into two sections. The first section is completed by the lender from information supplied by the applicant and is signed by the applicant, authorizing the financial institution to release the information to the lender. The second section of the form is to be completed by the financial institution. The financial institution is asked to give information about the deposit accounts and outstanding loans of the applicant. In the section dealing with deposit accounts, the financial institution is asked to give the current balance and also the average balance for the previous two months. There is reason for such a request. For example, if the present balance in the account is $10,000 and the average balance for the previous two months has been only $3000, the lender will ask the applicant to explain the reason for the radical increase. The applicant can do this by writing a source of funds letter. A sample of such a letter will be given later, in Figure 14–18. In item 12a, the institution is asked to give any additional information that may aid the lender in determining the credit worthiness of the applicant. This should include information about loans which have been paid in full.

The FHA/VA form entitled "Request for Verification of Deposit," Figure 14–15, requests similar information as the Fannie Mae form, but once again the form is somewhat different. As with the employment verification form, the lender is once again required to certify that the verification was sent directly to the bank and that the form did not pass through the hands of the applicant or any other interested party.

Mortgage Verification and/or Rental Verification

If the applicant has made mortgage payments, the lender will wish to verify the mortgage as to the type of mortgage, the original date and amount of the mortgage, and the payment record of the applicant. If the applicant and/or coapplicant have rented previously, the lender will verify with the landlord, rental agent, or manager of the property the dates of the rental period and the manner of payment of the applicant or coapplicant. An example of a

Figure 14-12.   Fannie Mae Request for Verification of Employment

Federal National Mortgage Association

REQUEST FOR VERIFICATION OF EMPLOYMENT

INSTRUCTIONS: LENDER- Complete items 1 thru 7. Have applicant complete item 8. Forward directly to employer named in item 1.

EMPLOYER-Please complete either Part II or Part III as applicable. Sign and return directly to lender named in item 2.

PART I · REQUEST

1. TO (Name and address of employer)	2. FROM (Name and address of lender)		
3. SIGNATURE OF LENDER	4. TITLE	5. DATE	6. LENDER'S NUMBER (optional)

I have applied for a mortgage loan and stated that I am now or was formerly employed by you. My signature below authorizes verification of this information.

7. NAME AND ADDRESS OF APPLICANT (Include employee or badge number)	8. SIGNATURE OF APPLICANT

PART II · VERIFICATION OF PRESENT EMPLOYMENT

EMPLOYMENT DATA	PAY DATA		
9. APPLICANT'S DATE OF EMPLOYMENT	12A. CURRENT BASE PAY (Enter Amount and Check Period) ☐ ANNUAL ☐ HOURLY ☐ MONTHLY ☐ OTHER $ _____ ☐ WEEKLY (Specify)	12C. FOR MILITARY PERSONNEL ONLY	
		PAY GRADE	

10. PRESENT POSITION	12B. EARNINGS			TYPE	MONTHLY AMOUNT
	TYPE	YEAR TO DATE	PAST YEAR	BASE PAY	$
11. PROBABILITY OF CONTINUED EMPLOYMENT	BASE PAY	$	$	RATIONS	$
13. IF OVERTIME OR BONUS IS APPLICABLE, IS ITS CONTINUANCE LIKELY?	OVERTIME	$	$	FLIGHT OR HAZARD	$
				CLOTHING	$
	COMMISSIONS	$	$	QUARTERS	$
OVERTIME ☐ YES ☐ NO BONUS ☐ YES ☐ NO	BONUS	$	$	PRO PAY	$
				OVER SEAS OR COMBAT	$

14. REMARKS (if paid hourly, please indicate average hours worked each week during current and past year)

PART III · VERIFICATION OF PREVIOUS EMPLOYMENT

15. DATES OF EMPLOYMENT	16. SALARY/WAGE AT TERMINATION PER (Year) (Month) (Week) BASE _____ OVERTIME _____ COMMISSIONS _____ BONUS _____
17. REASON FOR LEAVING	18. POSITION HELD

19. SIGNATURE OF EMPLOYER	20. TITLE	21. DATE

The confidentiality of the information you have furnished will be preserved except where disclosure of this information is required by applicable law. The form is to be transmitted directly to the lender and is not to be transmitted through the applicant or any other party.

PREVIOUS EDITION WILL BE USED UNTIL STOCK IS EXHAUSTED

FNMA Form 1005
Rev. June 78

Figure 14–13.   *FHA/VA Request for Verification of Employment*

Figure 14–14.   Fannie Mae Request for Verification of Deposit

Figure 14–15. FHA/VA Request for Verification of Deposit

Form Approved
OMB No. 63R-1062

VETERANS ADMINISTRATION AND U.S. DEPARTMENT OF HOUSING AND URBAN DEVELOPMENT
HUD COMMUNITY PLANNING AND DEVELOPMENT
HUD HOUSING - FEDERAL HOUSING COMMISSIONER
REQUEST FOR VERIFICATION OF DEPOSIT

PRIVACY ACT NOTICE STATEMENT - This information is to be used by the agency collecting it in determining whether you qualify as a prospective mortgagor for mortgage insurance or guaranty or as a borrower for a rehabilitation loan under the agency's program. It will not be disclosed outside the agency without your consent except to financial institutions for verification of your deposits and as required and permitted by law. You do not have to give us this information, but, if you do not, your application for approval as a prospective mortgagor for mortgage insurance or guaranty or as a borrower for a rehabilitation loan may be delayed or rejected. This information request is authorized by Title 38, U.S.C., Chapter 37 *(if VA)*; by 12 U.S.C., Section 1701 et seq., *(if HUD/FHA)*; and by 42 U.S.C., Section 1452b *(if HUD/CPD)*.

INSTRUCTIONS

LENDER OR LOCAL PROCESSING AGENCY: Complete Items 1 through 8. Have applicant(s) complete Item 9. Forward directly to the Depository named in Item 1. DEPOSITORY: Please complete Items 10 through 15 and return DIRECTLY to Lender or Local Processing Agency named in Item 2.

PART I - REQUEST

1. TO *(Name and Address of Depository)*	2. FROM *(Name and Address of Lender or Local Processing Agency)*

I certify that this verification has been sent directly to the bank or depository and has not passed through the hands of the applicant or any other party.

3. Signature of Lender or Official of Local Processing Agency	4. Title	5. Date	6. Lender's Number *(Optional)*

7. INFORMATION TO BE VERIFIED

Type of Account and/or Loan	Account/Loan in Name of	Account/Loan Number	Balance
			$
			$
			$
			$

TO DEPOSITORY: I have applied for mortgage insurance or guaranty or for a rehabilitation loan and stated that the balance on deposit and/or outstanding loans with you are as shown above. You are authorized to verify this information and to supply the lender or the local processing agency identified above with the information requested in Items 10 through 12. Your response is solely a matter of courtesy for which no responsibility is attached to your institution or any of your officers.

8. NAME AND ADDRESS OF APPLICANT(S)	9. SIGNATURE OF APPLICANT(S)

TO BE COMPLETED BY DEPOSITORY

PART II - VERIFICATION OF DEPOSITORY

10. DEPOSIT ACCOUNTS OF APPLICANT(S)

Type of Account	Account Number	Current Balance	Average Balance for Previous Two Months	Date Opened
		$	$	
		$	$	
		$	$	
		$	$	

11. LOANS OUTSTANDING TO APPLICANT(S)

Loan Number	Date of Loan	Original Amount	Current Balance	Installments (Monthly/Quarterly)	Secured by	Number of Late Payments within Last 12 Months
		$	$	$ per		
		$	$	$ per		
		$	$	$ per		

12. ADDITIONAL INFORMATION WHICH MAY BE OF ASSISTANCE IN DETERMINATION OF CREDIT WORTHINESS: *Please include information on loans paid-in-full as in Item 11 above)*

13. Signature of Depository Official	14. Title	15. Date

The confidentiality of the information you have furnished will be preserved except where disclosure of this information is required by applicable law. The completed form is to be transmitted directly to the lender or local processing agency and is not to be transmitted through the applicant or any other party.

Replaces Form FHA-2004-F, which is Obsolete

VA 26-8497a/HUD-92004-F-6234 (7-80)

Figure 14-16.   Mortgage Verification Form

MORTGAGE VERIFICATION

APPLICANT _____   ADDRESS _____
CO-APPLICANT _____   ADDRESS _____
LOAN NUMBER _____   DATE _____

Since the previous/present mortgagor has applied for a new loan through this company, the current status of the mortgage on the subject property is required. We will appreciate your answering the questions listed below Please return this letter in the enclosed self-addressed envelope provided.

As per your request, the following information is furnished in strict confidence and is not to be construed as a pay-off figure.

Approved:
Applicant _____   Co-applicant _____

Yours very truly
Loan Processor

1. Original Mortgagor _____   Date of Mortgage _____
2. Original Amount and Term: $ _____   Years _____
3. Type of Mortgage: Conv _____   VA _____   FHA _____
4. Present Unpaid Balance: $ _____ ; Payment Experience:
             Prompt _____   Slow _____   Unsatisfactory _____

   If the above loan is an FHA or VA loan now owned by persons other than above, please give the following information:

5. Date of Assumption _____   Name of Assumptor _____
6. Payment experience of the assumptor _____
7. Status of Loan _____

Date _____

_____
Mortgagee

_____
Signature and Title

Source: Mercantile Mortgage Corporation of Texas, Houston, Texas

mortgage verification letter is shown in Figure 14-16 and a sample rental verification letter is shown in Figure 14-17.

Credit Verification

The credit of an applicant is verified by the lender by ordering a credit report from the local credit-reporting agency as was discussed in Chapter 13. The report will give the applicant's payment history on accounts or loans held by members of the credit-reporting agency. By federal law, the applicant and coapplicant are not allowed to view their credit reports furnished to the mortgage lender. It should also be noted that if the lender rejects the application and it, along with all of the supporting data, is transferred to another mortgage lender, the credit report may not be transferred and a new report will have to be ordered from the credit-reporting agency. If the applicant or coapplicant wishes to inquire

into his or her credit, he must go personally to the credit reporting agency and request to view the information contained in his file. The applicant or coapplicant will not be allowed to view the actual file, but will be able to see an abstract of the information in the file. The cost of these reports is usually paid by the applicant or coapplicant.

Source of Funds Letter

As mentioned earlier in the section on bank account verification, if the balance in a checking or savings account has had a marked increase in the past two months, the lender may request that the applicant or coapplicant furnish information as to the source of funds for the increase. If the source of funds is the sale of property, the applicant and coapplicant must supply a letter stating the source and furnish a copy of the settlement statement covering the transfer of the property. An

Figure 14–17.   Rental Verification Form

RENTAL VERIFICATION

APPLICANT _____   ADDRESS _____

CO-APPLICANT _____   ADDRESS _____

The above mentioned persons have applied for a new mortgage through this mortgage company, and have indicated that they have been a renter/leaser from your organization.

We would appreciate your answering the questions listed below and returning the same to us in the self-addressed envelope provided. Your prompt consideration to this matter will be greatly appreciated.

Approved:

APPLICANT _____   CO-APPLICANT _____

DATE _____   DATE _____

_____

As per your request, the following information is furnished:

1. How long has the applicant/co-applicant been renting _____, leasing _____?

2. Amount of monthly rent $_____   Does this rent or lease payment include utilities?
    Yes _____   No _____

3. Manner of payment:
                     Prompt_____   Slow _____   Unsatisfactory _____

Date _____   _____
                                   Manager/Landlord

Source: Mercantile Mortgage Corporation of Texas, Houston, Texas

---

example of such a letter is shown in Figure 14–18.

If the additional funds were derived from a gift, then the lender may ask the applicant or coapplicant to furnish a letter stating that the money deposited was a gift and the giver does not expect the funds to be repaid. A form for such a letter is shown in Figure 14–19.

LOAN PACKAGING OR COLLATION

After the loan application is completed and the supporting documents that will accompany the application are received, the mortgage lender will then start to gather the information required for underwriting. This collection of information is sometimes referred to as *loan packaging*. The loan package required by lenders will vary, but in the following section we will review some of the standard items that can make up a loan package.

Conventional Loan Packaging

Since many conventional lenders have their own requirements, any of the following items may be included in the conventional loan package.

1. Submission letter (This is a cover letter outlining the items enclosed in the loan package. Usually, the letter will outline the terms and loan-to-value ratio of the mortgage. If the mortgage is one to be purchased by Fannie Mae, they require a form entitled Transmittal Summary, in place of the submission letter.)

2. Loan application

3. Standard factual credit report (This credit report should be current. Many lenders require the report to be less than ninety days old and provided by an approved credit-reporting agency. Many lenders,

Figure 14–18.   Source of Funds Letter

```
                          EXAMPLE

                   SOURCE OF FUNDS LETTER



                           Date



XYZ Mortgage Company
123 Main Street
Houston, Texas 77001


Gentlemen:
     This is to certify that the $11,500.00 that I have deposited
to our account at the First State Bank of Bellaire, Bellaire,
Texas, was recently deposited.  This money was realized from the
sale of my home located at 3456 Limping Lane, La Grange, Texas.
This sale was closed on February 15, 1982 at American Title,
La Grange, Texas.  A copy of the closing statement is attached.


                           Sincerely,


Applicant_____    Co-applicant_____
```

Source: Mortgage Bankers Association of America, Washington, D.C.

Figure 14–19.   Gift Letter and Receipt Acknowledgment

EXAMPLE

<u>GIFT LETTER</u>

To Whom it may concern:

I,_____, do hereby certify that I have made a
gift of $_____ to my <u>(relationship)</u>, to be used
for the purchase of the property located at_____.

I hereby further certify there is no repayment expected or implied
on this gift either in the form of cash or services in the future
from<u>   (applicant)   </u> or <u>   (co-applicant)   </u>.

Date_____   _____
                                        Donor

<u>RECEIPT ACKNOWLEDGEMENT</u>

We or I _____, _____ hereby
certify that we or I have received a gift in the amount of $_____
_____ from _____ my <u>(relationship)</u>
and that it is to be applied toward the purchase of the property
located at _____.

Date_____   _____
                                        Applicant

                           _____
                                        Co-applicant

Source: Mortgage Bankers Association of America, Washington, D.C.

including Fannie Mae/FHLMC, FHA, and VA, have a list of approved credit-reporting agencies. It should be noted that if the credit report is from an agency that is not approved by the lender, the loan package may be rejected or the lender will order a credit report from the approved agency. In either case, processing or approval time will be increased.)

4. Verification of deposits

5. Verification of employment

6. If the applicant is self-employed, the following information will be supplied in lieu of the verification of employment:

   a. Business credit report

   b. Signed federal income tax returns for the past two years

   c. If available, an audited profit-and-loss statement and balance sheets for the past two years

7. Verification of previous mortgage and payment record or rental verification with payment record

8. Property appraisal on the lender's approved form

9. Floor plan and plot sketch

10. Photographs of the property. (Many lenders require several pictures of the property showing the front, back, and a view looking both ways from the front.)

11. A copy of the earnest money contract

12. If PMI is required by the lender, a copy of the PMI commitment

Federal Housing Administration Loan Packaging

An FHA loan package may include the following items:

1. Loan application, page 1 of FHA Form 92900

2. The conditional commitment, FHA Form 92800, page 5

3. A copy of the earnest money contract

4. A credit report which is less than 90 days old from an FHA-approved credit reporting agency

5. Verification of employment

6. Verification of deposits

7. Other documents that may be included:

   a. Source of funds letter

   b. Gift letter

   c. If the applicant is self-employed, a business credit report, signed federal income tax returns for the past two years and, if available, profit-and-loss statement and balance sheets for the current period of operation

   d. A letter from the mortgage company or lender explaining or giving support to the application for mortgage insurance

Veterans Administration Loan Packaging

A VA loan package may include the following items:

1. Transmittal letter, outlining the loan and the documents that are included in the package (In some areas, the VA guaranty section requires that the documents be in a specific order.)

2. Certificate of Eligibility

3. Loan application, VA Form 26-1802a

4. Copy of the earnest money contract

5. Credit report from an approved credit-reporting agency

6. Verification of employment

7. Verification of deposits

8. A copy of the Certificate of Reasonable Value, VA Form 26-1843

9. Borrower's statement of liability (This is a statement signed by the veteran stating that if the VA approves the application for home loan guaranty, the veteran is obligated to repay the mortgage.)

Once the loan package is completed, the next step is for the package to be forwarded to the lender for underwriting, or if the originating mortgage company or financial institution has the ability or authority, the loan package will be approved or underwritten by the originator.

LOAN UNDERWRITING OR APPROVAL

Loan underwriting is the analysis or evaluation of the risk involved with a loan and matching the risk to the proper return.

Areas of Concern

Many lenders now use the concept that the property is the primary concern in the underwriting process. The reason for this was the introduction of the long-term self-amortizing mortgage. Many lenders use the theory; if the borrower defaults, will we be able to sell the property for a sufficient amount to recapture the amount of the mortgage? But it should be noted that the borrower is still of concern to the lender. This analysis of the risk is sometimes referred to as the analysis of the "Four Cs": character, capacity, capital, and collateral. One can see that the majority of the Four Cs relate to the applicant and the final C relates to the property. Let us examine the Four Cs.

Character   This is an analysis of the applicant and coapplicant's trustworthiness, their reputations, and most of all, their demonstration to meet their financial obligations. The lender uses the credit report and the verification of payment record on the previous mortgage or payment of rent as a good indicator of a person's sense of obligation. If the person is self-employed, the lender will review the payment record of the applicant or coapplicant in relation to the financial obligation of the business. Lenders will take note of whether the applicant or coapplicant will pay himself or herself first and let the obligation of the company go without payment.

Capacity   This is the analysis of the earning ability of the applicant or coapplicant. In this analysis, the lender will look not only at the present earning ability, but will try to evaluate the future capability of the applicants. The lender will take into consideration the training, educational experiences, and need for the skills possessed by the applicants. For example, if

the applicant is a master plumber, the lender is somewhat assured that the applicant's skills will be in demand in the future.

Capital   This analysis looks at the cash and assets of the applicant and coapplicant, in particular to see if the assets of the applicant and coapplicant exceed the liabilities. In addition, some lenders take into consideration the type of assets owned and, if the applicant and coapplicant need to sell any of these assets, how quickly can they be converted to cash.

Collateral   The last of the Four Cs is the property that will be used to secure the mortgage. As stated earlier in this section, many lenders place more emphasis on this aspect of underwriting. Here the underwriter will review the property as to location, neighborhood, supply and demand in the area, construction, and marketability in case of foreclosure. The underwriter will take into consideration the purchase price of the property in relationship to the average sales price for other properties in the area. If the applicant is marginal, but is buying the property several thousand dollars below the average sales price in the area, the lender may look favorably upon the application and approve the loan.

How Loans Are Underwritten

Because loan underwriting has been discussed in an earlier chapter, this will be a brief review.

Mortgage companies   Usually these types of lenders do not have the ability to approve or underwrite mortgages. They usually process the mortgage and after the packaging of the mortgage, review the information. If they feel the application meets the underwriting requirements of the investor, the package will be sent to the investor for approval. It should be noted that through a delegated underwriter program some mortgage companies have the ability to give in-house approval on conventional loans. If the mortgage is to be either insured by FHA or guaranteed by VA, once again the lenders will process the application, and if the mortgage company feels the application meets the underwriting guidelines of FHA or VA, the package may be forwarded to the nearest insuring office of FHA or the loan guaranty section of the nearest VA office. Some of the underwriting guidelines of Fannie Mae/FHLMC, FHA, and VA have been discussed in Chapter 3.

Regulated lenders   These types of lenders are regulated by an agency of either the federal government or a state government. These lenders in some cases have the ability to give in-house approval on loans insured by FHA or guaranteed by VA. If the institution (such as a savings and loan association) has this ability, then after the loan application is completed, after all of the supporting documents are received, and after the S and L feels that the mortgage meets the underwriting requirements of either FHA or VA, the institution may approve the application and FHA or VA must either issue the insurance or the guaranty on the mortgage. Usually the institution is more strict than FHA or VA. If the mortgage is borderline, it will normally be forwarded to FHA or VA for approval. In regard to conventional mortgages, if the institution is lending its own funds, it will approve or disapprove the loan upon the packaging of the materials and the submitting of the loan package to the loan committee. This committee usually meets once a week to review all of the completed and packaged loans and to approve or disapprove them. If the mortgage is to be sold to Fannie Mae, the mortgage will be approved in-house. Once again, all mortgages that are sold to Fannie Mae will have to be approved by the loan committee.

REVIEW QUESTIONS

1. Define the term *underwriting*.

2. Explain the first step in loan processing.

3. Outline the information that a lender may wish to verify.

4. Outline the major sections of the Fannie Mae, FHA, and VA loan applications.

5. Outline the provisions of the Real Estate Settlement Procedures Act regarding the taking of loan applications.

6. Outline some of the information a lender may not ask at the time of loan application.

15 Loan Closing

LEARNING OBJECTIVES

In this chapter we will examine the process of concluding the real estate transaction. This process is sometimes referred to as the *closing* or *loan closing*.

Upon completion of this chapter, you should be able to do the following:

★ Outline the requirements of the Real Estate Settlement Procedures Act in regard to loan closing.

★ Outline the procedures in closing after the approval of the property and the borrower.

★ Describe the basic closing requirements of the mortgage lender.

★ List some of the basic closing costs.

★ Complete the HUD Form 1

DEFINITION

Loan closing can be defined as the conclusion of the real estate transaction. This conclusion can include any of the following: the delivery of a deed, the transfer of title to real property through a tax free exchange, or the signing of a note and deed of trust by the purchaser/borrower.

Our discussion of the closing process will only reflect actions taken if the purchase of the property is to be financed by someone other than the purchaser—normally a mortgage lender.

OVERVIEW OF THE CLOSING PROCESS

All parties to the transaction—buyer, seller, buyer's agent, seller's agent, and the person who will conduct the closing—usually meet and exchange the necessary documents to insure the speedy and legal transfer of the title of the subject property. The agent for the buyer or seller can either be the real estate broker who represented the party in the negotiation of the earnest money contract or an attorney. In Texas the transfer agency or escrow agent is a title company. Usually, the title company that conducts the closing will issue the title policy on the property. In most cases, the title company will not charge a fee to conduct the closing. The title company that handles the closing will also have been the escrow agent listed in the earnest money contract.

The final step in closing after all of the documents have been signed by all of the parties is the *funding* of the transaction. In funding, the buyer delivers to the seller the money or additional money that will equal the price for the property agreed upon in the earnest money contract. The money can be in the form of a cashier's check from the buyer (if the buyer has sufficient funds to pay cash for the property) or in the form of a check from the mortgage lender to whom the buyer made application and was approved. If this latter method is the case, the buyer will have addi-

407

tional documents to execute and to have acknowledged. Some of these additional documents will be reviewed later in this chapter.

In regard to the actual funding of the transaction, there are two basic methods: table funding and funding at a later date.

Table Funding

Table funding is the receiving of funds at the time of closing, or "at the table," by all parties to the transaction who are to receive funds. This means that the closing agent will have all of the checks prepared for the title insurance, the inspections, the attorneys who have drawn the papers, and most important, the real estate firms involved in the transaction. For table funding to occur, all of the documents in the transaction, all of the instructions supplied by either the mortgage lender or the taxing authorities, and any other documents and items that could affect the title to the property must be in order.

Funding at a Later Date

Funding at a later date refers to a transaction that will not be funded until a specific date or after some specific actions have been taken. Usually the reason for funding at a later date is that the mortgage lender wishes to review the completed closing package or wants to review all of the documents involved in the transaction. This can take as little as 24-hours from the time the completed loan package is delivered to the mortgage lender or as long as months, but the lender usually will fund the mortgage in 48 hours after the package is received, if all of the documents are in order. We will review later in the chapter the mortgage lender's instructions and mortgage package.

REAL ESTATE SETTLEMENT PROCEDURES ACT (RESPA)

As mentioned in the last chapter, the Real Estate Settlement Procedures Act (RESPA) was passed to standardize the settlement or closing of real estate transactions, and in that chapter we saw how the law affects the application procedure.

It should be noted at this time that after the initial passage of RESPA, there was a great deal of opposition to the act not only from the lenders, but from the closing agents and homebuyers. After lengthy hearings, Regulation X of the act was revised and the revi-

sions became law in 1976. The revised RESPA has 9 basic requirements.

1-2. The first two of the requirements were discussed in the previous chapter. They require the lender to provide the applicant with the Good Faith Estimate of Costs and the HUD booklet on settlement costs.

The remainder of the provisions cover the actual closing of the transaction:

3. *Uniform Settlement Statement.* RESPA requires the use of the Uniform Settlement Statement, otherwise known as either HUD Form 1 or the closing statement. This statement will be reviewed later in this section.

4. *Selection of the title company.* RESPA makes it illegal for the seller to condition the sale of the property that will be purchased with the assistance of a federally related mortgage loan, upon the buyer's selection of the title company. This means that the seller cannot force the buyer to use a specific title company.

5. *Kickbacks.* RESPA prohibits anyone involved in the transaction from receiving or giving a fee, kickback, or anything of value for the promise of future business. It also makes the acceptance or offer of a fee illegal when no service has been rendered. It should be noted that this requirement does not prohibit a person who actually provides a service in the transaction from collecting a fee or payment for services. It does prohibit, for example, a title or mortgage company from making an agreement with a real estate agent or firm, so that for every closing or applicant the agent or firm sends, the agent or firm will receive something of value.

6. *Escrows.* RESPA prohibits the lender from collecting excessive amounts to be placed in escrow accounts. The act allows the lender to collect sufficient amounts to make necessary payments plus two months of escrow deposits. Thus, at the time of closing the mortgage lender usually requires the collection of 2 months of escrow payments for taxes, insurance (homeowners), PMI premiums, and any other fee or assessment that will affect the title to the property. The lender will collect the first year's insurance premium for both homeowners, and

PMI if required, for a total of 14 months for each.

7. *Preparation of the uniform settlement statement and truth-in-lending statement.* The lender is prohibited from charging a fee for the preparation of these 2 statements. It should be noted that only the lender is prohibited from charging a fee for the preparation of the statements.

8. *Loans to fiduciaries.* Institutions insured by either FDIC or FSLIC must require that the borrower disclose the identity of the person or company that is receiving the beneficial interest in a loan made to a fiduciary. *Fiduciary* is the holding by a person or organization of something in trust. Thus, if you are purchasing a piece of property from a person or organization that is holding the property in trust, the institution will require the person or organization holding the property to identify the person or persons that will ultimately benefit from the proceeds of the mortgage.

9. *Preview of settlement statement.* The final provision of RESPA allows the borrower or his or her agent to view the Uniform Settlement Statement one business day prior to the closing and see the amount which the borrower may be required to pay at the time of closing. This reviewing of the Uniform Settlement Statement is a good idea not only for the borrower, but also for the real estate agent who represents the borrower. This will allow the borrower to have either sufficient cash or a cashier's check to pay the required amount. If the agent reviews the Uniform Settlement Statement prior to closing, he or she can see if the buyer is paying the proper items and amounts outlined in the earnest money contract. Thus, there will be no surprises at the time of closing.

Uniform Settlement Statement

As was mentioned in the previous section, RESPA requires the use of a Uniform Settlement Statement in the settlement or closing of the sale of any one- to four-family residential property, sale of a lot with a mobile home, or sale of a lot on which a home can or is planned to be built. The Uniform Settlement Statement, or HUD Form 1, is illustrated in Figures 15–1 and 15–2.

Let us review some of the major sections of the form. The first section of the form, items A through I, are self-explanatory, identifying

the parties to the closing or settlement and the type of mortgage involved in the transaction. Item J summarizes the borrower's portion of the transaction, whereas item K summarizes the seller's portion of the transaction.

The second page of the statement is a detailed outline of the money to be paid at the time of the closing and who is to pay each of the charges. You will notice that the page is divided into seven sections, starting with a section showing the real estate commission and to whom the commission is to be paid. The second section sets forth the items that are to be paid in conjunction with the origination and processing of the mortgage. Not all of these fees will be paid to the lender. For example, the appraisal fee will usually be paid to an appraiser, and the cost of the credit report will be paid to the local credit bureau. The next section, Items Required by the Lender to be Paid in Advance, is self-explanatory. The fourth section, Reserves Deposited with Lender, shows a breakdown of prepaids collected. The next section, Title Charges, has to do with the closing title search, document preparation, issuance of the title insurance, and other fees involved with the actual closing of the transaction. When the documents are filed—like all documents relating to the transfer of real property—the charges for such recording will be indicated in section six. Since tax stamps are not used in Texas, there will be no charge on line 1202 or 1203, but there may still be a charge for tax certificates. The tax certificates, from the taxing authorities that have jurisdiction over the subject property, state that the taxes are current. These certificates, for example, may be issued by the city, county, and school district. The last section has space for other settlement charges, which can include those listed, as well as other types of inspections and repairs.

TRUTH-IN-LENDING LAW

The Truth-in-Lending law, passed by the U.S. Congress in 1968, became effective July 1969. It requires that a Truth-in-Lending Statement be given to a borrower providing certain information about the mortgage or loan. The information may include, but is not limited to, the annual percentage rate (APR), the finance charge, the dollar amount the credit will cost the borrower, the number of payments, and late charges and how they will be calculated.

Then, in March 1980, the Congress passed the Depository Institutions Deregulation and

Figure 15–1. HUD Uniform Settlement Statement, page 1

Form Approved
OMB No. 63-R1501

A.	U.S. DEPARTMENT OF HOUSING AND URBAN DEVELOPMENT	B. TYPE OF LOAN:

B. TYPE OF LOAN:
1. ☐ FHA 2. ☐ FMHA 3. ☐ CONV. UNINS.
4. ☐ VA 5. ☐ CONV. INS.
6. FILE NUMBER   7. LOAN NUMBER
8. MORTG. INS. CASE NO.

SETTLEMENT STATEMENT

C. NOTE: This form is furnished to give you a statement of actual settlement costs. Amounts paid to and by the settlement agent are shown. Items marked "(p.o.c.)" were paid outside the closing; they are shown here for informational purposes and are not included in the totals.

D. NAME OF BORROWER	E. NAME OF SELLER	F. NAME OF LENDER

G. PROPERTY LOCATION	H. SETTLEMENT AGENT	I. SETTLEMENT DATE:
	PLACE OF SETTLEMENT	

J. SUMMARY OF BORROWER'S TRANSACTION		K. SUMMARY OF SELLER'S TRANSACTION	
100. GROSS AMOUNT DUE FROM BORROWER:		400. GROSS AMOUNT DUE TO SELLER:	
101. Contract sales price		401. Contract sales price	
102. Personal property		402. Personal property	
103. Settlement charges to borrower *(line 1400)*		403.	
104.		404.	
105.		405.	
Adjustments for items paid by seller in advance:		Adjustments for items paid by seller in advance:	
		406. City/town taxes to	
		407. County taxes to	
106. City/town taxes to		408. Assessments to	
107. County taxes to		409. Maintenance to	
108. Assessments to		410. Commitment Fee to	
109. Maintenance to		411. to	
110. School Taxes to		412. to	
111. to		420. GROSS AMOUNT DUE TO SELLER:	
112. to			
120. GROSS AMOUNT DUE FROM BORROWER:		500. REDUCTIONS IN AMOUNT DUE TO SELLER:	
200. AMOUNTS PAID BY OR IN BEHALF OF BORROWER:		501. Excess deposit (see instructions)	
201. Deposit or earnest money		502. Settlement charges to seller *(line 1400)*	
202. Principal amount of new loan(s)		503. Existing loan(s) taken subject to	
203. Existing loan(s) taken subject to		504. Payoff of first mortgage loan	
204. Commitment Fee		505. Payoff of second mortgage loan	
205.		506.	
206.		507.	
207.		508.	
208.		509.	
209.			
Adjustments for items unpaid by seller:		Adjustments for items unpaid by seller:	
210. City/town taxes to		510. City/town taxes to	
211. County taxes to		511. County Taxes to	
212. Assessments to		512. Assessments to	
213. School/Taxes to		513. Maintenance to	
214. to		514. School/Taxes to	
215. to		515. to	
216. to		516. to	
217. to		517. to	
218. to		518. to	
219. to		519. to	
220. TOTAL PAID BY/FOR BORROWER:		520. TOTAL REDUCTION AMOUNT DUE SELLER:	
300. CASH AT SETTLEMENT FROM/TO BORROWER:		600. CASH AT SETTLEMENT TO/FROM SELLER:	
301. Gross amount due from borrower *(line 120)*		601. Gross amount due to seller *(line 420)*	
302. Less amounts paid by/for borrower *(line 220)* ( )		602. Less total reductions in amount due seller *(line 520)* ( )	
303. CASH (☐ FROM) (☐ TO) BORROWER:		603. CASH (☐ TO) (☐ FROM) SELLER	

HUD-1 (Rev. 5-76)

Figure 15–2. HUD Uniform Settlement Statement, page 2

L. SETTLEMENT CHARGES	PAID FROM BORROWER'S FUNDS AT SETTLEMENT	PAID FROM SELLER'S FUNDS AT SETTLEMENT
700. TOTAL SALES/BROKER'S COMMISSION Based on price $ @ % =		
Division of commission *(line 700)* as follows:		
701. $ to		
702. $ to		
703. Commission paid at settlement		
704.		
800. ITEMS PAYABLE IN CONNECTION WITH LOAN.		
801. Loan Origination fee %		
802. Loan Discount %		
803. Appraisal Fee to		
804. Credit Report to		
805. Lender's inspection fee		
806. Mortgage Insurance application fee to		
807. Assumption Fee		
808. Commitment Fee		
809. FNMA Processing Fee		
810. Pictures		
811.		
900. ITEMS REQUIRED BY LENDER TO BE PAID IN ADVANCE.		
901. Interest from to @ $ /day		
902. Mortgage insurance premium for mo. to		
903. Hazard insurance premium for yrs. to		
904. Flood Insurance yrs. to		
905.		
1000. RESERVES DEPOSITED WITH LENDER		
1001. Hazard insurance mo. @ $ per mo.		
1002. Mortgage insurance mo. @ $ per mo.		
1003. City property taxes mo. @ $ per mo.		
1004. County property taxes mo. @ $ per mo.		
1005. Annual assessments (Maint.) mo. @ $ per mo.		
1006. School Property Taxes mo. @ $ per mo.		
1007. Water Dist. Prop. Tax mo. @ $ per mo.		
1008. Flood Insurance mo. @ $ per mo.		
1100. TITLE CHARGES:		
1101. Settlement or closing fee to		
1102. Abstract or title search to		
1103. Title examination to		
1104. Title insurance binder to		
1105. Document preparation to		
1106. Notary fees to		
1107. Attorney's fees to to		
(includes above items No.:		
1108. Title insurance to		
(includes above items No.:		
1109. Lender's coverage $		
1110. Owner's coverage $		
1111. Escrow Fee		
1112. Restrictions		
1113. Messenger Service		
1200. GOVERNMENT RECORDING AND TRANSFER CHARGES		
1201. Recording fees: Deed $ Mortgage $ Releases $		
1202. City/county tax/stamps: Deed $ Mortgage $		
1203. State tax/stamps: Deed $ Mortgage $		
1204. Tax Certificates		
1205.		
1300. ADDITIONAL SETTLEMENT CHARGES		
1301. Survey to		
1302. Pest inspection to		
1303.		
1304.		
1305.		
1400. TOTAL SETTLEMENT CHARGES *(entered on lines 103, Section J and 502, Section K)*		

SELLER'S AND/OR PURCHASER'S STATEMENT

Seller's and Purchaser's signature hereon acknowledges his/their approval of tax prorations, and signifies their understanding that prorations were based on figures for preceding year, or estimates for current year, and in event of any change for current year, all necessary adjustments must be made between Seller and Purchaser direct; likewise any DEFICIT in delinquent taxes will be reimbursed to Title Company by the Seller.

We approve the foregoing settlement statement, in its entirety, authorize payments in accordance therewith and acknowledge receipt of a copy thereof.

Signature_____   _____

_____   _____
     Seller   Purchaser

_____
     Escrow Officer   HUD-1 (Rev. 5-76)

Monetary Control Act (Public Law 96-221), which contained Title VI and is entitled the Truth-in-Lending Simplification and Reform Act. The purpose of this act was to make sweeping revisions to the truth-in-lending law. Even though the effective date of the act was not until October 1, 1982, the act required the Federal Reserve to adopt a final rule to implement the act no later than April 1, 1981.

The act made major changes to many areas covered by the original law. One of the types of transactions affected was the real estate transaction. Some of the major changes affecting real estate transactions are as follows:

1. The sale of rental property not to be owner occupied is excluded and no Truth-in-Lending Statement is required

2. The term *refinancing* was redefined to include any and only those loans or mortgage agreements that pay off existing debt with the execution of a new mortgage or loan

3. Any points paid by the seller when calculating the finance charges are excluded from the calculation of finance charges, but any points paid by the buyer are still included

As with the previous rules, the extension of agriculture credit is exempt. Agricultural credit includes credit for the purpose of purchasing real property without or with improvements, including a home, if the property is to be used primarily for agriculture purposes.

In addition to these changes, the rules adopted by the Federal Reserve also contained suggested formats for several loan disclosure forms. Some of these relate to real estate transactions and are illustrated in Figures 15-3, 15-4, 15-5, and 15-6.

In addition to the suggested forms, the Federal Reserve has proposed several clauses to be used with the Variable Rate and the Demand Feature Model Disclosures. The Federal Reserve has also published suggested clauses for use with mortgages that include an assumption provision and/or a clause stating that the APR does not include any required deposit. These suggested clauses are illustrated in Figure 15-7.

In regard to the time of disclosure or the supplying of the Truth-in-Lending statement for a new loan, section 226.19 of Regulation Z, is rather explicit. The lender is required, on those transactions subject to RESPA, to supply to the borrower the information required by Regulation Z, either by delivering to the borrower or by placing it in the mail within three working days or prior to the closing of the loan, whichever is earlier.

If the real estate transaction involves an assumption, lenders are also required to make a disclosure. According to the regulation, an assumption occurs when the lender or creditor expressly agrees in writing with the person assuming the residential loan to become the primary or responsible party for the repayment of the loan. Then the lender is required to supply a new disclosure to the person assuming the loan prior to the assumption of the loan. The disclosure will be based on the remaining loan amount.

In this discussion of truth-in-lending, we have referred to the *annual percentage rate* (APR). This rate can be different from the interest rate quoted by the lender as the rate of the mortgage for which the borrower is making application. The reason for the difference is that the APR includes not only the face rate of the mortgage, but also all fees and/or discount points paid by the buyer. This difference in interest rate may cause some borrowers to become alarmed. In reviewing the model disclosure statements, in particular Figure 15-4, there is no mention of the note rate; only the APR is shown.

If you are working with a homebuyer and you have been quoted a qualifying rate of 11.5 percent and at closing the homebuyer is shown an APR of 15 percent, this could possibly frighten the buyer into not closing. In order to lessen the shock of the difference, you should ask the lender for the APR for a typical transaction at the time the lender quotes the interest rate, then, with that information you can advise your client of the difference and explain the difference before going to loan application and/or closing.

The agencies that have responsibility for the enforcement of truth-in-lending (Regulation Z) are listed in Figure 15-8.

This completes our examination of the major federal legislation that has an effect on the closing of the real estate transaction.

SETTING THE CLOSING

How is the date of the closing determined? The date is established by two factors: (1) the negotiation of the earnest money contract and (2) loan approval. With regard to negotiation of the earnest money contract, all of the standard real estate contracts promulgated by the Joint Committee of the Texas Real Estate

Figure 15–3. **Loan Model Form**

ANNUAL PERCENTAGE RATE The cost of your credit as a yearly rate.	FINANCE CHARGE The dollar amount the credit will cost you.	Amount Financed The amount of credit provided to you or on your behalf.	Total of Payments The amount you will have paid after you have made all payments as scheduled.
%	$	$	$

You have the right to receive at this time an itemization of the Amount Financed.
☐ I want an itemization.   ☐ I do not want an itemization.

Your payment schedule will be:

Number of Payments	Amount of Payments	When Payments Are Due

Insurance
Credit life insurance and credit disability insurance are not required to obtain credit, and will not be provided unless you sign and agree to pay the additional cost.

Type	Premium	Signature
Credit Life		I want credit life insurance. _____ Signature
Credit Disability		I want credit disability insurance. _____ Signature
Credit Life and Disability		I want credit life and disability insurance. _____ Signature

You may obtain property insurance from anyone you want that is acceptable to (creditor). If you get the insurance

from (creditor), you will pay $ _____.

Security: You are giving a security interest in:
☐ the goods or property being purchased.
☐ (brief description of other property).

Filing fees $ _____   Non-filing insurance $ _____

Late Charge: If a payment is late, you will be charged $ _____ / _____% of the payment.

Prepayment: If you pay off early, you
☐ may   ☐ will not   have to pay a penalty.
☐ may   ☐ will not   be entitled to a refund of part of the finance charge.

See your contract documents for any additional information about nonpayment, default, any required repayment in full before the scheduled date, and prepayment refunds and penalties.

_____
e means an estimate

Source: U.S., Federal Reserve System, *Final Rule; Truth-in-Lending; Revised Regulation Z, Appendix H,* April 1, 1981, p. 66.

Figure 15–4.   Mortgage with Demand Feature

Mortgage Savings and Loan Assoc.
Date: April 15, 1981

Glenn Jones
700 Oak Drive
Little Creek, USA

ANNUAL PERCENTAGE RATE The cost of your credit as a yearly rate.	FINANCE CHARGE The dollar amount the credit will cost you.	Amount Financed The amount of credit provided to you or on your behalf.	Total of Payments The amount you will have paid after you have made all payments as scheduled.
14.85%	$156,551.54	$44,605.66	$201,157.20

Your payment schedule will be:

Number of Payments	Amount of Payments	When Payments Are Due
360	$558.77	Monthly beginning 6/1/81

This obligation has a demand feature.

You may obtain property insurance from anyone you want that is acceptable to Mortgage Savings and Loan Assoc. If you get the insurance from Mortgage Savings and Loan Assoc. you will pay $ 150 — 1 year

Security: You are giving a security interest in:
☒ the goods or property being purchased.
☐ _____

Late Charge: If a payment is late, you will be charged $ N/A / 5 % of the payment.

Prepayment: If you pay off early, you may have to pay a penalty.

Assumption: Someone buying your house may, subject to conditions, be allowed to assume the remainder of the mortgage on the original terms.

See your contract documents for any additional information about nonpayment, default, any required repayment in full before the scheduled date, and prepayment refunds and penalties.

_____
e means an estimate

Source: U.S., Federal Reserve System, *Final Rule; Truth-in-Lending; Revised Regulation Z*, April 1, 1981, p. 74.

Figure 15–5. Variable-Rate Mortgage

State Savings and Loan Assoc.

Anne Jones
600 Pine Lane
Little Creek, USA

Account number: 210802-47

ANNUAL PERCENTAGE RATE The cost of your credit as a yearly rate.	FINANCE CHARGE The dollar amount the credit will cost you.	Amount Financed The amount of credit provided to you or on your behalf.	Total of Payments The amount you will have paid after you have made all payments as scheduled.
15.07 %	$157,155.20	$44,002—	$201,157.20

Your payment schedule will be:

Number of Payments	Amount of Payments	When Payments Are Due
360	$558.77	Monthly beginning 6-1-81

Variable Rate:
The annual percentage rate may increase during the term of this transaction if the prime rate of State Savings and Loan Assoc. increases. The rate may not increase more often than once a year, and may not increase by more than 1% annually. The interest rate will not increase above 19.75 %. Any increase will take the form of higher payment amounts. If the interest rate increases by 1 % in one year, your regular payment would increase to $ 594.51

Security: You are giving a security interest in the property being purchased.

Late Charge: If a payment is late, you will be charged 5% of the payment.

Prepayment: If you pay off early, you ☒ may ☐ will not have to pay a penalty.

Assumption: Someone buying your house may, subject to conditions, be allowed to assume the remainder of the mortgage on the original terms.

See your contract documents for any additional information about nonpayment, default, any required repayment in full before the scheduled date, and prepayment refunds and penalties.

―――――――
e means an estimate

Source: U.S., Federal Reserve System, *Final Rule; Truth-in-Lending, Revised Regulation Z; Appendix H,* April 1, 1981, p. 75.

Figure 15–6.   Graduated-Payment Mortgage

Convenient Savings and Loan   Account number : 4862-88

Michael Jones
500 Walnut Court, Little Creek USA

ANNUAL PERCENTAGE RATE The cost of your credit as a yearly rate.	FINANCE CHARGE The dollar amount the credit will cost you.	Amount Financed The amount of credit provided to you or on your behalf.	Total of Payments The amount you will have paid after you have made all payments as scheduled.
15.37%	$177,970.44	$43,777	$221,548.44

Your payment schedule will be:

Number of Payments	Amount of Payments	When Payments Are Due		
12	$446.62	monthly beginning	6	1	81
12	$479.67	"	"	6	1	82
12	$515.11	"	"	6	1	83
12	$553.13	"	"	6	1	84
12	$593.91	"	"	6	1	85
300	varying from $637.68 to $627.37	"	"	6	1	86

Security: You are giving a security interest in the property being purchased.

Late Charge: If a payment is late, you will be charged 5% of the payment.

Prepayment: If you pay off early, you
☒ may   ☐ will not   have to pay a penalty.
☒ may   ☐ will not   be entitled to a refund of part of the finance charge.

Assumption: Someone buying your home cannot assume the remainder of the mortgage on the original terms.

See your contract documents for any additional information about nonpayment, default, any required repayment in full before the scheduled date, and prepayment refunds and penalties.

_____
e means an estimate

Source: U.S., Federal Reserve System, Final Rule; Truth-in-Lending, Revised Regulation Z; Appendix H, April 1, 1981, p. 76.

Figure 15–7. Model Clauses

H-4—Variable Rate Model Clauses

The annual percentage rate may increase during the term of this transaction if:
(the prime interest rate of _(creditor)_ increases.)
(the balance in your deposit account falls below $ _____ .)
(you terminate your employment with _(employer)_ .)

(The interest rate will not increase above _____%.)
(The maximum interest rate increase at one time will be _____%.)
(The rate will not increase more than once every _(time period)_ .)

Any increase will take the form of:
(higher payment amounts.)
(more payments of the same amount.)
(a larger amount due at maturity.)

Example based on the specific transaction
(If the interest rate increases by _____ % in _(time period)_,
(your regular payments will increase to $ _____ .)
(you will have to make _____ additional payments.)
(your final payment will increase to $ _____ .))

Example based on a typical transaction
(If your loan were for $ _____ at _____% for _(term)_ and the rate increased to _____% in _(time period)_,
(your regular payments would increase by $ _____ .)
(you would have to make _____ additional payments.)
(your final payment would increase by $ _____ .))

H-5—Demand Feature Model Clauses

This obligation (is payable on demand.)
(has a demand feature.)
(All disclosures are based on an assumed maturity of one year.)

H-6—Assumption Policy Model Clause

Assumption: Someone buying your house (may, subject to conditions, be allowed to) (cannot) assume the remainder of the mortgage on the original terms.

H-7—Required Deposit Model Clause

The annual percentage rate does not take into account your required deposit.

Source: U.S., Federal Reserve System, Final Rule; Truth-in-Lending, Revised Regulation Z; Appendix H, April 1, 1981, p. 68.

Figure 15–8.   Federal Enforcement Agencies

The following list indicates which federal agency enforces Regulation Z for particular classes of businesses. Any questions concerning compliance by a particular business should be directed to the appropriate enforcement agency.

National Banks

Office of Customer and Community Programs
Comptroller of the Currency
Washington, D.C. 20219

State Member Banks

Federal Reserve Bank serving the district in which the State member bank is located.

Nonmember Insured Banks

Federal Deposit Insurance Corporation Regional Director for the region in which the nonmember insured bank is located.

Savings Institutions Insured by the FSLIC and Members of the FHLBB System (Except for Savings Banks Insured by FDIC)

The Federal Home Loan Bank Board Supervisory Agent in the district in which the institution is located.

Federal Credit Unions

Regional office of the National Credit Union Administration serving the area in which the federal credit union is located.

Creditors Subject to Civil Aeronautics Board

Director, Bureau of Consumer Protection
Civil Aeronautics Board
1825 Connecticut Avenue, N.W.
Washington, D.C. 20428

Creditors Subject to Packers and Stockyards Act

Nearest Packers and Stockyards Administration area supervisor.

Federal Land Banks, Federal Land Bank Associations, Federal Intermediate Credit Banks and Production Credit Associations

Farm Credit Administration
490 L'Enfant Plaza, S.W.
Washington, D.C. 20578

Retail, Department Stores, Consumer Finance Companies, All Other Creditors, and All Nonbank Credit Card Issuers (Creditors operating on a local or regional basis should use the address of the FTC Regional Office in which they operate.)

Division of Credit Practices
Bureau of Consumer Protection
Federal Trade Commission
Washington, D.C. 20580

Source: U.S., Federal Reserve System, *Final Rule; Truth-in-Lending, Revised Regulation Z; Appendix I*, April 1, 1981, p. 77.

Commission and the State Bar of Texas contain a statement that closing will occur on or before the specified date in the contract. The loan approval factor is noted in all of the standard Texas contract forms in that the closing portion of the contracts contains the following wording: "if necessary to complete loan requirements, the Closing Date shall be extended daily up to 15 days." It is important, then, for real estate professionals to be familiar with the time necessary for loans to be processed in their area of operation in order to schedule a realistic number of days from the time the earnest money contract is effective until the scheduled day of closing. This time frame will vary not only with the area of the state, but also with the type of mortgage and the complexity of the application and information to be verified.

MORTGAGE LENDERS CLOSING PROCEDURES

After approval of both the property and the borrower is received by the mortgage lender or the mortgage company from the loan committee and/or the investor, the application and all of the supporting documents are transferred to the closing department of the mortgage lender or mortgage company. The closing department then initiates actions that will prepare the mortgage for closing through the closing agent. The following are usually some of the major actions taken, but not necessarily in the order listed.

Commitment for Title Insurance

The mortgage lender or mortgage company will order the Commitment for Title Insurance. This is sometimes referred to as the Title Report.

The Commitment for Title Insurance is usually issued by the title company that will issue the title policy on the property that is serving as security for the mortgage. The form is prescribed by the Texas State Board of Insurance and contains three basic schedules. The information contained in each of the schedules is shown in Figures 15–9, 15–10, and 15–11.

Survey

The mortgage lender or mortgage company will, after the approval, also request a survey of the property in question. The survey that is usually ordered by the mortgage lender or the

Figure 15-9.   Schedule A—Commitment for Title Insurance

SCHEDULE A

1 GF NUMBER	2 COMMITMENT NO.	3 EFFECTIVE DATE OF COMMITMENT
	2 COMMITMENT NO.	

_____ o'clock _____ m

1. Policies or Policy to be issued:
   (a) Form T-1: Owner Policy of Title Insurance
       Proposed Insured:

   4
   Amount:_____

   (b) Form T-2: Mortgagee Policy of Title Insurance
       Proposed Insured:

       Proposed Borrower:

   4
   Amount:_____

   (c) Form T-13: Mortgagee Title Policy Binder on Interim Construction Loan
       Proposed Insured:

       Proposed Borrower:

   4
   Amount:_____

   (d) Other:

       Proposed Insured:

   4
   Amount:_____

2. The estate or interest in the land described or referred to in this Commitment and covered herein: (Fee simple, leasehold, easement, etc. − identify or describe)

3. Record Title thereto at the effective date hereof appears to be vested in:

4. The land referred to in this Commitment is described as follows:

Figure 15–10.   Schedule B—Commitment for Title Insurance

G.F. Number:

SCHEDULE B

Schedule B of the policy or policies to be issued will also contain the following exclusions and exceptions:

The policy will be subject to the Conditions and Stipulations thereof, the terms and conditions of the instrument creating the estate insured, if any, shown in Schedule A, and to the following matters which will be additional exceptions from the coverage of the policy:

1. The following restrictive covenants of record itemized below, but in any mortgagee policy of title insurance or mortgagee title policy binder on interim construction loan, the Company will guarantee that any such restrictive covenants have not been violated so as to affect, and that a future violation thereof will not affect the validity or priority of the Insured mortgage (insert specific recording data or state "None of Record"):

2. Any discrepancies, conflicts, or shortages in area or boundary lines, or any encroachments, or any overlapping of improvements.

3. Taxes for the year 19_____ and subsequent years, and subsequent assessments for prior years due to change in land usage or ownership.

4. Usury or claims of usury. (Mortgagee Policy or Mortgagee Title Policy Binder on Interim Construction Loan only.)

5. Any right of rescission contained in any CONSUMER CREDIT PROTECTION or TRUTH-IN-LENDING laws. (Mortgagee Policy or Mortgagee Title Policy Binder on Interim Construction Loan only.)

6. No materials have been furnished or any labor performed in connection with the construction contemplated hereunder prior to the execution, acknowledgment, and delivery of the lien instrument described under Schedule A hereof, if the land described under Schedule A forms any part of the homestead of the owner. (may be deleted if satisfactory evidence is furnished before binder is issued.) (Mortgagee Title Policy Binder on Interim Construction Loan only.)

7. The following lien(s) and all terms, provisions and conditions of the instrument(s) creating or evidencing said lien(s):

8. (INSERT HERE ALL OTHER SPECIFIC EXCEPTIONS AS TO SUPERIOR LIENS, EASEMENTS, OUTSTANDING MINERAL AND ROYALTY INTERESTS, ETC.)

Figure 15-11. *Schedule C—Commitment for Title Insurance*

SCHEDULE C

G.F. Number:

Schedule B of the policy to be issued will also contain exceptions with respect to the following matters supposed to affect title to the hereinabove described property unless the following matters are disposed of to the satisfaction of the Company at or prior to the date of the issuance of the policy:

1. Instrument(s) creating the estate or interest to be insured must be approved by the Company, executed and filed for record.

2. Satisfactory evidence that no person occupying the property or any portion thereof owns or claims any interest therein, either personally or by right of another, adverse to the present record owner as shown in Schedule A.

3. Payment of the full consideration to, or for the account of, the grantors or mortgagors.

4. Payment of all taxes, charges and assessments levied or assessed against the subject estate or interest, which are currently due and payable.

5. Satisfactory evidence that all improvements and/or repairs and/or alterations thereto are completed and accepted by the owner and that all contractors, subcontractors, laborers and materialmen have been paid in full, and no mechanic's, laborer's or materialmen's liens have attached.

6. Any defect, lien, encumbrance or other matter affecting or supposed to affect title to the estate or interest to be insured which may be filed or which may arise subsequent to the effective date hereof.

7. If a mortgagee policy of title insurance is to be issued, satisfactory evidence that restrictions and restrictive covenants, if any, have not been violated so as to affect, and that a future violation thereof will not affect the validity or priority of the insured mortgage.

mortgage company is not a true survey but a drawing or copy of the plat of the property and usually carries the following certification:

> I certify that the above is an accurate plat of the property of (the name of the present owner is inserted), known as, *(the street address is inserted)*, the correct map of which is recorded in *(the recording information is inserted)*, as inspected under my supervision. There were no encroachments at the time of this inspection. This plat is not to be used for construction purposes.
>
> > *(Signed by licensed surveyor)*
> > Name of Surveyor
> > State Registration Number

In addition to the above certification, the following note is usually included on the plat:

> NOTE: This is a plat to be used for loan purposes and is not a boundary or staked survey.

This survey will show all improvements to the property including buildings, driveways, and sidewalks. The plat will also show all of the recorded easements and building lines. This is the type of survey that is usually used in conjunction with loans on residential property located inside recorded subdivisions. If the property is not located inside a city subdivision or the property involves more than a normal subdivision lot, the mortgage lender or the title company may require an "on-the-ground staked boundary survey with full field notes." This is a true survey where the surveyor sends a crew to the property and the property and all improvements are physically located.

Document Preparation

After the commitment for title insurance and survey are received, the closing department will request the attorney firm that represents the mortgage lender or mortgage company to "draw" or prepare the following documents:

1. The note on the lender's prescribed form. If the mortgage is to be sold to Fannie Mae or FHLMC, the standard note for Fannie Mae/FHLMC will be completed. If the mortgage is to be either insured by FHA or guaranteed by VA, the attorney will use the authorized Note.

2. In addition to the note, the attorneys will draw the accompanying deed of trust using the lender's approved form.

One additional document that will be prepared for, or by, the closing department is the Truth-in-Lending Statement.

After all of the documents are prepared along with all of the necessary forms, the mortgage lender prepares the closing package, and this, along with specific instructions, is sent to the title company for the closing.

CLOSING INSTRUCTIONS

The most important document in the closing package to the agent of the title company closing the transaction is the closing instructions. These are the instructions given to the closing agent by the mortgage lender or the mortgage company listing the things that are to be done or checked by the closing agent. The closing instructions will be different for conventional mortgages, for FHA-insured mortgages, and for VA-guaranteed mortgages. A sample of closing instructions for a conventional mortgage is illustrated in Figures 15-12 and 15-13.

The instructions are divided into six sections. The first section, which is not numbered, deals with the funding of the mortgage, whether it is to be table funded or funded at a later date. The instructions on page 1 give the closing agent instructions on closing the loan and tell how the title policy is to be issued. The last instructions on page 1 deal with the hazard insurance policy. The instructions mandate a minimum rating for the company issuing the policy and state that certain types of policies are not acceptable to the lender. Also the instructions state that the policy may be furnished by an agent of the purchaser's choice.

Page 2 of the instructions (Figure 15-13) begins with an outline of the charges that the borrower will pay. The final portion of page 2 gives instructions as to what the closer is to furnish to the mortgage lender or mortgage company.

CLOSING COSTS

We will now examine some of the more common closing costs or fees that are connected with the application for, the processing of, and the closing of the mortgage.

Application fee   This fee is collected at the time of the application. The amount of the fee will vary with the type of mortgage applied for. The application fees for a mortgage insured by FHA or guaranteed by VA are set

Figure 15–12. *Conventional Mortgage Closing Instructions, part 1*

Closing Instructions: **Conventional Loan**

MERCANTILE MORTGAGE CORPORATION   **(713) 522-8903**

Date of Instructions: _____ Closing Date: _____ Closer: _____
Title Company: _____ Mortgagor: _____
GF #: _____ _____
Loan Amount: $ _____ Address: _____
Maturity: _____ months _____
Interest Rate: _____ % Appraised Lot Size: _____
P & I Payments: $ _____ (If less than this, contact us before proceeding with closing)

The following instructions are to be observed and followed implicitly by you in closing the above referenced loan. Should you not be able to meet the requirements set forth below, contact us before proceeding with the closing of the loan.

( ) Mercantile Mortgage Corporation will fund this loan upon receiving the instruments later referred to in these instructions, in form and content acceptable to us.

[handwritten: Table — Funding]

(✓) A Check in the amount of $ _____ is attached, and is to be disbursed by you at closing, if all conditions of closing and our written instructions are followed correctly. Please note: Items marked with an asterisk (*) apply only to our requirements as applied to disbursement at closing, and are not applicable if this loan is not "table funded".

I. In closing this loan, please observe the following:

(a) If the loan is not closed completely by buyer and seller within seven days from date of instructions, do not proceed with closing without permission from Mercantile Mortgage Corporation.

(*) A funding number must be obtained prior to disbursement of proceeds by calling Mercantile Mortgage Corporation. When funding number is issued and loan is closed, the documents referred to in Section V must be in the office of Mercantile Mortgage Corporation within 24 hours. The funding number is _____ , obtained from _____ at MERCANTILE MORTGAGE CORPORATION on _____.

(b) The closing must be in accordance with the enclosed earnest money contract as to sales price and downpayment.

(c) In examining the title and survey, if you find any easements more than twelve feet wide, any violation of restrictions, encroachments, or any exceptions of an unusual nature, e.g., a pipeline easement, advise us immediately and secure our approval before proceeding.

(d) All papers in connection with this loan are to be drawn by an attorney approved by Mercantile Mortgage Corporation.

(e) All documents must be signed as the names appear on the note and deed of trust, and all documents must be signed in the same manner.

(f) If the property is located in a water district, we must be forwarded a copy of the required affidavit.

(g) Any erasures, riders, gummed supplements or strikeovers on papers to be signed must be initialed by all parties.

(h)

II. Please issue your mortgagee's title policy observing the following:

(a) Policy must insure the deed of trust as a first lien, and the name of the insured must be: MERCANTILE MORTGAGE CORPORATION, Houston, Texas.

(b) Policy must not contain any exceptions to areas, boundaries, and encroachments, and must set out restrictions as "none of record" EXCEPT (list exceptions in usual manner), etc. The survey exception must be deleted and initialed.

(c) We will allow an exception to restrictive covenants provided they are not violated to date, and that future violation(s) will not affect the validity of the insured deed of trust. This loan is not to be closed if the restrictions contain a right of reversion.

(d) There is to be no secondary financing in connection with this loan, nor any outstanding liens, judgments, taxes or assessments.

(e) The policy must describe this new lien completely and accurately, reciting the county clerk's filing or recording dates for this deed of trust, and it must be dated even with, or after, the recited filing date.

(f) The policy must not contain any exceptions except those shown on your Mortgagee's Information Letter from which our closing preparations have been made.

(g) All taxes must be guaranteed prior to the current year. If this loan is closed after September 30, taxes must be guaranteed through the current year. The tax exception must show "taxes not yet due and payable".

(h) All easement exceptions must give size, location, purpose and recording, and must agree with the survey.

(i) All Maintenance charges must be subordinated to all valid purchase money liens. A 60-day letter is not acceptable. Next due date must be given.

(j)

III. Please examine the hazard insurance policy, observing the following:

1. Policy may be furnished by Agent of purchaser's choice.

2. The name(s) of the mortgagor(s) and legal description of the security property must be identical to those in the loan instruments; the street address must agree with the survey.

3. The insuring company must have a "BEST" rating of at least A + AA.

4. Reciprocal or assessment hazard insurance companies are not acceptable.

Source: Mercantile Mortgage Corporation of Texas, Houston, Texas

*Figure 15-13.   **Conventional Mortgage Closing Instructions, part 2***

III. (Continued)

5. The amount of the fire and extended coverage and PLF # 148 must be in the minumum amount of the loan as set out above, with loss payable clause to: MERCANTILE MORTGAGE CORPORATION AND/OR ASSIGNS, P. O. Box 40281, Houston, Texas 77040.

6. The invoice or receipt must be marked "PAID" and bear the statement, "This policy will not be cancelled for one year for non-payment of premium" and must be signed by the issuing agent.

7.

IV. Please make the following collections from the appropriate parties:

NOTE TO CLOSER: PURCHASER MUST PAY PREPAID ITEMS.
PURCHASER MUST NOT PAY MORE THAN _____ POINTS. SEE ATTACHMENT FOR
ALLOWABLE CLOSING COSTS.

Title Co.
use

( ) 1. _____ % Origination fee from buyer/seller . . . . $ _____
( ) 2. _____ % Loan Discount from buyer/seller . . . . _____
( ) 3. Private mortgage insurance examination fee . . . . _____
( ) 4. Credit Report . . . . _____
( ) 5. Photographs . . . . _____
( ) 6. Completion Photographs . . . . _____
( ) 7. Appraisal fee . . . . _____
( ) 8. Amortization schedule . . . . _____
( ) 9. Inspection fee . . . . _____
( ) 10. Two months' hazard insurance for deposit to escrow . . . . _____
( ) 11. Two months' flood insurance for deposit to escrow . . . . _____
( ) 12. Taxes from November 1 to date of 1st payment . . . . . . _____
( ) 13. Maintenance fee charges from December 1 to date of first payment . . _____
( ) 14. Preliminary interest from date of disbursement check to a date 30 days prior to first installment date . . . . _____
( ) 15. Attorney's fee for legal papers per invoice . . . . _____
( ) 16. Long distance calls . . . . _____
( ) 17. Processing fee . . . . _____
( ) 18. Warehouse fee . . . . _____
( ) 19. FNMA underwriting fee . . . . _____
( ) 20. Tax service fee—Seller . . . . _____
           TOTAL FEES DUE FOR IMPOUNDS AND LENDER CHARGES . . . . $ _____
( ) 21. First year's hazard insurance premium . . . . _____
( ) 22. First year's flood insurance premium . . . . _____
( ) 23. PMI INS premium . . . . _____
( ) 24. _____ . . . . _____
           TOTAL FEES AND CHARGES . . . . $ _____

( ) __WE REQUIRE FLOOD INSURANCE COVERAGE IN THE AMOUNT OF__ $ _____

V. When you have completed Sections I through IV and have filed the deed of trust of record, please forward the following to MERCANTILE MORTGAGE CORPORATION for disbursement:

( ) 1. Copy of mortgagee's title policy.
( ) 2. Original and two certified copies of note.
( ) 3. Two certified copies of deed of trust with filing receipt.
( ) 4. Two Certified copy of warranty deed.
( ) 5. Tax information sheet, signed by closer, showing all taxing authorities, their mailing address(es), tax account number(s) and amount of last taxes paid.
( ) 6. Oringial hazard insurance policy with receipted invoice (see instructions above) and copy of premium note if applicable.
( ) 7. Statement of cost of loan, in triplicate, which has been executed by purchaser and wife, exactly as name appears on note, properly acknowledged by closer.
( ) 8. Two certified copies of both the buyer's and seller's closing statement, executed by the closer.
( ) 9. Affidavit (our form) executed in duplicate by the purchasers.
( ) 10. Original and one copy of the PMI payment authorization form, if applicable.
( ) 11. FNMA form 1009, properly executed by purchasers and/or vendors.
( ) 12. Two copies of the survey, properly certified by a registered engineer. Be sure survey information agrees exactly with legal papers. It must reflect the borrower's name, property address, current date, house and lot dimensions, directional arrows, and distance to nearest intersection. Easements shown on survey must agree with those shown on mortgagee's title policy. Check lot, block, name of addition, and map references, making sure they agree with legal papers.
( ) 13.

( ) ( ) (*) FINAL INSPECTION OF SECURITY IF REQUIRED ON THIS LOAN. DO NOT FUND UNLESS NOTIFIED BY MERCANTILE MORTGAGE CORPORATION THAT INSPECTION IS IN FILE.

If disbursement check is not attached for funding at closing, disbursement will be made only after we have had an opportunity to check the entire file and after repairs and requirements have been complied with. Disbursement is subject to compliance with any requirements called for by the MERCANTILE MORTGAGE'S INVESTOR. If this loan is not closed and all requirements fully complied with within 7 days, any commitment by MERCANTILE MORTGAGE CORPORATION to close this loan is void.

                                    MERCANTILE MORTGAGE CORPORATION

Source: Mercantile Mortgage Corporation of Texas, Houston, Texas

by the agency involved. If the application is for a conventional mortgage, there is no standard fee, and therefore the real estate professional should have information on the fees charged by the conventional lenders in the area. The application fee usually covers those items that the mortgage lender or the mortgage company will have to pay during the processing of the application. These items include, but are not limited to (1) the credit report fee, and (2) the cost of the appraisal. The application fee for a conventional mortgage application can range from $150 to $250, with the average at $200. The application fee set by FHA was $218 and VA was $153 in late 1984.

Origination fee   This is the fee that the lender will charge for the taking of the application and the processing of the loan application. Once again this fee for an FHA-insured loan and a VA-guaranteed mortgage is set by the agency. It is now 1 percent of the mortgage amount. For conventional mortgages, the fee can vary with the lender, but once again averages 1 percent of the loan amount. This fee has remained rather constant at 1 percent. Since the amount of the mortgage has been increasing as the cost of housing has increased, the amount of money generated has also increased, and many lenders feel that the fee has almost kept up with the cost of application and processing.

Attorney's fee   This is a fee charged by the attorney involved with the transaction. If the mortgage is a simple conventional Fannie Mae/FHLMC mortgage, there is only one attorney involved, the attorney for the mortgage lender. The fee charged will vary with each lender. Therefore, it is a good practice to be familiar with the fees charged by the lenders in your area.

Loan discounts   These are the points charged by the investor who will buy the mortgage. If the mortgage is conventional or FHA, either the buyer or seller can pay the points, but if the mortgage is guaranteed by VA, only the seller is allowed to pay the points.

Copy cost of deed restrictions   This is the cost to the title company for the copy of the deed restrictions covering the subject property. These restrictions can be very important if the property is located in a planned unit development, condominium, subdivision, or area without zoning. These restrictions will outline what the owner may do with the property in regard to any addition to the property, fencing of the property, and many other aspects of land use and improvements.

Survey   The cost of required surveying varies from area to area within a state and can be paid by either the buyer or seller.

Real estate commission   This is of vital importance to the real estate salesperson. As we learned earlier, this is the first item of page 2 of the Uniform Settlement Statement. The commission is usually paid by the seller and is agreed upon at the time the property is listed by the owner.

Cost of amortization schedule   This cost is usually paid for by the buyer and it pays for the preparation of a schedule of payments showing the breakdown of the amount of each payment that will be credited to principal reduction and the payment of interest. It should be furnished to a buyer for federal income tax purposes. The schedule is normally prepared by the lender or mortgage company.

Recording fees   These fees are self-explanatory and are listed on the second page of the Uniform Settlement Statement. They cover the recording of the required documents to transfer title to the property and to secure the first-lien mortgage.

Private mortgage insurance   This is the cost of the PMI coverage required by the conventional lender and is usually paid by the buyer since it is insurance on the mortgage that was applied for by the buyer.

Interest charges   Since most mortgages are not closed on the last day of the month, the lender will require that the borrower pay interest at the time of closing for the period between the time of closing and the first of the next month. Since only interest is charged on the mortgage after the money is used, the lender will collect the money outlined and no other payment is due until the first of the following month. For example, a closing was held on the 17th of the month. The mortgage amount was $70,000, the interest rate was 12 percent, and the month had 30 days. The lender will figure the amount of interest charged each day and multiply that rate times the mortgage to get the amount of interest to be collected each day. Since the mortgage was closed on the 17th, interest will be collected beginning on the 18th through the last day of the month, or 13 days. To calculate the interest, the mortgage amount is multiplied by the interest rate ($70,000 × 12% = $8400). The $8400 represents the interest that would be paid in a year. Then to get the amount of interest paid in one month, the $8400 is divided by 12 months, or $8400/12 = $700. To get the daily amount of interest, the $700 is divided by the days in the month; in this example, 30: $700/30 = $23.33 per day. The total amount of interest to be collected, therefore, would be the daily interest rate times the number of days from closing to the first day of the next month, or $23.33 × 13 = $303.29.

This completes our discussion of some of the major charges and fees that can or will be collected in connection with the loan application, processing, and closing. Additional charges or fees could include:

Inspections

Insurance (homeowners)

Pre-paids of insurance, taxes, and any other fee or assessment that may affect the title to the property

DISBURSEMENT OF FUNDS

As mentioned earlier, the final step in loan closing is the funding to all parties involved in the transaction. This is done by the closing agent, usually in the form of a cashier's check.

SAMPLE CLOSING STATEMENT

Now that the closing statement's process and cost have been reviewed, let us complete a sample closing statement. For this example, the information in Figure 15–14 will be used to complete HUD Form 1. In the example, we will use a 360-day year because the Texas Real Estate Commission uses this value for testing purposes. But be sure to remember to use a 365-day year when working with a buyer.

Always start with page 2 of the form (Figure 15–15). Starting with line 700, Total Sales Broker's Commission based on price, enter $45,000 @ 6%. When you multiply $45,000 times 6 percent, you will get $2,700. Since normally the seller pays the real estate commis-

Figure 15–14.   Sample Closing Problem

Sales Price	$45,000.00
Loan to be made by First Mortgage	$36,000.00
Escrow Deposit: Title Company	$ 1,000.00
Owners Title Policy	$ 383.00
Mortgagee Title Policy (Buyer)	$ 50.00
Real Estate Commission @ 6%	$ 2,700.00
Recording Fee—Buyer (Deed: $5.00; D.T.: $9.00)	$ 14.00
Origination Fee (Buyer)—1 point	$ 360.00
Mortgage Discount (Buyer)—1 point	$ 360.00
Mortgage Discount (Seller)—1 point	$ 360.00
Escrow Fee (Buyer)	$ 25.00
Escrow Fee (Seller)	$ 25.00
Credit Report (Buyer)	$ 70.00
Appraisal (Buyer)	$ 200.00

The mortgage company requires that taxes and insurance be paid monthly along with the payments. The insurance policy, which the buyer must furnish, has an annual premium of $246.00 and is a one year policy dated on the date of closing, February 14. The interest rate on the loan is 12.25% and the First Mortgage Company requires that interest be paid in advance up to 30 days prior to the first payment. The loan company will pay taxes in October, and the taxes are $864.00 per year. The first payment will be on April 1.

The seller owes liens totaling $14,983.75 plus interest at 7% from February 1 through the date of closing. The loan must be paid off at the closing.

Attorney's fees for the Note and Deed of Trust is $100.00 paid by the purchaser and $20.00 to the seller for the Deed.

The survey required by the loan company costs $120.00.

All the remaining funds will be in cash at closing.

Prepare a Closing Statement for the buyer and seller.

Include one month hazard insurance for escrow.

Figure 15–15.   HUD Form 1, page 2

Form Approved OMB No. 63-R1501

L. SETTLEMENT CHARGES		PAID FROM BORROWER'S FUNDS	PAID FROM SELLER'S FUNDS
700.	TOTAL SALES' BROKER'S COMMISSION Based on price $ *45,000* @ *6* %		
	Division of commission (Line 700) as follows:		
701.	$ To		
702.	$ To		
703.	Commission paid at settlement		2700.00
800.	ITEMS PAYABLE IN CONNECTION WITH LOAN.		
801.	Loan Origination fee *1* % *of* *36,000* To Lender	360.00	
802.	Loan Discount *2* % *of* *36,000* To Lender	360.00	360.00
803.	Appraisal/Application Fee To Lender	200.00	
804.	Credit Report To Lender	70.00	
805.	Inspection fee To Lender		
806.	Mortgage Insurance Application Fee To Lender		
807.	Assumption Fee To		
808.	Photos To Lender		
809.	Amortization Schedule To Lender		
810.	Tax Research Fee To Lender		
811.			
812.			
813.			
900.	ITEMS REQUIRED BY LENDER TO BE PAID IN ADVANCE.		
901.	Interest from *2/15* to *3/1* *16* @ $ *12.25* /day	196.00	
902.	Mortgage insurance premium for mo. to		
903.	Hazard insurance premium for *1* yrs. To *XYZ Insurance*	246.00	
904.	Flood insurance yrs. To		
905.			
906.			
907.			
1000.	RESERVES DEPOSITED WITH LENDER		
1001.	Hazard insurance *1* mo. @ $ *20.50* /mo.	20.50	
1002.	Mortgage insurance mo. @ $ /mo.		
1003.	**City**, tax mo. @ $ /mo.		
1004.	**School** tax *5* mo. @ $ *72.00* /mo.	360.00	
1006.	**County** tax mo. @ $ /mo.		
1007.	**Flood insurance** mo. @ $ /mo.		
1008.	mo. @ $ /mo.		
1009.	mo. @ $ /mo.		
1010.			
1100.	TITLE CHARGES:		
1104.	Title Insurance binder to		
1105.	Document preparation to		
1107.	Attorney's Fees to	100.00	20.00
1108.	Title insurance to	50.00	383.00
1109.	Lender's coverage $		
1110.	Owner's coverage $		
1111.	**Escrow Fee to**	25.00	25.00
1112.	**Restrictions to:**		
1113.	Tax Certificates to		
1114.	Delivery Service to		
1115.			
1116.			
1117.			
1118.			
1119.			
1120.			
1121.			
1200.	GOVERNMENT RECORDING AND TRANSFER CHARGES		
1201.	Recording fees: Deed $ *5.00* Mortgage $ *9.00* Releases $ Affidavits $	14.00	
	D/T To Sec. Assumption $ UCC $ Assnm't $		
1300.	ADDITIONAL SETTLEMENT CHARGES		
1301.	Survey to	120.00	
1302.	Pest inspection to		
1303.			
1304.			
1305.			
1306.			
1307.			
1308.			
1309.			
1310.			
1400.	TOTAL SETTLEMENT CHARGES (entered on lines 103 and 502, Sections J and K)	2121.50	3488.00

sion, it will be charged to the seller. In order to charge it to the seller, it will be entered in the column Paid from Seller's Funds (line 703). These are the only entries in this section.

All of the items in the section dealing with Items Payable in Connection with Loan are 800 numbers. In checking our sample closing problem, the loan origination (line 801) is to be paid by the borrower. The fee is normally 1 percent of the loan amount, or in this case $360.00. This amount is entered on line 801, under the borrower's column. In the sample problem, there are two points of discount charged. The borrower and seller each paying 1 point. Once again each point has a value of 1 percent of the loan amount or $360.00, and that would be entered in both of the columns on line 802. Line 803, Appraisal/Application Fee, is a charge for an appraisal. The borrower, according to Figure 15–14, is to pay for the appraisal. Thus the amount of the appraisal will be entered on line 803, under the borrower's column. Line 804, Credit Report, indicates the charge for a credit report. Since it is to be paid by the borrower, the $70.00 will be entered on line 804 in the borrower's column. In reviewing the sample problem, there are no entries for lines 805 through 813.

The next section, Items Required by Lender To Be Paid in Advance, contains lines 900 through 907. Line 901 deals with the amount of the interest that will be collected at closing. This is the interest on the money from the date of closing to the first day of the following month. You will note that the loan will close on the 15th of February with the first payment due on April 1. Since interest is paid in arrears, the April 1 payment will pay the interest charges for March. Thus, the amount of interest that is to be collected will be for the period from February 14 to March 1, or 16 days. Remember this example uses a 360-day year with each month having 30 days. Now the daily amount of the interest must be calculated as follows:

1. First calculate the amount of interest that will be paid for a full year on the original loan amount or:

   Loan amount × annual interest rate
   36,000 × 12.25 percent = $4,410.00

2. Then calculate the daily interest rate:

   $$\frac{\text{Amount of Annual Interest}}{\text{Number days in a year}}$$
   $$\frac{\$4,410.00}{360} = \$12.25 \text{ per day}$$

3. Then multiply the amount of interest per day by the number of days:

   $$\$12.25 \times 16 = \$196.00$$

This amount is entered on the closing statement as shown in Figure 15–15.

In reviewing the sample problem, there is no mention of any private mortgage insurance so line 902 is left blank. Then going to the next line in this section or line 903, Hazard Insurance, the sample problem is reviewed and it is found that there is a requirement for hazard insurance and the buyer must supply a policy at closing. The problem states the premium is $246.00. This amount will be entered on line 903 under the borrower's column. There are no entries for the remainder of the section.

The next section is Reserves Deposited with Lender (sometimes called *prepaids*). In reviewing the sample problem, there is a requirement that 1 month or one twelfth of the cost of hazard insurance be placed in escrow or be prepaid. The amount is to be entered on line 1001. You will note that this section is blanked out in the seller's column; thus entries may be made only in the borrower's column. To calculate this amount, the annual hazard premium is divided by 12:

$$\frac{246.00}{12} = \$20.50$$

Once again, there is no mention of mortgage insurance so there would be no entry on line 1002, Mortgage Insurance. Lines 1003 through 1006 deal with taxes. In reading the problem, the taxes are due January 1, but are paid by the mortgage company in October. The reason the taxes are paid in October is that there is a discount if the taxes are paid early. The maximum discount occurs if the taxes are paid in October, prior to the due date in January. In reviewing the sample problem, the closing date of the loan is February 14, with the first payment due April 1. Since the mortgage company requires that one twelfth of the taxes and insurance be paid monthly along with the payments of principal and interest, the borrower will make tax escrow payments with the April, May, June, July, August, September, and October payment, or a total of 7 monthly payments toward the taxes. Since 12 months will be due in October, the lender will collect 5 months for taxes at closing. Thus, with the 7 monthly payments made and the 5 months collected at closing, there will be a total of 12 months in the account or the total amount of the taxes. How much will the lender collect at closing?

1. To calculate the amount for 1 month's escrow for taxes, the amount of the taxes is divided by 12:

$$\frac{\$864.00}{12} = \$72.00 \text{ per month}$$

2. Then multiply the number of months to be collected by the amount per month:

$$\$72.00 \times 5 = \$360.00$$

This amount will be entered in the borrower's column as per Figure 15–15. This completes the entries in this section.

The next section, Title Charges, covers, as the name implies, those charges that are in conjunction with the issuance of title insurance and the closing of the loan. The first several lines have no entries. In reviewing the sample problem there are attorney's fees for the drawing of the note and deed of trust. The fees total $120.00: $100.00 to be paid by the borrower and $20.00 to be paid by the seller. These amounts are entered in the proper column for line 1107, Attorney's Fees. The next line, 1108, deals with the cost of title insurance. Normally the seller supplies to the purchaser a title policy ensuring a clear title to the property. This policy is called the Owners Title Policy. The cost of this policy in the sample problem is $383.00 and will be entered on line 1108 in the seller's column. Then there is a charge for a Mortgagee Title Policy. This is the policy the borrower supplies to the lender. This cost is entered on line 1108 in the borrower's column. If there is a charge made by the escrow agent for their services, that charge is entered on line 1111, Escrow Fee. In reviewing the sample problem, there are such charges. The total amount of the charge is $50.00, with the buyer and seller both paying $25.00. This is entered in both the seller's and borrower's column for this line.

The next section, 1200, Government Recording and Transfer Charges, is the section where all of the recording fees are entered. In reviewing the problem, there is a total of $14.00 in recording fees; $5.00 to record the deed and $9.00 to record the deed of trust. These are to be paid by the borrower. Therefore, the total $14.00 will be entered on line 1201 in the borrower's column.

The final section of this page is 1300, Additional Settlement Charges. Note that there are only two printed entries: line 1301, Survey,

and 1302, Pest Inspection. All of the remaining lines are left blank so any other charges that do not appear above may be added. The only charge that is listed in the sample problem that has not been entered is the cost of the survey of $120.00 and is usually paid by the borrower, unless otherwise specified in the contract. With this fact in mind, the $120.00 is entered on line 1301 in the borrower's column.

Now each of the columns is totaled and entered on line 1400. The total for the borrower's column is $2,121.50 and the total for the seller's column is $3,488.00. Now that this page is complete, the front side can now be completed.

The front side, or page 1 of the form, is shown in Figure 15–16. You will note that the top part of the form will identify the type of loan, the borrower, the seller, the lender, property location, settlement agent, place of settlement, and the settlement date. Then the page is divided into two distinct halves: one is the Summary of the Borrower's Transaction; the other half is a Summary of the Seller's Transaction. This example will start with the borrower's summary.

In the first section, Gross Amount Due from Borrower, the contract sales price of the property is entered on line 101, or $45,000. Line 103, Settlement charges to borrower (line 1400), is the total from the indicated line on page 2 of the form, $2,121.50. In the problem there was no mention of any escrow or reserves transferred, so there will be no entry on line 104. According to the problem, there were no adjustments for items paid by the seller in advance, so lines 106 through 111 are left blank. Now this section is totaled. The two items are added and $47,121.50 is entered on line 120 of the borrower's summary.

The next portion of the borrower's summary is Amounts Paid by or in Behalf of Borrower. On line 201 is the line where the borrower's earnest money is shown. According to the sample problem, the borrower put up $1,000 of earnest money. That amount is entered on line 201. As per the information supplied, the borrower is securing a $36,000 loan, thus that amount will be entered on line 202, Principal Amount of New Loan.

You will note that this section is divided into two parts, the second part is Adjustments for Items Unpaid by the Seller. The only items that appear are taxes on lines 210, 211, and 212. On the previous sheet, the borrower was charged for 5 months of taxes plus the borrower will make 7 monthly payments that will contain escrow payments for taxes. In other words, the borrower would be charged for a

Figure 15–16.   HUD Form 1, page 1

HUD-1 Rev. 2/79 7

Page 1 Form Approved
OMB No. 63-R 1501

U.S. DEPARTMENT OF HOUSING AND URBAN DEVELOPMENT

B. TYPE OF LOAN

1. ☐ FHA   2. ☐ FMHA   3. ☐ CONV. UNIS.
4. ☐ VA   5. ☐ CONV. INS.

6. FILE NUMBER
GF

7. LOAN NUMBER

8. MORTG. INS. CASE NO.

SETTLEMENT STATEMENT

C. NOTE: This form is furnished to give you a statement of actual settlement costs. Amounts paid to and by the settlement agent are shown. Items marked "(p.o.c.)" were paid outside the closing; they are shown here for informational purposes and are not included in the totals.

D. NAME OF BORROWER	E. SELLER	F. LENDER	
G. PROPERTY LOCATION	H. SETTLEMENT AGENT	PLACE OF SETTLEMENT	I. SETTLEMENT DATE

J. SUMMARY OF BORROWER'S TRANSACTION		K. SUMMARY OF SELLER'S TRANSACTION	
100. GROSS AMOUNT DUE FROM BORROWER:		400. GROSS AMOUNT DUE TO SELLER:	
101. Contract sales price	45,000.00	401. Contract sales price	45,000.00
103. Settlement charges to borrower (Line 1400)	2,121.50	403. Reserves transferred	
104. Reserves transferred		404.	
105.		405.	
Adjustments for items paid by seller in advance:		Adjustments for items paid by seller in advance:	
106. City. tax to		406. City. tax to	
107. School tax to		407. School tax to	
108. County tax to		408. County tax to	
109. Assessments to		409. Assessments to	
110.		410.	
111.		411.	
120. GROSS AMOUNT DUE FROM BORROWER:	47,121.50	420. GROSS AMOUNT DUE TO SELLER:	45,000.00
200. AMOUNTS PAID BY OR IN BEHALF OF BORROWER:		500. REDUCTIONS IN AMOUNT DUE TO SELLER:	
201. Deposit or earnest money	1000.00	502. Settlement charges to seller (Line 1400)	3488.00
202. Principal amount of new loan(s)	36,000.00	503. Existing loan(s) taken subject to/assumed	
203. Existing loan(s) taken subject to/assumed		504. Payoff of first mortgage loan	14,983.75
204.		505. Payoff of second mortgage loan	
205.		506. Deposit or earnest money	
206.		507. Interest 14 days	40.74
207.		508.	
208.		509.	
Adjustments for items unpaid by seller		Adjustments for items unpaid by seller	
210. City. tax to		510. City. tax to	
211. School tax 1-1 to 2-15	105.60	511. School tax 1-1 to 2-15	105.60
213. County tax to		513. County tax to	
214.		514.	
215.		515.	
216.		516.	
217.		517.	
218.		518.	
219.		519.	
220. TOTAL PAID BY/FOR BORROWER	37,105.60	520. TOTAL REDUCTION AMOUNT DUE SELLER	18,618.09
300. CASH AT SETTLEMENT FROM/TO BORROWER		600. CASH AT SETTLEMENT TO/FROM SELLER	
301. Gross amount due from borrower (Line 120)	47,121.50	601. Gross amount due to seller (Line 420)	45,000.00
302. Less amounts paid by/for borrower (Line 220)	37,105.60	602. Less reductions in amount due seller (Line 520)	18,618.09
303. CASH (☐ FROM) (☐ TO) BORROWER	10,015.90	603. CASH (☐ TO) (☐ FROM) SELLER	26,381.91

The undersigned understands the Closing or Escrow Agent has assembled this information representing the transaction from the best information available from other sources and cannot guarantee the accuracy thereof. Any real estate agent or lender involved may be furnished a copy of this Statement.

The undersigned understands that tax and insurance prorations and reserves were based on figures for the preceding year or supplied by others or estimates for the current year, and in the event of any change for current year, all necessary adjustments must be made between Purchaser and Seller direct.

The undersigned hereby authorizes DALLAS TITLE CO. to make expenditures and disbursements as shown above and approves same for payment.

We acknowledge receipt of a copy of the SETTLEMENT STATEMENT.

_____   _____
Purchaser   Seller

_____   _____
Purchaser   Seller

Mailing Address After Closing

We hereby certify that this is a true and correct Statement of the transaction as closed.

Escrow Officer _____

full year of taxes even though the borrower did not live in the property for the full year. The seller owned the property from January 1 to February 15, therefore the borrower should be credited for the time the seller owned the property. This is the section of the form that is used to credit the borrower. You will note on the page that lines 210, 211, and 212 have been bracketed and the time period that the seller had title to the property is indicated. Thus, the seller had title to the property for 45 days. To determine the amount that should be credited to the borrower, the annual taxes of $864.00 is divided by 360 or:

$$\frac{\$864.00}{360} = \$2.40 \text{ per day}$$

Then, the $2.40 is multiplied by the number of days, in this case that is 45 days:

$$\$2.40 \times 44 = \$105.60$$

This amount is entered on the form as indicated. Now all of the entries in the section are added together for a total of $37,105.60. This is the amount that is either paid by the borrower or for the borrower.

The amount the borrower will need to bring to the closing is calculated in the next section, Cash at Settlement from/to Borrower. In this case it will be from the borrower. The first line in the section, line 301 (Gross amount due from borrower), is the amount shown back on line 120 on the form or $47,121.50. Thus, that amount is entered on line 301. In the next line in the section, line 302 (Less amounts paid by/for borrower) is entered the amount shown back on line 220. That amount, $37,105.60, is entered on line 302. Line 302 is subtracted from Line 301 with the difference being the amount of cash that the borrower must bring to closing. In this example, that amount is $10,015.90.

Section K, Summary of Seller's Transaction, is, as its name implies, the seller's portion of the transaction and will show the amount of money that the seller will receive from the sale of his or her home. The first portion is entitled Gross Amount Due to Seller, line 401. Contract sales price is the sales price of the property, or $45,000. That amount is entered on line 401. In reviewing the sample problem, there are no more entries for this portion. So, on line 420 (Gross Amount Due Seller) the $45,000 is entered. Portion 500, Reductions in Amount Due to Seller, is where all of the items that must be paid by the seller are listed and totaled. First, on line 502, the settlement

charges to the seller are entered. This amount is taken from line 1400 of the seller's column. In this example, that amount is $3,488. The next line that will apply to the example is line 504, Payoff First Mortgage Loan. In reviewing the sample problem, the existing lien with interest must be paid at closing. Thus, the amount of the loan, $14,983.75, is entered on line 504. There is no second, so line 505, Pay Off Existing Second Lien, will be left blank. The same is true for line 506, Deposit or Earnest Money. Now on line 507, the amount of the interest on the loan will be entered. Since the seller made the February payment that covered interest for January, the seller will owe interest on money that was used from February 1 to February 14, that is, 14 days. To calculate that amount, we would do the following:

1. Multiply the loan amount by the annual interest rate to calculate the interest for 1 year:

$$\$14,983.75 \times 7\% = \$1,048.86$$

2. Then the daily interest rate must be calculated. This is done by dividing the annual rate by 360 days:

$$\frac{\$1,048.86}{360} = \$2.91$$

3. Then the $2.91 is multiplied by 14 days.

$$\$2.91 \times 14 = \$40.74$$

This amount is then entered on Line 507. As with the borrower's summary, this portion of the seller's summary is divided into two sections. The second section is Adjustments for Items Unpaid by the Seller. Since the borrower is credited for the taxes for the time the seller is in the house, the seller must be charged a like amount. This is the area that the charge is made to the seller and it is indicated as per Figure 15–16 on line 511. In reviewing the sample problem, there are no more entries to be made so all of the entries in the 500 series of numbers are totaled and entered on line 520, Total Reduction Amount Due Seller. The total of all of the entries is $18,618.09.

The final calculation is to calculate the amount of cash the seller will receive. This calculation is done in the final portion of the seller's summary starting with line 601, Gross Amount Due Seller. On this line, the dollar amount shown on line 420 is entered. For this example, that amount is $45,000 or the amount the seller would get if he or she had no loans on the house or any settlement costs. Since this is not the case, there must be some payments. The amounts of those payments are subtracted from the $45,000. This is accomplished by making an entry on line 602, Less Reductions in Amount Due Seller. Here the amount shown on line 520 is entered and subtracted from line 601. The difference is entered on line 603; Cash (to) (from) Seller. Thus, in this example, the seller will receive a check from the title company for $26,376.55.

REVIEW QUESTIONS

1. List 2 of the provisions of the Real Estate Settlement Procedures Act that affect the closing of the real estate transaction.

2. Name and explain some of the procedures or actions taken by the mortgage lender or mortgage company after the approval of the property and purchaser.

3. List and explain 5 basic closing costs related to the closing of a real estate first lien mortgage.

4. Briefly outline the process of closing the real estate transaction.

5. List some of the basic information contained in the Truth-in-Lending Statement.

6. What are the major sections of a commitment for title insurance?

7. What is meant by the term *closing instructions?*

PROBLEMS

1. Using the information supplied in the sample closing problem below, completely prepare a closing statement for the buyer and seller.

2. What is the total settlement charge for the borrower? For the seller?

Sample Closing Statement

Sales price	$74,550.00
Loan to be made by ABC Mortgage	$70,800.00
Escrow deposit: Title company	$ 1,000.00
Owner's title policy	$ 546.00
Mortgagee title policy	$ 40.00
Real estate commission @ 6%	$ 4,473.00
Recording fee buyer deed $5.00 and deed of trust $9.00	$ 14.00
Origination fee	$ 708.00
Copy of restrictions (Buyer)	$ 6.00
Escrow fee (Buyer)	$ 25.00
Escrow fee (Seller)	$ 25.00
Tax research fee (Seller)	$ 27.50
Credit report (Buyer)	$ 70.00
Appraisal fee (Buyer)	$ 125.00
Final inspection fee (Buyer)	$ 35.00
Survey (Buyer)	$ 120.00
Private mortgage insurance	$_____

The mortgage company requires that taxes and insurance be paid monthly along with the payments. The insurance policy, which the buyer must furnish, has an annual premium of $325.00, and is a 1-year policy dated on the date of closing, June 1. (Remember to collect one month for escrow.) The interest rate on the loan is 13.50% and the mortgage company requires that interest be paid in advance up to 30 days prior to the first payment. The loan company will pay taxes in October and the taxes are $969.15. The first payment will be due on August 1. The seller owes liens totaling $41,500 and the loan must be paid off at closing. Attorney's fees for the note and deed of trust paid by the buyer are $90.00 and the seller's deed is $30.00.

Prepare a closing statement for the buyer and seller. PMI, first-year premium is 1.25% and renewal premium is 0.35%. Closing will be at 9 AM.

16   Creative Financing Methods

LEARNING OBJECTIVES

In this final chapter we will examine some of the creative methods that may be used to finance the residential real estate transaction. Upon completion of this chapter, you should be able to do the following:

★ Define *wraparound mortgage*.

★ Name the three types of wraparound mortgages.

★ Explain owner financing.

★ Explain the Federal National Mortgage Association's Home Seller Loan Program.

DEFINITION

Creative financing can be defined as the financing of the real estate transaction using methods that are not normally available through the traditional sources of mortgage financing.

However, since the real estate market has been plagued by high interest rates and rapid inflation of the price of housing, the use of creative financing has become rather commonplace, and some creative methods have now actually become common. Some of these methods were discussed in Chapter 3.

The following creative financing methods are by no means the only ones available, but they are some of the more commonly used.

WRAPAROUND MORTGAGE

As discussed in Chapter 2, a *wraparound mortgage* is the structuring of secondary financing to include an existing mortgage on real property. This structuring is done in a way that virtually makes the wraparound mortgage a first-lien mortgage. Because of the structuring of the wraparound mortgage, it is sometimes called the all-inclusive mortgage. If the wraparound mortgage is executed using a deed of trust, it is sometimes referred to as an all-inclusive deed of trust mortgage.

There are three types of wraparound mortgages.

Additional fund wrap   This is the most common wraparound mortgage. It is used when the existing financing has a below-market interest rate or the existing mortgage includes a restrictive or no prepayment provision. The additional fund wrap combines the mortgage balance with the additional funds that are to be advanced. We will give an example of this type of wrap later in the chapter.

Simultaneous wrap   This type of wrap can be used to reduce the loan-to-value ratio of a first lien mortgage. For example, the purchaser of an office building can only secure an

80 percent mortgage, but would like to reduce this ratio. Thus, the purchaser arranges for a wrap mortgage that is equal to 10 percent of the value. This reduces the purchaser's equity position to only 10 percent. The wrap is negotiated simultaneously with the first-lien mortgage.

Extended-term wrap   This type of wrap is used only to extend the term of existing financing. The only reason for the extension is to improve the cash flow on a piece of income-producing property.

Residential Use of a Wrap

The wraparound mortgage has been used for years in the financing of commercial properties. Now it is a possible method of financing the sale of residential properties. With the advent of the higher interest rates in late 1979, the wrap has become a popular alternative means of financing, but its use has been somewhat limited by the implementation of the *call* or *due-on-sale clause* in many conventional mortgages. Since neither the FHA-insured mortgage nor the VA-guaranteed mortgage has such a provision, the wraparound mortgage is a logical method for financing a transaction involving an existing FHA or VA mortgage.

With this in mind, the Mortgage Guaranty Insurance Corporation has devised a mortgage that combines the advantages of the wraparound mortgage and the safety of an insured conventional mortgage. They call this mortgage "the Magic-Wrap."

The Federal Home Loan Bank Board has realized the importance of the wraparound mortgage as a possible method of fostering homeownership for the first-time homebuyer. The Depository Institutions Deregulation and Monetary Control Act of 1980 (Section 501) states that any federally related mortgage loan, secured by a first lien on residential real property, made after March 31, 1980, is exempt from state usury ceilings. The FHLBB, under this act, has regulations that would permit some lenders to issue wraparound mortgages that would not be subject to the restraint of state usury laws, provided that certain conditions are met.

The FHLBB believes that the wraparound would provide a money-saving alternative to the prospective homebuyer and has taken the position that the wraparound meets the first lien requirement of the 1980 Deregulation Act if (1) The wraparound lender agrees to continue to pay the monthly payments on the existing mortgage on the home to be purchased at the original interest rate of the existing mortgage; and (2) the wraparound lender agrees to make any additional payments needed to meet the purchase price of the home to be purchased.

This agreement means that the term of the original mortgage will continue to be met, the seller will be paid for the sale of the property, and the homebuyer is able to purchase and take advantage of a below-market interest charged by the wraparound lender. Note that if the wraparound lender will not make the wraparound mortgage at a below-market interest rate, the advantage of the wraparound mortgage may be lost.

The FHLBB regulations require that the wraparound lenders meet the following criteria to ensure that they can protect their investments and satisfy their commitment to the borrowers:

1. The wraparound lender shall at all times have sufficient funds available to satisfy all prior liens on the security property.

2. The borrower will reimburse the lender for sums advanced in order to secure or protect the wraparound lender's investment. For example, if private mortgage insurance is required, the borrower would have to pay the premiums.

Note that the FHLBB has limited these regulations to the financing of residential properties.

A Wraparound Mortgage Example

Let us assume that a family wishes to buy a home with a purchase price of $125,000 and an existing mortgage of $80,000 with an interest rate of 9.5 percent. The seller is requiring a down payment of 10 percent, or $12,500.

If the buyer had to execute a new mortgage for the balance of $112,500 at, say, an interest rate of 14 percent, the monthly principal and interest payment would be $1333.

Let us assume that the seller would allow the purchaser to execute a wraparound mortgage with a lender that would agree to continue to pay the monthly payments on the original $80,000 at 9.5 percent. Thus, the amount of the wraparound mortgage would be $80,000 plus the remainder of the seller's equity of $32,500, or a total of $112,500. Let us also assume that the wraparound lender would charge 11.5 percent interest. The principal and interest payments to the borrower would be reduced to approximately $1114 per month.

With the use of the wraparound mortgage, all parties gain advantages. The seller is able to sell his house, the purchaser is able to buy the house with a reduced payment, and the lender is able to make a return on not only the amount advanced, but also on the original mortgage amount. How is this so? First, the wraparound lender is paying an interest rate of 9.5 percent on the original financing, but since it is included in the wraparound, the lender is collecting 11.5 percent, thus making a spread of 2 percent. The wrap lender is collecting a full 11.5 percent on the $32,500 loaned the purchaser to pay the seller's equity in full.

BLENDED YIELD MORTGAGE

The blended yield mortgage (BYM), sometimes called a consolidated mortgage or blended mortgage, can be defined as a first-lien mortgage secured by real property that combines an existing first-lien mortgage and any type of secondary financing that may be used to achieve a sale of real property. In other words, the BYM is used when a sale of real property would normally involve a second or wraparound mortgage. The normal operation of a BYM is that the lender holding the first lien on the property will allow the property to be sold and will take an average of the interest rate on the existing mortgage and the present yield on secondary financing or first-lien mortgage in the market and will refinance the purchase of the property at an interest rate below the prevailing market rate. A good example of the blended yield mortgage or blended mortgage is the Fannie Mae Resale/Refinance Program. This program is discussed in detail in Chapter 10.

The blended mortgage has advantages for both lenders and borrowers. The most obvious to lenders is that they are able to get low-yielding mortgages out of their portfolios. This type of mortgage slows the use of the wraparound mortgage or the second mortgage, which retains the low-yield mortgage.

The primary advantage to the borrower/coborrower is that he or she may purchase the property of his or her choice at a below-market interest rate. This rate may cost the borrower/coborrower less per month than making a combined monthly payment on an existing first and a new second mortgage. An example of such a situation is shown in Figure 10-4 in Chapter 10.

BALLOON MORTGAGE

A *balloon mortgage* is usually used for the financing of raw land or income-producing properties. The purpose of the balloon mortgage is to allow low monthly payments with a large payment due at the term of the mortgage. For example, a person wishes to purchase a parcel of vacant land with the hopes of selling the property in, say, 3 years. The cost of the property is $50,000 and the purchaser would like to be able to pay as little as possible monthly. So the seller agrees to a balloon mortgage with the following terms:

1. The purchaser is to make a down payment of 10 percent, or $5000

2. The note will be executed with monthly payments based on an amortization schedule as if the mortgage were to be paid out in 20 years, but the remaining principal is due and payable at the end of 5 years or upon sale of the property

Thus, the purchaser is able to pay a lesser amount per month while trying to sell the property, with one large, or balloon, payment due at the term of the mortgage or at the sale of the property.

The balloon mortgage also can allow the purchaser of property to pay interest only for a specific term (for example, 3 years) at the end of which the full principal amount of the mortgage is due.

Federally chartered thrifts were allowed to make the balloon mortgage, but due to the changing real estate market and the high interest rates, the FHLBB saw a need to liberalize this rule. After publishing the rule for public comment on July 14, 1981, and receiving comments, the Board issued its Final Rule revising the authority of Federal thrifts to make the balloon mortgage, effective October 21, 1981.

This revision made sweeping changes in the authority. Before this change, the thrifts could only make balloon loans for a maximum term of 5 years and with a maximum loan-to-value ratio of 60 percent. This would require the borrower to make a down payment of 40 percent. The revision now allows a maximum term of 40 years and allows a loan-to-value ratio of up to 95 percent.

The revision also allows the thrifts to adjust the interest rate on the balloon mortgage. The rule regarding the adjustment of the interest rate is the same as that of the ARM reviewed in Chapter 3.

The revised rule does contain a disclosure requirement. According to the revised rule, the application and the loan contract is to contain a disclosure notice. The form and content of this notice is shown in Figure 16–1. The other required notice is at the time of a rate or payment change. The rule states that this notice must be given at least 45 days, but not more than 90 days, prior to the maturity of the balloon mortgage. The notice must contain the following:

1. The maturity date

2. The amount due at maturity

3. Whether, and under what conditions, the mortgage will be refinanced

The board feels that this revised rule gives the federal thrifts the flexibility to structure the balloon mortgage to make it attractive to the prospective homebuyer. The FHLBB feels that the balloon mortgage will offer borrowers the advantage of a fixed-rate mortgage without being tied to a long-term mortgage that has a high interest rate.

The balloon mortgage may provide an excellent vehicle for a client who is being transferred into your area and knows that he or she will be there for a limited period, say up to 4 years. The balloon will allow this person the advantages of a short-term fixed rate mortgage with all of the monies paid to the lender being tax deductible. This type of mortgage is, however, not suitable for the person who is purchasing a home in which he or she plans to spend many years.

PARTICIPATION MORTGAGE

In this type of financing, the lender will participate in the property, in either the appreciation of the property upon its sale, or in the revenue generated by the property.

Until recently, the participation mortgage was limited to income-producing properties. With the advent of the shared appreciation mortgage, however, lenders are now sharing in the appreciation, or profit, from the sale of residential property. The other type of participation by the lender is limited to the income-producing property. Here the lender will make a mortgage financing, for example, an office building and in return the borrower must give the lender a share of the income derived from the property. For example, a lender may agree to make a 75 percent mortgage at an interest rate of 11.5 percent for twenty years. The lender will receive 15 percent of the net income before federal taxes and depreciation. Let us say the building has a net income of $20,000 before taxes and depreciation. The lender would not only receive the interest income from the mortgage, but would receive $3000 of the net income of the building.

EQUITY PARTICIPATION MORTGAGE

As mentioned in the previous section, the participation mortgage was limited to the financing of commercial real estate transactions. However, with the continuing high interest rates in the 1980s, the participation mortgage became an alternative way to finance residential real estate. These mortgages were called by many titles, one of the most common being Shared Equity Mortgage (SEM). This type of residential creative financing involves the borrower/coborrower who will occupy the property and an investor who will not occupy the property. It should be noted that the investor may or may not be the institution making the first-lien loan.

The SEM is designed for a builder, developer, or seller of single-family dwellings who knows of individuals or businesses interested in getting the tax advantages of investing in nonowner-occupied 1- to 4-family dwellings. Once the builder, seller, or developer finds a person or persons who would like to purchase a dwelling but does not have the necessary income or down payment to qualify for the mortgage on his or her own, the seller contacts one of the parties that would like to invest in one of these dwellings. Then the owner/occupant and the investor split the down payment and all of the costs of ownership. The percentage paid by the 2 parties is set by the SEM documents. If it is a 50/50 split, the borrower will put up half of the down payment, pay half of the closing costs, and pay half of the monthly payment. Normally, the investor has no right to occupy the property, but shares half of all tax benefits derived from the payment of interest on the mortgage and can also take depreciation on his or her half of the dwelling since he or she does not occupy the unit.

The borrower also can claim a tax deduction for his portion of the interest paid. The occupant of the unit will also pay a rental fee to the investor/nonowner occupant.

The term of an SEM ranges from 3 to 5 years and the procedure followed at the end of the SEM term is outlined in the original loan

Figure 16–1.   Balloon Disclosure

To be Included in Loan Application and Loan Contract:

THIS LOAN IS PAYABLE IN FULL AT THE END OF _____ YEARS. YOU MUST REPAY THE ENTIRE PRINCIPAL BALANCE OF THE LOAN AND UNPAID INTEREST THEN DUE. THE LENDER IS UNDER NO OBLIGATION TO REFINANCE THE LOAN AT THAT TIME. YOU WILL THEREFORE BE REQUIRED TO MAKE PAYMENT OUT OF OTHER ASSETS YOU MAY OWN, OR YOU WILL HAVE TO FIND A LENDER WILLING TO LEND YOU THE MONEY AT PREVAILING MARKET RATES, WHICH MAY BE CONSIDERABLY HIGHER OR LOWER THAN THE INTEREST RATE ON THIS LOAN. IF YOU REFINANCE THIS LOAN AT MATURITY, YOU MAY HAVE TO PAY SOME OR ALL CLOSING COSTS NORMALLY ASSOCIATED WITH A NEW LOAN, EVEN IF YOU OBTAIN REFINANCING FROM THE SAME LENDER.

SOURCE: "Rules and Regulations," *Federal Register*, October 23, 1981, vol. 26, no. 205, p. 51896.

documents. Normally there are three options available at the end of the term: (1) the owner/occupant can pay off the remaining principal balance by refinancing or from the sale of other assets; (2) the SEM may be renegotiated and run for another specific number of years; or (3) the home can be sold and the profits distributed as per the original loan documents. For the occupant, the third method is obviously the least desirable; the first is the best option in most cases.

As one can see, the SEM is a very involved type of mortgage that can have many pitfalls for both the investor and the owner/occupant. Before working with any builder, seller, or developer using the SEM you should have all of the documents reviewed by an attorney or have your client, prior to signing any SEM documents, take the documents to an attorney.

OWNER FINANCING

This is a method of financing the real estate transaction in which the seller actually finances the purchase of the property. It can be used when the property is free of all existing debt. The importance of this type of financing has been shown by some real estate commissions' promulgation of a standard contract for an all-cash sale or owner-financed sale of property. Realizing the importance of this method of financing, the Federal National Mortgage Association has created a mortgage purchase program that will allow the homeowner who finances the sale of his or her property by taking back a first-lien mortgage to sell this mortgage to Fannie Mae.

Home Seller Loan Program (Fannie Mae)

Under Fannie Mae's program, a home seller could contract with a Fannie Mae-approved lender to perform the services associated with the origination and processing of the loan and collection of the monthly payments.

The mortgage will be underwritten using the standard Fannie Mae Note and Deed of Trust. This will allow the seller wishing to finance the purchase of a home to use the services of a professional lender and have the ability to convert the first-lien mortgage to cash at any time during the term of the mortgage.

When the seller is ready to convert the mortgage to cash, he or she will contact the lender, who will in turn arrange with Fannie Mae to purchase the mortgage. The purchase

price of the mortgage would be based on the current mortgage rates. For example, the seller would negotiate with the buyer a first-lien mortgage with an interest rate of 12.5 percent face rate. Then, 2 years later, the seller wishes to be cashed out of the mortgage and arranges with the Fannie Mae-approved lender to sell the mortgage to Fannie Mae. If the current mortgage market rate was 12.5 percent, the seller would be able to sell the mortgage at par or for the full amount, less some fees. But if the mortgage market rate was more than 12.5 percent, the seller would have to pay discount points in order to bring the yield of the mortgage to the current mortgage market rate. This is one of the major drawbacks to the program. However, it does give the seller an opportunity to finance the sale of his or her home with liquidity.

SECOND MORTGAGES

Second mortgages have been used extensively to aid in the financing of real estate by assumption. Either the seller or a financial institution can execute a second mortgage for a portion of the down payment.

As the name implies, the mortgage executed is an inferior mortgage to the first-lien mortgage held by the original lender, as was mentioned earlier in this text. For example, a person wishes to purchase a piece of property by assuming the existing mortgage. (Not all existing conventional mortgages may be assumed without prior approval of the lender.) The purchase price of the property is $80,000, the balance on the existing mortgage is $50,000 with an interest rate of 9.5 percent, and the lender will require the interest rate to increase to 10.5 percent. The seller's equity in the property is $30,000, or the difference between the purchase price and the remaining principal balance of the existing mortgage. The purchaser agrees to the sales price, but only wishes to give the seller $20,000 in cash and to arrange for a second mortgage in the amount of $10,000.

At this point the seller has a choice. Does the seller wish to make the second to the purchaser or to have the purchaser go to a financial institution that specializes in second mortgages? If the seller selects to originate or carry the second, the purchaser would then make the payments directly to the seller. Thus, the seller would get $20,000 in cash, as well as principal reduction and interest on the $10,000 second mortgage.

LAND LEASING

A new method that has been used to finance the real estate transaction is *land leasing,* which is to separate the land from the home, thus making the cost of the house less. Under this method, the house, if financed using some type of first-lien mortgage, and the land is placed on a 99-year lease to the party or parties that purchase the home. It has been proposed that the ground lease be an escalating type lease that will allow for the initial lease payments to be at a lower amount for a specific number of years, say 3 years.

For example, if a person wished to purchase a home costing $84,500 including the land, financing 90 percent of the purchase price over thirty years at 12 percent interest, the payment for principal and interest would be $782.04. If the land was separated from the house, the payment could be lowered. For this example, let us say the land is valued at $18,000. The actual value of the house would then be $66,500. The principal and interest payment on 90 percent, or a mortgage of approximately $59,900 at 12 percent, would be $616.37, or $165.67 a month less. For our purposes, let us say that the cost of the land lease would be approximately $100 per month for the first three years. The buyer's total monthly payment then would be $716.27. The lease payment would escalate by an amount agreed upon between the parties to the lease. At the end of the first 3-year period, the income of the purchaser should have increased to a level that equals or exceeds the increase in the lease payments.

REVIEW QUESTIONS

1. Define *wraparound mortgage.*

2. Name and explain the types of wraparound mortgages.

3. Explain how owner financing may be used.

4. Explain the Federal National Mortgage Association Home Seller Loan Program.

5. Explain how a balloon mortgage can be used to finance a residential transaction.

6. What is meant by the term *second mortgage?*

7. Contact lenders or developers in your area to see what additional types of creative financing they have developed.

Monthly Payment Factors
for $1000 Loan Amounts

Interest rate	15 years or 180 months	20 years or 240 months	25 years or 300 months	30 years or 360 months
7.000	8.9882	7.7530	7.0678	6.6530
7.125	9.0583	7.8282	7.1477	6.7372
7.250	9.1286	7.9038	7.2281	6.8218
7.375	9.1992	7.9797	7.3088	6.9067
7.500	9.2701	8.0559	7.3899	6.9921
7.625	9.3413	8.1325	7.4714	7.0779
7.750	9.4128	8.2095	7.5533	7.1641
7.875	9.4845	8.2868	7.6355	7.2507
8.000	9.5565	8.3644	7.7182	7.3376
8.125	9.6288	8.4424	7.8012	7.4250
8.250	9.7014	8.5207	7.8845	7.5127
8.375	9.7743	8.5993	7.9682	7.6007
8.500	9.8474	8.6782	8.0523	7.6891
8.625	9.9208	8.7575	8.1367	7.7779
8.750	9.9945	8.8371	8.2214	7.8670
8.875	10.0684	8.9170	8.3065	7.9565
9.000	10.1427	8.9973	8.3920	8.0462
9.125	10.2172	9.0778	8.4777	8.1363
9.250	10.2919	9.1587	8.5638	8.2268
9.375	10.3670	9.2398	8.6502	8.3175
9.500	10.4423	9.3213	8.7370	8.4085
9.625	10.5178	9.4031	8.8240	8.4999
9.750	10.5936	9.4852	8.9114	8.5915
9.875	10.6697	9.5675	8.9990	8.6835
10.000	10.7461	9.6502	9.0870	8.7757
10.125	10.8227	9.7332	9.1753	8.8682
10.250	10.8995	9.8164	9.2638	8.9610
10.375	10.9766	9.8999	9.3527	9.0541
10.500	11.0540	9.9838	9.4418	9.1474
10.625	11.1316	10.0679	9.5312	9.2410
10.750	11.2095	10.1523	9.6209	9.3348
10.875	11.2876	10.2370	9.7109	9.4289
11.000	11.3659	10.3219	9.8011	9.5232
11.125	11.4446	10.4070	9.8916	9.6178
11.250	11.5234	10.4926	9.9824	9.7126
11.375	11.6026	10.5783	10.0734	9.8077
11.500	11.6819	10.6643	10.1647	9.9029
11.625	11.7615	10.7506	10.2562	9.9984
11.750	11.8413	10.8371	10.3480	10.0941
11.875	11.9214	10.9238	10.4400	10.1900
12.000	12.0017	11.0109	10.5322	10.2861
12.125	12.0822	11.0981	10.6247	10.3824
12.250	12.1630	11.1856	10.7174	10.4790
12.375	12.2440	11.2734	10.8104	10.5757
12.500	12.3252	11.3614	10.9035	10.6726
12.625	12.4067	11.4673	11.0156	10.7697
12.750	12.4884	11.5381	11.0905	10.8669
12.875	12.5703	11.6268	11.1843	10.9644
13.000	12.6524	11.7158	11.2784	11.0620
13.125	12.7348	11.8049	11.3726	11.1598
13.250	12.8174	11.8943	11.4670	11.2577
13.375	12.9002	11.9839	11.5616	11.3558
13.500	12.9832	12.0737	11.6564	11.4541
13.625	13.0664	12.1638	11.7515	11.5525
13.750	13.1499	12.2541	11.8467	11.6511
13.875	13.2335	12.3445	11.9420	11.7498

Interest rate	15 years or 180 months	20 years or 240 months	25 years or 300 months	30 years or 360 months
14.000	13.3174	12.4352	12.0376	11.8487
14.125	13.4015	12.5261	12.1334	11.9477
14.250	13.4858	12.6172	12.2293	12.0469
14.375	13.5703	12.7085	12.3254	12.1461
14.500	13.6550	12.8000	12.4216	12.2456
14.625	13.7399	12.8917	12.5181	12.3451
14.750	13.8250	12.9836	12.6146	12.4448
14.875	13.9104	13.0756	12.7114	12.5445
15.000	13.9959	13.1679	12.8081	12.6444
15.125	14.0816	13.2603	12.9054	12.7445
15.250	14.1675	13.3530	13.0026	12.8446
15.375	14.2440	13.4458	13.0999	12.9448
15.500	14.3399	13.5388	13.1975	13.0452
15.625	14.4264	13.6320	13.2951	13.1456
15.750	14.5131	13.7253	13.3929	13.2462
15.875	14.5999	13.8189	13.4908	13.3468
16.000	14.6870	13.9126	13.5889	13.4476
16.125	14.7743	14.0064	13.6871	13.5484
16.250	14.8617	14.1005	13.7854	13.6493
16.375	14.9493	14.1946	13.8839	13.7504
16.500	15.0371	14.2890	13.9824	13.8515
16.625	15.1603	14.4214	14.1207	13.9932
16.750	15.2132	14.4782	14.1800	14.0540
16.875	15.3015	14.5730	14.2789	14.1553
17.000	15.3900	14.6680	14.3780	14.2568
17.125	15.4787	14.7631	14.4771	14.3583
17.250	15.5676	14.8584	14.5764	14.4599
17.375	15.6566	14.9538	14.6758	14.5615
17.500	15.7458	15.0494	14.7753	14.6633
17.625	15.8351	15.1451	14.8749	14.7651
17.750	15.9247	15.2410	14.9746	14.8669
17.875	16.0144	15.3370	15.0744	14.9689
18.000	16.1042	15.4331	15.1743	15.0709

The factors were calculated using a Texas Instruments Business Analyst II using the following keys:

PV	$1000 (or Loan Amount)
%i	Annual Interest Rate divided by 12
N	Term of Loan in Months
2nd PMT	Compute Payment

Outstanding Loan Balance Factors—Section 245, Plan III

PLAN III GRADUATED PAYMENT MORTGAGE (SECTION 245)
WITH INCREASING PAYMENTS FOR 5 YEARS AT 7.50 PERCENT EACH YEAR

OUTSTANDING PRINCIPAL BALANCE FACTORS
(PER THOUSAND DOLLARS OF ORIGINAL LOAN PROCEEDS)

FOR 30 YEAR MORTGAGES WITH ANNUAL CONTRACT INTEREST RATES OF

INSTALL-MENT NUMBER	7.75	8.00	8.25	8.50	8.75	9.00	9.25	9.50	9.75	10.00
1	1001.0866	1001.1566	1001.2250	1001.2919	1001.3572	1001.4212	1001.4837	1001.5448	1001.6046	1001.6630
2	1002.1803	1002.3209	1002.4584	1002.5929	1002.7244	1002.8530	1002.9788	1003.1018	1003.2221	1003.3398
3	1003.2810	1003.4929	1003.7003	1003.9031	1004.1015	1004.2956	1004.4855	1004.6712	1004.8529	1005.0306
4	1004.3888	1004.6728	1004.9507	1005.2226	1005.4887	1005.7490	1006.0037	1006.2530	1006.4969	1006.7355
5	1005.5038	1005.8606	1006.2097	1006.5515	1006.8859	1007.2133	1007.5337	1007.8473	1008.1542	1008.4546
6	1006.6260	1007.0562	1007.4774	1007.8897	1008.2934	1008.6886	1009.0754	1009.4542	1009.8250	1010.1881
7	1007.7554	1008.2599	1008.7538	1009.2375	1009.7111	1010.1749	1010.6291	1011.0738	1011.5094	1011.9360
8	1008.8922	1009.4715	1010.0390	1010.5948	1011.1392	1011.6724	1012.1947	1012.7063	1013.2075	1013.6984
9	1010.0362	1010.6912	1011.3330	1011.9617	1012.5776	1013.1811	1013.7724	1014.3517	1014.9193	1015.4755
10	1011.1877	1011.9191	1012.6359	1013.3383	1014.0266	1014.7011	1015.3622	1016.0101	1016.6451	1017.2675
11	1012.3466	1013.1551	1013.9477	1014.7246	1015.4861	1016.2326	1016.9643	1017.6817	1018.3849	1019.0743
12	1013.5130	1014.3994	1015.2686	1016.1208	1016.9563	1017.7755	1018.5788	1019.3664	1020.1388	1020.8963
13	1014.2840	1015.2388	1016.1748	1017.0924	1017.9921	1018.8741	1019.7388	1020.5867	1021.4180	1022.2331
14	1015.0600	1016.0837	1017.0872	1018.0710	1019.0354	1019.9809	1020.9078	1021.8165	1022.7075	1023.5811
15	1015.8410	1016.9342	1018.0059	1019.0565	1020.0864	1021.0960	1022.0858	1023.0562	1024.0075	1024.9403
16	1016.6271	1017.7905	1018.9310	1020.0490	1021.1450	1022.2195	1023.2729	1024.3056	1025.3181	1026.3108
17	1017.4183	1018.6524	1019.8623	1021.0485	1022.2114	1023.3514	1024.4691	1025.5649	1026.6393	1027.6928
18	1018.2145	1019.5201	1020.8001	1022.0551	1023.2855	1024.4918	1025.6746	1026.8342	1027.9713	1029.0863
19	1019.0159	1020.3936	1021.7444	1023.0688	1024.3675	1025.6408	1026.8893	1028.1136	1029.3141	1030.4914
20	1019.8225	1021.2728	1022.6951	1024.0897	1025.4573	1026.7984	1028.1134	1029.4031	1030.6678	1031.9082
21	1020.6343	1022.1580	1023.6523	1025.1179	1026.5551	1027.9646	1029.3470	1030.7027	1032.0325	1033.3368
22	1021.4513	1023.0491	1024.6162	1026.1533	1027.6609	1029.1396	1030.5900	1032.0127	1033.4083	1034.7773
23	1022.2736	1023.9460	1025.5867	1027.1960	1028.7747	1030.3234	1031.8427	1033.3330	1034.7952	1036.2298
24	1023.1012	1024.8490	1026.5638	1028.2462	1029.8967	1031.5161	1033.1049	1034.6638	1036.1935	1037.6944
25	1023.5011	1025.3138	1027.0961	1028.8358	1030.5484	1032.2276	1033.8751	1035.4914	1037.0773	1038.6334
26	1023.9035	1025.7816	1027.6241	1029.4316	1031.2049	1032.9445	1034.6512	1036.3256	1037.9684	1039.5803
27	1024.3086	1026.2526	1028.1597	1030.0307	1031.8661	1033.6668	1035.4333	1037.1663	1038.8667	1040.5350
28	1024.7162	1026.7267	1028.6990	1030.6339	1032.5322	1034.3944	1036.2214	1038.0138	1039.7723	1041.4977
29	1025.1265	1027.2039	1029.2420	1031.2415	1033.2031	1035.1275	1037.0156	1038.8679	1040.6853	1042.4685
30	1025.5395	1027.6844	1029.7887	1031.8534	1033.8789	1035.8662	1037.8159	1039.7288	1041.6056	1043.4473
31	1025.9551	1028.1680	1030.3392	1032.4695	1034.5596	1036.6103	1038.6223	1040.5965	1042.5335	1044.4342
32	1026.3734	1028.6549	1030.8935	1033.0901	1035.2453	1037.3600	1039.4350	1041.4710	1043.4689	1045.4294
33	1026.7944	1029.1450	1031.4516	1033.7150	1035.9360	1038.1154	1040.2540	1042.3525	1044.4119	1046.4329
34	1027.2181	1029.6384	1032.0136	1034.3444	1036.6318	1038.8764	1041.0792	1043.2410	1045.3625	1047.4447
35	1027.6445	1030.1350	1032.5793	1034.9783	1037.3326	1039.6432	1041.9109	1044.1365	1046.3209	1048.4650
36	1028.0738	1030.6350	1033.1490	1035.6166	1038.0385	1040.4157	1042.7489	1045.0391	1047.2871	1049.4938
37	1028.0402	1030.6608	1033.2329	1035.7575	1038.2352	1040.6671	1043.0539	1045.3965	1047.6960	1049.9530
38	1028.0063	1030.6867	1033.3174	1035.8994	1038.4334	1040.9204	1043.3612	1045.7569	1048.1082	1050.4161
39	1027.9723	1030.7128	1033.4025	1036.0422	1038.6330	1041.1756	1043.6709	1046.1200	1048.5237	1050.8830
40	1027.9381	1030.7390	1033.4881	1036.1861	1038.8340	1041.4327	1043.9830	1046.4860	1048.9426	1051.3538
41	1027.9036	1030.7655	1033.5744	1036.3311	1039.0366	1041.6917	1044.2975	1046.8550	1049.3650	1051.8285
42	1027.8689	1030.7921	1033.6612	1036.4770	1039.2405	1041.9527	1044.6145	1047.2268	1049.7907	1052.3072
43	1027.8340	1030.8189	1033.7486	1036.6240	1039.4460	1042.2157	1044.9339	1047.6016	1050.2199	1052.7899
44	1027.7988	1030.8459	1033.8366	1036.7720	1039.6530	1042.4806	1045.2557	1047.9794	1050.6526	1053.2765
45	1027.7635	1030.8730	1033.9253	1036.9211	1039.8615	1042.7475	1045.5800	1048.3601	1051.0889	1053.7673
46	1027.7279	1030.9004	1034.0145	1037.0712	1040.0715	1043.0164	1045.9068	1048.7439	1051.5286	1054.2621
47	1027.6920	1030.9279	1034.1044	1037.2224	1040.2831	1043.2873	1046.2362	1049.1307	1051.9720	1054.7611
48	1027.6560	1030.9556	1034.1948	1037.3747	1040.4962	1043.5603	1046.5680	1049.5206	1052.4189	1055.2642

NOTE: DUE TO THE ROUNDING INVOLVED IN COMPUTING ACTUAL PAYMENTS, ACTUAL OUTSTANDING BALANCES
WILL TEND TO BE LOWER THAN THOSE COMPUTED USING THE ABOVE FACTORS.

THE HIGHEST OUTSTANDING BALANCE AND FACTORS ARE UNDERLINED.

PLAN III GRADUATED PAYMENT MORTGAGE (SECTION 245)
WITH INCREASING PAYMENTS FOR 5 YEARS AT 7.50 PERCENT EACH YEAR

OUTSTANDING PRINCIPAL BALANCE FACTORS
(PER THOUSAND DOLLARS OF ORIGINAL LOAN PROCEEDS)

INSTALL-MENT NUMBER	FOR 30 YEAR MORTGAGES WITH ANNUAL CONTRACT INTEREST RATES OF									
	7.75	8.00	8.25	8.50	8.75	9.00	9.25	9.50	9.75	10.00
49	1027.1192	1030.4701	1033.7595	1036.9884	1040.1579	1043.2689	1046.3225	1049.3198	1052.2620	1055.1500
50	1026.5789	1029.9813	1033.3212	1036.5994	1039.8171	1042.9753	1046.0751	1049.1175	1052.1037	1055.0349
51	1026.0352	1029.4893	1032.8798	1036.2077	1039.4739	1042.6795	1045.8258	1048.9136	1051.9442	1054.9188
52	1025.4879	1028.9941	1032.4355	1035.8131	1039.1281	1042.3816	1045.5745	1048.7081	1051.7834	1054.8017
53	1024.9372	1028.4955	1031.9880	1035.4158	1038.7799	1042.0813	1045.3213	1048.5009	1051.6213	1054.6837
54	1024.3828	1027.9936	1031.5375	1035.0157	1038.4291	1041.7789	1045.0662	1048.2921	1051.4579	1054.5647
55	1023.8249	1027.4883	1031.0839	1034.6127	1038.0757	1041.4741	1044.8091	1048.0817	1051.2931	1054.4446
56	1023.2634	1026.9797	1030.6272	1034.2069	1037.7198	1041.1671	1044.5500	1047.8695	1051.1270	1054.3236
57	1022.6982	1026.4677	1030.1673	1033.7982	1037.3613	1040.8578	1044.2889	1047.6557	1050.9596	1054.2016
58	1022.1294	1025.9523	1029.7043	1033.3866	1037.0001	1040.5461	1044.0258	1047.4402	1050.7908	1054.0786
59	1021.5569	1025.4334	1029.2381	1032.9721	1036.6364	1040.2322	1043.7607	1047.2230	1050.6206	1053.9545
60	1020.9807	1024.9111	1028.7687	1032.5546	1036.2699	1039.9158	1043.4935	1047.0041	1050.4490	1053.8294
61	1019.8628	1023.8334	1027.7302	1031.5541	1035.3064	1038.9883	1042.6008	1046.1453	1049.6230	1053.0352
62	1018.7377	1022.7485	1026.6845	1030.5466	1034.3359	1038.0537	1041.7012	1045.2796	1048.7902	1052.2343
63	1017.6052	1021.6564	1025.6316	1029.5319	1033.3583	1037.1122	1040.7947	1044.4071	1047.9507	1051.4268
64	1016.4655	1020.5570	1024.5715	1028.5100	1032.3736	1036.1636	1039.8812	1043.5277	1047.1043	1050.6125
65	1015.3184	1019.4503	1023.5041	1027.4808	1031.3817	1035.2079	1038.9607	1042.6413	1046.2511	1049.7915
66	1014.1639	1018.3362	1022.4294	1026.4444	1030.3826	1034.2450	1038.0330	1041.7479	1045.3910	1048.9636
67	1013.0020	1017.2147	1021.3472	1025.4006	1029.3761	1033.2749	1037.0983	1040.8474	1044.5238	1048.1288
68	1011.8325	1016.0857	1020.2577	1024.3495	1028.3624	1032.2975	1036.1563	1039.9398	1043.6496	1047.2870
69	1010.6555	1014.9492	1019.1606	1023.2909	1027.3412	1031.3128	1035.2070	1039.0251	1042.7683	1046.4383
70	1009.4709	1013.8051	1018.0560	1022.2248	1026.3126	1030.3208	1034.2504	1038.1030	1041.8799	1045.5824
71	1008.2786	1012.6534	1016.9438	1021.1511	1025.2765	1029.3212	1033.2865	1037.1737	1040.9842	1044.7194
72	1007.0787	1011.4940	1015.8240	1020.0699	1024.2329	1028.3142	1032.3151	1036.2370	1040.0813	1043.8493
73	1005.8710	1010.3268	1014.6964	1018.9810	1023.1816	1027.2996	1031.3363	1035.2929	1039.1710	1042.9719
74	1004.6555	1009.1519	1013.5611	1017.8843	1022.1227	1026.2774	1030.3499	1034.3414	1038.2533	1042.0871
75	1003.4321	1007.9691	1012.4181	1016.7800	1021.0560	1025.2476	1029.3559	1033.3823	1037.3282	1041.1951
76	1002.2008	1006.7785	1011.2671	1015.6677	1019.9816	1024.2100	1028.3542	1032.4156	1036.3955	1040.2955
77	1000.9616	1005.5799	1010.1082	1014.5476	1018.8994	1023.1646	1027.3448	1031.4412	1035.4553	1039.3885
78	999.7144	1004.3734	1008.9414	1013.4196	1017.8092	1022.1114	1026.3276	1030.4591	1034.5074	1038.4739
79	998.4591	1003.1588	1007.7665	1012.2836	1016.7111	1021.0503	1025.3026	1029.4693	1033.5519	1037.5517
80	997.1958	1001.9361	1006.5836	1011.1395	1015.6050	1019.9813	1024.2697	1028.4716	1032.5885	1036.6218
81	995.9242	1000.7052	1005.3925	1009.9873	1014.4908	1018.9042	1023.2288	1027.4661	1031.6174	1035.6842
82	994.6445	999.4661	1004.1933	1008.8270	1013.3685	1017.8190	1022.1799	1026.4525	1030.6383	1034.7387
83	993.3565	998.2188	1002.9858	1007.6585	1012.2380	1016.7257	1021.1229	1025.4310	1029.6513	1033.7854
84	992.0601	996.9632	1001.7700	1006.4816	1011.0993	1015.6243	1020.0578	1024.4013	1028.6563	1032.8241
85	990.7554	995.6992	1000.5458	1005.2965	1009.9523	1014.5145	1018.9845	1023.3635	1027.6532	1031.8548
86	989.4423	994.4267	999.3133	1004.1029	1008.7969	1013.3964	1017.9028	1022.3175	1026.6419	1030.8775
87	988.1207	993.1458	998.0722	1002.9009	1007.6331	1012.2700	1016.8129	1021.2632	1025.6224	1029.8919
88	986.7905	991.8564	996.8226	1001.6904	1006.4608	1011.1351	1015.7145	1020.2006	1024.5946	1028.8982
89	985.4518	990.5583	995.5644	1000.4713	1005.2799	1009.9916	1014.6077	1019.1295	1023.5585	1027.8962
90	984.1044	989.2516	994.2976	999.2435	1004.0905	1008.8396	1013.4924	1018.0500	1022.5140	1026.8859
91	982.7483	987.9362	993.0221	998.0071	1002.8923	1007.6790	1012.3684	1016.9619	1021.4610	1025.8671
92	981.3835	986.6120	991.7378	996.7619	1001.6855	1006.5096	1011.2358	1015.8652	1020.3994	1024.8398
93	980.0098	985.2790	990.4447	995.5079	1000.4698	1005.3315	1010.0944	1014.7599	1019.3292	1023.8040
94	978.6273	983.9371	989.1426	994.2450	999.2452	1004.1446	1008.9443	1013.6457	1018.2503	1022.7595
95	977.2358	982.5862	987.8317	992.9732	998.0118	1002.9487	1007.7853	1012.5228	1017.1627	1021.7064
96	975.8354	981.2264	986.5117	991.6923	996.7693	1001.7439	1006.6173	1011.3910	1016.0662	1020.6445

NOTE: DUE TO THE ROUNDING INVOLVED IN COMPUTING ACTUAL PAYMENTS, ACTUAL OUTSTANDING BALANCES
WILL TEND TO BE LOWER THAN THOSE COMPUTED USING THE ABOVE FACTORS.

THE HIGHEST OUTSTANDING BALANCE AND FACTORS ARE UNDERLINED.

PLAN III GRADUATED PAYMENT MORTGAGE (SECTION 245)
WITH INCREASING PAYMENTS FOR 5 YEARS AT 7.50 PERCENT EACH YEAR

OUTSTANDING PRINCIPAL BALANCE FACTORS
(PER THOUSAND DOLLARS OF ORIGINAL LOAN PROCEEDS)

FOR 30 YEAR MORTGAGES WITH ANNUAL CONTRACT INTEREST RATES OF

INSTALL-MENT NUMBER	7.75	8.00	8.25	8.50	8.75	9.00	9.25	9.50	9.75	10.00
97	974.4259	979.8574	985.1826	990.4024	995.5178	1000.5301	1005.4404	1010.2502	1014.9608	1019.5737
98	973.0073	978.4794	983.8444	989.1033	994.2572	999.3071	1004.2544	1009.1003	1013.8464	1018.4940
99	971.5795	977.0922	982.4970	987.7951	992.9873	998.0750	1003.0592	1007.9414	1012.7229	1017.4053
100	970.1425	975.6957	981.1404	986.4775	991.7082	996.8336	1001.8548	1006.7733	1011.5904	1016.3075
101	968.6963	974.2899	979.7744	985.1507	990.4198	995.5829	1000.6412	1005.5959	1010.4486	1015.2005
102	967.2407	972.8747	978.3990	983.8144	989.1220	994.3228	999.4182	1004.4093	1009.2975	1014.0844
103	965.7757	971.4501	977.0142	982.4687	987.8147	993.0533	998.1857	1003.2132	1008.1371	1012.9589
104	964.3012	970.0160	975.6198	981.1134	986.4979	991.7743	996.9438	1002.0077	1006.9673	1011.8241
105	962.8172	968.5724	974.2159	979.7486	985.1715	990.4857	995.6923	1000.7926	1005.7880	1010.6798
106	961.3237	967.1191	972.8023	978.3741	983.8354	989.1874	994.4311	999.5679	1004.5990	1009.5260
107	959.8205	965.6561	971.3790	976.9898	982.4896	987.8793	993.1602	998.3335	1003.4005	1008.3626
108	958.3075	964.1834	969.9459	975.5957	981.1339	986.5615	991.8796	997.0893	1002.1922	1007.1894
109	956.7849	962.7009	968.5029	974.1918	979.7684	985.2338	990.5890	995.8353	1000.9740	1006.0065
110	955.2523	961.2084	967.0500	972.7779	978.3929	983.8961	989.2885	994.5714	999.7460	1004.8137
111	953.7099	959.7061	965.5872	971.3540	977.0074	982.5484	987.9780	993.2974	998.5080	1003.6110
112	952.1575	958.1937	964.1143	969.9200	975.6118	981.1906	986.6574	992.0134	997.2599	1002.3983
113	950.5951	956.6712	962.6312	968.4759	974.2060	979.8226	985.3266	990.7192	996.0017	1001.1755
114	949.0226	955.1386	961.1380	967.0215	972.7900	978.4443	983.9855	989.4147	994.7333	999.9424
115	947.4400	953.5957	959.6345	965.5568	971.3636	977.0557	982.6341	988.1000	993.4545	998.6991
116	945.8471	952.0426	958.1206	964.0818	969.9268	975.6567	981.2723	986.7748	992.1654	997.4455
117	944.2439	950.4791	956.5964	962.5963	968.4796	974.2472	979.9000	985.4391	990.8658	996.1814
118	942.6304	948.9052	955.0617	961.1003	967.0218	972.8271	978.5171	984.0929	989.5557	994.9067
119	941.0065	947.3208	953.5164	959.5937	965.5	971.3963	977.1235	982.7360	988.2349	993.6215
120	939.3720	945.7259	951.9605	958.0764	964.0,	969.9549	975.7192	981.3683	986.9033	992.3255
121	937.7270	944.1203	950.3939	956.5483	962.5843	5 ,026	974.3041	979.9898	985.5610	991.0187
122	936.0714	942.5040	948.8165	955.0095	961.0835	967.0394	972.8781	978.6005	984.2077	989.7010
123	934.4051	940.8769	947.2283	953.4597	959.5718	965.5653	971.4410	977.2001	982.8434	988.3724
124	932.7281	939.2390	945.6242	951.8990	958.0491	964.0801	969.9930	975.7886	981.4681	987.0327
125	931.0402	937.5902	944.0190	950.3272	956.5152	962.5838	968.5337	974.3659	980.0816	985.6818
126	929.3414	935.9303	942.3978	948.7443	954.9702	961.0762	967.0632	972.9320	978.6838	984.3197
127	927.6316	934.2594	940.7655	947.1501	953.4139	959.5573	965.5813	971.4868	977.2747	982.9462
128	925.9108	932.5774	939.1219	945.5447	951.8462	958.0271	964.0881	970.0301	975.8541	981.5612
129	924.1789	930.8842	937.4671	943.9279	950.2671	956.4854	962.5833	968.5618	974.4219	980.1647
130	922.4358	929.1796	935.8008	942.2996	948.6765	954.9321	961.0669	967.0820	972.9782	978.7566
131	920.6814	927.4637	934.1231	940.6599	947.0743	953.3671	959.5389	965.5904	971.5227	977.3368
132	918.9157	925.7364	932.4339	939.0085	945.4605	951.7904	957.9990	964.0870	970.0554	975.9051
133	917.1386	923.9975	930.7330	937.3454	943.8348	950.2019	956.4473	962.5717	968.5761	974.4615
134	915.3501	922.2471	929.0205	935.6705	942.1973	948.6015	954.8836	961.0445	967.0849	973.0058
135	913.5499	920.4850	927.2962	933.9837	940.5479	946.9891	953.3079	959.5051	965.5815	971.5381
136	911.7382	918.7111	925.5600	932.2850	938.8864	945.3646	951.7200	957.9535	964.0659	970.0581
137	909.9147	916.9254	923.8119	930.5743	937.2128	943.7279	950.1199	956.3897	962.5380	968.5657
138	908.0795	915.1278	922.0518	928.8515	935.5271	942.0789	948.5075	954.8135	960.9977	967.0609
139	906.2324	913.3182	920.2796	927.1164	933.8290	940.4175	946.8826	953.2248	959.4448	965.5436
140	904.3734	911.4966	918.4952	925.3691	932.1185	938.7437	945.2452	951.6235	957.8794	964.0137
141	902.5024	909.6628	916.6985	923.6094	930.3956	937.0574	943.5952	950.0095	956.3012	962.4710
142	900.6193	907.8168	914.8895	921.8372	928.6601	935.3584	941.9324	948.3828	954.7102	960.9154
143	898.7240	905.9585	913.0680	920.0525	926.9119	933.6466	940.2569	946.7432	953.1063	959.3469
144	896.8165	904.0878	911.2340	918.2551	925.1511	931.9220	938.5684	945.0906	951.4893	957.7653

NOTE: DUE TO THE ROUNDING INVOLVED IN COMPUTING ACTUAL PAYMENTS, ACTUAL OUTSTANDING BALANCES
WILL TEND TO BE LOWER THAN THOSE COMPUTED USING THE ABOVE FACTORS.

THE HIGHEST OUTSTANDING BALANCE AND FACTORS ARE UNDERLINED.

PLAN III GRADUATED PAYMENT MORTGAGE (SECTION 245)
WITH INCREASING PAYMENTS FOR 5 YEARS   AT 7.50 PERCENT EACH YEAR

OUTSTANDING PRINCIPAL BALANCE FACTORS
(PER THOUSAND DOLLARS OF ORIGINAL LOAN PROCEEDS)

FOR 30 YEAR MORTGAGES WITH ANNUAL CONTRACT INTEREST RATES OF

INSTALL-MENT NUMBER	10.25	10.50	10.75	11.00	11.25	11.50	11.75	12.00	12.25	12.50
1	1001.7201	1001.7760	1001.8306	1001.8840	1001.9363	1001.9874	1002.0374	1002.0862	1002.1341	1002.1809
2	1003.4549	1003.5675	1003.6776	1003.7853	1003.8907	1003.9938	1004.0947	1004.1934	1004.2900	1004.3845
3	1005.2045	1005.3747	1005.5411	1005.7040	1005.8634	1006.0194	1006.1721	1006.3215	1006.4678	1006.6110
4	1006.9691	1007.1977	1007.4214	1007.6403	1007.8547	1008.0645	1008.2699	1008.4710	1008.6679	1008.8608
5	1008.7487	1009.0366	1009.3185	1009.5944	1009.8646	1010.1291	1010.3882	1010.6420	1010.8905	1011.1340
6	1010.5436	1010.8917	1011.2325	1011.5664	1011.8933	1012.2136	1012.5273	1012.8346	1013.1358	1013.4308
7	1012.3537	1012.7629	1013.1638	1013.5564	1013.9411	1014.3180	1014.6873	1015.0492	1015.4039	1015.7516
8	1014.1794	1014.6506	1015.1123	1015.5647	1016.0080	1016.4426	1016.8685	1017.2860	1017.6953	1018.0966
9	1016.0206	1016.5547	1017.0783	1017.5914	1018.0944	1018.5875	1019.0710	1019.5451	1020.0100	1020.4660
10	1017.8775	1018.4756	1019.0618	1019.6367	1020.2003	1020.7530	1021.2951	1021.8268	1022.3483	1022.8601
11	1019.7503	1020.4132	1021.0632	1021.7007	1022.3259	1022.9393	1023.5409	1024.1313	1024.7106	1025.2791
12	1021.6392	1022.3678	1023.0825	1023.7836	1024.4715	1025.1465	1025.8088	1026.4588	1027.0969	1027.7233
13	1023.0325	1023.8164	1024.5853	1025.3395	1026.0793	1026.8051	1027.5173	1028.2161	1028.9020	1029.5753
14	1024.4377	1025.2777	1026.1016	1026.9096	1027.7021	1028.4797	1029.2425	1029.9910	1030.7256	1031.4465
15	1025.8549	1026.7518	1027.6314	1028.4941	1029.3402	1030.1703	1030.9846	1031.7837	1032.5678	1033.3373
16	1027.2843	1028.2388	1029.1750	1030.0931	1030.9936	1031.8771	1032.7438	1033.5942	1034.4287	1035.2478
17	1028.7258	1029.7388	1030.7323	1031.7068	1032.6626	1033.6002	1034.5202	1035.4229	1036.3087	1037.1781
18	1030.1797	1031.2520	1032.3037	1033.3352	1034.3471	1035.3399	1036.3140	1037.2698	1038.2079	1039.1286
19	1031.6460	1032.7783	1033.8891	1034.9786	1036.0475	1037.0962	1038.1253	1039.1352	1040.1264	1041.0994
20	1033.1248	1034.3181	1035.4887	1036.6371	1037.7638	1038.8694	1039.9544	1041.0193	1042.0646	1043.0907
21	1034.6162	1035.8713	1037.1026	1038.3107	1039.4962	1040.6596	1041.8014	1042.9222	1044.0225	1045.1028
22	1036.1204	1037.4381	1038.7310	1039.9997	1041.2449	1042.4669	1043.6665	1044.8441	1046.0004	1047.1358
23	1037.6374	1039.0186	1040.3740	1041.7042	1043.0099	1044.2916	1045.5498	1046.7853	1047.9985	1049.1900
24	1039.1674	1040.6129	1042.0317	1043.4243	1044.7915	1046.1337	1047.4516	1048.7459	1050.0170	1051.2656
25	1040.1604	1041.6589	1043.1296	1044.5730	1045.9900	1047.3811	1048.7468	1050.0880	1051.4051	1052.6988
26	1041.1620	1042.7141	1044.2373	1045.7323	1047.1998	1048.6404	1050.0547	1051.4435	1052.8074	1054.1470
27	1042.1720	1043.7784	1045.3549	1046.9022	1048.4209	1049.9118	1051.3755	1052.8127	1054.2240	1055.6102
28	1043.1908	1044.8521	1046.4826	1048.0828	1049.6534	1051.1953	1052.7091	1054.1955	1055.6551	1057.0886
29	1044.2182	1045.9352	1047.6203	1049.2742	1050.8976	1052.4912	1054.0558	1055.5921	1057.1007	1058.5825
30	1045.2544	1047.0278	1048.7683	1050.4765	1052.1533	1053.7995	1055.4157	1057.0027	1058.5612	1060.0919
31	1046.2994	1048.1299	1049.9265	1051.6899	1053.4209	1055.1203	1056.7889	1058.4274	1060.0365	1061.6171
32	1047.3534	1049.2417	1051.0951	1052.9144	1054.7003	1056.4538	1058.1755	1059.8663	1061.5269	1063.1581
33	1048.4164	1050.3632	1052.2742	1054.1501	1055.9918	1057.8000	1059.5757	1061.3196	1063.0325	1064.7152
34	1049.4885	1051.4945	1053.4638	1055.3971	1057.2953	1059.1592	1060.9897	1062.7875	1064.5535	1066.2885
35	1050.5697	1052.6357	1054.6641	1056.6556	1058.6110	1060.5314	1062.4174	1064.2701	1066.0900	1067.8782
36	1051.6601	1053.7869	1055.8751	1057.9256	1059.9391	1061.9167	1063.8592	1065.7674	1067.6422	1069.4845
37	1052.1687	1054.3438	1056.4792	1058.5760	1060.6350	1062.6570	1064.6430	1066.5939	1068.5105	1070.3936
38	1052.6815	1054.9055	1057.0888	1059.2324	1061.3373	1063.4043	1065.4345	1067.4286	1069.3876	1071.3123
39	1053.1988	1055.4721	1057.7038	1059.8948	1062.0462	1064.1589	1066.2337	1068.2716	1070.2736	1072.2405
40	1053.7205	1056.0436	1058.3243	1060.5633	1062.7618	1064.9206	1067.0407	1069.1231	1071.1687	1073.1784
41	1054.2466	1056.6202	1058.9503	1061.2379	1063.4841	1065.6896	1067.8557	1069.9831	1072.0729	1074.1260
42	1054.7772	1057.2018	1059.5820	1061.9187	1064.2131	1066.4661	1068.6786	1070.8517	1072.9864	1075.0836
43	1055.3124	1057.7885	1060.2193	1062.6058	1064.9490	1067.2499	1069.5096	1071.7290	1073.9092	1076.0511
44	1055.8521	1058.3803	1060.8623	1063.2991	1065.6918	1068.0413	1070.3487	1072.6151	1074.8414	1077.0287
45	1056.3964	1058.9774	1061.5111	1063.9988	1066.4415	1068.8402	1071.1960	1073.5100	1075.7831	1078.0164
46	1056.9454	1059.5796	1062.1657	1064.7050	1067.1983	1069.6468	1072.0517	1074.4139	1076.7344	1079.0145
47	1057.4991	1060.1871	1062.8262	1065.4175	1067.9622	1070.4612	1072.9157	1075.3268	1077.6955	1080.0229
48	<u>1058.0575</u>	<u>1060.7999</u>	1063.4926	1066.1367	1068.7332	1071.2833	1073.7882	1076.2488	1078.6664	1081.0419

NOTE: DUE TO THE ROUNDING INVOLVED IN COMPUTING ACTUAL PAYMENTS, ACTUAL OUTSTANDING BALANCES
WILL TEND TO BE LOWER THAN THOSE COMPUTED USING THE ABOVE FACTORS.

THE HIGHEST OUTSTANDING BALANCE FACTORS ARE UNDERLINED.

PLAN III GRADUATED PAYMENT MORTGAGE (SECTION 245)
WITH INCREASING PAYMENTS FOR 5 YEARS AT 7.50 PERCENT EACH YEAR

OUTSTANDING PRINCIPAL BALANCE FACTORS
(PER THOUSAND DOLLARS OF ORIGINAL LOAN PROCEEDS)

INSTALL-
MENT   FOR 30 YEAR MORTGAGES WITH ANNUAL CONTRACT INTEREST RATES OF

NUMBER	10.25	10.50	10.75	11.00	11.25	11.50	11.75	12.00	12.25	12.50
49	1057.9851	1060.7683	1063.5009	1066.1838	1068.8184	1071.4056	1073.9467	1076.4427	1078.8948	1081.3041
50	1057.9121	1060.7364	1063.5092	1066.2314	1068.9043	1071.5291	1074.1068	1076.6386	1079.1256	1081.5690
51	1057.8384	1060.7043	1063.5176	1066.2795	1068.9911	1071.6537	1074.2684	1076.8364	1079.3588	1081.8368
52	1057.7641	1060.6718	1063.5261	1066.3279	1069.0787	1071.7796	1074.4317	1077.0362	1079.5943	1082.1073
53	1057.6892	1060.6391	1063.5346	1066.3769	1069.1671	1071.9066	1074.5965	1077.2380	1079.8323	1082.3806
54	1057.6137	1060.6061	1063.5432	1066.4262	1069.2564	1072.0349	1074.7629	1077.4418	1080.0727	1082.6567
55	1057.5375	1060.5728	1063.5519	1066.4761	1069.3465	1072.1643	1074.9310	1077.6476	1080.3155	1082.9358
56	1057.4606	1060.539'	1063.5607	1066.5263	1069.4374	1072.2951	1075.1007	1077.8555	1080.5608	1083.2177
57	1057.3831	1060.505.	1063.5696	1066.5771	1069.5292	1072.4271	1075.2721	1078.0655	1080.8086	1083.5026
58	1057.3050	1060.471.	1063.5785	1066.6283	1069.6218	1072.5603	1075.4452	1078.2776	1081.0589	1083.7905
59	1057.2261	1060.4367	1063.5875	1066.6800	1069.7153	1072.6948	1075.6199	1078.4918	1081.3118	1084.0813
60	1057.1466	1060.4019	<u>1063.5966</u>	<u>1066.7321</u>	<u>1069.8097</u>	<u>1072.8307</u>	<u>1075.7964</u>	<u>1078.7082</u>	<u>1081.5673</u>	<u>1084.3752</u>
61	1056.3832	1059.6683	1062.8919	1066.0553	1069.1599	1072.2070	1075.1979	1078.1340	1081.0167	1083.8472
62	1055.6132	1058.9283	1062.1809	1065.3723	1068.5040	1071.5773	1074.5935	1077.5541	1080.4604	1083.3138
63	1054.8367	1058.1818	1061.4634	1064.6830	1067.8420	1070.9416	1073.9833	1076.9685	1079.8985	1082.7748
64	1054.0535	1057.4288	1060.7396	1063.9875	1067.1737	1070.2998	1073.3670	1076.3769	1079.3308	1082.2302
65	1053.2637	1056.6691	1060.0093	1063.2855	1066.4992	1069.6518	1072.7448	1075.7795	1078.7574	1081.6799
66	1052.4671	1055.9029	1059.2724	1062.5771	1065.8184	1068.9977	1072.1164	1075.1761	1078.1781	1081.1238
67	1051.6637	1055.1299	1058.5289	1061.8622	1065.1312	1068.3372	1071.4819	1074.5666	1077.5928	1080.5620
68	1050.8534	1054.3502	1057.7788	1061.1408	1064.4375	1067.6705	1070.8412	1073.9511	1077.0016	1079.9943
69	1050.0362	1053.5636	1057.0220	1060.4127	1063.7373	1066.9973	1070.1942	1073.3294	1076.4044	1079.4207
70	1049.2120	1052.7702	1056.2583	1059.6780	1063.0306	1066.3177	1069.5408	1072.7014	1075.8011	1078.8412
71	1048.3808	1051.9698	1055.4879	1058.9365	1062.3173	1065.6316	1068.8811	1072.0672	1075.1916	1078.2556
72	1047.5425	1051.1624	1054.7105	1058.1882	1061.5972	1064.9389	1068.2149	1071.4267	1074.5759	1077.6639
73	1046.6970	1050.3480	1053.9261	1057.4331	1060.8704	1064.2396	1067.5422	1070.7798	1073.9538	1077.0660
74	1045.8443	1049.5264	1053.1348	1056.6711	1060.1368	1063.5336	1066.8629	1070.1263	1073.3255	1076.4619
75	1044.9844	1048.6976	1052.3363	1055.9020	1059.3963	1062.8208	1066.1769	1069.4664	1072.6907	1075.8515
76	1044.1170	1047.8616	1051.5307	1055.1260	1058.6489	1062.1012	1065.4843	1068.7998	1072.0495	1075.2348
77	1043.2423	1047.0183	1050.7179	1054.3428	1057.8945	1061.3746	1064.7848	1068.1266	1071.4017	1074.6116
78	1042.3601	1046.1676	1049.8978	1053.5524	1057.1330	1060.6411	1064.0785	1067.4467	1070.7473	1073.9820
79	1041.4704	1045.3094	1049.0703	1052.7548	1056.3643	1059.9006	1063.3653	1066.7599	1070.0862	1073.3457
80	1040.5730	1044.4437	1048.2355	1051.9499	1055.5885	1059.1530	1062.6451	1066.0663	1069.4184	1072.7029
81	1039.6680	1043.5705	1047.3931	1051.1375	1054.8054	1058.3983	1061.9178	1065.3658	1068.7437	1072.0534
82	1038.7553	1042.6896	1046.5432	1050.3178	1054.0149	1057.6362	1061.1834	1064.6582	1068.0622	1071.3970
83	1037.8348	1041.8010	1045.6857	1049.4905	1053.2170	1056.8669	1060.4419	1063.9436	1067.3737	1070.7339
84	1036.9064	1040.9047	1044.8206	1048.6557	1052.4117	1056.0903	1059.6931	1063.2218	1066.6782	1070.0639
85	1035.9701	1040.0005	1043.9476	1047.8132	1051.5988	1055.3061	1058.9369	1062.4928	1065.9755	1069.3868
86	1035.0257	1039.0883	1043.0669	1046.9629	1050.7783	1054.5145	1058.1733	1061.7565	1065.2657	1068.7027
87	1034.0734	1038.1682	1042.1782	1046.1049	1049.9500	1053.7153	1057.4023	1061.0129	1064.5487	1068.0115
88	1033.1128	1037.2401	1041.2816	1045.2390	1049.1141	1052.9084	1056.6237	1060.2618	1063.8243	1067.3131
89	1032.1441	1036.3038	1040.3770	1044.3652	1048.2702	1052.0938	1055.8375	1059.5032	1063.0926	1066.6074
90	1031.1671	1035.3594	1039.4642	1043.4834	1047.4185	1051.2713	1055.0436	1058.7370	1062.3533	1065.8944
91	1030.1818	1034.4066	1038.5433	1042.5935	1046.5588	1050.4410	1054.2419	1057.9631	1061.6066	1065.1739
92	1029.1880	1033.4456	1037.6141	1041.6954	1045.6910	1049.6028	1053.4323	1057.1816	1060.8522	1064.4460
93	1028.1858	1032.4761	1036.6767	1040.7891	1044.8151	1048.7565	1052.6149	1056.3922	1060.0901	1063.7104
94	1027.1750	1031.4982	1035.7308	1039.8745	1043.9310	1047.9021	1051.7894	1055.5949	1059.3202	1062.9672
95	1026.1555	1030.5116	1034.7764	1038.9515	1043.0386	1047.0395	1050.9559	1054.7896	1058.5425	1062.2162
96	1025.1274	1029.5165	1033.8135	1038.0200	1042.1378	1046.1686	1050.1142	1053.9763	1057.7568	1061.4575

NOTE: DUE TO THE ROUNDING INVOLVED IN COMPUTING ACTUAL PAYMENTS, ACTUAL OUTSTANDING BALANCES
WILL TEND TO BE LOWER THAN THOSE COMPUTED USING THE ABOVE FACTORS.

THE HIGHEST OUTSTANDING BALANCE FACTORS ARE UNDERLINED.

PLAN III GRADUATED PAYMENT MORTGAGE (SECTION 245)
WITH INCREASING PAYMENTS FOR 5 YEARS AT 7.50 PERCENT EACH YEAR

OUTSTANDING PRINCIPAL BALANCE FACTORS
(PER THOUSAND DOLLARS OF ORIGINAL LOAN PROCEEDS)

INSTALL-
MENT
FOR 30 YEAR MORTGAGES WITH ANNUAL CONTRACT INTEREST RATES OF

NUMBER	10.25	10.50	10.75	11.00	11.25	11.50	11.75	12.00	12.25	12.50
97	1024.0904	1028.5126	1032.8419	1037.0800	1041.2286	1045.2894	1049.2642	1053.1548	1056.9631	1060.6908
98	1023.0446	1027.5000	1031.8617	1036.1314	1040.3108	1044.4017	1048.4059	1052.3252	1056.1613	1059.9161
99	1021.9899	1026.4785	1030.8727	1035.1741	1039.3845	1043.5056	1047.5392	1051.4872	1055.3513	1059.1334
100	1020.9262	1025.4481	1029.8748	1034.2080	1038.4495	1042.6009	1046.6641	1050.6409	1054.5331	1058.3425
101	1019.8534	1024.4086	1028.8680	1033.2331	1037.5057	1041.6875	1045.7803	1049.7861	1053.7064	1057.5434
102	1018.7714	1023.3601	1027.8521	1032.2492	1036.5530	1040.7653	1044.8880	1048.9227	1052.8714	1056.7359
103	1017.6802	1022.3024	1026.8272	1031.2563	1035.5914	1039.8343	1043.9868	1048.0507	1052.0278	1055.9200
104	1016.5796	1021.2354	1025.7931	1030.2543	1034.6208	1038.8944	1043.0769	1047.1700	1051.1757	1055.0957
105	1015.4697	1020.1591	1024.7497	1029.2431	1033.6411	1037.9455	1042.1580	1046.2805	1050.3148	1054.2627
106	1014.3502	1019.0733	1023.6969	1028.2227	1032.6523	1036.9875	1041.2302	1045.3821	1049.4451	1053.4211
107	1013.2213	1017.9781	1022.6348	1027.1929	1031.6541	1036.0203	1040.2932	1044.4747	1048.5666	1052.5707
108	1012.0826	1016.8733	1021.5631	1026.1536	1030.6466	1035.0438	1039.3471	1043.5582	1047.6791	1051.7115
109	1010.9343	1015.7588	1020.4818	1025.1048	1029.6297	1034.0580	1038.3917	1042.6326	1046.7825	1050.8433
110	1009.7761	1014.6346	1019.3908	1024.0464	1028.6032	1033.0628	1037.4270	1041.6977	1045.8768	1049.9660
111	1008.6080	1013.5005	1018.2901	1022.9784	1027.5671	1032.0579	1036.4528	1040.7535	1044.9618	1049.0796
112	1007.4300	1012.3565	1017.1795	1021.9005	1026.5212	1031.0435	1035.4691	1039.7998	1044.0375	1048.1840
113	1006.2419	1011.2025	1016.0589	1020.8127	1025.4656	1030.0194	1034.4757	1038.8366	1043.1037	1047.2791
114	1005.0437	1010.0384	1014.9283	1019.7150	1024.4001	1028.9854	1033.4727	1037.8637	1042.1604	1046.3647
115	1003.8352	1008.8642	1013.7876	1018.6072	1023.3246	1027.9415	1032.4597	1036.8811	1041.2075	1045.4408
116	1002.6164	1007.6796	1012.6367	1017.4892	1022.2390	1026.8876	1031.4369	1035.8887	1040.2449	1044.5073
117	1001.3872	1006.4847	1011.4754	1016.3610	1021.1432	1025.8236	1030.4041	1034.8864	1039.2724	1043.5640
118	1000.1475	1005.2793	1010.3038	1015.2225	1020.0372	1024.7495	1029.3611	1033.8741	1038.2900	1042.6110
119	998.8971	1004.0634	1009.1216	1014.0735	1018.9207	1023.6650	1028.3080	1032.8516	1037.2976	1041.6480
120	997.6362	1002.8368	1007.9289	1012.9140	1017.7939	1022.5701	1027.2445	1031.8189	1036.2951	1040.6749
121	996.3644	1001.5995	1006.7255	1011.7439	1016.6564	1021.4647	1026.1706	1030.7759	1035.2823	1039.6918
122	995.0818	1000.3514	1005.5113	1010.5630	1015.5083	1020.3488	1025.0862	1029.7224	1034.2592	1038.6984
123	993.7882	999.0923	1004.2862	1009.3713	1014.3494	1019.2221	1023.9912	1028.6584	1033.2256	1037.6946
124	992.4836	997.8223	1003.0501	1008.1687	1013.1797	1018.0847	1022.8855	1027.5838	1032.1815	1036.6804
125	991.1678	996.5411	1001.8030	1006.9551	1011.9990	1016.9364	1021.7689	1026.4984	1031.1267	1035.6556
126	989.8408	995.2487	1000.5447	1005.7303	1010.8072	1015.7770	1020.6414	1025.4022	1030.0611	1034.6202
127	988.5025	993.9450	999.2751	1004.4944	1009.6043	1014.6065	1019.5029	1024.2950	1028.9847	1033.5739
128	987.1527	992.6299	997.9942	1003.2470	1008.3901	1013.4249	1018.3532	1023.1767	1027.8973	1032.5168
129	985.7914	991.3033	996.7018	1001.9883	1007.1644	1012.2319	1017.1922	1022.0473	1026.7988	1031.4486
130	984.4185	989.9651	995.3978	1000.7180	1005.9274	1011.0274	1016.0199	1020.9065	1025.6891	1030.3694
131	983.0338	988.6151	994.0821	999.4361	1004.6787	1009.8115	1014.8361	1019.7544	1024.5680	1029.2789
132	981.6374	987.2534	992.7546	998.1424	1003.4183	1008.5838	1013.6407	1018.5907	1023.4355	1028.1770
133	980.2289	985.8798	991.4152	996.8368	1002.1460	1007.3444	1012.4336	1017.4154	1022.2915	1027.0636
134	978.8085	984.4941	990.0639	995.5193	1000.8619	1006.0932	1011.2147	1016.2283	1021.1357	1025.9387
135	977.3759	983.0963	988.7004	994.1897	999.5657	1004.8299	1009.9839	1015.0294	1019.9682	1024.8020
136	975.9311	981.6863	987.3247	992.8480	998.2574	1003.5545	1008.7410	1013.8185	1018.7887	1023.6535
137	974.4740	980.2639	985.9367	991.4939	996.9368	1002.2669	1007.4859	1012.5955	1017.5972	1022.4930
138	973.0044	978.8291	984.5363	990.1274	995.6038	1000.9670	1006.2186	1011.3602	1016.3936	1021.3205
139	971.5222	977.3817	983.1233	988.7484	994.2583	999.6546	1004.9388	1010.1126	1015.1776	1020.1357
140	970.0274	975.9217	981.6977	987.3567	992.9002	998.3296	1003.6465	1008.8525	1013.9493	1018.9386
141	968.5198	974.4489	980.2593	985.9523	991.5294	996.9920	1002.3416	1007.5798	1012.7084	1017.7290
142	966.9994	972.9632	978.8080	984.5350	990.1457	995.6415	1001.0238	1006.2944	1011.4548	1016.5068
143	965.4659	971.4645	977.3437	983.1048	988.7491	994.2781	999.6932	1004.9961	1010.1884	1015.2719
144	963.9194	969.9527	975.8663	981.6614	987.3393	992.9016	998.3495	1003.6849	1008.9092	1014.0241

NOTE: DUE TO THE ROUNDING INVOLVED IN COMPUTING ACTUAL PAYMENTS, ACTUAL OUTSTANDING BALANCES
WILL TEND TO BE LOWER THAN THOSE COMPUTED USING THE ABOVE FACTORS.

THE HIGHEST OUTSTANDING BALANCE FACTORS ARE UNDERLINED.

PLAN III GRADUATED PAYMENT MORTGAGE (SECTION 245)
WITH INCREASING PAYMENTS FOR 5 YEARS AT 7.50 PERCENT EACH YEAR

OUTSTANDING PRINCIPAL BALANCE FACTORS
(PER THOUSAND DOLLARS OF ORIGINAL LOAN PROCEEDS)

FOR 30 YEAR MORTGAGES WITH ANNUAL CONTRACT INTEREST RATES OF

INSTALL-MENT NUMBER	12.75	13.00	13.25	13.50	13.75	14.00	14.25	14.50	14.75	15.00
1	1002.2267	1002.2715	1002.3154	1002.3583	1002.4003	1002.4415	1002.4817	1002.5212	1002.5598	1002.5977
2	1004.4770	1004.5676	1004.6563	1004.7431	1004.8281	1004.9114	1004.9930	1005.0728	1005.1511	1005.2278
3	1006.7513	1006.8886	1007.0230	1007.1548	1007.2838	1007.4102	1007.5340	1007.6553	1007.7743	1007.8908
4	1009.0497	1009.2347	1009.4159	1009.5935	1009.7675	1009.9381	1010.1052	1010.2690	1010.4297	1010.5871
5	1011.3725	1011.6062	1011.8353	1012.0597	1012.2798	1012.4955	1012.7069	1012.9143	1013.1177	1013.3172
6	1013.7200	1014.0035	1014.2813	1014.5537	1014.8208	1015.0827	1015.3396	1015.5915	1015.8387	1016.0813
7	1016.0925	1016.4267	1016.7544	1017.0757	1017.3909	1017.7001	1018.0035	1018.3011	1018.5933	1018.8800
8	1018.4901	1018.8761	1019.2547	1019.6261	1019.9905	1020.3481	1020.6990	1021.0435	1021.3816	1021.7136
9	1020.9133	1021.3521	1021.7827	1022.2052	1022.6199	1023.0269	1023.4266	1023.8189	1024.2043	1024.5827
10	1023.3622	1023.8549	1024.3385	1024.8133	1025.2794	1025.7370	1026.1865	1026.6279	1027.0616	1027.4877
11	1025.8371	1026.3848	1026.9226	1027.4507	1027.9693	1028.4788	1028.9792	1029.4709	1029.9541	1030.4290
12	1028.3383	1028.9422	1029.5353	1030.1178	1030.6901	1031.2525	1031.8051	1032.3482	1032.8821	1033.4070
13	1030.2362	1030.8851	1031.5223	1032.1481	1032.7628	1033.3666	1033.9600	1034.5431	1035.1162	1035.6796
14	1032.1542	1032.8490	1033.5312	1034.2011	1034.8591	1035.5055	1036.1405	1036.7645	1037.3778	1037.9806
15	1034.0927	1034.8342	1035.5623	1036.2773	1036.9795	1037.6693	1038.3469	1039.0128	1039.6672	1040.3103
16	1036.0517	1036.8410	1037.6159	1038.3768	1039.1242	1039.8583	1040.5796	1041.2882	1041.9847	1042.6692
17	1038.0316	1038.8694	1039.6921	1040.5000	1041.2935	1042.0729	1042.8387	1043.5912	1044.3307	1045.0576
18	1040.0325	1040.9199	1041.7913	1042.6470	1043.4876	1044.3133	1045.1246	1045.9219	1046.7055	1047.4758
19	1042.0546	1042.9925	1043.9136	1044.8182	1045.7068	1046.5799	1047.4377	1048.2808	1049.1095	1049.9242
20	1044.0983	1045.0876	1046.0593	1047.0138	1047.9515	1048.8729	1049.7783	1050.6683	1051.5431	1052.4033
21	1046.1636	1047.2054	1048.2288	1049.2341	1050.2219	1051.1926	1052.1467	1053.0845	1054.0066	1054.9133
22	1048.2509	1049.3462	1050.4222	1051.4794	1052.5183	1053.5394	1054.5432	1055.5300	1056.5004	1057.4547
23	1050.3604	1051.5101	1052.6398	1053.7500	1054.8411	1055.9136	1056.9681	1058.0050	1059.0248	1060.0279
24	1052.4923	1053.6975	1054.8819	1056.0461	1057.1904	1058.3155	1059.4219	1060.5099	1061.5803	1062.6333
25	1053.9697	1055.2183	1056.4453	1057.6511	1058.8364	1060.0016	1061.1474	1062.2742	1063.3825	1064.4728
26	1055.4628	1056.7556	1058.0258	1059.2742	1060.5012	1061.7074	1062.8935	1064.0598	1065.2069	1066.3353
27	1056.9718	1058.3095	1059.6239	1060.9155	1062.1851	1063.4332	1064.6602	1065.8669	1067.0537	1068.2211
28	1058.4968	1059.8802	1061.2395	1062.5754	1063.8883	1065.1790	1066.4480	1067.6959	1068.9232	1070.1305
29	1060.0380	1061.4680	1062.8730	1064.2538	1065.6110	1066.9452	1068.2570	1069.5469	1070.8157	1072.0638
30	1061.5956	1063.0729	1064.5246	1065.9512	1067.3535	1068.7320	1070.0874	1071.4204	1072.7314	1074.0212
31	1063.1698	1064.6953	1066.1944	1067.6677	1069.1159	1070.5397	1071.9396	1073.3165	1074.6708	1076.0031
32	1064.7606	1066.3352	1067.8826	1069.4035	1070.8985	1072.3684	1073.8138	1075.2355	1076.6339	1078.0097
33	1066.3684	1067.9929	1069.5895	1071.1588	1072.7015	1074.2185	1075.7103	1077.1776	1078.6212	1080.0415
34	1067.9933	1069.6686	1071.3152	1072.9338	1074.5252	1076.0902	1077.6293	1079.1433	1080.6329	1082.0986
35	1069.6354	1071.3624	1073.0599	1074.7288	1076.3698	1077.9837	1079.5710	1081.1327	1082.6693	1084.1815
36	1071.2950	1073.0745	1074.8239	1076.5440	1078.2356	1079.8992	1081.5359	1083.1461	1084.7307	1086.2904
37	1072.2443	1074.0631	1075.8511	1077.6090	1079.3376	1081.0376	1082.7099	1084.3551	1085.9740	1087.5674
38	1073.2036	1075.0625	1076.8896	1078.6860	1080.4522	1082.1893	1083.8979	1085.5787	1087.2326	1088.8603
39	1074.1732	1076.0727	1077.9396	1079.7750	1081.5797	1083.3544	1085.0999	1086.8171	1088.5067	1090.1695
40	1075.1531	1077.0938	1079.0012	1080.8764	1082.7200	1084.5331	1086.3163	1088.0705	1089.7964	1091.4949
41	1076.1434	1078.1259	1080.0745	1081.9901	1083.8734	1085.7255	1087.5471	1089.3390	1091.1020	1092.8370
42	1077.1442	1079.1693	1081.1597	1083.1163	1085.0401	1086.9318	1088.7925	1090.6228	1092.4237	1094.1958
43	1078.1557	1080.2239	1082.2568	1084.2552	1086.2201	1088.1523	1090.0527	1091.9221	1093.7615	1095.5716
44	1079.1779	1081.2900	1083.3661	1085.4069	1087.4136	1089.3869	1091.3278	1093.2372	1095.1158	1096.9647
45	1080.2109	1082.3677	1084.4876	1086.5716	1088.6208	1090.6360	1092.6181	1094.5681	1096.4868	1098.3751
46	1081.2550	1083.4570	1085.6214	1087.7494	1089.8418	1091.8996	1093.9238	1095.9151	1097.8746	1099.8031
47	1082.3101	1084.5581	1086.7678	1088.9404	1091.0768	1093.1780	1095.2449	1097.2784	1099.2795	1101.2491
48	1083.3764	1085.6711	1087.9269	1090.1449	1092.3260	1094.4713	1096.5817	1098.6582	1100.7017	1102.7130

PLAN III GRADUATED PAYMENT MORTGAGE (SECTION 245)
WITH INCREASING PAYMENTS FOR 5 YEARS AT 7.50 PERCENT EACH YEAR

OUTSTANDING PRINCIPAL BALANCE FACTORS
(PER THOUSAND DOLLARS OF ORIGINAL LOAN PROCEEDS)

FOR 30 YEAR MORTGAGES WITH ANNUAL CONTRACT INTEREST RATES OF

INSTALL-MENT NUMBER	12.75	13.00	13.25	13.50	13.75	14.00	14.25	14.50	14.75	15.00
49	1083.6716	1085.9985	1088.2857	1090.5344	1092.7455	1094.9201	1097.0592	1099.1637	1101.2345	1103.2727
50	1083.9699	1086.3294	1088.6485	1090.9283	1093.1699	1095.3742	1097.5424	1099.6753	1101.7740	1103.8393
51	1084.2714	1086.6639	1089.0153	1091.3266	1093.5991	1095.8336	1098.0313	1100.1931	1102.3201	1104.4131
52	1084.5761	1087.0020	1089.3861	1091.7294	1094.0332	1096.2984	1098.5260	1100.7172	1102.8728	1104.9940*
53	1084.8840	1087.3438	1089.7610	1092.1368	1094.4723	1096.7685	1099.0266	1101.2475	1103.4324	1105.5822
54	1085.1952	1087.6893	1090.1401	1092.5487	1094.9164	1097.2442	1099.5331	1101.7843	1103.9989	1106.1777
55	1085.5097	1088.0385	1090.5233	1092.9653	1095.3656	1097.7254	1100.0457	1102.3276	1104.5723	1106.7807
56	1085.8276	1088.3915	1090.9108	1093.3865	1095.8200	1098.2122	1100.5643	1102.8775	1105.1527	1107.3912
57	1086.1488	1088.7484	1091.3025	1093.8125	1096.2795	1098.7047	1101.0891	1103.4340	1105.7403	1108.0093
58	1086.4734	1089.1091	1091.6986	1094.2433	1096.7443	1099.2029	1101.6201	1103.9972	1106.3352	1108.6352
59	1086.8015	1089.4737	1092.0991	1094.6789	1097.2145	1099.7070	1102.1575	1104.5672	1106.9373	1109.2688
60	<u>1087.1331</u>	<u>1089.8422</u>	<u>1092.5039</u>	<u>1095.1195</u>	<u>1097.6900</u>	<u>1100.2169</u>	<u>1102.7012</u>	<u>1105.1441</u>	<u>1107.5468</u>	<u>1109.9105</u>
61	1086.6270	1089.3572	1092.0393	1094.6744	1097.2638	1099.8088	1102.3105	1104.7702	1107.1891	1109.5683
62	1086.1155	1088.8670	1091.5694	1094.2242	1096.8326	1099.3959	1101.9152	1104.3919	1106.8270	1109.2218
63	1085.5986	1088.3714	1091.0944	1093.7691	1096.3966	1098.9782	1101.5152	1104.0089	1106.4604	1108.8710
64	1085.0762	1087.8705	1090.6142	1093.3088	1095.9555	1098.5556	1101.1105	1103.6213	1106.0894	1108.5158
65	1084.5483	1087.3641	1090.1287	1092.8433	1095.5093	1098.1281	1100.7009	1103.2291	1105.7137	1108.1562
66	1084.0148	1086.8523	1089.6377	1092.3726	1095.0581	1097.6956	1100.2865	1102.8321	1105.3335	1107.7921
67	1083.4755	1086.3349	1089.1414	1091.8966	1094.6017	1097.2581	1099.8672	1102.4303	1104.9486	1107.4234
68	1082.9306	1085.8119	1088.6396	1091.4152	1094.1400	1096.8155	1099.4429	1102.0236	1104.5589	1107.0501
69	1082.3799	1085.2832	1088.1322	1090.9284	1093.6731	1096.3677	1099.0135	1101.6120	1104.1645	1106.6722
70	1081.8233	1084.7488	1087.6193	1090.4361	1093.2008	1095.9146	1098.5791	1101.1955	1103.7652	1106.2895
71	1081.2608	1084.2086	1087.1007	1089.9383	1092.7231	1095.4563	1098.1395	1100.7739	1103.3610	1105.9020
72	1080.6923	1083.6626	1086.5763	1089.4349	1092.2399	1094.9927	1097.6946	1100.3472	1102.9518	1105.5097
73	1080.1178	1083.1107	1086.0462	1088.9259	1091.7512	1094.5236	1097.2445	1099.9154	1102.5376	1105.1125
74	1079.5371	1082.5527	1085.5102	1088.4111	1091.2569	1094.0491	1096.7891	1099.4784	1102.1183	1104.7104
75	1078.9504	1081.9888	1084.9683	1087.8905	1090.7569	1093.5690	1096.3282	1099.0360	1101.6939	1104.3032
76	1078.3573	1081.4187	1084.4204	1087.3641	1090.2512	1093.0833	1095.8619	1098.5884	1101.2642	1103.8909
77	1077.7580	1080.8424	1083.8665	1086.8317	1089.7397	1092.5920	1095.3900	1098.1353	1100.8293	1103.4735
78	1077.1523	1080.2599	1083.3064	1086.2934	1089.2223	1092.0949	1094.9125	1097.6767	1100.3890	1103.0508
79	1076.5402	1079.6711	1082.7402	1085.7490	1088.6991	1091.5920	1094.4294	1097.2126	1099.9433	1102.6229
80	1075.9215	1079.0759	1082.1677	1085.1984	1088.1698	1091.0833	1093.9405	1096.7429	1099.4921	1102.1896
81	1075.2963	1078.4743	1081.5889	1084.6417	1087.6344	1090.5686	1093.4458	1096.2675	1099.0354	1101.7509
82	1074.6645	1077.8661	1081.0037	1084.0787	1087.0929	1090.0479	1092.9452	1095.7864	1098.5731	1101.3067
83	1074.0259	1077.2514	1080.4120	1083.5094	1086.5453	1089.5211	1092.4387	1095.2995	1098.1050	1100.8569
84	1073.3806	1076.6300	1079.8138	1082.9337	1085.9913	1088.9882	1091.9262	1094.8067	1097.6313	1100.4016
85	1072.7284	1076.0019	1079.2090	1082.3515	1085.4310	1088.4491	1091.4076	1094.3079	1097.1517	1099.9405
86	1072.0692	1075.3669	1078.5975	1081.7627	1084.8643	1087.9037	1090.8828	1093.8031	1096.6662	1099.4737
87	1071.4031	1074.7251	1077.9793	1081.1674	1084.2910	1087.3519	1090.3518	1093.2922	1096.1747	1099.0011
88	1070.7299	1074.0763	1077.3542	1080.5653	1083.7112	1086.7937	1089.8145	1092.7751	1095.6772	1098.5225
89	1070.0495	1073.4205	1076.7223	1079.9565	1083.1248	1086.2290	1089.2708	1092.2518	1095.1736	1098.0380
90	1069.3619	1072.7576	1076.0833	1079.3408	1082.5316	1085.6577	1088.7206	1091.7221	1094.6638	1097.5474
91	1068.6670	1072.0875	1075.4373	1078.7181	1081.9317	1085.0797	1088.1640	1091.1861	1094.1477	1097.0506
92	1067.9647	1071.4102	1074.7842	1078.0885	1081.3249	1084.4950	1087.6007	1090.6435	1093.6253	1096.5477
93	1067.2550	1070.7255	1074.1239	1077.4518	1080.7111	1083.9035	1087.0307	1090.0945	1093.0965	1096.0385
94	1066.5377	1070.0334	1073.4562	1076.8079	1080.0903	1083.3050	1086.4539	1089.5387	1092.5612	1095.5229
95	1065.8128	1069.3338	1072.7812	1076.1568	1079.4623	1082.6996	1085.8703	1088.9763	1092.0193	1095.0008
96	1065.0801	1068.6267	1072.0988	1075.4984	1078.8272	1082.0871	1085.2798	1088.4071	1091.4707	1094.4723

NOTE: DUE TO THE ROUNDING INVOLVED IN COMPUTING ACTUAL PAYMENTS, ACTUAL
OUTSTANDING BALANCES WILL TEND TO BE LOWER THAN COMPUTED USING THE ABOVE
FACTORS.

THE HIGHEST OUTSTANDING BALANCE FACTORS ARE UNDERLINED.

PLAN III GRADUATED PAYMENT MORTGAGE (SECTION 245)
WITH INCREASING PAYMENTS FOR 5 YEARS AT 7.50 PERCENT EACH YEAR

OUTSTANDING PRINCIPAL BALANCE FACTORS
(PER THOUSAND DOLLARS OF ORIGINAL LOAN PROCEEDS)

FOR 30 YEAR MORTGAGES WITH ANNUAL CONTRACT INTEREST RATES OF

INSTALL-MENT NUMBER	12.75	13.00	13.25	13.50	13.75	14.00	14.25	14.50	14.75	15.00
97	1064.3398	1067.9118	1071.4088	1074.8325	1078.1848	1081.4675	1084.6823	1087.8310	1090.9154	1093.9371
98	1063.5915	1067.1892	1070.7112	1074.1592	1077.5351	1080.8406	1084.0776	1087.2479	1090.3532	1093.3953
99	1062.8353	1066.4588	1070.0059	1073.4783	1076.8779	1080.2064	1083.4658	1086.6578	1089.7842	1092.8466
100	1062.0710	1065.7205	1069.2928	1072.7897	1076.2131	1079.5649	1082.8467	1086.0606	1089.2081	1092.2911
101	1061.2987	1064.9742	1068.5718	1072.0934	1075.5408	1078.9158	1082.2203	1085.4561	1088.6250	1091.7287
102	1060.5181	1064.2198	1067.8429	1071.3892	1074.8607	1078.2592	1081.5864	1084.8443	1088.0347	1091.1592
103	1059.7292	1063.4572	1067.1059	1070.6772	1074.1729	1077.5949	1080.9451	1084.2252	1087.4371	1090.5826
104	1058.9320	1062.6864	1066.3608	1069.9571	1073.4771	1076.9228	1080.2960	1083.5986	1086.8322	1089.9989
105	1058.1262	1061.9072	1065.6074	1069.2289	1072.7734	1076.2430	1079.6393	1082.9643	1086.2199	1089.4078
106	1057.3120	1061.1195	1064.8458	1068.4925	1072.0617	1075.5552	1078.9748	1082.3225	1085.6000	1088.8093
107	1056.4890	1060.3234	1064.0757	1067.7478	1071.3418	1074.8593	1078.3024	1081.6729	1084.9726	1088.2033
108	1055.6573	1059.5186	1063.2971	1066.9948	1070.6136	1074.1554	1077.6220	1081.0154	1084.3374	1087.5898
109	1054.8168	1058.7051	1062.5099	1066.2333	1069.8771	1073.4432	1076.9335	1080.3500	1083.6944	1086.9686
110	1053.9674	1057.8828	1061.7141	1065.4632	1069.1321	1072.7227	1076.2369	1079.6765	1083.0435	1086.3396
111	1053.1089	1057.0515	1060.9094	1064.6845	1068.3786	1071.9938	1075.5319	1078.9949	1082.3846	1085.7028
112	1052.2413	1056.2113	1060.0959	1063.8970	1067.6165	1071.2564	1074.8186	1078.3051	1081.7176	1085.0580
113	1051.3645	1055.3620	1059.2734	1063.1006	1066.8457	1070.5104	1074.0969	1077.6069	1081.0424	1084.4052
114	1050.4784	1054.5034	1058.4417	1062.2953	1066.0660	1069.7558	1073.3665	1076.9003	1080.3589	1083.7442
115	1049.5828	1053.6356	1057.6010	1061.4809	1065.2774	1068.9923	1072.6275	1076.1851	1079.6670	1083.0749
116	1048.6778	1052.7583	1056.7509	1060.6574	1064.4797	1068.2198	1071.8798	1075.4613	1078.9665	1082.3973
117	1047.7631	1051.8716	1055.8914	1059.8245	1063.6729	1067.4384	1071.1231	1074.7288	1078.2575	1081.7112
118	1046.8387	1050.9753	1055.0225	1058.9824	1062.8569	1066.6479	1070.3574	1073.9874	1077.5398	1081.0165
119	1045.9045	1050.0692	1054.1439	1058.1307	1062.0315	1065.8481	1069.5827	1073.2371	1076.8132	1080.3131
120	1044.9604	1049.1533	1053.2557	1057.2695	1061.1966	1065.0391	1068.7988	1072.4777	1076.0778	1079.6009
121	1044.0062	1048.2275	1052.3577	1056.3986	1060.3522	1064.2205	1068.0055	1071.7091	1075.3332	1078.8799
122	1043.0419	1047.2917	1051.4497	1055.5178	1059.4981	1063.3924	1067.2028	1070.9312	1074.5796	1078.1498
123	1042.0673	1046.3457	1050.5317	1054.6272	1058.6342	1062.5547	1066.3906	1070.1440	1073.8166	1077.4106
124	1041.0824	1045.3895	1049.6036	1053.7266	1057.7605	1061.7072	1065.5688	1069.3472	1073.0443	1076.6622
125	1040.0871	1044.4229	1048.6652	1052.8158	1056.8767	1060.8498	1064.7372	1068.5408	1072.2625	1075.9044
126	1039.0811	1043.4459	1047.7165	1051.8948	1055.9827	1059.9824	1063.8957	1067.7246	1071.4711	1075.1371
127	1038.0645	1042.4583	1046.7573	1050.9634	1055.0786	1059.1049	1063.0442	1066.8986	1070.6699	1074.3603
128	1037.0370	1041.4599	1045.7874	1050.0215	1054.1641	1058.2171	1062.1826	1066.0626	1069.8589	1073.5737
129	1035.9987	1040.4508	1044.8069	1049.0690	1053.2391	1057.3190	1061.3108	1065.2165	1069.0380	1072.7773
130	1034.9493	1039.4307	1043.8156	1048.1059	1052.3035	1056.4104	1060.4286	1064.3602	1068.2069	1071.9709
131	1033.8888	1038.3996	1042.8133	1047.1319	1051.3572	1055.4912	1059.5360	1063.4935	1067.3657	1071.1545
132	1032.8169	1037.3573	1041.8000	1046.1469	1050.4000	1054.5613	1058.6328	1062.6163	1066.5140	1070.3278
133	1031.7338	1036.3037	1040.7754	1045.1508	1049.4319	1053.6205	1057.7188	1061.7286	1065.6520	1069.4909
134	1030.6390	1035.2387	1039.7396	1044.1436	1048.4527	1052.6688	1056.7940	1060.8301	1064.7793	1068.6434
135	1029.5327	1034.1622	1038.6923	1043.1250	1047.4622	1051.7059	1055.8581	1059.9208	1063.8959	1067.7854
136	1028.4146	1033.0740	1037.6334	1042.0949	1046.4604	1050.7319	1054.9112	1059.0005	1063.0016	1066.9166
137	1027.2847	1031.9740	1036.5629	1041.0533	1045.4472	1049.7464	1053.9531	1058.0691	1062.0964	1066.0370
138	1026.1427	1030.8621	1035.4805	1039.9999	1044.4223	1048.7495	1052.9835	1057.1264	1061.1800	1065.1464
139	1024.9886	1029.7381	1034.3862	1038.9347	1043.3857	1047.7409	1052.0025	1056.1723	1060.2524	1064.2447
140	1023.8222	1028.6020	1033.2798	1037.8576	1042.3372	1046.7206	1051.0098	1055.2067	1059.3133	1063.3317
141	1022.6434	1027.4536	1032.1612	1036.7682	1041.2766	1045.6883	1050.0053	1054.2294	1058.3627	1062.4072
142	1021.4522	1026.2927	1031.0302	1035.6667	1040.2040	1044.6440	1048.9888	1053.2403	1057.4005	1061.4713
143	1020.2482	1025.1192	1029.8868	1034.5527	1039.1190	1043.5876	1047.9603	1052.2393	1056.4264	1060.5236
144	1019.0315	1023.9331	1028.7307	1033.4262	1038.0216	1042.5188	1046.9196	1051.2261	1055.4403	1059.5640

PLAN III GRADUATED PAYMENT MORTGAGE (SECTION 245)
WITH INCREASING PAYMENTS FOR 5 YEARS AT 7.50 PERCENT EACH YEAR

OUTSTANDING PRINCIPAL BALANCE FACTORS
(PER THOUSAND DOLLARS OF ORIGINAL LOAN PROCEEDS)

FOR 30 YEAR MORTGAGES WITH ANNUAL CONTRACT INTEREST RATES OF

INSTALL-MENT NUMBER	15.25	15.50	15.75	16.00	16.25	16.50	16.75	17.00	17.25	17.50
1	1002.6347	1002.6711	1002.7067	1002.7415	1002.7757	1002.8092	1002.8421	1002.8743	1002.9058	1002.9368
2	1005.3030	1005.3766	1005.4488	1005.5196	1005.5890	1005.6570	1005.7238	1005.7892	1005.8534	1005.9164
3	1008.0051	1008.1171	1008.2270	1008.3347	1008.4404	1008.5440	1008.6457	1008.7455	1008.8434	1008.9395
4	1010.7416	1010.8931	1011.0416	1011.1874	1011.3304	1011.4707	1011.6085	1011.7436	1011.8763	1012.0066
5	1013.5128	1013.7048	1013.8932	1014.0781	1014.2595	1014.4377	1014.6125	1014.7843	1014.9529	1015.1185
6	1016.3193	1016.5529	1016.7822	1017.0073	1017.2283	1017.4454	1017.6586	1017.8680	1018.0737	1018.2758
7	1019.1614	1019.4378	1019.7091	1019.9756	1020.2373	1020.4945	1020.7471	1020.9953	1021.2393	1021.4791
8	1022.0397	1022.3599	1022.6745	1022.9835	1023.2871	1023.5855	1023.8787	1024.1670	1024.4504	1024.7291
9	1024.9545	1025.3198	1025.6787	1026.0314	1026.3782	1026.7190	1027.0541	1027.3836	1027.7077	1028.0265
10	1027.9064	1028.3179	1028.7224	1029.1201	1029.5111	1029.8956	1030.2738	1030.6458	1031.0119	1031.3720
11	1030.8958	1031.3547	1031.8060	1032.2498	1032.6864	1033.1159	1033.5384	1033.9542	1034.3635	1034.7663
12	1033.9232	1034.4308	1034.9301	1035.4214	1035.9047	1036.3804	1036.8486	1037.3095	1037.7633	1038.2101
13	1036.2335	1036.7782	1037.3139	1037.8408	1038.3592	1038.8693	1039.3713	1039.8654	1040.3518	1040.8307
14	1038.5732	1039.1559	1039.7289	1040.2925	1040.8469	1041.3924	1041.9292	1042.4575	1042.9775	1043.4894
15	1040.9426	1041.5643	1042.1756	1042.7769	1043.3683	1043.9502	1044.5228	1045.0863	1045.6409	1046.1869
16	1043.3421	1044.0038	1044.6544	1045.2944	1045.9238	1046.5432	1047.1526	1047.7523	1048.3426	1048.9238
17	1045.7722	1046.4748	1047.1658	1047.8454	1048.5140	1049.1718	1049.8191	1050.4561	1051.0832	1051.7006
18	1048.2331	1048.9778	1049.7101	1050.4305	1051.1392	1051.8365	1052.5228	1053.1982	1053.8632	1054.5178
19	1050.7253	1051.5130	1052.2878	1053.0500	1053.8000	1054.5379	1055.2642	1055.9792	1056.6831	1057.3762
20	1053.2491	1054.0810	1054.8994	1055.7045	1056.4968	1057.2765	1058.0440	1058.7996	1059.5435	1060.2762
21	1055.8051	1056.6822	1057.5452	1058.3944	1059.2301	1060.0527	1060.8625	1061.6599	1062.4451	1063.2185
22	1058.3935	1059.3170	1060.2258	1061.1201	1062.0004	1062.8671	1063.7204	1064.5607	1065.3884	1066.2038
23	1061.0148	1061.9858	1062.9415	1063.8822	1064.8083	1065.7201	1066.6181	1067.5026	1068.3740	1069.2325
24	1063.6694	1064.6891	1065.6929	1066.6811	1067.6541	1068.6124	1069.5563	1070.4863	1071.4025	1072.3055
25	1065.5456	1066.6013	1067.6404	1068.6634	1069.6706	1070.6624	1071.6393	1072.6017	1073.5499	1074.4842
26	1067.4456	1068.5382	1069.6135	1070.6720	1071.7143	1072.7406	1073.7514	1074.7471	1075.7281	1076.6947
27	1069.3698	1070.5000	1071.6125	1072.7075	1073.7856	1074.8473	1075.8929	1076.9229	1077.9376	1078.9375
28	1071.3184	1072.4873	1073.6377	1074.7701	1075.8851	1076.9830	1078.0643	1079.1295	1080.1789	1081.2130
29	1073.2917	1074.5001	1075.6895	1076.8602	1078.0129	1079.1481	1080.2660	1081.3673	1082.4524	1083.5216
30	1075.2902	1076.5390	1077.7682	1078.9782	1080.1696	1081.3429	1082.4985	1083.6369	1084.7586	1085.8639
31	1077.3141	1078.6042	1079.8742	1081.1244	1082.3555	1083.5679	1084.7621	1085.9386	1087.0979	1088.2404
32	1079.3636	1080.6961	1082.0078	1083.2993	1084.5710	1085.8235	1087.0573	1088.2730	1089.4709	1090.6516
33	1081.4393	1082.8151	1084.1695	1085.5031	1086.8165	1088.1101	1089.3846	1090.6404	1091.8780	1093.0979
34	1083.5413	1084.9613	1086.3595	1087.7363	1089.0924	1090.4282	1091.7443	1093.0413	1094.3197	1095.5798
35	1085.6700	1087.1354	1088.5783	1089.9993	1091.3991	1092.7781	1094.1370	1095.4763	1096.7964	1098.0980
36	1087.8257	1089.3374	1090.8262	1092.2925	1093.7370	1095.1604	1096.5631	1097.9457	1099.3088	1100.6529
37	1089.1358	1090.6800	1092.2006	1093.6982	1095.1735	1096.6271	1098.0596	1099.4714	1100.8633	1102.2356
38	1090.4625	1092.0398	1093.5930	1095.1227	1096.6295	1098.1140	1099.5769	1101.0188	1102.4401	1103.8414
39	1091.8061	1093.4173	1095.0037	1096.5662	1098.1052	1099.6214	1101.1155	1102.5880	1104.0395	1105.4706
40	1093.1667	1094.8125	1096.4330	1098.0289	1099.6008	1101.1495	1102.6755	1104.1795	1105.6620	1107.1236
41	1094.5447	1096.2257	1097.8810	1099.5111	1101.1167	1102.6986	1104.2573	1105.7935	1107.3077	1108.8007
42	1095.9401	1097.6572	1099.3480	1101.0131	1102.6532	1104.2690	1105.8612	1107.4303	1108.9772	1110.5022
43	1097.3533	1099.1072	1100.8343	1102.5351	1104.2104	1105.8610	1107.4874	1109.0904	1110.6706	1112.2286
44	1098.7844	1100.5760	1102.3400	1104.0774	1105.7887	1107.4748	1109.1364	1110.7740	1112.3884	1113.9801
45	1100.2338	1102.0637	1103.8656	1105.6402	1107.3884	1109.1109	1110.8083	1112.4814	1114.1308	1115.7572
46	1101.7015	1103.5706	1105.4111	1107.2239	1109.0098	1110.7695	1112.5037	1114.2131	1115.8983	1117.5602
47	1103.1879	1105.0969	1106.9769	1108.8288	1110.6531	1112.4508	1114.2226	1115.9692	1117.6913	1119.3895
48	1104.6932	1106.6430	1108.5633	1110.4550	1112.3187	1114.1553	1115.9656	1117.7502	1119.5100	1121.2455

PLAN III GRADUATED PAYMENT MORTGAGE (SECTION 245)
WITH INCREASING PAYMENTS FOR 5 YEARS AT 7.50 PERCENT EACH YEAR

OUTSTANDING PRINCIPAL BALANCE FACTORS
(PER THOUSAND DOLLARS OF ORIGINAL LOAN PROCEEDS)

FOR 30 YEAR MORTGAGES WITH ANNUAL CONTRACT INTEREST RATES OF

INSTALL-MENT NUMBER	15.25	15.50	15.75	16.00	16.25	16.50	16.75	17.00	17.25	17.50
49	1105.2790	1107.2545	1109.1998	1111.1160	1113.0037	1114.8639	1116.6972	1118.5044	1120.2862	1122.0433
50	1105.8723	1107.8738	1109.8447	1111.7858	1113.6981	1115.5822	1117.4390	1119.2692	1121.0736	1122.8529
51	1106.4732	1108.5012	1110.4980	1112.4646	1114.4018	1116.3103	1118.1911	1120.0448	1121.8723	1123.6742
52	1107.0816	1109.1366	1111.1599	1113.1525	1115.1150	1117.0485	1118.9537	1120.8314	1122.6825	1124.5075
53	1107.6978	1109.7803	1111.8305	1113.8495	1115.8379	1117.7968	1119.7270	1121.6292	1123.5043	1125.3530
54	1108.3218	1110.4323	1112.5099	1114.5558	1116.5706	1118.5555	1120.5111	1122.4383	1124.3379	1126.2108
55	1108.9538	1111.0927	1113.1982	1115.2715	1117.3133	1119.3245	1121.3061	1123.2588	1125.1836	1127.0811
56	1109.5938	1111.7616	1113.8956	1115.9967	1118.0659	1120.1041	1122.1122	1124.0910	1126.0414	1127.9641
57	1110.2419	1112.4392	1114.6021	1116.7316	1118.8288	1120.8945	1122.9296	1124.9350	1126.9115	1128.8600
58	1110.8983	1113.1255	1115.3179	1117.4764	1119.6020	1121.6957	1123.7583	1125.7909	1127.7941	1129.7689
59	1111.5629	1113.8207	1116.0430	1118.2310	1120.3857	1122.5079	1124.5987	1126.6589	1128.6894	1130.6911
60	1112.2361	1114.5248	1116.7777	1118.9957	1121.1800	1123.3313	1125.4508	1127.5392	1129.5976	1131.6268
61	1111.9088	1114.2119	1116.4785	1118.7098	1120.9067	1123.0702	1125.2013	1127.3010	1129.3701	1131.4095
62	1111.5774	1113.8949	1116.1754	1118.4200	1120.6297	1122.8055	1124.9484	1127.0594	1129.1393	1131.1891
63	1111.2417	1113.5738	1115.8683	1118.1264	1120.3490	1122.5371	1124.6919	1126.8143	1128.9052	1130.9655
64	1110.9018	1113.2486	1115.5572	1117.8288	1120.0644	1122.2651	1124.4319	1126.5658	1128.6677	1130.7386
65	1110.5576	1112.9192	1115.2420	1117.5273	1119.7760	1121.9893	1124.1682	1126.3138	1128.4268	1130.5085
66	1110.2090	1112.5855	1114.9227	1117.2217	1119.4837	1121.7098	1123.9009	1126.0581	1128.1825	1130.2749
67	1109.8560	1112.2475	1114.5992	1116.9121	1119.1875	1121.4264	1123.6298	1125.7989	1127.9346	1130.0380
68	1109.4984	1111.9051	1114.2714	1116.5984	1118.8872	1121.1391	1123.3550	1125.5360	1127.6832	1129.7976
69	1109.1364	1111.5583	1113.9393	1116.2804	1118.5829	1120.8478	1123.0763	1125.2694	1127.4282	1129.5537
70	1108.7697	1111.2071	1113.6029	1115.9583	1118.2744	1120.5525	1122.7937	1124.9990	1127.1695	1129.3062
71	1108.3984	1110.8513	1113.2620	1115.6318	1117.9618	1120.2532	1122.5072	1124.7247	1126.9071	1129.0551
72	1108.0223	1110.4909	1112.9167	1115.3010	1117.6449	1119.9498	1122.2166	1124.4466	1126.6409	1128.8004
73	1107.6415	1110.1259	1112.5668	1114.9657	1117.3238	1119.6422	1121.9220	1124.1646	1126.3708	1128.5419
74	1107.2558	1109.7561	1112.2124	1114.6260	1116.9983	1119.3303	1121.6233	1123.8785	1126.0969	1128.2797
75	1106.8653	1109.3816	1111.8533	1114.2818	1116.6684	1119.0142	1121.3205	1123.5884	1125.8191	1128.0137
76	1106.4698	1109.0022	1111.4895	1113.9330	1116.3340	1118.6937	1121.0134	1123.2942	1125.5373	1127.7438
77	1106.0692	1108.6179	1111.1209	1113.5795	1115.9951	1118.3688	1120.7020	1122.9958	1125.2514	1127.4699
78	1105.6636	1108.2287	1110.7475	1113.2214	1115.6516	1118.0395	1120.3863	1122.6932	1124.9614	1127.1920
79	1105.2528	1107.8344	1110.3692	1112.8584	1115.3035	1117.7056	1120.0661	1122.3863	1124.6672	1126.9101
80	1104.8367	1107.4350	1109.9859	1112.4906	1114.9506	1117.3671	1119.7415	1122.0750	1124.3688	1126.6241
81	1104.4154	1107.0305	1109.5975	1112.1179	1114.5930	1117.0240	1119.4124	1121.7594	1124.0662	1126.3339
82	1103.9888	1106.6208	1109.2041	1111.7402	1114.2305	1116.6762	1119.0787	1121.4392	1123.7591	1126.0395
83	1103.5567	1106.2057	1108.8055	1111.3575	1113.8631	1116.3236	1118.7403	1121.1146	1123.4477	1125.7408
84	1103.1191	1105.7853	1108.4017	1110.9697	1113.4907	1115.9661	1118.3972	1120.7853	1123.1318	1125.4377
85	1102.6760	1105.3595	1107.9926	1110.5767	1113.1133	1115.6037	1118.0493	1120.4514	1122.8113	1125.1303
86	1102.2272	1104.9282	1107.5781	1110.1785	1112.7308	1115.2363	1117.6965	1120.1127	1122.4862	1124.8183
87	1101.7727	1104.4913	1107.1582	1109.7750	1112.3431	1114.8639	1117.3389	1119.7693	1122.1565	1124.5018
88	1101.3125	1104.0487	1106.7328	1109.3661	1111.9501	1114.4864	1116.9762	1119.4210	1121.8220	1124.1806
89	1100.8464	1103.6005	1106.3017	1108.9517	1111.5519	1114.1036	1116.6085	1119.0677	1121.4827	1123.8548
90	1100.3744	1103.1464	1105.8651	1108.5318	1111.1482	1113.7156	1116.2356	1118.7094	1121.1385	1123.5242
91	1099.8964	1102.6865	1105.4227	1108.1063	1110.7391	1113.3223	1115.8575	1118.3461	1120.7894	1123.1888
92	1099.4123	1102.2207	1104.9744	1107.6752	1110.3244	1112.9236	1115.4742	1117.9776	1120.4353	1122.8486
93	1098.9220	1101.7488	1104.5204	1107.2383	1109.9041	1112.5194	1115.0855	1117.6039	1120.0761	1122.5033
94	1098.4256	1101.2708	1104.0603	1106.7956	1109.4781	1112.1096	1114.6914	1117.2249	1119.7117	1122.1530
95	1097.9228	1100.7867	1103.5942	1106.3469	1109.0464	1111.6942	1114.2917	1116.8405	1119.3420	1121.7976
96	1097.4136	1100.2963	1103.1220	1105.8923	1108.6088	1111.2730	1113.8865	1116.4507	1118.9671	1121.4371

PLAN III GRADUATED PAYMENT MORTGAGE (SECTION 245)
WITH INCREASING PAYMENTS FOR 5 YEARS AT 7.50 PERCENT EACH YEAR

OUTSTANDING PRINCIPAL BALANCE FACTORS
(PER THOUSAND DOLLARS OF ORIGINAL LOAN PROCEEDS)

INSTALL-MENT NUMBER	FOR 30 YEAR MORTGAGES WITH ANNUAL CONTRACT INTEREST RATES OF									
	15.25	15.50	15.75	16.00	16.25	16.50	16.75	17.00	17.25	17.50
97	1096.8980	1099.7996	1102.6436	1105.4316	1108.1653	1110.8461	1113.4757	1116.0554	1118.5868	1121.0712
98	1096.3758	1099.2964	1102.1589	1104.9648	1107.7158	1110.4133	1113.0591	1115.6545	1118.2010	1120.7001
99	1095.8469	1098.7868	1101.6678	1104.4918	1107.2602	1109.9746	1112.6367	1115.2478	1117.8096	1120.3235
100	1095.3114	1098.2705	1101.1703	1104.0124	1106.7984	1109.5298	1112.2084	1114.8355	1117.4127	1119.9414
101	1094.7690	1097.7477	1100.6663	1103.5267	1106.3303	1109.0789	1111.7741	1114.4172	1117.0100	1119.5538
102	1094.2198	1097.2180	1100.1557	1103.0344	1105.8560	1108.6219	1111.3337	1113.9931	1116.6015	1119.1605
103	1093.6635	1096.6815	1099.6383	1102.5357	1105.3752	1108.1585	1110.8872	1113.5630	1116.1872	1118.7614
104	1093.1002	1096.1381	1099.1142	1102.0302	1104.8879	1107.6888	1110.4345	1113.1267	1115.7669	1118.3566
105	1092.5298	1095.5877	1098.5832	1101.5181	1104.3940	1107.2126	1109.9755	1112.6843	1115.3406	1117.9458
106	1091.9521	1095.0301	1098.0452	1100.9991	1103.8934	1106.7298	1109.5100	1112.2356	1114.9081	1117.5291
107	1091.3670	1094.4654	1097.5002	1100.4731	1103.3860	1106.2404	1109.0381	1111.7805	1114.4694	1117.1063
108	1090.7745	1093.8933	1096.9480	1099.9402	1102.8717	1105.7443	1108.5595	1111.3190	1114.0244	1116.6773
109	1090.1745	1093.3139	1096.3885	1099.4002	1102.3505	1105.2414	1108.0743	1110.8510	1113.5731	1116.2420
110	1089.5669	1092.7270	1095.8217	1098.8529	1101.8223	1104.7315	1107.5823	1110.3763	1113.1152	1115.8005
111	1088.9515	1092.1325	1095.2475	1098.2984	1101.2869	1104.2147	1107.0835	1109.8950	1112.6507	1115.3524
112	1088.3283	1091.5303	1094.6657	1097.7364	1100.7442	1103.6907	1106.5777	1109.4068	1112.1796	1114.8979
113	1087.6972	1090.9203	1094.0763	1097.1670	1100.1942	1103.1595	1106.0648	1108.9116	1111.7017	1114.4367
114	1087.0581	1090.3025	1093.4792	1096.5900	1099.6367	1102.6210	1105.5447	1108.4095	1111.2169	1113.9687
115	1086.4109	1089.6767	1092.8742	1096.0053	1099.0717	1102.0752	1105.0174	1107.9002	1110.7252	1113.4940
116	1085.7554	1089.0428	1092.2613	1095.4128	1098.4990	1101.5218	1104.4828	1107.3838	1110.2264	1113.0123
117	1085.0916	1088.4007	1091.6404	1094.8124	1097.9186	1100.9608	1103.9407	1106.8600	1109.7204	1112.5236
118	1084.4194	1087.7503	1091.0113	1094.2040	1097.3303	1100.3921	1103.3910	1106.3288	1109.2072	1112.0278
119	1083.7386	1087.0915	1090.3739	1093.5875	1096.7341	1099.8155	1102.8336	1105.7900	1108.6865	1111.5248
120	1083.0491	1086.4243	1089.7282	1092.9627	1096.1298	1099.2311	1102.2685	1105.2437	1108.1584	1111.0144
121	1082.3510	1085.7484	1089.0740	1092.3296	1095.5173	1098.6386	1101.6955	1104.6896	1107.6227	1110.4966
122	1081.6439	1085.0637	1088.4112	1091.6881	1094.8965	1098.0380	1101.1144	1104.1276	1107.0793	1109.9712
123	1080.9278	1084.3702	1087.7397	1091.0381	1094.2672	1097.4291	1100.5253	1103.5577	1106.5281	1109.4381
124	1080.2027	1083.6678	1087.0594	1090.3793	1093.6295	1096.8118	1099.9279	1102.9797	1105.9690	1108.8973
125	1079.4683	1082.9563	1086.3701	1089.7118	1092.9832	1096.1860	1099.3222	1102.3936	1105.4018	1108.3486
126	1078.7246	1082.2356	1085.6719	1089.0354	1092.3280	1095.5517	1098.7081	1101.7991	1104.8265	1107.7919
127	1077.9715	1081.5056	1084.9644	1088.3500	1091.6641	1094.9086	1098.0854	1101.1962	1104.2428	1107.2271
128	1077.2088	1080.7661	1084.2477	1087.6554	1090.9911	1094.2567	1097.4539	1100.5847	1103.6509	1106.6540
129	1076.4363	1080.0171	1083.5216	1086.9515	1090.3090	1093.5958	1096.8137	1099.9646	1103.0504	1106.0726
130	1075.6541	1079.2585	1082.7859	1086.2383	1089.6177	1092.9258	1096.1645	1099.3358	1102.4412	1105.4827
131	1074.8619	1078.4900	1082.0406	1085.5156	1088.9170	1092.2466	1095.5063	1098.6980	1101.8233	1104.8842
132	1074.0597	1077.7116	1081.2855	1084.7832	1088.2068	1091.5581	1094.8389	1098.0511	1101.1966	1104.2770
133	1073.2473	1076.9232	1080.5204	1084.0411	1087.4870	1090.8601	1094.1622	1097.3951	1100.5608	1103.6609
134	1072.4245	1076.1245	1079.7454	1083.2891	1086.7575	1090.1525	1093.4760	1096.7298	1099.9159	1103.0359
135	1071.5913	1075.3156	1078.9602	1082.5270	1086.0180	1089.4351	1092.7802	1096.0551	1099.2617	1102.4017
136	1070.7475	1074.4962	1078.1646	1081.7548	1085.2686	1088.7080	1092.0748	1095.3708	1098.5981	1101.7582
137	1069.8930	1073.6662	1077.3587	1080.9723	1084.5090	1087.9708	1091.3594	1094.6769	1097.9249	1101.1054
138	1069.0276	1072.8255	1076.5421	1080.1793	1083.7392	1087.2235	1090.6341	1093.9731	1097.2421	1100.4431
139	1068.1512	1071.9739	1075.7148	1079.3758	1082.9589	1086.4659	1089.8987	1093.2593	1096.5495	1099.7711
140	1067.2637	1071.1114	1074.8767	1078.5616	1082.1680	1085.6978	1089.1530	1092.5354	1095.8469	1099.0893
141	1066.3649	1070.2377	1074.0276	1077.7365	1081.3664	1084.9193	1088.3969	1091.8013	1095.1342	1098.3976
142	1065.4547	1069.3527	1073.1673	1076.9004	1080.5540	1084.1300	1087.6303	1091.0568	1094.4113	1097.6957
143	1064.5329	1068.4563	1072.2957	1076.0532	1079.7306	1083.3299	1086.8529	1090.3017	1093.6780	1096.9837
144	1063.5994	1067.5483	1071.4127	1075.1946	1078.8960	1082.5187	1086.0647	1089.5359	1092.9341	1096.2612

Source: U.S., Department of Housing and Urban Development, The Graduated Payment Mortgage Program—A HUD Handbook, 4240.2 Rev.

Appendix C

Factors for Calculating Monthly Payments— Section 245, Plan III

Plan III Graduated Payment Mortgage (Section 245) With Increasing Payments for 5 Years at 7.50 Percent Each Year

Factors for computing monthly installment to principal and interest (per thousand dollars of original loan proceeds)

For 30-year mortgages with annual contract interest rates of

Year	7.75	8.00	8.25	8.50	8.75	9.00	9.25	9.50	9.75	10.00
1	5.3717	5.5101	5.6500	5.7915	5.9344	6.0788	6.2246	6.3719	6.5204	6.6704
2	5.7746	5.9233	6.0738	6.2258	6.3795	6.5347	6.6915	6.8498	7.0095	7.1706
3	6.2077	6.3676	6.5293	6.6928	6.8580	7.0248	7.1934	7.3635	7.5352	7.7084
4	6.6732	6.8452	7.0190	7.1947	7.3723	7.5517	7.7329	7.9158	8.1003	8.2866
5	7.1737	7.3585	7.5454	7.7343	7.9252	8.1181	8.3128	8.5094	8.7079	8.9081
Remaining payments	7.7118	7.9104	8.1113	8.3144	8.5196	8.7269	8.9363	9.1476	9.3609	9.5762

Year	10.25	10.50	10.75	11.00	11.25	11.50	11.75	12.00	12.25	12.50
1	6.8216	6.9740	7.1277	7.2826	7.4387	7.5960	7.7543	7.9138	8.0743	8.2358
2	7.3332	7.4971	7.6623	7.8288	7.9966	8.1657	8.3359	8.5073	8.6798	8.8535
3	7.8832	8.0594	8.2370	8.4160	8.5964	8.7781	8.9611	9.1453	9.3308	9.5175
4	8.4744	8.6638	8.8548	9.0472	9.2411	9.4364	9.6332	9.8312	10.0306	10.2313
5	9.1100	9.3136	9.5189	9.7257	9.9342	10.1442	10.3556	10.5686	10.7829	10.9986
Remaining payments	9.7932	10.0121	10.2328	10.4552	10.6793	10.9050	11.1323	11.3612	11.5916	11.8235

Year	12.75	13.00	13.25	13.50	13.75	14.00	14.25	14.50	14.75	15.00
1	8.3983	8.5618	8.7263	8.8917	9.0580	9.2252	9.3933	9.5621	9.7318	9.9023
2	9.0282	9.2040	9.3808	9.5586	9.7374	9.9171	10.0978	10.2793	10.4617	10.6450
3	9.7053	9.8943	10.0843	10.2755	10.4677	10.6609	10.8551	11.0502	11.2464	11.4434
4	10.4332	10.6363	10.8407	11.0461	11.2528	11.4604	11.6692	11.8790	12.0898	12.3016
5	11.2157	11.4341	11.6537	11.8746	12.0967	12.3200	12.5444	12.7699	12.9966	13.2243
Remaining payments	12.0569	12.2916	12.5277	12.7652	13.0040	13.2440	13.4852	13.7277	13.9713	14.2161

Year	15.25	15.50	15.75	16.00	16.25	16.50	16.75	17.00	17.25	17.50
1	10.0736	10.2456	10.4183	10.5918	10.7660	10.9408	11.1163	11.2924	11.4692	11.6465
2	10.8291	11.0140	11.1997	11.3862	11.5734	11.7613	11.9500	12.1393	12.3294	12.5200
3	11.6413	11.8401	12.0397	12.2402	12.4414	12.6435	12.8463	13.0498	13.2541	13.4590
4	12.5144	12.7281	12.9427	13.1582	13.3745	13.5917	13.8097	14.0285	14.2481	14.4685
5	13.4530	13.6827	13.9134	14.1450	14.3776	14.6111	14.8454	15.0807	15.3167	15.5536
Remaining payments	14.4619	14.7089	14.9569	15.2059	15.4559	15.7069	15.9589	16.2117	16.4655	16.7201

Note: Because of rounding, utilization of these factors can result in small differences in the actual outstanding balances and mortgage insurance premiums.

SOURCE: U.S. Department of Housing and Urban Development, *The Graduated Payment Mortgage Program — A HUD Handbook* 4240.2 Rev.

Appendix

D

Growing Equity Mortgage
with increasing payments for 10 years at 2.00 and 3.00 percent each year

---

Section 203(B) Growing Equity Mortgage
With Increasing Payments for 10 Years at 2.00 Percent Each Year

Monthly Installment Per Thousand Dollars of Original Loan Proceeds

For 30-Year mortgages with annual contract interest rates of

Year	7.75	8.00	8.25	8.50	8.75	9.00	9.25	9.50	9.75	10.00
1	7.164122	7.337646	7.512666	7.689135	7.867004	8.046226	8.226754	8.408542	8.591544	8.77571
2	7.307405	7.484399	7.662919	7.842918	8.024344	8.207151	8.391289	8.576713	8.763375	8.95123
3	7.453553	7.634087	7.816178	7.999776	8.184831	8.371294	8.559115	8.748247	8.938643	9.13025
4	7.602624	7.786768	7.972501	8.159771	8.348528	8.538720	8.730297	8.923212	9.117415	9.31286
5	7.754677	7.942504	8.131951	8.322967	8.515498	8.709494	8.904903	9.101676	9.299764	9.49911
6	7.909770	8.101354	8.294590	8.489426	8.685808	8.883684	9.083001	9.283710	9.485759	9.68909
7	8.067965	8.263381	8.460482	8.659215	8.859524	9.061358	9.264661	9.469384	9.675474	9.88288
8	8.229325	8.428648	8.629692	8.832399	9.036715	9.242585	9.449955	9.658772	9.868984	10.08053
9	8.393911	8.597221	8.802286	9.009047	9.217449	9.427436	9.638954	9.851947	10.066363	10.28215
10	8.561790	8.769166	8.978331	9.189228	9.401798	9.615985	9.831733	10.048986	10.267691	10.48779
Remaining payments	8.733025	8.944549	9.157898	9.373012	9.589834	9.808305	10.028368	10.249966	10.473044	10.69754
Term in months	251	249	246	244	242	240	237	235	233	231

Year	10.25	10.50	10.75	11.00	11.25	11.50	11.75	12.00	12.25	12.50
1	8.961013	9.147393	9.334814	9.523234	9.712614	9.902914	10.094097	10.286126	10.478964	10.672578
2	9.140233	9.330341	9.521510	9.713699	9.906866	10.100973	10.295979	10.491848	10.688544	10.886029
3	9.323038	9.516948	9.711940	9.907973	10.105003	10.302992	10.501899	10.701685	10.902314	11.103750
4	9.509499	9.707287	9.906179	10.106132	10.307104	10.509052	10.711937	10.915719	11.120361	11.325825
5	9.699689	9.901432	10.104302	10.308255	10.513246	10.719233	10.926176	11.134034	11.342768	11.552341
6	9.893682	10.099461	10.306389	10.514420	10.723511	10.933618	11.144699	11.356714	11.569623	11.783388
7	10.091556	10.301450	10.512516	10.724708	10.937981	11.152290	11.367593	11.583849	11.801016	12.019056
8	10.293387	10.507479	10.722767	10.939202	11.156740	11.375336	11.594945	11.815525	12.037036	12.259437
9	10.499255	10.717629	10.937222	11.157986	11.379875	11.602842	11.826844	12.051836	12.277777	12.504626
10	10.709240	10.931981	11.155966	11.381146	11.607473	11.834899	12.063381	12.292873	12.523332	12.754718
Remaining payments	10.923425	11.150621	11.379086	11.608769	11.839622	12.071597	12.304648	12.538730	12.773799	13.009813
Term in months	229	227	224	222	220	218	216	214	212	210

Year	12.75	13.00	13.25	13.50	13.75	14.00	14.25	14.50	14.75	15.00
1	10.866932	11.061995	11.257735	11.454122	11.651125	11.848718	12.046871	12.245559	12.444757	12.644440
2	11.084271	11.283235	11.482890	11.683204	11.884148	12.085692	12.287808	12.490470	12.693652	12.897329
3	11.305956	11.508900	11.712548	11.916868	12.121831	12.327406	12.533565	12.740280	12.947525	13.155276
4	11.532075	11.739078	11.946799	12.155206	12.364267	12.573954	12.784236	12.995085	13.206476	13.418381
5	11.762717	11.973859	12.185735	12.398310	12.611553	12.825433	13.039921	13.254987	13.470605	13.686749
6	11.997971	12.213337	12.429449	12.646276	12.863784	13.081942	13.300719	13.520087	13.740017	13.960484
7	12.237931	12.457603	12.678038	12.899201	13.121059	13.343580	13.566733	13.790489	14.014818	14.239693
8	12.482689	12.706755	12.931599	13.157186	13.383481	13.610452	13.838068	14.066298	14.295114	14.524487
9	12.732343	12.960890	13.190231	13.420329	13.651150	13.882661	14.114829	14.347624	14.581016	14.814977
10	12.986990	13.220108	13.454036	13.688736	13.924173	14.160314	14.397126	14.634577	14.872637	15.111277
Remaining payments										
	13.246730	13.484510	13.723116	13.962511	14.202657	14.443521	14.685068	14.927268	15.170090	15.413502
Term in months										
	208	206	204	202	200	198	196	194	193	191

Source: U.S., Department of Housing and Urban Development, Memorandum from the Office of the Assistant Secretary for Housing—Federal Housing Commissioner, June 4, 1982, Appendix B.

Year	15.25	15.50	15.75	16.00	16.25	16.50	16.75	17.00	17.25	17.50
1	12.844585	13.045169	13.246171	13.447570	13.649346	13.851481	14.053956	14.256753	14.459858	14.663252
2	13.101477	13.306073	13.511094	13.716521	13.922333	14.128510	14.335035	14.541889	14.749055	14.956517
3	13.363506	13.572194	13.781316	13.990852	14.200780	14.411081	14.621735	14.832726	15.044036	15.255648
4	13.630776	13.843638	14.056943	14.270669	14.484795	14.699302	14.914170	15.129381	15.344917	15.560761
5	13.903392	14.120511	14.338082	14.556082	14.774491	14.993288	15.212454	15.431968	15.651815	15.871976
6	14.181460	14.402921	14.624843	14.847204	15.069981	15.293154	15.516703	15.740608	15.964851	16.189415
7	14.465089	14.690979	14.917340	15.144148	15.371381	15.599017	15.827037	16.055420	16.284148	16.513204
8	14.754391	14.984799	15.215687	15.447031	15.678808	15.910998	16.143577	16.376528	16.609831	16.843468
9	15.049479	15.284495	15.520001	15.755972	15.992385	16.229217	16.466449	16.704059	16.942028	17.180337
10	15.350468	15.590185	15.830401	16.071091	16.312232	16.553802	16.795778	17.038140	17.280868	71.523944
Remaining payments										
	15.657477	15.901988	16.147009	16.392513	16.638477	16.884878	17.131694	17.378903	17.626486	17.874423
Term in months										
	189	187	186	184	182	181	179	178	176	175

Source: U.S., Department of Housing and Urban Development, Memorandum from the Office of the Assistant Secretary for Housing—Federal Housing Commissioner, June 15, 1982.

Section 203(B) Growing Equity Mortgage
With Increasing Payments for 10 Years at 3.00 Percent Each Year

Monthly Installment per Thousand Dollars of Original Loan Proceeds

For 30-year mortgages with annual contract interest rates of

Year	7.75	8.00	8.25	8.50	8.75	9.00	9.25	9.50	9.75	10.00
1	7.164122	7.337646	7.512666	7.689135	7.867004	8.046226	8.226754	8.408542	8.591544	8.775716
2	7.379046	7.557775	7.738046	7.919809	8.103014	8.287613	8.473557	8.660798	8.849290	9.038987
3	7.600418	7.784508	7.970187	8.157403	8.346105	8.536241	8.727764	8.920622	9.114769	9.310157
4	7.828430	8.018044	8.209293	8.402125	8.596488	8.792329	8.989596	9.188241	9.388212	9.589461
5	8.063283	8.258585	8.455572	8.654189	8.854382	9.056098	9.259284	9.463888	9.669859	9.877145
6	8.305181	8.056342	8.709239	8.913815	9.120014	9.327781	9.537063	9.747805	9.959954	10.173460
7	8.554337	8.761533	8.970516	9.181229	9.393614	9.607615	9.823175	10.040239	10.258753	10.478663
8	8.810967	9.024379	9.239632	9.456666	9.675423	9.895843	10.117870	10.341446	10.566516	10.793023
9	9.075296	9.295110	9.516821	9.740366	9.965685	10.192719	10.421406	10.651690	10.883511	11.116814
10	9.347555	9.573963	9.802325	10.032577	10.264656	10.498500	10.734048	10.971240	11.210016	11.450319
Remaining payments										
	9.627982	9.861182	10.096395	10.333554	10.572596	10.813455	11.056070	11.300377	11.546317	11.793828
Term in Months										
	221	219	217	215	212	210	208	206	204	202

Year	10.25	10.50	10.75	11.00	11.25	11.50	11.75	12.00	12.25	12.50
1	8.961013	9.147393	9.334814	9.523234	9.712614	9.902914	10.094097	10.286126	10.478964	10.672578
2	9.229843	9.421815	9.614858	9.808931	10.003992	10.200002	10.396920	10.594710	10.793333	10.992755
3	9.506739	9.704469	9.903304	10.103199	10.304112	10.506002	10.708828	10.912551	11.117133	11.322538
4	9.791941	9.995603	10.200403	10.406295	10.613235	10.821182	11.030093	11.239928	11.450647	11.662214
5	10.085699	10.295471	10.506415	10.718484	10.931632	11.145817	11.360995	11.577125	11.794167	12.012080
6	10.388270	10.604335	10.821607	11.040038	11.259581	11.480192	11.701825	11.924439	12.147992	12.372443
7	10.699918	10.922466	11.146256	11.371239	11.597369	11.824598	12.052880	12.282172	12.512431	12.743616
8	11.020916	11.250140	11.480643	11.712377	11.945290	12.179336	12.414467	12.650638	12.887804	13.125924
9	11.351543	11.587644	11.825063	12.063748	12.303649	12.544716	12.786901	13.030157	13.274438	13.519702
10	11.692089	11.935273	12.179815	12.425660	12.672758	12.921057	13.170508	13.421061	13.672672	13.925293
Remaining payments	12.042852	12.293331	12.545209	12.798430	13.052941	13.308689	13.565623	13.823693	14.082852	14.343052
Term in months	200	198	196	194	192	190	188	186	185	183

Year	12.75	13.00	13.25	13.50	13.75	14.00	14.25	14.50	14.75	15.00
1	10.866932	11.061995	11.257735	11.454122	11.651125	11.848718	12.046871	12.245559	12.444757	12.644440
2	11.192940	11.393855	11.595467	11.797745	12.000659	12.204179	12.408277	12.612926	12.818100	13.023773
3	11.528728	11.735671	11.943331	12.151678	12.360679	12.570304	12.780525	12.991314	13.202643	13.414487
4	11.874590	12.087741	12.301631	12.516228	12.731499	12.947414	13.163941	13.381053	13.598722	13.816921
5	12.230828	12.450373	12.670680	12.891715	13.113444	13.335836	13.558859	13.782485	14.006684	14.231429
6	12.597753	12.823884	13.050801	13.278466	13.506848	13.735911	13.965625	14.195959	14.426884	14.658372
7	12.975685	13.208601	13.442325	13.676820	13.912053	14.147988	14.384594	14.621838	14.859691	15.098123
8	13.364956	13.604859	13.845594	14.087125	14.329415	14.572428	14.816132	15.060493	15.305482	15.551067
9	13.765904	14.013005	14.260962	14.509739	14.759297	15.009601	15.260616	15.512308	15.764646	16.017599
10	14.178882	14.433395	14.688791	14.945031	15.202076	15.459889	15.718434	15.977677	16.237585	16.498127
Remaining payments	14.604248	14.866397	15.129455	15.393382	15.658138	15.923686	16.189987	16.457008	16.724713	16.993070
Term in months	181	179	177	176	174	173	171	169	168	166

Source: U.S., Department of Housing and Urban Development. Memorandum from the Office of the Assistant Secretary for Housing—Federal Housing Commissioner. June 4. 1982. Appendix B.

Year	15.25	15.50	15.75	16.00	16.25	16.50	16.75	17.00	17.25	17.50
1	12.844585	13.045169	13.246171	13.447570	13.649346	13.851481	14.053956	14.256753	14.459858	14.663252
2	13.229923	13.436524	13.643556	13.850997	14.058827	14.267025	14.475574	14.684456	14.893653	15.103150
3	13.626820	13.839620	14.052863	14.266527	14.480591	14.695036	14.909842	15.124990	15.340463	15.556244
4	14.035625	14.254809	14.474449	14.694523	14.915009	15.135887	15.357137	15.578739	15.800677	16.022932
5	14.456694	14.682453	14.908682	15.135358	15.362459	15.589964	15.817851	16.046102	16.274697	16.503620
6	14.890394	15.122926	15.355943	15.589419	15.823333	16.057663	16.292386	16.527485	16.762938	16.998728
7	15.337106	15.576614	15.816621	16.057102	16.298033	16.539392	16.781158	17.023309	17.265826	17.508690
8	15.797219	16.043913	16.291120	16.538815	16.786974	17.035574	17.284593	17.534008	17.783801	18.033951
9	16.271136	16.525230	16.779853	17.034979	17.290583	17.546642	17.803131	18.060029	18.317315	18.574969
10	16.759270	17.020987	17.283249	17.546029	17.809301	18.073041	18.337224	18.601830	18.866834	19.132218
Remaining payments	17.262048	17.531617	17.801746	18.072410	18.343580	18.615232	18.887341	19.159884	19.432839	19.706185
Term in months	165	163	162	160	159	158	156	155	154	152

Source: U.S., Department of Housing and Urban Development, Memorandum from the Office of the Assistant Secretary for Housing—Federal Housing Commissioner, June 15, 1982.

Appendix

E

HUD-FHA Mortgage Insurance Programs

Section	Nature of Program (Selected)	Eligibility	Information Source
202	Long-term direct loans to eligible, private nonprofit sponsors finance rental or co-operative housing facilities for elderly or handicapped persons. The current interest rate is based on the average rate paid on federal obligations during the preceding fiscal year. (Until the program was revised in 1974, the statutory rate was 3 percent.) Participation in the Section 8 rental housing program is required for a minimum of 20 percent of the Section 202 units.	Private, nonprofit sponsors may qualify for loans. Households of one or more persons, the head of which is at least 62 years old or is handicapped, are eligible to live in the structures.	HUD area offices or local lenders.
203 (i)	By insuring commercial lenders against loss, HUD encourages them to invest capital in the home mortgage market. HUD insures loans made by private financial institutions for up to 97 percent of the property value and for terms of up to 30 years. The loans may finance homes in rural areas (except farm homes). Less rigid construction standards are permitted in rural areas.	Any person able to make the cash investment and the mortgage payments.	HUD area offices or local HUD-approved lenders.
207	HUD insures mortgages made by private lending institutions to finance the construction or rehabilitation of multifamily rental housing by private or public developers. The project must contain at least eight dwelling units. Housing financed under this program, whether in urban or suburban areas, should be able to accommodate families (with or without children) at reasonable rents.	Investors, builders, developers, and others who meet HUD requirements may apply for funds to an FHA-approved lending institution after conferring with their local office. The housing project must be located in an area approved by HUD for rental housing and in which market conditions show a need for such housing.	HUD area offices.

Section	Nature of Program (Selected)	Eligibility	Information Source
213	HUD insures mortgages made by private lending institutions on cooperative housing projects for five or more dwelling units to be occupied by members of nonprofit cooperative ownership housing corporations. These loans may finance: new construction, rehabilitation, acquisition, improvement or repair of a project already owned, and resale of individual memberships; construction of projects composed of individual family dwellings to be bought by individual members with separate insured mortgages; and construction or rehabilitation of projects that the owners intend to sell to nonprofit cooperatives.	Nonprofit corporations or trusts organized to construct homes for members of the corporation or beneficiaries of the trust; and qualified sponsors who intend to sell the project to a nonprofit corporation or trust.	HUD area offices or local lenders.
221(d) (3) and (4)	To help finance construction or substantial rehabilitation of multifamily (5 or more units) rental or cooperative housing for low- and moderate-income or displaced families, HUD conducts two related programs. Projects in both cases may consist of detached, semi-detached, row, walk-up, or elevator structures. The insured mortgage amounts are controlled by statutory dollar limits per unit which are intended to assure moderate construction costs. Units financed under both programs may qualify for assistance under Section 8 if occupied by eligible low-income families. Currently, the principal differences between the programs are two: HUD may insure 100 percent of total project cost under Section 221(d)(3) for nonprofit and cooperative mortgagors but only 90 percent under Section 221(d)(4) irrespective of the type of mortgagor; and statutory unit limit mortgage amounts are less for Section 221(d)(3) than for Section 221(d)(4).	Section 221(d)(3) mortgages may be obtained by: public agencies, nonprofit, limited-dividend or cooperative organizations; private builders or investors who sell completed projects to such organizations. Section 221(d)(4) mortgages are limited to profit-motivated sponsors. Tenant occupancy is not restricted by income limits, except in the case of tenants receiving subsidies.	HUD area offices.
223(f)	HUD insures mortgages to purchase or refinance existing multifamily projects originally financed with or without Federal mortgage insurance. HUD may insure mortgages on existing multifamily projects under this program that do not require substantial rehabilitation. Project must contain eight or more units, and must be at least three years old.	Investors, builders developers, and others who meet HUD requirements.	HUD area offices or local lenders.
231	To assure a supply of rental housing suited to the needs of the elderly or handicapped, HUD insures mortgages to build or rehabilitate multifamily projects consisting of eight or more units.	Investors, builders, developers, public bodies, and nonprofit sponsors may qualify for mortgage insurance. Persons at least 62 years old are eligible to rent such units.	HUD area offices or local lenders.

Section	Nature of Program (Selected)	Eligibility	Information Source
232	HUD insures mortgages to finance construction or renovation of facilities to accommodate 20 or more patients requiring skilled nursing care and related medical services, or those in need of minimum but continuous care provided by licensed or trained personnel. Nursing home and intermediate care services may be combined in the same facility covered by an insured mortgage or may be separate facilities. Major equipment needed to operate the facility may be included in the mortgage.	Investors, builders, developers, and private nonprofit corporations or associations, which are licensed or regulated by the State to accommodate convalescents and persons requiring skilled nursing care or intermediate care, may qualify for mortgage insurance. Patients requiring skilled nursing or intermediate care are eligible to live in these facilities.	HUD area offices or local lenders.
234(c)	HUD insures mortgages made by private lending institutions for the purchase of individual family units in multifamily housing projects. Sponsors may also obtain FHA-insured mortgages to finance the construction or rehabilitation of housing projects which they intend to sell as individual condominium units under Section 234(d). A project must contain at least four dwelling units; they may be in detached, semi-detached, row, walkup, or elevator structures. A condominium is defined as joint ownership of common areas and facilities by the separate owners of single dwelling units in the project.	Any qualified profit-motivated or nonprofit sponsor may apply for a blanket mortgage covering the project after conferring with his local FHA insuring office; any credit-worthy person may apply for a mortgage on individual units in a project.	HUD area offices.
244	HUD insures 80 percent of the losses on mortgages made by State housing finance agencies to finance multifamily projects. This guarantee makes it easier for the State agencies to obtain credit in the private market through the issuance of State bonds. The remaining 20 percent of the risk is borne by the agencies themselves and, indirectly, by investors in the bonds.	State housing finance agencies.	See administering office.

Source: From *Programs of HUD*, U.S. Department of Housing and Urban Development, HUD-214-4-PA(3), November, 1978.

Appendix

F

Farmers Home Administration Loan Programs

Type of Loan	Purpose of Loan	Who May Apply	Where to Apply
Operating	Operating loans to family farms for land improvement, equipment, labor, and development resources necessary to successful farming, including the development of recreational enterprises to be operated as part of farms.	Operators of not larger than family farms.	Local Farmers Home Administration Office.
Farm Ownership	To develop and buy family farms	Farmers and ranchers who are or will become operators of not larger than family farms.	Same
Conservation	Soil and water conservation loans to develop, conserve and make better use of their soil and water resources.	Individual farm operators and owners.	Same
Water and Waste Disposal Programs	Loans and grants for the construction of rural community water and waste disposal systems.	Public bodies and non-profit organizations.	Same
Other Community Facilities	Insured loans for construction of rural community facilities other than water and waste disposal systems.	Same	Same
Irrigation	Loans to develop irrigation systems, drain farmland, and carry out soil conservation measures.	Groups of farmers and ranchers.	Same
Grazing Areas	Loans to develop grazing areas for mutual use.	Same	Same
Rural Housing	To construct and repair needed homes and essential farm buildings, purchase previously occupied homes or buy sites on which to build homes.	Farmers and other rural residents in open country and rural communities of not more than 20,000.	Same
Rural Rental Housing	Loans to provide rental housing for the rural elderly and for younger rural residents of low and moderate income.	Individuals, profit corporations, private nonprofit corporations, public bodies.	Same
Cooperative Housing	Loans to develop cooperative housing for the rural elderly and younger rural residents of low and moderate income.	Consumer cooperatives, housing cooperatives and nonprofit corporations that can legally operate as housing cooperatives.	Same
Housing for Labor	Loans to finance housing facilities for domestic farm labor.	Individual farmers, groups of farmers, and public or private nonprofit organizations.	Same
Labor Housing Grants	Grants to help finance housing facilities for domestic farm labor.	Public bodies or broadly-based nonprofit organizations.	Same
Disaster	Emergency loans in designated areas where natural disasters such as floods and droughts have brought about a temporary need for credit not available from other sources.	Farmers	Same

Type of Loan	Purpose of Loan	Who May Apply	Where to Apply
Economic Emergency	Loans to farmers in economic distress due to general lack of commercial credit resources or adverse economic factors such as high production costs and low prices for farm goods.	Same	Same
Watershed	Watershed loans to help finance projects that protect and develop land and water resources in small watersheds.	Local organizations.	Same
Business and Industry	Guarantee of loans by private lenders to business and industries in rural areas and towns of up to 50,000 population to create or preserve employment for rural people.	Business concerns.	Same
Industrial Development Grants	Preparation of improvement of industrial site areas in rural countryside and rural towns of not more than 10,000.	Local public bodies.	Same

SOURCE: *Handbook for Small Business*, 4th ed., 1979, Select Committee on Small Business—United States Senate, p. 19.

Federal Home Loan Mortgage Corporation Approved PMI Companies

AMI Mortgage Insurance Company
P.O. Box 50005
San Jose, CA 95150

Commonwealth Mortgage Assurance
Company
8 Penn Center
Philadelphia, PA 19103

Foremost Guaranty Corporation
P.O. Box 7062
Madison, WI 53707

General Electric Mortgage Insurance
Corporation of Florida
P.O. Box 30006
Tampa, FL 33630

General Electric Mortgage Insurance
Corporation of North Carolina
5401 Six Forks Road
P.O. Box 177800
Raleigh, North Carolina 27619

Home Guaranty Insurance Corporation
180 East Belt Boulevard
Richmond, VA 23224

Integon Mortgage Guaranty Corporation
P.O. Box 3199
Winston-Salem, NC 27102

Investors Mortgage Insurance Company
225 Franklin Street
Boston, MA 02102

Liberty Mortgage Insurance Corporation
P.O. Box 7066
Madison, WI 53707

Mortgage Guaranty Insurance
Corporation
MGIC Plaza
250 East Kilbourn Avenue
Milwaukee, WI 53202

Old Republic Mortgage Assurance Company
1320 Fenwick Lane
Silver Spring, Maryland 20910

PAMICO Mortgage Insurance Company
1750 Walton Road
Blue Bell, PA 19422

PMI Mortgage Insurance Co.
601 Montgomery Street
San Francisco, CA 94111

Republic Mortgage Insurance Company
P.O. Box 2514
Winston-Salem, NC 27102

*Also known as RMIC Insurance Company
for mortgages on properties located in
Texas only.*

Ticor Mortgage Insurance Company
6300 Wilshire Boulevard
Los Angeles, CA 90048

United Guaranty Residential Insurance Company
P.O. Box 21367
Greensboro, NC 27420

Verex Assurance, Inc.
P.O. Box 7066
Madison, WI 53707

SOURCE: U.S. Federal Home Loan Mortgage Corporation, *Sellers' Guide: Conventional Mortgages*, Exhibit V, p. 237.

Appendix H

Samples of Completed Appraisal Forms

RZS **ROBERT L. STANLEY** *and Associates*   RESIDENTIAL APPRAISAL REPORT   File No.

To be completed by Lender

Borrower	John Smith Census Tract 000 Map Reference XYZ
Property Address	702 Banning Ct.
City	Houston County Harris State Texas Zip Code
Legal Description	Lot 100, Block 4, Darrington Place, Section 6, Harris County, Texas

Sale Price $ N/A   Date of Sale   Loan Term   yrs   Property Rights Appraised [X] Fee [ ] Leasehold [ ] DeMinimis PUD

Actual Real Estate Taxes $ (yr) Loan charges to be paid by seller $ Other sales concessions

Lender/Client ABC Mortgage Company   Address 6500 Smith Street, Houston, Texas

Occupant Vacant   Appraiser R.L. Stanley & Assoc. Instructions to Appraiser Estimate market value as of date of Inspection.

NEIGHBORHOOD

				Good	Avg.	Fair	Poor
Location	[ ] Urban [X] Suburban	Rural	Employment Stability **	[ ]	[X]	[ ]	[ ]
Built Up	[ ] Over 75% [X] 25% to 75%	Under 25%	Convenience to Employment	[ ]	[X]	[ ]	[ ]
Growth Rate [ ] Fully Dev.	[X] Rapid [ ] Steady	Slow	Convenience to Shopping	[ ]	[X]	[ ]	[ ]
Property Values	[X] Increasing [ ] Stable	Declining	Convenience to Schools	[ ]	[X]	[ ]	[ ]
Demand/Supply	[ ] Shortage [X] In Balance	Over Supply	Adequacy of Public Transportation	[ ]	[ ]	[X]	[ ]
Marketing Time	[X] Under 3 Mos [ ] 4-6 Mos	Over 6 Mos	Recreational Facilities	[ ]	[X]	[ ]	[ ]

Present Land Use *50 % 1 Family 0 % 2-4 Family 0 % Apts 0 Condo 5 % Commercial   Adequacy of Utilities [ ][X][ ][ ]
   0 % Industrial 40 % Vacant 5 % School   Property Compatibility [ ][X][ ][ ]

Change in Present Land Use [ ] Not Likely [ ] Likely (*) [X] Taking Place (*)   Protection from Detrimental Conditions [ ][X][ ][ ]

(*) From Vacant To SFD   Police and Fire Protection [ ][X][ ][ ]

Predominant Occupancy [X] Owner [ ] Tenant [ ] Vacant   General Appearance of Properties [ ][X][ ][ ]

Single Family Price Range $ 100,000 to $ 150,000 Predominant Value $ 130,000   Appeal to Market [ ][X][ ][ ]

Single Family Age New yrs to 4 yrs Predominant Age 1 yrs

Note: FHLMC/FNMA do not consider race or the racial composition of the neighborhood to be reliable appraisal factors.

Comments including those factors, favorable or unfavorable, affecting marketability (e.g. public parks, schools, view, noise) No public transportation is available; however, this is typical of the area and has no effect on the subject's marketability. Good location with excellent access to I-10, shopping, schools, and employment centers along I-10. Subject neighborhood is approximately 24 miles west of downtown Houston. * Immediate neighborhood is 100% deed restricted to Single Family Dwellings. ** "Average" rating compares subject to competing neighborhoods and homes.

SITE

Dimensions 73.72 x 117.0 x 86.86 x 123.5   9635+ Sq Ft or Acres [X] Corner Lot

Zoning classification Deed - Single Family Dwelling   Present improvements [X] do [ ] do not conform to zoning regulations

Highest and best use [X] Present use [ ] Other (specify)

	Public	Other (Describe)	OFF SITE IMPROVEMENTS	
Elec	[X]		Street Access [X] Public [ ] Private	Topo Generally level, slopes to street for drainage
Gas	[X]		Surface Concrete	Size Comparable to others in area
Water	[X]		Maintenance [X] Public [ ] Private	Shape Rectangular
San Sewer	[X]		[X] Storm Sewer [X] Curb/Gutter	View Good view site, typical of area
	[X] Underground Elect & Tel		[ ] Sidewalk [X] Street Lights	Drainage Appears to be adequate

Is the property located in a HUD Identified Special Flood Hazard Area? [X] No [ ] Yes

Comments (favorable or unfavorable including any apparent adverse easements, encroachments or other adverse conditions) Standard utility easement located at rear of property with no effect on the subject's marketability, use, enjoyment, and/or stated value. Subject is located 2 blocks north of Carmel Independent School District High School with no adverse effect on the subject's marketability.

IMPROVEMENTS

[X] Existing [ ] Proposed [ ] Under Constr No. Units 1 Type (det. duplex, semi/det., etc.) Detached Design (rambler, split level, etc.) French Exterior Walls Brick Veneer

Yrs. Age: Actual New Effective New to New No. Stories 2

Roof Material Wood Shingle   Gutters & Downspouts [X] None Adequate roof overhang   Window (Type) Aluminum   Insulation [ ] None [ ] Floor

   [ ] Storm Sash [ ] Screens [X] Combination   [X] Ceiling [ ] Roof [X] Walls

[ ] Manufactured Housing

BSMT

Foundation Walls	0 Basement [ ] Outside Entrance [ ] Sump Pump [ ] Finished Ceiling [ ] Finished Walls
Concrete	[ ] Concrete Floor % Finished [ ] Finished Floor
[X] Slab on Grade [ ] Crawl Space	Evidence of [ ] Dampness [ ] Termites [ ] Settlement

Comments New construction with no evidence of settlement at time of inspection.

ROOM LIST

Room List	Foyer	Living	Dining	Kitchen	Den	Family Rm	Rec Rm	Bedrooms	No. Baths	Laundry	Other
Basement											
1st Level	1	Study	1	1		1		1	1½	1	Breakfast area
2nd Level							1	3	2		

Finished area above grade contains a total of 10 rooms 4 bedrooms 3½ baths Gross Living Area 3301 sq. ft. Bsmt Area 0 sq. ft.

INTERIOR FINISH & EQUIPMENT

Kitchen Equipment [ ] Refrigerator [X] Range/Oven [X] Disposal [X] Dishwasher [X] Fan/Hood [ ] Compactor [ ] Washer [ ] Dryer [X] Microwave

HEAT Type GFWA Fuel N.G. Cond Good AIR COND [X] Central [ ] Other [X] Adequate [ ] Inadequate

					Good	Avg.	Fair	Poor
Floors	[ ] Hardwood [X] Carpet Over Conc. [X] Vinyl			Quality of Construction (Materials & Finish)	[X]	[ ]	[ ]	[ ]
Walls	[X] Drywall [ ] Plaster [X] Panel, wallpaper			Condition of Improvements	[ ]	[X]	[ ]	[ ]
Trim/Finish	[X] Good [ ] Average [ ] Fair [ ] Poor			Room sizes and layout	[ ]	[X]	[ ]	[ ]
Bath Floor	[ ] Ceramic [X] Carpet			Closets and Storage	[ ]	[X]	[ ]	[ ]
Bath Wainscot	[ ] Ceramic [X] Marble			Insulation—adequacy	[ ]	[X]	[ ]	[ ]

Special Features (including energy efficient items) Intercom, crown moldings, marble entry floor, block panel & dec. beam ceiling in family room, wet bar

					Good	Avg.	Fair	Poor
				Plumbing—adequacy and condition	[ ]	[X]	[ ]	[ ]
ATTIC [X] Yes [ ] No [ ] Stairway [X] Drop-stair [ ] Scuttle [ ] Floored				Electrical—adequacy and condition	[ ]	[X]	[ ]	[ ]
Finished (Describe) Unfinished [ ] Heated				Kitchen Cabinets—adequacy and condition	[ ]	[X]	[ ]	[ ]
CAR STORAGE [X] Garage [ ] Built-in [ ] Attached [X] Detached [ ] Car Port				Compatibility to Neighborhood	[ ]	[X]	[ ]	[ ]
No. Cars 2 [X] Adequate [ ] Inadequate Condition Good				Overall Livability	[ ]	[X]	[ ]	[ ]
				Appeal and Marketability	[ ]	[X]	[ ]	[ ]

Yrs Est Remaining Economic Life 50 to 55 Explain if less than Loan Term

FIREPLACES, PATIOS, POOL, FENCES, etc. (describe) Deluxe 8' fireplace, 1950 open patio, 650 covered walk, 6' wood fence at rear of lot. Subject has extra landscaping at builder cost of $2,000.00

COMMENTS (including functional or physical inadequacies, repairs needed, modernization, etc.) None required to meet minimum property standards; however, some paint and trim work remain to be completed by the builder and is covered by builder warranty. Appraisal made subject to completion of builder's final items in good workmanlike manner.

FHLMC Form 70 Rev. 7/79   ATTACH DESCRIPTIVE PHOTOGRAPHS OF SUBJECT PROPERTY AND STREET SCENE   FNMA Form 1004 Rev. 7/79

Source: Robert L. Stanley and Associates, Appraisers; Houston, Texas.

VALUATION SECTION

Purpose of Appraisal is to estimate Market Value as defined in Certification & Statement of Limiting Conditions (FHLMC Form 439/FNMA Form 1004B). If submitted for FNMA, the appraiser must attach (1) sketch or map showing location of subject, street names, distance from nearest intersection, and any detrimental conditions and (2) exterior building sketch of improvements showing dimensions.

COST APPROACH

Measurements	No. Stories	Sq. Ft.
33.5 x 50.0 x	1st Floor	= 1,675.0
33.5 x 50.0 x	2nd Floor	= 1,675.0
x x		=
x x		=
x x		=

Total Gross Living Area (List in Market Data Analysis below) 3350+

Comment on functional and economic obsolescence: None observed.

ESTIMATED REPRODUCTION COST – NEW – OF IMPROVEMENTS:

Dwelling 3350 Sq. Ft. @ $ 35.50 =	$ 118,925
Sq. Ft. @ $ =	
Extras 650 covered walk =	400
6' wood fence =	1,600
Special Energy Efficient Items =	
Porches, Patios, etc. 1950 patio =	275
Garage/Carport 471 Sq. Ft. @ $8.00 =	3,768
Site Improvements (driveway, landscaping, etc.) =	4,000
Total Estimated Cost New =	$ 128,968
Less Physical Functional Economic	
Depreciation $ -0- $ -0- $ -0- = $ (-0-)	
Depreciated value of improvements =	$ 128,968
ESTIMATED LAND VALUE (If leasehold, show only leasehold value) =	$ 30,000
INDICATED VALUE BY COST APPROACH	$ 158,968

The undersigned has recited three recent sales of properties most similar and proximate to subject and has considered these in the market analysis. The description includes a dollar adjustment, reflecting market reaction to those items of significant variation between the subject and comparable properties. If a significant item in the comparable property is superior to, or more favorable than, the subject property, a minus (-) adjustment is made, thus reducing the indicated value of subject; if a significant item in the comparable is inferior to, or less favorable than, the subject property, a plus (+) adjustment is made, thus increasing the indicated value of the subject.

MARKET DATA ANALYSIS

ITEM	Subject Property	COMPARABLE NO. 1	Adjustment	COMPARABLE NO. 2	Adjustment	COMPARABLE NO. 3	Adjustment
Address	702 Banning Ct.	1103 Castle		20638 River Court		20743 Banning Drive	
Proximity to Subj.		4 blocks south		1 block north		1 block southwest	
Sales Price	$ N/A	$ 146,900		$ 155,000		$ 152,000	
Price/Living area	$ N/A	$ 48.16		$ 47.69		$ 44.06	
Data Source	Inspection	Agent		Agent		Agent	
Date of Sale and Time Adjustment	8/80	6/80	+2900	7/80	+1550	6/80	+3000
Location	Good	Equal		Equal		Equal	
Site/View	9635+ Inside	Superior Corn.	-2000	Similar Inside		Similar Inside	
Design and Appeal	Good	Equal		Equal		Equal	
Quality of Const.	Excellent	Equal		Equal		Equal	
Age	1980	1980		1980		1980	
Condition	Good	Equal		Equal		Equal	
Living Area Room Count and Total	Total 10 / B-rms 4 / Baths 3½	Total 9 / B-rms 4 / Baths 2½	+1000	Total 10 / B-rms 4 / Baths 3½		Total 10 / B-rms 4 / Baths 3½	
Gross Living Area	3350 Sq.Ft.	3050 Sq.Ft.	+7500	3250 Sq.Ft.	+2500	3450 Sq.Ft.	-2500
Basement & Bsmt. Finished Rooms							
Functional Utility	Good	Equal		Equal		Equal	
Air Conditioning	Central A/C	Equal		Equal		Equal	
Garage/Car Port	D 2	Equal		Equal		Equal	
Porches, Patio, Pools, etc.	Patio Extra Landscape	Patio Inferior	+2000	Patio Inferior	+2000	Patio Inferior	+2000
Special Energy Efficient Items							
Other (e.g. fireplaces, kitchen equip., remodeling)	RO,VH,GD,DW,MW CH FP	Equal		Equal		Equal	
Sales or Financing Concessions	Conventional	20% Down Conventional		20% Down Conventional		30% Down Conventional	+1500
Net Adj. (Total)		☒ Plus ☐ Minus $ 11,400		☒ Plus ☐ Minus $ 6,050		☒ Plus ☐ Minus $ 4,000	
Indicated Value of Subject		$ 158,300		$ 161,050		$ 156,000	

Comments on Market Data: All comparable sales were given weighted consideration in value analysis and indicated values support final value conclusion within 1.9% range. Adjustment of 1% per month for time is supported by additional data maintained in appraiser's office.

INDICATED VALUE BY MARKET DATA APPROACH $ 158,000

INDICATED VALUE BY INCOME APPROACH (If applicable) Economic Market Rent $ ____ Mo. x Gross Rent Multiplier ____ = $ N/A

This appraisal is made ☐ "as is" ☐ subject to the repairs, alterations, or conditions listed below ☒ completion per plans and specifications.

Comments and Conditions of Appraisal: Income Approach is not considered applicable in the appraisal of single family dwellings since they are not typically purchased for their income producing capabilities. Appraisal made subject to completion of final paint and trim items by builder - Estimated cost - $1,000.00.

Final Reconciliation: Market and Cost Approaches both given weighted consideration in the appraisal of new construction such as the subject property and are supportive of the final value conclusion.

Construction Warranty ☒ Yes ☐ No Name of Warranty Program GHBA Warranty Coverage Expires 1 year

This appraisal is based upon the above requirements, the certification, contingent and limiting conditions, and Market Value definition that are stated in

☐ FHLMC Form 439 (Rev. 10/78)/FNMA Form 1004B (Rev. 10/78) filed with client ____ 19 ____ ☐ attached

I ESTIMATE THE MARKET VALUE, AS DEFINED, OF SUBJECT PROPERTY AS OF August 12, 19 80 to be $ 158,000.00

Appraiser(s) Robert L. Stanley, Jr., SRA, ASA

Review Appraiser (If applicable) ☒ Did ☐ Did Not Physically Inspect Property

FHLMC Form 70 Rev. 7/79   REVERSE   FNMA Form 1004 Rev 7/79

Source: **Robert L. Stanley and Associates, Appraisers; Houston, Texas.**

APPRAISAL REPORT—INDIVIDUAL ☒ CONDOMINIUM OR ☐ PUD UNIT   File No. ____

Borrower/Client John A. Doe   **Census Tract** 000   **Map Reference** XYZ

Unit No. 1106 W   **Address** 1550 West Street   **Project Name** The Hamilton

City Houston   **County** Harris   **State** Texas   **Zip Code** ____

Legal Description Unit 1106 W. The Hamilton   **Property Rights Appraised** ☒ Fee ☐ Leasehold

Actual Real Estate Taxes $____ (yr) Loan charges to be paid by seller $____ Other sales concessions ____

Lender ABC Mortgage Company   **Lender's Address** 6500 Smith St., Houston, Texas

Occupant ____   **Appraiser** ____   **Instructions to Appraiser** Estimate market value as of date of inspection.

1073A Required ☐

NEIGHBORHOOD

Location	☐ Urban ☒ Suburban ☐ Rural	
Built Up	☒ Over 75% ☐ 25% to 75% ☐ Under 25%	
Growth Rate	☐ Fully Developed ☒ Rapid ☐ Steady ☐ Slow	
Property Values	☒ Increasing ☐ Stable ☐ Declining	
Demand/Supply	☐ Shortage ☒ In Balance ☐ Over Supply	
Marketing Time	☒ Under 3 Mos. ☐ 4-6 Mos. ☐ Over 6 Mos.	

Present Land Use 10% 1 Family 0% 2-4 Family 30% Apts. 20% Condo 30% Commercial 0% Industrial 10% Vacant

Change in Present Land Use ☐ Not Likely ☒ Likely (*) ☐ Taking Place (*)   (*) From Vacant To Comm/MFD

Predominant Occupancy ☐ Owner ☐ Tenant 5% Vacant

Single Family Price Range $55,000 to $65,000 **Predominant Value** $60,000

Single Family Age 15 yrs to 20 yrs **Predominant Age** 15 yrs.

Describe potential for additional Condo/PUD units in nearby area Average potential for const. of new condo/PUDs or conversions.

Describe type of buyers most attracted to this area Single and married, middle to upper middle income class. Mixture of white collar, skilled blue collar and young professionals.

Comments including factors affecting marketability (e.g. public parks, schools, view, noise) Excellent proximity to schools, churches, shopping, recreational and employment facilities. Few SFDs in immediate neighborhood.

Note: FNMA does not consider the racial composition of the neighborhood to be a relevant factor and it must not be considered in the appraisal.

NEIGHBORHOOD RATING

	Good	Avg.	Fair	Poor
Employment Stability	☐	☒	☐	☐
Recreational Facilities	☐	☒	☐	☐
Adequacy of Utilities	☐	☒	☐	☐
Property Compatibility	☐	☒	☐	☐
Protection from Detrimental Cond.	☐	☒	☐	☐
Police and Fire Protection	☐	☒	☐	☐
General Appearance of Properties	☐	☒	☐	☐
Appeal to Market	☐	☒	☐	☐

	Distance	Access or Convenience
Public Transportation	1 blk	☒ ☐ ☐ ☐
Employment Centers	6 blks	☒ ☐ ☐ ☐
Neighborhood Shopping	1 blk	☒ ☐ ☐ ☐
Schools	1 mi.	☐ ☒ ☐ ☐
Freeway Access	5 blks	☒ ☐ ☐ ☐

PROJECT SITE

Area 4.41 sq. ft. or acres. **Completed project density (or when completed as planned)** 51.7 units/acre

Zoning classification Deed - Condo   **Present improvements** ☒ do ☐ do not conform to zoning regulations

Highest and best use: ☒ Present use ☐ Other (specify)

	Public	Other (Describe)
Elec.	☒	____
Gas	☒	____
Water	☒	____
San. Sewer	☒	____
	☐ Underground Elect. & Tel.	

OFF SITE IMPROVEMENTS
Street Access: ☒ Public ☐ Private
Surface Concrete
Maintenance: ☒ Public ☐ Private
☒ Storm Sewer ☒ Curb/Gutter
☒ Sidewalk ☒ Street Lights

Ingress and Egress (Adequacy) Good
Topography Level - wooded
View Amenity Good view site, highrise building
Drainage and Flood Conditions Appears to be adequate
Is property located in a HUD identified Special Flood Hazard Area? ☒ No ☐ Yes

COMMENTS (Including any easements, encroachments or adverse conditions) Standard utility easement located at rear of property with no effect on the subject's marketability, use, enjoyment, and/or stated value.

PROJECT IMPROVEMENTS

☒ Existing Approx. Year Built 19 64
☐ Built as Condo/PUD ☒ Converted (19 79)

TYPE ☐ Proposed ☐ Under Construction
PROJECT ☒ Elevator ☐ Walk-up No. of Stories ____
☐ Row or Townhouse ☐ Other (specify)
☒ Primary Residence ☐ 2nd home or recreational 6 in subject

Approx. No. units for sale in subject project 32 in both phases; bldg.
If project completed: No. phases 2 No. bldgs. 2 No. units 228
Units in Subject Phase: Total 114 Completed 114 Sold 108 Rented 0
Exterior Walls Brick Veneer   **Roof Covering** B.U. Tar & Gravel
Security Features Controlled access, lobby w/cameras, 24 hr. security guard.
Elevator(s): Number 4 Automatic Yes Adequacy and Condition Good   **Availability of Off-Site Parking** Good
Parking: Total No. spaces 360+ Ratio 1.58 spaces/unit Type Cov/Uncov. No. spaces for guest parking Adeq. open parking
Describe other Common Elements or Recreational Facilities 2 club areas, 2 pools, 2 tennis courts, 2 laundry rooms, landscaped walkways
Are any of the common elements, recreational facilities, or parking leased? No If yes, attach addendum describing rental, terms and options
Unit Location: Type Building High-rise   **Floor No.** 11 **Unit livable area** 675 sq. ft.

PROJECT RATING

	Good	Avg.	Fair	Poor
Location	☐	☒	☐	☐
General Appearance	☐	☒	☐	☐
Density (Units per Acre)	☐	☒	☐	☐
Unit Mix	☐	☒	☐	☐
Quality of Construction (Material & Finish)	☐	☒	☐	☐
Condition of Exterior	☒	☐	☐	☐
Condition of Interior	☒	☐	☐	☐
Amenities and Recreational Facilities	☐	☒	☐	☐
Appeal to Market	☐	☒	☐	☐

Room List	Foyer	Living	Dining	Kitchen	Bedrooms	Baths	Family Rm	Rec. Rm	Laundry	Balcony	Other
Basement											
1st Level		AREA	1	1	1						
2nd Level											

SUBJECT UNIT

Kitchen Equipment: ☐ Refrigerator ☒ Range/Oven ☒ Disposal ☒ Dishwasher ☒ Fan/Hood ☐ Compactor ☐ Washer ☐ Dryer ☐
HEAT: Type Wall **Fuel** Elect. **Cond.** Good **AIR COND.:** ☒ Central ☐ Other ☒ Adequate ☐ Inadequate
Parking for unit: No. 1 **Type** Uncovered ☒ Assigned ☐ Owned **Convenience to unit** Average

Floors ☐ Hardwood ☒ Carpet Over Conc ☒ VA
Interior Walls ☒ Drywall ☐ Plaster ☒ Wallpaper
Trim/Finish ☐ Good ☒ Average ☐ Fair ☐ Poor
Bath Floor ☒ Ceramic Carpet over tile
Bath Wainscot ☐ Ceramic ____
Insulation ☐ None ☒ Floor ☐ Ceiling ☐ Roof ☒ Walls
Ins. Material Batt **Est. Adequacy** Average
Soundproofing: Vertical Batt **Horizontal** Concrete
Est. Adequacy of Soundproofing Average to Good
Window (Type): Alum. ☐ Storm Sash ☐ Screens ☒ Combination
0 % Basement ☐ Concrete Floor % Finished (describe)

UNIT RATING

	Good	Avg.	Fair	Poor
Location within project or view	☒	☐	☐	☐
Room sizes and layout	☐	☒	☐	☐
Adequacy of closets and storage	☐	☒	☐	☐
Kitchen equipment, cabinets & workspace	☐	☒	☐	☐
Qual. of Const. (Material & Finish)	☐	☒	☐	☐
Condition of Improvements	☐	☒	☐	☐
Plumbing—adequacy and condition	☐	☒	☐	☐
Electrical—adequacy and condition	☐	☒	☐	☐
Overall livability	☐	☒	☐	☐
Appeal and Marketability	☐	☒	☐	☐

Est. Effective Age, Approx. 5 to 10 yrs. Est. Remaining **Economic Life, Approx.** 40 to 45 yrs.

COMMENTS: (Special features, functional or physical inadequacies, modernization or repairs needed, etc.) Well designed, functional, floor plan. Subject is currently being renovated to include new carpet, wallpaper, and new kitchen appliances.

THIS FORM MUST BE REPRODUCED BY SELLER/SERVICERS   1 of 2   FNMA FORM 1073 Feb. 78

Source: Robert L. Stanley and Associates, Appraisers, Houston, Texas.

Cost Approach (to be used only for detached, semi-detached, and town house units):

Unit area & reproduction cost new: _____ sq. ft. @ $ _____ per sq. ft. = $ ___N/A___

   less depreciation attributed to all causes: . . . .   _____

Depreciated value of improvements: . . . .   _____

Add: Land value and value of all amenities attributable to unit . . . .   _____

Total indicated value: . . . . $ ___N/A___

Comments regarding estimate of depreciation and value of land and amenity package: __The Cost Approach is not considered applicable in the appraisal of single condo units such as the subject property.__

Unit Charge $ __70.00__ /Mo. x 12 = $ __840__ /yr. ($ __1.24__ /Sq. Ft./year of livable area).   Ground Rent (if any) $ __N/A__ /yr.

Project operating expense and replacement budget:

  To properly maintain the project and provide the services anticipated, the budget appears: ☐ High ☒ Adequate ☐ Inadequate

  Compared to other competitive projects of similar quality and design subject unit charge appears: ☐ High ☒ Reasonable ☐ Low

Management Group: ☐ Owners Association   ☐ Management Agent (Identify)   ☐ Developer   ☐ Other __ACME Management__

Quality of Management and its enforcement of Rules and Regulations appears: ☐ Superior ☒ Good ☐ Adequate ☐ Inadequate

Comment __Typical management policies for this type project.__

Special or unusual characteristics in the Condo/PUD Documents or otherwise known to the appraiser, that would affect marketability (if none, so state) __None noted upon examination of appropriate documents.__

The appraiser, whenever possible, should analyze two comparable sales from within the subject project. However, when appraising a unit in a new or newly converted project, at least two comparables should be selected from outside the subject project. The appraiser should remember that, in the following analysis, the comparable should always be adjusted to the subject unit and not vice versa. If a significant feature of the comparable is superior to the subject unit, a minus (−) adjustment should be made to the comparable; if such a feature of the comparable is inferior to the subject, a plus (+) adjustment should be made to the comparable.

LIST ONLY THOSE ITEMS THAT REQUIRE ADJUSTMENT

ITEM	Subject Property	COMPARABLE NO. 1	+(−)$ Adjustment	COMPARABLE NO. 2	+(−)$ Adjustment	COMPARABLE NO. 3	+(−)$ Adjustment
Address-unit no. / Project name	1550 West Unit 1106 W.	Unit 1502 W		Unit 1202 W		Unit 1606 W	
Proximity to Subj.		Same project		Same project		Same project	
Sales Price	$ 44,000	$46,000		$44,500		$45,750	
Price/Living area	$ 65.19	$68.1		$65.93		$67.78	
Data Source	Inspection	Sales Office		Sales Office		Sales Office	
Date of Sale and Time Adjustment	9/80	7/80	+900	4/80	+2200	6/80	+1400
Location	Good	Equal		Equal		Equal	
Site/View	Good 11th Fl.	Good 15th Fl.	−2000	12th Floor	−500	16th Floor	−2500
Design and Appeal	Good	Equal		Equal		Equal	
Quality of Const.	Good	Equal		Equal		Equal	
Age	1964	Equal		Equal		Equal	
Condition	Good	Equal		Equal		Equal	
Living Area, Room Count and Total (Total / B-rms / Baths)	3 / 1 / 1	3 / 1 / 1		3 / 1 / 1		3 / 1 / 1	
Gross Living Area	675 Sq.ft.	675 Sq.ft.		675 Sq.ft.		675 Sq.ft.	
Basement & Bsmt. Finished Rooms	None	Equal		Equal		Equal	
Functional Utility	Good	Equal		Equal		Equal	
Air Conditioning	Wall	Equal		Equal		Equal	
Storage	None	Equal		Equal		Equal	
Parking facilities	1 uncov.	Equal		Equal		Equal	
Common elements and Rec. facilities	Pool, tennis courts, laundry	Equal		Equal		Equal	
Mo. Assessment	70.00	Equal		Equal		Equal	
Leasehold/Fee Simple	Fee	Equal		Equal		Equal	
Terms of Sale or Financing	Conventional	VA		Conventional		Cash	+1000
Net Adj. (Total)		☐ Plus; ☒ Minus $ 1100		☒ Plus; ☐ Minus $ 1700		☐ Plus; ☒ Minus $ 100	
Indicated Value of Subject		$ 44,900		$46,200		$ 45,650	

Comments on Market Data __Comparable #2 given greater weight in value conclusion due to more comparable location within project and terms of sale. Market Data indicates adjustment of $500 per floor due to view amenities. Cash Sale #3 discounted by seller.__

                                               $ 46,000.00

(If applicable) Economic Market Rent $ _____ /Mo. x Gross Rent Multiplier $ __N/A__

This appraisal is made ☒ "as is" ☐ subject to the repairs, alterations, or conditions listed below

Comments and Conditions of Appraisal: __Income Approach is not considered applicable in the appraisal of single family dwellings since they are not typically purchased for their income producing capabilities. Seller's costs are typical of today's market and have no effect on the appraisal value.__

Final Reconciliation: __Market Approach is considered the only applicable approach in the appraisal of single condominium units such as the subject property.__

This appraisal is based upon the above requirements, the certification, contingent and limiting conditions, and Market Value definition that are stated in FNMA Form 1004B filed with client _____ 19 ___ ☐ attached

I ESTIMATE THE MARKET VALUE, AS DEFINED, OF SUBJECT PROPERTY AS OF __September 10,__ 19__80__ to be $ __46,000.00__

Appraiser(s) _____   Review Appraiser (if applicable) _____

      Robert L. Stanley, Jr., SRA, ASA   ☒ Did ☐ Did Not Physically Inspect Property

FNMA FORM 1073
Feb. 78

Source: Robert L. Stanley and Associates, Appraisers, Houston, Texas.

Worksheets for Borrower Qualification

CONVENTIONAL LOAN QUALIFYING

1

Gross Monthly Income		*Proposed Monthly Payment*	
Borrowers Income	$_____	Principal & Interest	$_____
Co-Borrower Income	$_____	Private Mort. Insurance . . .	$_____
Overtime	$_____	Taxes	$_____
Part-time	$_____	Homeowners Insurance	$_____
Other	$_____	Home Owners Assoc.	$_____
Total Income	$_____	Total First Mortgage Pymt . . .	$_____

Total Mortgage Pymt $ _____ divided by total Income $_____ equals _____ % (cannot exceed 28%).

2

Obligations (Debts Lasting over 10 months)

Balance	*Owed To*	*Purpose*
$_____ @mo.	_____	_____
$_____ @mo.	_____	_____
$_____ @mo.	_____	_____
$_____ @mo.	_____	_____
$_____ @mo.	_____	_____
$_____ @mo.	_____	_____

Total Obligations $_____ + Total Mortgage Payment $_____ = Total Fixed Payment

$_____ Divided by Gross Income $_____ = _____ % (cannot exceed 36%)

3

Move-In Costs		*Source: Down Payment and Closing Costs*	
Sales Price	$_____	Banks	$_____
Loan Amount	$_____	Savings	$_____
Required Down Pymt	$_____	Net from sale of Real Est	$_____
Closing and Prepaids	$_____	Other (List)	$_____
Other	$_____		
Total Move-In	$_____	Total Available	$_____

The Total Available should equal or exceed the Total Move-In Costs.

U.S. DEPARTMENT OF HOUSING AND URBAN DEVELOPMENT HOUSING — FEDERAL HOUSING COMMISSIONER **MORTGAGE CREDIT ANALYSIS WORKSHEET**	CASE NUMBER

SECTION I — LOAN DATA

1. NAME OF BORROWER AND CO-BORROWER	2. AMOUNT OF MORTGAGE $	3. CASH DOWN PAYMENT ON PURCHASE PRICE $

SECTION II — BORROWER'S/CO-BORROWER'S PERSONAL AND FINANCIAL STATUS

4. BORROWER'S AGE	5. OCCUPATION OF BORROWER	6. MIP	7. TOTAL MIP	8. CURRENT MONTHLY RENTAL OR OTHER HOUSING EXPENSE

9. IS CO-BORROWER EMPLOYED?	10. CO-BORROWER'S AGE	11. OCCUPATION OF CO-BORROWER	12. MIP FINANCED	13. OTHER DEPENDENTS (a) Ages_____ (b) Number_____

SECTION III — ESTIMATED MONTHLY SHELTER EXPENSES (This Property) | 14. TERM OF LOAN (Months) | 16. SETTLEMENT REQUIREMENTS

FUTURE MONTHLY PAYMENTS

15.		16.
(a) Principal and Interest	$	(a) Existing Debt (Refinancing ONLY) $
(b) FHA Mortgage Insurance Premium	$	(b) Sale Price (Realty ONLY) $
(c) Ground Rent (Leasehold ONLY)	$	(c) Repairs and Improvements $
(d) TOTAL DEBT SERVICE (A+B+C)	$	(d) Closing Costs $
(e) Hazard Insurance	$	(e) TOTAL ACQUISITION COST (A+B+C+D) $
(f) Taxes, Special Assessments	$	(f) Mortgage Amount $
(g) TOTAL MTG. PAYMENT (D+E+F)	$	(g) Borrower(s)' Required Investment (E minus F) $
(h) Maintenance and Common Expense	$	(h) Prepayable Expenses $
(i) Heat and Utilities	$	(i) Non-Realty and Other Items $
(j) TOTAL HSG. EXPENSE (G+H+I)	$	(j) TOTAL REQUIREMENTS (G+H+I) $
(k) Other Recurring Charges (explain)	$	(k) Amount paid ☐ cash ☐ other (explain) $
(l) TOTAL FIXED PAYMENT (j+K)	$	(l) Amt. to be paid ☐ cash ☐ other (explain) $
		(m) TOTAL ASSETS AVAILABLE FOR CLOSING $

SECTION IV — MONTHLY EFFECTIVE INCOME | **SECTION V — DEBTS AND OBLIGATIONS**

		ITEM	✓	Monthly Payment	Unpaid Balance
17. Borrower's Base Pay	$	25. State and Local Income Taxes		$	$
18. Other Earnings (explain)	$	26. Social Security/Retirement			
19. Co-Borrower's Base Pay	$	27. Child Care Expense/Support			
20. Other Earnings (explain)	$	28. Operating Exp.,Other R.E.			
21. Income, Real Estate	$	29.			
22. TOTAL MONTHLY EFFECTIVE INCOME	$	30.			
23. Less Federal Tax	$	31.			
24. NET EFFECTIVE INCOME	$	32.			

SECTION VI — BORROWER RATING

34. Borrower Rating		33. TOTAL	$	$
35. Credit Characteristics				
36. Adequacy of Eff. Income				
37. Stability of Eff. Income				
38. Adequacy of Available Assets				

39. FINAL ☐ Approve Application ☐ Reject Application

SECTION VII—RATIOS
40. Loan to Value Ratio ____%
41. Total Payment to Rental Value ____%
42. Debt Service to Rental Income ____%
43. ☐ Ratio of Net Effective Income to: Total Housing Expense ____% Total Fixed Payment ____%

44. REMARKS (Use reverse, if necessary)   First Time Home Buyer? ☐ Yes ☐ No

45. SIGNATURE OF EXAMINER	46. DATE

FORWARD TO MANAGEMENT SYSTEMS WITH HUD-92800-8   HUD-92900-WS (5-81)

LOAN ANALYSIS

	LOAN NUMBER

SECTION A — LOAN DATA

1. NAME OF BORROWER	2. AMOUNT OF LOAN $	3. CASH DOWN PAYMENT ON PURCHASE PRICE $

SECTION B — BORROWER'S PERSONAL AND FINANCIAL STATUS

4. APPLICANT'S AGE	5. OCCUPATION OF APPLICANT	6. NUMBER OF YEARS AT PRESENT EMPLOYMENT	7. LIQUID ASSETS (CASH, SAVINGS, BONDS, ETC.) $	8. CURRENT MONTHLY RENTAL OR OTHER HOUSING EXPENSE
9. IS SPOUSE EMPLOYED? ☐ YES ☐ NO	10. SPOUSE'S AGE 11. OCCUPATION OF SPOUSE		12. NUMBER OF YEARS AT PRESENT EMPLOYMENT	13. AGE OF OTHER DEPENDENTS

SECTION C — ESTIMATED MONTHLY SHELTER EXPENSES (This Property) / SECTION D — DEBTS AND OBLIGATIONS (Itemize and indicate by (√) which debts considered in Section E, Line 41)

	ITEMS	AMOUNT		ITEMS	√	MO. PAYMENT	UNPAID BALANCE	
14.	TERM OF LOAN YEARS		23.			$	$	
15.	MORTGAGE PAYMENT (Principal and Interest)	$	24.					
16.	REALTY TAXES		25.					
17.	HAZARD INSURANCE		26.					
18.	SPECIAL ASSESSMENTS		27.					
19.	MAINTENANCE		28.					
20.	UTILITIES (Including heat)		29.					
21.	OTHER (HOA, Condo Fees, etc.)		30.	JOB RELATED EXPENSE				
22.	TOTAL	$	31.	TOTAL		$	$	

SECTION E — MONTHLY INCOME AND DEDUCTIONS

	ITEMS		SPOUSE	BORROWER	TOTAL	
32.	GROSS SALARY OR EARNINGS FROM EMPLOYMENT		$	$	$	
33.	DEDUCTIONS	FEDERAL INCOME TAX				
34.		STATE INCOME TAX				
35.		RETIREMENT OR SOCIAL SECURITY				
36.		OTHER (Specify)				
37.		TOTAL DEDUCTIONS	$	$	$	
38.	NET TAKE HOME PAY					
39.	PENSION, COMPENSATION OR OTHER NET INCOME (Specify)					
40.	TOTAL (Sum of Lines 18 and 19)		$	$	$	
41.	LESS THOSE OBLIGATIONS LISTED IN SECTION D WHICH SHOULD BE DEDUCTED FROM INCOME					
42.	TOTAL NET EFFECTIVE INCOME				$	
43.	LESS ESTIMATED MONTHLY SHELTER EXPENSE (Line 22)				$	
44.	BALANCE AVAILABLE FOR FAMILY SUPPORT				$	

45. PAST CREDIT RECORD ☐ SATISFACTORY ☐ UNSATISFACTORY	46. DOES LOAN MEET VA CREDIT STANDARDS? (GIVE REASONS FOR DECISION UNDER "REMARKS," IF NECESSARY, E.G., BORDERLINE CASE) ☐ YES ☐ NO

47. REMARKS (Use reverse, if necessary)

SECTION F — DISPOSITION OF APPLICATION

☐ Recommend that the application be approved since it meets all requirements of Chapter 37, Title 38, U.S. Code and applicable VA Regulations and directives.

☐ Recommend that the application be disapproved for the reasons stated under "Remarks" above.

48. DATE	49. SIGNATURE OF EXAMINER

50. FINAL ACTION ☐ APPROVE APPLICATION ☐ REJECT APPLICATION	51. DATE	52. SIGNATURE AND TITLE OF APPROVING OFFICIAL

VA FORM OCT 1974 26-6393

HUD-FHA Effective
Income Guidelines

SECTION 2. EFFECTIVE INCOME

3-8. *BORROWERS WHO MUST SIGN THE NOTE.* The borrower or borrowers whose income is used as effective income, shall be required to sign the note which establishes the intent of the borrower or borrowers to assume responsibility for repayment of the debt. All sources of income must be considered to determine what income can be considered as effective and what income is to be used as a compensating factor.

3-9. *EFFECTIVE INCOME.* The determination as to whether the income of borrowers or co-borrowers qualifies as effective income depends upon facts presented with the application for mortgage insurance. The mortgagee shall indicate on the Form HUD-92900 those persons who are individually or jointly responsible for the mortgage debt and subject to mortgage credit analysis. The income of the borrower, co-borrower, or both is to be analyzed by the Mortgage Credit Examiner to determine whether or not the income claimed can be expected to continue through the first five years of the mortgage loan in accordance with the instructions in this Handbook, and shall apply to every borrower, co-borrower or both regardless of sex, marital status, race, color, religion or is in any way handicapped.

   a. *The fact that a spouse* may require maternity/paternity leave at some future time which would cause a temporary halt to his/her income shall not be considered. Inquiry regarding family planning shall not be made.

   b. *Borrowers, co-borrowers* or both shall be considered on the basis of their financial capacity, financial stability and creditworthiness. If they are jointly responsible for the debt, their combined income is used in determining effective income, regardless of the relationship of the individuals requesting consideration for an individual mortgage loan.

   c. *Individuals may take title* as co-borrowers for the exclusive purpose of sharing equity although they have no interest, beyond a monetary one, in the applicant or the property. A high ratio mortgage will be available in those instances in which HUD reviews the shared equity agreement and determines that the occupant mortgagor's interests are adequately protected. HUD need not review agreements in those transactions in which the mortgage amount is limited to 85 percent of that available to an owner-occupant.

   d. *If more than one borrower* is submitted for consideration, it may be necessary, in order to clearly identify all factors to be considered in the analysis, for the mortgagee to provide a separate Form HUD-92900 for each. If all the information necessary for a complete analysis can be included on one Form HUD-92900, a second Form HUD-92900 should not be submitted.

3-10. *CO-SIGNERS.* Co-signers are sometimes proposed in connection with a loan application for the purpose of strengthening the transaction. The important consideration in determining the extent to which the income of a co-signer can be recognized is the interest in the transaction and availability of income for the transaction. The interest, in turn, will depend upon the relationship to the borrower and whether or not the co-signer occupies or receives any benefits from the property. Established charitable groups, associations or corporations may also be considered acceptable as co-signers. A vested interest in title shall not be required. The co-signer's income shall be considered only to the extent of the amount of the monthly mortgage payment.

   a. *Co-signers* sign the note but do not sign the mortgage.

   b. *It is not intended* that a co-signer make the monthly payment on the mortgage instead of the borrower. The co-signer makes the monthly mortgage payment only in the event the borrower cannot make it because of temporary adversity. If the adverse circumstances continue, the co-signer will be expected to continue the payments until such time as the borrower can resume paying regularly or some disposition is made of the property.

3-11. *OCCUPATIONAL INCOME.* All of the borrower's occupational income shall be considered when establishing the borrower's effective income. In all cases, the effective income must be limited to the amount that will be reasonably expected to continue during the early period of the mortgage risk. If the borrower indicates the intent to retire, the income is the amount of retirement benefits and other income that will prevail after retirement, such as benefits under various retirement plans, the social security, annuities, or other pension plans.

3-12. *OVERTIME/PART-TIME AND OTHER EARNINGS.* Income received for overtime/part-time work, bonuses, incentive plans, etc., are included as effective income if it can be established that such earnings are characteristic of the employer, kind of employment, and will continue during the early period of mortgage risk. Based on continually updated data maintained in the Single Family Mortgage Credit Branch, the Loan Examiner shall include in effective income any supplementary income that the borrower can reasonably expect to receive. No limit is applied to the number of hours of overtime that can be worked. The Loan Examiner shall not arbitrarily reduce overtime earnings based on the premise the borrower cannot work the hours claimed.

   a. *The kind of employment* in particular areas provides the Loan Examiner with evidence that overtime is common to that particular industry and the borrower regularly works extra hours. Data maintained at the Field Office based on local industry practices will assist the Loan Examiner in arriving at a decision that overtime is a regular feature of the particular employer and, therefore, can be counted as effective income.

b. *The kind of work* or profession provides the Examiner evidence that overtime is a regular feature of a particular occupation. The Loan Examiner can assume that the individual that has a history of fiscal responsibility will work overtime if the need arises. Therefore, if overtime or supplementary income is claimed, the Examiner may use it as Effective Income.

3-13. *INCOME FROM COMMISSIONS, FEES OR TIPS.* In determining the Effective Income of a commission salesperson or a person deriving income from fees or tips, the principles applicable to self-employed applicants should be applied. A verification of commissions or fees may be available; however, individuals, such as attorneys, appraisers, accountants, houseworkers, consultants, etc., who collect fees from various employers may not be able to provide a verification of income earned.

a. *In instances where borrowers* claim income from fees paid by various individuals, the Loan Examiner shall refer to data maintained by the Mortgage Credit Staff that provides statistical information on the average earnings of people working on a fee basis. The income claimed by the borrower shall not be discounted, if statistical data will support the amount of income that can be assured the borrower for repayment of the debt. Earnings in excess of the average claimed by the borrower shall be counted as a compensating factor and shall be used in qualifying the borrower.

b. *Borrowers whose income* is derived from commissions, for example, insurance sales, real estate sales, business machine sales, and stock and bond sales, are able to provide some verification of a record of earnings. The Loan Examiner shall include in Effective Income an annual average earned in commissions and compute the monthly Effective Income on the average earnings.

c. *Income from tips* is difficult to verify. The file must contain evidence of average earnings or indicate the level of annual earnings maintained by the applicant over a two-year period.

3-14. *INCOME FROM A BUSINESS OWNED BY BORROWER.* When a substantial portion of the borrower's income is derived from a business which he/she owns or in which he/she is one of the principal owners, the amount of Effective Income will generally be the amount which he/she takes out of the business in the form of salary or withdrawals, provided this amount does not exceed his/her portion of the net profits of the business. Capital amounts withdrawn cannot be considered as Effective Income. The determination of the probable earning capacity of the business from which the borrower derives income will be estimated in the same manner as that of a corporation or partnership. It is particularly important in cases of small individually owned businesses to obtain current financial statements containing sufficiently complete information as to the earnings and financial condition of the business to determine the amount of borrower's Effective Income.

3-15. *IN THE EVENT THE BUSINESS* is small and the borrower does not have a sophisticated bookkeeping system, other methods of verifying income shall be applied. It is the responsibility of the mortgagee to submit all information pertinent to the analysis of income. The loan examiner shall conduct an in-depth analysis of the actual expenditures of the borrower to determine if the borrower could pay all debts on the income claimed. The Mortgage Credit sections shall maintain data on approximate earnings of small businesses, and self-employed individuals, e.g., taxi drivers, barber shops., etc. This can be used to arrive at the approximate earning expectation of the self-employed borrower. Although income tax returns can be accepted in lieu of other evidence of income from self-employed individuals or individuals owning their own business, it is important that the deductions for tax purposes be analyzed since these deductions do not always represent cash expenditures but are used to reduce the tax liability of the tax payer.

3-16. *INCOME OF CORPORATE OR PARTNERSHIP BORROWER.* When the borrower is a corporation or a partnership operating under a trade name, the amount of the Effective Income ordinarily will be based upon the demonstrated earning power of the business. The estimate should reflect the net income from normal operations before any charges for debt principal of any kind and income taxes. The operating statement should be analyzed in connection with the balance sheet to see that adequate charges to reserves have been made. The operating statement should cover a fiscal period of recent date and the balance sheet should be as of the date of the closing of that fiscal period. In cases involving operative-builder corporations or partnerships to be formed or recently formed, where an operating statement is not available, an estimate of Effective Income shall not be made.

a. *A commercial credit report covering* the business should be available when estimating the amount of Effective Income of a corporation or partnership. These reports will sometimes indicate that operating statements for previous fiscal periods should be obtained, for comparative purposes, to aid in estimating the income available over a period of time.

b. *Generally, commercial credit* reports indicate the trend of earnings of the business and sometimes will show a comparison of earnings for at least a two-year period. If the report does not contain this information but indicates the business to be in a healthy financial condition, additional statements for previous fiscal periods need not be included.

c. *It is not necessary* to order a commercial report for a business with modest capital and earning capacity such as a small grocery, filling station, beauty or barbershop.

3-17. *INCOME FROM SOURCES OTHER THAN OCCUPATION.* Whenever it constitutes a significant portion of total income, net income from sources other than that of the borrower's occupation shall be analyzed to determine the amount which may be included as Effective Income.

a. *Elimination of Income-Producing Assets.* Income-producing assets, such as stocks, bonds, income property, or any asset which, if sold to complete the mortgage loan transaction, reduces the amount of available future income that can be assured the borrower for repayment of the debt shall not be included as Effective Income. The borrower should not be required to sacrifice future income by selling assets since the assets may be better used as collateral for a loan to cover the cash investment.

b. *Income from Room and Board and Travel Expenses.* Income from room and board, amounts received for automobile and other travel expenses, VA benefits and similar items shall be considered Effective Income, provided the documentation in the file substantiates the continuity and regularity of this source of income. In the case of automobile or travel expenses, VA school education benefits, and similar types of reimbursement, allowance must be made for the expenses to be paid out of the money received. If the regularity of this type of income is not sufficiently documented, it shall be considered a compensating factor in qualifying the borrower.

c. *Income from Contributions.* Contributions reported as income by the borrower may be considered as Effective Income if they are derived from members of the borrower's family who are financially able to continue making such contributions.

d. *Income for Repayment of Principal of Capital Investment.* Amounts received in repayment of the principal of a capital investment shall be considered as Effective Income if the income is regularly received, such as continuing income from annuities or trusts.

e. *Disability Compensation.* Payments on account of disability of the borrower shall be included as part of Effective Income if payments are likely to continue through the early period of mortgage risk. Payments received on account of temporary disability shall be used as a compensating factor.

f. *Income from Real Estate.* Income and debts on improved real estate need special consideration. A schedule of all other real estate owned should be submitted in which the gross income, taxes and operating expenses, and the net income on real estate owned by the borrower are itemized. The Net Rental Income from such real estate should be entered in the "Gross Monthly Income" section of the application. Before recognizing this net income as stable income, the underwriter must relate the type of property to the net income; generally, the gross income from a single family property will only offset any mortgage payments and operating expenses, with the owner's profit being received through appreciation, debt reduction, refinancing or sale. If a multifamily or income-producing property, the underwriter should be familiar with the rental demand for the type of property in the area and the pattern of operating costs. Increasing vacancy rates and operating costs can materially off-set the net income and marketability of a property. The obligation arising from ownership of rental properties shall not be included in recurring charges but is charged to gross rents prior to establishing net actual income.

(1) If the real estate holdings are non-income producing, but the borrower has substantial equity in properties which are readily marketable, the monthly obligations are not to be considered as consumer debt or unsecured debt. In this instance, the borrower can liquidate the real estate and be relieved of the installment obligation without the credit position being jeopardized.

(2) If the subject property is to be rented, the gross rental income from the unit(s) to be rented minus a reasonable deduction for probable losses due to vacancies and uncollected rents, taxes, maintenance and operating expenses is considered as Effective Income.

(3) If the subject property is to be occupied by the applicant as a secondary home on a seasonal or part-time basis, no income from any anticipated rental of the property shall be considered as Effective Income.

g. *Income Received from Local, State or Federal Assistance Programs.* Income received under a welfare program of a governmental agency shall be included in the estimate of Effective Income provided there is reasonable expectation that payments or the equivalent are expected to continue for the first five years of the mortgage term, and the income is received on behalf of the applicant's immediate family.

h. *Payments to Foster Parents.* An activity of this type must be treated as a form of self-employment. Income shall qualify as Effective Income if the activity gives evidence of continuing.

i. *Alimony, Child Support and Separate Maintenance Agreements.* Income in this category shall be considered to the extent the payments are likely to continue. The lender must advise the applicant that income from alimony, child support or separate maintenance need not be revealed if the borrower does not wish to have such income considered as a basis for repaying the debt. This advice is contained in Block 23, Item E of the Form HUD-92900. Factors to be considered in determining the likelihood of consistent payments are whether the payments are made pursuant to a court order, the length of time the payments have been received, the regularity of the payments, availability of procedures to enforce the payment and the creditworthiness of the payor, including the credit history of the payor, if available, under the Fair Credit Reporting Act or other applicable laws. A statement from the payor indicating the intent to continue and the fact that payments have been regularly made in the past shall be accepted and considered evidence of regularity of payments. The agreement to make the payments may be made between the parties without legal assistance. An agreement of this nature shall be considered evidence of the intent to make regular payments for the maintenance of the family.

3-18. *NET EFFECTIVE INCOME.* In analyzing a borrower's financial capacity, it is realistic to recognize that only the Net Income, after deducting the estimated Federal Income Tax, will be available for mortgage payments. Even in those cases in which the borrower's income, by reason of its nature, is not subject to income tax withholding (e.g., investment and certain business income), the borrower must accumulate funds to pay the Federal Income Tax owed. A reasonable estimate may be made by calculating the tax through use of a table showing Federal Income Tax withholding rates applicable to income received monthly. The withholding tax used in the calculation may not represent the borrower's actual liability and future tax liability may be less because of the deduction available through homeownership or other benefits. Any possible reduction in tax liability may be considered a compensating factor.

SOURCE: U. S. Department of Housing and Urban Development, *Mortgage Credit Analysis for Mortgage Insurance on One- to Four-Family Properties*—A HUD Handbook, 4155.1 Rev, 5/83, pp. 3-8 to 3-15

Glossary

A

Abstract of title. A short version of the history of title to a piece of property, tracing the ownership or title. It covers the period from the origin of the parcel of land or property to the present day. This history is based on the information filed or recorded in the county clerk's records in the county in which the property is located.

Acceleration clause. A provision or covenant in a written mortgage, deed of trust, note, bond, or conditional sales contract which states that, in the event of default, due to nonpayment or if other terms of the written agreement are not met, the remaining unpaid principal balance is due and payable at once.

Accretion. An addition to the land, usually through natural causes such as wind or water flow.

Acknowledgment. A declaration made by a person to a notary public or other public official authorized to take such a statement, that the document was executed by him or her and that the execution was a free and voluntary act.

Adjustable Rate Mortgage (ARM). A mortgage that allows the lender to adjust the rate of interest and/or payment, usually every first, third or fifth year.

Alternative mortgage. Sometimes referred to as an AMI, a mortgage in which one of the four basic characteristics of the mortgage changes over the life of the mortgage, such as the interest rate, amount of the principal, repayment term, or amount of the payment.

Amortization. The reduction of a financial obligation by regularly scheduled payments.

Annual Percentage Rate (APR). The cost of credit expressed as a yearly rate. This includes not only the note rate but also certain fees and charges.

Appraisal. An estimate of value of an adequately described piece of real property, as of a specific date, supported by the analysis of relevant data by a trained professional, and usually in written form.

Appreciation. An increase in the value of real or personal property.

Assessed valuation (assessed value). For real estate purposes, the estimate of a property's value strictly for the purpose of taxation. Usually determined by a governmental unit, i.e., county government or municipal utility district (MUD).

Assessment. The valuation and listing of property by a taxing authority for the purpose of apporting or establishing the tax upon the property.

Assignee. The person or corporation to whom an interest in real property has been assigned or transferred.

Assignment of mortgage. The documented transfer of ownership of a mortgage from one lender to another lender or party.

Assignor. The person or corporation who assigns or transfers an interest in property, mortgage, or rents.

Assumption of mortgage. The transfer of title to property whereby the purchaser assumes the primary liability for the repayment of an existing mortgage on said property. The original purchaser, unless released in writing, remains also liable for the original mortgage if the purchaser for some reason defaults and is unable to repay the debt in full.

Attachment. Property seized by court order pending the outcome of a lender's or creditor's suit.

B

Balloon mortgage. A type of mortgage where the periodic payments of principal and interest are not sufficient to fully repay the loan by the end of the term of the mortgage. The balance of the loan mortgage is due and payable at a specific time, usually at the end of the term.

Balloon payment.   The payment that is due sometime in the future that will be sufficient to pay back the unpaid principal amount of a balloon mortgage.

Basis point.   One one-hundredth of one percent of interest.

Bill of sale.   A written instrument whereby a person or corporation transfers title to personal property to another person or corporation.

Blanket.   The coverage of one or more pieces of property by one instrument such as a blanket insurance policy. Sometimes this is referred to as a master policy.

Blanket mortgage.   A single mortgage that covers more than one piece of real property.

Blended yield mortgage.   First-lien mortgage secured by real property that combines the yield on an existing mortgage and the yield on any type of secondary financing used to achieve a sale of real property.

Break-even point.   The point at which the property's income from rentals and any other source equals operating expenses and debt service.

Broker (real estate).   Any person, corporation, association, firm, or partnership who for a fee will sell or exchange real property on the behalf of a seller and who holds a valid license to sell or exchange property. The broker will represent the seller and will be paid by the seller upon closing and funding of the transaction.

Buy-down mortgage.   A fixed-rate, fixed-term mortgage where the effective interest rate to the borrower is lowered by the use of an escrow account, sometimes referred to as a 3-2-1 mortgage.

BYM.   An acronym for blended yield mortgage.

C

Call clause or provision.   A provision in a note, mortgage, or deed of trust giving the lender the right to declare the remaining unpaid balance due and payable on a specified date or upon a special event, such as the death of a comaker on a note.

Capitalization.   A method to establish the value of an income producing property, based on the income stream of the property.

Cash flow.   The net income or spendable cash generated by an income-producing property after deducting all expenses and debt service from the gross income generated by the property.

Cash flow after taxes.   The amount of cash remaining after all taxes have been paid.

Certificate of commitment.   A form issued by the Veterans Administration upon approval of a mortgage application for the VA's loan guarantee (VA form 26-1866a, p.3).

Certificate of Eligibility.   A certificate issued by the VA that establishes a veteran's eligibility for and the amount of guarantee available to the veteran.

Certificate of occupancy.   A written statement from a governmental agency stating that a structure, either new or substantially rehabilitated, is fit for occupancy.

Certificate of Reasonable Value (CRV).   VA Form 26-1843. When completed, it establishes the value and maximum loan amount the VA will guarantee for a specific property.

Certificate of title.   A document prepared by either a title company or an attorney stating that the person or corporation selling a piece of property has clear, marketable, and insurable title to said property.

Chain of title.   A history of all documents pertaining to the transfer of title to a specific piece of property, beginning with the earliest and ending with the latest transfer.

Chattel.   An item of personal property.

Chattel mortgage.   Any type of debt instrument that applies to any item of personal property.

Clear title.   A title to a piece of real property with no defects, sometimes referred to as encumbrances or clouds.

Closed period.   A period of time in a note, mortgage, or any other debt instrument when the debt may not be prepaid.

Closing.   The consummation of a transaction.

Closing costs.   Sometimes referred to as settlement costs, these are the monies paid by either the buyer or seller at the time of closing of the transaction. These may include but are not limited to origination fee, title insurance, discount points, attorney's fees, and prepaid items.

Closing instructions.   A list of instructions issued by the mortgage company or lender to a settlement agent listing all of the instructions to be followed in closing a particular mortgage.

Cloud on title.   Any claim or encumbrance revealed by a title search that may affect the title to a piece of real property.

Commercial paper.   Unsecured corporate debt issued for a period of 1 to 12 months by corporations to meet short-term money needs.

Commitment.   A written agreement between a lender and a borrower that mortgage money will be available at some time in the future when all of the terms of the commitment are met. This can also be an agreement between a corporation in the secondary market (such as FNMA) who agrees to purchase mortgages that meet the underwriting guidelines of the corporation, and a mortgage lender.

Commitment fee.   A fee paid by the borrower to the lender for a commitment either to loan money or to purchase mortgages.

Common areas.   Those areas in a condominium or planned unit development that are held by the homeowners association for the benefit and use of all of the tenants and/or home or unit owners (for example, swimming pools, tennis courts, and parking areas).

Community property.   Any type of property either personal or real that by law belongs equally to both husband and wife when acquired by either using joint funds.

Condemnation.   The process by which private property is taken by a governmental agency or body for public use.

Conditional commitment (FHA).   A promise from the agency to insure to the lender the repayment of a mortgage, meeting FHA insurance requirements.

Condominium.   A multi-unit project of either offices or family units where the family or individual holds title to the unit occupied and a pro rata share ownership in all of the common areas.

Constant, mortgage.   The percent of the original unpaid principal balance of a mortgage that is repaid annually. This is expressed as a percentage, for example, 11.25 percent. Thus for an original balance of $75,000, $8437.50 would be repaid each year.

Construction loan.   A short-term loan for specifically constructing houses or commercial property. Sometimes this is referred to as interim financing.

Contiguous.   Adjoining.

Contingent interest.   An interest charge that is assessed by a lender making a mortgage equal to a specific percentage of the property's net appreciation.

Contract for deed.   A written sales agreement whereby the seller agrees to deliver to the buyer a deed to the property only after all of the required payments have been made.

Conventional loan.   Any loan secured by real property that is neither insured nor guaranteed by a government agency.

Conveyance.   Any written instrument that is evidence of the transfer of title to some interest in real property from one individual or corporation to another individual or corporation. This can be in the form of a deed, mortgage, or lease.

Cooperative (co-op).   A multifamily building or group of buildings in which the owners buy shares in the corporation that holds title to the property. The shares of stock allow the persons purchasing the stock to occupy units in the building. The cost of operation of the cooperative is prorated by the number of shares a person owns in the corporation.

Correspondent.   In lending terms, this means a person or company that represents or services mortgage loans for the person or company that actually owns the mortgages.

Covenant.   An agreement between the borrower and the lender as set forth in a mortgage or deed of trust. Sometimes these are referred to as uniform and nonuniform covenants as in the Fannie Mae/FHLMC Mortgage/Deed of Trust.

D

DD-214.   A form issued by one of the armed forces of the United States that establishes a veteran's time of service and is sometimes a requirement for the issuance of a Certificate of Eligibility.

Debenture.   An unsecured debt obligation.

Debt coverage ratio.   The ratio of the net effective income of a property to the debt service. For example, if the annual debt service on a property is $12,000 and the net effective income is $24,000, the debt coverage ratio is 2.

Debt service.   The amount of money paid annually to repay the principal and the interest on a debt.

Deed.   A written instrument that transfers the ownership of land from one individual or corporation to another. This is usually a general warranty deed but may take the form of a special warranty deed or a sheriff's deed.

Deed of trust.   This is the written instrument that is used in place of a mortgage. The title to the property is transferred, in trust, to a third party. When the debt is paid in full, the trustee transfers the title to the borrower. In the case of default by the borrower, the trustee, at the lender's request, will institute foreclosure proceedings.

Default.   Failure to live up to the terms of an obligation or debt.

Deficiency Judgment.   Filed by a lender against a borrower if the amount realized by the lender from forced sale is less than the amount owed by the borrower.

Delinquent.   The status of an obligation or debt if a payment is not received by the due date.

Depreciation.   The loss of value of improvements to real property. This can be from age, physical deterioration, functional obsolescence, or economic obsolescence.

Devise.   A gift of real property by a will.

Devisee.   The person or persons who receive the property from a will.

Disclosure statement.   A statement required by Regulation Z (Truth-in-Lending Law) from the lender to the borrower.

Discount.   The amount at which an investor will purchase a mortgage. This amount is usually less than the face amount of the mortgage and is expressed as a percentage.

Discount point.   See *Point.*

E

Earnest money.   A sum of money given usually by the buyer to bind the sale, or to show good faith in the completion of the transaction.

ECOA.   An abbreviation for the Equal Credit Opportunity Act, a federal law that requires all lenders to make credit available without regard to sex, race, color, religion, national origin, age, marital status, or receipt of public assistance.

Effective rate.   See *Yield.*

Encumbrance.   A "cloud" or claim against the title to real property usually done by filing a lien against a piece of real property.

EPM.   An acronym for equity participation mortgage.

Equity participation mortgage.   A first-lien mortgage involving an owner/occupant and an investor who share the cost of ownership, equity, and tax benefits.

Equity.   In real estate, the difference between the fair market value and the indebtedness against the property.

Equity participation.   The participation or sharing of the ownership in a piece of property by the lender.

Escalator clause.   Sometimes referred to as escalation, this is a clause in a mortgage that allows the lender to increase the interest rate. In terms of leases, this clause allows the property owner or his agent to increase or decrease the rent as required by operating costs.

Exception.   Sometimes referred to as an encumbrance. In a title policy this is an item not covered by the policy. In legal descriptions it refers to any property or piece of property to be excluded.

F

Fair market value.   See *Market value.*

Farmers Home Administration (FmHA).   An arm of the Department of Agriculture whose primary purpose is to furnish mortgage money to the rural areas of the United States.

Fed.   An abbreviation for the Federal Reserve Board.

Fee simple.   Sometimes referred to as fee simple absolute; the most comprehensive method of owning property, whereby the owner may dispose of the real property by trade, sale, or will as the owner chooses.

FHA.   An abbreviation for the Federal Housing Administration, a division of the Department of Housing and Urban Development. FHA's main purpose is to issue mortgage insurance on mortgages made by private lenders.

FHA mortgage.   A mortgage made by a private lender according to the underwriting guidelines of FHA, who then will issue insurance to protect the lender from default by the borrower.

FHLMC.   An abbreviation for the Federal Home Loan Mortgage Corporation, sometimes referred to as "The Mortgage Corporation."

FNMA.   An abbreviation for the Federal National Mortgage Association. Its purpose is to raise money in the capital markets and issue commitments to purchase mortgages from approved lenders.

Foreclosure.   A legal process instituted by the lender through a mortgage or deed of trust to terminate the borrower's interest in a property after the default of the borrower.

G

GEM.   An acronym for the growing equity mortgage.

GI-guaranteed loan.   A loan where part of the repayment is guaranteed by the Veterans Administration.

GNMA.   An abbreviation for the Government National Mortgage Association, created by the division of FNMA by the Congress in 1968.

Graduated payment adjustable mortgage.   A hybrid mortgage that combines the rate adjustment features of the renegotiable rate mortgage (RRM) with the graduated payment feature of the graduated payment mortgage (GPM).

Graduated payment adjustable rate mortgage.   A hybrid mortgage that combines the rate adjustment feature of the adjustable mortgage loan (ARM) with the graduated payment feature of the graduated payment mortgage (GPM).

Graduated payment mortgage.   A mortgage where the initial monthly payments start at a level below a standard mortgage and an increase or are graduated at a specific rate at specific time intervals.

Grantee.   A buyer.

Grantor.   A seller.

Gross income.   The total amount of income produced by a property from all sources (for example, rents, parking, and fees).

Gross rent multiplier (GRM).   The relationship of the monthly rent of a property to the sales price. It may be expressed as: sales price/gross monthly rent = GRM.

Gross stable monthly income.   The total monthly income of an applicant without deductions.

Growing equity mortgage.   A fixed rate first lien mortgage in which the monthly payments increase at a specified rate per year for a specific number of years. All increases are credited to principal reduction.

Guaranteed loan.   A loan that is guaranteed by an agency of either the federal or a state government (for example, FHA, FmHA, or a State Agriculture Department).

H

Homeowners association.   An organization of homeowners in a particular subdivision, planned unit development, or condominium development or project formed for the specific purpose of maintaining common areas and providing other services for the residents of the area.

Homestead.   Land and the improvements thereon which the owner has declared as his or her homestead; protected by the laws of some states from forced sale by certain creditors of the owner or owners.

HUD.   The Department of Housing and Urban Development created by the passage of the Urban Development Act of 1965.

I

Improvements.   As related to real estate, the additions to raw land that increase the value of the land, such as the addition of a house to a lot.

Income property.   Real property that is developed for the specific purpose of producing income for the owner.

Index.   In conjunction with the ARM, is the measurement of the interest rate. A change in the index will cause a change in the interest rate.

In-house approval.   The ability of a lender to approve a loan application without having to submit it to an investor or lender for approval.

Institutional lender.   A lender that makes real estate mortgages or any other type of mortgage and holds the mortgage in its own portfolio.

Interest rate.   The sum, expressed as a percentage, that is charged for the use of loaned funds.

Interest.   A term that is sometimes substituted for interest rate. Also means a share of the ownership in a property.

Investor.   The person supplying the funds to make mortgages and for whom the mortgage banker or financial institution services the mortgage.

J

Joint note.   A note or mortgage that is signed by two or more people who are equally liable for the repayment of the note or mortgage.

Joint tenancy.   Title to real property held equally by two parties, with right of survivorship.

Junior mortgage.   A mortgage that is inferior to a prior mortgage.

L

Late charge.   An additional fee charged by the lender to the borrower if the payment is not paid on time.

Lessee.   Renter or tenant.

Lessor.   Landlord or owner.

Level payment mortgage.   A type of mortgage where the monthly payment remains constant for the life of the mortgage.

Leverage.   The ability to borrow a larger amount of money than the borrower has invested in the property.

Lien.   A claim or encumbrance by a creditor against a piece of property used as security for a debt.

Loan closing.   See *Closing.*

Loan origination.   The solicitation of mortgage loans by a lender or their agent. This process sometimes includes the taking of the loan application.

Loan processing.   The gathering of the information that will enable the lender or the lender's agent either to approve or disapprove the loan, based on the applicant and the property.

Loan submission.   The delivery of a completed loan package to a potential lender for approval.

Loan-to-value ratio.   The relationship of the amount of loan to the value of the property. Usually expressed as a percentage, such as 95 percent.

M

Market value.   The price at which a seller is willing to sell and a buyer is willing to pay.

Maturity.   In reference to mortgages or any type of debt, the date in the debt that the last payment is due.

Mechanic's lien.   Sometimes referred to as a material and mechanic's lien (M & ML). A statutory claim against the property of others in favor of persons who have either provided materials or done work on improvements to real property.

Mortgage.   A written document pledging property as security for a debt or the fulfillment of an obligation. Upon the repayment of the debt or fulfillment of the obligation, the mortgage is void.

Mortgage banker.   A company, individual, or corporation that originates mortgages and then sells the mortgages to an investor and services the mortgages for the investor.

Mortgage broker.   A company, individual, or corporation that is paid a fee to bring together those needing loanable funds with those that have loanable funds.

Mortgagee.   The lender of money.

Mortgage insurance premium.   A fee paid to FHA for the mortgage insurance issued by FHA.

Mortgage portfolio.   The mortgages held by a lender or an investor; or the mortgages serviced by a mortgage banker.

Mortgagor.   The borrower of money.

N

NCUA.   An acronym for National Credit Union Administration.

Negative cash flow.   In reference to income-producing properties, occurs when the total annual cash outlay is more than the cash received from the property.

Net appreciated value.   The value established in regard to the shared appreciation mortgage.

Net effective income.   The income base used by FHA. It is the gross stable monthly income less federal income tax withholding.

Net income.   In reference to income-producing properties, it is the gross income of the property less operating expenses and a factor for vacancy and credit loss.

Net operating income (NOI).   See *Net income.*

Net profit.   The cash remaining after all expenses and taxes are paid.

Note.   A written document creating a debt.

Notice of default.   A legal notice filed by the trustee in a deed of trust that the property is to be sold at a trustee's sale.

O

Offeree.   One receiving an offer.

Offeror.   One making an offer.

Open end mortgage.   A mortgage that has no due date and that allows the lender to advance additional funds without rewriting the mortgage.

Operating expenses.   The costs of doing business.

Origination fee.   A charge collected by a company or lender to cover the cost of processing and taking a mortgage application. Usually expressed as a percentage of the mortgage amount.

P

Package mortgage.   A mortgage including not only the real estate, but some of the appliances and other items that are part of the structure.

Packing and shipping.   The grouping of mortgages that meet a particular investor's guidelines. The group or package is then shipped to the investor.

Participation loan.   A mortgage with more than one lender. This type of mortgage is primarily used to finance large commercial projects.

Permanent investor.   A lender that provides long-term financing.

Personal property.   Usually any item that is not considered real property or a fixture to real property.

PITI.   An abbreviation for principal, interest, taxes, and insurance charges which are collected monthly as the mortgage payment.

Plat.   A map of a subdivision or PUD, usually recorded in the county clerk's office.

Point.   Usually expressed as a percentage of the loan amount. Thus, one point equals one percent of the loan amount.

Prepaid items.   An advance payment of taxes, hazard insurance, and mortgage insurance, if the mortgage is insured by FHA or a private mortgage insurance company. This payment is collected at the time of closing and is held in escrow by the lender or the servicing agent for the lender.

Prepayment penalty.   A fee collected by the lender as per the loan agreement for the repayment of a mortgage prior to the maturity date.

Prepayment privilege.   The right of the borrower to prepay the loan or mortgage prior to the maturity date.

Price level adjusted mortgage.   Sometimes abbreviated PLAM, this is a mortgage in which the interest rate as well as the principal amount is adjusted periodically.

Principal balance.   In pertaining to mortgages, the remaining balance of the mortgage less any interest or fees.

Private mortgage insurance.   Mortgage default insurance issued in the name of the lender by an approved private mortgage insurance company.

Processing.   See *Loan processing*.

Pro forma statement.   The projected income and expenses of an income-producing property, usually for a period of one year.

PUD.   An abbreviation for planned unit development, a large area that has a comprehensive land development plan and usually contains roads, homes, and common areas. The most common PUDs are large townhouse developments.

Purchase money mortgage.   A mortgage that is executed by the purchaser of the property as part of the sales price, naming the seller as mortgagee.

Q

Quickclaim deed.   A written instrument that conveys whatever rights the grantor may presently have in the subject piece of property.

R

Rate.   Another term for interest rate.

Real estate.   Real property and all improvements.

Realtor®.   A licensee, either a broker or salesperson, who is a member of a local real estate board that is affiliated with the National Association of Realtors®.

Recordation.   The act of filing a legal document in the office of the county clerk.

Redemption.   The acquiring of property taken by court or sold at auction by the original owner.

Redemption period.   The period of time the owner may repurchase property by paying all judgments and fees against the property.

Refinance.   The paying off of one indebtedness on a piece of property, using the proceeds from another mortgage or loan on the same property as security.

Release of lien.   Upon payment of a debt in full, the written instrument that is filed to release the property from the lien.

Renegotiable rate mortgage.   Sometimes referred to as a rollover mortgage, this is a series of short-term loans issued for a term of three to five years each, secured by a long-term mortgage.

RESPA.   The Real Estate Settlement Procedures Act, a federal law that sets standards for the settlement or closing of the real estate transaction.

Restrictions.   Legal limitations contained in the deed regarding the use of the real property.

S

Secondary financing.   A second mortgage on a piece of real property.

Secondary mortgage market.   An unorganized market in which mortgages are bought and sold.

Second mortgage.   See *Junior mortgage.*

Seller-servicer.   The name given by FNMA to an approved lender.

Separate property.   Property of a married person that was acquired prior to marriage or by gift or as a result of a bequest.

Settlement costs.   See *Closing costs.*

Shared appreciation mortgage.   A mortgage on residential real estate in which the lender agrees to share in the property's appreciation and in return offers the borrower a below-market interest rate.

Sheriff's deed.   A deed to property given by a sheriff when property is purchased at a court-ordered sale for back taxes.

Situs.   Location.

Spot loan.   A single loan on a single house. Sometimes the term is used to refer to mortgages solicited from a real estate firm.

Subordination.   The act of making one debt inferior to another when both debts are on the same property.

Sweat equity.   A term used by FHA for value added to property by the efforts of the homebuyer. It refers to the sweat and toil of the homebuyer.

Syndication.   A group of people organized for the specific purpose of purchasing "in total or an interest in" real estate.

T

Take-out loan.   A commitment of permanent financing upon completion of the structure. It is called a take-out because it takes the interim lender out of the structure.

Term.   The period or length of a mortgage or lease.

Title.   Written evidence to one's right to, or ownership in, a specific piece of property.

Title defects.   See *Exception.*

Trust deed.   See *Deed of trust.*

Trustee.   The third party to a deed of trust to whom the title to the property is transferred in trust.

U

Underwriting.   The evaluation or analysis of the risk involved with a loan and matching the risk to the proper return.

Unsecured loan.   A loan made by an individual, firm, or corporation that is not secured by property, personal or real.

Usury.   Charging an interest rate more than is allowed by law.

V

VA.   Veterans Administration, a federal agency created by the Servicemen's Readjustment Act of 1944. The purpose of the VA is to administer the veterans benefit programs.

Variable rate mortgage.   A mortgage with the characteristic of an interest rate that may vary at a specific time, as little as one month, based on a specific index.

VA loan.   See *GI-guaranteed loan.*

Vendee.   Purchaser.

Vendor.   Seller.

Veterans entitlement.   In mortgage lending, the amount of VA loan guarantee that is available to a veteran.

W

Warehousing.   In reference to mortgage bankers, the borrowing of funds for a short term in order to fund a mortgage or loan prior to the lender or investor actually purchasing the mortgage or loan.

Warranty deed.   See *Deed.*

Wrap or wraparound mortgage.   A mortgage used to finance real property which will include an existing first lien mortgage.

Y

Yield.   As it applies to mortgage financing, the return or annual income generated by a mortgage. Usually expressed as a percentage.

Index

Italicized numbers indicate illustrations.

A

Accelerated amortization, 159
Acceleration-upon-sale provision. *See* Due-on-sale clause
Acquisition cost, FHA, 146, 358–61
Action! Mortgage, 82, *83*
Actual cash method, 79
Additional fund wraparound mortgages, 433
Adjustable mortgage loans (AMLs), 47, 54, 84. *See also* Adjustable-rate mortgages (ARMs)
Adjustable-rate deed of trust rider, FNMA/FHLMC, 71, *72–73*, 256, *267–72*
Adjustable-rate mortgages (ARMs), 16, 47–78
    COC, 46–53, *50*, *51–53*
    credit union, 134
    FHLBB, 46–47, 54–56
    FHA, 166–70, *169*
    FHLMC purchases of, 285–87
    FNMA purchases of, 254–55, 274
    interest rate determination for, 71–78
    NCUA, 47, 56–57
    private mortgage insurance for, 222–24, *225*
    savings and loan association, 112
    secured by energy-efficient property, 357
    standard instruments for, 57–71, *59–70*
Adjustable-rate note, FNMA/FHLMC, 58, *59–70*
Adjustable-rate rider, 71, *72–73*
Adjusted incomes, FmHA, 196
Administrator of National Banks, 114
Adverse action
    defined, 376
    notice of, 376, *377*
Age of applicant, and income stability, 345–46
Alimony, and borrower qualification, 347, 349
All-inclusive mortgages. *See* Wraparound mortgages
Alternative mortgage instruments (AMIs), 14–16, 46–101
    and Alternative Mortgage Transaction Parity Act, 135
    savings and loan association, 111, 113
Alternative Mortgage Transaction Parity Act, 135

American Institute of Real Estate Appraisers (AIREA), 316
AMIs. *See* Alternative mortgage instruments
AMLs. *See* Adjustable mortgage loans
Annual disclosure, 170
Annual percentage rate (APR), 412
Anticipation, 317
Application fee, 422–25
Application for Property Appraisal and Commitment, HUD, 334–36, *335*, *337*
Application for Release from Personal Liability, VA, 190, *191*
Appraisal Review Journal, 343
Approval of Purchaser and Release of Seller, FHA, 175, *177*
Assumptions, 18
    adjustable-rate mortgage, 49, 55
    conventional mortgage, 213–14
    FHA mortgage, 139, 154, 174–75, 213
    FHLMC multifamily purchase program, 290
    financed by tax-exempt bonds, 207
    and FNMA/FHLMC deed of trust, 29
    and loan disclosure, 412
    and second mortgages, 18, 438
    VA mortgage, 180, 190–95, 213
    VHAP mortgage, 199
Attorney's fee, 425

B

Balance available for family support, 367–70
Balloon mortgages, 435–36
    adjustable-rate, 53
    disclosure for, 436, *437*
    and FHA, 138
    multifamily, FNMA purchases of, 274
    savings and loan association, 112, 435
Bank accounts and loans, verification of, 395, *398*, *399*
Banking Act of 1933, 113

Banking Department of Texas, 115
Bank of North America, 2
Bankruptcy, and credit history, 351
BDMs. *See* Buydown mortgages
Blanket mortgages, with release clause, 17
Blended-yield mortgages (BYMs), 435
Board of Directors, Federal Reserve
System, 2–5
Board of Governors, Federal Reserve
System, 5, 118–19
Bond-type securities, GNMA, 309–10
Bonuses, as stable monthly income, 346
Borrower qualification, 344–73
   conventional mortgage, 352–57, 371–72
   FHA, 139, 352, 357–66, 372
   for self-employed individuals, 371–73
   Texas Housing Agency, 370–71
   VA, 180, 352, 366–70, 372–73
   worksheets for, *354, 355, 359, 360,* 470–72
Borrower's statement of liability, 404
Budget mortgages, 16–17
Building associations, 107
Buydown mortgages (BDMs), 78–80
   FHLMC, 285–86, 287
   FNMA, 235–39, *237–38,* 253, 255
   HUD, 150–51, 168
   VA, 187
Buydown period, 78

C

Call option rider, 214, *215*
Canada, and renegotiable-rate mortgage,
98–99
Capacity, and loan underwriting, 405
Capital, and loan underwriting, 405
Capitalization rate, 321
Capitalized interest, 55
Carry-over provision, 56
Carryover requirements, FHA adjustable-rate
mortgage, 167–68, *169*
Catch-up payment, 55

Certificate of Commitment, FHA and VA,
391, *393, 394*
Certificate of Eligibility, VA,
181–85, *182*
Certificate of Reasonable Value (CRV), VA,
186, 196, 336, 338
Certificates of deposit, 6, 9
Change, as principle of value, 320
Character, and loan underwriting, 405
Child support, and borrower qualification,
347, 349
City housing agencies, 208–9
Clear Lake City, 131
Closing costs, 422–26
   FHA, 146, *148, 149,* 422–25
   sources of funds for, 347–48, 357
   VA, 179, 422–25
Closing instructions, 422, *423–24*
Closing statement. *See* Uniform Settlement
Statement
COC. *See* Controller of the Currency
Collateral, and loan underwriting, 405
Collation. *See* Loan packaging
Commercial banks, 113–15
   alternative mortgage instruments of, 135
   loan warehousing by, 130
   mortgage debt held by, 105, 106
   and secondary market, 228
   as supervised lenders, 180
Commercial property loans, 107, 120
Commissions
   real estate, 425
   as stable monthly income, 346
Commitment for Title Insurance, 418, *419–21*
Commitments
   FHLMC, 128, 290–302, 303–5
   FNMA, 128, 275–80
   mortgage banker, 128
Community Development Block Grants, 122
Community Property Law, 20
Community reinvestment, 118–26
Community Reinvestment Act (CRA), 118–23,
126
Community Reinvestment Act (CRA)
statement, 119–21, *120*
Comparables, 320–21

Comp books, 314–16, *315*
Comptroller of the Currency (COC)
    adjustable-rate mortgages of, 46–53
    bank regulations of, 114
    and Community Reinvestment Act, 118
Concurrent first lien, 199
Condemnation, 28, 38, 41
Conditional Commitment, FHA, 336
Conditioning of property sale, 408
Condominium units
    FHA insurance for, 141, 153, 161–64, *165*, 167
    FNMA/FHLMC appraisal report for, 322, *327–28*
    FNMA/FHLMC rider for, 29, *30*
    FNMA programs for, 239–43
Conduit program, 312
Conformity, 317
Congress, U.S., and real estate industry, 8
Consolidated mortgages, 435
Construction mortgages, 18, 53, 112, 114, 115
Consumer loans, 120
Contingent interest, 91
Contract for deed, 18–19
Contribution, 317–20
Conventional Mortgage Pass-Through Securities, 231–33
Conventional mortgages, 14, 211–21. *See also* Standard mortgages
    borrower qualification for, 352–57, 371–72
    closing instructions for, 422, *423–24*
    closing costs for, 425
    as federally related mortgages, 380
    FHLMC purchases of, 281, 284–86, 290–92, 307
    FNMA purchases of, 233–39
    GNMA purchases of, 307
    packaging of, 401–4
    VHAPs with, 199, *202–3*
Convertible adjustable-rate mortgage note, FHLMC, 71, *74–76*
Copy cost of deed restrictions, 425
Cosigner on note or loan, and borrower qualification, 348
Cost method, 320–21, 322
Cost of amortization schedule, 425

Cost of funds index, 95
County housing agencies, 208–9
Creative financing, 433–39
Credit history, and borrower qualification, 349–52
Credit Report, Standard Factual Data, 349, *350*, 400, 401–4
Credit reporting agencies, 351, 400
Credit Union Act of Texas, 134
Credit Union Department of the State of Texas, 134
Credit unions, 104, 132–34
    alternative mortgage instruments of, 135
    borrower qualification for, 348

D

Dallas County Housing Finance Corporation, 208–9
Debentures
    FHLMC, 284
    FNMA, 231, *232*
Deed of trust, defined, 13–14, 19
Deed of trust mortgages, 19
Deed restrictions, copy cost of, 425
Deep buydowns, 78
Defense Department Form 214, 181–85
Delegated Underwriter Program, 405
Demand adjustable-rate mortgages, 53
Demand deposits, 113
Demand feature, loan disclosure form for mortgage with, 412, *414*
Department of Housing and Urban Development (HUD), 8. *See also* Federal Housing Administration (FHA); Uniform Settlement Statement
    Conditional Commitment of, 336
    and FHA, 136
    and FNMA, 229, 230–31
    and GNMA, 302
    mortgage banking regulation by, 128
    and Office of Interstate Land Sales

Registration, 19
offices of, 137
Settlement Costs of, 381
Depository Institutions Deregulation and Monetary Control Act, 5, 10, 11, 57, 112, 409–12, 434
Depreciation
and cost method, 320
as deduction in loan qualification, 371, 372
Derogatory credit information, 351
Desire to pay, 348
Direct Endorsement Program, FHA, 140
Disaster housing mortgages, 307–9
Discount points, 140, 180, 212–13, 285, 425
Discount rate, Federal Reserve, 6–8
Disintermediation, 103
Displaced families, homeowner assistance for, 151–52
Distributive shares for FHA insurance terminations, 142, *144*
Dividend income, as stable monthly income, 346–47
Divorce covenant, 20
Dollar, stabilization of, 7–8
Down payments. *See also specific mortgages*
conventional mortgage, 213
FHA mortgage, 139, 146–49
and maximum sales price, 344
source of funds for, 347–48, 357
and VA mortgage, 179
VHAP mortgage, 199
Draws, 18
Due-on-sale clause
FHA, 207–8, *208*
FNMA enforcement of, 213, 243, 274–75
VA, 207, *207*
and wraparound mortgages, 434
Due-on-transfer rider, FNMA/FHLMC, 245, *252*, 288–90, *301*

E

Early-ownership mortgages (EOMs), 89–91
Earnest money contract, negotiation of, 412–18

Easy money, 7–8
Economic obsolescence, and cost method, 320
Effective lending territory, 120
Emergency Home Finance Act of 1970, 222, 281
Emergency Home Purchase Act of 1974, 306
Emotional needs for housing, 348
Employment
and income, verification of, 395, *396, 397*
pattern of, 345
stability of, 345–46
Energy addendum, 329, *330–31*
Energy-efficient property
and borrower qualification, 352, 357
determinants for, 329
FNMA program for, 273
Energy escrow account, 273
Equal Credit Opportunity Act (ECOA), 129, 346, 347, 376, 381
Equity participation mortgages, 436–38
Escrow accounts
buydown mortgage, 78–80, 150–51
and deed of trust, 28, 38, 41
energy, 273
FHA mortgage, 138
and RESPA, 408–9
Escrow advance mortgages, 81, 82
Existing boundaries, 120
Extended-term wraparound mortgages, 434

F

Fair Credit Reporting Act, 129, 349, 351
Fair market value, 322
Fannie Mae. *See* Federal National Mortgage Association (FNMA)
Farm Credit Act of 1971, 209
Farmers Home Administration (FmHA), 8, 462–63
loan application form of, 386–95, *390, 392*
Section 502 rural housing mortgages of, 123, 196–97
Fast-and-dirty method, 79
Federal Credit Union Act of 1934, 132

Federal Deposit Insurance Corporation (FDIC), 113, 117, 118–19
Federal Farm Loan Act of 1916, 209
Federal financial supervisory agencies, Community Reinvestment Act, 118, 121
Federal Home Loan Bank Act, 107
Federal Home Loan Bank Board (FHLBB), 107
   and adjustable-rate mortgages, 46–47, 54–56
   and balloon mortgages, 435–36
   and Community Reinvestment Act, 118, 122
   and graduated-payment adjustable-rate mortgages, 46, 83–85
   and graduated-payment mortgages, 46, 80–82
   lending regulations of, 112–13
   and private mortgage insurance, 222
   and reverse-annuity mortgages, 46, 99–100
   and shared-appreciation mortgages, 46, 91
   and variable-rate mortgages, 46–47, 96, 97
   and wraparound mortgages, 434
Federal Home Loan Bank System
   and FHLMC, 281–84
   mortgage debt held by, 106
   mutual savings banks in, 117
   organization of, 107, *108*, *109*
Federal Home Loan Mortgage Corporation (FHLMC), 107, 281–302
   areas served by, 282
   borrower qualification guidelines of, 352–57
   commitments of, 128, 290–302, *303–5*
   and condominium mortgage insurance, 164
   funds sources for, 281–84
   history of, 281
   mortgage purchase programs of, 284–90
   offices of, *283*
   and prepayment penalties, 214
   and private mortgage insurance, 223, 464
   purposes of, 229, 281
   underwriting guidelines of, 212, 221, 284
Federal Home Loan Mortgage Corporation (FHLMC) instruments and forms
   adjustable-rate deed of trust rider, 71, *72–73*, 256, *267–72*
   adjustable-rate note, 58, *59–70*

   condominium rider, 29, *30*
   convertible adjustable-rate note, 71, *74–76*
   due-on-transfer rider, 245, *252*, 288, 288–90, 301
   home improvement note, 245, *246–47*
   loan application, 381–86, *383*, *385*, *387*
   multifamily deed of trust, 288, 290, *293–300*
   multifamily note, 288–90, *289*, *291–92*, *302*
   planned unit development rider, 29–32, *31*
   property appraisal report, 322–32, *323–28*
   purchase money deed of trust, 245, *248–51*
   standard deed of trust, 22–32, *24–27*
   standard note, 20–22, *21*, *23*
   2- to 4-family rider, 32, *33*
Federal Housing Administration (FHA), 8. *See also* Department of Housing and Urban Development (HUD)
   and buydown funds, 79
   certificate of commitment of, 391, *393*
   due-on-sale clause of, 207–8, *208*
   effective income guidelines of, 473–75
   history and purposes of, 136–37, 221
   and mortgage company underwriting, 405
   mortgage insurance premium rider of, *38*, 39
   and regulated lenders, 405
   property appraisal/commitment forms of, 332–41, *335*, *337*
   Section 245 deed of trust of, 161, *163*, 170–74, *171–72*
   Section 245 note of, 161, *162*, 170–74, *173*
   standard deed of trust of, 32–38, *35–37*
   verification request forms of, 395, *397*, *399*
Federal Housing Administration (FHA) mortgages, 14, 136–75, 459–61
   advantages/disadvantages of, 139–40
   alternative mortgage instruments for, 166–70
   application for, 386–95, *388*, *390*, *392*
   assumptions of, 139, 154, 174–75, 213
   borrower qualification for, 139, 352, 357–66, 372
   closing costs for, 146, *148*, 149, 422–25
   and Community Reinvestment Act, 122–23
   condominium-unit, 141, 153, 161–64, *165*, 167
   and conventional mortgages

compared, 211–21
as federally regulated mortgage loans, 380
FHLMC purchases of, 281
FNMA purchases of, 233, 234
general rules for, 137–38
GNMA purchases of, 307, 309
growing-equity, 89, 157–61, 187–88
low-and-moderate-income family, 122, 151–54
mobile home or manufactured housing, 164–66
and mortgage banking, 128
mortgage insurance premium for, 137, 141–43, *145*
and mutual savings banks, 117
negotiated interest rate of, 140–41
packaging of, 404
and private mortgage insurance compared, 222, 225, 226
reforms in, 138–39
Section 203(b), 144–50, *147*, 164–66
Section 221(d)(2), 151–53
Section 234(c), 141, 161–64
Section 235(i), 153–54
Section 245, 80, 122, 154–61, *155*, *158*, 170–74
and Texas Veterans Housing Program, 199
veterans', 149–50
and wraparound mortgages, 434
Federal Land Banks, 8, 209–10
Federally related mortgage loans, 380
Federal National Mortgage Association (FNMA), 8, 229–80
    borrower qualification guidelines of, 352–57, 371–72
    commitments of, 128, 275–80
    and condominium mortgage insurance, 164
    due-on-sale policy of, 213, 243, 274–75
    and federal government, relationship between, 230–31
    funds sources for, 231–33
    and GNMA, relationship between, 302, 306, 307
    history of, 229–30
    home seller program of, 438
    mortgage debt held by, 106
    mortgage purchase programs of, 234–74
    mortgage ratios and standards of, 129
    offices of, 221
    and prepayment penalties, 214
    and private mortgage insurance, 222, 223, 224
    purpose of, 137, 230
    Refinance/resale program of, 234–35, *244*, 254, 275, 435
    and regulated lenders, 406
    underwriting guidelines of, 212, 221, 233–34
Federal National Mortgage Association (Fannie Mae) instruments and forms
    adjustable-rate deed of trust rider, 71, *72–73*, 256, *267–72*
    adjustable-rate note, 58, *59–70*
    call option note, 214, *215*
    condominium rider, 29, *30*
    due-on-transfer rider, 245, *252*, 288, 290, *301*
    graduated payment note, 256, *258–66*
    growing-equity note, 91, *92–93*
    home improvement note, 245, *246–47*
    loan application, 381–86, *383*, *385*, *387*
    multifamily deed of trust, 288, 289, 290, *293–300*
    multifamily note, 288-90, *289*, *291–92*, *302*
    planned unit development rider, 29–32, *31*
    property appraisal report, 317, 322–32, *323–28*
    purchase money deed of trust, 245, *248–51*
    standard deed of trust, 22–32, *24–27*
    standard note, 20–22, *21*, *23*
    2- to 4- family rider, 32, *33*
    verification request, 395, *396*, *398*
Federal Reserve Bulletin, 5, 6
Federal Reserve Statistical Release, 71, 77
Federal Reserve System, 2–8, *3*, *4*
    loan disclosure forms of, 412, *413–17*
    and FNMA obligations, 230
    Treasury Constant Maturities of, 9–10
Federal Savings and Loan Insurance Corporation (FSLIC), 107, 109, 118–19

Fed fund rate, 9
FHA. *See* Federal Housing Administration
FHLBB. *See* Federal Home Loan Bank Board
FHLMC. *See* Federal Home Loan Mortgage Corporation
Fiduciaries, loans to, 409
Financial Statement, VA, 190, *193–94*
First Bank of the United States, 2
First Mortgage of Texas, 131
502 loan program, FmHA, 123, 196–97
Fixed-debt reverse annuity mortgages, 100, 101
Fixed-rate mortgages. *See* Standard mortgages
FLIP Mortgage Corporation, 82
FmHA. *See* Farmers Home Administration
FNMA. *See* Federal National Mortgage Association
Foreclosure
    and HUD buydown program, 151
    loan priority in, 18
    and simple assumption, 175
    and temporary mortgage assistance payments program, 161
    trustee's role in, 14, 19
Form 1, HUD. *See* Uniform Settlement Statement
Forward commitment program, 206
"Four Cs" of loan underwriting, 405
Freddie Mac. *See* Federal Home Loan Mortgage Corporation (FHLMC)
Freddie Mac Commitment Activity, 292, *303–5*
Functional obsolescence, and cost method, 320
Funding, 407–8
Funding fee, VA, 180

G

Garn-St. Germain Depository Institutions Act, 49, 112, 114, 135

GEMs. *See* Growing-equity mortgages
Gift letter and receipt acknowledgment, 401, *403*
Ginnie Mae. *See* Government National Mortgage Association
Ginnie Maes. *See* Mortgage-backed securities (MBS) program
Gold, price of, 7
Good faith estimates, 381, *382*
Government National Mortgage Association (GNMA), 8, 302–12
    adjustable-rate mortgage requirement of, 167
    funds sources for, 306
    history of, 229, 302
    mortgage-backed securities program of, 231–33, 306, 309–12, *311*
    mortgage debt held by, 106
    offices of, 306
    purposes of, 230, 302–6
    special assistance programs of, 306–9
Government Services Agency, 8
GPARMs. *See* Graduated-payment adjustable-rate mortgages
GPMs. *See* Graduated-payment mortgages
Graduated-payment adjustable-rate mortgages (GPARMSs), 82–85
    disclosure for, 85, *86–88*
    on energy-efficient property, borrower qualification for, 357
    FHLBB, 46, 83–85
Graduated-payment mortgages (GPMs), 16, 80–82
    disclosure for, 80, *81*, 416
    FHA, 80, 141, 154–57, 170
    FHLBB, 46, 80
    FNMA purchases of, 255–73
    GNMA purchases of, 310
    savings and loan association, 80–82, 112
    VA, 186–87
Great Depression, 107, 113, 127–28, 136, 196, 221
Gross monthly income
    for conventional mortgage qualification, 353–56

for self-employed individuals, 371
for Texas Housing Agency qualification, 370-71
Gross rent multiplier (GRM), 321-22, 332
Growing-equity mortgages (GEMs), 16, 85-91
   certification for, 159, *160*
   and conventional mortgages compared, 89, *90*
   factors for, 456-58
   FHA, 89, 157-61, 187-88
   note for, 91, *92-93*
   VA, 89, 187-88
Guaranteed mortgage certificates, 284
Guarantee fee, 180

H

Hazard Insurance Schedule, 361, *362*
High-cost areas, 152, 153, 164
Highest and best use, 317
Home Energy Checklist, 338-41, *339-40*
Home improvement loans, 120, 121, 123
Home Mortgage Disclosure Act (HMDA), 123-26
Homeowner's Fact Sheet, 143, *145*
Homeownership, underlying desire for, 348
Homeowners Loan Corporation (HOLC), 128, 136, 229
Home seller loan program, FNMA, 438
Homestead, defined, 19
Homestead Act, 19-20, 243
Housing, emotional needs for, 348
Housing and Community Development Act, 11, 118, 123, 234, 286. *See also* Community Reinvestment Act
Housing and Home Finance Agency, 229
Housing and Urban-Rural Recovery Act, 139-66 passim
Housing bond mortgages, 14
Housing rehabilitation loans, 120, 121
Houston Area Teachers Credit Union, 132

HUD. *See* Department of Housing and Urban Development

I

Immediate delivery program, 290-92
Important Notice, VA, 190, *195*
Income. *See also* Gross monthly income; Net effective income
   and employment, verification of, 395, *396*, *397*
   long-term debt to, ratio of, 129, 352, 356
   to payment, ratio of, 129, 352, 356
   stable monthly, 345-47
Income and debt analysis. *See* Borrower qualification
Income limits
   FmHA, 196
   Texas Housing Agency, 205
Income method, 320, 321-22, 332
Indexed mortgages, 170
Inflation, 7
Installment debts, and borrower qualification, 348
Institutional lenders, 103-17
Insurance companies. *See also* Life insurance companies
   mortgage lending by, 128
   and prepayment penalties, 214
   and secondary market, 228
Insurance sales, by mortgage bankers, 131
Interest charges, 425-26
Interest income, as stable monthly income, 346-47
Interest rate(s). *See also specific mortgages*
   and alternative mortgage instruments, 46, 135
   and annual percentage rate, difference between, 412
   conventional mortgage, 212-13
   and creative financing, 433, 434, 436

and Federal Reserve System, 5, 7–8
FHA, 138, 139, 140–41
FmHA, 197
indicators of, 9–10
nominal, 101
and real estate market, 8–9
and usury laws, 10–12, *11*
VA, 179
Interest-rate-capped mortgages, 56
Interest-rate indexes
adjustable-rate mortgage, 48, *50*, 54, 56–57, 58, 71–78, 167
graduated-payment adjustable mortgage, 84
renegotiable-rate mortgage, 99
variable-rate mortgage, 94–95
Interim construction loans. *See* Construction mortgages
Intermediate theory, 14
Intermediation, 103
Interstate Land Sales Full Disclosure Act, 19
Investment property, NOO loans on, 285

J

Junior mortgages. *See* Second mortgages

K

Kickbacks, 408

L

Land leasing, 439
Leasehold estates loans, 116
Lender, defined, 10–11

Letter appraisals, 316
Level buydown plan, 253
Liabilities, and borrower qualification, 348–49
Lien theory, 14, 19
Life insurance companies, 115–116. *See also* Insurance companies
conventional loans of, 211, 212
mortgage debt held by, 105, 106, 107, 115
as supervised lenders, 180
Loan Analysis Form, VA, 367, *368*, *369*
Loan application, 129, 375–95
basic information on, 375–76
FHA/VA, 386–95, *388*, *390*, *392*
FNMA/FHLMC, 381–86, *383*, *385*, *387*
legislation affecting, 376–81
Loan approval. *See* Loan underwriting
Loan closing, 407–32. *See also* Closing costs; Closing instructions; Uniform Settlement Statement
date of, 412–18
legislation affecting, 408–12
methods of, 407–8
by mortgage bankers, 129–30
procedures in, 418–22
Loan disclosure
adjustable-rate mortgage, 49–53, *51–53*, 55–56, 57
balloon mortgage, 436, *437*
Federal Reserve forms for, 412, *413–17*
FHA, 140–41, *141*, 168–70, *169*
graduated-payment adjustable-rate mortgage, 85, *86–88*
graduated-payment mortgage, 80, *81*
Home Mortgage Disclosure Act format for, 123–26, *124–25*
renegotiable-rate mortgage, 99, *100*
reverse-annuity mortgage, 100
shared-appreciation mortgage, 94, *95*
variable-rate mortgage, 97, *98*
Loan fee. *See* Origination fee
Loan guaranty. *See* Veterans entitlement
Loan limits. *See also specific mortgages*
conventional, 212
FHA, 137–38, 144–46

VA, 196
VHAP, 199
Loan maturity extension, 97, 99
Loan origination, by mortgage bankers, 129
Loan packaging
    conventional, 401–4
    FHA, 404
    and shipping, by mortgage bankers, 129, 130
    VA, 404–5
Loan participation program, FNMA, 276
Loan processing, by mortgage bankers, 129
Loan servicing, by mortgage bankers, 129, 130
Loan solicitors, 129
Loan-to-lenders program, 206
Loan-to-value ratios. *See also specific mortgages*
    balloon mortgage, 435
    commercial bank, 114
    conventional mortgage, 211, 212
    credit union, 132, 134
    FHA, 138, 139, 141
    FHLMC requirement for, 284, 285
    FNMA requirement for, 233
    life insurance company, 116
    and private mortgage insurance, 211, 222, 226
    savings and loan association, 111–13
    and simultaneous wrap, 433–34
    VA, 185
Loan underwriting, 405–6
    conventional mortgage, 221
    defined, 129, 405
    private mortgage insurance company guidelines for, 225–26
Loan warehousing, by mortgage bankers, 129, 130
Long-term debt
    FHA definition of, 358
    FNMA/FHLMC definition of, 356
    to income, ratio of, 352, 356–57, 371
    private mortgage company definition of, 225–26
    VA definition of, 366–67
Low-and-moderate income families
    and Community Reinvestment Act, 118–22
    FHA programs for, 122, 151–54
    and FNMA, 230

M

MAGIC Payment Mortgage, 82
Magic-Wrap, 434
Maintenance and repair schedule, monthly, 362, *364*
Management and liquidation function of GNMA, 306
Mandatory delivery commitments, 275–76
Manufactured housing loans
    FHA, 164–66
    FNMA program for, 256–73
    VA, 188
Market data method, 320–21, 322
Market value. *See also* Property appraisal
    defined, 314
    basic principles of, 317–20
    methods of determining, 320–22
Maximum sales price, determination of, 344
MGIC. *See* Mortgage Guaranty Insurance Corporation
MIP. *See* Mortgage insurance premium
Mobile home loans, 164–66, 189, 196, 273
Modification and Assumption Agreement with Release, 214, *218–20*
Modified pass-through securities, GNMA, 309
Money supply
    control of, 5, 6–8
    measurement of, 6
Monthly payment factors, 16–17, 440–41, 455
Mortgage(s). *See also specific mortgages*
    categories of, 14
    commercial bank, 113–15
    and Community Property Law, 20–21
    credit union, 132–34
    deed of trust versus, 13–14, *15*
    defined, 13
    history of, 13
    and Homestead Act, 19–20
    life insurance company, 115–16
    mutual savings bank, 116–17

savings and loan association, 110-13
standard instruments for, 20-41
types of, 14-19
Mortgage-backed securities (MBS)
program, 134, 306, 309-12, *311*
Mortgage bankers. *See* Mortgage companies
Mortgage Bankers Association of America, 10
Mortgage brokers, 131
Mortgage companies, 127-32, 180, 405
Mortgage Corporation. *See* Federal Home
Loan Mortgage Corporation (FHLMC)
Mortgage Credit Analysis Worksheet, HUD,
358-66, *359, 360*
Mortgage debt, amount and distribution of,
104-7
Mortgage guarantee companies, 127-28
Mortgage Guaranty Insurance Corporation
(MGIC), 82, 221-22, 227, 312, 434
Mortgage insurance premium (MIP), 137,
141-43, *142, 143, 145*
Mortgage insurance premium rider, HUD, 38,
39
Mortgage payment to income, ratio of, 129,
352, 356
Mortgage-rate index, 95
Mortgage verification letter, 395-400, *400*
Multifamily purchase program
    FHLMC, 287-90, 292-302
    FNMA, 274-75
Multiple pool, 233
Mutual mortgage insurance, 137
Mutual savings banks, 104, 105, 106, 116-17

N

Naked title, 14
Narrative appraisal, 316-17
National Association of Home Builders
(NAHB) Thermal Performance Guidelines,
357
National Association of Realtors, 316
National Association of Review Appraisers
(NARA), 343
National Bank Act of 1863, 113
National Credit Union Administration (NCUA)
    adjustable-rate mortgages of, 47, 56-57
    organization of, 132, *133*
National debt, 104
National Housing Act, 107, 136, 137, 144-70
passim, 229, 302
National Mortgage Association of
Washington, 229
Negative amortization
    of adjustable-rate mortgages, 49, 55, 58,
    224, 255, 287
    of FHA graduated-payment mortgages,
    154-55
    of FHLBB graduated-payment adjustable-
    rate mortgages, 83, 84-85
Negatively Amortizing Loans chart, 224
Neighborhood Reinvestment Corporations,
Title IV, 122
Net appreciated value, 91-94
Net effective income, 358
    determination of, 364-65
    ratio of total fixed payments to, 366
    ratio of total housing expense to, 366
Net operating income (NOI), 321
Net selling value, 91
Net yield, 255. *See also* Yield(s)
New England Mutual, 2
New York Housing Finance Agency, 199
Nominal interest rate, 101
Noninstitutional lenders, 127-35
Nonuniform covenants, 22, *26-27*, 28-32
NOO loans, 285, 286
Norwest Mortgage, 312
Notice of adverse action, 376, *377*
Notice of sale, 29

O

Office of Interstate Land Sales Registration,
19
Omnibus Reconciliation Act of 1980, 206
Open-end mortgages, 18
Open Market Committee, 5-6
Operating income, FNMA, 239, *240-41*

Optional delivery program, 292
Origination fee, 130–31, 214, 245, 425
Outstanding loan balance factors, 442–54
Overtime, and borrower qualification, 346
Owner financing, 438

P

Package mortgages, 17
Packaging. *See* Loan packaging
Participation certificates (PCs), 284
Participation mortgages, 436
Participation sale, 114
Pass-through securities, GNMA, 309. *See also* Guaranteed mortgage certificates; Mortgage-backed securities (MBS) program; Participation certificates (PCs)
Payment-capped mortgages, 56, 287
Pension funds, 134, 231
Physical deterioration, and cost method, 320
Planned unit developments (PUDs), 32
    FHLMC program for, 284
    FNMA/FHLMC appraisal form for, 322, *327–28*
    FNMA/FHLMC rider for, 29–32, *31*
    FNMA program for, 234, 239–43
Pledged savings account mortgages (PSAMs), 81–82, 235
PMI. *See* Private mortgage insurance
Points. *See* Discount points
Pool of mortgages, 233, 309
Pre-loan disclosure, 168–70
Premiums, private mortgage insurance, 223–25, *224, 225*
Prepayment fees
    adjustable-rate mortgage, 49, 50, 54–55
    conventional mortgage, 214
    and FHA, 139
    FHLMC multifamily purchase program, 288, 290
    and VA, 180
Presbyterian Annuity and Life Insurance Company, 2
Present value of money (PVM), 79–80

Price-level adjusted mortgages (PLAMs), 101
Primary lenders, 228
Primary market, 228
Prime rate, 5, 9, 18, 48
Principles of value, 317–20
Prior approval purchase program, 292
Private mortgage insurance (PMI), 211, 221–27
    calculation of, 222–23, 356
    FHLMC requirement for, 284
    FNMA requirement for, 234
    RFC requirement for, 312
Proforma statement, 321
Promissory note, defined, 13
Property
    FHA minimum standards for, 138–39, 140
    improvements to, 317–20, 329
    survey of, 418–22, 425
    types of covered by private mortgage insurance, 222
Property appraisal, 314–43. *See also* Market value
    formats for, 316–17
    organizations for, 314–16, 343
    sample forms for, 465–69
    standard reports for, 322–41
PSAMs. *See* Pledged savings account mortgages
Purchase-money mortgages, 18, 19–20. *See also* Owner financing

Q

Qualification. *See* Borrower qualification

R

Real estate
    development and sales of, and mortgage banking, 131
    history of, 1–2

Real estate commissions, 425
Real Estate Settlement Procedures Act
(RESPA), 129, 376–81, 408–9
Reconstruction Finance Corporation, 229
Recording fees, 425
Referral fees, and RESPA, 380
Refinance/resale program, FNMA, 243–45,
244, 254, 275, 435
Regulated lenders, 406
Regulation 4314, VA, 188
Regulation X. *See* Real Estate Settlement
Procedures Act (RESPA)
Regulation Z. *See* Truth-in-Lending Law
Rehabilitation Loan Agreement, 121
Rehabilitation Mortgage Plan, FNMA, 253–54
Reinstatement of entitlement, 189–95
Release, 29
Release clause, blanket mortgages with, 17
Release of liability
    assumptions with, 174–75
    VA mortgage, 189–95
Renegotiable-rate mortgages (RRMs), 16,
98–99
    disclosure for, 99, *100*
    and FHLBB, 46–47, 54, 83, 99
Rental income, as stable monthly income, 347
Rental verification letter, 395–400, *401*
Report appraisals, 316, 317
Repossessions, and credit history, 351
Request for Credit Approval of Substitute
Mortgagor, 174–75, *176*
Request for Determination of Reasonable
Value, VA, 334–36, *335, 337*
Request for Reconsideration of Appraisals,
HUD/VA, 341, *342*
Request for Verification of Deposit, 395, *398,
399*
Request for Verification of Employment, 395,
396, 397
Request Pertaining to Military Records, VA,
181, *184*
Reserve requirements, 5, 6–8
Residential Appraisal Report, FNMA/FHLMC,
317, 322–32, *323–24, 330–31*
Residential Funding Corporation (RFC),
312–13
Residual income method, 358, 366

Resort dwellings, FNMA program for, 235
RESPA. *See* Real Estate Settlement
Procedures Act
Retirement income, as stable monthly income,
347
Reverse-annuity mortgages (RAMs), 46,
99–101
RFC. *See* Residential Funding Corporation
Rising debt reverse annuity mortgages,
100–101
Rollover mortgages. *See* Renegotiable-rate
mortgages (RRMs)
RRMs. *See* Renegotiable-rate mortgages
Rural area, defined, 197
Rural housing mortgages, FmHA Section 502,
123, 196–97

S

Safe rate, 10, 78
Salaries, and stable monthly income, 346
Sales-comparison method. *See* Market data
method
Sales data books, 314–16, *315*
SAMs. *See* Shared-appreciation mortgages
Satisfactory Completion Certificate, 332, *333*
Savings and loan associations, 107–13
    alternative mortgage instruments of, 135
    community investment by, 122
    conventional mortgages of, 211, 221
    mortgage debt held by, 104–7
    number and assets of, 109, *110, 111*
    and secondary market, 228
    short-term lending by, 131
    as supervised lenders, 180
Savings and Loan Department of Texas,
109–10, 111–12
Schedule A, 170–74, *174*
Secondary market, 137, 228–313
    and commercial bank mortgage
    lending, 114
    and mortgage banking, 128–29
Secondary Mortgage Enhancement Act of
1984, 245

Second Bank of the United States, 2
Second home
 NOO loans for, 285
 VA loans for, 188-89
Second jobs, as stable monthly income, 346
Second mortgages, 18, 438
 FNMA purchase program for, 245-53
 savings and loan association, 112, 113
Self-employed individuals, 371
 borrower qualification for, 371-73
 withholding rate for, 365
Seller Warranty and Indemnification
Agreement, Texas Veterans Housing
Assistance Program, 199, *204*
Serviceman's Readjustment Act, 179, 180
Settlement costs, and RESPA, 380, 381
Settlement Costs (HUD guide), 381
Shared-appreciation mortgages (SAMs),
91-94, 436
 disclosures for, 94, *95-96, 97*
 FHA, 170
 FHLBB, 46, 91
Shared-equity mortgages (SEMs), 436-38
Short-term discount notes, FNMA, 231
Short-term obligations, FHLMC, 284
Simple assumption, 174-75
Simultaneous wraparound mortgages, 433-34
Single-Family Mortgage Purchase Program,
Texas Housing Agency, 205-6, 370
Single-user pool, 233
Small Business Administration, 8, 123
Small Residential Income Property Appraisal
Report, FNMA/FHLMC, 322, *325-26*
Social security tax, 365
Society of Real Estate Appraisers (SREA),
314-16, 321
Source of funds letter, 400-401, *402*
Special assistance function (SAF) of GNMA,
302-9
Spot loans, 129, 242
Stable monthly income, 345-47
Standard Factual Data Credit Report, 349,
350, 400, 401-2

Standard mortgages, 14-19. *See also*
Conventional mortgages
 adjustable-rate mortgage conversions to, 71
 and growing-equity mortgages compared,
 89, *90*
 offers of, and variable-rate mortgages, 97
 and shared-appreciation mortgages
 compared, 94
Standard Plans (ARM), 254
Standby commitments, 276-80
State housing agencies, 199-208
Statement of Purchaser or Owner Assuming
Loan, VA, 190, *192*
State usury laws, 10-12
Step mortgages. *See* Buydown mortgages
(BDMs)
Stockholders, as self-employed individuals, 371
Straight pass-through securities, GNMA, 309
Submission letter, 401
Substantial rehabilitation, 153
Substitution, 317
Supervised lenders, VA, 180
Supply and demand
 law of, 9
 and market value, 317
Survey of property, 418-22, 425

T

Table funding, 408
Tandem programs, GNMA, 307, *308*
Taxes, monthly escrow for, 361, *363*
Temporary mortgage assistance payments
program (TMAP), 161
Texas Family Farm and Ranch Security
Program, 209
Texas Housing Agency (THA), 205-6
 borrower qualification guidelines of, 370-71
 maximum sales price of, 205, *206*
 Single Family Mortgage Purchase Program
 of, 205-6, 370

Texas Savings and Loan Association, 109
Texas Veterans Housing Assistance Program (VHAP), 198–99, *200–204*
Texas Veterans Land Program, 197–98
3-2-1 mortgages. *See* Buydown mortgages (BDMs)
Tight money, 7–8
Time deposits, 113
Title companies, 228, 407, 408
Title Insurance, Commitment for, 418, *419–21*
Title policy, 134
Title theory, 14
Total fixed payments to net effective income, ratio of, 366
Total housing expense
    defined, 358
    to net effective income, ratio of, 366
Treasury, U.S.
    auction of bills of, 10
    Constant Maturities of, 9–10, 71–78
    and GNMA, 306
    and HUD, 230–31
    securities of, as interest-rate index, 9–10, 58, 71–78, 167
Treasury backstop authority, 230
Trustee, 14, 19
Truth-in-Lending Law, 57, 409–12, *418*
Truth-in-Lending Simplification and Reform Act. *See* Depository Institutions Deregulation and Monetary Control Act
Truth-in-Lending Statement, 409–12, 422
2- to 4-family rider, FNMA/FHLMC, 32, *33*

U

Underwriting. *See* Loan underwriting
Uniform covenants, 22, *25*, 28
Unscheduled payment increase provision, 53
Uniform Settlement Statement
    format of, 409, *410–11*
    and RESPA, 408
    sample, 426–32, *427*, *430*
Urban Development Action Grants, 122
Urban Homesteading, 122
Usury laws, 10–12
Utilities, average monthly expenses for, HUD table for, 362, *365*

V

VA. *See* Veterans Administration
Variable-rate mortgages (VRMs), 94–98
    disclosure for, 97, *98*, 412, *415*
    and FHLBB, 46–47, 83, 97
Verification forms, 395–401, *396–401*
Veterans, FHA 203(b) program for, 149–50
Veterans Administration (VA), 8
    and buydown funds, 79
    certificate of commitment of, 391, *394*
    and condominium mortgage insurance, 164
    deed of trust of, 41, *42–44*
    due-on-sale clause of, 207–8, *207*
    Form 26-1880 of, 367, *368, 369*
    Loan Analysis Form of, 367, *368, 369*
    and mortgage company underwriting, 405
    note of, 38–41, *40*
    property appraisal commitment forms of, 332–41, *335, 337*
    purpose of, 179
    and regulated lenders, 406
    residual income method of, 358, 366
    verification request forms of, 395, *397, 399*
Veterans Administration (VA) guaranteed mortgages, 14, 179–96
    advantages/disadvantages of, 179–80
    application for, 386–95, *388, 390, 392*
    borrower qualification for, 180, 352, 366–70, 372–73
    buydown, 187
    closing costs for, 179, 422–25

and Community Reinvestment Act, 123
and conventional loans compared, 211–21
eligibility for, 180–85
as federally related mortgage loans, 380
FHLMC purchases of, 281
FNMA purchases of, 233, 234
GNMA purchases of, 307, 309
graduated-payment, 186–87
growing equity, 89, 187–88
manufactured housing, 188
maximum loan and term for, 296
mobile home, 189, 196, 273
and mortgage banking, 128
and mutual savings banks, 117
packaging of, 404–5
standard home, 185, 196
and Texas Veterans Housing Assistance
Program, 199
and wraparound mortgages, 434
Veterans entitlement, 185
partial use of, 188–89
reinstatement of, 189–95
Veterans Housing Act of 1974, 190
Veterans Housing Amendments Act of 1976,
180–81
Veterans Housing Assistance Act, 198

VHAP. *See* Texas Veterans Housing
Assistance Program
VRMs. *See* Variable-rate mortgages

W

Wall Street Journal, The, 9, 10
Warehouse fee, 130
Welfare assistance, as stable monthly income
347
Wisconsin Insurance Commission, 221
Wraparound mortgages, 18, 433–35
commercial bank, 115
savings and loan association, 112

Y

Yield(s)
FHLMC, 287, 292–302
FNMA, 255, 275, 276, *277–79*
in real estate financing, 8